The Creative COOKING COURSE

Edited by Charlotte Turgeon

WEATHERVANE BOOKS · NEW YORK

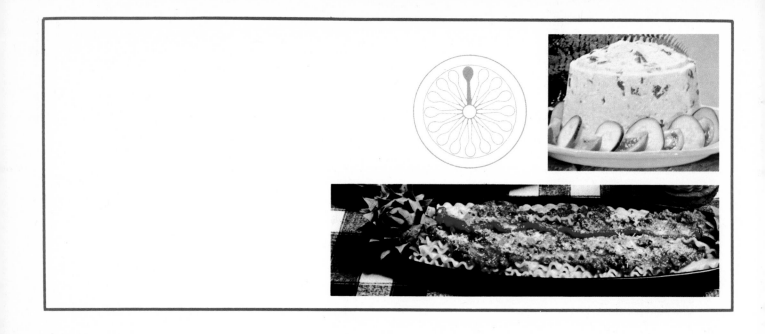

Photographic compilation copyright © MCMLXXV, MCMLXXIII
by the Creative Homemakers Academy
All rights reserved under the International Copyright Union by
Ottenheimer Publishers, Inc.

This 1982 edition is published by Weathervane Books,
distributed by Crown Publishers, Inc., by arrangement with Ottenheimer
Publishers, Inc.

Manufactured in Hong Kong.

Library of Congress Cataloging in Publication Data
Main entry under title:

The Creative cooking course.

    1. Cookery. I. Turgeon, Charlotte Snyder, 1912-
TX715.C92132   1982   641.5   82-7053
                         AACR2

ISBN: 0-517-17250X
h g f e d c

Foreword

Welcome to The Creative Cooking Course!

You are now beginning an adventure in creative cooking. In the series of carefully organized lessons that follow, you will learn through progressive steps how to cook with authority, with flair, with creativity.

The Creative Cooking Course is designed to teach you classic cookery. You will become familiar with many classic recipes and techniques of both Occidental and Oriental cooking. You will, for example, learn to prepare Basic sauces of French *haute cuisine: vinaigrette, Béchamel, velouté,* Hollandaise. You will discover how to make breads, pasta, puff pastry, engraved aspic, Belgian soufflé omelets, *pâté maison.* The methods of preparation for these dishes have been simplified in many instances, not to change the authenticity of the dish, but to fit them into the active life of the modern, creative homemaker.

Throughout The Creative Cooking Course you will find recipes and techniques marked with the Cooking Course symbol — The Creative Home-maker's Wheel of Spoons. The colored spoon in the larger Wheels serves as a marker for one of the sixteen divisions of the Course. The boxed, black Wheel of Spoons is used to identify a Basic recipe or technique. All of the Basic recipes or techniques will be used many times in vary-ing combinations during the Course . . . study them carefully! As you gain familiarity with the Basic recipes, subsequent lessons will become easier for you.

The General Information section of this Course explains the basics of Creative Cookery. Read the first two pages of this section to under-stand the concept and principles of the Course.

Creative Cooking can be fun! It is even more fun when you enter your kitchen with confidence, with the knowledge that you know exactly what to do and how to do it. This Course will give you that confidence. So, enjoy the Course. Work hard, work carefully, but above all . . . enjoy what you're doing. Good cooking!

The Directors
The Creative Cooking Academy

Contents

general information

table of contents

the basics
add up to
creative cookery

Cooking can be an exciting, creative adventure. With imagination, it can become one of the most satisfying arts. A wonderful part of it is it's easy to master! The more you learn, the simpler it becomes.

THE CREATIVE COOKING COURSE, beginning with the Basics of everyday cooking, brings you a once-in-a-lifetime opportunity to learn to cook with efficiency, authority, flair and creativity—in your own kitchen, at your own pace and with family and friends enjoying your acquired artistry with food.

Your Course will provide many ways to save time and effort, not to mention money, while increasing your abilities—and it's entertaining as well. We will share with you professional methods made easy and culinary know-how accumulated over the years. We will not only tell you in clear detail, we'll show you with full-color photographs how to do everything from stuffing and trussing poultry to preparing the most elegant Marie Louise Crème imaginable. You will begin to feel we're right in the kitchen with you.

In many ways, our method of instruction is more useful and effective than a demonstration-cooking course. Our clear, full-color instructions are permanent—there for your easy reference time and again. In addition the only timetable you have to meet is your own.

We will show you new techniques and tricks of the trade used by master chefs to economize and cut time, enforcing each one with a score of recipes on which you can practice your skills. You will learn how to make every dish, no matter how simple, appear on a grand scale. You'll learn efficient kitchen arrangement including the best use of equipment.

Starting with the very BASICS of food preparation, we will help increase your knowledge, confidence and expertise to a plateau many cooks long for, but few obtain. As these BASICS appear throughout the Course, they will be marked with the Creative Homemaker's Wheel of Spoons. Take note of them and carefully follow the instructions. They are like golden threads linking everything of importance in accomplished—and enviable—cooking.

New techniques and skills will be introduced. You will learn through our clear, step-by-step instructions and photographs while actually preparing a dish that can be served the same day. Your newly acquired skills will be put to use in making more elaborate dishes. Your knowledge and confidence will increase through our planned sequence of instructions, as we show you how to un-complicate even the most detailed recipes. Advanced methods will become as easy as BASICS.

Among the skills you will master are how to bake, baste, blanch, blend, boil, braise, broil, cream, cut-in, canelle, dredge, fillet, fold-in, fry, glaze, grill, jell, knead, lard, mix, mold, parboil, parch, sauté, scald, scallop, score, skin, scramble, skewer, steam, stew, whisk and whip—a tongue-twister of talents.

Before long, you will know how to bake an elegant soufflé . . . make flaming crêpes and roast to perfection . . . prepare delicious pastries and elaborately decorate a cake . . . mold a glistening salad . . . blend a magnificent sauce . . . create mouth-watering hors d'oeuvres . . . and bake tempting homemade bread.

All of these dishes will be possible because of the logical order in which we present the recipes and our step-by-step photographs and illustrations. Simply begin with the BASICS, build from there and you'll soon be hearing the accolades of your family and compliments of your friends (perhaps a little envy, too).

The vivid color photographs will show you how our completed dishes look. You might want to make yours look different. We encourage using your imagination, allowing your dishes to reflect your personal taste, which may or may not be the same as ours. As you progress through The Creative Cooking Course, you will gain the confidence you need to become an independent artist with food. That confidence should lead you to add your interpretation to our recipes as well as old favorites.

Your culinary repertoire will include BASIC techniques and recipes for *eggs and cheese; beef; pork; lamb; game and variety meats; fish and shellfish; pasta, cereals and grains; breads;* and *beverages.* In addition, there are *desserts; soups, appetizers and hors d'oeuvres; salads and relishes; sauces; poultry;* and *vegetables.* A separate category carries general information about *kitchen equipment, table setting and garnishing,* completing the knowledge required to succeed at cooking.

A GROWING COLLECTION

The material for each category is flagged by a colored square at the top corner of every page. You have an entire, definitive encyclopedia of creative cooking. In short, a delightful storehouse of culinary enjoyments.

We welcome you in sharing an exciting adventure— THE CREATIVE COOKING COURSE!

EXPLANATION OF COOKING SCHOOL SYMBOL

Our Creative Homemaker's Wheel of Spoons is your guide to the BASICS. Look for it beside the title of every BASIC recipe and technique. It signals a fundamental you should learn.

a cook's tools of the trade and how to use them

Let's sit down in your kitchen for a few minutes and think about the BASIC relationship between good food and proper utensils. Consider the many tools a creative cook uses to prepare a delicious meal. Without them, otherwise pleasurable tasks can become chores. And we all know that the right equipment always enhances the skills of any artisan.

On the following pages, we will share with you our collection of the kitchen utensils that lend a special flair to our techniques and make our work in the kitchen much easier.

As you acquire BASIC culinary knowledge and experience in this course, you'll also learn to use the equipment best suited for developing your skills. For instance, look at our shiny metal spatula pictured on page 4. It's great for turning bacon and small pieces of meat browning in a frying pan. And do you recall how expertly we frosted and iced our Basic Close-Textured Sponge Cake with the same spatula? (Desserts, pg. 7.)

You may or may not have many of the items shown on the next page. They simply represent our "suggestions" for kitchen equipment to help you improve your culinary expertise. We know that buying a kitchen full of Cook's Tools is a major investment both in terms of time and money, but it can also be a lot of fun and bring personal satisfaction. Good tools are well worth the time it takes to find them and the money spent on them. Two items which we have not pictured but consider very necessary are a heavy, shallow roasting pan with rack and a double boiler of good quality.

Buy kitchen equipment carefully. Before making a purchase, browse through restaurant supply stores, specialty food stores and the housewares and cutlery sections of better department stores. Be sure to select utensils that are sturdy, durable and comfortable to handle. After all, chefs depend on their implements year after year, and so should you.

Of course, it is possible to start cooking with basic and often improvised equipment — such as a glass jar instead of a rolling pin — while building your collection of professional implements over the years.

Sturdy, high quality metal or wood implements generally have a longer life span than those made of light metal or plastic, which often bend or break. Stainless steel combines the durability of metal with the easy care of plastic. As an added feature stainless steel tools retain their shiny, new appearance for many years.

It is very important to select the equipment sizes best suited for your needs. And if you have an automatic dishwasher, remember to choose utensils that are safe in extremely hot water.

The utensils shown in our first photograph of cook's tools are a mingling of the familiar with the not-so-familiar. The list is not meant to be comprehensive — frankly, we don't want to bore you with an exhaustive catalog of mixing bowls, measuring cups and spoons, pots, pans and the like.

Instead you will see some of the multi-purpose tools that have worked best in our own kitchen. We'll briefly explain what to do with each and later on feature in step-by-step pictures some gourmet items — specialized cooking implements to help you add a professional, creative touch to your own culinary efforts.

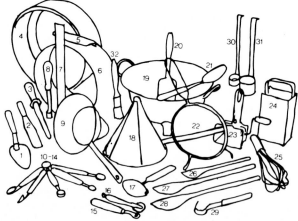

cooking utensils for your kitchen

1. *Metal pie server.* An invaluable tool for serving pie or any other wedge-shaped foods from a shallow dish.

2. *Metal spatula.* Use this tool to loosen cakes from the sides of a baking pan, to turn small pieces of food in a frying pan, to ice cakes and to smooth frostings.

3. *Sharpening Steel.* Often called a butcher steel, it will restore the sharp edge to your knives.

4. *Wooden drum sieve* or *tamis* (TA mee). A professional cook's fine-meshed sieve used as a sifter of flour and sugar or as a strainer for smooth sauces. The derivation of the word *tamis* is French — from *tamiser* (Ta mee zay) meaning to "sieve very finely." Originally fine worsted or a blend of woolen and cotton cloths (called tammy cloths) were rubbed together to strain liquids and to smooth sauces. Our drum sieve has finely woven horsehair as the straining fiber.

5. *Stanley knife.* Perched on the drum sieve in the foreground, this knife with a razor-sharp triangular blade is actually a carpenter's tool. It's great for scoring the outer skin of pork roasts and hams.

6. *Wooden drum sieve.* A smaller version of the sieve described in no. 4.

7. *Transparent plastic ruler.* Used to measure the width of pastry and bread doughs.

8. *Apple corer.* A handy tool especially designed for removing the centers or cores from apples — done in one easy step.

9. *Fine metal sieve* or *passoire* (PA swar). Similar in function to the drum sieve, it is used to purée fruits and vegetables and to strain stock, bouillon and soups.

10-14. *Oval* and *round melon scoops,* sometimes called Parisian cutters. They have sharp edges to help you make perfectly shaped balls from melons, potatoes, carrots, etc. To use, press the scoop into raw peeled vegetables or fruits, then turn the cutter with a twist of your wrist.

15. *Lemon stripper* or *canelle* (CANel) *knife.* You will love to make decorative border garnishes or long strips of fruit and vegetable peel with this marvelous utensil.

16. *Wooden wheel.* Often used for the cutting of pasta and pastry.

17. *Sieve roller.* This sturdy, wooden, lemon-shaped tool revolves and pushes simultaneously, pressing any substance through a drum sieve with amazing speed.

18. *Chinois* (sheen WA). A sieve especially good for smoothing finished sauces and other creamy mixtures and, like the *passoire,* is also good for pureeing foods.

19. *Colander.* You undoubtedly recognize this familiar utensil used for draining, straining and rinsing various kinds of food.

20. *Rubber spatula.* Reach for this handy tool whenever you have bowls or utensils to scrape, ingredients to fold in or blend, or icing to spread. We recommend a rubber rather than a plastic spatula because it is more pliable.

21. *Slotted metal (or wooden)* spoon. A very special spoon to help you remove vegetables, meats and other foods from a container and drain the liquid off at the same time.

22. *Strainer.* With this handy wire-meshed tool resting securely on the rim of a bowl or pot, both hands are free to stir liquid or solid foods through the mesh.

23. *Parsley mill* or *Mouli-grater.* A versatile tool for grating parsley and other fresh herbs. It works as well for cheese, nuts and hard-cooked eggs.

24. *Food grater.* Grate everything from cheese to onions, potatoes and cabbage with this four-sided utensil. Stainless steel will insure easy care and long wear.

25. *Wire whisk or whip.* Similar in shape to inflated balloons but made of wire (often with flexible handles), whisks are the best utensils for whipping cream and egg whites. They're also good for beating omelet ingredients and mixing sauces.

26-28. *Wooden spoons.* Excellent for stirring hot mixtures. Unlike metal spoons, they do not conduct heat or discolor mixtures containing eggs. The unusual design of these spoons makes them well suited for scraping bits of food stuck to the bottoms of pans.

29. *Butter curler.* A hooked gadget to help you make decoratively fluted butter curls. Dip it into cold water then pull it over a 1/4-pound stick of butter.

30-31. *Long-handled ladles.* Ideal for dipping and skimming liquids, these ladles can also be used to measure fluid quantities as well.

32. *Paint brush.* Yes, that's right, a paint brush. It's the best tool we've found for applying glazes or removing excess flour from working surfaces. Wash it in warm soapy water and rinse it thoroughly after each use.

home bakery equipment

Equipment plays such an important part in making the art of bread baking an enjoyable pastime you will probably want to own some of the tools pictured here. If you have difficulty finding some of them, check with a local baker. He'll probably direct you to his own supply house where you'll find all the equipment you want — and more. ·

Reading from left to right . . .

Back row: *Bread basket of plaited rushes.* This particular bread basket is impractical for most of today's home baking needs, but we included it to show how a day's yield of baked goods was stored in olden times. (Nowadays we wrap each loaf individually in aluminum foil.) *Sweeping brush.* Professional bakers and pastry cooks use this type of brush to sweep surplus flour from their working surface.

Second row: *Earthenware crock.* For bread making, no other mixing container quite compares with our earthenware. It is deep enough for mixing large batches of dough, and it holds enough heat to allow yeast doughs to rise properly. Recommended for all bulk mixtures except those containing onion or garlic. *Stainless steel pot.* An unbreakable substitute for the earthenware crock and much easier to clean. *Pyramid of bread pans.* An assortment of loaf pans for a variety of breads. They're also good for baking meat loaves, bread puddings and cakes and for molding gelatin mixtures. *Long loaf pan.* A jumbo-sized loaf pan for baking a long sandwich loaf.

Third row: *Brioche mold.* A decorative mold for creating an elegant brioche yeast bread and other sweet breads for special occasions. In addition to this particular size, there are other flared, fluted brioche molds available. *Decorative ribbed saddle mold.* Although we've pictured this mold in the Home Bakery section, it is actually quite versatile. It can be used for meat loaves as well as for breads and cakes. *Rolling pin.* Unlike rolling pins with handles, this old-fashioned one is thicker and longer to help you work with large amounts of dough. *Drum sieve.* Use this tool to sift large quantities of flour quickly. However, an ordinary metal, triple-screened flour sifter is easier to handle and store. *Pastry brush.* You saw a similar, soft-bristled paint brush in our first section on Cook's Tools. We prefer paint brushes to pastry brushes for sweeping up surplus flour because they are softer and less costly. *Oval fluted mold.* It produces decoratively shaped breads and is often used to mold *pâtés*. The sides have a spring opening for easy release of the bread from the mold; this type of mold is known as *spring-form.*

In front: *Sweeping brush.* Another type of baker's brush. Like the one hanging on the wall, it is used to sweep away excess flour.

pastry cook's tools

The next group of exciting Cook's Tools contains assorted rings, cutters and pans for making a variety of sweet and savory pastry dishes. In addition to the equipment illustrated below, you will also find flan rings and tart pans of varying sizes and shapes — some oblong, some square and some adjustable.

Baking sheet. A heavyweight sheet for baking flans, cookies and biscuits. Select a baking sheet that will neither warp nor bend under the weight of a full-sized tart or flan. Jelly roll pans, providing they are large enough, may also be used.

Tartlet pan. Our special fluted pan holds eight tartlets. Individual tartlet pans, ranging from about 2 to 4 inches in diameter, are also available. Muffin or cupcake pans make exceptionally good substitutes.

Tart pan. Tart pans have removable bottoms for easy handling of the finished tarts. In the most versatile tart pans, the 8-inch and 10-inch sizes, you can bake a Quiche Lorraine as well as many sweet and savory tarts.

Plain and fluted flan rings. A circular, bottomless, roughly 1-inch deep strip of metal which, when placed on a baking sheet, supports a pastry shell. All you do is remove the ring after baking and slip the completed flan onto a plate for serving. The fluted flan ring will help evenly scallop the edges of your pastry.

Plain and fluted pastry cutters. Available in a wide range of sizes, these cutters allow you to cut pastry dough into many shapes for many types of treats.

Pie pans. Your collection of pastry cook's tools should most definitely include at least one 9-inch and one 10-inch pie pan of metal or ovenproof glass. These will permit your piecrusts to brown to a delicate golden color.

garnishing with fruits and vegetables

There is something about an elegant appearance that makes good food more delicious. That's why you hear "oohs" and "ahs" when a hostess presents a beautiful array of refreshments even before the guests taste them. Tantalizing food displays are often the products of hostesses who make the most of garnishing. If you have ever been envious of cooks with this knack of making food so appealing, there's no reason to be any longer. Our step-by-step illustrations on garnishing will help you make your own beautiful and tempting creations to impress your friends the next time you entertain.

Let's begin this exciting area of cooking with fruit and vegetable garnishes. We've pictured a collection of border garnishes on page 10 to give you an idea of what decoration can do for your special dishes. For another idea, turn to page 11 in Salads. There you'll find a mouth-watering Russian salad garnished with a circle of green peas. These are just samples of what you'll find as you progress. Throughout your cooking course, we'll give you many opportunities to experiment with a variety of garnishes and we'll also teach you to use specialized gourmet equipment to make your job easier and your foods more attractive.

FRUIT AND VEGETABLE GARNISHES

Color is an important key to attractive garnishing and fresh fruits and vegetables give you a wonderful spectrum of colors to work from. They also supply great flavor accents to most any food.

When you choose citrus fruits for garnishing, you'll find it easy and fun to make decorative shapes with both the fruit and peel using only a small kitchen knife, a lemon stripper and miniature canapé cutters. We're going to demonstrate amazing garnishing techniques with the orange, but you'll probably want to try out your new abilities on other citrus fruits such as kumquats, grapefruit, tangerines, lemons and limes.

As for oranges, we know how easy it is to become confused with the many varieties available today. In most cases the type of oranges you buy will depend on your intended use. When you're planning to use the colorful peel, for example, you'll want to buy thick-skinned oranges. For the most attractive fruit sections, the juicy, thin-skinned ones are best, especially the seedless navel oranges or Temple oranges.

Give your imagination a free reign when selecting vegetables for garnishing — many varieties can be made into creative food decoration. In the next few pages we'll be showing you some unusual garnishes with such vegetables as carrots, potatoes, turnips and mushrooms.

Other vegetables that can be made into distinctive garnishes (and, incidentally these are best served raw) are celery, cucumbers, green peppers, onions, tomatoes, and radishes. There are a couple of important things you'll want to be especially careful of with vegetable garnishes: if the vegetable is to be cooked, it should not be overcooked to the point of losing its decorative shape or design; and if the vegetable is to be used raw, keep it chilled to make sure that it retains a fresh, crisp, and unwilted appearance.

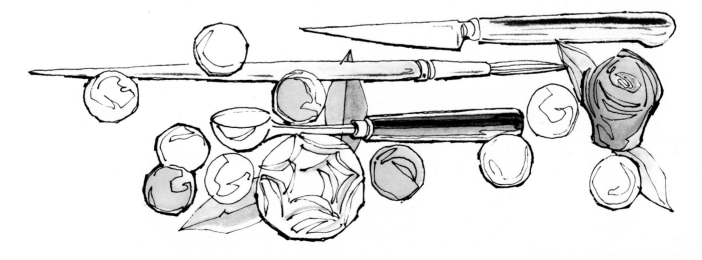

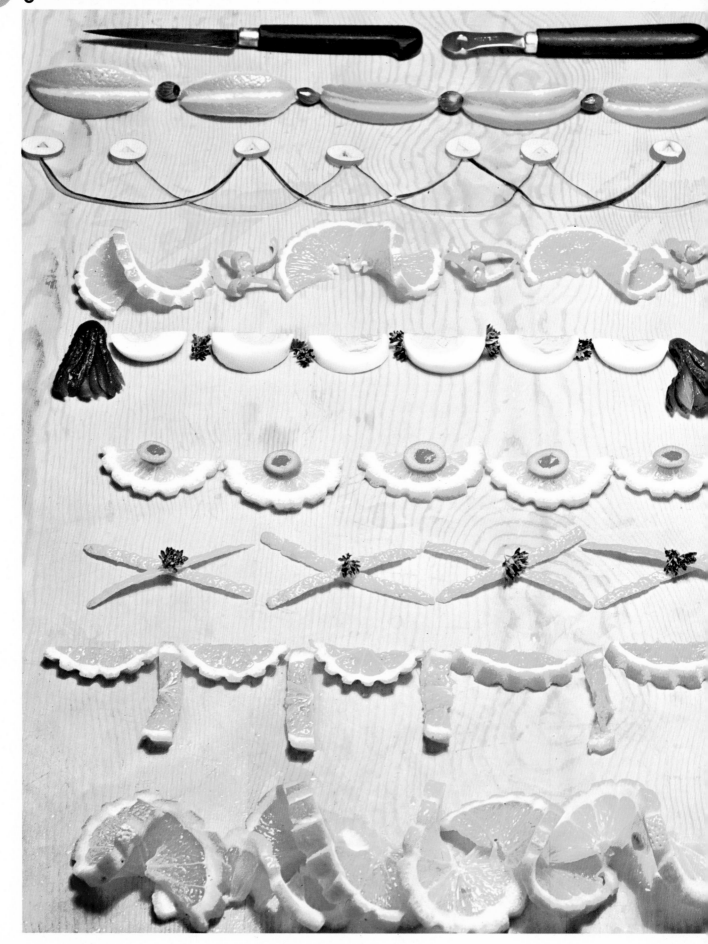

using the lemon stripper

Here is one of our prized culinary implements, one that you'll use often for garnishing and food decoration. It's called a lemon stripper or canelle knife. The lemon stripper has a flat, hollow circle of metal with a small protruding flange or lip on one side. With it you can strip the peel or skin from citrus fruits and vegetables to make many decorative garnishes like the ones on this page. The motion you use is one of pulling the stripper across the skin of the fruit or vegetable and thereby removing a uniform strip of peel. Below in our step-by-step illustrations, we're going to show you how to handle the lemon stripper and what interesting garnishes you can make with it.

1 Here is a close-up shot of the lemon stripper and some examples of stripped orange peels that we have tied into knots.

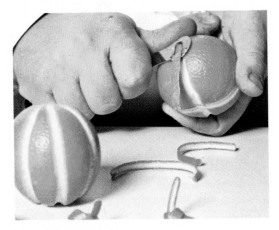

2 To strip the peel from your orange, place the protruding edge of the lemon stripper firmly against the orange. Then, applying sufficient pressure, draw the lemon stripper toward your thumb. You must continue to press firmly while you are stripping or you won't obtain a thick enough peel.

3 To make this first simple garnish pull the lemon stripper around the orange from the top to the bottom until there are eight equal petals or divisions. The orange in the foreground shows what yours should look like. Tie the curly strips of peel into knots and you can use them as a separate garnish we call Lovers' Knots.

4 Now turn the orange on its side and cut thin slices.

5 Halve the slices if you would like to use them as a border garnish. In this picture you can see quite clearly the uniformly turreted edges of each slice.

6 This is our first example of a fairly simple border garnish that is made by knotting the peels and alternating them with orange slices.

7 Here we are showing you another type of decorative border garnish made by interspersing slices of hard-boiled eggs between the orange slices.

8 Now we're going to show you how to remove the colorful peel from an orange in one unbroken strip, leaving the strip attached to the base of the orange for a very elegant garnish. Beginning at the top of the orange just below the stem end, pull the lemon stripper around the fruit as evenly as possible until you come to within one inch of the base. Now slide the lemon stripper right back along the whole strip of peel until it slides off the end.

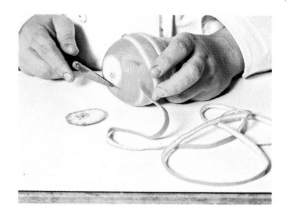

9 Turn the orange on its side and cut a slice from the base so that the fruit will stand steadily. You can see quite clearly here that we have left roughly one inch of uncut peel on the bottom with the strip still attached to the orange.

10 Here we are creating a festive maypole effect with the peeled oranges. For demonstration purposes we are placing the stripped oranges around another orange (with a ring-ended skewer driven through it) but the maypole is actually intended to encircle a roasted duck, orange gelatin salad or dessert. Bring the four peeled strands up through the ring of the skewer and pull them so that the ends dangle down.

how to cut
skinless citrus fruit sections

Have you ever wondered what kitchen magic is performed by master chefs in stylish restaurants to create delicate, delicious and fantastically beautiful fresh fruit cups and garnishes? One of our students said the other day that she had never understood how these chefs managed to remove the peeling from citrus fruits without making a grand mess. She said her mother would spend days before Thanksgiving and Christmas just trying to accomplish this feat for her ambrosia and fruit salads.

Well, like all sleight of hand tricks, the real key is in knowing and mastering the basic techniques. If you don't know the proper methods, you could end up with an endless process like our student's mother and maybe a real mess on your hands, not to mention a couple of nicked fingers. But don't lose heart. Solving this dilemma is not as difficult as you might have imagined.

All you need is a small, very sharp kitchen knife, a pair of relatively steady hands, that old standby patience, and our easy step-by-step instructions. Before you know it, you'll be removing the outer skin from citrus fruits without undue trouble. And you'll be creating fruit cups and fruit garnishes which would turn even master chefs — not to mention your neighbors — green with envy.

1 Starting at the stem end with a very sharp knife, cut the skin and pith away from the fruit, leaving a clean surface.

2 Run the blade of your knife right up against the little wall of skin that divides each fruit section.

3 Then reverse the knife to free the fruit section from its surrounding membrane.

how to
make an orange basket

We are very enthusiastic over what we have termed "fun foods", those great dishes that are especially fun to make, fun to serve and fun to eat. Orange baskets perfectly fit this category. These versatile fruit delicacies will make any meal more appealing. We've topped them with dressing and served them as salads, added creamy sauces and served them as desserts and placed them decoratively on platters of fresh game birds and fish.

Now, by following our step-by-step illustrations on the following page, you can show off your artistic ability by serving them at parties, brunches and luncheons. Delight the neighborhood children by serving Orange Baskets at Halloween and birthday parties or impress your entire family by garnishing your Thanksgiving turkey with this attractive display of fruit.

1 Begin by cutting off a thin slice of rind from the stem end of the orange so the fruit will rest steadily on a flat bottom. Make a cut slightly off center and about one third through the orange just as we are showing you above.

2 From the picture above you can see how you must cut through the side of the orange until the knife intersects with the first cut you made and the section comes out easily. Cut an identical section from the opposite side, thereby making the framework of the basket and handle.

3 To complete the basket handle, run the tip of your knife through the flesh in the center and around the top under the peel. Be careful not to cut through the handles.

4 Now cut wedges out from the top surface of the basket all the way around.

5 With a fine skewer or thick darning needle pierce the top center of the handle very carefully and insert an orange leaf, as we have done, or use parsley, rosemary or any other herb.

6 Your finished basket should look like this. It can be used as a delightful and imaginative decoration for sweet or savory dishes or as the serving dish for salads, desserts or vegetables.

simple border garnishes

Now we'll show you how to put your new skills with the lemon stripper to work to make a variety of decorative border garnishes. All of the simple border garnishes pictured on this page are appropriately named: they are not only simple to make from ingredients commonly found in the kitchen, but the only tools you'll require are a small knife and a lemon stripper. There are no limits to the types and border garnishes you can invent with these two implements. We've pictured many of our favorites so that you can see how we try to coordinate colors and textures to produce a total effect. We expect that very soon you'll be creating your own border garnishes to highlight many of your dishes from trays of hors d'oeuvres to desserts.

1 You make this border garnish with stripped, unpeeled orange sections and ripe olives arranged side by side.

2 Here we are showing you thin strands of stripped cucumber skin that we draped and topped with radish slices.

3 This border garnish consists of orange slices that have been split and twisted until they stand partially upright. Between each orange slice we've placed Lovers' Knots that are made by twisting and tying the orange peels.

4 For this border decoration we used halved slices of hard-boiled egg and small tufts of parsley. The gherkin tassels, which are described on the next page, add more color to the garnish.

5 To make this border garnish you simply place halved lemon slices end to end and a sliced stuffed olive in the center of each slice.

6 You can always use the strips of peel from any citrus fruit to make a separate border garnish. Crisscross lemon peels and set a tuft of parsley in the center of each cross.

7 You make this garnish by cutting off two crescent-shaped pieces from a whole orange slice. For a more interesting garnish, place the central piece that remains between each crescent.

8 This elegant garnish consists of double, partially upright twists of orange and lemon slices slipped inside each other.

how to cut vegetables with a ball decorating cutter

Now is the time to get out those wonderful, decorative melon scoops that were described to you earlier in this section under Cook's Tools (pg. 3). Sometimes called Parisian cutters, these scoops are most often used to make perfectly shaped melon balls (and ovals) for fresh fruit salads. Here we will use them on vegetables where you have so many varieties to choose from and practice with. Don't restrict yourself to the carrots and potatoes pictured here, but try this technique with cucumbers, beets, sweet potatoes and turnips.

First you will have to peel your vegetables and wash them thoroughly in cold running water. Then press the little scoop firmly down into your chosen vegetable, give it a turn of the wrist and withdraw the scoop. Remember to press down and in on the first movement to obtain a perfectly shaped ball. We admit that you'll have to practice to become really good, so don't be discouraged before you master the technique.

Once you have scooped out all the needed vegetable balls, you will cook them. The simplest method is to boil them in enough water to cover. It is difficult for us to tell you exactly how long to cook these vegetables because the times will vary with the size balls you have made. You'll want to watch the cooking time closely, however, so that the vegetables don't become mushy from overcooking. The second method is a variation of the first that you may also want to try: boil the vegetables until they are tender-crisp and thoroughly drain them. Place them in a deep fat frying basket and brown them in hot oil at 390 degrees for 2 to 3 minutes. The great French Chef Escoffier devised yet another cooking method that entails steaming the vegetables and rolling them in consommé that has been reduced to a thick syrup. Then, to serve them, he merely sprinkled them with chopped parsley.

HOW TO TURN A MUSHROOM

Here is a garnishing trick with mushrooms that will help you create an elegant, eye-appealing decoration or side dish. You'll be surprised how easy the technique is to learn. As you can see, we are using the tip of a small kitchen knife to cut little curved grooves in a clean, unskinned mushroom. We sauté the mushrooms in a little oil or butter for serving. Be certain to save the trimmings to add to your soup pot.

CUTTING SHAPES IN COOKED CARROTS.
Pictured above are the colorful results of one of our favorite garnishing techniques: cutting decorative shapes from cooked carrots. It is one of the easiest decorations we know and one that always brings many compliments. We suggest using any of these shapes when you want to make an interesting combination vegetable dish or decorate a roast or salad.

First you must peel then boil the carrots until they are tender-crisp (if you cook them too long, the carrots will become mushy and will fall apart when you cut them). Allow them to cool thoroughly and, with a small sharp knife, slice the carrots to the desired thickness. Depending on the intended use, we usually slice our carrots approximately 1/4 inch thick.

In the little metal box in this picture is a complete set of miniature canapé cutters which we used for our array of carrot shapes. At the top of the picture you can see our special tulip cutter and, in the middle, our heart-shaped cutter.

Back Row. A tassel flower. To create this flower you vandyke (cut into "V" shapes) the edges of a round slice of carrot and add the fringe, which is made by splitting sections of chives or green onions. Complete the garnish with a small round sliver of black olive placed in the center of the flower. *A daisy flower.* Using one of our miniature cutters, we stamped out seven little petals and arranged around a center of sliced, stuffed green olive.

Second row. Scalloped flower. Cut a large thin slice of carrot and scallop the edges with a small sharp knife. Then place a thin slice of stuffed green olive in the center. *Rosette.* This is a more detailed version of the scalloped flower. Using the scalloped flower as the base, cut a short stump from the base of a carrot and pare away a few layers of petals. (For instructions on how to make vegetable flowers, see pages 17 and 18 of this section.)

Third row. Here we are showing you another delightful garnish that can be used as a border decoration or for any other purpose you can devise. We stamped out a row of little hearts with our miniature cutter and simply placed one up and one down.

Front row. With our tulip cutter we made a row of upright and upside-down tulips.

HOW TO SHAPE TOMATO FLOWERS. Beginning at the top, peel a ripe tomato in a continuous circular strip, just as you would peel an apple. Turn the peeled strand skin side in and curl enough around to form a fat little bud. Pinch the bud firmly at the base and use the remainder of the strand (which lies in the foreground of our picture) to wind around the bud for a second and third set of petals.

HOW TO CUT GHERKIN TASSELS. Split the gherkin lengthwise almost through to the broad end and withdraw the knife. Then, working from the cut end, make as many thin slices as you can. Press them with your thumb and they will fan out to give you a tassel exactly like ours.

vegetable flowers

Envision yourself as a sculptor when you are creating vegetable flowers because your guests are certainly going to consider your finished product a work of art. Never limit yourself to only the vegetables with which we demonstrate. We're presenting techniques with the tur- and carrot mainly because they can be eaten raw, but you might want to experiment with a beet or sweet potato. Remember that white potatoes tend to lose their color quickly in the air. Have fun doing these and please do not think you have failed if you don't create a master-piece on the first try.

1 Here you can see the turnip and the stump of carrot we will be using to make vegetable flowers. Take special note of the particular shapes we are showing here: the carrot section remains wide at the top and slopes inward toward the base; the turnip is pared to a uniformly round, shallow shape.

2 Beginning at the extreme outside and fairly low on each vegetable, cut off a petal. It may be difficult for you to see the location of the petals on the turnip, but the first cuts on the carrot are clearly visible. Pare away some of the flesh from behind both sides of each petal so that it stands away from the vegetable. Continue sculpting around the vegetable until both are completely petaled.

3 You can even highlight the petals of the turnip with food coloring as we are doing above. With a little water-diluted food coloring in the color of your choice, very lightly brush the top of each petal. Since the deep orange color of the carrot does not react well with food coloring, we recommend that you leave it as is.

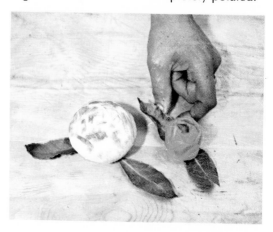

4 When you are ready to arrange your vegetable flowers on a serving dish, tuck bay leaves underneath them for a perfect finishing touch.

equipment for cakes and puddings

Selecting the right shape and size pan is important in achieving elegance in your cakes and steamed puddings. We all know the familiar 8 or 9-inch heavy aluminum layer pans, but on these pages you'll learn about more exotic types of pans you may want to try. You'll also find pointers for taking care of your equipment.

Pictured on this page is a sampling of the types of pans and molds you'll find helpful in your baking. Don't be upset if you presently find your shelves sadly lacking. And don't worry if you can't rush right out and buy all of them right away. But whenever you see an item or a shape that appeals to you, consider adding it to your supply. You'll hardly miss the money, and you'll find the equipment a valuable investment in creative cookery.

Look at the numbered illustration to identify the various utensils: **1.** You remember *flan rings* from our lesson on pastry, but did you know they can also be used for baking certain layer cakes? We tell you how to line them for cakes on the next page. **2.** The *flute-edged sponge cake pan* makes an especially decorative cake which can be covered with any number of delicious toppings. **3.** The *heart-shaped cake pan* is good for special occasions and

holidays. **4.** The *brioche pans* which we used in the Breads section (pgs. 12 & 13) to make *brioches* can also be used to make deep sponge cakes and sweet breads. We show a hollow-centered pan inside a standard *brioche* pan. **5.** The *springform cake set* is one of the most versatile pieces of equipment you'll find anywhere. The reinforced spring clip on the side makes the contents easy to remove, and it comes with three bottoms: plain, fluted and tubed. **6.** The *Madeleine plaque* or *shell pan* is used to make tea cakes, cookies and pastries. **7-9.** *Star, round* and *heart-shaped cutters* design canapés, cookies or decorative pastry. **10.** The *Savarin mold* is used for sponge cakes and gelatins as well as the classic Savarin (Breads, pg. 14). **11.** The *cooling rack* is a must for proper cooling of your baked goods. **12.** *Sponge flan pans* turn out attractive cakes with a depressed top to pile high with a tasty filling. They can also be bought in individual serving sizes. **13-17.** *Animal, tree* and *character cutters* make perfect cookies and treats for children's parties. **18.** The *heart-shaped frame*, like the flan ring in no. 1, may be used for cakes if you follow the lining procedure on next page. **19-21.** Another multipurpose pan, the *sliding-based cake pan*, comes in deep and shallow sizes. It is good for raised meat pies, *Quiche Lorraine* and rich fruitcakes, as

well as layer and angel cakes. In smaller sizes it is superb for cheesecake. **22.** The *solid-based cake pan* is ideal for baking deep cakes and for steamed puddings.

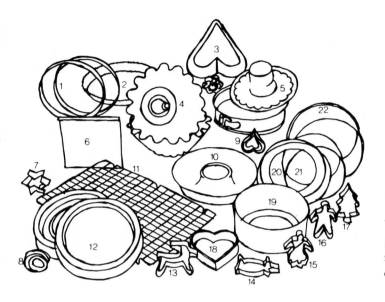

PREPARING THE PAN

The kind of cake you bake and the type of pan you use will determine how you prepare the pan. Although your recipe will give you general instructions, we will explain the various methods of preparation here so that you'll understand the reasoning behind the instructions.

The most common method of preparation is to *oil and lightly flour* the pan. Cakes which contain little or no fat, such as most sponge cakes, will have this requirement. If the cake is supposed to lie flat to stack in layers or to make a jelly roll, don't oil the sides. The grease will hold the edges down so that, instead of being flat, your lovely cake will be rounded across the top. On the other hand, a rounded top is characteristic of tube cakes such as pound or bundt cakes, so you may oil the sides for easier removal. If you are making a chocolate or other dark cake, dust the pan with cocoa instead of flour to assure no traces of white. Some cakes containing large proportions of butter may not require any pan preparation.

Recipes for richer cakes may instruct you to *line* the cake pan for best results. In most instances, waxed paper cut to fit the bottom of the pan and lightly oiled will suffice.

To line a pan for a fruitcake, place the base of the pan on brown paper and trace around it with a pencil. Cut a circle 1 inch outside the tracing line. Cut slits ½ inch apart from the edges of the circle to the tracing line. Next, cut a strip of paper which is the same depth as the pan and long enough to go around the sides of the pan with an overlap of 1 inch. Grease both the circle and the strip,

and place the circle inside the pan, allowing the slit ends to fold up at the bottom. Place the strip of paper around the sides of the pan inside the circle, overlapping the ends to fit.

You may also use a flan ring to bake cakes in, provided the batter is relatively thick. Cut 4 thicknesses of waxed paper into a circle 1 inch larger than the diameter of the ring, as explained above. Cut slits to the diameter line and place the circle inside the ring, which has been placed on a baking sheet. Lightly oil the waxed paper and you're ready to pour the batter in.

Pans with fluted sides may require a combination of lining and oiling. Cut waxed paper to fit the flat areas and lightly oil the fluted areas.

The new non-stick coatings for pans sometimes make any preparation unnecessary. Follow the manufacturer's instructions. Another recent boon is a non-greasy spray-on coating to prevent sticking.

HOW TO BUY CAKE PANS

When you buy your pans, always shop for quality rather than quantity, even if you must put off buying some of them. Select heavier stainless steel or aluminum pans over lightweight aluminum, which tends to buckle when subjected to heat. Buying good cooking utensils pays off in the long run, because they seemingly last forever.

If you prefer a thin, lightly browned crust for your cakes, choose a pan that is shiny on the upper surface and slightly dulled beneath. If you prefer heavier, browner crusts, use ovenproof glass pans which absorb and hold more heat. When you use these pans *reduce the oven temperature* by 25 degrees.

CARE OF BAKING UTENSILS

As any artist respects and takes care of his implements, so good cooks should. Your cooking utensils are the tools of your craft — the implements with which you create culinary works of art.

When you first buy a cake pan or mold (this also applies to cast iron skillets and the like), wipe it out carefully, then oil or grease it well, using a paper towel if you like. Put it into a warm oven and heat it for about an hour to temper it. Remove the pan from the oven and wipe off the grease with a paper towel. After you use it, wipe it out thoroughly with a paper towel or soft cloth as soon as you remove the cake. You should always keep your baking utensil scrupulously clean, but if possible avoid immersing in water. If you must wash it, wipe the pan very dry and put it in a warm place for several hours before placing it in the cupboard. This procedure prevents rust and spotting.

The ability to create something beautiful can fill a real need for imaginative people. And who among us doesn't feel the creative urge at some time or other? Creating a beautiful cake can be a most satisfying experience. With a simple icing bag and a couple of icing tubes you can easily make elaborate designs right from the start. And each decorating endeavor can produce a different elegant result.

The visual beauty of a cake is certainly a joy to any cook. While the actual existence of a cake is brief — it ends when you slice and serve it — its sight will thrill those who see it.

Cake decorating is an art, and as in most arts, it can easily be learned by any willing student. In the Desserts section of this lesson, beginning on page 35, you'll learn two simple decorating techniques which can be used to produce a variety of designs.

On this page we have assembled for you a representative sampling of cake decorating equipment. Some of the items — spatulas, greaseproof paper, food colorings and the like — are probably already in your kitchen. Others you may want to buy. If you purchase a medium-priced decorating set, it should include two icing bags with fittings and several tubes for piping. (You'll find instructions for making your own paper icing bags on the next page.) If you do not have an icing turntable, improvise by placing a flat plate over a large mixing bowl. This will hold your cake up off the counter to make decorating easier. A clear plastic ruler may be used to draw across icing — or to level and even it — if you do not have an icing comb. Probably the only items you'll have to purchase before your first successful attempt at cake decorating are the writing tubes to fit inside the icing bags.

MAKING YOUR OWN ICING BAGS

A problem you might encounter when decorating with frosting containing large amounts of butter is having the heat of your hands melt the butter slightly. When the frosting gets too thin, put it — bag and all — into the refrigerator for about 3 minutes. If you're in a hurry, you can put it in the freezer for about 45 seconds, but the icing in the metal tube will have to be squeezed out before you begin decorating again.

You can buy nylon icing bags for your cake decorating, but if you'd like to make your own, the instructions on next page will show you how to make them from greaseproof paper. We suggest 3 possible sizes, starting with 8-inch, 10-inch or 12-inch squares of paper. The 8-inch bags are handy when you have several colors of icing in small amounts. The larger bags are better for big jobs.

Assorted Icing and Decorating Equipment.

1. Greaseproof paper (sometimes called delicatessen paper or parchment paper) for lining pans and making paper icing bags. **2.** Regular icing turntable. **3.** Straight edge. **4.** Cake spatula for spreading icing. **5.** Deluxe professional icing turntable with adjustable tilt and clips to hold the cake steady. **6.** Cake decorator's special equipment box containing two smoothing "combs" (one straight-edged and one with ridges) to even out icing, a set of metal icing tubes, a box of special powdered food coloring, and four bottles of liquid food colorings (two inside and two in front of the box). **7.** Icing pins used when piping icing flowers. **8.** Classic column stands for tiered cakes. **9.** Homemade paper icing bags.

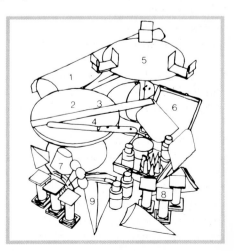

How to make a paper icing bag

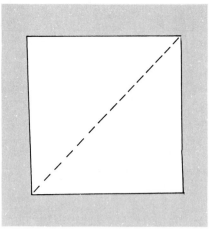

1 Cut 8-, 10- or 12-inch squares from thick greaseproof paper and cut the squares into triangles.

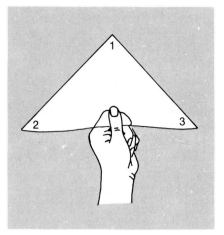

2 Hold the triangle in your left hand with your thumb in the middle of the longest side.

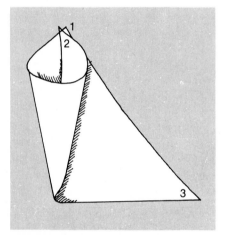

3 Make a sort of cone by bringing point 2 up to point 1 and hold with your right hand.

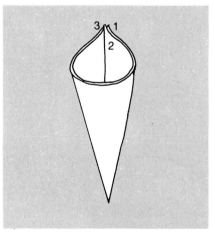

4 Bring point 3 around the cone with your left hand and hold it behind 1 and 2 with right hand.

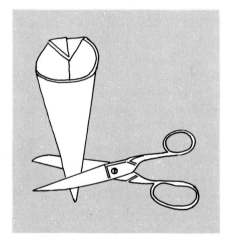

5 Fold down the point to hold the bag together, and cut off the tip.

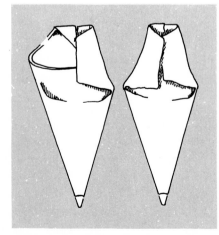

6 Drop in a decorating tube and half fill the bag with icing. Fold the two sides in towards the middle.

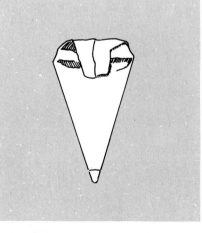

7 Fold the top down to seal in icing. Now you may decorate.

table settings

A good hostess knows that the effort she puts into finishing touches makes the difference between the ordinary and the elegant. Chopped chives for the soup or chocolate leaves on chocolate cake — these extras add much more than the little effort required in their preparation would make it appear.

In much the same way, the good hostess should see that the atmosphere is pleasant and relaxed so that mealtime becomes an occasion to be enjoyed and savored — a retreat from the tensions of the day. Otherwise all her careful meal planning and food preparation were in vain.

Pleasant surroundings include not only your own attitude as hostess, which sets the tone of the meal, but also the appearance of the table itself. The table should be covered with a tablecloth or, especially in summer when a bare table gives the impression of coolness, attractive place mats and a runner down the center of the table. A pretty bowl — a vase of flowers, or a seasonal motif — will do much for atmosphere.

You'll find, too, if you make it a practice to set an attractive table even for family occasions, you will gain confidence in your entertaining.

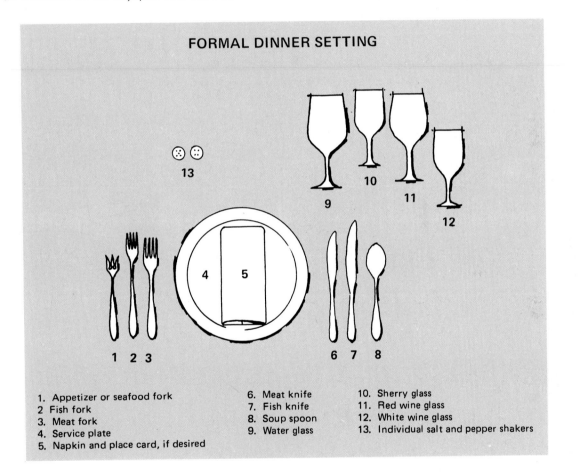

FORMAL DINNER SETTING

1. Appetizer or seafood fork
2. Fish fork
3. Meat fork
4. Service plate
5. Napkin and place card, if desired
6. Meat knife
7. Fish knife
8. Soup spoon
9. Water glass
10. Sherry glass
11. Red wine glass
12. White wine glass
13. Individual salt and pepper shakers

Illustrated above is the formal dinner setting, rarely used in its entirety now except for diplomatic affairs but nice to know about. The formal setting is the basis in varying degrees of informal placement. The table is covered with a lace or linen cloth that hangs 9 to 15 inches over the table on all sides. Napkins are folded once the long way and twice the short way to form a rectangle as illustrated.

The silver is placed about one inch from the table edge. About 18 to 24 inches of dining space is allowed each guest. The diner uses the pieces on the outside first, working his way in as the meal progresses. As a general rule, not more than three pieces of silverware are set to each side of the service plate. In the above illustration, provision has been made for seafood appetizer, soup, fish, and meat courses. A butter plate is optional. In some parts of the country, the salad course replaces one or the other of these courses. Formal dinners are served by servants who clear the utensils, plates and glasses after each course. Any time the plate is removed and the next course is not served immediately, a service plate is set in front of the guest, except after the meat course when only the water glass remains. The table is cleared of crumbs and the dessert course is served.

The setting for a formal luncheon is much the same as for a formal dinner, with silverware laid 1 inch from the table edge and 18-24 inches of space allowed each diner. Whereas at a formal dinner no food is on the table when guests are seated, at a luncheon the seafood appetizer might be already placed on the service plate, requiring that the napkin be beside the forks.

A butter plate and knife, absent in a formal dinner setting, are placed above the forks, and smoking accessories may be added at the discretion of the hostess. The salad

knife and fork may be omitted if there is no salad course. If your local preference is for salads before the main course, reverse the positions of the salad and luncheon knives and forks.

An informal dinner setting, which is appropriate for almost all occasions, is similar to the formal luncheon setting. The seafood appetizer may be on the plate when the diners are seated. A water glass is placed in position 12 and the wine glass in position 13.

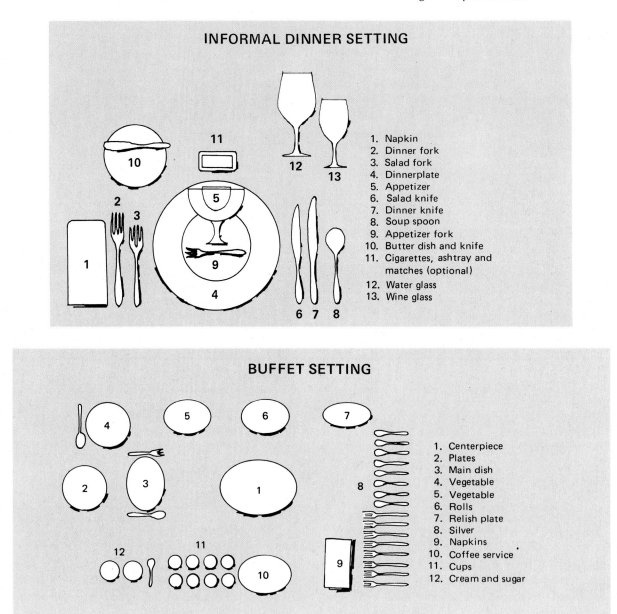

INFORMAL DINNER SETTING

1. Napkin
2. Dinner fork
3. Salad fork
4. Dinnerplate
5. Appetizer
6. Salad knife
7. Dinner knife
8. Soup spoon
9. Appetizer fork
10. Butter dish and knife
11. Cigarettes, ashtray and matches (optional)
12. Water glass
13. Wine glass

BUFFET SETTING

1. Centerpiece
2. Plates
3. Main dish
4. Vegetable
5. Vegetable
6. Rolls
7. Relish plate
8. Silver
9. Napkins
10. Coffee service
11. Cups
12. Cream and sugar

Today's more casual life-styles and small apartments make buffet service a lifesaver for large parties. And it can be as formal or informal as you like — linens, glasses, flatware, dishes and table appointments determine the formality of the occasion. Guests may be seated at one large table or several smaller tables, or they may be scattered about the party room, the latter being more casual.

As illustrated above, food, dishes, silver, napkins and coffee are spread on a large table. Each guest helps himself, beginning by picking up a plate and proceeding clockwise around the table, ending by selecting his silver and napkin. If the buffet table is against one wall, the coffee, cups, cream, sugar, silver, and napkins may be set up at a smaller table.

LUNCHEON SETTING

This table supports our contention that the most important thing for you to remember is that dishes and silverware be attractively arranged and the atmosphere relaxed. The centerpiece of irises, begonias, and pink carnations is low enough so that it won't interfere with conversation, and the pink of the flowers is picked up in the water-lily-folded napkins (see next page). Combining crystal and silver goblets adds a note of elegance to the more informal china.

how to
fold a napkin water lily

1 The water lily is an attractive variation for napkin treatment. Fold the four corners to the center, making a reduced square. You may iron the edges down to make the napkin easier to work with if you prefer.

2 Again bring the corners to the center, reducing the square a second time.

3 Holding the corners at the center, turn the napkin over and bring the corners to the center of the opposite side.

4 Hold the corners firmly at the center with your left hand, reach underneath with your right hand, and pull the folded inner corners one by one around to the top to form peaks.

5 Lock in the peaks by again reaching underneath and pulling out the four single layer corners that remain, working them upward and inward.

6 The water lily is completed. The effect will be softer, as in the picture on the preceding page, if you don't iron the edges down. However, ironing makes the napkin easier to work with at first.

decorative shapes in butter

The Scandinavians were the first people to use fresh butter as food. They, in turn, introduced it to the rest of Europe. Today butter is a part of almost everyone's diet. All U.S. butter is at least 80% pure butter fat and comes in three grades, AA grade, B grade and C grade. However, C grade is lower in butter fat and used mainly in baking and food processing plants.

One of the exciting things about butter is the many different ways it can be served. Aside from the standard way, in little square pats on a butter dish, there are butter balls, curls, flowers and butter trees. Although we take butter for granted at most meals, these various decorative ways of serving it add a special flair to even the smallest detail of your meal. An iced bowl of butter curls on the table, a delicate looking butter tree on a silver stand, a butter plate set with pretty butter flowers can give even the most basic meal an elegant look.

In this section we show you how to create these butter showpieces and give you recipes for making the simplest, most delicious flavored butters ever.

1 Take a plain metal butter curler and pull it across a very firm stick of butter. Place each completed curl in a bowl of ice water. The ice will help the butter curls to keep their shape.

2 After the butter curls have set in cold water, they look like the one pictured here. Your next step is placing them in a pretty bowl to serve at the table.

butter curls

These delicate curls have been created with a metal butter curler from sweet butter. They were placed in a bowl of ice water to chill firm for serving. Here you see them in a beautiful red glass bowl, certain to add flair to your meal. Place a few ice cubes in the bottom of the bowl and a little iced water around the curls to keep them firm and cold while on the table. This is one of the easiest ways to serve butter.

sculpturing a butter tree

1 Take two to four sticks of butter and dip first in warm, then in cold water. Then stick together and form a cone shape.

2 Place the butter cone in a serving dish. Use a butter curler to ridge the cone by pulling it lightly up from the bottom of the cone.

3 Hold the butter curler at a sloping angle and push it into the butter cone around an inch above the stand or tray on which the cone sits. Then bend the curler slightly out to form a petal. Leave about 1/4 inch space between each petal and keep working in the same manner around and around the cone towards the peak.

4 Here we show you three tiers of petals completed. You can see how they alternate in their position, one above the other.

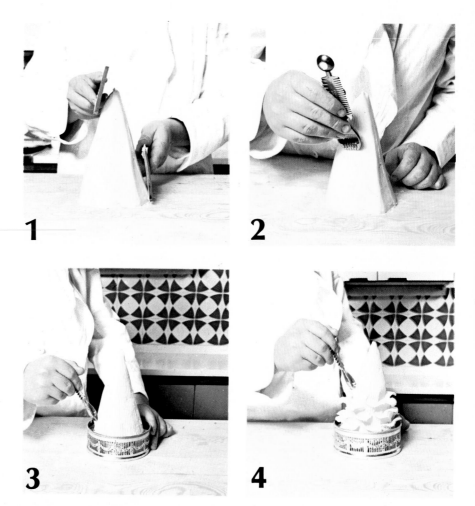

1

2

3

4

5 In this picture we have reached the top of the cone. Now the final peak is split in two with the butter curler. The butter tree is now completed . . . refrigerate until serving time.

5

After forming each petal, the curler should be dipped into a pan of boiling water before going to the next petal.

how to make
butter flowers

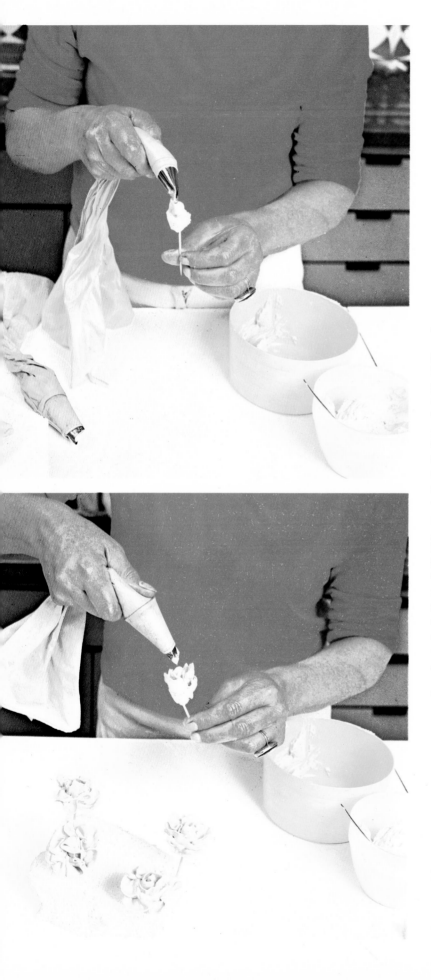

1 To create butter flowers, you'll need creamy savory butter, toothpicks, 1 inch square cubes of stale bread and a nylon icing bag fitted with a number 103 or a number 104 petal tube. Push the stale bread cube on the end of the toothpick. Then fill the icing bag with your choice of a basic or savory butter, page 30. Hold the toothpick between the thumb and forefinger of your left hand and the icing bag tightly in the other as shown in picture number 1. With the fat end of the tube pointing downward, pipe a flower as follows: Make a bulb about 1/2 inch high. This is used as a base to pipe the flower on. Always hold the tube stationary, turning the bread cube as the butter is forced out of the tube. Encircle the entire bulb with petals, working the tube in a curving, downward motion toward you from the top to the base of the bulb. Continue until the bulb is covered, which requires about five petals, each overlapping the previous one. If in the middle of this process the butter gets warm and begins to melt, put the icing bag and the half finished flower in the refrigerator for a few minutes.

2 Holding the tube at a slight angle as shown in picture number 2, pipe on several outer petals which slant outward to give the flower an open effect. After the flowers are completed, place them in the refrigerator until firm and cold. Then lift the set butter flowers off the stale bread cubes and serve them as a garnish on savory items or on butter plates.

basic savory butters

BASIC GARLIC BUTTER

½ c. butter, softened
2 sm. cloves of garlic, pressed
1 tsp. fresh, finely chopped parsley
½ tsp. salt.

Cream the butter until light; add the remaining ingredients. Mix until well blended. Store in the refrigerator in an airtight container until needed.

BASIC PARSLEY BUTTER

½ c. butter, softened
Dash of freshly ground pepper
¼ c. fresh, finely chopped parsley

Cream the butter until light. Stir in remaining ingredients and mix until well blended. Store in the refrigerator in a tightly covered container. This may be used on various meat and vegetable dishes.

SAVORY MINT BUTTER

½ c. butter, softened
⅛ tsp. white pepper
2 tbsp. finely chopped mint leaves

Cream butter in a small mixing bowl with electric mixer until light. Stir in the pepper and mint leaves, mixing well. Store in tightly covered container in refrigerator. Mint butter is very delicious with lamb and pork dishes.

SAVORY PAPRIKA BUTTER

½ c. butter, softened
1 tsp. paprika
1 tbsp. Chablis

Cream butter until light with electric mixer. Add remaining ingredients; beat until well mixed. Store in refrigerator in tightly covered container until needed. Excellent for piping into Butter Flowers, page 29.

SAVORY ANCHOVY BUTTER

4 anchovy fillets, drained
½ c. butter, softened
10 drops of hot sauce

Mash the fillets into fine particles. Cream the butter until light, using an electric mixer. Add fillets and hot sauce, then beat until well combined. Several drops of food coloring may be added to tint as desired. Store in an airtight container for use as needed. Spread on cut out shapes of bread. Bake in a preheated 375-degree oven for 10 minutes or until golden. May also be used as a spread on Baked Croutons (Breads, pg. 16).

how to cut decorative lemon shapes

A few years ago someone came up with the term "appestat" to describe the appeal of food apart from satisfying actual hunger. It is well known that attractive dishes seem to taste better than bland-looking ones. Some *haute cuisine* chefs have been known to take this realization to extremes, as when they prepare foods shaped like landscapes, buildings or animals, for formal dinners, adding cardboard arches, plastic stands and the like. While the creativity of the chef is given free rein — and the food may even taste good — most people find food that looks like food more satisfying. And as you learned on pages 9 to 18, food can be made more appealing with garnishes "good enough to eat."

The lemon is a perfect example of a food which adds eye appeal while retaining its useful function. Lemon is often served in slices and wedges to be squeezed over entrées such as fish, lamb or poultry, or to perk up iced beverages. On this page, you'll find a suggestion for making lemon pieces more convenient for squeezing while at the same time making them more decorative.

Lemon juice can also be used to accent the flavor of soups and fruits, and since it's low in sodium, it can also be used to add flavor to salt-free diets. It may be used to replace oil in salad dressings for fewer calories, and it is the most concentrated natural source of Vitamin C.

2 Coil the strip of lemon peel around and pull the end up through the loops as in the one at left.

1 Cut the lemon in half and slice a fraction off the base so it will set flat. With a canelle knife, cut a narrow strip of peel 4 inches long from the cut end. Remove the knife, but leave strip attached to lemon.

3 Vandyke (cut in V-shapes) the edges of the remaining peel, (as shown in illustration on page 14) for a more attractive finish. The completed lemon should look like the one at right.

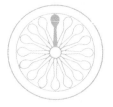

how to use a mandoline or vegetable slicer

A vegetable slicer is a kitchen tool you'll find indispensable once you've tried it. It ensures that your slices and strips of fruits and vegetables for salads, appetizers and side dishes are uniform in size and shape, and it cuts down enormously on preparation time.

There are many types of vegetable slicers on the market, and care should be taken to select a good one. Be especially sure the blades are sharp. Our favorite slicer is the classic mandoline (MAN-DOH-LEEN-AY). Relatively simple in construction, the mandoline has two blades which can be adjusted for rough-chopping, ridges, *julienne* strips, waffle-cut and thin or thick slices. The most satisfactory type is made of stainless steel and has very sharp blades.

The mandoline is pictured below, along with foods chopped in a variety of shapes and sizes. Although it is called a vegetable slicer, the mandoline is also useful for chopping fruits, hard-boiled eggs and cheese.

2 The mandoline may be used to slice cheese or hard-boiled eggs as well as vegetables. Here, the blades have been adjusted for very thin slices which we have rolled decoratively. To make *julienne* of raw vegetables, slice thin slices — vertically — into straw-sized strips.

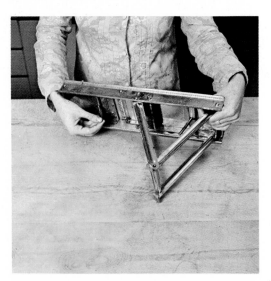

1 Here is a close-up of one type of vegetable slicer — the mandoline. It is made of stainless steel. Notice the two handles by which you adjust the blades. For best results, practice the various cuts and shapes with a peeled raw potato to get accustomed to using the implement. Cucumbers, celery, peeled Jerusalem artichokes and carrots are effective when cut *julienne* style.

3 Here is an assortment of possible shapes for fruits and vegetables sliced with the mandoline. The French salad basket is filled with rough-chopped lettuce. Below it is a dish holding sliced cucumber and Jerusalem artichoke. Reading clockwise, the other dishes contain green beans, cheese in 3 thicknesses, potatoes cut into waffled and ridged slices, straw or matchstick potatoes, and chopped apples for salads.

equipment for making ice creams and ices

A feature of this lesson is to show you how to make superb ice cream and fruit ices. This requires certain equipment which we would like to tell you about in advance. Excitement over homemade ice cream for dessert is practically universal. Although commercially prepared ice creams and ices are readily available, most people feel that they can't compare, for flavor and richness, with the homemade variety that "everyone took turns cranking!"

From the simple fruit juice ices the Chinese enjoyed centuries ago, ice cream has evolved to a frozen sweet dessert made from cream, sugar, flavorings and usually eggs. There are three basic types of ice cream: French, American and Philadelphia (Desserts,

pg. 67). All three varieties of ice cream, plus fruit ices, frozen custards, sherbets, frappés and mousses can be made in a refrigerator or freezer. However, there is no doubt that the home ice cream maker produces superior ice creams and ices. Therefore, we are recommending recipes for both methods. There are two types of home ice cream makers: manual and electric. These are specially designed to make a smooth, velvety ice cream. Both produce the same quality ice cream, but, of course the electric ice cream maker is much less work.

REFRIGERATOR OR DEEP FREEZER

All of these desserts can be made in a freezer or a refrigerator freezing compartment. They do, however, require occasional stirring. Ice creams made in this manner should be a rich mixture with a creamy custard base. Ice creams and ices are usually beaten with a wire whisk or rotary beater several times during the freezing process. This should be done when the mixture has frozen enough to form a thick mush around the edge of the pan. Beating during the freezing process will break up the ice crystals and insure a smooth finished product.

HOME ICE CREAM MAKER

The traditional ice cream maker, either electric or manual, consists of three main parts: the outer wood or plastic bucket which holds the ice, the inner metal can which holds the cream mixture, and the turning crank. The inner metal can is held in position by the dasher which is attached to the crank frame. The dasher is a paddle that fits inside the can. This churns the ice cream during the freezing stages to speed the freezing process and keep the mixture smooth and creamy.

When using the ice cream maker, place the dasher in the can, add the cooled cream or ice mixture, then place the top on. The can should not be more than three-quarters full to allow for expansion. Set the filled can into place and attach the crank.

To obtain a smooth texture, free of lumped ice crystals, ice cream made in a manual ice cream maker must be turned slowly and steadily. After freezing to a mush (about 10 minutes) the crank may be turned more rapidly until it is extremely difficult to turn. The mixture is then frozen properly.

To obtain a low freezing temperature, surround the can with cracked ice and coarse rock salt alternately, shaking down firmly. The proportion of rock salt to crushed ice should be one part salt to eight parts ice. Now begin to turn the crank or switch on the motor for the electric type. Do not open during the freezing unless necessary to add an ingredient and be careful to keep the salt water level below the top of the can or it might seep into the cream mixture.

When the ice cream is frozen, remove the crank and enough of the ice so that the top of the can is clear. Wipe the top quickly with a damp cloth to remove any salt. At this point you need a large bowl (to receive the dasher), and a long handled spoon and a piece of aluminum foil. Remove the top; grasp the dasher firmly and pull, holding the can down in the ice with the other hand. Scrape the ice cream from the dasher back into the can (the cream may be served immediately, however it is better to pack it down and let it *set*, covered in the ice, for at least an hour). Place the large piece of foil over the can opening, then place the top on over the foil. Drain off a small amount of the melted salt water and then place additional ice in the bucket to cover the can completely. Cover the top of the bucket with a thick stack of newspapers or burlap to insulate and keep the mixture as cold as possible. Lastly, place the crank on top of the newspapers to weight everything down. After an hour or two, the ice cream will be set to a firm consistency and ready to serve with pride.

Any remaining ice cream may be stored in a freezer. It should be packed in waxed or plastic cartons, then sealed completely. If the ice cream is frozen in a mold or the classic *bombe* mold, lightly oil the container — exactly as for molding cream salads (Salads, pg. 2). To insure easy unmolding in a pan which is not specially designed for molding ice cream, you may also line the container with a large piece of clear plastic wrap.

Please be warned: lightly wrapping the top of the container with foil is of no use. If the entire container is not wrapped, the ice cream will turn icy. A hard crust of ice or ice crystals will form each time the ice cream is returned to the freezer after a portion is removed.

ICE CREAM EQUIPMENT

1. Tin *Bombe* Mold. **2.** Cone-Shaped Pudding Mold. **3.** Classic Copper *Bombe* Mold. **4.** Electric Ice Cream Maker. **5.** *Brioche* Mold. **6.** *Savarin* Mold. **7.** Ice Cube Tray. **8.** Loaf Pan. **9.** Round Cake Pan. **10.** Charlotte Mold.

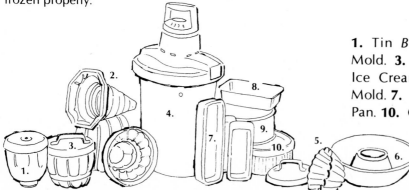

the fundamentals of
fondue cookery

Tired of being alone in the kitchen? Why not make fondue right at the dinner table? There's no need to wait for company to come — surprise and delight your family with a fondue dinner. It's sure to provide pleasure and excitement even for the youngest members of the family.

The word *Fondue* comes from the French word *fondre* which means "to melt". According to legend, the original fondue was developed in Switzerland during the 18th century. The Swiss baked bread and made cheese during the summer and fall months, and stockpiled a supply which had to last throughout the long winter. Needless to say, before the next summer arrived, the cheese and bread had become very hard and difficult to chew. Some ingenious Swiss peasant decided to try melting the cheese and dunking the stale bread into the melted cheese mixture. Presto, the first fondue!

This lesson includes recipes for two different kinds of fondue — Cheese and Italian Vegetable Fondue. Cheese Fondue is, of course, the classic one. The basic cheese fondue is made from two different types of Swiss cheese: a mild type, Emmenthaler, and the more robust, Gruyère. If a very mild fondue is desired, use only Emmenthaler; a heartier mixture may be made entirely of Gruyère.

Cheese for fondue may be diced or shredded. Toss the cheese bits with the flour called for in the recipe (generally a couple of tablespoons.) Try to obtain the type of cheese called for in the recipe — not all cheeses lend themselves to a smooth, non-lumpy fondue. To add interest to the flavor, rub the fondue pot lightly with half a clove of garlic before adding the specified amount of wine. Take care in choosing the type of wine to be used. The best choice is a light, dry, white wine such as Sauterne, Rhine, Reisling or Chablis. Heat the wine in the fondue pot until it just begins to bubble — then add the cheese, a handful at a time, stirring constantly with a wooden spoon. When all the cheese has been added and has melted to a smooth consistency, additional flavorings such as nutmeg and freshly ground pepper may be added. The fondue is then ready for dunking.

Cubes of crusty French or Italian bread are speared on long-handled forks. Each diner dips his bread into the cheese mixture, swirls it around and then eats the tasty morsel. A good chilled wine and crisp, green salad are perfect accompaniments. The prize of the evening goes to the person who, by luck and skill, manages to keep from dropping even one piece of bread into the pot. His reward might be a bottle of wine or the honor of eating

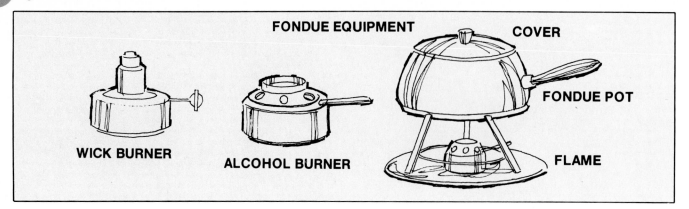

FONDUE EQUIPMENT — COVER — WICK BURNER — ALCOHOL BURNER — FONDUE POT — FLAME

the cheese crust left in the bottom of the fondue pot — it's the best part!

Fondue *Bourguignonne* consists of pieces of meat speared on a fork and cooked in hot oil. Some people use a mixture of peanut oil and butter; others prefer plain salad oil, coconut oil or olive oil. Olive oil imparts a pleasant flavor. Unfortunately, olive oil smokes quickly when heated, so it is not always the best type to use unless a recipe specifically calls for it. Tender cuts of beef such as tenderloin, sirloin or porterhouse are preferred for beef fondue although other cuts may be used if they are first tenderized. Veal is likely to be tough unless the cut is the tenderloin. If pork is used, caution the guests that it must be thoroughly cooked without even a hint of pink on the inside. Allow five to seven ounces of meat per person for fondueing.

Seafood may also be used for fondue. The most popular seafood fondue is shrimp — allow about two pounds of raw, shelled shrimp for four people. For other seafoods including fish, allow the same proportions.

The meat or seafood to be used in fondue may be placed in a bowl at either end of the table or served individually as part of each place setting. An attractive way of garnishing the uncooked meat is to line the bowls with salad greens. Each place setting should include a salad fork and dinner fork as well as a fondue fork. At least one dinner plate is needed for each place setting.

It is customary to include four to six different sauces in which to dunk the cooked meat or seafood (suitable dunking sauces can be found in the Sauces section). The best sauces for meat are those with a spicy, flavorful taste such as barbecue sauces (Sauces, p. 8) or Paprika-Tomato Sauce (Sauces, p. 15). For seafood, a tartar, Maureen or Rémoulade Sauce provides a savory dip. Especially recommended is Gorgona Sauce, a marvelous cold dunking sauce for shrimp.

FONDUE EQUIPMENT

There are three different types of fondue pots. One is metal and the other two are earthenware. Cheese fondue is traditionally prepared in a *caquelon*, or *pôelon* which

is a round, heavy pottery dish with a wide mouth and heavy pottery handle. A smaller version of the *caquelon* is generally used for dessert fondues such as chocolate fondue. The third type or metal fondue pot is wider at the bottom than the top and deeper than those made of pottery. The metal fondue pot is essential when making meat or vegetable fondue. The hot oil in which the meat or vegetables cook must reach a temperature of 360° F. which would crack a pottery fondue dish.

The heat source for fondue cookery depends on the type of fondue being served. Dessert fondue requires little heat. It may be heated on the stove over very low heat, then poured into the fondue pot. A candle warmer is all that is needed to keep it sufficiently warm. Meat, Vegetable and Cheese Fondue all require more intense heat than the dessert type. For these, use an alcohol lamp, canned heat or an electric fondue pot. Alcohol lamps are generally of two types. One has a wick which is raised and lowered by a screw. The other has cotton wool in the base of the lamp which is saturated with alcohol and then ignited. The degree of heat is controlled by a cover which opens and closes vents on the sides of the lamp. Never fill the lamp more than half-full of fuel. Denatured alcohol is the best type to use — it is less expensive, has less odor and produces the most intense heat. One tablespoon of alcohol will burn for about 12 minutes. Canned heat is self-contained and may be used in place of an alcohol lamp. A three-ounce can burns for approximately 50 to 60 minutes and a seven-ounce can will burn for 4 hours. Canned heat may be stored, covered and reused later. If you have an electric fondue pot, be sure to read manufacturer's directions before using.

When selecting fondue equipment, look for a sturdy, well-constructed pot with a tray to catch spills and protect the surface on which it is placed when in use. In general, one pot will serve up to four people. Fondue forks have two or three tines and long handles with wooden ends to prevent them from becoming too hot to handle. The best kind of forks are color-coded, so everyone will recognize his own fork when it is in the pot. Fondue plates are also available. These may be made of plastic, metal or china and are divided into several compartments to hold various sauces.

presenting
food for gifts

Many times while frantically trying to think of gifts for friends and relatives, we overlook one of the easiest, most economical and unique gifts — home-cooked food. Home-cooked delicacies can be so simple to prepare, and yet so welcomed by friends, neighbors and family. At Christmas, an array of homemade sweet breads in a frilly box is as decorative as it is delicious. Steamed puddings, such as Christmas Plum Pudding and Escoffier's Steamed Chocolate Pudding, in the Desserts section make excellent holiday gifts. Try decorating tin and cardboard containers with unusual wrappings, perhaps add your own original label, then fill the container with a specialty from your kitchen.

Candies make excellent Christmas, Valentine and anniversary presents. What could be a more wonderful gift than homemade bread, coffee cake, rich cream filled pastries, homemade candy or a beautifully decorated chocolate cake? There simply isn't a more personal way to tell someone how much you care than by presenting her something wonderful from your own kitchen. Homemade foods prepared with such pride and care are never forgotten.

food for gifts

These candies are so colorful and professional looking they might be mistaken for part of the decorations. Although beautiful, they will never last long as decorations because their homemade flavor is irresistible. Sweet breads, cakes, pastries and puddings are other wonderful gifts for festive occasions. Tinted cellophane and bright colored bows make perfect wrappings.

BRANDY BUTTER

1 c. unsalted butter, softened
4 c. confectioners' sugar, sifted
1 tsp. orange flower water *(Desserts, pg. 7)*
1 tsp. rose water *(Desserts, pg. 7)*
6 tbsp. brandy
3 drops of green food coloring

Place the butter in a large mixer bowl and cream thoroughly with the electric mixer. Add 1 cup sugar and cream again. Add another cup of sugar, the orange flower water and the rose water. Cream until well combined and fluffy, then add the remaining sugar gradually, beating constantly, until smooth and fluffy. Beat in the brandy slowly. Add the food coloring and beat until the color is evenly distributed. Spoon or pipe onto serving dish. Chill until ready to serve. Serve as a spread with steamed puddings, fruitcakes or fruit breads. This makes about 3 cups of butter.

HOW TO CREAM

The term cream means to beat or whip an ingredient or mixture to a creamy, smooth consistency. Electric mixer, whisk or wooden spoon may be used to cream.

brandy butter

Brandy Butter, a delightful accompaniment to steamed puddings, is sophisticated in its simplicity. Its workable texture enables you to design it in any fashion you desire. Blanched almonds, glacé cherries and angelica may be used as decorative garnish. For gift-giving, chill the Brandy Butter and use transparent cellophane for wrapping.

kitchen planning

Do you ever lift stacks of pans in order to reach the one you need? Are there dark corners in your kitchen where you must combine braille technique with location familiarity in order to perform everyday tasks? Do you feel as though you've walked a mile in the course of preparing an evening meal, crossing your kitchen again and again?

These are a few of the problems that can be solved with proper kitchen planning. The kitchen, more than any other room in the house, deserves consideration of storage, appliances, and accessories for accessibility and working ease.

In this section we will analyze the tasks that are performed in the kitchen, explore organizational techniques, and suggest ways to make *your* kitchen more efficient and pleasant through the storage-by-use approach. No expensive, out-of-reach ideas are to be offered here; instead you will find practical suggestions that can be put into use immediately. You may well find that by "investing" three or four hours rearranging your kitchen equipment today, you will save that many hours of extra work and motion every week from now on!

If you had to take an inventory of the activities you perform in the kitchen, a general listing would include: preparing of and cooking food; meal planning; food storing; setting, serving, and clearing the table; washing and drying dishes and utensils, and general kitchen cleaning.

All the activities related to food preparation in the kitchen center around one or more of the three basic kitchen tools — the stove, the sink, and the refrigerator. The most advantageous arrangement of these appliances, in terms of motion and step saving, is a triangle connecting the three, with the perimeter of the triangle not exceeding 22 feet. Of course, this is the ideal, and not always possible with the variety of kitchen floor plans available. However, whatever the floor plan, there is room for efficiency if the appliances are carefully located.

There are four basic floor plans into which all kitchens generally may fit. The one-wall kitchen, in which all appliances are lined side by side, is the least desirable arrangement. However, the most can be made of it by locating the sink between the stove and refrigerator, with counter space by each.

The corridor kitchen (or pullman-style plan) places appliances and work space along two paralleled walls with an aisle between. The refrigerator and stove should be on one side, the sink opposite. More efficient than the one-wall plan, the main drawback of this layout is that such a kitchen often serves as a passageway and receives a great deal of traffic flow. To alleviate this problem, it should be closed at one end.

Another common pattern is the L-shaped kitchen. For maximum facility the sink should be in the corner of the "L" with the refrigerator to one side, the stove to the other, and, of course, counter space beside each.

Finally, the U-shaped kitchen, using the traditional and time-tested triangle arrangement, is the most efficient floor plan. The sink is at the bottom of the "U" and the stove and refrigerator opposite each other on the "arms" of the letter.

A cooking island is often the ideal solution to kitchen space problems. It provides extra work and storage areas while utilizing vacant floor space.

Although a kitchen is a workshop where efficiency is of primary importance, there is no reason to overlook the value of a cheerful decor. Ample lighting, a pretty view, polished surfaces, and a restful color scheme actually ward off fatigue by making the hours spent there more pleasant.

THREE WORK CENTERS

As well as her kitchen floor plan, every homemaker's work pattern is different. However, we offer the following arrangement suggestions as guidelines to using the storage-by-use approach. After you've read our suggestions, examine your own way of doing things, then decide where you first use particular items, and where they will be more efficiently stored in your kitchen.

The basis of the storage-by-use plan is the analyzing of kitchen activities in relation to the major appliances — refrigerator, sink, stove — around which each task centers, then storing the utensils needed to perform each task in the area where it will be first used.

A work counter is needed beside each major appliance. A cook needs space to put hot dishes from the oven, space to handle dishes and prepare vegetables to be cooked, and space to place foods as they are removed from the refrigerator. The appliances and their work counters form a logical division of a kitchen into three work centers: the Refrigerator and Preparation Center; the Sink Center; and the Cook and Serve Center.

Since uncooked foods generally are drawn from the refrigerator, studies have revealed that a counter by the refrigerator will accommodate almost three-fourths of a homemaker's food preparation activities. For this reason we named this area the Refrigerator and Preparation Center. All that is needed for baking or cooking is located here where foods are prepared for these operations.

Ideally the refrigerator latch is on the side where the work counter is located, so foods won't have to be carried around the door to the counter. This center should contain small appliances (mixer, blender, automatic can opener), cutting board, and canisters.

To keep small appliances handy, they can be stored at the rear of the counter where they will be ready for use. Since most work is done at the front of a 24-inch work counter, the rear space under overhanging cabinets is usually ideal for this use. When it is not possible to store small appliances on the counter, or if the homemaker feels better when counters can be left completely clear after cleanup, an alternative is to use pullout or swingout shelves in base cabinets for this purpose. Remember that plenty of electrical outlets are needed in this center so that appliances may be quickly and easily used.

The utensils needed for mixing foods for baking should also be stored in the Preparation Center — either in handy drawers or on hooks at the back of the counter. These would include utensils such as, measuring and mixing spoons, egg beater, whisk, cookie and biscuit cutters, knives, pastry blenders, spatula. In the cabinet space above this center, measuring cups and mixing bowls can be stored, as well as herbs, spices and seasonings. Cake, muffin, and pie pans, sifter, rolling pin, cookie sheet, custard cups, and jelly roll pan can handily be stored in the cabinet below this work space.

The sink is most logically located between the preparation counter and the stove because water is needed often at both. At best, the storage drawers for the Refrigerator and Preparation Center will be next to the Sink Center so that certain implements, for example, paring knives, may be reached from either center.

At the Sink Center, a homemaker washes and dries dishes and utensils, washes fruits and vegetables and disposes of garbage. The sink should definitely have counter space on both sides so that dirty dishes may be stacked on one side, the clean ones placed on a drain board on the other. A double sink with a sprayer is an added aid, especially if there is no dishwasher. If there is a dishwasher, it should be right next to the sink. For right-handed persons, it is best located to the left of the sink; vice-versa for left-handed people.

Other necessities in this work center are drawer storage for dishcloths and towels, rubber gloves, vegetable brush, and paring knife; and door storage for detergent, scouring powder, steel wool, and sponges. Either a garbage disposal or a covered garbage can and wastebasket may be located under the sink. Cabinet space for dishes and glasses, strainers, double boiler, saucepans, and colander should also be located near the Sink Center.

The remaining area is the Cook and Serve Center located around or near the stove. We have combined these since most foods go from the oven to a serving counter. Ample counter space on either side of the stove and oven will enable the homemaker to set out serving dishes, plates, and cooking utensils. This counter may be a convenient place to put the toaster, coffee maker, and waffle iron. Salt, pepper, and items used with boiling water (such as instant coffee, tea, rice, spaghetti) could be in nearby cabinets, along with canned goods. Spoons, cooking thermometers, spatula, potato masher, pancake turner and pot holders should be placed either on the wall or in a drawer in this area. Cabinets beneath or beside the stove should be used to store frypans, lids, teakettle, platters, wire racks, and saucepans. It's a good idea to divide pots and pans into those which are frequently used, and those which are used only occasionally, and store them separately. This eliminates needless searching through tall stacks of pans each time a particular utensil is desired.

An eating area should be near the Cook and Serve Center if possible . . . inside the kitchen but outside the work area. The majority of families in this country eat one or more meals each day in the kitchen, and really no kitchen is complete without at least a snack counter. Informal eating areas, in or adjacent to the kitchen, save extra steps at mealtime, are handy for after-school snacks, and can provide extra work surface. Big windows and a perky color scheme can make this eating area pretty and pleasant.

type of cabinets

In the perfect kitchen, a cook will have access to several countertop materials, each suited to particular uses. There should be a chopping board for meat and vegetable cutting, a heatproof counter of tile or stainless steel by the stove, a marble surface for pastry and cleanable, long-wearing surfaces everywhere else (such as formica or laminated plastic counters).

For most women, work counters should be about 36 inches in height for comfort while performing preparation procedures. (To figure this more exactly, deduct about 7 inches from the measure of the distance from your bent elbows to the floor.) Proper counter height can contribute immeasurably to a cook's well-being.

Where counter space is limited, or to cut a large kitchen "down to size," a cooking island is a wonderful solution — with the added advantage of taking the cook's face away from the wall. As well as turning empty floor space into work space, an island may also provide extra storage.

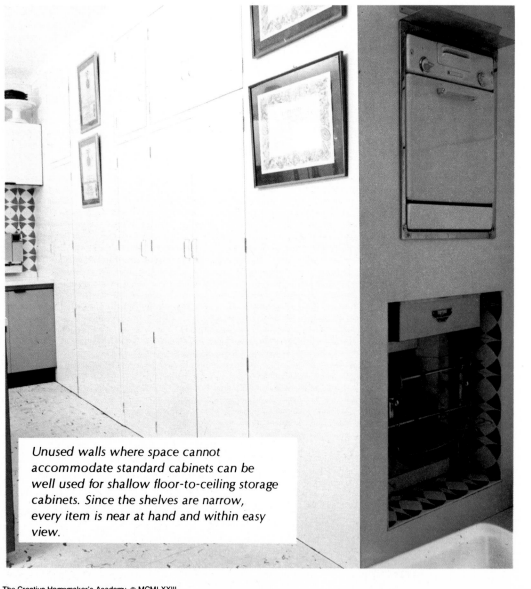

Unused walls where space cannot accommodate standard cabinets can be well used for shallow floor-to-ceiling storage cabinets. Since the shelves are narrow, every item is near at hand and within easy view.

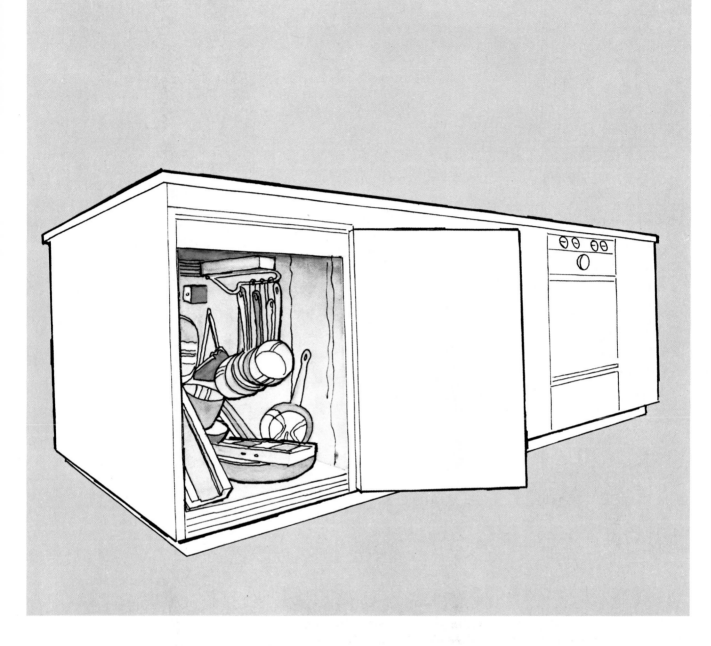

If extra counter space is needed in several areas of the kitchen, but there is no space for it, a small island may be mounted on rollers. Then it can be wheeled about the kitchen to the area where it is needed at the time.

Wall and base cabinets are the two main categories of kitchen storage. The minimum amount of cabinet storage recommended by the Federal Housing Authority for a three bedroom house is 15½ feet (each) of base and wall storage. This estimate refers only to that space that is within arm's reach in height. Things used every day should be stored in lower cabinets; high cabinets should be used only for seasonal storage or infrequently used items. Adjustable shelves are an advantage so that cabinets may from time to time be adapted to changing needs.

To make the fullest use of the cabinet space in your kitchen we suggest the "divide and conquer" approach — that is, divide your storage cabinets to conquer space problems. The easiest and most economical way to accomplish this is with commercial "storage helpers" that are available in department and variety stores. Bins made of rubber-coated metal mounted on wooden rollout trays store vegetables neatly and accessibly. Plastic rollout trays may hold canned goods, or if you prefer, a rotating lazy Susan brings those hard-to-get-at cans from the back of the cabinet into easy grasp. By inserting vertical plastic dividers in the storage shelves, baking pans and sheets may be stored on end, record-style; you can then pull out the desired pan without disturbing any others. Drawer dividers, cup hooks, plate racks, and silverware trays are other organization aids that will shorten work time.

FINISHING TOUCHES

Although there is nothing like the tempting, alluring aroma of an appetizing meal in the making, too frequently that aroma is not the only thing produced in the process! Heat, smoke, odors, and grease are often unwanted by-products. In this day of environmental consciousness, homemakers certainly don't want to "pollute" their homes. The solution is efficient kitchen ventilation. A hood with an exhaust fan should cover the entire width of the cooking area and have proper ducting through the shortest, most direct route to outdoors. For older homes or apartments where installation of a ducted system is impractical, non-ducted range hoods are available. These have either chemically treated filters or an activated charcoal system.

Although facility should not be sacrificed to decorator tricks, there is no reason for an efficient kitchen to be less than a showplace as well. In fact, a well-planned kitchen contributes to faster cleanups and a tidy appearance that will enhance the decorative touches you add! The color scheme should be restful. Orange and red are hot colors that will make the kitchen, which is often full of heat, seem even hotter. Ice blue gives a feeling of chill in the winter. Colors in between on the color spectrum such as green or yellow, are better choices.

Finally, all these suggestions are useless if a kitchen does not have proper lighting. Good lighting is absolutely necessary to assure efficiency and avoid fatigue. You should never have to work in your own shadow. Overhead light to illuminate work paths should be supplemented with spot lighting on work centers. While reducing the possibility of burns and cuts, well-planned lighting will add cheer to the efficient kitchen of a creative homemaker.

oriental cookery

The perfect preparation of oriental cuisine is considered to be an ancient and honorable art. Americans who wish to acquaint themselves with the techniques of oriental cookery will find that the basic philosophy of this elegant cuisine is a reflection of the culture and customs of the Orient, which dates back centuries in time. Each dish must be artfully presented, giving pleasure to the eye, nose and palate.

Becoming adept at cooking oriental food is not difficult if one conscientiously observes a few simple rules. One basic principle of oriental cooking is rapid cooking at high temperatures. Once the cooking is started, it is advisable not to look away from the pot even for a moment since the ingredients may become overcooked in just an instant. Accordingly, the preliminary preparation (which sometimes is very time consuming and involved) of the food to be cooked must be completed before beginning the actual cooking process. In addition, to ensure the characteristic crispness of well-prepared oriental food, careful attention must be paid to the length of cooking time specified in the recipes.

Rice affected by the weather or [spoiled] . . . must not be eaten, nor fish that is not sound, nor meat that is high. He must not eat anything discolored or that smells bad. He must not eat what is overcooked, nor what is undercooked, nor anything that is out of season. He must not eat what has been crookedly cut, nor any dish that lacks its proper seasoning. The meat that he eats must at the very most not be enough to make his breath smell of meat rather than of rice. As regards wine, no limit is laid down; but he must not be disorderly.

— Confucius (Born 551 B.C.)

BASIC KITCHEN EQUIPMENT
FOR ORIENTAL COOKING

During the past several thousand years, oriental chefs have designed and perfected their kitchen equipment, achieving a maximum of efficiency and usefulness. These illustrations are examples of some of the most basic tools, and while oriental cooking can be successfully executed using western-style utensils, some of their oriental counterparts are fairly inexpensive and very useful for cooking a wide variety of foods.

1. Wok. Oriental chefs fry almost exclusively with vegetable oil. It attains the high heat necessary to seal in flavor and nutrients and it preserves the color of the food. The *wok* is the classic "frying pan" used for sautéing, frying and deep frying (including tempura). It is made of metal and is available in various sizes, ranging from 10 inches in diameter to the very large commercial *woks* used in restaurants. A *wok* has a conical shaped bottom and a metal ring is used to hold it firmly in place over the stove burner.

2. Cooking chopsticks do not conduct heat and are used to stir-fry vegetables, meat and fish in a *wok*.

3. Chinese Cleavers are very useful for chopping and slicing food. Some Western chefs feel that the cleaver is far more efficient than even a French chef's knife for performing these tasks.

4. Chopping block. This item is very necessary to use with the cleaver, although a wooden cutting board may be substituted.

5. Strainers. These brass strainers are used for draining deep-fried foods such as tempura. The bamboo handles do not conduct heat.

6. Mongolian firepot. This unusual brass pot has a chimney extending from a brazier on the bottom. Its main function is to keep food hot, though it is sometimes used for cooking.

7. Hibachi. This popular "portable stove" is a cast iron brazier for hot coals, with a grill on top to broil food.

8. Electric rice cooker. Rice, of course, is the main staple of oriental food. An ordinary saucepan with a lid may be used to cook rice but the wonders of modern technology have produced this automatic rice cooker which guarantees "perfect rice every time." It is as indispensable to oriental households as electric coffee pots are to Americans.

9. Soy Sauce or Shoyu. The use of the soybean is very prevalent in oriental cooking. This exceedingly useful vegetable is one of the chief sources of protein in oriental diets. Soybeans are also used to produce cooking oil, soybean milk (an excellent substitute for cow's milk) bean curd (a firm custard-like cheese made from soybean milk) and of course, the ubiquitous *shoyu* or soy sauce, used to season and enhance the flavor of many, many oriental dishes.

The Creative Homemaker's Academy © MCMLXXIII
Selected Illustrations © B.P.C. Publishing Limited MCMLXX

the basics of carving

Since the time of ancient Rome, the art of carving has been of recognized importance. It was practiced by men of high rank who took pride in being appointed official carvers at ceremonious affairs. Throughout history, kings frequently appointed a number of noblemen to be in charge of carving. King Edward IV had four "Carvers-In-Ordinary" and one "Carver-In-Chief."

Even before the use of individual plates, forks, knives and napkins, carving was a very important ritual. The carver held fowl or large joints of meat with his hand and carved slices and presented them to guests on the flat of the knife. The guests took the slices and ate them with their hands.

Today carving is still considered an art which every homemaker takes pride in mastering for many worthwhile reasons. Carving helps set a gracious dining atmosphere and makes the guests feel honored. Properly done, it makes meat servings more attractive and more appetizing.

Proper carving insures more tender meat because slicing correctly across the grain naturally makes the individual servings easier to cut and eat. It also has economical advantages because well-carved meat and poultry yields more servings.

To aid successful carving, use care in selecting meat for the occasion, always considering how it is to be served. It is very easy to find meat that will be easy to carve due to today's modern packing and retailing. Boneless smoked hams, pork loin roasts and standing rib roasts are plentiful and a pleasure to carve.

Make sure you have the proper equipment for carving. Of course the finest steel carving knife is preferred, and well worth the extra cost, as the blade can be honed to razor sharpness. The standard carving set pictured on page 48 includes a curved blade knife from 8 to 9 inches long, a matching fork and a steel for sharpening. These three pieces are well suited to all medium-sized cuts of meat.

Another set, pictured on the same page, is especially desirable for large meat cuts, such as standing rib roasts and whole or half hams. It contains a roast slicer with a long flexible blade especially suited for carving across large surfaces of meat, and a fork or carver's helper with widely spread tines to hold a large piece of meat steady.

For smaller pieces of meat, you may wish to purchase a small 6 or 7 inch, curved edge knife and a fork with narrow tines, both of which are ideal for cutting steaks, chops and poultry.

Always keep carving knives sharpened with a good electric knife sharpener or a roller sharpener. Better yet, have your carving knife ground and sharpened by a professional knife sharpener. To test for proper sharpness, hold a piece of paper with one hand and, using your carving knife, slice through the paper with the other. A sharp knife will cut through the paper like a razor, whereas a dull one will only tear it.

Electric knives have become popular as an aid to perfect carving. The two stainless steel blades in an electric knife are extremely sharp and operate with a fast back and forth action (1800 to 2200 cutting strokes per minute). There is no need to "saw" or use pressure with this appliance. It glides through meat, poultry and other foods with minimal effort.

The blades of an electric knife never need sharpening if given proper care. If, however, they do become dull, return them to the dealer. He will either have them sharpened or replace them for you.

The blades are easily removed for washing, and the attractive plastic handles may be sponged clean as needed.

To insure safety, always disconnect the cord from the electric outlet when the knife is not in use.

After selecting the best meat and carving equipment, be sure to cook the meat properly. Even the best carving equipment will not successfully slice meat that is improperly prepared. If a roast is cooked at too high an oven temperature, its outer crust may be difficult to carve. Or if the meat is overcooked, it will fall apart no matter how sharp the knife.

Meat should be allowed to "repose" after it is removed from the oven in order to "firm up," thus making carving easier. Let a rare rib roast remain loosely covered in an open oven or other warm place for 20 or 30 minutes before carving. For a medium or well-done roast, about 15 minutes is adequate.

Remove strings or skewers just before carving, except those on a rolled boned roast: one or two strings may be left during carving to hold the shape.

When you're ready to carve, place the meat on a large platter, roomy enough to accommodate the roast and the cut slices. Make sure that garnishes, gravy boats and vegetable dishes are well out of the way. It is perfectly acceptable to have a smaller platter nearby to hold meat slices and garnishes if the carving platter is not large enough.

Be comfortable while carving. Stand or sit, but give yourself plenty of elbow room. You may wish to use a small auxiliary table for carving if the dinner table does not allow enough room.

Make sure you anchor the meat firmly with the tines of the fork, then slice across the grain. The short meat fibers will help retain the juices in the meat. For perfect results, follow the step-by-step illustrations on pages 49 and 50.

Make the slices uniform in size and thickness by keeping the knife angle the same with each slice. Carve enough slices for everyone for one serving, arranging them attractively on the platter. Then serve them on warm plates, not forgetting to divide and serve garnishes, vegetables and stuffings.

You will feel much more confident while carving before dinner guests if you practice often at family dinners. Encourage other family members to learn this valuable art also.

PORK LOIN ROAST

1 Before roast is brought to table, remove back bone leaving as little meat on it as possible. Place roast on platter with rib side facing carver so he can see angle of ribs and can make his slices accordingly.

2 Insert fork in top of roast. Make slices by cutting closely along each side of rib bone. One slice will contain the rib; the next will be boneless.

SHANK HALF OF HAM

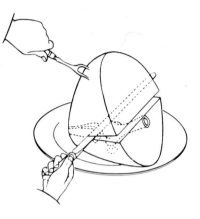

1 With shank at carver's left, turn ham so thick cushion side is up. Cut along top of leg and shank bones and under fork to lift off boneless cushion.

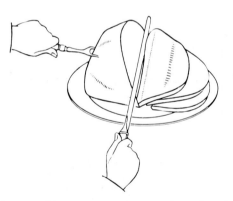

2 Place cushion meat on carving board and make perpendicular slices as illustrated.

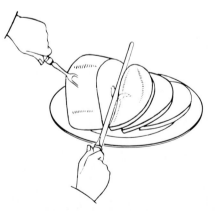

3 Cut around leg bone with tip of knife to remove meat from this bone. Turn meat so that thickest side is down. Slice in same manner as cushion piece.

The standard set includes a knife with a curved blade from 8 to 9 inches long, a matching fork and a steel. This set is especially desirable for medium-sized pieces of meat, but it may be used for other cuts when necessary.

WHOLE HAM

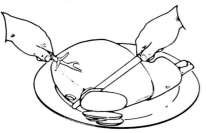

1 Ham is placed on platter with decorated or fat side up and shank to carver's right. Location of bones in right and left hams may be confusing so double check location of knee cap which may be on near or far side of ham. Remove two or three lengthwise slices from thin side of ham which contains knee cap.

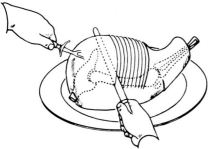

2 Make perpendicular slices down to leg bone or lift off boneless cushion similar to method illustrated for picnic shoulder.

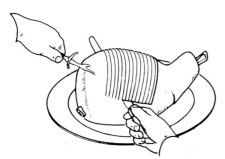

3 Release slices by cutting along leg bone.

BEEF STANDING RIB ROAST

1 When necessary, remove wedge-shaped slice from large end so roast will stand firmly on this end. Insert fork below top rib. Carve across "face" of roast to rib bone.

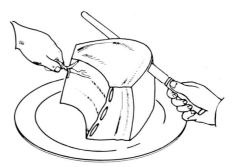

2 Cut along rib bone with tip of knife to release slice.

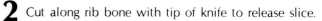

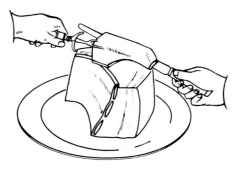

3 Slide knife back under slice and, steadying it with fork, lift slice to side of platter or auxiliary platter.

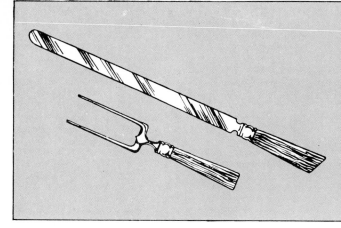

The roast slicer and carver's helper work well together, but they are seldom sold as a set. They come in various sizes and shapes and are designed for use with standing rib roasts, whole or half hams and other large cuts of meat. A good roast slicer has a long flexible blade especially suited for carving across large surfaces of meat. The blade should be a minimum of 11 inches in length. The widely spread tines in the carver's helper will help to hold a large roast steady.

LAMB LEG ROAST

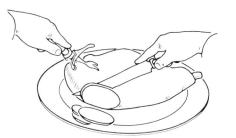

1 With lower leg bone to right, remove two or three lengthwise slices from thin side of leg. This side has the knee cap.

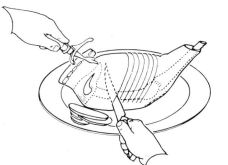

2 Turn roast up on its base and, starting where shank joins the leg, make slices perpendicular to leg bone or lift off cushion similar to method shown for picnic shoulder.

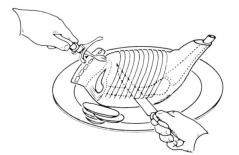

3 Loosen slices by cutting under them, following closely along top of leg bone. Lift slices to platter for serving.

BEEF BLADE POT ROAST

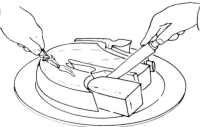

1 Cut between muscles and around bones to remove one solid section of pot-roast at a time.

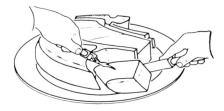

2 Turn section just removed so meat fibers are parallel to platter. This makes it possible to carve across grain of meat.

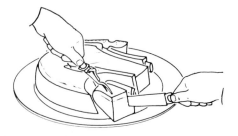

3 Holding meat with fork, carve slices about ¼ inch thick.

The Creative Homemaker's Academy © MCMLXXIII
Selected Illustrations © B.P.C. Publishing Limited MCMLXX

appetizers & soups

table of contents

basic stock for soups

It's important that you learn stock making because you'll be relying on this skill not only in this soups lesson, but in later ones, and in making salads and sauces as well. You'll make basic simple aspic in the salads section and basic velouté sauce in the sauces section—both of which use stock.

Stock is a rich liquid obtained by slowly simmering meat bones, scraps, seasonings and often vegetables in water, then skimming off the fat and straining the liquid. In this lesson we will make beef stock and chicken stock.

In the stock making process every last bit of savory flavor and the valuable vitamins and minerals are extracted from the beef and chicken leaving a full-bodied, nutritious liquid. Strength, thickness and body are added by a gelatinous substance the meat bones contain. Both beef and chicken stocks are used as a base for soups, stews, sauces, gravies, aspics, and many vegetable dishes.

It is very easy to make a good stock: basic equipment and ingredients are used, and while cooking, the stock requires very little attention. The only equipment required is a large, heavy pot, kettle or Dutch oven; a large spoon or ladle for skimming fat as the stock simmers; a baster (a long, narrow, transparent tube with a rubber bulb at the end) for skimming fat when the stock is done; and a fine-meshed metal sieve to strain the finished stock. Avoid using a cooking pot made of aluminum—it may adversely affect the clearness of your stock.

In making stock it's best to use *uncooked* beef or poultry trimmings and bones. They provide more flavor and nourishment than cooked meat. The meat may be either fresh or frozen. You could save beef scraps, bones and chicken parts in your freezer until you have enough to make stock. Before making beef stock, brown the meat in a very hot oven to add flavor. Chicken pieces should be chopped finely.

You'll want to use at least as much meat as bones. With too many bones the stock may become "gluey"—good only as a base for thick sauces and gravies. Finally, don't try mixing leftover cooked meat and bones with uncooked. It clouds the stock.

For seasoning, we suggest a *bouquet garni* (BOO kay GAHR nee) consisting of several complementary, preferably fresh, herbs—usually parsley stalks with leaves, sprigs of thyme and bay leaves, with an optional sprig of marjoram. Don't use powdered herbs—they cloud the stock. Tie them together with string or put them into a small cheesecloth bag for easy handling. For extra flavor in our basic beef stock, we'll add a large onion stuck with 10 cloves. Many beef and chicken stocks are made with the addition of vegetables. If you later decide to experiment with vegetables, remember *not* to use starchy root vegetables such as potatoes—they may sour the stock or cloud the liquid—and they don't freeze well. Also, some vegetables are too strongly flavored to be used in stock: for example; turnips, cauliflower and cabbage.

The procedures for making both beef and chicken stocks are similar. Place the beef or chicken meat and bones and the seasonings in your stock pot. Cover the ingredients completely with *cold* water. It helps draw out the flavor, vitamins and minerals. Slowly bring the mixture to a boil over medium heat. A heavy scum will form on top. Skim off the scum with a large spoon or ladle. By now the liquid in the pot will have reduced. With the liquid still at the boiling point, again add enough cold water to cover the ingredients in the pot. Reduce the heat, and from this point on do not allow the stock to return to a boil. Reboiling will cause fat particles to be incorporated into the stock, producing a cloudy liquid. Just let the stock simmer for several hours with a slight bubble over steady, low heat.

During the process you may find it necessary to skim the stock occasionally with a spoon or ladle to remove fat, or to add boiling water to keep the ingredients covered. Keep the stock pot *partially covered* during simmering time. An airtight cover may cause the ingredients to boil; no covering at all will cause rapid evaporation.

The last two steps are skimming and straining. An effective method of removing fat from stock is to chill it in the refrigerator. The fat will accumulate on the top and become firm, at which time it is easily removed. When you are in a rush, simply use a baster to draw off the fat from the top of the stock. To remove any remaining fat particles, glide an absorbent piece of paper towel across the surface. Finally, strain the stock through a fine-meshed metal sieve, and it will be ready for use.

If you want to store the stock for a few days or perhaps several weeks, it can be refrigerated or frozen. First make sure the stock is thoroughly cool. Then, for refrigeration, pour it into a jar (or jars, depending on quantity) and seal tightly. For freezer storage, place the stock in airtight pint or quart containers that will hold up under freezing; seal. If you do refrigerate before using the stock, you can skip the skimming step with the baster. When chilled, the fat will rise to the surface, forming a solid protective coating for the liquid underneath. You won't have to remove the firm fat layer until you're ready to reheat and use. Before using refrigerated or frozen stock, it should be heated to the boiling point.

CLARIFYING STOCK

To clarify four to six cups stock pull away inner skins from 2 eggshells; wash the eggshells and crush into 4 to 6 cups hot stock. Add 2 egg whites. Beat with rotary beater, over moderate heat, for about 4 minutes or until thick foam forms on top. Foam must be thick and high. Remove beater and bring mixture to a boil without stirring. Reduce heat to low and simmer for 10 minutes. Remove from heat and let stand for 3 minutes. Place a piece of wet muslin in large sieve. Pour the stock mixture slowly and steadily through the muslin, letting drain well. This procedure makes your stock sparkling clear for use in those special aspics. Clarification is not a substitute for skimming, but an optional addition to it.

The Creative Homemaker's Academy © MCMLXXIII
Selected Illustrations © B.P.C. Publishing Limited MCMLXX

BASIC CHICKEN STOCK

1 4-lb. hen
1 lb. chicken wings
2 tbsp. salt
4 peppercorns
5 qt. water
½ bay leaf
Pinch of thyme
6 green onions with tops
4 lg. carrots, quartered
2 stalks celery with leaves, cut in 2-in. pieces
1 lg. onion, studded with 3 cloves

Place the chicken, salt, peppercorns and water in a stock pot. Bring to a boil over medium heat, removing scum from the surface. Cover the pot and reduce the heat. Simmer for 1 hour, skimming frequently. Add remaining ingredients; cover and cook for about 2 hours and 30 minutes. Skim off fat; season to taste with additional salt and pepper. Remove chicken and vegetables from stock. Strain stock through wet muslin. Chill and remove fat before using.

BASIC BEEF STOCK

3 lb. beef brisket
2 lb. med. soupbones
5 qt. water
4 green onions and tops
1 lg. onion, studded with 10 cloves
1 celery stalk and leaves
1 Bouquet Garni (opt.)
2 tbsp. salt

Place beef and bones in large baking pan. Bake at 400 degrees for about 1 hour or until well-browned on both sides. Remove from pan and place in a large stock pot. Drain off fat from baking pan; add 1 cup water to pan and scrape up brown bits from bottom. Pour into stock pot. Add remaining water and remaining ingredients except salt. Bring slowly to a boil, removing scum as it accumulates on surface. Cover and simmer for 1 hour. Add the salt. Simmer for 3 hours longer. Remove meat and vegetables. Strain through wet muslin. Chill and remove fat before using.

BOUQUET GARNI

1 parsley stalk
1 bay leaf
2 sprigs of thyme
1 sprig of marjoram (opt.)

Combine all ingredients in a small piece of muslin or a double thickness of cheesecloth; tie securely with string.

CLEAR TOMATO SOUP

1 lb. very ripe tomatoes
3 pt. Basic Chicken Stock *(Soups, pg. 2)*
1 tsp. dried basil
1 tsp. salt
⅛ tsp. white pepper

Cut the tomatoes in large chunks; place in small saucepan. Add ½ cup stock and the basil. Simmer for 20 minutes. Force the tomato mixture through a sieve into a bowl. Let set for several minutes. Pour the remaining stock in a medium saucepan; add all the tomato mixture except the sediment in the bottom of the bowl. Add salt and pepper. Simmer until soup is reduced to about 2 pints. Float a basil leaf on top if available.

SPECIAL ONION SOUP

2 lb. onions, peeled and sliced
¼ c. cooking oil
3 tbsp. butter
4 med. tomatoes, peeled and cut in eighths
¼ c. flour
1 tsp. dry mustard
1 tsp. salt
⅛ tsp. white pepper
½ c. sauterne
5 c. Basic Beef Stock *(Soups, pg. 2)*
2 eggs
¼ c. port

Prepare as shown in our step-by-step illustrations on the following page.

preparation of special onion soup

1 In a frying pan or skillet, fry the peeled, sliced onions with the given oil and butter. Cook over low heat for about 15 minutes or until the onions are almost tender.

2 Just before the onions are completely tender, add the prepared tomatoes. The tomatoes take only a fraction of the cooking time needed for the onions (3 to 5 minutes to heat through).

3 Add the flour, mustard and a light seasoning of salt and white pepper.

4 Now add the sauterne and slightly increase the heat. Stir the mixture until the sauterne is absorbed and the mixture becomes thick and smooth.

5 Add 1 cup of stock gradually, stirring constantly. Transfer the mixture into a large saucepan, scraping the frying pan or skillet.

6 Now add the remaining beef stock to the mixture in the saucepan. Stir over medium heat until completely blended. Then simmer for 30 minutes.

7 Using a wire whisk, whip the whole eggs with the port in your chosen serving dish—we are using a soup tureen. Our picture shows how to hold a wire whisk to obtain maximum strength for whipping.

8 Finally, pour the contents of the saucepan into your serving dish, whipping it into the egg and port mixture as you pour. We have to admit here that our student cook called in an extra helper to hold the pan so that she'd be free to whip!

appetizing canapés

The only trouble with appetizers is trying to list the many different kinds and then neatly categorizing them — canapés, hors d'oeuvres and cocktails.

A list of possible appetizers would be almost unlimited and any kind of categorization would be, at best, immaterial to our purposes and your needs. What we want to do is to show you how to prepare all kinds of appetizers creatively and to serve them artfully. We believe that's what you're interested in accomplishing, too.

The term "appetizers" includes any kind of easily handled food or snack served in small portions. They are commonly offered before main meals to excite — not satisfy — the appetite, and at parties and receptions.

Fruit juices, seafood cocktails and first-course soups can be appetizers, the same as open-faced sandwiches, bite-sized kabobs, crackers with spreads, dips, relishes and salted nuts. Practically the only requirements of appetizers are attractive appearance and inviting flavor.

The choice of appetizers to preface a main meal should partially depend on the food to follow. Choose appetizers that complement rather than compete with your main dishes.

Try not to repeat the same ingredients in hors d'oeuvres and main meals. If your salad is tomato aspic, don't serve tomato juice beforehand.

If the meal is large and filling, select light appetizers; serve more substantial ones before less hearty dinners.

There will be many recipes for creative appetizers in future lessons. We begin our adventure with our easy-to-prepare Stuffed Olive Canapés.

STUFFED OLIVE CANAPÉS

1 loaf sliced bread
Butter
5 oz. cream cheese, softened
1/8 tsp. freshly ground pepper
1/4 tsp. celery salt
1/4 tsp. lemon juice
1/2 tsp. half and half cream
1 bunch parsley
1 can pitted black olives, drained
1 sm. bottle pitted green olives

Preheat broiler. Dip a 1½-inch fluted, cookie cutter in water and cut 24 rounds from bread slices. Wet the cutter several times as you are cutting the bread. Spread both sides of each bread round with butter. Place rounds on a large baking sheet. Broil on each side until lightly browned. Reduce oven temperature to 225 degrees. Bake the rounds until they are crisp and dry croutons. Blend the cream cheese with a fork until fluffy. Stir in pepper, celery salt, lemon juice and half and half until smooth. Stir in additional half and half if cream cheese mixture is too stiff for easy spreading. Remove stems from the parsley, then chop the leaves finely. Spread 1 side of each crouton with cream cheese mixture. Spoon remaining cream cheese mixture into pastry bag fitted with a medium-sized star tube. Pipe a small dot of cream cheese mixture in the center of each crouton. Place olives securely in the cream cheese mixture. Pipe a rosette into and on top of each olive. Cut remaining olives into petal shapes, then insert them into stuffed olives. Sprinkle parsley thickly onto each crouton base as shown in the illustration. These may be chilled for a short time until ready to serve. Too long a period of refrigeration will cause croutons to become soggy.

stuffed olive canapés

Stuffed Olive Canapés are among those much appreciated appetizers that can be partially made in advance and assembled when ready for serving. Canapés are most attractive when they are uniform in appearance. To achieve this, we suggest using the assembly line method of preparation, completing one step at a time on all canapés before proceeding to the next step.

liptauer cheese

This recipe for Liptauer Cheese attractively combines cream cheese, butter and flavorings. We've found it to be immensely popular among guests because it has excellent flavor. Cooks like it because it is easy to make and simple to serve.

Liptauer Cheese is an appetizer *dip*, a soft, smooth and creamy mixture to be scooped up on crackers, potato chips, pretzels, bread or raw vegetable slices. You can make Liptauer Cheese ahead of time and store it in the refrigerator until ready to serve. Just be sure to take it out of the refrigerator and let it stand at room temperature for about 45 minutes before serving. Refrigeration hardens Liptauer Cheese, and this period allows it to soften to dipping consistency.

Don't throw away Liptauer Cheese left over from a party. It can be spread on crackers or biscuits and, if desired, softened for an emergency canapé or fast snack.

liptauer cheese

We shaped our Liptauer Cheese into a neat rectangle and roughed swirls into it with a fork. Then we added an attractive border garnish of pretzels — you may substitute rye bread triangles.

LIPTAUER CHEESE

½ c. salted butter, softened
4 oz. cream cheese, softened
1 tsp. (heaping) caraway seeds
1 tsp. pickled capers, drained
1 tsp. (heaping) Dijon mustard
1¼ tsp. paprika
1 boned anchovy fillet
Pretzels

Cream the butter in a small mixing bowl with an electric mixer until light and fluffy. Add the cream cheese and continue beating until smoothly blended. Chop caraway seeds in blender, then add to butter mixture. Chop the capers finely and add to mixture. Add the mustard and paprika. Rinse, dry and chop the anchovy, then stir into the cheese mixture and blend well. Shape into a neat rectangle on serving plate and border with pretzels. Serve with additional pretzels or crackers.

cheese mousse

A *mousse* (which, by the way, is pronounced MOOSE rather than MOUSE and means "frothy" or "foamy" in French) is a rich, sweet or savory mold commonly made from a whipped cream mixture, often containing gelatin. The whipped cream contributes to its light, fluffy texture, while the gelatin allows it to retain a firm and stable shape. The savory Cheese Mousse given here calls for gelatin, so you might want to review the section on Working with Gelatin (Salads, pgs. 1-2) before trying your hand at this recipe.

Our Cheese Mousse, which should be served chilled, makes an elegant and refreshing appetizer. If you choose to serve it with bread rounds or crackers, be sure to supply a small spreading knife. In our picture we've teamed the Cheese Mousse with pretzels, using them not only as a side dish, but also as an attractive top and side garnish.

With its very distinctive taste, this Cheese Mousse always makes a conversation dish. We think you will find it excitingly different.

CHEESE MOUSSE

3/4 c. milk
2 med. eggs, separated
5 oz. Parmesan cheese, finely grated
1/3 c. cottage cheese
Grated rind and juice of 1 med. lemon
1/2 c. whipping cream, stiffly beaten
1 env. unflavored gelatin
1/3 c. water
1/4 tsp. salt
1/8 tsp. white pepper
Generous dash of nutmeg
Dash of paprika
2 drops of hot sauce

Heat milk to lukewarm. Blend egg yolks slightly in mixing bowl with electric mixer. Pour milk gradually into yolks, beating at low speed until blended. Stir in Parmesan and cottage cheeses, blending well. Stir in lemon juice and rind. Fold whipped cream into egg yolk mixture. Soften gelatin in water; dissolve over low heat. Pour into cream mixture gradually, stirring until blended. Beat egg whites until stiff, then fold into gelatin mixture. Add seasonings. Turn into oiled, 1-quart ring mold. Chill until set. Unmold on platter. Serve with crackers or pretzels.

cheese mousse

This light, fluffy Cheese Mousse is a star attraction wherever it is served. We garnished the top with stem pretzels and accompanied it with another dish of pretzels. It is also good with bread rounds or any of the vast array of crackers now available at the supermarkets.

SANDWICH KEBABS

2 loaves thin-sliced sandwich bread
Softened butter
Basic Blender Mayonnaise *(Sauces, pg. 3)*
Smoked salmon slices
Salami
Dijon mustard
Braunschweiger (Liver Sausage)
Large stuffed Spanish olives, sliced
Fresh parsley sprigs

Cut bread into rounds using a wet 2-inch plain or fluted cutter. Butter all the rounds on one side, then spread thinly with mayonnaise. Arrange a slice of salmon over buttered side of 1 round and spread with mayonnaise. Place second bread round on top of salmon, buttered-side up. Trim salami to fit the bread round. Place on the round and spread with mustard. Top with third bread round. Spread on braunschweiger. Spread with mustard. Top with another bread round and arrange olive slices on round. Top with last bread slice, buttered side down. Insert bamboo skewer in center of the sandwich kebabs to hold securely. Garnish with parsley sprigs. Repeat until all ingredients are used. Thinly sliced breast of chicken, turkey, tongue and ham may be used in kebabs. Four-tier kebabs may be made and secured with wooden picks. Cover with a damp cloth if made ahead of serving time.

sandwich kebabs

Alternating bread and meat slices skewered on wooden cocktail picks and garnished with parsley. Sandwiches can be made in advance of serving and wrapped in a slightly dampened kitchen towel to preserve freshness and moisture.

hot cheese canapés

Appetizers, as mentioned on page 5, should excite, not satisfy, the appetite. Most hostesses serve them shortly before a meal as a preview of good food to come.

Although all good tasting appetizers are a welcome sight to guests, hot appetizers seem to have a special appeal and win many compliments. Many of them, including the Hot Cheese *Canapés* that are presented in this section, can be prepared in advance, stored in the refrigerator, and baked immediately before serving. Such an advantage enables the hostess to spend less time in the kitchen and more time with the guests.

hot cheese canapés

These Hot Cheese Canapés are ready to be served as a tempting appetizer. Emmenthal cheese has been melted inside crisp puff pastry to create an irresistible delicacy.

HOT CHEESE CANAPÉS

¼ c. dry English mustard
½ **recipe Basic Puff Pastry** *(Desserts, pg. 22)*
Swiss cheese, very thinly sliced
1 egg
Salt and pepper to taste

Mix mustard with small amount of cold water to make a smooth paste. Cut cheese into 3 x ½-inch strips. Beat egg and season with salt and pepper. Roll out pastry, the final or 6th rolling, on a well-floured board until thin; cut into 4 x 3-inch rectangles. Brush the mustard on 4-inch side of each pastry rectangle and place 1 piece of cheese over mustard. Brush all edges with cold water and roll as for jelly roll. Place on a lightly floured baking sheet; brush tops with egg. Bake in preheated 375-degree oven for about 20 minutes or until cheese is melted and *canapés* are golden brown. Serve immediately. This will make about 3½ dozen.

potted herb cheese

POTTED HERB CHEESE

3 c. grated Cheddar cheese
1 tbsp. whipping cream
2 tbsp. sherry
6 tbsp. butter
1 tsp. chopped chives
1 tsp. tarragon leaves
1 tsp. sage
1 tsp. thyme

1 tsp. parsley flakes
Basic Clarified Butter *(Sauces, pg. 13)*

Place all the ingredients except clarified butter in the top of a double boiler over hot water. Stir over medium heat until the cheese and butter melt and the mixture is thoroughly blended. Pour into pint jar; chill until cold. Cover with a 1/4-inch deep layer of clarified butter. Cover and store in refrigerator. Let come to room temperature and serve with fingers of hot buttered toast or tiny, hot biscuits.

potted herb cheese

Potted Herb Cheese, an old English recipe, is packed in glass jars with well-fitting lids. Glass canisters, crockery or mason jars are also suitable containers. Here the cheese jars are placed inside black wedge-wood dishes and surrounded with crustless sticks of hot toast.

bleu cheese

Cheese has a zesty flavor that most of us find desirable in a variety of dishes — from meats and vegetables to scrumptious desserts. In this section, we introduce to you some very unusual ways to serve cheese as an appetizer.

Bleu cheese has a particularly tangy flavor that perks up the appetites of your guests. (If you are confused about the spelling of "bleu," it is simply the French spelling for blue. You will find both spellings of this cheese in supermarkets. Both indicate the same product.)

Bleu cheese is soft-crumbly, sharp-flavored and veined with a greenish-blue color. This comes from a blue mold formed during fermentation. Because of the similarity between the appearance and taste of bleu cheese and Roquefort cheese, many people are under the impression that they are the same. However, French law requires that only the cheese made from ewe's milk (the milk of a mature female sheep during the lambing season) in the Roquefort area of France be labeled Roquefort Cheese. Bleu cheese, on the other hand, is made in many countries including the United States and, although it is similar in flavor to Roquefort, it is made from cow's milk.

CREAMED BLEU CHEESE

6 oz. bleu cheese, crumbled
¾ c. butter
⅛ tsp. white pepper
Ground pistachio nuts

Cream the bleu cheese until light and smooth. Cream the butter in a separate bowl until fluffy. Combine the cheese and butter and blend well. Add the pepper, mixing thoroughly. Line a small decorative mold with about 3 thicknesses of cheesecloth, leaving enough over the rim to bring over the top. Press the cheese mixture firmly into the mold, then bring the corners of the cheesecloth up over the top. Store in refrigerator overnight. Grasp the corners of the cheesecloth and lift the cheese mixture out of the mold. Remove the cheesecloth and turn into a serving dish. Sprinkle pistachio nuts thickly over the top. Let set at room temperature to soften. Serve with fresh celery sticks, cauliflowerets or assorted crackers.

creamed bleu cheese

This delicious Creamed Bleu Cheese was set in a small jelly mold. To make sure the molding container will yield a perfect mold, line it with cheesecloth to prevent sticking hazards. Milled or finely chopped pistachio nuts sprinkled over the top give the cheese an added flavor appeal.

yogurt cocktails

Yogurt has become a very popular dairy food in the United States only in recent years. However, centuries ago people in other countries, while trying to find a way to preserve milk, discovered if they clabbered and fermented it, the resulting yogurt lasted much longer. Yogurt can be made from cow's milk, ewe's milk, goat's milk and camel's milk, although dairy producers in the United States make it from cow's milk only.

Yogurt became well known in the United States a few years ago as a popular health food because it contains the same nutrients as milk with less fat calories. A glass of milk has 170 calories while an equal amount of yogurt has only 125. But plain yogurt did not receive the popularity of fruit yogurt. By adding strawberry preserves and other fruit to yogurt, dairy producers found a greater market for this low-calorie dairy product. Americans now consume over a million cups a year.

yogurt cocktails

These creamy Yogurt Cocktails topped with peach slices, whipped cream and cherries are ready to be served as appetizers, dessert or even as a light meal. The combined fruit flavors of grapes, pears, peaches and pineapple along with creamy yogurt make this dish a refreshing delight.

Yogurt has such a refreshing taste and may be served in a variety of ways. Dieters frequently make yogurt a complete meal. Some prefer it as a light dessert or as a between-meal snack. Others think that yogurt cocktails make excellent appetizers and, in this section, we offer you an excellent recipe for yogurt cocktails. Bits of juicy fruit, creamy yogurt and a few hints on decorative design will help to create a delicious appetizer.

YOGURT COCKTAILS

1 med. can sliced peaches
1 c. quartered seedless grapes
2 8-oz. cartons yogurt
2 peeled sliced pears
1 sm. can pineapple chunks
½ c. cream, whipped (opt)
4 maraschino cherries

Reserve 8 peach slices for decoration. Place a layer of grapes in 4 parfait glasses. Cover with a layer of yogurt, then add layers of pears, peaches and pineapple alternately with yogurt until the last layer of yogurt comes within ¾ inch of the top of each glass. Pipe a spiral of whipped cream over the yogurt in each glass, then top with a cherry. Push 2 reserved peach slices onto each glass. Fruits may be layered in sherbet glasses, if desired.

pickled eggs

The process of pickling in this country dates back to the colonial days. Early settlers were forced to find ways of preserving food in abundant times to last through periods when food was not so plentiful. Early American homes were equipped with kettles, stone and earthen jars, pickle dishes and an abundance of other utensils needed for pickling. Now however, pickling is no longer just a way to preserve food — modern cooks often spend hours pickling and preserving because the finished products are so delectable.

There is such a demand for the sweet and sour flavors of pickled foods that modern food stores are well stocked with herbs, spices, seeds and other seasonings needed for making pickles and relishes. Many unusual foods find their way into pickle jars — tiny ears of corn, pods of okra, cauliflower, Brussels sprouts — and the results are almost invariably a hit.

Pickled eggs are popular favorites in British pubs, having been enjoyed for centuries. The recipe on this page is exceptionally simple — and it doesn't take hours! In fact, it only takes moments of your time to create these delicacies. Try serving them at your next party, and notice how many people ask for your "secret."

PICKLED EGGS

Place as many eggs as you wish to pickle in a heavy saucepan and cover with water. Salt the water heavily. This will make the shells easy to remove. Bring to a boil over medium heat. Reduce heat to maintain a slow boil and cook the eggs for 15 minutes. Remove from heat and cool under cold running water. Remove shells and place eggs in pickling jar. Add water to cover 1 to 2 inches above eggs. Remove eggs carefully and let dry on paper toweling. Measure water from jar in order to replace the same amount with a mixture of 3/4 red wine vinegar and 1/4 water. Place vinegar mixture in a saucepan. For each quart of vinegar mixture, 1 small dried red pepper, 1 clove of garlic, 4 peppercorns, 2 whole cloves and a 1-inch piece of gingerroot, quartered. Bring to a boil. Reduce heat and simmer for 5 minutes. Let cool to room temperature. Place eggs in pickling jar. Pour vinegar mixture over eggs and cover tightly. Let stand for at least 1 week. The eggs, as they pickle, will produce a strong odor. Open everyday during first week to let fumes escape. After a week or so this odor will disappear and they will have a most delectable pickled aroma.

pickled eggs

The unusual flavor combination of these pickled eggs makes them a favorite for picnics and patio parties.

choux pastry canapés

CHEESE CHOUX PASTRY PUFFS

1 c. water
½ c. butter
1 c. sifted all-purpose flour
⅛ tsp. salt
2 generous pinches of nutmeg
2 generous pinches of pepper
½ c. freshly grated Parmesan cheese

Combine water and butter in heavy saucepan and place over medium heat. Cook until butter is melted and water comes to a boil. Combine flour, salt, nutmeg and pepper. Stir vigorously into butter mixture with a wooden spoon until dough is smooth and leaves side of pan, forming a ball. Remove from heat and add eggs, one at a time, stirring after each addition until well mixed. Add cheese and beat until smooth. Cover lightly and cool to room temperature. Spoon dough into icing bag with No. 6 piping tube affixed. Pipe into 1½-inch puffs onto lightly greased baking sheet, holding bag in an upright position. Bake in preheated 450-degree oven on shelf above center for 8 minutes. Reduce oven temperature to 350 degrees and bake for 20 minutes longer or until dry and browned. Remove from baking sheet immediately and let cool on racks. Fill as desired. You may use an electric mixer to beat in eggs, if desired. This makes about 4 dozen puffs.

DAUPHINE POTATOES

½ recipe Cheese Choux Pastry Puffs mixture
1 recipe Basic Duchess Potato Mixture, chilled (Vegetables, pg. 3)
Sifted all-purpose flour
1 egg, beaten
Fine bread crumbs
Vegetable oil

Stir pastry mixture and potato mixture together until well combined. Cover with plastic wrap and refrigerate until thoroughly chilled. Shape into 1½-inch balls and place on a baking sheet, then return to the refrigerator until cold. Roll balls in flour; dip in egg, then coat with bread crumbs and place on baking sheet. Chill until ready to cook. Fry about 8 balls at a time in deep hot oil until well browned on all sides and cooked through. Keep hot until ready to serve.

ROQUEFORT CANAPÉS

½ c. butter, softened
1 4-oz. package Roquefort cheese
2 tbsp. port
⅛ tsp. white pepper
24 Cheese Choux Pastry Puffs
Sliced blanched almonds

Place the butter in a small mixer bowl and crumble the cheese into the bowl. Add the port and pepper; beat with electric mixer until smooth and fluffy. Spoon filling into icing bag with No. 62 tube affixed. Remove tops from cheese puffs and pipe in filling petal fashion, as shown in our illustration. Arrange 3 or 4 almond slices in filling.

The Creative Homemaker's Academy © MCMLXXIII
Selected Illustrations © B.P.C. Publishing Limited MCMLXX

miniature savory bouchées

The French term *"vol-au-vent"* literally means "flying with the wind" or "light as wind," both of which are very appropriate for this puff pastry shell. Its texture is delicately light and hollow.

Smaller forms of *vol-au-vents* are called *bouchées* or *petits bouchées*. There are step-by-step illustrations for making *bouchées* in Desserts, page 66.

Although the word "pastry" ordinarily suggests desserts, we would like to stress that these delicious patties, which contain no sugar, make excellent appetizers when filled with bits of fish, meat, poultry, rich sauces or other savory delights. These *bouchées* take much care and patience in making, so it is best to make them a day ahead and store them in an airtight container. Then they may be heated and filled before serving. The filling we use is a rich, delectable combination of chicken, white wine, cream, olives and mushrooms. Compliments are sure to abound anytime these are served.

miniature savory bouchées

Bite-sized bouchées have been stuffed with a savory chicken mixture and topped with diced vegetables and a slice of stuffed olive.

MINIATURE SAVORY BOUCHÉES

1 recipe Basic Puff Pastry (Desserts, pg. 22)
3 tbsp. butter
3 tbsp. all-purpose flour
1/3 c. Chablis
1/3 c. milk
1/3 c. half and half cream
1 c. chopped white chicken
1 3-oz. can chopped mushrooms, drained
1/4 tsp. salt
Dash of white pepper
2 tbsp. cooked green peas
Sliced stuffed green olives

Roll out and assemble pastry according to the step-by-step illustrations for *vol-au-vents* and *bouchées* (Desserts, pgs. 65 and 66), using a 2¼-inch cutter for bases and rings and a 1½-inch cutter for centers. Bake in preheated 425-degree oven for 10 minutes. Reduce oven temperature to 350 degrees and bake for about 17 minutes longer or until golden brown. Remove to cooling racks and cool for about 5 minutes. Cut around inside circle with tip of a sharp knife and remove tops, then centers. Melt the butter in a saucepan and stir in the flour until smooth. Stir in the Chablis and cook, stirring, until slightly thickened. Stir in the milk and half and half cream and cook until thick, stirring constantly. Add the chicken and mushrooms and heat through. Spoon into *bouchées* and garnish with peas and olive slices. May use diced, cooked carrots and diced, cooked green beans for garnish, if desired. Serve immediately.

tomato coulis soup

Two bowls of steaming homemade soup are attractively presented with baked strips of fluted puff pastry (Desserts, pg. 22) — a delightful combination. The soup is made with Tomato Coulis Sauce (Sauces, pg. 14).

TOMATO COULIS SOUP

1 recipe Tomato Coulis Sauce *(Sauces, pg. 14)*
3 10½-oz. cans beef broth
1 tsp. paprika
1 tsp. dried basil leaves (opt.)

Combine all ingredients in a heavy saucepan. Bring just to a boil, stirring occasionally. This may be served with croutons *(Breads, pg. 16)* or puff pastry strips. This makes about six 1-cup servings.

greek lemon soup

This is a highly favored Greek regional soup called Avgolémono. The tangy flavor of lemons transforms chicken stock into a delicate and unusual soup. The appealing garnish is croutons and slivers of boiled egg whites. Serve this beautiful soup for a special luncheon.

GREEK LEMON SOUP

2 qt. Basic Chicken Stock *(Soups, pg. 2)*
⅓ c. long grain rice, rinsed
3 eggs, separated
2 tbsp. lemon juice

Pour the stock into a 4-quart saucepan and bring to a boil. Reduce heat and simmer for 5 to 10 minutes. Add the rice and cook for 15 to 20 minutes or until rice is tender. Remove from heat and cool slightly. Beat the egg yolks until thick and lemon colored, then add the egg whites. Beat until foamy, adding the lemon juice slowly and beating constantly. Pour ½ cup of the broth into the egg mixture very slowly, beating constantly to keep foamy, then beat in 1½ cups broth gradually. Pour the egg mixture slowly into the remaining broth in saucepan, stirring constantly. Reheat slowly but do not boil. Serve immediately. This makes about 6 servings.

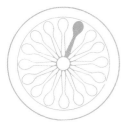

italian vegetable fondue

Italian Vegetable Fondue is a famous specialty of the Piedmont region of Italy. In its native land, it is called *bagna cauda*, which means "hot bath". The "hot bath" is olive oil and butter seasoned with garlic, anchovies and truffles. Since truffles are difficult to obtain in the United States and are quite expensive, the recipe we use does not include them.

Traditionally this Italian fondue is prepared at the table in an earthenware crock and served as an antipasto — literally, "before the pasta". Antipasto is the equivalent of *hors d'oeuvre* or appetizer. A variety of vegetables such as carrots, celery, finocchio, tomatoes, radishes and cardoons (an Italian vegetable, somewhat bitter in taste and related to celery) are dunked into the deliciously seasoned oil and eaten with the fingers.

In Italy this is a traditional Christmas Eve delicacy, but it would make a marvelous summer buffet or patio party appetizer. Italian Vegetable Fondue may be prepared in a fondue pot (General Information, pg. 35) or in the top of a double boiler — just make sure it is a heavy one.

On the next page you'll find a traditional Swiss Fondue which is made with Swiss cheese and Sauterne. The classic fondue, which originated in Switzerland, consisted of dunking bread cubes into a cheese mixture. As its popularity became widespread, people began experimenting with different kinds of foods. Now, in addition to bread, several types of raw or parboiled vegetables and even cooked or cured meats are served with the fondue. Foods you may want to try include rolled slices of pepperoni, boiled shrimp, parboiled or raw cauliflowerets, raw or sautéed mushrooms, carrots, radishes, artichoke hearts and cherry tomatoes.

ITALIAN VEGETABLE FONDUE

1¼ c. olive oil
3 cloves of garlic sliced
½ tsp. freshly ground pepper
2 2-oz. cans anchovy fillets

Pour the oil into the fondue pot, then add the garlic and pepper. Chop the anchovies and add to the fondue pot with the anchovy oil. Heat until bubbly. Serve as dipping sauce for fresh vegetables such as radishes, carrot sticks, small green onions and celery strips.

italian vegetable fondue

Bagna Cauda, as this pungent dipping sauce is called, is a tangy blend of oil, spices and anchovies. Cooked in the traditional earthenware pot over a brazier, the fondue is accompanied by a bowl of crunchy, fresh vegetables for dipping.

swiss fondue

SWISS FONDUE

¾ lb. Swiss cheese
1 tbsp. all-purpose flour
1¼ cloves of garlic
1¼ c. Sauterne
Dash of pepper
Dash of nutmeg
3 tbsp. Kirsch brandy
Salt to taste

Cut the cheese into thin strips and place in a bag. Add the flour and toss well until cheese is coated.

Split the garlic clove in half and rub the inside of the fondue pot well with the cut sides of both halves. Press the remaining ¼ clove of garlic and place in the fondue pot, then add the Sauterne. Place over the flame and heat until bubbles start to rise. Do not cover or boil. Add the cheese gradually and cook over a low flame, stirring constantly, until melted. Stir in the pepper, nutmeg and kirsch. You may add warmed Sauterne if mixture becomes too thick. Serve with French bread cubes, cauliflowerets, mushrooms and rolled pepperoni slices for dipping.

FONDUE FRIBOURG

1⅓ c. Chablis or other dry white wine
½ lb. Swiss cheese, shredded
1 tsp. potato flour or cornstarch
¼ tsp. ground nutmeg
⅓ c. kirsch brandy
4 egg yolks
⅔ c. whipping cream
⅛ tsp. salt

Pour Chablis into fondue pot and place over low heat. Add cheese and stir with a wooden spoon until cheese is melted as the cheese will tend to lie on the bottom of the pot. Stir potato flour and nutmeg into the kirsch, then add to cheese mixture. Stir for about 2 minutes or until well blended. Beat egg yolks with a fork, then add cream and salt, stirring until blended. Add egg mixture gradually to cheese mixture, stirring constantly. Do not let mixture boil. Continue stirring for about 5 minutes or until mixture thickens and is very smooth. Additional salt may be added to taste if desired. Serve with cubes of day-old French bread. For serving techniques, see General Information, page 36.

swiss fondue

This classic version of the cheese fondue relies on Swiss cheese and Sauterne for its delicacy and taste. Accompanying it are rolled pepperoni slices, cauliflowerets, sautéed mushrooms, bread and a light, white wine.

gazpacho

It is not difficult to sing praises of Gazpacho — a light, cool, refreshing soup from the Andalusian region of Spain. It is interesting to know that the Spanish call Gazpacho "salad". However, to an American it is a soup. Developed in a hot weather climate, this soup is perfect for summer days, yet it is surprisingly filling. Gazpacho contains few calories, since its ingredients are little more than light, raw vegetables. It's sure to be a favorite with weight watchers.

As with many traditional dishes, the Gazpacho recipe varies with the inspiration of the cook and the ingredients on hand. Some prefer to blend the vegetables and serve the Gazpacho as a drink — while others chop the vegetables and serve them in side bowls. Still others, as our recipe illustrates, use chopped vegetables in the soup.

Minestrone, featured on the following page, is a thick, hearty Italian soup which, along with a simple salad and beverage, can constitute an entire meal. Like Gazpacho, it is a term whose interpretations vary from region to region and even from cook to cook. Minestrone, though, always implies vegetables and a starchy supplement such as pasta (Pasta, pg. 9) or cubed potatoes, dried beans or rice. The contents of a particular Minestrone may depend on the regional produce available and the cook's expertise and taste. This recipe contains a colorful variety of diced vegetables, tiny bits of ham and vermicelli. Minestrone is traditionally sprinkled with fresh, grated Parmesan cheese when served.

GAZPACHO

1 c. finely chopped peeled tomatoes
½ c. finely chopped green sweet peppers
½ c. finely chopped celery
½ c. finely chopped cucumber
¼ c. minced onion
2 tsp. chopped parsley
1 tsp. chopped chives
1 sm. clove of garlic, pressed
2 tbsp. tarragon vinegar
2 tbsp. olive oil
1 tsp. salt
¼ tsp. pepper
½ tsp. Worcestershire sauce
2 c. tomato juice

Combine all the ingredients in a glass bowl and blend well. Cover tightly and refrigerate for at least 4 hours. Serve in chilled cups with Fried Croutons, (Breads, pg. 16). You may liquefy in blender if desired. This will make about 6 servings.

gazpacho

The version of this hot weather cooler presented here has been placed in a blender for several seconds to make a vegetable cocktail; however, as the recipe explains, Gazpacho may also be served in bowls, with vegetables chopped instead of blended.

minestrone

MINESTRONE

¾ c. dried Great Northern beans
1 recipe Basic Beef Stock *(pg. 2)*
4 med. onions, finely chopped
3 cloves of garlic, crushed
1½ c. shredded cabbage
2 celery hearts, finely chopped
1 lg. potato, diced
2 c. diced fresh green beans
2 med. leeks, finely chopped
½ c. diced ham
4 stalks parsley, stems removed
2 tsp. salt
½ tsp. pepper
5 med. tomatoes, skinned and chopped
½ c. water
⅛ tsp. nutmeg
⅛ tsp. basil
¾ c. 1-inch pieces vermicelli

Place the dried beans in a bowl and cover with water. Let soak for at least 1 hour, or, while preparing the vegetables. Drain and place in a stockpot. Add the stock, onions, garlic, cabbage, celery, potato, green beans, leeks, ham, parsley, salt and pepper. Bring to a slow rolling boil and skim off any scum. Cover and simmer for 2 hours and 30 minutes. Combine the tomatoes, water, nutmeg and basil in a medium saucepan and simmer until tender. Pour into blender container and purée, or force through a strainer. Then add to the stockpot. Add the vermicelli and cook until the vermicelli is tender. Serve hot with Parmesan cheese sprinkled over top. This makes about 5 quarts.

minestrone

A traditional Italian vegetable soup, Minestrone is shown here in an earthenware bowl, served with breadsticks and, in the background, freshly grated Parmesan cheese.

cream of broccoli soup

To be served cold, this soup has been garnished with tiny Toasted Bread Cups filled with sour cream and sprinkled liberally with parsley. If the soup is served hot, a sliver of butter may be added to each bowl.

CREAM OF BROCCOLI SOUP

1 10-oz. package frozen chopped broccoli
1 recipe Basic White Sauce *(Sauces, pg. 4)*
3 c. Basic Chicken Stock *(pg. 2)*
Salt and pepper to taste
1 egg yolk
½ c. half and half cream
1 tbsp. melted butter

Cook the broccoli according to package directions and drain. Place in the blender container and purée. Combine the white sauce and chicken stock in the top of a double boiler and heat, stirring until blended and smooth. Stir the broccoli into the hot sauce mixture. Season with salt and pepper. Beat the egg yolk with a fork, then blend in the cream. Stir the egg mixture slowly into the broccoli mixture and heat, stirring constantly. Do not allow to boil. Cover and keep warm until serving time. Add the butter just before serving. This soup may be served hot or cold. The egg, cream and butter may be omitted for a less rich soup, if desired. Garnish the cold soup with toasted bread cups filled with sour cream. Two cups of cooked fresh broccoli may be substituted for frozen broccoli if desired. This makes about 6 servings.

To Make Toasted Bread Cups:
Cut bread slices with a wet 3-inch cutter and fit into small tart or tassie pans. Bake in a preheated 350-degree oven until dry and lightly browned.

vichyssoise

Vichyssoise, the classic leek and potato soup, was created in 1910 by chef Louis Diat to celebrate the opening of the roof garden at the old Ritz-Carlton Hotel in New York City. This creamy soup is undoubtedly the most famous of all cold soups.

VICHYSSOISE

2 lbs. leeks
2 lbs. potatoes
6 to 8 c. Basic Chicken Stock *(pg. 2)*
2½ c. milk
1¼ c. whipping cream
Salt and white pepper to taste
Chopped chives

Trim the green tops from the leeks, then slice the bottoms thinly. Peel the potatoes and dice coarsely. Place leeks and potatoes in a Dutch oven or large, heavy saucepan. Pour in enough chicken stock to cover. Simmer covered until vegetables are very tender. Purée the potato mixture, a small amount at a time, in the blender. Return to the Dutch oven and stir in the milk and cream. Season with salt and pepper, then heat, stirring constantly until just blended. Chill until ready to serve. Sprinkle chopped chives over each serving. May be served hot, if desired. This makes 6 to 8 servings.

SPINACH SOUP

2 10-oz. packages frozen chopped spinach
1 tbsp. lemon juice
3 tbsp. butter
3 tbsp. all-purpose flour
2 c. milk
¼ c. freshly grated Romano cheese
⅛ tsp. nutmeg
Salt and pepper to taste

Cook the spinach according to package directions. Place the spinach and lemon juice in a blender container and process until puréed. Melt the butter in a large saucepan, then stir in the flour to make a smooth paste. Add the milk gradually, stirring constantly, and cook until thickened. Stir in the cheese, nutmeg and spinach. Cook until heated through. Season with salt and pepper. More milk may be added if a thinner soup is desired. Two pounds of fresh spinach, cooked and chopped, may be substituted for the frozen spinach, if desired. This makes about 4 to 6 servings.

spinach soup

Served in attractive earthenware soup cups, Spinach Soup, or Velouté d'Epinards as it is known to French chefs, is a combination of a rich, velvety cream sauce with spinach and cheese. The addition of a generous tablespoon of thick cream to each cup adds a rich flavor. In the background on the wooden platter are extremely thin triangles from trimmings of Basic Cold Yeast Dough (Breads, pg. 20-21) which have been baked and sprinkled with paprika.

cream of corn soup

This soup is equally delicious refrigerator cold during the hot summer, or piping hot on a crisp winter day. The sunshine yellow soup shown in orange containers is served with bread sticks. Cream of Corn Soup makes an excellent first course when served with Beef Aspic (Salads, pg. 8) and Stuffed Eggs (Salads, pg. 8).

CREAM OF CORN SOUP

1 1-lb. can cream-style corn
2 c. Basic Chicken Stock *(pg. 2)*
¾ c. half and half cream
½ tsp. celery salt
Salt and white pepper to taste

Combine all ingredients in a large saucepan and heat through. This makes about 6 servings.

LIMA BEAN SOUP

2 10-oz. packages frozen baby lima beans
2 c. Basic Chicken Stock *(pg. 2)*
1/2 tsp. savory
4 c. Béchamel Sauce *(Sauces, pg. 4)*
3/4 c. half and half cream
Salt and white pepper to taste

Combine the beans, stock and savory in a sauce-pan and cover. Bring to a boil, then reduce heat and simmer for 20 minutes or until tender. Purée the beans with the stock in a blender, 1/3 at a time. Stir the beans into the hot *Béchamel* Sauce. Stir in the cream and season with salt and pepper. Simmer, stirring, until heated through. This makes about 10 to 12 servings.

lima bean soup

This pale green soup is garnished with a pat of butter, a spoonful of rice and a few baby lima beans scattered over the top of each serving. Hot biscuits or Baked Croutons (Breads, pg. 16) make a delicious accompaniment.

grilled appetizer sandwiches

Hot cheese finger foods are among the most desirable appetizers, and the Grilled Appetizer Sandwiches presented here are a perfect example. They are easily made with sandwich bread, mustard, cheese and butter. The following recipe makes twelve sandwiches, but of course you may vary the amount to suit any occasion. They can be made in a variety of shapes and sizes. These bubbly cheese delights are delicious and ready to serve in a jiffy.

GRILLED APPETIZER SANDWICHES

8 slices sandwich bread
Dijon mustard
1 6-oz. package sliced Emmenthal
    or Swiss Cheese
Melted butter

Cut bread into 24 fancy shapes, using small, wet cutters. Spread with mustard. Cut cheese slices into fancy shapes matching the bread. Assemble into 12 sandwiches, using 2 pieces of cheese in each sandwich.

CREAM HERB SAUCE

1 tsp. fennel seed
5 parsley stalks
2 bay leaves
4 peppercorns
¼ tsp. thyme leaves
1½ c. whipping cream
½ tsp. salt
¼ tsp. white pepper
2 tsp. chopped chives
1½ tsp. grated lemon peel

Place the fennel seed, parsley, bay leaves, peppercorns and thyme in a small muslin bag to make a *Bouquet Garni* (page 2). Pour the cream in a saucepan and add the salt and pepper. Add chives and the *Bouquet Garni* to the cream. Bring to a boil, then reduce heat and simmer for 20 to 25 minutes or until thickened. Remove the *Bouquet Garni* and stir in the lemon peel. Serve hot or cold as a dipping sauce for Grilled Appetizer Sandwiches or vegetables. This makes about 1 cup of sauce.

1 Grease a hot griddle or large heavy skillet with fresh pork fat or melted butter. Place sandwiches on griddle, then brush tops with melted butter.

2 Grill sandwiches until browned, then turn to brown other side.

3 Arrange cheese trimmings on top of each sandwich and drizzle or brush with additional butter.

4 Remove from heat and slide griddle under broiler. Broil for several minutes or until cheese is bubbly.

TOMATO DUNKING SAUCE

1 8-oz. carton sour cream
1 c. chili sauce
1 tbsp. lemon juice
1/2 tsp. garlic salt
1/4 tsp. white pepper
1 1/2 tsp. Worcestershire sauce
1/4 tsp. red hot sauce
Dash of salt

Combine all ingredients and mix well. Serve as a dipping sauce for Grilled Appetizer Sandwiches or various seafoods. This makes 2 cups of sauce.

miniature egg and asparagus open sandwiches

Take extra minutes to apply pale golden aspic jelly "wash" to these pretty appetizers. These little sandwiches are refrigerated until serving time. Garnish with Gherkin Tassels (General Information, pg. 17).

MINIATURE EGG AND ASPARAGUS OPEN SANDWICHES

½ **recipe Basic Emergency Aspic *(Salads, pg. 4)***
10 slices thin-sliced pumpernickel or whole wheat bread
½ **c. Basic Blender Mayonnaise *(Sauces, pg. 3)***
10 slices Monterey Jack cheese
6 hard-boiled eggs
20 small gherkins
1 1-lb. can white asparagus tips

Prepare aspic substituting chicken consommé for the beef consommé and let chill until syrupy. Remove the crusts from the bread, then cut into 2 rectangles. Spread generously with mayonnaise, then top with a rectangle of cheese. Cut eggs crosswise into ¼-inch slices. Place 3 slices on each rectangle. Cut gherkin tassels as instructed in General Information, page 17. Place 1 tassel and 1 asparagus spear on each sandwich. Place sandwiches on rack over jelly roll pan. Spoon aspic carefully over each sandwich, coating evenly. Place rack on a cookie sheet. Place in the refrigerator and chill until firm. Return excess aspic in jelly roll pan to remaining aspic, but do not stir. Chill aspic as needed to keep at syrupy stage. Repeat coating and chilling several times until sandwiches are thickly glazed. Refrigerate until ready to serve. Garnish serving tray with any remaining asparagus. This will make about 20 rectangles.

The Creative Homemaker's Academy © MCMLXXIII
Selected Illustrations © B.P.C. Publishing Limited MCMLXX

introducing pâtés

What is a *pâté*? So many people ask this question. A *pâté* (French for pie or paste) can be an elegant fine meat loaf baked with or without a pastry crust (see French Lining Pastry, Pork, page 7). When *pâté* is prepared in this manner it may be served as a first course of a formal dinner, or as the entrée for a luncheon or light supper. A *pâté* can also be a savory mixture of seasoned meat or fish. It is delicious as an appetizer, snack or as an accompaniment for a green salad. In this particular type of *pâté*, the meat is so finely ground that it has the consistency of paste.

Pâtés are not particularly difficult to make and the creative homemaker can develop her very own version of *pâté*. An excellent *pâté* mixture is not the most economical dish to prepare. The ingredients may include some or all of the following: ground pork, pork fat, ground beef or veal, Cognac, Port or Madeira, spices, strips of meat, game or liver and frequently, truffles. The meats are sometimes marinated in Cognac before sautéing and grinding or blending. After these meats have been smoothly blended, many recipes call for the addition of ground pork fat to be incorporated into the mixture. This ground fat helps to keep the *pâté* moist and sweet, and also lightens the texture.

The mixture is then ready to be poured into the prepared baking pan or "terrine." This pan may be a *pâté* mold (which can be purchased in most gourmet shops) or it can be any ovenproof dish or pot of the appropriate size. The pan may be lined with a pastry crust, or if preferred, with strips of pork fat, bacon or salt pork.

The *pâté* is then ready to be baked in a moderate oven. Usually, the baking mold is placed in a larger baking dish to which water is added, then placed in the oven. The length of baking time depends upon the size mold used and the recipe. After it has been baked, the *pâté* is cooled, then well-chilled which helps to bring out the flavors. Some experts feel that the pastry crust of a *pâté* is not meant to be eaten but merely to encase the *pâté* mixture as a protection against loss of juices and flavor. Others hold the opinion that the pastry is edible and therefore, to be eaten with the *pâté*. Properly refrigerated, a *pâté* will keep for about 10 days. It may also be frozen; but the original smooth texture will be partially lost in the process. A *pâté* which has been frozen and thawed has a somewhat damp quality and is not as light and creamy as it was prior to the freezing.

ovenproof dish

Virtually any type of ovenproof dish may be adapted to baking a pâté. Here is a display of some of those dishes called terrines that are made especially for pâtés. Not pictured but also available are oval or rectangular springform pans which are excellent for baking pâtés.

SIMPLE PÂTÉ MAISON

6 slices salt pork
6 slices bacon, diced
1½ c. chopped onions
1 lb. calves liver
1 lb. chicken livers
1¾ tsp. salt
1 tsp. pepper
3 egg yolks
2 eggs
¼ c. Maderia
½ tsp. chervil
½ tsp. tarragon leaves
½ tsp. nutmeg
¼ tsp. allspice

Rinse the salt pork slices in cold water to remove some of the salt. Drain thoroughly. Line a 7-inch soufflé mold with salt pork slices. Cook the diced bacon in a skillet until the fat is rendered. Sauté the onions in the bacon fat until tender and lightly browned. Cut the calves liver into 1-inch pieces and halve the chicken livers. Add the livers, 1 teaspoon salt and ½ teaspoon pepper to the onion mixture. Sauté until all the pink has disappeared from the livers. Place the liver mixture in the blender container, a small amount at a time. Blend until thoroughly puréed, adding egg yolks, eggs and Madeira. Spoon the liver mixture into a large bowl. Stir in remaining salt, pepper and spices. Pour the liver mixture into the prepared mold and cover with aluminum foil. Place the mold in a larger baking dish and add water halfway to the top of mold. Bake in a preheated 375-degree oven for 2 hours. Cool the *pâté* well and invert onto a serving platter. Refrigerate for at least 8 hours to chill thoroughly. The *pâté* may be sliced thinly and served with French bread, crackers or as a separate course with a green salad. This makes about 30 servings when used as a spread.

simple pâté maison

Nearly every restaurant in France has its own version of Pâté Maison or "house specialty." A fine, light pâté, it is accompanied here by gherkins and cocktail onions, a classic combination.

EMERGENCY PÂTÉ

2½ lb. braunschweiger (liver sausage)
1 c. butter, softened
½ c. finely minced onion
¼ c. minced chives
⅓ c. brandy or bourbon

Combine the braunschweiger and butter in a mixer bowl and beat with an electric beater until well blended. Add the remaining ingredients and mix thoroughly. Pack into a small crock or mold. Chill until firm. Unmold onto serving dish and garnish with chopped parsley, pitted ripe olives and cherry tomatoes. This makes about 5½ cups of *pâté*.

HOT CHICKEN LIVER AND SAUSAGE PÂTÉ

2 tbsp. butter
½ lb. chicken livers
1 tsp. salt
¼ c. Madeira
2 tbsp. Cognac
3 eggs
2 tbsp. all-purpose flour
¼ tsp. rosemary
½ tsp. allspice
½ tsp. freshly ground pepper
1 lb. mild sausage

Melt the butter in a skillet, then add the chicken livers. Sauté until all the pink disappears. Cool for about 10 minutes. Combine chicken livers, salt, Madeira, Cognac, eggs, flour and seasonings in blender container. Blend for about 3 minutes or until the mixture is thoroughly puréed. Blend the puréed mixture and the sausage thoroughly. Spoon the chicken liver mixture into a 7-inch *pâté* mold and cover tightly. Place mold in a larger baking dish and add hot water to half the depth of the mold. Bake in a preheated 350-degree oven for 1 hour and 45 minutes. Unmold onto a serving platter and slice to serve. May be chilled and served cold. This makes about 8 to 10 servings.

hot chicken liver and sausage pâté

An especially flavorful spread, this Hot Chicken Liver and Sausage Pâté is shown here two ways: encased in a light, flaky pastry crust and baked plain with a film of melted pork fat over the surface to help seal in the juices and flavor.

CHICKEN PÂTÉ CREAM

Bacon fat
2 tbsp. butter
1½ lb. chicken livers
½ lb. unsalted pork fat, ground
2 tbsp. dry sherry
2 tbsp. brandy
½ tsp. freshly ground pepper
3 green onions or shallots, chopped
1 clove of garlic, minced
1½ tsp. salt

Coat a 7-inch soufflé mold well with cold bacon fat. Melt the butter in a skillet. Sauté the livers until all the pink has disappeared. Combine livers, pork fat, sherry, brandy, pepper, onions, garlic and salt and mix well. Place the liver mixture in the blender container, a small amount at a time, and blend until thoroughly puréed. The blending may take longer than usual as the pork fat is not easily puréed. Spoon the liver mixture into the prepared mold and cover with aluminum foil. Place the mold in a baking dish. Pour hot water halfway the depth of the mold. Bake in a preheated 350-degree oven for 1 hour. Remove from oven and let cool. Invert onto a serving platter and chill in the refrigerator overnight. Serve with French bread or crackers. This makes about 2 cups of *pâté*.

chicken pâté cream

This pâté, with its delicate blend of flavors, is heavenly when accompanied by freshly baked croissants and sweet butter. It may be done in an elaborate manner, covered with a layer of aspic and garnished with stuffed olives. Or, it may simply be baked, chilled and served by itself with a tiny sprig of parsley to add a touch of color.

HOT PÂTÉ WITH GARLIC BREAD

½ lb. finely ground lean beef
½ lb. finely ground lean pork
½ lb. mild pork sausage
2 cloves of garlic, pressed
2 tbsp. grated onion
¼ tsp. basil
¼ tsp. marjoram
¼ tsp. thyme
¼ tsp. oregano
1 tsp. salt
½ tsp. freshly ground pepper
½ c. Basic Beef Stock *(pg. 2)*
3 tbsp. sherry
1 tbsp. brandy
Hot Garlic Loaf *(Breads, pg. 17)*

Combine the beef, pork and sausage and grind through a food chopper 3 times. Add the garlic, onion, basil, marjoram, thyme, oregano, salt and pepper. Mix with a wooden spoon until thoroughly blended. Add the stock, sherry and brandy and blend until smooth. Turn into a buttered 1-quart earthenware mold and cover. Set in a baking pan, then pour in boiling water to half the depth of the mold. Bake in a preheated 325-degree oven for 1 hour and 15 minutes. Increase oven temperature to 350 degrees. Remove cover and bake for 30 minutes longer or until brown. Slice and serve with Hot Garlic Loaf. This makes about 3 cups *pâté*.

hot pâté with garlic bread

A hearty and very aromatic snack or appetizer, Hot Pâté with Garlic Bread will satisfy even the most robust appetite. A red wine would be a pleasant addition to this simple fare.

giblet soup

A full-flavored soup which puts to use the frequently discarded giblets of a holiday turkey, chicken or goose. Long slow simmering of the giblets in stock helps to heighten the flavors. The meat is puréed, returned to the stock and blended well to produce a smooth nutritious result. It may be garnished with toasted croutons.

GIBLET SOUP

½ lb. chicken gizzards
¼ lb. chicken livers
1 lb. chicken necks
Basic Seasoned Flour *(pg. 32)*
Bacon drippings
2½ qt. water
4 stalks celery with leaves
1 bay leaf
10 peppercorns
Salt
1½ tbsp. butter
½ c. chopped onions
1 c. chopped tomatoes
½ c. diced carrots
½ c. chopped celery
¼ tsp. pepper
1 tbsp. lemon juice

Dredge the gizzards, livers and necks in flour. Heat bacon drippings in a large heavy kettle until hot, then add the giblets and brown on all sides. Add water, celery stalks, bay leaf, peppercorns and 1 teaspoon salt. Bring to a boil, then cover and boil gently for 1 hour and 30 minutes. Strain stock and set giblets aside to cool. Heat butter in the kettle, then add the onions and sauté until golden. Chop the gizzards and livers. Add strained stock, gizzards, livers, tomatoes, carrots, chopped celery, pepper and salt to taste. Cover and boil gently for 30 minutes or until vegetables are tender. Stir in the lemon juice. Meat from necks may be added, if desired. The soup may be frozen. This makes about 6 servings.

BASIC SEASONED FLOUR

4 c. all-purpose flour
¼ c. salt
2 tbsp. freshly ground pepper
2 tbsp. dry English mustard
1 tbsp. paprika
1 tsp. basil
1 tsp. chervil
1 tsp. thyme
1 tsp. parsley flakes

Sift flour, salt, pepper, mustard and paprika together. Stir in the herbs and store in an airtight container for use as needed. This makes about 4½ cups of seasoned flour.

shrimp party crêpes

shrimp party crêpes

A variation of the Shrimp and Cream Cheese Crêpes (Seafoods, page 19,) these miniature crêpes will add to the festive air of any special celebration. Perfect to serve as that extra special hors d'oeuvre, they make life easy for the busy hostess — they may be prepared ahead and reheated just before serving.

SHRIMP PARTY CRÊPES

1 lb. fresh small shrimp
1 tbsp. lemon juice
3 tbsp. freshly grated Parmesan cheese
1 tbsp. chopped chives
2 tbsp. Basic Mayonnaise *(Sauces, pg. 3)*
3 tbsp. sour cream
1/8 tsp. salt
White pepper to taste
1 recipe Savory Crêpe Batter *(Desserts, pg. 102)*
Melted butter

Prepare shrimp according to instructions for Boiled Shrimp (Seafood, pg. 14). Combine the boiled shrimp, lemon juice, cheese, chives, mayonnaise, sour cream, salt and pepper in a mixing bowl. Mix thoroughly. If you do not have a small 5 or 6-inch *crêpe* pan, use a small skillet with sloping sides. Place 1 tablespoon *crêpe* batter in center of hot greased *crêpe* pan or skillet and shake gently in circular motion to spread batter to make miniature *crêpes*. The *crêpes* may be irregularly shaped but can be trimmed neatly with scissors. Place a small amount of the shrimp filling in each *crêpe*. Fold over and place in jelly roll pan. Brush with butter. Just before serving, place in the broiler 6 to 8 inches from the source of heat and broil for several minutes or until lightly browned. Remove to serving dish, then garnish with additional chives and serve immediately. This makes about 16 *crêpes*.

FRESH SHRIMP PÂTÉ

1 lb. fresh small shrimp
1 3-oz. package cream cheese, softened
1/2 c. Basic Mayonnaise *(Sauces, pg. 3)*
2 tbsp. lemon juice
1 tbsp. chili sauce
1 tbsp. grated horseradish
1/2 tsp. salt
White pepper to taste
1 sm. green onion, minced
2 hard-boiled eggs, riced

Prepare the shrimp according to instructions for Boiled Shrimp (Seafood, pg. 14). Place the shrimp, a small amount at a time, in the blender container and process until chopped. Place the cream cheese and mayonnaise in a medium-sized bowl and mix with a wooden spoon until smooth. Add the shrimp and remaining ingredients and mix until well combined. Place in the blender container and process until puréed. Mound onto a serving dish, smoothing it with a knife, then cover and chill thoroughly. Garnish with parsley and serve with assorted crackers. This makes about 2 cups of *pâté*.

shrimp bisque

No other type of cooking is as basic to good meal planning as homemade soup. This flavorful Shrimp Bisque tastes as good as its fragrant odor suggests.

POTTED SHRIMP

1 lb. fresh shrimp
1½ c. butter
3 bay leaves, halved
12 peppercorns
½ tsp. salt
1 sm. clove of garlic, pressed

Prepare shrimp according to instructions for Boiled Shrimp (Seafood, pg. 14). Clarify butter according to instructions (Sauces, pg. 13). Place half the boiled shrimp in a 2-cup container and add half the bay leaves, peppercorns and salt. Add the remaining shrimp, bay leaves, peppercorns and salt. Combine the clarified butter and garlic and pour over the shrimp. Cover tightly and refrigerate overnight. Serve hot, in a chafing dish, with French bread or crackers. This makes about 2 cups of Potted Shrimp.

SHRIMP BISQUE

1 lb. fresh small shrimp
1 recipe Mirepoix (*Sauces, pg. 5*)
¼ tsp. salt
⅛ tsp. freshly ground pepper
2 tbsp. brandy
1 c. Sauterne
1¼ c. Basic Chicken Stock (*pg. 2*)
¾ c. half and half cream

Shell and devein the shrimp. Prepare the Mirepoix in a heavy, medium-sized saucepan. Add the shrimp and sauté, stirring frequently, until the shrimp turn pink and lose all transparency. Season with salt and pepper. Add the brandy and Sauterne, then simmer for 10 minutes. Remove about ¼ of the shrimp and set aside for garnish. Remove the bay leaf and discard. Cool the remaining shrimp mixture thoroughly, then place in the blender container. Process until puréed. Pour into a heavy saucepan and add the stock. Simmer for 5 minutes, then add the cream slowly, stirring constantly, and simmer until heated through. Serve immediately or keep hot in top of double boiler over hot water. Ladle into serving bowls and garnish with reserved shrimp. This makes about 4 servings.

potted shrimp

One of the simplest and most delicious ways to serve boiled shrimp is to marinate them in clarified butter. The shrimp are first boiled in court bouillon and then placed with seasonings in a clean jar and covered with clarified butter. The mixture is refrigerated overnight, allowing the flavors to blend. These Potted Shrimp are wonderful served hot in a chafing dish, accompanied with small slices of French bread or crackers.

creamed shrimp soup

Shrimp may be used in a wide variety of ways, from the simplest *hors d'oeuvres* to the most elaborate entrée. Creamed Shrimp Soup is but another example of the versatility of this popular seafood.

The preparation of this rich, full-bodied soup is not difficult even for the novice cook. But it is important to use fresh, top quality ingredients to produce a perfect result. An excellent creamed soup must have a good stock and real cream, not milk thickened with flour. Some cooks like to add a beaten egg yolk which adds extra body and richness.

CREAMED SHRIMP SOUP

1 lb. fresh small shrimp
¼ c. butter
¼ c. all-purpose flour
2 c. Basic Chicken Stock (pg. 2)
2 c. half and half cream
Salt to taste
½ tsp. white pepper

Prepare shrimp according to instructions for Boiled Shrimp (Seafood, pg. 14). Melt butter in a large saucepan and stir in the flour to make a smooth paste. Add chicken stock, stirring constantly, then cook until thick and smooth. Stir in cream, shrimp and seasonings and cook over low heat until heated through, stirring frequently. Garnish with finely chopped parsley. Canned chicken stock may be substituted for Basic Chicken Stock if desired. This makes 4 to 6 servings.

creamed shrimp soup

Serve Creamed Shrimp Soup, a smooth, savory velouté with shrimp, for an elegant beginning of a gourmet meal. Your family and guests will be impressed with your artful ability to add subtle seasonings and they'll never suspect how quick and simple this soup is to make.

crab soup

CLASSIC CRAB SOUP

5 c. Basic Fish Stock *(Seafood, pg. 5)*
1 lb. fresh crab meat
¾ c. dry white wine
Salt and freshly ground pepper to taste
¾ c. half and half cream
1 tbsp. brandy

Heat the fish stock just to boiling point in large
heavy saucepan. Add crab meat, wine and
seasonings and simmer for several minutes or until
crab meat is heated through, stirring constantly.
Stir in cream and brandy, then heat for 1 minute
longer. This makes 4 to 6 servings.

SIMPLE CRAB SOUP

1 recipe Basic Béchamel Sauce *(Sauces, pg. 4)*
1 can tomato soup
½ c. clam juice
3 c. half and half cream
1 lb. fresh crab meat
¼ c. sherry

Pour *Béchamel* sauce, tomato soup, clam juice and
cream into heavy saucepan. Cook over low heat
until well combined, stirring constantly. Stir in crab
meat and sherry, then cook until heated through.
This makes 4 to 6 servings.

crab soup

We have provided recipes for two
versions of this Crab Soup. Classic
Crab Soup is for those cooks equipped
with both ample time and fresh crab
in the shell. Simple Crab Soup is less
elaborate, designed for the chef who
is in a hurry and forgot to store extra fish
stock in the freezer.

clam chowder

NEW ENGLAND CLAM CHOWDER

1 qt. shucked clams with liquor
3 slices salt pork, diced
2 sm. onions, minced
2 med. potatoes, diced
1 bay leaf
1 c. water
3 c. milk, scalded
1½ c. half and half cream
¼ c. butter
Salt and freshly ground pepper to taste

Drain the clams, reserving the liquor, then chop coarsely. Fry the salt pork slowly in a kettle until all the fat is rendered. Add the onions and sauté until golden. Add potatoes, bay leaf and water, then simmer until the potatoes are tender. Strain the reserved clam liquor, then stir into the potato mixture with the milk, cream, butter and chopped clams. Add seasonings, then simmer for 15 minutes. Add more seasonings, if needed. Remove bay leaf before serving. This makes 6 to 8 servings.

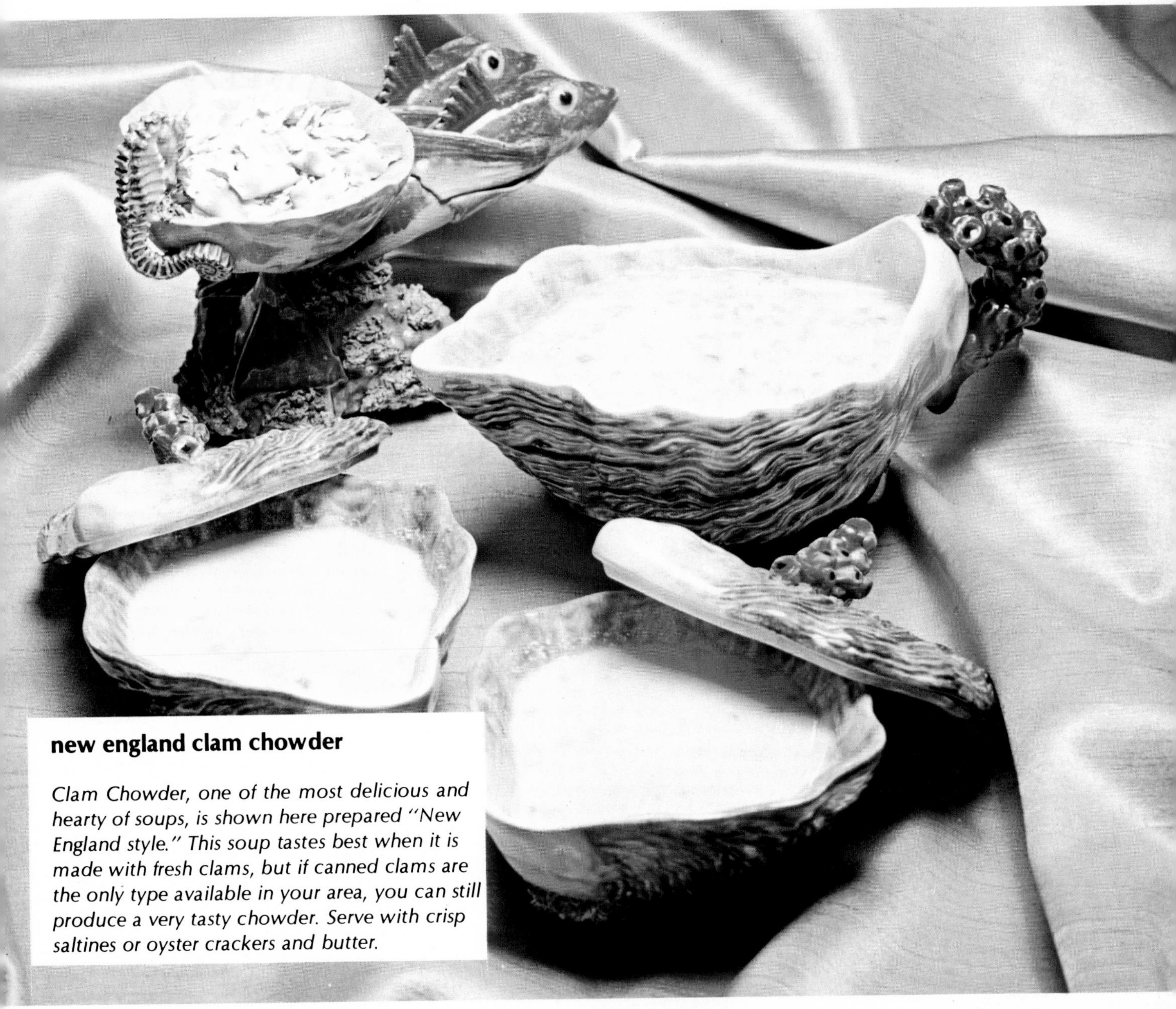

new england clam chowder

Clam Chowder, one of the most delicious and hearty of soups, is shown here prepared "New England style." This soup tastes best when it is made with fresh clams, but if canned clams are the only type available in your area, you can still produce a very tasty chowder. Serve with crisp saltines or oyster crackers and butter.

MINIATURE SEAFOOD TARTLETS

½ recipe Basic Savory Short Pastry *(Desserts, pg. 12)*

Roll out the pastry thin and cut 24 circles with a 2½-inch cookie cutter. Fit the circles in miniature cupcake pans, then prick bottoms and sides. Bake in a preheated 400-degree oven for about 15 minutes or until browned. Remove from pans and cool. Fill each pastry cup with about 1 teaspoon of one of the suggested fillings and garnish as desired. Serve immediately after filling. The remaining pastry scraps may be formed into a ball and rolled out, then cut for additional tartlets or cut into ¾-inch wide and 3-inch long strips. Sprinkle strips with cayenne pepper or garlic salt and bake. Serve as cheese straws.

SUGGESTED FILLINGS FOR 24 TARTLETS:

SALMON FILLING

1 7¾-oz. can red salmon
1 3-oz. package cream cheese, softened
¼ c. Basic Mayonnaise *(Sauces, pg. 3)*
2 tsp. lemon juice
4 drops of hot sauce
1 tsp. finely minced green onion
¼ tsp. dry mustard
¼ tsp. curry powder
Salt and pepper to taste

Place the salmon in a strainer and drain thoroughly, then remove the bones. Flake the salmon with a fork. Combine all ingredients and mix until smooth. Chill overnight before using. One cup of crab meat may be substituted for salmon. This makes about 1¼ cups of filling.

LOBSTER FILLING

1 3-oz. package cream cheese, softened
1 c. finely diced cooked lobster
1 tbsp. Basic Mayonnaise *(Sauces, pg. 3)*
2 tsp. lemon juice
½ tsp. capers
Salt and pepper to taste

Combine all ingredients and mix well. Chill before using.

CLAM-CHEESE FILLING

1 8-oz. package cream cheese, softened
⅓ c. clam juice
½ tsp. onion salt

Combine all ingredients and beat until smooth.

BASIL MEATBALL APPETIZERS

¼ c. whipping cream
3 tbsp. water
¼ c. fine Holland rusk crumbs
1 tsp. dried basil or 2 tsp. fresh basil
¼ tsp. cayenne pepper
1 tsp. salt
¾ lb. ground beef
¼ lb. ground lean pork
2 tbsp. grated onion
Butter

Combine the cream and water in a small bowl, then add the crumbs. Mix until the crumbs are moistened. Combine the basil, cayenne pepper, salt, beef, pork and onion in a mixing bowl and mix thoroughly. Add the crumb mixture and mix until well blended, then shape into 1-inch balls. Sauté in a small amount of butter in a frypan until browned on all sides. Shake the frypan occasionally to keep balls round. You may serve this in a chafing dish, if desired. This makes 16 to 20 appetizers.

basil meatball appetizers

Basil Meatball Appetizers have three virtues to their credit — flavor, ease of preparation, and economy. These herb-flavored hors d'oeuvres are best served hot for occasions (such as cocktail parties) when an entire meal is not served.

SHALLOW-FRIED MUSHROOMS AND CREAM

¼ c. butter
¼ lb. fresh mushrooms, sliced
¼ c. dry white wine
½ c. beef broth
½ c. half and half cream
¼ c. chopped chives
Salt and freshly ground pepper to taste
5 Grilled Appetizer Sandwiches *(pg. 24)*

shallow-fried mushrooms and cream

If you would like to prepare an appetizer of gourmet quality, serve Shallow-Fried Mushrooms and Cream. Succulent mushrooms in a rich, savory sauce (made from broth, wine, cream and chives) is spooned over little grilled sandwiches. These delicious flavors come together with perfection to produce a really memorable appetizer. And, like Basil Meatballs, hot canapés are substantial and filling — ideal for a brunch or cocktail party.

1 Melt the butter in a skillet over low heat. Add the mushrooms to the butter.

2 Sauté until the mushrooms absorb the butter, turning frequently.

3 Pour in a small amount of the wine at a time, allowing mixture to maintain a steady simmer. Repeat the procedure using the broth.

4 Pour the cream slowly over the mushrooms.

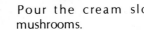

5 Cook over low heat, stirring to blend thoroughly.

6 Stir in the chives and season with salt and pepper.

7 Simmer, stirring frequently, until the sauce is creamy and thickened. Serve on Grilled Appetizer Sandwiches and garnish with parsley. This makes 5 servings or 20 small canapés.

appetizer sandwiches

In the foreground, from left to right, is The Cucumber Sandwich, The Orange-Leek Sandwich, The Avocado Sandwich and The Shrimp Sandwich. The Olive Sandwich is in the background.

appetizer sandwiches

THE OLIVE SANDWICH

2 c. well-drained pitted California ripe olives
1 lg. round loaf French bread, split
Soft butter
12 thin slices Monterey Jack cheese
18 slices dry salami
1 lg. green sweet pepper, cut in rings

Slice the olives. Hollow out a portion of the soft crumbs from both halves of the bread loaf and spread the halves with butter. Cover the bottom half with the cheese, salami, green pepper and olives and top with the remaining half of the bread loaf. Wrap tightly in waxed paper and let stand in the refrigerator for at least 2 hours for flavors to blend. Cut in small slices to serve. This makes 8 servings.

THE CUCUMBER SANDWICH

2 cucumbers
1½ tsp. salt
6 slices whole wheat bread
6 tbsp. soft butter
3 hard-boiled eggs, sieved
12 canned pitted California ripe olives, halved
Sour Cream Whip (below)
Sliced green onions

Peel the cucumbers, then cut in very thin slices and sprinkle with salt. Chill for at least 30 minutes, then squeeze out the excess moisture. Spread the bread with butter, then arrange the cucumbers, sieved eggs and olives on the bread. Top with Sour Cream Whip and sprinkle with the green onions. Cut into quarters to serve. This makes 6 open-faced sandwiches or cut in small pieces makes an excellent canapés.

SOUR CREAM WHIP

¾ c. sour cream
1 tsp. lemon juice
1 tbsp. thinly sliced green onions
½ tsp. salt

Combine the sour cream, lemon juice, green onion and salt in a small bowl and mix well. This makes about ¾ cup of Sour Cream Whip.

THE AVOCADO SANDWICH

½ c. soft butter
1 tbsp. crumbled basil
6 slices corn bread or Cornmeal Muffins
    (Breads, pg. 40)
6 slices bacon
1 ripe avocado, sliced
12 cherry tomatoes, halved
12 canned pitted California ripe olives
Salt and pepper to taste
1 lime

Combine the butter and basil and blend well, then spread over the corn bread. Cut the bacon slices in half and fry until crisp. Arrange the bacon strips, avocado slices, tomato halves and ripe olives on the corn bread, then sprinkle with salt and pepper. Cut the lime into 6 wedges and garnish each sandwich with a wedge. Lime juice may be squeezed over sandwiches. This makes 6 open-faced sandwiches. You may cut each sandwich into quarters, if desired.

THE SHRIMP SANDWICH

½ lb. fresh shrimp
Dry sherry
3 tbsp. lemon juice
4 slices light rye bread
3 tbsp. soft butter
4 oz. cream cheese
12 canned pitted California ripe olives
2 tbsp. chopped parsley
Pepper to taste

Prepare the shrimp according to instructions for Boiled Shrimp (Seafood, pg. 14). Add 3 tablespoons sherry and the lemon juice to the shrimp and toss until coated. Let stand for 30 minutes. Spread the bread with the butter. Soften the cream cheese to room temperature, then mix with 2 teaspoons sherry. Spread the cream cheese mixture on the buttered bread. Drain the shrimp and cut the olives in half, then arrange over the cream cheese. Sprinkle the parsley and pepper over the top. Cut into quarters. This makes 16 canapés.

THE ORANGE LEEK SANDWICH

6 tbsp. soft butter
2½ tsp. ground coriander
3 slices dark rye bread
1 7-oz. can tuna, drained and flaked
9 pitted California ripe olives, quartered
1 orange, peeled and thinly sliced
3 tsp. thinly sliced leeks

Combine the butter and coriander in a small bowl and blend well, then spread on one side of the bread slices. Arrange the tuna, olives, orange and leek slices on the bread. Cut into quarters. This makes 12 canapés.

miniature party crêpes

MINIATURE PARTY CRÊPES

2 recipes Savory Crêpe Batter (Desserts, pg. 102)
1 c. ground ham
¼ c. Mustard Mayonnaise (Sauces, pg. 3)
Finely chopped parsley
Melted butter
½ c. Cheese Filling (Pasta, pg. 12)
½ c. Cheese Sauce Supreme (Breads, pg. 36)

Place 1 tablespoon of the batter in the center of a hot greased *crêpe* pan and shake gently in circular motion to spread batter to make miniature *crêpes*. Cook for several seconds or until edges begin to dry, then turn and cook for several seconds on the other side. Continue until all batter is used. Place on sheets of waxed paper. Trim any irregularly shaped *crêpes* neatly with scissors. Combine the ham with the mayonnaise and mix thoroughly. Shape the ham mixture into small rolls. Place the ham rolls in the centers of ⅓ of the *crêpes*. Fold sides over ham roll and secure with wooden picks, then dip the ends in chopped parsley. Place the rolls on a baking sheet and brush with melted butter. Place the Cheese Filling in a pastry bag with the large star tube affixed. Fill ⅓ of the remaining *crêpes* by coiling a double-folded *crêpe* around a finger to form a cornet, then pipe Cheese Filling into one side. Secure with wooden picks and place on baking sheets. Brush with melted butter. Spoon about 1 teaspoon of Cheese Sauce Supreme on each of the remaining *crêpes*. Fold over, then place on the baking sheet and brush with melted butter. Broil about 8 inches from the source of heat until lightly browned. Arrange on heated serving platter and serve on small party plates. This makes about 32 *crepês*.

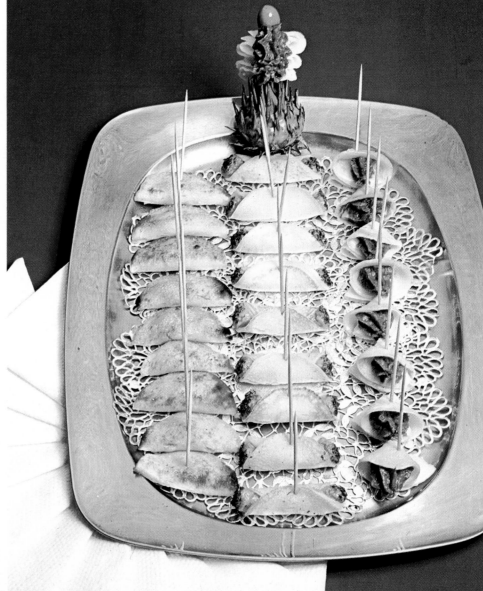

miniature party crêpes

Savory Crêpe Batter (Desserts, pg. 102) has many delicious guises, three of which are illustrated by our array of appetizers. All begin with a simple round crêpe. Then the fillings and manner of folding are varied. From left to right, in the first vertical row are Miniature Party Crêpes filled with a smooth, savory cheese sauce. The second row is rolled crêpes containing ham; stuffed crêpe cornets with a cheese-spinach filling form the third row.

FRIED CHEESE PROFITEROLES

⅓ c. all-purpose flour
⅓ c. freshly grated Parmesan cheese
¼ c. butter, softened
2 eggs
Paprika

Blend the flour with the cheese. Combine the butter with ½ cup of water in a small saucepan, then bring to a boil, stirring until the butter melts. Add the flour mixture all at once and stir vigorously with a wooden spoon until mixture is smooth and leaves side of pan, forming a ball. Remove from heat. Add 1 egg and beat for 1 minute until well mixed. Repeat the procedure with the remaining egg and beat until smooth and thickened. Let stand, covered, at room temperature until completely cool. Do not refrigerate. Spoon the mixture into a pastry bag with a ½-inch writing pipe affixed. Pipe ½-inch pieces or drop by teaspoonfuls into 350-degree oil in deep fat fryer. Fry until golden, then drain well on absorbent toweling. Sprinkle with paprika. This makes 40 to 50 small puffs.

fried cheese profiteroles

Fried cheese and *chou* pastry puffs, or profiteroles, are elegant, delicate tasting appetizers. These little pastry puffs are made from a Basic *Chou* Pastry (Desserts, pg. 56) to which grated cheese is added. They are delicious prepared and served immediately or they may be frozen and reheated for last-minute entertaining.

fried cheese profiteroles

Fried to a golden brown perfection, these profiteroles are served piping hot in a serving dish. Care must be taken when preparing these little puffs as overfrying will ruin both texture and color. Serve them with a dish of grated cheese for extra flavor.

CHEESE STRAWS

2 c. grated sharp Cheddar cheese
1 c. all-purpose flour
1/2 tsp. salt
1/8 tsp. cayenne pepper
1/2 c. butter, melted

Combine the cheese, flour, salt and cayenne pepper in a mixing bowl, blending well. Add the melted butter, stirring with a wooden spoon until blended. The dough will be stiff. Place the dough in a pastry bag with a large star tube affixed. Pipe onto a baking sheet in 1 1/2-inch strips. Bake in a preheated 400-degree oven for about 10 minutes or until lightly browned. Cool on wire rack, then store in airtight container until ready to use. This makes about 30 to 35 Cheese Straws.

CAULIFLOWER CREAM SOUP

1 med. cauliflower
1 med. potato
1 lg. tomato
4 c. milk
4 minced green onions or scallions
1 tbsp. minced parsley
1/2 tsp. savory
2 tsp. salt
1/4 tsp. white pepper
1 c. whipping cream

Separate the cauliflower into flowerets. Peel and dice the potato, then skin and chop the tomato. Combine the milk, cauliflower, potato, tomato, green onions, parsley and seasonings in a heavy kettle. Simmer until the vegetables are tender. Pour the soup through a colander, draining off the liquid. Reserve the liquid. Place 1/3 of the vegetables in the blender container with enough of the liquid to blend easily, then process until puréed. Repeat process with the remaining vegetables. Return the purée and remaining liquid to the kettle, then stir in the cream gradually. Place over low heat and heat through, stirring frequently. You may serve with a bowl of grated Parmesan cheese to sprinkle over the top. This makes 6 servings.

cauliflower cream soup

Cauliflower Cream Soup is an unusual, delicately flavored soup. This tantalizing soup is suitable for either simple or grand occasions yet it is simple to prepare. This may be served hot or cold. You may serve grated Parmesan cheese to sprinkle over the hot soup for added flavor.

GREEN SPLIT PEA SOUP

1 1-lb. package green split peas
1 ham hock
12 green onions or scallions
1 c. diced carrots
1 c. diced celery
1 slice of lemon
½ tsp. white pepper
Salt to taste
1 bay leaf

Place the peas in a colander and rinse thoroughly with cold water. Rinse the ham hock with cold water. Place the peas, ham hock and 2½ quarts of water in a large kettle or saucepan. Slice the green onions, using about 6 of the green tops. Add the onions, carrots, celery, lemon, seasonings and bay leaf to the peas mixture. Bring to a boil, then reduce heat. Simmer, uncovered, for 2 hours, stirring frequently to prevent sticking and adding more water as needed. Caution must be taken to avoid scorching as the soup thickens. Remove the ham hock, lemon slice and bay leaf when the soup is done. Cut the ham from the ham hock, discarding skin and bone. Dice the ham coarsley and return it to the soup. Soup may be puréed, if a creamier soup is desired. This makes 6 to 8 servings.

WHITE ONION SOUP WITH PASTA

4 lg. white onions, peeled
2 c. Béchamel Sauce *(Sauces, pg. 4)*
1½ c. Basic Chicken Stock *(pg. 2)*
Salt and freshly ground pepper to taste
⅔ c. freshly grated Parmesan cheese
1 3-oz. package star pasta
1 tbsp. melted butter

Steam the onions until tender according to the instructions for steaming (Vegetables, pg. 7). Cool, then chop coarsely. Combine the onions with the *Béchamel* Sauce in a saucepan. Stir in the stock, then heat through. Season with salt and pepper and stir in 2 tablespoons of the cheese. Cook and drain pasta according to instructions (Pasta, pg. 9). Toss with the butter and serve with the soup and remaining cheese. This makes about 4 servings.

green split pea soup

This inviting split pea soup is a dream of ease to prepare. Dried peas are simply washed, then simmered with ham hock, green onions and other savory seasonings. A sprinkling of toast crumbs atop each bowl of soup provides a nice garnish. Serve with homemade bread and a wedge of cheese for a very special treat.

HORS D'OEUVRE EGGS

2 English Muffins *(Breads, pg. 40)*
Butter
4 hard-boiled eggs
Basic Blender Mayonnaise *(Sauces, pg. 3)*
Salt and freshly ground pepper to taste
2 or 3 drops of hot sauce
Paprika Mayonnaise *(Sauces, pg. 3)*

Split the English Muffins and cut each half with a 1¾-inch cookie cutter. Spread a thin layer of butter on the cut side of each round. Place on a baking sheet and toast until lightly browned. Peel the eggs and cut away the pointed ends just to the egg yolks. Remove the yolks, place in a small bowl and mash. Add enough blender mayonnaise to moisten. Season with salt, pepper and hot sauce and mix until smooth. Stuff the egg whites with the egg yolk mixture, then place, cut side down, on the muffin rounds. Pipe rosettes of Paprika Mayonnaise around base of the eggs. Garnish eggs with parsley sprigs. This makes 4 servings.

variations of
hors d'oeuvre eggs

2

4 sm. thin-skinned oranges
4 hard-boiled eggs
2 tbsp. Emergency Pâté (pg. 29) or canned pâté
1 tsp. sherry
1 tsp. whipping cream
Salt and freshly ground pepper to taste
Basic Blender Mayonnaise (Sauces, pg. 3)

Cut the peeling of each orange, Vandyke fashion, ³/₄ of the way to the base, then remove the pulp down to the base of each petal. Peel the eggs. Cut away the pointed ends just to the egg yolks and reserve. Remove the egg yolks from the egg whites. Place the yolks in a small bowl and mash. Add the pâté, sherry, cream, salt and pepper and blend until smooth. Stuff egg whites with the sherry mixture. Cut reserved ends of the egg whites Vandyke fashion. Place the eggs in the orange cups, cut side down, and place the egg white points on top of the eggs. Pipe mayonnaise rosettes at the base of each petal. This makes 4 servings.

3

4 hard-boiled eggs
¹/₄ c. Basic Emergency Aspic (Salads, pg. 4)
¹/₂ c. Basic Mornay Sauce (Sauces, pg. 11)
4 Vol-Au-Vent Shells (Desserts, pg. 65)
¹/₄ c. (about) cooked green peas

Peel and chill the eggs. Chill by stirring the aspic over a bowl of ice until syrupy. Spread the cold Mornay sauce on the inside of the Vol-Au-Vent Shells. Place the eggs, pointed ends down, in the shells. Spoon the aspic over the eggs, then place the peas around top of the shells. Chill until the aspic is firm. Frozen patty shells, baked and centers removed, may be substituted for Vol-Au-Vent Shells. This makes 4 servings.

4

8 ¹/₂-in. slices rye bread
4 hard-boiled eggs
1 tbsp. freshly grated Parmesan cheese
¹/₂ tsp. dry mustard
Salt and freshly ground pepper to taste
Basic Blender Mayonnaise (Sauces, pg. 3)
4 tsp. Emergency Pâté (pg. 29) or canned pâté
8 Gherkin Tassels (General Information, pg. 17)

Cut the bread with an oval 2 x 2³/₄-inch cookie cutter. Place the bread ovals on a baking sheet and toast until well browned. Peel the eggs and cut in half lengthwise. Remove the egg yolks, place in a small bowl and mash. Add the cheese, mustard, salt, pepper and enough mayonnaise to moisten, then mix well. Place the egg yolk mixture in the egg white cavities. Spread 1 teaspoon of pâté on each bread oval. Place egg halves, cut side down, on pâté on bread ovals, then garnish with Gherkin Tassels. This makes 8 servings.

5

4 ¹/₂-in. slices pumpernickel bread
4 hard-boiled eggs
2 tbsp. finely ground shrimp
¹/₂ tsp. paprika
Dash of lemon juice
Salt and freshly ground pepper to taste
Basic Blender Mayonnaise (Sauces, pg. 3)

Cut the bread slices with a 2-inch round cookie cutter. Place the bread rounds on a baking sheet and toast until well browned. Peel the eggs and cut in half lengthwise. Remove the egg yolks, place in a small bowl and mash. Add the shrimp, paprika, lemon juice, salt, pepper and enough mayonnaise to moisten, then mix well. Place the egg yolk mixture in a pastry bag with large star tube affixed and pipe a small mound onto each bread round. Press 2 egg white halves into each mound, having rounded ends together and pointed ends slightly extended. Pipe remaining egg yolk mixture between egg white halves. This makes 4 servings.

6

4 sm. tomatoes, skinned (Vegetables, pg. 27)
2 hard-boiled eggs
1 3-oz. package cream cheese, softened
¹/₂ tsp. celery salt
1 tsp. onion juice
Salt and freshly ground pepper to taste
Basic Blender Mayonnaise (Sauces, pg. 3)
4 thin slices pimento-stuffed olives

Slice the top off the stem end of each tomato, then scoop out the pulp, leaving a shell. Invert tomato shells onto a rack to drain. Peel the eggs. Cut a thin slice off both ends of each egg and reserve. Cut the eggs in half and remove the egg yolks. Chop the egg whites fine. Place the egg yolks in a medium-sized bowl and mash. Add the cream cheese, celery salt, onion juice, salt and pepper and mix well. Stir in enough mayonnaise to moisten, then fold in the egg whites. Spoon the egg mixture into the tomato shells, mounding top of each. Cut the reserved egg white slices Vandyke fashion and place 1 slice on mound of each tomato. Place an olive slice on each egg white slice. This makes 4 servings.

7

4 ¹/₂-in. slices cucumber
4 hard-boiled eggs
1 tbsp. caviar
2 tbsp. whipped cream
Salt and freshly ground pepper to taste

Canelle the cucumber slices as shown in Illustration No. 1 (Salads, pg. 10). Peel the eggs and cut thin slice from round end of each egg. Cut the eggs in half lengthwise. Remove the egg yolks, place in a small bowl and mash. Add the caviar, whipped cream, salt and pepper and mix until smooth. Spoon the egg yolk mixture into the egg white cavities, spreading thin layer over cut surfaces, then press 2 egg halves together. Remove any filling from outside surface of the eggs. Place the eggs, cut end down, on the cucumber slices. Garnish with pimento strips. This makes 4 servings.

egg and anchovy mousse

This highly flavored Egg and Anchovy Mousse is tempting both in eye and taste appeal. The mousse has been easily shaped into a mound and placed on an elegant serving plate. Savory Paprika Butter has been piped into frilly petals and delicate leaves to add a gourmet touch to this rich appetizer spread.

anchovies

From ancient days to modern times, anchovies have been highly prized as a seafood delicacy. By definition, anchovies are a very small herring-like fish common to Mediterranean waters.

The use of anchovies dates back to both Roman and Greek cultures. Greek fishermen netted anchovies along with sardines and tuna. As their civilization progressed, fresh fish became a luxury. Neighboring Romans found a more sophisticated method of using anchovies which laid the basis for our modern usage of anchovies in sauces and meat dishes. These ancient connoisseurs combined anchovies with other fish and oysters. The mixture was covered with salt, dried in the sun, and combined with herbs and spices. It was enjoyed by weatlhy Romans as a kind of appetizer.

The use of anchovies today is almost unlimited. When added to salads, anchovies lend a zesty tang. For special occasions, anchovies served with assorted crackers are excellent *hors d'oeuvres*. When mixed into a paste, anchovies make a delicious spread or a tasty garnish for the relish tray. Nibblers in a hurry will also enjoy a snack of anchovies right from the tin.

EGG AND ANCHOVY MOUSSE

6 hard-boiled eggs
2 2-oz. cans anchovy fillets
3¼ tsp. lemon juice
½ c. butter, softened
¼ tsp. white pepper
¼ c. Basic Blender Mayonnaise *(Sauces, pg. 3)*

Cut the eggs into slices and process through a ricer or a food mill. Drain the anchovy fillets well on absorbent paper, then place them on a chopping block. Sprinkle with ¼ teaspoon of lemon juice. Mash into a smooth paste. Place the butter in a mixer bowl and beat with an electric mixer until light and fluffy. Add the anchovy mixture gradually, beating well after each addition. Add the eggs, 2 tablespoons at a time, mixing well. Stir in the pepper and mayonnaise and beat until well blended. Spoon the egg mixture onto a serving plate and shape into a mound with a knife. Chill overnight for flavors to blend. Make a pattern with fork tines around side. You may garnish the top with Savory Paprika Butter (General Information, page 30). Serve as a spread with toast rounds or crackers. This makes about 25 to 30 servings.

JAPANESE VEGETABLE SOUP

1 lb. lean pork
1 carrot
12 dried mushrooms
4 c. Basic Chicken Stock (Soups, pg. 2)
1 4-oz. can bamboo shoots, drained
1 tbsp. soy sauce
1/2 c. chopped fresh spinach leaves
1 tsp. powdered ginger

Cut the pork and carrot into julienne strips. Place the dried mushrooms in a small bowl. Add enough of the chicken stock to cover and let stand for 1 hour. Remove the mushrooms from the stock and slice, then place in a large saucepan. Add the stock from the bowl, remaining stock and the pork and bring to a boil. Reduce the heat to low and simmer for 10 minutes. Add the carrot, bamboo shoots and soy sauce and cook for 5 minutes longer. Stir in the spinach and ginger and boil rapidly for 2 minutes. This makes about 1 1/2 quarts of soup.

SOUPS IN ORIENTAL COOKERY

Soups play a very important role in Oriental Cookery. Like many other areas of Chinese and Japanese cuisine, soups may generally be characterized by their variety and elegant simplicity — eye appeal is considered to be as important as taste.

There are three basic types of soups in oriental cuisine. The clear soup which is most often served at the beginning of a meal is similar to consommé or bouillon. The second type is thicker, somewhat sweeter and is called miso soup. It is usually flavored with red or white soybean paste. The third variety of soup is quite thick, very much like a stew and is served as a hearty main course for lunch or dinner.

One of the most important ingredients necessary for the preparation of a perfect soup, whether a clear broth or a thick miso, is called dashi. This tea-colored mixture is a combination of clear fish broth and shoyu, (soy sauce). Dashi is considered to be an indispensable part of oriental soup-making and a reasonable facsimile may be achieved by combining beef or chicken stock, clam juice and soy sauce to taste.

ORIENTAL CLAM SOUP

2 c. chicken broth
2 c. clam juice
2 c. minced clams
1/4 c. minced onion
2 tbsp. chopped fresh parsley
2 tbsp. soy sauce
1 tbsp. sake

Combine the chicken broth and clam juice in a large saucepan. Add the clams and onion and bring to a boil. Reduce heat and simmer for 10 minutes. Add the parsley, soy sauce and sake and cook for 2 minutes longer. Serve in soup bowls. This makes about 6 servings.

SALTED ALMONDS

2 c. shelled almonds
1/4 c. salad oil
Salt to taste

Pour the almonds into boiling water in a large saucepan. Remove from heat and let stand for about 5 minutes or until skins are soft. Drain, then remove the skins from almonds. Spread the almonds on a cookie pan and let stand until dry. Sprinkle with the oil and stir until the almonds are coated evenly. Sprinkle with salt and stir again. Bake in a preheated 350-degree oven until lightly browned, stirring frequently. Cool, then store in an airtight container.

watercress and potato soup with salted almonds

One of the most delicious of the light oriental soups is Watercress and Potato Soup, a tasty combination of savory broth, potatoes and watercress. Serve with salted almonds for a simple but elegant first course.

EGG SOUP

2 c. Basic Beef Stock *(pg. 2)*
2 tbsp. cornstarch
3 c. clam juice
2 tbsp. soy sauce
2 eggs, beaten
1/3 c. chopped green onions

Combine 1/4 cup of the stock with the cornstarch and blend until smooth. Pour the remaining stock and the clam juice into a large saucepan and place over medium high heat. Stir in the cornstarch mixture and soy sauce and bring to a boil, stirring constantly. Pour the eggs carefully onto the surface of the boiling soup and cook until the eggs are set. Ladle into soup bowls and sprinkle with the green onions. This makes about 5 servings.

WATERCRESS AND POTATO SOUP

1 1/2 lb. potatoes
1 1/4 c. Basic Chicken Stock *(pg. 2)*
3 1/2 c. milk
2 c. watercress leaves
Salt and freshly ground pepper to taste
1/4 c. butter

Peel and chop the potatoes, then cook according to the steaming instructions (Vegetables, pg. 7). Combine the stock and milk in a large saucepan and place over medium heat. Add the watercress leaves. Bring to a boil, then reduce the heat and simmer until the watercress leaves are tender. Strain the stock mixture and return the liquid to the saucepan. Place the watercress in a blender container and process until puréed. Add to the stock mixture. Place the potatoes in the blender container and process until puréed, then stir into the stock mixture. Season with salt and pepper. Reheat and add the butter, stirring until melted. Ladle into soup bowls and garnish with watercress leaves. Serve with Salted Almonds. This makes 6 to 8 servings.

EGG ROLLS

2 eggs
2¾ c. water
2 c. all-purpose flour
4 tbsp. peanut oil
2 c. bamboo shoots, chopped
3 c. fresh bean sprouts or 1
    1-lb. can bean sprouts
3 tbsp. soy sauce
2 tbsp. minced green onion or scallions
½ c. slivered dried mushrooms
1 tbsp. sherry
2 tbsp. cornstarch
1 tsp. salt
1 lb. ground pork
1 tbsp. minced fresh gingerroot

Beat the eggs and water together with a whisk until blended, then add the flour, mixing until smooth. With a pastry brush, brush a thin layer of the batter into a 5-inch square in a hot, lightly greased 7-inch skillet. Brush in a small amount of batter crosswise if holes appear in the batter. Cook for about 1 minute or until just set. Repeat until all batter is used, stacking the pancake squares on a platter. Heat 2 tablespoons of the oil in a large skillet. Add the bamboo shoots and bean sprouts (canned bean sprouts must be drained) and sauté, stirring constantly, until heated through. Add 2 tablespoons of the soy sauce and sauté for about 30 seconds longer. Remove the bean sprout mixture from the skillet and set aside. Add 1 tablespoon of the oil to the same skillet and sauté the onion and mushrooms for about 5 minutes or until onion is just tender. Remove the onion mixture from the skillet and set aside. Combine remaining soy sauce, sherry, 1 tablespoon of the cornstarch and salt in a bowl. Add the pork and mix well. Add the remaining oil to the skillet and sauté the pork mixture for about 15 minutes or until the pork is cooked, stirring frequently. Add the bean sprout mixture, the onion mixture and gingerroot and cool. Combine remaining cornstarch and ½ cup of cold water. Place 1½ teaspoons of the filling across the bottom end of each pancake square about 1 inch from the edge. Moisten the side edges of the squares with the cornstarch mixture, then fold the bottom edge over the filling. Fold in the right and left sides about 1 inch, then moisten the top edge with the cornstarch mixture. Roll up the squares, sealing well. Fry in 390-degree oil in a deep fat fryer until golden brown, then drain well on paper toweling. You may serve these with Duk Sauce (Sauces, pg. 31). The Egg Rolls may be frozen before frying. One pound of cooked, cleaned, minced shrimp may be used instead of the pork. This makes 45 to 50 rolls.

ANCHOVY-PUFF PASTRY FISH

10 anchovy fillets
Basic Puff Pastry trimmings *(Desserts, pg. 22)*
1 recipe Anglais Glaze *(Breads, pg. 6)*
10 capers

Drain the anchovy fillets well on paper toweling. Place the pastry trimmings together on a lightly floured surface and roll out as thin as possible. Cut into 1¼ x 3½-inch pieces. Cut 20 fish shapes from the pastry strips, using the pattern made from the illustration. Brush 10 of the pastry fish with the glaze. Place 1 anchovy fillet down center of each glazed fish as shown on dotted line of pattern, splitting the end with a sharp knife and curving for the tail. Top the anchovy-filled pastry with the remaining pastry fish, pressing the edges together to seal well. Brush tops with the glaze and place the capers on the fish for eyes, pressing in gently. Place on a lightly floured baking sheet. Bake in a preheated 400-degree oven for 12 to 15 minutes or until lightly browned. Serve hot. This makes 10 appetizers.

HOW TO CUT PASTRY FISH:
Cut a cardboard pattern from this diagram.

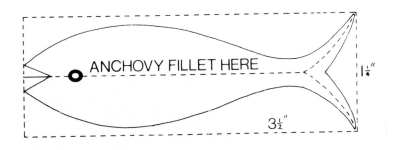

ANCHOVY FILLET HERE

1¼"

3½"

SCALLOPS IN SOY SAUCE

1 c. soy sauce
2 tbsp. sugar
2 tsp. minced gingerroot
1 tbsp. lemon juice
½ tsp. monosodium glutamate
1 lb. scallops

Combine the soy sauce, sugar, gingerroot, lemon juice and monosodium glutamate in a saucepan and bring to a boil. Cut the scallops into bite-sized pieces. Add the scallops and cook over moderate heat until all the liquid has evaporated. Serve hot with wooden picks. This makes about 25 pieces.

SCALLOPS IN WINE

1½ lb. fresh scallops
1 c. dry white wine
¼ c. vegetable oil
2 tsp. grated onion
1 tsp. sugar
¼ tsp. salt
⅛ tsp. crushed dried rosemary leaves
⅛ tsp. freshly ground pepper
2 tbsp. melted butter
1 tbsp. lemon juice

Place the scallops in a skillet and pour the wine over the scallops. Bring to a boil, then reduce the heat and simmer for 6 minutes. Drain the scallops and reserve the liquid. Cut the scallops into bite-sized pieces if large and place in a bowl. Combine the reserved liquid, oil, onion, sugar, salt, rosemary and pepper and pour over the scallops. Marinate in the refrigerator for several hours, stirring occasionally. Drain the scallops and reserve the marinade. Place the scallops in the blazer pan of a chafing dish. Combine the reserved marinade, butter and lemon juice in a saucepan and heat through. Pour over the scallops. Keep warm over hot water. Serve with wooden picks. This makes about 50 appetizers.

ROCK LOBSTER APPETIZERS

12 2-oz. frozen rock lobster-tails
6 tbsp. butter
6 tbsp. all-purpose flour
1½ c. half and half cream
1 tsp. grated lemon rind
1 tsp. paprika
2 eggs, separated
Salt and freshly ground pepper to taste
½ c. freshly grated Cheddar or Parmesan cheese

Drop the frozen lobster-tails into a kettle of boiling, salted water and bring to a boil again. Drain the lobster-tails immediately and drench with cold water. Remove the underside membrane with scissors and pull out the lobster meat, reserving the shells. Dice the lobster meat. Melt the butter in top of a double boiler over boiling water and stir in the flour until smooth. Add the cream gradually, stirring constantly, and cook until thickened. Add the lemon rind and paprika. Stir a small amount of the sauce into the beaten egg yolks, then stir the mixture back into the sauce. Cook for 2 minutes longer, stirring constantly. Season with salt and pepper. Combine the lobster meat and half the sauce, mixing well. Spoon the lobster mixture into the reserved shells and place the shells on a baking sheet. Heat the remaining sauce, add the cheese and stir until it is melted. Cool slightly and fold in the stiffly beaten egg whites. Spoon the egg white mixture over the lobster mixture in the shells. Bake in a preheated 350-degree oven for 25 to 30 minutes or until puffed and lightly browned. Serve in a chafing dish over hot water. This makes 12 appetizers.

rock lobster appetizers

This tempting array of hors d'oeuvres and appetizers is certain to be the center of attention at a party.

portuguese cucumber soup

Chilled cucumber soup, laced with fresh tomatoes, onions, garlic and lemon juice, is ideal for a summer luncheon. Basic Chicken Stock and a little white wine give this colorful soup added flavor.

portuguese cucumber soup

Cucumbers, with their cool, refreshing taste, blend well with many foods, for example tomatoes, onions, lettuce, garlic, peppers, radishes and cabbage, all of which are delicious in tossed salads. However, tomatoes, onions and garlic, along with fresh cucumbers, also make delectable ingredients for a light, refreshing, chilled soup.

Portuguese Cucumber Soup, made with chicken stock and wine seasoned with lemon juice or wine vinegar, is an excellent choice for a light luncheon. Served chilled, it is perfect for mid-summer meals. Make the most of its attractive appearance by serving it in clear glass soup bowls.

PORTUGUESE CUCUMBER SOUP

3 lg. cucumbers
4 tomatoes, skinned (*Vegetables, pg. 27*)
1 sm. red sweet pepper
1 sm. green sweet pepper
1 glove of garlic, pressed
2 tbsp. finely chopped onion
5 c. Basic Chicken Stock, clarified (*pg. 2*)
½ tsp. salt
1 tbsp. fresh lemon juice
½ c. dry white wine

Peel the cucumbers and remove the seeds, then grate the pulp coarsely. Place in a large glass bowl. Chop the tomatoes and add to the bowl. Remove the seeds and membranes from the peppers and chop coarsely. Add to the bowl. Add the remaining ingredients and mix. Chill before serving. Serve with Fried Croutons (Breads, pg. 16). This makes about 6 servings.

SAVORY SWISS ROLL

½ c. sifted all-purpose flour
⅔ c. freshly grated Parmesan cheese
1 tbsp. chopped parsley
3 eggs
½ recipe Emergency Pâté *(pg. 29)*
  or 3 lg. cans pâté
1 8-oz. package cream cheese, softened
⅓ c. Piquant Mayonnaise *(Sauces, pg. 3)*

Prepare the jelly roll pan and paper according to the illustrations No. 1 through No. 3 (Desserts, pg. 3). Combine the flour, cheese and parsley in a small bowl and mix well. Place the eggs in a small mixer bowl and beat with an electric mixer for about 4 minutes or until thick and lemon colored. Shake the flour mixture lightly over the eggs and fold in completely with a rubber spatula. Pour into the prepared pan, then spread evenly to the corners of the pan. Bake in a preheated 425-degree oven for 9 minutes or until golden brown. Turn out onto the prepared paper and cool slightly. Remove the waxed paper carefully and trim the edges. Spread softened pâté over the top, covering completely. Roll as for a jelly roll, starting with the long side. Place the cream cheese in a small mixer bowl and beat until fluffy. Add the mayonnaise and beat until well combined. Place the cheese mixture in a pastry bag with a medium-sized star tube affixed. Pipe rows of rosettes over top and around ends as shown in the illustration. Garnish between rows with chopped parsley. Cut into slices to serve. This makes about 20 servings.

savory swiss roll

This Savory Swiss Roll is a discovery for those who prefer a savory rather than a sweet refreshment. The decorative parsley hints of its "non-sweet" taste.

savory pastry sandwich

This attractive hors d'oeuvre sandwich is deliciously filled with layered olive-egg and chicken salad mixtures. Beautifully garnished with cream cheese mixture, sliced olives and gherkins, it is an excellent beginning for a bridge luncheon or patio brunch.

SAVORY PASTRY SANDWICH

1 recipe Basic Cold Yeast Dough (Breads, pgs. 20-21)
1 recipe Pecan-Chicken Salad Filling
1 recipe Olive-Egg Salad Filling
1 3-oz. package cream cheese, softened
½ recipe Mustard Mayonnaise (Sauces, pg. 3)

Cut the chilled dough into thirds. Roll out ⅓ of the dough on a floured board to about ⅜-inch thickness. Cut two 12 x 3 ½-inch strips and place on a baking sheet. Repeat the process with the two remaining balls of dough. Bake in a preheated 400-degree oven for 10 minutes or until golden brown. Transfer with wide spatulas to racks to cool. Place 1 baked layer on a serving platter and spread with 1 ½ cups of Pecan-Chicken Salad Filling. Top with second layer and spread with 1 ½ cups of Olive-Egg Salad Filling. Repeat, using 2 more layers, then top with the fifth baked layer. Combine the cream cheese and mayonnaise in a small mixing bowl, stirring until smooth and of spreading consistency. Frost the top layer with the mayonnaise mixture. Chill for several minutes, then make ridges in frosting, using the tines of a fork. Decorate with gherkin slices, sliced pimento-stuffed green olives and finely chopped parsley, if desired. Chill until ready to serve, then cut carefully into wedges. Cut the remaining baked layer crosswise into narrow strips and spread with the remaining fillings for open-faced finger sandwiches, if desired. This makes 4 to 6 servings.

PECAN-CHICKEN SALAD FILLING

3 c. finely diced cooked chicken
1 c. minced celery
½ c. ground pecans
⅓ c. Basic Mayonnaise (Sauces, pg. 3)
¼ c. sour cream
1 tsp. salt
⅛ tsp. onion salt
2 tbsp. lemon juice

Combine the chicken, celery and pecans in a large bowl. Mix the remaining ingredients, then add to the chicken mixture and stir until well combined. Chill thoroughly. This makes about 5 cups of filling.

OLIVE-EGG SALAD FILLING

10 hard-boiled eggs, finely chopped
1 c. finely chopped pimento-stuffed olives
Salt to taste
¾ c. Basic Mayonnaise (Sauces, pg. 3)

Combine the eggs, olives and salt in a mixing bowl. Add the mayonnaise and mix well. Chill thoroughly. This makes about 4 ½ cups of filling.

stuffed grape leaves

These Stuffed Grape Leaves are filled with a mixture of rice, onions and tomato purée. Their sausage-like shapes and their savory flavor make them a perfect hors d'oeuvre.

In Turkey, Stuffed Grape Leaves, better known as *dolmas*, are made by combining mixed vegetables (eggplants, tomatoes, artichokes and zucchini) together with minced lamb or ground beef, rolled up and baked in grape leaves. However, by general definition, *dolmas* are any stuffed foods. They may be vegetable shells, made of eggplant, green pepper or zucchini, stuffed with a meat and vegetable mixture. Or they may be a savory mixture rolled up in edible leaves, such as grape, cabbage or fig leaves. They are frequently served as a main course. In this section, *dolmas* are made with a seasoned mixture of rice, onions and tomato purée, rolled up in grape leaves. These sausage-like rolls are then baked and served as a hot hors d'oeuvre for a cocktail party.

STUFFED GRAPE LEAVES

Olive oil
2 lb. ground lamb or chuck
1 ½ c. chopped onions
1   15-oz. can tomato sauce
¼ c. lemon juice
¼ c. chopped fresh parsley
¼ c. currants
½ c. pine nuts
½ tsp. cinnamon
1 tsp. paprika
½ tsp. allspice
1 recipe Risotto *(Cereals, pg. 2)*
2   1-qt. jars grape leaves

Heat ⅓ cup of oil in a large frying pan. Add the lamb and cook over medium heat, stirring constantly, until the lamb loses red color. Add the onions and cook, stirring, until the lamb is lightly browned. Add the tomato sauce, lemon juice, parsley, currants, pine nuts, cinnamon, paprika and allspice and mix well. Reduce the heat and simmer until most of the liquid has evaporated. Stir in the Risotto until well mixed, then cool. Wash the grape leaves in hot water, then cut off the stems and open the leaves. Shape 1 to 2 teaspoons of lamb mixture, according to the size of leaves, into rolls and place near the stem end of the leaves. Fold over sides of the leaves, then roll up from the stem end. Grease a large casserole heavily with olive oil and place a layer of grape leaves over the bottom of the casserole in layers. Cover the casserole. Bake in a preheated 350-degree oven for 45 minutes. Serve hot or cold. If served cold, do not uncover until the *dolmas* have cooled to prevent discoloration of leaves. This makes 70 to 80 *dolmas*.

avocado appetizer

As a first course appetizer, the avocado can be served in many ways. The nutlike, buttery flavor of avocados blends readily with a wide assortment of other flavors. These avocados have been halved and filled with four delicious mixtures. In a clockwise presentation, the first pair has been filled with a Vinaigrette dressing spiced with herbs. The second pair has been filled with shrimp in a special mayonnaise sauce. An unusual scoring technique has been used on the third pair which is filled with Madeira sauce. Flaked fresh crab meat fills the fourth pair of avocados which is bordered with rosettes of mayonnaise.

AVOCADO APPETIZERS

4 lg. avocados
Lemon juice
4 tbsp. Vinaigrette Aux Fines Herbes *(Sauces, pg. 2)*
4 tbsp. Madeira
1 c. Basic Mayonnaise *(Sauces, pg. 3)*
⅛ tsp. hot sauce
1 tsp. paprika
Salt to taste
1 c. fresh crab meat, flaked
1 c. cooked small shrimp

Cut the avocados and remove the seeds according to the instructions (Salads, pg. 15), then brush the cut sides of the avocados with lemon juice. Spoon 2 tablespoons of the vinaigrette into each cavity of 2 avocado halves. Spoon 2 tablespoons of the Madeira into each cavity of 2 more of the avocado halves. Place the mayonnaise in a mixing bowl. Add the hot sauce, paprika, salt and 2 teaspoons of lemon juice and mix well, then divide in half. Add the crab meat to ½ of the mayonnaise mixture and stir until combined. Mound the crab meat mixture on 2 more of the avocado halves and garnish each mound with 1 of the shrimp. Add the remaining shrimp to the remaining mayonnaise mixture and mix well. Place half the shrimp mixture on each of the remaining avocado halves. Place the halves on a serving platter as shown in the illustration, then garnish as desired. Each guest can make his own choice. This makes 8 servings.

assorted canapés

The *canapé* has long been the standard way to open the first course of a dinner party or to greet guests for any festive affair. The variety of *canapés* is endless and is limited only by the hostess' imagination.

Canapés may be served warm from the oven or well chilled. The smaller, less complicated ones are served as an accompaniment to drinks at cocktail parties. Many savory *canapés* can double as both a first course at dinner or as a part of the meal itself or as a savory after dinner in the British manner.

Although not mandatory, a wise hostess knows that serving a large assortment of *canapés* which differ in both appearance and flavor is very elegant and distinctive. The preparation of *canapés* need not be expensive because their primary function is to tempt and interest the appetite of guests. As an added advantage, many types of *canapés* can be prepared wholly or partially in advance of serving time. They may be refrigerated or put in plastic wrap to preserve freshness.

Imagination plays the largest role in creating *canapés* which are both tasty and colorful. Fillings and spreads may range from sweet to savory. Sweet fillings utilize such ingredients as sweet pickles, relishes, nuts, cream, and citrus flavorings. The heartier *canapés* may be spread or filled with mayonnaise, pork, beef, fish, caviar, eggs, vegetables, or cheese.

Canapés may also be varied by different decorating and garnishing techniques. As bread is most commonly used as the base of a *canapé*, all different kinds may be served toasted or plain. This bread can be cut into different shapes and sizes to add an extra flair to the *canapé*. Favorite shapes are the rectangle, square, and the plain and scalloped circle. *Canapés* may be served as either an open-faced, closed or rolled sandwich.

For the *canapé* tray, a variety of garnishes add a special finishing beauty. These may range from a few sprigs of fresh parsley to the fancifully canelled Lemon Pig's Ears (General Information, pg. 31). As a creative cook, you will enjoy the variety of delicious *canapés* which we present in this section.

The Creative Homemaker's Academy © MCMLXXIII
Selected Illustrations © B.P.C. Publishing Limited MCMLXX

SUGGESTIONS FOR CANAPÉ FILLINGS OR SPREADS

1 Use braunschweiger topped with pickle relish.

2 Try pickled herring, cut julienne-style, topped with thin onion rings, then spread with horseradish mixed with a small amount of whipping cream.

3 Mix finely diced roast pork with Hot Sweet and Sour Barbecue Sauce (Sauces, pg. 8).

4 Mix finely diced luncheon meat, minced cucumber, minced tomato and minced pimento with Basic Mayonnaise (Sauces, pg. 3).

5 Try Savory Paprika Butter (General Information, pg. 30) mixed with grated cheese and freshly ground pepper.

6 Use caviar mixed with lemon juice and Basic Parsley Butter (General Information, pg. 30).

7 Mix Spanish Sauce (Sauces, pg. 14) with scrambled eggs.

8 Try cream cheese blended with sherry, ground walnuts and minced celery hearts.

9 Use thick Basic Mornay Sauce (Sauces, pg. 11) mixed with crab meat and a small amount of anchovy paste.

10 Mix finely chopped, cooked shrimp with Basic Blender Mayonnaise (Sauces, pg. 3) and a dash of hot sauce.

11 Use flaked salmon mixed with sour cream and minced dill pickle.

12 Mix puréed cooked spinach with finely diced ham, cream cheese and celery salt.

13 Try finely diced, cooked chicken and minced tomato folded into scrambled eggs.

14 Mix finely chopped, hard-boiled egg and cooked pork sausage with half Basic Mayonnaise (Sauces, pg. 3) and half Basic Vinaigrette (Sauces, pg. 2).

ASSORTED CANAPÉS

On opposite ends of a serving platter are 2 decorative lemon halves (General Information, pg. 31). Below the left-hand lemon is a rectangular slice of thin, buttered bread covered with smoked salmon, then garnished with a lengthwise slice of hard-boiled egg and topped with a caper. The next sandwich, going clockwise, is a fluted circle of thin, buttered bread topped with an identically shaped slice of salami, with an asparagus tip garnished with a strip of pimento on top. Next to this sand-wich is a fluted circle of thin bread with cream cheese mixed with whipping cream piped over the bread, then topped with an English walnut half and sprinkled with paprika. These 3 sandwiches are re-peated all around the edge of the platter. Down the center of the platter are circles of bread covered with caviar and piped around the edges with the cream cheese mixed with whipping cream, then garnished with thin slices of gherkins. To the left of the platter are 2 containers, one with red caviar, and the other with black caviar.

assorted canapés

The simplicity of this tray provides just the right contrast for the elegance of these assorted canapés. Perched on the outside of the tray are two cleverly canelled Lemon Pig's Ears. The instructions for these canapés are not given with definite amounts for ingredients as you may prepare them in as small amounts as you desire, then decide on your favorites. Ingredients used require only minutes of preparation. Such delicious items as asparagus, pimento, cream cheese, caviar, smoked salmon and red caviar are quickly assembled for tempting canapés. Individual bowls of red caviar and black caviar accompany the canapé tray and make this assortment of appetizers suitable for the most special occasions.

greek
appetizers

greek fish appetizers

Greek Fish Appetizers are fun to serve as conversation food as well as being very delicious. This Greek meze or hors d'oeuvres is made from a combination of whitefish and seasonings. The mixture is shaped into little balls and fried to the golden brown perfection shown here. The finished appetizers are impaled on picks. The bowl of sweet and spicy Pimento Escoffier provides a perfect accompaniment for these zesty little appetizers.

GREEK FISH APPETIZERS

All-purpose flour
1 tsp. salt
1/8 tsp. paprika
3 tbsp. vegetable oil
1 c. milk
1/2 tsp. Worcestershire sauce
2 tsp. grated onion
2 c. cooked flaked whitefish
1 egg
Fine dry bread crumbs

Mix 6 tablespoons of flour, the salt and paprika in a small saucepan. Stir in the oil and mix until smooth. Add the milk and mix well. Cook over low heat, stirring constantly, until thick and smooth. Remove from the heat, then stir in the Worcestershire sauce, onion and whitefish. Refrigerate until chilled. Beat the egg with 2 tablespoons of water. Shape the whitefish mixture into small balls, using 1 teaspoon for each, then roll in flour. Dip in the egg, then roll in bread crumbs. Cook in deep fat at 350 degrees until well browned, then drain on paper toweling. Place on a serving plate and insert the end of a small skewer or pick in each ball. Serve with Pimento Escoffier (Vegetables, pg. 31). This makes about 48 appetizers.

CLAM BALLS

3 cans minced clams
3 stalks celery, minced
1 onion, ground
Salt and freshly ground pepper to taste
6 hard-boiled eggs, diced
1/2 lb. moist bread crumbs

Drain the clams, reserving 2 cups of broth. Add water to make 2 cups of broth if needed. Combine the celery, onion and 1 1/2 cups of clam broth in a saucepan, then simmer until the vegetables are tender. Add the clams, salt and pepper to the vegetable mixture, then simmer for about 10 minutes. Add the eggs, remaining broth and bread crumbs, mixing well. Shape the clam mixture into small balls and chill thoroughly. Fry in deep fat at 350 degrees until browned. Serve immediately with wooden picks. This makes 30 to 40 small balls.

BAKED ITALIAN CROSTINI

24 slices sandwich bread
1 recipe Basic Béchamel Sauce (Sauces, pg. 4)
1/4 lb. fresh mushrooms, minced
1 tbsp. anchovy paste
Freshly grated Parmesan cheese

Cut 2 crescents from each bread slice, using a wet crescent cookie cutter. Place on a baking sheet. Bake in a preheated 450-degree oven until golden on top. Combine the sauce, mushrooms and anchovy paste, mixing well. Spread the sauce mixture on the untoasted side of the crescents and sprinkle liberally with Parmesan cheese. Place on an oven-proof serving dish. Bake in 400-degree oven until bubbly and browned. You may garnish these with olive slices or rolled anchovies with capers. This makes 48 crescents.

italian crostini

baked italian crostini

These attractive arrangements of Baked Italian Crostini make flavorful hot canapés. Popular in Italy as fried cheese sandwiches, these little bread crusts have been spread with a luscious combination of Béchamel sauce, mushrooms and anchovy paste. The bread squares are then topped with a generous sprinkling of Parmesan cheese, then browned until the cheese is bubbly. The bread shapes may be cut into crescents or squares prior to frying.

sardines with chopped cooked eggs

For an easy-to-prepare appetizer, few items are as versatile as sardines. By definition, a sardine is any one of the several varieties of tiny fish which can be served fresh or preserved. Sardines may either be salted, preserved in brine, or canned in oil, mustard or tomato sauce. As the name indicates, sardines derived their origin from the little fish common to Sardinia. For particular palates, only the best brand of canned sardines should be purchased. In contrast to their less expensive counterparts, best quality sardines are characterized by their tiny size and are packed in the finest oil available to protect their superlative flavor.

SARDINES WITH CHOPPED EGGS

1 flat can sardines in mustard
2 flat cans sardines in oil
4 hard-boiled eggs
Fresh parsley

Place the sardines in mustard in a small bowl and mash, then place off center on a large serving plate. Drain the sardines in oil, then place them on the plate in a fan shape as shown in the illustration. Separate the egg yolks and egg whites and chop each fine. Mound the egg whites on the left of the sardines to the center of the plate. Hold a knife in the center of the plate against the egg whites, then mound the egg yolks on the right half of the plate. Remove the knife. Place a border of parsley around the sardines. Garnish with cancelled lemon slices and strips of lemon peel (General Information, pg. 11). Serve with Basic Vinaigrette (Sauces, pg. 2). This makes about 4 servings.

sardines with chopped eggs

This colorfully assembled dish of sardines and chopped eggs makes a perfect last minute appetizer. Eggs have been hard-boiled, the whites and yolks separated and then chopped. Carefully selected sardines have been drained and garnished with parsley. Canelled slices of lemon border the dish.

COLD BEET SOUP WITH SOUR CREAM (BORSCHT)

2   1-lb. cans diced beets, drained
3 c. Basic Beef Stock *(pg. 2)*
1 tsp. wine vinegar
¼ c. Burgundy
1 tbsp. onion juice
¼ tsp. white pepper
2 tsp. celery salt
¼ c. orange juice
1 carton sour cream
1 tbsp. finely minced parsley

Combine half the beets and a small amount of the stock in a blender container and process until the beets are puréed. Repeat the process, using the remaining beets and a small amount of the stock. Combine the puréed beets mixture, the remaining stock, vinegar, Burgundy, onion juice, seasonings and orange juice and chill for several hours. Serve in individual soup bowls with a dollop of sour cream, sprinkled with parsley. Two pounds of fresh, cooked beets may be substituted for the canned beets. This makes 8 to 10 servings.

QUICK BORSCHT

1   ¼-in. thick lemon slice
1¾ c. sour cream
¼ tsp. salt
½ sm. onion, chopped
1 c. diced cooked beets
1 c. crushed ice

Cut the rind from the lemon and remove any seed. Place all the ingredients except the ice in the blender container and blend for 20 seconds. Add the ice and blend for 30 seconds longer. Serve in soup cups and garnish with a small dollop of additional sour cream. This makes about 4 servings.

cold beet soup

If you are looking for a soup with a foreign flavor, borscht or beet soup is an excellent one. The varieties of borscht are almost endless. This hearty soup dish is common to the Slavic countries, having originated in Russia and Poland. The recipes for borscht include a hefty meat and cabbage borscht from the Ukraine and a clear all beet borscht common to Poland. Most recipes for borscht include vinegar, vegetables, flavorings, salt, and pepper. These soups may be served either hot or cold. For extra flavor almost all versions of borscht are served with sour cream or a boiled potato.

cold beet soup with sour cream

This colorful cold beet soup is an appetizing way to begin any meal. Cooked or canned beet root has been cut, combined with seasonings, and placed in a blender. The mixture is then chilled until serving time. After the soup has been poured into bowls, a dollop of sour cream is added to each. A lavish sprinkling of freshly milled parsley perfectly complements the finished cold soup.

iced green bean soup

For an unusual first course appetizer, these bowls of Iced Green Bean Soup will certainly please the palate. Fresh green beans have been simmered with seasoning and stock until tender. Heavy cream is stirred in to add richness and flavor. Although this delicious soup is usually served icy cold, it is equally good piping hot.

ICED GREEN BEAN SOUP

1 lb. fresh green beans
6 c. Basic Chicken Stock (pg. 2)
1/2 tsp. thyme
1/4 tsp. savory
1 clove of garlic, pressed
1/2 c. whipping cream
Salt and freshly ground pepper to taste

Snap the ends from the green beans and cut the beans into large pieces. Combine the beans and stock in a large saucepan, then add the thyme, savory and garlic. Bring to a boil, then reduce heat and cover. Simmer until the beans are tender. Drain and reserve the liquid. Pour the reserved liquid back into the saucepan and boil until reduced to 4 cups. Place the beans in a blender container and process until pureed. Stir into the liquid in the saucepan and mix well. Bring to a boil, then stir in the cream and bring just to a boil. Remove from heat and season with salt and pepper. Cool, then chill until cold. The soup is equally delicious when served hot. Two 1-pound cans of green beans, drained, may be substituted, if desired. This makes 6 to 8 servings.

SENATOR'S SOUP

2 lb. dried navy beans
1 1/2 lb. smoked ham hocks
1 onion, chopped
1 tbsp. butter
Salt and freshly ground pepper to taste

Rinse the beans in hot water, then place in a soup kettle. Add 4 quarts of hot water and the ham hocks. Cover and boil slowly for 3 hours or until beans are very tender, adding more water, if needed. Sauté the onion in the butter until lightly browned, then add to the soup. Season with salt and pepper. This makes about 12 servings.

BLACK BEAN SOUP

2 c. dried black beans
1/4 lb. lean salt pork
2 med. onions
3 whole cloves
1/2 lb. diced lean beef
1/4 tsp. mace
1/8 tsp. cayenne pepper
1/2 c. diced carrot
Salt and pepper to taste
1/2 c. sherry
3 hard-boiled eggs, sliced
1/2 lemon, thinly sliced

Rinse the beans, then place in a large saucepan and cover with water. Soak for 1 hour, then drain off the water. Rinse the salt pork and slash to the rind several times. Add to the beans. Dice 1 onion and add to the beans. Stick the cloves in the remaining onion and add with the beef, mace, cayenne pepper and carrot. Pour in 4 quarts of water. Cover and simmer for 3 hours or until the beans are very tender. Season with salt and pepper. Remove the piece of salt pork. Process the soup in the blender container until puréed. Stir in the sherry just before serving. Pour into a heated tureen, then arrange the egg and lemon slices on the top. This makes 8 to 10 servings.

FRESH POTATO SWIRL SOUP

3 c. finely chopped onion
2 tbsp. butter
4 c. thinly sliced potatoes
¼ c. finely chopped fresh celery
3 c. chicken broth
1 tsp. salt
¼ tsp. white pepper
1 c. chopped fresh watercress
2 tbsp. chopped fresh parsley
½ c. water
1 c. whipping cream

Sauté the onion in the butter in a medium-sized saucepan until transparent. Add the potatoes, celery, broth, salt and pepper. Cover and simmer for about 25 minutes or until the vegetables are very tender. Process the mixture in the blender until puréed. Place 1 cup of the puréed mixture in a saucepan and add the watercress, parsley and water. Cover and simmer for 15 minutes. Place in the blender and process until puréed. Add ¾ cup of the cream to the potato mixture and the remaining ¼ cup cream to the watercress mixture. Chill both mixtures. Pour the potato mixture into a tureen, then pour the watercress mixture into the potato mixture and stir to swirl. This makes about 6 servings.

fresh potato swirl soup

This garden fresh soup is a delicious combination of creamy potatoes, green watercress and parsley. The unusual color effect has been achieved by preparing the potato and watercress bases separately. At the last moment prior to service, the watercress and parsley mixture is then gently swirled through the potato mixture to add a contrast in both color and flavor.

OYSTER BISQUE

1 qt. fresh oysters
3 c. Basic Chicken Stock *(pg. 2)*
1½ c. fine bread crumbs
⅓ c. finely chopped onion
1 c. finely diced celery
Salt and white pepper to taste
1 qt. milk, scalded
2 tbsp. butter
¼ c. sherry

Drain the oysters and reserve the liquid. Chop the oysters. Pour the chicken stock in a soup kettle. Add the reserved oyster liquid, bread crumbs, onion, celery, salt and pepper. Boil slowly, stirring frequently, for about 30 minutes. Process in the blender container until onion and celery are puréed, then return to the soup kettle. Add the oysters and heat thoroughly, but do not overcook. Stir in the milk, butter and sherry and heat through. Serve immediately. This makes 6 to 8 servings.

jerusalem artichoke soup

Steamed fresh Jerusalem artichokes combine with a simple roux base to create this creamy soup. This gently seasoned appetizer has a most unusual, rich flavor. A matching bowl filled with freshly grated Parmesan cheese and a few crisp grisini (Italian breadsticks) accompany this delightfully different soup.

JERUSALEM ARTICHOKES

Although the plant known as Jerusalem artichoke originated in North America, it was imported to France early in the seventeenth century. It was in this country that the Jerusalem artichoke gained its first real popularity through the skill of the master chef Parmentier.

In contrast to its name, the Jerusalem artichoke is a member of the sunflower family. It is a tall plant with an edible tuber similar to a potato. The Jerusalem artichoke has a sweet, watery taste and can be boiled or eaten raw. The name Jerusalem is a corruption of the Italian word *girasole* which translated means sunflower.

The best Jerusalem artichokes are available at the beginning of winter and spring. They should be used as soon as possible, as flavor quickly diminishes. Jerusalem artichokes are very firm in consistency and resemble globe artichokes only in flavor. Jerusalem artichokes may be used in salads and soups as well as making crisp pickles.

JERUSALEM ARTICHOKE SOUP

1 lb. Jerusalem artichokes
2½ c. Basic Chicken Stock *(pg. 2)*
2 tbsp. butter
2 tbsp. all-purpose flour
2½ c. milk
1½ tsp. salt
¼ tsp. white pepper
⅓ c. freshly grated Parmesan cheese

Steam the artichokes according to instructions for steaming (Vegetables, page 7). Cool and remove the skins with the tip of a sharp knife. Combine the artichokes and ¾ cup of the stock in the blender container and process until puréed. Melt the butter in the top of the double boiler over boiling water, then stir in the flour quickly. Cook, stirring, until smooth and bubbly. Stir in the milk gradually and cook, stirring constantly, until slightly thickened. Combine the milk mixture, puréed artichokes, remaining stock and seasonings in a heavy saucepan. Cook over low heat, stirring occasionally, for about 5 minutes. Stir in the cheese just before serving. Serve with additional cheese to sprinkle over the soup. This makes about 6 servings.

french
onion soup

There are so many wonderful recipes for onion soup, it is rather difficult to say there is one better than all others. However, our recipes are certainly among the best.

Onion soup may have as its base beef stock, chicken stock or even a simple canned consommé. Its color varies with the base used, and its texture with the ingredients. French Onion Soup is made with homemade Basic Beef Stock (pg. 2) which gives this soup a rich brown color. A generous amount of onions give it just the right pungency, and a topping of *croûtes* and melted Swiss cheese add an unusual flavor combination.

FRENCH ONION SOUP

½ c. butter
8 c. thinly sliced onions
1½ tsp. salt
3 tbsp. all-purpose flour
8 c. Basic Beef Stock *(pg. 2)*
Freshly ground pepper to taste
6 to 8 ½-inch slices of French bread
6 to 8 thin slices of Swiss cheese

Melt the butter in a large, heavy kettle over medium heat. Add the onions and salt and cook over low heat, stirring frequently, for about 20 minutes or until the onions are golden brown. Sprinkle the flour over the onions and stir until well blended. Remove from heat. Pour the stock into a large saucepan and bring to a boil over high heat. Stir into the onion mixture and mix well. Reduce the heat and cover. Simmer for 40 minutes, skimming off excess fat occasionally, then season with the pepper and additional salt, if needed. Prepare the slices of bread according to the instructions for Baked *Croûtes* (Breads, pg. 16), then place 1 slice of cheese on each *croûte*. Ladle the soup into individual ovenproof soup bowls and top each serving with a *croûte*. Place soup bowls on a broiler pan 8 inches from the source of heat and broil for 2 minutes or until the cheese is golden brown. Serve immediately. One cup of freshly grated Parmesan cheese may be used instead of the Swiss cheese slices. This makes 6 to 8 servings.

french onion soup

Savory French Onion Soup with croûtes coated in melted Swiss cheese makes a taste-tempting appetizer. Serve the soup piping hot while the cheese croûte is still bubbly.

cream of chicken soup

CREAM OF CHICKEN SOUP

4 c. Basic Chicken Stock *(pg. 2)*
2 c. finely chopped celery
1 sm. clove of garlic, pressed
¾ c. half and half cream
Salt and freshly ground white pepper to taste
2 c. minced cooked chicken
½ c. finely grated Parmesan cheese

Pour the stock into a large saucepan and bring to a boil. Add the celery and garlic and simmer for 10 minutes or until tender. Pour into a blender container and process until puréed, then return to the saucepan. Add the cream, salt and pepper, and bring just to the boiling point. Stir in the chicken and cheese and heat, stirring, until the cheese is melted and the soup is well blended. Serve in soup bowls. A dash of whipping cream may be poured into the center of each serving, if desired. This makes about 8 servings.

cream of chicken soup

Delicious homemade chicken stock is the base for this creamy, rich chicken soup. It is made with a hearty mixture of minced chicken, celery, cream and grated Parmesan cheese.

danish smørrebrød

Outstanding food preparation is part of Danish life-style. The Danes even have an organization entitled *Ekkodamark*, whose sole duty is to promote Danish food and demonstrate extravagant recipes to Danish homemakers.

One of the best known Danish creations is *Smørrebrød*, which literally translated means "buttered bread." However, it means much more than that. *Smørrebrød* is a lavish array of Danish open-faced sandwiches made with single slices of bread and piled high with various combinations of meats and garnishes.

Open-faced sandwiches are a traditional Danish lunch, but they also make perfect appetizers and *hors d'oeuvres*. You may, of course, use your choice of firm bread, cut in a variety of sizes and shapes with any combination of toppings. Black bread is most frequently used. Sour rye, which is also a Danish favorite, is available in the United States, but if it is not available in your area, dark pumpernickel makes an excellent substitute. The following recipe for Danish Open Sandwiches will give many suggestions for preparing these marvelously different appetizers.

DANISH OPEN SANDWICHES WITH MEAT

1 Beginning at the top center is a slice of toasted Danish black bread spread with butter, then covered with a lettuce leaf. A slice of roast pork is added and the sandwich is garnished with a stuffed prune, a broiled mushroom strip and a twisted orange slice.

2 The next sandwich, moving clockwise, is a slice of toasted brown bread spread with butter and topped with 4 slices of garlic bologna. Four asparagus tips, 2 broiled, fresh mushrooms caps and a radish rose (Cereals, pg. 21) are placed on top.

3 Next to this sandwich is one made of a slice of toasted rye bread spread with butter and topped with 3 folds of salami, leaving 1 corner of the bread exposed. A dollop of Basic Mayonnaise (Sauces, pg. 3), placed in the exposed corner, is topped with a smoked oyster or sardine, then garnished with a pimento slice and an onion ring.

4 The next sandwich is one made of a slice of toasted pumpernickel bread spread with butter. Two folded slices of barbecued pork are placed on the bread, then 2 broiled, whole, fresh mushrooms, capers and a gherkin tassel (General Information, pg. 17) are added.

5 The next sandwich is made of a slice of toasted firm white bread spread with butter and topped with 2 slices of fried bacon, 2 rolled pastrami slices, and a gherkin tassel.

6 The next sandwich is one made of a slice of toasted cheese bread spread with butter and covered with a slice of luncheon ham. A dollop of mayonnaise is placed in 1 corner, then a radish rose is pressed into the mayonnaise. Another slice of luncheon ham is added, then the ham is garnished with 2 hard-boiled egg quarters. These sandwiches are repeated around the tray.

7 Two of the sandwiches in the center of the tray are made of slices of toasted whole wheat bread spread with butter, then topped with chicken spread. Canelled cucumber slices and hollowed-out tomato halves filled with mayonnaise and sprinkled with chopped chives are placed on the chicken spread.

8 The remaining sandwiches are made of 4 toasted crackers spread with butter and topped with lettuce, then covered with tuna. The tuna is garnished with chopped hard-boiled eggs, chopped chives and chopped dill.

Mayonnaise may be used instead of butter for spreading on the bread, if desired. This makes 18 sandwiches.

danish open sandwiches with meat

These attractive appetizer sandwiches contain a delicious assortment of bacon, sausages, pork, liver, salami, mushrooms, onions, asparagus, radishes, prunes, oranges, boiled eggs and lettuce leaves.

avocado
appetizer

Avocados, as we have mentioned many times before, have such a blendable taste and texture, they can be combined and served in a variety of appetizing ways. Here we are introducing Avocado Cream, which is a most versatile appetizer. It can be used as a dip, a salad, topping, or even a spread for small crackers or bread rounds. For a creative *hors d'oeuvre*, pipe it in rosettes on different flavored crackers.

AVOCADO CREAM

2 ripe avocados
1/4 c. lime or lemon juice
Dash of hot sauce
Dash of paprika
1 c. whipping cream, whipped

Cut the avocados in half lengthwise, twisting gently to separate the halves. Insert a sharp knife directly into the seed and twist to lift out. Peel and quarter the avocados. Place in a blender container and add the lime juice, hot sauce and paprika, then process until puréed. Place in a bowl and fold in the whipped cream. Place in a serving bowl, then place on a large serving plate and garnish with tomato wedges and corn or taco chips. This makes 3 cups of cream.

avocado cream

Here, a bowl of Avocado Cream is pictured with two ideal accompaniments, taco chips and fresh tomato wedges. This is just one of many ways to serve this delicious appetizer.

CREAM CHEESE-STUFFED CELERY

1 8-oz. package cream cheese, softened
2 tsp. celery salt
1 1/2 tsp. freshly ground white pepper
1/8 tsp. cayenne pepper
1/4 c. Basic Mayonnaise (Sauces, pg. 3)
2 tsp. sherry
1 lg. bunch of celery
Paprika

Place the cream cheese, celery salt, white pepper, cayenne pepper, mayonnaise and sherry in a medium-sized bowl and blend thoroughly. Cut the root end from the bunch of celery and separate the stalks, reserving the heart of the celery. Wash the celery stalks and trim into uniform lengths, then drain well. Place the cream cheese mixture in a pastry bag with a large star tube affixed and pipe into the celery stalk cavities. Sprinkle with paprika and chill thoroughly. Place the reserved celery heart in the center of a large serving plate and arrange the stalks around the celery heart like the spokes of a wheel. This makes 10 to 12 servings.

shellfish trio

Shellfish Trio is made with three seafood favorites: shrimp, clams and oysters, served on a bed of cracked ice.

Preserving freshness is always an important point to remember in preparing seafood because fish, especially shellfish, is very perishable. If not cooked immediately, it must be packed in ice or refrigerated. If it is to be stored for more than two or three days, it is best to freeze it.

It is important to the festive appearance of this dish that you serve both hard shell clams and oysters on the half shells. If you buy fresh or frozen oysters and clams without the shells, ask for empty shells at a local fish market. Wash thoroughly before using them. Most fish markets will open oysters for you. If not possible, teach yourself to open them with a special oyster knife.

To prepare fresh dug clams for Shellfish Trio, scrub them thoroughly with a stiff brush and rinse 3 times. Then open them as you would oysters — this takes practice. If fresh clams are not available, double the number of oysters used.

Boil and chill fresh shrimp before serving (Seafoods, pg. 14) and serve oysters raw on the half shell. Place all three on a bed of crushed ice in a serving dish and serve them with a choice of cocktail sauce and lemon wedges. For individual servings, place some of each on a plate with cocktail sauce and lemon wedges.

shellfish trio

These icy cold shrimp, clams and oysters are a delicious Shellfish Trio. Keep the shellfish icy cold on a bed of cracked ice. Serve with lemon wedges and one or several favorite seafood cocktail sauces.

SHELLFISH TRIO

2 lb. jumbo shrimp
1 ½ c. catsup
¾ c. chili sauce
⅓ c. lemon juice
3 tbsp. Worcestershire sauce
Hot sauce to taste
¼ c. grated onion
¼ c. grated horseradish
3 doz. hard shell clams
1 c. cornmeal
3 doz. large oysters on half shell

Prepare the shrimp according to the instructions for Boiled Shrimp (Seafood, pg. 14), removing the shells and leaving the tails intact. Chill the shrimp. Combine the catsup, chili sauce, lemon juice, Worcestershire sauce, hot sauce, onion and horseradish in a bowl and mix well. Cover the sauce and chill. Scrub the clams and open the shells with an oyster knife and refrigerate. Place the chilled oysters, clams and shrimp on a bed of ice in a serving dish and serve with the cocktail sauce and Hot Garlic Loaf (Breads, pg. 17). This may be served with additional lemon wedges and horseradish. This makes about 100 appetizers.

festive seafood cocktail

Two seafood delicacies on ice, boiled shrimp and lobster, are combined for this seafood cocktail. Serve this compatible twosome in a decorative serving dish, with the accompanying seafood cocktail sauce.

festive seafood

FESTIVE SEAFOOD COCKTAIL

3 lb. Boiled Shrimp *(Seafood, pg. 14)*
1 ½ c. catsup
2 tbsp. fresh lemon juice
1 tbsp. Worcestershire sauce
1 ½ tsp. sugar
Dash of hot sauce
Salt and freshly ground pepper to taste

Place the shrimp in the refrigerator and chill thoroughly. Combine the remaining ingredients for the sauce and mix thoroughly. Chill well. Arrange the shrimp in cocktail icers, then spoon the sauce over the shrimp. This makes about 6 servings.

SHRIMP DIP

1 8-oz. package cream cheese, softened
3 tbsp. milk
2 tbsp. grated fresh onion
½ tsp. Worcestershire sauce
1 c. boiled shrimp, finely chopped

Combine the cream cheese and milk in a small mixer bowl and beat with an electric mixer until smooth. Add the onion and Worcestershire sauce and beat until fluffy. Stir in the shrimp. Serve with dipping chips or crackers. This makes about 3 cups of dip.

DELICIOUS SHRIMP FONDUE

1 clove of garlic, halved
2 cans cream of shrimp soup
1 c. milk
4 c. freshly grated Swiss cheese
½ c. vermouth
Freshly ground pepper to taste
Paprika to taste

1 recipe Boiled Shrimp *(Seafood, pg. 14)*
1 sm. loaf of French bread, cut into 1-in. cubes

Rub a fondue pot with the cut side of the garlic. Pour the soup and milk into the fondue pot and cook over low heat, stirring frequently, until hot. Add the cheese and vermouth, then stir until melted. Season with pepper and paprika, then place over low fondue burner. Spear the shrimp and bread cubes with fondue forks. Dip into the cheese mixture, then cool slightly before eating. This makes 10 to 12 servings.

NEW ORLEANS SHRIMP

4 c. water
4 green onions, finely chopped
1 sm. clove of garlic, pressed
Salt and freshly ground pepper to taste
1 sm. bay leaf
4 celery heart stalks, finely chopped
1 lb. medium shelled deveined shrimp
2 tbsp. olive oil
¼ c. lemon or lime juice
¼ c. chili sauce
¼ c. catsup
1 tbsp. freshly grated horseradish
1 tbsp. prepared mustard
1 tsp. paprika
Dash of cayenne pepper

Pour the water into a medium-sized saucepan and bring to a boil. Add ½ of the green onions, the garlic, salt, pepper, bay leaf and celery and cover. Simmer for 15 minutes, then add the shrimp and simmer for 5 minutes longer. Drain the shrimp mixture and remove the bay leaf. Place the shrimp mixture in a medium-sized bowl and cool. Place the remaining green onions, olive oil, lemon juice, chili sauce, catsup, salt, horseradish, mustard, paprika and cayenne pepper in a small bowl and mix well. Pour over the shrimp mixture and mix until well blended. Cover and place in the refrigerator to marinate in the sauce overnight. Serve the shrimp and sauce in a glass bowl placed in a bowl of cracked ice. Serve with cocktail picks.

danish sandwiches

Danish Open Fish Sandwiches are made in the typical Danish *smørrebrød* fashion (Danish Open Sandwiches with Meat, pg. 71): elaborate, decorative and delicious. Follow the suggested recipes to create these delectable seafood appetizers.

DANISH OPEN FISH SANDWICHES

Danish black bread
Butter
Canned Danish cod roe
Finely chopped hard-boiled egg whites
Finely chopped hard-boiled egg yolks
Brown bread
Basic Mayonnaise *(Sauces, pg. 3)*
Smoked salmon
Canned asparagus spears
Twisted lemon slices
White bread
Lettuce leaves
Breaded fried flounder fillets
Thin cucumber slices
Tomato wedges
Pumpernickel bread
Small canned sardines in olive oil, drained
French bread
Small cooked shrimp, shelled and deveined
Whole wheat bread
Canned chunk-style tuna, drained
Thin radish slices
Pickled herring
Carrot sticks
Chopped chives

1 The first sandwich in the foreground is a slice of black bread spread with butter with a diagonally halved slice of cod roe placed at 2 opposite corners. Four small, fluted circles are cut from another slice of cod roe. Two circles are sprinkled with egg whites and the other 2 with egg yolks, then the circles are placed diagonally in the center of the sandwich.

2 The next sandwich is a slice of buttered brown bread spread with mayonnaise with 3 rolls of smoked salmon placed on the mayonnaise. An asparagus spear is placed between each roll, then the sandwich is garnished with a twisted lemon slice.

3 The third sandwich is a slice of buttered white bread covered with lettuce leaves, then with flounder. The sandwich is garnished with a lemon slice, cucumber slices and tomato wedges. You may serve with mayonnaise, if desired.

4 The next sandwich is made from a slice of pumpernickel bread that has been cut into a square and spread with butter, then sardines are placed over the butter. Egg whites are sprinkled diagonally over half the sandwich, then egg yolks are sprinkled over the other half. Mayonnaise is piped in between the egg white and egg yolk seam.

5 The fifth sandwich is a slice of French bread cut into a square and spread with butter, then covered with lettuce leaves. Shrimp are placed over the lettuce. Dollops of mayonnaise are placed in 2 opposite corners and the sandwich is garnished with a lemon slice.

6 The next sandwich is made from a slice of buttered whole wheat bread covered with lettuce leaves. Chunks of tuna are placed on 2 opposite sides of the sandwich, then overlapping slices of radish are placed in a row toward the center of the sandwich next to each row of tuna. Overlapping slices of cucumber are placed in a row in the center of the sandwich, then mayonnaise is piped down the center of the cucumber row and garnished with radish slices. An asparagus spear is placed to the inside of each row of tuna.

7 The seventh sandwich is the same as sandwich No. 5.

8 The last sandwich is made of a slice of buttered brown bread with a square of pickled herring in the center. Mayonnaise is piped on all the bread outside the herring. Carrot sticks are placed on the herring, then the herring is sprinkled with chives.

danish cheese sandwiches

DANISH CHEESE SANDWICHES

Dark rye bread
Butter
White Cheddar process cheese slices
Unskinned tomato
Pimento-stuffed olive slices
Danish black bread
Roquefort cheese wedges
Pitted black olives
Whole wheat bread
Caraway Swiss cheese slices
Heart of lettuce leaves

1 The sandwiches on the round platter are made of rye bread slices spread with butter, then covered with slices of Cheddar cheese. The cheese is decorated with tomato slivers and half slices and with green olive slices.

2 The outer sandwiches on the panel board are made of buttered black bread slices with 4 wedges of Roquefort cheese, topped with 2 black olives on each slice.

3 The inner sandwiches on the panel are made of buttered whole wheat bread covered with slices of caraway Swiss cheese, then an overlapping row of green olives placed down 2 sides of each sandwich. A rolled slice of the Swiss cheese is placed diagonally across each sandwich, then the sandwiches are garnished with lettuce leaves and tomato slivers.

danish cheese sandwiches

In the culinary style of the Danes, these cheese sandwiches are appetizingly beautiful. The cheese toppings are made with processed cheese and Roquefort cheese. They are garnished with green and black olives, lettuce and tomato slivers.

CAVIAR AND SALMON CHECKERBOARD

Brown bread slices, ¼ in. thick
White bread slices, ¼ in. thick
Softened butter
8 oz. black caviar (sturgeon or cod)
¼ lb. very thinly sliced smoked salmon
1 lemon, cut in half

Trim the crusts evenly from brown and white bread. Butter the slices, then cut forty 1 ¼-inch squares from the brown bread and forty-one 1 ¼-inch squares from the white bread. Spread caviar on each of the brown bread squares. Cut forty-one 1 ¼-inch squares from the smoked salmon, then place 1 square of the salmon on each of the white bread squares. Arrange the squares on a large serving platter as shown in the illustration and garnish the edges of the checkerboard with parsley. Squeeze lemon juice over all the squares just before serving. This makes 81 appetizers.

EGG AND SARDINE CHECKERBOARD

White bread slices, ¼ in. thick
Softened butter
1 hard-boiled egg, mashed
Blender Mayonnaise *(Sauces, pg. 3)*
1 can sardines in olive oil, well drained
Basic Vinaigrette *(Sauces, pg. 2)*
Kitchen Bouquet

Trim the crusts evenly from the bread slices, then spread with butter. Then cut fifty 1¼-inch squares from the bread. Mix the egg with just enough mayonnaise for spreading consistency. Place the sardines in a small bowl and mash them stirring in just enough vinaigrette to make a spreading consistency. Add just enough Kitchen Bouquet to give a dark brown color. Spread the egg mixture on half the bread squares and spread the sardine mixture on the remaining bread squares. Arrange the squares on 2 small platters as shown in the illustration and garnish the edges of the checkerboards with parsley. This makes 50 appetizers.

When serving the caviar and smoked salmon, do not forget to squeeze the lemon juice over the checkerboard just before serving. Black cods' roe may be substituted for the caviar.

caviar and salmon checkerboard

This extravagant checkerboard is made by alternating smoked salmon and caviar on small squares of brown and white bread. The smaller checkerboards in the background are much less costly, yet have the same effect. They are made with eggs and sardines. All are bordered with tiny parsley sprigs.

ZUPPA PAVESE

4 med. croûtes *(Breads, pg. 16)*
5 c. Basic Chicken Stock *(Soups, pg. 2)*
4 eggs
6 tbsp. freshly grated Parmesan cheese

Prepare the *croûtes*. Pour the stock into a large, shallow saucepan and bring to a simmer. Poach the eggs in the stock, one at a time, according to the instructions (Eggs, pg. 24). Trim the edges of the eggs to make them evenly round and keep the eggs warm in hot, not boiling, water. Strain the stock. Place a *croûte* in each of 4 heated soup bowls, then place a poached egg on each *croûte*. Sprinkle 1 ½ tablespoons of the cheese on each egg. Ladle the stock into the bowls and garnish with chopped parsley, if desired. This makes 4 servings.

zuppa pavese

Zuppa (Italian for soup) Pavese is a classic dish which is extremely popular throughout Italy. It is prepared by placing a poached egg atop a toasted croûte in a serving bowl and sprinkling it with freshly grated Parmesan cheese. The hot chicken stock is ladled into the bowl and the Zuppa Pavese is ready to be served.

FRESH PEA SOUP

4 sm. onions, finely chopped
½ c. butter
2 lg. potatoes, cut into cubes
2 lb. fresh green peas, shelled
3 tsp. salt
2 c. milk
½ tsp. pepper
½ c. half and half cream

Sauté the onions in ¼ cup of the butter in a saucepan over medium heat until tender, but not brown. Add the potatoes and 1 cup of boiling water and cover. Cook until the potatoes are tender. Combine the peas, 1 teaspoon of the salt and 1 cup of boiling water in a saucepan and cover. Cook over medium heat until the peas are tender. Place the potato mixture and the peas in a blender container and process until puréed. Pour the mixture into a large saucepan, then stir in the milk, remaining salt, pepper, remaining butter and cream until blended. Place over low heat until heated through, adding more milk if soup is too thick. Serve in soup bowls and garnish with hard-boiled egg white cut into designs, if desired. This makes 6 servings.

BRUSSELS SPROUTS SOUP

½ lb. fresh Brussels sprouts
1 recipe Basic White Sauce *(Sauces, pg. 4)*
¼ c. freshly grated Parmesan cheese
Milk
Salt and freshly ground pepper to taste
2 tsp. butter

Cook the Brussels sprouts in boiling, salted water until tender, then drain. Place in a blender container and process until puréed. Stir into the white sauce, then add the cheese and cook over low heat, stirring constantly, until the cheese has melted. Add enough milk to thin to desired consistency, then season with salt and pepper. Ladle into 4 heated soup bowls and place ½ teaspoon of the butter in the center of each serving. This makes 4 servings.

turkish hors d'oeuvres

Turkish Spinach And Cream Cheese *Hors D'oeuvres* or *Burek*, as they are called in their native land, are little pillows of very thin, flaky *phyllo* dough filled with a savory mixture of finely chopped or puréed spinach and cream cheese. Because *Burek* are traditional, there are undoubtedly countless variations of these delicious little morsels. Any thin, flaky pastry dough — strudel pastry, puff pastry or *phyllo* dough (available in Greek specialty shops) — may be used for the little pastry envelopes. The following recipe uses strudel pastry. The spinach must be very finely chopped or puréed and feta cheese may be substituted for the cream cheese, if preferred. These pastries may be prepared in advance and heated just before serving.

TURKISH SPINACH AND CREAM CHEESE HORS D'OEUVRES (BUREK)

1   8-oz. package cream cheese, softened
1 c. finely chopped cooked spinach
Half and half cream
Salt and white pepper to taste
Dash of hot sauce
1 recipe Basic Strudel Pastry *(Desserts, pg. 205)*
Anglais Glaze *(Breads, pg. 6)*

Combine the cream cheese, spinach and enough cream to moisten, then mix until the cheese mixture is fluffy and well combined. Stir in the seasonings. Cut the strudel pastry into 2½ to 3-inch squares and place 1 teaspoon of the cheese filling in 1 corner of each square. Fold over the pastry to make a triangle and seal the edges with the tines of a fork. Place the triangles on a baking sheet and brush with the glaze. Bake in a preheated 425-degree oven for 10 minutes. Reduce the oven temperature to 350 degrees and bake for 10 minutes longer or until golden. These *hors d'oeuvres* can be frozen before baking. This makes about 50 *hors d'oeuvres*.

turkish spinach and cream cheese hors d'oeuvres

These special Turkish hors d'oeuvres are an uncommon presentation for cocktail parties. You may serve them often, as they are not difficult to make. They may also be made ahead of time and reheated just before serving.

The Creative Homemaker's Academy © MCMLXXIII
Selected Illustrations © B.P.C. Publishing Limited MCMLXX

tomato soup

Ukranian Tomato Soup, a rich tomato and vegetable soup based on a hearty beef stock, is a Russian regional dish. It is blended until smooth in an electric blender and then further enriched with sour cream. When serving, it is customary to spoon some cooked rice into each soup dish before adding the soup. Each portion may then be garnished with toasted croutons and freshly milled parsley or dill.

ukranian tomato soup

Ukranian Tomato Soup is similar to Borscht, which also originated in Russia. This is a hearty soup; a steaming bowl full will provide a flavorful beginning to a winter meal.

UKRANIAN TOMATO SOUP

2 lg. beef bones
1 lg. carrot, finely chopped
1 lg. onion, finely chopped
1 c. shredded cabbage
4 c. Basic Beef Stock *(pg. 2)*
2 lb. ripe tomatoes, skinned *(Vegetables, pg. 27)*
2 tsp. salt
1 tsp. sugar
½ tsp. freshly ground pepper
¼ c. all-purpose flour
1 c. sour cream
1 c. Basic Boiled Rice *(Cereals, pg. 3)*

Combine the beef bones, carrot, onion, cabbage and stock in a soup kettle and bring to a boil. Reduce the heat and simmer for 1 hour, skimming the surface occasionally. Chop the tomatoes and add to the soup, then stir in the seasonings. Simmer for 45 minutes longer, then remove the bones from the soup. Pour the soup into a blender container and process until puréed. Return the soup to the kettle and place over low heat. Blend the flour with the sour cream, then stir into the soup and bring just to a boil. Spoon the rice into 4 soup bowls and ladle the soup over the rice. Sprinkle the soup with chopped dill or parsley, if desired. This makes 4 servings.

clear niçoise soup

This clear soup is very simple and quick to make, especially if you have prepared stock on hand. The pungent flavors of olive oil and garlic enrich the savory broth. The addition of a lightly poached egg to each serving makes this soup a filling dish. Toasted croutons may be served in a separate bowl to sprinkle in the soup, if desired.

CLEAR NIÇOISE SOUP

4 c. Basic Beef Stock *(Soups, pg. 2)*
2 tbsp. olive oil
½ tsp. salt
2 peppercorns
2 cloves of garlic, chopped
1 bay leaf
2 sprigs of parsley
4 poached eggs *(Eggs, pg. 24)*
½ tsp. dried thyme

Combine the stock, olive oil, salt, peppercorns, garlic, bay leaf and parsley in a large saucepan. Bring to a boil, then reduce the heat and simmer for 15 minutes. Remove the peppercorns, bay leaf and parsley, then ladle the soup into 4 soup bowls. Place 1 egg in each soup bowl and sprinkle the soup with thyme. This makes 4 servings.

salads & relishes

table of contents

the basics of working with gelatin

A common lament often heard among cooks is "My gelatin simply will not gel!" We promise to dispel many of the perplexities long associated with gelatin-making by sharing with you some hints and tricks and by giving you practice with five different salad recipes. By the time you master our BASIC techniques and recipes, you'll find yourself expressing surprise and delight at the simplicity and ease of gelatin cooking. And, you'll never be driven to make the above complaint, because you'll have success every time.

We'll be working with plain, unflavored, unsweetened gelatin, a colorless, odorless, tasteless powder made from pure animal protein. You can buy it packaged in envelopes, each one containing about ¼ of an ounce, or 1 tablespoon of gelatin. Gelatin softens in a cold liquid, dissolves in a hot liquid or mixture, and becomes firm when chilled. When combined with sweet, savory or creamy mixtures it creates a variety of interesting salads, as well as desserts.

If you handle gelatin carefully and correctly from initial softening to final unmolding, it will always come out perfectly. And what's correct handling, you're probably asking. It depends on the recipe you're using. However, we can make a few general statements to help you know what to expect.

The recipe will tell you to *soften* gelatin. Do this by sprinkling it on cold liquid (most often this will be water), then letting it stand two to three minutes until the gelatin absorbs the moisture. It must be softened before being mixed with other ingredients; if it isn't, it tends to form lumps. After this step the recipe will direct you to do one of several things to completely dissolve the softened gelatin. For example, it might tell you to add a hot liquid and stir until the gelatin dissolves. Or, using a double boiler, dissolve it over hot water, then add the specified liquid or mixture, stirring well; or place the softened gelatin in a saucepan over low heat, stirring constantly until it is dissolved and you have a hot syrup.

The general procedure, then, involves softening the gelatin and then dissolving it, although specific steps and kinds of liquids and mixtures vary according to the recipe. Again, rely on the recipe. It will bring you success.

The equipment required varies according to your recipe. You may need a double boiler or a saucepan. You'll need some kind of mold—the dish or pan you pour the mixture into to give it its shape. You can buy special fluted or scalloped decorative molds of different sizes and shapes, or simply use a square cake pan, loaf pan, mixing bowl or similar cooking utensil. A word of caution when you choose your mold: tin might change the color of chocolate and acidic mixtures. For these foods you'd be wise to use glass, china or aluminum molds.

PREPARING YOUR MOLD

When working with gelatin, prepare your mold by brushing it with oil or moistening it with cold water. It depends on the type of mixture: for creamy solid or non-clear mixtures, use oil; for clear jelly or aspic, use water. Oil is not brushed on molds for clear gelatins because it makes the surface blurry. If the oil slides down the sides and collects in a stubborn little puddle on the bottom, immediately before you pour the mixture into the mold work a brush upward from the bottom of the mold. The water or oil contributes to easy unmolding after it sets.

SUCCESSFUL UNMOLDING

Here's the common, successful unmolding procedure: First dip the mold in *warm* water to the depth of the gelatin for about 15 seconds. Don't use hot water. It will melt the gelatin. Loosen the gelatin at various points around the edge of the mold with the tip of a paring knife. Place your serving dish on top of the mold; carefully turn it over. Gently shake the mold and, finally, carefully lift it from the firm mixture. If it doesn't come out readily, repeat the procedure.

You might want to dampen slightly the serving plate and the exposed surface of the gelatin with cold water before unmolding. This will make it easy to slide the gelatin to the center of the serving plate.

The Creative Homemaker's Academy © MCMLXXIII
Selected Illustrations © B.P.C. Publishing Limited MCMLXX

HAWAII SALAD

1 c. milk
1 vanilla pod
¼ c. flour
½ c. sugar
3 egg yolks
1 No. 303 can crushed pineapple
3 env. unflavored gelatin
2 tsp. lemon juice
½ c. whipping cream

Combine the milk and vanilla pod in a small sauce-pan; cook over medium heat to just below boiling point. Combine flour and sugar in a medium mixing bowl; blend well. Add the egg yolks and beat well with electric mixer. Remove the vanilla pod from the milk and pour the milk slowly into flour mixture into top of double boiler. Cook over boiling water, stirring constantly, until custard is thick and smooth. Drain the pineapple, reserving juice. Soften gelatin in ¼ cup cold water. Pour ½ cup of the reserved pineapple juice and lemon juice into a small saucepan; place over low heat until hot. Remove from heat and add the softened gelatin, stirring until dissolved. Place pineapple pulp in blender container; blend until puréed. Stir puréed pulp into custard. Whip cream just until soft peaks form. Stir gelatin mixture into custard, then fold in the whipped cream. Pour into an oiled mold; place in refrigerator until firm. Will keep well up to 3 days. One teaspoon vanilla extract may be substituted for vanilla pod. Add vanilla extract to the cooked custard.

basic aspic

The two recipes here give you practice working with plain gelatin and also introduce a popular type of savory gelatin salad—aspic. Aspics are jellied molds usually made from clarified stock, consommé, unflavored gelatin and other ingredients. Whether simply engraved with a special design (as our picture on page 5 shows) or filled with meat, poultry, fish or vegetables, aspics make stunning and refreshing luncheon, buffet and supper dishes.

Our first recipe, Basic Simple Aspic, uses Basic Beef Stock, (Soups, pg. 2). Since it should have a sparkling transparency, clarified stock should be used. Our recipe instructions will tell you how to clarify the stock to make Basic Simple Aspic. We'll show you how to engrave this aspic on the next page.

kle the gelatin over stock. Stir in vinegar, sherry, thyme, parsley, peppercorns and egg whites. Cook, stirring constantly, over moderate heat until the gelatin dissolves. Beat with a rotary beater, still over moderate heat, for about 4 minutes or until thick foam forms on top. Foam must be thick and high. Remove beater and bring the mixture to a boil without stirring.. Reduce heat to low and simmer for 10 minutes. Remove from heat and let stand for 3 minutes. Place a piece of wet muslin in large sieve. Pour the stock mixture slowly and steadily through the muslin, letting drain well. Add lemon juice. Use as desired for various congealed molds, glazes or coatings.

Our second recipe, Basic Emergency Aspic, is designed for speedy preparation. You can skip the stock clarification procedure because ready-to-use, canned consommé, a stock already clarified, is substituted for homemade stock. This aspic is best used to coat meat, seafood, vegetables and eggs.

BASIC SIMPLE ASPIC

5 c. Basic Beef Stock *(Soups, pg. 2)*
2 eggshells
2 env. unflavored gelatin
2 tbsp. wine vinegar
2 tbsp. sherry
⅛ tsp. thyme
½ tsp. parsley flakes
5 peppercorns
2 egg whites
½ tsp. lemon juice

Measure 5 cups stock into a large saucepan to clarify stock, pull away inner skins from eggshells, then wash the eggshells and crush into stock. Sprin-

BASIC EMERGENCY ASPIC

2 env. unflavored gelatin
2 c. canned beef consommé
2 tbsp. lemon juice
¼ c. sherry
¼ tsp. salt

Soften gelatin in ½ cup cold water. Combine the consommé and 2 cups cold water in a medium-sized saucepan and bring to a boil. Add the softened gelatin, stirring until dissolved. Remove from heat. Add lemon juice, sherry and salt, stirring until well blended. Use as desired for various congealed molds, glazes or coatings.

engraving in aspic

Here you see how to engrave Basic Simple Aspic. Our recipe on page 4, combined with our engraving techniques, provides an impressive, decorative gelatin salad. We're using bits of carrots, peas and tarragon leaves for decoration. If you wish to make our suggested design but don't have tarragon leaves, substitute strips of gherkins

or string beans. Of course, you're not restricted to these foods. You might want to experiment with pimento-stuffed olive slices, slivered green pepper, or scraps of cooked egg. Just remember to prepare the ingredients before you begin the procedure. You won't have time to slice and chop as you decorate.

The aspic must be partially congealed, or at the consistency of uncooked egg whites before you begin the engraving procedure. Refrigerate it to get a workable thickness. About 15 minutes did the trick for us.

For equipment you'll need a 1-quart glass mold and large, clean tweezers. A *glass* mold allows you to examine your design as you work. The tweezers will help you position the design.

1 Have ready a chilled glass mold. Pour into it a small amount of the partially congealed aspic, or enough to thinly coat the sides and bottom of the mold. Set aside the remaining partially congealed aspic. Then roll, tip and tilt the mold to cover it completely with aspic. Above, in the right foreground, you see the "base" design we've made—it will, of course, be on top after unmolding!

2 Here our base design in the aspic coating is positioned. Next we spoon additional aspic from our partially congealed reserve to form a layer of aspic over the design to keep it in place.

3 We're placing our side decoration of small V's (example shown in left foreground of picture). When our side design is completed, we'll fill the mold with the remaining partially congealed aspic. Then the engraved aspic will be refrigerated until set and ready for unmolding. Served with homemade mayonnaise (Sauces, pg. 2), it makes a distinctive and delicious salad.

engraved aspic mold

Unusual molded salad made from Basic Simple Aspic and decorated with nothing more extravagant than bits and strips of carrots, scraps of hard-boiled egg, peas and string beans.

layering in gelatin

To give you additional experience our Layered Orange Gelatin is ideal for illustrating the procedure of dissolving gelatins and combining with remaining ingredients.

In our step-by-step pictures you see how to layer the Basic Orange Gelatin with fruit sections for a sweet, attractive, molded salad. The gelatin must be thickened or partially congealed for the layering procedure.

1 Moisten your mold with cold water for easy removal of the set mixture. Pour a layer of thickened or partially congealed gelatin into the mold.

2 Arrange the desired fruit on the partially set layer. We have chosen bright mandarin orange segments matching the colors. Refrigerate until set.

3 Pour a second layer of thickened gelatin over the fruit segments. Refrigerate until the second layer sets. Continue, alternating layers of fruit with layers of thickened gelatin, each time allowing the mixture to set under refrigeration. When the mold is almost filled, finish with a gelatin layer.

LAYERED ORANGE GELATIN

1 11-oz. can mandarin oranges
⅝ c. sauterne
2 3-oz. packages orange-flavored gelatin
1 env. unflavored gelatin
2 c. hot water
1 c. cold water

Drain the oranges well; reserve ½ cup liquid. Combine oranges with 2 tablespoons sauterne. Combine orange-flavored gelatin and unflavored gelatin in large bowl and mix well. Add hot water and stir until gelatin is dissolved. Stir in the remaining sauterne, reserved liquid and cold water. Chill until thick syrupy stage. Pour about ½ cup gelatin in 1½-quart mold rinsed in cold water. Arrange orange segments petal-fashion in gelatin. Chill until set. Spoon layer of thickened gelatin about 1 inch over oranges. Arrange layer of orange segments around edge of mold. Chill until set. Spoon another layer of gelatin over oranges. Repeat layers. Chill until set. For a tangier flavor, fresh tangerine segments may be substituted for mandarin oranges.

4 Here you see the completed mold with all the layers in position.

apricot cream salad

*A sweet, creamy, molded gelatin salad
made with puréed apricots. We've topped
and bordered it with bright apricot halves
filled with sweetened cream cheese.*

APRICOT CREAM SALAD

1 8-oz. package dried apricots
3 tbsp. confectioners' sugar
1 tsp. lemon juice
1 c. half and half
2 env. unflavored gelatin
1 c. whipping cream
Salad oil
4 oz. cream cheese, softened
16 canned apricot halves, well drained

Place the dried apricots in a small saucepan and
rinse with cold water. Drain off water. Cover apricots with warm water and simmer for about 15
minutes or until the apricots are soft, adding more
water if necessary. Place the apricots and liquid,
2 tablespoons of confectioners' sugar and lemon
juice in an electric blender and purée until smooth.
Pour the apricot purée into a medium-sized mixing
bowl, let stand until cool. Add the half and half,
mixing well. Place the gelatin in a small heavy
saucepan and add 4 tablespoons water to soften.
Place saucepan over low heat and stir until gelatin
is dissolved. Stir gelatin into the apricot mixture
and mix thoroughly. Whip cream with electric
mixer until stiff; fold into the apricot mixture.
Spread salad oil evenly over all surfaces of 1-quart
salad mold and pour the apricot cream into the
mold. Refrigerate until congealed. Dip the mold
into hot water for 30 seconds or until the apricot
cream will unmold easily. Turn out on serving
plate. Keep refrigerated until ready to serve. Mix
the cream cheese and remaining confectioners'
sugar together until smooth and well blended.
Spoon a dollop of cheese in the center of 8 of the
canned apricot halves. Top with remaining halves.
Place remaining cheese in icing bag with a large
writing pipe. Pipe cheese around centers of apricots as shown. Serve with Apricot Cream Salad.

beef aspic.

A main-dish salad of molded beef with vegetables. We are serving it bordered by an unusual version of stuffed eggs, for which we give you the recipe.

BEEF ASPIC

3 lb. round steak
1 lb. diced carrots
1 lb. thinly sliced onions
1 tsp. Worcestershire sauce
½ c. tomato purée
1½ tsp. salt
½ tsp. white pepper
1 c. Burgundy
2¾ c. (about) Basic Beef Stock *(Soups, pg. 2)*
1 tsp. paprika
4 env. unflavored gelatin

Trim all fat from steak; cut into ½-inch cubes. Place in a 4-quart casserole. Add the carrots, onions, Worcestershire sauce, tomato purée, salt, pepper and Burgundy; mix well. Add about 2½ cups stock or enough to cover. Bake, covered, at 250 degrees for about 2 hours or until steak is tender. Remove from oven; stir in paprika. Soften

the gelatin in ¼ cup Beef Stock in small saucepan. Place over low heat, stirring constantly, until dissolved. Stir into the steak mixture, mixing well. Let stand until cool. Turn into oiled 3-quart mold. Chill until firm. Lift off any congealed fat that may have accumulated on top. Dip mold into hot water for several seconds to loosen Aspic; turn out onto serving platter.

STUFFED EGGS

2 eggs
½ tsp. anchovy paste
White pepper to taste
1 tbsp. Basic Mayonnaise *(Sauces, pg. 2)*
½ tsp. tomato purée
1 to 2 drops of red food coloring

Place the eggs in cold salted water and bring to a boil. Boil for 9 minutes. Plunge into cold water. Remove shell under running water, then cool eggs. Cut in half, lengthwise. Turn the yolks into a small bowl and mash with a fork until fine. Add the anchovy paste, white pepper, mayonnaise and tomato purée, stirring until smooth. Transfer small amount of egg yolk mixture to a small bowl and add enough food coloring to obtain a slightly deeper shade than desired. Blend into remaining egg yolk mixture until of desired shade. Pipe or spoon into the egg white halves.

The Creative Homemaker's Academy © MCMLXXIII
Selected Illustrations © B.P.C. Publishing Limited MCMLXX

introducing vegetable salads

Pictured on this page is a basket of *crudités*, fresh raw vegetables for salads. This idea originated in the sidewalk cafés of France, where proprietors hung these huge white wicker baskets of crisp, fresh vegetables outside on latticed beams. We've found this charming, old-world custom readily adaptable for informal entertaining, as you'll see in the box below.

But this appealing, if somewhat unorthodox, method of serving salads is only the beginning! As you progress in your CREATIVE COOKING COURSE, you'll learn many techniques for creating vegetable salads ranging from Cucumber Cups to Caesar Salads.

First let's discuss some of the basics of working with vegetables in salads. Use fresh vegetables unless we tell you that canned or frozen ones may be substituted.

Salad greens are the basis for many vegetable salads. From the old standby Iceberg lettuce to the lesser known escarole and dandelion greens, they appear in assorted shades of green and a variety of leaf shapes. Some are found in supermarkets throughout the year. But whenever a recipe specifies a type of salad green you can't find, your produce manager can usually get it for you. Frankly, there are so many combinations of greens and other vegetables for salads that you could give your imagination free rein for two weeks and never repeat your ingredients!

The main attribute of our *crudités* basket, besides its good taste, is that its vegetables look so delicious and appealing. To achieve this same taste-tempting effect, buy only select produce. Avoid vegetables with excessive moisture, soft spots or bruises, as these spoil quickly.

HINT FOR ENTERTAINING

To bring a touch of the charming sidewalk cafés of France to your patio party or informal buffet, prepare a basket of fresh, raw, well-cleaned vegetables like the one in the picture. You might include tomatoes, carrots, radishes, celery, onions and cabbage. Be adventurous; almost any vegetable will be great. Place the basket, a chopping board, a sharp knife and bowls of sauces and dressings on a centrally located table. Let each guest serve himself from the basket, chopping his favorites.

Wash your salad vegetables thoroughly in cold water, shake off excess water and refrigerate them in plastic bags. Don't prepare them too far ahead of serving time since they're highly perishable, and to avoid wilting, don't add your salad dressing until the last minute.

VEGETABLE RELISH TRAY

1 head cauliflower
Grated white cabbage
Thin cucumber slices
Carrot curls
Green and red pepper strips
Radishes
Green onions
Tomatoes

Wash the cauliflower thoroughly. Trim leaves and remove the core. Break off each section resembling a flower. Place the cauliflowerets in the center of round tray to resemble a complete head. Make a circle of cabbage around the cauliflowerets. Surround the cabbage with the cucumber slices. Make thin strips down length of carrot with vegetable peeler. Roll up strips and secure with toothpicks. Place in ice water until crisp and curled. Place the carrot curls at intervals over the cabbage. Make a scalloped pattern with the pepper strips and set a radish in each scallop. Place green onions in bunches in about 4 places around edge of tray. Place a small tomato between the onions. Serve with Basic Vinaigrette (Sauces, pg. 2).

French *crudités* basket

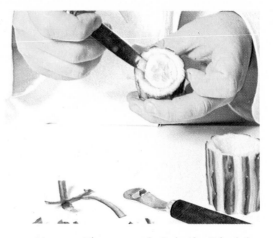

1 Cut a whole cucumber into unpeeled segments like the ones shown above. Then, pulling your lemon stripper (canelle knife) from top to bottom, make decorative stripes on the segments.

2 Now, with a grapefruit knife (ideal for use here because of its slightly bent, serrated blade) hollow each cucumber segment to make a "cup."

cucumber cups

Create your own serving "cups" for delicious salad mixtures by hollowing out vegetables such as tomatoes, green peppers and cucumbers. You'll enjoy the color and serving variety these vegetable "cups" offer. And you'll find dozens of delectable salad mixtures to go inside them as we progress through the course. On this page we'll use cucumbers and show you how to make salad cups that are a delight to the eye.

The best cucumbers to buy are the medium-sized ones. They should be smooth and firm to the touch and bright green in color. To make our cucumber cups, you'll need a grapefruit knife and a lemon stripper, which you should feel comfortable with after studying our section on garnishing (General Information, pgs. 11-12).

SAVORY BLEU AND COTTAGE CHEESE FILLING

1 c. cream-style cottage cheese
½ c. sour cream
1 4-oz. package crumbled bleu cheese
2 tbsp. minced onion
1 2-oz. jar pimento, chopped
2 tbsp. Worcestershire sauce
¼ tsp. salt
2 drops of hot sauce

Combine the cottage cheese and sour cream in a small bowl and blend well. Add the bleu cheese, onion, pimento, Worcestershire sauce, salt and hot sauce and mix well. Fill cucumber cups with cheese filling. Set on toast rounds or cucumber slices to form bottoms. Garnish with thin cucumber slices and pieces of tomatoes.

cucumber cups

Garnishing your salad cups with slices of raw vegetables is part of the fun of making them. We've garnished these with thin cucumber slices and pieces of tomato. To flute the edges on your tomato slices, cut them with a highly unorthodox, but oh so effective utensil — pinking shears. We've included one of our favorite cheese recipes as a suggested filling for Cucumber Cups. But feel free to fill them with any complementary salad mixture that strikes your fancy.

russian salad

Made from diced, cooked vegetables and unflavored gelatin. We shaped it in a round ring mold, filled the center with cooked carrots, peas and green beans, garnished the top with peas on fluted pieces of potato, and arranged a single row of peas around the base.

Our Russian Salad is a prime example of how the varied tastes, textures and colors of several ingredients can make an intensely interesting salad blend. It includes diced (cut into small cubes) and cooked green beans, carrots, turnips, potatoes and peas. If desired, canned or frozen vegetables may be substituted for fresh ones. Dice the vegetables raw for easier cutting. Place them in separate saucepans in a small amount of water and then simmer them until just tender. Remember, when potatoes are overcooked they tend to crumble and flake, and you want them as firm as possible for this salad.

RUSSIAN SALAD
²/₃ c. diced cooked potatoes
²/₃ c. diced cooked carrots
²/₃ c. cooked green peas
²/₃ c. diced cooked turnips
²/₃ c. cooked French-style green beans
1 c. Basic Blender Mayonnaise (*Sauces, pg. 3*)
2 tbsp. strained lemon juice
2 tbsp. strained orange juice
¼ c. cold water
1 env. unflavored gelatin

Combine potatoes, carrots, peas, turnips, and beans in a medium-sized bowl. Add the mayonnaise, then toss to coat vegetables well. Combine the juices and water in a small saucepan, then add gelatin. Stir over hot water until dissolved. Add to vegetable mixture, stirring until thoroughly mixed. Pour into an oiled ring mold and chill until firm. Unmold onto serving platter and fill center with diced, cooked vegetables, if desired. Garnish with additional green peas.

tomato wheels

TOMATO WHEELS

6 lg. firm ripe tomatoes
1 3-lb. box American processed cheese
1 8-oz. package cream cheese, softened
Half and half cream or Basic Mayonnaise
(Sauces, pg. 3)
2 tbsp. onion juice
½ tsp. paprika
¼ c. chopped walnuts

Almost no vegetable is as versatile for salad making as a ripe juicy tomato. Tomato lovers always seem to be looking for delicious new ideas for serving them. We are particularly pleased with our attractive Tomato Wheels. We've found them to be a great buffet salad because each tomato wheel lends itself beautifully to easy individual serving.

Tomato Wheels are really quite simple and fun to make. All you need is a very sharp knife, a pastry cutter and a little patience.

To make them we cut whole fresh tomatoes halfway down to form eight wedge-shaped petals and fill the centers with a delectable cheese mixture. These wheels are delicious with almost any type of filling.

Cut each tomato almost halfway down four times to make eight pointed topped petals like a flower. Trim out a portion of each center. Slice the cheese thinly; cut eight 1-inch rounds with a fluted pastry cutter for each tomato. Combine the cream cheese with just enough cream to make a smooth mixture. Add the onion juice, paprika and walnuts and mix well. Spoon the cream cheese mixture into the tomatoes. Place a cheese circle into each petal division. Garnish with parsley sprigs.

tomato wheels

You'll enjoy making and serving these beautiful tomatoes which have been decoratively cut to form containers for salad mixtures. We've fluted the cheese circles with a pastry cutter, tucked them around the sides and spooned a marvelous nut-cheese filling into the center.

The Creative Homemaker's Academy © MCMLXXIII
Selected Illustrations © B.P.C. Publishing Limited MCMLXX

cold ham mousse

COLD HAM MOUSSE

2 c. canned chicken broth
3 env. unflavored gelatin
2 tbsp. lemon juice
½ c. Sauterne
¼ tsp. salt
4 c. ground cooked ham
3 green onions, minced
1 tbsp. dry English mustard
½ tsp. white pepper
1 c. whipping cream, whipped

Remove all fat from chicken broth. Soften 1 envelope gelatin in ¼ cup cold water; stir into 1 cup hot chicken broth until dissolved. Add lemon juice, ¼ cup Sauterne and salt; mix well. Place this aspic in refrigerator until partially congealed. Coat side and bottom of chilled 1½-quart mold with a thin layer of aspic; refrigerate until aspic is firm. See Engraving in Aspic, pages 4-5. Coat again and refrigerate mold until ready to fill. Put ham and onions through finest blade of food chopper 5 times. Soften remaining envelopes of gelatin in remaining chicken broth in small saucepan. Place over low heat and stir constantly until gelatin is dissolved. Combine ham mixture, mustard, pepper and hot chicken broth; mix well. Process in blender to purée. Cool ham mixture, stirring occasionally, then fold in whipped cream. Pour into prepared mold; chill until firm. Unmold mousse in center of chilled serving plate. Garnish with ham bits, ham rolls filled with Cream Cheese Mixture topped with parsley, and halved hard-boiled eggs topped with piped Cream Cheese Mixture. Aspic may be engraved as explained on pages 4 and 5, if desired.

CREAM CHEESE MIXTURE

1 3-oz. package cream cheese
1 tbsp. Basic Blender Mayonnaise (Sauces, pg. 3)

Place cream cheese in a small mixing bowl; bring to room temperature. Add mayonnaise and stir until well blended. More mayonnaise may be added for a softer spreading consistency, if desired.

cold ham mousse

The perfect dish for a special occasion luncheon, Cold Ham Mousse was chilled thoroughly before being turned out of its mold. It is garnished with rolled ham slices and hard-boiled eggs piped with Cream Cheese Mixture in 2 colors.

french
potato salad

Potato Salad is an irresistible all-American favorite which is served with baked ham, grilled steaks or hot dogs.

Here we offer an enticingly different variation with a foreign flair — French Potato Salad. Its flavor is enhanced by the addition of both ripe and green olives, chicken stock, chives and just a hint of garlic. It will be a bonus to any meal — from a formal buffet to a picnic.

french potato salad

Brightly garnished with black olives, chopped parsley and a sprinkling of paprika, French Potato Salad, nestled in leafy green lettuce, is a "taste surprise" and an attractive looking dish.

FRENCH POTATO SALAD

3 lb. potatoes
1 clove of garlic, halved
2 tsp. Dijon mustard
3 tbsp. tarragon vinegar
1/3 c. olive oil
1 end slice of bread
1 c. hot Basic Chicken Stock *(Soups, pg. 2)*
Salt and pepper to taste
1 tbsp. chopped chives
12 lg. pitted ripe olives, quartered
12 lg. pitted green olives, quartered
Paprika

Cook the potatoes in water to cover until tender. Remove from water and let stand until cool enough to handle. Peel the potatoes, then cut into 1/2-inch cubes. Rub the inside of a large salad bowl with garlic half, then discard. Place the mustard in the salad bowl, then add the vinegar and oil, beating constantly with a wooden spoon until well mixed. Crush the remaining half clove of garlic through a garlic press onto the crumb side of bread crust. Spread the garlic evenly over bread, then cut bread into very small cubes. Place in salad bowl; toss until well moistened. Add the potatoes. Pour the chicken stock over the potatoes and toss lightly until well combined. Season with salt and pepper; add the chives and olives and toss again. Cover securely with plastic wrap and refrigerate for 8 hours or overnight. Sprinkle with paprika before serving.

GARLIC

Garlic is an accomodating seasoning that can be used in almost all savory dishes, but it must be prepared properly so it will blend smoothly with the other ingredients. The best method is to use a garlic press. The press crushes out the juice which you scrape off and use, discarding the tough pulp. If you don't have a garlic press, chop the peeled garlic clove on a flat surface with the tip of a small kitchen knife; then mash until it is completely broken down — add this mashed pulp to the oil or other liquid ingredients in your recipe.

avocado salad vinaigrette

For a decidedly different approach to the sometimes overlooked salad, we have used avocado halves as sauceboats for Basic Vinaigrette (Sauces, pg. 2) which will be spooned over the other ingredients. To create the "layered look" here, we began at the top with frills of fresh-washed watercress, diced green onions and strips of red sweet pepper. Overlapping these ingredients are slices of avocados. This salad provides a perfect opportunity for you to use your imagination. You might choose a different arrangement for your ingredients or even substitute different vegetables in your garnishing.

avocado salad

Avocados contradict all warnings not to eat fruit that has green or blackened skin or is green inside. That's exactly how avocados are at their best! They may be any color between green and black, any shape between pear and round, and any texture between smooth and pebbly. Any combination of these differences will have the same light green pulp and the same buttery, nutlike flavor.

In selecting your fruit, remember to choose avocados that are firm and show no signs of withering. Plan ahead and buy firm avocados several days before they are to be served, since they come to a perfect softness if left at room temperature for a few days. Test the fruit for ripeness by cupping it between both palms. If it yields to pressure, it is ready to eat. Store the avocado in the refrigerator if it ripens before the day of preparation. For tossed avocado salads, it is best to use the "almost ripe" ones that will not mush when tossed.

When preparing the avocado for use, halve it lengthwise and twist the halves slightly to separate. Strike the seed with the sharp edge of a knife; twist and lift the seed out.

To peel an avocado half, use the tip of a knife to loosen the skin. Starting at the stem end, lift or strip skin away. In order to keep its fresh color, brush the surface with lemon or lime juice. To store a cut avocado half in the refrigerator, replace the seed and wrap it in airtight wrap.

There seems to be no limit to the uses of avocado. The fruit is ready to eat with salt and lemon or lime juice. A half makes a neat cup for seafood or fruit salad. The avocado can also be mashed, molded, sliced and diced, and featured in salads, soups, spreads and dips.

AVOCADO SALAD VINAIGRETTE

1 recipe Basic Vinaigrette *(Sauces, pg. 2)*
8 green onions or scallions
¹/₂ lg. red sweet pepper
2 avocados, peeled
Lemon juice
Watercress or chopped romaine

Prepare Basic Vinaigrette, substituting ¹/₂ cup tarragon wine vinegar for the red wine vinegar. Trim onions, leaving about 2 inches of the green stems; cut into ¹/₂-inch lengths. Remove seeds and white membrane from red sweet pepper, then cut into thin lengthwise slices. Cut avocados in half and remove seeds. Cut 1 avocado into lengthwise slices; dip halves and slices into lemon juice to prevent discoloration. Arrange watercress, red sweet pepper, onions and avocado on serving dish as shown in our illustration. Shake vinaigrette to blend, then fill avocado halves with the sauce. This makes 2 servings.

rice salad vinaigrette

Rice Salad Vinaigrette is a main dish salad which demonstrates how our Golden Threads of basics can work for you. Although it appears to be an intricate undertaking for even a master chef, it is a breeze to prepare because it's based on techniques you've already mastered.

You've learned about rice in this lesson (Pasta and Cereals) and you're familiar with such basic sauces as Basic Vinaigrette and Basic Mayonnaise (Sauces, pgs. 2 and 3). Combined with selected, flavorful vegetables, your BASICS provide the makings of a hearty, savory, yet cool entrée. Add diced chicken — leftovers are great for this — and you've got the perfect main attraction for a club luncheon. Best of all, Rice Salad Vinaigrette is one of those dishes that tastes even better if the flavors are allowed to blend in the refrigerator overnight, so you can prepare it well in advance. Just reserve the tomatoes and pimentos and add them at serving time.

A side dish salad, Celery with Rémoulade Sauce, adds a bright touch of color with its sprinkling of paprika. Basic Rémoulade Sauce (Sauces, pg. 11) envelopes tiny, crisp-tender matchsticks of celery hearts in this lovely salad. (The procedure of cutting vegetables or meats into matchstick-sized slivers is called "julienning," (Vegetables, pg. 18). Both these tasty salads may be served on a bed of garden-fresh lettuce.

RICE SALAD VINAIGRETTE

Butter
Salt
2 c. converted rice
2 c. chopped fresh mushrooms
3 c. diced cooked chicken
12 pitted green olives, halved
12 pitted black olives, halved
1 8½-oz. can green peas, drained
1 c. Basic Blender Mayonnaise (Sauces, pg. 3)
½ c. Basic Vinaigrette (Sauces, pg. 2)
Grated rind of 1 orange
2 lg. tomatoes, cubed
1 canned pimento, julienned
Pepper to taste

Combine 4¼ cups water, 2 tablespoons butter and 2 teaspoons salt in a large heavy saucepan; bring to a boil. Add the rice slowly, stirring constantly. Cover and cook for 15 minutes, then stir. Cover and cook for 10 minutes longer or until water is absorbed. Chill thoroughly. Sauté mushrooms in ½ cup butter until soft and tender. Combine rice, mushrooms, chicken, olives, peas, mayonnaise, vinaigrette and orange rind in a large salad bowl. Toss carefully to combine all ingredients well. Cover securely with plastic wrap, then refrigerate overnight. Remove from refrigerator, then add the tomatoes and pimento. Season to taste with salt and pepper. Toss with 2 forks until well mixed. Place in a large serving bowl; garnish with watercress or romaine. Serve immediately with the Celery with Rémoulade Sauce.

CELERY WITH RÉMOULADE SAUCE

1 c. julienned celery
¼ c. Basic Rémoulade Sauce (Sauces, pg. 11)
2 tbsp. whipping cream
Paprika

Place celery in small bowl. Combine rémoulade sauce and whipping cream; stir with a wooden spoon until blended. Pour over celery, then toss until celery is coated. Refrigerate until ready to use. Sprinkle with paprika before serving.

rice salad vinaigrette and celery with rémoulade sauce

This hearty salad attracts attention with its combination of diced chicken, bits of savory vegetables and fruit such as black and green olives, pimento, mushrooms, peas, tomatoes, tangy grated orange rind and fluffy rice. Also pictured are tiny celery hearts tossed with Basic Rémoulade Sauce (Sauces, pg. 11) and liberally sprinkled with paprika.

introducing fruit salads

fresh fruit bowl

This creative fruit arrangement is not only a bright decoration for the dining table, but also an invitation to enjoy the mélange of flavors and refreshing taste of oranges, pears, grapes, bananas and apples.

The Koran says it wasn't an apple at all with which the serpent tempted Eve in the Garden of Eden, but a banana. Whatever the case, we may be sure that our earliest ancestors depended on the wild fruits for a good deal of their subsistence. And it wasn't long before they began cultivating them to be sure of a steady supply.

Historians say, as early as 2000 B.C., people were eating apples, apricots, bananas, dates, figs, grapes, mangoes, mulberries, peaches, pears, quinces and watermelons. The ancient Romans, great appreciators of food, knew of 36 varieties of apples and 40 varieties of pears; the best news a Roman general could bring back to the Empire was the finding of a new exotic fruit.

But the variety of fresh fruits available to the Romans was miniscule compared to the selections in our present-day supermarkets. Modern rail and truck transportation make it possible for people in Chicago to enjoy California avocados and people in Boston to have Florida oranges even in the mid-winter. Fresh fruits are among the best sources of the body's necessary vitamins and minerals, especially Vitamins A and C, and they are a healthy source of natural sugar.

Eating fruit straight from the fruit bowl is only one of the many ways to enjoy fruits. At one time or another they find their way into virtually every course of every meal: from an appetizingly glazed grapefruit at breakfast or a salad of mixed tropical fruits at luncheon, to a dessert of Peach Melba at dinner. In addition, the methods of preparation are infinitely varied. They may be stuffed, fried, baked, poached, preserved or combined in many dishes.

On these pages we share a selection of tempting fruit dishes which make particularly good salads — but don't be shy about serving them as light luncheon entrées or elegant desserts.

preparing an apple for stuffed apples

One of the most popular and versatile fruits is the apple. There are literally thousands of apple recipes. Baked, fried, stewed, spiced or candied apples are delicious.

Our European ancestors who settled America were so devoted to the delicious taste of apples that they brought with them seeds and grafted trees. They took apple seeds and trees with them across the Mississippi Valley and, eventually, to the Pacific. Among them was a missionary named John Chapman who later became legend. Known as Johnny Appleseed, he roamed the frontier settlements in the 19th Century planting apple orchards.

Today there are more than 7000 varieties of apples, all of which resulted from years of systematic hybridization, budding and grafting. Because of these years of effort, we can always purchase colorful, juicy, sweet apples. You will probably want to choose cooking apples such as Greenings or Northern Spy for the following recipe. Varieties of eating apples include Jonathans and Red or Golden Delicious; McIntoshes and Winesaps can be used for both purposes.

STUFFED APPLES

4 apples
1/2 c. peeled, seeded, quartered grapes
1 orange, sectioned and chopped
1 pear, peeled and chopped
1/4 c. chopped pecans
2 tbsp. Creme de Noyaux liqueur (optional)

Prepare the apples according to our step-by-step illustrations. Combine grapes, orange, pear and pecans and stir in *Noyaux*. Spoon into centers of apples and arrange remaining fruit mixture around apples. Serve with Basic Blender Mayonnaise (Sauces, pg. 3) and cheese wedges if desired.

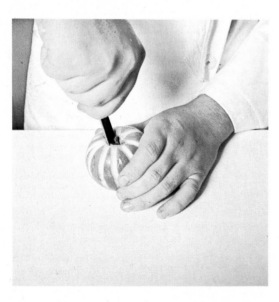

1 In this picture, the apple has been stripped with a lemon stripper, (canelle knife) and to prepare it for fruit stuffing, the core has been removed with an apple corer.

2 Here the hollow center is filled with sweetened white grapes and skinless orange segments. Of course, there are an endless number of delicious fillings such as chopped pecans, Basic Blender Mayonnaise (Sauces, pg. 3) or a choice of other fruits.

stuffed lemon apples

Lemon is a popular fruit with such a definite flavor accent that a very small portion of juice will season seafood, salads and meats and will distinctly flavor drinks. But its use is certainly not limited to flavoring. It is used in a number of salad dressings and sauces, in which it acts as a combining agent as well as a flavoring.

The zesty flavor of lemons and sweet flavor of apples combine to make the following recipe a very special salad dish. Lemon gelatin along with cherries and sweet white wine make Stuffed Lemon Apples irresistible.

STUFFED LEMON APPLES

3 tbsp. vinegar
7 apples
¾-in. strip lemon peel
1 c. sugar
1 c. Sauterne
1 3-oz. package lemon gelatin
½ c. golden raisins
¼ c. chopped red candied cherries

Combine 6 cups water and vinegar in a large bowl. Peel and core 6 apples and place in vinegar solution to prevent darkening. Mix 2 cups water, lemon peel, sugar and ¾ cup Sauterne in large, shallow pan until sugar is dissolved. Bring to a boil, reduce heat and simmer for 10 minutes. Arrange apples in pan and simmer over very low heat for about 15 minutes or until almost tender on bottom. Turn carefully with forks and cook for 10 to 15 minutes or until tender, but not mushy. Remove apples carefully to serving dish. Chill thoroughly. Prepare the gelatin according to package directions, substituting remaining Sauterne for ¼ cup cold water. Chill until partially set. Peel and core remaining apple and chop finely. Place in small saucepan and add the raisins and cherries. Cover with some of the remaining sugar syrup in which apples were cooked, and cover. Cook over low heat until raisins are plump and apple is tender; chill thoroughly. Fill apple centers with raisin mixture. Spoon about ¾ of the gelatin over apples and chill until set. Chill remaining gelatin until set, then beat with a fork until coarsely chopped. Spoon around edge of serving dish. Serve with Basic Blender Mayonnaise (Sauces, pg. 3).

stuffed lemon apples

Lemon apples are not only a delicious combination of flavors, but also a beautiful blend of colors. The filling includes the rich flavors of cherries, lemon and white wine. The beaten lemon gelatin bordering the serving dish, lends a jewel-like finish.

iced grapefruit

Iced Grapefruit eliminates the problem most often associated with serving grapefruit — the inevitable squirt in the eye. Grapefruit sections are removed, then replaced in the shells. With the tiniest hint of liqueur sprinkled over the fruit and served on ice it is delicious. To avoid spilling the juice into the ice, put the grapefruit shells into small bowls and then place into larger bowls of cracked, tinted ice. Or use a dish especially suited for this, called an "icer."

ICED GRAPEFRUIT

2 seedless ruby red grapefruit
2 tbsp. grenadine cordial

Cut off ⅓ of each grapefruit from the stem end. Cut around core with grapefruit knife and remove core. Cut around individual segments, making sure knife extends underneath in order to flip out each segment. Place segments in a bowl and set aside. Drain juice from shells into bowl. Remove all membrane from the grapefruit shells, then vandyke the edges. Stir grenadine cordial gently into grapefruit juice and segments. Spoon mixture into the grapefruit shells. Place shells in bowls in nests of green-tinted crushed ice and serve. White grapefruit may be used with green *Creme de Menthe* if desired.

apples poached in cider

APPLES POACHED IN CIDER

3 tbsp. vinegar
10 sm. apples
1 10-oz. jar apple jelly
1¾ c. apple cider

Mix vinegar and 6 cups water in a large bowl. Peel apples and place in vinegar solution to keep from discoloring. Combine ¾ cup warm water with the jelly and stir until broken up and partially dissolved. Arrange the apples in a large skillet and pour jelly mixture and cider over apples. Cook over very low heat until apples are almost tender on bottom. Turn carefully with 2 forks and simmer until tender but not mushy. Remove apples to a serving dish. Cook cider mixture until reduced to thick syrup. Spoon syrup over apples and chill well before serving. Food coloring, such as yellow, red or green, may be added to syrup to make a more eye-appealing dish. This dish is delicious as a salad, meat accompaniment or may be served with cheese as a dessert.

apples poached in cider

These rich, glossy apples were prepared with apple jelly and cider. The cooked cider, which becomes a thick, rich syrup, has been spooned lavishly over the apples to give the shiny appearance. The cider may be tinted with yellow, red or green food coloring before coating the apples to give a more festive appearance.

mixed fruit salad

This refreshing fruit salad is made with an irresistible combination of fruits, walnuts and honey. Piquant Stuffed Eggs are a delicious blend of eggs, Basic Blender Mayonnaise, tomato juice, grated Parmesan cheese and toasted almonds.

PIQUANT STUFFED EGGS

1 tbsp. almonds
6 hard-boiled eggs
3 tbsp. Basic Blender Mayonnaise (Sauces, pg. 3)
4 tsp. tomato juice
1½ tbsp. freshly grated Parmesan Cheese
⅛ tsp. white pepper
¼ tsp. salt

Spread the almonds on a cookie sheet and place in the oven. Toast the almonds lightly at 350 degrees for about 10 minutes. Remove from oven and place in blender; grind or chop finely. Peel eggs and cut about ⅓ of the rounded end off of each egg. Remove yolks and place in small mixing bowl, then mash with fork until fine. Add remaining ingredients and mix until smooth. Pipe or fork back into egg whites, bringing the filling up to a peak. Place cut-off ends to one side of filling as shown in illustration. Place eggs in lettuce-lined egg cups.

MIXED FRUIT SALAD

2 tbsp. honey
¼ c. lemon juice
2 thin-skinned oranges
¾ c. chopped dates
½ c. chopped walnuts
5 bananas

Combine honey and lemon juice in a small saucepan. Cook over low heat, stirring, until honey is dissolved. Peel oranges and remove sections over a bowl to retain all juice. Squeeze out juice from orange membranes. Drain juice from orange sections and combine with dates and walnuts. Slice bananas into serving dish and pour honey mixture over bananas to coat well. Spoon date mixture over bananas. Arrange orange segments over and around salad. Chill well before serving.

avocados and strawberries

Devotees of the flavor of avocados claim this fruit is limited only by the user's imagination. In the recipe on this page, we used our imagination and discovered that the buttery smoothness of avocados, when combined with the tart sweetness of strawberries, creates a most delicious flavor and an eye appealing salad. For a review of information on buying and preparing avocados, refer to page 15.

Strawberries are extremely nutritious, containing both citric acid, found in lemons, and malic acid, found in apples. This combination produces their irresistible tart-sweet taste.

When buying strawberries, examine carefully for over-ripeness or rough handling. Green or white tips, unless typical of the variety, indicate lack of flavor. Always treat strawberries as gently as possible. Store in the refrigerator without washing. When preparing for serving, dip the berries in a bowl of water and drain in a colander. Do not *soak* them as this seems to dilute the flavor. To bring out their true berry flavor, leave at room temperature for about a half hour before serving.

AVOCADO AND STRAWBERRY SALAD

½ c. almonds
1 8-oz. package cream cheese, softened
¾ c. confectioners' sugar
2 ripe avocados
Lemon juice
1 pt. fresh strawberries, cleaned
⅓ c. fresh orange juice

Spread the almonds on a cookie sheet and toast them lightly in 350-degree oven for about 10 minutes. Then place in blender and grind or chop finely. Combine the cream cheese and ½ cup confectioners' sugar in a small mixing bowl and beat until fluffy. Stir in the almonds. Shape into cone in center of serving dish. Peel the avocados, cut in half and remove seeds. Coat avocados generously with lemon juice to prevent darkening. Place 2 halves on opposite sides of cream cheese cone. Arrange strawberries between avocado halves over cone. Slice remaining avocado and place around edge of serving dish, garnishing with any remaining strawberries. Combine remaining confectioners' sugar with the orange juice and 1 tablespoon lemon juice for sauce. Dust the strawberries with additional confectioners' sugar. Spoon small amount of orange sauce over each serving.

avocado and strawberry salad

This decorative avocado and strawberry salad includes cream cheese and toasted almonds. To add extra flavor to individual servings, serve with orange sauce.

pepper salad

PEPPER SALAD

2 med. green sweet peppers
3 lg. firm ripe tomatoes
Salt and freshly ground pepper to taste
1/2 c. olive oil
1 to 2 tbsp. red wine vinegar
1 1/2 tsp. chopped chives
1 1/2 tsp. chopped parsley

Cut the peppers in half and remove the seeds and membrane. Cut into thin lengthwise slices. Slice the tomatoes thinly. Arrange the tomatoes and peppers in a serving dish and sprinkle with salt and pepper. Pour the oil evenly over all. Sprinkle the vinegar, chives and parsley over the top. This makes about 6 servings.

pepper salad

A taste of Italy comes through in this colorful pepper salad. An attractive and tasty accompaniment for any cold meat, game or poultry, this is an ideal warm weather salad. There is very little preparation required which is a boon when there is little time to devote to cooking.

caesar salad

SPECIAL SALADS

A familiar dilemma is what to feed a hungry crowd when the cupboards are nearly bare. This is what prompted a restaurant owner from Tijuana, Mexico to create this salad from the few ingredients he happened to have on hand. Caesar salad consists of a variety of salad greens, eggs, garlic, salad oil, lemon juice, croutons and cheese. Anchovies were not among the original ingredients, but have become a popular addition and are often included.

This salad, when properly assembled, is one of the most delicious of all tossed green salads. The ingredients may be prepared well in advance, which is a nice con- venience when preparing a company dinner. The salad greens should be washed, drained and chilled for several hours before serving. When preparing salad greens for tossed salads, always tear the greens into bite-sized pieces rather than cutting them. Cutting tends to bruise the tender leaves. The croutons may be made several days ahead and the garlic should steep in the oil for at least 1 hour for good flavor.

If the man of the house enjoys being in the spotlight, let him assume the role of chef and toss this impressive salad for family and guests. He can show off his culinary expertise by preparing the dressing at the table; most men are uninhibited with seasonings and can come up with some very original combinations. Supply him with all the ingredients, making sure that everything is fresh and crisp (even the Parmesan cheese should be freshly grated). Place everything on a tray at the table along with a capacious salad bowl and large wooden salad servers. The rest is up to him!

CAESAR SALAD

1 c. peanut oil
1 clove of garlic, crushed
2 c. bread cubes
2 heads romaine
1 head Boston lettuce
1 bunch watercress
3/4 c. freshly grated Parmesan cheese
1/2 tsp. salt
1/4 tsp. dry mustard
1/4 tsp. freshly ground pepper
1/3 c. lemon juice
2 eggs, lightly beaten
Dash of Worcestershire sauce
1 2-oz. can anchovy fillets

Pour the peanut oil into a jar and add the garlic. Cover and let stand for at least 1 hour. Sauté the bread cubes in 1/4 cup of the garlic oil until golden brown. Drain on absorbent paper. Tear the romaine, Boston lettuce and watercress into a large salad bowl. Combine the cheese, salt, mustard and pepper. Sprinkle the cheese mixture over the greens gradually, tossing to mix well. Beat the lemon juice gradually into the eggs, then add the Worcestershire sauce. Pour 1/3 of the egg mixture and 1/3 of the remaining oil mixture over the salad, then toss gently. Repeat 2 more times, adding the anchovies and croutons during the last tossing. Serve immediately. This makes about 12 servings.

caesar salad

This inspired version of tossed green salad is the perfect accompaniment to grilled meats or roasts. All ingredients may be prepared well ahead of serving time and the only last minute requirement is to combine the salad greens with the dressing and croutons.

engraved chicken aspic

An engraved aspic salad adds an elegant and festive touch to any buffet dinner or holiday feast. Its preparation requires extra time and patience but the spectacular results make the effort well worthwhile.

Engraved Chicken Aspic is a lovely summertime dish and is fun to make. It consists of a molded chicken salad topped with the engraved chicken aspic.

The basic technique for engraving in aspic was introduced on page 4. It is simply a process of coating a mold with slightly congealed aspic, and while the aspic is still only partially set (about the consistency of uncooked egg whites) arrange colorful designs in the aspic with various garnishes of your choice.

These garnishes may be any type of vegetable which lends itself to the recipe and which can be cut into attractive shapes for use in the engraved design. Green or black olives, strips of cucumber, green beans, celery slices and green peas are all adaptable for use in engraving aspic. Fresh green leaves such as tarragon and parsley also contribute a pleasing effect. Be sure to consider color when choosing garnishes — small cutouts of pimento or carrot might add just the right contrast to an otherwise drab color scheme.

The designs may be intricate, extremely simple or even amusing. By using a little imagination and spending a little extra time, an ordinary molded salad or mousse can be transformed into a real work of art.

ENGRAVED CHICKEN ASPIC

½ recipe Basic Emergency Aspic (pg. 4)
Pimento pieces
Ripe olive pieces
Canelled peel of cucumber
Stuffed green olive slices
6 egg yolks
3 c. milk
2 env. unflavored gelatin
1½ c. chicken broth
3 c. diced cooked chicken
½ c. minced celery
½ c. chopped pecans
1 c. Basic Blender Mayonnaise (Sauces, pg. 3)
½ tsp. white pepper
¼ tsp. paprika
2 tsp. celery salt
½ tsp. curry powder
Salt to taste

Prepare the Basic Emergency Aspic, substituting chicken consommé for the beef consommé. Pour aspic into a 3-quart mold to about ½-inch depth. Chill until partially congealed. Chill remaining aspic in a shallow dish until firm. Engrave, using pimento, ripe olives, cucumber peel and green olives according to the step-by-step illustrations on page 5. Chill until very firm. Beat the egg yolks well, then add the milk gradually, beating constantly. Pour into top of double boiler and cook over hot water, stirring constantly, until the mixture coats a spoon. Remove from heat. Soften gelatin in ½ cup cold broth, then dissolve in 1 cup hot broth. Stir gelatin mixture into the custard, mixing well. Stir in chicken and remaining ingredients. Let cool. Turn the chicken salad carefully into the mold and let chill until firm. Unmold on serving plate. Break up firm aspic with a fork and arrange around the base of the salad. Garnish with cooked and boned breasts of chicken piped with Basic Blender Mayonnaise and decorated with cucumber slices and pimento pieces. This will make 12 servings.

pallas athene salad

PALLAS ATHENE SALAD

5 med. tomatoes
1 tsp. oregano
Salt and pepper to taste
2 med. green sweet peppers
24 sm. Greek olives
Small curd cottage cheese
Sour cream

Cut the tomatoes into wedges and place in a bowl. Sprinkle with oregano, salt and pepper. Toss lightly. Cut the peppers in half and remove the seeds and membrane. Cut into thin lengthwise slices. Arrange tomatoes, peppers and olives on a lettuce-lined serving dish. Spoon dollops of cottage cheese and sour cream on top.

TOSSED ESCAROLE-ENDIVE SALAD

1 head escarole
1 head endive
1/4 lb. Roquefort cheese
1 Bermuda onion, thin sliced
Basic Vinaigrette *(Sauces, pg. 2)*
Salt and freshly ground pepper to taste

Wash escarole and endive thoroughly in cold water. Shake off excess water. Tear greens into bite-sized pieces, then place in a plastic bag and chill for 1 hour. Place greens in a salad bowl. Crumble Roquefort cheese over greens and add onion slices. Add enough Basic Vinaigrette to moisten greens thoroughly. Sprinkle with salt and pepper, then toss lightly until greens are coated with vinaigrette. This makes 8 servings.

pallas athene salad

The simplicity of this combination of lettuce, tomatoes, green peppers, olives, cottage cheese and herbs will appeal to anyone on a busy schedule. Almost no preparation is required — only the assembling of the ingredients just before serving.

SEA BREEZE SPINACH MOLD

1/4 c. cold water
1 10 1/2-oz. can beef broth
2 env. unflavored gelatine
1/4 tsp. salt
2 tbsp. lemon juice
1 c. Basic Blender Mayonnaise *(Sauces, pg. 3)*
1 med. onion, quartered
1 10-oz. package frozen chopped spinach, thawed
4 hard-cooked eggs, quartered
1/2 lb. cooked bacon, crumbled

Pour the cold water and 1/4 cup beef broth into blender container and sprinkle with gelatin. Let stand until the gelatin is softened. Heat the remaining beef broth in a saucepan to boiling point. Add to the blender container and cover. Process at low speed until gelatin is dissolved, using a rubber spatula to push gelatin granules into the broth mixture. Add the salt, lemon juice and mayonnaise and process until well blended. Add the onion and cover. Process at high speed until onion is chopped. Add the spinach and eggs and cover. Process at high speed just until eggs are chopped. Stir in the bacon and turn into a 6-cup mold. Chill until firm. Unmold and garnish with cherry tomatoes. This makes 8 servings.

sea breeze spinach mold

Make-ahead recipes end the last minute mealtime rush. This refreshing spinach salad is ideal for a summertime luncheon or supper. Its preparation is not complicated and it may be made the day before it is to be served.

The Creative Homemaker's Academy © MCMLXXIII
Selected Illustrations © B.P.C. Publishing Limited MCMLXX

egg salad

Simple egg salads and pickled relishes are often underrated. Although they can be spectacular in flavor and eye appeal, the typical epicurean dismisses both as suitable only for children's picnics or Wednesday night "hurry-up" dinners.

Although the egg is plain and simple and very fashionable at picnics, it is often considered the last resort at the dinner table. But an ingenious and appreciative cook will give herself free rein to vary the many ways of garnishing the egg.

The word "relish" means a number of nice things such as pleasure, enjoyment, zest or an attractive quality. Relish can also be any number of pickled or preserved foods that are often served as an accompaniment to meats or main dishes. Vegetable relishes are prepared from chopped or small vegetables. They may be either sweet or sour, spiced or unspiced. Fruit relishes consist of chopped or small fruits usually preserved with sugar, spices and vinegar. Home-prepared vegetable and fruit relishes will add enjoyment and zest to any meal.

A cocktail party food tray with flavor and eye-appeal can be prepared by combining vegetable pickles, spiced and pickled fruits with club crackers and several types of mellow cheeses. For a tempting buffet, broaden the selection of relishes and add an egg dish, some cold luncheon meats and warm rye bread.

LUNCHEON EGG SALAD

2¼ c. Basic Mayonnaise *(Sauces, pg. 3)*
1¼ c. chili sauce
¾ c. catsup
9 hard-cooked eggs, chopped
1½ c. diced celery
½ c. minced green pepper
1 tsp. sugar
½ tsp. Worcestershire sauce
Salt and pepper to taste
3 tbsp. gelatin
¾ c. cold water
Avocado and mandarin orange slices
4 tbsp. Basic Vinaigrette *(Sauces, pg. 2)*

Combine first 9 ingredients. Soften gelatin in a small amount of cold water. Place in a small saucepan over low heat and dissolve stirring constantly. Stir into egg mixture. Pour into a ring mold and chill until firm. Unmold on lettuce and fill center with avocado and orange slices mixed with Vinaigrette. Crab meat and shrimp may be added to egg mixture, if desired. Yield: 12-16 servings.

EGG SALAD

4 hard-cooked eggs
1 c. julienne carrots *(General Information, pg. 32)*
1 c. shredded fresh spinach
4 med. tomatoes, skinned
Mustard Mayonnaise *(Sauces, pg. 3)*

Slice the eggs and place in center of salad plates. Arrange the carrots and spinach around the eggs. Cut the tomatoes into thin wedges and place around outer edge. Garnish with rosettes of Mustard Mayonnaise. Serve with additional Mustard Mayonnaise. This makes 4 servings.

egg salad

During the warm summer months, a main dish salad for luncheon or supper is always welcome. Easy to serve and quick to prepare, sliced eggs are arranged on plates with a border of matchstick-thin slices of raw carrots, shredded spinach and tomatoes. Serve with Mustard Mayonnaise to make a satisfying and wholesome salad.

DEVILED EGGS IN CLEAR TOMATO ASPIC

2 c. tomato juice
2 env. unflavored gelatin
2½ c. Basic Chicken Stock *(Soups, pg. 2)*
3 peppercorns
1 bay leaf
1 tbsp. lemon juice
½ tsp. celery salt
1 recipe Piquant Stuffed Eggs *(pg. 21)*

Place the tomato juice in a Dutch oven or heavy saucepan, then sprinkle the gelatin over juice and let stand 3 minutes to soften. Add the stock, peppercorns, bay leaf, lemon juice and celery salt. Bring to a boil. Clarify the mixture according to the Clarifying Stock directions in Appetizers and Soups, page 2. Chill clear aspic until syrupy. Prepare the Piquant Stuffed Eggs according to directions but cutting in half lengthwise to fill. Place halves together after filling to form a whole egg. Pour about ¼-inch of aspic into 6 oval molds. Chill until firm. Place the eggs on the firm aspic, then spoon 2 tablespoons of liquid aspic over each egg. Chill until firm. Pour in remaining aspic to top of mold and chill until firm. Unmold when ready to serve and garnish with Savory Paprika Butter (General Information, page 30).

deviled eggs in clear tomato aspic

The things you can do with the simple egg is limitless. This clear aspic is made with clarified tomato juice.

vegetable pickles

vegetable pickles

With the back-to-natural-food movement gathering steam, what could be more natural than to apply your culinary ingenuity and expertise to something deceptively simple. Vegetable Pickles — actually pickled vegetables are delicious for a buffet, with sandwiches or served with crackers as hors d'oeuvres.

VEGETABLE PICKLES

2 lb. carrots
2 heads cauliflower
4 lb. very small fresh cucumbers
2 lb. fresh green peas
2 lb. small young onions
3 qt. vinegar
5 c. sugar
1/2 c. prepared mustard
1/2 c. curry powder
1 c. flour

Prepare the vegetables as for cooking, cutting the carrots in thick slices and separating the cauliflower into flowerets. Soak each vegetable separately in salted water to cover using 3 tablespoons salt to each quart of water. Let the vegetables stand overnight, then drain. Pour the vinegar into a large kettle and bring to a boil. Add the sugar and the vegetables, a small amount at a time, allowing vinegar mixture to remain at the boiling point. Combine the mustard, curry and flour with enough water to make a paste, then add to the boiling mixture. Place the vegetables and liquid in stone jars and cover the tops with waxed paper. Tie the waxed paper securely. Allow the vegetables to stand for about 1 week or until fermentation has ceased. Pack vegetables in hot sterilized jars and cover with the vinegar. Place lids on the jars and screw bands tight. Process for 30 minutes in boiling water.

PICKLED FIGS

5 qt. firm ripe figs
1 c. soda
4 to 5 c. sugar
2 1/2 c. vinegar
1 tsp. salt
1/4 tsp. ground nutmeg
2 tsp. whole cloves
2 tsp. whole allspice
1 med. piece of gingerroot
3 sticks cinnamon
Green food coloring

Place figs in a large bowl, then sprinkle with the soda and add 6 quarts boiling water. Let stand for 5 minutes, then rinse the figs thoroughly in cool water and drain. Combine 2 1/2 cups sugar and 2 quarts water in a kettle and bring to a boil. Add the figs and cook for 30 minutes or until tender. Add remaining sugar, vinegar, salt and nutmeg. Tie the whole spices in a bag and drop into the syrup. Cook until the figs are clear. Let stand in a cool place overnight. Add the coloring, if desired. Pack the figs to within 1/2-inch of the top of pint fruit jars. Bring the syrup to a boil and pour over the figs. Place the lids on the jars and screw bands tight. Process for 15 minutes in boiling water. This makes about 6 pints.

pickled fruit

SPICED KUMQUATS

1 qt. kumquats
3 c. sugar
1 c. vinegar
1 stick cinnamon
1 tbsp. whole cloves
1 tbsp. whole allspice

Wash and slit kumquats, then place in kettle. Cover with water and bring to a boil. Cook for 10 minutes, then drain. Combine the sugar, vinegar and 3 cups water in a large saucepan and bring to a boil. Tie the spices in a small piece of muslin and drop into the syrup. Cook for 5 minutes. Add the kumquats and cook for 10 minutes, then discard the spice bag. Let the kumquats stand overnight. Bring to a boil and cook until the syrup is thick. Pack the kumquats into hot sterilized jars and cover with syrup. Place the lids on the jars and screw bands tight. Process the jars for 10 minutes in boiling water.

CRISP WATERMELON RIND

5 lb. watermelon rind
1 tbsp. salt
8 tsp. alum
9 c. sugar
1 qt. cider vinegar
2 lemons, thinly sliced
4 2-in. cinnamon sticks
2 tsp. whole allspice
2 tsp. whole cloves

Cut off and discard the green and red portion from watermelon rind, leaving only the white inner rind. Cut the rind into 1-inch pieces, to measure 4 quarts. Place the rind in a large enamel or stainless steel pot. Add water to cover and stir in the salt. Bring to a boil, then reduce heat and simmer for 15 to 20 minutes or until rind can be easily pierced with a fork. Remove from heat and stir in the alum. Cool, then cover and let stand for 24 hours. Pour off the water, then rinse and drain well. Add the sugar, vinegar, lemon slices and cinnamon sticks. Tie the allspice and cloves in a cheesecloth bag and add to rind mixture. Mix well, then bring just to a boil, stirring constantly. Remove from heat and cool, uncovered. Cover and let stand for 24 hours longer. Drain off the syrup into a large saucepan and bring just to a boil. Pour over the rind and cool. Cover and let stand for 24 hours longer. Heat the rind in the syrup, but do not boil. Remove and discard the spice bag. Pack the rind and cinnamon in hot, sterilized jars. Heat the syrup to boiling, then fill jars with boiling syrup. Seal immediately. Store for at least 4 weeks or longer before serving. This makes 4 quarts.

PICKLED CRAB APPLES

4 lb. ripe crab apples
4 1/2 c. sugar
2 1/2 c. vinegar
2 c. water
1 tsp. salt
1/2 tbsp. whole cloves
1/2 tbsp. allspice
1 1 1/2-in. piece of gingerroot
2 sticks cinnamon
Red food coloring

Wash and rinse the crab apples, then drain. Remove the blossom end and prick the crab apples with a large needle. Place sugar, vinegar, water and salt in a saucepan or kettle. Tie the spices in a muslin bag and drop into the kettle. Cook, stirring, until the sugar dissolves. Add one layer of crab apples and boil gently for 7 minutes. Remove from kettle and place in a large bowl. Repeat until all the crab apples are cooked, then add a few drops of color to the syrup. Pour the syrup over the crab apples, then add the spice bag. Cover and let stand in a cool place for 24 to 48 hours. Pack the crab apples to within 1/2 inch of the top of hot, sterilized fruit jars. Heat the syrup to boiling and pour over the crab apples. Place the lids on the jars and screw bands tight. Process pints and quarts for 20 minutes in boiling water. This makes 4 to 6 pints.

pickled fruits

Spiced Kumquats, Pickled Crab Apples, Pickled Figs, and Watermelon Rind make an appetizing and interesting variation in color, texture and taste. Serve all three with a meat entrée for a flavorful and cool contrast. The recipe for Pickled Figs is on page 29.

spiced mandarin oranges

SPICED MANDARIN ORANGES

1 sm. tangerine or orange
2 11-oz. cans mandarin oranges
1 2-in. piece of stick cinnamon
1/4 c. water
1/3 c. (firmly packed) brown sugar

Cut the peeling from the tangerine in paper-thin strips with a paring knife or lemon stripper. Squeeze the juice from the tangerine and strain. Combine the peeling and juice with the remaining ingredients in a medium-sized heavy saucepan. Simmer for 15 minutes. Remove from heat and remove the peeling and cinnamon. Chill thoroughly. Serve in small dishes. This makes about 4 servings.

MANGO CHUTNEY

25 mangos
2/3 tsp. nutmeg
2/3 tsp. cloves
1 1/2 tsp. allspice
2/3 tsp. ginger
5 c. vinegar
4 lb. brown sugar
2 tbsp. chopped chili peppers
1 clove of garlic, minced
1/2 lg. onion, chopped
1/4 c. chopped gingerroot
1 c. currants
1 c. seedless raisins
1/4 c. chopped preserved ginger

Peel and slice the mangos. Combine the nutmeg, cloves, allspice and ginger with the vinegar and brown sugar in a large preserving kettle or large saucepan. Mix well. Add peppers, garlic, onion and gingerroot, then bring to a boil. Boil for 10 minutes. Add currants, raisins and preserved ginger. Boil for 15 minutes longer. Add mangos and reduce heat. Simmer, stirring occasionally, for 30 minutes. Ladle into hot, sterilized pint jars and seal. This makes about 10 to 12 pints of chutney.

spiced mandarin oranges

Let the yellow and orange colors of late fall remind you that it's a good time to prepare Spiced Mandarin Oranges. This tangy delicacy is excellent served with game and wild fowl dishes so popular in the fall and winter months.

GRAPEFRUIT SALAD

2 firm thin-skinned grapefruit
1 c. diced cold cooked potatoes
1/2 c. diced unpeeled cucumber
Juice of 1 sm. orange, strained
2 tbsp. Basic Blender Mayonnaise *(Sauces. pg 3)*
1 tbsp. sour cream
2 tsp. lemon juice
1/8 tsp. paprika

Cut small slice from stem end of grapefruit to prevent tipping. Slice off 1/3 of the tops of the grapefruit and reserve the tops. Cut the edges of the grapefruit in Vandyke fashion with kitchen shears or small sharp knife. Remove the grapefruit sections carefully, using small sharp knife and fingers. Remove any excess pith from the shells and all pith and membrane from the grapefruit sections. Drain the sections thoroughly. Combine the grapefruit sections, potatoes and cucumber in a medium bowl. Boil the orange juice in a small pan until reduced to 1 teaspoon of liquid and let cool. Add the mayonnaise, sour cream, lemon juice, paprika and orange juice to grapefruit mixture and toss lightly. Chill thoroughly. Spoon the grapefruit mixture into shells. Garnish tops of grapefruit with decorative leaves or parsley and attach at a slight angle over salad-filled shells with toothpicks. This makes about 2 servings.

CREAM CHEESE WITH APRICOTS

8 fresh apricots
4 oz. cream cheese, softened
1 tbsp. whipping cream
Watercress

Split apricots almost in half and remove stones. Drain thoroughly. Combine cream cheese and cream, mixing until smooth. Place in icing bag with a large star tube affixed. Pipe cream cheese between apricot halves. Arrange watercress in serving dish, then place filled apricots on watercress. Basic Cream Cheese (Eggs and cheese, pg. 16) may be used in place of bought cream cheese. Garnish with additional watercress. This makes 8 servings.

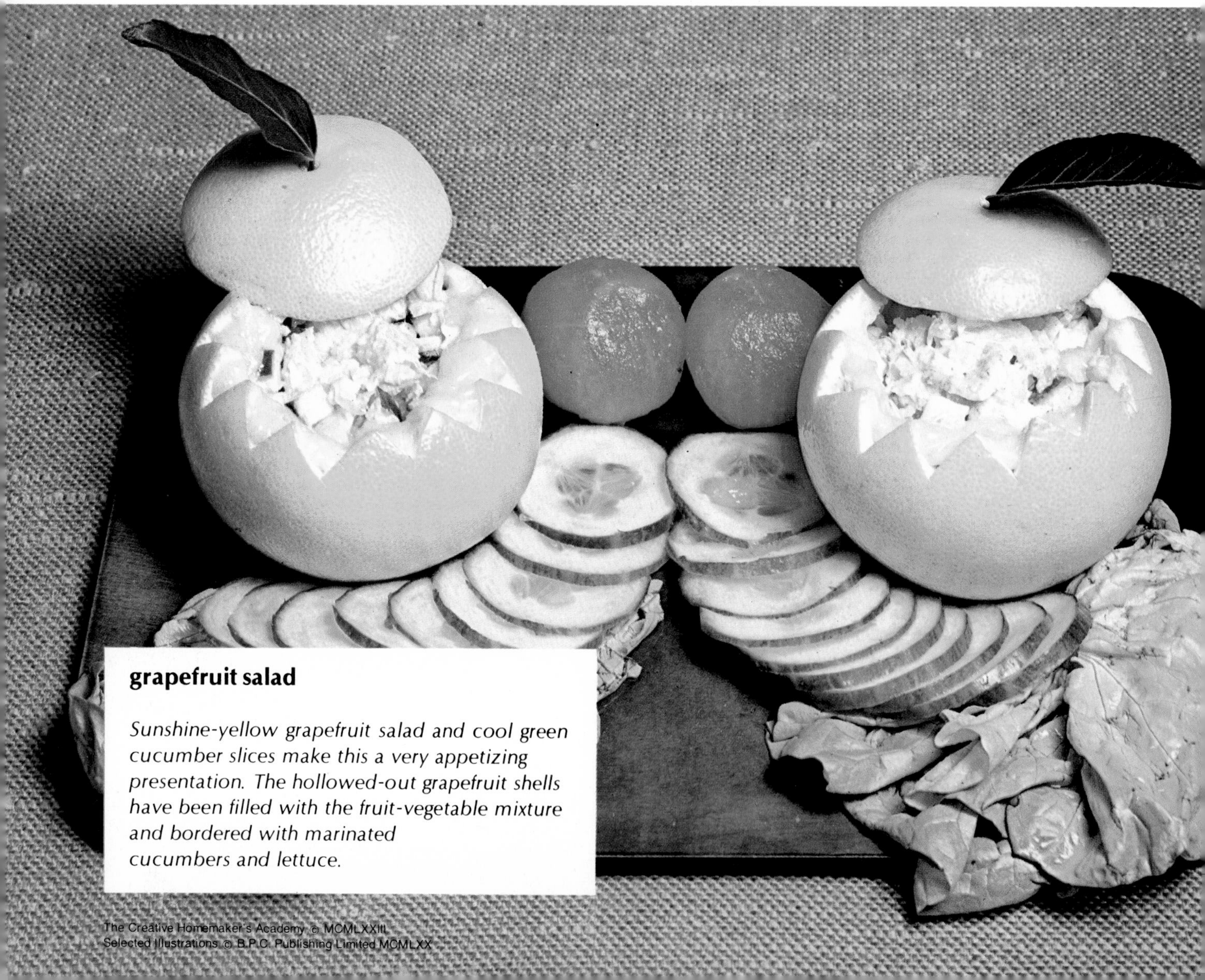

grapefruit salad

Sunshine-yellow grapefruit salad and cool green cucumber slices make this a very appetizing presentation. The hollowed-out grapefruit shells have been filled with the fruit-vegetable mixture and bordered with marinated cucumbers and lettuce.

CREAMY GOLDEN WALDORF

1 6-oz. package lemon gelatin
¼ tsp. salt
⅔ c. hot water
Lemon juice
3 med. golden Delicious apples
½ c. mayonnaise
1 c. heavy cream, whipped
1 c. finely chopped celery
1 c. finely chopped walnuts
Salad greens

Dissolve the gelatin and salt in hot water in a bowl, then stir in 2 tablespoons of lemon juice. Chill until thickened. Pare 2 apples partially, then core and dice. The skin will add color to the salad. Core and cut remaining apple into thin slices. Sprinkle diced

creamy golden waldorf

Golden delicious apples peek out of a layer of whipped cream and gelatin. High in fruit and flavor appeal, this molded salad will soon become a family favorite.

and sliced apples with lemon juice to prevent discoloration. Arrange apple slices, skin side down, around bottom of an 8-cup mold. Blend the mayonnaise into thickened gelatin and fold in the whipped cream. Fold in the diced apples, celery and walnuts gently, then spoon carefully over apple slices. Chill until firm. Unmold onto salad platter and garnish with salad greens. This makes 6 to 8 servings.

slimming vegetable salad

This attractive salad is simply an array of fresh crisp vegetables (and an excellent dish for weight watchers). It is a combination of shredded celery, cucumber slices, finely grated fresh cabbage and shredded fresh carrots.

SLIMMING VEGETABLE SALAD

Shredded carrots
Grated cabbage
Shredded celery
Thinly sliced cucumber

Arrange carrots around the edge of a serving dish. Place a circle of cabbage next to the carrots. Fill center with celery, then arrange a circle of cucumber slices around the celery. Garnish with carrot and turnip flowers (General Information, pg. 18). May serve with green pepper strips, fresh green onions and cherry tomatoes may be added, if desired. Serve with Basic Rémoulade Sauce (*Sauces, pg. 11*) or other favorite dressings.

beet and onion salad

The blend of colors is as attractive as the blend of flavors in this pungent Beet and Onion Salad.

BEET AND ONION SALAD

2 lb. fresh beets
2 tsp. salt
1 recipe Vinaigrette Aux Fines Herbes (*Sauces, pg. 2*)
2 white onions, peeled

Cut tops from beets, leaving at least 3 inches of stalk to prevent bleeding. Place in large kettle and add water to cover. Add salt and bring to a boil. Cook about 60 minutes or until tender, then drain and cool. Cut off tops and slip skins from roots. Cut into medium-thick slices and place in a bowl. Pour vinaigrette over beets and toss lightly. Cover and chill for several hours, tossing occasionally. Cut onions into thin slices and separate into rings. Remove beets from vinaigrette with a slotted spoon and place in a serving dish. Arrange onion rings over top. Garnish with chopped parsley. This makes 6 to 8 servings.

CUCUMBER GONDOLA SALAD

3 long straight cucumbers
1½ c. chopped cooked shrimp
¼ c. finely chopped celery
2 tbsp. minced green onion
2 tsp. minced parsley
1 tsp. fresh tarragon leaves or ⅛ tsp. dried tarragon leaves
½ tsp. salt
⅛ tsp. white pepper
¼ c. Basic Mayonnaise *(Sauces, pg. 3)*
21 lg. pitted ripe olives
3 whole pimentos
6 radishes

Slice off ⅓ of the cucumbers lengthwise, then cut long strips of peeling from the cut off portions for garnish. Dice enough of this portion of cucumber to make ¼ cup. Scoop the pulp from the larger portions of cucumber carefully, leaving shells ¼ inch thick. Combine the shrimp, diced cucumber, celery, onion and parsley in a medium bowl, then sprinkle with the tarragon, salt and pepper. Add the mayonnaise and toss lightly until just blended. Fill the cucumber shells with the shrimp mixture, heaping along the entire length of the cucumber. Cut olives into quarters, lengthwise, to form petals, then cut pimentos into an equal number of matching petals. Arrange the pimento and olive petals alternately along sides of cucumbers. Arrange strips of peeling over salad as shown in the illustration. Place cucumber gondolas on a bed of lettuce and garnish with radishes. Serve with Basic Vinaigrette (Sauces, pg. 2). This makes 6 servings.

IRIS SALAD

1 clove of garlic, pressed
¾ c. wine vinegar
Salt and pepper to taste
⅛ tsp. paprika
¾ c. salad oil
2 tbsp. minced green sweet pepper
2 tbsp. minced red sweet pepper
1 tbsp. minced pitted green olives
1 tbsp. chopped sweet pickle
1 sm. head lettuce
6 ½-in. thick tomato slices
3 hard-boiled eggs, sliced
¼ c. chopped slivered almonds

Combine the garlic, vinegar, salt, pepper, paprika and oil in a jar and add green and red peppers, olives and pickles. Shake until well blended, then chill thoroughly. Arrange a bed of lettuce on a large platter. Place tomato slices over the lettuce, then top with egg slices. Sprinkle with almonds and pour the dressing over all. Serve immediately. This makes 6 servings.

cucumber gondola salad

Cucumber and shrimp are combined with bright colorful garnishes to make this an attractive and refreshing salad.

pâté in aspic

Simplicity and skill go hand in hand in creating a good *Pâté* in Aspic salad. The key to proper preparation rests in using the right approach. A basic *pâté* recipe should be chosen, prepared, and refrigerated in a plain mold. The aspic recipe and molding technique should also be kept simple (*Salads*, pg. 4). Prepare this salad well ahead of time for service and refrigerate until just ready to serve. This salad can be made suitable for any occasion by the imaginative use of garnishes.

PÂTÉ IN ASPIC

1 recipe Simple Pâté Maison (*Appetizers, pg. 28*)
½ recipe Basic Simple Aspic (*Salads, pg. 4*)
12 to 20 radishes, sliced
1 lg. unpeeled cucumber, sliced

Prepare the *pâté* according to the instructions, then cover and chill overnight. Unmold on a wire rack over a shallow pan. Chill the aspic by stirring it over ice until just syrupy. Spoon a small amount of aspic carefully over top, covering top and side evenly. Pour excess aspic from pan back into remaining aspic. Place *pâté* in the refrigerator for 15 minutes or until coating is firm. Keep the aspic at syrupy stage by chilling as necessary. Repeat procedure 4 or 5 times or until desired thickness of aspic is obtained. Cut 7 radish slices into halves and arrange in a circle on top of *pâté*. Spoon aspic over top to set radish slices. Chill until ready to use. Place the *pâté* on serving dish and arrange cucumber slices around the *pâté*. Top with the remaining radish slices. Garnish with slightly fringed green onion. This makes 8 to 10 servings.

pâté in aspic

This tempting salad will add special appeal to a buffet dinner. The pâté peeks through the shimmering firmness of the aspic mold, and a festive use of vegetable garnishes adds a colorful trim.

RUSSIAN EGG SALAD

4 English muffin halves
Butter
4 hard-boiled eggs
16 thin unpeeled cucumber slices
1 c. cooked mixed vegetables
½ c. Basic Rémoulade Sauce *(Sauces, pg. 11)*
Basic Mayonnaise *(Sauces, pg. 3)*

Toast the muffins in a 200-degree oven for 30 minutes or until golden brown and dry. Cut a 1-inch circle from the center of each muffin. Spread each muffin with butter. Cut each egg, from pointed end to just below the center, to form 4 petals. Place 1 egg in the center of each muffin, then arrange cucumber slices between egg petals. Combine the mixed vegetables with just enough rémoulade sauce to moisten, then spoon vegetable mixture around the eggs. Pipe with green-tinted mayonnaise. Garnish with watercress, fresh parsley, and stuffed green olives, if desired. Serve immediately. This makes 4 servings.

russian egg salad

Pert little boiled egg salads may be served as a main dish luncheon salad. Deceptively easy to prepare, the egg salads rest on English muffin rounds surrounded with mixed vegetables in rémoulade sauce. These salads are most attractive garnished with fresh parsley, watercress, and olives.

CHICKEN SALAD WITH BACON

1 sm. head iceberg lettuce
1 sm. red sweet pepper, cut in strips
1 cucumber, thickly sliced
1 c. small whole mushrooms
2 c. coarsely chopped chicken
2 hard-boiled eggs, quartered
4 slices crisp-fried bacon, halved
2 tbsp. wine vinegar
6 tbsp. salad oil
Salt to taste
¼ c. mashed Roquefort cheese

Tear the lettuce into large pieces and place in a salad bowl. Add the red pepper, cucumber, mushrooms and chicken, then toss lightly. Top with the eggs and bacon. Combine the vinegar, oil, salt and cheese and blend thoroughly. Serve with the salad. This makes 4 servings.

chicken salad with bacon

A hearty, make-ahead dish, Chicken Salad With Bacon combines the meal's salad, vegetable and meat courses in one bowl — convenient for picnic or a quick luncheon dish.

CURRIED CHICKEN WITH GRAPES

3 c. diced cooked chicken
1½ c. thinly sliced celery
1 c. seedless green grapes
2 tbsp. lemon juice
1¼ tsp. salt
¼ tsp. freshly ground pepper
1½ tsp. curry powder
½ c. Basic Mayonnaise *(Sauces, pg. 3)*
3 tbsp. slivered toasted almonds

Combine the chicken with celery, grapes, lemon juice, salt, pepper, curry powder and mayonnaise in a large bowl and toss lightly until just blended. Chill for about 2 hours to blend flavors. Place the salad on a bed of lettuce on a serving plate, then sprinkle with the almonds. This makes 6 servings.

FROZEN EMPRESS SALAD

1 1-lb. can apricot halves
1 1-lb. can cling peach slices
1 3-oz. package strawberry gelatin
2 tbsp. lemon juice
1 8-oz. package cream cheese, softened
½ Basic Mayonnaise *(Sauces, pg. 3)*
1½ c. miniature marshmallows
½ c. sliced maraschino cherries
½ c. whipping cream, whipped

Drain the apricots and peaches, reserving 1¼ cups of juice, and cut the apricots and peaches into small pieces. Dissolve the gelatin in 1 cup of hot water, then stir in reserved juice and lemon juice. Chill until thickened. Blend the cream cheese and mayonnaise until smooth, then stir into the gelatin. Place the bowl in a larger bowl of ice, then chill, stirring frequently, until thickened. Fold the apricots, peaches, marshmallows and cherries into the gelatin mixture, then fold in the whipped cream carefully. Spoon the salad into a 2-quart mold and freeze for at least 6 hours or overnight. Unmold on serving plate and garnish with watercress. This makes 10 to 12 servings.

SORRENTO SALAD

3 c. diced cooked chicken
1 c. chopped celery
¼ c. chopped red sweet pepper *(opt.)*
½ tsp. salt
½ tsp. pepper
⅔ c. bleu cheese dressing
2 c. orange sections
2 c. grapefruit sections
½ c. diced avocado
1 avocado, cut in wedges
Orange or grapefruit juice
Salad greens

Combine the chicken, celery and red pepper in a bowl, then sprinkle with salt and pepper. Add the bleu cheese dressing and toss to mix well. Chill thoroughly. Dice enough orange and grapefruit sections to make ½ cup of each. Add to chicken mixture. Coat diced avocado and avocado wedges with orange juice. Add the diced avocado to the chicken mixture. Line a large salad bowl with salad greens and spoon the salad into the bowl. Arrange remaining orange and grapefruit sections and the avocado wedges around the salad. Serve with additional bleu cheese dressing. This makes 6 servings.

sorrento salad

Colorful Sorrento Salad combines chicken, vegetables, and fruit for an unusual taste treat. Additional flavor and texture has been added by using crisp red peppers and sharp bleu cheese dressing. For a finishing touch, a petal border of crisp green lettuce surrounds the salad bowl.

attractive fruit salads

Fruit Salads is an inclusive title for many delicious dishes. They serve as a first course, a main course or as a refreshing dessert after a heavy dinner. Creating a super fruit salad requires both variety and imagination. Don't settle for a slice of canned pineapple with the usual toppings. So many kinds of exotic fruits are in plentiful supply that it's not difficult to create exciting and different tasting salads.

Fruit salads may be varied according to season and menu. Fresh fruit supply is greater in the summer, but a wide range is available year-round. Always select fruit which is firm, well shaped and colored, and free of telltale bruises. New flavors are often discovered by trying some of the unusual fresh foreign fruits which are frequently available in supermarkets. For homemakers in a hurry or for last minute ideas, canned fruit can be a lifesaver.

As a complement to any dinner or lunch, fruit salads are appetizing and especially healthful for calorie counters. Fruit salads complement almost any meat, but are especially delicious with any kind of fowl. You'll enjoy serving fruit salad with the game bird recipes featured in this lesson.

PINEAPPLE-BLACKBERRY AND STRAWBERRY SALAD

1 lg. pineapple
2 c. blackberries
1 c. strawberries
Sifted confectioners' sugar
Kirsch

Remove the crown from the pineapple, cutting evenly so that it will sit evenly. Place it on a large circular serving platter at center back. Cut the pineapple lengthwise into 3 sections, having the center section 1½ inches wide, and reserve the center section. Remove the pineapple from each remaining section, leaving a shell, then dice the pineapple. Vandyke the edges of the pineapple shells and fill the shells with diced pineapple. Place on the platter, cut ends next to the crown, at angles toward outside. Pare the reserved pineapple slice and cut lengthwise to remove the core, leaving 2 slices. Cut both slices in half lengthwise. Place 1 slice of pineapple lengthwise over diced pineapple in each shell. Cut remaining slices in half crosswise and place in center at right angles to lengthwise slices of pineapple. Fill sections of pineapple slices alternately with half the blackberries and the strawberries. Arrange the remaining blackberries on the platter between the pineapple shells. Sprinkle fruits generously with confectioners' sugar. Moisten with a small amount of kirsch and chill until the sugar has dissolved. This makes about 8 servings.

pineapple-blackberry and strawberry salad

This luscious fruit salad is laden with appealing freshness. As colorful as it is appetizing, the skillful arrangement of pineapple, strawberries, and blackberries makes a real creation. The burst of fresh pineapple leaves and garden petunias adds a perfect bouquet touch to this tempting salad. Other fruits in season may be substituted.

MACÉDOINE FRUIT SALAD

2 bananas, sliced
Lemon juice
Sifted confectioners' sugar
2 apples, cut in wedges
1 pt. strawberries
4 peaches, sliced
3 oranges, sectioned *(General Information, pg. 13)*
3 pears, sliced
2 c. pitted cherries
1/2 c. Grand Marnier

Place a layer of banana slices in a straight-sided clear glass jar and sprinkle generously with lemon juice, then cover lightly with confectioners' sugar. Arrange the remaining fruits in layers, sprinkling each layer with lemon juice and confectioners' sugar. Pour the Grand Marnier over the top. Chill overnight for flavors to blend. Serve cold in crystal icers or sherbets. Any variety of fresh fruits in season may be used. This makes about 10 servings.

STUFFED APPLE-JERUSALEM ARTICHOKE SALAD

6 lg. red apples
Juice of 1 med. orange
3 med. Jerusalem artichokes
1/4 c. finely chopped celery
2 tbsp. coarsely chopped walnuts
3 tbsp. Basic Mayonnaise *(Sauces, pg. 3)*
1/2 tsp. celery salt

Remove the apple cores with a corer, then cut a thin slice about 1 1/2 inches in diameter from the stem end of the apple. Scoop out the apple pulp with the corer or a sharp knife, leaving a shell about 1/2 inch thick. Chop the removed apple pulp coarsely and drop immediately into the orange juice to prevent discoloration. Grate the artichokes coarsely and drop into the orange juice. Add the celery, walnuts, mayonnaise and celery salt, then toss with a fork to mix well. Pack the salad mixture into the hollowed out apples and chill until serving time. This makes 6 servings.

macédoine fruit salad

As a method of preparing fruit salad, you'll find macédoine fruits interesting and flexible. By way of translation, this means a mixture of fruits. This technique involves using fresh fruit attractively sliced and steeped in a marinade of liqueur and sugar. Although Macédoine Fruit Salad is almost always served cold, you might try it flambéed for a special occasion. The fruits are best when prepared in advance and allowed to manufacture the delicious juices. Serve in an attractive dish to enhance the simple elegance of this delicious fruit salad favorite.

The Creative Homemaker's Academy © MCMLXXIII
Selected Illustrations © B.P.C. Publishing Limited MCMLXX

fruit salad with a flair

As variety is the spice of life, a variation of ingredients is a must when preparing fruit salad with a flair. An unusual assortment of fruits and flavorings will add a distinctive taste to any salad. Here, brandy and wine blend with fruits in a truly marvelous way, as the brandy lends a heady contrast to the tartness of the fruits. The brandy, wine and fruit mixture should be chilled overnight for best results.

BRANDIED FRUIT SALAD

3 tbsp. strained lemon juice
3 lg. apples
3 ripe pears
2 lg. oranges
1/2 lb. fresh pitted Queen Anne cherries
1/2 lb. seedless white grapes
1 sm. honeydew melon
3/4 c. confectioners' sugar
1 c. Sauterne
1/2 c. brandy

Combine the lemon juice and 3 tablespoons of cold water in a large salad bowl. Peel, core and dice the apples and pears. Place the apples and pears in lemon juice mixture, turning to coat well. Let stand for 20 minutes. Peel the oranges and separate into skinless segments (General Information, pg. 13). Combine the orange segments, cherries and grapes with the apple mixture in the salad bowl. Peel and slice the melon into narrow strips. Add the melon to the other fruits. Sift the sugar over the fruits. Mix the Sauterne and brandy and pour over the fruits. Chill overnight. Serve in individual bowls. This makes 12 servings.

TOMATO ASPIC

3½ c. tomato juice
2 env. unflavored gelatin
2 tbsp. celery seed
1 tsp. salt
1 tsp. sugar
2 tbsp. Worcestershire sauce
¼ tsp. hot sauce
¼ c. lemon juice

Pour 1 cup of the tomato juice into a small saucepan. Sprinkle the gelatin on the tomato juice in the saucepan and let stand for 5 minutes to soften. Add the celery seed and place the saucepan over low heat. Stir until the gelatin is dissolved, then remove from the heat and strain the liquid through a fine sieve into a small bowl. Stir in the remaining tomato juice and other ingredients and pour into a lightly oiled 1½-quart mold. Chill until firm. Unmold onto a serving plate and garnish with salad greens. Serve with Basic Mayonnaise (Sauces, pg. 3).

MOLDED ASPARAGUS SALAD WITH DRESSING

2 env. unflavored gelatin
1 tbsp. sugar
½ c. lemon juice
½ tsp. salt
¼ c. chopped pimentos
1 1-lb. can asparagus tips, drained
2 tsp. grated onion
1 c. chopped celery

Soften the gelatin in ½ cup of water. Combine the sugar, 1 cup of water and lemon juice in a saucepan and bring to a boil. Remove from heat, add the gelatin and salt and stir until dissolved. Chill until partially set. Fold in the pimentos, asparagus tips, onion and celery and spoon into a 1-quart ring mold. Chill until firm, then unmold onto a serving plate. This makes 4 servings.

SOUR CREAM DRESSING

1 c. sour cream
¼ c. lemon juice
1 tsp. sugar
½ tsp. salt
Cayenne pepper to taste
¼ tsp. celery salt
½ tsp. paprika
1 tsp. dry mustard
¼ tsp. garlic salt

Combine all the ingredients in a small mixer bowl and beat until smooth. Spoon into the inside of asparagus salad ring. This makes 1¼ cups of dressing.

tomato aspic

This unusually molded Tomato Aspic is filled with sharp, tomato flavor. The lacy bed of green lettuce which surrounds it provides an excellent contrast to the ripe redness of the aspic. This cool salad may be served with Basic Mayonnaise and fresh vegetables for a delicious combination.

MOLDED EGG SALAD

3 env. unflavored gelatin
3/4 c. cold water
3 c. boiling water
2 tbsp. sugar
3/4 c. lemon juice
6 hard-boiled eggs
1/2 c. Basic Blender Mayonnaise *(Sauces, pg. 3)*
1/4 c. chopped parsley
1/2 c. chopped celery
1/2 c. chopped green olives
Salt and white pepper to taste

Sprinkle the gelatin over the cold water in a bowl. Add the boiling water, sugar and lemon juice and stir until the gelatin and sugar are dissolved. Cut the eggs in half and remove the yolks. Mash the yolks in a small bowl and mix with 1/3 of the gelatin mixture. Stir in the mayonnaise and pour into a decorative nonmetal mold. Chill until firm, then sprinkle with the chopped parsley. Chill the remaining gelatin until thickened. Chop the egg whites and add to the thickened gelatin. Add the celery, olives, salt and pepper and stir until well mixed. Spoon over the parsley in the mold, then chill until firm. Unmold onto a serving plate and garnish with hard-boiled egg slices and parsley sprigs. Top may be garnished with green peas and mushrooms, if desired. This makes 6 servings.

molded egg salad

Rich in flavor and appeal, Molded Egg Salad will please even the most particular gourmet. A simple gelatin base is used to which eggs, mayonnaise and seasonings are added. As this dish requires several different steps in preparation, it is best when fixed ahead of time and served for a special occasion. Garnishes of hard-cooked eggs, parsley, mushrooms, and green peas are artistically arranged on both the sides and top of the mold.

fruited rice salads

An unusual combination of fruit, celery, seasonings, and rice blend to make these Fruited Rice Salads a real taste delight. Plump, bright oranges have been scooped out to form shells for the rice filling. Vandyking the edges of the oranges adds an extra flair to the salads.

FRUITED RICE SALADS

1/2 c. diced celery
1/4 c. minced onion
2 tbsp. butter
2 tsp. grated orange rind
1/2 tsp. poultry seasoning
1 c. orange juice
1 c. water
1/3 c. raisins or currants *(opt.)*
1 c. long grain rice
6 Vandyked orange shells (opt.)

Sauté the celery and onion in the butter in a medium-sized saucepan until tender. Stir in the orange rind, seasoning, juice, water, raisins and rice and bring to a boil. Stir well, then reduce heat and cover. Simmer for 25 minutes or until rice is tender and liquid is absorbed. Cool, then chill well. Spoon into orange shells or onto individual salad plates lined with lettuce leaves. This makes 6 servings.

AMBROSIA CONSERVE

2 med. oranges
1 lg. ripe pineapple
6 cooking apples
2 c. water
1 c. raisins
6 c. sugar
1 c. flaked coconut

Remove the outer peeling of the oranges with a vegetable peeler and cut the peeling into thin slivers with a knife or scissors. Remove the white membrane from the oranges, then section the oranges and remove the seeds. Cut the oranges in small pieces. Pare the pineapple and remove the core, then cut in small cubes. Peel, core and chop the apples. Combine the orange rind and pulp, pineapple, apples and water in a large kettle. Bring to a boil. Reduce the heat and simmer, covered, for 10 minutes. Add the raisins and sugar and cook over moderate heat, stirring, until the sugar dissolves. Add the coconut and boil rapidly, stirring constantly, for 20 to 30 minutes or until the mixture sheets from a spoon. Remove from the heat and skim off the foam quickly. Ladle immediately into hot sterilized pint jars, filling to within 1/8 inch of tops. Cover tightly and invert jars for several seconds, then stand the jars upright to cool. This makes 4 pints of conserve.

QUINCE JELLY

6 lb. quinces
Sugar
Melted paraffin

Quarter the quinces and remove the cores with a very sharp knife. Place the quinces in a large kettle, adding enough water to cover and bring to a boil. Reduce the heat and simmer for about 45 minutes or until the quinces are tender. Strain the liquid through a jelly bag or cloth into a large bowl, but do not squeeze the bag. Measure the liquid and place in a large kettle. Add 3/4 cup of sugar for every cup of liquid. Bring to a boil over medium heat, stirring, until the sugar is dissolved. Reduce heat and simmer for about 20 minutes or to 220 degrees on a candy thermometer. Remove from heat and skim thoroughly. Ladle into hot, sterilized 6-ounce jelly glasses, then cover with paraffin. This makes 8 to 10 glasses.

ambrosia conserve

A traditional favorite, Ambrosia Conserve may be served as an accompaniment to meat, game or poultry. Fresh fruits have been simmered with raisins, sugar, and coconut to form a superb conserve. When made in your own kitchen, Ambrosia Conserve is a gourmet, homemade treat you may serve with pride.

chinese fruit salad

Does a good cook ever resort to opening cans for dinner? Of course! The recipe for Chinese Fruit Salad calls for litchi nuts, longans, and water lily roots, all of which come in cans obtainable in specialty or oriental food stores. Chinese Fruit Salad is an appetizing combination of these unusual flavors and textures.

chinese fruit salad

Here is a pretty and practical way to serve Chinese Fruit Salad; use the melon halves as your container, heaping the fruit in the hollowed melon halves. To offset the sweetness of the salad, we suggest lemon slices and almonds or white nuts as accompaniments.

CHINESE FRUIT SALAD

1   4-oz. jar ginger in syrup
1   8-oz. can kumquats
1   11-oz. can litchi nuts in syrup
1   20-oz. can longans
1   16-oz. can mangos
1   12-oz. can water lily roots
1 round watermelon, chilled
1   18-oz. can white nuts or 1 c. slivered almonds
1 lemon, sliced

Drain the ginger, kumquats, litchi nuts, longans, mangos and water lily roots. Place in a large bowl and mix well. Chill until cold. Cut the watermelon in half and remove the meat and seeds. Cut the melon meat into cubes or balls. Cut a slice off the base of each watermelon half and place each half in a serving dish. Place the melon cubes back into the shells. Pile the ginger mixture on watermelon cubes. Serve with the white nuts and lemon. This makes about 12 servings.

FRUIT AND CRAB SALAD

1   6-oz. package lemon gelatin
½ tsp. crushed rosemary
1 c. fresh orange sections
1 c. fresh grapefruit sections
1 lb. fresh crab meat or 2   6-oz. packages frozen
     Alaskan King crab, thawed
½ c. chopped onion
1 tbsp. chopped fresh parsley
 3 drops of hot sauce
⅓ c. Basic Mayonnaise *(Sauces, pg. 3)*
1 tsp. prepared mustard
¾ c. sliced celery

Dissolve the gelatin in 2 cups boiling water. Add 2 cups cold water, then chill until partially set. Fold in the rosemary and orange and grapefruit sections and spoon into 1½-quart ring mold. Chill until firm. Drain the crab and cut into large pieces, then place in a medium-sized bowl. Mix the onion with the parsley, hot sauce, mayonnaise, mustard and celery. Pour over the crab and toss until mixed. Chill. Unmold the gelatin mixture onto a large serving plate, then fill center with the crab mixture. Garnish with salad greens and serve immediately. This makes 6 servings.

fruit and crab salad

Refreshingly cool . . . elegantly beautiful . . . absolutely delicious! This describes Fruit and Crab Salad. A lemon gelatin ring, filled with orange and grapefruit sections, encases a tangy crab mixture — a mutually complementary flavor combination that will delight those to whom it is served.

The Creative Homemaker's Academy © MCMLXXIII
Selected Illustrations © B.P.C. Publishing Limited MCMLXX

fresh crab salad

Seafood salads, because they are so filling and refreshing, are often a meal in themselves. This Fresh Crab Salad makes a delicious light lunch.

FRESH CRAB SALAD

Fresh crab meat has a delicate flavor that is easily overwhelmed. Understanding this, we have added very little seasoning to Fresh Crab Salad: only a little mayonnaise, a small amount of pimento for color, and celery for texture. The result, in its simplicity, is most pleasing. In the event you are fortunate enough to have fresh-caught crabs, you may want to refer to "How To Clean Crabs" on page 8 of the Seafood section.

FRESH CRAB SALAD

1 lb. fresh crab meat, flaked
1/2 c. minced celery
1 tsp. grated onion
1 tbsp. minced pimento
1/4 tsp. salt
2 tbsp. lemon juice
Basic Blender Mayonnaise (Sauces, pg. 3)
Lettuce leaves
2 tbsp. minced parsley

Combine the crab meat, celery, onion and pimento in a bowl. Sprinkle with salt and lemon juice and toss to mix. Add just enough mayonnaise to moisten, then mix well. Spoon the crab meat mixture onto a bed of lettuce leaves and sprinkle with the parsley. Garnish with thin slices of cucumber and Tomato Flowers (General Information, pg. 17). Serve with additional mayonnaise. This makes 4 servings.

FRESH SHRIMP AND PORK SALAD

2 cloves of garlic, pressed
1 tsp. freshly ground pepper
1/2 tsp. ground coriander
2 tsp. honey
1 tsp. salt
1 tsp. chili powder
1/4 c. red wine vinegar
1/4 c. lime juice
1 med. cucumber
2 c. diced cooked pork
2 c. chopped cooked shrimp

Combine the garlic, pepper, coriander, honey, salt and chili powder in a jar. Add the vinegar and lime juice, then cover. Shake vigorously until blended. Peel the cucumber, then cut into thin slices. Place the pork, shrimp and cucumber in a large bowl. Add the vinegar mixture and toss lightly to mix. Garnish with sprigs of mint. This makes about 6 servings.

fish aspic

Basic Fish Wine Aspic is a versatile variation of Basic Simple Aspic and may be used in virtually any fish or seafood recipe that calls for a clear aspic. It is important to have a well-seasoned fish stock (Seafood, pg. 5) in order to bring out the full flavor of the fish or shellfish to be covered with the aspic. If there isn't time to prepare a fish stock "from scratch," an emergency version may be quickly made by simmering equal parts of bottled clam juice, water, a little white wine, a few parsley sprigs and a sliced onion for 30 minutes, then strain it. If a stronger fish flavor is desired, increase the amount of clam juice to taste. This stock will not be as subtle and delicate as Basic Fish Stock, but it is a perfectly acceptable substitute in an emergency.

BASIC FISH WINE ASPIC

2 env. unflavored gelatin
3½ c. Basic Fish Stock *(Seafood, pg. 5)*
¼ c. Sauterne
¼ c. lemon juice

Soften the gelatin in ½ cup water for 5 minutes. Heat the fish stock in a medium-sized saucepan. Add the gelatin and heat, stirring, until the gelatin is dissolved. Stir in the Sauterne. Clarify the gelatin mixture according to the instructions for Clarifying Stock (Soups, pg. 2), then stir in the lemon juice. Use as desired for various congealed molds, glazes or coatings.

CRAB ASPIC

1 recipe Basic Fish Wine Aspic
½ lb. fresh lump crab meat
1   2½-oz. jar button mushrooms, drained
2 hard-boiled eggs
½ c. cooked green peas

Chill the aspic until syrupy. Rinse an 8 x 4-inch loaf pan with cold water, then pour in a ½-inch layer of aspic. Keep the remaining aspic at syrupy stage by placing it over a bowl of ice and stirring occasionally. Chill aspic in pan until partially congealed. Arrange crab meat around the edges of the pan, then place a row of mushrooms across the center. Place 1 egg, round side down, in the center of each square as shown in the illustration. Spoon a ½-inch layer of the aspic over the top carefully and chill until firm. Combine the remaining aspic, peas and any remaining crab meat and mushrooms and spoon over the congealed layer. Chill until firm. Unmold the Crab Aspic onto a bed of lettuce and serve with Basic Mayonnaise (Sauces, pg. 3). Cooked lobster, shrimp or fish may be substituted for the crab meat, if desired. This makes 4 to 6 servings.

crab aspic

Crab Aspic is a distinctively flavorful salad. The clear aspic shows morsels of crab meat, hard-boiled eggs, mushrooms, and peas. Substituting lobster for the crab meat creates an equally delicious variation.

ORANGE AND AVOCADO SALAD

¹/₄ c. fresh lemon juice
2 avocados
3 fresh oranges
³/₄ c. Basic Mayonnaise
   (Sauces, pg. 3)
¹/₄ c. fresh orange juice
¹/₂ tsp. paprika
Lettuce leaves

Pour the lemon juice into a shallow bowl. Peel the avocados and cut crosswise into ¹/₄-inch slices, removing the seeds as sliced. Dip the slices into the lemon juice to keep from turning dark. Peel the oranges and cut crosswise into ¹/₂-inch slices, then remove the seeds. Mix the mayonnaise, orange juice and paprika to make orange mayonnaise. Line a serving bowl with lettuce leaves. Place alternate layers of orange slices and avocado slices on the lettuce, ending with avocado slices. Serve with the orange mayonnaise. One cup of Basic Vinaigrette (Sauces, pg. 2) may be substituted for the orange mayonnaise. This makes 6 servings.

orange and avocado salad

If you have never before tried these flavors in combination, you are in for a delightful surprise when you prepare Orange and Avocado Salad. Top it with orange mayonnaise.

basic savory mousse

Basic Savory Mousse is pictured here in two sizes. The seafood border demonstrates that the flavor of the mousse is highly compatible with salmon, shrimp, and crab.

BASIC SAVORY MOUSSE

4 egg yolks
½ tsp. salt
¼ tsp. white pepper
¼ tsp. paprika
¼ tsp. onion salt
½ tsp. celery salt
1¼ c. milk
1 env. unflavored gelatin
¼ c. water
¾ c. half and half cream
1 recipe Shrimp Filling
2 egg whites

Place the egg yolks, salt, pepper, paprika, onion salt and celery salt in the top of a double boiler. Beat with a whisk until just mixed. Add the milk and beat until well blended. Place over hot, not boiling, water and cook, stirring constantly, until thick. Don't worry if the eggs curdle slightly. Soften the gelatin in the water, then stir into the hot mixture until the gelatin is dissolved. Stir in the cream and the filling. Place the egg whites in a small mixer bowl and beat with an electric mixer until stiff. Fold into the gelatin mixture. Turn into a wet 1-quart mold and chill until firm. A thin aspic-like layer forms on bottom of the mold and gives the mousse a glazed top when unmolded. Unmold on a serving dish and serve with Basic Mayonnaise (Sauces, pg. 3). The Salmon Filling or Crab Filling may be used in place of the Shrimp Filling. This makes about 6 servings.

SHRIMP FILLING

1 c. ground cooked shrimp
2 tsp. anchovy paste
2 hard-boiled eggs, riced or mashed

Combine all the ingredients and mix well.

SALMON FILLING

1 7-oz. can red salmon
1 tsp. anchovy paste

Drain and flake the salmon, removing all the bones and skin. Add the anchovy paste and mix well.

CRAB FILLING

½ lb. fresh crab meat
2 tsp. anchovy paste
¼ c. freshly grated Parmesan cheese

Pick over the crab meat and remove any shell. Combine with the remaining ingredients and mix well.

AVOCADO MOUSSE

½ c. cold water
1 env. unflavored gelatin
½ c. boiling water
1 tsp. salt
1 tsp. onion juice
2 tsp. Worcestershire sauce
2 tbsp. lemon juice
2 c. puréed avocados
½ c. whipping cream, whipped
½ c. Basic Blender Mayonnaise (Sauces, pg. 3)

Pour the cold water into a large bowl. Sprinkle the gelatin on the water and let soften for 5 minutes. Add the boiling water and stir until the gelatin is dissolved. Add the salt, onion juice, Worcestershire sauce, lemon juice and avocados and mix well. Chill in the refrigerator until slightly thickened. Fold in the whipped cream and mayonnaise, then turn into an oiled 6-cup mold. Chill until firm. This makes 6 to 8 servings.

autumn vegetable molds

Autumn vegetable molds are small egg and vegetable aspics, perfect in appearance and taste for fall dinners. However, do not let this title discourage you from serving them any time of the year. The delicious flavors of zucchini, cucumbers, boiled eggs and Basic Blender Mayonnaise are too good to be limited to a single season and these vegetables are available fresh or fresh-frozen throughout the year. Before preparing autumn vegetable molds, refer to the special instructions for engraving aspics on page 5.

Chill the aspic by stirring over a bowl of ice until syrupy. Rinse 8 individual molds and a 2-cup mold with cold water. Place a parsley sprig in the center of the bottom of each mold, then pour 1 tablespoon of the aspic over each sprig carefully. Chill until firm. Fill each mold with aspic to a depth of 1 inch and chill until firm. Peel and dice the zucchini. Cook in a small amount of water for 7 minutes or until tender, then drain well. Place in a large bowl. Peel the cucumber and grate coarsely. Add to the zucchini. Add the eggs and sweet pepper and mix well. Mix the cream and mayonnaise until blended. Soften the gelatin in 1/4 cup of cold water in a small saucepan. Place over low heat and stir until the gelatin is dissolved, then cool slightly. Beat into the mayonnaise mixture. Add the mayonnaise mixture to the zucchini mixture and mix well. Season with salt and pepper. Spoon into the individual molds to fill 3/4 full, then smooth the tops. Place remaining zucchini mixture in the larger mold, then smooth the top. Chill until firm. Pour enough remaining syrupy aspic over the individual molds to fill, then pour remaining aspic into the larger mold. Chill until firm. You may serve these on lettuce. The whole salad may be prepared in a 2-quart mold, if desired. This makes 10 servings.

AUTUMN VEGETABLE MOLDS IN ASPIC

1/2 recipe Basic Simple Aspic
    (pg. 4)
9 sprigs of parsley or tarragon
4 med. zucchini
1 med. cucumber
2 hard-boiled eggs, chopped
1/2 med. red sweet pepper, diced
1/4 c. half and half cream
1 c. Basic Mayonnaise *(Sauces, pg. 3)*
1 env. unflavored gelatin
Salt and freshly ground pepper to taste

autumn vegetable molds in aspic

These attractively arranged vegetable molds are made with zucchini, cucumbers, boiled eggs, red sweet peppers and Basic Mayonnaise (Sauces, pg. 3). If fresh zucchini and peppers are not available, you may use frozen zucchini and substitute a small jar of pimento for the red sweet pepper.

molded fruit salad
molded vegetable salad with shrimp

Here are two examples of the versatility of congealed salads. Pictured in the foreground is a congealed salad with shrimp and, in the background, a light congealed fruit salad. Either salad may be served as a main dish.

CONGEALED SALADS

Congealed salads are a most desirable accompaniment to any meal because they are colorful, light-textured and refreshing. They can be molded in many decorative shapes and sizes, so appealing for special occasions. And, because they can be prepared ahead of time, they are usually preferred for large dinners.

Fruits, vegetables, meats and seafood are all delicious in congealed salads. In this section, we are introducing Molded Fruit Salad and savory Molded Vegetable Salad with Shrimp. Both are particularly good tasting when topped with any of the Basic Mayonnaise Variations like Piquant Mayonnaise (Sauces, pg. 3) or Curry Mayonnaise (Sauces, pg. 3).

MOLDED FRUIT SALAD

2 3-oz. packages cherry gelatin
1 c. fresh seedless grapes, halved
2 c. fresh cantaloupe balls
½ c. fresh cherries, pitted

Place the gelatin in a large bowl. Add 2 cups of boiling water and stir until the gelatin is dissolved. Stir in 2 cups of cold water, then chill until slightly thickened. Add the grapes, cantaloupe and cherries and mix well. Place in a lightly oiled 2-quart mold and chill until firm. Unmold onto a serving plate. This makes about 8 servings.

MOLDED VEGETABLE SALAD WITH SHRIMP

1 lb. cooked fresh shrimp
12 sm. fresh radishes
1 lg. fresh carrot
1 stalk celery
2 3-oz. packages lime gelatin

Peel and devein the shrimp, then chill. Remove the tips and stems from the radishes, then cut the radishes into flower and other fancy shapes (General Information, pg. 18). Place in a large bowl of ice water and refrigerate. Slice the carrot lengthwise with a vegetable peeler and place the slices in a bowl of warm water until pliable. Wrap each slice around a knife handle and secure with a toothpick. Place in the bowl of ice water with the radishes and refrigerate for 1 hour. Cut the celery stalk into 2-inch lengths, then slice each piece lengthwise into very thin slits ¾ of the way down. Place in a large bowl of ice water and refrigerate for about 1 hour or until the celery forms fan shapes. Place the gelatin in a medium-sized bowl. Add 2 cups of boiling water and stir until the gelatin is dissolved. Stir in 2 cups of cold water and chill until syrupy. Drain the celery well. Pour half the gelatin into a lightly oiled 2-quart mold and push the celery fans into the gelatin. Chill until firm. Drain the radishes and carrot curls well and remove the toothpicks from the carrot curls. Add the radishes and carrot curls to the remaining gelatin and mix carefully to keep the carrot curls intact. Spoon over the gelatin mixture in the mold and chill until firm. Unmold onto a serving plate and garnish with the shrimp. This makes about 8 servings.

SALAD MIMOSA

1 1-lb. can tiny green peas
1 1-lb. can French-style green beans
1½ c. chopped celery
3 c. diced cooked potatoes
1½ c. chopped green onions
Basic Blender Mayonnaise
    (Sauces, pg. 3)
4 hard-boiled eggs
½ c. chopped mushroom stems and pieces
½ c. chopped green olives

Drain the peas. Drain the green beans and chop coarsely. Mix the peas, celery, potatoes, beans, and onions separately with just enough mayonnaise to coat evenly. Place the peas, celery, half the potatoes, beans, onions, then the remaining potatoes in a round glass bowl. Remove the egg yolks from the egg whites and chop. Chop the egg whites separately. Cover the peas with the mushrooms. Place half the egg whites over the celery and half the egg yolks over the first wedge of potatoes. Cover the beans with the olives. Place the remaining egg whites over the onions and remaining egg yolks over the second wedge of potatoes, then garnish with tomato. Serve with mayonnaise. This makes about 10 servings.

TROPICAL LAMB SALAD

So many times homemakers end up with leftover meats just too good to throw away, and a delicious way — one way too rarely thought of is to use them in salads. When you have leftover leg of lamb, try the following Tropical Lamb Salad. Served with an appropriate hot soup, such as Cream of Broccoli Soup (Appetizers and Soups, pg. 20), this makes an elegant light meal.

TROPICAL LAMB SALAD

2 bananas, peeled
2 tbsp. lemon juice
¾ c. sliced celery
2 c. diced cooked lamb
1½ tsp. prepared mustard
¼ c. Basic Blender Mayonnaise
    (Sauces, pg. 3)
¼ c. whole pimento-stuffed olives
¼ c. salted toasted almonds
½ tsp. salt

Slice the bananas into a large bowl. Add the lemon juice and toss lightly to coat the banana slices. Add the celery and lamb. Mix the mustard and mayonnaise and spoon over the lamb mixture. Add the olives, almonds and salt, then toss until all the ingredients are coated. Chill for at least 30 minutes. Serve on lettuce or watercress. This makes about 4 servings.

SALAD MARGUERITE

1 1-lb. can asparagus tips, drained
1½ c. cooked cauliflowerets
1½ c. diced fresh tomatoes, drained
1½ c. diced green sweet pepper
1½ c. diced cooked potatoes
1½ c. diced cooked carrots
1 recipe Basic Mayonnaise
  (Sauces, pg. 3)
4 hard-boiled eggs, chilled
½ tsp. Dijon mustard
Salt to taste
½ tsp. paprika

Arrange the asparagus tips, cauliflowerets, tomatoes, sweet pepper, potatoes and carrots in a round glass bowl. Spread 1½ cups of mayonnaise in an even layer over all the vegetables. Slice both ends of egg white from each egg, so that each slice is 1 inch wide on the cut side. Cut each end piece with a ¾-inch round fluted *canapé* cutter. Cut lengthwise through each egg with a sharp knife to form 2 halves. Place the egg yolks in a small bowl. Cut the egg whites into petal shapes to resemble daisy petals, then place in the center of the mayonnaise, pointed sides out and edges slightly overlapping, in the shape of a flower. Place the fluted egg white rounds, cut side up, at even intervals halfway between the center flower and the edge of the bowl and press lightly into the mayonnaise. Mash the egg yolks. Add the mustard, salt, paprika and just enough of the remaining mayonnaise to moisten, then mix well. Shape eight ½-inch balls from the egg yolk mixture, then flatten slightly. Place 1 ball in the center of each fluted round. Shape enough of the remaining egg yolk mixture into a large bowl for the center of the flower, then flatten to resemble the center of a daisy. Place in the center of the petals and score the top with the sharp knife. Garnish with fresh bay leaves or parsley around the inside of the glass bowl rim, if desired. This makes about 10 servings.

TOMATO RELISH

3 c. chopped fresh tomatoes
2 c. chopped onions
1 c. whole pitted black olives
1 c. chopped green sweet peppers
1 tbsp. sliced black olives
1 recipe Vinaigrette Aux Fines Herbes *(Sauces, pg. 2)*

Place 1 cup of the tomatoes in a tall, narrow serving container. Add ½ cup of onions, then add ½ cup of whole olives. Place ½ cup of the green pepper over the olives and add ½ cup of onions. Add 1 cup of the tomatoes, then add ½ cup of onions. Place remaining whole olives over the onions, then add the remaining green peppers. Add the remaining onions and place the remaining tomatoes on the top. Garnish with the sliced olives. Pour the Vinaigrette Aux Fines Herbes over the tomato mixture, then cover. Chill overnight. Remove the cover and drain the tomato mixture just before serving. This makes 8 to 10 servings.

tomato relish

These attractive layers of fresh tomatoes, chopped onions, black olives and green sweet peppers have been chilled overnight in delicious Vinaigrette Aux Fines Herbes (Sauces, pg. 2).

AL FRESCO OLIVE SALAD

4 c. diced carrots
2 c. diced potatoes
1½ c. canned pitted ripe olives
1 tbsp. butter
¼ c. chopped green onions
1 sm. clove of garlic, pressed
½ c. California Dressing

Cook the carrots and potatoes in boiling, salted water until just tender. Do not overcook. Drain and cool, then place in a large bowl. Cut the olives into quarters. Melt the butter in a small saucepan. Add the green onions and garlic and cook over low heat until tender, but not brown. Add to the carrot mixture, then add the olives and dressing and mix lightly. Spoon into an oiled 8-cup mold and press down lightly. Cover and refrigerate overnight. Unmold onto a serving plate and garnish with additional ripe olives, carrot curls and watercress. Serve with remaining dressing. This makes 8 to 10 servings.

CALIFORNIA DRESSING

⅔ c. vegetable oil
⅓ c. garlic wine vinegar
1½ tsp. seasoned salt
¼ tsp. seasoned pepper
½ tsp. paprika
½ tsp. sugar
2 tbsp. crumbled bleu cheese
2 pimentos, mashed

Place all the ingredients in a small bowl, then beat well. This may be processed in a blender, if desired. This makes about 1¼ cups of dressing.

CABBAGE-OLIVE SALAD

1 sm. can pimentos, drained
1 med. head of cabbage, chopped
1 green sweet pepper, chopped
12 pimento-stuffed olives, sliced
1 sm. onion, grated
½ c. sugar
½ c. wine vinegar
½ c. vegetable oil
1 tsp. salt
1 tsp. prepared mustard
1 tsp. celery seed

Chop the pimentos. Place the pimentos, cabbage, green pepper, olives and onion in a large bowl and mix well. Combine the sugar, vinegar, oil, salt, mustard and celery seed in a small saucepan and stir until mixed. Bring to a boil, then pour over the cabbage mixture. Cover and chill for at least 24 hours. Mix well before serving. This makes 6 to 8 servings.

OLIVE-CHEESE SALAD

1 lg. head of lettuce
1 sm. can pimentos, drained
½ lb. Cheddar cheese
½ lb. sliced salami
2 sm. cans anchovies, drained
1 med. can ripe olives, drained
1 med. jar pimento-stuffed olives, drained
½ lb. bleu cheese, cubed
2 lg. onions, sliced
Vinegar and oil dressing

Tear the lettuce into bite-sized pieces and cut the pimentos and Cheddar cheese into strips. Cut the salami into wedges. Place the lettuce in a large salad bowl. Add the pimentos, anchovies, ripe and stuffed olives, *bleu* cheese, Cheddar Cheese, salami and onions and toss until mixed. Add just enough dressing to coat all the ingredients and toss well. This makes 8 to 10 servings.

al fresco olive salad

The term Al Fresco *means "in the open air," which appropriately describes this refreshing salad. Pitted, ripe olives, fresh carrots, potatoes, green onions, minced garlic and a delicious California Dressing give this chilled salad mold its delectable flavor. Garnish with crisp carrot curls and whole ripe olives.*

mushroom salad

Congealed Mushroom Salad is a "show off" dish for those very special occasions. Although its preparation involves much time, it can be prepared a day ahead and simply unmolded when you're ready to serve it.

MUSHROOM SALAD

1½ lb. medium fresh mushrooms
1 c. Sauterne
1 c. Basic Chicken Stock (Soups, pg. 2)
1 recipe Basic Emergency Aspic (pg. 4)
1 recipe Basic Béchamel Sauce (Sauces, pg. 4)
⅓ c. freshly ground Parmesan cheese
½ c. whipping cream
3 eggs, separated
1 c. diced cooked ham
1½ env. unflavored gelatin
Salt and freshly ground pepper to taste
1 2½-oz. can pâté
1 tbsp. Basic Blender Mayonnaise (Sauces, pg. 3)

Wash and stem the mushrooms, then drain well. Combine the mushrooms, stems, Sauterne and stock in a saucepan and bring to a boil. Reduce the heat and simmer for 5 minutes or until the mushrooms are tender. Drain the mushrooms and reserve the liquid. Pour a ⅛-inch layer of aspic into a wet 8-inch soufflé dish. Arrange whole mushrooms around the edge and place 1 mushroom in the center. Slice 4 mushrooms in half lengthwise and place, cut side down, around center mushroom as shown in the illustration. Chill until the aspic is firm and the mushrooms set. Pour 1¼ cups of the remaining aspic carefully over the mushroom layer. Chill until firm. Prepare the Béchamel sauce, using only 1 cup of milk and all of the reserved Sauterne mixture. Stir in the cheese and whipping cream until well blended. Beat egg yolks slightly, then stir a small amount of the hot mixture into the egg yolks. Stir the egg yolks into the hot mixture and cook over low heat until smooth and well blended. Chop ½ of the remaining whole mushrooms and all of the stems coarsely and stir into the hot mixture. Add the ham, blending well. Heat through, then remove from heat. Soften the gelatin in ¼ cup water and stir into the mushroom mixture until dissolved. Season with salt and pepper, then let cool to room temperature. Beat the egg whites until stiff peaks form, then fold gently into the mushroom mixture. Spoon carefully over the aspic in the soufflé dish and chill until firm. Blend the pâté with the mayonnaise until smooth. Unmold the salad onto a round, rimmed serving dish and pour the remaining aspic around the base of the salad. Place the remaining whole mushrooms, top side down, in the aspic around the salad. Pipe the pâté mixture into the mushroom caps. Dust lightly with paprika, if desired. Chill until firm. This makes 8 to 10 servings.

smoked salmon rolls

The process of smoking gives salmon and many other varieties of fish a delicious flavor. Fish are generally cured in a brine solution before being smoked. Then they are placed above a dampened wood fire, usually made with hickory, and allowed to absorb the aroma of the smoke for a specified length of time.

Most smoked varieties of fish are available packaged or canned, and ready to eat when purchased. Combined with light foods, they make delicious salads. And they are quite good panfried, poached or cooked in a hearty casserole.

In the following recipe, we have combined smoked salmon with asparagus tips, mayonnaise, lemon and parsley, all of which make an unusually delectable salad. For a very attractive serving, we have rolled the salmon over asparagus tips and bordered them with fresh, green parsley.

SMOKED SALMON ROLLS

20 slices smoked salmon
20 canned asparagus spears, drained
½ c. Basic Mayonnaise (Sauces, pg. 3)
6 lemon wedges

Wrap the salmon slices around the asparagus spears. Arrange on a serving dish. Pipe the mayonnaise over the rolls. Add the lemon wedges to the dish and garnish with parsley. Chill well before serving. This makes 5 or 6 servings.

smoked salmon rolls

These attractive delicacies, bordered with fresh, green parsley and lemon slices may be served as a first course at dinner or as a luncheon salad. This shows the versatility of this dish. Pipe a decorative ridge of mayonnaise over the rolls for flavor and eye appeal.

red pepper salad

It's so nice to know that even though red sweet peppers are seasonal, this delectable salad is not! Green sweet peppers, in no way, diminish the taste of this dish, so feel absolutely free to use green ones when red peppers are not available. Before preparing this beautiful salad, made with rice, olives, onions, cream cheese, cabbage and a vinaigrette sauce (Sauces, pg. 2), refer to the information on sweet peppers (Vegetables, pg. 29).

red sweet pepper salad

These stuffed red sweet peppers on beds of fresh green lettuce, are a tantalizing salad for any meal. Garnish them with bits of chives, green and black olives. Although red sweet peppers make a more colorful base for this dish, green sweet peppers are equally suitable in taste.

RED SWEET PEPPER SALAD

6 lg. red sweet peppers
1 c. brown rice
1 3-oz. package cream cheese
2 tbsp. minced green onion
¼ c. Vinaigrette Aux Fines Herbes *(Sauces, pg. 2)*
Salt and freshly ground pepper to taste
6 sm. thin onion rings
6 green stuffed olives
2 tbsp. minced chives
1 head of lettuce
18 whole black olives

Cut the tops from the red peppers and remove the seeds and membranes. Rinse and invert on paper toweling to drain. Cook the rice according to the instructions for Basic Boiled Rice (Cereals, pg. 3), increasing the cooking time to 45 minutes or until tender, then drain. Dice the cream cheese. Combine the cream cheese with the rice in a large bowl and toss lightly. Fold in the green onion, vinaigrette, salt and pepper. Spoon the rice mixture into the red pepper shells, then place an onion ring on top of each. Place a green olive in the center of each onion ring. Sprinkle with the chives and chill until ready to serve. Arrange the stuffed peppers on beds of lettuce and garnish each serving with 3 ripe olives. This makes 6 servings.

herbed asparagus salad

Cottage cheese, with its refreshing flavor, makes an ideal light lunch, snack or salad. Because it blends so easily with an endless variety of fruits and vegetables, we can serve it often in a number of different combinations. In the following recipe, we have flavored cream-style cottage cheese with basil leaves, salad oil, chives and green onions, and combined it with cooked, fresh, marinated asparagus. Bits of chives and strips of pimento add flavor and a decorative touch.

HERBED COTTAGE CHEESE AND ASPARAGUS SALAD

1/4 c. olive or vegetable oil
4 tsp. wine vinegar
2 tsp. finely chopped fresh basil
3/4 tsp. salt
1/4 tsp. freshly ground pepper
1 1/2 lb. cooked fresh asparagus (*Vegetables, pg. 73*)
1 lb. cream-style cottage cheese
1 tbsp. finely chopped chives or green onion tops
10 pimento strips

Combine the oil, vinegar, basil, 1/2 teaspoon salt and pepper for the dressing in a jar and shake well. Place the asparagus in a dish and spoon the dressing over the top. Let stand for at least 30 minutes to marinate. Combine the cottage cheese, chives and the remaining 1/4 teaspoon of salt and mix well. Arrange the asparagus around the outside of a large round platter, then spoon the cheese mixture into the center. Arrange the pimento strips over the asparagus and sprinkle the cheese with additional chives. This makes 6 servings.

FRESH SPINACH SALAD

1 1-lb. package fresh spinach
3 tbsp. olive oil
2 tsp. lemon juice
1 egg
1/2 tbsp. sugar
1/2 tsp. salt
1/4 tsp. paprika
1/4 tsp. mustard
1 tsp. Worcestershire sauce
Garlic salt to taste
1/4 c. catsup
1 c. vegetable oil
1/4 c. wine vinegar
1/3 c. warm water

Wash the spinach and drain well, then cut into strips. Place in a large bowl. Sprinkle with olive oil and lemon juice and chill. Place the eggs, sugar, salt, paprika, mustard, Worcestershire sauce, garlic salt and catsup in a blender container and blend for 10 seconds. Add the salad oil alternately with the vinegar, blending constantly, then blend until thickened. Add the warm water gradually, blending constantly. Place the spinach in a salad bowl. Pour enough of the dressing over the spinach to coat well, then toss lightly. You may garnish with tomato wedges, asparagus tips and hard-boiled egg slices, if desired. This makes about 6 servings.

herbed cottage cheese and asparagus salad

This colorful, inviting dish may be served as a main dish salad. Display it in a large circular dish, garnished with bits of chives and strips of pimento. Its cool, refreshing taste will be welcomed by gourmet weight watchers!

charcuterie salad

If the term *charcuterie* is unfamiliar to you, it simply means cold cuts and cold meat slices, such as salami and pastrami, usually sold in delicatessens and special meat shops. One such meat included in the following recipe is *mortadella*, a large type of Italian sausage, especially good served as an *hors d'oeuvre*.

Charcuterie Salad is actually a number of small, decorative, cold-cut sandwiches, combined with bits of cooked green peas and lettuce, and attractively garnished with petals of a skinned tomato. Although these savory delights make an ideal salad, you may also wish to serve them on an *hors d'oeuvre* tray.

CHARCUTERIE SALAD

6 thin slices cooked chicken
6 thin slices cooked ham
6 thin slices mortadella
Basic Mayonnaise *(Sauces, pg. 3)*
Prepared mustard
¾ c. cooked green peas
1 tomato, skinned *(Vegetables, pg. 27)*
Lettuce

Cut circles from the chicken, ham and mortadella with a 4-inch fluted cookie cutter. Spread a thin layer of mayonnaise over the chicken circles, then cover with the ham circles. Spread a thin layer of mustard over the ham circles, then cover with the mortadella circles. Place 2 tablespoons of the peas in the center of each mortadella circle and spoon 1 tablespoon of mayonnaise over each mound of peas. Cut the top off of the tomato, then remove the seeds and pulp, leaving a ½-inch shell. Cut 6 wedges from the tomato shell to resemble petals and place 1 tomato petal on top of each salad. Garnish each with a lettuce leaf. Place the salads in a serving dish and place lettuce leaves around the salads. Serve with paper-thin cucumber slices and brown bread. This makes 6 servings.

charcuterie salad

The elegant design of these tiny cold-cut sandwiches makes them an attractive snack, salad or hors d'oeuvre. This easy-to-prepare Charcuterie Salad will add unsurpassed eye and taste appeal to any occasion.

FRESH VEGETABLE SALADS

A gelatin salad is one of the easiest and most convenient dishes to prepare — it can be made a day or two in advance and forgotten until time to unmold. The following recipe for Carrot Carousel is a perfect blend of sweet, crushed pineapple, tangy orange juice and crisp, grated, raw carrots. The combination of ingredients has an interesting texture as well as a nice flavor, which contrasts well with savory soups or main dishes.

The following Broccoli Salad may utilize leftover cold cooked broccoli for all or part of the 1½ pounds required in the recipe. All ingredients may be prepared and measured ahead of time but do not pour the dressing on the broccoli until serving time.

Cauliflower Salad and Dilled Cucumbers And Sour Cream are two quick, crisp salads which are delightful in flavor.

CARROT CAROUSEL

1½ c. cold orange juice
2 env. unflavored gelatin
½ c. boiling orange juice
¼ tsp. salt
1 c. Basic Blender Mayonnaise (Sauces, pg. 3)
1½ c. cubed carrots
1 13½-oz. can crushed pineapple

Pour ½ cup of cold orange juice into a blender container, then sprinkle the gelatin over the orange juice and let stand for 5 minutes. Add the boiling orange juice and process at low speed until the gelatin is dissolved, using a rubber spatula to push the gelatin granules into the mixture. Add the remaining cold orange juice, salt and mayonnaise and blend well. Add the carrots and cover, then process at high speed until the carrots are finely grated. Stir in the undrained pineapple and pour into a 6-cup mold. Chill until firm. Unmold onto a serving plate and garnish with carrot curls. Instructions for carrot curls are in Raw Vegetable Relish Tray recipe (Salads, pg. 9). This makes 8 servings.

BROCCOLI SALAD

1½ lb. fresh broccoli spears
¼ c. vegetable oil
6 tbsp. cider vinegar
½ c. apple juice
Salt and pepper to taste
6 lettuce leaves
2 hard-boiled eggs, chopped

Cook the broccoli in a small amount of boiling, salted water until tender, then drain and cool. Place in a shallow dish. Place the oil, vinegar, ¼ cup of water, apple juice, salt and pepper in a small bowl and mix well. Pour over the broccoli, then marinate in the refrigerator, carefully turning the broccoli occasionally, for at least 2 hours. Place the broccoli in the lettuce leaves on individual salad plates, then sprinkle the eggs over the top. Garnish with tomato wedges. This makes 6 servings.

CAULIFLOWER SALAD

1 head of cauliflower
¼ c. minced green onions
½ c. minced celery leaves
½ c. sour cream
½ c. Basic Vinaigrette (Sauces, pg. 2)
2 tsp. caraway seed
Salt to taste
Lettuce leaves

Separate the cauliflower into flowerets and place in a large bowl, then chill. Place the onions, celery leaves, sour cream, vinaigrette, caraway seed and salt in a small bowl and mix until blended. Add the onion mixture to the cauliflowerets and mix well. Line a salad bowl with lettuce, then place the salad in the bowl over the lettuce. This makes about 8 servings.

DILLED CUCUMBERS AND SOUR CREAM

2 cucumbers
1 c. sour cream
2 tsp. grated onion
2 tbsp. lemon juice
1 tbsp. wine vinegar
½ tsp. dillseed
1 tsp. salt
Lettuce leaves

Peel the cucumbers, then slice paper-thin. Place in a bowl and chill well. Place the sour cream, onion, lemon juice, vinegar, dillseed and salt in a medium-sized bowl and blend thoroughly. Add the cucumbers and toss lightly until coated. Line a salad bowl with lettuce, then add the cucumber mixture. This makes 4 servings.

carrot carousel

Here is a molded gelatin salad that is appropriate for many menus — from a light luncheon to a dinner party. A tangy combination of crushed pineapple, orange juice and carrot makes a pretty as well as a delicious salad.

tossed green salad

There is an art to the preparation of an impeccably crisp, ice cold, tossed green salad which has been seasoned to perfection with an excellent dressing. In order to achieve this culinary ideal, a few basic rules must be conscientiously observed. Always wash the greens in cold water and tear into bite-sized pieces. As stated before, do *not* cut the greens with a knife — cut edges will discolor and wilt, resulting in pieces that are limp and unattractive. Drain the greens on paper toweling, then store them in an airtight container in the refrigerator until *just before* ready to serve. *Never* toss the salad with dressing prior to serving time in order to avoid a limp salad. Always combine the salad and dressing in a well-chilled salad bowl. Romaine is a popular salad green. In the following Fresh Romaine And Lettuce Salad you may prefer to increase the romaine and use less lettuce.

FRESH ROMAINE AND LETTUCE SALAD

1 lg. head of lettuce
1 lg. head of romaine
1 med. clove of garlic
2/3 c. salad oil
1/3 c. grated Parmesan cheese
1/3 c. crumbled bleu cheese
1 tbsp. Worcestershire sauce
1/4 c. fresh lemon juice
3/4 tsp. salt
1/4 tsp. freshly ground pepper
1 1/2 c. Fried Croutons (*Breads, pg. 16*)

Tear the lettuce and romaine into bite-sized pieces into a large salad bowl and chill. Peel the garlic and cut into quarters. Pour the oil into a jar, then drop the garlic into the oil and cover. Let stand at room temperature for 30 minutes. Sprinkle the cheeses over the lettuce mixture. Remove the garlic from the oil, then add the Worcestershire sauce, lemon juice, salt and pepper to the oil. Cover and shake well. Pour the oil mixture over the lettuce mixture and toss until blended. Sprinkle the croutons over the salad and toss lightly. Serve immediately. This makes 6 to 8 servings.

TUNA CREAM WITH LEMON MAYONNAISE

2 c. milk
2 c. tomato juice
¼ c. all-purpose flour
3 eggs, separated
2 env. unflavored gelatin
½ tbsp. anchovy paste
1   7-oz. can light tuna, drained
1 lg. tomato, skinned (Vegetables, pg. 27)
½ c. minced celery
1 tsp. salt
½ tsp. white pepper

Combine the milk and tomato juice in a saucepan. Place the flour in a small bowl and stir in enough of the milk mixture to make a smooth pouring consistency. Beat the egg yolks, then beat in the flour mixture. Sprinkle the gelatin over the remaining milk mixture to soften, then place the mixture over medium heat and stir until the gelatin is dissolved. Add a small amount of the hot milk mixture to the anchovy paste in a small bowl, stirring until it is of pouring consistency. Combine the egg and the anchovy mixtures, then add to the milk mixture, mixing well. Cook over medium heat, stirring constantly, until slightly thickened. Chill until partially congealed. Flake the tuna with a fork. Remove the seeds from the tomato, then chop finely. Stir the tuna, tomato, celery, salt and pepper into the gelatin mixture, mixing well. Beat the egg whites until stiff. Fold ¼ of the egg whites into the tuna mixture thoroughly, then fold in the remaining egg whites. Spoon into a wet ring mold and spoon the remaining mixture into 4 wet individual molds and chill until firm. Unmold onto a serving plate as shown in the illustration. Serve with green-tinted Special Lemon Mayonnaise (Sauces, pg. 33). This makes 10 servings.

tuna cream with lemon mayonnaise

This savory mold is a combination of tuna and tomato flavors. Special Lemon Mayonnaise (Sauces, pg. 33) is a delicious addition to this salad. Chill the salad in an attractive mold, and reserve enough to make smaller molds for added decoration.

LOBSTER SALAD

2   1 to 1 ¼-lb. live lobsters
2 recipes Basic Court Bouillon for Seafood
        (Seafood, pg. 10)
3 c. diced cooked new potatoes
1 tbsp. diced red pimento
1 ¼ c. cooked green peas
Basic Mayonnaise (Sauces, pg. 3)
1 lg. heart of lettuce

Cook the lobsters in a court bouillon according to
the instructions (Seafood, pg. 12). Split and clean
the lobsters according to the step-by-step illustrations (Seafood, pg. 11). Remove the lobster meat,
reserving the shells, claws and legs for garnish, if
desired. Chop the meat of 1 lobster. Place
the meat in a large bowl. Add the potatoes, pimento and 1 cup of peas and toss lightly. Add enough
mayonnaise to moisten and mix until all ingredients are combined. Mound the salad in a serving
dish. Tear the lettuce and place around the edge of
the dish, then place the remaining peas on the
salad around the inside edge of the lettuce. Place
the remaining lobster meat on top of the salad, then
garnish the salad with the reserved shells, claws
and legs. Pipe a border of mayonnaise around the
outside of the lettuce. Chill thoroughly. The coral
may be chopped and added to the salad, if desired.
This makes about 6 servings.

AVOCADO AND SHRIMP SALAD

½ lb. Boiled Shrimp (Seafood, pg. 14)
½ c. water
Juice of ½ lemon
2 ripe avocados
¼ c. Paprika Mayonnaise (Sauces, pg. 3)
4 drops of hot sauce .
1 heart of lettuce

Cook and chill the shrimp. Mix the water and
lemon juice. Peel the avocados and cut in half, then
remove the seeds. Place the avocado halves in a
shallow dish that will just hold the halves and pour
the lemon juice mixture over the avocados. Let
stand for 10 minutes, spooning the liquid in the
dish over the avocados frequently. Remove the
avocado halves from the liquid. Place the halves on
a board, cavity side down, and slice very thinly
without separating the slices. Run a wide spatula
under each half and place it back in the lemon
juice mixture. Mix the shrimp, mayonnaise and hot
sauce. Shred the lettuce and place it in the bottom
of 4 glass salad bowls. Place ¼ of the shrimp mixture in each bowl over half the lettuce. Halve each
sliced avocado and place a section in each bowl,
fanning the avocado slices as they are placed. Chill
until served. This makes 4 servings.

lobster salad

*This delicious seafood-vegetable
salad, a refreshing meal in itself, is
made with lettuce, diced
potatoes, peas, Basic Mayonnaise
(Sauces, pg. 3) and fresh, cooked
lobster.*

MOLDED APPLE SALADS

In order to turn out a flawlessly molded gelatin salad, one must take care in preparing the molds (page 2) before filling with the salad mixture. As you peel the apples, place the pieces in a solution of water and lemon juice to prevent discoloration.

APPLE-LIME MOLDS

1 ½ tbsp. unflavored gelatin
⅓ c. fresh lime juice
½ c. sugar
⅛ tsp. salt
1 tsp. grated lime rind
2 med. Red Delicious apples

1 c. whipping cream, whipped
Green food coloring
Whole strawberries
Mint sprigs

Soften the gelatin in the lime juice. Combine 1 ¼ cups of water with the sugar and salt in a saucepan and bring to a simmer. Stir in the gelatin mixture until dissolved, then add the lime rind. Chill until thickened. Pare and dice 1 apple, then fold the apple and whipped cream into the gelatin mixture. Add enough food coloring for desired tint. Spoon the gelatin mixture into seven 5-ounce oiled molds and chill until firm. Remove the core from the remaining apple and cut the apple into thin wedges. Unmold the salad onto a serving dish and garnish with the apple slices, strawberries and mint sprigs. This makes 7 servings.

apple-lime molds

Here is a festive, colorful salad with as much appeal to the eye as the palate. A make-ahead salad to include on the menu for a special dinner, these Apple-Lime Molds may, if desired, be prepared in one large mold instead of small, individual ones.

APPLE-GRAPE SLAW

1/4 c. honey
1 tbsp. wine vinegar
1 tsp. horseradish
1/2 tsp. salt
1   8 1/2-oz. can crushed pineapple
1 sm. green cabbage
3 Washington State Red Delicious apples
1/2 c. chopped cashew nuts
1 c. halved Tokay grapes, seeded
2 tbsp. lemon juice
1/2 c. water

Combine the honey, vinegar, horseradish, salt and pineapple in a bowl for the dressing. Place in a jar and cover, then chill. Remove 5 of the outer leaves of the cabbage and sprinkle with several drops of cold water. Place the leaves in a plastic bag and place in the refrigerator until crisp. Shred the remaining cabbage and place in a large bowl. Core and dice 2 unpeeled apples into the shredded cabbage. Add the cashew nuts and 1/2 cup of the grapes. Shake the dressing and pour over the salad, tossing well. Line a salad bowl with the crisp cabbage leaves and fill with the apple mixture. Core and slice the remaining unpeeled apple into 10 slices. Combine the lemon juice and water and dip the apple slices into the lemon mixture to prevent discoloration. Arrange the remaining grapes in the center of the salad, then insert the apple slices around 1 end of the grapes to resemble a cluster of grapes and leaves. This makes 6 to 8 servings.

CURRIED CHICKEN SALAD

3 tbsp. instant minced onion
3 tbsp. water
2 tbsp. butter
1 1/4 tsp. curry powder
1/3 c. Basic Mayonnaise (Sauces, pg. 3)
1 tbsp. lemon juice
1/2 tsp. salt
Dash of cayenne pepper
3 c. diced cooked chicken
1   1-lb. 4-oz. can pineapple chunks, drained
1/2 c. coarsely chopped nuts
1/3 c. golden raisins
1 red apple, cored and diced
Lettuce
2 tbsp. shredded coconut

Combine the minced onion and water in a small bowl and let stand for 10 minutes. Melt the butter in a small skillet over medium heat, then stir in the onion and curry powder. Sauté, stirring constantly, for 3 to 5 minutes, then cool. Combine the curry mixture with the mayonnaise, lemon juice, salt and cayenne pepper and blend thoroughly. Combine the chicken, pineapple, nuts, raisins and apple in a large bowl, then add the curry dressing, tossing gently until mixed. Line a salad bowl with lettuce, then add the salad and sprinkle with the coconut. Turkey may be used instead of chicken. This makes 6 servings.

curried chicken salad

For a main course dish with distinction, choose Curried Chicken Salad to highlight a carefree, prepare-ahead meal. The flavors of chicken or turkey, pineapple, nuts, raisins and apples are combined in a tangy, curried mayonnaise dressing.

MIXED FRUIT SALAD

This salad tastes best when fresh fruits are used, so it is more frequently seen as a summertime salad. However, canned fruits may be substituted for fresh, when necessary. When preparing the fruits, make certain that all traces of pith and membrane are removed from the orange and grapefruit sections (General Information, pg. 13). If fresh peaches are used, be sure to sprinkle the slices well with lemon juice to prevent them from turning dark. This salad may be made several hours in advance and should be thoroughly chilled before serving.

HONEY AND FRUIT SALAD

1 c. fresh grapefruit sections
1 c. fresh orange sections
1 c. sliced bananas
1 c. fresh pineapple chunks
1 c. sliced fresh peaches
1 c. chopped pecans
1 8-oz. package cream cheese, softened
1/4 c. honey
Juice of 1/2 lemon
1 c. whipping cream
8 lettuce leaves

Combine the fruits in a large colander and drain well, reserving the juices for another occasion. Place in a large bowl. Add the pecans and mix well, then chill. Place the cream cheese in a small bowl and mash. Blend in the honey and lemon juice until smooth. Pour the cream into a small mixer bowl and beat with an electric mixer until soft peaks form, then fold in the cream cheese mixture. Place the lettuce leaves on 8 salad plates and spoon the fruit mixture equally onto the lettuce leaves. Spoon the cream cheese mixture over each salad and garnish with mint leaves and strawberries, if desired. This makes 8 servings.

BAKED GRAPEFRUIT

Hot Baked Grapefruit is a versatile dish. It may be served in a variety of ways. It is a very good first course appetizer accompanied by a glass of Madeira or sherry. For a breakfast menu, you may wish to use more brown sugar than the recipe calls for. Continental recipes for baked citrus fruits call for a dollop of sour cream after baking.

HOT BAKED GRAPEFRUIT

3 grapefruit
6 tsp. Madeira or dry sherry
6 tbsp. brown sugar
Butter
6 maraschino cherries

Cut each grapefruit in half and Vandyke the edges. Remove the centers and loosen all sections from the skin with a grapefruit knife. Place the grapefruit halves in a shallow baking dish. Sprinkle each half with 1 teaspoon of the Madeira and 1 tablespoon of the brown sugar, then dot with butter. Bake in a preheated 350-degree oven, 1 rack above center, for 25 to 30 minutes or until the grapefruit are heated through and the tops are golden. Place a cherry in the center of each grapefruit half, then place the grapefruit on a serving platter. This makes 6 servings.

hot baked grapefruit

Hot Baked Grapefruit is a delicious addition to any menu, particularly breakfast or brunch. Here each serving has been garnished with candied cherries and fresh orange leaves.

fresh tomato accordions

This very colorful and attractive salad is full of flavor. The secret is the homemade mayonnaise which is served with the salads. It is ideal to include on a summertime menu.

TOMATO SALADS

These Fresh Tomato Accordions may be served as a main course when accompanied by a clear or cream soup and piping hot bread. Consisting of fresh (vine ripe, if possible) tomatoes, shrimp and hard-boiled eggs, this dish is a boon to today's busy homemaker —everything may be done well in advance except for the easy final assembling. This should be done just before serving time, but will take only a few minutes. To add extra color, serve this cool, tempting salad on crisp lettuce leaves. Tuna, crab, lobster or even chicken may be used in place of the shrimp.

SEAFOOD AND ASPARAGUS

Seafood and Fresh Asparagus Salad combines the flavors of cooked shrimp (Seafood, pg. 14), crab, lobster (Seafood, pg. 12) and asparagus (Vegetables, pg. 73), all of which are marinated in Basic Vinaigrette (Sauces, pg. 2). Avocado and crisp lettuce add flavor, texture and color.

FRESH TOMATO ACCORDIONS

6 firm tomatoes
6 hard-boiled eggs, sliced
Lettuce leaves
1 c. Boiled Shrimp, diced *(Seafood, pg. 14)*
½ c. sliced celery
Fresh parsley
1 recipe Basic Mayonnaise *(Sauces, pg. 3)*

Cut a thin slice from the stem end of each tomato. Stand the tomatoes upright on the cut ends and cut 5 deep slits in each tomato with a sharp knife. Fill the slits with egg slices. Line a large platter with lettuce leaves, then arrange the tomatoes on the lettuce. Toss the shrimp with the celery, then mound in the center of the platter. Garnish the platter with parsley. Serve the salad with the mayonnaise. This makes 6 servings.

SEAFOOD AND FRESH ASPARAGUS SALAD

1 lb. fresh asparagus
1 ¼ c. Basic Vinaigrette *(Sauces, pg. 2)*
½ c. fresh avocado strips
2 tbsp. fresh lemon juice
1 c. Boiled Shrimp *(Seafood, pg. 14)*
1 c. cooked lobster chunks *(Seafood, pg. 12)*
1 c. lump crab meat
Fresh lettuce leaves

Cook the asparagus according to the step-by-step illustrations (Vegetables, pg. 73), then drain. Place in a shallow dish and add ½ cup of the vinaigrette. Chill thoroughly. Combine the avocado and lemon juice in a small bowl and chill well. Combine the shrimp, lobster and crab meat in a bowl and add the remaining vinaigrette, then chill. Arrange the lettuce leaves on a serving tray. Drain the shrimp mixture and combine with the avocado, then place in the center of the tray. Drain the asparagus and arrange at each end of the tray. This makes about 6 servings.

eggs & cheese

table of contents

introducing egg cookery

Eggs are the original packaged food, so high in protein, vitamins and minerals they actually constitute a complete food. Americans, on a yearly average, consume about 314 eggs per person. This does not mean that each of us eats an egg for breakfast 314 days a year — eggs cooked alone are only a fraction of the many uses of this versatile food.

Eggs serve as a *thickening agent* in custards, soups and sauces, and, as you learned when we made sponge cakes (Desserts, pg. 1), beaten egg whites are a *leavening agent*. Emulsions such as mayonnaise use eggs as a *stabilizer* to keep the oil in suspension. Eggs are also used as binders, either internally to hold preparations such as meatballs together or externally to hold bread crumbs, flour or cornmeal on foods for frying.

For use as a *glaze*, eggs are beaten with a little water and brushed over the top of breads and pastries.

BUYING EGGS

Eggs are standard graded according to size and quality. Sizing is based on their weight per dozen. Eggs come in jumbo, extra large, large, medium, small and peewee sizes. Most recipes are based on medium or large eggs, so if you use a different size, adjust the recipe. All our recipes use large eggs.

Grades of eggs, according to quality, include *Fancy Grade* (or *Grade AA*), *Grade A*, *Grade B* and *Grade C*. The whites in *Fancy Grade* eggs stand up well when they are fried. The yolk is round, firm and centered when the eggs are boiled. As the grades get lower, the egg whites get thinner and the yolks slightly flatter and less well centered. *Fancy Grade* and *Grade A* eggs are best for frying, poaching and boiling, when appearance is important, but the lower grades are acceptable for cooking.

Eggshells may be either brown, white or spotted with no difference in taste or quality.

STORING AND COOKING EGGS

Always keep eggs refrigerated and covered. If not covered, they will absorb other refrigerator odors. Since quality deteriorates at high temperatures and long storage times, do not keep a supply that will last longer than 3 weeks. The yolk will stay centered if it is stored broad

the key to savory omelets

end up. Separated eggs will keep in the refrigerator for 2 days — store yolks and whites in airtight containers. If storing just the yolk, cover with a little cold water first.

Eggs are very easily overcooked . . . and ruined! Cook eggs with care over low heat. Classic methods of cooking eggs are soft- and hard-boiled, coddled, poached, scrambled, shirred and fried.

Omelets are among the cook's best friends. If unexpected guests drop by at mealtime, it is so easy to make an impressive omelet with ingredients on hand that no one need ever know this meal wasn't planned. The varieties of ingredients for your omelet are as limitless as your imagination. One restaurant in New York lists 553 types of omelets on the menu — and the proprietor claims this is only the beginning of the possibilities!

In addition to plain omelets — eggs, butter, salt and pepper — there are three other categories: omelet *garnie*, which is served with vegetables as garnish; omelet *fourré*, or combination omelet containing a filling; and omelet *sucrée*, or dessert omelet, made with sugar, fruits or jams and often a liqueur. The omelet *sucrée* will be discussed later in the Desserts section of your Creative Cooking Course.

There are also several variations in method for making omelets which have evolved in different countries. On the following pages, these methods are presented, beginning with the simple, Basic French Omelet.

While omelets are very easy to prepare, you may need a few practice sessions to learn exactly when they are ready and how to fold them perfectly. With the aid of the helpful step-by-step instructions on pages 4 and 5, you will soon be turning out perfect omelets.

The criteria for perfect omelets are that they be moist-cooked inside, plump in the middle and golden brown on the outside. The method of preparation is very much like scrambled eggs at first. However, making an omelet is a gently folding process, not a vigorous stirring one.

THE OMELET PAN

The making of an omelet does not require special equipment. While you may buy a classic omelet pan, you'll see on the next page that an ordinary frying pan may be used. A copper, enamel or teflon skillet is best; *cast iron* is too heavy to manipulate properly. The pan should be relatively small, no more than 10 inches at the top, with sides slanting out so the finished omelet will slide out easily. It's best to use the omelet pan only for omelets.

The hinged omelet pans are an unnecessary frill, because it is so easy to make a true omelet folding after cooking.

To season a new pan for cooking omelets, place the pan over *very* low heat and half fill with coarse salt. French *gros sel* is best, but ice cream salt is an acceptable substitute. Leave the pan over low heat for several hours until the salt has turned a dirty beige. Discard the salt and, while the pan is still hot, polish with a clean cloth.

Now it's ready to make non-stick omelets. *Never scour* an omelet pan — just rinse it thoroughly and wipe carefully with a clean cloth.

If you prefer to use an ordinary frying pan for cooking omelets, put the pan over low heat and leave for 7 minutes. Then take a small piece of raw, unsalted pork fat and rub over the side and bottom of the hot pan until it sizzles.

If an omelet pan is used properly it will give many years of good service. It will eventually begin to get dark, but this is by no means a sign of disgrace. The French call such pans *culotté*, meaning they have blackened from serving their owners well.

how to prepare omelet pans

1 As you can see, we are using an old, well-worn frying pan to demonstrate how to prepare an ordinary pan for omelets. (Complete instructions for making an omelet are in the step-by-step illustrations on the next two pages.)

2 Immediately before making each omelet, heat the pan on low heat for 7 minutes. Rub the hot base firmly with a small piece of unsalted pork fat until it sizzles. Then wipe out excess with paper toweling.

3 Toss in the amount of butter required in your recipe. Allow it to melt and turn slightly golden at the edges. Pour in the prepared egg mixture and cook according to the instructions on the next page.

4 Here is a perfect omelet made in an ordinary skillet.

5 Turn the omelet out onto an oval platter.

how to make
basic french omelet

The Basic French Omelet is a classic recipe. Pictured on these two pages are step-by-step instructions for making this omelet; however, many other types follow this basic cooking method. Unless your recipe instructs otherwise, use these pictures as a general guide for all omelets.

When mixing this omelet, use a fork or a whisk — not an electric mixer. Beat the eggs about 30 to 45 strokes until well mixed but not watery. As mentioned earlier, omelet cooking begins much like scrambled eggs. Pour the mixture into the heated pan, which contains melted butter, and wait for the edges to begin to thicken — a matter of a few seconds. Pull these edges toward the middle lightly with a fork, allowing the soft part to run into the spaces. Meanwhile, shake the pan slightly to keep the eggs from sticking. When the entire bottom is thickened and the top is still moist, remove from heat and allow the mixture to "set" for 5 seconds more and your omelet is cooked.

Now loosen the edges with the fork and fold one-third of the omelet over the center. When you develop more skill and confidence in making omelets, you may prefer to fold it as many chefs do, by shaking the pan just so — as in step No. 8 on the next page. Then hold the pan at a narrow angle toward the serving dish and flip the omelet out, completing another fold as you do so forming a sort of envelope. If you prefer, double the omelet in the first fold rather than attempting a second fold.

One thing to remember about cooking an omelet is that the entire process is quick, not more than 6 minutes for the 6-egg omelet on this page. The greatest risk is destroying flavor by overcooking. The heat of the pan and the eggs will cause them to continue cooking for a few seconds after they are removed from the heat. The omelet should still be creamy inside when it is eaten.

As an omelet gets cold, it begins to get tough, so always prepare it as close to serving time as possible. And this might also be a good time to dispense with the custom of waiting until everyone is served before eating, especially if you are making individual omelets.

BASIC FRENCH OMELET

6 eggs
4 tbsp. butter
Salt and pepper to taste

1 Break the eggs into a glass or stainless steel bowl. Place a 9-inch omelet pan over very low heat. The omelet pan should be hot when butter is added.

2 Beat the eggs lightly with a fork until well mixed.

3 Cut 3 tablespoons butter into tiny pieces and drop into the beaten eggs. Season lightly with salt and pepper.

4 Mix again to distribute the butter.

5 Increase the heat under the omelet pan to medium hot, then add 1 tablespoon butter and swirl the pan around until butter is melted and just beginning to turn brown.

6 Pour the egg and butter mixture into the hot pan.

7 Work with the side of a fork and lightly pull the thickened edge away from side of pan, allowing the still soft parts to flow underneath.

8 Cook until bottom is set but the top is still moist, then loosen the edges one last time, hold the skillet handle with both hands and shake the pan to flip over 1/3 of the omelet.

9 If you find it difficult to maneuver the fold by shaking, use a fork or spatula to make fold.

10 Hold the pan and the dish at a sharp angle and slide half the omelet onto the dish, then flip the remaining half over the top.

OMELET GARGAMELLE

2 c. chopped fresh mushrooms
2 or 3 green onions, minced
5 tbsp. vermouth
¾ c. half and half cream
Salt and pepper to taste
1 tsp. cornstarch
1 recipe Basic French Omelet *(pg. 4)*
1 tbsp. grated Parmesan cheese
3 thin slices Swiss cheese
Paprika

Combine the mushrooms and onions in small heavy saucepan, then stir in the vermouth and ¼ cup of the cream. Simmer for 5 minutes. Season with salt and pepper. Add a small amount of the pan liquid to the cornstarch and stir until smooth, then stir back into pan. Cook, stirring, until thickened. Set aside. Prepare omelet according to the step-by-step illustration, pages 4 and 5, until bottom is set and top is still moist. Spoon half the mushroom mixture over half the omelet. Slide half the omelet onto an ovenproof platter, then flip over the remaining half. Cover with remaining mushroom mixture. Pour the remaining cream over top. Sprinkle with the Parmesan cheese and arrange Swiss cheese over all. Sprinkle with paprika. Place in preheated broiler and broil until cheese is melted and browned on top. Serve at once. This will make 3 servings.

MENU
TOMATO COULIS SOUP
(SOUPS, pg. 16)
*****OMELET GARGAMELLE**
COLD-STUFFED PEPPER DISH
(VEGETABLES, pg. 29)
PROFITEROLES IN CHOCOLATE SAUCE
(DESSERTS, pg. 59)

omelet gargamelle

This elegant, savory omelet is filled and topped with a mushroom and vermouth mixture, covered with cheese slices and cream, then broiled very quickly.

omelet with chicken livers

Made from the Basic French Omelet, this delectable dish was filled with cooked chicken livers, covered with a rich sauce and garnished with additional chicken livers.

Little Fried Croutons (Breads, pg. 16) may be added as a garnish. These are very delicious with the sauce juices surrounding this omelet.

OMELET WITH CHICKEN LIVERS

2 tbsp. butter
1/2 c. finely chopped onions
1/2 lb. chicken livers, quartered
1/2 c. beef consommé
1/4 c. sherry
1/2 c. half and half cream
1/2 tsp. salt
Pepper to taste
1 recipe Basic French Omelet (pg. 4)
Fresh parsley, finely chopped

Melt the butter in a medium-sized saucepan over medium heat. Add onions and livers and cook, stirring occasionally, until browned. Add consommé and sherry. Simmer for about 10 minutes or until livers are tender. Remove livers with a slotted spoon and keep warm. Add the cream to pan juices slowly, stirring constantly. Increase heat and cook until sauce is thick and creamy. Season with salt and pepper. Prepare the omelet according to the step-by-step illustrations, pages 4 and 5, and turn out onto heated platter. Pour sauce over omelet. Arrange livers over the top and sprinkle with parsley. Serve at once. This will make 2 to 3 servings.

crab-filled omelet

CRAB-FILLED OMELET

¹/₂ lb. crab claw meat
4 tbsp. butter
1¹/₂ tbsp. lemon juice
¹/₈ tsp. white pepper
2 tbsp. all-purpose flour
³/₄ c. Sauterne
³/₄ c. half and half cream
1 recipe Basic French Omelet *(pg. 4)*

Pick over the crab meat to remove any shell. Melt 2 tablespoons butter in a small saucepan, then add half the crab meat, lemon juice and pepper. Heat through, then keep warm. Melt the remaining butter in a saucepan and stir in the flour. Cook, stirring constantly, until lightly browned. Add the Sauterne slowly, stirring constantly until smooth. Stir in the remaining crab meat, then add the cream slowly,

crab-filled omelet

Here the classic Basic French Omelet has been filled with a crab mixture and covered with a sauce using additional crab meat. The crab claws make an especially attractive garnish.

stirring constantly. Cook until thickened. Stir 2 tablespoons crab-cream mixture into the crab-lemon mixture. Cook the omelet until ready to fold. Remove from heat, then spread the crab-lemon mixture over ¹/₂ of the omelet. Slide out of omelet pan onto heated platter and flip over. Cover with the remaining crab-cream sauce and garnish with finely chopped parsley. Serve immediately. This makes 3 to 4 servings.

savory bread omelet

This omelet is filled with toasty croutons and grated hard cheese. Serve this hearty dish with grilled meats or as a substitute for potatoes. It may also be served as a main dish for supper.

SAVORY BREAD OMELET

3 eggs
Salt and pepper to taste
1½ tsp. finely chopped fresh parsley
1 tbsp. butter
½ c. Fried Croutons (Breads, pg. 16)
2 tbsp. grated Parmesan cheese

Beat the eggs lightly with a fork. Season with salt and pepper, then add the parsley. Beat again. Melt the butter in a 9-inch omelet pan until butter just begins to brown around edge. Add the egg mixture and reduce heat. Lift around edge with fork or spatula and tilt pan to allow egg to run underneath. Cook until browned and set on bottom but top is still moist. Sprinkle the croutons to within 1 inch of the edge, then sprinkle with 1 tablespoon cheese. Flip over and slide onto a heated plate. Sprinkle with the remaining cheese and serve immediately. This makes 1 to 2 servings.

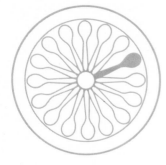

belgian soufflé omelets

So far we have described only the Basic French Omelet and some of its variations. Now we will introduce to you another BASIC in the realm of omelet cookery — the Belgian soufflé omelet. This dish is also known as the puffy omelet.

The chief difference in the two types is whether the eggs are separated or beaten whole. In the Belgian soufflé omelet, the eggs are separated and the whites beaten stiffly. A small amount of water is also added to the egg yolk. This mixture produces a fluffy, soufflé-like omelet.

On these two pages are three savory variations of the Belgian omelet — Soufflé Omelet Mornay using Basic Mornay Sauce (Sauces, pg. 11), Omelet Mousseline with Soubise Sauce (Sauces, pg. 14) and Cheese Soufflé Omelet. Later, in the Desserts section, you will use Basic Belgian Soufflé Omelet to produce elegant fruit-filled dessert omelets.

The procedure for making the puffy omelet is somewhat different from the method used on page 4 and 5. If time permits, separate the eggs while they are cold, then bring to room temperature and beat the whites until they are very stiff. The egg yolks are beaten separately, then blended lightly into the egg whites. The mixture should resemble a pale yellow foam.

When cooking the omelet, begin as before by heating the pan over low heat, then adding butter. When the butter is melted, increase the heat only a fraction and pour in the egg mixture. This omelet, unlike the French is only partially cooked on top of your stove. As you will find in the recipes, the final stage of cooking is done in the oven.

SOUFFLÉ OMELET MORNAY

4 eggs, separated
4 tbsp. cold water
Salt and pepper to taste
2 tbsp. butter
½ recipe Basic Mornay Sauce (Sauces, page 11)

Place the egg yolks in a small bowl and beat lightly with a fork. Add the water and beat until blended. Season with salt and pepper. Beat the egg whites until very stiff. Fold the egg yolk mixture slowly into the egg whites until mixture is a pale yellow foam. Place the butter in a heated 9-inch omelet pan until butter just begins to brown. Pour the egg mixture into the pan and cook slowly, pulling the edge away from side of pan and leveling the top to the side with a spatula. Pierce through the omelet with the tip of the spatula occasionally to allow the heat to rise through the omelet. Cook until the base is a light golden brown and set but top is still foamy. Remove from heat and place, about 6 to 8 inches from source of heat, in preheated broiler. Broil for about 4 minutes or until top is lightly browned. Fold the omelet in half and turn out on heated platter. Spoon the hot Mornay sauce over top and serve immediately. This makes 2 servings.

OMELET MOUSSELINE WITH SOUBISE SAUCE

4 eggs, separated
Salt and white pepper to taste
2 tbsp. whipping cream
1 tbsp. butter
1 recipe Basic Soubise Sauce (Sauces, pg. 14)
6 slices crisp-fried bacon

Combine egg yolks, salt, pepper and cream in a small mixing bowl and beat with a wire whisk until well mixed. Whip egg whites in a medium mixing bowl with an electric mixer until very stiff. Fold egg yolk mixture slowly into egg whites. Melt butter in a heated 9-inch omelet pan until butter just begins to brown. Pour in the eggs and cook slowly, pulling the eggs away from the side of the pan and leveling the top to the side with a spatula. Pierce through the omelet with the tip of the spatula occasionally to allow the heat to rise through the omelet. Cook until the base is set and a light golden brown and the top is still foamy. Remove from heat and place in preheated broiler about 6 to 8 inches from the source of heat. Broil for 4 minutes or until top is lightly browned. Fold omelet in half and slide onto heated platter. Pour half the Soubise sauce over the omelet and crumble the bacon over the sauce. Serve immediately with remaining Soubise sauce. This makes 2 to 3 servings.

CHEESE SOUFFLE OMELET

6 tbsp. butter
1 c. finely grated sharp Cheddar cheese
1 c. whipping cream
Salt
White pepper
5 eggs, separated
5 tbsp. cold water

Heat 4 tablespoons butter in the top of a double boiler over hot water until bubbly. Add cheese and stir until smooth. There may be a small amount of melted butter around the edge but this will blend in with the cream. Pour in cream very slowly, stirring constantly until smooth and creamy. Stir in 1/8 teaspoon salt and a dash of pepper and keep warm. Beat the egg yolks and water in a small bowl with a fork until blended. Season with salt and pepper to taste. Beat egg whites in a large bowl until very stiff. Fold egg yolk mixture into the egg whites until mixture is a pale yellow foam. Heat remaining butter in a preheated, 9-inch omelet pan until butter just begins to brown. Pour the egg mixture into the pan and cook slowly, pulling the edge away from the side of the pan and leveling the top to the side with a spatula. Pierce through the omelet occasionally with the tip of the spatula to allow the heat to rise through the omelet. Cook until the base is a light golden brown and set but the top is still foamy. Place in a preheated broiler 6 to 8 inches from the source of heat. Broil for 4 minutes or until top is lightly browned. Invert onto heated platter. Pour the cheese sauce over omelet. Return to broiler and broil until sauce is browned. Serve immediately. This will make about 3 servings.

cheese soufflé omelet

This beautiful omelet tastes as good as it looks, not due to expense or difficulty of preparation but to a blend of delicious flavors.

spinach omelet

SPINACH OMELET

1 10-oz. package frozen spinach
1 tbsp. lemon juice
6 eggs
¾ c. freshly grated Parmesan cheese
½ c. ground veal
½ tsp. salt
⅛ tsp. white pepper

Cook the spinach according to package directions. Drain and squeeze dry. Place in blender container with lemon juice and purée. Place the eggs in a medium-sized bowl and whip with a wire whisk until well blended. Add remaining ingredients and stir until mixed. Turn into a generously buttered 6-inch soufflé dish. Place in a preheated 300-degree oven on center shelf. Bake for 1 hour to 1 hour and turn out onto heated platter. Garnish with thinly sliced cucumber rings, if desired. This makes 4 servings.

FINNISH OMELET

1 c. Béchamel Sauce (*Sauces, pg. 4*)
1 c. finely chopped, cooked ham
4 eggs, separated
6 tbsp. milk
Salt and white pepper to taste

Combine the *Béchamel* Sauce and the ham. Spread in a well-buttered 9-inch round cake pan. Combine the egg yolks, milk, salt and pepper in a small bowl. Beat with a wire whisk until well combined. Beat the egg whites with an electric mixer or a wire whisk until very stiff. Fold the egg yolk mixture slowly into the egg whites. Spoon into pan over ham mixture and level off top. Bake in a preheated 450-degree oven for 10 minutes. Reduce temperature to 350 degrees and bake for 10 minutes longer or until eggs are set. This will make 2 servings.

spinach omelet

Deliciously different, this Italian omelet, unlike the Belgian omelet does not use separated eggs. Unlike most omelets, it is baked. Sliced fresh cucumbers provide an attractive garnish.

basic flat spanish omelet

The Basic Flat Spanish Omelet unlike the Basic French Omelet, is flipped over flat in the pan rather than folded.

The Basic Flat Spanish Omelet is cooked over relatively low heat in garlic oil instead of butter. When the omelet has completely set, place a heatproof plate over the pan, turn the pan and plate over so the omelet lands on the plate. Then slide the omelet back into the pan and allow to cook for a few more seconds. Be very careful not to add more oil in the pan than the recipe specifies in order to avoid having any excess spill when the pan is flipped.

This basic omelet can be livened up considerably by adding potatoes, olives, cooked vegetables or diced sausage as soon as the eggs are poured into the pan. On the next page is a Rolled Spanish Omelet made with 3 plain Spanish Omelets spread with sieved spinach, cooked potatoes and Tomato Fondue Sauce (Sauces, pg. 15). This rich, savory dish also utilizes Basic Béchamel Sauce (Sauces, pg. 4).

Omelet Pipérade is an egg recipe from the Basque Country. The Basques, a distinctive, peasant people of the Pyranees mountains, have contributed much to the culinary world.

OMELET PIPÉRADE

1 green sweet pepper
4 slices Canadian bacon
1 tbsp. Garlic Oil *(Sauces, pg. 10)*
¾ c. skinned, seeded, chopped tomatoes
4 eggs
Salt and pepper to taste

Skin the green pepper, (*Vegetables, pg. 30*), then slice thinly. Brown the bacon lightly in a skillet, then keep warm. Heat the oil in a frypan, then add the pepper and fry, stirring frequently, until tender and lightly browned. Add the tomatoes and simmer, stirring occasionally, until mixture is well done. Break in the eggs, then stir until the eggs are thoroughly broken down and blended with the green pepper mixture. Season with salt and pepper. Cook until eggs are of desired doneness. Serve on the bacon. This will make 2 servings.

BASIC FLAT SPANISH OMELET

6 eggs
Salt and pepper to taste
1 tbsp. Garlic Oil *(Sauces, pg. 10)*
¼ c. sliced ripe olives
¼ c. thinly sliced pepperoni
½ c. thinly sliced, cooked potatoes

Using a fork, beat the eggs vigorously in a small bowl. Season with salt and pepper. Heat the oil in a 9-inch omelet pan. Add the eggs, then sprinkle the olives, pepperoni and potatoes over the eggs. Cook over medium heat, pulling the eggs away from side of pan to allow eggs to flow underneath. Cook until set on bottom but still moist on top. Slide omelet out onto plate, then invert back into omelet pan. Cook for several seconds longer until eggs are set. Turn out onto heated platter and serve immediately. Any hard, garlic-flavored sausage may be substituted for the pepperoni. This omelet is delicious served with Tomato Fondue Sauce, (Sauces, pg. 15). This makes about 3 servings.

basic flat spanish omelet

Basic Flat Spanish Omelet is accented with the addition of sliced sausages, ripe olives and potatoes. It is served flat.

rolled spanish omelet

rolled spanish omelet

This "omelet cake" consists of three layers of flat spanish omelet spread with sieved spinach, Tomato Fondue Sauce, and Béchamel Sauce. The layers are rolled around each other before serving.

ROLLED SPANISH OMELET

1 recipe Tomato Fondue Sauce *(Sauces, pg. 15)*
1 recipe Béchamel Sauce *(Sauces, pg. 4)*
2 c. cooked, fresh or frozen spinach
1½ tbsp. lemon juice
Salt and pepper to taste
9 eggs
3 tbsp. butter
¾ c. thinly sliced cooked potatoes

Prepare the sauces and set aside. Drain spinach well, then place in blender container and chop. Place in a small saucepan and add the lemon juice. Season with salt and pepper. Heat thoroughly. Heat the tomato sauce and the *Béchamel* Sauce in separate saucepans. Place an ovenproof platter in a warm oven. Beat 3 eggs in a small bowl with a fork. Season with salt and pepper. Melt 1 tablespoon butter in a 9-inch omelet pan. Add the eggs and cook, pulling the eggs away from side of pan to allow eggs to flow underneath. Cook until set on bottom but still moist on top. Slide omelet out onto plate, then invert into omelet pan. Cook for several seconds longer or just until set. Slide out of pan onto 1 side of heated platter. Return to warm oven. Cook a second 3-egg omelet as before until bottom is just set. Add the potatoes and cook until the potatoes have set in the eggs. Slide out onto plate and invert back into omelet pan. Cook until bottom is set. Slide out onto other side of heated platter with omelet edges touching and return to warm oven. Cook the third omelet as before, and when done on both sides, slide out onto separate plate. Study the illustration of the finished omelet as you proceed with the folding. Remove omelets from oven and spread with *Béchamel* Sauce. Spread the omelet on the plate with tomato sauce, then fold into thirds. Place tomato sauce omelet over center of other 2 omelets and spread with *Béchamel* Sauce. Spoon spinach in a row along sides of the tomato sauce omelet. Fold potato omelet over top of tomato omelet and spread with *Béchamel* Sauce. Fold remaining side over top. Serve immediately with any remaining *Béchamel* or Tomato Fondue Sauce, if desired. This makes about 6 servings.

many varieties of cheese

1. Cheddar
2. Colby
3. Monterey Jack
4. Pasteurized
5. Cheese food
6. Cheese spread
7. Cold pack
8. Gouda and Edam
9. Camembert
10. Muenster
11. Brick

12. Swiss
13. Limburger
14. Bleu or Blue
15. Gorgonzola
16. Provolone
17. Romano
18. Parmesan
19. Mozzarella and Scarmorze
20. Cottage
21. Cream

MANY VARIETIES OF CHEESE

Like the wine connoisseur, it's said that the true cheese enthusiast derives pleasure from simply reading about cheese. For most of us, however, the joy of cheese is in the tasting. An English gourmet and cheese authority, Ernest Oldsmeadow, gives the advice that "the only way to learn about cheese is to eat it." For some 4,000 years or more people have been doing just that.

According to legend, the world's first cheese was discovered by a traveling Arab merchant who stopped in the desert for lunch. His meal consisted of dried dates and goat's milk which was carried in a sack-like container made of a sheep's stomach. To the great surprise of the merchant, the milk had changed from a cool, sweet liquid to curds and whey, a chemical reaction caused by the intense heat of the desert at midday, the jolting of the pack animal and the small amount of rennet left in the milk container. The whey, a milky liquid, satisfied the traveler's thirst and the curds, his appetite — thus, cheese was discovered.

Since that first chance encounter with cheese, cheesemakers have found hundreds of ways to make different types of cheeses. The final appearance, taste and aroma of the cured cheese is determined by the type of milk used, the curing period, methods used in handling and the type of bacterial growth which is allowed to ferment in the cheese.

There are some 350 different varieties of cheeses, all of which offer a great deal of eating pleasure. Most of these are not widely known and are produced in a relatively small area for a local market. The United States, which is the largest producer, is also the largest importer of cheeses. Some of the better known imported cheeses and the countries from which they originated are:

Camembert — a famous French dessert cheese. It is soft, with a pungent flavor.

Edam and *Gouda* are two Dutch cheeses that have similar texture and a mild, slightly salty flavor. All of them are best when brought to room temperature before serving. They may be served with crackers or fruit.

Provolone — popular in southern Italy, is a firm, smooth, pear-shaped cheese which is usually smoked. A table cheese when partially cured, it is especially good for grating when it is fully cured and dried.

Parmesan and *Romano* are used for grating, primarily on Italian dishes, cooked foods or adding to sauces.

Caciocavallo — a spindle-shaped Italian cheese very similar to Provolone.

Emmenthal and *Gruyère* — two Swiss cheeses, immediately recognizable by large "eyes." These are gas holes which develop in the curd as the cheese ripens. Both have a mild, nutlike flavor.

Mozzarella and *Scarmorze* — fresh, unsalted, white and moist are from the cheese-producing country of Italy. Both have a delicate flavor and may be eaten sliced or used in baking.

Roquefort — the original French version of blue-veined cheese. Only cheese made from ewe's milk in the Roquefort district of France, and cured in the caves of that district, may be called Roquefort. The flavor is sharp and lightly peppery. *Blue* or *Bleu* (Bleu is the French spelling) has the same characteristics as Roquefort; however, it is made from cow's milk. *Gorgonzola* is the Italian equivalent of *Bleu*.

Liederkranz — sounds very German in origin; however, it is definitely American. Liederkranz, a native product of Monroe, New York, is a soft, surface-ripened cheese, creamy white and mildly pungent. *Limburger* is produced in Belgium, resembles Liederkranz in texture, but has a much stronger flavor and aroma.

Cheshire and *Stilton* are two well known English cheeses. *Cheshire* is a hard cheese of crumbly texture, much the same as Cheddar. *Stilton* is a rich, blue-veined cheese made of cows milk. It is often mixed with wine or brandy and is often served as a dessert cheese.

All of these cheeses are *natural* cheeses. They are made directly from fresh milk, with or without aging and "ripening" by bacterial action or molds. In recent years, especially in America, *process cheese*, *cheese food* and *process cheese spread* have come into the kitchen and are used extensively. All three types are produced from natural cheese and are blended for uniformity of flavor and texture. They are processed in jars and cans or sliced and wrapped in plastic wrap.

Refrigeration is a must for any type of cheese — natural, processed or cheese food. The only exception is grated cheese, such as Parmesan, when it is bought in a shaker-storage container. Hard cheeses, such as Cheddar or Swiss, should be wrapped tightly in foil or plastic wrap to prevent drying. Soft, uncured cheeses (cottage and cream) do not keep well. Both should be stored in the containers they were packed in or wrapped tightly in foil. The Basic Cream Cheese, page 17, will keep for at least a week in the refrigerator and should be wrapped in foil. Basic Sweet Cream Cheese may be used to make classic *Coeur 'a la Crème*, which is served as a dessert cheese with fruits or jam.

BASIC CREAM CHEESE

Prepare as for Basic Sweet Cream Cheese below, omitting the vanilla pod and 2 tablespoons sugar. This delicious cheese may be used in any recipe requiring cream cheese. This makes about 1 ½ pounds cream cheese.

BASIC SWEET CREAM CHEESE

2½ c. half and half cream
2½ c. whipping cream
1 vanilla pod
¼ c. sugar
¼ rennet tablet
2 tbsp. buttermilk

1 Combine the creams, vanilla pod and sugar in a large, heavy saucepan, then heat until scalded. Remove the vanilla pod and let cream mixture cool to lukewarm. Dissolve the rennet in 1 tablespoon water and stir into the cream mixture. Add the buttermilk and pour into a large glass bowl. Let set in a cool place but not in refrigerator for 4 to 5 hours or until cooled and set.

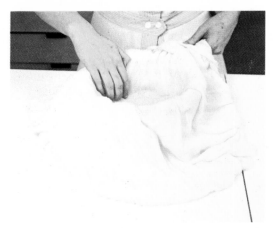

2 Place a colander in a bowl and line the colander with a large piece of muslin.

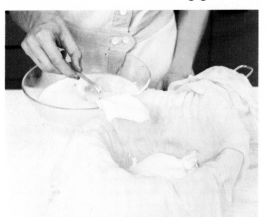

3 Spoon the cream mixture carefully into the muslin.

4 Tie the ends of the muslin together into a knot, then secure the knot over a hook in a cool place. Place a bowl under the bag, then let the cheese drip for 48 hours. Do not refrigerate. Turn cheese into a bowl.

FOR COEUR À LA CRÈME

5 Spoon cheese into 6 cheesecloth-lined *coeur ʼa la crème* molds or a cheesecloth-lined sieve, then fold cheesecloth over top. Place on jelly roll pan and refrigerate for at least 8 hours. Remove from molds, then remove cheesecloth. Arrange cheese hearts on platter and serve with fresh fruits mounded in center.

introducing quiches

Quiche is France's sophisticated answer to Italy's pizza. Where pizza is made with a yeast dough and a hot, spicy topping, a quiche is a flaky pastry shell with a creamy custard filling.

The word quiche (pronounced KĒĒSH) is derived from the French-German dialect spoken in the northeastern region of France and can be traced back to the German word *kuchen*, "cake." A quiche is any type of pie which is made in a flan ring and consists essentially of a stiff pastry shell which may be baked blind before filling (Desserts, pg. 14). It is then filled with a cream custard to which various other ingredients may be added. Quiches may be prepared using cheese, meats, seafood, onions or chopped crisp vegetables or a combination of any of these ingredients, which may be added to the filling itself or spread on the bottom of the pastry shell before the filling is spooned on top.

From Lorraine, a province in eastern France bordering on Germany, comes one of the most famous quiche dishes. Quiche Lorraine is a savory pie filled with bacon, custard and topped with cheese. As a matter of interest, the medieval or original Quiche Lorraine was a custard base poured into a hollowed-out bread shell containing a few pieces of meat. It was a rather bland mixture, unlike the savory custard filling of today.

An excellent brunch or luncheon dish, quiches, and Quiche Lorraine in particular, acquired a sudden popularity several years ago. Hot or cold, this French peasant pie is appropriate served at a dinner for four or a cocktail party for 40. When serving large numbers, the smaller, tart-like quiches make excellent *hors d'oeuvres*.

SUNDAY LUNCH MENU

GRAPEFRUIT SALAD
(Salads, pg. 32)

CHEESE-BACON QUICHE LORRAINE

ARTICHOKES IN LEMON BUTTER
(Vegetables, pg. 51)

PORT WITH WALNUTS
(Beverages, pg. 21)

CHEESE-BACON QUICHE LORRAINE

1 unbaked 8-in. pie shell
4 slices bacon
1 med. onion, sliced
3/4 c. milk
2 eggs, beaten
1/2 c. grated Cheddar cheese
1/2 tsp. salt
1/4 tsp. pepper
2 tbsp. chopped parsley
Pinch of sugar
Pinch of nutmeg
Dash of red pepper
Paprika

Chill the pie shell or place in the freezer for 5 minutes. Fry the bacon in a skillet until crisp. Remove from the skillet, then drain and crumble. Cook the onion in bacon drippings in the skillet until transparent, stirring frequently. Combine the milk, eggs, 1/4 cup cheese, salt, pepper, parsley, sugar, nutmeg and red pepper in a large mixing bowl. Stir in the bacon and onion and pour into the pie shell. Sprinkle with remaining cheese, then with paprika. Bake at 350 degrees for 25 to 35 minutes or until a knife inserted in the center comes out clean. This makes 6 servings.

CHEESE QUICHE

1/2 recipe Basic Savory Short Pastry
** (Desserts, pg. 12)**
4 slices crisp-fried bacon
3 eggs
3/4 c. half and half cream
3/4 c. milk
2/3 c. freshly grated Parmesan cheese
1/4 tsp. white pepper
1/2 tsp. salt
Thinly sliced Emmenthal cheese

Roll out the pastry on a floured board to 1/8-inch thickness and fit into a 9-inch flan pan. Bake blind as instructed (Desserts, pg. 14) at 400 degrees for 20 minutes. Crumble bacon into crust. Beat eggs until frothy, then stir in the cream, milk and Parmesan cheese. Add seasonings, then pour egg mixture into crust. Bake in a preheated 400-degree oven for 5 minutes. Reduce temperature to 300 degrees and bake for 25 to 30 minutes longer or until firm in center. Cut cheese slices in triangles and arrange on top in a circle with the slices slightly overlapping. Return to oven and bake until the cheese is melted. Loosen crust carefully and remove the ring. Serve immediately. This makes 4 to 6 servings.

cheese quiche

Cheese Quiche is a regional favorite of France. Two provinces, Lorraine and Alsace, lay claim to the origin of the quiche, which was a medieval peasant favorite. This quiche makes an excellent "last minute" dish. It can be served as an accompaniment at dinner or supper or as an entrée.

CHEESE AND LEEK FLAN

½ recipe Basic Savory Short Pastry (Desserts, pg. 12)
4 large leeks
½ recipe Basic Mornay Sauce (Sauces, pg. 11)
2 eggs, beaten
¾ c. half and half cream
¾ c. freshly grated Parmesan cheese
Salt and white pepper to taste
1½ tbsp. butter

Roll out the pastry on a floured board to ⅛-inch thickness and fit into a 9-inch flan pan. Bake blind as instructed (Desserts, pg. 14) at 400 degrees for 20 minutes. Wash and trim leeks, leaving 2 to 3 inches of the green tops. Place in a pan and cover with slightly salted boiling water. Cover and cook until tender. Drain and let cool slightly. Cut off green tops and chop fine. Sprinkle in crust. Cut the white portions into thin slices and arrange over chopped leeks. Combine Mornay sauce, eggs, cream, cheese and seasonings and blend well. Pour over the leeks and dot with butter. Bake in a preheated 400-degree oven for 5 minutes. Reduce oven temperature to 300 degrees and bake for 25 to 30 minutes longer or until firm in center. Serve with additional Mornay sauce, if desired. This makes 6 servings.

WHITE CHEESE FLAN

¹/₂ recipe Basic Savory Short Pastry
     (Desserts, pg. 12)
4 3-oz. packages cream cheese, softened
2 tbsp. whipping cream
3 eggs
¹/₄ tsp. salt
White pepper to taste
4 tsp. cornstarch
1¹/₂ tsp. lemon juice
1 c. finely grated Gruyére or Emmenthal cheese

Roll out the pastry on floured surface to ¹/₈-inch thickness. Cut and place in two 9-inch flan pans. Prepare for baking blind as instructed in Desserts, page 14. Bake in a preheated 350-degree oven for 15 to 20 minutes or until crust is lightly browned. Beat the cream cheese with the whipping cream in a large mixing bowl until smooth and well blended. Add the eggs, one at a time, beating well after each addition. Blend in the salt, pepper, cornstarch and lemon juice, then beat until smooth. Stir in half the Gruyére cheese and pour into prepared flan shells. Sprinkle remaining Gruyére cheese on top. Bake in preheated 400-degree oven for 20 minutes or until filling is set and lightly browned. This makes 8 to 10 servings.

CHEESE GRIDDLE OMELETS

4 eggs, separated
White pepper to taste
¹/₂ c. freshly grated Parmesan cheese
Salt to taste
Butter

Beat the egg yolks until thick and lemon colored, then stir in the pepper and cheese. Season with a very small amount of salt as the Parmesan cheese imparts a salty flavor. Beat the egg whites in a large bowl until stiff peaks form. Push the egg whites to one side of the bowl, then turn the cheese mixture into the bowl next to the egg whites. Fold and cut the cheese mixture into the egg whites with a rubber spatula until well blended. Melt a small amount of butter on a griddle over medium high heat. Spoon half the cheese mixture onto the hot griddle to form an oblong loaf, then repeat with remaining cheese mixture. Reduce heat to medium low. Shape omelets into neat ovals with a table knife and cook until bottoms are lightly browned and set. Turn the omelets with a spatula and cook until lightly browned and set. Drizzle with melted butter. This makes 2 servings.

white cheese flan

This golden cheese pie, so light, yet filling, makes a delicious hot first course for a buffet or a cold entrée for a family supper dish. White Cheese Flan is quite simple to prepare and can be served very elegantly with a chilled, well-tossed avocado salad or a steaming bowl of shrimp bisque.

PARMESAN CHEESE PUFF

1 box 6-count frozen patty shells, thawed, or ½
    recipe Basic Puff Pastry *(Desserts, pg. 22)*
1 beaten egg, strained
Paprika
¼ c. butter, softened
2 tbsp. all-purpose flour
1 c. milk
2 egg yolks, lightly beaten
½ c. freshly grated Parmesan cheese
Salt and white pepper to taste
¼ c. whipping cream, whipped

Prepare pastry according to step-by-step instructions or place the patty shells side by side in 2 rows on floured surface. Roll out pastry to a 10-inch square. Follow step-by-step illustrations for cutting and preparing. Bake in a preheated 425-degree oven for 10 minutes. Reduce oven temperature to 350 degrees and bake for 25 minutes longer.

For Sauce:

Melt the butter in the top of a double boiler over hot water. Stir in the flour until smooth. Mix the milk and egg yolks together, then add to the butter mixture gradually, stirring constantly. Cook, stirring, until thick and smooth. Add the cheese, salt and pepper, then stir until well combined. Cool slightly. Fold in whipped cream. Spoon onto pastry puff and swirl with tines of fork. Cut into 8 wedges. Serve hot or cold. This makes 8 servings.

parmesan cheese puff

This is a delightful puff pastry base which is accompanied with a superb Parmesan cheese sauce. The sauce is mounded in the center of the golden-browned, flaky pastry shell. The "puff" has been sprinkled with paprika to add a special color contrast.

1 Place a flat 7½-inch plate or circle of cardboard in center of pastry. Cut half circles around plate with a fluted 3-inch cookie cutter, using a rotating motion.

2 Pull outside pastry away, using the sharp point of a knife, if needed.

3 Prick inside of ring generously with tines of fork.

4 Place on wet baking sheet. Brush with the strained egg and sprinkle edge generously with paprika.

cheese yorkshire pudding

There is a Latin maxim "de gustibus non est disputandum," which means "there is no disputing concerning tastes." For a hostess who is unsure of her guests culinary preferences, this dish with a continental flair is sure to please everyone. Sample these menu companions — a glowing Burgundian Roast Sirloin of Beef (Beef, pg. 2), Cheese Yorkshire Pudding and a hearty red Beaujolais.

CHEESE YORKSHIRE PUDDING

2 eggs
1 c. milk
3 tbsp. bacon or roast drippings
1 c. sifted all-purpose flour
½ tsp. salt
1 c. finely grated Gruyère cheese

Beat the eggs in a medium mixing bowl until very thick and lemon colored. Add the milk gradually, then add the bacon drippings and blend thoroughly. Add the flour and salt gradually and beat until smooth. Fold in half the cheese. Pour into a well-greased 1-quart baking dish, then sprinkle the remaining cheese over top. Bake in a preheated 450-degree oven for 25 minutes or until golden brown. Serve immediately. This makes 4 to 6 servings.

WELSH RAREBIT

Butter
¼ **c. flour**
1 tsp. dry mustard
¾ **c. beer or ale**
1¼ **c. milk**
1¼ **c. grated sharp Cheddar cheese**
1 tbsp. wine vinegar
1 tbsp. Worcestershire sauce
Salt and white pepper to taste
6 slices bread

Melt ¼ cup butter in a heavy saucepan over low heat, then increase the heat to medium. Add the flour and mustard and stir until smooth. Add the beer and bring to a boil, stirring constantly. Add the milk alternately with the cheese, bringing to a boil after each addition and stirring until smooth. Add the vinegar, Worcestershire sauce, salt and pepper and mix well. Keep warm. Spread butter liberally on each slice of bread and place the bread on a cookie sheet. Broil until toasted. Place each slice of bread on a heatproof plate and spoon the cheese sauce over each slice. Dot each serving with a small amount of butter. Broil until sauce is bubbly and brown, then garnish with parsley sprigs. This makes 6 servings.

welsh rarebit

The English cousin to the Swiss fondue, Welsh Rarebit was originally a mixture of three types of cheese, stout ale, plenty of pepper and mustard. Traditionally it was brought to the tables steaming hot in earthenware dishes.

HOW TO POACH AN EGG

Place egg in shell in simmering water for 10 seconds before poaching. Break egg into a cup and slip carefully into enough simmering poaching liquid to cover. Simmer for 4 to 5 minutes or until the white is firm and a film has formed over the yolk. Remove egg with a slotted spoon and serve immediately or place in a bowl of cold water to stop the cooking process. Remove egg from water and trim off uneven edges with a sharp knife. Eggs may be prepared ahead, kept in the cold water and refrigerated for several hours. Place eggs in hot, salted water for about 30 seconds or until heated through. Drain well before serving. Eggs may be poached in a variety of liquids including milk, tomato sauce, vegetable or chicken stocks, half white wine and half water or lightly salted water with 1 tablespoon vinegar added for each quart of water used.

cheese soufflé

cheese soufflé in pastry

At last golden-light cheese soufflé that doesn't collapse within seconds of being removed from the oven. In a word, delicious!

CHEESE SOUFFLÉ IN PASTRY

Leftover puff pastry trimmings
1 egg, beaten
3 tbsp. butter
3 tbsp. all-purpose flour
1 c. milk
⅓ c. freshly grated Parmesan cheese
½ tsp. salt
Dash of nutmeg
4 egg whites, stiffly beaten

Roll out pastry on a lightly floured surface to ⅛-inch thickness and cut into four 6-inch squares. Line 4 baking cups with pastry, arranging the 4 points above the edge of each cup, then brush with beaten egg. Melt the butter in a saucepan over medium heat. Add the flour and stir until smooth. Add ¼ cup milk, stirring constantly until mixture clings together and forms a ball. Add the remaining milk gradually and cook, stirring constantly, until smooth and thickened. Add the cheese and seasonings and cook, stirring until well combined. Cool thoroughly. Fold in ¼ of the egg whites carefully, then fold in the remaining egg whites gently. Spoon soufflé into pastry-lined cups. Bake in a preheated 425-degree oven for 35 minutes or until soufflé is set. Serve hot. This makes 4 servings.

cheese soufflés
in tomato cases

cheese soufflés in tomato cases

*What a beautiful color contrast! Glossy red
tomatoes are baked with a pale yellow-white
cheese soufflé filling. Individual soufflés make a
very satisfying accompaniment for
a cold meat salad.*

CHEESE SOUFFLÉS IN TOMATO CASES

8 med. firm ripe tomatoes
1 recipe Cheese Soufflé mixture *(pg. 25)*

Cut small slice from blossom end of the tomatoes
and scoop out the seeds and pulp, leaving shells.
Invert tomato shells on a wire rack and drain
thoroughly. Prepare soufflé mixture, omitting the
pastry. Spoon soufflé mixture into tomato shells
and place in a baking dish. Bake in a preheated
400-degree oven for 30 minutes or until soufflés
have risen and tops are brown. Serve immediately.
This makes 8 servings.

italian pizza

This is, without a doubt, one of the most unusual pizzas that the inventive cook will ever have the pleasure of preparing. To provide a different but very pleasant flavor, fresh tomatoes are scattered over the top. Instead of the usual dill, tomato paste and mozzarella cheese, this marvelous pizza is a combination of flavorful Greek olives, Emmenthal cheese and marjoram.

ITALIAN PIZZA

½ recipe Rough Puff Pastry *(Desserts, pg. 27)*
1 2-oz. can anchovy fillets
1 8-oz. package thinly sliced Emmenthal
    or Swiss cheese
2 c. chopped skinned firm tomatoes
½ c. quartered black Greek olives
½ c. quartered green Greek olives
Salt and pepper to taste
2 tbsp. marjoram
12 capers
½ c. tomato purée
1 tbsp. Garlic Oil *(Sauces, pg. 10)*

Roll the pastry out on a floured surface to a 14-inch wide and ⅛-inch thick circle. Place the pastry on a 12-inch pizza pan and trim edge. Bake blind as instructed (Desserts, pg. 14) in a preheated 400-degree oven for 8 to 10 minutes or until lightly browned. Cool slightly. Drain the anchovies and split fillets in half lengthwise. Roll half the fillets into coils and chop the remaining fillets. Arrange the cheese slices over the pastry. Spread the tomatoes over the cheese slices and sprinkle with half the black and green olives. Sprinkle with salt, pepper and marjoram. Arrange the chopped anchovies and capers on pizza. Pour the tomato purée into an icing bag with a medium plain tube affixed. Pipe a lattice design of tomato purée over top of pizza. Arrange remaining black and green olives and anchovy coils over surface. Drizzle pizza with Garlic Oil. Bake in a preheated 400-degree oven for 30 minutes. This makes 8 servings.

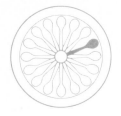

giving a cheese and wine party

Thousands of years before Omar Khayyam poetically paired a jug of wine with a loaf of bread, fermented grape juice had been linked with food. The one food that goes exceptionally well with wine is cheese.

Even during the times of David and Solomon, friends gathered to enjoy the two most natural food and drink combinations. Wine and cheese can be most enjoyable at home with a congenial gathering of friends.

For those who are discovering the many delicious varieties of fine aged cheese and wines, a cheese-wine-tasting party is a particular delight. Cheese is the perfect accompaniment to wine tasting, as it removes any trace of the wine and refreshes the palate. In return, wine brings alive the special mildness or sharpness and aroma of a fine cheese.

TASTING SESSIONS

One way for the novice to become familiar with the various types of cheese is to plan a tasting party. Because of the tremendous variety of cheeses and wines, a cheese-wine-tasting party can be tailored to fit the pocketbook and taste preferences. For a group of novices, it is especially important to avoid overbuying both wines and cheeses. Too many varieties are more apt to confuse than to clarify. The purpose of the party is to provide new taste experiences, not a complete meal. Provide plain crackers, French or Italian bread. For a simple party, choose four to six differing cheeses, ranging from mild to sharp, soft to hard.

Among the ripened and unripened varieties of soft cheeses, Demi-Sel is a popular cheese with a mild flavor. Other soft-textured cheeses are Brie, Camembert, cream, Muenster, Mysost and Neufchatel.

A second grouping, several of which should be included in the tasting session, are the semisoft cheeses. Included in this group are Gruyère, Port du Salut, Trappist and Edam. All of these cheeses have an excellent, rich flavor and slice easily. A bleu or Roquefort is essential to any

tasting session. Both are blue-veined cheeses with a slightly nutty flavor which is very appealing.

The hard cheeses constitute a third group. Cheddar, Caciocavallo, Swiss, Cheshire and Monterey Jack are several outstanding examples of prime hard cheeses.

At least six ounces of cheese should be allowed for each person. However, to avoid wasting cheese, try not to buy equal quantities of each kind, as many guests will find one or two of the cheeses more popular than the others. Most people prefer mild foods, so be sure to include a popular mild cheese in greater quantity.

For a cheese-wine-tasting party where most of the guests are knowledgeable about cheese, emphasis can be placed on a greater variety of imported cheeses. Depending upon the number of guests, this occasion can offer the hostess the opportunity to introduce some of the rarer cheeses from Greece, Norway, Denmark or Eastern Europe. Limited numbers of these cheeses are imported into the United States and may be purchased through specialty shops or ethnic delicatessens. Quite often cheeses such as Norwegian Gammelost, Gjetost and Primost, Italian Scanno and Scarmorze or Swiss Sapsago must be ordered from a specialty cheese store.

PRESENTATION

The best way to serve cheese is to place each block or wedge on ceramic platters or wooden cutting boards. These should be placed well apart from each other so that everyone will be able to easily sample them. A slab of marble makes a very elegant server if one is accessible.

Group similar cheeses together — strong, aromatic cheese tends to overshadow a milder cheese when it is placed in the same vicinity. All cheeses, with the exception of cottage and cream cheese, should be served at room temperature. This may take two to three hours for a hard cheese or as little as thirty minutes for a soft cheese such as Camembert. All cheeses should be unwrapped for easier handling and the rind cut away from a portion of a cheese such as Saint Paulin or Gouda.

WINES

For such a tasting party, serve each grouping of cheese with an appropriate wine. As a simple rule of thumb, white wines and light rosés go well with cream, processed and semihard cheeses. Red wines go best with bleu, Brie and Camembert cheeses. By keeping the number of wines to four or five, guests are not apt to be bewildered at the choices. Include one sweet, a dry white, a rosé and a dry red wine. You may prefer a tawny Port or a sweet red wine instead of a rosé. Champagne can be served throughout the tasting session or served as a finale.

For a more expansive party, each cheese may be matched to a particular wine. Limits should still be observed, however, and certainly no more than a maximum

of eight wines should be served. To accompany the cream cheese, serve a Reisling from California or Alsace, a Chablis or Graves. The flavor of semisoft cheese is accented by a Travel rosé or Pouilly-Fuisse white. Brie and Camembert are two soft cheeses that combine well with a smooth red wine such as Beaujolais or a Bordeaux Pomerol or St. Emilion. Bleu and highly flavorful or aromatic cheeses need a great, robust red such as *Côtes du Rhône* (Châteaneuf-du-Pape), a *Côte De Nuits* (Chambertin or Nuits-Saint-Georges), a California Cabernet Sauvignon or Pinot Noir.

At a tasting session where the guests must concentrate on an unusual variety of a large number of cheeses (12 to 15), it is best to serve just one wine. And, of course, the appropriate wine to serve is champagne.

Champagne should be served chilled and kept chilled during the entire party. White and rosé wines should be chilled before serving. Two hours in the refrigerator is usually sufficient. Red wine is best when served cool or at moderate room temperature. Draw the cork of the red wine at least an hour before serving time to allow the wine to breathe. Allow approximately one bottle of wine per three guests.

CHEESE SELECTION AND ARRANGEMENT

Purchase the following cheeses in amounts suitable to the size of the party:

Edam — semisoft and mild
Gouda — semihard and mild
Brie — semisoft and mild
Swiss — hard and sweet to nutlike
Provolone — hard and sharp (smoked)
Camembert — soft and pungent
Caraway (Kuminost) — hard and spicy
Bleu — semisoft and piquant
Port du Salut — semisoft and robust
Roquefort — soft and sharp
Cheddar — semisoft and mild or sharp.

Peel Edam and cut several wedges from it. Arrange in center of a large serving tray. Cut Gouda into wedges, leaving wax coating on. Fan out cheese wedges, alternating with thick slices of tart, unpeeled apples. Slice sections from brie cheese. Arrange block and slices at side of tray. Overlap slices of Swiss cheese and pile Provolone, cut into sticks, next to it. Cube Port du Salut cheese and pile it in any open space, preferably near the caraway and bleu. Garnish tray with fresh parsley or celery tops. Add chilled grapes in two colors and crisp apples. Fruit may be placed on the tray, if there is room, or next to it on the serving table. Serve a variety of crackers along with rye bread rounds and thin slices of French or Italian bread.

CONTINENTAL CHEESE-WINE-TASTING PARTY

Start this party off properly by sending invitations to each guest. Soak labels off wine bottles and paste them on pieces of construction paper cut into shapes of wine bottles. Outline the labels and letter the invitations in India ink. At the head table or in the center of the buffet table, place a wine rack with empty bottles, grape clusters and wax-dripped candles in wine bottle holders. On a sideboard, place bottles, candles, European menus or other memorabilia from an European vacation. Red and white tablecloths and white napkins, reminiscent of an Italian *bistro*, and stemmed glasses can decorate the tables. All of the bread and crackers may be served in wooden bowls, on cutting boards or in wicker baskets. Guests are free to sample an assortment of red and white wines. Some of the white wines might include Reisling, Semilon, Sauterne and white Burgundy. Red wines might include Chianti, Burgundy and Red Bordeaux or California Pinot Noir served with a Cheddar fondue and garlic bread cubes. Rosé or Cold Duck blends deliciously with various cheese balls. Dessert wines, such as Cream Sherry, Port or Dubonnet, may be served with grapes and a mild white cheese. Along with the assorted dessert wines and cheeses, a nut or fruit bread may be served.

WINE-TASTING AND FONDUE PARTY

This is the kind of spontaneous party that one can arrange so successfully. Each guest is asked to bring a bottle of wine and a covered dish. One couple might bring a bottle of Chianti and a salad; another, a bottle of Chablis and Cheese Bread (Breads, pg. 7). A third couple might bring Resiling and marinated cubes of meat for the meat fondue. The hostess can prepare a cheese fondue (Appetizers, pg. 18) at the buffet table and serve it with bread cubes as an *hors d'oeuvre*. The wine may be placed on one table and the food on another to facilitate a smooth flow of guests at the buffet table.

GARDEN CHEESE AND WINE-TASTING PARTY

A garden setting with flickering candles is appropriate for a tasting party. Place checkered tablecloths on tables grouped throughout the patio area. Candleholders can be made in advance, using wine bottles that are dipped with colored wax. The hostess might like to confine the wines to light rosés from different countries: French, American, Italian, German and Portuguese. Before tasting the wines and cheeses, the host or one of the guests may give a short talk on the art of wine sampling. Just for fun, blindfold several of the guests, have them sample two different wines and guess what kind each is.

egg flan

The interesting Egg Flan presented here comes from the Basque Country, an area in the Western Pyrenees Mountains in Northern Spain, bordering on France. The peasants who inhabit this area have contributed many dishes to gourmet cuisine, some of which we have introduced previously. One of the most appealing things about this dish, other than its irresistible flavor combination of eggs, tomatoes, pimentos and ham, is the interesting cheese rose used as the garnish.

EGG FLAN

½ recipe Basic Savory Short Pastry (*Desserts, pg. 12*)
4 med. tomatoes, skinned (*Vegetables, pg. 27*)
¼ c. olive oil
¼ c. coarsely chopped pimentos
1 clove of garlic, pressed
Salt and freshly ground pepper to taste
5 eggs
1 c. finely diced smoked ham
2 tbsp. milk

Roll out the pastry on a lightly floured surface to ⅛-inch thickness, then prepare for baking in a 9-inch flan ring according to the step-by-step illustrations (Desserts, pg. 13). Bake blind according to illustrations No. 1 through No. 3 (Desserts, pg. 14) in a preheated 400-degree oven for 10 minutes. Reduce the oven temperature to 375 degrees and bake for 15 minutes longer or until golden brown, then continue with illustration No. 4. Cut the tomatoes into quarters and remove the seeds. Chop the tomato pulp coarsely. Pour the oil into a large skillet and place over medium heat. Add the chopped tomatoes, pimentos, garlic, salt and pepper and cook, stirring occasionally, until the tomatoes are tender and the liquid has evaporated. Place in a blender container and process until puréed. Pour back into the skillet and place over low heat. Place 3 of the eggs in a small mixing bowl and beat until well blended, then add the ham. Stir the ham mixture into the tomato mixture and cook, stirring constantly, until the eggs are just set. Turn into the pastry ring and smooth the top. Place the 2 remaining eggs and milk in the small mixing bowl and beat until well blended. Pour over the tomato mixture. Bake in a preheated 425-degree oven until the eggs are set and well browned. Serve hot or cold and garnish with a cheese flower (Pork, pg. 10). This makes 6 servings.

egg flan

This attractive dish is a simple Egg Flan, filled with diced ham, tomatoes, pimentos and eggs, all in a hot pastry case. Although the decorative rose is optional, we urge you to try it.

eggs ardennaise

EGGS ARDENNAISE

All-purpose flour
8 eggs
Salt and white pepper to taste
¼ c. whipping cream, whipped
1 c. freshly grated Parmesan cheese
2 tbsp. butter
Vegetable oil

Fill a large cake pan with flour and level the top. Separate the eggs, dropping the egg whites into a large mixer bowl and leaving each egg yolk in an eggshell half. Place each eggshell half upright in the pan of flour to keep them separated. Add salt and pepper to the egg whites and beat with an electric mixer until the egg whites form stiff peaks. Fold in the whipped cream, then fold in the cheese. Grease a deep ovenproof platter or a shallow baking dish with the butter. Turn the egg white mixture into the platter and level the top. Make 8 evenly spaced indentations in the egg white mixture, using the oiled base of a round soup spoon. Slide 1 of the egg yolks into each indentation and sprinkle with salt, then cover the platter with a tent of aluminum foil. Bake in a preheated 350-degree oven for 15 minutes or until the egg yolks are set. Remove the foil and bake until the egg white mixture is lightly browned. This makes 8 servings.

eggs ardennaise

This fluffy dish looks as pretty as a dessert course. However, it is a simple attractive way to serve the morning eggs. The eggs are separated and the whites whipped with a small amount of grated cheese and seasonings. The yolks are then carefully placed on the beaten egg whites and baked. This recipe makes an ideal dish for a Sunday morning brunch.

SPANISH EGGS

2 c. Basic Beef Stock (*Soups, pg. 2*)
3 lg. tomatoes
¼ c. butter
1 c. finely diced lean pork
2 c. finely diced ham
½ c. minced onion
¼ c. all-purpose flour
Salt and freshly ground pepper to taste
5 eggs

Pour the beef stock into a small, heavy saucepan and simmer until reduced by half. Skin the tomatoes (Vegetables, pg. 27) and scoop out all the seeds with a spoon. Chop the tomato pulp coarsely. Melt the butter in a heavy saucepan, then add the pork, ham and onion. Cook over low heat, stirring constantly, until lightly browned. Combine enough of the stock with the flour to make a smooth, thin paste, then stir the paste into the ham mixture. Add the remaining stock and tomatoes, blending thoroughly. Add the seasonings and simmer until thickened and heated through, stirring frequently. Pour into a greased casserole, spreading the mixture evenly. Break the eggs carefully into the casserole, spacing them decoratively, and sprinkle lightly with salt. Bake, covered, in a preheated 350-degree oven for about 20 minutes or until the eggs are set. Garnish with finely chopped parsley, if desired. This makes 5 servings.

spanish eggs

The surface layer of baked eggs conceals a combination of pork, ham, butter, tomatoes, onions and Basic Beef Stock (Soups, pg. 2). Border these Spanish Eggs with a ring of parsley, and serve them at brunch or supper.

new potato omelet

If you have never before tried the combined flavors of eggs and potatoes, New Potato Omelet will be a delightful surprise. Refer to the step-by-step pictures on How to Prepare Your Omelet Pan (Eggs, pg. 3).

NEW POTATO OMELET

1 ½ c. diced new potatoes
1 ¼ tsp. salt
¼ c. butter
4 slices bacon, diced
4 eggs
1 tbsp. freshly ground parsley
¼ tsp. white pepper

Place the potatoes and ¼ teaspoon of the salt in a saucepan and cover with water. Bring to a boil, then reduce the heat and simmer until the potatoes are just tender. Drain the potatoes thoroughly and reserve 1 tablespoon of the potatoes. Cook the remaining potatoes in 2 tablespoons of the butter in a skillet until golden brown, stirring frequently, then remove from the skillet. Drain on paper toweling and keep warm. Cook the bacon in the same skillet until crisp, stirring frequently, then remove from the skillet. Drain on paper toweling and keep warm. Place the eggs in a bowl and beat lightly with a fork. Stir in the reserved potatoes, parsley, remaining salt, and white pepper. Cook the omelet according to the step-by-step instructions of page 5. Place on ½ of a heated plat-

ter. Mix the potatoes and bacon and place on the other half of the platter. Garnish with parsley. This makes 2 servings.

AVOCADO OMELET

1 lg. ripe avocado
1 tbsp. lemon juice
Salt and pepper to taste
¼ tsp. cayenne pepper
6 eggs
2 tbsp. butter

Pare the avocado and cut into strips, then sprinkle with the lemon juice, salt, pepper and cayenne pepper. Combine the eggs, 2 tablespoons of water, salt and pepper in a bowl and beat lightly. Melt the butter in a 9-inch omelet pan over low heat. Add the avocado and stir until coated with butter. Increase the heat to medium. Add the eggs and cook according to the step-by-step illustrations No. 7 through No. 10 on page 5. Garnish with red sweet pepper strips, if desired. This makes 4 to 6 servings.

EGG-CHEESE AND MUSHROOM VOL-AU-VENTS

½ recipe Basic Puff Pastry (*Desserts, pg. 22*)
½ lb. fresh mushrooms, finely chopped
½ c. dry white wine
Dash of freshly ground pepper
1 recipe Basic Mornay Sauce (*Sauces, pg. 11*)
3 hard-boiled eggs, finely chopped
Salt to taste

Prepare 6 *vol-au-vent* shells according to the step-by-step illustrations (*Desserts, pg. 65*). Place the mushrooms in a medium-sized saucepan. Add the wine and pepper and bring to a boil. Reduce the heat and simmer for 1 minute, then set aside. Prepare the Mornay sauce, using the ingredient amounts for thick sauce, then stir in the mushrooms and liquid. Add the eggs and salt and mix well. Place the *vol-au-vent* shells on a serving plate and fill each shell just to the top with the sauce. Garnish the plate with watercress. Pour the remaining sauce into a sauceboat and serve with the *vol-au-vents*, as each serving may need more sauce. The sauce and the *vol-au-vent* shells may be prepared ahead, then reheated. This makes 6 servings.

BRAZILIAN OMELET

½ lb. lean ground beef
1   1-lb. can tomatoes
1 sm. green sweet pepper, cut in strips
1 tbsp. chopped canned green chilies
1 tsp chili powder
1¾ tsp. salt
¼ tsp. sugar
6 eggs, separated
Dash of pepper
1½ tbsp. butter

Brown the beef in a skillet and drain off excess fat. Stir in the tomatoes, sweet pepper, chilies, chili powder, ¾ teaspoon of the salt and the sugar, then simmer, stirring occasionally, for 30 minutes. Beat the egg yolks with the remaining salt and pepper until thick and lemon-colored. Beat the egg whites until stiff peaks form, then fold the egg yolks into the egg whites. Melt the butter in a 9-inch omelet pan. Pour the egg mixture into the pan and spread evenly. Cook over low heat for 10 minutes or until set in center. Bake in a preheated 325-degree oven for 10 minutes or until a knife inserted in the center comes out clean. Turn the omelet out onto a platter. Serve with the sauce. This makes 4 to 6 servings.

egg-cheese and mushroom vol-au-vents

These beautifully golden vol-au-vent shells contain a flavorful combination of eggs, Mornay sauce and mushrooms. This dish is ideal for brunch or a light supper, and it also makes an excellent appetizer.

CREAMY EGG AND SAUSAGE QUICHE

$1/2$ recipe Basic Savory Short Pastry (Desserts,
   pg. 12)
1 lb. pure pork sausage links
5 eggs
1 $1/4$ c. half and half cream
Salt and white pepper to taste

Roll out the pastry on a floured board to $1/8$-inch
thickness and fit into a 9-inch flan pan. Bake blind as instructed (Desserts, pg. 14) in a preheated 400-degree
oven for 20 minutes. Bake the sausages according to
directions (Variety Meats, pg. 8). Cut the sausages into 1-
inch pieces and stand around the edge of flan. Place any
remaining sausage pieces in the center of the flan. Beat
eggs until frothy, then stir in the cream and seasonings.
Pour carefully into the crust. Bake in a preheated 400-
degree oven for 5 minutes. Reduce the oven temperature
to 300 degrees and bake for 25 minutes longer or until the
egg mixture is set. This makes 4 to 6 servings.

creamy egg and sausage quiche

A favorite twosome, eggs and sausage, are
combined here in Creamy Egg and Sausage
Quiche. This dish is bordered with bite-
sized pieces of sausage placed inside the
savory short pastry flan.

cheese-croissant bake

Since *croissants* stay fresh only a few hours, it's nice to know the leftover ones, even after they are stale, can be used to prepare this delicious Cheese-*Croissant* Bake.

cheese-croissant bake

Here is one way to use up leftover croissants (crescent rolls). Combine them with seasonings, eggs, milk, and grated Parmesan cheese for a cheesy, bread custard dish. Either bought rolls or your own homemade ones (Breads pg. 22) may be used.

CHEESE-CROISSANT BAKE

3 eggs
1 egg yolk
3 c. milk
¾ c. freshly grated Parmesan cheese
¼ c. fine soft bread crumbs
½ tsp. onion salt
⅛ tsp. white pepper
6 stale croissants

Place the eggs and egg yolk in a large bowl and beat until well blended. Pour the milk into a saucepan and bring just to the boiling point. Stir a small amount of the milk into the eggs, then add the remaining milk gradually, stirring constantly. Stir in the cheese, bread crumbs and seasonings. Place the *croissants* in a deep 6-cup soufflé dish and pour the egg mixture over the *croissants*. Let stand at room temperature for 1 hour or until the *croissants* are soaked. Bake in a preheated 375-degree oven for 7 minutes. Reduce the oven temperature to 325 degrees and bake for about 1 hour longer or until the egg mixture is set. This makes 6 servings.

cheese and egg soufflé

This Cheese and Egg Soufflé is an interesting variation of the previously introduced Cheese Soufflé (pg. 25). Eggs are added to the soufflé mixture and baked. Pictured above is the finished soufflé. Pictured below is a single serving, in which the texture of the delicately cooked eggs can be seen.

CHEESE AND EGG SOUFFLÉ

3 tbsp. butter
3 tbsp. all-purpose flour
1 c. milk
½ c. freshly grated Parmesan cheese
Salt to taste
Dash of nutmeg
4 egg whites, stiffly beaten
4 eggs

Melt the butter in a saucepan over medium heat. Add the flour and stir until smooth. Add ¼ cup of the milk, stirring constantly until mixture clings together and forms a ball. Add the remaining ¾ cup of milk gradually and cook, stirring constantly, until smooth and thickened. Add the cheese and seasonings and cook, stirring, until well combined. Cool thoroughly. Fold ¼ of the egg whites thoroughly into the cheese mixture, then fold in the remaining egg whites gently. Turn half the soufflé mixture into a buttered 7-inch soufflé dish, then make 4 indentations in the soufflé mixture, using a lightly oiled tablespoon. Break the eggs, one at a time, into a small dish and pour carefully into the indentations. Sprinkle the eggs lightly with salt, then pour in the remaining soufflé mixture. Smooth the top toward the center to form a small dome. Bake in a preheated 425-degree oven on 1 shelf above center for 15 to 20 mintues or until the soufflé is puffed and browned. Serve immediately. Each serving may be sprinkled with additional Parmesan cheese, if desired. This makes 4 servings.

stuffed eggs in sauce

stuffed eggs in tomato fondue sauce

Stuffed eggs are usually thought of as hors d'oeuvres, but here is a pleasant change-of-pace dish featuring stuffed eggs in a tangy Tomato Fondue Sauce. They are shown surrounded by a border of fluffy Duchess potatoes (Vegetables, pg. 3), which is an optional garnish.

STUFFED EGGS IN TOMATO FONDUE SAUCE

8 hard-boiled eggs
5 tbsp. melted butter
1 tbsp. freshly minced parsley
1 ½ c. fine soft bread crumbs
Half and half cream
4 sm. fresh mushrooms, finely chopped
Salt and freshly ground pepper to taste
1 recipe Tomato Fondue Sauce *(Sauces, pg. 15)*

Cut the eggs into halves lengthwise, then cut a small sliver from the base of each egg white half to steady when placed in the platter. Remove the egg yolks and place in a medium-sized bowl, then mash. Add the butter and parsley and mix until blended. Combine the bread crumbs with enough cream to work to a smooth paste, then add to the egg yolk mixture, blending well. Stir in the mushrooms and season with salt and pepper. Mound the egg yolk mixture in the egg white cavities, then arrange in a greased, shallow baking platter. Pour the fondue sauce around the eggs and cover lightly with aluminum foil. Bake in a preheated 350-degree oven for 10 minutes, then remove the foil and bake for 5 minutes longer. You may pipe hot Basic Duchess Potato Mixture (Vegetables, pg. 3) around the edge of the platter before serving. Garnish the eggs with additional minced parsley. This makes 8 servings.

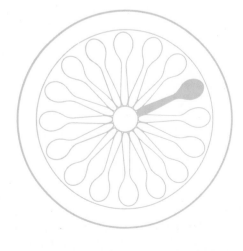

eggs with vegetables

spanish eggs with vegetables

Spanish Eggs With Vegetables is a continental version of an American favorite, hash and eggs. In this recipe, diced sausage or ham is combined with potatoes, tomatoes and sweet pepper. Individual serving dishes are then filled with the mixture, topped with raw eggs and baked until the eggs are set.

One of the most economical and adaptable foods known to man is eggs. One dozen eggs may be used to stretch a small amount of meat or fish into enough food for six hungry people. The versatility of eggs lends them to combinations with virtually every type of food we have at our disposal, ranging from fish (as in a salmon mousse) to ice cream.

One of the most delicious ways to use eggs to their best advantage is to combine them with vegetables. This may be done in a variety of ways: soufflés, omelets, quiches, etc. Even a tasty Spanish version of hash, consisting of diced meat and vegetables (see following recipe), is infinitely better when topped with an egg. The following two recipes are classic examples of excellent egg and vegetable combinations. These dishes are perfectly suited to brunch, light supper or after-theater menus. A tossed green salad and hot rolls are ideal accompaniments.

After preparing these recipes, the imaginative homemaker can invent her own original combinations of eggs and vegetables according to her own preferences and/or the fresh vegetables available during the time of year it happens to be.

SPANISH EGGS WITH VEGETABLES

1 sm. onion or shallot, finely chopped
1 tbsp. butter
1 med. cooked potato, diced
1 clove of garlic, pressed
2 med. tomatoes, skinned (*Vegetables, pg. 27*)
1 red sweet pepper, chopped
½ c. chopped chorizo sausage
Salt and pepper to taste
2 eggs

Sauté the onion in the butter in a small, heavy skillet until tender, then stir in the potato, garlic, tomatoes, sweet pepper and chorizo sausage. Cook over medium heat, stirring constantly, until heated through. Add the salt and pepper. Turn the potato mixture into 2 small ovenproof bowls and make an indentation in the center of each. Place an egg in each indentation, then cover the bowls lightly with foil. Bake in a preheated 350-degree oven for 10 minutes or until the egg is set, but not hard. Garnish with chopped parsley or chives, if desired. Diced ham may be substituted for the chorizo sausage. This makes 2 servings.

FRITTATA DI ZUCCHINI

½ c. thinly sliced zucchini
2 slices of onion
2 tbsp. butter
3 eggs
3 tbsp. water
¼ tsp. basil or thyme
½ tsp. salt
⅛ tsp. freshly ground pepper
2 tbsp. diced fresh tomato
1 tbsp. grated Parmesan or Romano cheese

Sauté the zucchini and onion in 1 tablespoon of the butter in a small skillet until tender. Combine the eggs, water, basil, salt and pepper in a bowl and beat just until the egg yolks and egg whites are blended. Melt the remaining butter in an omelet pan. Add the zucchini mixture to the egg mixture and pour into the hot omelet pan. Cook according to the step-by-step illustrations No. 6 through No. 8 on page 5, omitting the folding. Sprinkle the tomato and Parmesan cheese over the omelet, then broil 6 inches from source of heat until the cheese melts and top is lightly browned. This makes 2 servings.

frittata di zucchini

Here is an Italian variation on the omelet theme using fresh zucchini, diced tomato and a sprinkling of freshly grated Parmesan or Romano cheese. This dish is excellent to serve as a light supper accompanied by a salad and hot garlic bread.

SOFT-COOKED EGGS IN CROUSTADE

1 Croustade *(Breads, pg. 16)*
6 eggs
½ recipe Basic Soubise Sauce *(Sauces, pg. 14)*
½ recipe Basic Mornay Sauce *(Sauces, pg. 11)*

Prepare the *Croustade* from a large, round loaf of bread. Place the eggs in a saucepan and cover with cold water. Bring to a boil, then reduce heat and cover. Simmer for 4 minutes. Cool the eggs in cold water until easily handled, then remove the shells from the eggs. Pour half of the Soubise sauce into the *Croustade*, then stand the eggs on end in the cavity. Cover with the remaining Soubise sauce and garnish the *Croustade* with parsley and the eggs with dill sprigs. Place in a serving dish and serve with the Mornay sauce. This makes 6 servings.

soft-cooked eggs in croustade

An out-of-the-ordinary way to serve eggs is to present them, covered with a flavorful sauce, in their own edible container fashioned out of a round loaf of bread. The eggs are shown here garnished with parsley and dill for an attractive touch of color. A bowl of Mornay sauce may be passed separately.

beef

table of contents

the key to cooking beef

If the members of your family are like the majority of Americans, nothing pleases them more at dinner than a sizzling T-bone steak or a juicy beef roast. This country produces more beef than any other in the world and the average adult American consumes between 80 and 100 pounds a year.

Perhaps the reason for beef's popularity is the wide range of cuts available — enough to suit every pocketbook and please every palate. The cost of a cut of beef is generally based on its tenderness rather than its taste, so if you compensate by cooking a less expensive cut properly, it can be as tender and tasty as a more expensive cut. On these pages you'll learn to cook the various cuts of beef as well as to make your selection in the supermarket.

You've probably noticed the purple USDA mark (stamped with harmless vegetable coloring) on the outside of a cut of beef — this indicates that the grade of beef has met the standards of the United States Department of Agriculture. The grades you'll find most often in the supermarket are USDA Choice and USDA Good. A higher grade, Prime, is usually sold only to restaurants, and two lower grades, Standard and Commercial, are seldom found in any of the supermarkets.

The amount of fat marbled through the lean meat determines the cut's juiciness. When you buy Choice cuts, the lean meat should be a deep, rich red and well-marbled with fat. The outer rim of surrounding fat should be cream-colored. USDA Good is moderately-priced beef with less fat. It's not as juicy as Choice.

When you get the beef home you can store it in the coldest part of the refrigerator for up to 5 days (except ground beef which should be used within 24 hours). To store beef for longer periods, freeze it. It may be frozen in transparent wrap from the supermarket, but if it is wrapped in butcher paper, rewrap it tightly in clear plastic wrap or freezer paper. It will keep in your home freezer from 6 to 12 months.

burgundian roast sirloin

This roast is served on a plate with ridges and a pool to collect the meat juices. We have cut a slice from the beef and allowed it to roll back so that you can see the quality of the meat, the crispness of the skin around it, and the texture and color of our slightly rare roast beef. We serve Caramelized Potatoes (Vegetables, pg. 11) with this roast.

artichokes, watercress or parsley, and Caramelized Potatoes (Vegetables, pg. 11).

COOKING METHODS

There are two basic methods for cooking beef: dry heat and moist heat. Dry heat cooking, including broiling, open roasting and pan-frying (or pan-broiling), uses little if any liquid and is suitable for only the better cuts of roasts such as sirloin tip, rump and rib. Braising, boiling and stewing are moist heat methods requiring the addition of a liquid. Under heat, the liquid produces steam which tenderizes the connective tissues in less tender cuts of beef.

Before we present our cooking techniques in more detail, we would like to encourage you to purchase a good meat thermometer. This instrument eliminates guesswork. By indicating the internal temperature of meat, the thermometer will always tell you when meat is prepared exactly the way you want it.

The first cooking technique you'll learn is the dry heat method of roasting, which you'll promptly put to use on our recipe for Burgundian Roast Sirloin. In roasting this very juicy, tender cut of beef, you'll want to keep its natural good flavor. Some people still prefer to sear a roast, either in a heavy pan or at a very high temperature in the oven. However, the American Meat Institute recommends placing the roast on a rack in a roasting pan and roasting at 325 degrees for 18 to 20 minutes per pound depending on desired doneness. Insert a meat thermometer in the thickest part, being sure it doesn't rest against a bone, and continue as the recipe instructs.

BURGUNDIAN ROAST SIRLOIN

1 5-lb. sirloin tip roast
1 recipe Marinade for Beef *(Sauces, pg. 5)*

Place the roast in a shallow dish and cover it with the beef marinade. Marinate it in the refrigerator overnight or at room temperature for several hours. Turn the roast several times while marinating in order to soak it completely. Place the roast on a rack in a shallow roasting pan, then pour 1 cup of water in the pan. Set a meat thermometer to the temperature for desired doneness, then insert the thermometer in the roast. Bake in a preheated 325-degree oven until the thermometer dial reaches the desired temperature. Add a small amount of water as needed to prevent the roasting pan from becoming too dry.

MENU
CUCUMBER CUPS
(Salads, pg. 10)
BURGUNDIAN ROAST SIRLOIN
BROCCOLI WITH HOLLANDAISE SAUCE
(Vegetables, pg. 10)
CARAMELIZED POTATOES
(Vegetables, pg. 11)
ORANGE MERINGUE
(Desserts, pg. 34)

netted beef roast

This marvelously easy-to-prepare roast is attractively surrounded by fried potatoes, Caramelized Onions (Vegetables, pg. 11), and French-cut green beans.

netted beef roast

If you want to make sure your boned roasts are as attractive as they are delicious, try one of these techniques. The first one is done by slipping a net of elasticized string around the roast to hold the meat's shape while it cooks. Many large supermarkets and meat markets now have the equipment needed to net meats. This is one of the valuable new techniques for cooking meats. A second technique, which can be done easily in your own kitchen, is to wrap your roast in one thickness of cheesecloth and secure with heavy string. This method is used for open dry heat roasting. The third technique is simply rolling the roast and tying it in shape with heavy string. We have used the first and third techniques for the two recipes that follow.

NETTED BEEF ROAST

1 5-lb. netted sirloin tip roast

Place the roast on a rack in a shallow roasting pan. Pour 1 cup cold water around the roast. Bake in a preheated 450-degree oven for 15 minutes. Turn the roast over and bake for 15 minutes longer. This will sear the meat and seal in the juices. Reduce oven temperature to 400 degrees. Insert a meat thermometer in the roast. Bake until the meat thermometer dial reaches the temperature for desired doneness. Add water as needed. Roast may be turned once during baking for even browning. To remove netting, snip with scissors and peel away from roast.

ROLLED BONED ROAST

1 5-lb. rolled sirloin tip roast

Place the roast on a rack in a shallow roasting pan. Pour 1 cup of cold water into the pan. Bake in a preheated 450-degree oven for 15 minutes. Turn the roast over and bake for 15 minutes longer. This will sear the meat and seal in the juices. Reduce oven temperature to 400 degrees, then insert a meat thermometer in the roast. Bake to desired doneness as indicated on the meat thermometer, adding water as needed. Pan drippings may be served with the roast.

rolled boned roast

This rump, a roast cut from the top part of the leg, has been tied and roasted, then cut so that you can see the color of the slices. Potatoes, leeks and peas form their own garnish. Our recipe tells you how to prepare this roast.

SCANDINAVIAN BEEF POT ROAST

1 3½-lb. pot roast
Salt and pepper
Ginger
¼ c. olive oil
3 lg. onions
1 garlic clove
½ c. Burgundy
2 c. weak tea
12 diced pitted prunes
1 4½-oz. can olives, drained
1 2-oz. can mushrooms, drained
Beurre Manié

Sprinkle the roast generously with salt, pepper and ginger. Pour the oil in a shallow frying pan over medium heat. Peel and thinly slice the onions. Peel and crush the garlic. Sauté the onions and garlic in the hot oil until the onions are soft and golden. Place the prepared roast in a Dutch oven or deep casserole. Pour the onion mixture on top and add the Burgundy. Bake, covered, in a preheated 300-degree oven for 2 hours. Cover the prunes with hot strained tea. Allow the prunes to stand until cold, then drain away all but ¾ cup of liquid. Add the ¾ cup liquid, prunes and olives to the roast and cover. Bake for about 2 hours longer or until the roast is tender. Lift the roast onto a serving platter and surround it with the mushrooms, prunes and olives. Stir the pan liquid into a saucepan and bring the liquid to a boil. Thicken with *Beurre Manié*. Sauce may be poured over the roast or served separately as an accompaniment.

BEURRE MANIÉ

Beurre Manié is a classic recipe used to thicken sauces and gravies.

Combine 2 tablespoons soft butter and ¼ cup all-purpose flour in a small bowl. Mix the butter and flour until well blended. Roll the mixture into small balls. Add balls into boiling liquid, one by one, stirring constantly with a whisk. Add as many balls as needed for desired thickness.

scandinavian beef pot roast

We have arranged our pot roast in a copper sauté pan so that you can see it surrounded by its delicious liquor. To please the eye, sprinkle the top of both roast and sauce with finely chopped parsley.

how to cut and wrap fillets

When you want to serve that beef delicacy called *filet mignon*, you can justify such luxury with the classic treatment we're about to show you. (We would like to mention here the reason for the two different spellings of *fillet*. *Filet* is the French spelling always required when used with another French word such as *mignon*. *Fillet* is the accepted spelling of any piece or slice of boneless meat, or fish.)

You will find that one middle-cut beef fillet will yield an average of ten *fillets* — the steaks that are wrapped with fat to make *filet mignon*. It takes less than five minutes to cut them with a long, sharp, pointed French knife like the one we use in the illustrations below. Allow about another ten minutes to cut the pork fat, then about five minutes more for trimming and tying the pork fat around the fillets. Your cooking time will be approximately ten minutes, depending on the thickness of the steaks and the cooking method. You will then be ready to serve *filet mignon* for ten people.

Your butcher can sell you unsalted pork fat needed to prepare *filet mignon* or you can use strips of bacon. Either is acceptable. Wrapping and tying with fat is called barding, and it is one of the classic cooking techniques. We will introduce it to you here and will use it later to prepare breasts of game, poultry, and perhaps fillets of fish.

You will find recipes for cooking your prepared *filet mignon* on page 6.

1 Get everything ready before you start so that you will not have to search frantically for needed equipment. Shown from right to left, we have trussing string, including one ball of red that looks like a *filet*, but isn't. The real *filet* is in the middle of the picture. The knife for cutting pork strips is resting on the pork; an already cut strip lies between the knife and kitchen scissors you'll need for trimming and cutting string.

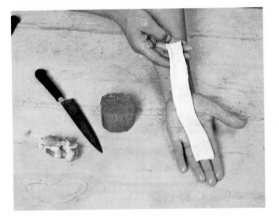

3 We have cut a strip of raw, unsalted pork fat the same length as the circumference of the trimmed *filet* and the same width as its depth. You can just as easily use bacon. On the left of this picture you can see how the fat and skin of the *filet mignon* have been trimmed away to make a perfect round. In the middle is the trimmed steak.

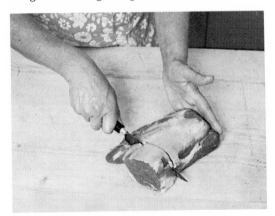

2 Here we are cutting a *filet* from a beef fillet. Our slice is 1 ½ inches thick, the minimum size for a good *filet mignon*.

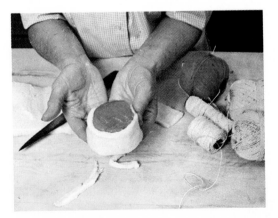

4 Look closely to see exactly how to wrap the fat or bacon around each piece of the meat.

5 If your strip is a bit too long, trim it carefully so that the two edges meet exactly.

6 Tie the trussing string we showed you in the first picture around the middle of the wrapped *filet mignon*. Make a double knot and cut the string close to the knot. Now you're ready to grill.

the art of grilling steaks

In the coldest part of winter, you may see a neighbor wrapped up in woolens making brief trips to his patio where billowing smoke rises from a barbecue grill. This is someone who is dedicated to the flavor of grilled meat. Maybe you aren't quite this dedicated, but when the weather is pleasant, there is nothing quite so appetizing as smelling the charcoal aroma of steaks or hamburgers while you watch them sizzle on an open grill.

For outdoor grilling, as well as for the previous alternate cooking methods covered, we suggest that searing the meat first will seal in the natural juices. A simple grilling for 2 to 3 minutes-on-each-side procedure will accomplish this. Be especially careful not to pierce the meat while cooking or the juices will escape.

If the weather is inappropriate for outdoor grilling and you don't have an indoor grill, try broiling, which is actually a method of grilling steaks in the oven. The broiling recipes will give you specific instructions for searing and cooking steaks.

BROILED FILET MIGNON

Place 1 1/4-inch thick *filets* on the rack in a broiling pan. Set the oven at broil and preheat for several minutes. Place the broiling pan in the highest position in broiler and allow 2 to 3 minutes on each side to sear the *filets*. Lower the pan to the middle position and broil for 2 minutes on each side for rare, 3 minutes and 30 seconds for medium and 4 minutes for well done.

MAÎTRE D'HÔTEL BUTTER

1/2 c. softened butter
Strained juice of 1/2 lemon
Salt and pepper to season
1 heaped tbsp. chopped parsley leaves

Blend all the ingredients in a small mixing bowl. Shape the mixture into a round or square pat and refrigerate it until ready to use. Cut into desired shapes and serve on *filets* as shown.

GRILLED FILET MIGNON

Place the grill rack about 4 inches above red hot coals. Place 1 1/2-inch thick *filets* on the grill and sear for about 2 to 3 minutes on each side, then cook for 2 minutes and 30 seconds on each side for medium rare.

GRILLED SIRLOIN STEAK

Place the grill rack about 4 inches above red hot coals. Sear a 1 1/4-inch thick sirloin steak for about 5 minutes on each side, then grill for 3 minutes on each side for medium rare.

how to lard fillets

Larding is another classic technique to add fat while enhancing the juicy flavor of your fillet. By inserting unsalted pork fat into the beef with a hollow pointed larding needle like the one we use below, your beef will cook beautifully. The compliments you receive will more than make up for the extra time you spend preparing this luxurious dish. You can produce a masterpiece every time by following these simple illustrations.

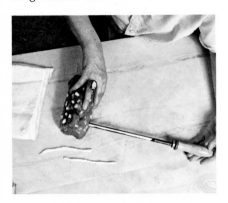

1 Cut long, narrow strips of fat as you see in the foreground of our picture. Fit a strip of fat into the groove of the larding needle and press down very securely at the tip of the needle. Push the needle through the piece of meat.

2 Pull the fat away from the needle — it comes away very easily. Here we're holding up the two ends of the strip so you can see clearly what it should look like.

3 Remove the larding needle, leaving in the fat. With kitchen scissors, trim off the ends so that only a tiny piece sticks out of each side. We suggest you lard about half an inch from the bottom of the fillet and allow about two inches between each insertion. Make another row half an inch above the first and continue with as many rows as the thickness of your fillet allows.

trimmed filet mignon

Here we show you our finished filets mignons served on croutons or toast rounds. Maître d'Hôtel Butter on top adds to the steaks' appearance and flavor. Our method for making stuffed tomatoes and straw potatoes will be given later. One filet mignon has been left with its encircling strip of fat while the other has the fat removed.

grilled hamburgers deluxe

These hamburgers are sizzling in a large oval iron pan supported by a home-made grill made of scrap iron rods. (We have found that neither the elaborateness nor simplicity of a grill affects the delicious flavor of hamburgers.) You'll find recipes for our Barbecue Sauces in Sauces, page 8.

grilled hamburgers

Hamburgers are a very popular, all-American food, perhaps because they are pleasing both to the taste and to the budget. When cooked properly, grilled hamburgers particularly appeal to our palates and can be a delicious part of any meal.

Before presenting our recipe for grilled hamburgers, we would like to give you a few hints on buying and storing hamburger meat. Look for the best quality meat that is rich, red and only slightly flecked with white. If it is light pink or almost white it probably contains too much fat.

Hamburger meat should be cooked within 24 hours after purchasing as it tends to spoil rapidly. If you don't plan to use it that quickly, you should freeze it.

A good way to be constantly prepared for unexpected guests is to form patties of hamburger meat, wrap them individually and freeze them. When company drops in, you can take your frozen patties out of the freezer, season them, and broil them in a short period of time. Hamburger is one of the only meats that can be cooked from a frozen state without losing its juiciness.

GRILLED HAMBURGERS DELUXE

1 tbsp. butter
1½ tsp. olive oil
1 med. onion, minced
1 lb. extra lean ground beef
3 drops of hot sauce
1 tbsp. Worcestershire sauce
1 tsp. salt
½ tsp. freshly ground pepper
2 egg yolks, lightly beaten
⅔ c. soft bread crumbs

Melt the butter with olive oil in a small frying pan. Add the onion and sauté until golden. Combine the ground beef, onion, hot sauce, Worcestershire sauce, salt and pepper in a bowl and mix well. Add the egg yolks and bread crumbs, mixing until well combined. Shape the meat into 4 patties, 3 inches in diameter and about ½ inch thick. Place the patties on a grill rack about 4 inches above the hot charcoal (or under a preheated broiler). Sear the meat quickly on both sides. Raise the grill rack to 6 to 8 inches above the coals and cook for 5 minutes on each side. Serve with Basic Barbecue Sauce. (Sauces, pg. 8).

shallow-fried round steak

Round steak can be delicious when correctly prepared. Of course the quality of the steak is important and you should purchase a cut from the bottom round of beef. Ask your butcher for a medium-sized steak cut about ½ inch thick. Although it is not as tender as other more expensive cuts of meat, round steak can be made succulent and tender in Marinade For Beef (Sauces, pg. 5). This technique not only tenderizes the steak but adds extra flavor. To cook round steak, gently sauté in a small amount of butter until done.

SHALLOW-FRIED ROUND STEAKS

1 1½-lb. boneless round steak, cut about ½ in. thick
1 recipe Marinade For Beef (Sauces, pg. 5)
2 tomatoes
Olive oil
Salt and freshly ground pepper to taste
¼ c. butter
2 tbsp. beef extract
Cooked and Uncooked Sautéed Potatoes (Vegetables, pg. 71)
3 tsp. finely chopped chives
Chives Butter

Cut the steak in half and place in a shallow dish. Pour the marinade over the steaks and refrigerate for at least 24 hours, turning occasionally. Drain the steaks and set aside. Remove stem end from the tomatoes and cut tomatoes in half. Place in a shallow baking pan, cut side up, and brush lightly with oil. Broil the tomatoes 6 inches from source of heat until tender and lightly browned, then sprinkle with salt and pepper. Keep warm. Place the butter in a large frypan over high heat until bubbly and light brown. Place the steaks in the butter and cook for 30 seconds. Turn and cook for 30 seconds longer. Reduce heat to low and cook steaks for 2 minutes on each side. Spoon the beef extract over the steaks and cook for 1 minute longer. The steaks will be medium rare. Place on a meat platter, then place the tomatoes around the steaks. Place the potatoes on the outside of the steaks. Sprinkle 1 teaspoon of chives on 4 pats of Chives Butter and place 2 pats on each steak. Sprinkle remaining chives on the potatoes and tomatoes. You may garnish with watercress, if desired. This makes 2 to 4 servings.

CHIVES BUTTER

½ c. unsalted butter, softened
¼ c. finely chopped chives
Salt and freshly ground pepper to taste

Place the butter and chives in a bowl and beat until creamy. Add the salt and pepper and mix well. Cover the top of a small plate with plastic wrap. Place the Chives Butter on the plastic wrap and shape into a ½-inch deep circle. Refrigerate until hard, then cut into circles with a 1-inch *canapé* or cookie cutter. Remove the plastic wrap from the plate and push out the circles from the plastic wrap side. Chives Butter may be kept in a covered container in the refrigerator for at least 10 days.

shallow-fried round steaks

Shallow-Fried Round Steaks, are browned to perfection with proper cooking. Natural meat juices are retained by sautéing quickly. The platter includes broiled tomatoes, sautéed potatoes, dots of Chives Butter, and fresh watercress.

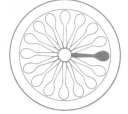

steak diane

An increasingly popular dish, Steak Diane may be included on special menus. Beef is a standard American favorite and the unusual preparation of this savory steak dish makes it irresistible. Well marbled beef should be selected and cut into ½-inch thick steaks. Pounding the meat tenderizes and prepares it for quick cooking. If you prefer to use a less expensive cut of beef than sirloin strip, marinate the steak for several hours or overnight before cooking. Cook Steak Diane quickly to retain tenderness and succulence.

STEAK DIANE

3 strip sirloin steaks, cut ½ in. thick
2 tbsp. butter
2 tbsp. cooking oil
2 tbsp. brandy
2 tbsp. minced shallots or green onions
1 tbsp. freshly chopped parsley
1 10½-oz. can chilled beef consommé
Salt and pepper to taste
1 tsp. Worcestershire sauce

1 Pound the steaks with a mallet or wine bottle to ¼-inch thickness. Pierce the steak with tines of fork on one end and roll up the steaks.

2 Unroll 1 steak into the sizzling butter and oil in a heavy skillet. Cook for 1 minute on each side, then remove to a heated platter.

3 Place the remaining steaks, one at a time, in the hot oil mixture, and cook for 1 minute on each side. Return the steaks on the platter to the skillet.

4 Turn the heat to high and pour the brandy over the steaks. Ignite the brandy, shaking the pan until the flame is extinguished. Reduce the heat and cook for 1 minute longer.

5 Add the shallots and cook for 2 minutes. Sprinkle with parsley, stirring well.

6 Add the consommé, one spoonful at a time, to the steak mixture in the skillet. Bring to a boil, then spoon about 2 tablespoons of the pan liquid onto a warm platter. Remove the steaks to the platter and keep warm.

7 Cook the pan liquid vigorously until reduced by half. Season with salt and pepper, then stir in the Worcestershire sauce. Spoon the sauce over the steaks and serve immediately. You may serve the steaks with French-Fried Potatoes, (Vegetables, pg. 64), if desired. This makes 6 servings.

steak diane

Superbly different, Steak Diane will tempt the most satiated appetite. Carefully chosen beef has been pounded, then cooked quickly to perfection. When prepared according to directions, the result is a beef dish well worth the extra effort. Steak Diane is shown served in its own seasoned juices and dotted with fresh parsley sprigs. It may be accompanied by French fries as pictured, or by your favorite cooked vegetable or green salad. Always serve Steak Diane on a heavy, preheated platter to keep the juices hot and heighten the full flavor.

beef stroganoff

An international favorite, Beef *Stroganoff* has long pleased the palates of gourmet diners. As the name indicates, the recipe began in prerevolutionary Russia, *Stroganoff* being the surname of one of St. Petersburg's prominent families of merchant noblemen. Surprisingly, the method of preparation is French — the only Russian contribution to the dish is sour cream!

Although many variations exist, there are two ingredients which are basic to the preparation of good *Stroganoff* — lean strips of beef and sour cream. Other ingredients may be varied, but the end result should be *rare* beef strips served in a rich, creamy sauce.

beef stroganoff

A subtle blending of choice ingredients combine to make Beef Stroganoff a very special dish. The meat has been simmered in a distinctive sauce of mushrooms, herbs, wine, onions and sour cream. Served with hot buttered rice, Beef Stroganoff is an epicurean delight.

BEEF STROGANOFF WITH RICE

3 tbsp. all-purpose flour
1 tsp. salt
¼ tsp. freshly ground pepper
1 1½-lb. sirloin steak, cut ½ in. thick
2 tbsp. olive oil
4 tbsp. butter
½ c. chopped onion
1 clove of garlic, pressed
½ lb. fresh mushrooms, sliced
½ c. sherry
½ c. beef bouillon
1 tsp. chopped chervil
Grated rind of 1 lemon
½ tsp. paprika
1 c. sour cream
1 recipe Basic Boiled Rice *(Cereals, pg. 3)*
¼ c. melted butter
2 tsp. finely chopped fresh parsley

Mix flour, salt and pepper. Slice steak into 2-inch strips and dredge with seasoned flour. Heat oil and 2 tablespoons of butter in frypan until piping hot. Add steak and cook, stirring constantly, until lightly browned. Do not overcook, as steak should be rare. Remove steak from frypan and reduce heat to low. Add remaining butter to frypan, then add onion, garlic, and mushrooms. Cook, stirring constantly, for 3 minutes or until onion and mushrooms are tender, but not brown. Return steak to frypan, add sherry, bouillon, chervil, lemon rind and paprika and mix well. Season with additional salt and pepper, if needed. Simmer for 5 minutes or until most of the liquid has evaporated. Stir in sour cream and heat through, but do not boil. Remove from heat and keep warm. Mix rice with melted butter and shape into an even border around a serving dish. Sprinkle with parsley. Place the Beef Stroganoff inside the rice border. This makes 6 servings.

INFORMAL DINNER PARTY MENU

IRIS SALAD
(Salads, pg. 35)

BOEUF BOURGUIGNONNE
(pg. 13)

PROVENÇAL TOMATOES   **SAUTÉED POTATOES**
(Vegetables, pg. 71)   *(Vegetables, pg. 71)*

ALMOND MACAROONS with
LUXEMBOURG SAUCE
(Desserts, pg. 129)
(Sauces, pg. 20)

SUGGESTED WINE:

SECOND COURSE —
RED BURGUNDY or CALIFORNIA PINOT NOIR

DESSERT —
CHAMPAGNE

boeuf bourguignonne

Another popular favorite is *Boeuf Bourguignonne* — a French dish both in origin and preparation. *Boeuf Bourguignonne* is actually a stew or ragoût, as it is known to the French housewife, and consists of cubed beef, simmered in a wine and stock.

BOEUF BOURGUIGNONNE

¼ lb. slab bacon, rind removed
1 tbsp. olive oil
2 tbsp. all-purpose flour
1 tsp. salt
¼ tsp. pepper
2 lb. boneless beef chuck, cut in 2-in. cubes
½ c. sliced onion
2 to 3 c. Basic Beef Stock *(Soups, pg. 2)*
1½ c. Burgundy
1 tbsp. tomato paste
1 clove of garlic, pressed
1 Bouquet Garni *(Soups, pg. 2)*
12 sm. onions
½ lb. fresh mushrooms, thickly sliced
2 tbsp. butter

Cut the bacon into small cubes and sauté in olive oil in a large frypan over medium heat until brown, stirring constantly. Remove the bacon and place in a large casserole. Mix the flour, salt and pepper and dredge the beef with seasoned flour. Place in the frypan and add the sliced onion. Cook, stirring frequently, until brown. Remove from frypan and place in the casserole with bacon. Pour 2 cups of beef stock and the Burgundy into the frypan and add the tomato paste and garlic. Bring to a boil, stirring to remove browned particles from frypan, then pour over the beef mixture. Add the Bouquet Garni and enough beef stock to just cover. Bake in a preheated 325-degree oven for 3 to 4 hours or until the beef is tender. Prepare the whole onions and mushrooms while the beef mixture is baking. Cook the onions in boiling, salted water until almost tender, then drain. Cook the onions and mushrooms in the butter in a frypan until golden, stirring constantly. Remove beef mixture from the oven and remove cover. Drain the liquid into a saucepan and skim off fat. Liquid should be thick enough to coat a spoon. Add beef stock if too thick or cook over high heat to reduce to sauce consistency if too thin. Season with additional salt and pepper, if needed. Remove Bouquet Garni from the beef mixture and stir in the mushroom mixture. Pour the sauce over the beef mixture and simmer for several minutes or until heated through. Serve with boiled potatoes, buttered noodles or cooked rice. This makes 6 servings.

FILETS MIGNONS WITH MADEIRA SAUCE

Through the magic of sauces, even a fine cut of beef can be made better. The basis for the dish is *Filet Mignon*, a rather expensive cut of beef which should be selected with great care. Correct preparation of the *Filets Mignons*, before cooking will insure best results (Beef, pg. 5). The success of this dish depends upon simmering the meat juices with other ingredients to make the delicious sauce. This step imparts a very special flavor to the beef and makes *Filets Mignons* With Madeira Sauce a tantalizing dish any cook may serve with pride.

FILETS MIGNONS WITH MADEIRA SAUCE

4 slices day-old bread
6 tbsp. butter
4 slices tomato, cut ¾ in. thick
Olive oil
Salt and freshly ground pepper to taste
4 filets mignons *(Beef, pg. 5)*
4 slices pitted black olive
2 tbsp. brandy
½ c. beef bouillon
1 tbsp. tomato paste
¼ c. Madeira
1 tsp. cornstarch
2 tbsp. finely minced fresh parsley
Truffles *(opt.)*

Cut out the center of each bread slice with a 3-inch round cookie cutter. Sauté the bread rounds in 4 tablespoons of hot butter until lightly browned on both sides, then keep warm. Place the tomato slices in a baking pan and brush lightly with oil. Broil until lightly browned and sprinkle with salt and pepper. Place on a serving platter and keep warm. Melt the remaining butter with 1 tablespoon oil in a large frypan over medium high heat until the foam subsides. Add the *filets* and cook for 3 minutes on each side or until medium rare. Remove frypan from heat and remove *filets* immediately. Remove the strings and strips of fat from *filets*. Season *filets* with salt and pepper and place on the tomato slices. Place a bread round on each *filet* and top with an olive slice. Keep warm. Increase heat to high and place the frypan over the heat. Pour the brandy into the frypan and ignite. Shake the frypan until flame burns out. Add the beef bouillon and tomato paste and boil, stirring to remove browned particles from bottom of frypan, until liquid is reduced to ¼ cup. Mix the Madeira with the cornstarch and stir into the frypan. Add the parsley and simmer for 1 minute. Season with salt and pepper, if needed. Pour over the *filet* stacks, top with truffles and serve immediately. This makes 4 servings.

hamburgers à la lindstrom

HAMBURGERS À LA LINDSTROM
1 lb. lean ground beef
1½ tsp. salt
Freshly ground pepper to taste
3 egg yolks
3 tbsp. pickled beet juice
¼ c. water
3 tbsp. chopped pickled beets
3 tbsp. chopped pickles
3 tbsp. finely chopped onion
2 tbsp. capers
2 to 3 tbsp. butter

Hamburger needn't always be served smothered with catsup and mustard inside a toasted bun. Break the hamburger habit with Hamburgers 'A La Lindstrom, a Swedish dish that will satisfy your taste buds without straining your budget. A good grade of beef is preferable for this recipe; calorie counters may prefer to use ground chuck or ground round. Texture is added to the meat base by combining it with egg yolks. Finely chopped onion, pickled beets, pickles and capers add both flavor and volume to the mixture. Shaped into round, plump patties and fried until brown and juicy, these hamburgers bring a touch of Sweden to an American favorite.

1 Assemble all ingredients before preparing the hamburgers.

2 Place the ground beef in a bowl and add the salt and pepper.

3 Add the egg yolks to the beef and mix with a wooden spoon until combined.

4 Pour in the beet juice and water, a small amount at a time, mixing well after each addition. Mixture will be very moist.

5 Stir in the beets, pickles, onion and capers, then shape into 4 patties. Score tops of patties. Slide the patties, with a spatula, into the hot butter in a large frypan.

hamburgers à la lindstrom

Sizzled to perfection, Hamburgers À La Lindstrom are packed with flavorful goodness. Their full-bodied texture and rich color are enhanced by skillful blending of ingredients. Served with creamy mashed potatoes and a tossed green salad Hamburgers À La Lindstrom make an inexpensive and ordinary meal an impressive one.

6 Cook over medium heat until hamburgers are of desired doneness. Serve with mashed potatoes and a green salad. This makes 4 servings.

beef buffins

A few extra ingredients have transformed ground beef and English muffins into tempting Beef Buffins. Egg, parsley, bread crumbs, and tomato purée are mixed with ground beef, shaped into round patties and perfectly fried until golden brown. Placed between hot, buttered English muffins and served with crispy onion rings, ground beef becomes Beef Buffins — perfect for patio party fare.

BEEF BUFFINS

4 English muffins
Butter
1 lb. ground chuck
1 tbsp. finely chopped fresh parsley
Salt and freshly ground pepper to taste
1 egg, beaten
1 c. soft bread crumbs
1 tbsp. tomato purée

Cut the English muffins in half and spread cut surfaces with butter. Place, cut side up, on a baking sheet and toast until golden brown. Keep warm. Combine the ground chuck, parsley, salt, pepper, egg, bread crumbs and tomato purée and mix well. Shape into 4 patties the same diameter as the muffins. Fry in a hot, lightly greased skillet to desired doneness, then place between muffin halves. Place on a platter and garnish with watercress. Serve with Crispy Fried Onion Rings (Vegetables, pg. 48) and mustard. This makes 4 servings.

vienna steaks

Still another way to lift ground beef out of the ordinary into the extraordinary. Lean ground beef, mixed with bacon, onion, egg, and seasonings, is formed into cutlet shapes. Coated with bread crumbs, the cutlets fry to a crisp, golden brown. Vienna Steaks are shown accompanied by Crispy Fried Onion Rings.

VIENNA STEAKS

2 lb. lean ground beef
2 thick slices bacon, finely minced
½ c. finely minced onion
2 eggs
1 tsp. cinnamon
1 clove of garlic, crushed
Salt and freshly ground pepper to taste
All-purpose flour
2 c. fine bread crumbs

Combine the beef, bacon, onion, 1 egg, cinnamon, garlic, salt and pepper and mix well. Form around wooden skewers into flat cutlet shapes, leaving 1 inch of skewers at narrow end exposed, then dredge with flour. Beat remaining egg with 2 tablespoons of water. Dip the cutlets into egg mixture, then coat with bread crumbs. Cook in small amount of fat in a frypan over medium heat for 4 to 5 minutes or until brown. Turn and brown on other side. Remove from frypan and place paper frills (Poultry, pg. 15) over exposed skewers. Place the cutlets in a serving dish and serve with Crispy Fried Onion Rings (Vegetables, pg. 48). Sprinkle with chopped fresh parsley, if desired. This makes 10 servings.

SUKIYAKI

3 lb. sirloin steak
3/4 c. soy sauce
3/4 c. beef broth
1/4 c. dry sherry or sake
2 tbsp. sugar
1/4 tsp. freshly ground pepper
1 tsp. monosodium glutamate
Salt to taste
1/2 c. vegetable oil
1 1/2 c. sliced onions
3/4 c. sliced celery
1 c. sliced bamboo shoots
1 c. sliced fresh mushrooms
3/4 c. sliced green onions

Cut the steak into thin diagonal strips. Combine the soy sauce, broth, sherry, sugar, pepper, monosodium glutamate and salt in a small mixing bowl. Heat the oil in a wok or deep skillet. Add the steak and stir-fry as shown in the illustrations on page 18 until browned. Push the steak to one side of the wok, then pour 1/2 cup of the soy sauce mixture over the steak. Add the sliced onions, celery, bamboo shoots and mushrooms to the wok and stir-fry for 3 minutes. Pour the remaining soy sauce mixture over the celery mixture. Add the green onions and stir-fry for 3 minutes longer. The vegetables should be crisp-tender. Stir the steak into the vegetable mixture. Serve the Sukiyaki with thin, cooked noodles. Thin strips of carrot and Chinese cabbage may be included in the celery mixture, if desired. This makes about 6 to 8 servings.

BURMESE GINGER BEEF

1 c. minced onions
2 cloves of garlic, pressed
1 tsp. chili powder
2 tsp. turmeric
2 tsp. ginger
1 tsp. salt
3 lb. lean stew beef
8 med. fresh tomatoes
1/2 c. peanut oil
4 c. Basic Beef Stock *(Soups, pg. 2)*

Combine the onions, garlic, chili powder, turmeric, ginger and salt in a bowl, mixing well. Cut the beef into 1 1/2-inch cubes and place in a shallow non-metal dish. Sprinkle with the onion mixture, then refrigerate for 3 hours, stirring occasionally. Peel the tomatoes and cut into large pieces. Heat the oil in a skillet. Add the beef and stir-fry, as illustrated on page 18, until browned on all sides. Place the beef in a casserole and add the skillet drippings, tomatoes and beef stock. Bake, covered, in a preheated 325-degree oven for about 2 hours or until the beef is tender. Serve with Basic Boiled Rice (Cereals, pg. 3) and garnish with red sweet pepper strips. This makes about 6 to 8 servings.

burmese ginger beef

Burmese Ginger Beef is an example of a type of oriental cooking, with characteristic seasonings such as ginger, garlic, peanut oil and turmeric. Serve it with Basic Boiled Rice (Cereals, pg. 3) garnished with red sweet pepper strips.

CHINESE STIR-FRIED BEEF AND MUSHROOMS

½ lb. dried Chinese mushrooms
3 lb. lean sirloin steak
¼ c. all-purpose flour
½ c. sherry
½ c. soy sauce
1 tbsp. sugar
¾ c. olive oil
1 1¾-in. slice gingerroot, minced
1 c. chopped onions
2 c. Basic Beef Stock *(Soups, pg. 2)*
Salt to taste

Soak the mushrooms in water for 30 minutes, then drain well and set aside. Cut the steak into thin strips. Combine the flour, sherry, soy sauce and sugar in a deep bowl. Add the beef and marinate for at least 15 minutes, stirring frequently. Heat ½ cup of the oil in a wok or deep skillet. Add the gingerroot and stir-fry for 1 minute. Add the beef and marinade and stir-fry until the beef loses its red color, then remove the beef from the wok. Add remaining oil to the wok. Add the onions and stir-fry until almost tender. Add the mushrooms and stir-fry until soft. Return the beef to the wok and stir-fry for about 2 minutes. Add the stock and bring to a boil, then reduce the heat. Add the salt and cook, covered, for 3 minutes longer. Place the beef mixture in a serving dish. You may serve this dish with soft-fried noodles (Pasta, pg. 22). This makes about 6 to 8 servings.

chinese stir-fried beef and mushrooms

Chinese Stir-Fried Beef and Mushrooms is made with lean beef and dried Chinese mushrooms. Chopped onions, sherry, minced gingerroot, and other seasonings add a distinctive flavor. Serve this combination with rice or soft-fried noodles, (Pasta, pg. 22).

1 Place the amount of oil or other fat that is listed in a recipe's ingredients in a wok or deep skillet. Heat to a moderately hot temperature.

2 Add the ingredients to be fried in the order listed in the recipe and swirl gently to the edge of the wok with a slotted spoon. Draw the ingredients back to the center of the wok and cook until the mixture is bubbly. Repeat the process until each addition is cooked according to the recipe's directions.

The Creative Homemaker's Academy © MCMLXXIII
Selected Illustrations © B.P.C. Publishing Limited MCMLXX

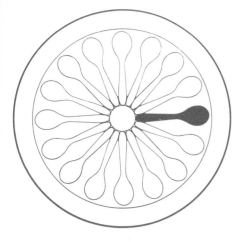

introducing veal

Veal, the tender meat of a young calf, is a very soft, fine-grained meat with practically no fat in its tissue. Because of this lack of fat, cooking methods usually include added fat in some form. Some veal is cooked with strips of bacon across it. Steaks, chops and cutlets are frequently dipped in beaten eggs and crumbs, and deep-fried or braised.

If, in the past, you have tried European veal recipes, you may have been somewhat discouraged when you went to the market for a specified cut. Some cuts of veal available in Europe may not be available in American markets. For example, *collop*, *escalope* and *scaloppine* (boneless pieces of veal cut from either the rib eye muscle or the loin), are not the most familiar cuts in America, though they are obtainable in some areas. American cuts are chiefly cutlets, steaks and roasts. However, you may purchase veal round steak 1/2-inch thick and pound it with a meat mallet until it is similar to the European type which is 1/4-inch thick, to suit certain recipes. We will demonstrate this technique in our following veal recipes which call for veal scallops.

VEAL LOAF WITH TOMATO FONDUE SAUCE

1 recipe Tomato Fondue Sauce *(Sauces, pg. 15)*
1 lb. ground veal or beef
2 c. soft fine bread crumbs
Salt and pepper to taste
1 tsp. crushed dried tarragon leaves
1/2 tsp. dried thyme
1 tsp. minced fresh parsley
3 eggs, separated

Prepare the sauce. Place the ground veal and bread crumbs in a large mixing bowl and mix well. Add the salt, pepper, tarragon, thyme, parsley and egg yolks and mix until well blended. Beat the egg whites until very stiff peaks form, then fold 1/4 of the egg whites thoroughly into the veal mixture. Fold in the remaining egg whites gently and place in a buttered soufflé dish or casserole. Place in a pan of hot water. Bake in a preheated 350-degree oven for about 1 hour or until well browned. Let stand for 10 minutes, then unmold onto a serving platter. Serve with the heated Tomato Fondue Sauce. This makes about 6 servings.

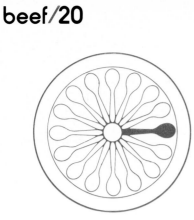

pounding and dividing veal scallops

1 Cut each veal scallop in half with a sharp knife.

2 Dip a meat mallet into cold water so that the surface of the veal will not be broken. These mallets are of several designs.

3 Pound the veal with the meat mallet until tender. The scallops may be pounded just as well before cutting as after.

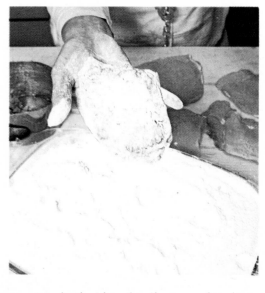

4 Dip both sides of each piece of veal into flour to coat well.

miniature veal scallops
with mushrooms and olives

*This special dish is made with taste-tempting
Mirepoix (Sauces, pg. 5) and small scallops of
veal floured and fried in butter. Top with Baked
Croûtes (Breads, pg. 16), and black olives. Fresh
watercress or fresh parsley may be used for garnish.*

MINIATURE VEAL SCALLOPS
WITH MUSHROOMS AND OLIVES

8 Baked Croûtes (Breads, pg. 16)
2 lg. veal scallops or cutlets
6 tbsp. butter
1 recipe Mirepoix (Sauces, pg. 5)
8 broiled fresh mushroom caps
Basic Garlic Butter (General Information, pg. 30)
8 black pitted olives

Prepare the *croûtes* and set aside. Prepare the veal
scallops according to the step-by-step illustrations
on page 20, cutting each scallop into fourths instead of halves. Melt the butter in a large frypan
over medium heat. Add the veal scallops and cook
until brown on both sides, adding more butter, if
needed. Spoon the Mirepoix over the scallops and
reduce the heat to low, then cook until all liquid in
the frypan has evaporated. Place the veal scallops
on a serving platter, then place a *croûte* on each
scallop. Place a mushroom cap on each *croûte* and
pipe garlic butter onto the mushrooms. Place an
olive in the butter on each mushroom. Garnish the
platter with watercress. This makes 4 servings.

ITALIAN VEAL AND HAM ROLLS

3 veal scallops or cutlets
3 thin slices of cooked ham
1 ¹/₂-in. thick slice of Gruyère or Swiss cheese
Poultry seasoning to taste (opt.)
3 tbsp. olive oil
2 tbsp. butter
¹/₄ c. dry white wine
1 c. beef broth
1 tbsp. tomato purée
Salt and freshly ground pepper to taste

Pound and divide the veal scallops according to
the step-by-step directions on page 20. Cut the
ham slices in half, then cut the cheese slice into 6
equal parts. Place a ham slice on each piece of veal
and sprinkle with poultry seasoning. Place a piece
of cheese at one end of each stack, then roll as for
jelly roll and secure with wooden picks. Heat the
oil and butter in a skillet. Place the rolls in the
skillet and cook over medium heat until brown on
both sides, turning with metal tongs. Mix the wine,
broth and tomato purée, then pour over the rolls.
Simmer until the veal is tender. Remove the rolls
and place them in a serving dish. Season the sauce
with salt and pepper, then simmer until thickened.
Pour over the rolls. Serve with buttered, toasted
French bread slices sprinkled with freshly grated
Parmesan cheese. This makes 6 servings.

foil-baked veal scallops

FOIL-BAKED VEAL SCALLOPS WITH SAUCE

4 thin veal scallops or cutlets
Olive oil
Salt and pepper to taste
8 tbsp. grated fresh onion
½ lb. fresh mushrooms, minced
Chablis
Sauce

Prepare and bake the veal scallops according to the step-by-step illustrations. Pour the Sauce over the scallops and serve immediately. This makes 4 servings.

SAUCE

¾ c. half and half cream
2 egg yolks, slightly beaten
Salt and white pepper to taste

Combine the cream and egg yolks in the top of a double boiler, blending well, then stir in the pan juices. Place over simmering water and stir just until thick. Season with salt and pepper.

2 Sprinkle each scallop with 2 tablespoons of grated onion and ¼ of the mushrooms. Fold up the sides of the rectangle and pinch the corners together tightly. Place the foil containers on a baking sheet.

1 Cut 4 rectangles of aluminum foil about 8 inches longer than each scallop and brush the foil generously with olive oil. Season the scallops with salt and pepper, then place 1 scallop in the center of each rectangle.

3 Pour enough Chablis over each scallop to moisten well. Bake in a preheated 375-degree oven for 20 minutes. Add more Chablis to each scallop and bake for 20 minutes longer or until the veal is tender. Remove from the oven. Lift the scallops from the foil and place in a lightly buttered serving dish. Pour the pan juices into a small saucepan for use in the Sauce.

foil-baked veal scallops with sauce

Veal scallops, dry white wine, mushrooms and onion are cooked together in these delectable Foil-Baked Veal Scallops. Border them with Beignet Potatoes (Vegetables, pg. 99) and fresh, green parsley.

MENU

FRENCH ONION SOUP
(Soups, pg. 69)

FOIL-BAKED VEAL SCALLOPS WITH SAUCE

ACORN SQUASH WITH SLICED APPLES
(Vegetables, pg. 104)

HORSERADISH BREAD
(Breads, pg. 60)

BROCCOLI SALAD
(Salads, pg. 61)

MACAROON MOUSSE
(Desserts, pg. 207)

Suggested Wines:
White Bordeaux or
California Sauvignon Blanc

VEAL SCALLOPS WITH MUSHROOM SAUCE

1/4 lb. fresh mushrooms, thinly sliced
1/2 c. dry white wine
Freshly ground pepper to taste
4 veal scallops or cutlets
All-purpose flour
3 tbsp. butter
3 tbsp. olive oil
2 tbsp. grated onion
1 1/2 c. Basic Chicken Stock (Soups, pg. 2)
Salt to taste

Place the mushrooms in a small saucepan. Add the wine and pepper and simmer until the mushrooms are tender. Set aside. Pound and divide the veal scallops according to the step-by-step illustrations on page 20, then dredge with flour. Heat the butter and oil in a large skillet over high heat. Add the onion and stir well. Add the veal and cook for 1 minute. Turn and cook for 1 minute longer, then

veal scallops with mushroom sauce

Veal scallops, deliciously flavored with a sauce of mushrooms, onion, stock and dry white wine, are in the center of this dish. Decorative Duchess Potatoes (Vegetables, pg. 3) and diced carrots garnish the veal and provide an attractive color contrast.

reduce heat to low. Add the stock and simmer for 2 minutes, then turn the veal. Add the mushrooms mixture and simmer for 2 minutes longer. Lift the veal and let drain over the skillet. Place in a serving dish and keep warm. Increase the heat under the skillet and cook the mushroom mixture until slightly thickened. Season with salt, then pour the sauce around the veal. Garnish with diced, cooked carrots and Duchess potatoes (Vegetables, pg. 3). This makes 8 servings.

veal rolls

Veal rolls or *Paupiettes* are very thin slices of meat stuffed with ground or finely minced meat and rolled up before cooking. The French term *Paupiette* actually means "big cork," which these rolls resemble when cooked.

These veal rolls are filled with a mixture of minced veal, ham, garlic and herbs. For cooking, each roll is secured with string. To make them exceptionally delicious, they are served in a mixture of puréed vegetables, flavored with dry white wine and beef broth.

VEAL ROLLS IN SAUCE (PAUPIETTES)

4 veal scallops or cutlets
1/2 lb. ham, finely diced
1 clove of garlic, pressed
1/2 tsp. marjoram
1/2 tsp. rosemary
Salt and pepper to taste
Butter
1 tbsp. olive oil
1 lg. carrot, finely chopped
1 lg. onion, finely chopped
1/2 c. dry white wine
1/2 c. beef broth
1/2 tsp. thyme
1 bay leaf
4 parsley stalks
1 tbsp. all-purpose flour

Pound the scallops as instructed on page 20 and trim into uniform rectangles. Mince the scallop trimmings. Combine the trimmings, ham, garlic, marjoram, rosemary, salt and pepper, then spread evenly over the scallops. Roll the scallops as for jelly roll and tie with string or secure with skewers. Melt 4 tablespoons of butter with the oil in a frypan. Add the carrot and onion, then cook until golden, stirring frequently. Stir in the wine and the broth, then add the thyme, bay leaf, parsley stalks, salt and pepper. Stir to mix well, then pour into a baking dish. Place the veal rolls in the sauce, then cover. Bake in a preheated 350-degree oven, one shelf below center, for 1 hour and 30 minutes. Remove the casserole from the oven and lift out the veal rolls to a serving dish. Remove the string and keep the veal rolls warm. Remove the bay leaf and parsley stalks from the sauce, then pour the sauce into the blender container. Process the sauce until puréed. Melt 1 tablespoon of butter in a saucepan, then stir in the flour to make a smooth paste. Pour in the sauce, stirring constantly, and bring to a boil. Reduce the heat and simmer until the sauce thickens. Pour over the veal rolls and garnish with finely chopped parsley. Serve with boiled new potatoes or rice. This makes 4 servings.

veal rolls in sauce

These flavorful veal rolls, frequently called Paupiettes, are highly seasoned and placed in a sauce made with cooked, puréed vegetables, stock and dry white wine. The dish is sprinkled with fresh, green parsley and bordered with new potatoes.

beef wellington

It is a mystery who first baked a fillet of beef in pastry; the Irish, English or the French, but it is certainly no mystery why this dish has remained popular throughout the years. The delectable combination of tender beef and crusty pastry is a festive dish for any occasion.

Marinating the beef a day before cooking in Burgundy, olive oil, parsley stalks, tarragon, thyme and bay leaf will give it a very desirable flavor. French Lining Pastry is used in this recipe for Beef Wellington though puff pastry is used in some recipes. You will find French Lining Pastry practical in several ways; it is more easily prepared, it holds its shape well and is equally delicious with meats.

Always pay close attention to cooking instructions so that the beef will be cooked to desired doneness. There are two cooking times given — one for a medium rare, pink beef and a 10 minute longer period for medium done.

BEEF WELLINGTON

1 2-lb. beef fillet
1 recipe Marinade for Beef *(Sauces, pg. 5)*
1 recipe French Lining Pastry *(Pork, pg. 7)*
¼ lb. fresh mushrooms, sliced
1 recipe Anglais Glaze *(Breads, pg. 6)*

Trim any gristle and surplus fat from the fillet, then place in a medium-sized mixing bowl. Pour the marinade over the fillet and cover the bowl with plastic wrap. Marinate the fillet for about 4 hours, turning occasionally. Remove the fillet from the marinade and drain well. Roll out the pastry on a well-floured board to ⅛-inch thickness. Cut into a rectangle wide enough to overlap the fillet by 1½ inches and long enough to cover the ends well. Place the pastry rectangle carefully over a shallow baking dish. Arrange half the mushrooms lengthwise down the center of the pastry, then place the fillet over the mushrooms. Arrange the remaining mushrooms over the fillet. Wrap, glaze, then decorate the fillet for baking according to the step-by-step instructions. Bake in a preheated 400-degree oven for about 40 minutes for a medium rare fillet or 50 minutes for medium doneness. Serve immediately. This makes 4 to 6 servings.

WRAPPING FILLET OF BEEF

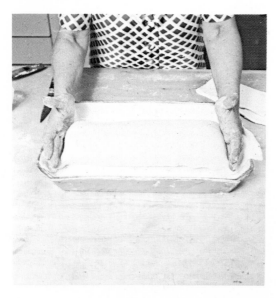

1 Lift one long side of the pastry over the fillet and brush the edge with cold water. Lift the opposite side over the top of the pastry and press gently to seal.

2 Wet the short ends and press together, sealing well. Trim off the excess pastry.

3 Brush the pastry wrapped fillet with *Anglais* Glaze.

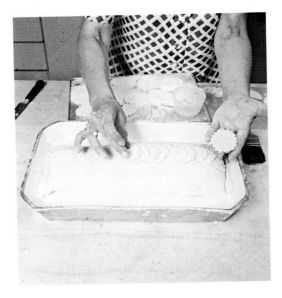

4 Cut the pastry trimmings into decorative rounds, crescents or into 3/8-inch strips for braiding (Breads, pg. 9). Place over the seam on the top of the pastry. Brush the trim with glaze. Any unused trim may be glazed and baked separately until golden brown.

beef wellington

Golden pastry envelopes a juicy fillet of beef, highly flavored with Burgundy, mushrooms and herbs. Each serving will slice beautifully and combine the flavors of juicy beef, mushrooms and flaky pastry. Garnish this creation with bits of pastry cut in small, decorative shapes.

broiled sirloin in sauce

This recipe for steak combines the delicious flavors of thick juicy sirloin steak with a rich sauce made with beef stock, mushrooms and Marsala wine. For an added attraction, garnish this beef creation with canelled lemon slices (General Information, pg. 11).

steak in savory marsala sauce

These broiled sirloin steaks are in a savory sauce made with Marsala wine, Basic Beef Stock (Soups, pg. 2), onion and mushrooms. Garnish this dish with colorful, canelled lemon slices. (Garnishes, General Information, pg. 11).

STEAK IN SAVORY MARSALA SAUCE

1 1½-in. sirloin steak
1 med. onion, grated
3 tbsp. all-purpose flour
1½ c. Basic Beef Stock *(Soups, pg. 2)*
½ c. Marsala wine
½ lb. fresh mushrooms, sliced
Salt and pepper to taste
4 canelled lemon slices *(General Information, pg. 11)*

Trim the steak and slash the fat at 1-inch intervals. Broil the steak about 6 inches from the source of heat for 8 minutes. Turn and broil for 7 minutes longer to achieve medium-rare doneness. Place the steak on a serving platter and keep warm. Pour ¼ cup of the pan juices into a heavy saucepan. Add the onion to the hot juices and sauté for about 4 minutes, stirring frequently. Stir in the flour to make a thick paste, then stir in the stock and Marsala. Cook until thickened and the flavors are blended. Add the mushrooms and seasonings and cook the sauce for 3 minutes longer. Cut the steak diagonally into ½-inch slices. Pour the sauce over the steak and garnish with lemon slices. This makes about 4 servings.

STUFFED BONELESS BEEF ROAST

1 3½-lb. beef brisket
4 slices of bacon, diced
1 c. chopped onions
8 c. stale bread cubes
1 tsp. oregano
¼ c. finely chopped parsley
2 eggs, lightly beaten
Salt and freshly ground pepper to taste

stuffed boneless beef roast

This boneless beef brisket is filled with a rich stuffing made with bread crumbs, herbs, bacon and eggs. The border of grilled tomatoes is a delicious accompaniment to the roasted beef.

Have the butcher cut a large pocket in the brisket. Sauté the bacon for about 3 minutes, then add the onions and cook, stirring frequently, until lightly browned. Combine the bread cubes with the bacon mixture in a large mixing bowl and toss lightly. Add the oregano, parsley and eggs and toss with a fork until well combined. Season with salt and pepper, then sprinkle about 3 tablespoons of water over the stuffing if the mixture seems too dry. Pack the stuffing evenly into the pocket of the brisket. Secure the opening with skewers. Score the top of roast lightly, then sprinkle with pepper and rub into the roast. Place in a lightly greased, shallow baking pan. Cover loosely with aluminum foil. Bake in a preheated 350-degree oven for 1 hour and 45 minutes. Remove the foil and bake for 30 minutes longer. Remove from oven and place on a serving platter, then pour pan juices over the top of the roast, if desired. You may double the recipe for the stuffing and bake additional amount separately, if desired. Serve with Broiled Tomatoes Napoli (Vegetables, pg. 100). This makes 8 to 10 servings.

SCANDINAVIAN BEEF ROLL WITH PEAS

1 recipe Basic Savory Short Pastry *(Desserts, pg. 12)*
1 lb. ground sirloin
¼ lb. fresh mushrooms, chopped
¼ c. grated Spanish onion
1 sm. clove of garlic, pressed
1 tsp. freshly minced parsley
½ c. grated Cheddar cheese
Salt and freshly ground pepper to taste
Egg Wash *(Breads, pg. 6)*
2 c. cooked green peas

Divide the pastry in half. Roll out ½ of the pastry on a lightly floured surface to an 11 x 6-inch rectangle for the base, then roll out the remaining pastry to an 11 x 8-inch rectangle for the top, trimming the rectangle with a sharp knife. Place the pastry base in a jelly roll pan. Place the ground sirloin in a medium-sized mixing bowl. Add the mushrooms, onion, garlic, parsley, cheese, salt and pepper and mix well. Shape into a 9 x 4-inch loaf and place in the center of the pastry base, leaving a 1-inch border. Brush the edge of the pastry with cold water. Cover the meat loaf with the top pastry, pushing the pastry against the meat loaf, then pinch the pastry edges together. Brush the pastry with Egg Wash. Bake in a preheated 350-degree oven for 45 minutes to 1 hour or until golden brown. Remove with 2 wide spatulas to a long platter. Cut in half and push halves to each end of the platter, then place the peas in the center of the platter. Garnish with carrot sticks. This makes about 4 servings.

scandinavian beef roll with peas

We have cut this Scandinavian Beef Roll in half to show its filling made with ground sirloin, mushrooms, Cheddar cheese, onion, garlic and parsley. The pastry covering is flavored with Parmesan cheese. Scandinavian Beef Roll is served here with a mound of sweet, green peas garnished with strips of fresh carrots.

hungarian goulash with rice

The name goulash is derived from a Hungarian word meaning herdsman — and the dish is the herdsman's stew. This goulash is made of delicious beef chunks in a seasoned mixture of onions, tomato purée, beef stock and wine vinegar. For a delectable, hearty meal, serve it over Basic Boiled Rice (Cereals, pg. 3).

HUNGARIAN GOULASH WITH RICE

3 lb. stew beef
¼ c. olive oil
1½ lb. onions, thinly sliced
4 tbsp. paprika
2 tbsp. tomato purée
Salt and freshly ground pepper to taste
Pinch of marjoram
2 tbsp. wine vinegar
1 tsp. caraway seed *(opt.)*
Basic Beef Stock *(Soups, pg. 2)*
1 recipe Basic Boiled Rice *(Cereals, pg. 3)*

Cut the stew beef into large chunks. Heat the olive oil in a large skillet over low heat. Add the onions and cook, stirring frequently, until golden brown. Add the paprika, ¼ cup water and beef and cook, stirring, until the water evaporates. Add the tomato purée, salt, pepper, marjoram, vinegar and caraway seed and mix well. Turn into a large casserole and add enough stock to cover all the ingredients, then cover. Bake in a preheated 325-degree oven for 2 hours and 30 minutes or until the beef is tender, then remove the cover and garnish with chopped parsley. Serve with the rice. This makes about 6 servings.

STEAK AND VEGETABLE STEW

1 1½-lb. boneless round steak
3 tbsp. butter
3 tbsp. vegetable oil
4 green onions, thinly sliced
8 round radishes, thinly sliced
½ c. diced green or red sweet pepper
1½ c. thinly sliced onions
1½ c. thinly sliced cabbage
1 Bouquet Garni (Soups, pg. 2)
Salt and freshly ground pepper to taste

Remove all of the fat from the steak, then cut the steak into small cubes. Melt the butter with the oil in a large skillet over high heat. Add the steak and cook, stirring constantly, until the steak loses red color. Remove from the skillet with a slotted spoon and place in a large casserole. Reduce the heat under the skillet to medium, then add all of the vegetables to the butter mixture remaining in the skillet and cook, stirring constantly, until wilted. Turn into the casserole and add the Bouquet Garni, salt and pepper. Add enough boiling water to cover all ingredients, then cover the casserole. Bake in a preheated 325-degree oven, 1 rack below center, for about 3 hours or until the steak is tender. Remove the Bouquet Garni and skim grease from the top of the casserole. The liquid may be thickened with cornstarch, if desired. Serve with French bread. The stew may be chilled after baking and the fat removed from the top, then reheated. This makes about 6 servings.

steak and vegetable stew

This flavorful stew, filled with steak, fresh vegetables and herbs, makes a nourishing light meal. This simple dish is made complete with the accompanying fresh French bread.

carbonnade flamande

Carbonnade de Boeuf Flamande, or Beef Casserole with Beer is a classic Belgian dish. The Belgians commonly use *lambic* for this recipe. This is a highly intoxicating sour-tasting beer which they feel adds a very distinctive flavor to beef. However, Americans usually substitute a strong-flavored beer or ale.

CARBONNADE DE BOEUF FLAMANDE (BEEF CASSEROLE WITH BEER)

4 c. Basic Beef Stock *(Soups, pg. 2)*
5 lb. lean stew beef
1 ½ c. Basic Seasoned Flour *(Appetizers, pg. 32)*
¼ c. vegetable shortening
1½ c. minced onions
24 sm. whole onions or shallots, peeled
Salt and freshly ground pepper to taste
4 c. strong beer or ale

Pour the stock into a saucepan and boil until reduced to ¾ cup of liquid. Cut the beef into large chunks. Place the seasoned flour in a plastic bag. Add the beef and shake until coated. Remove the beef and reserve the remaining seasoned flour. Melt the shortening in a heavy skillet. Add the beef and cook until brown, stirring with a wooden spoon. Remove the beef from the skillet and set aside. Coat the minced onions with the reserved seasoned flour, then brown in the skillet, adding shortening, if needed. Arrange half of the minced onions in a casserole and cover with half of the beef. Cover the beef layer with the remaining minced onions and top with the remaining beef. Add the whole onions, then season with salt and pepper. Pour the stock and beer over the beef mixture. Bake, covered, in a preheated 350-degree oven, 1 rack below center, for 2 hours or until the beef is tender. Place in a serving dish. Garnish with fresh parsley, if desired. This makes about 8 servings.

carbonnade de boeuf flamande

This is a very hearty casserole made with beef, onions, stock and beer. New potatoes make an excellent vegetable accompaniment.

HUNGARIAN STEAK

Hungarian Sirloin Steak is simply made with sirloin steak and Basic *Velouté* Sauce (Sauces, pg. 4) with chopped mushrooms. This dish is garnished with two previously introduced recipes: crescents of puff pastry cut from Basic Puff Pastry (Desserts, pg. 22); and *Beignet* Potatoes (Vegetables, pg. 99).

HUNGARIAN SIRLOIN STEAK

1 ½ c. Basic Velouté Sauce *(Sauces, pg. 4)*
½ c. butter
1 lg. onion, minced
¾ c. dry white wine
2 tbsp. brandy
¼ lb. fresh mushrooms, finely chopped
½ c. half and half cream
2 tbsp. paprika
Salt and freshly ground pepper to taste
6   8-oz. sirloin steaks

Prepare the *Velouté* sauce. Melt half of the butter in a large skillet. Add the onion and sauté, stirring constantly, until tender. Pour the wine into the onion mixture and simmer until the liquid has almost evaporated. Heat the brandy and pour over the onion mixture. Ignite the brandy and let it burn until the flame dies. Combine the sauce and the mushrooms with the onion mixture. Stir in the cream, paprika, salt and pepper and heat through. Keep warm. Melt the remaining ¼ cup of butter in a separate skillet and cook the steaks in the butter to desired doneness. Arrange the steaks on a heated serving platter and pour the sauce over the steaks. Garnish with crescents made from Basic Puff Pastry trimmings (Desserts, pg. 22) and *Beignet* Potatoes (Vegetables, pg. 99). This makes 6 servings.

DANISH MEAT PATTIES

1 lb. lean ground beef
1 med. onion, coarsely chopped
2 tbsp. all-purpose flour
¼ c. club soda
1 egg, beaten
1 tsp. salt
½ tsp. freshly ground pepper
2 tbsp. vegetable oil
2 lb. small new potatoes
2 tbsp. melted butter
3 tbsp. chopped chives

Combine the ground beef and onion in a large bowl, blending well. Stir in the flour, club soda, egg and seasonings. Chill for 1 hour. Shape into six 4 x 2 x 1-inch thick oval patties, then dredge with additional flour. Heat the oil in a large skillet. Add the patties and cook over moderate heat until browned and cooked through, turning once. Drain well on paper toweling and keep warm. Cook the potatoes in boiling, salted water until tender while the patties are cooking. Drain the potatoes, then remove the skins. Arrange the patties and potatoes on a heated serving platter, then pour the melted butter over the potatoes and sprinkle with chives. Serve with Tomato Fondue Sauce (Sauces, pg. 15) or sour cream, if desired. This makes 6 servings.

danish meat patties

Danish Meat Patties should be made with a good quality of lean ground beef. The unusual ingredient in this recipe is club soda. New potatoes, sprinkled with chives, are particularly delicious served with these meat patties. A sauce or sour cream may be served with the patties.

BEEF FONDUE

1 ¾ c. Basic Blender Mayonnaise (*Sauces, pg. 3*)
1 ¼ c. pickle relish
1 tbsp. minced capers
1 c. minced onions
1 c. Basic Mustard Sauce (*Sauces, pg. 12*)
1 c. minced black olives
1 c. Tomato Coulis Sauce (*Sauces, pg. 14*)
1 2-lb. beef tenderloin, cut into cubes
Peanut oil
Salt and freshly ground pepper to taste

Combine ¾ cup of the mayonnaise, ¼ cup of the pickle relish and the capers and place the mixture in a small serving bowl. Place the onions, mustard sauce, olives, remaining mayonnaise, remaining relish and Tomato Coulis Sauce in matching serving bowls. Place the beef on a platter and place on the table as shown in the illustration. Place the onion, the mustard sauce, olives, relish mayonnaise, mayonnaise, pickle relish and Tomato Coulis Sauce around the platter. Fill a fondue pot ¾ full with oil and place over high heat on the stove until hot. Place over the fondue burner. Spear the beef cubes with fondue forks and cook in the hot oil until of desired doneness. Season with salt and pepper, then eat with the desired accompaniments. This makes 6 servings.

beef fondue

Beef Fondue is as easy to prepare as it is delicious. Appropriate accompaniments pictured here are finely chopped raw onion, Basic Mustard Sauce (Sauces, pg. 12), finely chopped black olives, Basic Blender Mayonnaise (Sauces, pg. 3) with pickle relish and finely minced capers and Tomato Coulis Sauce (Sauces, pg. 14).

CORNISH BEEF PASTIES

1 recipe Basic Savory Short Pastry *(Desserts, pg. 12)*
1 c. finely diced potatoes
1 c. finely diced rutabaga
½ lb. ground round steak
¼ c. minced onion
Salt and freshly ground pepper to taste
1 egg, slightly beaten

Roll out the pastry on a lightly floured surface to ⅛-inch thickness, then cut six 6-inch circles from the pastry, marking the center of each circle lightly. Cook the potatoes and rutabaga in boiling, salted water in separate saucepans until crisp-tender, then drain. Combine the potatoes and rutabaga and spread ⅙ of the mixture over half of each circle, leaving a ½-inch edge to seal. Combine the steak, onion, salt and pepper and mix well. Spread ⅙ of the steak mixture evenly over the potato mixture on each circle. Moisten the edge of each circle of pastry with cold water, then bring the unfilled pastry half over the filled half. Pinch the edges of the pasties together very firmly, then place the pasties on a greased baking sheet, sealed edges up. Brush the tops of the pasties with the egg. Bake in a preheated 400-degree oven for 10 minutes, then reduce the oven temperature to 350 degrees and bake for about 25 minutes longer or until well browned. Serve with Basic Peperonata Sauce (Sauces, pg. 12) or Basic Dill Sauce (Sauces, pg. 28). This makes 6 large pasties.

cornish beef pasties

Savory short pastry envelopes a delicious mixture of ground steak, diced potatoes and rutabagas to make these delicious individual meat pies.

pork

table of contents

the art of
cooking pork

Pork has long been traditional in Western eating habits. A common centerpiece at medieval feasts was a roasted wild boar with an apple in its mouth, surrounded by mountains of vegetables.

Americans have taken this heritage of pork cooking and improved upon it, as you'll soon see. In this section you will learn how to prepare succulent roasts and mouth-watering baked hams that will make your menu more interesting and delicious.

Rotisserie cooking—a modern refinement of ancient spit cooking—is a popular treatment for pork. Using this method you'll learn how to cook a roast to perfection and save time for other activities. In addition, there are ideas for combining meat with other ingredients for savory ham and pork pies, all with easy how-to-do-it instructions and pictures that show how the finished dishes look.

Nutritious pork is noted for its high vitamin B content, including more thiamine (an essential for normal functioning of the nervous system) than any other food source. Pork protein is high quality, and the meat, when properly cooked, is quite digestible.

On the following pages you will find information on the types of cuts available, some cooking tips for perfect pork every time, and the most effective way for scoring a roast.

TO MARKET, TO MARKET . . .

Let's make a trip to the supermarket to learn a few things about pork products usually carried there. You will find pork available in both fresh and cured forms. In times past the cured form was necessary due to lack of refrigerated transportation. We now can enjoy fresh pork at any time of the year. Cured products are also available at all times due to the popularity of their tastes.

In preparing fresh pork, the meat is dressed and chilled at the packing plant, then divided into the various market cuts. (The trimmed-off fat is used to make lard and other types of shortenings.)

Because of the tangy flavor that curing and smoking impart, the demand for pork processed by these methods is high. First the meat is cured with brine; for limited amounts of pork, notably some picnics and hams, this is the end of the processing. However, the majority of the cured cuts are then smoked. Some of these, such as bacon, need additional cooking after purchase; others are ready to eat, as with fully cooked or canned hams.

. . . TO BUY A FAT PIG

Thanks to modern breeding techniques, the old description, "fat as a pig," is outdated. Hogs are now bred for leanness, and packers trim the meat more closely, making pork more suitable for healthful weight control.

Don't let the vast array of pork cuts lining the meat shelves cause you to give up in dismay and settle for pot-luck. First, learn a little anatomy. By familiarizing yourself with the portions of the hog from which the different cuts come, you will become proficient at identifying at least the more common cuts.

Starting at the front of the animal, shoulder cuts include the Boston shoulder or Boston butt and blade steaks or pork cutlets; picnic shoulders or callie hams (incorrectly called picnic *hams*) are from the upper part of the front legs. From the loin area on the back come the blade loin, rib (for crown roasts and rib chops), center loin and sirloin cuts, as well as Canadian bacon. The lower side produces spareribs, salt side and bacon. The hind legs yield cured and smoked hams and pork leg roasts, also called fresh hams.

In contrast with other meats, there are no pork grades to identify quality to consumers. The reasons are that most commercial hogs are butchered at about the same age, $5\frac{1}{2}$ to $6\frac{1}{2}$ months, and there is little difference in overall quality due to age. Some packers, particularly those selling smoked pork products, indicate the quality of the

cuts through different brand names. However, all the pork found on the meat counter has been inspected.

You will find that cuts from the back are more tender than those from the neck and legs. But in selecting cuts for their tenderness, keep in mind that tender cuts are not necessarily more nutritious.

Appearance should be considered when buying fresh pork. Look for a firm white layer of external fat — one of the reasons for pork's delicious flavor — and grayish pink or pale rose-colored meat. It should be firm and fine-grained. Cured ham is better if water has *not* been added. However, if it has been, the label will be marked "water added."

While we're here in the supermarket, let's talk about quantity — how much to buy per serving. In buying trimmed meats, allow $\frac{1}{4}$ to $\frac{1}{3}$ lb. per serving of boneless cuts such as boned roast. For meat with some bone — hams, chops, etc. — buy $\frac{1}{3}$ to $\frac{1}{2}$ lb. per serving. For bony cuts such as ribs, allow $\frac{3}{4}$ to 1 lb.

HOME AGAIN, HOME AGAIN . . .

When you store the meat, keep in mind that pork does not keep as long as some other meat products — beef, for example. Cured pork will keep in the coldest part of the refrigerator up to a week; salt pork keeps 2-3 weeks. Bacon may be frozen for up to 3 weeks, while cured ham will keep in your home freezer for 1-2 months. Do not keep them frozen longer, as the salt used in curing may cause the fat to become rancid. Canned cured pork may be stored in the refrigerator for as long as a year.

The transparent wrap used on packaged meats in the supermarket is designed for both refrigerator and freezer storage for short periods. To store fresh pork wrapped in butchers' paper, loosen the wrapper and place the meat in the coldest part of the refrigerator. Chops and spareribs keep 3 days; roasts, 3-4 days. To freeze fresh pork, be sure it is wrapped in moisture and vapor-proof paper. Do not salt the meat before freezing. Uncooked cuts keep 2-3 weeks in the freezer compartment of your refrigerator and 2-4 months in your home freezer. Cooked cuts will keep 2-3 months in the home freezer.

When defrosting the meat, it is best to thaw it in the refrigerator overnight. If you are in a hurry, place it in a watertight wrapper in cold water or in a closed, double paper bag at room temperature. You may also cook it while it is frozen, although the cooking time will be increased by about half.

The most important thing to remember in cooking pork is that it must be well done. However, overcooking reduces juiciness. We want to stress that the best way to ensure doneness is by using a meat thermometer. When the meat is done, it should register 190 degrees for fresh pork leg and shoulder cuts, and 160 degrees for cured hams and Canadian bacon. Fully cooked cured ham need only be cooked to 140 degrees. If you don't have a thermometer, follow your recipe for cooking time and pierce the meat with a cooking fork; when the juice runs clear, the meat is done.

. . . JIGGETY JIG

Now let's get right into the subject of preparing pork. You'll soon be cooking it like a professional, scoring it as if you'd been doing it all your life and serving a variety of pork cuts in dozens of delicious ways.

baked crusted ham

Here is tempting Baked Crusted Ham on a platter garnished with garden-fresh vegetables — sliced cucumber crescents, watercress and endive. Green-tinted, raw turnip flowers (General Information, pg. 18) and bay leaves adorn the crust to make this a special occasion dish. For family occasions it may be served ungarnished, accompanied by Périgord Potatoes (Vegetables, pg. 16), pictured here fresh from the oven.

BAKED CRUSTED HAM

1 8 to 10-lb. smoked ham butt
5 c. apple cider
5 c. cold water
8 peppercorns
1¼ c. (packed) dark brown sugar
2 tbsp. molasses
1 6-oz. package blanched almonds, ground
⅓ c. Basic Hot Huntington Sauce, *(Sauces, pg. 10)*
Grated rind and juice of 1 orange
All-purpose flour

Place ham in a large kettle. Pour in the cider and water, then add the peppercorns. Cover and bring to a boil. Cook at a medium boil for 2 hours or until tender. Remove ham from broth and continue boiling broth for about 30 minutes or until reduced to 5 cups liquid. Trim skin and fat evenly from ham and place ham in a baking dish. Place brown sugar in small mixing bowl; stir in the molasses, almonds, sauce and orange rind and juice. Blend in enough flour to make a thick paste. Spread the paste mixture over the top of the ham. Spoon excess fat from ham broth, then pour 1 cup broth around the ham in the baking dish. Bake in preheated 400-degree oven for 45 minutes or until thoroughly browned. Place on serving platter and let stand for 20 minutes. Score top of ham as shown in our illustration and garnish as desired.

scoring pork roasts

A successful pork roast, when sliced, will reveal juicy, succulent lean meat surrounded by a crisp — though never dry — thin layer of fat. Your reputation as a successful cook will soar with a well-cooked pork roast.

A good pork roast needs proper scoring, a technique which allows the fat of the outer layer to pour out into the pan while sealing in the juices of the lean meat.

When you buy the pork roast, don't let the butcher score it for you. Those shallow little cuts he makes will never do! It's easy to score your own roast. We suggest you do it with a handyman's tool — the Stanley knife. A Stanley knife consists of a large, easy-to-hold handle and a sharp, triangular, replaceable blade. Make the cuts 1/4 inch apart and deep enough to cut through the outer skin and fat.

SCORED FRESH PORK ROAST

1 5-lb. fresh pork roast
Salt and freshly ground pepper

Score the roast using a Stanley knife according to our step-by-step illustrations. Sprinkle the roast generously with salt and pepper, then place in a shallow baking dish. Insert a meat thermometer into the center of the roast without touching the bone. Bake in a preheated 350-degree oven for about 3 hours or until thermometer reaches 190 degrees. Remove roast from oven and let stand for several minutes before carving.

1 This is what the majority of butchers call scoring — cuts too shallow and too far apart. The fat has been removed from the roast in these pictures for clarity of detail.

2 Here is how pork should be scored, with cuts 1/4 inch apart and deep enough to slice through the skin into the underfat. Note the use of our favorite unorthodox kitchen implement, the Stanley knife, a real cook's treasure for scoring meats.

scored fresh pork roast

The key to preparing a pork roast which draws raves is to score it properly, being careful not to cut into the lean meat and cook until it is well done. Use the drippings for gravy. The pork roast is served here with oven-browned potatoes.

The Creative Homemaker's Academy © MCMLXXIII
Selected Illustrations © B.P.C. Publishing Limited MCMLXX

ham with cumberland sauce

The Ham with Cumberland Sauce, pictured on this page, keynotes a meal plan suitable for the most elegant of dinner parties or turns a family meal into a special occasion.

Build your menu beginning with an avocado salad featuring Basic Vinaigrette (Sauces, pg. 2). To this, add elegant Risotto (Cereals, pg. 2) and delicately steamed French-Style Green Beans (Vegetables, pg. 19). They provide complementary taste, texture and color to the entrée.

End your meal with the light, easy-to-prepare Ice Cream-Filled Party Cake (Desserts, pg. 44), and sit back to enjoy the praise. You'll command respect for your culinary flair with dishes that please the eye as well as the palate.

MENU

Avocado Salad Vinaigrette
(Salads, pg. 15)

Ham with Cumberland Sauce
(Pork, pg. 5)

Risotto
(Pasta and Cereals, pg. 2)

French-Style Green Beans
(Vegetables, pg. 19)

Ice Cream-Filled Party Cake
(Desserts, pg. 44)

HAM WITH CUMBERLAND SAUCE

1 No. 2 can apricot halves
1 recipe Basic Cumberland Sauce (Sauces, pg. 10)
1 6-lb. smoked ham

Drain apricot halves and place in Basic Cumberland Sauce in small bowl. Cover with plastic wrap and let stand in refrigerator for 48 hours. Insert a meat thermometer into the center of the ham without touching the bone. Place ham in a shallow baking dish. Bake in a 350-degree oven for about 2 hours or until thermometer reaches 160 degrees. Remove meat thermometer, then trim off rind and excess fat. Place the ham on a serving platter. Arrange the apricots around the ham, then pour the Cumberland sauce over the ham and apricots.

ham with cumberland sauce

Pork lends itself to the accent of other flavors such as sweet and sour sauces. The flavor of this ham is complemented by the tangy addition of Basic Cumberland Sauce (Sauces, pg. 10), a combination of citrus fruits, currant jelly and wine. And the ham looks as good as it tastes, garnished with fine strips of orange peel from the sauce. The halved apricots — fresh if possible — were soaked in the Cumberland sauce for 48 hours to give the entire dish a delightful citrus-y flavor.

rotisserie barbecued pork roast

DISTINCTIVE . . ? SUCCULENT . . ?

The special taste that rotisserie cooking imparts can hardly be described adequately unless you've tasted it. It suffices to say that the flavor of rotisserie cooking is more popular today — both outdoors over coals and indoors with an electric rotisserie — than it has been since cavemen tediously turned their game over a campfire.

A separate rotisserie is especially convenient when you are preparing other foods in your oven and time is important. Rotisserie cooking does not require constant attention. The heated metal spit helps distribute the heat from the inside of the meat, while the constant rotation of the meat over, under or in front of the heat ensures even cooking and self-basting from the outside layer of fat. And, since the spit turns automatically, this method of cooking leaves you free to do other things.

Pork is an excellent choice for rotisserie cooking. You will find this method enhances its natural good flavor. Just be sure to cook it well done — even the most obsessive of underdone meat eaters won't fancy pink-in-the-middle pork roast.

rotisserie-barbecued pork roast

Our succulent pork roast was basted during the last 15 minutes with Hot Sweet and Sour Barbecue Sauce (Sauces, pg. 8). However, the natural flavor that rotisserie cooking imparts makes serving the roast just as it is a delicious alternative. This cut was machine netted at the supermarket, but you may also buy them hand-tied with string. The roast is held on a spit with the heat behind it and a trough underneath to catch the natural juices. You may skim the fat off and serve the pan juices over the sliced meat.

ROTISSERIE-BARBECUED PORK ROAST

1 6-lb. boned pork loin roast
Salt and freshly ground pepper to taste
1 recipe Hot Sweet and Sour Barbecue Sauce
    (Sauces, pg. 8)

Balance roast on spit and secure for rotisserie roasting. Rub seasonings into roast; insert meat thermometer in thick part of roast without touching metal spit. Cook according to manufacturer's directions until pork is well done and thermometer reaches 170 degrees, basting with barbecue sauce during last 15 minutes of cooking time. Remove from spit and serve with remaining Hot Sweet and Sour Barbecue Sauce, if desired.

pork pie

Pork combines extremely well with other flavors, as you will discover in the assembly of pork combination recipes prepared for you — pork with apple cider, rosemary, eggs, vegetables and cheese, all equally delicious. Also, a French Lining Pastry, especially suitable for meat pies, is introduced here.

PORK PIE

3 lb. ground lean pork
2 c. diced onions
4 cooking apples, peeled and diced
2 tsp. mace
2 tsp. salt
1 tsp. freshly ground pepper
2 eggs, beaten
2 c. fine fresh bread crumbs
1 recipe French Lining Pastry
3 hard-boiled eggs, halved
1 recipe *Anglais* Glaze *(Breads, pg. 6)*

Place pork in a Dutch oven. Cook over medium heat, stirring constantly until fat is rendered. Drain off fat. Stir in onions, apples, mace, salt and pepper. Stir in eggs and bread crumbs; mix well. Roll out pastry, ¼ inch thick, on floured surface. Line 10 x 4-inch loaf pan with removable sides or 9-inch springform pan with the pastry; seal edges together to prevent leaking. Place in jelly roll pan. Pack half the pork mixture in pan; arrange egg halves, cut side down, on pork mixture. Pack in remaining pork mixture. Moisten rim of pastry with cold water; fit on top pastry. Pinch edges together. Roll out pastry trimmings. Cut part of the trimmings into 1-inch wide strips to fit around edge of pie; make diagonal cuts at 1-inch intervals, not cutting all the way through strips. Moisten edge of pastry in pan with water; place strips around edge. Cut remaining trimmings into a 2-inch strip about 6 inches long; cut fringe as shown in our step-by-step illustrations. Brush uncut part of strip with *Anglais* Glaze and roll up to form a tassel. Cut a hole in center of top pastry; insert tassel. Brush top and tassel with *Anglais* Glaze. Bake in preheated 400-degree oven for 15 minutes. Reduce oven temperature to 350 degrees; bake for 1 hour longer. Let cool slightly. Place on serving dish; remove sides of pan. May serve with Basic Peperonata Sauce, if desired (Sauces, pg. 12).

FRENCH LINING PASTRY

4 c. all-purpose flour
1¼ c. butter
1 egg
1 tsp. salt
¾ c. cold water

Sift flour into a mound on working surface and hollow out a well in the center with your fingertips. Place butter, egg, salt and half the water in center of ring; work up the center mixture with 2 table knives or pastry scrapers with cutting motion. Work in flour carefully from inside of ring, adding more water as needed. Mix until all flour is added and dough holds together. Gather dough into a ball. Wrap securely and refrigerate for at least 1 hour. This pastry will keep for 1 week.

pork pie

We are serving a tasty pork pie on a long platter garnished with two skewers of decoratively cut tomatoes. The plate in front holds the ingredients used in making the pie. The sturdiness of the French Lining Pastry (especially fine for meat pies) and the juiciness of the interior produces a superb dish.

pork
pie

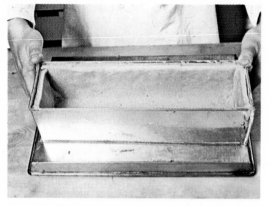

1 So that you can remove the finished pie from the pan, you'll need a springform loaf pan (ours is 10 x 4 x 4 inches) which comes in two sections locking together with pins. Line the pastry around the sides and bottom. Place the pan on a baking sheet. Reserve all the pastry trimmings.

2 Shown here is half the filling layered into the pan, with the halved hard-boiled eggs on top.

3 Add remaining filling to within ½ inch of rim and pack firmly. Press the pastry edges down over the meat mixture and brush them lightly with cold water. The pastry top in the foreground which has been cut to 10 x 4 inches from part of the rerolled pastry trimmings, should now be placed over the top. Pinch the edges together with thumb and forefinger to seal.

4 To make the pastry tassel, cut a 2-inch wide by 6-inch long strip of fairly thinly rolled pastry and "fringe" it with approximately 1½-inch deep cuts, spreading slightly as in the photo. Brush the uncut side of the pastry strip with *Anglais* Glaze (Breads, pg. 6), using a 1½-inch paint brush.

5 Now roll the pastry strip to make the tassel. Brush top of pie with *Anglais* Glaze and cut a hole in the center as the recipe directs.

6 Place the tassel over the hole in the center to conceal it. Give the entire dish a final light brushing with *Anglais* Glaze and bake as the recipe instructs.

pork casserole with cider

This savory pork casserole gets its delicious flavor from the blend of rosemary and apple cider with the pork. Use fresh rosemary if at all possible or use the dried leaf rosemary.

PORK CASSEROLE WITH CIDER

3 lb. lean cubed pork
3/4 c. all-purpose flour
1/2 c. cooking oil
3 c. apple cider
6 sm. carrots, sliced
3 leeks or 1 medium-sized onion, chopped
3/4 tsp. rosemary
2 tsp. salt
1 tsp. freshly ground pepper

Dredge pork with flour. Heat oil in a large frying pan until sizzling. Add pork and cook until browned, stirring occasionally. Remove pork with a slotted spoon and place in casserole. Drain excess oil from frying pan, then pour the cider into frying pan. Heat cider, stirring to remove browned particles from bottom of pan. Add carrots, leeks and rosemary to pork, then stir in hot cider. Season with salt and pepper. Cover. Bake in preheated 325-degree oven for 2 hours or until pork is tender.

ham & herb pie

HAM AND HERB PIE

**1 recipe Basic Savory Short Pastry
(Desserts, pg. 12)**
³/₄ c. finely diced cooked ham
2 eggs
1¹/₄ c. milk
2 tsp. onion juice
¹/₈ tsp. white pepper
¹/₂ tsp. salt
¹/₂ c. freshly grated Parmesan cheese
1 tsp. finely chopped chives
1 tsp. finely chopped parsley
¹/₈ tsp. dried tarragon leaves
Pinch of thyme leaves

Roll out ¹/₄ of the pastry ¹/₈ inch thick on a floured surface, then fit into 9-inch flan pan. Trim off excess pastry with rolling pin. Prick bottom of pastry lightly with fork but not quite all the way through. Refrigerate remaining pastry for future use. Spread ham evenly over pastry. Combine the eggs and milk in medium mixing bowl and beat with a fork until well mixed. Add remaining ingredients and

ham and herb pie

We have garnished this eye-appealing dish with a Gruyère cheese "rose," using oiled, dried bay leaves for the base and paper-thin slices of cheese cut into petals for the flower. Start at the center and press one or two tiny cheese petals together for the bud and work outward, placing inside a circle made with the bay leaves.

beat until combined. Pour carefully over ham. Place flan pan on a cookie sheet. Bake in a preheated 400-degree oven for 5 minutes. Reduce oven temperature to 325 degrees and bake for 1 hour longer or until center is set. Cool on rack for 15 minutes then remove flan ring. If desired, garnish with cheese rose. To make the cheese rose, use thin slices of Gruyère cheese, trimmed round into a petal shape. Start building rose by putting 2 petals together to make a bud, then add petals until you achieve the rose effect. Arrange oiled bay leaves on pie, then place cheese rose on leaves for desired effect. This will make about 4 servings.

LIME SPARERIBS

4 lb. spareribs
1 c. chopped onions
1 clove of garlic, pressed
1 c. sliced fresh mushrooms
¼ c. olive oil
2 tbsp. red wine vinegar
2 tbsp. honey
¼ c. lime juice
1 tbsp. prepared mustard
2 tsp. salt
Freshly ground pepper to taste
¼ c. soy sauce
⅔ c. water
½ c. chili sauce

Cut the spareribs into serving pieces and place in a baking pan. Sauté the onions, garlic, and mushrooms in the oil in a saucepan until tender. Add the vinegar, honey, lime juice, mustard, salt, pepper, soy sauce, water and chili sauce and mix thoroughly. Pour the sauce over the spareribs. Bake in a preheated 325-degree oven for 1 hour or until the spareribs are tender, basting frequently with sauce in the pan. This makes 8 servings.

sweet and sour pork and lime spareribs

Sweet and Sour Pork and Lime Spareribs give an oriental touch to a menu. In the foreground are pork spareribs with mushrooms in a tangy lime sauce, and behind it, pork cubes in rich sweet and sour sauce.

SWEET AND SOUR PORK

1½ lb. lean pork, cut in 1-in. cubes
3 tbsp. dry white wine
3 tbsp. soy sauce
2 med. carrots
1 lg. red sweet pepper
4 tbsp. olive oil
1 slice gingerroot, minced
1 med. onion, chopped
¼ lb. fresh mushrooms, sliced
½ c. beef broth
Salt to taste
1 recipe Basic Chinese Sweet And Sour Sauce *(Sauces, pg. 31)*

Place the pork in a shallow dish. Combine the wine and soy sauce and pour over the pork, turning to coat all sides. Marinate for at least 15 minutes, stirring frequently. Cut the carrots into *julienne* strips, (General Information, pg. 32). Remove the seeds from the sweet pepper and cut the pepper into thin rings. Heat 2 tablespoons of the oil in a wok or deep skillet over medium heat and stir in the gingerroot. Add the pork and stir-fry according to the illustrations (Beef, pg. 18) for about 5 minutes. Remove the pork and set aside. Add the remaining oil to the wok. Add the carrots, sweet pepper, onion and mushrooms and stir-fry for about 5 minutes or until the carrots and sweet pepper are crisp-tender. Add the pork and stir-fry for about 5 minutes longer. Add the broth and salt and mix well. Stir in the sweet and sour sauce and bring to a boil. Reduce the heat to low and cover the wok. Cook for 2 minutes longer. Serve with rice and fried slivers of heart of palm, if desired. This makes 4 servings.

CHINESE SPARERIBS WITH GLAZED FRESH PEPPERS

4 lb. spareribs
Salt
1 pineapple
2/3 c. (packed) brown sugar
3 tbsp. cornstarch
1 tsp. dry mustard
1 tsp. ginger
2 c. fresh orange juice
1/3 c. fresh lemon juice
1/3 c. soy sauce
2 tbsp. butter
1/2 lb. small fresh mushrooms
1/2 c. chopped fresh onion
1 green sweet pepper, cut into squares
1 red sweet pepper, cut into squares

Cut the spareribs into serving pieces. Place the spareribs, bone side down, in a shallow baking pan and sprinkle with salt to taste. Bake in a preheated 350-degree oven for 1 hour, then drain off the excess fat. Pare the pineapple. Cut the pineapple in half lengthwise and remove the core. Cut the pineapple into cubes. Combine the brown sugar, 1/2 teaspoon salt, cornstarch, mustard and ginger in a medium-sized saucepan and stir in the orange and lemon juices and soy sauce. Bring to a boil and cook until thickened, stirring constantly, then remove from the heat. Melt the butter in a skillet. Add the mushrooms and sauté for 5 minutes, stirring frequently. Pour the sauce over the spareribs, then add the onion, green and red peppers, pineapple and mushrooms. Bake for 30 minutes longer, basting occasionally with sauce in the pan. This makes 4 to 6 servings.

ORIENTAL MENU

CLAM SOUP
(Soups, pg. 53)

EGG ROLLS
(Appetizers, pg. 53)

*SWEET AND SOUR PORK
(Pork, pg. 11)

RAJAHMUNDRY RICE
(Cereals, pg. 22)

FAR EASTERN FRESH POLE BEANS
(Vegetables, pg. 79)

POACHED EMPRESS PEACHES
(Desserts, pg. 155)

JAPANESE TEA
(Beverages, pg. 36)

chinese spareribs with glazed fresh peppers

This dish is high in color as well as flavor. Fresh mushrooms and pineapple are combined in a delicious sweet and sour sauce which covers the spareribs.

PORK FILLETS IN PUFF PASTRY

2   8-in. long pork fillets
1/2 c. finely minced green onions
3/4 c. apple cider or juice
2 tbsp. olive oil
1/2 tsp. salt
1/4 lb. fresh mushrooms, sliced
1/2 tsp. crushed thyme
1 lg. stalk celery, minced
12 peppercorns
5 parsley sprigs
1 recipe Basic Puff Pastry (Desserts, pg. 22)
1 egg white, slightly beaten
1 c. chicken broth
Freshly minced parsley to taste

Place the pork in a shallow glass dish. Combine the green onions, cider, oil, salt, mushrooms, thyme, celery, peppercorns and parsley sprigs, blending thoroughly, then pour over the pork fillets. Marinate for at least 12 hours, turning the fillets occasionally, then remove fillets from the marinade and drain well. Remove the mushrooms from the marinade with a slotted spoon and drain thoroughly. Reserve the marinade. Roll out the pastry on a floured surface to a 1/4-inch thick rectangle, then trim to 20 x 16 inches. Place the mushrooms down the center of the length of the pastry the width of the 2 fillets to within 4 inches of each end, then place the fillets side by side over the mushrooms. Cut triangular notches from the corners of the pastry and dampen all the edges of the pastry with water. Bring the ends of the pastry over the pork, overlapping 2 inches, then bring the sides of the pastry over the pork loosely, sealing all of the edges securely. Place the pastry-covered pork, seam side down, on a jelly roll pan. Decorate the top with pastry trimmings, if desired. Bake in preheated 350-degree oven for 1 hour and 45 minutes. Remove from the oven and brush the crust generously with the egg white. Bake for 5 minutes longer or until the crust is golden. Remove from the oven and let stand for 5 to 10 minutes. Pour the reserved marinade into a blender container and process until smooth. Pour into a saucepan and stir in the stock. Bring to a boil, then reduce heat. Simmer for 4 minutes. Place the pork on a platter and sprinkle with the minced parsley. Cut the pork into diagonal slices and serve with the sauce. This makes about 6 servings.

pork fillets in puff pastry

These succulent fillets of pork and fresh mushrooms were marinated in a savory cider and oil mixture, then baked in a light casing of puff pastry. Artichoke bottoms, piped with potatoes, border the fillets.

Mustard Ham is another delicious, innovative
to serve a cured ham. A tangy mustard sau
prepared and spread over the baked ha
sprinkling of bread crumbs overall forms a c
golden brown crust. For homemakers in a hur
precooked cured ham or a canned ham ma
used in this rec

mustard ham

After a cured ham (that is, one that has been preserved by salting) is baked, it can be used as the basis for a zesty new pork dish, Mustard Ham. Mustard, egg yolks, and cornstarch are mixed to a smooth batter, and generously spread over the ham. After a final sprinkling of bread crumbs, the ham is slipped into the oven for a few minutes until it turns a beautiful, golden brown. The finished ham has a crisp crust with a mustard tang that accents the ham very well.

BAKED CURED HAM

1   12-lb. uncooked cured ham

Place the ham, fat side up, on a rack in a roasting pan. Insert a meat thermometer in the thickest part of the ham without touching the bone. Bake in a preheated 275 to 300-degree oven for 6 hours or until the meat thermometer registers 160 degrees. This makes 24 servings.

MUSTARD HAM

1 12-lb. Baked Cured Ham
4 tbsp. dry English mustard
1 tbsp. cornstarch
2 egg yolks
2 tbsp. Dijon mustard
Fine dry bread crumbs

1 Assemble all of the ingredients, along with a very sharp knife.

2 Remove the rind from the ham with the knife, then cut off most of the fat evenly. Place the ham in a roasting pan.

3 Mix the dry mustard and cornstarch in a small bowl. Add the egg yolks and Dijon mustard and mix until smooth.

4 Spread the mustard mixture over the ham down to the roasting pan, using a metal spatula.

5 Sprinkle the bread crumbs over the mustard mixture. Bake in a preheated 425-degree oven for about 20 minutes or until browned. This makes 24 servings.

baked cured ham

Although Baked Cured Ham In Brown Sauce looks elegant and expensive, it isn't really extravagant in terms of cost. When soup is made from the leftover ham bone and trimmings, the price of the ham becomes most reasonable.

This is a marvelous dish to serve when entertaining because, once prepared, it can easily be kept warm. The ham may be covered with a foil tent, and left in the oven with the heat reduced to about 200 degrees. The sauce can be poured into the top of a double boiler, covered, and kept hot over low heat. This will leave the hostess free to serve dinner in a leisurely fashion.

BAKED CURED HAM IN BROWN SAUCE

1   6-lb. butt end ham
1 tbsp. dark molasses
1 tbsp. brown sugar
15 whole cloves
6 c. all-purpose flour
2 ¼ c. water
1 recipe Basic Brown Sauce *(Sauces, pg. 5)*

Remove most of the rind from the ham. Rub the ham with the molasses and sprinkle with the brown sugar. Stud the ham fat with cloves. Place the flour in a large mixing bowl and add the water gradually, mixing with a wooden spoon or your hands until a stiff dough is formed. Roll the dough out on a lightly floured surface into a ³/₄-inch thick square large enough to completely cover the ham. Place the ham, fat side up, in the center of the square and moisten the edges of the dough. Bring the edges of the dough up to cover the ham, pressing the moistened edges firmly and trimming off any excess dough. Place the ham on a rimmed baking sheet. Bake in a preheated 350-degree oven for about 3 hours. Cool the ham until able to handle, then break off the flour casing with a hammer. Place the ham on a platter, then cut into thick slices. Spoon the brown sauce over the ham slices before serving. This makes about 12 servings.

baked cured ham in brown sauce

The cook will receive enthusiastic praise when Baked Cured Ham in Brown Sauce is served. Its unusual flavor makes it a memorable dish. Surprisingly, half of a small ham, as shown, will yield servings for twelve people, which is more than its appearance would suggest.

The Creative Homemaker's Academy © MCMLXXIII
Selected Illustrations© B.P.C. Publishing Limited MCMLXX

HAM WITH TOASTED ALMONDS AND PRUNES

½ c. **Basic Hot Huntington Sauce** (*Sauces, pg. 10*)
Grated rind of 1 orange
1   **4-oz. package blanched almonds, ground**
1   **1-lb. box pitted prunes**
1 **can beef broth**
1   **6-lb. buffet ham**
2   **4-oz. packages sliced almonds**

Combine the sauce, orange rind and ground almonds in a small mixing bowl to make a thick paste. Place the prunes in a saucepan and pour in the broth. Bring to a boil, then reduce the heat. Simmer for 20 minutes or until the prunes are tender and plump. Place the ham on a heatproof serving platter, then spread the almond paste over the ham. Cover the paste with sliced almonds, patting gently to form a crust. Bake in a preheated 375-degree oven for 20 minutes or until the almonds are toasted to a golden brown. Serve hot or cold with the pitted prunes and sauce. Prunes may be split and garnished with additional sliced almonds, if desired. This makes 15 to 18 servings.

PORK LOIN WITH PRUNES

18 sm. pitted prunes
1   5-lb. boned rolled pork loin, tied
Salt and freshly ground white pepper to taste
3 tbsp. all-purpose flour
1¾ c. chicken broth
3 tbsp. sherry *(opt.)*

Place the prunes in a bowl and cover with water. Soak for 30 minutes, then drain the prunes. Stuff the loin according to step-by-step illustrations. Season the pork loin with salt and pepper. Place the loin in a greased baking pan, then pour 2 cups of hot water into the pan. Bake in a preheated 350-degree oven for about 3 hours or to 190 degrees on a meat thermometer. Place the remaining prunes in a small saucepan and cover with water. Bring to a boil, then reduce the heat. Simmer for about 20 minutes or until just tender, then drain. Place the pork loin on a heated serving platter and garnish with the cooked prunes. Keep warm. Spoon 3 tablespoons of the pan drippings into a small saucepan. Add the flour and cook, stirring constantly, until smooth and brown. Add the broth gradually and cook until thickened, stirring constantly. Stir in the sherry, then season with salt and pepper. Pour into a sauceboat and serve with pork loin. This makes 15 servings.

pork loin with prunes

The flavor of pork is perfectly complemented by the sweetness of fruit, and this combination is illustrated by Pork Loin With Prunes.

how to stuff a pork loin

1 Drive a larding needle through the center of the pork loin, then pull out the needle and the pork it now contains.

2 Enlarge the needle cavity with a long, sharp knife. Push enough soaked prunes into the cavity to fit closely together and fill the space completely.

MENU FOR AN UNUSUAL DINNER PARTY

PORTUGUESE CUCUMBER SOUP
(Appetizers & Soups, pg. 55)

PORK LOIN WITH PRUNES
(Pork, pg. 18)

POMMES NOUVELLES
(Vegetables, pg. 95)

FRENCH-STYLE GREEN BEANS
(Vegetables, pg. 19)

GREEN GRAPE GELATIN
(Desserts, pg. 176)

SUGGESTED WINE:
FRENCH OR CALIFORNIA PINOT NOIR

pork chops
with mushrooms

PORK CHOPS WITH MUSHROOMS COOKED IN FOIL

1 tsp. beef stock base
1 tsp. rosemary
¼ c. red wine
Butter
4 lg. lean pork chops
½ lb. fresh mushrooms, sliced
Salt and pepper to taste

Dissolve the beef stock base in ½ cup of boiling water in a small bowl, then stir in the rosemary and wine. Cut 4 pieces of aluminum foil large enough to enclose each chop loosely. Grease the center of the dull side of each piece of foil generously with butter, then place a chop on each buttered area. Arrange the mushrooms equally over each pork chop. Spoon 3 tablespoons of the wine mixture carefully over each chop and season with salt and pepper. Bring 2 edges of the foil together over each chop, then fold over and crease several times to form a tent and, seal tightly, leaving about 2 inches of air space. Fold and crease the sides of each package and place the packages in a shallow baking dish. Bake in a preheated 400-degree oven for about 1 hour or until the chops are tender. This makes 4 servings.

pork chops with mushrooms cooked in foil

A cooking "pouch" made from aluminum foil is the secret of flavorful Pork Chops With Mushrooms Cooked in Foil. To avoid excess oiliness, buy well-trimmed, lean chops for this dish.

GERMAN-BAKED APPLES STUFFED WITH PORK

6 lg. firm cooking apples
1/4 tsp. crumbled dried thyme leaves
1/2 tsp. salt
1/4 tsp. freshly ground pepper
1 1/2-in. slice bread
1 1/2 tbsp. minced green onion
1/4 c. melted butter
1/2 lb. lean ground pork
1/2 c. apple juice

Cut through the peeling around each apple halfway down from the stem end. Core the apples to within 1/2 inch of the base, then cut out the center of the apples with a grapefruit knife, leaving a 1/2-inch thick shell. Place the scooped out apple in a bowl and add the seasonings. Trim the crust from the bread. Place the bread in a blender container, then process into crumbs, and add to the apple mixture. Stir in the onion and melted butter. Cook the pork in a skillet, stirring constantly, until tender, but not brown, then drain off any excess fat. Add to the apple mixture and mix well. Place the pork mixture in the apple centers. Place the apples in a baking pan and pour the apple juice into the pan. Bake in a preheated 350-degree oven for about 45 minutes or until the apples are tender. Cut away the peeling from each apple down to the cut line, then place the apples in a serving dish. Serve with *Petites Pyramides* of Duchess Potatoes (Vegetables, pgs. 3 and 5) and pickles. This makes 6 servings.

german-baked apples stuffed with pork

Pork and apples are a traditional combination, but German-Baked Apples Stuffed With Pork is a new way to present this popular duo. Duchess Potatoes (Vegetables, pg. 3) are a decorative tasty accompaniment.

PORK PIE

The traditional Old English Pork Pie, in olden times, often included rabbit meat as well as pork along with red wine, onions and herbs. This particular pork pie makes a complete meal. It is delicious accompanied by a fruit salad such as Stuffed Lemon Apples (Salads, pg. 19) or Macédoine Fruit Salad (Salads, pg. 40.) Serve a red Bordeaux type wine with this dish.

OLD ENGLISH PORK PIE

1 lb. ground lean pork
1/8 tsp. sage
1 egg, lightly beaten
Salt
Freshly ground pepper
1/2 c. all-purpose flour
1 lb. lean pork
8 slices of bacon, diced
1 c. chopped Spanish onion
2 tbsp. butter
1/2 tsp. thyme leaves
1/4 tsp. cinnamon
2 tbsp. finely chopped parsley
1 1/4 c. red wine
1 1/4 c. beef broth

1/2 **recipe Basic Savory Short Pastry** (*Desserts, pg. 12*)
Anglais Glaze (*Breads, pg. 6*)

Combine the ground pork, sage, egg, 1/2 teaspoon of salt and 1/4 teaspoon pepper in a mixing bowl and mix well. Shape into 1-inch balls. Combine the flour, 1/2 teaspoon of salt and 1/4 teaspoon of pepper. Dredge the balls with the flour mixture. Cut the pork into 1/2-inch strips, then dredge with the remaining flour mixture. Fry the bacon in a skillet until browned, then remove bacon with a slotted spoon and drain on paper toweling. Brown the pork balls, then the pork strips in the bacon drippings. Remove with a slotted spoon and place on paper toweling to drain. Sauté the onion in the butter until lightly browned. Combine the pork strips, onion, thyme, cinnamon, parsley, wine and broth in a 2-inch deep 9-inch casserole. Mix well, then arrange the pork balls over the top. Cover. Bake in a preheated 350-degree oven for 1 hour or until the pork is fork tender, adding more broth, if needed. Remove from the oven and cool thoroughly. Roll out the pastry on a lightly floured surface to 1/8-inch thickness and trim to fit the top of the casserole. Place on the cooled casserole, then brush with the glaze. Cut 1/2-inch strips of the remaining pastry and twist, then arrange the twists around the slightly moistened edge and center. Brush the trim with the glaze. Bake in a preheated 375-degree oven for 25 minutes or until browned. Serve immediately. This is an excellent do-ahead dish as the pie filling is cooked and cooled before the pastry topping is added and baked again. This makes about 10 servings.

old english pork pie

Under a crust of savory short pastry is a mixture of pork, onions, herbs and red wine. Meat pies, such as this, are traditional English holiday fare.

PORK ROLLS WITH CELERY

2 med. onions
3 med. tomatoes, skinned (*Vegetables, pg. 27*)
4 stalks of celery
¼ c. butter
8 lg. thin slices of pork shoulder
Salt and freshly ground pepper to taste
Grated rind of 1 lg. orange
1 ½ tsp. crushed rosemary
¼ c. vegetable oil
2 c. Basic Beef Stock (*Soups, pg. 2*)
1 tbsp. soy sauce

Chop the onions and tomatoes. Cut the celery stalks in half lengthwise, then cut into thin slices. Melt the butter in a large skillet. Add the onions, tomatoes and celery and cook over medium heat, stirring frequently, until the vegetables are just tender. Cut each slice of pork in half. Sprinkle the pork with salt, pepper, orange rind and rosemary, then roll up and secure with wooden picks. Brown the pork rolls in the oil in a separate skillet, then place over the vegetable mixture. Add the stock and soy sauce and cover. Simmer for 30 minutes, then garnish with parsley, if desired. Remove the picks before serving. This makes 8 servings.

HAM AND PISTACHIO NUT MOLD

4 c. minced cooked ham
¼ lb. fresh mushrooms, minced
4 c. bread crumbs
½ c. finely chopped pistachio nuts or pecans
½ c. tomato purée
½ recipe Basic Mornay Sauce (*Sauces, pg. 11*)
½ tsp. freshly ground pepper
2 eggs, lightly beaten

Combine the ham, mushrooms, bread crumbs and pistachio nuts in a large bowl and toss to mix well. Add

pork rolls with celery

Pungent onions, celery, tomatoes, grated orange rind and pork are combined to make these tempting pork rolls.

the tomato purée, Mornay sauce, pepper and eggs and blend thoroughly. Pack into a well-greased Savarin mold, leveling the top. Place buttered waxed paper over the top of the mold and cover with aluminum foil, then tie securely with string under the lip of the mold. Trim the edge of the foil to prevent any water from soaking up into the mold. Place on a rack in a steamer and pour boiling water to just below the rack, then bring to a boil over high heat. Cover the steamer and reduce the heat to medium. Steam for 1 hour. Remove the mold from the steamer, then remove the foil and buttered paper. Unmold onto a serving dish and fill the center with cooked green peas, if desired. This makes about 10 servings.

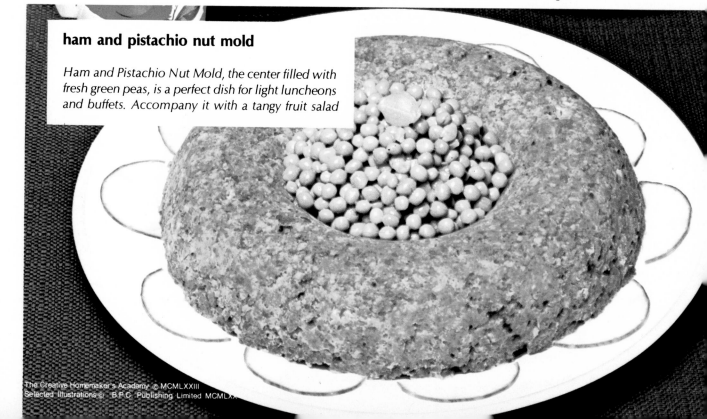

ham and pistachio nut mold

Ham and Pistachio Nut Mold, the center filled with fresh green peas, is a perfect dish for light luncheons and buffets. Accompany it with a tangy fruit salad

ham rolls

Cured ham and fresh spinach is a well liked meat-vegetable combination. Lean ham and fresh cooked spinach are combined with cheese, beef stock, wine and cream to make this a very flavorful dish. Before preparing this meat and vegetable combination, review the instructions for preparing fresh spinach (Vegetables, pg. 33).

HAM ROLLS WITH SPINACH

1 ½ lb. fresh spinach
¼ c. freshly grated Parmesan cheese
⅛ tsp. nutmeg
¼ c. whipping cream, whipped
1 tbsp. butter
Freshly ground pepper to taste
6 thin slices cooked ham

6 thin slices Emmenthal or Swiss cheese
1 c. Basic Beef Stock (Soups, pg. 2)
¼ c. Madeira wine
2 tsp. cornstarch

Clean and cook the spinach according to the instructions (Vegetables, pg. 33). Place the spinach in a colander over a bowl and press with the back of a wooden spoon, extracting and reserving the liquid. Place the spinach in a blender container and process until puréed. Combine the spinach, Parmesan cheese, nutmeg, whipped cream, butter and pepper, mixing well. Spread some of the spinach mixture over the ham slices and top with the Emmenthal cheese slices. Roll each ham slice up as for jelly roll and place in a buttered, heatproof platter. Arrange a border of the remaining spinach mixture around the ham rolls, using a fork to shape the design. Combine the reserved spinach liquid, stock and Madeira in a saucepan and bring to a boil. Blend the cornstarch with ¼ cup of cold water until smooth. Stir into the stock mixture and cook, stirring constantly, until thickened and clear. Pour over the ham rolls, then cover the dish loosely with aluminum foil. Bake in a preheated 300-degree oven for 20 to 25 minutes or until heated through. Garnish with broiled tomato slices and crescents made of puff pastry trimmings (Desserts, pg. 22), if desired. This makes 6 servings.

ham rolls with spinach

This special dish of ham with spinach is accented with flavors of Madeira and Parmesan cheese. This dish is garnished with slices of broiled fresh tomatoes and crescents of puff pastry (Desserts, pg. 22).

pork chops

pork chops with buttered noodles

Pork chops with pasta makes a delicious one-course meal. Rosemary and sage, two flavorful herb seasonings, add greatly to this dish. Sprinkle over all with sprigs of fresh, green parsley for color and flavor.

PORK CHOPS WITH BUTTERED NOODLES

4 loin pork chops, 1 in. thick
2 c. tortellini-shaped pasta
¼ c. butter
Salt and freshly ground pepper to taste
2 tsp. rosemary
1 tsp. sage

Place the pork chops on the rack in a broiler pan. Broil 8 inches from the source of heat for 20 to 30 minutes or until the chops are well done, turning once. Cook the pasta in a large saucepan of boiling, salted water until tender, then drain thoroughly. Melt the butter in the same saucepan. Add the pasta, salt, pepper, rosemary and sage and heat through, shaking the pan frequently. Place the pasta on a heated platter, then place the pork chops on the pasta. Garnish with crisp bacon and chopped parsley, if desired. This makes 4 servings.

PORK CHOPS IN PERUGINA

6 pork chops, ¾ in. thick
Salt and freshly ground pepper to taste
½ tsp. dry mustard
5 tbsp. butter
1 beef bouillon cube
1 ¼ c. boiling water
1 ½ lb. small potatoes

⅓ c. dry white wine
2 tbsp. all-purpose flour
½ c. half and half cream
½ c. small pimento-stuffed olives

Trim the excess fat from the pork chops. Combine the salt, pepper and mustard and sprinkle over the chops. Melt 3 tablespoons of the butter in a skillet, then add the chops and brown on both sides. Place the chops in a casserole. Dissolve the bouillon cube in the boiling water and pour over the chops. Bake in a preheated 350-degree oven for 45 minutes or until the chops are tender. Cook the potatoes in boiling, salted water until tender, then drain and peel. Melt the remaining 2 tablespoons of butter in the same skillet, then add the potatoes. Cook over medium heat, stirring occasionally, until well browned. Sprinkle with salt and pepper and place over the chops in the casserole. Add the wine to the flour gradually, stirring constantly until smooth. Add the cream gradually and stir the mixture into the pan drippings in the skillet. Bring to a boil and cook for 1 minute, stirring constantly. Add the olives and pour over the pork chops. Bake for about 15 minutes longer or until heated through. This makes 6 servings.

lamb

table of contents

introducing lamb

Why not give your family a special treat for dinner tonight! Prepare lamb for your main course. Chances are, if you're like most Americans, you forget about this flavorful and tender meat until the spring holiday season. Lamb is most plentiful in spring, but it is available all year, and your family is sure to be delighted anytime you prepare the delicious roasts, chops and casseroles you'll find in this section.

BUYING AND STORING LAMB

Let's first examine the different types of meat that come from the sheep. Mutton, coming from the mature animal, is usually too strong for American tastes, although "yearling mutton" — slaughtered at one to two years — is sometimes found in supermarkets. Most often you'll find "Genuine Spring Lamb," slaughtered at 3 to 6 months, or year-round lamb, 5 to 11 months. New Zealand lamb is considered especially fine. Quality grading for the consumer by the USDA is the same as for Beef.

In selecting your cuts, look for meat that is light pink to darker rose according to age. The texture should be fine and velvety, and the fat smooth, firm and white.

Unless you plan to use lamb within 3 to 4 days, it is best to freeze it. Before freezing, wrap the lamb in freezer paper and seal tightly. Follow the same procedures for defrosting lamb that you do for Pork (Pork, pg. 2).

COOKING LAMB

Lamb may be cooked by dry-heat or moist-heat methods. These cooking methods are discussed in detail in the Beef section, page 2. Since lamb is almost always tender, the method used for any cut depends on preference and the recipe being used. It should be cooked at a medium oven temperature to an internal temperature of 170 to 180 degrees. Lamb is almost always served either piping hot or chilled, rather than lukewarm.

boning a leg of lamb

BONING A LEG OF LAMB

Probably the most popular cut of lamb is the leg, which may be cooked with or without the bone in. Learning to remove the bone yourself is a proud accomplishment. Although frankly it's a feat of patience more than skill, we feel the admiring compliments make the effort well worthwhile, so we offer step-by-step instructions for removing the bone and stuffing the leg of lamb.

When buying leg of lamb, it is very important to ask the butcher to remove the gland near the shank. If it is left in, this gland gives the meat a strong taste.

First of all, never slit the leg of lamb straight down its length to remove the bone — boning is chiefly a job of excavation. You'll need a medium-sized thin knife or a boning knife, an extremely sharp smaller knife, a long needle, some strong thread and a thimble.

The sharp, pointed knife will be used for scraping and paring. The needle and thread will be used for sewing the ends of the boned roast together to hold the stuffing in during cooking. The thread will be removed before serving the roast.

Now you are ready to bone the lamb — so begin the process as if you were a veteran! Actually, it may be a little tedious the first time but with a little practice it becomes easy. After the lamb is cooked, it can be sliced in beautiful, uniform slices. Then the reason for boning becomes apparent and the extra effort so worthwhile.

MENU

ORANGE BASKETS
(General Information, pg. 13)
PROVENÇAL LEG OF LAMB, *page 5*
BASIC FRIED OVEN-COOKED RICE
(Cereals, pg. 2)
HERB BREAD
(Breads, pg. 17)
CHOCOLATE GÂTEAU
(Desserts, pg. 52)

1 Beginning at the broad end of the leg of lamb, push the end of the small sharp knife in around the bone. You can see better if you pare the flesh back a little. Start a paring/scraping movement to release the bone from the flesh.

2 Here you can see the broad end bone beginning to emerge as the flesh is pushed down.

The Creative Homemaker's Academy © MCMLXXIII
Selected Illustrations © B.P.C. Publishing Limited MCMLXX

3 The bone has been released from the meat about halfway down its length. The bone in a leg of lamb is in two parts, connected by a joint. So continue scraping until you reach the joint.

4 With the bone partially released at the broad end but still held at the opposite end, reverse the leg and start paring around the bone at the smaller end. Follow the same procedure of slipping the knife in against the bone and paring and scraping. Scrape as far down as possible at each end, meeting at the joint if you can.

5 Reverse the leg of lamb again. Grab the partially released broad end bone firmly in your left hand (if you are right handed), and roll the meat back to expose as much of the bone as possible. It will be almost rolled inside out when you finish. Continue scraping with the knife to release the bone.

6 Pull the bone out as the last tendons are removed from it. We have taken it out in one piece, but if it proves easier, separate the bones at the joint and remove them at each hand.

7 Unroll the meat and reshape it to the original. Sew the narrow opening together and fill the cavity, at the broad end, with stuffing. Still at the broad end, lap the top over the bottom flap and sew them together. Be sure to use a heavy knot when you begin and leave a long thread at the end, so that when you are ready to serve the roast, you only need to pull the string steadily from the knotted end to remove it. You may use metal skewers instead of thread if you prefer.

8 Here is the boned, stuffed leg of lamb ready for roasting. Sprinkle it with salt and pepper and place it on a rack in a broiler pan. Add a small amount of water to the bottom of the broiler pan to prevent the fat from burning.

lamb with soubise sauce

**BONED LEG OF LAMB WITH
SOUBISE SAUCE**

1½ c. bread crumbs
Pinch of rosemary
⅛ tsp. thyme leaves
1 egg, lightly beaten
Salt and pepper
1 5 to 6-lb. leg of lamb, boned
1 recipe Basic Soubise Sauce *(Sauces, pg. 14)*

Combine the bread crumbs, rosemary, thyme, egg,
¼ teaspoon salt, ¼ teaspoon pepper and ¼ cup
water. Mix until bread crumbs are moistened and
mixture holds together. Skewer or sew the small
end of leg together. Stuff bread mixture into large
opening. Skewer or sew opening together. Sprinkle
with additional salt and pepper. Insert meat thermometer in thickest part. Place on rack in broiler
pan. Roast in preheated 350-degree oven for about
2 hours or until thermometer reaches 180 degrees.
Remove from rack and place on heated platter.
Pour Basic Soubise Sauce over and around lamb.
Sauce may be served separately, if desired.

boned leg of lamb with soubise sauce

*This unusual dish makes excellent use of the
Golden Threads that are tying our lessons
together. The lamb roast was baked and covered
with creamy Basic Soubise Sauce (Sauces, pg.
14). You'll learn to make the croutons in the
Breads section, page 16. French Style Green
Beans (Vegetables, pg. 19) are served from the same
platter and garnished with a strip of canned
pimento. A border of chopped chives adds color
and a taste complement.*

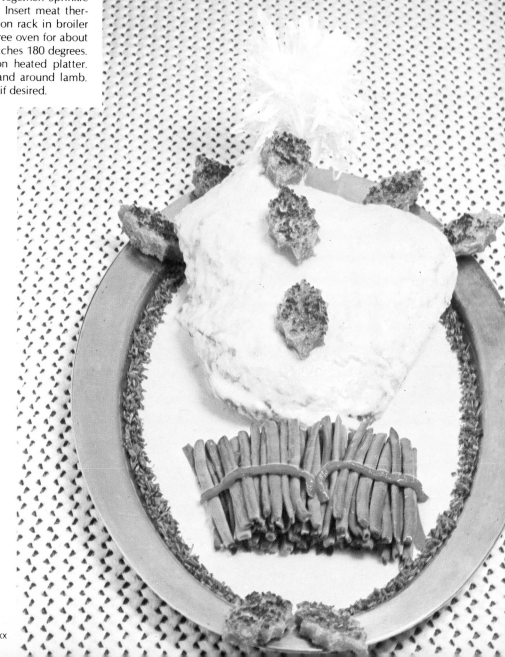

The Creative Homemaker's Academy © MCMLXXIII
Selected Illustrations © B.P.C. Publishing Limited MCMLXX

provençal lamb

PROVENÇAL LEG OF LAMB

1 med. eggplant
6 med. tomatoes, chopped
1 green sweet pepper, coarsely chopped
2 med. onions, thinly sliced
2 med. zucchini, thinly sliced
1 4 to 5-lb. leg of lamb
1 recipe Basic Garlic Butter *(General Information pg. 30)*
Salt and pepper to taste

Peel the eggplant, then slice thinly. Soak in salted water for at least 15 minutes. Drain well. Scatter eggplant, tomatoes, green pepper, onions and zucchini in a foil-covered broiler pan. Score the skin of the lamb lightly with a Stanley knife, then spread the lamb with Basic Garlic Butter. Place the lamb on top of vegetables. Insert meat thermometer in thickest part of lamb. Do not let the thermometer touch a bone. Bake in a preheated 350-degree oven for 30 minutes. Cover with foil and bake for about 2 hours longer or until thermometer reaches 180 degrees. Remove from oven and season with salt and pepper. Place the lamb on a large platter and arrange vegetable mixture around lamb. You may use one 10-ounce package frozen sliced zucchini if fresh zucchini is not available.

provençal leg of lamb

Here is the leg of lamb baked as shown in the step-by-step illustrations; ready to serve piping hot.

1 Remember the Stanley knife used to score a pork roast (Pork, pg. 4)? Here we use the same instrument to score the outer skin of a leg of lamb.

2 Remove the jointed tip from the end of the leg bone. Spread the scored skin thickly with Basic Garlic Butter (General Information, pg. 30).

3 Combine and mix the tomatoes, eggplant, mushrooms, green peppers, and onions. Spread them in foil-lined pan. Place the prepared leg of lamb on top, and bake as the recipe instructs. By the time the lamb is cooked, the vegetables below it are richly steeped in garlic butter and juices.

braised lamb chops with vegetables

These savory, braised lamb chops are served with new potatoes, braised tomatoes and fresh watercress. The pan juices from the lamb and tomatoes were poured over the finished dish. Notice the smooth texture of the potatoes which were steamed in their skins rather than peeled and boiled.

BRAISED LAMB CHOPS WITH VEGETABLES

3 tbsp. butter
1½ tbsp. Worcestershire sauce
6 lamb loin chops or steaks
¼ c. water
6 tomatoes, halved crosswise
12 new potatoes, boiled and peeled
Oregano to taste
½ recipe Basic Parsley Butter (*General Information, pg. 30*)
Salt and pepper to taste

Melt 1 tablespoon butter in a skillet. Add ½ tablespoon Worcestershire sauce and heat until sizzling. Place 2 chops in the butter mixture and brown quickly on both sides. Remove chops from skillet and repeat cooking procedure 2 more times, using remaining chops, butter and Worcestershire sauce. Return chops to skillet and add the water. Cover and cook over low heat for 15 minutes or until chops are tender. Remove the chops to a heated platter. Make 2 crosswise cuts on each tomato half; place in hot pan juices, cut side down. Sauté lightly on both sides. Arrange tomatoes and hot potatoes around chops on platter. Sprinkle tomatoes lightly with oregano and drizzle potatoes with parsley butter. Sprinkle chops lightly with salt and pepper. Garnish with watercress, if desired.

lamb with mushrooms and onions

This hearty lamb dish is sure to be a crowd pleaser. Combining cubed lamb with carrots, onions and button mushrooms, this casserole/stew is classically called Blanquette d'Agneau. The entire dish is sprinkled with parsley before serving. You might also serve additional croutons at table.

LAMB WITH MUSHROOMS AND ONIONS

3 lb. boned lamb shoulder
4 carrots
1 Bouquet Garni including 1 celery stalk with leaves
    (Soups, pg. 2)
2 14-oz. cans chicken broth
Salt to taste
1 lb. med. onions, peeled
1 lb. med. mushrooms, stems removed
1/4 c. butter
1/2 c. flour
2 egg yolks
1/2 c. whipping cream
2 tsp. lemon juice
1 tbsp. finely chopped parsley

Trim excess fat from lamb and cut lamb into 1/2-inch cubes. Peel carrots and quarter lengthwise, then cut the quarters in half. Place lamb in a Dutch oven and arrange carrots around lamb. Add Bouquet Garni; cover with broth and season with salt. Bring to a boil over high heat, removing any scum. Turn into a large casserole and cover. Bake in preheated 350-degree oven for 1 hour or until lamb is tender. Remove the Bouquet Garni and drain off the broth into a 3-quart saucepan. Keep lamb mixture warm. Place onions in the broth and cook until almost tender. Add mushrooms and cook for 7 minutes longer. Remove onions and mushrooms from the broth; keep warm with lamb mixture. Strain the broth and set aside. Melt butter in a medium saucepan. Add flour and cook, stirring constantly to make a light brown roux. Add broth gradually, stirring well after each addition; cook until smooth and thick. Combine egg yolks and cream, mixing well. Stir a small amount of the broth mixture into the egg mixture; add the egg mixture to the broth mixture slowly, stirring constantly. Place over very low heat until heated through and thickened, stirring constantly. Stir in lemon juice. Arrange the lamb and vegetables on a heated platter; pour suace over all. Sprinkle with parsley and garnish with triangular-shaped croutons. Serve immediately. This will make about 8 servings.

PENINSULA LAMB SHANKS

6 1-lb. lamb shanks
1 1/2 tsp. salt
1/4 tsp. pepper
3 tbsp. oil
3 tbsp. flour
1 14-oz. can chicken broth
1 med. onion, sliced
1 clove of garlic, finely minced
4 c. sliced celery
3 med. tomatoes, cut into wedges
1 tbsp. chopped parsley

Sprinkle the lamb shanks with the salt and pepper. Heat the oil in a Dutch oven. Add lamb shanks and brown well on all sides. Remove lamb shanks and set aside. Stir flour into oil and brown lightly. Blend in the broth and 1 3/4 cups water gradually and bring to boiling point. Return lamb shanks to Dutch oven and add the onion and garlic. Reduce heat and cover. Simmer for 1 hour and 15 minutes to 1 hour and 30 minutes or until lamb is tender. Remove lamb to a warm serving platter. Add the celery to liquid in Dutch oven and cook for 10 minutes. Add the tomatoes and parsley and cook for 5 minutes longer. Spoon over lamb shanks. Serve with Basic Boiled Rice or Mushroom Rissoto, if desired. This makes about 6 servings.

peninsula lamb shanks

A delicious, filling casserole, Peninsula Lamb Shanks can be a meal by itself — or better yet, serve it with Basic Boiled Rice or Mushroom Risotto (Cereals, pgs. 3 and 4). Here we present it in a Dutch oven surrounded by the vegetables which give it a blend of flavors.

MOROCCAN HARIRA

1 lb. lentils
¹/₂ lb. green onions
3 to 4 lb. lamb bones
3 qt. Basic Chicken Stock *(Soups, pg. 2)*
¹/₂ lb. diced lean lamb
6 sm. white onions, peeled
2 tbsp. lemon juice
1 tsp. saffron or curry powder
¹/₂ tsp. freshly ground pepper
Salt to taste

Soak the lentils in water to cover for 2 hours. Trim the onions and chop, using about 2 inches of the green tops. Place the lamb bones on the rack of a broiler pan. Bake in preheated 400-degree oven for 30 minutes or until well browned. Pour the stock in a stockpot and bring to a boil. Place the bones into the boiling stock. Reduce the heat and simmer for 1 hour. Remove the bones from stock and cool enough to remove any meat. Drain the lentils and add to the stockpot. Simmer for 15 minutes. Add the lamb and meat removed from the bones. Add the remaining ingredients and mix. Turn into a Dutch oven and cover. Bake in a preheated 350-degree oven for 1 hour and 30 minutes. Serve immediately. This makes 6 to 8 servings.

PIQUANT BARBECUED LAMB

1 5-lb. leg of lamb
Vegetable oil
Salt
1/2 tsp. freshly ground pepper
1/2 c. water
1/2 c. red wine
2 tbsp. wine vinegar
1 tbsp. Worcestershire sauce
1/4 c. lemon juice
1 tsp. dry mustard
Dash of hot sauce
1/4 tsp. paprika
1 clove of garlic, pressed
1 med. onion, grated

Rub the lamb with 1 tablespoon of oil, 1 table-spoon of salt and the pepper. Place on a grill over low coals and cook for about 1 hour, turning occasionally and brushing with oil. Combine the water, wine, vinegar, Worcestershire sauce, lemon juice, mustard, hot sauce, paprika, garlic, onion, 1 tablespoon of oil and 1/2 teaspoon of salt in a saucepan and bring to a boil. Brush the lamb with sauce and cook for about 1 hour longer or to desired degree of doneness, turning occasionally and brushing with the sauce. This makes about 10 servings.

roast lamb

The whole saddle of lamb is not usually found on the meat counter, so you should ask your butcher for this cut of lamb ahead of time. The saddle is the back portion of the lamb, and is ordinarily split in half and/or cut into chops for marketing. When the saddle is split, it is sold as a rack of lamb, as shown in the photograph of Lamb Rack With Orange-Filled Avocado on page 11. The meat from the saddle is very tender and flavorful, which makes this cut appropriate for special occasions. You must have the butcher loosen (or preferably remove) the chine bone from the saddle so that it can be carved between the lamb ribs.

roast saddle of lamb

Tender and succulent, Roast Saddle of Lamb is served here with conventional steamed side dishes: potatoes, carrots, Brussels sprouts, and cauliflower. The copper ladle alongside contains a savory gravy.

The Creative Homemaker's Academy © MCMLXXIII
Selected Illustrations © B.P.C. Publishing Limited MCMLXX

ROAST SADDLE OF LAMB

1 8-lb. saddle of lamb
2 tbsp. Basic Garlic Butter *(General Information, pg. 30)*
Salt and freshly ground pepper to taste
Beef consommé
2 tbsp. cornstarch

Rub the lamb with the garlic butter and season with salt and pepper. Prepare for roasting in a see-through bag according to the illustrations (Poultry, pg. 6) or roast in an open pan in a preheated 325-degree oven for 2 hours and 30 minutes to 3 hours or to 175 or 180 degrees on a meat thermometer according to desired doneness. Pour the lamb drippings from the bag into a large measuring cup and skim off the excess fat. Add enough consommé to make 2 cups of liquid and pour into a saucepan, then bring to a boil. Mix the cornstarch with 1/4 cup of water until smooth, then stir into the boiling liquid. Cook, stirring constantly, until thickened. Season with salt and pepper, then pour into a sauceboat. Place the lamb on a platter and serve with the gravy. The lamb may be served with steamed vegetables for a complete meal. This makes about 8 servings.

rack of lamb

LAMB RACK WITH ORANGE-FILLED AVOCADO

1 3 to 4-lb. rack of lamb
Salt and freshly ground pepper to taste
2 oranges
2 avocados
Lemon juice

Season the lamb with salt and pepper. Place the lamb, fat side up, in a shallow roasting pan. Cover the bone ends with aluminum foil to prevent burning before the lamb is done. Roast in a preheated 350-degree oven for 30 to 35 minutes per pound or 170 to 180 degrees on a meat thermometer, according to desired doneness, then remove the foil. Peel and section the oranges according to the step-by-step illustrations (General Information, pg. 13). Cut the avocados in half and remove the seeds. Brush the cut surfaces with lemon juice. Fill the cavities of the avocados with orange sections. Place the lamb on a serving platter and cover the bone ends with paper frills (Poultry, pg. 14). Arrange the avocados around the lamb and serve with Basic Vinaigrette (Sauces, pg. 2).

lamb rack with orange-filled avocado

A lamb rack is well suited for entertaining since this cut is particularly tender and easily carved. Served with orange-filled avocados and decorated with paper frills, the entire presentation is not only flavorful, but colorful, as well.

buckingham-glazed leg of lamb

BASILE LAMB

1 6-lb. leg of lamb
2 cloves of garlic
Salt and freshly ground pepper to taste
1/2 c. finely chopped celery
1/4 tsp. dried crumbled basil
1 lg. bay leaf
1 c. orange juice
3 tbsp. Triple Sec
6 slices bacon

Make several small cuts in the leg of lamb with a small paring knife. Cut the garlic in slivers and insert in the cuts. Rub the lamb with salt and pepper. Place the leg of lamb on a rack in a roasting pan. Combine the celery, basil and bay leaf with the orange juice, then add the Triple Sec and mix. Pour over the leg of lamb slowly. Place the bacon slices across the top of the lamb, then cover the roasting pan. Roast in a preheated 325-degree oven for 3 hours or 175 to 180 degrees on a meat thermometer according to desired degree of doneness. Baste frequently with the pan drippings. Uncover and bake for 15 minutes longer or until the lamb is browned. Remove from oven and let stand for 15 minutes before carving. Serve hot or cold garnished with mint. This makes 8 servings.

BUCKINGHAM-GLAZED LEG OF LAMB

1 6-lb. leg of lamb
Salt and freshly ground pepper to taste
1/2 c. dry sherry
1/2 c. red currant jelly
1/2 c. catsup
1/2 tsp. crushed marjoram leaves

Sprinkle the lamb with salt and pepper and place on a rack in a shallow roasting pan. Roast in a preheated 300 to 325-degree oven for 2 hours. Combine the sherry, jelly, catsup and marjoram in a small saucepan and heat, stirring constantly, until the jelly is melted. Brush on the lamb. Roast lamb for 30 to 60 minutes longer or 170 to 180 degrees on a meat thermometer, according to desired doneness, brushing with the sauce occasionally. Place the lamb on a platter and garnish with parsley and lemon wedges. Heat the remaining sauce and serve with the lamb. This makes about 8 servings.

buckingham-glazed leg of lamb

Here is a change-of-pace entrée: Buckingham-Glazed Leg of Lamb. A glaze made of currant jelly, sherry and catsup is used both as a basting sauce for the roast, and as an accompanying sauce.

The Creative Homemaker's Academy © MCMLXXIII
Selected Illustrations © B.P.C. Publishing Limited MCMLXX

spanish lamb casserole

Spanish Lamb Casserole is a version of classic Olla Podrida. Tender shoulder of lamb or mutton is surrounded by mixed vegetables and served with a delicious tomato sauce.

spanish lamb casserole

Cervantes, in his great novel, *Don Quixote*, mentions a hearty meat and vegetable stew called *Olla Podrida*. In this section, we introduce one of the many delicious variations of this classic Spanish dish. Our recipe for Spanish Lamb Casserole is an updated form of *Olla Podrida*, featuring shoulder of mutton or lamb, mixed vegetables, and tangy Tomato Fondue Sauce.

SPANISH LAMB CASSEROLE

1 3 to 4-lb. shoulder of lamb
¼ lb. pork fat, diced
2 cloves of garlic, pressed
3 med. carrots, sliced
1 lg. turnip, diced
1 sm. cabbage, shredded
1 lg. Spanish onion, sliced
3 leeks, sliced
1 ham hock
Salt and freshly ground pepper to taste
Pinch of saffron
1 16-oz. can garbanzos beans, drained
1 recipe Tomato Fondue Sauce *(Sauces, pg. 15)*
Cayenne pepper

Place the lamb in a large casserole. Bake in a pre-heated 450-degree oven for 30 minutes or until lightly browned. Cook the pork fat in a large frypan, stirring frequently, until lightly browned. Add the garlic, carrots, turnip, cabbage, onion and leeks. Sauté, stirring frequently, until the vegetables are lightly browned. Reduce the oven temperature to 325 degrees. Place the ham hock in the casserole with the lamb. Add the sautéed vegetables to the casserole, then add enough water to cover the vegetables. Cover and bake for 1 hour and 30 minutes. Uncover the casserole. Stir in the salt, pepper, saffron and garbanzo beans and bake for 30 minutes longer. Remove the ham hock. Place the lamb on one side of a large platter. Remove the vegetables with a slotted spoon and place around the lamb, reserving several carrot slices. Spoon some of the casserole liquid over the vegetables. Garnish the lamb with the reserved carrots. Serve with the fondue sauce and cayenne pepper. This makes about 10 servings.

SPRING DINNER MENU

FRESH SHRIMP PÂTÉ
(Appetizers, pg. 33)

with

MELBA TOAST
(Breads, pg. 38)

*BASILE LAMB
(pg. 12)

RICE WITH MUSHROOMS
(Pasta and Cereals, pg. 23)

FRESH ROMAINE AND LETTUCE SALAD
(Salads, pg. 62)

HOT CHOCOLATE SOUFFLÉ
(Desserts, pg. 170)

**Suggested wines: First course — DRY SHERRY
Second course — RED BORDEAUX or
CABERNET
SAUVIGNON**

moroccan couscous

Moroccan Couscous is a North African dish which is made with semolina, a rice-like grain. Couscous can be a somewhat confusing term: it refers not only to the complete dish (made of semolina, lamb and vegetables), but also to a particular kind of semolina.

In Morocco Couscous is served in two *tajines*, or covered earthenware cooking pots (see photograph): one is for the couscous semolina, the other for the lamb stew. Each diner ladles his own portions and tops it with a delicious raisin sauce. Couscous (the semolina) may be purchased, packaged in a box like rice, in some supermarkets or in gourmet food stores.

MOROCCAN COUSCOUS

1 med. eggplant
4 med. onions
1½ lb. lean lamb, cut into cubes
1 sm. head cabbage, coarsely chopped
½ c. butter
1 tsp. ground coriander
1 tsp. saffron
1 tsp. freshly ground pepper
4½ tsp. salt
4 med. carrots
3 lg. tomatoes, skinned *(Vegetables, pg. 27)*
1 red sweet pepper, cut into strips
2 c. couscous
2 c. Basic Chicken Stock *(Soups, pg. 2)*
1 c. raisins

Peel the eggplant. Slice lengthwise, then cut into strips. Prepare for cooking according to the step-by-step illustrations (Vegetables, pg. 13). Chop 2 onions fine. Combine the lamb, chopped onions, cabbage and ¼ cup of the butter in a large kettle and add enough water to cover. Stir in the coriander, saffron, pepper and 2½ teaspoons salt. Bring to a boil, then reduce heat and simmer for 30 minutes. Quarter the remaining onions. Scrape the carrots and cut crosswise into thirds. Cut the tomatoes into quarters. Add the quartered onions, carrots, tomatoes and sweet pepper to the lamb mixture and simmer for 20 minutes longer or until the lamb and vegetables are tender. Drain off most of the liquid and reserve. Keep the lamb mixture warm. Place the couscous in the top of a double boiler and stir in 2 cups of reserved liquid, chicken stock, remaining salt and remaining ¼ cup of butter. Place over boiling water and cook, stirring occasionally, for 5 minutes. Reduce heat to low and cover. Simmer for 15 minutes or until the liquid is absorbed. Remove from the water and stir lightly with a fork. Strain 1 cup of the reserved liquid and pour over the raisins in a small saucepan. Simmer, covered, for 5 minutes or until raisins are tender and plump. Heat the remaining reserved liquid and pour into a sauceboat. Place the couscous in a serving dish. Place the lamb mixture in a separate serving dish. Serve the couscous and lamb accompanied by the hot gravy and the raisin sauce. This makes 8 to 10 servings.

moroccan couscous

Illustrated here is the Moroccan manner of serving couscous in earthenware pots, or tajines. In the foreground is the lamb and vegetable stew, and behind it is a tajine heaped with grain-separate semolina. The brass vessel contains stock from the stew that may be spooned over the portion after the couscous is served. Another sauce, optional, but a delightful addition, is made with seeded raisins or sultanas, as seen in the containers on either side of the stew.

irish stew

IRISH STEW

3 lb. lamb
2 tbsp. vegetable oil
4 lg. onions, coarsely chopped
8 lg. potatoes, cut into cubes
1½ c. boiling water
½ tsp. hot sauce
1 tsp. salt
2 whole cloves
Flour

Cut the lamb into cubes, removing any fat or membranes. Heat the oil in a deep heavy skillet. Add the lamb and brown well. Add the onions, potatoes, water, hot sauce, salt and cloves. Cover the skillet and simmer for 2 hours, adding more boiling water, if needed, to keep the liquid at the same level. Remove the cloves. Drain the liquid from the skillet and measure. Pour into a large saucepan and bring to a boil. Mix 1 tablespoon of flour and 1 tablespoon of water together for each cup of liquid, blending well, then stir into the boiling liquid. Cook, stirring constantly, until thickened. Pour back into the skillet and heat through. This makes about 8 servings.

LAMB STEW WITH NOODLES

2 lb. boneless leg of lamb
¼ c. olive oil
1 2-oz. can anchovy fillets
½ tsp. basil
1 tsp. grated lemon rind
1 clove of garlic, pressed
2 tbsp. white wine vinegar
½ tsp. freshly ground pepper
1 c. beef consommé
2 tsp. cornstarch
3 c. cooked noodles

Trim any fat and membrane from the lamb, then cut the lamb into 1-inch cubes. Heat the oil in a heavy skillet. Add the lamb and cook over medium heat until well browned. Drain off excess oil. Drain the anchovy fillets and cut into small pieces. Add the anchovy pieces, basil, lemon rind, garlic, vinegar, pepper and consommé to the lamb, then cover. Simmer for about 1 hour or until the lamb is tender, adding boiling water, if needed, to keep the liquid measurement at 1 cup. Combine the cornstarch and 2 tablespoons of cold water, stirring to blend. Stir the cornstarch mixture into the stew, then cook, stirring constantly, until thickened. You may serve this over the noodles. This makes about 6 servings.

ROMANIAN LAMB STEW

3 lb. boned lamb shoulder
6 tbsp. olive oil
2 med. green sweet peppers
½ lb. green beans
1 sm. eggplant
¾ lb. yellow squash
1 c. sliced onions
1 c. sliced okra
3 med. tomatoes, sliced
2 tsp. salt
1 tsp. paprika
Cayenne pepper to taste

Trim any fat from the lamb and cut the lamb into 1-inch cubes. Heat 3 tablespoons of the oil in a skillet. Add the lamb and cook, stirring frequently, until browned. Cut the green peppers into strips. Trim the ends from the beans and cut the beans into small pieces. Peel the eggplant and cut into cubes. Cut off the ends of the squash, then cut the squash into cubes. Heat the remaining oil in a large saucepan. Add the onions, green peppers, eggplant, squash, beans and okra and sauté until the vegetables are lightly browned. Place alternate layers of the lamb, sautéed vegetables and tomato slices in a casserole, sprinkling each layer with salt, paprika and cayenne pepper. Bake, covered, in a preheated 350-degree oven for 1 hour or until the lamb is tender. This makes about 8 servings.

KORMA STEW

3 lb. boneless leg of lamb
1 c. yogurt
2½ tsp. salt
1 tbsp. curry powder
6 tbsp. olive oil
1 c. chopped onions
1 clove of garlic, pressed
1 tsp. dry mustard
½ tsp. freshly ground pepper
¼ tsp. cayenne pepper
½ tsp. ginger
¼ tsp. cinnamon
⅛ tsp. cloves
1½ c. water
1 tbsp. lemon juice
¼ c. flaked coconut

Trim any fat from the lamb, then cut the lamb into 1-inch cubes. Combine the yogurt, salt and curry powder in a mixing bowl. Stir in the lamb and marinate for at least 2 hours. Heat 3 tablespoons of the oil in a skillet. Add the lamb and brown well. Drain off any excess oil. Sauté the onions and garlic in the remaining oil in a separate skillet until tender. Stir in the mustard, pepper, cayenne pepper and spices and cook for 2 minutes. Add the lamb and cover tightly, then simmer for 20 minutes. Pour in the water, stirring well. Cover and simmer for 30 minutes or until the lamb is tender, adding water, if necessary. Add the lemon juice and coconut just before serving. Serve over rice, if desired. This makes about 6 servings.

lamb chops

There are several types of lamb chops, all of which are quite tender and, therefore, may be simply broiled, pan-broiled, or pan-fried. On an investigative trip to the grocer's meat counter, you will find that there are loin chops, English chops, shoulder or blade chops, rib chops, and round bone chops.

Of these, the loin chop is considered the most "choice" cut, because it is the tenderest and leanest. The loin section is split down the animal's backbone and sliced for single loin chops. If the entire loin section is kept whole, it may be sliced across to form double loin or English chops. A round bone identifies shoulder chops, which are cut from the arm side of the shoulder; these are usually fairly lean and there is little bone waste. Rib chops contain the backbone and sometimes a rib bone; the eye of the rib is meaty with fat and lean around it. Finally, the blade chops contain blade bone, backbone, rib and shoulder muscles.

Lamb Chop Dinner For Six, which follows, features loin lamb chops — and imagine the luscious flavor blend that results when they are cooked with baking apples, onions and carrots, with melted currant jelly overall!

LAMB CHOP DINNER FOR SIX

1 lb. small white onions
12 loin lamb chops, ¾ in. thick
Onion salt to taste
3 lg. baking apples
Juice of ½ lemon
1 lb. cooked sm. whole carrots
1 10-oz. jar currant jelly

Cook the onions in boiling, salted water until crisp-tender. Sprinkle the lamb chops with onion salt, then brown on both sides in a small amount of fat in a large skillet. Peel the apples and cut in half. Remove the cores and sprinkle the halves with lemon juice. Stand some chops around the side of a shallow casserole, then place the remaining chops on the bottom of the casserole. Arrange the apples around the standing lamb chops. Place onions over the chops in the center of the casserole. Arrange the carrots around and between the chops and apples. Melt the jelly, then spoon half the jelly over the casserole. Bake in a preheated 350-degree oven for 15 minutes. Brush all the ingredients with the remaining jelly and bake for 15 minutes longer or until the lamb and apples are tender. This dish may be made ahead, then covered with plastic wrap and stored in the refrigerator until baking time. This makes about 6 servings.

LAMB CHOPS WITH SPINACH DRESSING

1 med. onion, minced
2 tbsp. butter
6 lamb shoulder chops
2 tsp. salt
4½ c. chopped fresh spinach
4½ c. fine soft bread crumbs
¼ c. melted butter
2 eggs, well beaten
Celery salt to taste

Sauté the onion in the butter in a large skillet until soft, then remove from the skillet and set aside. Season the lamb chops with ½ teaspoon of salt and brown on both sides in the same skillet. Combine the spinach, bread crumbs, melted butter, onion, eggs, celery salt and remaining salt, then blend well. Place in a shallow baking dish and top with the lamb chops, then cover. Bake in a preheated 350-degree oven for 1 hour or until the lamb is tender. This makes 6 servings.

DEVILED LAMB SPARERIBS

4 lb. lamb spareribs
2½ c. lemon juice
2 cloves of garlic, pressed
4 tsp. salt
4 tsp. dry mustard
4 tsp. chili powder
2 tsp. ground cumin
1 tsp. dried thyme leaves
½ tsp. freshly ground pepper

Cut the spareribs into serving pieces. Combine the lemon juice, garlic, salt, mustard, chili powder, cumin, thyme and pepper in a small bowl and stir until well mixed. Pour over the lamb in a large, shallow pan. Marinate in the refrigerator for several hours or overnight, then drain and reserve the marinade. Place the lamb on a rack about 6 inches from hot coals and cook until tender, turning and basting frequently with the reserved marinade. This makes about 6 servings.

shish kebab

Shish Kebab was the invention of nomadic sheep herdsmen in the Near East, who found that they could conveniently roast lamb or mutton over their campfires by cutting the meat into small pieces and thrusting it on a skewer. The name for the meat dish came from two Turkish words: *shish*, which means skewer, and *kebap*, roast meat. The method of cooking is known in Russia as *shashlik* and in France as *en brochette*.

Through the years the term shish kebab (or kabob, as it is alternatively spelled) has been extended to the combination of any meat and vegetables cooked on a skewer. However, because of its beginnings, lamb is the traditional choice. For this reason, we introduce the shish kebab with three delectable recipes that feature lamb.

ARMENIAN SHISH KEBAB

1/2 c. vegetable oil
1/4 c. lemon juice
1 tsp. salt
1 tsp. marjoram
1 tsp. thyme
1/2 tsp. freshly ground pepper
1 clove of garlic, halved
1/4 c. chopped onion
2 tbsp. minced fresh parsley
2 lb. boneless leg of lamb, cut into 1 1/2-in. cubes
16 mushroom caps
4 tomatoes, quartered
2 green sweet peppers, cut into lg. squares
2 Spanish onions, cut into eighths

Combine the oil, lemon juice, salt, marjoram, thyme, pepper, garlic, chopped onion and parsley for marinade. Pour the marinade over the lamb cubes. Cover and refrigerate for 6 hours or longer. Remove the lamb from the marinade and drain on paper towels. Spear the lamb cubes, mushroom caps, tomato quarters, green pepper squares and onion quarters alternately on skewers. Broil over a barbecue grill or in the oven broiler, turning occasionally, until cooked to desired degree of doneness. Push foods off the skewers onto plates with the back of a fork to serve. Sixteen cherry tomatoes may be substituted for quartered tomatoes. This makes 8 servings.

HAWAIIAN SKEWERED SWEET AND SOUR LAMB WITH RICE

1 16-oz. can pineapple chunks
2 tbsp. soy sauce
1/4 c. lemon juice
1 clove of garlic, pressed
2 lb. boneless lamb, cut into 2-in. cubes
12 pitted black olives

Drain the pineapple, reserving the juice. Mix the reserved pineapple juice, soy sauce, lemon juice and the garlic in a large, shallow dish. Add the lamb cubes and marinate in the refrigerator for several hours or overnight. Remove the lamb from the marinade and drain. Reserve the marinade. Arrange the lamb cubes, olives and pineapple chunks alternately on skewers. Place the skewers on a rack in a broiler pan, then place the broiler pan 9 to 10 inches from the source of heat. Broil, turning and basting with the reserved marinade frequently, until the lamb is cooked to desired degree of doneness. Serve with Basic Boiled Rice (Cereals, pg. 3). This makes about 6 servings.

Pour the remaining marinade into a small, heavy saucepan and simmer until thick. This makes a Teriyaki Sauce to serve with the kebabs and rice.

PREPARING LAMB KEBABS

It is quite traditional for kebabs to feature lamb, but Hawaiian Skewered Sweet and Sour Lamb With Rice provides a slightly different approach to this venerable dish. Pineapple cubes and fatless lamb pieces are on the cutting board, ready to be skewered, cooked, and served with rice and Teriyaki Sauce.

shish kebab with rice pilaf

Pilaf is usually a highly seasoned long-grained rice that is cooked with stock (rather than water) so that the meat flavor is imparted to the grain. It is associated with the cuisine of Greece, the Near East and southern Asia, and in the various countries is alternately spelled *pilaw*, *pilau*, *pilaff*, *pilav*, and *pello*. It is an excellent substitute for potatoes or pasta to provide starch in your menus.

It is important to cook a pilaf slowly over very low heat, and the ratio of liquid to the amount of rice must be exact. We suggest referring to the illustrations for cooking Basic Fried Oven-Cooked Rice and Risotto (Cereals, pg. 2), since the same method is used in preparing the rice for Shish Kebab With Rice Pilaf.

shish kebab with rice pilaf

Pilaf is a highly seasoned rice that perfectly complements the succulence of lamb. Lamb cubes are skewered alternately with pieces of green pepper, tomato, and mushrooms to make the kebabs.

SHISH KEBAB WITH RICE PILAF

¼ c. tarragon vinegar
½ c. dry white wine
2 tbsp. vegetable oil
1 clove of garlic, pressed
2 tbsp. mixed pickling spice
¼ tsp. crushed rosemary
2 lb. boned lamb shoulder
2 green sweet pepper
2 firm tomatoes, quartered
8 med. mushrooms
¼ c. butter
1 c. rice
2 tbsp. minced onion
2 c. chicken broth

Combine the vinegar, wine, oil, garlic, pickling spice and rosemary in a jar, then cover and shake well. Cut the lamb into 1½-inch cubes and place in a shallow bowl. Pour the vinegar mixture over the lamb and marinate in the refrigerator for several hours or overnight. Drain the lamb, reserving the marinade. Cut the green pepper into 1½-inch squares. Alternate the lamb cubes, green pepper squares, tomato quarters and mushrooms on 4 large skewers and brush with the reserved marinade. Place on a rack in a broiler pan. Broil about 4 inches from the source of heat for 8 to 10 minutes on each side. Melt the butter in a saucepan. Add the rice and onion and cook, stirring constantly, until the rice is lightly browned. Add the chicken broth, then cover and simmer for 20 to 25 minutes or until the rice is tender and all the liquid is absorbed. Spoon into a serving dish and place the kebabs on the rice. This makes 4 servings.

TURKISH LAMB WITH RICE

¼ c. butter
2 lb. boned lamb, cut into cubes
3 med. onions, sliced
¼ tsp. cinnamon
¼ tsp. freshly ground pepper
1 tsp. salt
½ c. raisins
¾ c. chopped pitted prunes
2 c. cooked rice
1½ tbsp. melted butter
3 tbsp. lemon juice
1 tbsp. minced fresh parsley
½ c. chopped almonds

Melt the butter in a heavy skillet, then add the lamb. Sauté, turning to brown on all sides. Add the onions, cinnamon, pepper and 2 cups of water, then cover. Simmer for 2 hours and 30 minutes. Stir in the salt, then set aside to cool. Cover the raisins with boiling water and let stand for about 15 minutes or until plump, then drain. Drain the lamb, reserving the liquid. Add the raisins and prunes to the lamb and toss until well mixed. Place in a large casserole and cover with the rice. Pour the reserved liquid over the rice, then cover the casserole. Bake in a preheated 350-degree oven for 35 minutes or until the lamb is tender. Blend the melted butter and lemon juice and spoon over the rice. Sprinkle with the parsley and almonds. This makes 6 to 8 servings.

HEARTLAND LAMB

3 lb. lamb shoulder
1 tbsp. vegetable oil
¼ c. all-purpose flour
1 tbsp. sugar
2 tsp. salt
¼ tsp. freshly ground pepper
3 c. skinned diced tomatoes
2 med. onions, quartered
1 clove of garlic, pressed
3 whole cloves
¼ tsp. crushed rosemary
1 bay leaf
2 c. water
6 med. peeled potatoes, quartered
3 carrots, thickly sliced
1½ lb. rutabaga, cubed
1½ lb. fresh green beans, cut into 1-in. pieces

Cut the lamb into 1½-inch pieces, then brown in the oil in an ovenproof Dutch oven. Remove the lamb and drain off the excess fat. Combine the flour, sugar, salt and pepper and sprinkle over the lamb. Toss until well coated, then return to the Dutch oven. Add the tomatoes, onions, garlic, cloves, rosemary, bay leaf and water, then stir to mix well. Cover tightly. Bake in a preheated 350-degree oven for 30 minutes. Add the potatoes, carrots and rutabaga and bake for 30 minutes longer. Add the beans and bake for 30 minutes longer or until the lamb and vegetables are tender. This makes 8 to 10 servings.

LAMB WITH MUSHROOMS

3 lb. boned lamb shoulder
1 onion, diced
¼ c. bacon drippings
3 tbsp. all-purpose flour
1¼ c. beef consommé
Salt and freshly ground pepper to taste
1 c. skinned diced tomatoes
1½ c. sliced fresh mushrooms
1 tbsp. finely chopped fresh parsley

Cut the lamb into 1-inch cubes. Brown the lamb and onion in the bacon drippings in a large skillet. Remove the lamb and onion with a slotted spoon and place in a large casserole. Add the flour to the dripping in the skillet and cook, stirring, until brown. Add the consommé and cook, stirring, until thickened. Pour into the casserole, then season with salt and pepper. Stir in the tomatoes and mushrooms. Cover tightly. Bake in a preheated 350-degree oven for 1 hour. Remove the casserole from the oven and sprinkle with parsley. This makes about 6 servings.

LAMB CASSEROLE WITH SHERRY

4 c. diced cooked lamb
3 med. onions, sliced
4 med. potatoes, sliced
½ lb. fresh mushrooms, sliced
1 10-oz. package frozen green peas, thawed
¼ c. dry sherry
1 recipe Basic Brown Sauce (Sauces, pg. 5)

Arrange alternate layers of the lamb, onions, potatoes, mushrooms and peas in a large greased baking dish. Mix the sherry and brown sauce and pour over the top, then cover. Bake in a preheated 350 degree oven for 1 hour and 15 minutes. Uncover and bake for 15 minutes longer. One pound of fresh peas may be used in place of the frozen peas. This makes 6 servings.

paprika lamb

*Four mounds of Basic Boiled Rice are centered
in a rich, thick sauce of lamb, tomato purée and
paprika. The rice is sprinkled with additional paprika
and parsley garnishes the sauce that has been
drawn to the side of the dish.*

PAPRIKA LAMB

4 med. onions, minced
3 tbsp. butter
1 c. all-purpose flour
1 tsp. salt
1/2 tsp. freshly ground pepper
2 lb. boneless lamb, cut into cubes
2 tbsp. vegetable oil
1 1/3 c. Basic Lamb Stock *(pg. 21)*
3 tbsp. paprika
2 tbsp. tomato purée
3 tsp. wine vinegar

Sauté the onions in 2 tablespoons of the butter in a skillet
until tender, then remove from the skillet with a slotted
spoon and set aside. Combine the flour, salt and pepper
in a paper bag. Add the lamb and shake until well
coated. Add the remaining butter and oil to the skillet.
Add the lamb cubes and cook over medium heat until
brown, adding more oil, if necessary. Combine the lamb
and onions in a casserole. Pour the stock into the drippings in the skillet, then stir in the paprika, tomato purée
and vinegar. Heat through and pour over the lamb mixture. Bake, covered, in a preheated 325-degree oven for 1
hour or until the lamb is tender. Serve with mounds of
Basic Boiled Rice (Cereals, pg. 3). This makes about 6
servings.

LAMB WITH BROWN RICE

2 1/2 lb. boned lamb shoulder
1/2 c. all-purpose flour
1 c. brown rice
1/4 c. vegetable oil
1 onion, sliced
4 c. water
2 tsp. Worcestershire sauce
1 tsp. salt
1 tsp. thyme
1/2 tsp. freshly ground pepper

Cut the lamb in 1-inch cubes and dredge with 6 tablespoons of the flour. Place the rice in a large casserole.
Heat the oil in a large skillet, then add the lamb and cook
until brown on all sides. Remove the lamb with a slotted
spoon and place over the rice in the casserole. Place the
onion over the lamb. Sprinkle the remaining flour in the
skillet and cook, stirring, until brown. Add the water and
the seasonings and blend well. Pour over the lamb mixture, then cover tightly. Bake in a preheated 375-degree
oven for 2 hours, adding water, if needed. This makes
about 6 servings.

shepherd's pie

Shepherd's Pie is a traditional English dish — and an excellent example of British thriftiness, since the English often make it from leftovers. Similar to a hash, it is made of chopped cooked lamb or mutton and ham that is smothered in onion and topped with a delicious potato crust.

SHEPHERD'S PIE

2½ c. cubed cooked lamb
1 lg. onion, minced
2 tbsp. finely minced parsley
1 tsp. salt
¾ tsp. freshly ground pepper
4 slices lean bacon, minced
1 c. Basic Lamb Stock
1 recipe Basic Duchess Potato Mixture
　　(Vegetables, pg. 3)

Combine the lamb, onion, parsley, salt and pepper in a large bowl and mix well. Turn into a buttered 7 x 7 x 3-inch casserole. Combine the bacon and stock in a small saucepan over low heat. Bring to a boil and reduce the heat. Simmer for 5 minutes, then pour over the lamb mixture. Spread the potato mixture over the top evenly and score with a knife blade, then brush with the *Anglais Glaze*. Bake in a preheated 350-degree oven for 25 minutes or until lightly browned. The potato mixture may be piped on top, if desired. This makes 4 servings.

BASIC LAMB STOCK

2½ lb. lamb shoulder bones and
　　trimmings
1 tbsp. salt
1 tsp. peppercorns
2 c. coarsely chopped celery and leaves
1 lg. clove of garlic, halved
2 onions, quartered
2 carrots, coarsely chopped

Combine the bones and 2 quarts of water in a large heavy saucepan and bring to a boil. Reduce the heat and simmer for 15 minutes, skimming the top occasionally. Add the remaining ingredients and simmer for 1 hour and 30 minutes. Strain the stock through a fine sieve and cool. Remove any remaining fat. This makes about 1½ quarts of stock.

shepherd's pie

In Britain, Shepherd's Pie (also called cottage pie) is frequently seen on pub counters at midday. It is an old dish of rural invention, originally concocted to make use of leftover lamb or mutton.

italian lamb stew

Tomatoes, zucchini, olives, mushrooms, onions, garlic — vigorous flavors with the zest and liveliness typical of Italian ingredients — perfectly complement the lamb for this stew. It is a hearty one-dish meal that is delicious but easy on your marketing budget. Try serving this stew with a Hot Garlic Loaf (Breads, pg. 17) and Pepper Salad (Salads, pg. 23) for a meal that is truly *buonissimo*.

ITALIAN LAMB STEW

2 lb. lamb neck or shoulder slices
2 tbsp. vegetable oil
1 sm. onion, sliced
1 clove of garlic, pressed
1 20-oz. can tomatoes
1½ tsp. salt
¼ tsp. oregano leaves
⅛ tsp. freshly ground pepper
1 bay leaf
2 med. zucchini
¼ lb. small mushrooms, sliced
1 20-oz. can white kidney beans
½ c. small pitted ripe olives

Brown the lamb in the oil in a heavy Dutch oven. Pour off any excess drippings, then add the onion, garlic, tomatoes, salt, oregano, pepper and bay leaf. Cover and simmer for 45 minutes. Remove the bay leaf. Cut the zucchini into ½-inch slices, then add to the lamb mixture. Stir in the mushrooms. Cook for 15 minutes longer or until the vegetables and lamb are tender. Drain the kidney beans and add to the lamb mixture. Add the olives and cook for about 5 minutes longer. This makes about 8 servings.

LAMB BALLS EN BROCHETTE

¾ c. half and half cream
1 egg
1 c. soft bread crumbs
½ tsp. salt
½ tsp. garlic salt
¼ tsp. freshly ground pepper
¼ tsp. tarragon leaves
¼ tsp. ground savory
1½ lb. ground lamb
Brown Lemon Sauce
12 lg. fresh pineapple wedges
6 plum tomatoes
2 cucumbers, cut in ½-in. slices
1 recipe Basic Boiled Rice (Pasta, pg. 3)

Combine the cream and egg, then beat until well mixed. Add the crumbs and seasonings and let stand until the bread is completely moistened. Add the lamb and mix well. Shape into 18 balls, about 1½ inches in diameter, with moistened hands. Chill for several hours or overnight. Place the lamb balls on skewers. Grill, 4 to 5 inches from the source of heat, for 5 to 7 minutes on each side or to the desired degree of doneness. Brush frequently with the sauce. Place the pineapple, tomatoes and cucumbers on skewers and grill for 4 to 5 minutes on each side, brushing frequently with the sauce. Serve on a bed of rice with any remaining sauce. This makes 6 servings.

BROWN LEMON SAUCE

½ c. lemon juice
½ c. vegetable oil
¼ c. water
2 tbsp. dark brown sugar
1 tbsp. soy sauce
¼ tsp. ginger

Combine all ingredients and mix well. This makes about 1⅓ cups of sauce.

italian lamb stew

Lamb demonstrates its remarkable versatility in this Italian stew. Traditional Italian spices and ingredients provide the flair and taste associated with the great cuisine of that Mediterranean country.

LAMB KEBABS

Not only is lamb the traditional meat for kebabs, it is the most delicious. Festive Lamb Kebabs are excellent in flavor and are very tender. To make sure you are able to get plenty of all the vegetables, fruits and lamb on the skewers, you should choose long skewers.

FESTIVE LAMB KEBABS

3 lb. boneless lamb
1 c. dry white wine
½ c. lemon juice
¼ c. vegetable oil
2 cloves of garlic, pressed
1 tsp. oregano
½ tsp. thyme
½ tsp. basil
2 tbsp. Worcestershire sauce
Salt and freshly ground pepper to taste
1 lb. small white onions
3 med. green sweet peppers
12 bay leaves
1 med. fresh pineapple, peeled
Bottled kumquats
Bottled crab apples
1 lb. fresh mushrooms

Cut the lamb into 1 ¼-inch cubes. Combine the wine, lemon juice, oil, garlic, oregano, thyme, basil, Worcestershire sauce, salt and pepper in a large bowl. Add the lamb and refrigerate for several hours or overnight, stirring occasionally. Cook the onions in boiling, salted water for 5 minutes, then drain well. Cut each green pepper into 8 pieces and set aside. Soak the bay leaves in enough water to cover until well moistened, then drain. Remove the core from the pineapple and cut the pineapple into 24 wedges. Remove the lamb from the marinade with a slotted spoon, draining well, then reserve the marinade. Thread the lamb cubes, fruits, bay leaves and vegetables on 8 long skewers. Cook on a grill over white-hot coals for 12 to 16 minutes or to desired doneness, turning and brushing frequently with the reserved marinade. Serve hot. This makes 8 servings.

festive lamb kebabs

Lamb kebabs are not recommended for economy, but for unsurpassed flavor and succulence.

guard of honor

A Guard of Honor, by one definition, is a group of soldiers with crossed swords who greet distinguished persons or guests of honor. The following dish is called a Guard of Honor because it is made with two lamb racks arranged in similar fashion. This Guard of Honor greets distinguished persons and guests at the dinner table.

The finished Guard of Honor is pictured on page 25. Follow the step-by-step illustrations to prepare this continental lamb dish.

LAMB GUARD OF HONOR

2   7 to 9-bone lamb racks
Salt and freshly ground pepper to
taste

Have the butcher skin the lamb racks and cut through the bone between each rib at the large ends for easy carving. Prepare the racks according to the step-by-step illustrations. Season with salt and pepper. Bake in a preheated 375-degree oven for 30 to 35 minutes per pound or to desired degree of doneness. Remove the foil, then place the lamb on a serving platter. Wrap each bone in foil or place a paper frill (Poultry, pg. 14) on each bone tip. This makes 7 to 9 servings.

1 Place one rack, fat side up, on a board, then cut through the fat and meat 3 or 4 inches from the large end, using a sharp knife. Cut back the meat and fat to expose the bones.

2 Cut away the meat between the bones down to the cut line, exposing all of the bones.

3 Scrape off all surplus meat from the bones until completely cleaned. Repeat with the remaining rack.

4 Place the racks together, fat side out, alternating the bones the full length of the racks.

5 Place the racks in a greased roasting pan. Cut a piece of aluminum foil 3 inches longer than the exposed bones and fold in half. Crease the center lengthwise and place over the bones to prevent burning.

lamb guard of honor

This dish of distinction is made with a martial arrangement of baked lamb chops. It is garnished with fresh, green Brussels sprouts, green beans and fresh, red tomatoes.

BAKED RIBS OF LAMB

1   2 ½-lb. strip of lamb ribs
Salt and freshly ground pepper to taste
2 tbsp. vegetable oil
1 tbsp. soy sauce
1 tbsp. tomato purée
1 clove of garlic, pressed

Have the thick, bony side of the strip of lamb cut through in several places when you purchase the ribs. Sprinkle the ribs with salt and pepper and place on a rack in a roasting pan, meat side down. Bake in a preheated 350-degree oven for 30 minutes, then turn and bake for 30 minutes. Combine the oil, soy sauce, tomato purée, garlic, salt and pepper in a small bowl and brush all of the mixture over the ribs. Bake for 30 minutes longer. Cut the ribs into serving pieces. This makes about 4 servings.

baked ribs of lamb

These golden brown ribs of lamb were basted with a mixture of soy sauce, tomato purée and garlic. Cut them into serving pieces as shown.

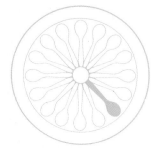

spit-roasted lamb

Tender lamb is perfect for rotisserie or spit roasting. A leg of lamb cooked done, remains succulent and tender. In the following recipe for Mint-Barbecued Leg of Lamb, a delicious mint mixture for basting gives a superb flavor to the grilled lamb.

MINT-BARBECUED LEG OF LAMB

½ c. butter
½ c. wine vinegar
¼ c. sugar
1 tbsp. Worcestershire sauce
¼ c. dried mint leaves
1   6-lb. leg of lamb
Salt and freshly ground pepper to taste

Combine the butter, vinegar, sugar, Worcestershire sauce and mint leaves in a small saucepan and cook over low heat, stirring constantly, until the sugar dissolves. Set aside. Place the leg of lamb on a rotisserie spit and insert a meat thermometer in thickest part of the lamb making sure it does not touch the bone. Cook for about 3 hours or to 180 degrees on the meat thermometer, basting frequently with the mint mixture during the last 30 minutes of cooking. Season with salt and pepper. Slice before serving. Serve any remaining mint sauce with the lamb. This makes about 8 servings.

mint-barbecued leg of lamb

This luscious barbecued lamb was basted with a delicious mint mixture. Serve it for festive outdoor dinners.

variety meats & game

table of contents

introducing variety meats

In contrast to the national appetite for pork and beef, the American taste for "variety meats" — also known as specialty cuts, remains amazingly undeveloped. Liver, tongue, tripe, sweetbreads and kidneys deserve to be re-introduced and better appreciated. Creative homemakers searching for new and different meat cuts to add variety to their menus, can discover the ease, convenience and adaptability of specialty cuts, sausage, frankfurters and preserved meats.

Variety meats, known as *offal* in culinary terms, are favored for their distinctive or finely subtle flavors and variety of textures. The glandular organ meats are very adaptable, combine well with other foods, and are enhanced by almost any seasoning or sauce. Being unusually rich in protein, vitamins and minerals, they are a wonderful staple food for weight watchers.

Once thought of as an economy meat, variety meat prices now compare with those of choice-grade red meats. Many types, such as brains, sweetbreads and kidneys (available through specialty stores and delicatessens) are considered great delicacies.

Most variety meats, other than those pickled in brine, are quite perishable and should be prepared the day they are bought.

Variety meats require different methods of preparation and cooking. Liver is the most delicate of the variety meats. It should be lightly browned, then cooked over medium heat. Many knowledgeable cooks assume wrongly that all organ cuts need braising or boiling to tenderize the meat.

Tender veal or lamb kidneys are usually broiled or sautéed. However, the tougher beef kidneys need to be braised before broiling or sautéing. Kidneys may or may not come encased in a thick fat covering. All fat and membrane should be trimmed off. The kidneys should then be seared in hot butter to seal in the juices and like liver, should be cooked gently until done.

Liver is a food always thought to be good for us, but seldom thought to be good tasting. Unfortunately, we think of it as we do other foods often treated with the same injustice: spinach, broccoli, prunes and many others that are always said to be filled with vitamins and iron, but never with flavor. Therefore, most of us think that when we do serve liver, we must be sure to disguise its "unpleasantness" with an overabundance of onions, heavy seasonings, spices, sauces or anything else that will help "sugarcoat the pill." However, liver has an unpleasant taste only when it is improperly cooked. A few

simple procedures introduced in this section will help you and your family discover the subtle, rich flavor of properly cooked liver.

To understand how delicious well-cooked (not over-cooked!) liver can be, try Liver with Bacon, cooked until done, but still juicy. Liver should be sautéed in butter or bacon drippings so a crust will form on the outside to seal in the juices.

Young beef liver is less expensive than calves liver and just as nutritious. Beef liver can be sautéed following the same methods used for calves liver. It will produce an excellent dish, provided it is not overcooked.

liver with bacon

LIVER WITH BACON

12 slices bacon
2 lb. ¹/₂-inch thick calves liver slices
Salt and pepper to taste

Fry bacon in a heavy pan until crisp. Remove to absorbent toweling to drain, then keep warm. Cook the liver in the bacon drippings over medium heat until browned on both sides and to desired degree of doneness. Remove to warm platter and sprinkle with salt and pepper. Serve with bacon. This makes 6 servings.

MENU FOR FAMILY DINNER

SPINACH SOUP
(Soups, pg. 22)

LIVER WITH BACON

CARROT BOATS
(Vegetables, pg. 43)

BAKED MASHED POTATO
(Vegetables, pg. 39)

CREAM CUSTARD AND FRUIT
(Desserts, pg. 84)

COFFEE

liver with bacon

Temptingly browned, sautéed calves liver is accented with bacon. Fresh frozen green beans and almond slivers or French Cooked Green Peas make a compatible contrast. This is accompanied by lettuce salad with Basic Vinaigrette (Sauces, pg. 2). Hot rolls complete the menu.

liver and bacon with bananas

Sautéed until nicely browned, tender calves liver is served with bacon rolls and baked bananas. The baked butter and crumb-coated bananas are a slightly sweet, delicious complement to the liver. Fluffy white rice served with this dish completes a main course. Try this unusual combination for a taste surprise.

LIVER AND BACON WITH BANANAS

4 firm bananas
Melted butter
3/4 c. soft bread crumbs
8 slices bacon
1 1/2 lb. sliced calves liver
Salt and pepper to taste
2 tbsp. all-purpose flour
2 tbsp. Madeira or dry sherry
1 1/2 c. beef broth

Peel the bananas and cut in half crosswise. Brush with melted butter, then coat with bread crumbs.

Place on rack in broiler pan. Fry the bacon in a large skillet until partially done. Remove to paper towel and roll the bacon into roll-ups immediately. Broil the bananas, about 6 inches from the source of heat, until browned. Turn bananas to brown on other side and add the bacon rolls to crisp. Keep warm. Fry the liver in the hot bacon drippings until browned on both sides and of desired degree of doneness. Season with salt and pepper. Place on warm platter. Stir the flour into the pan drippings until smooth. Add the Madeira and beef broth gradually, stirring constantly. Cook until smooth and thickened. Season with salt and pepper. Pour over liver. Arrange bananas and bacon around liver. Serve with cooked rice. This makes 4 servings.

BOILED CORNED BEEF

1 5-lb. corned beef round

Place corned beef in a Dutch oven or heavy pan and cover with cold water. Bring slowly to a boil. Simmer, covered, for 4 hours and 30 minutes to 5 hours or until tender. Remove corned beef from broth and let stand for 15 minutes before slicing. Cabbage wedges and potatoes may be cooked in the broth for old-fashioned Corned Beef and Cabbage.

corned beef hash

corned beef hash

Corned Beef is not actually a variety meat but we include it here because it is the same type simple family food as many of the variety meats. Le Melange Americain, as the French call Corned Beef Hash, is a typically American dish. Thrifty New Englanders prepared corned beef in numerous ways; one example is illustrated here. Other variations for hearty meals on snowbound evenings are the German inspired corned beef and cabbage, or the world famous "boiled dinner" — corned beef and vegetables.

CORNED BEEF AND CABBAGE HASH

¼ c. butter
¼ c. vegetable oil
3 c. thinly sliced onions
4 c. shredded cabbage
Salt
2 med. potatoes, diced
1 12-oz. can corned beef, flaked
2 tbsp. tomato purée
¼ tsp. freshly ground pepper

Heat the butter and oil in a large frypan. Add the onions and cook until transparent. Place cabbage in a saucepan, then add ½ cup water and ½ teaspoon salt. Cook over low heat until crisp-tender or about 12 minutes. Cook potatoes in a small amount of salted water until tender. Drain cabbage and potatoes well, then combine onions, cabbage, potatoes and corned beef. Stir in purée, and season with salt and pepper. Pack into a loaf pan. Bake in a preheated 375-degree oven for 30 minutes. Invert onto serving platter and serve with poached eggs, if desired. Two cups flaked, freshly cooked corned beef may be substituted for the canned corned beef. This makes 5 to 6 servings.

corned beef patties

Closely resembling croquettes, Corned Beef Patties offer a new recipe for a familiar variety meat. Shape into round patties, or prepare as shown. Surround the patties with a mixed vegetable dish of golden sweet corn and diced, green pepper then garnish with a narrow border of parsley. Four of the patties have been topped with poached eggs.

corned beef patties

CORNED BEEF PATTIES

3 c. riced potatoes
2 c. minced corned beef
¼ c. tomato purée
1 tsp. salt
½ tsp. white pepper
4 eggs
Fiour
Dry bread crumbs
¼ c. bacon drippings
¼ c. butter

Combine potatoes, corned beef, tomato purée, salt, pepper and 2 beaten eggs, then mix well. Shape into patties. Chill thoroughly. Dredge patties in flour, then dip in remaining beaten eggs. Coat well with bread crumbs. Melt the bacon drippings and butter in griddle over medium heat until hot. Fry patties slowly until browned on both sides. Serve immediately. This makes 8 to 10 servings.

CORNED BEEF LOAF

1 c. finely diced potatoes
1 c. finely diced carrots
1 c. green peas
4 c. finely diced corned beef
2 env. unflavored gelatin
1   10 ½-oz. can beef broth
2 tbsp. minced chutney
1 c. Basic Blender Mayonnaise *(Sauces, pg. 3)*
¼ tsp. dry mustard
¼ tsp. white pepper
Salt to taste

Potatoes and carrots should be diced to about the size of peas. Cook the potatoes, carrots and peas separately for about 12 minutes or until tender. Cool. Combine the vegetables and corned beef in a mixing bowl. Sprinkle the gelatin over the broth in a small saucepan and let soften for 3 minutes. Heat, stirring occasionally, until gelatin is dissolved. Cool, then add to corned beef mixture. Stir in the remaining ingredients until well blended. Turn into a 12 X 8-inch baking dish. Chill until firm. Cut into squares and serve on lettuce. Garnish with hard-boiled egg wedges, tomato wedges and black olives. This makes about 8 servings.

hot dog rolls

hot dog rolls with crispy onion rings

*The all-time favorite American dish,
devoured at fairs, race-tracks, baseball
parks, and enjoyed by all, THE Hot Dog.*

HOT DOG ROLLS WITH CRISPY-FRIED ONION RINGS

1 pkg. all-beef frankfurters
1 pkg. hot dog rolls, split
Prepared mustard
Swiss or American cheese slices
1 recipe Crispy-Fried Onion Rings
    (Vegetables, pg. 48)

Place frankfurters in steamer pan over hot water
and steam for 20 minutes or until heated through.
Spread the inside of the hot dog rolls with mustard,
then add a slice of cheese. Arrange on baking sheet
and cover with foil. Place in 200-degree oven to
warm. Place 1 frankfurter inside each bun when
ready to serve. Top with onion rings and serve with
desired accompaniments.

FRANKFURTERS WITH SAUERKRAUT

1 1-lb. can or bulk sauerkraut
1 sm. onion, minced
2 tbsp. bacon drippings
1½ tsp. caraway seed (opt.)
Freshly ground pepper to taste
1 med. potato, grated
1 lb. frankfurters

Place the sauerkraut in a colander, then rinse thoroughly with cold water and drain well. Sauté onion in bacon drippings in large frypan until transparent but not browned. Add sauerkraut, caraway seed, pepper, potato and 1 cup water. Simmer, covered, for 30 minutes or until liquid is absorbed. Place frankfurters in steamer pan over hot water and steam for 20 minutes. Turn sauerkraut into serving dish and arrange frankfurters on top. This makes 4 to 6 servings.

frankfurters with sauerkraut

Satisfy your family's hunger pangs with a hearty supper of Frankfurters and Sauerkraut, accompanied by potatoes cooked in their jackets. The piquant aroma is sure to tantalize even the most bored palate.

SAUSAGE AND RICE CASSEROLE

2½ c. milk
1 tsp. saffron shreds
24 pure pork sausage links
4 c. thin lengthwise-sliced onions
1¼ c. long grain rice
Salt and freshly ground pepper to taste
2 bay leaves
1¼ c. water

Heat ½ cup milk in a small saucepan until warm. Sprinkle with saffron and let steep for 30 minutes. Bake sausages according to directions on this page. Spread 1 cup onions in large casserole. Arrange 6 sausages over onions and sprinkle with ¼ of the rice. Season with salt and pepper. Repeat layers, then add 1 bay leaf. Repeat layers 2 more times, adding remaining bay leaf. Strain the saffron from the milk, then combine saffron-flavored milk, remaining milk and water. Pour over the rice to cover. Bake, covered, in preheated 325-degree oven for 1 hour. Stir rice mixture before serving, if desired. One tablespoon turmeric may be substituted for 1 teaspoon saffron if desired. This makes about 12 servings.

BAKED SAUSAGES

2 lb. pure pork link sausage

Place sausage on rack in broiler pan. Bake in preheated 350-degree oven for 20 minutes or until browned. Turn and bake for 15 minutes longer. Serve with Crisp Cabbage (Vegetables, pg. 45) and Baked Mashed Potatoes (Vegetables, pg. 39). This makes 6 servings.

sausage and rice casserole

Among the hearty dishes which so admirably satisfy large appetites at moderate cost, Sausage and Rice Casserole holds a prized place. The four main ingredients used in preparing this succulent dish are sausage, rice, onions and milk.

how to make sausage rolls

sausage rolls

Tangy sausage has been rolled in a casing of flaky puff pastry. In the background is a matching container of French Potato Salad (Salads, pg. 14) with tiny matchsticks of charcuterie and flavorful onions. Sausage Rolls may be served as a first course or as a luncheon dish along with a vegetable. Cut into bite-sized pieces they may be served as tempting hot hors d'oeuvres.

SAUSAGE ROLLS

2 12-in. country smoked pork sausage links
1 box 6-count frozen patty shells, thawed
1 recipe Anglais glaze *(Breads, pg. 6)*

Peel the casings from sausage, using a sharp knife.
Place 3 patty shells together in a row on a floured
surface. Roll out thin in 13-inch rectangle. Place 1
sausage link on pastry. Basic Puff Pastry (Desserts,
pg. 22) may be substituted for shells if desired.

1 Moisten edges with water.

2 Roll up and pinch edges together to
seal.

3 Prick top with tines of fork.

4 Cut into 3-inch lengths. Place rolls on
waxed paper and brush pastry with
glaze. Repeat procedure with remaining
sausage and pastry. Place rolls on cake racks
in jelly roll pan. Bake in a preheated 350-de-
gree oven for 30 minutes. This makes about
4 servings.

introducing
game birds

Whether or not there's a hunter in your family, game birds are a culinary pleasure that everyone can and should experience. So many game birds are now raised domestically for marketing, that you can enjoy them any day of the week.

The term "game bird" literally refers to any wild bird that can be eaten by man. However, it has been extended to include those ordinarily wild birds which have been domesticated for retail purposes . . . so that, whether the bird is in its wild state, or has been born in "captivity," it is still correctly called a game bird. Among those game birds which may be bought as well as hunted are the duck, goose, turkey, pigeon, quail, and partridge.

Game birds are an excellent choice for the homemaker who is seeking to enliven her party menus with an actual flavor adventure. Though various game birds are (unfairly) likened to chicken, each has a distinct flavor of its own. Many people avoid game birds because of their reputed strong, wild flavor, often called a gamey taste. However, not all game birds possess this gamey taste — in fact, quail and squab have a very delicate flavor. Those which do taste gamey, such as wild goose or duck, may be "tamed" either by marinating or by

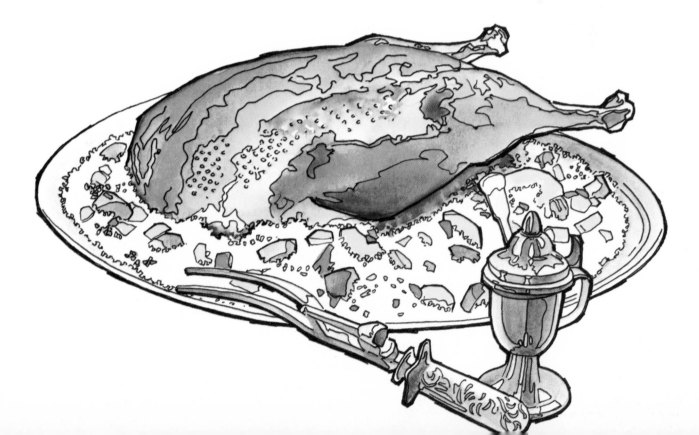

use of an appropriate stuffing. Either method of preparation will lessen the gaminess without masking the bird's distinctive flavor. Since the fowl's diet is the root of a gamey taste, generally domesticated game birds do not have an overpowering gamey flavor.

Duck is probably the most popular game bird for American tables. About 5 million a year are raised domestically in the U.S. alone. Almost all the domestic ducks sold here are very young birds, so that the terms duck and duckling can be used interchangeably. A duckling under 8 weeks of age is sold as a broiler or fryer; roaster ducklings are 8 to 16 weeks old.

Ducks are sold ready-to-serve, with the feet and head removed. When buying a fresh bird, choose a fairly long one with a broad breast. The breast and back should be rather fatty, soft and elastic. May through January is the season for fresh duck. Frozen duck is available year-round and is excellent.

Pheasant, a relative of the quail and partridge, is associated with high dining and opulent life-style. Its tender meat is prized as a delicacy. When shot as game, the wild birds have only a thin layer of fat, so that the breast should be covered with strips of bacon while roasting; the strips are removed the last half hour to allow the bird to reach a golden brown. This process is called barding.

Young pheasant are more tender than older ones, as is true of all game birds. Young pheasant may be identified by their short round claws. October to February is the hunting season for pheasant, but it may be purchased frozen, regardless of season, in specialty meat shops.

The game bird most highly rated by connoisseurs is the quail. Quail, even those which are wild, have a delicate, refined taste, devoid of gaminess. They are available at many markets, frozen in pairs, ready for roasting. You may also purchase smoked quail meat and canned whole quail stuffed with *paté de foie gras* in sherry sauce.

Squab are baby or nestling pigeons. Usually weighing about one pound, they are never more than four weeks old when sent to market, where they may be purchased frozen and ready to cook. The meat of this scarce bird is very tender, and therefore can be roasted on a spit or simply fried. If you prefer, they may be stuffed and oven-roasted.

Dove are also a species of the pigeon family and generally are not raised for commercial purposes. You must rely upon the hunting skills of a friend or relative if dove is to be on the menu.

If your local grocer does not ordinarily stock game birds, in most cases he will, upon request, special order the birds from a breeder. Other sources are specialty meat shops and ethnic food markets.

When you have chosen a game bird for your bill of fare, we recommend serving an accompanying wine. It is an accepted maxim among connoisseurs that wines belong with game. Red Bordeaux is excellent with game birds, although Red Burgundies may also be used. Nothing can better complement the succulence of roast duck than the forthright, robust flavor of a red wine. On the other hand, dove or quail, because of their delicate, light taste, may be served with either rosé or one of the less dominant, sweet white wines.

how to roast duck or goose

Roasting a duck or goose is surprisingly easy — and the succulently delicious result belies the simplicity of its preparation. To roast a goose, begin by removing the neck and giblets from the body cavity. Then wash the bird and dry with paper towels. As with a chicken or turkey, truss the goose (Poultry, pg. 3) and use a skewer to attach the neck skin to the back. Then set it in a roasting pan with rack.

Now thoroughly prick the skin all over with a large fork. Interestingly enough, this procedure eliminates any need for basting the goose during roasting. Fat will bubble up

through the holes and trickle down over the goose so that it, in effect, bastes itself.

A great deal of fat will be produced during cooking, so that after about an hour and a half the roasting pan will be half filled with drippings. Pour this off (but retain) and return the goose to the oven. The goose is done when the drumstick meat is soft.

A duck or duckling is also cooked in a roasting pan. The only difference in preparation for roasting is that the pricking is omitted. Instead, we recommend rubbing all over with honey. Then, to prevent the sugar in the honey from burning, place an aluminum foil tent over the bird for the final half hour of roasting. The cooked duck will be an appetizing deep chestnut brown when brought from the oven.

Now, what to do with the poured off goose or duck fat? Those drippings can be used to make a very excellent greasing agent. Use it as you would cooking oil to prevent foods from sticking to a dry-heated frying pan or griddle and to assure perfectly smooth surfaces on pancakes, potato cakes, *crêpes* . . . you name it. Simply let the drippings stand in the refrigerator, then skim off just the soft fat without a trace of the dark juices which will have jelled. For each 2 cups of perfectly clean fat, beat in one egg yolk. Brush the grid of your waffle iron with this mixture to guarantee perfectly formed waffles time and again. Under refrigeration, this fat may be kept for as long as two weeks.

3 Place the duck on a rack in a broiler pan. Coat the outside heavily with honey and secure the legs with string.

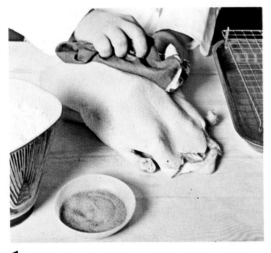

1 Dry the duck thoroughly with a cloth.

4 Roast in a preheated 350-degree oven for 1 hour, then reduce the oven temperature to 300 degrees and bake for 1 hour. Cover the duck with an aluminum foil tent and bake for 30 minutes longer.

2 Sprinkle the duck cavity with salt and pepper, then rub the outside with the seasonings.

5 Remove the duck and rack from the pan and pour off the fat. Prepare any desired sauce from the pan drippings. The roasted duck will be a very rich, chestnut brown.

roast duck with grapes

Roast Duck With Grapes is particularly notable for its unusual brown grape sauce, which must, without exaggeration, be pronounced "Heavenly!" Our illustration shows the honey-roasted duckling presented en croûte, but this is, of course, a purely optional garnish.

ROAST DUCK WITH GRAPES

1 4½-lb. duck
2¼ c. Basic Chicken Stock (Soups, pg. 2)
¼ c. white grape juice drink
⅛ tsp. salt
2 tbsp. cornstarch
2 c. seedless green grapes

Roast the duck according to instructions on page 13 and keep warm in a 150-degree oven. Combine the pan juices from the duck, chicken stock, grape drink and salt in the top of a double boiler. Dissolve the cornstarch in a small amount of additional grape drink and add to the sauce. Cook, stirring constantly, until thickened. Remove from the water and place over direct heat, then simmer until the volume is reduced to about 2 cups. Stir in the grapes and cook for about 1 minute longer. Place the duck on a serving platter and cover with some of the sauce. Garnish with additional grapes. Serve the remaining sauce in a sauce boat. This makes 4 to 5 servings.

AUTUMN DINNER PARTY MENU

ROAST DUCK WITH GRAPES

ORANGE RICE
(Pasta and Cereals, pg. 19)

FRESH ASPARAGUS WITH CREAM SAUCE
(Vegetables, pg. 74)

KNOT ROLLS
(Breads, pg. 11)

STRAWBERRY FRITTERS
(Desserts, pg. 135)

GERMAN CUSTARD
(Desserts, pg. 86)

**SUGGESTED WINE: CLARET
(RED BORDEAUX)
or CALIFORNIA MOUNTAIN RED**

The Creative Homemaker's Academy © MCMLXXIII
Selected Illustrations © B.P.C. Publishing Limited MCMLXX

WILD DUCK WITH WILD RICE

2 wild ducks, dressed
1 recipe Marinade For Game *(Sauces, pg. 5)*
Salt and freshly ground pepper to taste
¼ c. butter
1 apple, quartered
1 onion, quartered
1 carrot, quartered
3½ c. (about) Basic Chicken Stock *(Soups, pg. 2)*
1 Bouquet Garni *(Soups, pg. 2)*
2 green onions, finely chopped
1 c. wild rice
½ c. golden raisins
⅓ c. brandy

Place the ducks in a shallow oblong dish and pour the marinade over the ducks. Place in the refrigerator and marinate for about 12 hours, turning occasionally. Drain the ducks well and pat dry, then sprinkle inside and out with salt and pepper. Brown the ducks on all sides in butter in a large skillet. Place half the apple, onion and carrot in each duck cavity. Place the ducks in a casserole to fit snugly and add 1 cup of the chicken stock and the *Bouquet Garni*. Bake, covered, in a preheated 350-degree oven for 1 hour and 30 minutes or until the ducks are tender. Remove the ducks from the casserole, then discard the apple, onion and carrot. Place the ducks on a serving platter and keep warm. Skim the excess fat from the casserole liquid and remove the *Bouquet Garni*. Add enough chicken stock to make 2½ cups of liquid. Pour it into the top of a double boiler, then add the green onions and bring to a boil. Wash the rice well and drain. Stir into the stock mixture, then add the raisins and brandy and bring to a boil again, stirring frequently. Place over boiling water and cover. Cook for about 45 minutes or until rice is tender, stirring occasionally and adding chicken stock, if needed. Place the rice on the platter with ducks. Garnish with watercress and decorative orange slices (General Information, pg. 11). This makes 8 servings.

wild duck with wild rice

As an elegant entrée, succulent Wild Duck With Wild Rice is without equal. This dish may be flamed for added dining excitement and glamour. The two golden brown ducklings have been simply garnished with twisted orange peel, orange slices (General Information, pg. 11) and watercress — providing a scheme of earth colors that is so appropriate to this game dish.

duckling with oranges

Tangy orange sauce with a hint of brandy is the interesting "secret" of Duckling With Oranges. To guarantee soaring appetites, we suggest a beautiful presentation: decorate the bird with canelled orange strips, orange segments, and attractive orange baskets (General Information, pgs. 11-14).

DUCKLING WITH ORANGES

¼ c. olive oil
¼ c. butter
1 lg. duckling
Basic Seasoned Flour *(Appetizers & Soups, pg. 32)*
2 tbsp. wine vinegar
2 tsp. sugar
Strips of peel of 1 orange and 1 lemon *(General Information, pg. 11)*
Juice of 1 orange
Juice of ½ lemon
1 tsp. Curaçao
1 tsp. brandy

Heat the oil and butter in a large frypan. Dredge the duckling with Seasoned Flour. Place it in the frypan over medium high heat and brown on all sides. Place it in a casserole, pour the pan drippings over the duckling and cover. Bake in a preheated 350-degree oven for about 1 hour and 30 minutes or until duckling is tender. Remove the duckling from the casserole and place on a heated platter. Keep warm. Pour off the excess fat from the casserole drippings. Place the vinegar and sugar in a small saucepan. Cook over low heat, stirring, until sugar is dissolved. Stir in the drippings, orange and lemon strips, orange juice and lemon juice and cook over medium heat until liquid is reduced by half. Add the Curaçao and brandy and pour over the duckling. Garnish with a maypole effect of canelled strips, (General Information, pg. 12), orange baskets (General Information, pg. 13), orange segments and watercress. This makes about 4 servings.

QUAIL FOR SIX

6 1-in. thick slices sandwich bread
Melted butter
6 slices bacon
6 quail
2 juniper berries, crushed
2 tbsp. sherry
Salt and freshly ground pepper to taste
1 qt. Basic Beef Stock *(Soups, pg. 2)*
1 tbsp. cornstarch
¼ c. half and half cream
Chopped fresh parsley

Remove crusts from the bread slices. Cut a 1½-inch angle off each corner of each slice. Hollow out the slices by cutting ½ inch from edges of bread halfway to bottom, then remove inside bread to form the cases. Brush all surfaces of each case with butter and place the cases on a cookie sheet. Bake in a preheated 450-degree oven until well browned, then remove from oven. Reduce the oven temperature to 350 degrees. Dice the bacon and place in a casserole that will hold the quail snugly. Place the quail in the casserole in a single layer and sprinkle the crushed juniper berries over the quail. Add the sherry and season the quail with salt and pepper. Cover the casserole. Place in the oven and bake for 30 minutes or until the quail are tender. Pour the beef stock into a 1½-quart saucepan while the quail are baking and boil until reduced to 1 cup of stock. Place the bread cases on a serving platter, then place the quail on the bread cases. Keep warm. Strain the casserole liquid into stock in the saucepan and remove the excess fat from top. Place the saucepan over medium heat. Mix the cornstarch with the cream until dissolved. Stir into liquid in the saucepan and bring to a boil, stirring constantly. Pour over the quail and sprinkle with parsley. Garnish with watercress. This makes 6 servings.

quail for six

You will serve Quail For Six with justifiable pride. These very tender birds have a uniquely delicate and refined flavor that is considered by many connoisseurs to be superior to that of any other game bird. This — coupled with their costliness — creates an atmosphere of extravagant gourmet dining when quail is the entrée.

sauced dove breasts
on croutons

*This savory dish features tender
dove breasts set upon golden
brown croutons, covered with a rich
brown sauce. Artichoke bottoms
filled with baby green peas serve the
dual purpose of delicious
accompaniment and
pretty garnishment.*

SAUCED DOVE BREASTS ON CROUTONS

3 ¹/₂-in. thick slices sandwich bread
Melted butter
3 lg. dove breasts with wings
1 med. carrot
1 med. onion
1 stalk celery, cut in half
1 Bouquet Garni *(Soups, pg. 2)*
Salt and freshly ground pepper to taste
3 tbsp. butter
3 tbsp. olive oil
6 tbsp. all-purpose flour
¹/₄ c. Madeira
¹/₄ c. half and half cream
1 tbsp. beef extract

Remove crusts from the bread slices and cut each
slice in half. Brush with melted butter, then place
on a baking sheet and toast until brown for
croutons. Remove the tip from wing of each
dove. Cut each breast in half, then place in a large
saucepan. Add the carrot, onion, celery, *Bouquet
Garni*, salt, pepper and enough water to cover the
dove breasts and bring to a boil. Reduce the heat
and skim the liquid to remove any scum. Simmer
for about 30 minutes or until the dove breasts are
tender. Remove the breasts and place on paper
towels to drain. Strain the stock. Pour strained
stock back into the saucepan. Bring to a boil and
cook until stock is reduced to 1¹/₂ cups of liquid.
Place the butter and oil in a heavy skillet over
medium high heat until very hot. Place the dove
breasts in the butter mixture and cook until brown
on all sides. Remove the breasts from the skillet.
Add the flour to butter mixture in the skillet and
cook over medium heat, stirring constantly, until
dark brown. Add the stock and Madeira and cook,
stirring, until thick. Stir in the cream and beef extract, then bring to a boil. Remove from heat. Place
the croutons on a serving platter and place a dove
breast half on each rectangle. Pour the brown
sauce over all. Garnish with artichoke bottoms
filled with cooked peas, if desired. This makes 6
servings.

BAKED STUFFED SQUAB

6 dressed squab
1¹/₂ tsp. salt
1 c. chopped celery
¹/₂ c. chopped onion
3 tbsp. butter
1¹/₂ c. Basic Boiled Rice *(Cereals, pg. 3)*
6 tbsp. thawed frozen orange juice concentrate
1¹/₂ c. chopped fresh mushrooms
¹/₂ c. raisins
1 tbsp. finely chopped parsley
³/₄ tsp. marjoram
³/₄ c. vegetable oil

Sprinkle the squab cavities well with ³/₄ teaspoon
of the salt. Sauté the celery and onion in the butter
in a large skillet until golden, then stir in the rice, 3
tablespoons of orange juice concentrate, mushrooms, raisins, parsley, marjoram and the remaining salt. Blend thoroughly and heat through. Spoon
the rice mixture into squab cavities and truss
according to instructions (Poultry, pg. 3). Combine
the oil and the remaining orange juice and blend
well. Arrange squab on a rack in a roasting pan and
brush with the oil mixture. Bake in a preheated
375-degree oven for 45 minutes or until the squab
is tender, basting frequently with the remaining oil
mixture. Arrange the squab on a serving dish and
garnish with parsley and orange slices, if desired.
This makes 6 servings.

ROASTED PHEASANT WITH SOUBISE SAUCE

1 dressed pheasant
Salt and pepper to taste
4 slices bacon
6 sm. peeled white onions
10 med. mushroom caps
1 recipe Basic Soubise Sauce *(Sauces, pg. 14)*

Sprinkle the pheasant generously inside and out with salt and pepper. Wrap the bacon slices around the pheasant and secure each piece with string. Place on rack in a broiling pan. Roast in a preheated 350-degree oven for 1 hour and 30 minutes or until pheasant is tender. Baste at 15 minute intervals during the last 45 minutes of roasting. Place the onions in a steamer and steam for 15 minutes according to instructions for steaming (Vegetables, pg. 7). Add the mushrooms and steam for 5 minutes longer. Place the pheasant on a platter, then spoon the Soubise sauce over the top, covering completely. Arrange 4 mushroom caps down the center of the pheasant. Arrange the remaining mushrooms, stem side up, around the pheasant and place an onion in each mushroom. Serve any remaining sauce with the pheasant. This makes 4 to 6 servings.

roasted pheasant with soubise sauce

The distinctive flavor of game birds is often well accented by an appropriate sauce, as is true of Roast Pheasant With Soubise Sauce. The deliciously edible garnishes surrounding and covering the bird are steamed mushrooms and small white onions.

PHEASANT MUSCATEL

3 1½-lb. pheasant
½ lemon
Salt and freshly ground pepper to taste
½ c. butter, softened
3 oranges, cut in half
1 c. golden raisins
1 tsp. grated lemon peel
⅓ c. Muscatel
3 c. Basic Chicken Stock (Soups, pg. 2)
1 c. long grain rice
⅔ c. chopped pecans
2 tbsp. finely chopped fresh parsley

Cut the pheasant in half lengthwise. Rub the cut sides with the lemon and season with salt and pepper. Place the pheasant halves, skin side up, in a shallow, oblong baking dish and spread 1 tablespoon of butter over each half. Squeeze the juice carefully from the oranges, keeping the shells intact. Remove the pulp from the shells and reserve the orange shells. Remove the seeds from the juice, then combine the juice, raisins, lemon peel, Muscatel and 1 cup of chicken stock. Pour into the baking dish. Bake in a preheated 350-degree oven for 45 minutes, basting with the raisin mixture every 10 minutes. Remove from the oven and keep warm. Vandyke the edges of the reserved orange shells. Combine remaining chicken stock and rice in a 1½-quart saucepan and bring to a boil, stirring frequently. Reduce heat and cover. Simmer for about 15 minutes or until liquid is absorbed, then remove from heat. Add the remaining 2 tablespoons of butter, pecans, parsley and salt and stir until the butter is melted. Spoon into the orange shells. Place the pheasant on a serving platter and garnish with the rice cups. Pour the raisin mixture into a sauceboat and serve with the pheasant. This makes 6 servings.

FLOWERING PLUM CORNISH HENS

4 lg. Cornish hens
Salt and freshly ground pepper to taste
4 lg. oranges
1 1-lb. can purple plums
¼ c. butter
¼ c. minced onion
1 tsp. ginger
1 tsp. Worcestershire sauce
1½ tsp. prepared mustard
⅓ c. chili sauce
¼ c. soy sauce
1 6-oz. can frozen lemonade concentrate
¼ c. shredded coconut

Cut the Cornish hens in half lengthwise and sprinkle with salt and pepper. Slice the unpeeled oranges and remove the seeds. Place the slices in 2 shallow, oblong baking pans. Place 4 Cornish hen halves, skin side up, in each baking pan on the orange slices. Bake in a preheated 350-degree oven for 45 minutes. Drain the plums, then remove the seeds. Place the plums in a blender container and process until puréed. Melt the butter in a medium-sized saucepan. Add the onion and cook over low heat, stirring constantly, until the onion is golden. Add the ginger, Worcestershire sauce, mustard, chili sauce, soy sauce, lemonade and plums, then bring to a boil, stirring until the lemonade is thawed. Reduce the heat and simmer for 15 minutes, stirring occasionally. Spoon all of the sauce over the Cornish hens and bake for 30 to 45 minutes longer or until the hens are tender, basting with the plum sauce frequently. Remove the Cornish hen halves with orange slices to a serving platter and sprinkle with the coconut. Serve remaining sauce with the hens. This makes 4 to 6 servings.

CORNISH HENS WITH SOUTHERN DRESSING

¼ c. raisins
½ c. Sauterne
1 c. butter
1¼ c. chopped onions
2 c. crumbled Cornmeal Muffins (Breads, pg. 40)
1 tsp. salt
Freshly ground pepper to taste
¼ tsp. poultry seasoning
2 eggs, beaten
¾ c. chopped pecans
4 Cornish hens
Melted butter
1 c. wild rice or brown rice
1 lb. fresh mushrooms, sliced

Soak the raisins in the Sauterne overnight. Melt ¼ cup of butter in a small saucepan. Add ¼ cup of onions and sauté, stirring constantly, until tender. Place the crumbled muffins in a large mixing bowl. Add the sautéed onions, raisin mixture, ½ teaspoon salt, pepper, poultry seasoning, eggs and pecans and mix well. Brush cavities of the Cornish hens with melted butter. Stuff the hens with the corn bread dressing, then place on a rack in a shallow, oblong baking pan. Bake in a preheated 350-degree oven for 1 hour or until the hens are tender, brushing with melted butter every 15 minutes. Cook the wild rice while the Cornish hens are baking. Sauté remaining onions in ¼ cup of butter until tender, stirring constantly. Wash the rice well, then drain. Pour 3 cups of water into the top of a double boiler, then add remaining ½ teaspoon salt and bring to a boil. Stir in the rice gradually, then stir in the onions. Bring to a boil again. Place over boiling water, then cover and cook for 30 minutes. Sauté the mushrooms in remaining ½ cup of butter for 5 minutes, stirring frequently. Stir into the rice mixture and add more boiling water, if needed. Cover and cook for 15 minutes longer or until the rice is tender and water absorbed. Serve with the Cornish hens. This makes 8 servings.

The Creative Homemaker's Academy © MCMLXXIII
Selected Illustrations © B.P.C. Publishing Limited MCMLXX

GIANT HERO SANDWICH

1   3-oz. package cream cheese, softened
Basic Blender Mayonnaise *(Sauces, pg. 3)*
1 long loaf French bread
Prepared mustard
Ham slices
Salami slices
Sliced cooked pork
Bologna slices
Liver sausage slices
Swiss cheese slices
Fresh tomato wedges
Green and ripe olives
Sm. pickled onions
Gherkins
Endive
Watercress

Place the cream cheese in a small bowl, then stir in enough mayonnaise to make a smooth mixture of spreading consistency. Cut the bread in half lengthwise. Spread each half with the cheese mixture, then mustard. Arrange the remaining ingredients on the bottom half of the bread as shown in the illustration. Place the top half over the filling, then cut diagonally into 6 pieces to serve. This makes 6 servings.

SKEWERED PINEAPPLE-SALAMI SANDWICHES

1   16-oz. can sliced pineapple
6   3-in. thick slices sourdough bread
1/2 c. butter, softened
1/2 tsp. mixed Italian herbs
Dash of garlic powder
12 slices mozzarella cheese
12 slices salami
2 eggs
1/2 c. milk
3/4 c. freshly grated Parmesan cheese

Drain the pineapple. Cut 2 slits, 1 inch apart, in each bread slice from top to bottom, leaving bottom crust intact. Mix the butter, Italian herbs and garlic powder, then spread on the cut sides of each slit. Trim the mozzarella cheese slices to the same size as the salami slices. Place 1 cheese slice on each salami slice and roll as for jelly roll. Insert 1 pineapple slice in 1 slit and 2 salami-wrapped cheese slices in the other slit of each slice of bread. Secure each sandwich with 2 wooden picks. Place the eggs in a shallow bowl and beat well. Add the milk and mix until combined, then dip the sandwiches into the egg mixture to lightly moisten the surfaces. Place on a buttered baking sheet and sprinkle with the Parmesan cheese. Bake in a preheated 400-degree oven for about 15 minutes or until browned. Place in a serving dish and garnish with cherry tomatoes and parsley. This makes 6 servings.

TWO GIANT HOT SANDWICHES

Three meat favorites often used in sandwiches are pastrami, prosciutto, and salami. Pastrami is a highly flavored cut of beef which is rubbed with spices, smoked and cooked. "Italian Ham" or prosciutto is made from cured pork and can be eaten without further cooking. Salami is a dry sausage, also of Italian origin, made of finely chopped pork or beef seasoned with red wine and peppercorns. Sandwiches made from these meats are delicious with chilled wine or beer.

LONG SANDWICH WITH SALAMI

1 loaf Italian bread
12 salami slices
Butter
1/4 lb. fresh mushrooms, sliced
1/4 c. all-purpose flour
1 c. half and half cream
1/2 c. white wine
White pepper to taste
Celery salt to taste
3 tomatoes, skinned *(Vegetables, pg. 27)*
4 to 6 slices mozzarella cheese

Place the bread, cut side up, on a jelly roll pan. Bake in a preheated 425-degree oven until golden. Remove pan from the oven and keep oven hot. Arrange the salami slices on the toasted bread. Melt 1/4 cup of butter in a heavy saucepan. Add the mushrooms and sauté until golden. Remove the mushrooms with a slotted spoon and arrange over the salami. Add enough butter to the remaining butter in the saucepan to measure 1/4 cup, then place over low heat to melt. Stir in the flour to make a smooth paste. Add the cream, stirring constantly, then cook until thickened. Stir in the wine and seasonings, then cook, stirring, until the sauce is very thick and the flavors blended. Cut the tomatoes into thin slices. Spread the sauce over the mushrooms and salami, then arrange the tomatoes over the sauce so that the slices overlap slightly. Place the cheese slices over the top of the sand- wich, covering as evenly as possible. Bake until the cheese is melted. This makes 4 servings.

PROSCIUTTO UNDER COVER

1/2 loaf Italian bread
6 to 8 slices Port du Salut cheese or 1
    3-oz. package cream cheese
1/4 c. minced leek
12 slices prosciutto or pastrami
1 tbsp. capers
2 lg. eggs, separated
1 c. Basic Blender Mayonnaise *(Sauces, pg. 3)*

Slice the bread in half lengthwise and reserve the top half for use in Long Sandwich with Salami and Mushrooms. Place the remaining half, cut side up, on a baking sheet. Bake in a preheated 425-degree oven until golden. Arrange the cheese slices on the toasted bread, then sprinkle the leek over the cheese. Place the prosciutto slices over the cheese and sprinkle with capers. Beat the egg yolks slightly, then stir into the mayonnaise, mixing well. Beat the egg whites until stiff, but not dry. Fold 1/4 of the egg whites into the mayonnaise mixture thoroughly, then fold in the remaining egg whites carefully. Spread the mayonnaise mixture evenly over the sandwich. Bake in a preheated 400-degree oven for 8 to 10 minutes or until the topping is golden brown. Serve immediately. This makes 4 servings.

sausages lyonnaise with french mustard

Although this recipe comes from the Province of Touraine in France, it is highly popular in southern America among the Louisiana French. Sausage Lyonnaise, an excellent breakfast or supper dish, is made from smoked sausages called *andouille* (pronounced "ahn - dou - i), a well-known variety in Louisiana and various other southern locations. This highly seasoned, smoked sausage is often added to creole gumbo for a very exceptional flavor. If *andouille* sausages are not available in your area, you may substitute any highly seasoned, smoked sausage.

SAUSAGES LYONNAISE WITH FRENCH MUSTARD

1 tbsp. butter
1 lb. andouille or smoked pork sausage
1 recipe Basic Duchess Potato Mixture
    (Vegetables, pg. 3)
1 tbsp. finely chopped parsley

Melt the butter in a skillet over low heat, then add the sausage. Cook slowly, turning occasionally, for about 15 minutes or until lightly browned. Pipe the potato mixture into large mounds on the ends of a heatproof platter. Bake in a preheated 400-degree oven until lightly tinged with brown. Place the sausage in the center of the platter, then sprinkle with the parsley. Serve with French Mustard. This makes 4 servings.

FRENCH MUSTARD

½ c. dry mustard
¼ c. beer
½ tsp. salt
3 tsp. wine vinegar

Combine all ingredients in a small bowl and mix well.

sausage lyonnaise

Sausage Lyonnaise is made simply by browning andouille sausages over low heat, sprinkling them with bits of parsley, and serving them with potatoes. The white pot contains hot French mustard, which heightens the zesty flavor of these delicious sausages.

sausage and bacon pie

Sausage and Bacon Pie may be served either hot or cold — which makes it a very convenient entreé. The cut-away slice reveals the heartiness of this dish; its principle ingredients are sausage, bacon, onions and potatoes, encased in a flaky crust of pastry. Iced tomato soup with finely minced tarragon leaves is the side dish shown here and delightfully complements the pie.

SAUSAGE AND BACON PIE

1 recipe French Lining Pastry (Pork, pg. 7)
1 lb. cooked smoked pork sausage, sliced
2 c. sliced cooked potatoes
2 green onions, minced
2 tbsp. chopped chives
6 slices Canadian bacon, diced
Salt and freshly ground pepper to taste
¼ c. half and half cream
2 eggs, beaten

Roll out about ²/₃ of the pastry and fit it into a loaf pan, extending the pastry up and over the ends and sides. Trim off excess pastry. Combine the sausage, potatoes, onions, chives and bacon in a bowl and sprinkle with salt and pepper. Toss together lightly with 2 forks. Turn into the pastry-lined pan. Combine the cream and eggs and pour over the top. Lift the sausage mixture several times with a fork to allow the egg mixture to flow to bottom. Turn the edges of the pastry in and brush with water. Roll out to fit the top of the pan. Place on top, then pinch together to seal. Bake in a preheated 375-degree oven for about 45 minutes or until well browned. This makes 6 to 8 servings.

TRIPE À LA MODE DE CAEN

In 1066 William the Conqueror of Normandy held a feast for his knights before embarking for England and the Battle of Hastings. On that night, the entreé was a well-seasoned tripe dish that was destined in centuries to come to be regarded as a classic, *Tripe à la mode de Caen.*

A modern version of this most famous tripe dish in Europe is presented below — sparked with wine and the romance of its medieval origin. Tripe, the inner lining of the stomach of an animal (usually beef), is gourmet fare when prepared in this manner.

Interestingly, the gourmet status of tripe is guaranteed by an entire gastronomic order that is devoted to its recognition, *la Tripière d'Or et Membres de la Gastronomie Normande.* The existence of this order assures the dish of its place as an all-time classic — and gives us an inkling of the high opinion the Normans have of tripe.

If you are searching for an entreé that will bolster the budget and break the monotony of the usual daily fare, serve your family the meal that delighted the palates of Norman knights more than 900 years ago.

tripe à la mode de caen

Tripe à la Mode de Caen is the most famous tripe dish in Europe. It is served here in an earthenware cooking pot called a tripière, which has curved sides and a small opening. The flavorladen steam rising from the tripe is trapped by the curved sides of the pot, and is forced back into the food — increasing the flavor measurably.

TRIPE À LA MODE DE CAEN MADE WITH CANNED TRIPE

1 1-lb. can tripe
3/4 c. all-purpose flour
Vegetable oil
4 c. Basic Beef Stock (*Soups, pg. 2*)
1/2 tsp. salt
1/2 tsp. celery salt
1/4 tsp. onion salt
1/4 tsp. thyme
1/2 tsp. oregano
1 tbsp. A 1 Sauce
1 c. diced onions
1 1/2 c. diced carrots
1 1/2 c. diced potatoes

Remove the gelatin from the tripe and reserve. Wash the tripe and drain well. Remove all of the fat, then cut the tripe into large cubes. Place 1/2 cup of the flour in a bag. Add the tripe and shake until coated. Heat 6 tablespoons of oil in a large, heavy skillet over high heat until hot. Add the tripe and cook, stirring and turning occasionally, until well browned. Remove the tripe from the skillet and place in a large casserole. Pour 1/4 cup of oil into the same skillet and heat. Add the remaining 1/4 cup of flour to the oil and cook, stirring constantly, until dark brown. Add the beef stock all at once and cook, stirring constantly, until the mixture comes to a boil. Stir in the reserved gelatin, salt, celery salt, onion salt, thyme, oregano and A 1

Sauce, then remove from heat. Place the onions, carrots and potatoes in the casserole with the tripe and mix well. Pour the gravy over the tripe mixture and cover the casserole. Bake in a preheated 350-degree oven for 1 hour. Remove from oven and stir well, adding 1 cup of additional beef stock or water, if needed. Cover and bake for 15 minutes longer. Bovril or Kitchen Bouquet to taste may be added to the gravy before pouring over the tripe mixture if a darker shade is desired, but decrease the amount of salt. One pound of pickled tripe, soaked for 30 minutes and drained, may be substituted for canned tripe. This makes about 6 servings.

HOW TO BLANCH FRESH TRIPE:

Wash the fresh tripe thoroughly under cold running water. Place the tripe in a large saucepan and cover it with water. Bring to a boil for 5 minutes. Drain and rinse the tripe and repeat the boiling 2 more times. Drain the tripe and it is then ready to cook as your recipe directs.

charcuterie fans with choux pastry puffs

*Charcuterie meats (variety pork meats)
make an attractive cold luncheon platter
when the different cuts are shaped,
rolled and arranged in a pretty pattern.
This presentation of Charcuterie Fans
(the bread is on a separate serving dish)
also includes lettuce leaves dressed
with Basic Vinaigrette (Sauces, pg. 2) and
a border of butter curls.*

CHARCUTERIE FANS WITH CHOUX PASTRY PUFFS

2 recipes Basic Chou Pastry (Desserts, pg. 56)
3 c. torn lettuce leaves
½ recipe Basic Vinaigrette (Sauces, pg. 2)
1 hard-boiled egg, finely chopped
14 butter curls (General Information, pg. 27)
8 thin slices corned beef
12 slices cooked salami
24 slices liver sausage
3 lemon wedges
1 recipe Mustard Mayonnaise (Sauces, pg. 3)
Toasted sliced almonds

Prepare and bake the *chou* pastry, forming it into
3-inch long *éclair* shapes. Place the lettuce on one
side of a large serving plate. Mix the vinaigrette and
egg and pour over the lettuce. Place the butter
curls around the lettuce. Cut the corned beef slices
with a fluted round cookie cutter and overlap
around the butter curls. Overlap 9 of the cooked
salami slices halfway over the corned beef.
Overlap part of the liver sausage halfway over the
cooked salami. Coil remaining liver sausage slices
over 2 fingers to form horn shapes, then place halfway over the flat liver sausage slices. Coil the remaining cooked salami slices and place them over
the liver sausage horns. Place the lemon wedges in
the cooked salami horns. Split the puffs and spread
with mayonnaise. Place the halves back together,
then spread mayonnaise over the top of the puffs
and sprinkle heavily with almonds. Place the puffs
on a serving plate and serve with the meat plate.
Meats and lettuce may be served in the puffs as
sandwiches, if desired. This makes about 28 horns.

AUSTRIAN PANEL SANDWICH

1 8-oz. package cream cheese, softened
½ c. Basic Mayonnaise (Sauces, pg. 3)
¼ tsp. onion salt
¼ tsp. celery salt
9 lg. thin slices dark pumpernickel bread
6 slices salami
6 slices mortadella

Place the cream cheese in a small mixing bowl and
beat with an electric mixer until smooth and fluffy.
Add the mayonnaise, onion salt and celery salt,
then mix until well combined. Spread the cream
cheese mixture over all the slices of bread, then
stack 3 slices together to make 3 sandwiches. Fold
2 slices of salami and 2 slices of mortadella in half
for each sandwich, then arrange on the top of the
sandwiches. This makes 3 large sandwiches.

SWEETBREADS IN CREAM

1½ lb. sweetbreads
6 tbsp. all-purpose flour
Salt
¼ lb. fresh mushrooms, thinly sliced
¾ c. Chablis
½ c. chicken consommé
1 c. whipping cream
Freshly ground white pepper to taste
1 recipe Basic Duchess Potato Mixture
(Vegetables, pg. 3)

Place the sweetbreads in cold water and allow them to soak for at least 1 hour, then drain. Separate the sweetbreads into large pieces. Mix the flour with ½ cup cold water in a medium-sized saucepan until smooth. Stir in 5 cups of boiling water. This mixture is called a *blanc*. Add 1 tablespoon salt to the *blanc* and cook until thickened and clear. Add the sweetbreads and simmer for 15 minutes or until the sweetbreads are tender. Drain the sweetbreads. When they have cooled, remove the cartilage, tubes and connective tissue, then rinse in hot water to remove all the *blanc*. Drain well and pat dry. Place on an ovenproof platter and keep warm in the oven. Place the mushrooms in a small saucepan and pour the Chablis over the mushrooms. Bring to a boil and reduce heat. Simmer for 4 minutes. Remove the mushrooms with a slotted spoon and keep warm. Pour the consommé into the mushroom liquid and bring to a boil. Stir in the cream and bring to a boil again. Reduce the heat and simmer, without stirring, until the liquid is slightly thickened. Season with salt to taste and pepper. Stir in the mushrooms, then pour over the sweetbreads. Pipe the potatoes around the edge of the platter. Bake in preheated 400-degree oven until the potatoes are lightly tinged with brown. This makes 4 to 6 servings.

MENU FOR AN EARLY SUMMER EVENING

GREEK FISH APPETIZERS
(Appetizers, pg. 62)

WITH

PIMENTO ESCOFFIER
(Vegetables, pg. 31)

*****

SWEETBREADS IN CREAM

SWEET AND SOUR ASPARAGUS
(Vegetables, pg. 74)

*****

FROZEN RASPBERRY SOUFFLÉ
(Desserts, pg. 196)

WITH

ALMOND MACAROONS
(Desserts, pg. 129)

COFFEE AND LIQUEURS

SUGGESTED WINES:
**Greek Pallini,
California Emerald Dry or
Eastern Niagara**

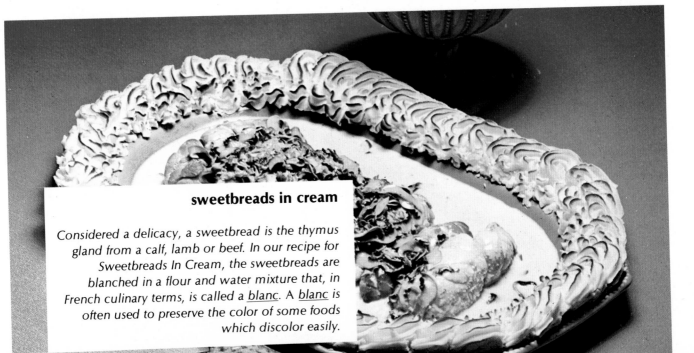

sweetbreads in cream

Considered a delicacy, a sweetbread is the thymus gland from a calf, lamb or beef. In our recipe for Sweetbreads In Cream, the sweetbreads are blanched in a flour and water mixture that, in French culinary terms, is called a <u>blanc</u>. A <u>blanc</u> is often used to preserve the color of some foods which discolor easily.

sweetbread and mushroom pie

Bubbly and golden brown when it comes from the oven, Sweetbread and Mushroom Pie is a savory open pie baked in puff pastry. A classic sauce, Basic Mornay (Sauces, pg. 11), unites the flavors of sweetbreads and mushrooms in this dish, and an additional sprinkle of Parmesan over the top accents the cheese flavor. Buttered corn and fresh, crisp lettuce are added for an appetizing and well-balanced family dinner.

SWEETBREAD AND MUSHROOM PIE

1 lb. sweetbreads
2 tbsp. vinegar
Salt
½ recipe Basic Puff Pastry *(Desserts, pg. 22)*
1 egg, well beaten
1 recipe Basic Mornay Sauce *(Sauces, pg. 11)*
¼ lb. fresh mushrooms, thinly sliced
Freshly ground white pepper to taste
¼ c. freshly grated Parmesan cheese
Egg Wash *(Breads, pg. 6)*

Soak the sweetbreads in cold water for 1 hour, then drain. Combine 1 quart of water, the vinegar and 1 teaspoon of salt in a saucepan and bring to a boil. Add the sweetbreads, then cover and simmer for 20 minutes. Remove the sweetbreads with a slotted spoon and place in a bowl of ice water. When chilled, separate into small pieces, remove the outer membrane and cut out the tubes. Roll out the pastry on a lightly floured surface to ⅛-inch thickness, then line a 2½-inch deep oval or rectangular baking dish with the pastry. Beat the egg quickly into the Mornay sauce. Add the mushrooms, sweetbreads, salt to taste and pepper and mix well. Turn into the pastry and sprinkle with the cheese. Bake in a preheated 425-degree oven, 1 shelf above the center, for 10 minutes. Reduce the oven temperature to 350 degrees and bake for 20 minutes longer or until the pastry is golden brown. Brush the edge of the pastry with Egg Wash and bake for 10 minutes longer or until the pastry is well browned. Garnish with toasted almonds, if desired. This makes about 6 servings.

SMOKED TONGUE WITH CREOLE SAUCE

1 2-lb. smoked beef tongue
1 lg. onion, chopped
1 carrot, chopped
2 stalks of celery, chopped
2 cloves
1 recipe Creole Sauce

Place the tongue in a large kettle and cover with water. Add the onion, carrot, celery and cloves, then cover and bring to a boil. Reduce the heat and simmer for about 2 hours or until fork-tender. Remove the tongue from the liquid and let cool. Peel off the outer skin and trim the base. Add enough tongue broth to the Creole Sauce to thin to desired serving consistency. Pour the Creole Sauce

into a serving platter to a depth of ¼-inch. Cut the tongue into thin slices, starting at the base and arrange the slices in the sauce. Cut the slices toward the tip at an angle so the pieces will not be too small. Serve with the remaining sauce. The tongue may be reheated in the liquid if desired. This makes 6 to 8 servings.

CREOLE SAUCE

4 med. onions
4 green sweet peppers
1 lb. fresh mushrooms
¼ c. olive oil
3 tbsp. sugar
1 bay leaf
1 tsp. allspice
¼ c. wine vinegar
2 1-lb. cans Italian tomatoes
Salt and cayenne pepper to taste

Slice the onions lengthwise into thin strips. Cut the peppers in half lengthwise and remove the seeds and membrane. Cut the halves into strips the same width as the onions. Cut the mushrooms with the stems attached into lengthwise slices about ⅛ inch thick. Sauté the vegetables lightly in the olive oil in a large saucepan over medium heat until wilted but not brown. Add the remaining ingredients and simmer, covered, over very low heat for 2 hours, stirring frequently and mashing the tomatoes. The sauce will be thick. This makes 3 to 4 cups sauce.

BEEF TONGUE WITH DILL SAUCE

1 2-lb. fresh beef tongue
1 med. onion
1 bay leaf·
1 stalk of celery, cut in half
4 peppercorns
Salt to taste
1 recipe Basic Dill Sauce *(Sauces, pg. 28)*

Place the tongue in a large saucepan and add enough water to cover. Add the onion, bay leaf, celery, peppercorns and salt, then bring to a boil. Reduce heat and cover. Simmer for about 2 hours or until the tongue is tender. Remove from the heat and let the tongue stand in the liquid until lukewarm. Remove the tongue from the liquid, then peel the skin from the tongue. Place the tongue on a serving platter and slice. Serve with the dill sauce. The tongue may be served cold. This makes 6 to 8 servings.

sautéed kidneys in cream

Kidneys, like liver, provides a high percentage of the vitamins required by the body — and couples economy and flavor with the nutrition it offers. The local market will probably carry kidneys from beef, lamb, pork and veal (the recipe below calls for veal kidney), all of which should be cleaned of their thin, white covering membranes as well as the tubes and white fatty centers prior to cooking.

SAUTÉED KIDNEYS IN CREAM

4 Baked Croûtes (*Breads, pg. 16*)
2 1-lb. veal kidneys
4 c. Basic Beef Stock (*Soups, pg. 2*)
¼ c. butter
¼ c. olive oil
¾ lb. fresh mushrooms, thinly sliced
¼ c. brandy
½ c. sherry
1 c. whipping cream
Salt and freshly ground pepper to taste

Prepare the Croûtes. Remove all membranes and cut away all the fat from the kidneys, leaving the kidneys in large pieces. Soak the kidneys in cold, salted water for 15 minutes. Drain and place in a large saucepan. Pour the beef stock over the kidneys and bring to a boil. Remove from the heat and let stand until cold. Drain the kidneys and reserve the liquid. Cut the kidneys into thin slices. Melt the butter with the oil in a large, heavy skillet over high heat. Add the kidneys and mushrooms and sauté, stirring constantly, for 1 minute to seal the juices in the kidneys. Pour the brandy over the kidney mixture and ignite. Shake the skillet over the heat for 30 seconds, then stop shaking the skillet and let the flames die. Add the reserved liquid and sherry to the skillet and bring to a boil. Reduce the heat and simmer for about 5 minutes or until the kidneys lose their pink color. Remove the kidney mixture from the skillet with a slotted spoon and keep warm. Increase the heat to high and pour the cream into the skillet. Boil until the creamy mixture is of sauce consistency. Lower the heat and add the kidney mixture, salt and pepper to the skillet. Heat through, then remove from the heat. Place the *croûtes* on a serving plate and spoon the kidney mixture and sauce over the *croûtes*. Garnish with chopped fresh parsley and Basic Duchess Potato Mixture (*Vegetables, pg. 3*). This makes 4 servings.

sautéed kidneys in cream

Sautéed Kidneys In Cream is a flambé dish. In this case, however, the purpose of flaming is culinary rather than aesthetic. Because the kidneys and mushrooms are sautéed in a butter and oil mixture, flaming brandy is used both to burn away the grease and at the same time to add flavor.

chinon rabbit with red wine

While most of the rabbit that comes to the table is the hutch or domestic rabbit, some wild rabbit is shot by hunters. Whether domestic or wild, young rabbit (about 3 to 4 months old) is the most tender. Domestic rabbit is almost entirely white meat with less fat than poultry. The meat is very succulent when prepared properly, though less delicate than poultry. Of course, wild rabbit has a more gamey flavor.

The rabbit recipe below is from Chinon, a town in the Province of Touraine, France, noted for its excellent cooking. Typical of the town, Chinon Rabbit With Red Wine is a simple but beautifully prepared dish.

chinon rabbit with red wine

Chinon Rabbit With Red Wine is shown here served in a rich brown sauce and garnished with a deep border of creamy duchess potatoes. Rabbit pieces were turned in flour, browned in bacon drippings and placed in a casserole with wine, stock and seasonings. This recipe (as you can see) creates an appetizing and attractive main dish, very appropriate for a cold winter evening or a hunter's breakfast!

CHINON RABBIT WITH RED WINE

1 rabbit, disjointed
Salt and pepper to taste
All-purpose flour
½ c. bacon drippings
1 c. red wine
1½ c. beef broth
1 Bouquet Garni (*Soups, pg. 2*)
1 lg. onion
3 cloves of garlic
¼ c. butter
12 sm. onions
3 tbsp. cornstarch
1 recipe Basic Duchess Potatoes (*Vegetables, pg. 3*)
2 tsp. Bovril or Kitchen Bouquet

Season the rabbit pieces with salt and pepper, then dredge with flour. Heat bacon drippings in a frypan, then add the rabbit pieces and brown on all sides. Remove the rabbit pieces and place in a baking dish. Add the wine, broth, *Bouquet Garni,* the large onion and garlic cloves and cover. Bake in a preheated 350-degree oven for 1 hour and 30 minutes or until the rabbit is tender. While the rabbit is baking, melt the butter in a heavy saucepan. Add the small onions and fry over medium heat until golden, stirring constantly. Add a small amount of water, then cover and simmer until onions are tender, stirring carefully several times. Remove the rabbit pieces from the baking dish and pile onto a large serving platter. Remove the onions from the saucepan, using a slotted spoon, and place over the rabbit pieces. Keep warm. Discard the *Bouquet Garni,* large onion and garlic cloves, then pour the pan juices into the saucepan. Combine a small amount of the pan juices with the cornstarch to make a smooth mixture, then stir the cornstarch mixture into the pan juices. Bring to a boil, stirring constantly. Reduce the heat and cook until the wine sauce is smooth and thick. Stir in Bovril and season to taste. Pour the sauce over the onions and rabbit. Pipe a border of duchess potatoes around the edge of the serving platter and serve immediately. This makes 4 to 6 servings.

normandy rabbit with cider

If you were to visit a farm kitchen in Normandy, you might find a potful of rabbit with cider in the oven, cooking away while the farmer's wife performs her morning chores. This highly seasoned rabbit stew, while originating with the peasantry, is a succulent dish that is fit for a king.

An oven-to-table casserole dish is satisfactory for this recipe. However, Normandy Rabbit With Cider may also be cooked in a Roman pot (Poultry, pg. 13), which is ideally suited to slow cooking. The following recipe uses a Roman pot.

normandy rabbit with cider

This is exactly the way Normandy Rabbit With Cider might be served in a Norman farm kitchen — taken directly from the oven to the table with additional cider served alongside. After the rabbit pieces were dredged with flour and fried until well browned, they were cooked in a casserole with onions and a cider mixture. This dish cooks slowly, so that once it is in the oven the cook is free.

NORMANDY RABBIT WITH CIDER

1 3-lb. rabbit
Basic Seasoned Flour *(Soups, pg. 32)* ·
½ c. vegetable oil
12 button mushrooms
½ tsp. chervil
¾ tsp. chopped chives
1¼ c. apple cider or juice
Salt and freshly ground pepper to taste

Prepare the Normandy Rabbit With Cider in a Roman pot, soaking and sealing the pot according to the instructions for Chicken With Saffron Rice (Poultry, pg. 14) or use a casserole. Cut the rabbit into serving pieces, then dredge with seasoned flour. Heat the oil in a large, heavy skillet. Add the rabbit and cook over medium high heat until well browned on all sides. Place the rabbit in the Roman pot or casserole and add the mushrooms, chervil and chives. Pour off all except 2 tablespoons of the drippings from the skillet. Add 1 tablespoon seasoned flour to the drippings in the skillet and cook, stirring constantly, until well browned. Add the cider and ½ cup water gradually, stirring constantly, and bring to a boil. Pour over the rabbit mixture and season with salt and pepper, if needed. Cover and seal. Bake in a preheated 350-degree oven for 1 hour and 30 minutes. Break the seal and remove the cover. This makes about 6 servings.

introducing venison

Venison, though the term is usually associated with deer meat, correctly applies to the meat of any antlered animal. Its tenderness depends upon the animal's age; its flavor upon its diet. The flavor has been described as a cross between beef and lamb, and it is influenced a great deal by proper aging. It is important that the carcass be aged *long* enough — depending upon the size and age of the animal, about 3 to 5 weeks in a temperature of 36 to 40 degrees — after which the animal may be prepared in cuts.

Venison is butchered in the same manner as beef, and like beef, the more tender cuts are the loin roasts, rib chops and loin steaks. These are often marinated and may, be cooked as you would corresponding beef cuts. Many people choose to marinate all venison to assure tenderness and diminish the gamey flavor. Actually there is very little fat but you should trim away as much of the fat as possible, since it has a strong taste and quickly becomes rancid.

GRAUSTARK VENISON

1 6-lb. leg of venison
Salt to taste
1 recipe Marinade For Game (*Sauces, pg. 5*)
6 strips of salt pork
3 lb. small potatoes
Butter
White pepper to taste
2 tbsp. minced fresh parsley
2   10-oz. packages frozen Brussels sprouts
¼ c. chopped walnuts
2 tbsp. all-purpose flour
1 c. beef broth

Season the venison with salt and place in a shallow pan. Pour the marinade over the venison, then refrigerate for 24 hours, turning occasionally. Remove the venison from the marinade, then strain the marinade and reserve. Place the venison on a rack in a shallow baking pan and place the salt pork over the venison. Bake in a preheated 450-degree oven for 25 minutes. Reduce the oven temperature to 325 degrees and bake for about 3 hours longer or until the venison is well done, basting occasionally with half the reserved marinade. Peel the potatoes and cut in half. Cook in boiling, salted water for about 15 minutes or until tender, then drain. Add 6 tablespoons of butter, salt, pepper and parsley and mix until the potatoes are coated. Keep warm. Cook the Brussels sprouts according to package directions until just tender, then drain. Melt ¼ cup

butter in a medium-sized saucepan. Add the Brussels sprouts and sauté for 5 minutes, stirring constantly. Add the walnuts and sauté, stirring, for 5 minutes longer. Keep warm. Place the venison on one side of a long, hot platter and keep warm. Pour the pan drippings into saucepan and add the remaining marinade. Bring to a boil. Blend 2 tablespoons of butter with the flour. Add to the marinade mixture and stir until blended. Add the broth slowly, stirring constantly, and bring to a boil again. Cook for 1 minute, then pour into a gravy boat. Place the potatoes on the other side of the platter and place the Brussels sprouts over the potatoes. Serve with the gravy. One pound of fresh, cooked Brussels sprouts may be used instead of the frozen variety. This makes 8 to 10 servings.

graustark venison

Graustark Venison features the leg portion of the animal, marinated in a mixture of dry red wine, onions, celery and seasonings. A marinade is almost essential for most venison cuts, to reduce the gamey taste and tenderize the meat. The wine marinade serves an additional purpose: it is part of a savory gravy to accompany the meat to the table. In the illustration, Brussels sprouts and potatoes are side vegetables — and to make the meal complete, a decanter of red wine is served.

CHILI DEER, VENISON LOAF, AND OZARK-STYLE VENISON STROGANOFF

As has been mentioned, deer is butchered into the same cuts as beef. This includes grinding the meat also, with the marked difference that ground venison is virtually all lean.

Two of the recipes on this page, Chili Deer and Venison Loaf, are made with ground venison. For those who have never tasted chili made with venison, Chili Deer is an interesting flavor adventure. Pork has been added because of venison's leaness, and the remaining ingredients are the traditional tomato, beans and pepper combination expected in a chili. Similarly, Venison Loaf resembles ground beef meat loaf — and the variation from beef to venison creates an entirely different taste from the popular beef standby.

The remaining recipe is Ozark-Style Venison Stroganoff, and as might be expected, the recipe calls for cubes of meat, mushrooms and sour cream. However, the unexpected variation of a tomato-based hot sauce provides a flavor complement to the venison.

CHILI DEER

5 lb. ground venison
1 lb. ground pork
3 lg. onions, finely chopped
4 cloves of garlic, pressed
2 sm. chili peppers, finely chopped
1/2 sm. box cumin seed
2 tbsp. red wine vinegar
1 c. catsup
1 c. tomato sauce
Salt to taste
4 1-lb. cans kidney beans

Place a large kettle or Dutch oven over high heat until hot. Add the venison and pork and cook until lightly browned, stirring frequently. Add the onions and garlic and cook, stirring, until the meats are well browned. Add the chili peppers, cumin seed, vinegar, catsup, tomato sauce, salt and 6 cups of water and mix well. Bring to a boil, then reduce heat and cover. Simmer for 1 hour or until most of the liquid has evaporated, stirring occasionally. Uncover and add the beans, then simmer until of desired consistency, stirring occasionally. This makes about 12 servings.

VENISON LOAF

2 lb. ground venison
2 lb. bulk pork sausage
2 med. onions, finely chopped
1 1/2 c. cracker crumbs
1 c. evaporated milk
3 eggs, lightly beaten
2 c. Basic Barbecue Sauce (Sauces, pg. 8)
1 tsp. salt
1/2 tsp. freshly ground pepper

Place the venison, sausage, onions and crumbs in a large bowl and mix well. Add the milk, eggs, 1 cup of the barbecue sauce, salt and pepper and blend well. Chill for 15 minutes. Shape into 2 loaves, then place the loaves in a large, greased baking pan. Bake in a preheated 350-degree oven for 30 minutes. Spoon the remaining barbecue sauce over the loaves and bake for 45 minutes longer. This makes 8 to 10 servings.

OZARK-STYLE VENISON STROGANOFF

1 1/2 lb. venison
1' recipe Marinade For Game (Sauces, pg. 5)
All-purpose flour
1/4 c. vegetable shortening
1 6-oz. can mushrooms
1 onion, finely chopped
1 clove of garlic, pressed
1 can cream of tomato soup
1/4 tsp. hot sauce
1 tbsp. Worcestershire sauce
1/2 tsp. salt
1 1/2 c. sour cream

Cut the venison in 1 1/2-inch cubes and place in a bowl. Pour the marinade over the venison and marinate for several hours, turning occasionally. Drain off the marinade. Dredge the venison with flour, then brown in the hot shortening in a skillet. Drain the mushrooms and reserve the liquid. Add the onion, garlic, and mushrooms to the venison. Combine the soup, reserved mushroom liquid, hot sauce, Worcestershire sauce and salt, then stir into the venison mixture. Simmer for 1 hour, stirring occasionally. Stir in the sour cream just before serving and heat through, but do not boil. Serve over rice or mashed potatoes. One-fourth pound fresh mushrooms, sliced and sautéed in butter, may be substituted for the canned mushrooms. This makes 6 servings.

MARENGO CASSEROLE

1   3-lb. venison roast
2 recipes Marinade For Game *(Sauces, pg. 5)*
1/2 lb. sliced salt pork
1 lb. small onions
1 lb. small fresh mushrooms
Butter
1 can beef consommé
1   8-oz. can tomato sauce
1/4 c. all-purpose flour
Salt and freshly ground pepper to taste
1 tbsp. dry sherry
1 tbsp. brandy

Place the venison in a shallow pan, then pour the marinade over the venison. Refrigerate for 12 to 24 hours, turning occasionally. Drain off the marinade, then strain and reserve. Wipe the venison dry and place on the rack in a roasting pan. Wash the salt pork and place over the venison. Pour 1 1/2 cups of water into the pan, then add 1 cup of the reserved marinade. Roast in a preheated 325-degree oven for 2 hours or until done, basting with the pan drippings occasionally. Peel the onions and cook in boiling, salted water until tender, then drain. Sauté the mushrooms in a small amount of butter until lightly browned. Remove the venison from the boiling pan and place on a cutting board. Let cool for 20 to 30 minutes, and cut into cubes. Place the venison in a large skillet and add the onions, mushrooms, consommé, tomato sauce and 1 cup of the pan drippings. Combine the flour with 1/4 cup of water and mix until smooth, then stir into the venison mixture. Season with salt and pepper, then add the sherry and brandy. Simmer, stirring frequently, for 15 minutes or until thickened. Serve with boiled potatoes and green beans, if desired. This may be made the day before serving and reheated. This makes about 6 servings.

marengo casserole

Hearty, stew-like Marengo Casserole will satisfy the appetite of the hunter who brought home the venison. The meat is tenderized in the game marinade, then wrapped in salt pork and baked until done. From this point, the dish becomes a top-of-the-stove casserole simmered with onions, mushrooms, consommé, tomato sauce and an optional dash of sherry and brandy. For convenience, and improved flavor, Marengo Casserole may be prepared the day before serving and reheated.

poultry

table of contents

buying poultry

In this section, you'll learn how to buy, prepare and serve poultry. As you progress, you'll find many places—here and in other sections—where you'll be called on to use your newly-found BASIC skills.

We begin with the simple but important technique of roasting, with variations. You'll also learn how to cut up and truss chickens and turkeys. We've chosen chickens and turkeys because they usually cost just pennies a serving, and when properly prepared yield moist, tender meat with a succulent flavor.

After you have mastered the art of buying, preparing and serving chicken and turkey, you'll learn about game birds, wild members of the poultry family such as ducks, quail and pheasant. A section in a later lesson will be devoted entirely to game birds.

BUYING POULTRY

Your best buys are whole birds. If you purchase poultry already cut up, it will cost at least two or three cents more a pound.

When you choose poultry, look for birds with short legs, plump bodies and unbruised skins. The skin should be moist-looking, smooth, fine-grained, thin and should show no tears or discoloration. If the pink flesh shows from underneath the skin, it is a young, prime bird.

Look for a fat layer between the flesh and the skin. One of the signs fat is present is a yellow edge around the tail and neck. It melts during cooking and provides a natural basting liquid, keeping the delicate meat from drying out.

Once you have found poultry that appears to be what you want, apply still another test. Press the tip of the breastbone. It should be soft and pliable. A flexible bone means the bird is young; it stiffens as the bird gets older.

If you have found a bird with good skin, a fat layer and a pliable breastbone, check it over once more to ensure the package is unbroken.

Throughout this Course, we recommend using fresh foods and seasonings. If you live near a poultry farm, by all means patronize it. But if you depend on your local supermarket, let your butcher know you are relying on him for top quality, fresh birds. He can supply you with chickens and turkeys virtually indistinguishable from those freshly-killed.

In the meat department of most supermarkets, chicken is packaged under a variety of names. Let's explore these terms to see what is meant by each one.

TYPES OF POULTRY

Broilers-fryers are among the most popular kinds of chicken. These young, very tender chickens usually weigh between 1½ and 3½ pounds. Available whole or cut-up, they are well suited for roasting, simmering, baking, frying, grilling or broiling.

Roasters are large chickens weighing 3½ to 8 pounds. Usually sold whole, they are best for roasting, as their name implies.

Stewing chickens are older, less tender birds than either broilers-fryers or roasters. Weighing from 2½ to 5 or more pounds, they are recommended for stewing in water or other liquid.

Capons are large birds usually weighing from 5 to 10 pounds. For those who don't know what a capon is, let's just say it is a male chicken that has been unsexed and therefore is neither hen nor rooster. Capons yield a large amount of tender, white meat and are best roasted.

Turkeys are available in sizes ranging from as small as 8 to as large as 24 pounds. The best buy, in terms of flavor and economy, are 16 to 24-pound turkeys. They yield more meat per pound, and it's moist and tender.

COOKING METHODS

The basic methods of cooking poultry are roasting, grilling, broiling, frying, *sautéing,* braising, stewing and baking. In this Course, you'll master each.

Roasting is a classic method of preparing poultry, and the first one you'll learn. The bird is usually placed in an open pan and usually a preheated oven.

In *grilling,* the bird is placed on a spit or a grill over coals. (You may be more familiar with this method under the name "barbecuing.")

Broiling is similar to grilling but is usually done indoors under an oven broiler.

In *frying* and *sautéing,* poultry is cooked in hot fat in a pan on the stove. More fat is used to fry than to *sauté.*

Braising is similar to frying, but the cooking is done in a small amount of fat plus another liquid.

Stewing is cooking the poultry in a large quantity of water. When the cooking is completed, you usually have a rich broth to serve with the chicken.

Roasting, grilling and broiling are called "dry heat" cooking methods because little or no liquid is used. Other methods described above are "moist heat" methods, requiring the use of some liquid. Some meats and fish are suitable for moist heat methods because of their physical characteristics, while others lend themselves better to dry heat methods.

trussing a bird

Our first BASIC technique, trussing, simply fastens the wings and legs so the bird keeps its shape while cooking. We have developed a technique that is very easily accomplished, using nothing more elaborate than fine, strong string. Furthermore, after cooking the string can be quickly removed without burning your fingers.

The five pictures below give you instructions. You'll be pleasantly surprised at how easy it is to learn.

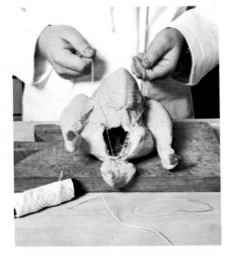

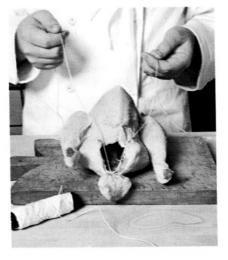

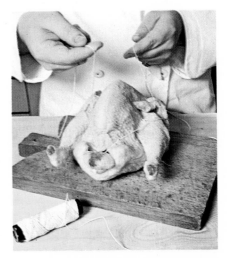

1 With the bird breast-side down, tie the string over the parson's nose—that's an old term for the tail end of the bird—leaving two long ends.

2 With the bird in the same position as for step 1, bring the string ends back toward you.

3 Wind the piece of string held in one hand around the wing on the same side of the bird. Repeat for the other side, and use the two stringholds to bring the wings against the bird's body.

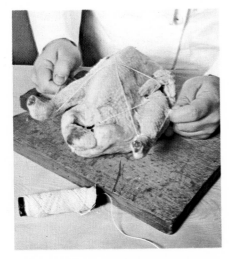

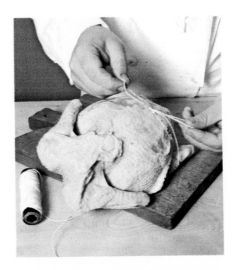

4 Now, cross the strings over the middle of the bird's breast. Bring each piece of string forward so that it goes under and over the leg tips as shown in the foreground of our picture. Pull both pieces of string tightly to draw the legs in against the body.

5 Turn the bird over and tie the string in a simple bow. After the bird is roasted, all you have to do is turn it over, pull the string ends, and the trussing will come apart.

basic open-roasting

Roasting is a popular method of cooking poultry. After you are familiar with the BASIC roasting technique, you'll be able to prepare chicken and turkey in a number of succulent dishes. What's more, you'll be at home with roasting the various meats and seafoods you'll encounter in subsequent lessons.

One reason for the popularity of roasting is its versatility. For instance, roast chicken can be served stuffed and hot, or cold and complemented with zesty vegetables. It can be dusted with paprika or other spices. You will find it can be prepared in many new and exciting ways.

Of all the different techniques for roasting, the one most often used and the simplest is probably classic open-roasting—the bird is cooked in an uncovered pan. The finished product will be exquisitely flavored with its own natural juices and the basting liquid of your choice. The fat layer mentioned earlier melts under heat, creating natural basting juices.

We emphasize that, if you open-roast, you must really baste—or brush the meat with this natural basting liquid, melted butter or other liquid to keep the food from drying out. The resulting juices are excellent to accompany a prime roasted fowl. And as a basis for gravy, they contribute rich flavor and color.

We will open-roast a capon, (a small turkey could be substituted). On following pages you'll also learn how to roast in foil and in a bag. Any of the three BASIC roasting techniques can be used to cook chicken or turkey.

To prepare your bird, rub the trussed chicken well with butter, cooking oil or chicken fat; sprinkle with salt and pepper. (See page 3 for illustrated instructions on how to truss.) Place the bird in an ungreased roasting pan, and add the amount of water specified in the recipe. This water, in combination with the fat that melts from beneath the chicken's skin and the fat that you rubbed it with, provides the basting liquid to keep your chicken moist throughout cooking.

Place the pan in a preheated oven and begin basting as your recipe directs. (We suggest you invest in a very inexpensive utensil marketed as a "baster," a rubber bulb attached to the end of a heavy plastic tube. Insert the tip of the tube into the liquid in the bottom of the pan, squeeze the bulb, then release it so the liquid is pulled into the tube. Lift the baster over the chicken and, slowly squeezing the bulb, cover the entire chicken with liquid.) It is desirable to repeat every fifteen to twenty minutes if possible.

Let the chicken cook as long as your recipe directs. To test for doneness, prick the skin of the thigh with a fork. If the juice runs clear, the bird is done. Or, jiggle the drumstick to see if the hip joint is loose. Remove it from the oven when thoroughly done and place it on a heated serving dish. Pour the pan juices into a saucepan and prepare the gravy as directed in the recipe or skim off some of the fat and strain the juices directly over the cooked chicken.

A word of warning. A solidly-frozen bird is unsuited for open-roasting. If you try to roast before thawing, you'll find a puddle of near-tasteless—and very unattractive—liquid in the bottom of the pan. The chicken won't have much flavor, either. If you have only a frozen chicken on hand and you want to roast it, bypass open-roasted in favor of a technique that will work—like the one on the next page.

NOTE:

We recommended above rubbing the chicken with salt and pepper. Some pepper comes already ground and has a distinctive flavor. But if you want to savor the full, richness of pepper, invest in a pepper mill and a bottle of peppercorns. Freshly ground pepper has a superb flavor that will greatly enhance many foods.

roasting in aluminum foil

Roasting in aluminum foil is a BASIC technique for preparing golden, moist, roasted chicken and turkey without basting. Unlike open-roasting, foil-roasting works as well with frozen poultry as with fresh.

Line the bottom and sides of a roasting pan with heavy-duty aluminum foil, which is not likely to tear during cooking. Reach into the stomach cavity of your bird and pull out the liver and gizzard. Freeze them to use later in stock and gravies. Rub the bird with melted butter, chicken fat or oil; lightly sprinkle with salt and pepper. After the chicken has been prepared, place it on the foil in the pan, and cover it loosely with a foil "tent."

Before you proceed, study the illustrations below. They show how your tent should look and how your chicken will look after cooking. Foil-roasting works successfully only if your tent covers loosely. While foil helps cook food, it can also act as an insulator and keep heat out. If you make a tight, form-fitting tent the inside of the chicken won't be done when the outside is.

Some cooks will tell you to fold the foil back from the bird during the last twenty minutes of cooking or the skin won't be crisp and brown. We've found this step totally unnecessary. The upper part of the bird will be richly browned when the cooking time is up, even though the bird remains under its tent the entire time.

1 Line the bottom and sides of a roasting pan with aluminum foil. Brush your chicken with fat and season as instructed above. Place the prepared chicken on foil in the pan, and make a tent similar to the one shown here. We are baking a 3-pound chicken at 350 degrees for 1 hour and 30 minutes or until golden brown.

2 If you've followed instructions, your chicken will look just like this. Neither basting nor browning the bird with foil turned back was necessary to produce this appetizingly golden chicken.

roasting in a see-through bag

The third BASIC roasting technique is in a see-through bag. Marketed under various brand names in most grocery stores, these bags are made of a special material that holds up under high temperatures. *Never* try to use cellophane bags—your lovely chicken or turkey will have a coating of melted plastic all over it!

See-through bags permit you to roast uniformly a golden, appetizing chicken or turkey. We found there was less shrinkage when we cooked in a see-through bag than in open roasting or in foil. Moreover, the bag kept spatters from dirtying the oven walls.

Before you use the roasting bag, familiarize yourself with the manufacturer's instructions. They will differ slightly. Follow our general instructions under the three pictures below, and your bird will be as attractive as ours. We used a turkey, but any of the three BASIC roasting methods is also suitable for chicken.

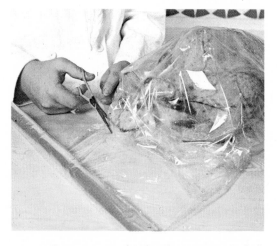

1 Prepare your bird as for roasting in foil: truss and brush it with melted butter, fat or cooking oil and season to taste. Put the bird inside the bag, following the manufacturer's instructions.

2 Wrap the package as the manufacturer instructs, being sure to punch holes in the top to allow steam to escape.

3 When your bird is taken from the oven it should be richly browned. Here is ours just cooked with the appetizing brownness showing through the bag.

ROASTING CHICKEN IN SEE-THROUGH OVEN BAGS

1 3½-lb. chicken
Cooking oil or butter
Sea salt or table salt
White pepper

Truss chicken. Brush the chicken with oil; sprinkle lightly with salt and pepper. Place the chicken in an oven bag and tie bag securely. Punch holes in bag according to manufacturer's directions. Place in shallow baking pan. Bake at 350 degrees for 1 hour and 15 minutes. Remove from oven, then let cool for at least 15 minutes. Remove from bag; save stock for future use.

piquant chicken

You can use chicken that has been open-roasted, foil-roasted, or cooked in a see-through bag for this dish. Sprinkle the chicken with paprika and place it on a bed of soft-fried red or green bell peppers. Top and tail it with cabbage and surround it with eggplant slices alternated with cheese-filled pastry. (You'll learn to prepare the vegetables and pastry in later lessons: if you want to wait until then to serve our suggestions, substitute a bed of parsley or a mixture of chopped sautéed onions, peppers and olives for the vegetables and pastry.

PIQUANT CHICKEN

4 lg. (green) bell peppers
1 sm. onion
⅛ tsp. thyme
⅛ tsp. basil
1 tsp. salt
⅛ tsp. white pepper
½ c. olive oil
1 baked chicken
12 pitted black olives
Paprika

Quarter the bell peppers and remove the seed and white inside portion. Grate the onion on a piece of waxed paper. Place bell peppers, onion with juice, thyme, basil, salt, pepper and olive oil in a small saucepan: cook until oil is bubbling. Simmer, covered, for about 15 minutes or until bell peppers are tender. Add the olives; cook and stir until heated through. Drain off the liquid, saving it to fry croutons, if desired. Sprinkle the hot chicken with paprika; set chicken on bed of bell pepper mixture. Red and yellow bell peppers may be used, if available, to add more color.

OPEN-ROASTED CAPON

1 7½ to 8-lb. capon or sm. turkey
Butter
Salt and freshly ground black peppercorns to taste
½ c. water

Rub the capon generously with butter, then season with a generous sprinkling of salt and pepper inside and out. Truss the capon as shown in step-by-step illustration on page 3. Place the capon in a foil-lined baking pan and place on middle shelf of oven at 400 degrees. Roast for 30 minutes, then spoon up pan juices and baste the capon thoroughly. Add the water to the pan. Reduce the oven temperature to 375 degrees. Place a small piece of foil over the breast of the capon and bake for about 2 hours longer, basting with pan juices frequently. Test the fattest part of the thigh by sticking with a slim skewer If juice is faintly pink, roast for about 15 to 20 minutes longer or until done. Serve with *Velouté* sauce (Sauces, pg. 4) if desired.

GRAVY

1½ to 2 c. hot water
3 tbsp. cornstarch

Remove the capon to a serving dish. Pour pan juices or broth into a saucepan and add enough water to the broth for desired taste. Combine the cornstarch with a small amount of broth and mix to a smooth liquid. Pour this into the broth and cook over medium heat, stirring constantly, until slightly thickened and rather clear, or for about 10 o 15 minutes.

open-roasted capon

Our golden brown roasted capon is surrounded by artichoke bottoms filled with tiny peas. In the silver bowl in the background is Velouté Sauce (Sauces, pg. 4). The silver pitcher contains the natural juices from the roasted bird.

cutting chicken into pieces

A simple but important procedure, cutting a whole chicken into serving pieces, can save you money. You'll need to know how to cut up chicken to prepare Oven-Baked Chicken with Mushrooms (page 11) and Sauté of Chicken with Cream Sauce (page 10). Follow the step-by-step pictures and instructions below.

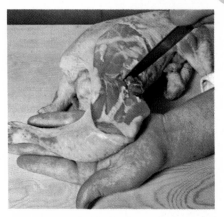

1 With a sharp knife, cut away the legs, keeping the thighs attached.

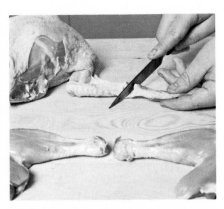

2 Cut off the wing tips. Skin the chicken.

3 Chop off the bone tips at the end of the legs. Using sterilized pruning shears or a similarly sharp cutting tool, cut straight through the center of the bird from the neck to the tail. In the foreground of this picture, see the severed wing tips, leg pieces and bone tips of legs.

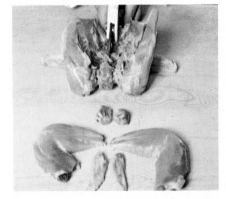

4 Cut off the tail of the bird. Finish separating the bird through the backbone.

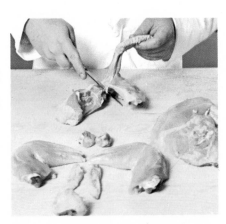

5 Remove wing from one breast as being done here. The other breast with the wing still attached and the previously severed pieces appear in foreground.

6 Now cut the other wing away as shown in the right background. (At the left in the background, you'll see the wing severed in step 5). Cut each leg away from the attached thigh, as shown.

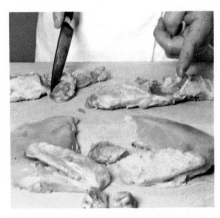

7 We indicate, with knife and finger, cavities from which oyster-shaped pieces of succulent meat have been removed.

sauté of chicken with cream sauce

This dish is made entirely in a frying pan. Our picture shows a formal serving with the chicken enclosed by an ornamental piping of Duchess potatoes (Vegetables, pg. 2) tinted green with food coloring. We've tucked peas into the four Duchess potato baskets. This decoration is, of course, purely optional.

MENU

Layered Orange Gelatin with Basic Mayonnaise
(Salads, pg. 6, Sauces, pg. 3)

Sauté of Chicken with Cream Sauce
(Poultry, pg. 10)

Lima Bean Casserole
(Vegetables, pg. 6)

Chocolate Chip Meringues
(Desserts, pg. 10)

SAUTÉ OF CHICKEN WITH CREAM SAUCE

1 3 to 4-lb. chicken
3 tbsp. butter
¼ c. cooking oil
½ c. dry white wine
1 c. Basic Chicken Stock *(Soups, pg. 2)*
1 tsp. dried thyme
½ c. heavy cream
1 tsp. salt
¼ tsp. pepper

Cut the chicken into serving portions. Melt the butter with the oil in a large heavy frying pan. Add chicken; fry over medium-heat for about 3 minutes or until golden. Add the wine, then bring to a simmer. Add the stock and thyme and simmer for about 20 minutes or until chicken is tender. Transfer chicken to a heated serving dish. Add the cream to the liquid in frying pan; boil until mixture is consistency of heavy cream. Add salt and pepper; mix well. Pour over chicken.

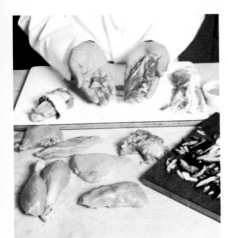

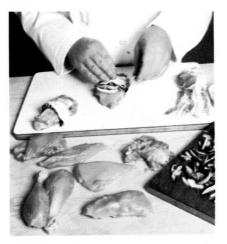

1 Assemble the ingredients for this recipe. In addition to the pieces of uncooked, skinned chicken and thinly sliced, unskinned mushrooms, set out pieces of chicken meat not specifically called for in the recipe. Tuck them under each portion of chicken.

2 Set each piece of chicken on a strip of bacon, top with mushrooms; season lightly with pepper. Then wrap the bacon slices completely around the chicken.

3 Pack the chicken into your greased baking dish and scatter the remaining mushrooms over the top. Bake, following recipe.

OVEN-BAKED CHICKEN WITH MUSHROOMS

1 3-lb. chicken
8 slices bacon
½ lb. fresh mushrooms, chopped
Pepper to taste
½ c. butter
½ tsp. salt
¼ c. flour
¾ c. Basic Chicken Stock *(Soups, pg. 2)*
¼ c. dry white wine
½ c. whipping cream

Preheat oven to 400 degrees. Skin the chicken; cut into 2 legs, 2 thighs and 4 breast pieces. Lay each piece of chicken on a bacon slice; sprinkle half the mushrooms over the chicken. Season each portion with pepper. Roll bacon around chicken; secure with toothpicks. Grease a shallow baking dish with ¼ cup butter. Place the bacon-wrapped chicken portions in the baking dish; dot with small pieces of remaining butter. Sprinkle with salt. Cover. Bake on middle shelf for 1 hour, basting occasionally. Remove cover; bake for 15 minutes longer or until bacon is brown. Place chicken portions on heated serving dish; cover. Keep warm. Drain liquid from baking dish into small saucepan. This should measure about ½ cup. Place flour in small bowl; add enough stock to make a smooth paste. Bring liquid in saucepan to a boil; stir in the flour paste. Add remaining stock gradually, stirring constantly. Stir in the wine and cream. Cook and stir until thick and smooth. Remove cover from serving dish; pour sauce over chicken portions.

oven-baked chicken with mushrooms

Bordered with piped Duchess potatoes (Vegetables, pg. 2), the chicken and mushrooms are smothered in sauce. We've used little bread croutons as a decorative garnish.

SCALLOPED CHICKEN

1 5-lb. stewing hen with giblets
1 carrot and 1 onion

Combine all ingredients except giblets in kettle; add 2 quarts salted water. Bring to a boil, then reduce heat and simmer, covered,for 1 hour and 30 minutes. Let chicken cool in broth. Cook giblets in small saucepan in salted water to cover for 30 minutes. Drain giblets. Remove chicken from broth; chill broth to solidify fat. Remove fat and set aside. Strip skin from meat; pull meat from bones. Grind skin and giblets separately; set aside.

Stuffing

1½ 1-lb. loaves day-old bread
1 onion, chopped
2 stalks celery with leaves, chopped
¼ c. minced parsley
½ c. butter or margarine
Salt and pepper to taste
1 tsp. poultry seasoning

Cut crusts from bread; crumble slices into large bowl. Sauté onion, celery and parsley in butter for 5 minutes. Add onion mixture, ground giblets, seasonings and 6 tablespoons chicken broth to bread; toss to mix well.

Sauce

1 c. sifted all-purpose flour
1 c. milk
2 tsp. salt
4 eggs, beaten

Heat 1 cup chicken fat in large saucepan; stir in flour to make a smooth paste. Add 4 cups chicken broth slowly, stirring constantly; mix in milk and salt. Cook until thick and bubbly, stirring constantly. Stir a small amount of the hot sauce into eggs, then stir eggs into hot sauce. Cook over low heat for 3 to 4 minutes longer, stirring constantly. Remove from heat; stir in the ground chicken skin. Spoon stuffing into 2 well-greased 9 x 12-inch casseroles. Arrange chicken chunks over stuffing; cover with sauce. Sprinkle buttered bread crumbs over top, if desired. Bake, covered, at 350 degrees until bubbly. Remove cover; bake for 10 minutes longer. May be frozen, then baked. Thaw before baking.

DEVILED CHICKEN

1 3-lb. chicken
Cooking oil or butter
Sea salt or table salt
White pepper

Preheat oven to 350 degrees. Line a shallow roasting pan with aluminum foil. Brush the chicken with oil; sprinkle lightly, inside and out, with salt and pepper. Place in the prepared pan. Cover loosely with aluminum foil; do not seal. Bake for about 1 hour and 30 minutes or until tender. Let cool enough to handle easily. Remove and discard the

DEVILED CHICKEN

Creamy Deviled Chicken covered with a tangy sauce made with various spices including garlic, white pepper, curry and bouquet garni.

skin. Separate the chicken into serving portions and arrange on a platter. Chicken may be removed from bones if desired and placed on platter. Cover lightly with aluminum foil and keep warm in 225-degree oven.

DEVIL SAUCE

3 to 4 sm. onions, minced
1 lg. clove of garlic, crushed
Bouquet Garni (Soups, pg. 2)
Basic Chicken Stock (Soups, pg. 2)
⅛ tsp. white pepper
3 tbsp. butter
3 tbsp. flour
¼ tsp. curry powder
1 tbsp. water
Several drops of Worcestershire sauce
1 tbsp. tomato purée

Place the onions, garlic, Bouquet Garni, 2 cups stock and pepper in small saucepan; simmer for 20 minutes. Force the onion mixture through a sieve into a bowl. Measure, then add enough stock to make 2 cups liquid. Melt the butter in a small saucepan; blend in flour. Add stock mixture gradually, stirring until smooth. Combine the curry powder and water, stirring, to make a smooth paste. Add curry paste, Worcestershire sauce and tomato purée to sauce. Cook, stirring frequently, until thick and smooth. Serve over warm chicken.

roman pot cookery

The interesting cooking vessel introduced in this section is called a Romertopf. Available information indicates that the Romertopf originated in ancient Rome. It is a porous, unglazed clay roasting pot and, due to the exceptional results it produces, is still popular today both in Europe and America. The Romertopf, more commonly called a Roman pot, cooks meat, fish and vegetables in their own juices, preserving the natural flavor and vitamins. Throughout roasting, meat stays remarkably moist and tender, yet when done, it is always a beautiful golden brown.

These clay Roman pots, because they are porous, permit easy, natural baking without adding any fats. Their special serrated bottoms keep the meat raised out of the liquid, and yet hold all the delicious juices.

Once you have invested in a Roman pot (which is usually moderately expensive), you certainly want to give it proper treatment. Before placing this pot in the oven, you *must* submerge both pot and lid in hot water for at least 10 minutes, or else your treasured Romertopf will crack.

One further note of importance for Roman pot cookery . . . when meat or poultry has cooked to desired doneness and is removed from the oven, remove the pot lid immediately, or the meat will continue to cook until the pot has cooled.

The Romertopf is wonderful for preparing many meats and vegetables and is especially good for preparing poultry.

CHICKEN WITH SAFFRON RICE

1 4 to 4½-lb. chicken
Butter
Salt and pepper to taste
2 tbsp. all-purpose flour
2 tsp. saffron shreds
2 c. long grain rice
1 recipe Tomato Fondue Sauce *(Sauces, pg. 15)*

Soak a large Roman pot in hot water to cover for 10 minutes, then drain. Brush the chicken with melted butter and season inside and out with salt and pepper Place in the Roman pot. Mix the flour with enough water to make a thick paste. Coat the rim of the Roman pot heavily with the paste and press on the lid. Place pot in a cold oven, then turn the temperature to 350 degrees. Bake for 2 hours. Remove pot from the oven and break the seal immediately, using the tip of a sharp knife. Place chicken on serving dish. One hour after the chicken has started cooking begin the preparation of the rice. Sprinkle the saffron over 1 cup warm water and let steep for 30 minutes. Strain the saffron from the water, then combine the saffron-flavored water, 3 cups water and 2 teaspoons salt in a large heavy saucepan. Add the rice gradually, stirring constantly Cover and cook over low heat for 18 to 20 minutes or until rice is tender and water is absorbed. Stir in ¼ cup butter until melted. Press rice firmly in 8 buttered molds, then turn out on serving dish around the chicken. Garnish the rice molds with stuffed olives. Pour the sauce around chicken and rice molds and serve immediately. This makes 8 servings.

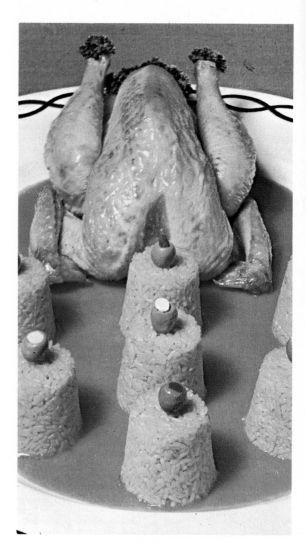

chicken with saffron rice

The tender, golden brown Chicken With Saffron Rice is an excellent example of Roman pot cookery. The perfect sauce accompaniment for such a classic combination is Tomato Fondue Sauce.

How To Make Paper Frills

You will need pieces of thick white paper cut lengthwise into 2½-inch wide strips. Double each piece over to give a folded strip of 1⅜-inch width. Snip the folded edge to half the overall depth in hair-thin loops. Unfold and bend back the reverse way, lay against the edge of a cocktail stick and roll up at a sloping angle so that the whole thing forms a spiral of frill all the way down. Secure with a little adhesive and the job is done.

To Fasten Frills

Wrap fold around turkey or chicken legs and fasten with tape.

SMALL DINNER PARTY MENU

CREAM OF BROCCOLI SOUP
(Soups, pg. 20)

***PORTUGUESE CHICKEN WITH RICE**
(Poultry, pg. 15)

TOSSED SALAD GREENS WITH VINAIGRETTE SAUCE
(Sauces, pg. 2)

ORANGE LEMON ICE
(Desserts, pg. 78)

**SUGGESTED WINE:
TRAMINER OR VINHOS VERDES**

COFFEE WITH BRANDY
(Beverages, pg. 25)

The Creative Homemaker's Academy © MCMLXXIII
Selected Illustrations © B.P.C. Publishing Limited MCMLXX

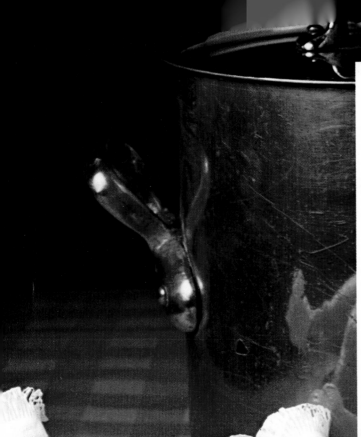

PORTUGUESE CHICKEN WITH RICE

2 c. chopped onions
Salt
Freshly ground pepper
3 c. chicken stock
¾ c. Sauterne
1¼ c. long grain rice
¼ c. melted butter
1 tsp. paprika
1 2½-lb. chicken
2 tbsp. all-purpose flour

Soak a large Roman pot in hot water to cover for 10 minutes. Combine the onions, 1½ teaspoons salt, ¼ teaspoon pepper, stock, Sauterne, rice, butter and paprika. Sprinkle the chicken lightly inside and out with salt and pepper. Place in the Roman pot, then spoon the rice mixture around the chicken. Blend the flour with enough water to make a thick paste. Coat the rim of the Roman pot heavily with the flour paste and press on the lid. Place pot on a baking sheet in a cold oven, then turn the temperature to 350 degrees. Bake for 2 hours. Remove the pot from the oven and break the seal immediately, using the tip of a thin sharp knife. The chicken and rice may be served in the pot or transferred to a serving platter. This will make 3 to 4 servings.

portuguese chicken with rice

Chicken stock, Sauterne and chopped onions are three divine flavors found in Portuguese Chicken With Rice. This delectable treat was baked in a sealed Roman pot for 2 hours.

CHICKEN FONDUE

1 2¹/₂-lb. chicken, disjointed
2¹/₂ c. Basic Chicken Stock (*Soups, pg. 2*)
4 green onions
¹/₂ tsp. tarragon leaves
1 clove of garlic, minced
¹/₂ c. finely chopped Gruyère cheese
2 tsp. all-purpose flour
¹/₄ c. brandy
3 egg yolks
³/₄ c. whipping cream

Place the chicken in a Dutch oven or large saucepan and cover with the stock. Trim the green onions, leaving about 2 inches of the tops, then chop coarsely. Add the onions, tarragon and garlic to the stock and bring to a boil. Reduce heat and simmer, covered, for 1 hour or until chicken is very tender. Remove the chicken from the stock. Strain the stock into a saucepan and bring to a boil. Reduce heat and simmer until stock is reduced to 2 cups of liquid. Remove skin and bone from chicken and cut chicken into small pieces. Place a small amount of chicken and a small amount of stock in the blender container and process until puréed. Repeat until all the chicken has been puréed, using only ¹/₂ of the stock. Heat the remaining stock, then add the cheese. Simmer, stirring constantly, until cheese is melted. Combine the flour with the brandy in a small bowl, then stir into stock until smooth and slightly thickened. Blend the chicken purée into stock. Combine the egg yolks and cream and beat until well mixed. Stir quickly into chicken mixture, blending until smooth. Serve in a fondue pot or chafing dish with squares of French bread. This makes 5 to 6 cups of fondue.

CHICKEN PEPERONATA

1 3¹/₂-lb. chicken
1 tbsp. olive oil
2 tsp. salt
1 8-oz. package pasta shells
¹/₂ c. melted butter
¹/₃ c. freshly grated Parmesan cheese
1 recipe Basic Peperonata Sauce (*Sauces, pg. 12*)

Bake the chicken in a see-through bag as instructed on page 6. Let cool until easily handled. Disjoint chicken, removing skin, if desired. Combine 2 quarts water, oil and salt in a kettle or large saucepan and bring to a boil. Add the pasta shells slowly and cook for about 12 minutes or to desired degree of doneness. Drain well, then place in mixing bowl. Drizzle with butter and sprinkle with cheese, then toss lightly. Place the chicken in the center of a large serving dish and arrange the shells around the chicken. Pour the hot peperonata sauce over the chicken. Serve with Mango Chutney (Salads, page 31) and additional Parmesan cheese, if desired. This makes 6 servings.

chicken peperonata

This casserole combines the juiciness of tender baked chicken with the tangy flavor of peperonata sauce. Chicken Peperonata may be served on a bed of buttered pasta with freshly grated cheese.

chicken
with
cheese

chicken with cheese

Chicken With Cheese is a simple baked chicken which is smothered with a delicious Swiss Fondue. The natural flavor of the cheese blends with the poultry for an irresistible flavor combination.

CHICKEN WITH CHEESE

1 3½-lb. chicken
1 recipe Swiss Fondue (Appetizers, pg. 18)
Chopped chives

Roast the chicken in aluminum foil as instructed on page 5. Prepare the fondue in a heavy saucepan over low heat instead of using a fondue pot. Remove chicken from foil and place on a serving dish. Pour the fondue over the chicken until well coated. Sprinkle with the chives. Serve with toasted bread cubes and the remaining fondue. This makes about 6 servings.

CHICKEN WITH RED WINE

1 3½-lb. fryer, disjointed
1 c. Basic Seasoned Flour *(Soups, pg. 32)*
½ c. butter
½ c. bacon drippings
20 sm. onions
3 tbsp. all-purpose flour
1½ c. Basic Chicken Stock *(Soups, pg. 2)*
2½ c. Beaujolais or other dry red wine
Salt and pepper to taste

Dredge the chicken pieces with seasoned flour. Place the butter and bacon drippings in a Dutch oven and heat until bubbly. Add the chicken, then sauté on all sides until golden. Remove the chicken. Add the onions and sauté until golden. Remove the onions and pour off all but 2 tablespoons of the pan drippings. Stir in the flour to make a smooth paste, then brown lightly. Add the stock slowly, stirring constantly, then stir in the Beaujolais. Season with salt and pepper. Return the chicken and onions to the sauce and cover. Simmer for about 35 to 45 minutes or until chicken is very tender, stirring occasionally. Remove the chicken and onions to a serving dish and pour the sauce over the top. You may thicken sauce with additional flour paste, if needed. Garnish with Baked Croutons (Breads, page 16), if desired. This makes 4 servings.

chicken with red wine

Tender pieces of chicken sautéed with button onions and covered with a flavorful wine sauce makes this presentation a gourmet delight. The finished dish may be garnished with small mushrooms or, as shown, with baked croutons.

CHICKEN PUFFS

6 frozen patty shells
2 1-lb. chicken breasts
2½ tbsp. butter
2 c. Basic Chicken Stock *(Soups, pg. 2)*
½ box long grain and wild rice
2 tbsp. cornstarch
2 tbsp. Sauterne
Salt and pepper to taste
¼ c. chopped onion
¼ c. chopped green pepper
¼ c. slivered almonds
1 4-oz. jar sliced mushrooms, drained
1 egg

Thaw the patty shells. Brown the chicken breasts in 2 tablespoons butter. Add the chicken stock and cook over medium heat until the chicken is tender. Remove the chicken from the broth and reserve broth. Remove the skin and bones from the chicken, then cut the chicken into small pieces. Place remaining butter in a saucepan and add 1¼ cups water. Stir in the long grain and wild rice and bring to a boil. Cover tightly. Cook over low heat for about 25 minutes or until all of the water is absorbed, then cool. Pour the reserved broth into a saucepan and bring to a boil. Mix the cornstarch and Sauterne and stir into the broth. Cook until thickened, then season with salt and pepper. Let cool. Combine the chicken, rice, half the broth mixture, onion, green pepper, almonds and mushrooms and mix well. Roll out each patty shell on a floured surface to a 6-inch square. Place ⅙ of the chicken mixture in the center of each square and fold pastry over, forming triangles. Dampen edges of the pastry and seal with a fork. Turn up-

side down onto a cookie sheet. Beat the egg with 2 tablespoons water, then brush on the triangles. Bake in a preheated 425-degree oven for 15 minutes or until brown. Heat remaining broth mixture and serve with the puffs. This makes 6 servings.

CHICKEN WITH BROCCOLI AND CORN

1 egg, beaten
½ tsp. salt
¼ tsp. pepper
1 8-oz. can cream-style corn
1 10-oz. package frozen chopped broccoli, thawed
3½ c. diced cooked chicken
2 c. herb-seasoned stuffing mix
¼ c. melted butter
¼ c. all-purpose flour
2 c. Basic Chicken Stock *(Soups, pg. 2)*
¼ tsp. sage

Combine egg, ¼ teaspoon salt, pepper, corn and broccoli in a mixing bowl. Stir just until mixed. Grease a 9 x 14-inch baking dish and spread the broccoli mixture in the dish. Top with the diced chicken. Combine stuffing mix and butter and sprinkle over the chicken. Mix flour with a small amount of the chicken stock to form a smooth paste. Combine flour paste, remaining stock, remaining ¼ teaspoon salt and sage in a small saucepan. Cook, stirring constantly, until thickened. Pour over chicken mixture. Bake in a preheated 325-degree oven for 25 to 30 minutes. Two cups of canned chicken broth may be substituted for chicken stock, if desired. This makes 6 to 8 servings.

sauced chicken
in vol-au-vent shells

The thought of serving leftovers is usually quite unappealing because most of us face one of two problems: either we don't have quite enough to make another meal, or we simply can't face our family again with the same old thing. However, there are some wonderful solutions to both of these problems. One creative and delightful way to serve leftovers, particularly leftover chicken and turkey, is with flaky puff pastry. Prepare this delicious Sauced Chicken and serve it in large vol-au-vent shells.

sauced chicken in vol-au-vent shells

Seven-inch vol-au-vent shells contain the delicious sauced chicken to make this dish something more than leftovers. Bits of parsley may be scattered over the top for added flavor and eye appeal.

SAUCED CHICKEN IN VOL-AU-VENT SHELLS

3 tbsp. butter
3 tbsp. all-purpose flour
1¼ c. chicken stock
2 tbsp. sherry
1 recipe Basic Brown Sauce (*Sauces, pg. 5*)
Salt and pepper to taste
3 c. cubed cooked chicken or turkey

Melt the butter in a heavy saucepan, then stir in the flour to make a smooth paste. Add the stock gradually, stirring constantly, and cook over low heat until thickened. Stir in the sherry and brown sauce, then season with salt and pepper. Fold in the chicken and heat through. Serve hot in two 7-inch puff pastry vol-au-vent shells (Desserts, page 65), patty shells or on toast points. This makes about 8 servings.

CHICKEN CURRY

1 2½-lb. chicken, disjointed
3 c. Basic Chicken Stock *(Soups, pg. 2)*
¼ tsp. ginger
1 tsp. salt
2 tbsp. olive oil
1½ c. chopped onions
2 cloves of garlic, pressed
1 tbsp. peanut butter
1 tsp. curry powder
1 c. coconut milk or milk
2 tbsp. flour
2 tbsp. lemon juice
¼ tsp. ground cardamom
¼ tsp. ground cloves
½ tsp. cinnamon

Remove the skin from the chicken. Pour the stock into a large skillet, then add the ginger, salt and chicken pieces. Cover and simmer for about 30 minutes or until the chicken is tender and the stock is reduced to about 2 cups liquid. Heat the oil in a small skillet and sauté the onions until tender and golden. Blend in the garlic, peanut butter, curry powder and coconut milk. Cook the onion mixture over low heat for about 4 minutes. Mix the flour and a small amount of water together until smooth. Remove chicken pieces from the stock. Add flour mixture to stock and cook over medium heat, stirring constantly, until smooth and thickened. Pour the onion mixture into the sauce and blend well. Stir in the lemon juice and remaining seasonings. Add the chicken pieces to the sauce and heat through gently. Serve the curry with Basic Boiled Rice (Cereals, page 3) and Mango Chutney (Salads, page 31). This makes 6 to 8 servings.

chicken curry

Chicken Curry is a far eastern poultry dish, highly seasoned with onion, garlic, curry and several other East Indian spices. Fluffy white rice and tart Mango Chutney make delicious accompaniments to Chicken Curry.

CHICKEN WITH CHOCOLATE

1 3-lb. chicken, disjointed
Salt and pepper
All-purpose flour
2 tbsp. butter
2 tbsp. olive oil
1½ c. Basic Chicken Stock *(Soups, pg. 2)*
½ oz. bitter chocolate, melted
½ tsp. cinnamon
½ c. chopped blanched almonds
½ c. finely chopped onions
1 c. grated carrots
½ c. raisins
12 pitted prunes

Season chicken with salt and pepper, then dredge with flour. Melt the butter and olive oil in a large skillet. Add the chicken and brown on both sides. Remove chicken to an ovenproof dish. Add 2 tablespoons of flour to pan drippings and cook until browned, stirring constantly. Add the stock gradually and cook, stirring constantly, until thickened. Blend in the chocolate and cinnamon, adding salt and pepper, if needed. Stir in the remaining ingredients, then pour over chicken. Bake, covered, in a preheated 325-degree oven for 45 minutes. Garnish with chopped parsley and blanched whole almonds. This makes 4 servings.

chicken with chocolate

Chicken With Chocolate is an interesting and delicious flavor combination, which, on very special occasions, may be combined with a bit of brandy and set aflame.

ROAST TURKEY WITH BLEU CHEESE SAUCE

1 12-lb. turkey
Salt and freshly ground pepper
Butter
20 med. onions, peeled
2 tbsp. soy sauce
½ c. chopped onions
1 c. half and half cream
3 tbsp. all-purpose flour
1 tbsp. red currant jelly
1 tbsp. bleu cheese

Cut the tips from the turkey wings. Rub the turkey generously inside and out with salt and pepper, then brush with melted butter. Tie the legs together and place on one side on rack in roasting pan. Place the wing tips, neck, heart, liver, gizzard and the onions around the whole turkey in the bottom of the pan. Roast in a preheated 350-degree oven for 30 minutes, then remove the turkey pieces. Roast the whole turkey for 30 minutes longer. Place the turkey pieces in a large saucepan and add 4 cups water and the soy sauce. Sauté the chopped onions in a small amount of butter until transparent, then add to the soy sauce mixture. Bring to a boil. Boil, uncovered, over medium heat until the liquid is reduced to about 2 cups of broth, then strain broth and set aside. Turn the turkey to the other side and brush with butter. Roast for 1 hour longer. Turn the turkey, breast side up, and roast for 1 hour longer or until brown and tender. Remove the turkey and onions to a serving platter. Pour the pan drippings into a bowl to cool. Remove the fat from the surface, and reserve 2 tablespoons, then strain the drippings. Combine 1 cup of pan drippings, the reserved broth and the cream. Place the reserved fat in a medium saucepan, then blend in the flour until smooth. Add the cream mixture gradually and cook, stirring constantly, until the sauce is smooth and thickened. Add the jelly and bleu cheese and cook, stirring, until blended. Carve the turkey and serve with the sauce and additional currant jelly. This makes about 10 servings.

TURKEY BEAULIEU

3 c. diced cooked turkey
½ c. finely chopped celery
½ c. finely chopped cucumber
¼ c. minced green onions
½ c. slivered almonds
1 tbsp. minced parsley
1 tsp. salt
¼ tsp. white pepper
½ c. Basic Mayonnaise *(Sauces, pg. 3)*
1 recipe Basic Duchess Potato Mixture
    (Vegetables, pg. 3)

Combine turkey, celery, cucumber, onions, almonds and parsley in a large bowl. Sprinkle with salt and pepper. Add mayonnaise and toss lightly until just blended. Spoon turkey mixture evenly into 6 ramekins, then pipe potatoes around edges. Bake in a preheated 400-degree oven for 10 minutes or until potatoes are lightly browned. Garnish with red sweet pepper strips, if desired. Serve immediately. Omit the potatoes and serve cold as a salad, if desired. This makes 6 servings.

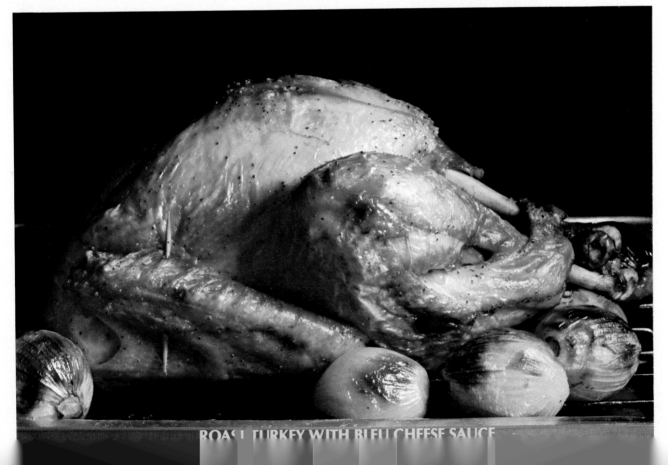

ROAST TURKEY WITH BLEU CHEESE SAUCE

CHICKEN BREASTS WITH ARTICHOKES

4 chicken breasts
Salt and pepper to taste
½ tsp. poultry seasoning
¼ tsp. monosodium glutamate
1 jar marinated artichoke hearts
1 c. white wine
½ c. Basic Chicken Stock, *(Soups, pg. 2)*
½ lb. fresh mushroom caps
1 tbsp. cornstarch

Remove the skin and bones from the chicken breasts, then sprinkle the breasts with salt, pepper, poultry seasoning and monosodium glutamate. Drain the artichoke hearts and reserve 3 tablespoons oil. Heat the reserved oil in a frypan. Place the chicken breasts in the oil and cook until brown. Add ½ cup wine and chicken stock, then cover tightly. Simmer for 35 to 45 minutes or until the chicken is almost tender. Add the mushroom caps, artichoke hearts and remaining wine and simmer for 15 to 20 minutes longer. Remove the chicken to a platter and keep warm. Mix the cornstarch with ¼ cup water and stir into the liquid in the frypan. Cook until thickened, stirring constantly, then pour over the chicken. This dish is delicious served with wild rice. Canned chicken broth may be substituted for the Basic Chicken Stock. One package frozen artichokes and 3 tablespoons butter may be used instead of the marinated artichokes.

BROWN CHICKEN FRICASSÉE

1 3-lb. chicken, disjointed
Salt and pepper to taste
½ c. butter
½ to 1 tsp. thyme leaves
½ to 1 tsp. leaf marjoram
1 lg. onion studded with 12 cloves
½ lemon
¾ c. Burgundy
⅛ tsp. nutmeg
⅛ tsp. mace
1 c. half and half cream
¼ c. all-purpose flour
3 egg yolks, beaten
¼ c. tomato purée (opt.)

Season the chicken with salt and pepper and place in a large saucepan. Add the butter, thyme, marjoram, onion, lemon, Burgundy, nutmeg and mace. Add enough water to cover. Bring to a boil, then reduce the heat. Cover and simmer for about 30 minutes or until chicken is very tender. Remove the chicken from the broth and discard the lemon and onion. Cool the chicken until easily handled. Remove the skin and bones, then dice the chicken coarsely or leave in large pieces. Mix enough cream into the flour to make a smooth thin paste, and stir into the broth. Combine the egg yolks with the remaining cream and blend into broth gradually, stirring constantly. Cook over medium heat, stirring constantly, until thickened but do not allow to boil. Stir in the tomato purée and add the chicken. Season with salt and pepper and heat through. Serve with rice or pasta and garnish with Baked Croutons (Breads, page 16). This makes 8 servings.

brown chicken fricassée

Poultry fricassées are perennial favorites. Brown Chicken Fricassée is made with bite-sized pieces of cooked chicken and covered with a luscious, savory sauce. This dish may be served with fried or baked bread croutons.

BROILED SPRING CHICKEN

2 sm. broilers
Salt and pepper to taste
¹/₂ c. melted butter
4 tbsp. lemon juice

Remove the wing tips from the broilers and split from the necks through the breasts, leaving backs together. Place on a chopping board and flatten with a rolling pin. Season with salt and pepper, then place, skin side up, on rack in broiler pan. Combine butter and lemon juice, then brush broilers with the butter mixture. Place broiler pan 3 or 4 inches from the source of heat and broil for 2 minutes. Lower pan to about 10 inches from the source of heat and broil for about 40 minutes or until broilers are tender, turning frequently and basting with butter mixture each time. Place on platter and garnish with endive. This makes about 2 servings.

broiled spring chicken

Broiled Spring Chicken is deceptively easy to prepare. The whole broilers are flattened, then placed on a rack and broiled with lemon butter. It is shown garnished with endive.

CHICKEN-PEPPER STEW

1 3-lb. broiler-fryer
5 lg. carrots
1 tbsp. salt
5 white peppercorns
5 whole allspice
1 bay leaf
3 whole cloves
1 leek, chopped
2 lg. onions, chopped
2 c. shredded cabbage
1 6-oz. can tomato purée (opt.)
½ tsp. minced chili pepper
1 c. ground peanuts
1 recipe Basic Boiled Rice (Cereals, pg. 3)

Place the chicken in a large saucepan and add enough water to cover. Bring to a boil, then skim well. Dice 1 carrot and add to chicken with the salt, peppercorns, allspice, bay leaf, cloves and leek. Cook for about 40 minutes or until chicken is tender. Remove the chicken from the broth and cool. Strain the broth and add enough water, if needed, to make 4 cups liquid. Reserve ½ cup broth for later use, then pour the remaining broth back into the saucepan. Grate the remaining carrots and add to the broth with the onions, cabbage, tomato purée and chili pepper. Bring to a boil, then reduce the heat and cook, stirring frequently, until thickened and vegetables are tender. Add the peanuts and cook for 15 minutes longer, stirring frequently. Remove the skin and bones from chicken and cut chicken into large pieces. Combine reserved broth with the chicken in a heavy saucepan and heat through. Place the chicken, vegetable mixture and the rice in separate serving dishes. Place the rice, then the chicken, then the vegetable mixture in soup bowls to serve. This makes about 6 servings.

chicken-pepper stew

Chicken-Pepper Stew, a delectable combination of chicken, vegetables, rice and spices, makes a perfect one-dish meal.

mulligatawny

Generously flavored and very exotic, Mulligatawny is an East Indian soup prepared from vegetables and chicken stock with bits of coconut and rice.

MULLIGATAWNY

2 tbsp. butter or oil
1 lg. onion, chopped
2 med. Winesap apples
1 lg. carrot
1 med. turnip
4 tomatoes
½ tsp. curry powder
¼ tsp. cayenne pepper
2 tbsp. instant flour
4 c. hot chicken stock
1 recipe Basic Boiled Rice (Cereals, pg. 3)

Melt the butter in a large heavy saucepan, then add the onion. Sauté until tender. Peel and chop the apples, carrot, turnip and tomatoes, then add to the onion. Sprinkle with the curry powder and cayenne pepper and cook until the vegetables are almost tender. Sprinkle the flour over the vegetables and mix well. Add the stock and cook for 10 minutes. Place a small amount of rice in each soup bowl and ladle the soup over the rice. Serve with freshly grated coconut and raisins. This makes about 6 servings.

chicken with boiled oranges

There are several easy ways to roast chicken for Chicken with Boiled Oranges. The recipe introduced here tells you to roast it in a see-through bag. However, you may use other methods such as aluminum foil, page 5, or the Roman Pot method, page 13, both of which are suitable. Any way you choose, you'll find that boiled oranges and tender roasted chicken make a delectable combination.

CHICKEN WITH BOILED ORANGES

1 3½ to 4-lb. chicken
3 thin-skinned oranges
2 tbsp. dry sherry
2 tbsp. brown sugar
4 tbsp. butter
3 tbsp. all-purpose flour
½ c. dry white wine
Grated rind of 1 sm. orange
1 c. half and half cream
Salt and freshly ground white pepper to taste

Roast the chicken according to the step-by-step illustrations and instructions on page 6 or by another preferred method. Keep warm after removing from the bag. Cook the oranges while the chicken is roasting. Place the oranges in a large saucepan of boiling water and cook for 25 minutes or until soft. Drain the oranges, then place them in ice water until cold. Drain and wipe the oranges dry, then cut each orange in half crosswise. Remove the seeds. Place the orange halves in a shallow baking pan and spoon 1 teaspoon of sherry over each half. Cover each half with 1 teaspoon of brown sugar, and dot each with ½ teaspoon of butter. Broil until brown and crusty. Keep warm. Melt remaining 3 tablespoons butter in a small saucepan over low heat. Add the flour and stir until smooth, but not brown. Stir in the wine gradually. Add the orange rind, then stir in the cream gradually. Cook, stirring constantly, until smooth and thickened. Remove from heat and season with salt and pepper. Place the chicken on a warm serving platter. Pour half the sauce over the chicken and pour the remaining sauce into a sauceboat. Place the oranges around the chicken, then garnish as desired. This makes 6 servings.

chicken with boiled oranges

Chicken with Boiled Oranges is served with a delightful sauce made of white wine and grated orange rind. The accompanying boiled oranges are flavored with sherry, sugar and butter and garnished here with heart-shaped croutons and sprigs of rosemary.

deep-fried sweet and sour chicken

Bite-sized pieces of chicken are cooked oriental style and served with Basic Sweet and Sour Sauce. This dish will be a favorite . . . perfect for a party buffet.

chinese chicken

Deep-Fried Sweet and Sour Chicken, a classic oriental dish, is similar to the Japanese Tempura (Seafood, pg. 28), which often uses shrimp and bits of vegetables. As with other deep-fried oriental foods, the secret is in the batter, and the secret of good batter is to avoid overmixing. To insure perfect results, follow the recipe closely.

DEEP-FRIED SWEET AND SOUR CHICKEN

1   4-lb. cooked chicken
2 tbsp. cornstarch
2 tbsp. soy sauce
1 tsp. salt
2 eggs
1 recipe Basic Sweet and Sour Sauce (*Sauces, pg. 31*)

Remove the skin and bone from the chicken and cut the meat into 1-inch cubes. Combine the cornstarch and soy sauce and mix well. Combine the salt and eggs in a mixer bowl and beat with a whisk or rotary beater until light, then stir in the cornstarch mixture until just mixed. Heat oil in a deep fat fryer to 375 degrees or until a small ball of flour mixed with water dropped into the oil floats to the top immediately. Dip the chicken cubes into the egg mixture and drain slightly. Drop the chicken, several cubes at a time, into the oil and fry until lightly browned, then drain on paper toweling. Place the chicken in individual serving dishes and spoon the sweet and sour sauce over the chicken. This makes 4 to 6 servings.

CHICKEN GO WAN

2 whole chicken breasts, boned
3/4 c. soy sauce
2 c. long grain rice
4 1/2 c. Basic Chicken Stock (*Soups, pg. 2*)
1 tsp. monosodium glutamate
1 c. sliced fresh mushrooms

Cut chicken into 1/2-inch cubes. Combine chicken cubes and soy sauce in a mixing bowl and let stand for at least 1 hour to marinate. Combine rice, chicken stock, monosodium glutamate and mushrooms in a Dutch oven, mixing lightly. Spoon chicken and soy sauce over top. Cover and cook over low heat for 30 minutes or until the chicken and rice are tender. Serve with cooked snow peas, if desired. This makes 4 to 6 servings.

CHINESE CHICKEN WITH SWEET PEPPERS

2 whole chicken breasts, boned
1 clove of garlic, pressed
4 tbsp. olive oil
3 tbsp. soy sauce
1/2 tsp. salt
1/2 tsp. pepper
2 tsp. cornstarch
2 green sweet peppers
1 red sweet pepper
8 green onions
3 celery stalks
1/4 tsp. sugar
1/4 c. cold water

Cut chicken into 1-inch pieces. Combine chicken, garlic, 1 tablespoon of oil, 2 tablespoons of soy sauce, salt, pepper and 1 teaspoon of cornstarch in a mixing bowl and let stand for at least 30 minutes to marinate. Cut the peppers into 1-inch pieces, removing seeds and membrane. Cut onions and celery in 1/2-inch pieces. Heat the remaining 3 tablespoons of oil in a wok. Add the peppers and stir-fry (Beef, pg.18) for 3 minutes. Add the onions and stir-fry for 2 minutes. Remove the peppers and onions, using a slotted spoon. Keep warm. Place the chicken in the hot oil in the wok and stir-fry for 5 minutes. Combine the remaining 1 tablespoon of soy sauce, remaining 1 teaspoon of cornstarch, sugar and water and pour over the chicken. Add the vegetables and combine carefully, cooking over low heat for about 3 minutes. This makes about 4 servings.

CHINESE LEMON CHICKEN

1   3-lb. chicken
1 1/2 tsp. salt
2 tbsp. soy sauce
2 tbsp. brandy
5 tbsp. safflower oil
1/2 tsp. powdered ginger
1/2 c. chicken broth
1/4 c. strained lemon juice
1/2 tsp. sugar

Rub the inside of the chicken with 1 teaspoon of the salt, then rub the outside with the soy sauce. Place in a deep dish and pour the brandy over the chicken. Marinate for 4 hours, turning the chicken frequently. Drain the chicken and reserve the marinade. Combine the oil and ginger in a wok, (General Information, pg. 46) over medium high heat. Add the chicken and brown on all sides, turning with a fork. Reduce the heat to low and add the reserved marinade, broth, lemon juice, sugar and remaining salt. Place a lid on the wok and simmer for about 15 minutes. Turn the chicken and simmer for 15 minutes longer or until the chicken is tender. Place on a heated platter and cut into serving pieces. Pour the pan drippings over the chicken and serve immediately. This makes about 4 servings.

russian chicken cutlets

These crusty Russian Chicken Cutlets are a generous and delectable mixture of chicken, mushrooms, cream and bread. Served with a rich lemony sauce, Russian Chicken Cutlets are considered haute cuisine.

RUSSIAN CHICKEN CUTLETS

2 slices sandwich bread
¼ c. half and half cream
2 to 2½ c. uncooked ground chicken
2 tsp. salt
¼ tsp. freshly ground white pepper
½ c. finely chopped fresh mushrooms
6 tbsp. butter
1½ c. sifted all-purpose flour
1 egg, well beaten
2 c. fine dry bread crumbs
Vegetable oil
2 tbsp. lemon juice
2 egg yolks, beaten
⅛ tsp. cayenne pepper

Remove crusts from the bread and place the bread in a large bowl. Pour the cream over the bread and let stand until all the liquid is absorbed. Add the chicken, 1 teaspoon salt, pepper, mushrooms and 2 tablespoons of softened butter and mix until well blended. Chill for at least 1 hour so that the mixture will be easy to handle. Shape into 12 cutlets as shown in the illustration. Coat each cutlet with flour, then dip into the egg. Coat with bread crumbs, pressing crumbs on firmly. Chill for 1 hour longer to set the coating. Fill a large heavy skillet ¼ inch deep with vegetable oil and place over medium heat until hot. Add the cutlets and fry until browned on both sides. Drain on paper toweling and keep warm. Combine the lemon juice and egg yolks in the top of a double boiler and blend thoroughly. Place over hot water and add 2 tablespoons of butter. Beat with a whisk until smooth and thoroughly blended. Cut remaining 2 tablespoons butter into small pieces, then add to the egg yolk mixture, 1 piece at a time, beating until smooth after each addition. Remove from water and stir in remaining salt and the cayenne pepper. Place in a sauceboat. Place the cutlets on a serving platter and serve with the sauce. This makes 12 servings.

chicken victoria

Chicken Victoria is a highly seasoned dish which is cooked and served with mushrooms and onions. Crisp croutons, sprinkled with Parmesan cheese, are served with the chicken and gravy.

CHICKEN VICTORIA

¼ c. butter
1 3 to 4-lb. chicken
2 tbsp. dried tarragon
Salt and freshly ground pepper to taste
1 clove of garlic, pressed
1 Bouquet Garni *(Soups, pg. 2)*
2 ½ c. Basic Chicken Stock *(Soups, pg. 2)*

½ lb. fresh mushrooms
1 recipe Beurre Manié *(Beef, pg. 4)*
8 sm. onions or shallots

Melt the butter in a roasting pan. Add the chicken and cook over moderate heat until brown on all sides. Sprinkle with tarragon, salt and pepper. Add the garlic and *Bouquet Garni*, then pour the stock into the pan. Cut the stems from the mushrooms and chop. Add the chopped mushrooms and mushroom caps to the pan. Add the *Beurre Manié*, then add the onions. Bake, covered, in a preheated 325-degree oven for about 1 hour and 15 minutes or until the chicken is tender, then remove the *Bouquet Garni*. Place the chicken in a serving dish and place the onions around the chicken. Pour the gravy over the chicken. Serve with Baked Croutons (Breads, pg. 16) sprinkled with freshly grated Parmesan cheese, if desired. This makes 6 servings.

chicken à la française

To give Chicken a la Française a special flavor, the birds are stuffed with a mixture of celery leaves and onion. Lemon juice, butter and seasonings are brushed in and over the chickens before cooking.

CHICKEN À LA FRANÇAISE

2 bunches of celery
2   3-lb. chickens
2 tbsp. lemon juice
2 ½ tsp. salt
¼ tsp. freshly ground pepper
¼ tsp. garlic powder
1 c. diced onions
2 tbsp. melted butter
1 ¾ c. Basic Chicken Stock *(Soups, pg. 2)*
2 tbsp. all-purpose flour
¼ c. water

Trim the stem ends of the celery, keeping the bunches intact. Cut the leaves off of the bunches of celery and reserve for stuffing. Cut each celery bunch lengthwise into 4 pieces and set aside. Brush the chickens inside and out with lemon juice. Combine the salt, pepper and garlic powder and rub in the cavities and on the skin of the chickens. Fill the chicken cavities with the reserved celery leaves and onions, then secure the openings with skewers. Place the chickens in a shallow dish and cover. Chill for 2 to 4 hours to blend the seasonings with the chickens. Place the chickens on a rack in a roasting pan and brush with the butter. Bake in a preheated 425-degree oven for 30 minutes or until browned. Arrange the celery bunch pieces around the chickens, then pour the stock into the pan. Cover the roasting pan. Reduce the oven temperature to 375 degrees and bake for 1 hour longer or until the chickens are tender. Remove the celery mixture from the chicken cavities and discard. Arrange the chickens on a heated serving platter and surround with the celery pieces. Drain 2 cups of the pan liquid into a saucepan and bring to a boil. Mix the flour and water until smooth, then stir into the pan liquid. Cook, stirring constantly, until thickened, then pour into a gravy boat. Serve with the chickens. This makes 8 to 10 servings.

CHICKEN WITH LOBSTER

8 chicken breast halves
1 ½ tsp. salt
¼ tsp. pepper
½ c. butter
2 tbsp. sherry
½ lb. fresh mushrooms, sliced
2 tbsp. all-purpose flour
1 ½ c. chicken broth
1 tbsp. tomato paste
1 bay leaf
2 tbsp. chopped chives
2   10-oz. packages frozen lobster-tails or ½ lb. cooked lobster meat
3 ripe tomatoes, skinned *(Vegetables, pg. 27)*

Sprinkle the chicken breasts with 1 teaspoon of the salt and ⅛ teaspoon of the pepper. Heat the butter in a skillet until foamy, then add the chicken. Sauté until golden. Spoon the sherry over the chicken, then remove from the skillet. Place in a shallow baking dish and cover with foil. Bake in a preheated 350-degree oven for 30 minutes or until tender. Add the mushrooms to the drippings in the skillet and sauté for about 5 minutes. Blend the flour into the mushroom mixture, then stir in the broth gradually. Simmer, stirring constantly, until thickened. Add the tomato paste, bay leaf, chives, the remaining ½ teaspoon of salt and the remaining ⅛ teaspoon of pepper. Simmer for 15 minutes. If using frozen lobster-tails, cook the lobster-tails according to the package directions, then remove the meat from the shells. Cut the lobster meat into bite-sized pieces. Add the lobster meat to the sauce. Quarter the tomatoes and add to the sauce. Simmer for about 8 minutes or until the tomatoes are tender. Arrange the chicken on a platter and top with the sauce. This makes 6 to 8 servings.

CHICKEN SAUTERNE

2   3½-lb. frying chickens, disjointed
6 tbsp. butter
1 lb. fresh mushrooms, sliced
3 tbsp. all-purpose flour
½ tsp. salt
½ tsp. paprika
1 tbsp. instant minced onion
¼ tsp. hot sauce
1 tbsp. Worcestershire sauce
½ tsp. celery salt
½ tsp. oregano
1 c. California Sauterne
1 c. half and half cream
1 c. cooked fresh green peas

Place the chickens in a kettle and cover with cold, salted water. Bring to a boil, then reduce the heat and simmer for 1 hour or until the chickens are tender. Remove the chickens from the broth, then cool. Reserve 1 cup of the broth. Remove the skin and bones from the chickens and discard. Cut the chicken into large chunks, then set aside. Melt the butter in a large saucepan, then add the mushrooms and cook, stirring constantly, until tender. Add the flour, salt and paprika and mix well. Stir in the onion, hot sauce, Worcestershire sauce, celery salt and oregano. Add the reserved stock and Sauterne and cook, stirring constantly, until smooth and thickened. Cool slightly, then stir in the cream. Stir in the peas and chicken and heat through. Serve over Basic Boiled Rice *(Cereals, pg. 3)*, if desired. This makes about 12 servings.

chicken lyonnaise

Mushroom caps are a perfect substitute for the very costly truffles which are used in classic Chicken Lyonnaise.

CHICKEN LYONNAISE

½ **lb. small fresh mushrooms**
12 med. carrots
8 to 10 med. potatoes
24 sm. onions or shallots
1   5-lb. stewing hen
1 Bouquet Garni *(Soups, pg. 2)*
Basic Chicken Stock *(Soups, pg. 2)*
Salt and freshly ground pepper

Cut off the mushroom stems and reserve for future use. Place the unpeeled mushroom caps in a colander and pour boiling water over the caps, then drain well. Peel the carrots and potatoes, then trim to approximately equal sizes. Peel the onions. Prepare and cook the chicken according to the step-by-step illustrations. Place the chicken on a heated platter, then arrange the vegetables around the chicken. Remove the *Bouquet Garni* from the stock and season the stock with salt and pepper. Boil the stock until reduced to 2 cups of liquid. Pour some of the stock over the chicken and vegetables. Pour the remaining stock into a sauceboat and serve with the Chicken Lyonnaise. Sliced truffles may be used in place of mushroom caps, if desired. Some of the cooked vegetables may be puréed and added to part of the stock before it is reduced. This makes a delicious soup. Serve grated Parmesan cheese and Baked Croutons (Breads, pg. 16) with the soup, if desired. This makes about 6 servings.

1 Place the chicken on a board, breast side up. Pinch the skin all over the breast of the chicken repeatedly to loosen the skin from the chicken meat.

2 Slip one hand under the skin to separate the skin from the chicken meat.

3 Push the mushrooms, cut side up, under the skin to cover the chicken breast completely.

4 Place the chicken in a baking pan or stockpot and add the carrots, potatoes, onions and *Bouquet Garni*. Add enough stock to just cover the chicken, then cover the baking pan. Simmer for about 2 hours or until the chicken is tender.

CREAMY PAPRIKA CHICKEN WITH SPAETZLE

2 sm. broilers with giblets
1 sm. whole onion, halved
Salt and pepper to taste
½ c. butter
¾ c. chopped onions
1 ½ tsp. paprika
3 tbsp. all-purpose flour
1 c. sour cream
Spaetzle

Place the chicken giblets, necks and wing tips in a saucepan and add 2 cups of water. Add the halved onion and season with salt and pepper. Bring to a boil, then cover and reduce the heat. Simmer for 1 hour. Strain the broth, then simmer until reduced to 1 cup. Cool. Cut the chickens into quarters and season with salt and pepper. Melt the butter in a large skillet, then add the chickens and cook until brown on all sides. Place the chickens in a baking dish. Pour about 2 tablespoons of the drippings into a small saucepan and add the chopped onions. Sauté until soft and transparent, then stir in the paprika. Spread the onion mixture over the chicken pieces. Cover with foil. Bake in a preheated 350-degree oven for about 1 hour or until the chickens are tender. Remove from the oven. Arrange the chickens on a heated serving dish and keep warm. Blend the flour into a small amount of the cooled broth to make a paste, then stir into the remaining broth. Pour into a saucepan and add the pan juices from the baking dish. Season with salt and pepper, if needed. Place over medium heat and cook, stirring constantly, until thickened. Remove from heat and stir in the sour cream. Pour the sauce around the chickens in the serving dish. Serve with Spaetzle or cooked rice. This makes 8 servings.

SPAETZLE

1 ½ c. all-purpose flour
¾ tsp. salt
⅛ tsp. nutmeg
2 eggs, lightly beaten
½ c. milk

Combine the flour, salt and nutmeg in a bowl. Stir in the eggs, then add the milk gradually, beating with a wooden spoon until smooth. Fill a large kettle half full with salted water. Bring to a rapid boil. Slide thin sheets of the dough off of a spoon with a spatula into the boiling water. Loosen with a slotted spoon if the Spaetzle sticks to the bottom of the kettle. Boil until the Spaetzle rises to the top of the water, then cook for 12 minutes longer or until tender. Remove with a slotted spoon and drain on paper toweling. To use a Spaetzle maker, place the dough in the maker. Place over the boiling water and turn the handle to press the dough through the holes. These noodles will need to boil for only 5 minutes. Drain in a colander. Place in sauce or toss with melted butter.

creamy paprika chicken with spaetzle

The interesting shaped morsels surrounding the golden brown chickens are called Spaetzle, which are Austrian dumplings.

CHICKEN SAUTÉ IN WINE

¼ c. finely diced salt pork
1   3 ½-lb. frying chicken
¼ c. butter
¼ c. vegetable oil
2 leeks
20 shallots or sm. onions
Salt and white pepper to taste
1 clove of garlic, pressed
3 tbsp. freshly minced parsley
¾ c. sweet white wine
¾ c. chicken broth
½ c. whipping cream
1   5-oz. can black mushrooms or button
      mushrooms, drained
1 recipe Basic Boiled Rice *(Cereals, pg. 3)*

Soak the salt pork in enough water to cover for 30 minutes, then drain well. Cut the chicken into serving pieces and remove the skin. Melt the butter with the oil in a large, heavy skillet over medium heat. Add the chicken and sauté on all sides until lightly browned, then drain off the excess fat. Set aside. Trim the green end from the leeks and discard, then cut the white part into thin slices. Combine the diced pork, sliced leeks and shallots in a saucepan over medium heat and cook, stirring constantly, until lightly browned. Add to the chicken, then add the salt, pepper, garlic, parsley, wine and broth. Cover and simmer for about 45 minutes or until the chicken is tender. Remove the chicken, pork and vegetables with a slotted spoon and place on a heated serving platter. Keep warm. Add the cream to the liquid in the skillet and simmer until of sauce consistency. Add half the mushrooms and heat through. Spoon the sauce over the chicken and vegetables, then border with the rice. Garnish with the remaining mushrooms. Fresh mushrooms, cooked with the diced pork mixture, may be used instead of the canned mushrooms. Remove from the pork mixture after browned, then add to the sauce the same as for black mushrooms. This makes 6 servings.

chicken sauté in wine

This tempting chicken is deliciously flavored with salt pork, wine, mushrooms and onions. Serve it with a border of Basic Boiled Rice (Cereals, pg. 3) or a dish of buttered noodles.

FLEMISH CHICKEN CASSEROLE

2 lg. carrots, sliced
2 green onions with tops, sliced
1 heart of celery, cut into julienne strips
4 sprigs of parsley
Salt and freshly ground pepper to taste
1   3 ½-lb. chicken with giblets
¼ c. butter
2 tbsp. vegetable oil
2 lg. onions, quartered
1 bay leaf
1 recipe Beurre Manié *(Beef, pg. 4)*
1 egg
¼ c. half and half cream
2 tbsp. freshly minced parsley

Combine the carrots, green onions, celery, sprigs of parsley, salt, pepper and the chicken liver and neck in a soup kettle and cover with water. Bring to a boil, then reduce the heat. Simmer until the vegetables are tender. Remove the liver and neck from the kettle and cool. Remove the meat from the chicken neck and discard the bones. Strain the liquid from the kettle and reserve. Place the vegetables, liver and neck meat in a blender container and process until puréed. Cut the chicken into serving pieces. Melt the butter with the oil in a heavy skillet. Add the chicken and fry until browned. Remove the chicken from the skillet and season with salt and pepper. Place the chicken in a large casserole and add the puréed mixture. Add the reserved liquid, quartered onions and bay leaf, then cover. Bake in a preheated 350-degree oven for about 1 hour or until the chicken is tender. Remove the chicken, onions, and bay leaf from the casserole with a slotted spoon and discard the bay leaf. Place the chicken and onions in a tureen. Add *Beurre Manié* to the casserole liquid and simmer, stirring constantly, until thickened. Beat the egg, then blend in the cream. Add to the sauce in the casserole slowly and simmer, stirring constantly, until heated through. Pour over the chicken mixture and sprinkle with the minced parsley. Serve in soup bowls. This makes about 6 servings.

flemish chicken casserole

Tender chicken, combined with fresh carrots, celery, onions, parsley, seasonings and a savory cream sauce makes this delicious Flemish casserole.

CHAUD-FROID SAUCE

As we have stated before (Sauces, pg. 21), the French term *chaud-froid* literally means "hot-cold" because this classic sauce is made hot and served cold. Review carefully all of the information given in Sauces, page 21.

Chaud-Froid Sauce may be decorated with bits of fruits or vegetables. As shown here, black olives are cut and designed to decorate Chicken in *Chaud-Froid* Sauce.

CHICKEN IN CHAUD-FROID SAUCE

3 cooked chicken breasts, halved
Pitted black olives or truffles
1 c. Chaud-Froid Sauce using chicken stock
  (Sauces, pg. 21)
1 c. Basic Emergency Aspic (Salads, pg. 4)
¾ c. Savory Pate de Foie Cream (Sauces, pg. 30)

Remove the skin and bones from the chicken breasts and trim the edges of the chicken evenly. Cut the olives into flower shapes as shown in the illustration. Coat the chicken breasts with the Chaud-Froid Sauce according to the instructions on How To Coat (Sauces, pg. 21). Garnish with the black olives and coat with clear aspic according to the same instructions. Arrange the chicken breasts on a serving platter. Place the pâté cream in a pastry bag with a small rosette tube affixed and pipe around the edge of the chicken breasts. Chill until ready to serve. This makes 6 servings.

napoleon's
chicken and
seafood
dish

chicken marengo

Shrimp, brandy, white wine and herbs add superb flavor to this dish. Serve with heart-shaped croutons and poached eggs.

The following chicken dish has a very distinguished history. It was created by Napoleon's chef after Napoleon defeated the Austrians in the Battle of Marengo.

After the tiring battle, Napoleon ordered his chef, Dunand, to prepare dinner. Dunand immediately sent his staff to search for provisions, and they returned with three eggs, four tomatoes, six crayfish, a small hen, some oil, garlic cloves and a saucepan. With all the ingredients and some borrowed brandy, Dunand created the dish he named Chicken Marengo. Since crayfish are not readily available to everyone, the following recipe uses shrimp as a very acceptable substitute.

CHICKEN MARENGO

2 3-lb. frying chickens
1/4 c. vegetable oil
1 onion, thinly sliced
3 tbsp. brandy
2 1-lb. cans Italian tomatoes, drained
1/2 c. dry white wine
2 cloves of garlic, pressed
1/2 tsp. dried thyme
1 bay leaf
4 sprigs of fresh parsley
1 c. Basic Chicken Stock *(Soups, pg. 2)*
1 tsp. salt
1/2 tsp. freshly ground pepper

1 c. small cleaned shrimp
1/2 lb. fresh mushrooms, sliced
1/4 c. butter
2 tbsp. lemon juice
2 tbsp. freshly minced parsley

Remove the skin from the chickens, then cut each chicken into quarters. Pour the oil into a large, heavy skillet and place over medium heat until hot. Add the onion slices and sauté, stirring frequently, until golden brown. Remove the onions from the skillet with a slotted spoon and set aside. Add the chicken to the oil remaining in the skillet and cook until browned on all sides. Heat the brandy and pour over the chicken. Ignite the brandy and flame, shaking the skillet until the flame dies. Place the tomatoes in a blender container and process until puréed. Add to the skillet. Add the wine, garlic, thyme, bay leaf, sprigs of parsley, stock, tomatoes, salt and pepper and sautéed onions. Cover the skillet and simmer for 1 hour or until the chicken is tender. Remove the chicken from the sauce and keep warm. Strain the sauce, if desired. Add the shrimp to the sauce and simmer for 5 minutes. Sauté the mushrooms in the butter in a saucepan until tender, then stir in the lemon juice. Add to the sauce and heat through. Arrange the chicken pieces on a heated serving platter and pour the sauce over the chicken. Sprinkle with the minced parsley. Garnish with Baked Croutons (Breads, pg. 16) and serve with poached eggs (Eggs, pg. 24), if desired. This makes 8 servings.

MENU
For A Bon Voyage Dinner

HONEY AND FRUIT SALAD
(Salads, pg. 67)

CHICKEN À LA KIEV

SPINACH SOUFFLÉ WITH SPICY SAUCE
(Vegetables, pg. 112)

CHOCOLATE ROULAGE
(Desserts, pg. 211)

FRENCH BREAD

SUGGESTED WINES:
California Chenin Blanc
or
French White Burgundy

DEMITASSE CAFÉ BRÛLOT
(Beverages, pg. 51)

russian chicken

Chicken À La Kiev, a popular Russian dish, is a simple but elegant recipe for boned chicken breasts. Each boned breast has a little pocket which is filled with a pat of butter, then carefully folded. Each piece is then rolled in flour, egg and bread crumbs, and fried in deep fat. The trick of the dish is sealing the butter within the chicken breast so it will not leak out during cooking.

CHICKEN À LA KIEV

6 boneless chicken breast halves, skinned
Salt and pepper to taste
Butter
All-purpose flour
2 eggs, well beaten
1 c. dry bread crumbs

chicken à la kiev

Chicken à La Kiev is beautifully shaped, coated with crumbs, then fried at an exact temperature for golden brown perfection. Fresh corn on the cob is served with this dish.

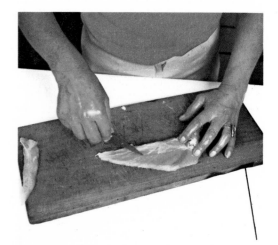

1 Lift the fillet, the strip of flesh on the inside of the breast, with the tip of a knife, then pull gently to remove. Set aside.

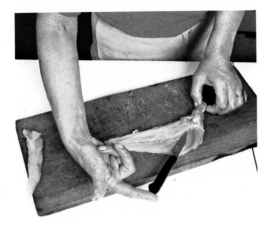

2 Place the knife flat against the center-line of the breast and cut a pocket on one side, being careful not to cut through the edge.

3 Cut a pocket in the opposite side.

4 Dip the fillet in cold water, then place flat on the cutting board. Dip the meat pounder or wine bottle in water, then pound the fillet gently until flattened out thin.

5 The pounded fillet is on the left and the breast with the pocket is on the right. Sprinkle both lightly with salt and pepper.

6 Cut a 1 tablespoon cube of butter from a cold stick of butter. Place in the center of the fillet.

7 Fold each side of the fillet over the butter to form a neat package.

8 Place the fillet with butter in the pocket of the breast.

9 Fold the edges over one another and press tightly.

10 Form into a tadpole shape with the hands by pressing together.

11 Dredge with flour until well coated, shaking off the surplus.

12 Dip into the beaten eggs.

13 Coat well with the bread crumbs. Chill until ready to fry. Heat deep fat to 325 degrees. Add the breasts and fry for about 10 minutes or until brown.

STEWED CHICKEN

Chicken Tourangelle is a French dish which comes from the area of Touraine, the home of many famous cooks and recipes. This outstanding dish is made with stewed, boned chicken, onions, mushrooms, grated orange rind, dry white wine and other delicious ingredients.

CHICKEN TOURANGELLE

1   4-lb. stewing chicken
2 lg. onions, quartered
1 Bouquet Garni *(Soups, pg. 2)*
2 c. Basic Chicken Stock *(Soups, pg. 2)*
6 to 8 med. mushrooms
½ c. dry white wine
½ c. whipping cream
Salt and freshly ground pepper to taste
Grated rind of ½ orange
1 recipe Basic Duchess Potato Mixture
   (Vegetables, pg. 3)
2 tbsp. toasted sliced almonds

Place the chicken, onions, Bouquet Garni and stock in a roasting pan and cover. Bake in a pre-heated 325-degree oven for 2 hours or until the chicken is tender. Remove the chicken from the roasting pan and cool until easily handled. Remove the skin and bones from the chicken and cut the chicken into serving pieces. Arrange on a heated platter and keep warm. Cut the stems from the mushrooms, then cut the caps in half. Add the mushroom caps and stems to the liquid in the roasting pan and bring to a boil over high heat. Boil until the liquid is reduced to 2 cups. Stir in the wine and cream and boil until reduced to 2 cups of liquid, then remove the *Bouquet Garni.* Season with salt and pepper and stir in the orange rind. Pour the sauce over the chicken. Place the potato mixture in a pastry bag with a large writing tube affixed and pipe around the chicken mixture. Do not glaze. Sprinkle the potato mixture with the almonds. This makes about 6 servings.

chicken tourangelle

This rich chicken dish, a French classic, is flavored with orange rind and dry white wine. Mushrooms and cream add richness. Border this dish with Duchess potatoes (Vegetables, pg. 3) and browned, flaked almonds.

BEST BARBECUED TURKEY

½ c. chopped onion
1 ½ tbsp. butter
1 ½ c. catsup
¼ c. (packed) brown sugar
1 clove of garlic, pressed
1 lemon, thinly sliced
¼ c. Worcestershire sauce
2 tsp. prepared mustard
1 tsp. salt
¼ tsp. freshly ground pepper
1   12-lb. fresh or frozen turkey
2 to 3 tbsp. barbecue salt or seasoned salt

Sauté the onion in the butter in a small saucepan until lightly browned. Add the remaining ingredients except the turkey and barbecue salt and simmer for 20 minutes. Remove the lemon slices. Store the sauce in a covered jar in the refrigerator if not used immediately. Thaw the turkey, if frozen. Rinse the turkey and pat dry. Start the charcoal briquette fire 20 to 30 minutes before cooking the turkey, allowing about 5 pounds of charcoal for the beginning fire. During the cooking period, push the burning charcoal to the center while adding more briquettes as needed around the edge. Sprinkle the cavity of the turkey with the barbecue salt. Truss the turkey as instructed on page 3. Insert the spit rod in front of the tail and run diagonally through the breastbone, then fasten tightly with the spit forks at both ends. Test for balance, readjusting the spit rod, if necessary. Insert a meat thermometer into the thickest part of inside thigh, making sure the thermometer does not touch the bone or spit rod and that the thermometer will clear the charcoal as the spit turns. Brush off the gray ash from the coals and push the coals back of the firebox. Place a drip pan made of heavy-duty foil directly under the turkey in front of the coals. Attach the spit and start the rotisserie. Cook for 25 minutes per pound or to 180 to 185 degrees on the meat thermometer, basting generously and frequently with the barbecue sauce during the last 30 minutes of cooking. This makes 10 to 12 servings.

OVEN-SMOKED TURKEY

1   10 to 12-lb. turkey
¼ c. vegetable oil
½ c. salt
3 tbsp. liquid smoke
1 c. red wine vinegar
¼ c. pepper
2 tsp. finely chopped parsley

Rinse the turkey, then pat dry with paper toweling. Combine the oil and salt to make a paste. Rub the inside cavity and the neck cavity with ¼ cup of the salt paste. Truss the turkey, then rub generously with additional oil. Place on one side on a rack in a roaster pan. Bake in a preheated 350-degree oven for 1 hour. Combine the remaining salt paste with the liquid smoke, vinegar, pepper and parsley. Baste the turkey with the vinegar mixture, using a basting brush, then turn to other side and baste that side. Bake for 30 minutes, then baste again. Bake for 30 minutes longer, then baste and turn breast side up. Baste the breast generously. Bake for 2 hours and 30 minutes longer or until tender, basting every 30 minutes. Let the turkey stand for at least 20 minutes before carving. Brush off some of the salt and pepper before carving. This makes 10 to 12 servings.

best barbecued turkey

What could be more delicious than tender Turkey roasted over a charcoal fire and basted with a tangy barbecue sauce — this is perfect for parties or family meals.

seafood

table of contents

introducing seafood

In many areas of the Western world, seafood was for years eaten only as a meat substitute on religious holidays. But gourmands of the Renaissance began to appreciate seafood for its own good taste, as the following menu shows. A royal banquet was held in France during Lent in 1571 to honor the new bride of Charles IX. The royal party and its hordes of courtiers went through 2 barrels of Brittany oysters, 50 pounds of whale meat, 200 crayfish, great platters of broiled lobster and steamed mussels, 400 herring (half fresh, half salted), 18 brill, 28 salmon, 10 turbot, 50 carp and 1,000 pairs of frogs' legs.

While tastes today do not run to such quantities, many American families are discovering seafood as a healthful, economical alternative for combating the monotony of a meat-oriented menu. Modern packing methods and refrigerated transportation make freshwater and saltwater fish and shellfish (all generically termed *seafood*) available even to people who live miles from an ocean, lake or river.

Seafoods are light in texture and bulk, yet surprisingly satisfying. While supplying an impressive assortment of health-giving vitamins, minerals and proteins which equal or exceed those contained in meats, they are exceptionally easy to digest. Learning how to buy properly, prepare tastefully and serve seafood with flair will be one of the nicest things you can do for your family.

In this section we've included an exciting array of seafood dishes to prepare while you master the BASICS of this important area of cooking. We will treat the varieties of shellfish individually, since each requires special techniques. However, preparation methods for fish are basically the same. The only difference is whether the fish is covered with scales or skin. Scales are *always* removed before cooking — some fish are skinned and others not. Rely on the recipe for instructions.

If you scale your own fish, soak it in water for a few minutes first, then lay it on a flat surface. Hold it firmly by the tail and, starting at the tail and working upwards toward you, scrape off the scales with a tablespoon.

BUYING FISH

Since seafood is an extremely perishable commodity, an important consideration in buying it is the reputation of your dealer for quality and freshness. And purchase seafood as near as possible to the day of preparation.

Unless you buy fresh fish directly off the boat, it will be packed in ice when you get it. Look for bright, clear, bulging eyes, reddish or pink gills, tight shiny scales, and firm elastic flesh that springs back when pressed.

Most seafood markets sell fish *drawn,* that is, with the entrails removed. However, if you're an angler or receive the bounties of such, you may remove the entrails yourself, always as soon as possible. After the head is removed (see first picture, pg. 2), slit the belly of the fish from the vent (anal opening) to the (now removed) head with a sharp knife. Scrape out the intestines with the knife and rinse fish thoroughly in cold water.

If your supply and selection of fresh seafood is limited, don't overlook the possibility of using frozen fish. A wide variety, already cleaned, boned, packed and quick-frozen at the point of supply, is available year-round. The flavor and texture are exceptionally well preserved during freezing. Check to see that the package is solidly frozen and contains no evidence of oiliness, discoloration or freezer burn.

COOKING METHODS

Now that you've learned the guidelines for buying fish, let's briefly review the seven BASIC methods of cooking seafood: *baking, broiling, grilling, deep-frying, sautéing, poaching* and *steaming.*

Baking, broiling and *grilling* are "dry heat" cooking methods, in which the seafood is exposed to the direct and intense heat of an oven or charcoal fire. When using dry heat, it is vitally important that the fish be frequently basted to preserve the natural juices.

The other cooking methods listed above are classed as "moist heat" because they require the use of some liquid. In *sautéing* and *deep-frying,* seafood is cooked in hot fat — more fat is needed to fry than to sauté. A seasoned liquid is used for *poaching* and *steaming.* The most important thing to remember, in preparing seafood by any method, is do not *over*-cook or use too high a temperature in poaching or steaming. A good guide to use (to avoid over-cooking fish) is to cook the fish for ten minutes per inch of the thickness of the fish.

how to fillet a fish

An important technique for your repertoire of seafood basics is filleting fish. The procedure, which is not difficult to master, involves skinning a fish and removing the boneless pieces of flesh from the sides. These individual portions of fish are both easy to prepare and easy to eat.

Although many kinds of fish are now available in fresh and frozen fillets, every cook should know how to fillet a whole fish for several good reasons. For one thing, a whole fish sells for less per pound than fillets. For another, if you catch your own, you'll obviously need to know how to prepare them. Also, with a whole fish you'll have the nutritious backbone and tail portions to add to fish stews, soups and stocks. Using these inedible portions as

the basis for other dishes will contribute to overall savings on your food bill as well as provide menu variety.

We are demonstrating the filleting process here with a whole drawn flounder, but you could easily use another fish. If you choose, say, mackerel, you may or may not remove the skin, as you prefer. If you use a scaly fish, such as red snapper, bass or trout, be sure to remove the scales.

Using a very sharp boning or filleting knife, work on a wooden cutting board or block to protect your countertop and to make your clean-up easier.

1 With a well-sharpened boning knife, remove the head with the pectoral fin attached, exactly as shown.

2 Next cut off the tip of the tail, about halfway down the tail fin.

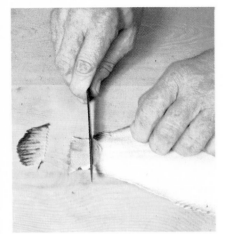

3 Slit the skin at the beginning of the tail section and cut around the edges of the fins so the skin can be removed more easily. If the fish is slippery and difficult to handle, drive an ice pick through the tail and into the wood to make it stay put.

4 Use the tip of your knife to separate the skin from the flesh. Get a firm grip on the loosened skin before you begin to pull it back toward the head of the fish. Your job will be easier if you push with your thumb nail as shown above, or run your fingertips between the skin and the flesh.

5 Continue pulling and easing the skin away from the flesh until you have removed the skin all the way to the head section.

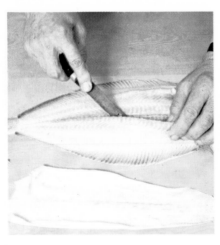

6 Now we can begin to fillet. Working from head to tail, run the tip of your knife down the center of the fish against one side of the spine bone.

7 Still using the tip of your knife, now held flat against the bone, separate the fillet from the bone by gradually stroking the fillet free with the knife.

8 In this picture you can see how we are successfully separating the fillet from one side of the spine bones. Note especially the angle of the knife.

9 After you have separated this fillet, remove the fillet from the opposite side of the spine bones. Then turn the flounder over, skin the underside, as we have previously explained, and remove the two remaining fillets.

BROILED RED SNAPPER IN CREAM SAUCE

1¼ c. Basic Fish Stock (*pg. 5)*
¾ c. Chablis or other dry white wine
¾ c. whipping cream
2 lb. red snapper or sole fillets
Butter
Salt to taste
1 tbsp. (heaping) minced parsley

Pour fish stock into a 2-quart saucepan and bring to a boil. Add the Chablis gradually and return to a boil. Add the cream gradually, stirring constantly, then simmer until sauce is reduced to measure ¾ cup. Place the fillets in a well-buttered shallow baking pan. Sprinkle with salt. Brush the fillets with melted butter. Broil for 5 minutes or until browned and tender. Add the parsley to the sauce and season with salt, if needed. Arrange the fillets in a serving dish and pour the sauce over the top. Serve with Duchess potatoes *(Vegetables, pg. 3)*.

steamed haddock with mediterranean sauce

The BASIC technique of steaming involves no more than cooking fish or shellfish over a boiling liquid for a specified length of time.

Learning how to steam fish correctly is easy with the proper equipment. If you don't have an oblong fish steamer (or poacher) with a perforated removable rack on which to place the fish, it's a simple matter to improvise with a Dutch oven, electric skillet or baking dish and a wire rack.

Our recipe calls for wrapping the haddock fillets in aluminum foil. Not only will this prevent their breaking apart during cooking, but it's the most efficient way to collect the juices for the sauce. However, when you are cooking a whole fish, you may omit the foil and simply place the fish in the steamer.

STEAMED HADDOCK WITH MEDITERRANEAN SAUCE

6 med. tomatoes
1/2 tsp. dried oregano
1/2 tsp. thyme
1/2 tsp. basil
1 tsp. chives
2 green onions, finely minced
1/3 c. vermouth
2 lb. haddock or cod fillets
Salt and freshly ground pepper to taste
1 tbsp. olive oil

Peel the tomatoes and chop coarsely. Combine the tomatoes, herbs, green onions and vermouth in a medium-sized saucepan. Simmer for 30 minutes

while preparing the haddock. Place the haddock on a large piece of aluminum foil. Season with salt and pepper. Fold the foil around the haddock securely. Place the haddock in a steamer over boiling water. Steam for about 20 minutes or until the fish begins to flake. Pour the juice from the foil packet into the tomato sauce. Rewrap the foil packet and keep the haddock warm in a very slow oven. Add the olive oil to the sauce and simmer for about 30 minutes longer or until thickened and considerably reduced in volume. Arrange the haddock on a heated platter. Pour the sauce over the haddock and serve.

Throughout this Course we will demonstrate the professional way to cook, which often requires exploding popular misconceptions. For instance, many cooks believe fish stock is difficult and time-consuming to prepare. If you glance at our recipe below, you'll see how easily and quickly you can make *our* Basic Fish Stock.

BASIC FISH STOCK

2 slices lemon
2 parsley stalks
1/4 med. onion
1 1/2 lb. inexpensive whitefish
1/2 c. vermouth
3 peppercorns

Place lemon, parsley, onion and fish in a 4-quart saucepan, then add the vermouth, peppercorns and enough water to cover. Cover the saucepan, and bring to a fast, rolling boil. Remove the cover and remove scum from stock. Add 1/2 cup cold water. Bring to a boil, then reduce the heat and boil slowly for about 15 minutes or until the lemon and onion are slightly transparent and the fish flakes easily. Strain thoroughly.

To keep a ready supply of stock, pour into pint jars, seal and freeze immediately.

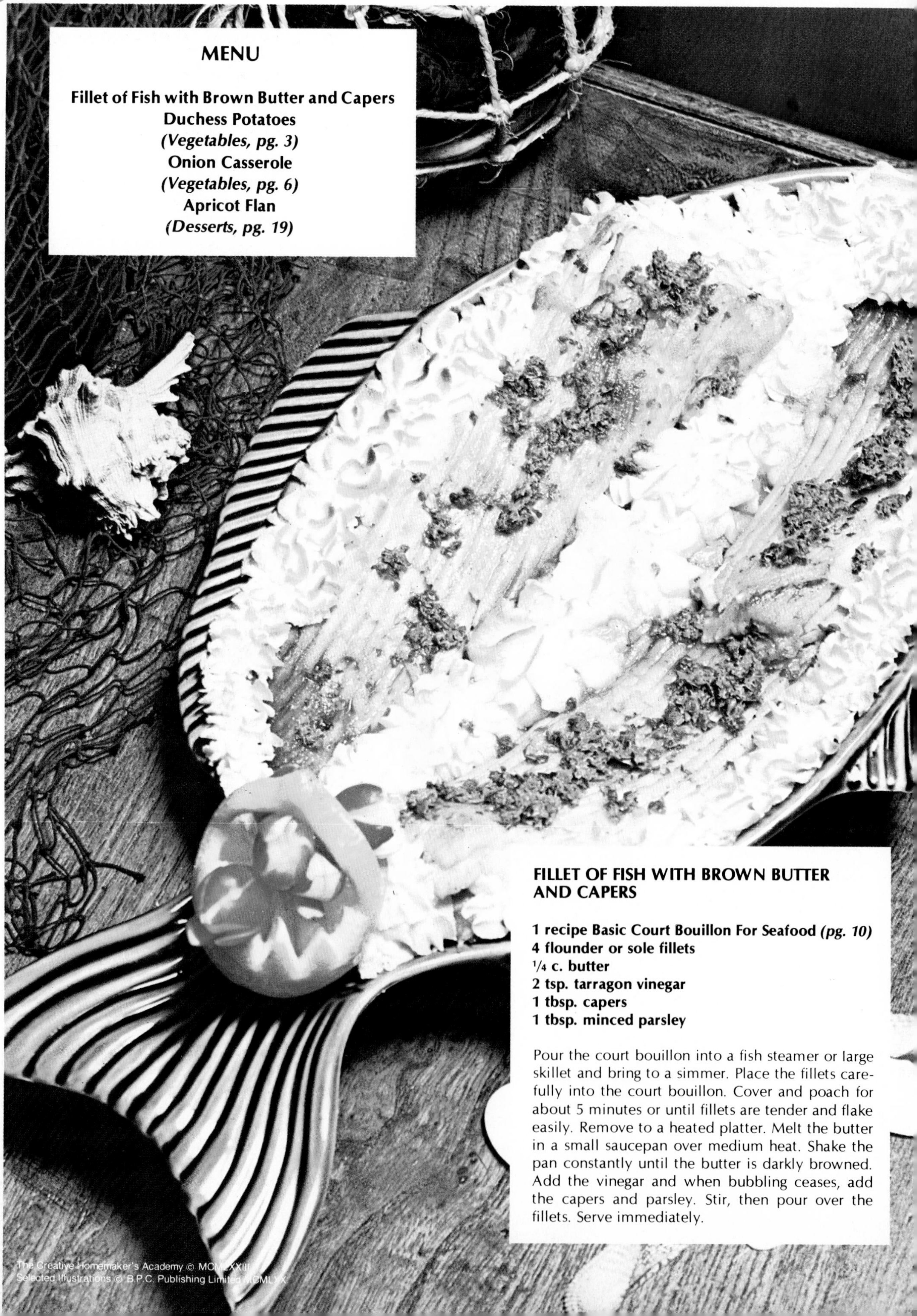

MENU

Fillet of Fish with Brown Butter and Capers
Duchess Potatoes
(Vegetables, pg. 3)
Onion Casserole
(Vegetables, pg. 6)
Apricot Flan
(Desserts, pg. 19)

FILLET OF FISH WITH BROWN BUTTER AND CAPERS

1 recipe Basic Court Bouillon For Seafood *(pg. 10)*
4 flounder or sole fillets
1/4 c. butter
2 tsp. tarragon vinegar
1 tbsp. capers
1 tbsp. minced parsley

Pour the court bouillon into a fish steamer or large skillet and bring to a simmer. Place the fillets carefully into the court bouillon. Cover and poach for about 5 minutes or until fillets are tender and flake easily. Remove to a heated platter. Melt the butter in a small saucepan over medium heat. Shake the pan constantly until the butter is darkly browned. Add the vinegar and when bubbling ceases, add the capers and parsley. Stir, then pour over the fillets. Serve immediately.

flounder with mayonnaise sauce

Flounder is probably the most popular flatfish. It is normally in plentiful supply year-round, either fresh or frozen. The flatfish family, including plaice, sole and fluke, is noted for its lean, tender flesh and almost-sweet taste.

Although many of these flatfish are marketed as sole — gray, lemon or American — they should not be confused with genuine Channel or Dover sole. The latter are imported, usually at great expense, from England, Belgium, Denmark and the Netherlands and are available in America only in frozen fillets.

Our recipe for Flounder with Mayonnaise Sauce beautifully illustrates the BASIC steps of baking fish. Even though many recipes do not specifically call for adding a liquid to the baking pan, we've found this step helps keep the fish moist during cooking. The liquid can also be incorporated into the sauce.

FLOUNDER WITH MAYONNAISE SAUCE

2 lb. flounder fillets
1 tbsp. butter
¼ tsp. salt
⅛ tsp. freshly ground pepper
Several sm. pieces of lemon peel
½ c. vermouth
1 recipe Basic Blender Mayonnaise (*Sauces, pg. 3*)
2½ tsp. grated orange rind
¼ c. orange juice

Cut the flounder fillets into 3-inch pieces. Place them in a shallow, buttered, heat-resistant dish, leaving a small amount of space between the pieces. Season with salt and pepper. Arrange the lemon peel over the fillets. Pour vermouth over the fillets, tilting the dish slightly so that each fillet has been drenched with vermouth. Cover the dish. Bake at 350 degrees for about 20 to 25 minutes or until the fish begins to flake. Pour the fish liquid into a small saucepan and keep the flounder warm. Bring the fish liquid to a boil over medium heat and cook for about 15 minutes or until reduced to 1 tablespoon. Reduced fish liquid will be thick. Fold the reduced liquid into the mayonnaise carefully, mixing well. Add the orange rind and juice to the mayonnaise mixture. Spoon the mayonnaise mixture over the fillets. Bake at 350 degrees for about 5 minutes or until heated through.

how to clean crabs

There are several popular varieties of crabs in the United States: *hard-shelled* or *blue crab* of the Atlantic; *dungeness crab* of the Pacific; *Alaskan king crab* and *soft-shelled crab*, which is really a hard-shelled crab undergoing a growing stage.' (Crabs grow by shedding their shells — molting — then manufacturing larger ones.) The meat of dungeness crab is sweeter than that of the blue crab and makes larger flakes. This makes dungeness especially good for salads, cocktails and creamed dishes. Blue crab is more distinct in flavor and is very good for more highly seasoned dishes.

Thanks to modern packing, refrigeration and transportation, the succulent meat of crabs is available in every area. Some of it is canned, some frozen and some packed in ice. All of it is good, and many cooks prefer to purchase these forms because the crabs are already cleaned. However, it's a lot of fun to catch, cook and clean your own. The next best thing is to buy live, active crabs.

The first step in preparing live, hard-shelled crabs is to plunge them headfirst into a large pot of vigorously boiling, salted water or court bouillon. Cover the pot tightly and simmer for 20 minutes. Our step-by-step pictures show you our method for cleaning a crab to obtain the maximum amount of meat. Allow the crab to cool before beginning the work illustrated below. We suggest nutcrackers or ordinary pliers for cracking the claws and a cocktail fork to help you scrape out the delicious morsels of meat.

NOTE:

Inside the main portion of the shell you will find more edible meat. Before you can get at it, you must first remove and discard the thin protective cartilage. This darker meat can be served separately or mixed with the white meat. Clean and wash the shell thoroughly and you can use it as a serving dish.

1 When the boiled crab is cool, break away all the claws — first the large ones and then the small.

2 Hold the crab shell exactly as we are here. Break the "apron" on the underside away from the body and pull the two halves of the shell apart.

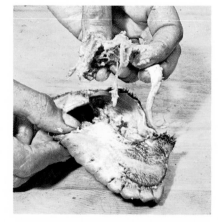

3 You can see quite clearly the spongy gray lungs, sometimes called "dead man's fingers," that were once attached to both parts of the shell. Discard all this inedible and unpalatable material, as well as any bits of splintered shell.

4 We are holding the portion of the body containing the edible white crab meat. Behind the body you see the large and small claws also containing white meat; use nutcrackers to open the shell and a cocktail fork or skewer to remove the meat.

stuffed blue crab

STUFFED BLUE CRAB

1 lb. crab meat
4 tsp. lemon juice
2 tsp. salt
½ tsp. freshly ground pepper
3 c. coarse bread crumbs
⅓ c. dry sherry
½ c. whipping cream, whipped
1 c. fine bread crumbs
¼ to ½ c. melted butter

Use 6 buttered crab shells for baking dishes if available or 6 buttered, individual ramekins. Combine the crab meat, lemon juice, salt, pepper, coarse bread crumbs, sherry and whipped cream. Mix well. Spoon the mixture into the ramekins, mounding the tops. Sprinkle the fine bread crumbs evenly over the tops, then drizzle generously with melted butter. Place on a baking sheet. Bake at 375 degrees, on middle shelf, for about 15 minutes or until lightly browned.

stuffed blue crab

Five piping hot toast rounds have been piled high with the crabmeat mixture and garnished with minced parsley. The remaining mixture has been returned to the clean body shell of the crab.

how to prepare cooked lobster

In New England it used to be, when you wanted lobster, you rowed far out to the cold, deep waters of the Northern Atlantic, baited your traps and dropped them. Then you had an arduous journey back to shore and, on the next day, an equally arduous return trip to collect your lobsters. If lucky, you would pull up the traps and find one or maybe two lobsters snapping at the slats trying to get out.

All of this is now left to the lobstermen. Many supermarkets and local seafood markets carry the average-sized, one- to two-pound lobsters year-round. Tender, white lobster meat has thus become popular fare throughout America.

Most people are familiar with the dark, mottled, blue-green *Maine lobster* or *"homard."* Although this cold water species is found chiefly along the coasts of Maine and Massachusetts, its habitat stretches from Labrador to South Carolina. The other major variety is the clawless *Rock lobster* or *"langouste,"* which has a reddish-orange or maroon shell. It dwells in the warm waters off Mexico, Southern California and South Africa.

In some parts of the country, notably the Deep South, crayfish are popular. This shellfish is best described as a smaller, freshwater version of the lobster.

For our demonstration on the next page and for the Lobster Mélanie recipe on page 12, we will be using a freshly cooked Maine lobster that we first boiled in Basic Court Bouillon for Seafood. Buying live lobsters has taught us to look for alert, active down-east lobsters heavy for their size. Their tails should snap back and forth under their bodies when the lobsters are handled. Make certain that the claws are shut with wooden pegs. Otherwise, you could receive a nasty wound.

Live lobsters should be cooked as soon as possible. However, they can be kept a short time in the refrigerator immersed in salt or fresh water, or they may be wrapped in a moist cloth.

True lobster fanciers insist vigorously that boiling is the best way to bring out the delicate flavor of this shellfish. Unlike baking or broiling, boiling helps preserve the natural juices. However, there is a running debate regarding the best way to boil a lobster. Some cooks claim it is easier and faster to plunge a live lobster into boiling water. Others believe that, at the moment of impact with the boiling water, the lobster tends to tighten its muscles and thereby toughen its flesh. They start their lobster in lukewarm water and bring to a vigorous boil. We have used both methods, but we prefer to place our lobster in lukewarm Basic Court Bouillon for Seafood and then increase the heat gradually to the boiling point. We believe that lobster cooked in court bouillon is even more flavorful than one cooked in water.

BASIC COURT BOUILLON FOR SEAFOOD

A court bouillon, sometimes called "Short Broth," is an aromatic, seasoned liquid in which vegetables, meats and seafoods are poached or boiled. Although technically *not* a broth or stock, court bouillon may be used as the basis for sauces and aspics. As the name "Short Broth" implies, the liquid is cooked only long enough to allow the flavors of the various ingredients to mingle.

Our Basic Court Bouillon for Seafood is made from water with herbs, fresh vegetables and wine vinegar added. We find it especially good for all seafood, not just lobsters.

The recipe for Lobster Mélanie (pg. 12) will give you complete instructions on how to boil a lobster in Basic Court Bouillon for Seafood. The step-by-step pictures will show you how to prepare cooked lobster.

BASIC COURT BOUILLON FOR SEAFOOD

2 med. carrots, grated
1 med. onion, minced
Generous pinch of leaf thyme
1/2 bay leaf
1/4 c. tarragon vinegar
1 qt. cold water
2 peppercorns

Place all the ingredients except the peppercorns in 2-quart saucepan. Bring to a boil, then reduce the heat and simmer for 15 minutes. Add the peppercorns, then simmer for 12 minutes longer. Cool to lukewarm, then strain.

1 Lay the cooked lobster on a wooden cutting board and tuck the tail underneath the body to prevent any shell sections from separating when the knife goes through. Insert the tip of a large, very sharp (not serrated edge) knife into the joint where the head and tail portions come together and split the tail section into two halves.

2 Turn the lobster around and cut through the remaining portion of the shell until the lobster is in two separate pieces.

3 Here we are pointing out the greenish-gray stomach pouch. Remove and discard this sac as well as the dark thread-like intestine running the length of the tail section. If you have cooked a female lobster, as we have, you'll see the bright red strip of eggs or "coral" along the outer side of the white tail meat. Save it for use in sauces or as a garnish.

4 Remove the tail meat in one piece with a skewer or cocktail fork. Scrape away all meat from the body of the lobster. Crack the claws with a hammer or nutcracker and, using the same cocktail fork, remove all the meat from the claws.

LOBSTER MÉLANIE

4 recipes Basic Court Bouillon for Seafood (pg. 10)
2   1 to 1¼-lb. live Maine lobsters
Butter
1½ c. whipping cream
¼ c. finely minced parsley
¾ c. Chablis or other dry white wine
Freshly ground pepper to taste
2½ c. fresh bread crumbs
¾ c. freshly grated Parmesan cheese
Salt to taste

Place the court bouillon in a deep kettle and heat to lukewarm. Turn off heat. Place the lobsters in kettle side by side, facing in opposite directions. Cover and let stand for 2 minutes. Turn on the heat to moderate and bring slowly to a boil. Boil the lobsters for 5 minutes or until red. Remove the lobsters from court bouillon and drain. Rinse with cold water and cool to room temperature. Place in the refrigerator until cold to firm the flesh. Split the lobsters in halves and clean as shown in our step-by-step illustrations on page 11. Place the coral in a small bowl. Remove all the flesh from the shells. Work 2 tablespoons butter into the coral to make a smooth paste. Work in 2 tablespoons of cream and 2 teaspoons of parsley. Break the claws from the shells. Crack the claws and remove all the meat.

Dice all the lobster meat coarsely, then pack it back into shells. Rub a baking pan generously with butter. Place the lobster shells in the baking pan side by side and head to head. Pour half the Chablis over the lobsters and the remaining Chablis into the pan. Season with pepper and sprinkle half the remaining parsley over the lobsters and in the pan. Sprinkle half the cheese over the lobsters, then sprinkle the remaining cheese in the pan. Reserve 1 heaping tablespoon of bread crumbs. Sprinkle the remaining crumbs over the lobsters and into the pan. Stir the remaining parsley into the remaining cream. Pour slowly over and around the lobsters, allowing the cream mixture to soak into the lobsters thoroughly. Spread the top of the lobsters with the coral mixture. Sprinkle with reserved bread crumbs and dot with small bits of butter. Cover lightly with foil and refrigerate until ready to bake. Bring the lobsters to room temperature. Sprinkle lightly with salt. Bake, covered, at 350 degrees for 30 minutes. Remove the foil and bake for 15 minutes longer. Increase oven temperature to 425 degrees and bake for 5 minutes or until lightly browned. For an easier and more perfect Lobster Mélanie, prepare the bread crumbs, mince the parsley and grate the cheese in a blender. (If coral is unavailable omit the steps concerning the coral paste.)

lobster mélanie

The four lobster halves are surrounded by a cream sauce and garnished with parsley, bread crumbs and coral paste in this most elegant of hot lobster dishes. We baked it in an oven-proof serving dish.

introducing shrimp

Shrimp, by far one of the most popular seafoods in the United States, may be prepared in a wide variety of ways — in salads, grilled, boiled, fried, stuffed and baked, sauced, in omelets and soufflés. The possibilities are endless. Most of the shrimp available in American markets are the large variety from the Gulf of Mexico, although the small Pacific shrimp are abundant on the west coast. The preferred way to purchase them is raw in the shell — when they're cooked and frozen, much of their delicate flavor is lost.

Shelling and deveining shrimp is a somewhat time consuming but necessary task, usually done before the shrimp are cooked. It is a simple operation — just grip the shell between the thumb and forefinger and pull — it will come off quite easily. The tails may be left on for certain types of recipes, especially barbecued or grilled shrimp. Although it is not essential, most people prefer to devein the shrimp after shelling them — they're less apt to be gritty and have a more pleasing appearance. Use a small sharp paring knife and cut along the curve in the back of the shrimp to remove the black vein.

CURRIED SHRIMP INDIENNE

1½ tsp. vinegar
1 clove of garlic, minced
1½ tsp. ground coriander
½ tsp. salt
½ tsp. turmeric
¼ tsp. cumin
¼ tsp. dry mustard
⅛ tsp. freshly ground pepper
⅛ tsp. ground ginger
1 sm. piece of stick cinnamon
Dash of cayenne pepper
1 cardamom seed
1 bay leaf
1 lb. fresh large shrimp, peeled and deveined
1½ tbsp. butter
½ c. chopped onions
½ green sweet pepper, chopped
½ c. Coconut Milk
1 tbsp. all-purpose flour
1½ tsp. lemon juice

Combine the vinegar, garlic, coriander, salt, turmeric, cumin, mustard, pepper, ginger, cinnamon, cayenne pepper, cardamom seed and bay leaf in a medium-sized bowl. Add the shrimp and mix well. Cover and refrigerate for 2 hours. Melt the butter in blazer pan of chafing dish over direct flame, then add the onions and green pepper. Cook, stirring occasionally, until tender. Add the shrimp mixture and cook, stirring occasionally, for 10 minutes or until shrimp are tender. Combine the Coconut Milk and flour, then stir into the shrimp mixture. Cook for about 3 minutes or until sauce thickens and comes to a boil. Stir in the lemon juice. Serve with rice, toasted coconut, plumped raisins, peanuts and chutney. This makes 4 servings.

COCONUT MILK

½ c. milk
½ c. grated coconut

Combine the milk and coconut in a small saucepan. Bring to a boil over medium heat and boil for 2 minutes. Strain and use milk as instructed, then reserve coconut for toasting.

To Toast Coconut:

Mix the coconut with 1 tablespoon of butter and 2 tablespoons of confectioners' sugar. Spread on baking sheet. Bake in preheated 350-degree oven for 8 to 10 minutes or until browned.

SHRIMP IN BREAD SHELLS

1 lb. fresh small shrimp
4 1½-in. slices French bread
1 egg, beaten
⅓ c. milk
2 tbsp. butter
2 tbsp. all-purpose flour
3 tbsp. sherry
1 c. half and half cream
1 tsp. finely chopped parsley
¼ tsp. salt
White pepper to taste

Prepare shrimp according to instructions for Boiled Shrimp. Trim the crust from the bread slices, then cut a circle about ¾ inch deep and ¾ inch in from side of bread. Pull out center gently to make a shell. Combine the egg and milk in a shallow bowl and beat lightly. Dip both sides of the bread shells quickly into the egg mixture and deep-fat fry in hot oil until brown on both sides. Drain on paper towels and keep warm. Melt the butter in the top of a double boiler, then add the flour. Cook, stirring constantly, until smooth. Stir in the sherry slowly, then the cream. Add the parsley and season with salt and pepper. Cook, stirring constantly, until thickened and smooth. Fill the shells with shrimp, then ladle the sauce over the shrimp. You may add shrimp to the sauce, if desired. This makes 4 servings.

BOILED SHRIMP

2 qt. water
1 tbsp. Worcestershire sauce
⅛ tsp. hot sauce
10 peppercorns
½ lemon, sliced
2 tsp. salt
2 bay leaves
1 sm. onion, halved
1 piece of celery with leaves
3 lb. fresh medium shrimp

Bring the water to a boil in a kettle, then add the remaining ingredients except the shrimp. Boil for 10 minutes. Add the shrimp, then bring to a slow boil and cook, stirring occasionally, for 5 minutes. Remove from the heat and cover. Let stand for 15 minutes. Drain in colander, then cool. Peel and devein. Use in recipes as instructed when boiled shrimp are needed. You may serve Boiled Shrimp with hot garlic butter, a rémoulade sauce or other seafood sauces, if desired. This makes about 5 cups of cooked and cleaned shrimp.

shrimp in bread shells

For a savory seafood course, serve Shrimp In Bread Shells shown here accompanied by its own sauce. The bread cases are cut from thick slices of fresh bread and deep-fried until they're golden brown. A chilled, dry white wine would complement this dish.

The Creative Homemaker's Academy © MCMLXXIII
Selected Illustrations © B.P.C. Publishing Limited MCMLXX

boiled shrimp

For casual entertaining, a large bowl of Boiled Shrimp is a good choice for a main course. Serve with individual bowls of hot melted butter flavored with garlic or a piquant seafood sauce and let everyone peel their own shrimp.

shrimp mousse

This attractive arrangement of light, delicately flavored shrimp mousse is an appropriate addition to any buffet or luncheon table. The individual portions of mousse have been garnished with capers and anchovy fillets and placed on a bed of cool, crisp lettuce. The cucumber and tomato sections add extra color.

SHRIMP MOUSSE

2¹/₂ lb. fresh shrimp
2 env. unflavored gelatin
¹/₂ c. cold water
5 hard-boiled eggs
1 sm. jar stuffed green olives
4 anchovy fillets (opt.)
1¹/₄ c. catsup
Grated rind and juice of 2 lemons
1 c. Basic Mayonnaise *(Sauces, pg. 3)*
¹/₄ tsp. salt

Prepare shrimp according to instructions for Boiled Shrimp, page 14. Soften gelatin in cold water, then place over hot water and stir until dissolved. Grind the shrimp, eggs, olives and anchovies through a food chopper. Combine catsup, dissolved gelatin, lemon rind and lemon juice, then stir in the shrimp mixture. Stir in mayonnaise and salt, then pour into individual molds or 1 large mold. Chill until firm. Unmold on salad greens and garnish with additional anchovies and cucumber slices. This makes about 6 to 8 servings.

shrimp-filled brioche

Every hostess appreciates the opportunity to impress her family and guests by serving unusual and attractive menus. Shrimp-Filled Brioche is a dish that is not only unique but also may be prepared in advance — the brioche may be prepared a day ahead. A medium-sized brioche is hollowed out and becomes the edible container for a delicious mixture of shrimp salad. (The center of the brioche may be crumbled and used for other recipes.) A light summer supper would be a suitable occasion to present this delightful salad.

shrimp-filled brioche

Here is a new and different way to serve shrimp salad: in its own edible container made from a hollowed-out brioche. A garnish of fresh boiled shrimp adds a pleasing effect.

SHRIMP-FILLED BRIOCHE

½ lb. fresh shrimp
½ c. minced celery
1 sm. cucumber, peeled and diced
½ c. cooked green peas
½ c. Basic Mayonnaise *(Sauces, pg. 3)*
2 tsp. lemon juice
3 or 4 drops of hot sauce
Salt and pepper to taste
1 Brioche For Savory Fillings *(Breads, pg. 12)*

Prepare the shrimp according to instructions for Boiled Shrimp, page 14, then chill. Combine shrimp, celery, cucumber and peas in a mixing bowl. Combine mayonnaise, lemon juice and hot sauce. Add the shrimp mixture and toss carefully. Season with salt and pepper, then pack into the brioche shell. Wrap tightly in foil and refrigerate until ready to serve. This makes 4 servings.

shrimp curry with eggs

Add spark to your menu by serving this spicy Shrimp Curry With Eggs. The tartness of an apple gives unexpected zest to the sauce. Bordered by fluffy rice, all that is needed is a salad to complete the meal.

SHRIMP CURRY WITH EGGS

¼ c. **Basic Clarified Butter** *(Sauces, pg. 13)*
1 med. **onion, grated**
1 med. **apple, peeled and grated**
¼ c. **cornstarch**
1 tbsp. **curry powder**
1 tsp. **paprika**
Freshly ground pepper to taste
4 c. **chicken consommé or broth**
1 lb. **fresh small shrimp, shelled and deveined**
1 recipe **Basic Boiled Rice** *(Cereals, pg. 3)*
6 **hard-boiled eggs, halved lengthwise**

Heat the butter in a large saucepan. Add the onion and apple and sauté for several minutes or until golden, stirring frequently. Combine the cornstarch, curry powder, paprika and pepper, and sprinkle over the onion mixture. Cook over low heat, stirring constantly, until thick and well mixed. Pour in consommé slowly, stirring constantly. Add the shrimp and simmer for about 15 minutes or until shrimp is tender and sauce thickened. Arrange the rice around edges of serving dish and place egg halves, cut side down, in center. Pour shrimp curry over the eggs. Serve with Mango Chutney (Salads, pg. 31), if desired. This makes 4 to 6 servings.

The Creative Homemaker's Academy © MCMLXXIII
Selected Illustrations © B.P.C. Publishing Limited MCMLXX

shrimp and cream cheese crêpes

SHRIMP AND CREAM CHEESE CRÊPES

1 lb. fresh shrimp
1 recipe Savory Crêpe Batter *(Desserts, pg. 102)*
1 8-oz. package cream cheese, softened
1 c. half and half cream
Salt and pepper to taste
Melted butter
Freshly grated Parmesan cheese

Shrimp and Cream Cheese *Crêpes* are another example of the innumerable ways in which shrimp may be served. Boiled fresh is preferred although frozen or canned shrimp may be used in this dish. A mild sauce of cream cheese and cream complements the flavor of the shrimp. The *crêpes* are made with Savory *Crêpe* Batter (Desserts, pg. 102).

SHRIMP AND CREAM CHEESE CRÊPES

Tiny pink shrimp combined with a creamy sauce fill these savory crêpes to provide the superb beginning of an elegant dinner.

Prepare the shrimp according to instructions for Boiled Shrimp, page 14. Cook the *crêpes* as instructed in the step-by-step illustrations No. 2 through No. 7, and keep warm. Place the cream cheese in a heavy saucepan and stir in half the cream. Cook over low heat until smooth, stirring constantly. Reserve 1/3 of the shrimp for garnish, then add the remaining shrimp to the cream cheese mixture and cook until heated through, stirring constantly. Season with salt and pepper. Spread cream cheese mixture over half of each *crêpe*, then fold other half over top. Arrange *crêpes* in buttered baking dish. Pour remaining 1/2 cup cream around the *crêpes* and drizzle tops with melted butter. Sprinkle generously with Parmesan cheese. Bake in a preheated 450-degree oven until brown and bubbly. Arrange the reserved shrimp over the *crêpes* and serve immediately. This makes 5 servings.

MIXED SEAFOOD CRÊPES

3 tbsp. butter
3 tbsp. all-purpose flour
⅓ c. dry white wine
1 c. Basic Fish Stock *(pg. 5)*
3 tbsp. tomato purée
¼ lb. fresh crab meat
½ c. whipping cream
½ c. small shrimp, shelled and deveined
¼ pt. fresh small oysters
1 tbsp. brandy *(opt.)*
1 tbsp. finely chopped parsley
Salt and freshly ground pepper to taste
6 Savory Crêpes *(Desserts, pg. 102)*

Melt the butter in the top of a double boiler over hot water. Stir in the flour to form a smooth paste. Blend in the wine slowly, then the stock, stirring constantly, until thickened. Add the tomato purée and crab meat and cook, stirring constantly, until well blended and bubbly. Blend in the cream slowly with a whisk and cook until heated through. Add the shrimp and oysters and cook, stirring constantly, until oysters curl and the shrimp are pink. Blend in the brandy and half the parsley, then season with salt and pepper. Cover each *crêpe* with the seafood mixture, then roll up carefully. Place in a baking dish and spoon remaining seafood over *crêpes*. Bake in a preheated 375-degree oven for about 7 minutes or until bubbly. Sprinkle with remaining parsley before serving. One-half cup bottled clam juice with ½ cup of water may be substituted for Basic Fish Stock. This makes 6 servings.

mixed seafood crêpes

Seafood lovers will appreciate the variety of shellfish in these Mixed Seafood Crêpes. The rich, creamy sauce contains wine, stock and cream all of which combine to bring out the delicate flavor of the fish. Economy-conscious homemakers can make use of leftovers in this recipe.

MIDSUMMER MENU

VICHYSSOISE
(Soups, pg. 21)

SEA BREEZE SPINACH MOLD
(Salads, pg. 26)

SHRIMP AND CREAM CHEESE CRÊPES
(pg. 19)

FRESH CORN ON THE COB
(Vegetables, pg. 62)

ELEGANT STRAWBERRY WHIP
Desserts, pg. 122)

SUGGESTED WHITE WINE:
Pinot Chardonnay, Sauvignon Blanc or Chenin Blanc

JAPANESE - STEAMED ROCK LOBSTER

3 8-oz. packages frozen South African rock
    lobster-tails
6 lg. mushrooms, cut into slices
6 scallions, cut into long thin strips
1 c. thinly sliced celery
1 bunch broccoli, trimmed and cut into flowerets
1 tbsp. soy sauce
1 env. dehydrated chicken broth
¼ c. water

Remove thin underside membrane from lobster-
tails with scissors. Push a bamboo skewer lengthwise through tail to prevent curling. Place a colander over boiling water in a large pot or use a
steamer. Place lobster-tails in a colander and place
vegetables on top and around tails. Combine soy
sauce, broth and water, then brush over the tails
and vegetables. Cover pot and let steam for 20
minutes or until vegetables are crisp tender and
lobster meat loses translucency and is opaque.
Serve with Basic Fried Oven-Cooked Rice,
(Cereals, pg. 2). This makes 6 servings.

CAPE COD TURKEY

1 lb. salt cod
4 lg. red or yellow onions, finely sliced
⅔ c. white vinegar
⅔ c. water
2½ tbsp. sugar
Salt and pepper to taste
4 lb. medium boiling potatoes
¾ lb. lean salt pork, finely diced

Cover the cod with cold water and let soak overnight. Drain and rinse well. Combine the onions,
vinegar, water, sugar, salt and pepper in a bowl
and let stand for about 2 hours before serving time.
Peel the potatoes and cut in half, then place in a 5-
quart boiler. Place cod over the potatoes and add
enough water to cover. Cover with lid and bring to
a boil. Reduce heat and simmer for about 40 minutes or until potatoes are tender. Place diced pork
in an iron skillet and cook slowly over medium
heat until golden brown. Pour the diced pork and
fat into a gravy boat. This is the sauce. Drain the
potatoes and cod and arrange on platter. Spoon the
pickled onions over the potatoes and cod. This
makes 4 to 6 servings.

japanese - steamed rock lobster

*This simple, beautifully prepared, lobster
dinner is for special occasions. The lobster-
tails are steamed with vegetables and
flavored in the Japanese manner.*

lobster soufflé

When a fine restaurant featuring haute cuisine prepares a lobster soufflé in the classic manner, the procedure begins with a live lobster and results in a glorious fluffy masterpiece. If that sounds too difficult and involved, you'll be glad to know that there is a much easier method for producing a perfectly acceptable lobster soufflé. Most of the ingredients can be found in the average American market and the recipe is almost as uncomplicated as the Basic Four-Egg Soufflé (Desserts, page 46).

The Creative Homemaker's Academy © MCMLXXIII
Selected Illustrations © B.P.C. Publishing Limited MCMLXX

LOBSTER SOUFFLÉ

1 9-oz. package frozen rock lobster tails
2 tbsp. Madiera
1 10½-oz. can she-crab soup or lobster soup
3 tbsp. all-purpose flour
2 tbsp. butter
3 egg yolks
¼ tsp. salt
⅛ tsp. cayenne pepper
6 egg whites

Cook the lobster according to package instructions. Remove shell and dice finely. Combine the lobster and Madiera in a small bowl and set aside.

1 Pour the soup into a medium-sized heavy saucepan and whisk in the flour. Bring to a boil, stirring constantly, then reduce heat and simmer for several minutes, stirring constantly.

2 Remove from heat and add the butter. Cool to lukewarm. Beat in the egg yolks with whisk.

3 Season with salt and cayenne pepper, then stir in the lobster mixture.

4 Beat the egg whites until stiff.

5 Fold ¼ of the egg whites into the lobster mixture until blended, then fold in the remaining egg whites carefully.

6 Turn into a well-buttered 6½ or 7-inch soufflé dish. Bake in a preheated 425-degree oven for 25 minutes. Serve immediately. This makes about 4 servings.

presenting escargots

Escargots (the French word for snails, pronounced es´car-gō) have been part of the European menu as far back in history as ancient Rome. Today, snails are fancy food — expensive but delicious — and usually reserved for very special occasions. These small mollusks have a one-part spiral shell; the best size for eating are those measuring 1 to 1½ inches in diameter.

Edible snails of either the water or land variety are found in various parts of Europe and the United States. They are also raised on snail farms. Connoisseurs consider those snails found in vineyards to be the best for eating.

Snails must be starved for a length of time before being consumed; they may have eaten plants harmless to themselves but poisonous to humans. It is recommended that only snails which have sealed themselves in their shells to hibernate be eaten. The most reliable way to obtain snails for eating is to purchase the canned variety, along with a package of cleaned empty snail shells which are ready to be stuffed. These are available at gourmet shops or the delicatessen section of many supermarkets.

STUFFED BAKED SNAILS

1 recipe Basic Parsley Butter *(General Information, pg. 30)*
2 cloves of garlic, pressed
2 doz. canned snails with shells

Let butter soften to room temperature and stir in garlic to blend well. Drain snails, then stuff each snail down into a shell. Fill shells with the softened butter and place in 4 snail baking dishes with shell openings upright. Bake in a preheated 375-degree oven for about 15 minutes or until butter is melted and bubbly. Serve immediately with slices of French bread to absorb the butter from the shells. This makes 4 servings.

stuffed baked snails

For sophisticated dining, choose Stuffed Baked Snails for the appetizer. They are shown here baked in a dish designed specifically for that purpose — it keeps the snails level and holds in the heat. If you do not have a snail dish, a cookie tin filled with crushed rock salt (as shown) will serve as a good substitute. For eating, the snail is gripped with special tongs and the meat is extracted with a snail fork or a cocktail fork.

introducing scallops

Coquilles Saint Jacques (pronounced kō·kē saṅ·zhäḱ) is the French name for scallops, the species of bivalve mollusks found along the coasts of France and the eastern United States. (This term may also refer specifically to a particular method of preparing scallops: serving them gratinéed in their shells with a creamy wine sauce.)

In the United States, scallops are usually sold already shelled, either fresh in bulk, or frozen. When buying fresh scallops, look for the small pink or tan bay scallops. These are more tender than the larger, firmer white sea scallops. To be sure that the scallops are fresh, they should have a mild, sweet odor; those sold in bulk should not have an accumulation of liquid. Allow ⅓ pound of sea scallops or ¼ pound of bay scallops per serving.

If you are able to buy scallops in their shells, first scrub the shells thoroughly, then put them in a 300-degree oven, deep side down, until they open. Remove the flesh and the coral matter (which is considered to be a great delicacy.) Both may be used in any scallop recipe. Clean the shells well and keep them for use as individual serving dishes for scallops.

COQUILLES SAINT JACQUES

1½ c. Sauterne
2 lb. fresh scallops
½ lb. medium mushrooms, sliced
6 green onions, finely chopped
6 tbsp. butter
3 tbsp. water
1 tbsp. finely chopped parsley
1 tbsp. lemon juice
¼ c. all-purpose flour
2 egg yolks
¼ c. whipping cream
½ tsp. salt
⅛ tsp. freshly ground pepper
1 recipe Basic Duchess Potato Mixture
 (Vegetables, pg. 3)

Bring the Sauterne to a boil in a medium-sized saucepan, then add the scallops. Reduce heat and simmer for about 3 minutes or until the scallops are tender. Drain and set aside. Reserve the broth. Combine the mushrooms, green onions, 2 tablespoons butter, water, parsley and lemon juice in a saucepan. Cover and simmer for about 10 minutes, stirring occasionally. Melt the remaining butter in a saucepan, then stir in the flour and cook, stirring constantly, until lightly browned. Stir in the reserved broth slowly and cook, stirring constantly, until thickened and smooth. Remove from heat. Combine the egg yolks and cream and beat well. Add part of the hot sauce to egg mixture very slowly, beating constantly with whisk, then beat the egg mixture into the remaining sauce. Season with the salt and pepper. Stir in the mushroom mixture, then the scallops. Spoon evenly into 8 scallop shells or small ramekins. Pipe duchess potato mixture around shell. Place shells in jelly roll pan. Bake in a preheated 400-degree oven for 15 to 20 minutes or until potatoes are lightly browned. Serve immediately. This makes 8 servings.

coquilles Saint Jacques

Scallops are generally served as a first course or as a light luncheon entrée. Here they are shown prepared in a classic recipe: Coquilles Saint Jacques. Scallops, mushrooms and a delicious sauce are gratinéed in scallop shells and broiled until bubbly.

SCALLOPS AND MUSHROOMS IN PASTRY

1 lb. scallops
½ lb. fresh mushrooms, sliced
½ c. half and half cream
⅓ c. Sauterne
¼ c. finely chopped parsley
1 tsp. salt
½ tsp. freshly ground pepper
1 recipe Basic Cold Yeast Dough *(Breads,*
pg. 20-21)
1 recipe Egg Wash *(Breads, pg. 6)*

Cut large scallops in quarters and smaller scallops in halves, then mix scallops and mushrooms together carefully. Combine the cream, Sauterne, parsley and seasonings in a small mixing bowl. Roll out prepared dough on a heavily floured surface to about ⅛-inch thickness. Cut into eight 7-inch circles, then fit the circles into 4½-inch tart pans. Divide scallop mixture equally into the pastry-lined tart pans, then spoon the cream mixture over the scallop mixture. Gather the edge of dough in each tart pan and pinch together over the scallop mixture, making a frill at the top and leaving a small hole in the center. Brush dough with Egg Wash. Bake in a preheated 400-degree oven for 25 minutes. Remove from tart pans to serve, if desired. May be served with Fennel Sauce (Sauces, pg. 24). This makes 8 servings.

scallops and mushrooms in pastry

The perfect luncheon requires an entrée which is attractive, good tasting and easy on the hostess. Scallops and Mushrooms In Pastry meets every one of those criteria. The scallops and mushrooms are encased in flaky croissant dough — unusual and especially delicious. These individual portions may be prepared in advance and reheated just before serving.

CODFISH CAKES WITH SHRIMP SAUCE

1 c. shredded cooked codfish
1 c. mashed potatoes
2 eggs, slightly beaten
½ tsp. freshly ground pepper
1½ c. fine bread crumbs
¼ c. butter
1 10½-oz. can cream of shrimp soup,
1 tbsp. soy sauce

Combine the codfish, potatoes, eggs and pepper and blend well. Shape the codfish mixture into 8 cakes and coat well with the bread crumbs. Melt the butter in a skillet. Fry the cakes in the butter until lightly browned on both sides, then arrange on a serving platter. Heat the soup and soy sauce in a saucepan over low heat, stirring frequently. Spoon the soup mixture over the codfish cakes and garnish with fresh dill sprigs and lemon wedges. This makes 8 servings.

codfish cakes with shrimp sauce

Seafood fanciers will be pleased when served Codfish Cakes With Shrimp Sauce. This quick and easy entrée may be quickly assembled with very little advance preparation necessary. Fresh dillweed adds attractive color as well as zest to the sauce.

CRAB IMPERIAL

1 green sweet pepper, minced
1 med. onion, minced
2 tsp. dry mustard
2 tsp. prepared horseradish
2 tsp. salt
½ tsp. freshly ground white pepper
2 eggs, beaten
1 c. Basic Mayonnaise *(Sauces, pg. 3)*
3 lb. lump crab meat
Paprika

Combine the green pepper, onion, mustard, horseradish, salt, white pepper and eggs and mix well. Blend in the mayonnaise thoroughly, then fold in the crab meat. Spoon the crab meat mixture into 8 large cleaned crab shells or ramekins. Coat with additional mayonnaise and sprinkle generously with paprika. Arrange the crab shells in a shallow oblong baking pan. Bake in a preheated 350-degree oven for 15 to 20 minutes or until heated through. This makes 8 servings.

fish tempura with sauces

French fries, English chips and Italian fritto misto are all examples of deep-fried foods. The Japanese, famous for their *tempura* cookery, first learned of this process of cooking from Portugese sailors in the sixteenth century. They not only borrowed the idea from their Portuguese visitors, but developed many refinements and improvements resulting in *tempura* as we know it today. Simply defined, *tempura* is a method of cooking raw fish, meat or vegetables by coating them with a thin cold batter and quickly deep-frying in hot oil. The crust is light and delicate and the texture of the food is chewy and crisp.

It is not a difficult procedure, but to ensure success when making *tempura*, there are several basic rules to keep in mind: 1. Meat and vegetables must be dry before dipping in batter. 2. The batter must be very cold and should be used immediately after it is made. 3. Allow batter-coated food to stand for a few minutes before frying. 4. Maintain temperature of oil between 350 to 375 degrees. 5. Skim off loose particles of food as they appear to keep the oil clean.

Almost any type of raw food may be cooked in *tempura* batter and by following the dictates of your imagination, you may create your own original combinations of fish, meat and/or vegetables to be prepared in this classic manner. Serve with savory dipping sauces and be prepared for lavish praise from those who are gathered around the table.

FISH TEMPURA WITH SAUCES

2 lb. fresh or frozen fish fillets
Salt to taste
1 lemon, halved
½ recipe Basic Tempura Batter
1 qt. vegetable oil
Green Mayonnaise Sauce
Chili-Horseradish Sauce
Yogurt and Green Onion Sauce

BASIC TEMPURA BATTER

2 c. sifted all-purpose flour
3 egg yolks
2 c. ice water

Sift the flour 3 times. Combine the egg yolks and water in a large bowl over ice and beat with a whisk until well blended. Add the flour gradually, stirring and turning the mixture from the bottom with a spoon. Do not overmix. The flour should be visible on top or the batter will become gummy. Keep the batter over ice while dipping and frying. Cold beer may be substituted for the water, if desired. This makes about 4½ cups of batter.

1 Thaw the fish, if frozen. Assemble the ingredients. Cut the fish fillets into bite-sized pieces and drain well on paper toweling. Season with salt and squeeze desired amount of lemon juice over the fish.

2 Test the consistency of the batter by spearing a piece of the fish with a fork and dipping into the batter. A very thin coating of batter should adhere to the fish. The batter may be thinned with additional water or thickened with additional flour, if needed. Place all of the fish in the batter. Remove the fish from the batter with a fork and drain slightly when ready to fry.

3 Heat the oil in a *tempura* pan, an electric skillet or a deep fat fryer to 360 degrees. Test a piece of fish by dropping into the oil and frying until quickly browned. Fry the fish, 4 or 5 pieces at a time, for about 5 minutes, turning to brown evenly.

4 Remove the fish from the oil with a slotted spoon and drain well on paper toweling. Keep warm until all fish is cooked. The fish may be garnished with parsley and lemon slices. Serve with Green Mayonnaise Sauce, Chili-Horseradish Sauce, and Yogurt and Green Onion Sauce.

three dipping sauces for tempura

CHILI-HORSERADISH SAUCE

1 c. Basic Mayonnaise *(Sauces, pg. 3)*
1/3 c. chili sauce
3 tbsp. prepared horseradish

Combine the mayonnaise, chili sauce and horseradish in a small bowl and mix well. Chill before serving. This makes about 1 1/2 cups of sauce.

GREEN MAYONNAISE SAUCE

1/2 c. frozen spinach, thawed
1 tbsp. chopped fresh parsley
2 tbsp. chopped chives
1 tsp. crumbled dried dillweed
1 c. Basic Mayonnaise *(Sauces, pg. 3)*

Drain the spinach well, then squeeze out any remaining moisture. Place the spinach, parsley, chives and dillweed in a blender container and process until puréed. Combine the purée and mayonnaise in a small bowl and mix well. Chill before serving. This makes about 1 1/2 cups of sauce.

YOGURT AND GREEN ONION SAUCE

1 c. yogurt
2 tbsp. finely minced green onion
2 tsp. curry powder
Salt to taste

Combine the yogurt, onion, curry powder and salt in a small bowl and blend well. Chill well before serving. This makes about 1 cup of sauce.

SHRIMP AND LOBSTER TEMPURA WITH SAUCE

4 frozen lobster-tails
2 doz. fresh shrimp
1 recipe Basic Tempura Batter (pg. 28)

Thaw the lobster-tails. Shell and devein the shrimp, leaving the tails intact. Slit the shrimp down the back without separating the halves and press flat. Remove the lobster meat from the lobster-tails and cut into cubes. Drain the shrimp and lobster meat thoroughly. Dip into the batter, then drain slightly. Fry as shown in the step-by-step illustrations for Fish Tempura on page 28. This makes 4 servings.

SAUCE

¾ c. Basic Fish Stock (pg. 5)
⅓ c. soy sauce
1 tbsp. sugar
½ tsp. monosodium glutamate
⅓ c. sake
1 tsp. ginger
¼ c. grated white radish

Combine the fish stock, soy sauce, sugar, monosodium glutamate and sake, stirring to mix well. Pour into individual serving bowls. Sprinkle each bowl with the ginger and radish just before serving. This makes about 1⅔ cups of sauce.

OYSTER PUFFS

4 eggs, separated
¼ c. finely chopped green onions
¼ tsp. freshly ground white pepper
1 tsp. salt
¼ c. sifted all-purpose flour
¼ c. ground almonds
1½ c. chopped oysters, drained

Combine the beaten egg yolks, onions, pepper, salt, flour and almonds in a medium-sized bowl. Beat the egg whites until stiff peaks form, then fold the egg whites and oysters into the egg yolk mixture. Drop the oyster mixture by tablespoonfuls into 370-degree fat in a deep fryer and fry until golden brown. Drain on paper toweling. Serve with Oyster Cocktail Sauce (Sauces, pg. 32) or Creole Rémoulade Sauce (Sauces, pg. 31). This makes about 20 puffs.

SHRIMP AND FRESH CELERY RING

1 c. fine dry bread crumbs
2 c. finely chopped fresh celery
2 tbsp. ground fresh parsley
¾ c. ground hazelnuts or almonds
¼ c. ground fresh onion
2 tbsp. ground green sweet pepper
3 lg. eggs, beaten
3 tbsp. melted butter
1½ tsp. salt
¼ tsp. freshly ground white pepper
⅛ tsp. ground mace
1½ c. milk
2 lb. cooked cleaned shrimp

Combine all the ingredients except shrimp in a large bowl and blend well. Turn into a well-buttered 8½-inch ring mold, then let stand for 30 to 45 minutes. Place the ring mold in a larger pan containing hot water. Bake in a preheated 350-degree oven for 1 hour. Remove from oven and let stand in the hot water for 15 minutes. Unmold onto a serving platter and fill with shrimp. The celery ring may be served hot or cold and may be accompanied with Piquant Mayonnaise, (Sauces, pg. 3). Tuna may be substituted for the shrimp. This makes 6 to 8 servings.

shrimp and fresh celery ring

This versatile cooked celery ring with its garnish of fresh shrimp is an ideal choice for a luncheon entrée. It may be prepared in advance and baked just before needed or, if desired, it may be baked a day ahead and served cold. Any type of seafood such as tuna or crab meat can be used in place of the shrimp.

STEAMED COD FILLETS WITH SPECIAL LEMON MAYONNAISE

Butter
4 frozen cod fillets, thawed
Salt to taste
1 recipe Special Lemon Mayonnaise (Sauces, pg. 33)

Grease the perforated base of a steamer pan with butter and place the cod fillets on the buttered surface. Cover the pan. Pour enough boiling water into the bottom pan to fill 1/2 full. Place the perforated pan over the bottom pan and steam for about 15 minutes or until the cod flakes easily when tested with a fork. Remove the cod fillets and cool, then remove any skin and bones. Season with salt. Place the fillets on a serving platter and spoon the mayonnaise around the fillets. Garnish with canelled lemon slices (General Information, pg. 11) and cloves. Serve with New Potatoes (Vegetables, pg. 95). This makes 4 servings.

steamed cod fillets with special lemon mayonnaise

Special Lemon Mayonnaise (Sauces, pg. 33), served here with cod fillets, is an ideal flavor combination. Border this combination with canelled lemon wedges.

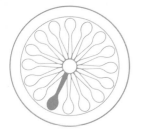

lenten mackerel

Mackerel is a delicious fish. It may be prepared in a number of different ways, accompanied by different sauces, or it is very delicious when simply grilled and served with butter.

Mackerel is available frozen and salted. Frozen mackerel can be easily defrosted by immersing it in cold water, then prepared like fresh mackerel. Salt mackerel should be soaked in fresh water for a 24-hour period before preparing.

The following recipe for Lenten Mackerel, a favorite French dish, is a hearty combination of tomatoes, onions, parsley, thyme, fish stock and dry white wine. For an equally delicious variation, you may substitute snapper steaks or cutlets for the mackerel.

LENTEN MACKEREL

4 med. tomatoes, skinned *(Vegetables, pg. 27)*
1 sm. onion, thinly sliced
4 peppercorns
2 strips of lemon peel
4 thick mackerel or snapper steaks
Leaves of 4 sm. sprigs of thyme
Leaves of 2 sprigs of fennel
Salt to taste
½ c. Basic Fish Stock *(pg. 5)*
½ c. dry white wine

Slice the tomatoes, then arrange the tomato slices and onion slices in a well-buttered, shallow baking pan. Add the peppercorns and lemon peel and arrange the mackerel steaks over the tomato mixture. Sprinkle with thyme and fennel leaves and season with salt. Pour the stock and wine into the baking pan, then cover. Bake in a preheated 325-degree oven for 20 to 25 minutes or until the mackerel flakes easily when pierced with a fork. One-half teaspoon of powdered thyme and 1 teaspoon of dried fennel may be substituted for the thyme and fennel leaves. This makes 4 servings.

lenten mackerel

Combined with whole, cooked tomatoes, onion, fish stock, lemon peel and dry white wine Lenten Mackerel is ready to be served in this beautiful copper dish.

boned mackerel with sauce

This dish of boned mackerel is stuffed with a seasoned mixture of bread crumbs, chives, parsley and bacon, then covered with a tart sauce containing wine vinegar and garlic.

boned mackerel with sauce

For the following recipe, Boned Mackerel with Lemon Sauce, you should use the smaller mackerel. Ask your fish dealer to remove the bones without cutting the fish in half. Then follow the instructions to create this savory dish made with bread crumbs, chives, bacon and lemon juice. The accompanying sauce, made with wine vinegar, garlic and lemons, gives the mackerel an outstanding flavor.

BONED MACKEREL WITH LEMON SAUCE

5 sm. mackerel, cleaned
1 c. fine soft bread crumbs
2 tbsp. chopped chives
2 tbsp. freshly minced parsley
1 slice of bacon, finely chopped
Gratted rind and juice of 1 lemon
Salt and freshly ground pepper to taste
Lemon Sauce

Have the fish dealer remove the heads and tails from the mackerel, then bone without cutting the mackerel in half. If this is not possible, cut off the head and tail and slit the fish down the underside. Remove the entrails and rinse the fish. Lay the mackerel open and lift out the bones in one piece, using a small, sharp knife. Combine the bread crumbs, chives, parsley, bacon, lemon rind and juice, salt and pepper in a bowl and mix well. Divide into 5 equal parts. Shape each part into a roll that will fit in the mackerel cavity, then place 1 roll inside each mackerel. Place each mackerel on a sheet of lightly oiled aluminum foil and wrap loosely, sealing the edges. Place the foil packets on a baking sheet. Bake in a preheated 375-degree oven for 20 to 25 minutes, depending upon the size, or until the mackerel is tender and flakes easily with a fork. Unwrap and arrange on a serving platter, then garnish with canelled lemon slices (General Information, pg. 11) and parsley sprigs. Pour half the Lemon Sauce over the mackerel, then serve the remaining Lemon Sauce in a sauceboat. Serve hot. This makes 5 servings.

LEMON SAUCE

1/2 tsp. freshly ground pepper
2 cloves of garlic, pressed
1 tbsp. dried tarragon
1 tsp. salt
2 tbsp. freshly minced parsley
2 lemons, cut into sections (*General Information, pg. 13*)
1 c. vegetable oil
1 tbsp. wine vinegar

Place the pepper, garlic, tarragon, salt and parsley in a blender container and blend. Add the oil very slowly with alternating drops of the vinegar, blending well after each addition. Place in the top of a double boiler. Cut the lemon sections into small pieces and add, along with any lemon juice, to the sauce. Mix well, then place over hot water until heated through. This makes about 1 1/4 cups of sauce.

HERB-STUFFED TROUT WITH SAUCE

6 dressed fresh trout
2 bay leaves, halved
1 sm. shallot, thinly sliced
4 peppercorns
2 or 3 sprigs of parsley
Salt
½ c. wine vinegar
½ c. water
1 ½ c. soft bread crumbs
1 egg, beaten
2 tbsp. freshly minced parsley
1 tbsp. chopped chives
Pepper to taste
Melted butter
1 tbsp. capers
1 sm. lemon, cut into sections *(General Information, pg. 13)*

Have the fish dealer remove the heads and tails from the trout, then bone without cutting in half. If preparing your own fish, prepare according to instructions for mackerel, page 33. Place the trout in a shallow glass container. Combine the bay leaves, shallot, peppercorns, parsley and 1 teaspoon of salt and sprinkle over the trout. Mix the vinegar and water and pour over the trout. Marinate in the refrigerator overnight. Drain the trout and reserve the marinade. Combine the crumbs, egg, 1 tablespoon of the parsley, chives, salt to taste and pepper in a bowl and mix well. Stuff the trout cavities with the dressing, then brush the trout with melted butter. Arrange the trout in a shallow baking dish and cover lightly with aluminum foil. Bake in a preheated 375-degree oven for about 20 minutes or until the trout flakes easily when pierced with a fork. Strain the reserved marinade and place in a small saucepan. Stir in the capers, remaining parsley, lemon sections and the marinade mixture. Heat through. Arrange the trout on a serving dish and pour the sauce over the trout. Serve hot. This makes 6 servings.

herb-stuffed trout with sauce

These trout were marinated overnight in a combination of herbs and seasonings, then stuffed with a seasoned dressing. Garnish this dish with crisp-fried potatoes.

LEMON TROUT WITH PARSLEY JELLY

4 fresh dressed trout
1/2 c. dry white wine
2 tbsp. vegetable oil
1 sm. onion, sliced
1/2 c. chopped green onions
1/2 bay leaf
1/2 tsp. salt
1/2 tsp. thyme
3 peppercorns
Juice of 1 lemon
3 c. Basic Fish Stock *(pg. 5)*
1 tbsp. butter
2 env. unflavored gelatin
3 tbsp. minced parsley

Place the trout in a buttered, shallow baking dish. Combine the wine, oil, onion slices, green onions, bay leaf, salt, thyme, peppercorns, lemon juice, fish stock and butter in a medium-sized saucepan and bring to a boil. Simmer for 15 minutes, then strain and pour over the trout. Cover with aluminum foil. Bake in a preheated 350-degree oven for about 20 minutes or until the trout flakes easily when pierced with a fork. Remove the baking dish from the oven and lift out the trout. Remove the skins from just below the heads to just above the tails, then place the trout in a deep platter. Soften the gelatin in 1/2 cup of cold water, then stir into the hot liquid in the baking dish until dissolved. Add the parsley and mix well, then pour over the trout. Cool, then chill until firm. Garnish with canelled lemon slices (General Information, pg. 11). You may serve this with Seafood Sauce Supreme (Sauces, pg. 33). This makes 4 servings.

lemon trout with parsley jelly

Fresh trout, flavored with dry white wine, onion and lemons, then set in parsley jelly are exceptionally delicious. Top them with sprigs of parsley and slices of lemon.

festive haddock fillets

Haddock, which is available fresh or frozen throughout the year, may be prepared in a variety of ways: broiled, pan-fried, steamed, baked or stuffed. The following recipe for Festive Haddock Fillets will demonstrate an easily prepared, inexpensive dish that is appealing enough for a party supper.

For convenience, this recipe calls for frozen haddock. The simple step-by-step illustrations will show how to combine the fish with dry bread crumbs, grated Parmesan cheese, chopped dill and cooked shrimp to make these fillets "company fare."

Festive Haddock Fillets may be accompanied by dry white Burgundy.

FESTIVE HADDOCK FILLETS

2   1-lb. packages frozen haddock fillets, partially thawed
2 tsp. salt
2 tbsp. melted butter
1 egg yolk, slightly beaten
Freshly ground pepper to taste
3 tbsp. fine dry bread crumbs
3 tbsp. freshly grated Parmesan cheese
¾ c. whipping cream
2 tbsp. chopped dill
1 lb. small cooked shrimp

1 Cut each package of haddock fillets lengthwise into 5 slices, then sprinkle slices with the salt.

2 Melt the butter in a small saucepan, then stir in the egg yolk and pepper. Brush the top of the haddock slices with half of the butter-egg mixture.

3 Combine the bread crumbs and cheese in a bowl. Place the haddock slices, buttered side down, in the crumb mixture.

4 Arrange the haddock slices, coated sides down, in a greased baking dish. Brush the tops of the haddock slices with the remaining butter mixture.

5 Sprinkle the haddock slices with the remaining crumb mixture. Bake in a preheated 425-degree oven for about 15 minutes or until lightly browned.

6 Bring the cream to a boil, then remove from heat and stir in the dill. Pour around the haddock slices.

7 Bake for about 10 minutes longer or until the haddock flakes easily when pierced with a fork. Add the shrimp and heat through. Sautéed mushrooms may be substituted for the shrimp. This makes 10 servings.

sole

fillets of sole

Here, Fillets of Sole are rolled around mushroom and shrimp stuffing, and topped with a colorful strip of red pimento. The accompanying sauce is made by thickening a mixture of fish stock, lemon juice and the remaining pan juices.

Sole is a delicious variety of the flat fish or flounder family. American sole is purchased as lemon sole or gray sole. Dover sole, imported from England, is sometimes found in city markets although it is very expensive. Sole may not always be available, therefore if you wish, you may substitute other flat fish such as small flounder or dabs, which are also very good and perfectly suitable for the following recipe.

FILLETS OF SOLE

12 sole fillets
½ lb. fresh mushrooms
1 med. onion, finely chopped
6 tbsp. butter
1 tbsp. minced parsley
Salt
¼ lb. cooked cleaned shrimp, finely chopped
6 tbsp. sifted all-purpose flour
3 tbsp. lemon juice
1 c. Basic Fish Stock *(pg. 5)*
Freshly ground pepper to taste
1 egg yolk, well beaten

Mince 3 of the sole fillets and chop half of the mushrooms. Sauté the onion in 1 tablespoon of the butter until soft, but not brown. Add the chopped mushrooms and sauté for 3 minutes longer.

Remove from the heat and add the parsley, ¼ teaspoon of salt, the minced sole and the shrimp. Combine ½ cup of water and 1 tablespoon of the butter in a small saucepan and bring to a boil. Stir in 4 tablespoons of the flour and 1 teaspoon of salt and beat with a wooden spoon until smooth. Remove from the heat. Add the shrimp mixture and mix thoroughly. Reserve 2 tablespoons of the mixture. Spread 1 side of the 9 remaining sole fillets with the remaining mixture, then roll up from the tail to the broad end and secure each roll with a wooden pick. Place the rolled fillets in a buttered baking dish. Melt the remaining 4 tablespoons of butter and pour over the fillets, then drizzle 2 tablespoons of the lemon juice over the fillets. Cover the baking dish with aluminum foil. Bake in a pre-heated 375-degree oven for about 20 minutes or until the fillets are tender. Place the rolled fillets on a hot serving dish and keep warm. Add the remaining 2 tablespoons of flour to the pan juices and mix well, then add the reserved parsley mixture. Add the fish stock gradually and cook over low heat, stirring constantly, until thickened. Slice the remaining ¼ pound of mushrooms and add to the sauce. Simmer for 4 minutes, then season with salt and pepper to taste. Remove from the heat. Add the remaining 1 tablespoon of lemon juice and the egg yolk and beat well. Pour into a gravy boat. Garnish the sole rolls with pimento and serve with the sauce. This makes 9 servings.

coulibiac

Coulibiac is a hot fish pie of Russian origin. For special occasions, it was made with sterlet, the most prized fish in Russia. For everyday meals, it was commonly made with salmon.

Our following recipe calls for red snapper fillets which are easily obtainable and very delicious in Coulibiac. If you wish, however, you may substitute cod or salmon fillets.

coulibiac

Here is a close-up look at Coulibiac, or Russian fish pie, showing the mixture of fish, rice, parsley, boiled eggs and mushrooms.

COULIBIAC

1 recipe Rough Puff Pastry *(Desserts, pg. 27)*
3 tbsp. vegetable oil
1 ½ lb. red snapper fillets, cut in pieces
½ recipe Basic Boiled Rice *(Cereals, pg. 3)*
3 tbsp. finely chopped parsley
¼ c. minced onion
Salt and freshly ground pepper to taste
¼ lb. fresh mushrooms, thinly sliced
3 hard-boiled eggs, finely chopped
6 tbsp. melted butter
½ c. Sauterne
Anglais Glaze *(Breads, pg. 6)*

Roll out half the pastry and line a 9 ½-inch baking dish. Heat the oil in a large skillet, then add the snapper pieces and cook for 2 to 3 minutes. Set aside. Spoon ⅓ of the rice over the pastry, then place ⅓ of the snapper over the rice. Sprinkle with ⅓ of the parsley and ⅓ of the onion and season with salt and pepper. Arrange ⅓ of the mushrooms over the onion and top with ⅓ of the chopped eggs. Repeat layers until all the ingredients are used. Pour the melted butter and Sauterne over the top. Roll out the remaining pastry and cut to fit the baking dish, using trimmings for pastry crescents. Place over the top and seal to the bottom pastry by pinching the edges together. Brush with the glaze. Decorate the top with pastry crescents and brush with the glaze. Bake in a preheated 400-degree oven for 45 to 50 minutes or until the top is golden brown. Serve with lemon butter, if desired. This makes 8 to 10 servings.

fish in potato baskets

Fish Fingers in Potato Baskets is a French version of the British Fish 'N Chips. When cooked, the fish fingers resemble goujon, a small gudgeon fish found in French rivers, which the French frequently use for this recipe. However, our recipe calls for flounder which is a good substitute, particularly when served with a favorite seafood sauce, such as Mexicali Sauce (Sauces, pg. 32) or Creole Rémoulade Sauce (Sauces, pg. 31).

FISH FINGERS IN POTATO BASKETS

8 Potato Baskets (Vegetables, pg. 68)
2 lb. flounder fillets
All-purpose flour
3 eggs, well beaten
Fine dry bread crumbs
1 recipe Mexicali Sauce (Sauces, pg. 32)

Prepare the Potato Baskets and keep warm. Cut each flounder fillet into small strips and roll in flour. Dip the strips into the eggs, then coat well with bread crumbs. Fry the strips in deep fat at 375 degrees until golden brown, then drain on paper toweling. Place in the Potato Baskets, then place on a platter. Garnish with parsley. Serve with the sauce. This makes 8 servings.

fish fingers in potato baskets

Strips of crispy-fried flounder piled in crunchy Potato Baskets (Vegetables, pg. 68) is a different and attractive way to serve fish and potatoes.

fried dabs with cream herb sauce

Dabs are a delicious species of the flounder family. These dabs are made with four whole dabs, fried and sprinkled with a mixture of bread crumbs, boiled eggs and freshly minced parsley. Accompany them with delicious Cream Herb Sauce (Appetizers, pg. 24), and serve them with French bread.

FRIED DABS WITH CREAM HERB SAUCE

4 whole dabs or small flounder fillets
All-purpose flour
2 eggs, beaten
Fine dry bread crumbs
2 hard-boiled eggs, finely chopped
1 tbsp. freshly minced parsley
1 recipe Cream Herb Sauce *(Appetizers, pg. 24)*

Wash the dabs and pat dry. Coat the dabs with flour, shaking off any excess, then dip into the beaten eggs. Coat generously with bread crumbs, patting the crumbs into the egg coating firmly. Fry the dabs in deep fat at 375 degrees until brown on both sides. Drain on paper toweling, then arrange on a heated serving platter. Sprinkle with the eggs, then the parsley. Serve with the sauce, and French bread. This makes 4 servings.

batter-fried fish with sauce

Basic *Béarnaise* Sauce (Sauces, pg. 23), world famous for its taste that goes well with a number of seafoods and meats, is served here with fried fish fillets. The fillets are dipped in an egg mixture, coated with dry bread crumbs and fried to a golden brown in peanut oil. They are then garnished with lemon wedges and parsley.

BATTER-FRIED FISH WITH BÉARNAISE SAUCE

1 lb. fish fillets
1 egg
2 tbsp. milk
¼ tsp. salt
½ c. fine dry bread crumbs
2 c. peanut oil
1 recipe Basic Béarnaise Sauce (Sauces, pg. 23)

Wash the fish fillets and pat them dry. Combine the egg, milk and salt in a bowl and beat until blended. Dip the fish into the egg mixture, then coat well with the crumbs. Pour the oil into a skillet and heat to 375 degrees. Fry the fish fillets in the oil until golden brown on both sides. Drain the fish on paper toweling. Place in a serving container and garnish with lemon wedges and parsley. Serve with the sauce. This makes 4 servings.

batter-fried fish with béarnaise sauce

These hot, crisp fish fillets are served with a classic sauce, Basic Béarnaise Sauce. Serve this combination fish and sauce with crisp, cold slaw for a delicious fish supper.

MENU FOR A GALA FISH FRY

COCKTAILS:
CARIBBEAN PUNCH
(Beverages, pg. 52)

SHELLFISH TRIO
(Appetizers, pg. 73)

BATTER-FRIED FISH

BASIC BÉARNAISE SAUCE
(Sauces, pg. 23)

PALLAS ATHENE SALAD
(Salads, pg. 26)

CORNMEAL MUFFINS
(Breads, pg. 40)

ORANGE-YOGURT CHIFFON PIE
(Desserts, pg. 209)

SUGGESTED WINES:
HERMITAGE BLANC
(RHONE WINE)
AMERICAN SAUVIGNON
BLANC

STUFFED PICNIC LOAF

1 lg. unsliced sandwich loaf of bread
1 env. unflavored gelatin
2 7-oz cans chunk-style tuna, drained and
    flaked
3/4 c. diced cooked potatoes
3/4 c. cooked green peas
3/4 c. chopped cooked green beans
3/4 c. diced cooked carrots
2 hard-boiled eggs, chopped
6 tbsp. half and half cream
1/2 tsp. freshly ground pepper
1 tsp. salt
2 tsp. paprika
1 c. Basic Mayonnaise (Sauces, pg. 3)

Slice the crust from one end of the sandwich loaf
and reserve. Scoop out the center of the loaf, leaving a 1/4-inch shell. Soften the gelatin in 1/4 cup of
water, then dissolve over hot water. Combine the
tuna, potatoes, green peas, green beans, carrots and
eggs in a large bowl and blend well. Stir in the
cream, pepper, salt, paprika, mayonnaise and
gelatin and blend thoroughly. Spoon the tuna mixture into the prepared shell and pack firmly. Cut off
the excess bread shell, if tuna mixture does not fill
the shell, then replace the reserved crust. Wrap the
loaf tightly with aluminum foil and refrigerate until
chilled. Cut into slices to serve. This makes 20 to 24
slices.

stuffed picnic loaf

*This savory picnic loaf was made with tuna,
diced vegetables, hard-boiled eggs and
delicious Basic Mayonnaise (Sauces, pg. 3).*

tuna soufflé

Before preparing delicious Windsor Tuna Soufflé, review
the "basics" for making a perfect soufflé (Desserts, pg. 45).
Remember that soufflés are made by adding sweet or savory mixtures to frothy, stiffly beaten egg whites so that the
finished product puffs and has a delicate airy texture.

WINDSOR TUNA SOUFFLÉ

3 tbsp. butter
3 tbsp. all-purpose flour
2 c. milk
1 tsp. salt
1/8 tsp. freshly ground pepper
1/8 tsp. nutmeg
3/4 c. freshly grated Parmesan cheese
3/4 c. Fried Croutons (Breads, pg. 16)
1 7-oz. can chunk-style tuna, drained and flaked
8 egg whites

Melt the butter in the top of a double boiler over boiling
water, then stir in the flour with a wooden spoon until
blended. Add the milk gradually and cook, stirring constantly, until slightly thickened. Add the seasonings and
cheese and cook, stirring, until the cheese is melted and
the mixture is well blended. Remove from the water and
cool thoroughly. Add the croutons and tuna and mix well.
Beat the egg whites in a medium-sized bowl until stiff
peaks form. Fold 1/4 of the egg whites into the tuna mixture, blending well, then add the remaining egg whites,
folding in carefully. Spoon the tuna mixture into a well-
buttered 7 1/2-inch soufflé dish, spreading the mixture
with a knife to the edge to seal well. Bake in a preheated
350-degree oven for 1 hour. Serve immediately. This
makes about 8 servings.

bouillabaisse

This elaborate French stew originated in Marseilles, France. The original recipe called for 12 different types of fish, some of which were frogfish, eel, lobster, redfish, whiting, haddock, codfish and turbot. All twelve were combined with many other ingredients including onions, leeks, tomatoes, saffron, garlic and minced parsley. There are many versions of this soup which do not have to include as many varieties of fish. For this recipe, we have chosen mackerel, halibut and flounder fillets to combine with vegetables, seasonings, lemon and dry white wine.

BOUILLABAISSE

1 lb. mackerel fillets
½ lb. halibut fillets
1 lb. flounder fillets
4 med. tomatoes, skinned *(Vegetables, pg. 27)*
4 med. potatoes
3 cloves of garlic
1 leek, sliced
2 sprigs of parsley
1 bay leaf
1 tsp. grated lemon rind
1 ½ tsp. salt
Freshly ground pepper to taste
¼ c. dry white wine
½ tsp. saffron or 1½ tbsp. tumeric
5 thick slices of bread
1 tbsp. olive oil

Cut the fish fillets into bite-sized pieces. Cut the tomatoes into wedges. Peel and slice the potatoes. Combine the fish fillets, tomatoes and potatoes in a soup kettle. Crush 1 clove of garlic and add to the kettle, then add the leek, parsley, bay leaf and lemon rind. Pour 6 cups of boiling water into the kettle, then add the salt, pepper and wine. Bring to a boil and cook for about 20 minutes or until the fish flakes easily when tested with a fork. Crush the remaining 2 cloves of garlic and blend in the saffron. Remove the crust from 1 slice of bread and soak the bread in a small amount of water. Squeeze the water from the bread, then mix the bread with the garlic mixture. Add the oil and ¼ cup of the stock from the fish mixture and mix well. Spread the oil mixture over the remaining bread slices and place the slices in 4 soup bowls. Ladle the soup over the bread slices. This makes 4 servings.

SHRIMP TARRAGON WITH PIMENTO RICE

2 tbsp. melted butter
3 tbsp. all-purpose flour
1 can cream of shrimp soup
½ c. chicken broth
½ c. Sauterne
2 tbsp. lemon juice
½ tsp. tarragon
½ tsp. seasoned pepper
½ tsp. salt
½ tsp. onion powder
1 ¼ lb. shelled deveined shrimp
Pimento Rice

Blend the butter and flour in a saucepan until smooth, then stir in the soup, broth, Sauterne, lemon juice, tarragon, seasoned pepper, salt and onion powder. Cook over medium heat until thickened, stirring constantly. Add the shrimp and cook for 5 to 10 minutes longer or until the shrimp are pink. Turn into a heated serving dish. Serve with Pimento Rice. This makes about 4 servings.

PIMENTO RICE

1 c. chopped onions
2 tbsp. butter
1 recipe Basic Boiled Rice *(Cereals, pg. 3)*
¼ c. diced pimento

Sauté the onions in the butter in a saucepan until tender, but not brown. Stir in the rice and pimento and simmer, stirring frequently, until heated through. This makes about 4 cups of rice.

bouillabaisse

This hearty, French fish stew, made with mackerel, halibut and flounder fillets, is combined with potatoes, tomatoes, leeks, parsley, garlic and seasonings. Serve it as a complete meal or as a first course for dinner.

SEAFOOD IN VOL-AU-VENT SHELLS

¼ c. chopped onion
1 c. sliced fresh mushrooms
¼ c. butter
¼ c. all-purpose flour
½ tsp. salt
⅛ tsp. freshly ground pepper
⅛ tsp. paprika
1 c. whipping cream
1 c. chicken broth
1 tbsp. Worcestershire sauce
2 egg yolks, beaten
2 c. cooked lobster *(pg. 10)*
2 c. cooked cleaned shrimp
2 tsp. sherry
12 Vol-Au-Vent Shells *(Desserts, pg. 65)*

Sauté the onion and mushrooms in the butter in a chafing dish pan over low heat until the onion is tender. Blend in the flour and seasonings and cook until bubbly. Remove the pan from the heat and stir in the cream, broth and Worcestershire sauce. Bring to a boil, stirring constantly, then reduce the heat and cook, stirring, for 1 minute longer or until thickened. Add a small amount of the hot mixture to the egg yolks, then stir the egg yolk mixture back into the hot mixture. Cut the lobster and shrimp into large pieces and stir into the sauce. Add the sherry and cook for 5 minutes longer, stirring frequently. Place the pan over hot water. Serve the seafood mixture in the *Vol-au-vent* Shells. This makes 12 servings.

seafood in vol-au-vent shells

Vol-au-vent shells make excellent containers for seafood mixtures. Displayed here is a taste-tempting mixture of lobster, shrimp, onions and mushrooms, spooned into savory, flaky pastry shells

baked clams

Baked Clams in Basic Mornay Sauce are served here on clam shells. If you do not have clam shells, you may use scallop shells. If neither are available, use individual baking dishes. Individual servings of this delicious seafood dish make a very attractive display.

baked clams in basic mornay sauce

Dry white wine, freshly grated Parmesan cheese and Basic Mornay Sauce (Sauces, pg. 11) give baked clams a gourmet taste. Make individual servings and garnish with bits of parsley.

BAKED CLAMS IN BASIC MORNAY SAUCE

1 pt. shucked clams
Dry white wine
1 recipe Basic Mornay Sauce *(Sauces, pg. 11)*
2 tbsp. fine dry bread crumbs
1 tbsp. freshly grated Parmesan cheese
2 tsp. chopped parsley
2 tsp. chopped chives
Butter

Mince the clams and place in a saucepan, then add just enough wine to cover. Simmer for about 5 minutes or until the wine has evaporated. Combine the clams and the sauce and mix well. Spoon the clam mixture into scallop shells or individual baking dishes. Blend the bread crumbs, cheese, parsley and chives and sprinkle over the clam mixture, then dot with butter. Place the shells on a baking sheet. Bake in a preheated 350-degree oven, 1 rack above center, for 15 minutes. This makes 8 servings.

pasta & cereals

table of contents

introducing rice

There is a fascinating body of fact and fancy surrounding one of mankind's most important staple food crops, rice. In ancient China the sowing of rice was part of an important and revered religious ceremony. And centuries ago in India, as legend has it, a special bladed knife was used to harvest rice so that the jealous "rice spirit" could not see the grain being cut from the stalk and, thus, "curse" the crop. Farmers believed that if they pacified the spirit in this way they would be blessed with a more abundant yield.

Many things have changed since Indian farmers wielded those legendary knives. But the dietary importance of rice has not altered in all those years. The chief source of food for over eighty percent of the world's population, rice is a highly nutritious and easily digested food.

KINDS OF RICE

For the peoples of the world who depend on rice as their staple food, *brown rice* is the most common kind. This whole, unpolished grain of rice with only the outer hull and a small amount of the bran removed has a delightful nutlike flavor and chewy texture. Available in America predominantly in health food stores, brown rice is both tasty and nutritious.

Milled white rice, the most common type of rice in this country, is usually grouped into long and short grain varieties. Short grain rice cooks up moist and tender and has a slight tendency to stick together. For these reasons, it is often preferred for sweet puddings, rice rings, and risottos (fried rice dishes). Long grain rice, like the Indian Patna, is the preferred type for boiling and serving with butter or gravy and with savory dishes such as curries.

Long grain *precooked rice* is a real timesaver in today's busy world. You can have it cooked and ready to serve in a matter of minutes. We will tell you in recipes you will meet later in your course when you can successfully substitute this convenience food.

Esteemed a gourmet's delight, and native only to North America, *wild rice* is the most luxurious grain in the world. Although it is priced in the bracket of truffles and caviar, it is worth the extra cost to enjoy its natural flavor and unusually firm, chewy texture.

COOKING RICE

A familiar distress call we hear quite often is: "My rice is a disaster, a gluey, stuck-together mush! What can I do?" Our recipes that follow will remedy that perplexing situation by giving exact instructions for cooking perfect rice.

1 For Basic Fried Oven-Cooked Rice, melt 4 tablespoons butter in a large skillet. When the butter begins to sizzle, add 1 cup long grain rice and one small onion, finely chopped. Cook this mixture over medium heat, stirring constantly.

2 When the butter has been absorbed and the rice glistens, turn the mixture into a 1½-quart casserole.

3 Pour in 2 cups hot stock and cover the casserole. Place the casserole in the oven, one shelf above center, at 425 degrees, for approximately 25 minutes.

4 For Risotto (re SOT to), instead of transferring the rice to a casserole, place it in a large iron skillet. Add 1 cup stock. When this has been completely absorbed, add more stock in ½-cup quantities until the last addition has been absorbed and rice is tender.

BASIC FRIED OVEN-COOKED RICE

4 tbsp. butter
1 c. long grain rice
1 sm. onion, finely chopped
2 c. hot Basic Chicken Stock (Soups, pg. 2)

Melt the butter in a frying pan. Add the rice and onion; cook over medium heat for about 5 minutes or until golden, stirring frequently. Turn the rice mixture into a 1½-quart casserole; stir in the stock. Cover. Bake in preheated 425-degree oven for 25 minutes or until the rice is tender and the stock is absorbed.

RISOTTO

4 tbsp. butter
1 c. long grain rice
2 c. Basic Beef or Chicken Stock (Soups, pg. 2)

Melt the butter in a heavy skillet. Add the rice and cook over medium heat, stirring constantly, until butter is absorbed. Pour in 1 cup stock and cook, stirring frequently, until stock has been absorbed. Add ½ cup stock and cook until absorbed. Add remaining stock; stir well. Cover and simmer until stock has been absorbed, stirring occasionally. Cooking time will be about 25 minutes after first addition of stock.

how to
insure grain-separate rice

1 When the boiled rice is done, pour it into a sieve and let the water drain through into a glass bowl or a saucepan.

2 See for yourself how perfectly the grains of rice separated. Pour it into a bowl and fluff with a fork.

BASIC BOILED RICE

5 c. water
2 tsp. salt
1 c. long grain rice

Bring water and salt to a hard rolling boil in a large saucepan. Add rice gradually, stirring constantly. Cover. Reduce heat and cook at a slow boil for 18 to 20 minutes or until rice is tender. Drain and serve hot. Do not rinse before serving, as this washes away vitamins and minerals.

alternate method

2 c. water
1 tsp. salt
1 c. long grain rice

Bring water and salt to a hard rolling boil in a 2-quart saucepan. Add rice gradually, stirring constantly. Cover. Reduce heat and cook at a slow boil for 18 to 20 minutes or until rice is tender and water is absorbed.

BASIC PARBOILED OVEN-COOKED RICE

2½ c. Basic Chicken Stock *(Soups, pg. 2)*
1 c. long grain rice
¼ c. butter

Bring the stock to a boil, then add the rice gradually, stirring constantly. Reduce heat and cook at a slow boil for 6 minutes. Pour into a 1½-quart casserole and cover. Bake in a preheated 375-degree oven for 25 minutes or until rice is tender and stock is absorbed. Remove from oven and stir in the butter until melted. Serve immediately.

mushroom risotto

MUSHROOM RISOTTO

3 tbsp. butter
1 sm. onion, thinly sliced
2 4-oz. cans sliced mushrooms
¾ c. Sauterne
2 c. yellow rice
4 c. Basic Chicken Stock *(Soups, pg. 2)*
½ c. grated Parmesan cheese

Melt the butter in a large, heavy skillet over low heat. Add the onion and cook, stirring constantly, until transparent but not brown. Drain the mushrooms. Add to onion and stir until mixed. Add the Sauterne and stir well. Simmer until most of the Sauterne has evaporated. Add rice and cook over low heat, stirring constantly, for 5 minutes. Add 1 cup chicken stock and mix well. Cook until stock has been absorbed by rice, stirring frequently. Add 1 cup chicken stock and cook, stirring frequently, until stock has been absorbed by rice. Add remaining stock, stir well, then cover. Simmer, stirring frequently, until stock has been absorbed. Cooking time is 25 minutes after first stock has been added. Remove from heat. Add the cheese and stir well. Cover and let stand for 3 minutes. Garnish with a large, sautéed mushroom and green pepper strips. Serve with additional grated Parmesan cheese and lemon juice, if desired.

mushroom risotto

The copper frying pan is piled high with glistening Mushroom Risotto. Though the dish needs no additional beautifying, we crowned it with a "turned" sautéed mushroom (General Information, pg. 16) and bordered it with sliced green pepper.

The Creative Homemaker's Academy © MCMLXXIII
Selected Illustrations © B.P.C. Publishing Limited MCMLXX

RICE WITH MORNAY SAUCE

1 recipe Basic Boiled Rice *(pg. 3)*
¼ c. butter
1 red sweet pepper, finely chopped
1 green sweet pepper, finely chopped
1 recipe Basic Mornay Sauce *(Sauces, pg. 11)*

Place the boiled rice in a mixing bowl. Add the
butter and stir until butter is melted and each grain
of rice is coated. Stir in the red and green peppers
until well mixed. Press the rice mixture firmly into
a large oiled mold and let stand for about 5
minutes. Invert onto serving dish and serve with
Mornay sauce.

rice with mornay sauce

*This simple dish is a delightful blend of rice
flecked with chopped red and green peppers and
zesty Basic Mornay Sauce (Sauces, pg. 11). The rice
mixture, incidentally, is pressed into greased
molds while still hot and turned out immediately.*

rice with toasted pine nuts

Pour 4 cups water into a large saucepan; add 2 teaspoons salt. Bring to a boil. Stir in rice gradually so that water continues to boil, then cover. Cook over very low heat for about 25 minutes or until all water is absorbed. Place in a large casserole; cover. Keep hot in a preheated 250-degree oven. Pour vinaigrette into a small saucepan. Add butter and place over low heat until melted. Add the paprika, chives, lemon juice, Garlic Oil and raisins; simmer for 5 minutes or until raisins are plump. Add the eggs to rice. Pour raisin mixture over rice; add pepper and remaining salt. Toss with 2 forks, then cover. Heat the olive oil in a small skillet. Stir in the pine nuts and cook over low heat, stirring constantly, until browned. Sprinkle over rice mixture and garnish with additional chives.

RICE WITH TOASTED PINE NUTS

3½ tsp. salt
2 c. long grain rice
¼ c. Basic Vinaigrette *(Sauces, pg. 2)*
¼ c. butter
1 tbsp. paprika
3 tbsp. chopped chives
Juice of 1 lemon
½ tsp. Garlic Oil *(Sauces, pg. 10)*
1 c. golden raisins
4 hard-boiled eggs, chopped
½ tsp. freshly ground pepper
1 tbsp. olive oil
¾ c. pine nuts

rice with toasted pine nuts

We have placed a layer of toasted pine nuts and chopped chives on a bed of boiled rice tossed with boiled eggs, raisins, and Basic Vinaigrette (Sauces, pg. 2) to make up this glamorous dish. Instead of pine nuts, which are sold as Indian nuts or pignolia in some locales, try substituting slivered almonds.

creole rice

CREOLE RICE

½ c. butter
1 clove of garlic, pressed
2 lg. onions, thinly sliced
1 lg. green or red sweet pepper, diced
1½ c. Basic Chicken Stock *(Soups, pg. 2)*
2 c. diced smoked ham
6 skinned tomatoes, diced
½ c. Sauterne
½ tsp. dried thyme
½ tsp. dried basil
1 tsp. paprika
6 drops of red hot sauce

1¼ c. long grain rice
1 tsp. salt
½ tsp. freshly ground pepper

Melt the butter in a Dutch oven and stir in the garlic. Add the onions and sweet pepper and sauté until tender but not browned. Stir in 1 cup of the stock and all remaining ingredients and cook for 3 minutes. Turn into a large casserole and cover. Bake in a preheated 400-degree oven for 25 minutes. Remove from oven and stir in the remaining stock. Cover and bake for 10 minutes longer or until rice is tender.

creole rice

*This rice casserole is liberally seasoned with
onions, garlic, peppers, liquid hot sauce,
tomatoes, and herbs. Tender morsels of diced ham
mingle with the grains of rice.*

spiced rice with oranges

The perfect accompaniment to pork or fowl, this dish combines rice with mushrooms, celery, carrots, cucumbers, green pepper and onions. Pictured in the foreground is tangy Paprika-Orange Sauce (Sauces, pg. 12).

SPICED RICE WITH ORANGES

2 c. sliced mushrooms
1 c. chopped onions
¾ c. finely chopped green sweet pepper
1 c. finely chopped celery
1 lg. carrot, grated
6 tbsp. olive oil
3 c. diced cooked chicken
½ cucumber, peeled and diced
1 10½-oz. can tomato purée
Salt and pepper to taste
3¾ c. **Basic Chicken Stock** *(Soups, pg. 2)*
1¼ c. long grain rice
1 recipe **Paprika-Orange Sauce** *(Sauces, pg. 12)*

Sauté the mushrooms, onions, green pepper, celery and carrot in 4 tablespoons olive oil in a Dutch oven until tender, stirring frequently. Add the chicken, cucumber, tomato purée, salt and pepper and ¾ cup chicken stock, stirring to combine. Cover; simmer for 5 minutes, stirring occasionally. Saute the rice in a frying pan in remaining olive oil until golden, stirring constantly. Turn rice into tomato mixture. Stir in remaining chicken stock; cover. Cook for about 30 minutes or until rice is tender and liquid is absorbed, stirring frequently. Turn into serving bowl; garnish edge with fresh orange slices. Serve with Paprika-Orange Sauce.

introducing pasta

In 1533 Catherine de Médici married the Dauphin of France who later became Henry II. When she left Italy to live in France, naturally her entourage included the finest of the Florentine chefs. Upon arrival in Paris, these Italian cooks realized that vast new areas of gastronomy were now open to them, as they began acquainting themselves with French cuisine. They, in turn, introduced innovations to the French: pastas, savoy cabbages, broccoli, haricot beans, artichokes, sweetbreads, truffles, grated Parmesan cheese, iced cream, and many more. Historians today acknowledge that the marriage of Catherine de Médici and Henry II was not only a political union, but, sparked by the arrival of the Italian chefs from Florence, it also marked the beginning of French *haute cuisine*.

The apparently simple cooking of Italy is sometimes more difficult to produce well than the more subtle and refined cuisine of France. The excellence of an Italian dinner depends on the excellence of the ingredients which go into it, while a pleasant French recipe might be successfully executed with the plainest of ingredients. The old saying that good cooking begins in the market is very apropos of Italian cuisine; a dish of pasta is only as good as the quality of the pasta itself. In this section, we will concentrate on recipes for pastas and sauces to serve with them.

Pasta is the generic Italian name for many noodle-like pastes or doughs which are made in a wide variety of shapes and sizes. There are over 500 different kinds. The ancient origins of pasta remain obscure to modern man. Except for parts of Northern Italy where polenta (cornmeal mush) and risotto (sautéed and steamed rice) prevail, the daily use of pasta has been enjoyed for centuries by both rich and poor Italians. Even though Marco Polo is often credited with introducing pasta to his countrymen from the Chinese (he brought back a dish known as Chinese Spaghetti), an ancient tool identified as a macaroni-maker is included in the fresco of an Etruscan tomb. There is evidence that ravioli and fettucini were being prepared in the middle ages. By the seventeenth century, demand for pasta was so great, assembly line production was required to fill the needs of the Italian villages and towns. At the back of the shops where the pasta was made, strong young men waded barefoot into the dough to knead it. The dough was then forced through a cylinder with a trafila on one end. The trafila was a metal plate with perforations to form the dough into one of the dozens of characteristic shapes of pasta. The preference for a particular shape varied markedly from one region to another. Each shape was said to have its own flavor even though they all were made from the same basic recipe!

Any cook with an eye to economy and a desire to serve hearty, satisfying meals would be wise to keep several different types of pasta in her cupboard. A minimum of meat, poultry, fish, leftovers, vegetables or cheese (along with a sprinkling of ingenuity) combined with these expansive starch products makes a tasty, nourishing meal. The variety of serving possibilities for a package of spaghetti or macaroni is endless — from a simple bowl of noodles dressed with oil and garlic as a side dish, to something as rich and filling as Spaghetti with Italian Meat Sauce (Sauces, pg. 18). If olive oil is used in a recipe, be sure to obtain the best grade available — an inferior type can spoil an otherwise perfectly prepared dish.

Cooking pasta in boiling water or broth is a very simple procedure, but attention must be given to a few basic rules:

1. The pot in which it is boiled must be large enough — for every 4 ounces of pasta to be cooked, a minimum of 1 quart of boiling, salted water is required. This is essential to keep the pasta from sticking together (and also, the more boiling water contained in the pot, the sooner it will return to the boiling point after the pasta is added).

2. The water must be well salted — about $1\frac{1}{2}$ teaspoons of salt for each quart of boiling water. It must be brought to a rolling boil and the pasta dropped in, a little at a time so the water remains as close to a full boil as possible. It must be stirred often to prevent the pasta from sticking together or to the pot in which it is cooked. Another very reliable method to prevent sticking is to add a tablespoon of cooking oil (butter or margarine can also be used) to the boiling water. After all the pasta has been dropped in, bring the water back to a vigorous boil and continue cooking, stirring occasionally.

It is not possible to give a fixed cooking time since this depends on the quantity, type and thickness of the pasta to be cooked. Taste preference is also a factor which determines cooking time. Most Italians prefer pasta *al dente*, that is, slightly chewy, (*al dente*, literally translated, means "to the tooth"). After it is cooked, remove from the heat and drain quickly in a colander. <u>Never</u> rinse the pasta with cold water after draining.

the many varieties of pasta

Cooking with pasta is undemanding, adaptable and inexpensive; these characteristics help modern cooks resist the pressures of rising food costs, shortened schedules and fast-paced living of today.

The following illustrations will give you some idea of the wide variety of pasta available in supermarkets and Italian grocery stores. This section will give recipes for some of them although bought pasta may be substituted.

Like cheese and egg dishes, a different pasta recipe could be served every day for a whole year without repeating a single recipe.

You can use your imagination to suggest many more uses for pasta than we have room for here. Most pastas are interchangeable with potatoes or rice as accompaniments for meat or fish dishes.

TYPES OF PASTA

Here is an array of 39 different types of pasta to give you an idea of the many different shapes and sizes:

Top Level

1. Cannelloni
2. Mafaldine
3. Mafalde
4. Lasagne Verde
5. Spaghetti
6. Lumace
7. Lasagne
8. Long Ziti
9. Lasgnette
   Pennini in bottom of same container

Bottom Level, Back Row

1. Spaghettini
2. Finely folded Tagliatelli Verde
3. Zitoni

4. Capellini
   In bottom of same container, Ruote
5. Lasagne Verde Grande
   In bottom of same container, Finely folded Vermicelli
6. Broad Tagliatelli
7. Wholemeal Spaghetti
   In bottom of same container Large Rigatoni
8. Tagliatelli
   In bottom of same container Spirali
9. Long Macaroni
10. Spaghetti

Saucers, back row

1. Rigatoni Regate
2. Penne
3. Farfalle
4. Ravioli
5. Tortellini
6. Conchiglie
7. Spirali
8. Mezzani

The small dishes containing minute pastas, which include Stellete, Pastine Semini, Acine di Pepe, Alfabeto and Anellini, are good to use in soups.

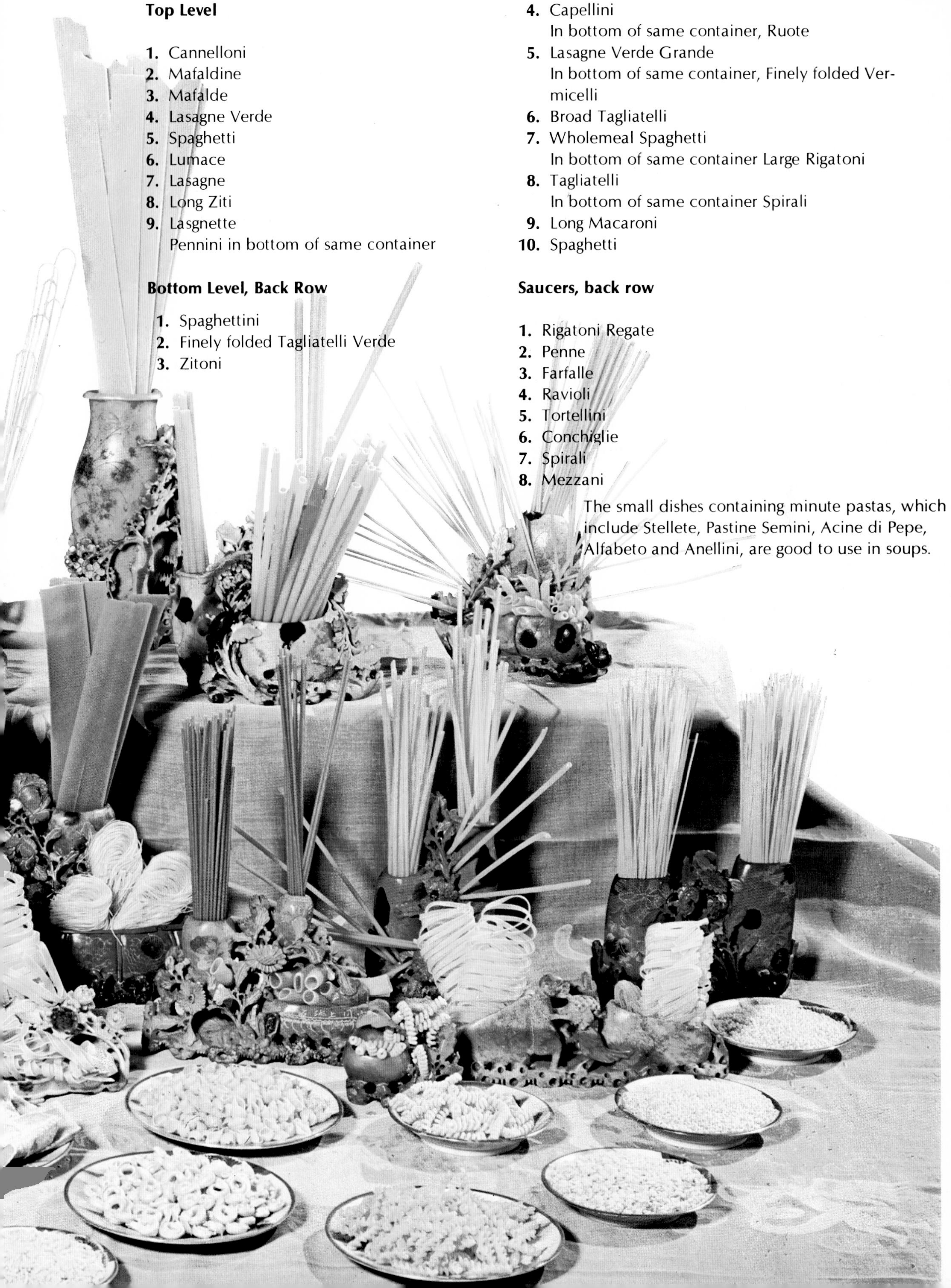

how to
make ravioli

The savory stuffed pillows of pasta dough called ravioli have been enjoyed by the Italians since the thirteenth century. According to legend, ravioli was created by Italian sailors who, on long voyages, had to utilize leftovers since every scrap of fresh food had to be used. After meals, whatever food remained was combined, chopped fine and stuffed into little envelopes of pasta dough and served at the next repast. These were called *rabiole*, a dialectical term for leftovers — things of little value.

Care must be taken to knead ravioli dough properly to develop the gluten which makes the dough elastic. The dough should be rolled out as thinly as possible using a small amount of flour — too much flour toughens the dough. If you prepare large amounts of ravioli, the uncooked ravioli may be frozen in a tightly sealed container for later use.

BASIC RAVIOLI

3½ c. sifted all-purpose flour
1 tbsp. salt
4 eggs
1 tbsp. olive oil
4 to 5 tbsp. water

Sift the flour with salt onto a large board or working surface. Make a well in the center and add the eggs, oil and half the water. Blend together, using 2 knives, drawing in the flour and adding the remaining water as needed. You may use pastry scrapers to finish blending in the flour. Gather the dough into a ball and knead for about 3 minutes or until smooth and elastic. Cover dough with a cloth and let rest for 30 minutes to remove elasticity. Divide the dough into 4 parts. Place 1 part on a lightly-floured board and roll out as thin as possible into a large rectangle. Lift the dough occasionally and turn over on floured surface during the rolling procedure to keep from sticking and insure a paper-thin pasta. Trim edges to make a uniform rectangle, using a plastic ruler and a sharp knife.

BEEF FILLING

2 tbsp. butter
2 tbsp. olive oil
⅓ c. diced salt pork
1½ c. minced onions
½ lb. Italian sweet sausage
¾ lb. lean ground beef
¼ c. chopped chicken livers
1 bay leaf
1 clove of garlic, pressed
Salt and freshly ground pepper to taste
1 1-lb. can tomatoes
1 tbsp. tomato paste

Combine the butter, olive oil and salt pork in a frypan. Cook, stirring occasionally, until salt pork is golden. Add the onions and sauté until lightly browned. Remove the casing from the sausage and add the sausage to frypan, then add the beef, livers and bay leaf. Cook slowly, stirring frequently, for 15 minutes. Add the garlic and season with salt and pepper. Cook, stirring, for 5 minutes longer. Add the tomatoes and simmer for 30 minutes or until thick, stirring occasionally. Remove from heat and stir in the tomato paste. Cool. Force through food grinder 2 times. Refrigerate until ready to fill ravioli.

CHEESE FILLING

1 10-oz. package frozen chopped spinach
½ c. ricotta or cottage cheese
⅓ c. freshly grated Parmesan cheese
Salt and pepper to taste
Pinch of nutmeg
1 tsp. basil or marjoram

Cook the spinach according to package directions. Drain thoroughly, pressing to remove all liquid. Combine all the ingredients in the blender container and purée. Set aside or refrigerate until ready to fill ravioli.

1 Mark off 1½-inch squares lightly using a pastry wheel or knife. Brush entire surface with cold water.

2 Place desired filling in a pastry bag with a ½-inch plain tube and pipe a small mound into the center of each square. Filling may be dropped from a teaspoon, if desired.

3 Dip knife into cold water and flatten filling tops slightly.

4 Roll out 2nd part of dough as directed, only slightly larger. Roll rectangle of dough onto rolling pin, then unroll carefully over filling.

5 Press between rows of filling, forming squares.

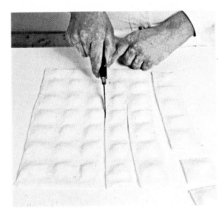

6 Cut between squares, using a sharp knife or pastry wheel. You may need to seal edges with tines of fork. Separate squares and let stand for at least 1 hour to dry before cooking.

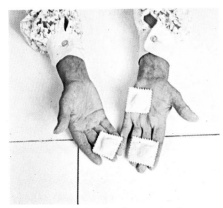

7 Drop into boiling salted water and cook for about 15 minutes or until tender. Pour gently into colander and drain. Place carefully into a serving dish, then drizzle with melted butter and sprinkle with Parmesan cheese. May be served with favorite sauce, if desired.

pasta shells with basic génoise sauce

SIMPLE ITALIAN SUPPER MENU:

PASTA SHELLS WITH BASIC GÉNOISE SAUCE

CAESAR SALAD
(Salads, Pg. 24)

HERB BREAD
(Breads, pg. 17)

ORANGE ICE CREAM
(Desserts, pg. 70)

SUGGESTED WINE: CHIANTI

PASTA SHELLS WITH BASIC GÉNOISE SAUCE

2 tbsp. salad oil
1 1-lb. package pasta shells
1 recipe Basic Génoise Sauce *(Sauces, pg. 17)*

Bring 4 quarts heavily salted water to a boil, then add the oil. Add the pasta shells slowly and cook for about 12 minutes or to desired degree of doneness. Drain well. Place shells and sauce in serving dish. Garnish with chopped, sweet basil and freshly grated Parmesan cheese. This makes 6 servings.

SPAGHETTI WITH SPECIAL GÉNOISE SAUCE

1½ tbsp. salad oil
1 7-oz. package spaghetti
1 recipe Special Génoise Sauce *(Sauces, pg. 17)*

Bring 6 cups heavily salted water to a boil, then add the salad oil. Add the spaghetti slowly and cook for about 12 minutes or to desired degree of doneness. Drain well and place in serving dish. Add the sauce and toss gently. This will make about 2 servings.

pasta shells with génoise sauce

This simple, yet elegant, presentation of pasta is the perfect dish to complement a colorful salad — one filled with salad greens, zesty onions, peppers and ripe tomatoes. A flavorful dressing for the salad might be Vinaigrette aux Fines Herbes (Sauces, pg. 2). The Basic Génoise Sauce is surrounded by large and small shell-shaped pasta which has been sprinkled with Parmesan cheese and sweet basil.

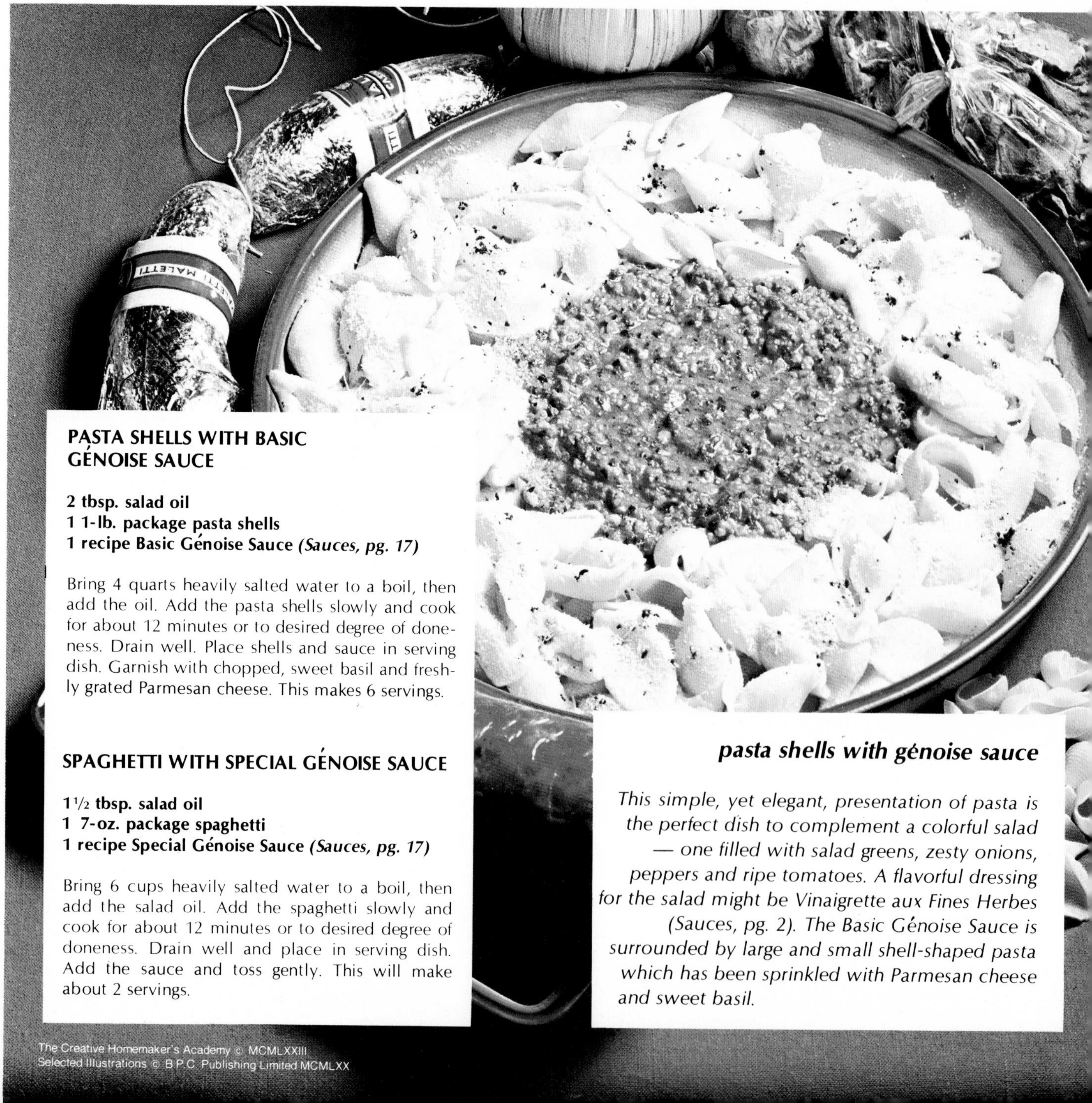

LASAGNE WITH ITALIAN MEAT SAUCE

2 tbsp. salad oil
1 1-lb. box lasagne
1 1-lb. package sliced mozzarella cheese
1 recipe Italian Meat Sauce (Sauces, pg. 18)
1 8-oz. can tomato purée

Bring 4 quarts heavily salted water to a boil, then add the oil. Add the lasagne slowly and cook for about 20 minutes or until tender. Drain well. Arrange lasagne, cheese and meat sauce in layers in a serving dish. Repeat layers until all ingredients are used, ending with meat sauce. Spoon tomato purée over top of meat sauce in decorative manner. Garnish with freshly grated Parmesan cheese. This will make about 6 to 8 servings.

lasagne with italian meat sauce

This main dish has both eye appeal and a wonderful flavor. The lasagna noodles pictured here both raw and cooked, are available in several different widths. The sauce is made from meat and dried or fresh mushrooms and is topped with cheese. Tomato puree is piped along the length of the finished recipe and for garnish, the Italian artichokes add just the right note of color contrast.

MEZZANI AND RUOTE WITH FRESH TOMATO SAUCE

3 tbsp. salad oil
1 6-oz. package mezzani
1 6-oz. package ruote
1 recipe Fresh Tomato Sauce (Sauces, pg. 18)

Bring 6 cups of heavily salted water to a boil in 2 separate pans. Add 1½ tablespoons oil to each pan. Add the mezzani slowly to 1 pan and the ruote to the other pan. Cook for about 14 minutes or to desired degree of doneness. Drain well and place in serving dishes. Pour half the sauce over each pasta. Serve with freshly grated Parmesan cheese. This will make about 6 servings.

mezzani and ruote with fresh tomato sauce

Two different shapes of pasta are pictured, both in their raw form as well as cooked. The "little wheels" are called ruote and the corkscrew shapes are known as mezzani. The cooked pastas are topped with the same Fresh Tomato Sauce (Sauces, pg. 18) which is seasoned with chives and basil. In keeping with Italian tradition, the ubiquitous bowl of grated Parmesan cheese is offered as an accompaniment.

PASTA WITH EGGS AND RED DEVIL SAUCE

1½ tbsp. salad oil
1 8-oz. package mezzani
1 tbsp. olive oil
1 tsp. finely chopped fresh sage or parsley
10 hard-boiled eggs, peeled
Red Devil Sauce

Bring 2 quarts of heavily salted water to a boil and add the salad oil. Add the mezzani slowly and cook for 14 to 16 minutes or to desired degree of doneness. Drain and place in serving dish. Add the olive oil and toss lightly. Sprinkle with sage. Cut the eggs in half lengthwise and place in a shallow serving dish. Pour the hot sauce over the eggs. Serve over the mezzani. This makes 4 to 6 servings.

RED DEVIL SAUCE

½ c. tarragon vinegar
1 tsp. dry mustard
1 tsp. paprika
½ tsp. white pepper
1 clove of garlic, sliced
¾ tsp. salt
2 bay leaves
¼ tsp. cayenne pepper
½ c. beef consommé
2 tbsp. butter
1 tbsp. Worcestershire sauce
1 15-oz. can tomato sauce

Combine the vinegar, mustard, paprika, white pepper, garlic, salt, bay leaves and cayenne pepper in a saucepan. Boil until mixture is reduced by one half. Strain through a fine sieve. Return to the saucepan and add the consommé, butter, Worcestershire sauce and tomato sauce. Simmer for 8 minutes. Keep warm. This makes about 2¾ cups sauce.

pasta with eggs and red devil sauce

For pasta and egg lovers, this "quick and easy" dish should hold special appeal. Hard-boiled eggs have been "deviled" in a piping hot tomato sauce. This dish can be served with the pasta on the side or, if you prefer, place the eggs and sauce over the mezzani noodles. Garnish with several sprigs of fresh herbs. Two everyday ingredients with extraordinary taste appeal!

The Creative Homemaker's Academy © MCMLXXIII
Selected Illustrations © B.P.C. Publishing Limited MCMLXX

HOMEMADE LASAGNE VERDE

1 10-oz. package frozen chopped spinach
Salt
2 c. all-purpose flour
3 eggs
4 tbsp. olive oil

Place spinach, 1/2 teaspoon salt and 1 tablespoon water in a heavy saucepan and place over low heat. Cook, covered, until spinach is tender and water is evaporated, stirring occasionally. Place spinach in blender container and process until puréed. Let cool. Sift the flour onto a cold surface and make a well in the center. Place the eggs, 1 tablespoon oil, 2 teaspoons salt and 3/4 cup spinach purée in the well. Work in with knives or pastry scrapers as shown in the illustrations for Basic Short Pastry (Desserts, page 11), then knead for 10 minutes. Cover the dough with a damp cloth and let rest for 30 minutes. Divide the dough in half, then roll out each half into a rectangle as thin as possible on a lightly floured surface. Cover with a cloth and let stand for 1 hour. Cut into 2-inch wide strips and place on dry towels. Let dry for 1 hour and 30 minutes. Thoroughly dried, lasagne may be stored in plastic bags in a dry place until ready to cook, if desired. One pound of fresh cooked spinach may be substituted for the frozen spinach. This makes enough pasta for an 8-serving recipe.

How To Cook Lasagne

Combine 6 quarts water, 1 tablespoon salt and remaining oil in a large kettle and bring to a boil. Add the lasagne gradually so that the water continues to boil. Boil rapidly for 10 minutes or to desired degree of doneness. Drain in colander and use as recipe directs.

GREEN RIBBON PASTA

1 recipe Homemade Lasagne Verde, cooked
1 recipe Bolognese Sauce (*Sauces, pg. 22*)
4 c. Béchamel Sauce (*Sauces, pg. 4*)
Freshly grated Parmesan cheese

Arrange a layer of lasagne in a large, well-buttered baking dish. Spoon a thin layer of *Bolognese* Sauce over lasagne, then spread with a layer of *Béchamel* Sauce. Repeat layers until all ingredients are used, ending with the *Béchamel* Sauce. Sprinkle the top generously with the Parmesan cheese. Bake in a preheated 375-degree oven until heated through and bubbly. This makes 8 servings.

corn and rice casserole

corn and rice casserole

Corn and rice in a casserole combine to make a satisfying vegetable course. Perfect as an accompaniment to grilled or barbecued meats, this make-ahead dish will be a boon to the busy homemaker. The sliced, hard-cooked eggs add an attractive edible garnish.

CORN AND RICE CASSEROLE

Salt
1½ c. long grain natural brown rice
1 1-lb. can cream-style corn
Butter
Pepper to taste
4 hard-boiled eggs, halved
Finely chopped fresh parsley
Paprika

Place 3 cups of water in a saucepan and add 1 teaspoon of salt. Bring to a hard boil. Add the rice gradually, stirring constantly. Cover and reduce the heat. Cook at a slow boil for about 40 minutes or until rice is tender, adding more boiling water if needed. Place the corn in a small saucepan, then add 2 tablespoons of butter and season with salt and pepper. Heat thoroughly. Turn the hot rice into a baking dish and make a well in the center to hold the corn. Spoon the corn into the well and arrange the egg halves in the corn. Sprinkle eggs and corn with parsley. Sprinkle the rice with paprika. Drizzle melted butter over the top. Bake in a preheated 350-degree oven only until heated through and corn is bubbly. Serve with Basic Mornay Sauce (Sauces, page 11) or Basic Soubise Sauce (Sauces, page 14). This makes about 6 to 8 servings.

GREEN RIBBON NOODLES WITH TOMATO SAUCE

1 12-oz. package green noodles
½ c. olive oil
4 c. chopped skinned seeded tomatoes
1 tsp. salt
⅛ tsp. sugar
⅛ tsp. freshly ground pepper
1 tsp. basil

Cook the noodles according to the package directions. Prepare the sauce while the noodles cook. Heat the oil in a frypan until sizzling, then stir in the tomatoes and seasonings. Cook for about 5 minutes or until tomatoes are tender, stirring occasionally with a wooden spoon. Drain noodles and arrange in a serving dish, then spoon sauce over the noodles. Serve immediately with freshly grated Parmesan cheese. This makes 8 servings.

ORANGE RICE

3 tbsp. butter
½ c. chopped onions
1 c. chopped celery
1 c. long grain rice
1 c. orange juice
Grated rind of 1 orange
1½ c. water
½ tsp. salt
⅛ tsp. thyme (opt)

Melt the butter in a medium-sized frypan, then add the onions and celery. Sauté until golden but not brown. Combine the celery mixture with the remaining ingredients in a baking dish, then cover. Bake in a preheated 350-degree oven for 30 minutes or until liquid is absorbed. Serve with Deviled Chicken (Poultry, page 12), if desired. This makes 4 to 6 servings.

MALAYSIAN RICE

½ c. melted butter
1 clove of garlic, pressed
½ tsp. ginger
Dash of cayenne pepper
½ tsp. salt
1 tsp. curry powder
2 tbsp. lemon juice
1 recipe Basic Boiled Rice *(pg. 3)*
1 c. freshly grated coconut

Combine the butter, garlic, ginger, cayenne pepper, salt, curry powder and lemon juice and mix well. Place the hot rice and coconut in a large bowl and toss with 2 forks to mix well. Drizzle the butter mixture over the rice mixture, then toss again until rice is well coated. Serve immediately. This makes 4 to 6 servings.

orange rice

Fluffy Orange Rice surrounds the Deviled Chicken to make an easy gourmet meal. Your family will applaud your clever ingenuity when you serve this attractive and tasty main course. And, what a way to use leftovers!

GREEN RICE

1 10-oz. package frozen chopped broccoli
2 c. milk
1/2 c. butter
1 onion, finely chopped
2 eggs
2 recipes Basic Boiled Rice (pg. 3)
1 tsp. salt
2 c. grated Cheddar cheese

Cook the broccoli according to package directions and drain. Place 1/2 of the broccoli and 1/2 cup of milk in the blender container and process until puréed, then process remaining broccoli with 1/2 cup of milk. Melt the butter in a small frypan, then add the onions and sauté until golden. Beat the eggs with the remaining milk. Combine all the ingredients in a well-buttered large casserole. Bake, covered, in a preheated 350-degree oven for 35 minutes. Remove cover and bake for 10 to 15 minutes longer. This dish may be prepared and frozen. Bring to room temperature before baking. This makes about 12 servings.

pakistani rice and lentils

What could be better than a rice dish which is so versatile it may be served with any type of meat, is simple to make, is very high in protein and is also unusually delicious? Pakistani Rice and Lentils combine all of these attributes.

PAKISTANI RICE AND LENTILS

1 c. lentils
2 c. long grain rice
1 c. chopped onions
5 c. chicken stock
1/3 c. melted butter
2 tsp. salt
1 tsp. turmeric

Soak the lentils in cold water to cover for 2 hours. Drain well. Combine the lentils, rice and onions in a large casserole. Stir in remaining ingredients, then cover. Bake in a preheated 425-degree oven for 25 minutes. Stir rice and lentils gently to mix well, then bake for 20 minutes longer or until the rice is tender and the liquid absorbed. One teaspoon of curry powder may be added, if desired. This makes 12 servings.

chinese fried rice with mushrooms

CHINESE-FRIED RICE

½ c. sliced dried mushrooms
¼ c. olive oil
¾ c. sliced green onions
2 c. long grain rice
4 c. Basic Chicken Stock *(Soups, pg. 2)*
⅛ tsp. dry mustard
1 tbsp. soy sauce
½ c. white bean curd, cut in cubes
¼ c. safflower oil
¾ c. cooked green peas

Soak the mushrooms in cold water for 5 minutes, then drain well. Heat the olive oil in a wok or deep skillet over medium heat. Add the onions and stir-fry as shown in the illustrations (Beef, pg. 18) until the onions are limp and transparent. Add the rice and stir-fry until the rice is golden. Add 1 cup of the stock and the mustard and stir-fry for 2 to 3 minutes or until the liquid is absorbed. Add another cup of the stock and the soy sauce and stir-fry until this liquid is absorbed. Add 1 more cup of the stock and reduce the heat to low. Stir in the bean curd, and cook, stirring occasionally, until the liquid is absorbed. Add the remaining stock, safflower oil, peas and mushrooms. Cover and cook, stirring occasionally, for about 20 minutes or until the rice is tender. Place in a serving dish and garnish with Chinese Radish Flowers. This makes about 10 to 12 servings.

chinese-fried rice with mushrooms in broth

A dinner featuring oriental food would not be complete without a dish of fluffy Chinese-fried rice. Green peas and sautéed mushrooms add texture and flavor while radish flowers provide a colorful effect. The accompanying Mushrooms In Broth are poured over the rice, with the resulting combination of flavors guaranteed to win the approval of family and guests.

MUSHROOMS IN BROTH

1½ c. sliced dried mushrooms
2 c. Basic Chicken Stock *(Soups, pg. 2)*
1 green onion
1 ½-in. slice gingerroot
¼ c. soy sauce
1 tsp. sugar
1 tsp. salt
1 tbsp. cornstarch

Soak the mushrooms in the stock for 30 minutes. Combine the mushrooms and stock with the onion and gingerroot in a wok or saucepan. Bring just to a boil, then reduce heat to low. Simmer, covered, for 1 hour. Remove the onion and gingerroot and stir in the soy sauce, sugar and salt. Blend the cornstarch with a small amount of the mushroom mixture, then stir into the mushroom mixture. Cook over medium heat, stirring constantly, until smooth and slightly thickened. This makes about 2½ cups.

CHINESE RADISH FLOWERS

10 med. radishes
1 tbsp. sugar
2 tsp. salt

Cut the tops and roots from the radishes, then wash and dry the radishes well. Cut ¹⁄₁₆-inch wide slashes across each radish ¾ of the way to the bottom, then cut the same number of slashes at right angles to the first slashes. Place the radishes in a jar. Mix the sugar and salt and pour over the radishes. Cover tightly with a lid, then shake the jar until all the radishes are coated. Chill for 24 hours, shaking the jar twice. Remove radishes from the jar and place on a flat surface, cut sides up. Press down in the center of each radish with thumb to create a flower effect. The radishes may be cut and placed in ice water, instead of salt mixture, for at least 2 hours or longer, if crispness is desired. This makes 10 radish flowers.

SOFT-FRIED NOODLES WITH MUSHROOMS

1 5-oz. package fine egg noodles
2 tbsp. safflower oil
1 c. bamboo shoots
1 c. sliced fresh mushrooms
1 c. sliced almonds
1/2 c. chicken broth
3 tbsp. soy sauce
1 tsp. salt

Cook the noodles in a large saucepan in boiling, lightly salted water for 8 minutes, then drain thoroughly. Heat the oil in a wok or large skillet over low heat, then add the noodles. Stir-fry as shown in the illustrations (Beef, pg. 18) for 4 minutes. Stir in the bamboo shoots, mushrooms and almonds and mix well. Stir in the broth, soy sauce and salt, then reduce heat to very low. Simmer, covered, for 20 minutes or until the liquid is almost absorbed. Serve with additional soy sauce, if desired. This makes 8 to 10 servings.

RAJAHMUNDRY RICE

4 c. hot cooked rice
1 tsp. curry powder
1/2 c. finely chopped cooked celery
1/2 c. toasted slivered almonds

Combine the rice, curry powder and celery in the top of a double boiler. Place over boiling water and heat through. Place in serving dish and sprinkle with almonds. Serve with pork, chicken or seafood.

deep-fried crispy noodles and soft-fried noodles with mushrooms

Both soft-fried and deep-fried noodles are made from the same basic ingredient: fine egg noodles or Chinese egg noodles. The crisp noodles are deep-fried twice in hot fat while the soft-fried noodles are boiled gently, then cooked in a wok with a delicately-flavored combination of mushrooms, bamboo shoots, almonds, and chicken stock. A bowl of preserved ginger may be offered as a condiment.

DEEP-FRIED CRISPY NOODLES

1 5-oz. package fine egg noodles
Vegetable oil

Place the noodles in a large saucepan in enough water to cover and bring to a boil. Cook, stirring occasionally, for 5 minutes, then drain well. Fill a deep fat fryer half full with oil and heat to 350 degrees. Drop the noodles into basket in the oil and cook for 2 minutes. Remove from the oil and drain well on paper toweling. Heat the oil to 375 degrees. Return the noodles to the deep fat fryer and cook until golden brown and crisp. Drain well on paper toweling, then separate the noodles, if necessary. This makes 4 to 5 cups of noodles.

rice with mushrooms

The most popular recipes are those which produce excellent results with minimal effort, and Rice with Mushrooms is such a recipe. To save time, use precooked rice. We give you a recipe using minute rice, however, if you prefer the regular long grain, follow the instructions for Basic Boiled Rice, page 3. The combined flavors of mushrooms and rice complement many entrées, and you can prepare this time-saving dish in a short 20 minutes.

RICE WITH MUSHROOMS

1 10½-oz. can beef consommé
1 c. packaged precooked rice
½ lb. fresh mushrooms
1 tbsp. lemon juice
¼ c. butter
¼ c. chopped onion
¼ c. chopped fresh parsley

Combine the consommé and 1¾ cups of water in a 1½-quart saucepan and bring to a boil. Add the rice and stir well. Reduce heat and cover. Simmer for about 15 minutes or until the rice is tender and all the liquid is absorbed. Meanwhile wash the mushrooms thoroughly under cold water and wipe them dry. Slice the mushrooms thin, then toss with the lemon juice. Melt the butter in a small saucepan, then add the mushrooms and onions and sauté for 5 minutes. Add the mushroom mixture and the parsley to the hot rice and toss well. This makes 6 servings.

EPICUREAN WILD RICE

Wild rice, which requires longer cooking than regular rice, has an interesting, rather exotic flavor which goes well with almost any meat dish. It is extravagantly expensive, but worth the cost for those very special occasions. Try the following Epicurean Wild Rice when you entertain guests for a truly memorable dinner.

EPICUREAN WILD RICE

⅓ c. butter
½ c. minced fresh parsley
½ c. chopped green onions or scallions
1 c. diagonally sliced celery
1¼ c. wild rice
1 can chicken consommé
1½ c. boiling water
1 tsp. salt
½ tsp. dried marjoram
½ c. sherry

Melt the butter in a large saucepan, then add the parsley, onions and celery and sauté until soft but not brown. Add the rice, consommé, water, salt and marjoram and cover. Bake in a preheated 350-degree oven for about 45 minutes or until the rice is tender, stirring occasionally and adding boiling water, if needed. Remove the cover and stir in the sherry. Bake for about 5 minutes longer or until the sherry is absorbed. This makes 6 servings.

rice with mushrooms

This quick and easy dish is Rice With Mushrooms, containing savory beef consommé, precooked rice, fresh mushrooms, onions and parsley, flavored with butter and lemon juice. Your dinner guests will never suspect this dish was completed in 20 minutes.

piquant vermicelli

Vermicelli is the thinnest type of pasta, even finer than spaghetti ("Many varieties of Pasta," pg. 10). In preparing delicious Piquant Vermicelli, cook until just tender, no longer.

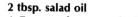

PIQUANT VERMICELLI

2 tbsp. salad oil
1 7-oz. package vermicelli
¼ lb. fresh mushrooms
¼ c. butter
1 tsp. crushed marjoram
2 tbsp. chopped fresh parsley
Salt and freshly ground pepper to taste

Bring 2½ quarts of salted water to a boil and add the oil. Cook the vermicelli in the boiling water for 7 to 8 minutes or until just tender, then drain thoroughly. Place in a serving bowl and keep warm. Wash the mushrooms carefully in cold water and drain, then slice thinly. Melt the butter in a small saucepan. Add the mushrooms and cook over low heat, stirring constantly, for about 3 minutes. Place over the vermicelli. Add the marjoram, parsley, salt and pepper and toss until well mixed. You may serve this with spareribs and Basic Barbecue Sauce (Sauces, pg. 8). This makes about 6 servings.

VENETIAN RICE AND PEAS

1 tbsp. olive oil
2 tbsp. butter
¼ c. finely chopped onion
1 slice bacon, diced
2 c. fresh green peas
1 c. long grain rice
2 c. Basic Chicken Stock (Soups, pg. 2)
Salt and freshly ground pepper to taste
1 tbsp. grated Parmesan cheese

Heat the oil and butter in a heavy frypan, then add the onion and bacon and cook over low heat for 3 minutes, stirring constantly. Add the peas and cook, stirring, for 5 minutes. Add the rice and stir until coated with the oil mixture. Stir in the chicken stock, salt and pepper and cover. Cook over low heat, stirring occasionally, for 15 to 20 minutes or until the rice is tender and all the liquid is absorbed. Add the cheese just before serving and toss to mix well. Drained canned peas, added during the last 5 minutes of cooking, may be substituted for fresh peas. This makes 6 to 8 servings.

vegetables

table of contents

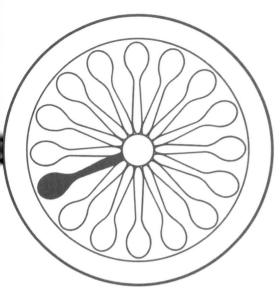

vegetables

"Eat your vegetables, dear."
Surely we can all remember similar coaxing from our earliest days as we furtively rolled green peas from one side of the plate to the other, camouflaging the fact that we hadn't eaten them. Later most of us learned that eating vegetables can be more than a duty—it can be a satisfying experience.

Vegetables can be appetizing as well as nutritious, and they needn't always be side dishes to "stretch the meat." They may be stars in their own rights, as you'll discover when you serve the elegant Duchess potatoes described in this lesson.

We will show you BASIC cooking methods which will contribute to more flavorful and distinctive vegetable dishes and will share with you a variety of ideas to avoid menu monotony. As we progress you will be introduced to a wide panorama of vegetables and cooking techniques. In later lessons, for example, you will learn the art of steaming green peas which doesn't cook out the nutrients, and how to create taste-tempting fritters from cauliflower, zucchini and eggplant. We will also show you how to prepare exotic-sounding but deceptively easy dishes such as baked mushrooms under glass.

Throughout your entire course you will learn new and unusual flavor combinations as well as variations on old favorites. These exciting aspects of vegetable cookery will give your family new appreciation for some of nature's most nutritious gifts.

vegetables/2

If we stop to think a minute, we realize most Americans eat potatoes at least once a day. Although there are hundreds of ways to prepare potatoes, usually they are boiled, roasted, fried, baked or just plain mashed. It's a pity potato monotony isn't minimized.

Let's expand one of the five overworked but undernourished methods listed above—mashed—with a simple basic recipe for Duchess potatoes. A variety of exciting potato shapes will soon be yours.

Duchess potatoes are simply cooked, mashed potatoes dried over low heat and mixed with egg yolk, softened butter and seasonings. But they can be served a number of ways. As a side dish, they can be shaped into small cakes, brushed with beaten, raw egg or glazing mixture, and baked. They may be piped into many different shapes, glazed and baked. Or, they may simply be piped and browned for a decorative border or garnish for other foods, especially meats. We'll concentrate in this lesson on the first two procedures, treating Duchess potatoes as a side dish vegetable. From our basic mixture, we'll make the seven different shapes shown on this page.

Special equipment needed includes an icing or pastry bag and a soft, sterilized brush for glazing before baking. If you'll glance at page 3 for just a minute, you'll see our display of 10-inch and 14-inch icing bags, the most useful sizes for the piping we'll do together. Nylon icing bags, or plastic-lined muslin bags, are more desirable than linen and other types. Nylon is easier to handle and easier to clean.

Between the two icing bags in the illustration we have lined up examples of metal and plastic pipes, either of which can be used in shaping Duchess potatoes. Finally, regarding the brush for glazing, please don't try to use just any one that's available—brushes with stiff bristles play havoc with delicate potato surfaces.

baked duchess potatoes

Seven classic shapes of baked Duchess potatoes. Left to right, from back to front: Galettes, Doigts, Petites Pyramides, Petits Pains, Brioches, Rosettes Longues and Couronnes. On pages 4 and 5 we show you how to shape each of these.

The Creative Homemaker's Academy © MCMLXXIII
Selected Illustrations © B.P.C. Publishing Limited MCMLXX

how to pipe duchess potatoes

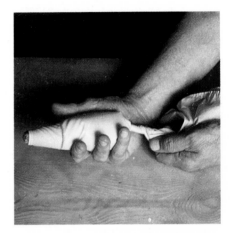Our step-by-step pictures show the special equipment you need for piping Duchess potatoes, proper preparation of the equipment and the best way we've found to handle it. If you've never before worked with an icing bag, follow our instructions to become familiar with one now; you'll be using it to make several of the shapes we showed you on the previous page.

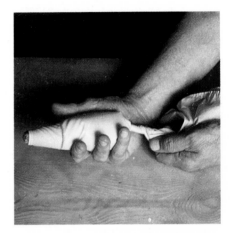

1 Here are two sizes of icing bags that will be used to pipe Duchess potatoes. As we mentioned earlier, we're displaying 10-inch and 14-inch bags. The picture also shows examples of metal and plastic pipes.

2 Prepare your equipment by slipping the chosen pipe into the icing bag and fitting it firmly at the narrow tapering end. This is how it should look.

3 Hold the bag as illustrated above for ease in piping. With one hand, cradle the filled bag, resting your thumb on top near the nozzle. Use this hand to squeeze the potato mixture·from the bag. Use your other hand to hold the empty, twisted portion of the bag for control. Some cooks say they obtain more control by placing their index finger where we've told you to place your thumb. Try this hold, and use it if you find it easier.

BASIC DUCHESS POTATO MIXTURE

1 lb. peeled potatoes, quartered
⅛ tsp. white pepper
1 tsp. (scant) salt
1 med. egg yolk
2 tbsp. butter, melted
Anglais Glaze

Steam the potatoes in a vegetable steamer with about 1 cup.water until soft. (Or, you may steam them in a pressure cooker according to manufacturer's directions.) Drain water from steamer. Force potatoes through ricer. Dry the riced potatoes in a pan over low heat, stirring constantly. Add the remaining ingredients except Anglais Glaze and mix well. Pipe or shape as desired. Brush on Anglais Glaze with pastry brush. Place on a baking sheet. Bake at 400 degrees for about 20 minutes or until edges are lightly browned.

ANGLAIS GLAZE

1 med. egg
1 tsp. olive oil
⅛ tsp. salt
⅛ tsp. white pepper

Combine all ingredients and beat well with a fork.

4 Hold the icing bag as shown in the previous picture and as shown above for horizontal or parallel-to-table types of piping. Maintaining the same hold, work vertically to make rosettes and garlands. This is only the beginning of the exciting techniques we'll build as we progress.

how to make seven classic shapes of duchess potatoes

An important thing to remember in using this BASIC recipe is that the final results of your Duchess potatoes depend on the care and attention you give to the important fourth step of preparation. If you are lax in drying out the sieved potatoes by stirring them in a pan over low heat, they'll be too moist. The otherwise fun and easy job of shaping them will be hard and the finished product less attractive. Be patient at this stage. Remember the drier and firmer the potatoes become at this point, the easier the following steps will be. Follow our recipe closely, and you'll be headed in the right direction.

When piping Duchess potatoes, remember the finished shape and design depend on how you hold the icing bag. After shaping and before baking the potatoes, we will glaze them with *Anglais* Glaze, which imparts a fine, rich sheen. You'll be meeting the versatile *Anglais* Glaze again where we introduce Breads. All of the potato shapes are baked at 400 degrees for about 20 minutes, or until the edges are lightly browned.

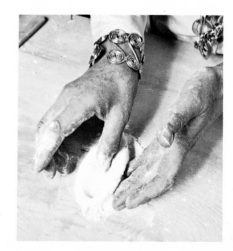

2 For *Petits Pains,* divide the Basic Duchess potato mixture into several lemon-sized portions. Roll the portions in flour. Then shape them with lightly floured thumb and fingers as shown above, working on a floured surface.

1 For *Couronnes,* again use your icing bag with large pipe. Partially fill the bag with potato mixture. Hold the bag at a slight angle, as shown above, to make little rings or garlands on your prepared baking sheet. Our experienced demonstrator uses only one hand for piping here—better use two until you have a lot of practice. Glaze potato shapes, sprinkle lightly with sliced almonds, and bake.

3 After molding the shapes for *Petits Pains,* indent around the inside edges with a table knife. Note especially the angle the knife should be held. Glaze and bake.

4 For *Galettes,* divide the Duchess potato mixture into orange-sized portions. Roll portions into balls, then roll again in sifted flour. Shape little flat, round discs on your floured baking sheet. Brush surplus flour away.

5 Brush shaped *Galettes* with *Anglais* Glaze. Use a fine, soft, sterilized brush.

6 Before baking *Galettes,* crisscross the top surface with a knife blade.

7 For *Brioches,* shape the potato mixture into small topknots and larger bases on a floured surface as shown above. We don't use a pipe in the icing bag. You can also make the shapes by hand rather than with an icing bag if you wish; just divide the potato mixture into an equal number of lemon-sized portions, then roll potato portions in flour to make large bases and small top-knots or balls.

8 Continuing with *Brioches,* tidy up each potato base and indent it with the thumb to cradle the small top-knot. The bottom of each top-knot is dipped in glaze before being placed onto the base. *Brioches* are now ready for surface glazing and baking as directed.

9 For *Petites Pyramides,* place some of your potato mixture in the icing bag fitted with a large pipe. Hold the icing bag vertically, as shown above, to pipe pyramid shapes like ours. Pipe the mixture right onto your lightly floured breadboard. Remove to lightly floured baking sheet with wide spatula. Brush pyramids with *Anglais* Glaze and bake. Follow the same procedure to make *Doigts,* or finger shapes, but instead of pyramids, pipe "fingers" about 3–4 inches long. As you pipe, turn the nozzle to create a "rope" effect as shown in our picture of *Doigts* on page 2. Do the same to make *Rosettes Longues,* but don't twist the nozzle.

vegetable casseroles

Now that you've learned piping and shaping Duchess potatoes, let's move on to the technique of cooking vegetable casseroles and two scrumptious recipes—Onion Casserole and Lima Bean Casserole. "Casserole" actually describes a type of deep, heavy baking dish with a tight-fitting lid that can withstand intense oven temperatures and yet still be used as a serving dish. The name of the dish is now used interchangeably with the food prepared in it. When we speak of a casserole, we are referring to a combination of two or more foods baked together, such as rice, meat, vegetables and seafood.

As long as your casserole dish meets the loose description, you can probably use it for any type of casserole recipe. However, when we call for a casserole dish with specific dimensions, we believe that particular size will best accommodate the amount of food you are cooking.

LIMA BEAN CASSEROLE

¼ lb. smoked slab bacon, diced
1 tbsp. melted shortening
6 sm. white onions, chopped
3 10-oz. packages frozen Fordhook lima beans
¾ c. fresh or frozen sliced carrots
1½ tsp. salt
Dash of sifted confectioners' sugar
2 c. boiling water
Bouquet Garni *(Soups, pg. 2)*
2 cloves of garlic, crushed

Sauté the bacon in a large skillet until brown; add shortening. Sauté the onions for about 1 minute with bacon in shortening and pan drippings. Add the carrots and sauté for 3 to 4 minutes longer. Add the lima beans, salt, sugar and boiling water. Turn into a 2-quart casserole; add the garlic. Stir gently until mixed well. Place Bouquet Garni in lima bean mixture. Bake at 350 degrees for about 1 hour or until carrots and onions are tender. Remove Bouquet Garni. Decorate with canned tomato wedges and serve immediately.

ONION CASSEROLE

8 med. onions, peeled
1 tbsp. sherry
2 c. Basic Chicken Stock *(Soups, pg. 2)*
1 tsp. Chinese brown gravy sauce
4 tsp. cornstarch

Place the onions in a casserole. Combine the sherry, stock and brown gravy sauce and mix well. Pour over onions; cover. Bake at 350 degrees for 2 hours or until onions are tender. Remove from oven. Remove the onions from casserole with slotted spoon and place in serving bowl. Place the cornstarch in a small bowl; stir in a small amount of the onion liquor to make a smooth liquid. Add the cornstarch mixture to remaining liquor and cook over low heat until thickened and transparent. Pour over onions and serve steaming hot.

vegetable cookery

In the past, the so-called "uncivilized peoples" had extensive knowledge of the native plants their land yielded. America's Great Lakes Indians, for example, used 130 species of plants for food and 275 for medicinal purposes.

At the time the American Indians were finding many uses for plants, people in Europe thought they were unwholesome as food. Tomatoes and potatoes were believed to cause leprosy.

It took centuries for legends about harmful and unwholesome plants to play out. Even when this happened, vegetables (edible plants) were considered unpalatable because cooks did not know how to make the most of their freshness and flavor. They usually smothered them in sauces or boiled them in soups.

Fortunately we know now that vegetables can be delicious and are good for us. We know that we do not have to purify them by boiling them for hours or smother them in soup to make them taste good.

Vegetables are a desirable and nutritious addition to any meal. There are many advantages to including them in the menu. They come in so many varieties of colors, textures and designs that we can choose, not only vegetables that add the taste we're looking for to balance a meal, but also a color or a design that will look particularly appealing with our other dishes.

Before we introduce you to some of our favorite methods of cooking vegetables, we'd like to give you a few helpful hints on buying them. Our first rule is to be particular. Linger at the market long enough to choose the very best produce. Try to keep in mind the vegetables in season because they will be fresher, more flavorful and less expensive. Vegetables out of season have to be shipped long distances and, unfortunately, are not as tasteful. (If you are looking for a vegetable that isn't in season or is simply not available on your shopping day, don't hesitate to choose frozen or canned vegetables. You'll always find explicit cooking instructions on the can or the package.)

After you have carefully selected the freshest and most colorful vegetables available, you'll certainly want to preserve their natural goodness throughout the cooking and serving procedure. Thus, we would like to give you a few tips that will help you make the most of the rich color and taste of the plants you have chosen.

There are two very important "don'ts" in preparing vegetables: don't overcook and don't keep vegetables warm too long before serving.

If you want your vegetables to look their delectable best and to retain their high food value, get the knack of "undercooking" — cooking vegetables as short a time as possible. We give recommended cooking times in our vegetable recipes which will help you become familiar with this procedure.

The length of cooking time will often depend on the cooking method you use. Vegetables can be prepared in a wide variety of ways. Let's go over the ones you will use most often.

BOILING

Boiling is the most widely used cooking method for vegetables and the one most often abused. We consider the following method the best way to preserve flavor, color and nutrition: spread your vegetables out in a skillet or shallow saucepan containing just enough water to barely cover. Then simmer them gently until just done, keeping an eye on the skillet to make sure that the water doesn't boil away.

STEAMING

If you have a vegetable steamer, you have all the equipment needed for this cooking method. A special rack in your cooker holds the vegetables out of the water while cooking. However, if you don't have a steamer, you can place your vegetables on a rack in a tightly covered saucepan filled with enough water to come just under the rack. In either container, the water turns to steam which seals in the natural goodness. However, be careful to watch your cooking time closely. Remember that overcooking can make your vegetables mushy and tasteless.

PRESSURE COOKING

We highly recommend using a pressure cooker to quickly steam fresh vegetables. In this sealed container the vegetables are cooked by very intense steam heat. The more steam you allow to build up, the greater the pressure, and as a result, the faster the vegetables cook. Because you use very little water in the pressure cooker, be certain to follow the manufacturer's directions and watch the cooking time closely.

BRAISING

Braising is another interesting way to cook vegetables. Gently simmer vegetables in a skillet containing just enough water, bouillon or broth to cover. Shake the pan occasionally. When all the liquid has cooked away and the vegetables are just barely tender, add a small amount of melted butter or cooking oil and saute the vegetables until done.

FRYING

Since frying methods vary slightly with each vegetable, we will give detailed instructions with each recipe.

BAKING

When you cook turnips, squash, sweet potatoes or unpeeled Irish potatoes in the oven, you are using a process known as dry baking. When you roast whole vegetables with meat or in gravy, you are using a process known simply as baking. We will be using both techniques throughout the course.

introducing tomatoes and onions

If you had asked someone centuries ago about the tomato, they might have told you it was a "love apple" or an aphrodisiac. If you had wanted an onion in ancient India, you would have been asked to go outside the city to eat it. But today you can enjoy these two vegetables without having the mayor reprimand you or the neighbors talk about you. The sweet taste of tomatoes blended with the pungency of onions makes a mouth-watering and appealing combination.

Tomatoes. Before you prepare our following recipe of Tomatoes with Onions and Cream, we would like to mention a few pointers on choosing good tomatoes. Always look for fresh, round, uniformly-shaped tomatoes. Avoid the ones that are puffy, bruised, yellowed or cracked. Remember that in most areas tomatoes are fresher in the summer months because they are widely grown and require only short shipping distances. The best tomatoes are those that are allowed to turn red and juicy on the vine before being picked.

Onions. You probably have little difficulty in finding flavorful onions year-round. Several varieties are available; globe onions are globular in shape and are yellow, red, white or brown. You'll find that they usually have a strong flavor. Bermudas are white, flat-shaped onions with a rather mild flavor. Green onions, also called scallions, have very small bulbs and are usually sold in bunches. They are more useful as seasoning agents. Frequently they are served raw on relish trays. We suggest globe onions for our following recipe.

TOMATOES WITH ONIONS AND CREAM

1 lb. peeled onions, thinly sliced
4 tbsp. olive oil
1/8 tsp. dried thyme leaves
1 bay leaf
2 tbsp. cornstarch
1 tsp. salt
4 firm, ripe tomatoes
1/4 c. whipping cream

Place the onions in hot oil in a shallow 9½-inch, heatproof casserole. Add the herbs and cover with the casserole lid or foil. Simmer until the onions are fork-tender. Make a paste with the cornstarch, salt and a small amount of the liquid from the simmered onions and add it to the remaining liquid in the casserole. Peel the tomatoes and cut them in half. Place the tomato halves, cut side up, over the onions. Simmer for about 7 minutes or until the tomatoes begin to appear limp. Turn the tomatoes over and simmer until tender. Add the cream and heat thoroughly. Do not boil. May be served with toast points.

tomatoes with onions and cream

Here we have pictured halved fresh tomatoes on onion slices, cooked until soft and tender, then covered with thick cream. We've surrounded this tomato and onion dish with triangular croutons.

introducing broccoli

Are you watching your weight or someone else's? If so you'll be very pleased to know that a two-thirds cup of cooked broccoli, including stalks and tops, has only 26 calories, but contributes half of the recommended daily allowance of vitamin A for adults. It contains about 1½ times the recommended adult daily allowance of vitamin C, and some of the B vitamins, calcium and potassium.

Although broccoli predates Christianity, it remained relatively unknown in the United States until the early 1920's when hotels and restaurants started serving it. Italians brought broccoli to this country over 100 years ago, and they were the only ones to cultivate and eat the vegetable for many years. During this time it was grown only in New York and Boston. In the 1920's broccoli underwent a trial planting in California's Santa Clara Valley where it quickly gained popularity. Now it is grown in areas all across the United States and available year-round, except during the hot summer months.

Broccoli is an excellent green vegetable to serve in the early fall and spring months, its primary growing seasons. It has a very rich color that is attractive at any meal. In order to make the most of its deep green color, make sure that you follow the cooking time suggestions closely because overcooking will make broccoli turn a much less attractive olive green.

When you shop for broccoli, look for firm, clean stalks and compact clusters of buds. Avoid buying plants that have yellowed or have tough, woody stalks. (If fresh broccoli is not available, don't hesitate to use frozen broccoli. You'll find that we have used it in two of the broccoli recipes that follow.)

Because broccoli is especially popular served with Hollandaise Sauce, you may want to review our lesson on making perfect Hollandaise Sauce (Sauces, pg. 7).

BROCCOLI SPEARS WITH HOLLANDAISE SAUCE

1 bunch fresh broccoli
½ tsp. salt
1 recipe Basic Hollandaise Sauce (Sauces, pg. 7)

Cut all but the smallest curly leaves away from the small heads and cut the broccoli stems ½ inch long. Cook in a small amount of boiling salted water for about 12 minutes or until tender. Drain well. Place in desired serving dish and cover with Hollandaise Sauce.

BROCCOLI CASSEROLE

1 pkg. frozen broccoli
1¼ c. milk
3 eggs, lightly beaten
½ tsp. salt
½ tsp. nutmeg
½ c. grated cheese

Preheat oven to 350 degrees. Cook the broccoli in a small amount of boiling water for 3 minutes, then drain. Pour the milk in a small saucepan and bring to a boil. Cool to lukewarm. Mix the eggs with the salt and nutmeg. Add the milk and cheese, beating constantly. Pour into a greased baking dish and add the broccoli. Bake for 30 to 40 minutes or until a knife inserted in the center comes out clean. Must be served hot.

BROCCOLI LOAF

1 pkg. frozen broccoli
2 tsp. lemon juice
1 tsp. salt
1 tbsp. butter
1 tbsp. flour
3 eggs, beaten
1 c. cream
1 c. Blender Mayonnaise (Sauces, pg. 3)

Combine the broccoli, lemon juice, ½ teaspoon salt and 1 cup boiling water in a saucepan. Cook for 3 minutes, then drain. Melt the butter in a saucepan, then stir in the flour and remaining salt. Combine the eggs, cream and mayonnaise and stir into flour mixture. Cook, stirring, until thickened. Combine the sauce and broccoli and pour into a loaf pan. Set the loaf pan in a pan with about 1 inch of water. Bake at 350 degrees for 30 to 45 minutes or until set. (Two cups fresh, cooked broccoli may be substituted for frozen broccoli.)

broccoli casserole

This simmering casserole just taken from the oven is filled with mouth-watering broccoli and melted cheese, a delicious combination for any meal. It should always be served piping hot.

caramelizing vegetables

Caramelizing is a very simple process which will make your vegetables, particularly potatoes and onions, taste absolutely delicious. By caramelizing, you envelop vegetables in a flavorful, syrup-like coating. The coating, which gives vegetables a subtly sweet taste and a rich shining brown color, is a simple mixture of brown sugar and *consommé*. Caramelized vegetables offer you an interesting accompaniment for many main dishes. Look for the picture of caramelized potatoes served with sirloin or beef in the Beef category, page 2, and discover how this interesting technique can add variety to your meals.

CARAMELIZED ONIONS

9 small skinned onions
1 c. beef consommé
1½ c. brown sugar
2 tbsp. sherry

Partially cover the onions in boiling, salted water. Cook until tender but firm. Place on a lightly buttered dish. Combine the consommé, brown sugar and sherry in a medium saucepan. Cook and stir over low heat until the sugar is dissolved and the mixture coats the spoon. Pour the mixture over the onions and serve.

CARAMELIZED POTATOES

12 medium potatoes
1½ c. beef consommé
¼ c. (firmly packed) brown sugar

Place the potatoes in boiling, salted water to cover and cook until fork-tender. Remove the skins. Combine the consommé and brown sugar in a medium saucepan. Cook and stir over low heat until the sugar is dissolved. Add several potatoes at a time to the consommé mixture, turning until the potatoes are coated. Remove to a warm serving platter and repeat the process until all the potatoes are coated. The platter may be kept warm in the oven at a very low temperature.

fried eggplant

fried eggplant

Sliced fresh eggplant is coated with flour batter, fried in hot oil, and then sprinkled with paprika and grated cheese.

Most cooks need no introduction to fried potatoes but the technique of frying most other vegetables is different. It yields delicious results and can be adapted to many vegetables such as tomatoes, onions, squash and okra. We particularly like it for eggplant with which we will demonstrate this basic frying technique.

Eggplant is a large, shiny, purple vegetable that is mild and delicately flavored. You'll find eggplant oblong or somewhat pear-shaped, varying in length from 2 inches to 12 inches.

Fresh eggplant is available year-round but you'll find it to be in greatest supply from July to September. When buying eggplant, look for firm, heavy vegetables with smooth, glossy and uniformly-dark skins. Steer away from those that are soft or dull-skinned or those with dark brown spots which indicate decay.

Buying firm, fresh eggplant is the first step toward successfully preparing this delicious vegetable. The following step-by-step illustrations show you how to prepare your eggplant for frying.

FRIED EGGPLANT

1 eggplant
¼ c. (about) flour
Cooking oil
Salt and pepper to taste
Paprika
Grated Parmesan cheese

Peel the eggplant and prepare for frying as shown in our step-by-step illustrations. Place the flour in a shallow bowl and stir in enough water to make the consistency of light cream. Immerse each eggplant slice in the batter, then fry in 375-degree oil until golden brown on each side. Season with salt and pepper. Sprinkle liberally with paprika and grated Parmesan cheese.

1 With a sharp knife cut the eggplant into thin slices (about ¼ inch) as shown above. Lay out the slices on a wooden board as shown here.

2 To remove bitterness from this otherwise delectable vegetable, sprinkle the top of each slice with table salt. Allow to sit for 30 minutes.

3 At the end of 30 minutes, wipe off the excess salt. Then soak the eggplant in a bowl of water for about 10 minutes. (Here you may want to place a bowl or plate on top of the soaking eggplant to keep the slices under water.) Then proceed according to recipe.

ratatouille

Relax. Ratatouille is much easier to prepare than to say. It's pronounced *ra ta TOO ya*. Here we will teach you how to make it as well as pronounce it. This vegetable concoction made with onions, tomatoes, eggplant and zucchini has an Italian flavor and is delicious as a hot vegetable side dish.

We have previously discussed onions, tomatoes and eggplant. Zucchini may be foreign to you. It is simply a variety of summer squash with an Italian name. It is similar in appearance to the cucumber, smooth, dark green and cylindrical in shape. Zucchini is available almost year-round with peak market supply in May and June. Buy firm, young zucchini that are not too large.

For buying suggestions on tomatoes, onions and eggplant, see Vegetables, pages 9 and 12.

RATATOUILLE

1 med. eggplant
1 lg. red sweet pepper
4 med. tomatoes
3 sm. zucchini
1/3 c. olive oil
2 med. onions, finely chopped
2 sm. cloves of garlic, pressed
2 tsp. minced parsley
1½ tsp. salt
¼ tsp. freshly ground pepper
1 tsp. sugar

Trim the stem from the eggplant but do not peel. Cut into ½-inch slices, then cut into cubes. Place the eggplant slices in a bowl with salted water to cover. Weight the eggplant down with a plate. Let soak for at least 15 minutes. Remove the seeds and membrane from the sweet pepper, then cut it into strips and chop coarsely. Peel the tomatoes and chop coarsely. Cut ends from the zucchini, then slice crosswise thinly. Heat oil in a Dutch oven until sizzling, then add onions, sweet pepper and zucchini. Cover and cook for 5 minutes, stirring occasionally. Combine the garlic and parsley, then stir into the onion mixture. Drain the eggplant thoroughly, then stir the eggplant into mixture. Cover and cook for 5 minutes. Add the tomatoes, salt, pepper and sugar, mixing thoroughly. Cover and cook for 5 to 10 minutes or until flavors blend. Serve hot.

ratatouille

A savory Mediterranean dish made from tomatoes, onions, eggplant and zucchini. The vegetables are gently cooked together in their own juices and seasoned to bring out their full flavors.

the versatile potato

cheese and potatoes rissolé

Another of the many examples of the versatility of the "humble tuber" is this crunchy-crisp on the outside yet soft and tender on the inside, sausage-shaped potato treat. A sprinkling of parsley flakes creates an interesting eye-appealing touch.

The potato wins hands down in a vegetable versatility contest. And well, it should! This "humble tuber" has proven itself an adaptable and delicious main dish accompaniment. In the first pages of this vegetables section you learned how to artfully pipe Duchess Potatoes and later how to caramelize potatoes. That was just the beginning of a whole exciting world of potato cookery.

On these pages we present you with two more potato recipes that are sure to impress. Like the decorative Duchess Potatoes, our recipes for Cheese and Potatoes Rissolé and Périgord Potatoes both begin with steamed white potatoes.

The first recipe, Cheese and Potatoes Rissolé, is pictured on this page. In making it you will learn an important culinary technique — rissolé (ris sow lay) — in which you fry steamed potatoes in deep fat until they are crisp and brown. Refrigerating the cooked potatoes before frying makes them easier to shape and handle.

The Périgord Potatoes is a fluffy, soufflé-like potato side dish. Combining stiffly whipped egg whites with sieved potatoes adds the delicate lightness to this vegetable. Turn to the Pork section, page 3, to see the attractive, finished dish.

For most potato dishes, any "old" potato will do very nicely! Offbeat and jocular as this remark may sound, it is actually a technical term describing late crop, fully mature potatoes. "New potatoes," harvested in spring and early summer, are available seasonally.

Although countless varieties of white potatoes fill the markets each year, there are only two major groupings that you need concern yourself with. *Mealy potatoes*, often called all-purpose potatoes, are best for baking and mashing. Included in this group are the well-known Idaho, Maine and Long Island varieties.

Waxy potatoes, like the Early Rose and Green Mountain varieties, hold their shape well during cooking and, as a result, are preferred for creaming, scalloping and in salads.

As we mentioned above, it doesn't really matter whether you use mealy or waxy potatoes in most cooking. However, in recipes calling for steam-cooked potatoes such as the two here, we prefer mealy potatoes since they cook up light and fluffy.

CHEESE AND POTATOES RISSOLÉ

2 lb. potatoes
Salt
¼ c. butter
6 egg yolks
½ tsp. white pepper

1 lb. Swiss cheese, grated
Sifted all-purpose flour
2 eggs
Soft bread crumbs

Pare the potatoes and cut into eighths. Place in a saucepan and cover with water. Add 1 tablespoon salt. Cover and bring to a boil. Reduce heat and simmer for 15 minutes or until tender. Drain potatoes; press through a food mill or mash well. Place in a dry saucepan and add the butter. Cook over low heat, stirring constantly, until butter is melted and mixture is dry. Place in a bowl; refrigerate until cool. Beat in egg yolks, pepper and salt to taste. Add the cheese and stir until well mixed. Chill well. Shape with hands into 4-inch sausage-shaped rolls; coat each roll well with flour. Beat the eggs with ¼ cup water until mixed. Dip potato rolls into eggs, then coat well with bread crumbs. Place on a cookie sheet and chill thoroughly. Fry in deep fat at 375 degrees until brown; do not overcook. Drain on paper toweling; place on a platter. Garnish with chopped parsley. These may be kept warm in a 200-degree oven until served, if desired. This recipe may be prepared and refrigerated for 24 hours before frying. This amount makes about 8 servings.

PÉRIGORD POTATOES

2 lg. potatoes
1½ tsp. salt
2 tbsp. grated onion
2 tbsp. butter
⅛ tsp. white pepper
3 eggs, separated

Peel potatoes and cut them into eighths. Place in a medium saucepan and cover with water; add 1 teaspoon salt. Bring to a boil, then reduce heat. Cover and simmer for 15 minutes. Drain. Place potatoes in large mixing bowl, then add onion and butter. Beat with electric mixer at low speed until potatoes are in small pieces. Beat at high speed until smooth, scraping side of bowl frequently. Add the pepper, egg yolks and remaining salt and beat until well mixed. Fold in stiffly beaten egg whites until well combined. Turn into well-buttered small soufflé dish. Bake in preheated 400-degree oven for 30 minutes or until brown. Serve immediately. This makes about 6 servings.

PURCHASING GUIDE

For all your cooking needs, firm, well-shaped potatoes that are free from cuts, growth cracks or surface defects are the most practical. And to eliminate paring away the valuable nutrients close to the skin, it's wise to select potatoes with small, shallow eyes.

The Creative Homemaker's Academy © MCMLXXIII
Selected Illustrations © B.P.C. Publishing Limited MCMLXX

cauliflower with mornay sauce

The "cabbage with a college education," as Mark Twain once called the cauliflower, does have a look of distinction. Its unusual white flowering curd should be clean, firm and compact with crisp, green outer leaves. Sometimes small leaves weave into the curd, but this doesn't affect desirability. Large or small heads of the same maturity are equally desirable. Avoid spotted or bruised curd unless it can be trimmed without too much waste.

We consider it a virtue to get the most out of anything we buy. Too often unknowing cooks take nice healthful vegetables and boil the nutrition and taste right out of them. In our recipe we steam the cauliflower until just tender which saves its nourishing juices. Cauliflower is a very tender vegetable and is frequently ruined by overcooking. Don't cook it until it's mushy! Undercook rather than overcook.

CAULIFLOWER WITH MORNAY SAUCE

1 lg. head cauliflower
Freshly grated bread crumbs
⅓ c. melted butter
1 recipe Basic Mornay Sauce (Sauces pg. 11)

Wash and trim the cauliflower, then separate into flowerettes. Place in a vegetable steamer and steam until tender. Arrange cauliflower around edge of baking dish. Sprinkle liberally with bread crumbs. Drizzle butter over bread crumbs. Spoon Mornay sauce into center of baking dish. Broil until crumbs are lightly browned.

cauliflower with mornay sauce

This dish overflows with nourishing taste appeal. A creamy cheese sauce enhances the circle of tender-crisp cauliflowerettes. Melted butter and bread crumbs are sprinkled over all to give that au gratin touch. (Surprised? To gratiné does not necessarily refer to cheese, for it actually means sprinkled with buttered bread crumbs and browned.)

green beans

Until the Spanish explorers discovered green beans in the Americas, nobody in Europe had ever tasted them. But the Indians had been eating them for hundreds of years.

Now, green beans are a popular vegetable in all Western cultures, although different localities have coined their own names for them. They are called string beans, snap beans, pole beans, French beans, wax beans and probably quite a few others. The name string beans evolved because earlier varieties had long fibrous strings, although a stringless variety was developed in the late 19th Century. The name snap bean comes from the characteristic "snap" when a good quality bean is broken. Green beans grow either on small bushes or on vines which are wrapped around poles; hence, the name pole beans. And the British term all varieties of the bean French beans, while to us, French beans are those cut *julienne* style. Wax beans are so called because of the color and sheen of the pods. Incidentally, just to confuse the issue, this variety of green bean is yellow!

But whatever you call them, when you begin to buy beans for our green bean dish, you should look for clean, firm, well-shaped beans with no scars. Many people like to test for the "snap" when choosing their beans, though some produce managers might frown on this practice. If the seeds inside the pod are rather large, the bean will probably be tough.

1 Don't purchase green beans that bend as easily as this one. A fresh bean, unless it is a tiny young one, should snap readily so this one is obviously too old. Don't wait until you get home to test for freshness. Make certain you are buying fresh produce for the best results.

2 Take a small bunch of beans and level them at one end so that the tips come together evenly.

3 Snip these evened tips. Level the other end of the bunch in the same way. The beans will be uniform in length and ready for cooking.

HOW TO FRENCH-CUT BEANS

Prepare the beans according to our step-by-step illustrations. Then place the beans, one at a time, on chopping board. Cut through each bean lengthwise, halfway between string sides, with a sharp paring knife. You will now have thin strips of beans. Foods prepared by this method are also called *julienne*.

FRENCH-STYLE GREEN BEANS

french green beans

2 lb. fresh green beans
1 sm. clove of garlic, crushed
¼ c. butter
2 tsp. salt
⅛ tsp. freshly ground pepper
2 tsp. finely chopped parsley

This luscious dish is the finished product from the beans we carefully trimmed. The sheen on these tender-crisp beans comes from the butter in which they were tossed. The garlic is invisible as we made sure it was crushed to a fine pulp (Salads, pg. 14). We also sprinkled the top with a touch of grated Parmesan cheese.

Prepare the beans according to our step-by-step illustrations, then French-cut them. Wash beans and place in top of a vegetable steamer. Pour water into base of steamer pan to just below level of top of steamer pan; bring to a boil. Add beans and cover. Cook for 30 minutes or until beans are crisp-tender. Remove top steamer pan from base. Pour water from base of steamer pan; turn beans into base. Add the garlic, butter, salt, pepper and parsley and mix well with a slotted spoon. Serve immediately. Beans may be cooked in a colander over large saucepan with boiling water, if steamer pan is not available. This makes about 6 servings.

green peas

Green peas are so familiar to most of us today, that it is hard to imagine they were once a novelty. Late in the 1600's, eating green peas became an aristocratic fad. According to a historical letter written by a member of the French court in 1696, some ladies, even after they had dined at the royal table, returned home to eat peas again before going to bed.

Although a fashionable novelty in western Europe in the late 1600's, some authorities claim peas were eaten as early as the Stone Age. Green peas were found in Egyptian tombs near the remains of Thebes. The Greek Theophrastus, father of botany, previous to his death in 287 B.C. frequently referred to peas as a common vegetable.

A short time before the birth of Christ, the Roman poet Virgil mentioned peas in his writings. Much later, during the Middle Ages, peas were a chief guard against famine, and medieval soldiers and sailors found them included in their rations. Peas in medieval England were so commonly used that they became synonymous with terms such as "pottage" and "porridge." Hence the nursery rhyme, "Pease porridge hot, pease porridge cold."

Unlike the ancients, who mainly used dried peas for food, some peoples in the Middle Ages ate fresh green peas. Their manner of eating them seems strange to most of us. They cooked the whole pod, dipped them in sauce and ate the peas from the pod. The French were the first to popularize shelling the peas before cooking, but even they regarded this as simply a fad at the time.

There are approximately 200 varieties of green peas. All are round, but some are wrinkled and others have smooth skins.

The recipes presented here represent the most common preparation of green peas in France and in America. The French have a way of steaming in lettuce leaves that seals in the delicate, natural flavor of the tiny peas. Americans sometimes enhance the flavor of the peas with a delicious sauce. The British simply boil the peas and add the various seasonings of their choice.

When buying fresh peas, select pods that are bright green, well-filled and velvety to the touch. Yellowing pods indicate over-mature, tough peas. Avoid mildewed,

FRENCH-COOKED GREEN PEAS

2 10-oz. packages frozen green peas
Outside lettuce leaves or garden lettuce, washed
1 tsp. salt
1/2 tsp. sugar
1/4 c. Sauterne

Thaw peas. Line a shallow 9 1/2-inch casserole with lettuce leaves; pour peas over lettuce. Sprinkle with salt and sugar and pour Sauterne over peas. Cover with lettuce leaves, then cover with lid. Bake in a preheated 350-degree oven for 45 minutes. Remove lettuce leaves before serving if desired. Three cups shelled, fresh green peas may be substituted for the frozen peas if desired. This makes about 4 servings.

french-cooked green peas

These plump, delicious green peas owe their success to the lettuce leaves they were steamed in, allowing them to cook without water and retain their valuable nutrients.

excessively swelled or speckled pods. Fresh peas begin to lose their sweetness after being picked, so use them as soon as possible. If you have to wait a short while before using them, refrigerate the peas still in their pods. Basic preparation is simply to shell the peas and wash them. Most commercial green peas are shelled by machinery in the field and are canned or frozen within a few hours. The frozen green peas are very good and offer an acceptable substitute when fresh peas are not available.

Green peas are among the most delicious of vegetables when they are properly cooked — and, as with most vegetables, this means don't overcook them. Whether we are going to envelop the peas in a sauce or serve them in their own juices, we prefer cooking them in a casserole lined with well-washed outer lettuce leaves. When the peas and seasonings are tucked inside, a top covering of lettuce is added before covering the casserole. After cooking, remove and discard the lettuce which will have turned an unattractive gray.

Another perfectly acceptable way of preparing green peas without rendering them tasteless is to use a vegetable steamer. Steaming retains color and nutrition in most vegetables. If you don't have one, improvise with a colander or large coarse strainer. Place peas in the colander and set it over water in a covered saucepan. The key to happy cooking is to choose the utensil and cooking method which best suits you.

CASSEROLE-COOKED GREEN PEAS IN CREAM

2 10-oz. packages frozen green peas
6 lg. outside lettuce leaves, washed
1 tsp. sugar
1½ tsp. salt
¼ tsp. freshly ground pepper
2 tbsp. Basic Chicken Stock *(Soups, pg. 2)*
2 sprigs of parsley
1 tbsp. butter
¼ c. half and half cream
¼ c. Basic Blender Mayonnaise *(Sauces, pg. 3)*

Thaw the peas. Line a shallow 9½-inch casserole with 4 lettuce leaves; pour peas over lettuce. Sprinkle the sugar, salt and pepper over peas. Spoon the chicken stock over peas and place parsley on top. Cover peas with remaining lettuce leaves, then cover with lid. Bake in a preheated 350-degree oven for 45 minutes; remove from oven. Remove lid. Remove the parsley and lettuce from casserole with a 2-pronged kitchen fork and discard. Drain pan juices from peas into a small saucepan; simmer until reduced to 1 tablespoon liquid. Add butter and stir until melted. Stir in the half and half cream, then stir into peas. Add mayonnaise and mix well. Garnish with an artichoke and cherry tomatoes sprigged with rosemary. Three cups shelled, fresh green peas may be substituted for the frozen peas if desired.

casserole-cooked green peas in cream

Serving green peas in a cream sauce is a favorite with most Americans. Ours here are brightly garnished with cherry tomatoes with rosemary sprigs and a small globe artichoke.

ratatouille tarts

Crisp tart shells are piled high with a savory mixture of tomatoes, onions, eggplant and zucchini, that has been gently cooked until tender. We sprinkled freshly grated Parmesan cheese on the top of each tartlet. The little petals are an added touch that were bought, not homemade. These are oven-baked potato crisps called "Chippers" which can be found in the snack section of your supermarket.

You were earlier promised that as you master the Basics presented in your Creative Homemaker's Cooking Course, your work in the kitchen would become not only easier, but more fun.

Here we have a perfect example of the Golden Threads of Basics that intertwine throughout this course. We have gone step-by-step through the procedure of making Basic Short Pastry to make a seemingly involved process easy to achieve. We discussed the various uses of pastry and then illustrated how to mix, roll and cut pastry for flans, pies and tarts. Here we will use this pastry procedure to prepare tart shells for an exciting and different dish.

You will use the recipe for Basic Savory Short Pastry (Desserts, pg. 12) to make Ratatouille Tarts. You will make up pastry tart shells and bake them blind (Desserts, pg. 14) so they will be crisp before adding the Ratatouille filling, page 14.

You will fill the shells with Ratatouille, the fresh vegetables mixture introduced on page 14 of this section.

Prepare it as you did before and spoon it into your tart shells when they come from the oven. While everything is still piping hot, sprinkle grated cheese, preferably Parmesan on top of each.

As you see, Ratatouille Tarts is a recipe that combines techniques and recipes that you have already learned.

RATATOUILLE TARTS

1 recipe Basic Savory Short Pastry
  (Desserts, pg. 12)
1 recipe Ratatouille (*pg. 14*)
Freshly grated Parmesan cheese

Roll out pastry on floured surface ⅛ inch thick. Cut into twelve 6½-inch circles; fit circles into 5-inch tart pans. Flute edges. Prepare for baking blind as explained in Desserts, page 14. Place tart pans on baking sheets. Bake at 400 degrees for 20 minutes or until browned. Remove peas and waxed paper from the tarts. Cool peas before storing for future use. Spoon hot Ratatouille into tart shells just before serving, then sprinkle generously with Parmesan cheese.

mushroom cookery

Mushrooms are and have always been considered a universal delicacy. Just about anyone will be pleased to hear you say they're on the dinner menu.

Mushrooms, technically a fungus, grow wild almost anywhere. There are over 40,000 known varieties of mushrooms in the world and over 1000 in the United States. However, this country cultivates only one in large quantities. These mushrooms are grown in Pennsylvania, New York, California and Illinois. Because of the carefully controlled process of cultivation, they are always available to us fresh, canned or dried.

There are hundreds of varieties of wild mushrooms which are edible and quite delicious. Here are pictured four varieties: Boletus Edulis, Lepiotus Procera, Cantharellus Cibarius and Boletus Rufus. This, perhaps, will give you an idea of the beauty of the colors and shapes of wild mushrooms. However, we don't recommend you pick your own unless you're in the company of an experienced mushroom horticulturist.

Boletus Edulis. Some mushrooms of the species *Boletus* are inedible. This edible variety has a cap from a light to brownish-black color. The foot has a much lighter color than the cap and can have a fine, whitish-grey or reddish-brown network of veins. Its taste resembles that of ripe hazelnuts.

Lepiota Procera. These edible mushrooms are scaly on both the cap and the foot. They have a delicious taste especially when sautéed in butter. The caps may be umbrella-shaped or hat-shaped.

Cantharellus Cibarius. The *Chanterelle* can be whitish-yellow but in damp weather may turn a butter or golden yellow. It has an aroma of fruit and spice and is delicious both sautéed and creamed.

Boletus Rufus. These edible mushrooms have thick stalks with caps which may be from a light to a dark reddish-brown. The foot has reddish-brown or black scales. The meat turns red, then black but is still edible.

bread shell with mushrooms

BREAD SHELL WITH MUSHROOMS

1 round loaf of bread
Melted butter
8 slices Canadian bacon
½ c. butter
1 lb. fresh mushrooms, sliced
¼ c. flour
1 tsp. dry English mustard
½ tsp. dried tarragon leaves
¼ c. sherry
1 ¼ c. Basic Chicken Stock *(Soups, pg. 2)*
¼ tsp. salt
⅛ tsp. pepper
¾ c. fine bread crumbs

bread shell with mushrooms

This delicacy is made by baking the inverted shell of a round loaf of bread to make a croustade. This vandyked bread shell is piled high with delectable mushrooms in a rich sauce topped with rolls of crispy-fried Canadian bacon. The stems are green onion tops which garnish and lend flavor.

Cut thin slice from top of bread, then invert. Cut circle from bottom of bread and pull out center crumb to form the shell. Vandyke or cut points around the edge with scissors as shown in the illustration. Brush inside and around points with melted butter. Place on baking sheet. Bake in a preheated 250-degree oven for 1 hour and 15 minutes. Increase oven temperature to 350 degrees and bake until brown. Fry the bacon in a large frypan until lightly browned. Remove from pan and cool until easily handled, then roll up and secure with wooden pick. Keep warm with bread shell. Melt the butter in the bacon drippings, then stir in the mushrooms. Cook over low heat, stirring until butter and drippings have been absorbed by the mushrooms. Combine the flour and mustard, then stir into the mushrooms. Add the tarragon and sherry, stirring until blended. Add the stock gradually and cook, stirring constantly, until thickened. Season with salt and pepper. Add the bread crumbs and stir until heated through and thickened. Garnish around edge of hot toasted bread with split tops of green onions. Turn hot mushroom mixture into shell. Remove picks from bacon and arrange bacon around top. Serve immediately. If the bacon is very lean, add 2 to 4 tablespoons of vegetable oil to butter, for cooking the mushrooms.

BAKED MUSHROOMS IN CHEESE SAUCE

8 lg. mushrooms
2 thick slices salt pork, diced
1 recipe Basic White Sauce *(Sauces, pg. 4)*
1 c. grated Romano cheese
¹/₃ c. finely minced green onions
1 ¹/₂ c. fine bread crumbs

Remove the stems from the mushrooms and chop coarsely. Fry the salt pork in saucepan over low heat until all the fat is rendered. Remove the pork from the pan. Add the chopped mushrooms and cook over medium heat until all the fat is absorbed, then set aside. Combine the white sauce and ³/₄ cup cheese, stirring until the cheese is melted. Stir in the green onions and the chopped mushrooms. Arrange the mushroom caps, round side down, in a 9 ¹/₂-inch shallow baking dish, then pour the cheese sauce over all. Sprinkle the bread crumbs over the cheese sauce and sprinkle the remaining cheese evenly over the bread crumbs. Bake in a preheated 350-degree oven for about 20 minutes or until the topping is browned. Parmesan or any hard cheese may be substituted for the Romano cheese.

baked mushrooms in cheese sauce

This simple dish blends the irresistible flavors of mushrooms and cheese. Our large mushroom caps are topped with a delicious cheese sauce.

mushroom soufflé

Here the mixture is divided into two portions and baked in shallow, heat-resistant dishes. No need to worry about this fluffy delicacy oozing over the sides. If it is prepared correctly, it will rise perfectly every time.

MUSHROOM SOUFFLÉ

2 c. finely chopped fresh mushrooms
1/2 c. vermouth
3/4 c. milk
3 tbsp. butter
3 tbsp. all-purpose flour
3/4 tsp. salt
1/4 tsp. white pepper
5 eggs, separated

Combine the mushrooms and vermouth in a small saucepan. Add the milk and bring to a boil. Reduce heat and simmer for 15 minutes. Melt the butter in a saucepan, then stir in the flour. Cook, stirring constantly, until golden. Stir in the mushroom mixture and cook, stirring constantly, for about 3 minutes or until thick. Remove from heat. Season with salt and pepper. Beat the egg yolks with a fork until light and lemon colored. Pour egg yolks slowly into mushroom mixture, beating vigorously with a wooden spoon. Bring just to boiling point, but do not boil. Remove from heat and stir constantly for several minutes or until cooled. Beat the egg whites until stiff but not dry. Fold about 1/3 of the egg whites thoroughly into the mushroom mixture, then add the remaining egg whites. Fold in lightly but thoroughly. Turn into a 7-inch, buttered and floured soufflé dish. Bake in a preheated 350-degree oven for 35 minutes or until puffed, browned and firm in center.

stuffed spanish tomatoes with croutons

This savory, vegetable side dish blends the flavors of juicy tomatoes, ham, sausage, mushrooms and cheese. The fried croutons add a special taste and lend a decorative appeal.

how to skin a tomato

Grasp the tomato with tongs and dip into boiling water for several seconds. Plunge immediately into cold water. Pull the skin from the tomato and cut out the hard stem end.

STUFFED SPANISH TOMATOES WITH CROUTONS

8 firm tomatoes, skinned
Butter
1/2 tsp. salt
2 tbsp. cooking oil
2 med. green onions, finely chopped
1 c. finely chopped fresh mushrooms
1 1/2 c. finely chopped cooked ham
1 c. chopped cooked chorizo sausages
1 tbsp. minced parsley
1/2 c. fine bread crumbs
1/4 c. freshly grated Parmesan cheese
1 recipe Tomato Coulis Sauce (*Sauces, pg. 14*)

Hollow out inside of tomatoes. Place the tomato shells upside down on paper towels and drain thoroughly, then arrange in a shallow baking dish. Place 1/4 teaspoon butter in each tomato and season with salt. Melt 2 tablespoons butter in a frypan, then add the oil. Add onions and fry over low heat for 3 minutes. Add mushrooms and cook for 2 minutes longer. Add the ham and sausages and heat through. Add half the parsley and mix well. Fill the tomato shells with the mushroom mixture. Combine the bread crumbs and cheese, then spoon over the mushroom mixture. Melt 2 tablespoons butter and drizzle over bread crumbs. Bake in preheated 400-degree oven for about 10 minutes or until topping is brown. Pour the sauce around the tomatoes, then sprinkle remaining parsley over all. Serve immediately.

onions monte carlo

This simple onion dish is made from the flavorful shallots pictured in the background and delicious clear beef broth which gives these pungent vegetables their glistening appearance.

ONIONS MONTE CARLO

2 10½-oz. cans beef broth
½ tbsp. dark brown sugar
½ c. golden raisins
2 lb. small peeled onions or shallots
2 tbsp. potato flour

Pour the beef broth into a small, deep, oven-proof dish, then stir in the brown sugar until mixed. Add raisins and onions. Cover. Bake in a preheated 325-degree oven for about 2 hours or until onions are tender. Remove from oven. Mix the potato flour with ½ cup hot beef broth; stir into broth in the ovenproof dish. Cook over low heat, stirring constantly, until thickened. Garnish with mixed chopped chives and chopped parsley, if desired. Two tablespoons cornstarch mixed with a small amount of cold water may be substituted for the potato flour, if desired.

sweet peppers

cold-stuffed pepper dish

A ham/egg mixture has been spooned into fresh green peppers to make this attractive dish. The three peppers in front are surrounded by canned or frozen mixed vegetables, while those in the background are served on beds of lettuce.

Sweet peppers are related only in name to the white and black pepper of the spice trade. They are mild-flavored green, red and sometimes yellow vegetables that add flavor and color to salads, meat and vegetable dishes.

However, they are related to other vegetable peppers such as cayenne, tabasco and paprika. Sweet peppers are about the size of apples and are often called bell peppers because of their shapes. Pimentos are somewhat heart-shaped but are basically interchangeable in flavor and use with other sweet peppers. Paprika, cayenne and tabasco are long, slender peppers, and the last two are quite pungent. Paprika, the spice, is made from the finely ground fruit walls of the mild paprika pepper.

These plants are called peppers because the early explorers who first found them in the New World assumed the hotter varieties must be related to the hot black and white spice pepper.

When shopping for sweet peppers, select those that are firm and well-shaped; avoid the shriveled, limp, tough or blemished ones. The color does not necessarily affect the taste of sweet peppers. Instead, it indicates a stage of maturity, green or yellow when immature and red when

ripe. Your choice may depend solely on color and eye-appeal for a particular dish. When preparing sweet peppers, remove the seeds and membranes, as they are much sharper-flavored than the outer flesh.

COLD-STUFFED PEPPER DISH

2 10-oz. packages frozen mixed vegetables
1 recipe Basic Vinaigrette *(Sauces, pg. 2)*
2 c. ground cooked ham
10 hard-boiled eggs, ground
½ c. pickle relish
Basic Blender Mayonnaise *(Sauces, pg. 3)*
Salt and pepper to taste
6 green sweet peppers

Cook the vegetables according to package directions and drain well. Mix the vegetables and the vinaigrette together in a bowl and cover. Let stand in refrigerator for at least 8 hours to marinate, stirring occasionally. Combine ham, eggs and pickle relish in a large bowl. Add enough mayonnaise to moisten to desired consistency. Season with salt and pepper and chill until ready to serve. Cut the tops from the peppers and remove the seeds and white membranes. Arrange on serving dish and fill with ham salad. Drain the vegetables and arrange around peppers. This will make about 6 servings.

how to peel sweet peppers

Pimentos are a type of sweet pepper, usually used after it has turned red with maturity. Either fresh or canned, they are used in a variety of ways.

Because of the bright red color and the clean, distinctive taste, canned pimentos are especially popular for adding contrast to salads and *hors d'oeuvres*. But they are probably best-known as the "stuffing" in stuffed olives and the "pimento" in pimento-cheese spread.

Canned pimentos needn't be limited to a secondary role, though, as you'll discover in the Tunisian Pimento Dish featured on this page. It's an unusual change-of-pace combination of pimentos, tomatoes and eggs, originated by the Tunisians of North Africa who are particularly fond of the taste of sweet peppers. Called *Chachouka* by the Tunisians, this dish is often served as an *hors d' oeuvre*. It makes an appetizing side dish for lamb and is an excellent choice for a brunch or buffet supper.

Included on this page are two step-by-step illustrations for peeling fresh sweet peppers. Many delicious dishes such as Pimento *Escoffier* require peeled peppers.

tunisian pimento dish

Bright red tomatoes and peppers combine to form this easy-to-prepare dish. A scrambled egg mixture is placed in a line down the center to garnish as well as to provide a taste complement.

1 Cut red or green peppers in quarters lengthwise and remove seeds and membrane. Place on a rack under a preheated broiler for 1 or 2 minutes.

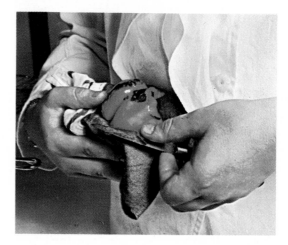

2 When the skins begin to darken and blister, remove the peppers. Let the peppers cool, then peel away the skins with a paring knife.

TUNISIAN PIMENTO DISH

2 tbsp. butter
2 c. drained chopped canned tomatoes
1 c. sliced canned pimento
salt
White pepper
1/8 tsp. basil leaves
3 eggs
3 tbsp. milk

Melt 1 tablespoon butter in a small saucepan. Add the tomatoes, pimento, 1/4 teaspoon salt, 1/8 teaspoon pepper and basil leaves. Simmer for 10 minutes. Combine the eggs and milk in a small bowl and season with salt and pepper to taste. Beat well with a fork. Melt the remaining butter in a small skillet. Add the egg mixture and cook, stirring constantly, until eggs are soft and creamy. Turn the pimento mixture onto a serving dish, then place the eggs on top. Serve with Baked Croutons (*Breads, pg. 16*) or toast points.

pimento escoffier on croutons

This tasty dish of red sweet peppers is presented on croutons with its sweet juices in a separate dish. Pimento Escoffier is a sweet, pungent dish, and when served on croutons, it is a most delicious accompaniment to meats and curries.

PIMENTO ESCOFFIER ON CROUTONS

1¼ lb. red or green sweet peppers
¼ c. olive oil
2 c. finely chopped onions
2 c. chopped skinned tomatoes
½ c. golden raisins

1 tsp. powdered ginger
1 c. (packed) brown sugar
1 c. red wine vinegar
1 clove of garlic, pressed
1 tsp. dried tarragon leaves
¼ tsp. salt
Baked Croutons *(Breads, pg. 16)*

Skin the peppers according to the step-by-step illustrations, page 30. Cut into thin strips. Heat the oil in a large heavy skillet, then add the peppers and onion. Sauté until lightly browned and limp. Cover and simmer for 15 minutes. Add the remaining ingredients except the croutons and mix well. Turn into a large casserole and cover. Bake in a preheated 350-degree oven for about 2 hours or until thick. Serve on large, round Baked Croutons. Excellent served with curried rice, curried meats or other meat and poultry dishes. This makes 8 to 10 servings.

eggplant and mushroom vol-au-vents

eggplant and mushroom vol-au-vents

Set on a bed of fresh watercress, these Eggplant and Mushroom Vol-Au-Vents make an impressive luncheon dish. The "tops" have been set inside behind the filling and covered with sauce.

EGGPLANT AND MUSHROOM VOL-AU-VENTS

1 lg. eggplant
2 tbsp. butter
1 c. chopped onions
2 c. chopped mushrooms
1 1-lb. can tomatoes, chopped
½ c. canned tomato sauce
1½ tsp. sugar
½ tsp. salt
⅛ tsp. pepper
1 bay leaf
1 c. grated sharp cheese
8 vol-au-vent shells (*Desserts, pg. 65*)

Peel the eggplant and cut into cubes. Soak in heavily salted water for at least 15 minutes. Drain, then place in large saucepan and cover with salted water. Cook over medium heat until tender, then drain. Melt the butter in a saucepan, then add the onions and sauté until golden. Add the mushrooms and sauté for about 3 minutes. Add the tomatoes, tomato sauce, sugar, salt, pepper and bay leaf. Stir well and simmer for 15 minutes. Add the eggplant and heat through. Let stand for at least 1 hour to blend flavors. Reheat just before serving and stir in the cheese. Serve in *vol-au-vent* shells. This makes 8 servings.

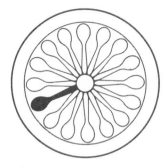

introducing
spinach

Spinach is one of the most praised as well as the most abused vegetables. It has long been popularized in the comic strips by the herculean feats of Popeye The Sailor. An English cookbook, published in 1599, hailed spinach as "wholesome greens for any age or condition, especially for youth". Its juice "cureth any wound received of a scorpion and is therefore of much request in Italy". While reserving judgment on its curing properties, spinach is, in fact, an excellent source of vitamin A, contains a fair amount of vitamin C and riboflavin. By itself, it is very low in calories — having only 21 calories per $1/2$ cup serving.

Although the culinary history of spinach is somewhat nebulous, its origin has been pinpointed to southwestern Asia. It was unknown to the ancient Greeks and Romans and the first written record of it was Chinese — it reached China around 647 A.D. Spinach plants have been known to exist in this country for centuries, but how their cultivation and use spread is still uncertain.

Spinach is an annual potherb with a short-term growth cycle. It requires specific climate and soil conditions for proper development of its tender green leaves. Cool weather and moist, sandy, well-limed soil are essential for the maturing of spinach plants — a process which takes about eight weeks. Spinach is grown during the winter in the south and during the spring and fall in other regions of the country.

Whether fresh, frozen or canned, spinach is a versatile vegetable which may be used in a wide variety of ways. Fresh and uncooked, its color and flavor is an excellent addition to tossed green salads; it may be used in addition to or as a substitute for lettuce. Cooked fresh spinach is best when it is gently steamed in only the water left clinging to its washed leaves. With the addition of a little butter or cream and salt, it is excellent served as the vegetable accompaniment to meat, poultry or fish. Frozen spinach may not contain quite as many vitamins and minerals as fresh, but it's still highly recommended for flavor and especially for convenience. Canned spinach is also a handy item to have on hand in the kitchen — it may be used in place of the fresh or frozen variety in many recipes.

Spinach combines well with many different seasonings. Allspice, basil, cinnamon, dill, marjoram, mint, nutmeg, oregano, rosemary, or sesame seed may be added to the cooking liquid, or to the dressing for a spinach salad. Creamy sauces can be used as toppings for cooked spinach or spinach casserole dishes. Most recipes with the word "Florentine" included in the title indicate the inclusion of creamed spinach with the ingredients. Chopped or sliced hard-boiled eggs make an excellent garnish for uncooked or cooked spinach.

When buying fresh spinach in bulk, choose large, crisp, dark leaves, avoiding those which are decayed, crushed or wilted. Examine spinach that is packed in clear plastic bags — the leaves may be broken but it should look crisp and green. Two pounds of leaf spinach will serve 4 people. Trim the roots and tough stems from the spinach and wash it in a sink of lukewarm water — the warm water sends the sand and dirt to the bottom of the sink. Repeat the process with cold water, lifting the leaves out of the sink several times to free them from the sand. Spinach which is already trimmed and packaged into plastic bags, should be lightly rinsed. It is then ready to cook or to store in a covered container in the refrigerator.

When ready to cook, put the washed leaves into a saucepan or vegetable steamer. Do not add more water than the recipe directs — the drops clinging to the leaves and the natural juice of the spinach will provide part of the moisture needed. Cook over low heat until leaves are thoroughly wilted and tender . . . about 10 minutes. Do not overcook — this will destroy important vitamins and minerals. Drain well and serve with butter and/or cream and salt, or blend and serve as a spinach purée.

PARMESAN SPINACH PURÉE

1½ to 2 lb. fresh spinach
2 tbsp. butter
1 tbsp. lemon juice
½ tsp. salt
¼ c. hot half and half cream
3 tbsp. freshly grated Parmesan cheese

Wash and remove stems from spinach. Place in a large pan and add ¼ cup water. Cover and cook over medium heat for 10 to 15 minutes or until spinach is tender, turning occasionally with a fork. Drain well, then place half the spinach in the blender container. Add the butter, lemon juice, salt and the remaining spinach. Process spinach until puréed, scraping sides with rubber spatula occasionally. Spoon into small mold and invert onto serving dish. Shape sides and level top with tines of fork. Make a well in the center and pour the hot cream in the well. Sprinkle cheese around side. Serve immediately. This makes about 4 servings.

parmesan spinach purée

Like other green vegetables, spinach is a rich source of vitamins and iron. Why not utilize these important nutrients and serve a Parmesan Spinach Purée as the vegetable course at your next meal? It is quick and easy to prepare (a boon to modern-day homemakers) and will make just an "ordinary dinner" an impressive one.

steamed spinach with egg sauce

STEAMED SPINACH WITH EGG SAUCE

2 10-oz. packages frozen chopped spinach
1 c. sour cream
1/2 c. freshly grated Parmesan cheese
2 tbsp. half and half cream
2 tbsp. melted butter
4 eggs, separated
4 c. bread crumbs
1/8 tsp. nutmeg
1 tsp. salt
1/4 tsp. white pepper
1 recipe Egg Sauce (*Sauces, pg. 18*)

The steamed spinach mold shown above is served with Egg Sauce for a wonderful flavor contrast. Similar to spinach soufflé, it is an ideal choice for a luncheon or light supper. It would also be an excellent side dish to accompany broiled chops. Add a salad and hot rolls for a well-balanced and tasty dinner.

Cook the spinach according to package directions, then drain thoroughly. Place in blender container and process until puréed. Place in a large mixing bowl. Add the sour cream, cheese, cream and butter and mix well. Mix in the beaten egg yolks. Add the bread crumbs and seasonings and blend thoroughly. Beat the egg whites until stiff but not dry. Fold 1/4 of the egg whites into the spinach mixture. Fold in the remaining egg whites gently. Turn into a well-buttered 7-inch soufflé dish. Cover tightly with foil. Bake in a preheated 350-degree oven for 50 minutes. Serve immediately with Egg Sauce. This makes about 8 servings.

SPINACH WITH BACON

1½ to 2 lb. fresh spinach
5 slices bacon
½ tbsp. bacon drippings
1 tbsp. lemon juice
½ tsp. salt
1 hard-boiled egg, chopped

Wash and remove stems from spinach. Place in a large pan and add ¼ cup water. Cover and cook over medium heat for 10 to 15 minutes or until spinach is tender, turning occasionally with a fork. Drain well. Cook the bacon until crisp and drain on paper towel. Place the spinach in a serving dish and crumble the bacon over the spinach. Add the drippings, lemon juice and salt, then toss with 2 forks until mixed. Sprinkle top with chopped eggs. This makes about 4 servings.

SPINACH TIMBALES

2 10-oz. packages frozen leaf spinach
4 slices bacon, diced
3 eggs, well beaten
Salt and white pepper to taste
2 tbsp. butter
2 tbsp. all-purpose flour
1 c. milk

Cook spinach according to package directions, then drain well. Place in a mixing bowl. Fry the bacon until crisp. Add the bacon and the drippings to the spinach and toss to mix well. Add the eggs and season with salt and pepper. Fill 6 well-buttered custard cups ⅔ full. Place cups in baking pan and pour in boiling water to a depth of 1 inch. Bake in preheated 350-degree oven for 40 minutes.

Melt the butter in top of double boiler, then blend in flour to make a smooth paste. Stir in the milk and cook, stirring constantly, until smooth and thick. Season with salt and pepper. Unmold spinach and serve with the sauce. Two cups of cooked, fresh spinach may be substituted for the frozen spinach if desired. This makes 6 servings.

SPINACH MADELEINE

2 10-oz. packages frozen chopped spinach
¼ c. butter
2 tbsp. minced onion
3 tbsp. all-purpose flour
½ c. evaporated milk
½ tsp. white pepper
⅛ tsp. cayenne pepper
¾ tsp. celery salt
¾ tsp. garlic salt
1 tbsp. lemon juice
1 tsp. Worcestershire sauce
1 6-oz. roll jalapeño cheese
1 egg, beaten
½ c. buttered toasted bread crumbs

Cook the spinach according to package directions, then drain well, reserving ½ cup liquid. Melt the butter in a medium saucepan, then add the onion and cook until soft. Add the flour, stirring until blended, then stir in the milk and reserved liquid. Cook, stirring constantly, until thickened. Stir in the seasonings. Cut the cheese into small pieces, then add to the sauce, stirring until the cheese is melted. Mix the egg into the spinach until well combined. Add the sauce and mix well. Place in a casserole and sprinkle bread crumbs over the top. Bake in a preheated 350-degree oven for 25 minutes. This will make 6 to 8 servings.

 # mushrooms

BUYING AND PREPARING MUSHROOMS

Mushrooms have so many uses in preparing delicious foods. Their unique flavor enhances everything from delicately sauced dishes to soups, gravies and stews. As a garnish for steaks and chops, mushrooms are without peer. Fresh uncooked mushrooms are excellent sliced thin and added to tossed green salads.

When buying fresh mushrooms, look for those with smooth, firm caps and beige-colored stems. They are freshest if they are slightly moist and the gills on the underside of the cap are not yet exposed. Avoid those with wrinkled caps or bruised skin. Many purists argue that mushrooms should never be washed in water, but simply wiped with a damp cloth. However, fresh mushrooms do tend to have a great deal of dirt and impurities embedded in their skin and we feel the best method of cleaning them is to wash them under cold, running water. Also, if mushrooms have been stored for a while, they may develop a strong, musty odor. This may be removed

by rinsing them in a weak solution of vinegar or lemon juice and water.

One of the most interesting ways to use fresh mushroom stems and pieces is to make a *Duxelles*, a concentrated mixture of finely chopped mushrooms cooked very slowly in butter until dark brown and all moisture evaporated. Refrigerate *Duxelles* in a sealed container; later, when making sauces or stuffings, add a spoonful or so for a wonderful essence-of-mushrooms flavor.

Perhaps the most elegant way to serve whole mushrooms is to steam them under a glass bell called a *cloche*. Cooking them in this manner gives the mushrooms a very tender texture; they do not dry out and they retain their natural flavor and aroma. The *cloche* can most likely be found in the gourmet shop of fine department stores. The *cloche*, or a comparable glass bell dome, ranges in sizes for individual servings and multiple servings. If they are not available in your area, any clear, ovenproof deep dish will serve the same purpose.

MUSHROOMS UNDER GLASS

4 slices bread
¹/₂ recipe Savory Anchovy Butter (General Information, pg. 30)
Mushroom caps
³/₄ c. whipping cream
Salt and white pepper to taste
Cayenne pepper to taste
Finely chopped parsley

Cut rounds from bread slices and toast until dry and golden brown. Butter the bottoms of 4 individual baking dishes with anchovy butter, then spread the toasted slices with the butter. Pile 3 or 4 mushroom caps on each toast round. Season the whipping cream with salt, white pepper and cayenne pepper, then spoon 3 tablespoons of the cream over each serving of mushrooms. Sprinkle with parsley and cover with glass bells. Bake in a preheated 350-degree oven for 15 to 20 minutes. Serve immediately and remove the bells at the table. This makes 4 servings.

mushrooms under glass

This is a very simple but impressive method of cooking and serving cultivated mushrooms. This delicious dish may be served as a separate vegetable course or as an accompaniment for grilled meats.

stuffed zucchini

stuffed zucchini

Serve an unusual and delightful variation of zucchini stuffed with a mixture of seasoned, ground lamb. The Stuffed Zucchini has been simmered in stock with carrots and shallots which garnish the finished platter. The stock is then reduced to a delicious sauce and poured over the vegetables. Extra sauce may be served separately.

STUFFED ZUCCHINI

6 carrots, sliced
12 shallots, peeled
4 c. beef broth
4 med. zucchini
2 slices bread
¼ c. milk
1 lb. ground lean lamb
1 tsp. thyme
2 tsp. salt
1 tsp. pepper
2 eggs, beaten
¼ c. tomato paste
Melted butter

Place the carrots, shallots, beef broth and 1 cup of water in a Dutch oven or heavy casserole. Bring to a boil and simmer until tender. Prepare the zucchini while the vegetables are cooking. Peel each zucchini, then cut in half lengthwise and hollow out the centers. Remove the crusts from the bread, then soak the bread in the milk. Combine the lamb and bread mixture in a mixing bowl. Add the seasonings, egg and tomato paste and mix well. Fill each zucchini half with the lamb mixture, then fit the halves together. Brush generously with melted butter and wrap each zucchini loosely in aluminum foil. Remove the carrots and shallots from the broth and set aside. Place the wrapped zucchini carefully in the broth and simmer, covered, for 1 hour. Remove the zucchini and return the carrots and shallots to the broth to reheat. Unwrap the zucchini and place in a serving dish. Arrange carrots and shallots around the zucchini and pour broth over the top. This will make about 8 servings.

stuffed baked potatoes

This attractive cold meat platter includes Stuffed Baked Potatoes as well as a wide variety of meats. When ready to serve, heat the stuffed potatoes in the oven before arranging them on the platter. Tiny gherkins and green olives add a pleasing color contrast.

STUFFED BAKED POTATOES

4 lg. baking potatoes
2 slices bacon
¼ c. milk
¼ c. melted butter
Salt and pepper to taste
2 tbsp. minced parsley

Scrub the potatoes, then grease with oil. Bake at 400 degrees for 1 hour or until soft. Fry bacon until crisp, then drain on absorbent toweling. Cut potatoes in half lengthwise. Scrape out the insides into a medium-sized bowl. Mash with a fork. Stir in milk, melted butter, salt and pepper. Crumble in the bacon, then add the parsley and mix well. Pack into shells and drizzle tops with additional melted butter. Place on a cookie sheet. Broil 5 inches from the source of heat until tops are browned. Serve immediately. This makes 8 servings.

baked mashed potatoes

Baked Mashed Potatoes are the perfect accompaniment to Baked Sausages (Variety Meats, pg. 8) and Crisp Cabbage. The potatoes are baked in their jackets until done. The cooked potato is carefully scooped out of the jackets, mashed with sour cream and tomato purée, then piped or spooned back into the jackets. The result is not only an unusual color but a delicious flavor.

BAKED MASHED POTATOES

8 med. potatoes
2 tbsp. butter
½ c. tomato purée
½ c. sour cream
Salt and pepper to taste
1 c. grated sharp Cheddar cheese

Bake well-greased potatoes in 400-degree oven for 45 minutes or until soft. Split lengthwise, then scoop out centers into mixing bowl. Set shells aside. Add butter, tomato purée and sour cream to the potatoes, then mash until well mixed. Season with salt and pepper, then stir in the cheese. Mound potato mixture into the shells and place shells on baking sheet. Broil 10 inches from the source of heat until potatoes are heated through. This makes 8 servings.

boiled potatoes
whipped potatoes
potatoes au gratin
hashed brown potatoes

BOILED POTATOES WITH CHEESE SAUCE

10 med. new potatoes
¹/₄ c. butter
¹/₄ c. all-purpose flour
2 c. milk
1 c. grated Cheddar cheese
Salt and pepper to taste

Scrape the potatoes. Cook in boiling, salted water until tender, then drain. Keep warm. Melt the butter in a saucepan. Add the flour and mix until smooth. Add the milk and cook, stirring constantly, until thickened. Remove from heat. Add the cheese and stir until melted. Stir in the salt and pepper. Place the potatoes in a serving dish and pour the cheese sauce over potatoes. This makes 4 to 6 servings.

WHIPPED POTATOES PAPRIKA

6 med. potatoes, cubed
1 3-oz. package cream cheese
¹/₄ c. butter
Salt and pepper to taste
Milk
Paprika

Cook the potatoes in boiling, salted water until tender, then drain. Add the cream cheese, butter, salt, pepper and enough milk for desired consistency. Beat with an electric mixer until smooth and fluffy. Place in a serving dish and sprinkle with paprika. Serve immediately. This makes 6 servings.

POTATOES AU GRATIN

4 c. sliced potatoes
6 tbsp. butter
6 tbsp. all-purpose flour
1 c. milk
1 c. cream
1 c. chicken broth
Salt and pepper to taste
Dry bread crumbs
Parmesan cheese

Cook the potatoes in boiling, salted water until partially done, then drain. Place in a casserole. Melt the butter in a saucepan, then stir in the flour to make a smooth paste. Add the milk, cream and chicken broth and cook, stirring constantly, until thickened. Add salt and pepper and pour over the potatoes. Bake at 350 degrees for 45 minutes. Sprinkle with bread crumbs and cheese and bake for 4 to 5 minutes longer or until browned. This makes 6 to 8 servings.

HASHED BROWN POTATOES

3 c. cubed cooked potatoes
1 tsp. salt
¹/₈ tsp. freshly ground pepper
1 tbsp. minced onion
¹/₄ c. butter

Sprinkle the potatoes with salt, pepper and onion. Heat the butter in a skillet. Add the potatoes and cook until brown, stirring frequently. Place in a serving dish and garnish with parsley. This makes about 4 servings.

**boiled potatoes with cheese sauce,
whipped potatoes paprika,
potatoes au gratin,
hashed brown potatoes**

*Among vegetables, versatility means potato!
Pictured here are four reliable potato recipes
guaranteed to spark any menu: Boiled Potatoes
with Cheese Sauce (excellent with your favorite
fish recipe), Whipped Potatoes Paprika (creamy
and smooth, they are the perfect accompaniment to any roasted meat with gravy), Potatoes Au
Gratin (great with Glazed Ham), and Hashed
Brown Potatoes (hearty food for hearty eaters —
they're superb with bacon and eggs or
breakfast steak).*

corned beef–stuffed potatoes

CORNED BEEF-STUFFED POTATOES

6 lg. baking potatoes
1½ c. minced corned beef
½ c. butter

Scrub the potatoes, then grease with oil. Bake at 400 degrees for 1 hour or until soft. Cut a thin slice from the top of each potato and scoop out the inside, leaving a ¼-inch wall. Mash the potatoes with a fork, then stir in the corned beef and butter. Pack into the shells and garnish with minced parsley. Serve immediately. Each potato may be topped with a poached egg and served as a main dish, if desired. This makes 6 servings.

corned beef-stuffed potatoes

A hearty, satisfying supper can be quickly assembled by stuffing hollowed-out, baked potato cases with a mixture of corned beef and mashed potato. Top each filled potato with a poached egg and garnish with snipped parsley, if desired. Serve with a green vegetable for a nourishing, well balanced meal.

CARROT BOATS

½ **recipe Basic Savory Short Pastry**
  (Desserts, pg. 12)
4 **c. diced carrots**
¼ **c. whipping cream**
¼ **c. melted butter**
Salt and pepper to taste
½ **tsp. nutmeg**

Roll pastry out thin on a floured surface and cut into 20 ovals to fit into small oval-shaped tartlet pans. Place into pans and prick bottoms generously. Place pans on baking sheet. Bake in preheated 425-degree oven for about 15 minutes or until browned. Let cool for 5 minutes, then remove shells from tartlet pans. Cook carrots in a small amount of boiling salted water until very tender. Drain carrots. Purée 1 cup of the carrots with 1 tablespoon of the cream and 1 tablespoon butter in blender container. Repeat process 3 more times. Season carrot mixture with salt, pepper and nutmeg. Spoon into pastry shells and garnish with quartered pitted black olives. Serve immediately. These may be made ahead and covered lightly with aluminum foil, then reheated. This recipe makes about 20 boats.

STUFFED MUSHROOMS

2 **10-oz. packages frozen chopped spinach or 2 c.**
  cooked fresh spinach
¼ **c. freshly grated Parmesan cheese**
2 **tbsp. melted butter**
⅛ **tsp. nutmeg**
Salt and pepper to taste
12 **lg. mushroom caps**
Olive oil
12 **blanched whole almonds**

Cook spinach according to package directions and drain thoroughly. Purée half the spinach at a time in a blender. Combine puréed spinach, cheese, butter, nutmeg, salt and pepper in top of double boiler and mix well. Cover and place over hot, but not boiling, water to keep warm. Brush entire surface of mushroom caps with oil, then place on baking sheet. Bake in preheated 375-degree oven for 10 minutes. Mound spinach mixture inside each mushroom. Garnish with almonds and serve immediately. This makes 6 servings.

STUFFED ARTICHOKE BOTTOMS

12 **canned artichoke bottoms**
½ **recipe Basic Mornay Sauce (Sauces, pg. 11)**

Place the artichoke bottoms and liquid in a saucepan and heat through. Drain and pat dry. Place on baking sheet, then spoon sauce onto the artichokes. Broil until sauce is bubbly and browned. Garnish with tomato petals and pieces of hard-boiled eggs. Serve this dish immediately. This makes 6 servings.

carrot boats, stuffed mushrooms, stuffed artichoke bottoms

Here is an attractive presentation of assorted vegetables served in individual portions. The Carrot Boats are small pastry shells filled with creamy puréed carrots garnished with pieces of ripe olive. Stuffed Mushrooms (a wonderful garnish for grilled steaks) are filled with spinach purée and topped with almond halves. Stuffed Artichoke Bottoms are filled with Basic Mornay Sauce (Sauces, pg. 11), lightly broiled and decorated with pieces of tomato. The amusing garnish in the center is nothing more than an onion ring basket containing an artichoke bottom, hard-boiled egg and tomato cap.

stuffed cabbage casserole

Here is a full-flavored, nourishing main course, especially suitable for a family supper. A meal in itself, this Stuffed Cabbage Casserole is a combination of cabbage, sausage, liver, Canadian bacon and vegetables. This recipe is one of those surprises — not exciting when read, but a real treat to taste and satisfies the most robust appetite.

stuffed cabbage

Modern homemakers, who are economy conscious, will do well to include cabbage in their menus. Lowly and plebian though it may seem, it is almost as versatile as the potato. It may be eaten raw in salads or cooked in almost any manner — boiled, steamed, braised, sautéed or baked. A small head of cabbage costs only pennies and makes about 4 servings.

The common *or green cabbage* is sold everywhere. During the summer months the tender young heads are bright green and fairly small (2 or 3 lbs.); the winter crop (also called late crop) is much lighter in color and larger — the heads weigh up to 6 lbs. *Savoy cabbage* is a curly leaf variety which has a more delicate flavor than that of green cabbage. *Red cabbage,* often used in German and Pennsylvania Dutch recipes must be cooked with some acid (such as vinegar, lemon juice or tart apple) added to the cooking liquid. Otherwise, its attractive red color will turn grayish-purple.

Never overcook cabbage. The old-fashioned method of boiling it for hours accounts for a strong cabbage odor which permeates the entire house. The result is a mushy, grayish, unappetizing vegetable completely lacking nutritive value. Cabbage, like most other green vegetables is best when cooked quickly in a small amount of liquid just to the tender but still slightly crisp stage. It is excellent served simply with butter, salt and pepper.

STUFFED CABBAGE CASSEROLE

1 lg. head cabbage
²/₃ c. long-grain rice
¹/₂ c. pure pork sausage
6 slices bacon, diced
³/₄ lb. calves liver, minced
¹/₄ c. olive oil
2 leeks
¹/₈ tsp. mace
¹/₈ tsp. nutmeg
Thyme leaves
Parsley
Salt and pepper to taste
1 egg, beaten
6 med. carrots
6 sm. turnips, peeled
6 med. onions, chopped
1¹/₂ lb. Canadian bacon, diced
Pinch of rosemary
1 bay leaf
2 c. beef broth
¹/₂ c. tomato sauce

Remove any undesirable outside leaves from cabbage. Immerse cabbage in boiling water to cover and remove pan from heat. Let stand for 10 to 15 minutes or until leaves are softened. Plunge into ice water to loosen leaves. Peel off 10 outside leaves carefully. Use remaining cabbage as desired. Cook the rice in 1¹/₃ cups boiling salted water for 5 minutes then drain. Combine the rice, sausage, bacon, liver and olive oil in a Dutch oven or heavy saucepan; fry for several minutes or until the liver is slightly tender. Mince the white part of the leeks to measure 1¹/₂ cups. Add leeks, mace, nutmeg, 1 teaspoon thyme leaves, 2 teaspoons minced parsley, salt, pepper and egg to the liver mixture and stir until well mixed. Spread liver mixture on the largest cabbage leaf, then place another large cabbage leaf over the liver mixture. Repeat process until all the liver mixture is used, progressing to smallest cabbage leaves and ending with 1 or 2 small unfilled cabbage leaves. Shape to resemble cabbage head. Tie cabbage head with string to hold shape. Help may be needed to hold cabbage head together while tying. Place stuffed cabbage upside down in roasting pan, then arrange carrots, turnips and onions around cabbage. Spoon the diced Canadian bacon over vegetables. Prepare a *Bouquet Garni*, (Soups, pg. 2) using a pinch of thyme leaves, several sprigs of parsley, rosemary and bay leaf. Drop into roasting pan. Combine beef broth and tomato sauce; pour over all ingredients. Bake, covered, 1 shelf below center of oven at 300 degrees for 3 hours. This makes about 6 to 8 servings.

RICE-STUFFED CABBAGE ROLLS WITH MELTED BUTTER

1 head cabbage
1 c. long grain rice
1 tbsp. butter
1 tbsp. paprika
1/4 c. currants
2 tbsp. finely chopped parsley
Melted butter

Place the cabbage in a steamer and steam for 1 hour and 30 minutes or until tender. Cook the rice in 3 cups boiling salted water for 18 minutes or until tender, then drain. Combine the rice, butter, paprika, currants and parsley, stirring until butter is melted. Remove the cabbage from the steamer and plunge into cold water to loosen leaves. Cut out any hard core and separate leaves. Place about 1 tablespoon rice mixture in each leaf. Overlap the sides and roll up. Place the rolls on a serving platter. Pour the melted butter over the cabbage rolls and serve immediately. This makes 6 to 8 servings.

CRISP CABBAGE

8 c. shredded cabbage
1 sm. onion, grated
1/2 tsp. sea salt
1 tsp. dillweed (optional)
1/4 c. dill pickle juice (optional)

Combine cabbage, onion and salt with 1 cup water in Dutch oven or heavy saucepan. Cook, covered, over low heat until cabbage is crisp-tender. Drain, if necessary. Stir in dillweed and pickle juice and serve immediately. An alternate method is to add butter or cream and pepper to the cooked cabbage, omitting the dillweed and pickle juice. This makes 4 to 6 servings.

rice stuffed cabbage rolls

Tender-steamed, young cabbage leaves wrapped around a savory mixture of rice and currants make a fancy vegetable course. Melted butter, offered in a separate bowl, enhances the flavor of this dish. Its unusual preparation will perk up a simple menu.

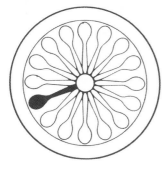

dried beans

INTRODUCING DRIED BEANS

The term *légume* refers to any vegetable or plant (such as peas, beans or lentils), that have shell-like pods containing seeds. In culinary terms, however, *legumes* usually means dried peas or beans that are used in soups and casseroles. These hearty staples are among man's oldest and most reliable foods. Even the most primitive people knew that dried beans would not spoil during the long cold winter months and could be used in place of fresh vegetables. *Légumes* are also a rich source of protein and thus, a nutritious substitute for meat.

Like pastas and rice, *légumes* have such a distinct though bland flavor that care must be taken in seasoning. Onion, garlic and cured, smoked or salted meat are frequent additions to recipes for dried beans. Various national or regional groups have their own special ways of flavoring. Mexicans prefer garlic and chili powder; Mediterranean people frequently use garlic and oregano; the British favor mustard and bay leaf; New Englanders are famous for their brown sugar and molasses beans. Whatever seasonings are used, be sure to cook the beans very slowly until thoroughly done. Long slow cooking at a low temperature blends the seasonings and intensifies the flavor.

Whether preparing dried beans (navy, Great Northern or kidney) for New England Baked Beans, Mexican-Style Beans, Pinto Bean Pot, or any other recipe calling for this type of *légume*, preparation is much the same. In the past, it was a traditional practice to soak beans hours or overnight. This is no longer necessary due to changes in the quality of available beans, drying methods used in preparing beans and the packaging itself. In fact, beans that are soaked overnight absorb a great deal of water and have a tendency to become very mushy when cooked. There is also the fact that soaking for more than 4 to 5 hours will cause fermentation.

First, you should always place dried beans in a colander and rinse them under cold running water. Then be sure to pick over the beans to remove any bits of pod or any damaged beans. Cover the beans with cold water and soak for about 4 hours or follow the instructions in the recipe used. The following recipes for several kinds of dried beans are all deliciously seasoned, each with a flair of inventiveness.

PINTO BEAN POT

2 c. dried pinto beans
1 sm. onion, chopped
1 1½-in. square salt pork, diced
½ tsp. salt
5 sm. dried chili peppers
1 6-oz. bottle cola beverage

Soak the beans in cold water to cover for 1 hour. Drain. Combine the beans, onion, salt pork, salt and chili peppers in a bean pot. Add water to cover, then stir in the cola beverage. Cover. Bake at 250 degrees for 8 hours. Stir 2 or 3 times and add water, if needed to keep beans covered. This makes about 8 servings.

MEXICAN-STYLE BEANS

2 lb. pinto beans
1 tbsp. salt
2 c. chopped tomatoes
2 lg. onions, diced
1 can green chilies, chopped
4 cloves of garlic, diced
1 can taco sauce
1 tsp. cumin
½ tsp. pepper

Rinse beans thoroughly, then drain and place in a large kettle. Add salt and enough water to cover beans by 2 inches. Bring to a hard boil. Cover and remove from heat. Let stand for 1 hour and 30 minutes. Stir in remaining ingredients. Simmer, covered, for about 4 hours or until beans are tender, adding water and salt, if needed. This makes about 25 servings.

SAVORY HOT BEANS

1 1-lb. package pinto beans
Salt
3 slices bacon, diced
2 med. onions, chopped
3 tbsp. catsup
2 tbsp. red hot sauce
2 tbsp. Worcestershire sauce
Pepper to taste

Rinse beans thoroughly and place in a large bowl. Fill bowl with water and let beans soak for about 3 hours. Drain beans, then place in a large kettle. Add enough water to cover beans 2 inches over top, then add 1 tablespoon salt. Bring to a boil. Cover and let simmer for 1 hour and 30 minutes or until tender, adding water if needed. Drain beans and set aside until ready to use. Fry the bacon in a Dutch oven or heavy saucepan until lightly browned. Add the onions and fry until transparent. Add the cooked beans, catsup and sauces, then season to taste. Simmer for about 30 minutes, stirring occasionally and adding water if needed. This makes about 10 servings.

NEW ENGLAND-BAKED BEANS

1 lb. dry navy beans
1 lg. onion, diced
½ tsp. salt
1 c. molasses
1 tsp. dry English mustard
1 tsp. Worcestershire sauce
1 c. (firmly packed) brown sugar
¼ lb, salt pork, sliced

Rinse and pick over the beans. Place beans in a large kettle and cover with water. Let soak for 4 hours. Drain and place the beans in a large kettle. Cover again with water. Bring to a boil, then cook covered for about 45 minutes or until beans are just tender. Drain, reserving the liquid. Combine the onion, salt, molasses, mustard, Worcestershire sauce and brown sugar. Place about ⅓ of the beans in a bean pot with a small amount of the reserved liquid. Cover with about ⅓ of the molasses mixture. Place several slices of pork on top. Repeat layers, adding part of the reserved liquid with each layer. Bake at 300 degrees for 5 to 6 hours or until tender, adding water as needed to keep beans covered. This makes 8 to 10 servings.

new england-baked beans

Virtually every New England housewife has her own favorite method of preparing baked beans. This is one of the authentic recipes for New England baked beans. Additional ingredients that may be added to vary this bean dish are: tomato sauce, cloves, and a bay leaf or a touch of ginger.

eggplant supreme

Eggplant Supreme is a zesty, vegetable dish, as tangy as it is colorful. The eggplant, actually a vegetable fruit, is surprisingly a cousin of the potato and tomato. Available the year round, it is an excellent choice as an out-of-the-ordinary treat that will add variety to any menu.

delicious eggplant supreme

EGGPLANT SUPREME

2 medium-sized eggplant
¼ c. salad oil
1 sm. onion, sliced
¼ c. green pepper strips
1 clove of garlic, minced
2 tomatoes, cut in wedges
1 tsp. oregano
1 tsp. basil
1 tsp. salt
Pepper to taste
¼ c. parsley sprigs

Cut the eggplant in half lengthwise and scoop out pulp, leaving ½-inch shells. Dice the pulp and set aside. Cook the eggplant shells in boiling, salted water until just tender, then drain. Place in a baking dish, cut side up. Heat the oil in a sauce-pan. Add the onion, green pepper, garlic, diced eggplant, tomatoes, oregano, basil, salt and pepper and cook for about 3 minutes or until heated through, stirring frequently. Spoon into eggplant shells and sprinkle with parsley. Bake at 350 degrees for 25 minutes. This makes 4 servings.

CRISPY FRIED ONION RINGS

2 lg. onions
1 c. self-rising flour

Peel onions and cut into medium-thick slices. Separate into rings. Combine the flour and enough water to make the consistency of heavy cream. Dip each ring in the batter and allow to drain slightly. Fry in deep hot oil until golden brown on both sides. This makes 6 servings.

introducing artichokes

Artichokes, with their intriguing clusters of leaves, have for years added irresistible flavor and eye appeal to cookery. They were among the most demanded and highest priced vegetables in Rome as early as the 5th Century A.D. From Italy, they gradually became popular in other countries, particularly France. The French settlers of the 1800's cultivated this much-desired vegetable in Louisiana, where it is still grown today.

Artichokes require a warm, humid climate for proper growth. Temperatures below 30 degrees cause the buds to turn black, and harvest has to be delayed until new ones form. Temperatures below 28 degrees usually destroy all growth above the ground. The special kind of climate needed for artichokes is found mainly in Louisiana and the mid-coastal region of California.

Fresh artichokes are available throughout the year, but they are most plentiful in April and May. When shopping for fresh artichokes, look for those that are compact and heavy in relation to size. The leaves should be fleshy and tight clinging. Spreading leaves that are discolored indicate that the vegetable is not tender.

Fresh artichokes should be used immediately. However, if temporary storage is necessary, the storing temperature should be about 32 degrees.

Artichoke hearts and bottoms are available canned, frozen or packed in oil or marinade. Marinated artichokes add a special, spicy flavor to tossed salads or can be served as an appetizer or on a relish tray.

Artichokes can be prepared and served in a variety of ways. They can be steamed or boiled, served hot or cold, dipped in melted butter, topped with seasoned sauce, or filled with a delicious meat or seafood mixture. The following recipes will give you many more creative ideas for preparing and serving artichokes.

how to
prepare artichoke vinaigrette

GLOBE ARTICHOKES VINAIGRETTE

4 fresh globe artichokes
Lemon juice
¾ tsp. salt
1 recipe Basic Vinaigrette *(Sauces, pg. 2)*

Wash artichokes, then cut off stems and remove small bottom leaves. Trim tips of leaves and cut off 1 inch from the tops of the artichokes. Dip cut portions of artichokes in lemon juice to prevent discoloration. Stand artichokes upright in a deep saucepan just large enough to hold snugly. Twine may be tied around large bottom leaves to hold closely together, if desired. Pour in boiling water to a depth of 3 inches and add salt. Cover and boil gently for 35 to 45 minutes or until base can be pierced easily with fork. More boiling water may be added, if needed. Remove artichokes with a slotted spoon and turn upside down to drain and let cool.

3 Grasp the top firmly and twist to loosen and remove leaves.

4 Set aside the cap of small, pale leaves.

1 Pull leaves apart gently.

2 Spread leaves open to find the peak of small, pale leaves covering the choke.

5 Remove the spiky choke from the artichoke bottom with a metal spoon. Invert the caps over the artichoke bottoms and fill with Basic Vinaigrette just before serving. This makes 4 servings.

ARTICHOKE HEARTS IN LEMON BUTTER

½ c. minced onion
½ clove of garlic, crushed
2 tbsp. butter
¾ c. chicken broth
2 15-oz. cans artichoke hearts, drained
3 tbsp. lemon juice
1½ tsp. salt
1 tsp. oregano
¼ tsp. grated lemon rind

Sauté the onion and garlic in butter in a medium saucepan until transparent, then add the broth and artichoke hearts. Season with the lemon juice, salt, oregano and lemon rind. Simmer for 10 minutes or until the artichokes are heated through. Two packages of cooked, frozen artichokes may be used in place of canned artichokes. This makes 6 to 8 servings.

ARTICHOKES SUPREME

12 artichokes
1 tsp. salt
1 clove of garlic, crushed
1 tbsp. salad oil
¼ c. lemon juice
2 c. chopped cooked shrimp
1 recipe Béchamel Sauce or Basic White Sauce (*Sauces, pg. 4*)

Prepare and cook artichokes as directed in Globe Artichokes Vinaigrette, page 50, adding salt, garlic, salad oil and lemon juice to the boiling water. Continue preparation as illustrated just through removing the choke. Place the artichokes in shallow, individual baking dishes and fill centers with shrimp. Spoon *Béchamel* Sauce over shrimp. Bake in a preheated 350-degree oven for 20 minutes or until heated through. This makes 12 servings.

globe artichokes vinaigrette

An attractive side dish, Globe Artichokes Vinaigrette is a fine accompaniment to any meat course.

italian potato gnocchi

For a pleasant change from the usual starch supplements, serve these light, cheesy Potato Gnocchi. Convenience is part of their appeal, as they may be prepared in advance and refrigerated for later use.

potato gnocchi

The Italians, who created so many of our American favorites like macaroni, spaghetti, ravioli and lasagna, also created delectable Potato Gnocchi (pronounced nyôk kē). Gnocchi is also made by combining pasta dough with cooked, sieved potatoes. These delicious, cheesy potatoes are shaped like small dumplings or flat cakes. The most popular method of cooking them is poaching; then they are covered with an Italian sauce and baked.

Something of a novelty on American menus, gnocchi is a very light potato which is delicious with any meal. Busy homemakers will be especially glad to know that it can be poached in advance and then refrigerated. When needed, just let the gnocchi come to room temperature, cover with sauce and brown under a broiler.

ITALIAN POTATO GNOCCHI

7 med. potatoes, peeled
¼ c. butter, softened
2 egg yolks, lightly beaten
1 c. all-purpose flour
Salt and white pepper to taste
¼ tsp. nutmeg
Melted butter
1 c. grated Gruyère cheese

Cube potatoes and cook in boiling, salted water until tender. Press the potatoes through a ricer into a large mixing bowl. Add the butter and mix until butter is melted, then let cool. Stir in the egg yolks, flour and seasonings with a wooden spoon, working until smooth. Shape the potato mixture into 1½-inch balls. Flatten the balls with the tines of a fork, dipping the fork in water occasionally. Fill a kettle ⅔ full with water and bring to a slow boil. Lower the cakes into simmering water with a slotted spoon and cook until the cakes rise to the top. Arrange the cakes in a greased baking dish and drizzle with melted butter. Sprinkle with cheese. Bake in a preheated 400-degree oven for 20 to 25 minutes or until golden. May increase oven temperature to brown tops. This makes 10 to 12 servings.

french potato fritters

A delightful variation of pancakes, these savory French Potato Fritters are a delightful way to serve potatoes. Delicious when served with meats or fish, they're easy, economical and best of all, a real crowd pleaser.

french potato fritters

French Potato Fritters are cooked, sieved potatoes mixed with a batter and cooked, very much like pancakes, on a hot griddle. Unlike fritters made with raw potato, French Potato Fritters are light and airy — and especially delicious when served with melted butter and freshly grated Parmesan cheese.

A convenient aspect of this dish is that the batter may be made in advance and refrigerated until needed. Then, about 30 minutes before you plan to fry the fritters, bring the batter to room temperature.

French Potato Fritters are a complementary side dish for ham, bacon, or sausage and eggs. Add hot rolls and coffee for a satisfying brunch or light supper.

FRENCH POTATO FRITTERS

1 lb. baking potatoes, peeled
2 eggs
1 egg yolk
1/4 c. whipping cream
2 tbsp. melted butter
1/2 tsp. salt
1/4 tsp. white pepper
1/2 tsp. onion salt
1 c. flour
1/2 c. milk

Cut potatoes into small cubes. Cook in boiling, salted water until tender, then drain. Press through ricer into mixing bowl, then cool. Combine the eggs, egg yolk and cream and beat well. Pour onto potatoes, then add the butter, salt, pepper and onion salt. Mix thoroughly. Sift the flour over the top and stir in with a wooden spoon until blended. Add enough milk to make a thick batter-like consistency. Drop from spoon onto well-greased griddle and smooth the top. Cook over medium high heat until brown, then turn and brown other side. Drizzle with additional melted butter or serve with freshly grated Parmesan cheese. This makes about 8 servings.

layered vegetable gâteau

This impressive vegetable course with its alternating layers of vegetables may accompany the most elegant entrée. Though it is somewhat time-consuming in its preparation, it can be made a day ahead, refrigerated, then baked just before serving. Truly company fare!

LAYERED VEGETABLE GÂTEAU

3 red or green sweet peppers
½ c. olive oil
6 tbsp. butter
4 c. finely chopped onions
3 c. coarsely chopped firm ripe tomatoes
4 c. diced unpeeled zucchini
1 lb. fresh mushrooms, sliced
4 c. fine soft bread crumbs
1½ c. freshly grated Parmesan cheese
Salt and pepper to taste
¼ c. finely chopped parsley
4 slices bread
1 recipe Tomato Fondue Sauce *(Sauces, pg. 15)*

Cut peppers in half lengthwise, then remove seeds and pith. Cut each half lengthwise into thirds. Chop half the peppers coarsely and reserve remaining pepper strips. Place ¼ cup olive oil and 2 tablespoons butter in a large, heavy skillet over medium heat. Sauté the onions in oil mixture until tender but not browned. Remove from skillet with slotted spoon and place in a sieve. Drain off excess oil into the skillet by shaking sieve and pressing onions gently with the spoon. Turn into a small ovenproof dish and keep warm in a preheated 150-degree oven. Sauté tomatoes lightly in remaining oil mixture, then repeat draining and warming procedure. Repeat sautéeing and draining procedures with zucchini, chopped peppers and mushrooms, adding butter and oil as needed. Keep warm. Sauté pepper strips in remaining oil and butter until tender, then drain on absorbent toweling and set aside. Center the rim of a springform pan in a shallow baking dish. Arrange mushrooms evenly inside springform rim. Sprinkle generously with bread crumbs, cheese, salt, pepper and parsley. Pat gently but firmly into place. Arrange layers of onions, tomatoes, chopped peppers and zucchini with generous sprinklings of crumbs, cheese, salt, pepper and parsley between each layer. Combine any remaining crumbs, cheese and parsley and sprinkle over top zucchini layer, pressing gently but firmly to make a smooth surface. Bake in a preheated 375-degree oven for 10 to 15 minutes or until golden brown. Remove crusts from bread slices, then cut each slice in half. Cut one end of each half into a point. Bake according to directions for Baked Croutons (Breads, pg. 16). Bring fondue sauce just to a boil. Add pepper strips, then heat through. Remove the springform rim and decorate edge of gâteau with the croutons, then spoon fondue sauce and pepper strips around base. Serve immediately. This makes 10 to 12 servings.

zucchini in bread crumbs with cheese

ZUCCHINI IN BREAD CRUMBS WITH CHEESE

2 lb. small zucchini
¼ c. butter
¼ c. salad oil
1½ c. cooked rice
½ c. freshly grated Parmesan cheese
½ c. grated sharp Cheddar cheese
Salt and pepper to taste
2 eggs, slightly beaten
Dry bread crumbs
Melted butter

Cut ends from zucchini and steam until tender, according to directions on page 7. Reserve 2 zucchini for garnish, then dice remaining zucchini. Combine butter and oil in a Dutch oven and heat until butter is melted. Add rice and diced zucchini, then sauté until golden, stirring frequently. Stir in the cheeses until melted and add seasonings. Let cool slightly, then stir in eggs quickly. Pour into a greased baking dish and sprinkle generously with bread crumbs. Slice reserved zucchini and arrange around the diced zucchini mixture. Drizzle melted butter over top. Broil about 6 inches from the source of heat until lightly browned and bubbly. This makes 6 to 8 servings.

zucchini in bread crumbs with cheese

The versatility of casseroles is again demonstrated by this combination of zucchini, rice, Parmesan cheese and bread crumbs. Today's busy homemakers will appreciate the convenience of this "prepare-ahead" dish. Teamed with broiled chops or steaks, its succulent flavor is one which your family is sure to applaud.

STUFFED ONIONS WITH ITALIAN MEAT SAUCE

6 lg. Spanish onions, peeled
½ lb. lean ground beef
½ tsp. thyme leaves
¼ c. tomato purée
1 egg yolk, beaten
Salt and pepper to taste
Salad oil
1 recipe Italian Meat Sauce *(Sauces, pg. 18)*

Place onions in boiling, salted water to cover and simmer for 30 minutes or until tender. Remove with a slotted spoon and let drain until cool. Hollow out onions, being careful to leave shells intact, then set shells aside. Chop onion centers finely. Sauté ground beef until lightly browned. Remove from pan with a slotted spoon and place in a mixing bowl. Add chopped onion, thyme, tomato purée, egg yolk and seasonings, then mix well. Spoon beef mixture into onion shells and place in baking dish. Brush onions lightly with oil and cover with foil. Bake in a preheated 350-degree oven for 15 minutes or until heated through. Heat meat sauce and pour into serving dish. Place onions in sauce. Garnish onions with sprigs of rosemary, if desired, and serve immediately. This makes 6 servings.

stuffed onions with italian meat sauce

The woman who cooks to please her family and friends can use this tantalizing vegetable course to her advantage. Steamed white onions with a mildly sweet flavor are hollowed out and filled with a savory mixture of ground meat and spices (a good way to utilize leftovers). Surrounded by a rich, bubbling Italian Meat Sauce, they make an ideal change-of-pace dish which will bring new flavor excitement to your dinner table!

fresh spring vegetables

Carrots, a member of the parsley family, have been used in a variety of ways throughout the centuries. They were first grown for food in Afghanistan and soon after were cultivated by the Chinese, Japanese and Indians. Europeans later found additional uses for the carrot. English women used the feathery leaves as adornments for their hair. Germans ground carrots into a fine powder and used it as a coffee substitute. With the establishment of the colonies, the carrot was brought to America.

Carrots are an important part of a well-balanced diet. One medium carrot furnishes more than a day's minimum requirement of vitamin A and contains only 21 calories. Raw, they are also of value in promoting good dental health (chewing carrots cleanses the teeth and exercises the gums and jaw muscles). The texture, color and flavor of carrots will add eye and taste appeal to any menu. Crisp carrot curls or sticks brighten the hors d'oeuvre and relish tray. Diced carrots lend body and seasoning to soups and stews. Frozen and canned carrots may be used as a quick yellow vegetable addition to any meal. Carrot soup, carrot soufflé, even carrot cakes are further examples of the versatility of this vegetable.

Fresh carrots, available year-round, are sold in bunches packaged in plastic bags. Carrots should be deep orange in color, moist, firm, smooth and well shaped. Small young carrots are more tender and better flavored than older larger ones. Fresh carrots should be washed, the tops removed, then placed in an airtight container in the refrigerator to preserve nutrients and moisture.

Before cooking, rinse the carrots and remove skin with a vegetable peeler. If left whole, carrots will cook to crisp tenderness in about 30 minutes using a moist cooking method. Sliced carrots require 20 to 30 minutes and diced pieces are fully cooked in 10 to 15 minutes.

CARROT-CHEESE RING

1½ c. milk, scalded
3 eggs, slightly beaten
2½ c. grated carrots
1 tbsp. minced onion
1 tbsp. melted butter
1 c. grated Cheddar cheese
1 tbsp. lemon juice
Pinch of marjoram
Salt and pepper to taste

Scald the milk in a double boiler. Add small amount of hot milk to eggs, stirring constantly. Stir egg mixture back into milk and cook, stirring constantly, until thickened. Add remaining ingredients and pour into a greased 1½ quart mold. Place in a baking pan and add enough water to fill to a depth of 1 inch. Bake in a preheated 325-degree oven for 45 minutes or until set. Unmold and fill center with green peas if desired. This makes 8 servings.

APPLE-GLAZED CARROTS

1½ tbsp. melted butter
3 tbsp. brown sugar
¼ c. applesauce
2 c. cooked sliced carrots

Combine the butter, brown sugar and applesauce in a small saucepan. Cook over low heat, stirring, until the brown sugar is melted. Place the carrots in a baking dish and pour the applesauce mixture over the top. Bake in a preheated 350-degree oven for 15 minutes or until heated through. This makes about 4 servings.

SAVORY CARROT STICKS

6 med. carrots, peeled
⅓ c. finely chopped onion
⅓ tbsp. butter
¼ tsp. thyme
Salt and pepper to taste
1 tbsp. finely chopped parsley

Cut the carrots into 2-inch sticks or julienne-style (General Information, page 32) and place in the top of a double boiler. Add the onion, butter, thyme and 1 tablespoon water. Cover and cook over boiling water for 30 minutes or until crisp tender. Season with salt and pepper. Turn into serving dish and sprinkle with the parsley. This makes about 4 servings.

CARROT LOAF

½ c. fine bread crumbs
2½ c. mashed cooked carrots
2 eggs
1 c. milk
1 tsp. sugar
½ tsp. salt
1 tsp. finely chopped onion
2 tbsp. melted butter
¾ c. chopped peanuts

Combine the crumbs and carrots and blend well. Beat the eggs and milk together. Add the egg mixture and remaining ingredients to the carrot mixture. Turn into greased molds or a shallow baking dish, then place in a pan of water. Bake in a preheated 350-degree oven for 30 minutes. Remove from molds or cut into squares to serve. This makes 6 to 8 servings.

creamed peppered carrots

creamed peppered carrots

Highlight your dinner table with color as well as flavor and offer Creamed Peppered Carrots for the yellow vegetable on your menu. If you wish to be very elaborate, serve them in small pastry boats as shown.

CREAMED PEPPERED CARROTS

4 c. diced carrots
¼ c. whipping cream
¼ c. melted butter
Salt to taste
1 tsp. freshly ground pepper

Cook the carrots in a small amount of salted water until very tender. Drain the carrots. Process ¼ of the carrots, ¼ of the cream and ¼ of the butter at a time in the blender until all is puréed. Add the salt and pepper to the purée. Spoon into a mound onto a heatproof serving dish and shape with the tines of a fork. Make a well in the center and pour additional cream into the well. Serve immediately or reheat in a 275-degree oven if necessary. This may be served in pastry boats (page 43), if desired. This makes 6 to 8 servings.

cauliflower

Cauliflower has a look of distinction. However, the more appealing aspect of cauliflower is its taste, which most of us discovered in Cauliflower with Mornay Sauce, page 17. The following recipes are three further examples of the good taste and versatility of this crunchy, white vegetable. Cheese, bread crumbs, eggs and parsley make Cauliflower Soufflé an excellent presentation. An unusual but delicious combination of flavors found in Cheese-Sesame Cauliflower is sour cream and sesame seed. The colorful and irresistible combination of Brussels sprouts, green peas, carrots and cauliflower make our Cauliflower And Vegetable Dish the perfect vegetable course.

CHEESE-SESAME CAULIFLOWER

1 med. cauliflower
Salt and pepper to taste
1 c. sour cream
1 c. shredded longhorn cheese
3 tsp. toasted sesame seed

Separate the cauliflower into flowerets and place in a vegetable steamer. Steam according to instructions on page 7. Remove from steamer and place half the cauliflower in a 1-quart casserole. Season with salt and pepper. Spread half the sour cream over the cauliflower, then sprinkle with half the cheese and half the sesame seed. Repeat layers. Bake in a preheated 350-degree oven for 5 to 10 minutes or until heated through. This makes about 4 to 6 servings.

CAULIFLOWER AND VEGETABLE DISH

1 cauliflower
1 pkg. frozen Brussels sprouts
1 pkg. frozen green peas
4 carrots, sliced
5 sm. beets
2 leeks, trimmed and sliced
2 parsnips, sliced
Melted butter
Lemon juice (opt.)

Cook the cauliflower in boiling water until tender, then drain thoroughly. Cook the Brussels sprouts and peas separately according to package directions, then pour off any remaining liquid. Cook the carrots, beets, leeks and parsnips separately in a small amount of boiling salted water until tender, then drain. Place the cauliflower in the center of a serving bowl and arrange the remaining vegetables around the cauliflower. Drizzle generously with melted butter and lemon juice and serve immediately. This may be served with Basic Hollandaise Sauce (Sauces, page 7), if desired. This makes 8 servings.

CAULIFLOWER SOUFFLÉ

3 tbsp. butter
3 tbsp. all-purpose flour
1 c. milk
½ lb. American cheese, diced
3 eggs, beaten
1½ c. chopped fresh cauliflower
1½ c. soft bread crumbs
1 tsp. finely chopped parsley
Salt and white pepper to taste

Melt the butter in a heavy saucepan over medium heat, then stir in the flour to make a smooth paste. Add the milk gradually, stirring constantly, and cook until sauce is thick and smooth. Add the cheese and stir until melted. Stir part of the cheese sauce into the eggs, then stir the eggs into the cheese sauce and cook for 1 minute longer. Combine the cheese sauce and remaining ingredients, then pour into a buttered ring mold. Place the mold in a baking dish and pour in boiling water to a depth of 1 inch. Bake in a preheated 325-degree oven for 1 hour or until set. Loosen side and invert onto serving plate. Fill the center with cooked peas or lima beans, if desired. This makes 4 to 6 servings.

cauliflower and vegetable dish

Every conscientious homemaker knows the importance of serving both a green and yellow vegetable every day to her family. Here's a vegetable medley which more than satisfies that requirement. It teams seven different vegetables together in a potpourri of nutrition and flavor. Melted butter and lemon juice add just the right zip for these vegetables.

STUFFED TOMATOES AND ZUCCHINI

4 med. zucchini
2½ c. fine soft bread crumbs
⅛ tsp. oregano
4 tbsp. melted Basic Garlic Butter *(General Information, pg. 30)*
¼ c. shredded Gruyère or Emmenthal cheese
Salt and pepper to taste
Freshly grated Parmesan cheese
4 firm ripe tomatoes
½ tsp. minced chives
1 tsp. finely chopped parsley
½ tsp. chopped tarragon
Melted butter

Trim the ends from the zucchini and cut in half lengthwise. Steam according to instructions on page 7. Remove from steamer and cool until easily handled, then scoop the pulp from centers into a bowl. Invert shells onto wire rack. Mash the pulp with a fork, and add 1 cup of crumbs, oregano, 2 tablespoons Basic Garlic Butter and the Gruyère cheese. Season with salt and pepper, then mix well. Spoon into the zucchini shells and sprinkle tops generously with Parmesan cheese. Place the stuffed shells in a jelly roll pan. Cut the tomatoes in half crosswise and scoop out centers into a bowl. Invert shells onto a wire rack to drain thoroughly. Drain the juice from the pulp and reserve the juice. Combine pulp, remaining bread crumbs and half the herbs and mix well. Add remaining Basic Garlic Butter and enough of the reserved tomato juice to moisten, then season with salt and pepper. Spoon into the tomato shells and sprinkle tops with remaining herbs. Place the stuffed tomato halves in a jelly roll pan. Drizzle zucchini halves and tomato halves generously with melted butter. Bake in a preheated 375-degree oven for 15 minutes or until heated through and golden. Serve immediately. This makes 8 servings.

cooking with corn

Few vegetables are as delicious or as universally popular as corn. As a year-round taste tempter, corn is as convenient as your market, pantry or freezer.

Fresh corn may be selected from several varieties of yellow and white. Hybrid yellow corn is tender when fully mature. This variety is sweeter and contains more starch than white corn. White corn is best before it reaches maturity. The kernels should be small, tender and very juicy.

When buying fresh corn, choose ears with husks that are crisp and green. Tassels should be moist and golden. Avoid pale, dry husks and corn with shriveled or over-developed kernels.

FRESH CORN-CHEESE QUICHE

4 ears of fresh corn
5 eggs
1½ c. half and half cream
¼ c. freshly grated Parmesan cheese
2 tbsp. finely chopped onion
2 tbsp. finely chopped pimento
1 tsp. salt
⅛ tsp. freshly ground pepper
1 unbaked 9-in. Basic Savory Short Pastry
    Pie Shell (Desserts, pg. 12)
6 slices bacon

Cut the kernels off the cobs and set aside. Beat the eggs in a large mixing bowl, then stir in the cream. Add the cheese, onion, pimento, salt and pepper and mix well. Stir in the corn kernels and pour into the pie shell. Bake in a preheated 400-degree oven for 25 minutes. Fry the bacon in a skillet over low heat until partially done, then drain. Arrange the bacon over the corn mixture and bake for 20 minutes longer or until a knife inserted in the center comes out clean. Garnish with fresh parsley. This makes 6 servings.

fresh corn-cheese quiche

This hearty corn casserole adds color and flavor to any menu. Note the golden cheesy texture which gives an appealing contrast to the crispy pie shell. Succulent bacon strips complement the cheese flavor. Topped with fresh green parsley, this tempting "quiche" is perfect for the family dinner table or for your most particular guest.

fresh corn on the cob and confetti corn

The ears of corn may be placed in a baking pan after the butter, salt and pepper have been added, then broiled until lightly browned. Do not place toothpicks or holders in the ends of corn until after broiling. This makes 6 servings.

FRESH CORN ON THE COB

6 ears of corn
Melted butter
Salt and pepper to taste

Husk the corn, then remove the silks. Rinse each ear under cold running water, rubbing with the hands or a brush to remove any remaining silks. Cut the stems off as close as possible to the cobs. Fill a kettle ¾ full with water and bring to a boil. Add the ears of corn, one ear at a time, and bring water back to a boil. Reduce heat and cover. Simmer for 8 to 10 minutes or until the corn is tender, then drain the corn. Brush with butter and sprinkle with salt and pepper. Force a round, wooden toothpick or corn holders into each end of each ear of corn to serve.

CONFETTI CORN

6 ears of corn
¼ c. butter
¼ c. chopped green sweet pepper
¼ c. chopped red sweet pepper
1 tbsp. finely chopped fresh parsley

Remove the husks and silks from the corn. Cook the corn in boiling water for 8 to 10 minutes or until tender, then drain. Cool until easily handled and cut kernels from the cobs. Melt the butter in a saucepan. Add the green pepper, red pepper and parsley and cook over low heat, stirring constantly, until peppers are tender. Stir in the corn and heat through. This makes 6 servings.

fresh corn on the cob and confetti corn

Variety is the key to vegetable dishes. Here fresh corn has been prepared in two different ways. Sliced right from the cob and gently cooked, corn kernels seasoned with sweet peppers and spices, make a zesty and colorful dish. Boiled Fresh Corn On The Cob is very succulent but for another taste treat, try grilled Fresh Corn On The Cob. Brush the boiled corn with melted butter and place it on the grill for several minutes until lightly browned.

fresh southern corn pudding

Dairy-fresh eggs, butter and milk are blended with fresh corn cut from the cob to make this moist, corn pudding. Topped with garden parsley and served right from the oven, this luscious corn pudding is hard to resist.

FRESH SOUTHERN CORN PUDDING

2 c. fresh corn, cut from cob
2 tsp. sugar
1 1/2 tsp. salt
1/8 tsp. pepper
3 eggs, lightly beaten
2 tbsp. butter
2 c. milk

Combine the corn, sugar, salt and pepper in a bowl. Add the eggs and mix well. Place the butter and milk in a saucepan and heat until the butter is melted. Blend with the corn mixture. Turn into a greased 1-quart casserole, then place the casserole in a pan of hot water. Bake in a preheated 350-degree oven for 1 hour or until a knife inserted in the center comes out clean. Garnish with fresh parsley. This makes 6 servings.

CORN CASSEROLE

8 ears of fresh corn
2 eggs, well beaten
2 tbsp. grated onion
1/4 c. melted butter
3/4 tsp. salt
Dash of pepper
3/4 c. milk

Remove the husks and silks from the corn. Cut off the tips of the kernels, then scrape the cobs to remove all corn. Add the eggs and onion and mix well. Stir in the butter, salt, pepper and milk, then place in a buttered baking dish. Bake in a preheated 350-degree oven for 40 minutes or until set in the center. This makes 8 servings.

BAKED CHEESE-CORN CUSTARD

2 green onions, finely minced
3 tbsp. butter
3 tbsp. all-purpose flour
1/2 tsp. salt
2 c. milk
1 c. grated Cheddar cheese
1 tsp. sugar
2 tbsp. minced pimento
1/2 tsp. marjoram
2 No. 2 cans whole kernel corn, drained
2 eggs, slightly beaten
1/2 c. bread crumbs
Paprika

Sauté the onions in the butter in a skillet until golden, then blend in the flour and salt. Add the milk gradually, stirring constantly, then cook and stir over medium heat until thickened. Blend in the cheese, then add the sugar, pimento and marjoram. Stir the corn into the cheese sauce until well mixed. Add the eggs and blend thoroughly. Pour into a shallow 2-quart casserole. Sprinkle with the crumbs and sprinkle lightly with paprika. Bake in a preheated 350-degree oven for 35 minutes. This makes 8 servings.

BAKED CORN FONDUE

1 1/2 c. hot milk
1 1/2 c. soft bread crumbs
1 17-oz. can cream-style corn
2 c. grated Cheddar cheese
1/8 tsp. salt
1/8 tsp. white pepper
3 eggs, separated

Combine the milk, crumbs, corn, cheese and seasonings in a large bowl and mix well. Beat the egg yolks well, then stir into the corn mixture. Beat the egg whites until stiff peaks form. Stir 1/4 of the egg whites into the corn mixture thoroughly, then fold in the remaining egg whites gently. Turn into a 1 1/2-quart casserole. Bake in a preheated 325-degree oven for 1 hour or until golden brown. This makes 4 to 6 servings.

french-fried potatoes

What goes better with hamburgers than French fries or with fish than chips? No matter what you call them, French fries are a delicious addition to any menu.

Even though French fries are available in frozen form, the most delicious ones are those prepared in your own kitchen. Cut them in lengthwise strips then place them in cold water approximately an hour before cooking. This insures crispness, prevents discoloration and removes some of the starch. After soaking the potato strips, drain and dry thoroughly just before frying. French fries should be cooked in hot, deep fat until crisp on the outside and mealy on the inside. They're done when they turn a golden brown color.

Before serving, drain French fries thoroughly on paper towels. Season them with salt and be sure to serve them hot to enjoy their peak flavor and crispness.

1 Peel and cut potatoes into strips, using the largest strip cutter on a mandoline or vegetable cutter. Let stand in cold water for at least 30 minutes. Dry thoroughly, then, place in frying basket.

2 Lower basket into hot oil in deep-fat fryer. Cook until the potatoes rise to the top of the oil and brown.

3 Remove the basket from the fryer and let the excess oil drain back into the fryer.

4 Turn potatoes out onto absorbent toweling and sprinkle with salt.

homemade french-fried potatoes

Delicious French fries are so much tastier and economical when prepared at home. Note the difference in the quantity of the two plates of French fries. The home cooked fries are certainly more appetizing in appearance. In spite of their convenience, frozen French fries lack the texture and flavor of homemade ones. Correct preparation yields French fries which are both nutritious and appealing.

homemade potato chips

Potato chips were created quite by accident. A fussy eater in a Saratoga, New York, restaurant angrily refused his French fries, complaining that they were not thin enough. The enraged chef quickly sliced a batch of potatoes as thin as paper. He dropped the slices in boiling fat and fried them quickly until crisp. The angry diner was delighted by the thin potatoes. "Saratoga Chips", as they were called, soon became a national food favorite. With popularity, the name was changed to the familiar "potato chips."

Although commercial potato chips which are quick fried in cottonseed oil and packaged are very good, those prepared in your own kitchen are unsurpassed in flavor.

HOMEMADE POTATO CHIPS

6 med. Idaho potatoes, peeled
Vegetable oil
Salt

Cut the potatoes very thin on the slicing blade of mandoline or vegetable cutter. Place in a large bowl of ice water. Let stand for at least 1 hour. Drain and dry thoroughly on paper towels. Arrange a layer in frying basket, then lower into the hot deep fat. Fry until lightly browned and crisp. Drain, then place on paper towels and sprinkle with salt. This makes about 6 to 8 servings.

homemade potato chips

There is an exciting burst of flavor in these light-as-air potato chips. From cutting board to table, these homemade chips are simple to prepare and a delight to serve. They are excellent as snacks and delicious served with your favorite dip.

CRISPY NIBBLES

2 lg. peeled Idaho potatoes
Lemon juice
½ c. vegetable oil
Salt and pepper to taste

Cut the potatoes with the mandoline, using the julienne blade or grate on coarse side of grater. Shape potatoes into patties and sprinkle with lemon juice. Slide a patty onto a pancake turner, then into the hot oil in a frypan. Cook until golden brown on both sides. Repeat until all the potatoes are used. Season with salt and pepper and serve immediately. This makes about 4 servings.

HOW TO CUT MATCHSTICK OR STRAW POTATOES

Cut potatoes for Crispy Nibbles by pushing the potato carefully down the smallest fluted side or julienne blade. The strips should be very fine.

how to make potato baskets

potato baskets

Fried to perfection, these crunchy Potato Baskets filled with matchstick potatoes taste as good as they look. Serve Potato Baskets with meats or fried fish for added flavor and flair.

1 Peel the potatoes. Push the potato downward over the fluted mandoline blade, or vegetable cutter, having the blade set to cut slightly thicker than 1/8 inch. Discard the first slice, then turn the potato halfway around and push over fluted blade again, making a waffle. Repeat until all potatoes are waffled, then soak in cold water for at least 30 minutes.

2 The special equipment used here is a pair of bird's nest frying baskets, sometimes referred to as "nids." These frying baskets are essential to make the delicate potato bird's nests; they are available in most gourmet cookware shops.

3 Separate baskets and heat thoroughly in hot vegetable oil or shortening. Arrange waffled slices in larger basket to completely line basket

4 Place hot smaller basket over waffle slices and clip together to hold firmly. Fry in hot oil for several minutes or until brown.

5 Remove from oil and unclip baskets. Lift out smaller basket, then tip larger basket to remove potatoes. Drain on absorbent paper.

cabbage leaf rolls

Here is one way serving leftovers can be popular. Diced ham or beef from the previous night's meal will be welcomed back to the table when served in Cabbage Leaf Rolls. This entrée is a meal in itself when served on a bed of noodles, preferably green.

CABBAGE LEAF ROLLS

1 med. firm head cabbage
2 c. ground cooked ham
1 c. mashed carrots
1 c. mashed potatoes
Salt and pepper to taste
Basic Beef Stock (*Soups, pg. 2*)
1 egg, lightly beaten
5 tbsp. butter
1 med. onion, finely chopped
2 tbsp. cornstarch
2 tbsp. dry Madeira
1 12-oz. package green noodles
1 tbsp. crushed thyme

Remove the core from the cabbage, then cover with boiling water. Let stand until leaves are easily detached, then remove 16 large leaves. Cut the coarse section from base of each leaf. Combine the ham, carrots, potatoes, salt, pepper, 2 tablespoons of stock and egg and blend thoroughly. Shape into 8 rolls. Place the rolls in the center of 8 cabbage leaves, then overlap edges, tucking in the top and bottom edges. Place, fold side down, on remaining cabbage leaves and repeat procedure, securing rolls with string. Steam for 45 minutes according to steaming instructions on page 7. Melt 2 tablespoons of butter in a skillet and sauté the onion until tender but not browned. Sprinkle with paprika and stir in 1³/₄ cups of stock. Dissolve the cornstarch in ¹/₄ cup of stock and add to the onion mixture. Cook, stirring constantly, until thickened. Stir in 1 tablespoon of butter and the Madeira. Prepare the noodles according to package instructions and drain well. Melt the remaining butter in saucepan, then stir in noodles and thyme, tossing to coat well. Place noodles in a shallow, heated serving dish and top with cabbage rolls. Garnish with peeled tomato strips as shown in the illustration and spoon a small amount of sauce over the cabbage rolls. Serve with the remaining sauce. An equal amount of ground, cooked beef may be substituted for the ham, if desired. This makes 8 servings.

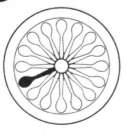

introducing celery

Subtle flavor for soups and stuffings . . . crisp, cold snack or appetizer . . . delicious boiled, fried or sautéed accompaniment for poultry or roasts . . . These are a few of the versatile uses of celery. This crunchy, stalked vegetable, so popular with dieters, is often overlooked as a side dish; however, as the following recipe for Sweet And Sour Celery And Onions will illustrate, it has a great deal of flavor potential.

Sold in bunches, celery is available year round. To prepare it for storage, remove the leaves from the stalks (saving the fresh green ones for soups and salads!), cut away coarse root ends, then wash the stalks thoroughly. Refrigerate in a plastic bag, or place stalks in a jar half filled with water. Either storage method will keep celery crisp for several weeks.

CELERY AMANDINE

2 tbsp. butter
1/3 c. blanched whole almonds
4 c. diagonally sliced celery
1 chicken bouillon cube, crushed
2 tbsp. minced onion
1 tsp. monosodium glutamate
1/2 tsp. sugar
1/8 tsp. garlic powder
1/8 tsp. ground ginger

Melt the butter in a skillet over low heat. Add the almonds and sauté until lightly browned. Add the celery, bouillon cube, onion, monosodium glutamate, sugar, garlic powder and ginger. Stir until well mixed. Cook for 10 minutes or until the celery is crisp-tender. This makes about 4 servings.

sweet and sour celery and onions

The flavor combination of celery, onions and bacon with a hint of vinegar and sugar is great! Diagonally cut celery is sautéed, just until crisp tender, in a small amount of the bacon drippings for added flavor.

AVERY ISLAND CELERY

4 tbsp. butter
1 onion, chopped
1 1-lb. 4-oz. can tomatoes
1/2 tsp. hot sauce
1 tsp. salt
1/4 tsp. sugar
1/4 tsp. dried thyme leaves or 1 tsp. fresh thyme
4 c. diagonally cut celery
1 10-oz. package frozen peas, thawed

Melt the butter in a large skillet. Add the onion and sauté until soft and transparent. Drain the tomatoes, reserving the liquid. Add hot sauce, salt, reserved tomato liquid, sugar, and thyme to the onion mixture. Bring to a boil and add the celery and peas. Cover and simmer for 5 minutes or until the celery is crisp-tender. Chop the tomatoes and add to the celery mixture. Heat through before serving. This makes 6 servings.

SWEET AND SOUR CELERY AND ONIONS

1 bunch fresh celery
6 slices bacon
1 c. sliced onion rings
3 tbsp. cider vinegar
1 tbsp. sugar
1/4 tsp. salt
1/4 tsp. white pepper

Trim the celery and cut ribs or stalks into 1-inch pieces. Fry the bacon in a large skillet until crisp. Remove the bacon and drain on paper towels. Drain all but 3 tablespoons bacon drippings from skillet, then add the celery and onion rings. Sauté for 5 minutes, stirring occasionally. Reduce the heat and cook, covered, for 12 to 15 minutes or until vegetables are crisp-tender. Stir in the vinegar, sugar, salt and white pepper and heat through. Spoon into a serving dish and crumble bacon over the top. This makes 6 servings.

cooked and uncooked sautéed potatoes

The procedure for sautéing both Cooked and Uncooked Potatoes is very similar — yet the slight difference is important! As shown in the how-to illustrations, that difference is raw potatoes must be sautéed slowly over *low* heat until soft, at which point the heat may be increased and the sautéing carried out exactly as with cooked potatoes.

Whether the cook begins with raw potatoes or previously cooked ones, the result is a crisp, brown-tinged side dish that is an ideal accompaniment to, for example, Shallow-Fried Round Steaks (Beef, pg. 9).

1 Slice both raw and cooked potatoes ¹/₁₆ inch thick. Pour enough oil in a skillet to just cover bottom and heat. Slide cooked potatoes into hot oil as shown on left. Place raw potato slices in skillet individually, as shown on right side, because moisture will cause raw potatoes to stick together.

2 Sauté the cooked potatoes over medium heat until lightly tinged with brown. Pour off excess oil, then brown evenly. Sauté the raw potatoes over low heat until soft, then drain off the excess oil and cook until brown.

3 Shake pan occasionally while potatoes are browning, then turn to brown other side. Turn out on paper towels to drain. Sprinkle with salt and pepper before serving.

provençal tomatoes

With little effort, a homemaker can give tomatoes a gourmet flair and sophistication. Halved tomatoes are spread with a paste made of bread crumbs, parsley, garlic and a few drops of olive oil. When broiled until soft, the result is called Provençal Tomatoes. These tomatoes have a robust flavor, making them a delicious combination with Steak Diane (Beef, pg. 10).

PROVENÇAL TOMATOES

4 med. tomatoes
2 cloves of garlic, pressed
½ c. fine soft bread crumbs
1 tbsp. minced parsley
Salt and pepper to taste
Olive oil

Cut tomatoes in half crosswise and make crisscross incisions ¼ inch deep in the top of each tomato half. Combine the garlic, bread crumbs, parsley, salt and pepper in a small bowl. Blend with a small amount of olive oil to make a paste. Spread the paste evenly over tomato halves. Brush lightly with olive oil and place on a broiler rack. Broil 8 inches from source of heat until tomatoes are heated through and the tops are golden brown. This makes 4 servings.

FRENCH WHITE BEAN CASSEROLE

French White Bean Casserole has all the flavor excitement and gusto to be expected of a dish that originated with the French peasantry. Basically, it is a mixture of dried white beans, ham, chicken, and salami, with a layer of bread crumbs over the top to form an attractive, light brown crust. This meaty dish is well suited to hearty man-sized appetites, and served with red wine, as shown, the casserole has a spirited, European air.

If a refresher in the handling of dried beans is needed, review the information on page 46 of the Vegetables section.

FRENCH WHITE BEAN CASSEROLE

1 1-lb. package Great Northern beans
2 tsp. salt
½ c. diced salt pork
1½ c. diced cooked ham
2 c. chopped onions
1½ c. diced carrots
2 c. diced skinned tomatoes (Vegetables, pg. 27)
3 sm. cloves of garlic, pressed
2 bay leaves
2 tbsp. chopped parsley
½ tsp. oregano
1 tsp. freshly ground pepper
4 c. Basic Chicken Stock (Soups, pg. 2)
½ lb. hard salami, slivered
2 c. diced cooked dark chicken meat
2 c. fine soft bread crumbs

Rinse the beans thoroughly in cold, running water. Then place the beans in a large saucepan and add enough water to cover. Bring to a boil and boil for 2 minutes. Remove from heat and let stand for 1 hour. Bring to a boil again before stirring in the salt. Reduce the heat and simmer for 1 hour and 30 minutes or until almost tender. Fry the pork over low heat until golden, then stir in the ham, onions, carrots and tomatoes. Add the garlic, bay leaves, parsley, oregano and pepper and blend thoroughly. Stir in the stock and bring to a boil. Reduce heat to low and simmer for 30 minutes. Drain the beans and place in a 4-quart casserole. Add the salami and chicken, then pour the sauce over all, stirring to blend thoroughly. Bake, covered, in a preheated 350-degree oven for 30 minutes, stirring at 10-minute intervals. Sprinkle the bread crumbs evenly over the top and pat gently. Reduce oven temperature to 300 degrees. Bake for 30 minutes longer or until the crumbs are browned. This makes 15 servings.

introducing fresh asparagus

Like onions, garlic and leeks, asparagus is a member of the lily family, with about 150 known species. The best known, especially to homemakers, is the garden asparagus with its delicious spring stalks.

In 1965, asparagus was among the 24 principal vegetable crops produced in the United States. One hundred and two million pounds were produced, of which 62.4 million were supplied by the chief asparagus producing state California.

Asparagus is divided into two general color categories. The more well-known and widely used is a dark, rich green. Much less prevalent is a light green or whitish type.

When buying fresh asparagus, always select spears that have firm, closed or compact tips. Avoid those which have tips partially opened, spread or wilted. They are likely to be too tough and fibrous.

As with all fresh vegetables, asparagus should be cooked as soon as possible in order to make the most of flavor and texture. Store it in the refrigerator for no longer than 2 or 3 days, and if possible prepare it on the day of purchase.

Fresh asparagus is best during the months from March through June, and it is especially abundant during the peak months of April and May. However, throughout the remaining months of the year, frozen and canned asparagus are adaptable to most asparagus recipes.

If you have avoided serving asparagus because you didn't know how to prepare it or your family didn't like it, the following easy step-by-step illustrations for steaming fresh asparagus plus our 4 asparagus recipes will expand your culinary resources for new and exciting asparagus dishes.

how to cook fresh asparagus

1 Trim bases of asparagus to make the spears equal lengths, then scrape lower portion of each spear lightly to remove tough fibers.

2 Remove the perforated container from a vegetable steamer. Place the asparagus spears, cut side down, in the container.

3 Place the perforated container in the steamer. Pour in enough boiling, salted water to fill just to the beginning of asparagus tips, then cover. Simmer until asparagus spears are tender.

fresh asparagus with cream sauce

The rich green color of fresh asparagus with a creamy sauce accompaniment make Fresh Asparagus with Cream Sauce an ideal vegetable presentation. The natural goodness of asparagus accented with a rich sauce made of cream, eggs, milk and butter make an irresistible flavor combination.

ASPARAGUS CASSEROLE WITH ALMONDS

1 14½-oz. can green asparagus spears or 1½ lb. fresh asparagus, steamed
3 hard-boiled eggs, chopped
6 slices crisp-fried bacon, crumbled
½ c. slivered almonds
Salt and freshly ground pepper to taste
1 10½-oz. can cream of mushroom soup
1 c. grated American cheese
½ c. fine bread crumbs

Drain the asparagus and place in a shallow baking dish. Sprinkle the eggs over the asparagus, then add the bacon and almonds. Sprinkle with salt and pepper. Cover with the soup and cheese, then sprinkle with the bread crumbs. Bake in a preheated 350-degree oven for 30 minutes or until bubbly and golden brown. This makes about 6 servings.

ASPARAGUS AND SHRIMP ORIENTAL

1 lb. fresh shrimp
1 can water chestnuts
1 c. sliced fresh mushrooms
1 med. onion, sliced
1 c. diagonally sliced celery
1 lg. can cut asparagus spears, drained or 1½ lb. fresh asparagus, steamed
1 11-oz. can mandarin orange sections, drained
2 tbsp. vegetable oil
½ tsp. salt
¼ tsp. freshly ground pepper
2 tbsp. sugar
2 tbsp. soy sauce
1 recipe Basic Boiled Rice (Cereals, pg. 3)

Prepare the shrimp according to instructions for Boiled Shrimp, (Seafood, pg. 14). Shell and devein the shrimp. Drain and slice the water chestnuts. Arrange the shrimp, chestnuts, mushrooms, onion, celery, asparagus and mandarin oranges on a large tray. Heat the oil in a chinese wok or electric skillet. Add the onion, celery, salt, pepper and sugar. Cook, stirring, until the vegetables are crisp-tender. Add the asparagus and shrimp, then place the mushrooms and water chestnuts over the shrimp. Sprinkle with the soy sauce and place the orange sections on top. Cover and cook until the mixture begins to steam. Reduce the heat and simmer for about 12 minutes. Serve on the rice. This makes about 6 servings.

FRESH ASPARAGUS WITH CREAM SAUCE

2 lb. fresh asparagus
¼ c. butter
¼ c. all-purpose flour
¾ c. milk
¾ c. half and half cream
2 hard-boiled eggs, minced
2 tbsp. fresh lemon juice

Cook the asparagus as shown in the step-by-step illustrations on page 73. Keep warm. Melt the butter in the top of a double boiler over hot water, then blend in the flour with a wooden spoon. Add the milk and cream gradually, stirring constantly, and cook over low heat until smooth and thick. Reserve 1 teaspoon of minced egg, then add the remaining egg to the sauce and mix well. Place the asparagus in a serving dish and sprinkle with the lemon juice. Pour the cream sauce in a gravy boat and sprinkle with the reserved egg. This makes 4 servings.

SWEET AND SOUR ASPARAGUS

2 lb. fresh asparagus
⅔ c. white vinegar
½ c. water
¼ c. salad oil
¼ tsp. salt
½ c. sugar
3 sticks cinnamon
1 tsp. whole cloves
1 tsp. celery seed

Prepare and cook the asparagus as shown in the step-by-step illustrations on pg. 73. Remove asparagus from steamer and set aside. Combine the vinegar, water, oil, salt, sugar, cinnamon, cloves and celery seed in a saucepan and bring to a boil. Place the asparagus spears in a shallow glass dish, then pour the vinegar mixture over the top. Cover and chill for 24 hours. Drain before serving. Equal amounts of canned, green asparagus spears may be substituted for the fresh asparagus. This makes about 6 servings.

vegetable fritters

Frying is a popular method of preparing fresh vegetables. Unfortunately, most homemakers seldom venture past French-fried potatoes, and miss the crispy goodness of other fried vegetables such as mushroom, cauliflower, eggplant and zucchini fritters. The French term for fritters is *beignets*, pronounced be-nay. With the simple Basic Fritter Batter, you can prepare delectable fritters with many different vegetables.

mushroom fritters with rémoulade sauce

Though these crispy mushroom fritters are a delightful vegetable dish, they are also excellent as an hors d'oeuvre. The creamy accompaniment is Basic Rémoulade Sauce, (Sauces, pg. 11), made with mayonnaise, mustard, capers, parsley, chives and anchovy paste.

BASIC FRITTER BATTER

1½ c. sifted all-purpose flour
1 tsp. salt
2 tbsp. oil
1 egg, well beaten

Sift the flour and salt together into a medium bowl. Add the oil, egg and about 1 cup of cold water or enough to make a thick batter. If the batter does not adhere to the vegetables, add 1 or 2 tablespoons of water to the batter. This makes about 2 cups of batter.

MUSHROOM FRITTERS WITH RÉMOULADE SAUCE

½ lb. small fresh mushrooms
1 recipe Basic Fritter Batter
1 recipe Basic Rémoulade Sauce *(Sauces, pg. 11)*

Remove the stems from the mushrooms. Dip the mushrooms in the batter to coat the entire surface. Drop into hot oil at 370 degrees in a deep fat fryer. Fry until lightly browned on all sides. Remove from fat and drain on paper toweling. Serve with Basic Rémoulade Sauce. Drained, canned button mushrooms may be coated with this batter and fried the same way, if fresh mushrooms are not available. This makes about 6 servings.

ASSORTED VEGETABLE FRITTERS

1 sm. eggplant
1 recipe Basic Fritter Batter (pg. 75)
1 zucchini, cut in ¼-in. slices
1 sm. cauliflower, separated into flowerets

Prepare the eggplant for frying according to the instructions on page 13. Dip the eggplant slices into the fritter batter, one piece at a time, then drop, several at a time, into hot oil at 370 degrees in a deep fat fryer. Brown on one side, then turn and brown the other side. Remove with a slotted spoon and drain on paper toweling. Place on an ovenproof platter and keep warm until all the vegetables are cooked. Dip the remaining vegetables in the batter and fry as for eggplant. Serve with Basic Dill Sauce (Sauces, pg. 28-29) or Hot Herb Cream, if desired. This makes about 6 to 8 servings.

HOT HERB CREAM

¾ c. half and half cream
1 tsp. basil leaves
1 tsp. chopped parsley
¼ tsp. thyme leaves
Salt and freshly ground pepper to taste

Combine all the ingredients in a small saucepan and bring just to a boil. Serve hot with the vegetable fritters for dipping. This makes about ¾ cup of sauce.

assorted vegetable fritters

Assorted Vegetable Fritters make an ideal vegetable dish for any meal. This selection includes cauliflower, eggplant and zucchini fritters attractively garnished with sprigs of parsley. These delicious, hot fritters may also be served for hors d'oeuvres.

potato flan

This flan is a delicious combination of potatoes, bacon, cheese and onion. Its decorative appearance, as well as its excellent flavor, make it a superb choice for a buffet dinner.

POTATO FLAN

5 or 6 med. potatoes
¹/₂ recipe Basic Savory Short Pastry *(Desserts, pg. 12)*
1 med. onion, finely chopped
6 slices cooked bacon, crumbled
Salt and pepper to taste
¹/₂ c. grated med. sharp Cheddar or Swiss cheese
1 egg
¹/₂ c. half and half cream

Cook the potatoes with the peeling in a pressure cooker for about 10 to 15 minutes. Cool and peel the potatoes. Roll out about ³/₄ of the pastry. Line an 8-inch flan pan or pie pan with the pastry, then prick the bottom generously with the tines of a fork. Cover the base of the pastry with the onion and bacon. Slice the potatoes and place in layers over the onion and bacon until the pastry shell is almost filled. Sprinkle with salt, pepper and cheese. Blend the egg and cream together thoroughly, then pour over the potatoes. Roll out the remaining pastry and follow the step-by-step illustrations for a trellis top. Place over the flan. Bake in a preheated 375-degree oven on the middle shelf for about 30 minutes or until pastry is golden brown. Slice and serve hot. This makes about 4 servings.

how to make trellised pastry

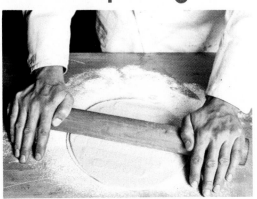

1 Roll out pastry and cut a circle the size of plastic cutter. Place the pastry over the indented side of cutter and roll over the top with rolling pin.

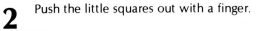

2 Push the little squares out with a finger.

3 Remove pastry carefully from cutter and place on baking sheet until ready to use.

4 Push out any remaining pastry squares from cutter. Little squares of pastry may be baked and served as tidbits.

onion flan

This beautiful dish is an Onion Flan, made of soft-fried, seasoned onions and anchovy fillets. The decorative squares are made with split anchovies and centered with black olives. The flavor of onions and anchovies is accented with garlic and butter. Serve this highly seasoned flan with your favorite wine.

ONION FLAN

½ **recipe Basic Savory Short Pastry** *(Desserts, pg. 12)*
¼ **c. butter**
2 **tbsp. olive oil**
5 **c. thinly sliced onions**
1 **clove of garlic, crushed**
16 **anchovy fillets**
24 **pitted black olives**

Roll out the pastry about ¼ inch thick to fit an 11-inch flan ring. Place in the ring and trim. Prick the bottom of the pastry generously with a fork. Combine the butter and oil in a large skillet and heat until the butter is melted. Add the onions and garlic and sauté over low heat, stirring frequently, until onions are transparent and golden. Turn into the pastry-lined flan ring. Cut the anchovy fillets in half, lengthwise, then arrange trellis fashion over the onion mixture. Press the olives into the squares. Bake in preheated 375-degree oven for about 30 minutes or until pastry is golden brown. Cut into wedges and serve immediately. This makes about 6 servings.

sweet-sour yams and pineapple

Boldly colorful, Sweet-Sour Yams and Pineapple is an eye-catching dish, well suited for a buffet. A glistening coat of syrup, made from pineapple juice and cornstarch, gives the vegetables an appealing sheen.

SWEET-SOUR YAMS AND PINEAPPLE

1 No. 2 can sliced pineapple
1 tbsp. cornstarch
¼ tsp. salt
3 tbsp. lemon juice
2   1-lb. cans yams, drained
4 green onions, diagonally sliced
½ c. diagonally sliced celery
½ c. green sweet pepper chunks
2 tbsp. vegetable oil

Drain the pineapple and reserve the syrup. Combine the cornstarch, reserved syrup and salt in a small saucepan and stir until blended. Bring to a boil over medium heat, stirring constantly, then cook until thickened. Stir in the lemon juice. Arrange the pineapple and yams in a casserole and pour the sauce over the yam mixture. Cover. Bake in a preheated 350-degree oven for about 25 minutes or until heated through. Sauté the onions, celery and green pepper in the oil in a skillet over medium heat for about 4 minutes or until crisp-tender. Stir into the yam mixture, then place in a serving dish. This makes 8 servings.

FAR EASTERN FRESH POLE BEANS

2 lb. fresh pole beans
2 tbsp. peanut oil
1 c. Basic Chicken Stock *(Soups, pg. 2)*
1 tbsp. cornstarch
Salt to taste

Cook the pole beans in boiling water until crisp-tender, then drain well. Heat the oil in a large skillet. Add the beans and cook, stirring constantly until heated through. Stir in the stock and cover. Cook over high heat for 3 minutes. Blend the cornstarch and 2 tablespoons of water until smooth. Push the beans to the side of the skillet, and stir the cornstarch mixture into the broth. Stir the beans into the broth and cook, stirring constantly, until the broth is slightly thickened and the beans are glazed. Season with salt. Place the beans in a serving bowl. Garnish with Sweet And Sour Pork (Pork, pg. 11) if desired. Serve pieces of candied ginger as an accompaniment. This makes 6 to 8 servings.

far eastern fresh pole beans

Irresistible hints of oriental cooking will tempt even the least enthusiastic vegetable eaters in your household. Far Eastern Fresh Pole Beans have been garnished with Sweet and Sour Pork and served with pieces of crystallized ginger as accompaniment.

how to grow your own bean sprouts

In the Far East where meat is considered a luxury, vegetables dominate the meals. (Even when meat is served, Orientals use it sparingly, cutting it up into small pieces and mixing it with vegetables.) For this reason, they have developed the art of preparing vegetables in a manner that will preserve the maximum taste and nutritive value.

One of the vegetables which serves as a source of protein is the mung bean. The sprouts of the small, green mung bean — which we simply refer to as bean sprouts — are typical of Chinese cuisine and a frequent ingredient in oriental recipes. Although canned bean sprouts are available, as with any food, fresh ones are much better. You can easily grow them at home, as we illustrate, and the experience is not only fun and interesting, but a rewarding one in terms of eating pleasure.

It takes only a few days for the beans to sprout. After you remove them from beneath the layers of toweling, rinse them in a pan of cold water. Stir them back and forth, and within minutes the husks will loosen and separate from the sprouts. Then they are ready to be cooked immediately, or stored in cold water for up to a week. During storage, the water should be changed daily.

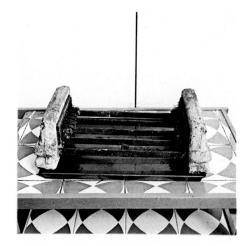

1 Bean sprouts are usually grown in a cellar. Here is an improvisation. A firm heavy rack is placed on a jelly roll pan on an out-of-the-way surface.

2 A fairly deep wooden box is placed over the rack and a piece of heavy burlap is tacked tightly over the surface of the box. The burlap is dampened thoroughly with water and sprinkled heavily with beans

3 The beans are watered thoroughly and a fruit crate is inverted over them.

4 The top and sides of the crate are covered completely with dripping towels to provide darkness and the necessary moisture. The beans are watered and the towel wet every day for 4 days.

5 The beans are just beginning to sprout.

6 The bean sprouts are ready to be washed after 7 days. The green beans and brown roots are discarded and the bean sprouts are ready to be cooked.

MANDARIN VEGETABLES

¼ c. olive oil
1 c. bean sprouts
¼ c. sliced bamboo shoots
¼ c. sliced fresh mushrooms
1 c. shredded cabbage
¼ c. sliced celery
½ c. green peas
3 tbsp. soy sauce
½ tsp. monosodium glutamate
½ tsp. sugar
Salt to taste

1 c. chicken broth
1 tbsp. cornstarch

Heat the oil in a large skillet over high heat. Add the bean sprouts, bamboo shoots, mushrooms, cabbage, celery and green peas and stir-fry as shown in the illustrations (Beef, pg. 18) for 2 to 3 minutes. Stir in the soy sauce, monosodium glutamate, sugar, salt and ¾ cup of the broth. Reduce the heat and simmer, covered, for 6 to 8 minutes. Mix the remaining broth with the cornstarch, then stir into the vegetable mixture. Cook for about 5 minutes longer or until the sauce is thickened, stirring occasionally. This makes 4 servings.

preparing vegetables

The most alluring and tantalizing aspect of an oriental dish is its texture, created in part by fresh, crisp vegetables. The Chinese cook their vegetables quickly and minimally, so that the original flavor, color, texture and crispness are not lost.

When you prepare Fresh Vegetables with Pork, the emphasis is on the first word of the title — use only the freshest mushrooms, celery, peppers and onions. The finished creation will be one upon which a Ming emperor would smile.

FRESH VEGETABLES WITH PORK

¼ c. butter
4 c. diagonally sliced celery
½ lb. fresh mushrooms, halved
1 med. green sweet pepper, sliced
1 med. red sweet pepper, sliced
1 med. onion, sliced
2 c. cubed cooked pork
1¼ c. Basic Beef Stock *(Soups, pg. 2)*
1 tbsp. cornstarch
3 tbsp. soy sauce
½ tsp. salt
½ tsp. ginger
½ tsp. freshly ground pepper

Melt the butter in a wok or medium-sized skillet. Add the celery and sauté for 5 minutes. Stir in the mushrooms, green and red pepper and onion and sauté for 5 minutes longer. Stir in the pork and stock and bring to a boil. Reduce heat and simmer for 5 minutes. Blend the cornstarch with the soy sauce, salt, ginger and pepper, then stir into the pork mixture. Cook, stirring constantly, for about 5 minutes or until heated through and thickened. Serve over rice, if desired. This makes 6 servings.

VEGETABLE TEMPURA

3 or 4 carrots
6 sm. white radishes
1 sm. eggplant
2 sweet potatoes
1 sm. cauliflower
3 or 4 stalks celery
12 sm. okra pods
12 lg. mushroom caps
1 recipe Basic Tempura Batter *(Seafood, pg. 28)*

Cut the carrots and radishes into bite-sized pieces. Peel the eggplant and sweet potatoes and cut into strips. Separate the cauliflower into flowerets and cut the celery into diagonal slices. Dry all of the vegetables thoroughly and chill well. Coat the vegetables with batter and fry as instructed in the step-by-step illustrations No. 2 through No. 4 (Seafood, pg. 28), placing the vegetables in the batter one type at a time. This makes 10 to 12 servings.

CHOW CHOY

¼ c. olive oil
½ to 1 tsp. cayenne pepper
1 clove of garlic, pressed
Salt to taste
4 c. Chinese cabbage or chopped celery
2 tbsp. soy sauce
2 tbsp. red wine vinegar
1 tsp. monosodium glutamate
1 tsp. sugar
1 tsp. sugar
3 green onions or scallions, chopped
1 tbsp. cornstarch

Heat the oil in a large skillet over medium heat. Stir in the cayenne pepper, garlic and salt. Add the cabbage and soy sauce and stir-fry as shown in the illustrations (Beef, pg. 18) for 2 minutes. Add the vinegar, monosodium glutamate, sugar and onions and stir-fry for 1 minute. Mix the cornstarch with 2 tablespoons water until smooth, then stir into the cabbage mixture. Stir-fry for 3 minutes longer or until the cabbage mixture is lightly browned. This makes about 4 servings.

fresh vegetables with pork

Fresh Vegetables with Pork is a nutritious, complete meal in one dish. Typical of cooking in China where meat is scarce, the cubed pork is used thriftily, but to its best advantage.

FRESH TOMATO-CORN CASSEROLE

6 med. fresh tomatoes
½ c. chopped fresh celery
½ c. chopped fresh green sweet pepper
½ c. chopped fresh onion
Salt to taste
2 c. fresh corn, cut from cob
3 hard-boiled eggs, sliced
2 c. Basic White Sauce (Sauces, pg. 4)

Peel and chop 5 of the tomatoes. Place in a saucepan and add the celery, green pepper and onion. Cook, stirring occasionally, for 15 minutes, then stir in the salt. Place half the mixture in a casserole, then add half the corn. Arrange the egg slices over the corn, then add half the white sauce. Add the remaining tomato mixture, then add the remaining corn. Cover with the remaining white sauce. Bake in a preheated 350-degree oven for about 45 minutes or until set. Slice the remaining tomato and arrange on the casserole. Broil until the tomatoes are hot. Garnish with parsley. This makes 6 servings.

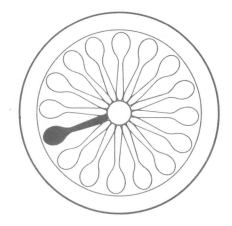

introducing
brussels sprouts

If you have ever referred to Brussels sprouts as "tiny cabbages," you were exactly right. They are one of many varieties of the cabbage family. Brussels sprouts are the buds which grow close to the stem of a tall, cabbage-like plant.

Fresh Brussels sprouts are marketed in the fall and winter months during their peak growing season. As with all fresh vegetables, it is very important to know how to pick the best and freshest produce. In selecting Brussels sprouts, choose those which are hard, small and compact. The larger, loose heads usually indicate age and a harsh flavor. Avoid those with yellow leaves because they are usually wilted.

Before preparation, Brussels sprouts should be washed thoroughly and soaked in heavily salted water for 10 to 15 minutes in order to remove dirt or any insects among the leaves. Then they may be cooked in boiling, salted water until just tender.

Brussels sprouts are delicious simply seasoned with salt, pepper and butter. They also combine well with other foods and sauces. Brussels sprouts with cheese and noodles is a particularly good combination and you will discover many more when you prepare the following recipes.

brussels sprouts with cheese-noodle ring

This attractive dish is a savory vegetable-pasta combination. The ring of noodles is made by baking tender, boiled noodles in a well-greased ring mold in a pan of hot water. The noodle ring is then unmolded, drizzled with melted cheese and filled with tender-cooked Brussels sprouts.

BRUSSELS SPROUTS WITH CHEESE-NOODLE RING

4 c. fresh Brussels sprouts
1¼ tsp. salt
3 tbsp. butter
⅛ tsp. freshly ground pepper
Cheese-Noodle Ring

Wash and trim the Brussels sprouts. Place in a saucepan containing 1 inch of boiling water and add the salt. Bring to a boil and cook for 5 minutes. Cover and reduce the heat. Simmer for 15 minutes or until the Brussels sprouts are crisp-tender, then drain. Add the butter and pepper and toss lightly until the butter is melted. Spoon most of the Brussels sprouts into the center of the Cheese-Noodle Ring and place the remaining Brussels sprouts around the ring. This makes 6 servings.

CHEESE-NOODLE RING

1 lb. wide noodles
3 tbsp. butter
2 c. grated Cheddar cheese
2 tsp. Worcestershire sauce

Cook the noodles in boiling, salted water until tender, then drain. Add the butter and toss until butter is melted. Pour into a well-greased ring mold and place the mold in a pan of hot water. Bake in a preheated 350-degree oven for 25 minutes. Unmold onto a serving plate. Melt the cheese in a double boiler and stir in the Worcestershire sauce, then pour over the noodle ring.

BRUSSELS SPROUTS IN SOUR CREAM

2 10-oz. packages frozen Brussels sprouts
¾ c. sour cream
½ c. toasted slivered almonds

¼ c. chopped pimento
1 tsp. sugar
½ tsp. freshly ground pepper
1 tsp. salt

Cook the Brussels sprouts in ½ cup of boiling, salted water for 7 to 9 minutes or until crisp-tender, then drain. Combine the Brussels sprouts, sour cream, almonds, pimento, sugar, pepper and salt in the top of a double boiler and toss lightly with a fork. Place over hot water for 7 minutes or until heated through. Turn into a serving dish and serve hot. This makes about 6 servings.

BRUSSELS SPROUTS IN CELERY SAUCE

8 c. fresh Brussels sprouts
2 tsp. salt
1½ c. diced celery
6 tbsp. butter
6 tbsp. all-purpose flour
Milk
Dash of freshly ground pepper

Remove and discard any wilted Brussels sprouts leaves, then wash and soak for 10 minutes in cold, salted water. Cook the Brussels sprouts in a small amount of water for 7 to 9 minutes or until tender, then drain. Pour 2¼ cups of water into a medium-sized saucepan and bring to a boil. Add 1 teaspoon of salt and celery and cook for 15 minutes. Drain the celery and reserve the liquid. Melt the butter in the top of a double boiler over boiling water, then stir in the flour with a wooden spoon until smooth. Combine the reserved liquid with enough milk to measure 4 cups. Stir into the flour mixture gradually and cook until smooth and thick, stirring constantly. Add the celery, remaining salt and pepper. Place the Brussels sprouts in a serving dish and pour the sauce over the Brussels sprouts. This makes 8 servings.

mushroom and tomato bake

The flavorful combination of mushrooms, tomatoes and hazelnuts and fried bread crumbs makes this an irresistible dish. Season this mixture with salt, pepper and marjoram, and top it with a bright red, skinned tomato.

MUSHROOM AND TOMATO BAKE

½ c. butter
4 c. fine soft bread crumbs
2 c. finely chopped hazelnuts or pecans
4 lg. tomatoes
½ lb. fresh mushrooms, chopped
Salt and freshly ground pepper to taste
1 tsp. dried crushed marjoram

Melt 6 tablespoons of the butter in a frypan. Add the bread crumbs and hazelnuts and cook over medium heat, stirring constantly, until crisp and golden. Set aside. Skin the tomatoes according to the instructions on page 27, then chop coarsely. Melt the remaining 2 tablespoons of butter in a frypan, then add the tomatoes and mushrooms and cook, stirring, until the tomatoes are soft. Place half the mushroom-tomato mixture evenly in 4 buttered individual baking dishes and season with salt, pepper and half the marjoram. Place half the bread crumb mixture evenly over each mushroom mixture, then repeat the layers. Bake in a preheated 375-degree oven for 30 minutes or until well browned. Garnish with additional skinned tomatoes. This makes 4 servings.

SPINACH SOUFFLÉ WITH HAM AND CHEESE SAUCE

2 c. chopped cooked spinach
½ c. milk
4 slices sandwich bread
½ c. softened butter
4 eggs, separated
3 tbsp. minced fresh parsley
1 c. sour cream
1 tsp. salt
½ tsp. freshly ground white pepper
½ recipe Basic Mornay Sauce (Sauces, pg. 11)
1 c. diced ham

Drain the spinach thoroughly, then place in a tea towel or piece of muslin and wring as dry as possible. Pour the milk over the bread and let stand until the milk is absorbed. Wring the bread as dry as possible and set aside. Cream the butter in a mixer bowl with an electric mixer until light, then add the egg yolks, one at a time, beating well after each addition. Beat in the parsley, spinach and bread mixture, then beat in the sour cream until thoroughly blended. Season with the salt and white pepper. Beat the egg whites until stiff peaks form. Fold ¼ of the egg whites into the spinach mixture, then fold in remaining egg whites until well blended. Spoon into a heavily greased pudding mold and cover tightly with the lid. Place in the steamer. Add boiling water to just below the rack. Bring to a boil, then cover the steamer. Reduce heat to low and steam for 1 hour and 45 minutes, keeping the water level just below the rack. Combine the Mornay sauce with the ham in the top of a double boiler over hot water and heat through. Unmold the spinach souffle and serve with the sauce. This makes 6 to 8 servings.

fresh green beans with cherry tomatoes

Fresh green beans seasoned and flavored with butter, black pepper and chopped parsley are accented with bright red cherry tomatoes. Use only fresh vegetables when preparing this dish.

LIMA BEAN-ASPIC FLAN

½ **recipe Basic Savory Short Pastry (Desserts, pg. 12)**
2½ **c. baby lima beans**
½ **tsp. celery salt**
1 **recipe Basic Emergency Aspic (Salads, pg. 4)**
2 **hard-boiled eggs**
1 **end slice of peeled tomato**

Roll the pastry out on a lightly floured surface to fit into a 12 x 8-inch rectangular flan pan or a round, 11-inch flan pan with a removable bottom. Fit the pastry into the pan carefully, then trim. Bake blind according to the step-by-step illustrations No. 1 through No. 3 (Desserts, pg. 14) in a preheated 400-degree oven for 10 minutes. Reduce the oven temperature to 375 degrees and bake for 15 minutes longer or until golden brown, then continue with step No. 4. Cook the beans in boiling salted water until tender, then drain. Add the celery salt and mix well, then cool. Chill the aspic by stirring over a bowl of ice until syrupy. Spoon the beans into the flan case. Pour half the aspic over the beans, then chill until set. Cut 10 petals lengthwise from the egg whites and arrange over the beans, forming 2 flowers. Cut 2 small circles from the tomato slices and place in the center of the petals as illustrated. Spoon the remaining aspic over the egg white flowers and lima beans and chill until set. This makes about 6 to 8 servings.

FRESH GREEN BEANS WITH CHERRY TOMATOES

1 **lb. fresh green beans**
1¼ **tsp. salt**
3 **tbsp. butter**
½ **tsp. sugar**
Pinch of freshly ground pepper
1½ **tbsp. chopped fresh parsley**
8 **cherry tomatoes, halved**

Wash the beans and remove the tips, then cut into 1-inch pieces. Place in a saucepan with 1 inch of boiling water and 1 teaspoon of salt. Cook for 5 minutes, then cover and cook over medium heat for 10 to 15 minutes or just until crisp-tender. Drain, if necessary. Add the butter, sugar, pepper, remaining salt and parsley and toss lightly until the butter is melted and the beans are coated. Place in a serving bowl and garnish with the cherry tomato halves. This makes about 6 servings.

lima bean-aspic flan

Lima Bean-Aspic Flan is a show-off dish, ideal for a party buffet or summer luncheon. The crusty case is made with Basic Savory Short Pastry (Desserts, pg. 12). It may be surrounded with lettuce leaves and asparagus tips. The beans, in clear aspic, are attractively garnished with boiled egg petals and tomato centers.

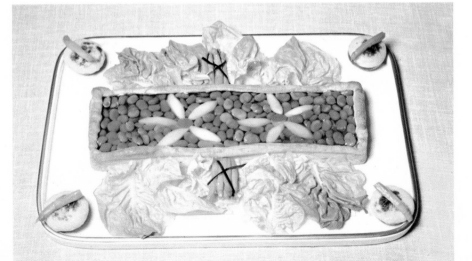

florence fennel

Sweet fennel, a member of the parsley family, is a very versatile plant. Its feathery leaves are used frequently as an herb in fish cookery; its seeds are used as an aromatic flavoring and its layered, flat root can be cooked and served as a vegetable as in the following recipe for Florence Fennel.

FLORENCE FENNEL

2 lg. bunches fennel
½ recipe Basic Mornay Sauce (Sauces, pg. 11)
½ c. freshly grated Parmesan cheese
½ c. fine fresh bread crumbs
¼ c. melted butter

Trim and wash the fennel thoroughly in cold water. Cook the stalks in boiling, salted water to cover for about 35 minutes or until just tender. Drain well, then cut into 2-inch lengths. Place ½ of the Mornay sauce over the bottom of a greased casserole. Place the fennel over the sauce and spoon the remaining Mornay sauce over the fennel. Mix the cheese and bread crumbs and sprinkle over the sauce. Pour the butter over the top. Bake in a preheated 350-degree oven for about 15 to 20 minutes or until lightly browned. This makes about 6 servings.

scalloped eggplant

Alternating layers of eggplant, fresh corn, ground beef, and spices make this eggplant dish a meal in itself. After baking to juicy tenderness, it is topped with wedges of ripe, fresh tomatoes.

SCALLOPED EGGPLANT

1 lg. eggplant
2 tbsp. olive oil
½ c. chopped onion
2 tbsp. chopped green sweet pepper
½ lb. ground lean chuck
1 ½ c. cut fresh corn
2 tsp. salt
½ tsp. oregano
½ tsp. freshly ground pepper
1 egg, lightly beaten
¼ c. grated American cheese

Cut the eggplant into 1-inch cubes. Place the eggplant in a bowl with salted water to cover. Weigh the eggplant down with a plate and let soak for 15 minutes, then drain. Cook in boiling, salted water for 10 minutes or until tender, then drain well. Pour the oil into a skillet and place the skillet over medium high heat. Add the onion, green pepper and ground chuck, and cook, stirring constantly, until the meat loses its red color. Add the corn and cook, stirring, for 5 minutes longer. Remove from heat and cool slightly. Add the eggplant, salt, oregano, pepper and egg and mix well. Stir in the cheese, then place in a greased 2-quart casserole. Bake in a preheated 350-degree oven for 30 minutes or until heated through. Garnish with fresh tomato wedges. This makes about 6 servings

creamed vegetable stew

Fresh vegetables and salt pork are combined, much like a chowder, to make this rich Creamed Vegetable Stew. Careful preparation will insure a colorful, superbly flavored stew.

CREAMED VEGETABLE STEW

Prepared in several simple steps, Creamed Vegetable Stew is a hearty way to warm the coldest day. Flour and milk are added to the salt pork and gently cooked until the mixture is thickened. It is important that the mixture not be boiled hard after the milk has been added to prevent scalding the mixture. When the vegetables are added to the pork, the stew should be maintained at a simmer to prevent the vegetables from becoming mushy.

CREAMED VEGETABLE STEW

1 c. diced carrots
1 c. cubed potatoes

½ c. diced green sweet pepper
½ c. sliced green onions
1 c. diced celery
Salt
½ lb. salt pork
½ c. all-purpose flour
4 c. milk

Place the carrots, potatoes, green pepper, onions and celery in a large saucepan and add 2 teaspoons of salt and enough water to cover the vegetables. Bring to a boil, then reduce the heat and simmer until the vegetables are tender. Drain and set aside. Wash the salt pork and remove the rind. Cut the salt pork into cubes and place in a large saucepan. Cook over medium heat until the cubes are brown, stirring frequently. Add the flour and mix well. Stir in the milk and bring just to a boil, stirring constantly. Reduce the heat and simmer until the mixture is thickened. Season with salt to taste. Add the vegetables and heat through. This makes about 8 servings.

DRIED PEAS AND BEAN DISHES

As has been stated before, for economy, nutrition, versatility and ease of preparation, few vegetables can compare with dried peas and beans. They may be purchased any time of year and stored for long periods of time without spoilage. Dried peas and beans may be prepared in a variety of ways by altering cooking methods and varying seasonings and spices. Since early colonial times, different sections of the country have developed traditional favorites.

Cranberry Baked Beans is a variation of the New England favorite Boston Baked Beans. This dish is made distinctive by adding cranberry juice and ginger to a basic baked bean recipe. Savory Black Bean Casserole is a hearty mixture of beans, green and yellow vegetables, and ham tidbits. When served over hot rice, this Southwestern bean dish is a meal in itself. Hopping John is a classic Southern dish which is traditionally served on New Year's Day for good luck.

CRANBERRY BAKED BEANS

1 ½ c. dried pea beans
1 ½ tsp. salt
2 c. cranberry juice cocktail
⅓ c. chopped onion
2 tbsp. molasses
1 tsp. dry mustard
⅛ tsp. ginger
¼ c. catsup
2 tbsp. dark brown sugar
¼ lb. salt pork, sliced

Place the beans, salt, cranberry juice and 2 cups of water in a large saucepan, then bring to a boil. Remove from heat and let stand for 1 hour. Bring to a boil again, then cover and simmer until the beans are tender, adding water if needed. Drain the beans and reserve the liquid. Combine the beans with the remaining ingredients except the salt pork. Place half the bean mixture in a bean pot or 2-quart casserole. Top with half the salt pork. Repeat the layers, then add 1 ½ cups of the reserved bean liquid. Bake, covered, in a preheated 250-degree oven for 5 to 7 hours. Uncover and bake for 1 hour longer, adding more reserved liquid, if needed to keep the beans from drying. This makes 6 to 8 servings.

SAVORY BLACK BEAN CASSEROLE

1 ½ c. dried black beans
1 c. chopped onions
½ c. chopped green sweet pepper
½ c. chopped carrot
2 cloves of garlic
2 whole cloves
1 bay leaf
1 tsp. salt
½ tsp. hot sauce
2 tbsp. vegetable oil
1 c. diced cured ham
1 recipe Basic Boiled Rice *(Cereals, pg. 3)*

Wash the beans, then place in a large saucepan. Add 4 cups of water and let stand for 1 hour. Do not drain. Reserve 2 tablespoons of the onions. Add the remaining onions, green pepper, carrot, garlic, cloves, bay leaf, salt and hot sauce to the beans, then bring to a boil. Reduce the heat and simmer for 1 hour or until the beans are tender but still whole, adding boiling water, if needed. Remove the garlic, cloves and bay leaf. Pour the oil into a small skillet and place over medium low heat. Add the ham and reserved onion and cook, stirring constantly, until lightly browned. Place the rice around the outside of serving bowl, then pour the bean mixture into the center of the bowl. Spoon the ham mixture onto the center of the bean mixture. This makes 6 servings.

HOPPING JOHN

1   8-oz. package dried black-eyed peas
1 ham hock, halved
1 sm. onion, chopped
1 tsp. salt
1 tsp. cayenne pepper
1 c. long grain rice

Soak the peas in cold water to cover for 1 hour, then drain. Place the ham hock in a large saucepan and cover with water. Cook for 30 minutes. Add the peas, onion, salt, cayenne pepper and enough water to cover. Cook, covered, for 45 minutes, adding water as needed. Stir in the rice, then cover. Cook for 30 minutes longer or until the rice and peas are tender. Remove the ham hock and discard the bone and fat. Stir the ham back into the Hopping John. May add 1 can of tomatoes, if desired. This makes about 6 servings.

hopping john

Hopping John is a delicious, Southern-style, vegetable dish, made with black-eyed peas and rice. It is particularly popular on New Year's Day.

LIMA BEANS

Lima beans, as with other vegetables, can be served with a flair. This dish, especially rich and filling, is easily prepared. First make the Rough Puff Pastry the day before. On serving day make the pastry case, prepare the special *thick* Basic Mornay Sauce, cook the beans, assemble all and viola! — an elegant vegetable dish.

LIMA BEANS IN PUFF PASTRY

1 recipe Rough Puff Pastry (Desserts, pg. 27)
1 recipe Basic Mornay Sauce (Sauces, pg. 11)
2 c. cooked baby lima beans

Roll out the pastry on a chilled floured surface to-1/2-inch thick rectangle, then trim to 14 x 7 inches. Set pastry trimmings aside for baking hors d' oeuvres or freeze for future use. Cut the rectangle in half, making two 7-inch squares, then place 1 square carefully on a lightly floured baking sheet. Prick thoroughly with the tines of a fork. Fold the remaining square in half, then cut an outer frame 1 inch wide as shown in illustration No. 2 on page 26 of the Desserts section. Moisten edges of the pricked square with cold water and place the frame carefully onto the moistened dough. Press the frame gently down onto the base and even the edges. Open the folded pastry and roll out slightly, keeping the pastry square. Place on another lightly floured baking sheet and prick thoroughly with the tines of a fork. Place the case and top in a pre-heated 425-degree oven. Bake for 10 minutes. Reduce the oven temperature to 350 degrees and bake the top for 5 to 10 minutes longer or until golden. Bake the case for 15 to 20 minutes longer or until golden. Cool on wire racks. Prepare the Basic Mornay Sauce, using the white sauce ingredients for thick sauce. Combine the beans and half the sauce in a heavy saucepan, then heat thoroughly, stirring frequently. Place the pastry case on a serving dish and pour the hot beans and sauce into the case. Cut pastry top in half and place over the beans as in the illustration. Serve with the remaining Mornay sauce. To double the amount of servings, double the amounts of beans and sauce and make a 10-inch pastry case. This recipe makes 4 servings.

lima beans in puff pastry

A golden case of Rough Puff Pastry is filled with lima beans and Basic Mornay Sauce. Although homemade puff pastry is more flavorful, the frozen (puff pastry) patty shells may be substituted.

ARTICHOKES

Once you have mastered the technique of preparing fresh artichokes (Vegetables pg. 50), you can vary the flavor of this tender vegetable by combining it with sauces. For a taste treat, steamed artichokes are served with a creamy Basic Hollandaise Sauce (Sauces, pg. 7). For the time conscious cook, artichokes are delicious when served with quick Blender Hollandaise Sauce (Sauces, pg. 7)

ARTICHOKES WITH HOLLANDAISE SAUCE

6 fresh artichokes
1 recipe Basic Hollandaise Sauce (Sauces, pg. 7)

Prepare and cook the artichokes according to the instructions and step-by-step illustrations for Globe Artichokes Vinaigrette on page 50, omitting the Basic Vinaigrette. Serve in individual dishes with the hollandaise sauce on the side for dipping. This makes 6 servings.

Artichokes with Cold Corn Salad is a western-style dish with both visual and flavor appeal. The artichokes may be prepared ahead of time, following basic directions for cooking artichokes (pg. 50). The artichokes are then stuffed with the chilled corn salad and topped with Chili Mayonnaise for extra flavor.

ARTICHOKES WITH COLD CORN SALAD

2   10-oz. packages frozen whole kernel corn
2/3 c. chopped green sweet pepper
3/4 c. sliced cooked carrots
2 tbsp. finely chopped onion
1/2 c. Basic Blender Mayonnaise (Sauces, pg. 3)
1 tsp. chili powder
1/8 tsp. seasoned salt
1/8 tsp. freshly ground pepper
6 fresh artichokes
Chili Mayonnaise

Cook the corn, then drain and cool. Place in a large bowl. Add the green pepper, carrots, onion, mayonnaise, chili powder, salt and pepper and mix well. Chill the mixture. Prepare and cook the artichokes according to the instructions and step-by-step illustrations for Globe Artichokes Vinaigrette on page 50, omitting the Basic Vinaigrette, then chill. Fill the artichokes with the corn salad and place on a serving platter. Serve with Chili Mayonnaise. This makes 6 servings.

CHILI MAYONNAISE

1 c. Basic Blender Mayonnaise (Sauces, pg. 3)
1 tsp. chili powder
1/2 tsp. seasoned salt
Dash of freshly ground pepper
1 tbsp. lemon juice

Place all of the ingredients in a small bowl and mix until blended, then chill.

new potatoes (pommes nouvelles)
potato-tuna chowder
cheese soufflé-stuffed potatoes

The versatile potato can be used in an almost
endless variety of ways. Pommes Nouvelles, the
French term for new potatoes, is a delicious dish
prepared in classic French style. Diced potatoes
and tuna are combined with stock and vegetables
for a hearty Potato-Tuna Chowder. This is served
in the large tureen. For a special mealtime
accompaniment, fluffy Cheese Soufflé-Stuffed
Potatoes garnished with fresh parsley is perfect —
and will also become a family favorite.

POTATO-TUNA CHOWDER

2 ½ c. diced potatoes
2 c. Basic Chicken Stock *(Soups, pg. 2)*
2 tbsp. fresh minced onion
½ tsp. salt
¼ tsp. sage
¼ tsp. paprika
Dash of white pepper
½ c. sliced fresh carrots
½ c. cut fresh green beans
½ sliced fresh celery
3 c. milk
1 7-oz. can chunk-style tuna, drained

Combine 1 cup of the potatoes, chicken stock,
onion and salt in a large saucepan and bring to a
boil. Reduce the heat and cover. Simmer for 10 to
15 minutes or until the potatoes are tender. Add
the sage, paprika and pepper, then mash the
potatoes. Add the remaining 1 ½ cups of potatoes,
the carrots, beans, celery and milk to the mashed
potatoes and bring just to a boil. Reduce heat and
simmer for about 15 minutes or until the vegetables are tender. Break the tuna into chunks and
add to the chowder. Simmer for 5 minutes longer.
This makes 4 to 6 servings.

NEW POTATOES
(POMMES NOUVELLES)

2 lb. new potatoes
2 c. Basic Chicken Stock *(Soups, pg. 2)*
½ tsp. salt
1 tbsp. butter
¼ tsp. white pepper
1 ½ tsp. cornstarch
2 tbsp. chopped fresh green onion tops or chives

Wash and scrape the potatoes. Place in a large
saucepan and add the chicken stock and salt. Bring
to a boil, then reduce heat. Cover and simmer for
15 to 20 minutes or until the potatoes are tender.
Drain the potatoes and reserve 1 cup of the stock.
Pour the reserved stock into a small saucepan and
add the butter and pepper. Bring to a boil. Mix the
cornstarch with 1 tablespoon of water, then stir
into the broth mixture. Cook for 1 minute or until
slightly thickened and transparent, stirring constantly. Place the potatoes in a serving bowl, then
pour the sauce over the potatoes. Garnish with the
chopped onion tops or chives. This makes 6 to 8
servings.

CHEESE SOUFFLÉ-STUFFED POTATOES

4 med. baking potatoes
¼ c. warm milk
1 tbsp. butter
1 tsp. salt
Dash of white pepper
2 eggs, separated
¼ c. grated Cheddar cheese

Wash the potatoes and dry thoroughly. Grease the
potatoes, then place in a baking pan. Bake in a preheated 425-degree oven for about 1 hour or until
the potatoes are soft. Remove from the oven, then
reduce the oven temperature to 350 degrees. Cut a
slice from the top of each potato. Scoop out the
potato pulp and place in a large bowl. Reserve the
shells. Add the milk, butter, salt and pepper to the
potato pulp and beat with an electric mixer until
fluffy. Add the egg yolks and cheese and beat until
mixed. Beat the egg whites until stiff peaks form,
then fold into the potato mixture. Fill the reserved
shells with the potato mixture and place in the
baking pan. Bake for 25 to 30 minutes or until
browned. Place on a serving platter and garnish
with fresh parsley, if desired. This makes 4 servings.

VEGETABLE KEBABS WITH SEASONED BUTTER SAUCE

2 med. zucchini
12 cherry tomatoes
6 lb. fresh mushrooms
½ c. melted butter
1 tbsp. parsley flakes
¾ tsp. onion powder
½ tsp. garlic powder
¼ tsp. pepper

Cut off the ends of the zucchini, then cut each zucchini into 6 slices. Arrange the tomatoes, zucchini and mushrooms on 6 skewers as shown in the illustration. Pour the butter into a small bowl. Add the parsley flakes, onion powder, garlic powder and pepper and mix well. Brush over the kebabs. Place on a grill over hot coals and cook for about 10 minutes or until the vegetables are tender, turning and brushing with the butter mixture frequently. This makes 6 servings.

butter beans in cream

*This flavorful vegetable dish is
made from dried butter beans
and an irresistible combination of
onions, garlic, carrots,
ham and cream. To add color,
sprinkle it with fresh parsley
before serving.*

BUTTER BEANS IN CREAM

1 lb. dried white butter beans
2 tsp. salt
1 onion
1 clove of garlic, pressed
2 sm. carrots, diced
1 c. diced ham
1 *Bouquet Garni (Appetizers, pg. 2)*
Freshly ground pepper to taste
¹/₂ c. half and half cream

Rinse the butter beans with cold water, then place
in a large saucepan and cover with cold water.

Bring to a boil, then remove from the heat and let
stand for 5 minutes. Drain, then cover again with
cold water. Add the salt, onion, garlic, carrots, ham
and *Bouquet Garni*. Bring to a boil, then cover and
let simmer for 1 hour and 30 minutes or until beans
are tender. Remove the onion, if desired, and the
Bouquet Garni, then season with the pepper. Stir
in the cream and serve immediately. This makes 8
to 10 servings.

pommes anna

Pommes Anna or Anna Potatoes, is an unusual potato dish introduced by the renowned French chef *Escoffier*, well known for hundreds of extravagant gourmet dishes.

The secret in preparing *Pommes Anna* is to slice the potatoes paper thin. Then follow instructions closely for seasoning and placing the slices in a casserole. If prepared properly, the slices will form a round shape while baking, and will retain this attractive shape when inverted onto a serving dish.

There is a baking utensil available which is especially designed for preparing *Pommes Anna*. However, made of copper, it is usually extravagantly expensive, and not at all necessary to the taste or appearance of these delectable potatoes. You may use any round, deep casserole, and a cover of aluminum foil, as we did in our following recipe.

POMMES ANNA

2 lb. potatoes
½ c. melted butter
¼ c. grated onion
Salt and white pepper to taste

Peel the potatoes and cut into paper-thin slices. Brush the bottom and side of a 6½ x 3-inch soufflé dish generously with butter. Arrange the potatoes, overlapping the slices, around the side of the soufflé dish to form a firm wall, then place an overlapping layer of potatoes in the bottom of the dish to cover. Brush lightly with butter and sprinkle lightly with onion, salt and pepper. Repeat the layers until all ingredients are used, then cover lightly with foil. Bake in a preheated 400-degree oven for 30 minutes. Remove the foil and bake for 30 minutes longer or until the top is well browned. Unmold on a heated serving platter. This makes 6 to 8 servings.

pommes anna

Here is an absolutely delicious way to serve potatoes. Pommes Anna is made of paper-thin potato slices, seasoned and baked to form this attractive shape. Cooked properly, the potatoes will be firm enough to slice.

potato puffs with almonds and beignet potatoes

Potato Puffs with Almonds (left) are made with a fluffy mixture of eggs, flour, potatoes and water, formed into balls and rolled in flaked almonds. Then each coated ball is fried in hot oil to a golden brown. Beignet Potatoes (right) are simply potato puffs without almonds.

POTATO PUFFS WITH ALMONDS

¼ c. butter
½ c. water
6 tbsp. all-purpose flour
2 eggs
3 c. riced or sieved cooked potatoes
1 tsp. salt
½ tsp. white pepper
1 c. sliced blanched almonds

Combine the butter and water in a small saucepan and place over low heat until the butter is melted and the water comes to a boil. Increase the heat to medium and add the flour. Remove from the heat and beat until smooth. Add the eggs, one at a time, beating well after each addition. Cover and let stand until cold. Do not refrigerate. Dry the potatoes in a pan over low heat, stirring constantly. Add the egg mixture, salt and pepper and blend thoroughly. Shape into walnut-sized balls, using 1 tablespoon of potato mixture for each, then roll in almonds until coated. Fry several balls at a time in hot, deep fat about 375 degrees until golden brown, then drain on paper toweling. This makes 20 to 25 potato puffs.

BEIGNET POTATOES

1 recipe Potato Puffs with Almonds mixture
1 c. finely diced cooked ham
All-purpose flour

Prepare the potato puffs as instructed, adding the ham to the potatoes with the egg mixture and seasonings. Shape into walnut-sized balls and roll in flour instead of the almonds. Fry several balls at a time in hot, deep fat about 355 degrees until golden brown, then drain on paper toweling. This makes 25 to 30 potato puffs.

mushroom-stuffed tomatoes

These elegant Mushroom-Stuffed Tomatoes are amazingly easy to prepare. Simply scoop out plump, fresh tomatoes, season with salt and place a fresh mushroom in each. Then brush with butter and bake in a buttered casserole for 20 minutes. Chopped parsley makes an ideal garnish.

MUSHROOM-STUFFED TOMATOES

6 firm fresh tomatoes
Salt to taste
6 lg. fresh mushrooms
2 tbsp. melted butter

Cut a slice from the top of each tomato, then scoop out enough pulp to insert a mushroom. Sprinkle cavities lightly with salt. Remove the stems from the mushrooms and place 1 mushroom in each tomato, cavity side up. Brush tops with the melted butter and arrange the tomatoes in a baking dish. Bake in a preheated 350-degree oven for 20 minutes or until the mushrooms are tender. Garnish with parsley, if desired. This makes 6 servings.

BROILED TOMATOES NAPOLI

4 lg. tomatoes
1 c. fresh bread crumbs
¼ c. melted butter
2 tbsp. freshly grated Parmesan cheese
½ tsp. Italian seasoning or oregano

Cut the tomatoes into thick slices and arrange in a shallow baking pan. Combine the crumbs, butter, cheese and seasoning, blending well, then spoon over the tomato slices. Broil 10 inches from the source of heat for 5 minutes or until heated through and golden brown. This makes 6 to 8 servings.

DEVILED TOMATOES

4 lg. tomatoes, halved
Salt and freshly ground pepper to taste
Cayenne pepper to taste
2 tbsp. buttered bread crumbs
2 tbsp. butter
½ tsp. prepared mustard
⅛ tsp. hot sauce
2 tsp. Worcestershire sauce
1 tsp. sugar
1½ tbsp. vinegar
1 egg yolk

Arrange the tomato halves in shallow baking pan, cut side up, then sprinkle lightly with the salt, pepper, cayenne pepper and bread crumbs. Melt the butter in a small saucepan, then stir in the mustard, hot sauce, Worcestershire sauce, sugar, vinegar and additional salt to taste. Beat the egg yolk lightly, then stir in a small amount of the vinegar mixture. Stir egg yolk into the vinegar mixture and simmer, stirring constantly, until smooth and thickened. Broil tomatoes 10 inches from the source of heat for 10 minutes or until heated through and crumbs are browned. Remove to a heated serving dish and top each tomato half with a spoonful of the hot sauce. This makes 8 servings.

MAIN DISH SOUP

French Peasant Soup is a main dish soup which is actually a hearty, healthy meal in itself. It is eaten in vast quantities by the simple peasant folk of France. They accompany it only with a little local wine, French bread and a bit of cheese or fruit.

Since this reputable French soup makes such a satisfying, hearty meal, we can hardly classify it as an appetizer, so we have included it here in Vegetables.

FRENCH PEASANT SOUP

1 1-lb. package dried Great Northern Beans
1 lb. salt pork, diced
1 lb. cured ham, diced
2½ c. diced carrots
1 c. sliced leek bulbs or onions
3 c. thinly sliced celery
4 c. chopped cabbage
Bouquet Garni *(Soups, pg. 2)*
1 clove of garlic, pressed
1 tsp. freshly ground pepper
½ tsp. turmeric
6 c. water

Place the beans in a saucepan and add enough water to cover, then bring to a boil. Let stand for 1 hour, then drain well. Rinse the salt pork well and soak in cold water for 30 minutes, then drain on absorbent paper. Fry the salt pork in a heavy iron skillet until lightly browned. Drain off excess fat, leaving a small amount in the skillet. Add the ham and cook, stirring frequently, until lightly browned. Place the pork mixture in a large casserole and add the vegetables. Add the *Bouquet Garni*, garlic and seasonings, mixing well. Pour enough water over the pork mixture to cover well, then cover the casserole. Bake in a preheated 300-degree oven for 3 hours and 30 minutes. This makes 15 to 20 servings.

french peasant soup

This hearty, delicious French Peasant Soup may be made in quantity and frozen in quart containers for convenient use. It is generously filled with pork, white beans, carrots, leeks and cabbage.

cabbage

Cabbage is one of the most economical vegetables on the market today, and can be served in many delicious ways. To make the most of the flavor and appearance of fresh cabbage, cook it quickly in boiling salted water until just tender. The cabbage will then retain its natural, green color and delectable flavor.

The following vegetable dish, Baked Stuffed Cabbage, is an elegant way to serve fresh cabbage. Follow the easy instructions carefully for perfect results.

BAKED STUFFED CABBAGE

1 2-lb. fresh green cabbage
4 slices of bacon
1 tbsp. chopped fresh onion
3 tbsp. all-purpose flour
Salt and freshly ground pepper to taste
1 c. milk
1 c. shredded Cheddar cheese
2 tbsp. chopped pimento-stuffed olives

Hollow out the center of the cabbage, leaving a shell about 1/2 inch thick. Set the shell aside and chop the remaining cabbage coarsely. Fry the bacon in a skillet until crisp, then remove from skillet and drain on paper toweling. Pour off all but 3 tablespoons of the drippings, then add the onion to the drippings. Sauté until the onion is tender. Blend in the flour and season with salt and pepper. Add the milk gradually and cook, stirring constantly, until thickened. Stir in the cheese until melted, then remove from the heat. Mix the sauce with the chopped cabbage, then crumble the bacon over the top. Add the olives and blend well. Place the cabbage shell on a large piece of aluminum foil. Spoon the cheese mixture into the shell. Wrap loosely and place on a baking dish. Bake in a preheated 350-degree oven for 30 minutes. This makes 6 servings.

baked stuffed cabbage

Baked Stuffed Cabbage is made with fresh, green cabbage and a savory stuffing of onions, Cheddar cheese, olives and crispy fried bacon. Serve it straight from the oven, piping hot.

cabbage roll

CABBAGE ROLL

1 med. head white cabbage
1 lg. Spanish onion
1 lb. lean ground beef
1 tsp. Worcestershire sauce
½ tsp. paprika
⅛ tsp. tarragon leaves
⅛ tsp. rosemary
⅛ tsp. thyme
2 garlic cloves, pressed
1 egg
½ c. tomato purée
1 c. soft bread crumbs
1½ tsp. salt
¼ tsp. freshly ground pepper
Melted butter

Immerse the cabbage in boiling water in a large kettle and boil for 5 minutes, turning several times. Plunge the cabbage into ice water, then peel off the limp outer leaves. Repeat the process, then drain all of the leaves. Chop enough of the remaining firm cabbage to measure 2 cups, then place in a large bowl. Peel and grate the onion, then add to the chopped cabbage. Add the ground beef, Worcestershire sauce, paprika, tarragon, rosemary, thyme, garlic, egg, tomato purée, bread crumbs, salt and pepper to the cabbage mixture and blend thoroughly. Place a long sheet of wide aluminum foil on a working surface, then cover with buttered waxed paper. Arrange the cabbage leaves in a 14 x 9-inch rectangle on the waxed paper. Shape the beef mixture into a roll about 12 inches long and place in the center of the cabbage leaves. Bring the leaves up around the beef roll and fit over each end, then brush with melted butter. Fit the waxed paper around the cabbage roll, then wrap up with foil. Fold up the ends to seal, then tie in the center and about 3 inches from the ends with string. Place in a large, oval roaster. Add enough boiling water to almost cover the cabbage roll, then cover the roaster. Simmer for 1 hour and 30 minutes. Remove the roll from roaster with tongs. Open one end of the foil and pour off the liquid. Remove the string and foil, then remove the waxed paper carefully. Slide onto a long, narrow serving dish and garnish with shreds of green onion, onion rings and pimento as shown in the illustration. The length of the roll may be varied according to available cooking pans. This makes about 10 servings.

cabbage roll

Although this cabbage roll may look somewhat complicated, it's actually quite simple to make. The roll is brushed with butter and garnished attractively with shreds of green onions, boiled eggs, bits of fresh tomato and pimento.

ASPARAGUS WITH ORANGE AND CASHEW CREAM SAUCE

2½ lb. fresh asparagus
1 fresh orange
1 recipe Basic Béchamel Sauce (Sauces, pg. 4)
Salt to taste
½ c. chopped cashew nuts

Steam the asparagus as instructed on page 73. Section the orange according to the step-by-step illustrations (General Information, pg. 13). Cut the orange sections into large pieces, then add to the *Béchamel* sauce and mix well. Arrange the asparagus in a serving dish and sprinkle with salt. Pour the sauce over the asparagus, then sprinkle with the cashew nuts. This makes 8 servings.

ACORN SQUASH WITH SLICED APPLES

3 fresh acorn squash
Salt to taste
2 or 3 fresh tart apples
Butter
6 tbsp. brown sugar
Nutmeg to taste

Cut the squash in half and remove the seeds. Place the squash, cut side down, in a shallow, greased baking dish and add ½ cup boiling water, then cover. Bake in a pre-heated 350-degree oven for 10 minutes. Remove from oven and remove the cover. Turn the squash, cut side up, and sprinkle with salt. Peel and core the apples, then cut into wedges. Fill the squash cavities with the apples and dot generously with butter. Sprinkle each squash half with 1 tablespoon of the brown sugar, then with nutmeg. Pour ½ cup boiling water into the baking dish and bake for 30 minutes longer or until the squash and apples are tender. This makes 6 servings.

asparagus with orange and cashew cream sauce and acorn squash with sliced apples

Here are two vegetable dishes, both delicious and unusual flavor combinations. Pictured on the left is Asparagus With Orange And Cashew Cream Sauce, and on the right, Acorn Squash With Sliced Apples.

BAKED TOMATO NEPTUNE

6 lg. firm tomatoes
¼ c. chopped green sweet pepper
¼ c. grated carrots
2 tbsp. minced fresh onion
¼ c. melted butter
¼ c. all-purpose flour
2 tsp. salt
2 tsp. sugar
¼ tsp. freshly ground pepper
¾ c. coarsely chopped cooked shrimp
1   8-oz. package frozen King crab meat, flaked
1 c. coarsely chopped cooked lobster
3 tbsp. dry sherry
2 tbsp. finely chopped parsley

2 tbsp. fine bread crumbs
1 tbsp. butter

Cut a ¼-inch slice from the stem end of each tomato. Scoop out the pulp, leaving a firm ¼-inch shell, and reserve the pulp. Sauté the sweet pepper, carrots and onion in the melted butter in a large saucepan for 5 minutes, then stir in the flour, salt, sugar and pepper. Add the reserved pulp and cook over medium heat, stirring constantly, until the mixture comes to a boil and thickens. Stir in the shrimp, crab meat, lobster, sherry and parsley. Spoon the mixture into the tomato cups and arrange the cups in a greased, shallow baking dish. Sprinkle with the crumbs and dot with the butter. Bake in a preheated 375-degree oven for 15 minutes or until heated through. Garnish tops with additional parsley, if desired. This makes 6 servings.

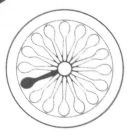

shrimp-stuffed potatoes

SHRIMP-STUFFED POTATOES

4 lg. baking potatoes
2 egg yolks
Half and half cream
4 tbsp. minced fresh parsley
2 tbsp. chopped chives
1 c. chopped cooked shrimp
½ c. grated Cheddar cheese

Place the potatoes in a baking pan. Bake in a pre-heated 375-degree oven for 1 hour or until the potatoes are tender. Do not turn off the oven. Cut a thin slice from 1 side of each potato and scoop out the pulp, leaving a firm shell. Reserve the shells. Place the pulp in a medium-sized mixer bowl and add the egg yolks, then beat with an electric mixer until smooth. Beat in enough cream to make the mixture light and fluffy. Fold in 2 tablespoons of the parsley, the chives and shrimp, then spoon the potato mixture into the reserved shells and sprinkle with the cheese. Return to the baking pan and bake about 20 minutes longer or until the cheese is melted and golden. Sprinkle each potato with ½ tablespoon of the remaining parsley. This makes 4 servings.

shrimp-stuffed potatoes

These baked potatoes contain a mixture of cream, shrimp, chives and Cheddar cheese. Sprinkle with fresh, minced parsley and serve piping hot.

ARTICHOKE HEARTS MORNAY WITH DUCHESS POTATOES

1 pkg. frozen rock lobster-tails
1 recipe Basic Garlic Butter *(General Information, pg. 30)*
2 cans artichoke hearts
1 recipe Basic Mornay Sauce *(Sauces, pg. 11)*
1 recipe Basic Duchess Potato Mixture *(pg. 3)*

Cook the lobster-tails according to package directions, then drain and cool. Remove the lobster meat from the shells and cut into bite-sized pieces. Place in a bowl. Melt the garlic butter, then pour over the lobster pieces. Marinate lobster, stirring occasionally, until ready to use. Drain the artichoke hearts thoroughly and arrange in a buttered 1 ½-quart baking dish. Pour the Mornay sauce over the artichoke hearts and pipe the duchess potato mixture around the edges of the baking dish. Drain the lobster and arrange over the Mornay sauce. Bake in a preheated 400-degree oven for 20 minutes or until the potatoes are browned and the sauce is bubbly. This makes about 6 servings.

artichoke hearts mornay with duchess potatoes

A garnish of cooked lobster-tails enhances the appearance and wonderful taste of Artichoke Hearts Mornay with Duchess Potatoes. Serve this "show-off" dish for any special occasion.

celery and cheese casserole

This celery casserole is colorful, delicious and simple to prepare. Bake and serve it in a brightly colored casserole.

CELERY AND CHEESE CASSEROLE

3 c. diagonally sliced fresh Florida celery
3 tbsp. butter
¼ c. water
½ tsp. crumbled dried tarragon leaves
2 tbsp. all-purpose flour
Salt to taste
½ c. milk
1 can cream of chicken soup
½ c. grated Cheddar cheese
¼ tsp. paprika

Combine the celery, 1 tablespoon of the butter, water and tarragon in a large saucepan and bring to a boil. Reduce heat and simmer, covered, for 10 minutes. Turn the celery mixture into a buttered 2-quart casserole. Melt the remaining 2 tablespoons of butter in the same saucepan over medium heat. Stir in the flour and salt and cook, stirring constantly, until lightly browned. Add the milk gradually and cook, stirring constantly, until the mixture is smooth and thick. Stir in the soup and heat through. Add the cheese and stir until melted. Pour over the celery mixture, blending lightly, then sprinkle with the paprika. Bake in a preheated 350-degree oven for 15 minutes or until heated through and bubbly. This makes 6 to 8 servings.

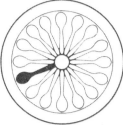

a special mushroom dish

Mushrooms and shrimp are more than just compatible — their combined flavors are memorable, and the following recipe is an excellent example. Mushroom-Shrimp Chowder is made with milk, fresh, boiled mushrooms, sautéed onions and fresh, cooked shrimp. For the very best in flavor, chill thoroughly before serving.

mushroom-shrimp chowder

Pictured on the cutting board are fresh mushrooms, shrimp and onion, three of the delicious ingredients in Mushroom-Shrimp Chowder.

MUSHROOM-SHRIMP CHOWDER

1 lb. fresh mushrooms, sliced
1 ½ c. water
2 ½ tsp. salt
¼ c. chopped fresh onion
¼ c. melted butter
¼ c. all-purpose flour
⅛ tsp. freshly ground pepper
2 ½ c. milk
½ c. whipping cream
2 c. chopped cooked shrimp

Combine the mushrooms, water and 1 teaspoon of the salt in a saucepan and bring to a boil. Reduce the heat and cover. Simmer for 10 minutes, then drain the mushrooms and reserve the liquid. Sauté the onion in the butter in a saucepan until tender. Add the flour, remaining salt and pepper and mix well. Stir in the reserved liquid gradually, blending until smooth, then add the milk gradually and cook, stirring constantly, until the mixture comes to a boil and thickens. Remove from the heat and stir in the cream, shrimp and mushrooms. Chill thoroughly before serving. Garnish with turned mushrooms (General Information, pg. 16) and parsley. This makes about 6 servings.

broccoli chowder

This chowder is an unusual and delicious way to serve broccoli. Its base is made of savory chicken stock, milk and cream. Fresh broccoli, chopped ham and grated Swiss cheese are combined in this rich base. With minimal effort, one can prepare this quick and easy dish in about fifteen minutes.

BROCCOLI CHOWDER

2 lb. fresh broccoli
3 c. Basic Chicken Stock (Soups, pg. 2)
3 c. milk
1 c. chopped cooked ham
2 tsp. salt
¼ tsp. freshly ground pepper
1 c. half and half cream
2 c. grated Swiss cheese
¼ c. butter

Wash the broccoli and remove any leaves and coarse stem ends. Place the broccoli in a large kettle and add half the stock. Bring to a boil, then reduce the heat and cover. Simmer for 7 minutes or until the broccoli is just tender. Remove the broccoli from the stock with a slotted spoon and chop coarsely. Add the remaining stock, milk, ham, salt and pepper to the stock in the kettle and stir well. Bring to a boil over medium heat, stirring occasionally. Stir in the cream, cheese, butter and broccoli and heat until the cheese is melted. Do not boil. This makes about 8 servings.

broccoli chowder

Flavorful Broccoli Chowder, made with fresh broccoli, is a dish you will serve often. Serve it for a light lunch or as a first course for dinner.

ranchero corn

Simply prepared Ranchero Corn, made with bacon, onion, sweet peppers and Cheddar cheese, is a perfect dish for outdoor meals and barbecues.

ranchero corn

RANCHERO CORN

6 slices bacon, diced
1   4 ½-oz. jar sliced mushrooms, drained
2 tbsp. finely chopped onion
2   12-oz. cans vacuum-packed golden whole kernel corn with sweet peppers, drained
¾ c. grated Cheddar cheese

Fry the bacon in a skillet over medium heat until cooked but not brown, then drain off the excess fat. Stir in the mushrooms and onion and sauté until the onion is tender. Blend in the corn and heat through. Sprinkle with the cheese and heat, without stirring, until the cheese is melted. This makes 6 servings.

SCALLOPED CORN WITH SWEET PEPPERS

1   1-lb. can whole kernel corn
Half and half cream
2 tbsp. butter
2 tbsp. all-purpose flour
1 tsp. salt
¼ tsp. freshly ground pepper
½ tsp. monosodium glutamate
1 tsp. celery salt
2 eggs, beaten
3 tbsp. chopped green sweet pepper
2 tbsp. chopped pimento
½ c. buttered bread crumbs

Drain the corn and reserve the liquid. Pour the reserved liquid into a measuring cup and add enough cream to make 1 cup of liquid. Melt the butter in a medium-sized saucepan over low heat, then stir in the flour, salt, pepper, monosodium glutamate and celery salt until smooth. Stir in the cream mixture gradually and cook, stirring constantly, until thickened. Stir a small amount of the hot sauce into the eggs, then stir the mixture back into the sauce and cook, stirring, until smooth. Stir in the corn, sweet pepper and pimento. Pour into a buttered baking dish and sprinkle with the bread crumbs. Place the baking dish in a shallow pan of water. Bake in a preheated 350-degree oven for 45 to 50 minutes or until set. This makes about 6 servings.

corn-chicken-carrot dinner

CORN-CHICKEN-CARROT DINNER

6 tbsp. butter
2 1-lb. chicken breasts, halved
4 med. carrots, thinly sliced
4 ears of corn, halved
2 tbsp. chopped chives
2 tsp. salt
1/8 tsp. garlic powder

A hearty combination of corn on the cob, carrot slices and pieces of chicken breast cooked together in an aluminum foil packet makes a meal in itself. All that is needed to complete the menu is a salad and hot rolls. A note to those who enjoy camping trips: when getting ready for your next outing, prepare this dish at home (except for the actual cooking) and carry it along with your other provisions in a portable cooler. Then, when ready, cook over a bed of coals and enjoy an easy no-mess meal which tastes even better around the campfire.

Melt 2 tablespoons of the butter in a skillet over medium heat. Add the chicken and cook until browned. Place each chicken half on a 12 x 18-inch piece of heavy-duty aluminum foil and arrange 1/4 of the carrots and corn around each chicken half. Add the remaining butter, chives, salt and garlic powder to the butter in the skillet and heat, stirring frequently, until the butter is melted. Pour over the chicken and vegetables on each piece of foil. Seal the foil pockets, using a double fold on top and sides. Place on a baking sheet. Bake in a preheated 350-degree oven for 1 hour and 15 minutes. Garnish with parsley. This makes 4 servings.

spinach soufflé

A perfectly prepared soufflé which is light, puffed and brown is easy to accomplish if the cook is careful to observe the few simple, basic rules for making soufflés (Desserts, pg. 45). The following recipe for spinach soufflé is an excellent choice to accompany broiled steak or lamb chops instead of potatoes or rice. A tangy, homemade tomato sauce may be served with the soufflé to enhance its subtle, delicate flavor. If desired, 2 pounds of fresh spinach may be used in place of the frozen type. Read the instructions on fresh spinach (pg. 33) for cooking directions and amounts.

SPINACH SOUFFLÉ WITH SPICY SAUCE

1   10-oz. package frozen chopped spinach
3 tbsp. butter
5 tbsp. cornstarch
3/4 tsp. salt
1/8 tsp. pepper
1 c. milk
4 eggs, separated
1/4 tsp. nutmeg
1   14-oz. can stewed tomatoes
1   3-oz. can mushrooms
1/4 tsp. dried basil leaves
Dash of Worcestershire sauce

Cook the spinach according to package directions, then drain well. Melt the butter in a small, heavy saucepan over medium heat, then stir in 3 table-spoons of the cornstarch, 1/2 teaspoon of the salt and the pepper until smooth. Stir in the milk gradually. Bring to a boil, stirring constantly, then cook for 1 minute. Remove from the heat. Beat the egg yolks slightly. Stir a small amount of the hot mixture into the egg yolks, then stir back into the hot mixture. Add the spinach and nutmeg and mix thoroughly. Beat the egg whites until stiff peaks form. Fold 1/4 of the egg whites into the spinach mixture, then fold in the remaining egg whites. Turn into a 1 1/2-quart soufflé dish. Bake in a preheated 375-degree oven for 30 to 35 minutes or until a knife inserted in the center comes out clean. Prepare the sauce while the soufflé is baking. Combine the tomatoes, mushrooms, basil, Worcestershire sauce, remaining 2 tablespoons of cornstarch and remaining 1/4 teaspoon of salt in a small saucepan. Bring to a boil over medium heat, stirring constantly, then cook for 1 minute. Serve the sauce with the soufflé. This makes 4 servings.

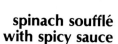

spinach soufflé
with spicy sauce

An entrée need not be costly to be impressive. A spinach soufflé is a lovely dish to serve for a luncheon or buffet supper. It is shown here accompanied with a spicy tomato sauce.

RED AND GREEN PEPPER POT

3 red sweet peppers
3 green sweet peppers
6 yellow onions
12 tomatoes
¼ c. butter
Salt and freshly ground pepper to taste

Cut the tops off the red and green peppers and remove the seeds and center membranes. Peel the onions and cut off the stem ends of the tomatoes. Slice the peppers into rings, then cut the onions and tomatoes into wedges. Melt the butter in a heavy skillet. Add the peppers and onions and sauté over low heat for 10 minutes, stirring frequently. Add the tomato wedges, then season with salt and pepper. Cook for 10 minutes longer, stirring frequently. This makes about 6 servings.

red and green pepper pot

A zesty combination of tomatoes, onions and red and green peppers makes an excellent change-of-pace vegetable course. This dish freezes well.

mushrooms, eggs and cheese

MUSHROOMS AND EGGS IN CHEESE SAUCE

1 ½ c. sliced fresh mushrooms
1 tbsp. lemon juice
¼ c. butter
½ c. chopped celery
½ c. chopped green sweet pepper
¼ c. chopped onion
2 tbsp. all-purpose flour
½ tsp. salt
Dash of freshly ground pepper
1 c. milk
1 c. shredded Cheddar cheese
¼ tsp. Worcestershire sauce
3 hard-boiled eggs
1 recipe Basic Boiled Rice *(Cereals, pg. 3)*
1 can chow mein noodles

Toss the mushrooms with the lemon juice. Melt the butter in a chafing dish pan or blazer pan over low heat. Add the mushrooms, celery, green pepper and onion and sauté until just tender, stirring constantly. Add the flour, salt and pepper and mix well. Stir in the milk gradually and cook over medium heat, stirring constantly, until thickened. Cook for 2 minutes longer, then remove from the heat. Add the cheese and Worcestershire sauce and stir until the cheese is melted. Reserve 1 egg yolk, then chop the remaining egg yolks and egg whites. Add the chopped eggs to the sauce and heat through. Do not boil. Sieve the reserved egg yolk and sprinkle over the center of the sauce mixture. Garnish with parsley, if desired. Place the chafing dish pan over low heat or over the *bain-marie* to keep warm. Serve the mushroom mixture over rice sprinkled with chow mein noodles. This makes about 6 servings.

Mushrooms and eggs combined in a delicious cheese sauce is a simple but memorable dish. It may be served over rice and chow mein noodles, or in patty shells it is ideal for a buffet dinner. It may be kept hot in a chafing dish over low heat or over a *bain-marie* (the French word for water bath) or double boiler, then served directly over the rice or in patty shells. Any type of entrée which has a cream or egg yolk-based sauce is best served from this type of utensil, as it will keep the food hot without overheating and causing the sauce to separate.

mushrooms, eggs and sherry

When planning the menu for your next "very special dinner," an excellent choice for the vegetable course would be Mushrooms A La Ritz. A delicate, sherry-flavored cream sauce containing sliced fresh mushrooms and hard-cooked eggs is ladled into *vol-au-vent* shells and each serving is garnished with celery leaves or fresh parsley.

Note: Homemade *vol-au-vent* shells (Desserts, pg. 65) are decidedly superior to the store-bought type, although the latter may be used for the sake of convenience. The mushroom and sauce mixture may be kept warm in a chafing dish or double boiler until time to serve. In order to prevent *vol-au-vents* from getting soggy, do not fill with the creamed mixture until just before serving.

MUSHROOMS À LA RITZ

6 Vol-au-vent Shells *(Desserts, pg. 65)*
6 tbsp. butter
¼ lb. sliced fresh mushrooms
1 tbsp. finely chopped onion
3 tbsp. all-purpose flour
¾ tsp. salt
Dash of ground red pepper
1 ½ c. half and half cream
6 hard-boiled eggs
4 tsp. dry sherry

Prepare the *vol-au-vents*. Melt 2 tablespoons of the butter in a small skillet. Add the mushrooms and onion and sauté for 5 minutes, stirring constantly. Heat the remaining butter in a medium saucepan, then stir in the flour, salt and red pepper until smooth. Add the cream gradually and cook, stirring constantly, until thickened and smooth. Dice 5 of the eggs and stir into the sauce. Add the mushroom mixture and sherry and heat through. Do not boil. Place the *vol-au-vents* on a serving plate, then spoon the mushroom mixture over the *vol-au-vents*. Cut the remaining egg into 6 wedges and place 1 wedge on the mushroom mixture in each shell. Garnish with parsley, if desired. One 6-count package of frozen patty shells, baked according to package directions, may be substituted for the *vol-au-vents*. This makes 6 servings.

mushrooms à la ritz

Mushrooms À La Ritz is an elegant vegetable course, guaranteed to draw compliments and praise. Everything may be prepared in advance, but the final assembly is done just before serving.

sauces

table of contents

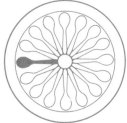

using sauces in creative cookery

Imagine a master chef scurrying around his kitchen, preparing a perfect meal. His tall white hat tips precariously as he adds the proper seasoning to the sautéed chicken and tastes with his big wooden spoon. He nods approval, then gets a quizzical look. Something is missing.

The chicken is cooked to perfection, the *hors d'oeuvres* are prepared, and the salad is a veritable garden delight. But it needs that special something which effectively says, "This meal was prepared by an artist." Suddenly he snaps his fingers and sets about preparing a cream sauce. Combined with his other careful preparations, the sauce supplies the flair—just the right touch of elegance.

This imaginary scene points out our ideas about the value of sauces. Sure, you can get by without them—many cooks do. But you want to add a uniqueness to your meals which will make them an occasion to remember.

In this lesson we will introduce a representative sampling of the BASIC sauces. You will learn how to complement other foods with sauces, to add texture and flavor contrast, and to vary the presentation of many type of foods.

If this sounds like a tall order, you'll be surprised at how easy it is when you follow our professional hints on saucemaking.

We have included representative sauces from the major categories, referred to as *sauces mères* or "mother sauces." The BASIC *sauces mères* include *vinaigrettes,* often called French dressings, that are based on oil and vinegar; emulsified sauces such as mayonnaise, which depend on the ability of egg yolks to absorb and disperse a fatty substance throughout, resulting in a creamy, semi-solid solution; *roux* sauces, including the Basic White Sauce or *Béchamel,* that are based on the thickening agents flour and butter in combination with milk or stock; and marinades, sauces in the sense that they impart a flavor to the food they accompany, though frequently are not served with the food itself.

Our final category—dessert sauces—exhibits considerably more variation in ingredients and techniques than *sauces mères.*

A BASIS FOR IMAGINATION

Because sauces add the touch that make your dishes stunning successes, we have tried to anticipate the most common pitfalls. The most frustrating problems for many cooks are seasonings and consistency. Gain experience and confidence with the herbs and spices we've suggested before adding your own innovations. As for consistency, we admit with candor that practice makes perfect—in no time you will become familiar with the ingredients and how they react with each other in sauces.

For best results with the sauces in the following section, we recommend long, slow simmering. You'll find other helpful suggestions throughout this section.

vinaigrette

Basic *Vinaigrette* sauce and its herb-seasoned variation, the *Vinaigrette aux Fines Herbes,* are primary dressings for salads in Europe; both are classically French and simply delicious. And they are among the easiest to prepare. They will work wonders on crisp salad greens as well as on asparagus, artichokes, broccoli and cauliflower. You can even use these dressings to flavor savory rice dishes or to marinate meats and fish.

The main ingredients in the basic *Vinaigrette* and *Vinaigrette aux Fines Herbes* are oil and red wine vinegar. We recommend red wine vinegar as superior to the malt and cider varieties. For a flavorful variation, you may want to substitute lemon juice for the wine vinegar; especially on fish and vegetables.

BASIC VINAIGRETTE

2 tsp. salt
½ tsp. freshly ground pepper
1 tsp. prepared mustard
1 c. olive oil
¼ c. red wine vinegar

Place the salt, pepper and mustard in a medium-sized bowl; then add several drops of olive oil. Blend with a wooden spoon. Add several drops of vinegar, blending well. Add remaining oil and vinegar gradually, stirring constantly, until the total amount is used. Store in covered jar in refrigerator. Shake well before using. Yield: 1⅓ cups.

VINAIGRETTE AUX FINES HERBES

1⅓ c. Basic Vinaigrette
½ tbsp. chopped onion
½ tbsp. parsley
½ tbsp. chopped tarragon
½ tbsp. chopped chives

Combine all ingredients in medium-sized bowl; blend well with a wooden spoon. Store in covered jar in refrigerator. Shake well before using. Fresh or dried herbs may be used.

basic mayonnaise

Mayonnaise, our next *sauce mère,* is widely used and enjoyed. Technically, mayonnaise is an uncooked emulsion prepared from egg (yolk or whole), oil, vinegar, lemon juice and spices. A step further: an emulsion is a liquid mixture in which a fatty substance is suspended in minute droplets.

Although this sounds complex, it isn't. If you'll bear with us, you'll learn why and how the ingredients combine to form such a mixture. There are two Basic Mayonnaise

recipes to gain experience from: Version 1 uses 4 egg yolks and is prepared with a whisk or hand mixer; Version II uses 2 whole egg and is prepared in an electric blender.

Egg yolks are essential in making mayonnaise. They absorb oil and bind it into a thick, creamy mixture forming the basis of the mayonnaise. The tiny droplets of oil dispersed throughout the mixture are each surrounded by egg yolk, thus forming an emulsion. The maximum amount of oil that a large egg yolk will absorb is approximately ¾ cup. When this limit is exceeded, the yolks become saturated and their binding properties break down. As a result, the mayonnaise either thins out or separates. Be sure all your ingredients are at room temperature before beginning your mayonnaise.

If the mayonnaise refuses to thicken or if the oil suddenly releases from suspension (and the yolks appear to form tiny lumps), it has "curdled" or "separated." Often mayonnaise will curdle if it undergoes a sudden change of temperature. If this occurs, *don't panic.* It's a simple matter to restore the creaminess and smoothness to curdled mayonnaise. Place 1 egg in the blender and blend for a few seconds or beat in a mixing bowl for about one minute. Begin adding the curdled mixture to the egg in a very small stream, beating all the time. Check for the desired consistency of the mayonnaise as you work.

STORING HOMEMADE MAYONNAISE

Glass or earthenware crocks, bowls or jars are fine for storing mayonnaise. Unlike metal containers, they guard against any slight discoloration of the sauce. Level off the mayonnaise in the container and cover the mayonnaise, but not the container, with a fitted piece of waxed paper rinsed under cold water. This professional trick is used to prevent a film from forming on any thickened sauce. For added protection, place a lid on the container.

It is best to store mayonnaise in the refrigerator. In spite of these precautions, however, your mayonnaise may curdle during storage. If so, allow the mayonnaise to come to room temperature, then follow the procedure we gave you for restoring curdled mayonnaise.

RECIPE VARIATIONS

We've experimented a bit to develop several tasty and colorful variations for our Basic Mayonnaise recipes. You can replace the vinegar with lemon juice. Or, you can flavor Basic Mayonnaise with paprika, curry powder, tomato paste or dry mustard to taste. A few drops of Tabasco sauce and lemon juice give you Piquant Mayonnaise. If you prefer mayonnaise with a thinner consistency, dilute it with a small amount of cream or half-and-half, and a dash of orange or lemon juice. This helps to thin the sauce, making the mayonnaise spreadable.

BASIC MAYONNAISE

4 med. egg yolks
1 tsp. salt
⅛ tsp. white pepper
2 c. vegetable oil
1 tbsp. wine vinegar

Place the egg yolks, salt and pepper in a medium bowl. Beat with electric hand mixer at medium speed until thick, pale and fluffy. Add 5 ounces oil in very thin stream, beating constantly, until thickened and oil is absorbed. Beat in the vinegar. Add the remaining oil slowly, beating constantly, until all the oil is blended into the mixture. Mayonnaise will be very thick. Place in refrigerator container. Cut waxed paper to fit over top; rinse in cold water. Place over mayonnaise; cover and refrigerate until ready to use. Yield: 1¾ cups.

VARIATIONS:

Beat 1 teaspoon paprika into 1¾ cups Basic Mayonnaise for Paprika Mayonnaise.

Beat 2 teaspoons curry powder into 1¾ cups Basic Mayonnaise for Curry Mayonnaise.

Beat 2 tablespoons tomato paste into 1¾ cups Basic Mayonnaise for Tomato Mayonnaise.

Beat 3½ teaspoons dry mustard into 1¾ cups Basic Mayonnaise for Mustard Mayonnaise.

Beat 1 teaspoon Tabasco sauce, 2 teaspoons heavy cream and 4 teaspoons lemon juice into 1¾ cups Basic Mayonnaise for Piquant Mayonnaise.

BASIC BLENDER MAYONNAISE

1 c. salad oil
1 tbsp. red wine vinegar
1 tbsp. lemon juice
1 egg
½ tsp. salt
⅛ tsp. paprika
¼ tsp. dry mustard
Dash of cayenne pepper

Pour ¼ cup of the oil into electric blender and add vinegar, lemon juice, egg and seasonings. Cover and blend for 5 seconds. Remove cover while blender is running and add the remaining oil in a thin steady stream. Turn off blender immediately after adding oil. Yield: 1½ cups.

basic white sauces

ROUX

The next sauces you'll learn to prepare are based on a thickening mixture of flour and butter called a *roux*—plus a flavored liquid. You'll later make more varied sauces based on this fundamental process. Basic White Sauce or *Béchamel* uses milk, Basic *Velouté* uses chicken stock, and Basic Brown Sauce uses beef stock. All three share a common technique of preparation: the butter and flour *roux* is cooked for several minutes until the mixture is bubbly and foamy. This step eliminates a raw, pasty flour taste and prepares the flour particles to absorb the flavored liquid.

We'll expand the ingredients you use for these sauces, but seldom will we vary the BASIC technique. For example, in a later lesson is *Mornay Sauce,* a Basic White Sauce made with grated cheese, commonly served with eggs, vegetables, chicken and fish. In addition, BASIC sauces will also be incorporated into many other tasty dishes, such as cream soups, scalloped and *au gratin* casseroles and soufflés.

Probably the most famous *roux,* White Sauce or *Béchamel,* was named for its originator, *Louis de Béchamel,* steward to Louis XIV who served it often on dishes he prepared for the French Court.

The most essential step in making a good white sauce is to prevent the flour and butter *roux* from browning —even slightly. Because of its color, it is sometimes called a blond *roux.* White pepper contributes to the appearance of White Sauce, as well as adding flavor.

A distinguishing feature of *roux* sauces, and in particular White Sauce, is that the consistency can be altered to suit the type of dish you are preparing. For instance, to vary the thickness of our Basic White Sauce either add more or less flour and butter than the recipe specifies.

USING THE PROPER EQUIPMENT

When making BASIC *roux* sauces, melt the butter in a *heavy* saucepan. This is particularly important. The heat is not uniformly conducted in a thin pan, and the sauce may scorch. We recommend heavy-bottomed enameled, stainless steel, oven-proof glass or porcelain or tin-lined copper saucepans. Aluminum tends to discolor sauces made with wine or eggs. To smooth and break up any lumps of flour in Basic White and *Velouté* sauces, use a wire whisk. A wooden spoon is fine for mixing the thicker Basic Brown Sauce.

Below is a chart giving the amount of flour and butter to use to vary the consistency. The amount of milk remains unchanged. Through repeated use you will become familiar with the differing thicknesses and will soon be making flawless White Sauces that *Béchamel* himself would have been proud to serve.

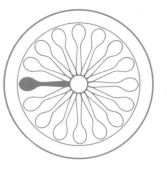

basic velouté sauce

THIN SAUCE

Consistency of coffee cream (for creamed vegetables; soup base)	2 tbsp. butter 2 tbsp. flour 2 cups milk Salt and pepper

MEDIUM SAUCE

General-purpose consistency of thick cream (for creamed and scalloped dishes)	3 tbsp. butter 3 tbsp. flour 2 cups milk Salt and pepper

THICK SAUCE

Consistency of batter (for *croquettes* and *soufflés*)	4 tbsp. butter 4 tbsp. flour 2 cups milk Salt and pepper

Basic *Velouté* and Basic Brown Sauce are cousins to Basic White Sauce. Their preparation is identical to that for White Sauce, although they depend for their flavor on a highly clarified and concentrated chicken or beef stock instead of milk. Like Basic White Sauce, Basic *Velouté* begins with a blond *roux*. For Basic Brown Sauce the *roux* is browned slightly to lend a darker hue and a nut-like flavor. Hence, it is often called a dark *roux*. Since you'll be meeting these sauces over and over again, it's best to understand them now.

FREEZER TIP . . .

As you've probably already guessed, *roux* sauces are exceptionally versatile—so versatile, in fact, we suggest keeping some in your freezer. For the Basic White and *Velouté* Sauces, you can make as much sauce as you need by doubling, tripling and quadrupling the recipe. Pour surplus amounts into freezer containers for storage. For the Basic Brown Sauce freeze only the *roux* with the brown stock added. When you need a batch of Basic Brown Sauce, simply thaw a pint freezer container of sauce, add tomatoes and *mirepoix* and cook as the recipe specifies.

If you want your White Sauce to have an appetizingly rich sheen, "finish" it in the classic French manner by beating in 1 tablespoon butter just before removing it from the heat. Store the unused portion in a small bowl. As you did for mayonnaise, cover the top of the mixture, not the bowl, with a fitted circle of waxed paper rinsed under cold water. Then cover the bowl with foil or plastic wrap. These precautions prevent a film from forming on top.

BASIC WHITE SAUCE OR BÉCHAMEL SAUCE

3 tbsp. butter
3 tbsp. flour
2 c. milk
¾ tsp. salt
¼ tsp. white pepper

Melt the butter in top of a double boiler over boiling water; stir in the flour with a wooden spoon until smooth. Add the milk gradually, stirring constantly; cook until sauce is thick. Stir in salt and pepper. Remove top of double boiler from water. Strain sauce through a fine sieve; use as desired. Pour any remaining sauce into a small bowl. Cover top of sauce with a circle of wet waxed paper; refrigerate for future use. Yield: 2 cups.

BASIC VELOUTÉ SAUCE

¼ c. butter
½ c. flour
6 c. clarified Basic Chicken Stock *(Soups, pg. 2)*
¼ c. sauterne

Melt the butter in a medium saucepan; blend in the flour gradually. Cook and stir for several minutes until smooth. Add stock gradually, stirring until smooth. Simmer over medium heat for about 1 hour, stirring frequently until reduced by ⅓. Sauce should be consistency of heavy cream. Add sauterne. Strain through a fine sieve.

BASIC BROWN SAUCE

Now for our special Basic Brown Sauce. To the dark *roux* and beef stock, add a vegetable and herb blend known as *Mirepoix* (MIR pwa). You will discover that *Mirepoix* is more than worth your time to prepare. It tremendously enriches the Basic Brown Sauce.

BASIC BROWN SAUCE

2 tbsp. butter
¼ c. flour
4 c. Basic Beef Stock *(Soups, pg. 2)*
1 c. chopped tomatoes
1 c. Mirepoix

Melt the butter in a small saucepan; blend in the flour to make a smooth paste. Cook and stir over low heat until mixture is browned. Add the stock gradually, stirring constantly, until smooth. Add the tomatoes; simmer for 3 minutes. Add *Mirepoix* and simmer until sauce is reduced by half, stirring occasionally. Strain sauce through a fine sieve and serve immediately.

MIREPOIX

2 tsp. butter
2 tsp. cooking oil
1 med. carrot, coarsely grated
1 med. onion, coarsely grated
1 stalk of celery, finely chopped
⅛ tsp. dried thyme leaves
1 bay leaf, crushed
2 tbsp. sherry

Melt the butter in a small heavy saucepan then add the oil. Add carrot, onion and celery; sauté until soft. Add the remaining ingredients; simmer until vegetables are tender. Yield: 1 cup.

marinades

Our next category of *sauces mères* is marinades, those flavorfully-seasoned, acid-based solutions in which meats, vegetables and seafoods are steeped or pickled. The word "marinate" comes from an old Spanish word meaning "to pickle." The acid in the solution, usually wine—Burgundy, claret, port or white wine—helps tenderize tough food fibers while imparting a new and different flavor. Marinades also enhance natural juiciness.

All our marinades are of the uncooked variety—which means speedy and uncomplicated preparation for you.

Three hints we would like to pass on: use a glass or stainless steel dish for marinating so the food absorbs only the flavors from the marinade; and, for basically the same reasons, we prefer a wooden spoon for stirring. Third, we recommend marinating food in the refrigerator. If you don't use your marinade as a flavorful basting or braising liquid during cooking, strain and refrigerate it for future use, or heat and serve it as a flavorful sauce. Here are our BASIC marinade recipes for beef, game, fish and lamb. These amounts should be doubled or increased for large amounts of meats or fish.

MARINADE FOR BEEF

1 c. Burgundy
½ c. olive oil
2 parsley stalks
2 sprigs of tarragon
2 sprigs of thyme
1 bay leaf

Combine all the ingredients in small container with lid. Cover and shake to mix well. One-eighth teaspoon dried tarragon leaves and thyme leaves may be substituted for the fresh tarragon and thyme.

MARINADE FOR FISH

1 c. dry white wine
4 peppercorns
2 tsp. slivered lemon peel
4 parsley stalks
¼ c. olive oil

Combine all ingredients in small container with lid. Cover and shake to mix well. Marinade may be stored in a covered container in refrigerator. Shake well before using.

MARINADE FOR GAME

¾ c. port
1¼ c. olive oil
3 sprigs of tarragon
2 parsley stalks
1 lg. celery stalk, coarsely chopped
1 sm. onion, thinly sliced
6 peppercorns
⅛ tsp. sage
1 tsp. slivered lemon peel

Combine all ingredients in small container with lid. Cover and shake to mix well. Marinate game according to recipe directions.

MARINADE FOR LAMB

Use our Beef Marinade recipe, simply substituting claret for the Burgundy.

dessert sauces

Let's consider a major category of dessert sauces — those made with cream. Included here are two good vanilla sauces and a Basic Orange Cream Sauce. You'll enjoy serving these luscious concoctions with fruits, cakes, puddings and sweet gelatins.

With minor variations, these recipes contain whipping cream for fluffiness, eggs for thickening, extra fine sugar, vanilla or orange flavoring, and our own suggestions for the addition of brandy or rum. And each one offers the opportunity to develop a new fundamental technique of cooking—working with cream. In later lessons you'll be using cream to prepare many fabulous savory sauces for meat, fish and vegetables.

The BASICS of whipping cream are very much the same as for whipping egg whites. Whipping cream is sometimes marketed as heavy cream; half-and-half or coffee cream will not stiffen sufficiently. Instead of your electric mixer, try whipping with a wire whisk, which allows you to incorporate the maximum amount of air into the cream. You'll find that not only is your whipped cream richer and lighter but it also holds up extremely well throughout preparation.

Begin preparing creamy dessert sauces by thoroughly chilling the mixing bowl, whipping utensil and whipping cream for about two hours. While these are chilling, prepare the recipe to the point of adding the whipped cream. Then whip the cream until it forms soft glossy peaks and has doubled in bulk. Because whipped cream is so delicate and loses body quickly, we advise whipping it as the final step before folding it into the other ingredients. And make certain these other ingredients are *not* hot; otherwise, the cream will lose its stiffness, thinning out.

BASIC VANILLA SAUCE

2 c. milk
1 vanilla pod
3 eggs
4 tbsp. sugar
¾ c. stiffly whipped cream

Pour the milk in a small heavy saucepan; add the vanilla pod. Heat to just under boiling point. Remove vanilla pod; wipe pod dry and store. Beat the eggs until lemon colored. Pour a small amount of hot milk over eggs, stirring constantly. Return to remaining hot milk in saucepan. Cook, stirring constantly, over low heat for about 20 minutes or until thick. Remove from heat; stir in sugar. Allow to cool. Fold in whipped cream gradually. One teaspoon vanilla extract may be substituted for vanilla pod. Add to custard after removing from heat.

LUXURIOUS SWEDISH VANILLA SAUCE

3 egg yolks
2 tbsp. extra fine sugar
1¾ c. whipping cream
1 vanilla pod

Beat the egg yolks and sugar to a smooth paste in medium-sized mixing bowl with wire whisk. Pour 1 cup whipping cream into small, heavy saucepan; add the vanilla pod. Place over low heat until just below boiling point. Stir hot cream slowly into egg yolk mixture, then pour into top of double boiler. Cook over boiling water until thick, stirring constantly with wooden spoon. Remove the vanilla pod and place double boiler top in bowl of ice cubes. Stir until lukewarm. Remove from ice. Beat remaining cream until stiff, then fold gently into sauce until well mixed. Refrigerate until ready to serve. One teaspoon vanilla may be substituted for vanilla pod. Add to custard after removing from heat. Yield: 2½ cups.

BASIC ORANGE CREAM SAUCE

Juice and grated rind of 2 oranges
3 tbsp. sifted confectioners' sugar
¾ c. whipping cream
¼ c. half and half

Combine the rind and juice in a small saucepan. Bring to a boil, then reduce heat to a slow boil. Cook until reduced to ⅓ its volume. Strain. Add sugar to liquid. Chill. Whip the cream with mixer until stiff. Add the half and half gradually, blending in gently with wooden spoon. Stir in the cold orange mixture until blended. Serve over fresh fruits, fruit pies or tarts.

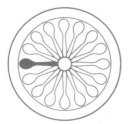

hollandaise sauce

Sauces are the *pièces de rèsistance* of French cooking and Hollandaise is one of the best. Because of its reputation, Hollandaise is feared by many cooks, but after you've studied our tips on making it, you'll find that it is really not as difficult to make as you may believe.

Golden rich Hollandaise is made of heated egg yolks into which butter has been added and flavored with lemon juice. Like mayonnaise, it belongs to the family of emulsified sauces that depend on the properties of egg yolks to achieve the proper thick and creamy consistency. To assure the egg yolks thickening into a smooth cream they must be heated slowly over low heat and stirred constantly. Too sudden heat will make them grainy and overcooking may cause you to have scrambled eggs. Make sure the water over which you are cooking is not boiling hot.

A flawless Hollandaise depends largely on how you add the butter. Egg yolks will absorb only a small quantity of butter at a time so it must be added very slowly and in small amounts. If too much is mixed in at one time (especially at first) the sauce won't thicken. If after the sauce is made you realize this has happened, put a teaspoon of lemon juice and a tablespoon of sauce into a mixing bowl which has been rinsed in hot water. Beat this with a wire whisk until the sauce creams and thickens, then add the rest of the sauce (half a tablespoon at a time) beating until each addition of sauce has thickened.

After you begin adding the butter if the yolks seem to be thickening too quickly or appear lumpy you can remedy this by immediately putting the bottom of the pan into cold water and beating the yolks to cool them. (Have a pan of cold water, with some ice cubes in it, ready just in case.) Continue beating after returning them to the heat. When you are able to see the bottom of the pan while beating the yolks and the sauce is the consistency of light cream and coats the whisk, the egg yolks have thickened to the proper stage.

When the total amount of butter is too much to be absorbed by the egg yolks, your sauce may congeal or curdle. To avoid this use the minimum amount of butter called for in the recipe. But, if in spite of your precautions it does, beat an ice cube or a tablespoon of cold water into the mixture to bring back its smooth texture.

Since proper heat regulation is so important when cooking Hollandaise, we recommend that you cook it in a double boiler over water or a saucepan set in a shallow frying pan partially filled with hot water. In this way the sauce cooks *in* the heat, so to speak, instead of *above* the heat, as it would in a double boiler. With this saucepan-in-frying pan method you can actually see that the water in the frying pan never boils. It is best to keep the water on *low* heat. If tiny bubbles begin to appear on the surface of the water, remove the sauce and quickly add one or two tablespoons of cold water.

After you have finished making your Hollandaise serve it warm, not hot, for if it is kept hot it will thicken and curdle. You can keep it perfectly for an hour or more by putting it over a pan of lukewarm water.

If you're really in a hurry and have a blender, you might want to try blender Hollandaise. It's virtually foolproof and a real time-saver. The consistency is somewhat thinner than Basic Hollandaise but it will thicken perfectly after you pour it over hot foods.

BASIC HOLLANDAISE SAUCE

1/2 c. butter
4 egg yolks, well beaten
2 to 2 1/2 tbsp. lemon juice
Pinch of white pepper
1/8 tsp. salt

Melt 2 tablespoons butter in the top of a double boiler, then pour gradually into the beaten egg yolks, stirring constantly. Return yolks to pan and place pan in or over hot water. Add the remaining butter by tablespoons; stir after each tablespoon until each is melted. Remove from the heat and stir in the lemon juice, pepper and salt.

BLENDER HOLLANDAISE SAUCE

1 egg
3 tbsp. lemon juice
1/4 tsp. salt
1/8 tsp. white pepper
1/2 c. butter

Combine egg, lemon juice and seasonings in blender container. Melt butter in small saucepan over medium heat until bubbling. Blend egg mixture in container until well mixed. Add bubbling butter gradually, blending until thickened and smooth. This makes approximately 3/4 cup sauce.

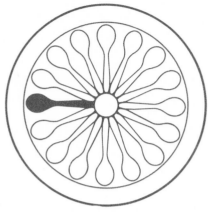

barbecue sauce

Regardless of whether you roast meat on a spit over an open fire, grill it over charcoal or cook it in an oven, you can turn it into delicious barbecue by basting it with a special sauce. This sauce is made by combining onion, garlic, catsup, and various seasonings and is named Basic Barbecue Sauce.

All over this country, people barbecue for private get-togethers and special events, on holidays and other important occasions. The Spanish word *"barbacoa"*, from which our word barbecue probably comes, means "a framework of sticks on which meat is roasted." It is a good guess that the first barbecue sauce was developed to enhance the flavor of meat roasted over such a structure. The sauce is almost as important to today's hostess as the wooden spit was to early barbecue cooks.

If you are planning a barbecue anytime soon, we know you want to make yours stand out. Because of this, we have included three distinctively delicious barbecue sauces. These recipes combine such ingredients as catsup, onion, vegetables and apples. They are guaranteed to turn meat or poultry into a real treat.

The first recipe we've included is for Basic Barbecue Sauce, which teams especially well with beef or chicken. The other two sauces, Hot Sweet and Sour Barbecue Sauce and Hot Apple Barbecue Sauce are culinary delights in themselves. Try them both on pork and chicken, the two meats we think they best compliment. Whichever you try, we know your barbecue will be a smashing success.

HOT SWEET AND SOUR BARBECUE SAUCE

⅓ c. salad oil
½ c. finely chopped celery
1 sm. green pepper, finely chopped
¾ c. (firmly packed) brown sugar
¾ c. red wine vinegar
2 tbsp. frozen minced chives
2 tsp. dry mustard
1 tbsp. Worcestershire sauce
2 tsp. sea salt or table salt
1 tsp. freshly ground pepper

Pour the olive oil in a small saucepan and add the celery and green pepper. Simmer, covered, for about 10 minutes or until vegetables are soft. Purée in a blender. Add the remaining ingredients and mix thoroughly. Sauce may be stored in a covered jar in the refrigerator. Sauce must be stirred before reuse to blend ingredients. Use as a basting sauce for barbecuing pork and chicken.

HOT APPLE BARBECUE SAUCE

2 c. applesauce
¼ c. onion juice
1 tsp. brown sugar
¼ tsp. dry mustard
2 tbsp. wine vinegar
¼ tsp. salt
⅛ tsp. pepper

Place the applesauce in a heavy pan and simmer until thick. Stir in the remaining ingredients until well mixed. Store, covered, in refrigerator. Heat before serving. This sauce is served with or over the meat — not as a basting sauce.

 ### BASIC BARBECUE SAUCE

½ c. butter
1 lg. onion, chopped
½ clove of garlic, crushed
1 14-oz. bottle catsup
2 tbsp. brown sugar
1 tbsp. Worcestershire sauce
⅓ c. red wine vinegar
1 c. water
¼ tsp. salt
¼ tsp. pepper
½ c. cola beverage

Melt butter in a saucepan. Add the onion and garlic and cook over low heat for about five minutes. Add the remaining ingredients except the cola beverage and simmer for about 20 minutes. Remove from heat and add the cola beverage. This sauce is excellent for meats and poultry.

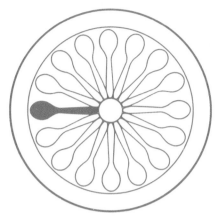

savory sauces

sauce accompaniments for cold cuts

In their own clear bottles, we present here the first three sauces you'll meet in this section. In front, accompanied by the oranges that provide its tang, is the delicious Basic Cumberland Sauce; behind it, in one bottle for serving and one for storing, you'll find the Basic Hot Huntington Sauce; similarly, the Garlic Oil on the right. All these sauces seemingly keep forever and would make ingenious gifts for special people on your list.

In this lesson we present you with another exciting array of sauces to show off and accent your cold cuts, salads, vegetables and entrées. The first three, Basic Cumberland Sauce, Basic Hot Huntington Sauce and Garlic Oil, are pictured on this page. All three keep their flavor when stored, so you can make a large batch at one time.

Our Basic Cumberland Sauce, which you'll first serve with smoked or cured ham (Pork, pg. 5), is a tasty combination of the sweet and sour flavors of currant jelly, wine and citrus fruits. Basic Cumberland Sauce is very much like a thin syrup, which may be served from a sauceboat at the table. We suggest you try it with fresh ham as well as the cured ham. Basic Hot Huntington Sauce is another variation of one of the *sauces mères – vinaigrette*. This sauce is quite simple to prepare and is a perfect complement to a delectable platter of cold cuts. This sauce, in contrast to the Cumberland, is a thick, brown sauce. As its name implies, it is hot and zesty . . . very delicious with meats and game.

You'll find any number of uses for the Garlic Oil presented here. You can even use it for flavoring to replace crushed garlic.

BASIC CUMBERLAND SAUCE

1 orange
1 lemon
1 12-oz. jar red currant jelly
⅛ tsp. onion juice
¼ tsp. cayenne pepper
¼ tsp. ginger
¼ c. port

Canelle the peeling from the orange and lemon. Cut into 4-inch lengths. Place in small saucepan and cover with water. Bring to a boil, then drain. Repeat boiling and draining 2 more times. Spoon jelly into a small saucepan and heat until melted. Add the drained peeling, onion juice, cayenne pepper and ginger. Simmer for 30 minutes or until peeling is transparent. Stir in the port and heat through. Store in refrigerator in covered container.

BASIC HOT HUNTINGTON SAUCE

¾ c. English mustard
3 tbsp. cold water
1½ c. (packed) dark brown sugar
1½ tbsp. salt
4½ tbsp. freshly ground pepper
½ c. red wine vinegar
1 c. olive oil

Mix the mustard and water to a smooth paste in a small container. Mix remaining ingredients except oil in a medium mixing bowl; stir in mustard mixture. Add the oil gradually, stirring constantly until well combined. Serve with pork or ham.

GARLIC OIL

5 lg. cloves of garlic
1 c. olive oil

Peel the garlic, then mash through a garlic press. Place in a 1 pint jar and pour the olive oil over garlic. Cover with jar lid and shake well. Let stand at room temperature for 1 week, shaking well once every day. Will keep indefinitely. One teaspoon oil may be substituted for 2 cloves of crushed garlic in any recipe.

mornay sauce
rémoulade sauce

Basic Mornay Sauce is one accompaniment no good cook should be without. One of the best-known cheese sauces, Basic Mornay Sauce is made from another Basic — Béchamel Sauce, page 4. You'll use it as an accompaniment for cauliflower (Vegetables, pg. 17), rice (Cereals, pg. 5) and later in a number of other dishes.

Basic Rémoulade Sauce is a cold sauce, highly spiced, which is often served with cold fish or meat. It is a prime ingredient in our tasty Celery Rémoulade (Salads, pg. 16).

BASIC MORNAY SAUCE

1 recipe Basic White Sauce (pg. 4)
2 tbsp. butter
1 c. grated Parmesan cheese

Prepare Basic White Sauce and remove from heat. Cut the butter into small pieces. Stir the Parmesan cheese and butter into white sauce, beating with wooden spoon until butter is melted. The amount of salt in white sauce may be decreased if desired, because Parmesan cheese sometimes imparts a salty flavor.

BASIC RÉMOULADE SAUCE

1 c. Basic Blender Mayonnaise (pg. 3)
1 tbsp. lemon juice
2 tbsp. finely chopped capers
2 tsp. Dijon mustard
1 tsp. minced parsley
2 tsp. chopped chives
¾ tsp. anchovy paste

Combine all ingredients in a small mixing bowl. Stir gently with a wooden spoon until blended. Place in airtight container and refrigerate.

a spicy touch

The three sauces on this page lend a spicy touch to the foods they accompany. Basic Peperonata is a sauce combining tomatoes, peppers and Spanish onion. It is especially good with poultry. Paprika-Orange Sauce is a piquant concoction that may be served with Spiced Rice With Oranges (Cereals, pg. 8). This sauce is a pretty, orange-red color and its flavor makes it a very versatile sauce. Our Basic Mustard Sauce is delightful with ham or cold cuts.

 ## BASIC PEPERONATA SAUCE

¼ c. butter
¼ c. olive oil
1 lg. Spanish onion, sliced
2½ c. diced green and red sweet peppers
1½ c. diced skinned tomatoes
2 tsp. Garlic Oil (*pg. 10*)
1 tsp. basil
1 tsp. salt
¼ tsp. freshly ground pepper

Heat butter and oil in a heavy frying pan until hot. Add the onion and sauté over low heat until lightly browned. Add the green and red peppers, tomatoes, Garlic Oil and basil; bring to a boil. Reduce heat and stir in salt and pepper. Cover and simmer for about 15 minutes or until vegetables are tender. Pour into blender container and blend until smooth. Store in covered container. Serve on pork pie and other meat dishes.

PAPRIKA-ORANGE SAUCE

5 c. Basic Chicken Stock (*Soups, pg. 2*)
1 tsp. paprika
Juice and grated rind of 1 lg. orange
⅛ tsp. white pepper
Salt to taste

Pour chicken stock into heavy saucepan; add paprika, orange juice and rind. Simmer for about 1 hour and 30 minutes or until liquid is reduced to 2 cups sauce. Season with pepper and salt; serve hot.

 ## BASIC MUSTARD SAUCE

2 tbsp. Dijon mustard
1 tbsp. dry English mustard
1 c. whipping cream

Combine mustards, mixing to a smooth paste. Whip the cream in a small bowl until soft peaks form. Stir a small amount of whipped cream into the mustard mixture, blending well. Beat the mustard mixture into the whipped cream just until blended. May serve as dip for vegetables or for meat fondues.

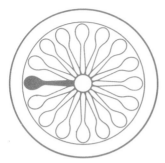

sour cream sauces

The sauces introduced on these two pages are very versatile, and you'll find any number of occasions to use them. The two sour cream sauces, Sauce Maureen and Cucumber Sauce, provide something different in a zippy complement to sliced cold meat and seafood. Basic Clarified Butter, which has the milk solids removed, is re-quired in the preparation of many dishes, but it is also good poured over foods, such as waffles, which are normally spread with butter. It is frequently used for sautéeing foods since it does not burn as quickly as regular butter. Tomato Coulis Sauce is a spicy, natural tomato purée that is used with many vegetables and meats — such as Stuffed Spanish Tomatoes With Croutons (Vegetables, pg. 27). Spanish Sauce, rich with the flavors of parsley, carrots, onions and white wine, is delicious served over rice.

CUCUMBER SAUCE

¾ c. grated cucumber
¾ c. sour cream
2 tbsp. red wine vinegar
½ tsp. salt
½ tsp. garlic salt
½ tsp. freshly ground pepper

Squeeze excess moisture from cucumber, then combine all ingredients in small mixing bowl. Cover; chill to blend flavors. Serve with cold meats and seafood. This makes about 1 ½ cups of sauce.

SAUCE MAUREEN

1 c. sour cream
1 tbsp. instant minced onion
1 tsp. curry powder
¼ tsp. salt
1 tbsp. lemon juice

Combine all ingredients in small mixing bowl. Cover; chill to blend flavors. Serve with cold meats and seafood. This makes about 1 cup of sauce.

sauce maureen

The pungent flavor of curry blended with sour cream, lemon juice and instant minced onion makes Sauce Maureen an outstanding one — and easy to prepare too! Try it with cold, sliced lamb or as a seafood sauce.

BASIC CLARIFIED BUTTER

1 c. butter

Place butter in a small saucepan and melt over very low heat. Remove from heat and allow to cool. Sediment will settle to the bottom of the pan and clear butter will rise to the top. Pour off the clear butter, leaving the sediment in pan. This will make about ¾ cup of clarified butter.

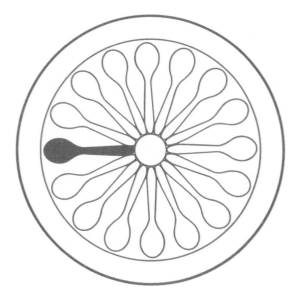

savory sauces

TOMATO COULIS SAUCE

2 c. chopped peeled tomatoes
1/8 tsp. thyme leaves
1/8 tsp. tarragon leaves
1/4 c. chopped chives
1 garlic clove, pressed
1/4 tsp. freshly ground pepper
1/2 tsp. salt
2 tbsp. olive oil

Combine all ingredients except olive oil in a 1 1/2-quart saucepan. Simmer until the tomatoes are tender, then turn into blender container and purée. Return to the pan and add the oil. Simmer for 3 minutes. May be served hot or cold. This makes 2 cups of sauce.

SPANISH SAUCE

2 tbsp. Garlic Oil *(Sauces, pg. 10)*
1 med. onion, thinly sliced
1 med. carrot, diced
2 tbsp. flour
1/2 c. Chablis
2 1/2 c. beef broth
1 bay leaf
1 clove
2 stalks parsley
1 1/2 tbsp. finely chopped fresh parsley
1 sm. piece of ham hock
Salt and pepper to taste

Heat the oil in a 2-quart saucepan, then add the onion and carrot. Sauté over low heat until tender. Blend in the flour. Add the Chablis and the broth gradually, stirring constantly. Add the remaining ingredients, then cover. Simmer gently for 1 hour and 30 minutes. Strain through sieve and discard vegetable mixture. This sauce may be served with beef and side dishes. Beef and rice may be cooked in this sauce for outstanding flavor.

basic soubise sauce

Basic Soubise Sauce is a delicate, onion-flavored sauce, easy to prepare and certain to add a special touch to anything you serve. And the list of foods that may be served with Basic Soubise Sauce is almost limitless — eggs, veal, poultry, lamb, vegetables, and foods which are gratinéed. Basic Soubise Sauce may be used with fish and in the egg category it will be presented with omelets.

BASIC SOUBISE SAUCE

4 c. thinly sliced onions
3 c. milk
3/4 c. whipping cream
1/2 tsp. salt
1/8 tsp. white pepper

Place the onions in a saucepan and cover with milk. Simmer until the onions are tender. Strain and return liquid to saucepan. Simmer until reduced to 3/4 cup liquid. Stir frequently as the liquid reduces and thickens. If liquid should curdle, then press through a sieve. Place onions in blender and purée. Combine reduced liquid, onion purée and cream in a saucepan and heat through, stirring constantly. Season with salt and pepper. This makes about 2 cups of sauce.

savory sauces

The term "fondue" in recent years has come to be associated with cheese sauces melted in an attractive pot over a flame. We *will* cover those specific types of fondues later, but the more general meaning of fondue is the one we're concerned with here. A fondue in this sense, is simply any food cooked in butter or vegetable oil over low heat until reduced to a pulp. It may then be puréed to a sauce consistency. Such is the category into which this spicy Tomato Fondue Sauce falls. This sauce is used when preparing the Rolled Spanish Omelet (Eggs, pg. 14). However, it is also delightful with many vegetables and meats, and may in fact, be used as a dip for these foods at informal gatherings.

Paprika Tomato Sauce is an unusual tasting blend of mint leaves and celery salt. It is delicious when served over omelets or pasta and is a delightful accompaniment for veal.

Mustard Cream Sauce is made from a *roux* base (page 3) and may be used to add color and flavor variety to vegetables such as broccoli and asparagus; it may also be used on seafoods.

The basic ingredient of Gorgona Sauce is fresh tomatoes. It is a marvelous cold dunking sauce for seafood or fresh vegetables. When making this sauce, it is very important that the olive oil be added to the egg yolk very slowly — a drop at a time if necessary — to avoid curdling.

The boiled eggs are added in a granular form by passing them through a "ricer" — a kitchen utensil built somewhat like a perforated basket with a snug plunger which, when pressure is exerted, forces the egg through the many holes.

TOMATO FONDUE SAUCE

2 tbsp. butter
2 tbsp. olive oil
3/4 c. finely chopped onions
1 1/2 c. peeled, seeded and chopped tomatoes
1 clove of garlic, crushed
1 tsp. finely chopped, fresh parsley.
1/2 tsp. paprika
Salt and pepper to taste
1 6-oz. can tomato paste

Melt the butter in a small saucepan and add the olive oil. Add the onions and sauté, stirring occasionally, until tender but not brown. Stir in the tomatoes, garlic, parsley and paprika. Cook until tomatoes are tender. Season with salt and pepper. Add the tomato paste and cook for 5 minutes longer. Purée in blender. This makes about 2 cups of sauce.

PAPRIKA-TOMATO SAUCE

2 tsp. paprika
1 1/4 c. beef broth
1 10 1/2-oz. can tomato purée
1/2 tsp. celery salt
1 tsp. finely chopped mint leaves

Mix the paprika with a small amount of the beef broth to make a smooth paste. Combine the remaining beef broth, tomato purée, celery salt and paprika paste in a small saucepan. Stir well and bring to a boil. Stir in mint. Serve as a pasta sauce or sauce for poultry and meats. This makes about 2 1/2 cups of sauce.

MUSTARD CREAM SAUCE

2 tbsp. butter
3 tbsp. all-purpose flour
1/2 tsp. salt
4 tsp. dry English mustard
1 c. boiling water
3 egg yolks
1/3 c. whipping cream
2 tbsp. lemon juice
1 tsp. finely chopped capers

Melt the butter in a heavy saucepan. Combine the flour, salt and mustard and stir into the butter to make a smooth paste. Add the boiling water gradually, stirring constantly, then cook until smooth and thickened. Combine egg yolks and cream and stir slowly into the mustard mixture. Cook until thick, stirring constantly. Combine lemon juice and capers and stir into mustard sauce. Serve with fish and vegetable dishes. This makes about 1 1/2 cups of sauce.

GORGONA SAUCE

1 1/2 cups chopped skinned tomatoes
1 egg yolk
2 tbsp. olive oil
1 1/2 tbsp. tarragon vinegar
10 anchovies, drained and mashed
2 green onions, minced
3 sm. sweet gherkins, minced
1 tsp. finely chopped fresh parsley
1/4 tsp. celery salt
1/4 tsp. salt
Dash of white pepper
6 drops of hot pepper sauce
1 hard-boiled egg, riced

Place tomatoes in a colander to drain all juice. Place egg yolk in a medium mixing bowl and beat lightly with a fork. Beat in the olive oil, several drops at a time, until thick. Add the vinegar slowly, beating constantly. Stir in the remaining ingredients in order listed and mix well. Purée the tomatoes in a blender, then stir into the sauce. Chill overnight to blend flavors. Serve with boiled shrimp or other seafood or use as a dipping sauce for fresh vegetables. This makes about 2 cups of sauce.

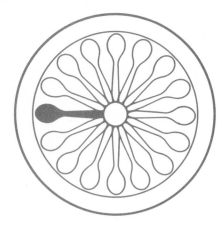

dessert sauces

Dessert is a favorite course for cooks because a well-planned dessert is sure to be appreciated by everyone. The sauce for most desserts is often the *pièce de résistance*. Being so variable and therefore creative, dessert sauces are the most fun to make.

On this page are several chocolate sauces which will glorify the plainest of desserts and even add to fancy ones. The Basic·Chocolate Sauce is an integral part of Profiteroles With Chocolate Sauce, (Desserts, pg. 59). This rich sauce is poured over tiny chou pastry cream puffs for a delightful dessert that's universally liked. The Chocolate Rum Sauce is made with cocoa, and the addition of rum gives it a rich, West Indies flavor and aroma.

Chocolate Cream Sauce is almost pudding-like in its consistency. In addition to serving it as a sauce, it may be frozen — in Basic Sweet Short Pastry tartlet shells, (Desserts, pg. 20) or in ice cube trays for "fudgesicles."

Caramel Glaze is similar to melted or caramelized sugar. It is an extremely hot mixture and therefore must be handled with caution. However, it is most interesting and fun to work with as you will find in making Caramel Glazed Cream Puffs. (Desserts, pg. 64).

BASIC CHOCOLATE SAUCE

¼ c. (firmly packed) brown sugar
2 c. chocolate chips
¼ c. water
½ c. butter
2 tsp. vanilla extract

Combine the brown sugar, chocolate and water in the top of a double boiler over boiling water and stir until smooth. Cut the butter into small pieces and beat into the chocolate mixture. Stir in the vanilla extract. Cover tightly and let stand over warm water until ready to serve. Cool and use as frosting, if desired. This makes 2 cups of sauce.

CHOCOLATE RUM SAUCE

2 c. sugar
¼ c. cocoa
Pinch of salt
1 tbsp. white corn syrup
½ c. milk
1 tbsp. butter
6 tbsp. rum

Combine sugar, cocoa and salt in a heavy saucepan and mix well. Stir in the corn syrup and milk until well blended. Place over medium heat and bring to a slow boil, stirring constantly. Boil for about 2 minutes or until all sugar is melted. Remove from heat and stir in the butter. Add the rum slowly, stirring until well blended. Serve hot or cold. This will make about 2½ cups of sauce.

CHOCOLATE CREAM SAUCE

1 4-oz. package sweet cooking chocolate
2 tbsp. sugar
3 tbsp. water
1 recipe Basic Vanilla Sauce *(pg. 6)*

Break the chocolate into small pieces and place in a small heavy saucepan. Add the sugar and water. Cook over very low heat until smooth, stirring occasionally. Let cool, then fold into the vanilla sauce. This thin pudding-like sauce may be served over cake or cream puffs. This makes about 2½ cups of sauce.

CARAMEL GLAZE

2 c. sugar
1 c. water

Combine the sugar and water in a heavy saucepan. Place over medium heat and stir only until sugar is melted. Let cook at a slow boil, without stirring, for about 30 minutes or until lightly golden and syrupy. Use immediately as individual recipes direct, because glaze hardens rapidly. Handle the hot glaze with caution.

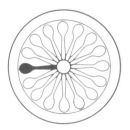

basic génoise sauce

Génoise sauce is a very old, classic sauce. Carême, the great French chef, included "Génoise au Vin de Bordeaux" in his book on the art of French cuisine of the 14th century. His recipe included red Bordeaux wine, herbs, spices, a rich brown stock, shallots, butter, truffles, mushrooms and a little thickening. The recipe for Basic Génoise Sauce is essentially the same as Carême's — well tried and truly delicious. This sauce is great with pastas but by no means limited to this use.

Combine butter and oil in a heavy frypan and heat until sizzling. Add the onions and cook for 3 minutes. Add the carrot, celery and the mushrooms, then cook, stirring frequently, for about 5 minutes. Stir in the veal and cook, stirring constantly, until well broken up and lightly browned. Add the tomatoes, stirring to mix well. Sprinkle the flour over the veal mixture and stir to mix well. Stir in wine gradually, then stir in the beef broth. Season with salt and pepper. Simmer for about 2 hours or until thick, stirring occasionally. This makes about 4 cups of sauce.

BASIC GÉNOISE SAUCE

2 tbsp. butter
½ c. olive oil
1½ c. finely chopped onions
1 carrot, grated
½ c. finely diced celery
½ lb. fresh mushrooms, finely chopped
1 lb. ground veal
2 c. chopped skinned tomatoes
2 tbsp. all-purpose flour
¾ c. dry red wine
1 c. beef broth
Salt and freshly ground pepper to taste

SPECIAL GÉNOISE SAUCE

2 tbsp. finely chopped basil leaves
2 cloves of garlic, pressed
½ tsp. salt
½ c. freshly grated Parmesan cheese
½ c. olive oil

Place the basil, garlic and salt in a wooden bowl and pound with a pestle or press to a paste with the back of a wooden spoon. Work in the cheese. Add the oil, a drop at a time, until well combined. Serve over favorite pasta. This makes about 1 cup of sauce.

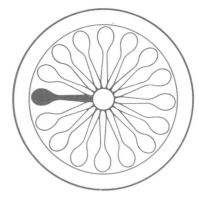

savory sauces

ITALIAN MEAT SAUCE

¼ c. butter
½ c. olive oil
1½ c. finely chopped onions
1 c. grated carrots
½ c. finely chopped celery
2½ c. finely chopped mushrooms and stems
2 tsp. finely chopped parsley
2 lb. lean ground beef
2 tbsp. all-purpose flour
2 tbsp. tomato pureé
1 c. red wine
3½ c. beef broth
Salt and freshly ground pepper to taste

Combine the butter and oil in large frypan and heat. Add the onions and sauté for 1 minute. Add the carrots, celery, mushrooms and parsley and cook, stirring frequently, for 5 minutes. Crumble in the ground beef and cook, stirring frequently, until lightly browned. Sprinkle the flour over the ground beef and stir until well blended. Stir in the tomato pureé. Add the wine gradually, stirring constantly. Add the beef broth and season with salt and pepper. Simmer, stirring occasionally, for about 1 hour or until thick. May be served with various pastas. This makes about 5 cups of sauce.

FRESH TOMATO SAUCE

2 tbsp. olive oil
2 tbsp. butter
1 clove of garlic, pressed
1 lg. green onion, minced
5 c. skinned, chopped ripe tomatoes
⅛ tsp. freshly ground pepper
1 tsp. basil
1 tsp. chopped chives
1 tsp. oregano
½ tsp. sugar
1 tsp. salt

Combine olive oil and butter in a saucepan and heat until butter is melted. Add the garlic and onion. Cook over medium heat for 5 minutes. Stir in the remaining ingredients and cook, stirring, for several minutes, until tomatoes are soft. Serve over favorite pasta. This makes about 4 cups of sauce.

PUNGENT GARLIC SAUCE

5 sm. cloves of garlic, pressed
2 eggs
1 egg yolk
½ tsp. salt
2 c. olive oil

Combine the garlic, eggs, egg yolk, salt and ¼ cup of oil in blender container. Cover and blend for about 5 seconds. Continue blending, adding the remaining oil very slowly as for mayonnaise. This is a thick mayonnaise-like sauce that may be served with pastas, vegetables or bread. This makes about 2½ cups of sauce.

WHITE CLAM SAUCE

¼ c. olive oil
¼ c. butter
3 tbsp. minced green onions
2 tbsp. finely chopped parsley
2 cloves of garlic, pressed
⅛ tsp. white pepper
2 8-oz. cans minced clams
¼ c. dry white wine

Combine the olive oil and butter in a saucepan and heat. Add the green onions, parsley and garlic and sauté without browning for 5 minutes or until onion is transparent. Drain the clams and reserve the juice. Stir the clams into the butter mixture and cook for 2 minutes. Add the reserved juice and the wine and simmer for 5 minutes. Serve over spaghetti or other pastas. This makes about 2½ cups of sauce.

EGG SAUCE

Grated rind of 1 lemon
1 tbsp. finely chopped parsley
2 hard-boiled eggs, chopped
Salt and white pepper to taste
1 recipe Basic White Sauce (pg. 4)
1 tbsp. butter

Fold the lemon rind, parsley, eggs and seasoning into the hot white sauce. Stir in the butter. May be served with vegetables or seafood. This makes about 3 cups of sauce.

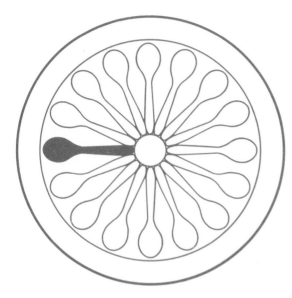

classic dessert sauces

SABAYON SAUCE

Sabayon is one of many sauces with a medieval heritage. One of the sweet Italian dishes introduced by Catherine de Médici to delight the French court, it is now a well known French dessert sauce. The Italian name for this sauce, *Zabaglione*, was gallicized to *Sabayon*.

Sabayon is a BASIC dessert sauce — one that is not difficult to prepare if the directions are followed explicitly. Keep in mind that the mixture containing sugar, egg yolks, water and wine is cooked in a *bain-marie* or double boiler saucepan. It must be cooked over very low heat and whisked vigorously until it is frothy, thick and creamy. *Sabayon* must never be allowed to boil.

This BASIC sauce is a fine emergency dessert and may be served in cups or glasses, warm or chilled. It may also be used as an accompaniment to bread pudding or fruit. *Sabayon* is delicious as a sauce with finger cookies or thin slices of sponge cake baked in the oven until dry and crisp.

BASIC SABAYON SAUCE

4 egg yolks
1 tbsp. cold water
3 tbsp. sugar
½ c. Sauterne

Combine the egg yolks and water in the top of a double boiler, then beat with a whisk until well mixed. Add the sugar gradually, beating constantly until dissolved. Add the Sauterne slowly, beating constantly, then place over hot, but not boiling, water. Cook for about 3 minutes or until thickened and of lightly whipped cream consistency, beating constantly. Remove from heat and beat for 1 minute longer. Prepare sauce substituting champagne for Sauterne for a special occasion. This makes about 1 cup of sauce.

LUXEMBOURG SAUCE

Luxembourg Sauce is very similar to Sabayon, in fact, BASIC *Sabayon* Sauce is the foundation for this more luxurious version. This sauce may be poured into a bowl and served at the table over a sweet cake or prepared and served in individual cups. It is very elegant served over summer fruits such as raspberries, pears, peaches and strawberries.

What makes Luxembourg Sauce so characteristic of a gourmet dessert is the method of preparation. The whole success of this delicate sauce depends upon whipping the thick, foamy *Sabayon* over a pan of ice until it is thoroughly cold. Never try to make this sauce with a thin *Sabayon* mixture. Luxembourg Sauce should be thick, creamy and cold before the whipped cream is added. The addition of whipped cream changes the color of the sauce from a golden velvet to a light beige, and the texture from a custard consistency to an airy sauce.

When making Luxembourg Sauce for grand occasions, such as wedding buffets, a promotion, or toasting the arrival of a new baby, replace the Sauterne given in BASIC *Sabayon* Sauce with champagne.

LUXEMBOURG SAUCE

1 recipe Basic Sabayon Sauce
¾ c. whipping cream, whipped

Prepare sauce according to recipe directions, then set top of double boiler in bowl of ice. Beat sauce with wire whisk until cold. Fold in whipped cream carefully until well blended, then turn into serving bowl. This makes about 2½ cups of sauce.

SAUCE MARASCHINO

1½ c. whipping cream
¼ c. maraschino liqueur
6 tbsp. confectioners' sugar

Whip the cream in a large bowl until foamy. Place bowl over a pan of ice, then add the liqueur slowly beating until blended. Add the sugar gradually, then beat cream until stiff. This sauce is very light. Serve over meringues and puddings, if desired. This makes about 3 cups of sauce.

CHOCOLATE SAUCE WITH HONEY

4 squares unsweetened chocolate
1 tbsp. Cointreau
Pinch of salt
¾ c. strained honey
⅓ c. chopped almonds, toasted

Combine the chocolate and Cointreau in the top of a double boiler and cook over hot water until the chocolate melts. Add the salt and honey and cook, stirring constantly, until smooth. Stir in the almonds, then cover. Remove from heat and allow to stand for 20 minutes. Serve warm over plain sponge cake, vanilla ice cream or cream-filled choux pastries. This makes about 1 cup of sauce.

ALMOND SAUCE

1 c. sugar
⅓ c. whipping cream
2 tsp. vanilla
½ c. (packed) brown sugar
⅓ c. butter
½ c. chopped almonds, toasted

Combine sugar, cream, vanilla, brown sugar and butter in the top of a double boiler. Cook over boiling water until butter is melted and sauce is smooth, stirring constantly. Remove from heat and stir in almonds, then let cool. Serve over pudding, fruit or ice cream. Sauce will become sugary if refrigerated. Cook over low heat, stirring constantly, to return to smooth consistency. This makes about 2 cups of sauce.

DATE-FIG SAUCE

½ c. pitted dates
½ c. fig preserves with syrup
1 c. chopped blanched almonds

Cover dates with boiling water and let soak for about 1 hour or until plump. Drain dates, then cut into small pieces. Combine dates, fig preserves and almonds and blend well. Serve with ice cream, bread pudding or baked custard, if desired. This makes about 2 cups of sauce.

chaud-froid sauce

Chaud-Froid (pronounced "sho-frwa") is a classic coating sauce. Delicious and elegantly beautiful, it is used over chicken, turkey, cold meats, ham and fish and other seafood. The French term literally translated means "hot-cold," a reference to the manner in which the sauce begins hot and ends cold.

Basically, *Chaud-Froid* Sauce is a form of aspic containing unflavored gelatin to set it. It also consists of stock from the food it is to coat; beef stock is used in a *chaud-froid* sauce for beef, fish stock for seafood in *chaud-froid* sauce, and so on. (In a later lesson we will give a beautiful recipe for Chicken In *Chaud-Froid* Sauce.) The color of the sauce will be either white or brown, dependent upon the stock.

In handling *Chaud-Froid* Sauce (as with any aspic glaze), it is vital that it be at the correct temperature to produce a syrupy consistency. If it is too cold, the sauce will become thick; if too warm, it will become thin — and either way it will not coat the meat smoothly. Over-thickening may be corrected by setting the sauce out at room temperature to soften; conversely, refrigeration will thicken a too-thin mixture.

It is very important to note that you only stir the sauce very gently. Stirring will cause air to be trapped within the sauce and bubbles will form on the surface. Such bubbles cannot be broken, for bursting one bubble will produce two in its place! Therefore, care must be taken to avoid their formation.

Several coatings are applied to the meat — about four to six — to form a shiny, smooth covering. (Between coatings the sauce is refrigerated.) The meat is placed on a wire rack while the coatings are poured over it, and the dripping sauce may be caught in a jelly roll pan beneath, to avoid waste. These drippings may be <u>slowly</u> poured back into the remaining sauce in the original container; however, you must discard the drippings if a bubble appears while pouring.

Because of their beauty — and because they may be conveniently stored in the refrigerator until serving time — *chaud-froid* dishes are particularly appropriate for buffets and festive dinners. The aspic coating lends itself to decorating to fit the occasion; black olives, truffles, pimentos, lemon rind, and other vegetables and fruits cut into various shapes and designs may be used. A *chaud-*

froid dish may even be decorated with nonedibles, such as flowers and leaves. After the decorations are placed, the entire production is covered with a thin layer of clear, syrupy aspic (as in Engraving, Salads, pg. 5) to set the design.

Mastering *Chaud-Froid* Sauce will enable you to create truly classic dishes. Patience and care in preparation will produce an entrée that is undoubtedly a masterpiece of culinary art.

CHAUD-FROID SAUCE

1 c. Basic Simple Aspic *(Salads, pg. 4)*
1¼ c. Basic Velouté Sauce *(pg. 4)*

Prepare the appropriate aspic, using Basic Beef, Chicken or Fish Stock depending upon which food you are coating. Prepare the *Velouté* sauce. Let the aspic and *velouté* sauce cool to room temperature. Stir the aspic into the *velouté* sauce very gently until well blended, avoiding making bubbles. Chill the sauce until syrupy before using to coat poultry, fish and meats. This makes 2¼ cups of sauce.

How To Coat:

Arrange the meat, poultry or fish to be coated on a wire rack in a jelly roll pan. Spoon a small amount of sauce carefully over top, covering evenly. Spoon the excess sauce from the jelly roll pan back into remaining sauce. Place the meat in the refrigerator for 15 minutes or until coating is firm. Keep sauce at syrupy stage by chilling if necessary. Repeat procedure 6 times or until desired thickness of coating is obtained. Arrange garnish over the final coat. Spoon clear syrupy aspic over the top to set garnish. Chill until ready to use.

FAR EASTERN CURRY SAUCE

¼ c. butter
⅓ c. finely chopped onion
¼ c. all-purpose flour
4 tsp. curry powder
2 tsp. sugar
1 tsp. salt
¼ tsp. ginger
⅛ tsp. white pepper
2 c. milk
2 tsp. lemon juice

Melt the butter in a medium saucepan over low heat. Add the onion and sauté, stirring occasionally, for about 5 minutes or until golden. Remove from heat. Combine the flour, curry powder, sugar, salt, ginger and pepper, and stir into the onion mixture. Return to heat and add the milk gradually, stirring constantly. Cook over medium heat, stirring constantly, until mixture comes to a boil. Reduce heat and simmer until thick, then stir in the lemon juice. This sauce may be served with poultry, rice or potatoes. This makes about 1½ cups of sauce.

bolognese sauce

Bolognese Sauce, another of the classics, is mildly spicy and particularly compatible with pasta. Appropriately, it is named for the Italian town Bologna, where pasta is a gastronomical specialty.

There are some notable variations from the usual in the list of ingredients for *Bolognese* Sauce. Most striking is the absence of quantities of tomato paste or sauce which ordinarily dominates Italian dishes. Instead, only three tablespoons of tomato purée are called for in the recipe. Another interesting difference that sets *Bolognese* apart from other Italian sauces is the inclusion of chicken livers — minced and browned, that lends a subtle flavor innovation. All stock may be used for the principal liquid in the sauce; however, we suggest that using vermouth or another white wine for half of the stock allowance will add an exciting zest to the taste.

BOLOGNESE SAUCE

¼ c. olive oil
4 slices bacon, diced
2 lg. onions, finely chopped
2 med. carrots, grated
½ c. diced celery
1 lb. lean ground beef
½ lb. chicken livers, minced
⅓ c. tomato purée
1½ c. vermouth or white Chianti
3½ c. beef stock
½ tsp. nutmeg
1 tsp. salt
½ tsp. pepper

Heat the oil in a large skillet. Add the bacon and cook until lightly browned. Add the onions, carrots and celery and cook, stirring, for 5 minutes. Crumble the beef over the vegetable mixture and break up with a wooden spoon. Cook, stirring occasionally, until all pink is gone from the beef. Add the chicken livers and cook, stirring, for about 3 minutes. Stir in the tomato purée, vermouth, beef stock and seasonings. Reduce heat and simmer for about 1 hour or until the sauce is thickened. This makes about 4 cups of sauce.

HICKORY BARBECUE SAUCE

¼ c. finely minced onion
1 tbsp. brown sugar
1 tbsp. mustard seed
2 tsp. paprika
1 tsp. oregano
1 tsp. chili powder
1 tsp. freshly ground pepper
½ tsp. salt
½ tsp. ground cloves
1 bay leaf
1 clove of garlic, pressed
1 c. catsup
½ c. water
¼ c. olive oil
¼ c. tarragon vinegar
2 tbsp. Worcestershire sauce
2 or 3 drops of liquid smoke (opt.)

Combine all the ingredients in a heavy saucepan and mix well. Simmer for about 25 minutes, stirring occasionally. Remove the bay leaf before serving. Serve with beef or pork. This makes about 2 cups of sauce.

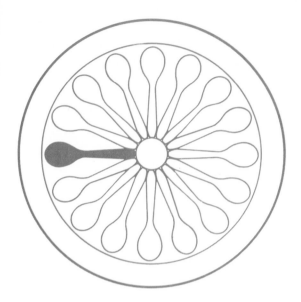

béarnaise sauce

Béarnaise sauce, according to many authors of culinary works, was named in honor of King Henry IV of France who was known as the "Great *Béarnais*". This sauce is certainly one of the best of the classic French sauces. *Béarnaise* is often unfairly described as mayonnaise with butter. Flavored with wine, vinegar, shallots and herbs, it is much more. Like Hollandaise, it is an emulsified sauce made with egg yolks and butter.

Béarnaise is thought to be difficult to prepare because it curdles easily if overheated. However, curdling can be prevented by simply paying close attention to suggested temperatures. By following our easy step-by-step instructions, you can produce perfect Basic *Bearnaise* Sauce. Serve it over grilled or sautéed meat, poultry, fish or any other appropriate dish.

BASIC BÉARNAISE SAUCE

½ c. butter
1 tbsp. minced green onion or shallots
¼ tsp. white pepper
½ tsp. tarragon leaves
½ tsp. chervil
2½ tbsp. red wine vinegar
2½ tbsp. Chablis or other dry white wine
3 egg yolks
2 tbsp. water
¼ c. finely chopped parsley
1 tsp. lemon juice
Salt to taste

1 It is important to have all ingredients measured and assembled before beginning the sauce.

2 Melt the butter in a small saucepan and keep warm.

3 Combine the onion, pepper, tarragon, chervil, vinegar and wine in the top of a double boiler and place over direct heat. Simmer until almost all the liquid has evaporated. Cool to lukewarm.

4 Beat the egg yolks with the water, then blend into the onion mixture. Place over hot water and cook, beating constantly with a whisk until thick. Remove from heat.

5 Add a tablespoon of butter at a time, whisking vigorously, until all butter is absorbed. The sauce will separate if the butter is added too fast or too much at a time.

6 Add the parsley and stir until well blended.

7 Stir in the lemon juice, then season with salt and additional pepper, if desired. Keep warm over hot water. This makes 1 cup of sauce.

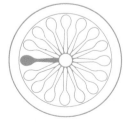

fennel sauce

FENNEL SAUCE

¼ c. butter
2 tsp. all-purpose flour
1 tsp. dry mustard
4 egg yolks, lightly beaten
6 sprigs of fennel leaves, finely chopped
2 tsp. finely chopped parsley
2 tsp. finely chopped chervil
4 green onions, finely chopped
1½ c. half and half cream

Salt and white pepper to taste
1 tbsp. strained lemon juice

Place the butter, flour, mustard, egg yolks, herbs and onions in the top of a double boiler. Cook, stirring, over hot water until blended. Add the cream gradually, stirring constantly. Cook and stir until the sauce thickens. Season with salt and pepper, then add the lemon juice. If fresh fennel is not available, ½ teaspoon dried fennel may be substituted. This makes about 2 cups of sauce.

dessert sauces

Dessert sauces have a way of making an average dessert something special. That's why they are more than worth the little effort it takes to prepare them. Introduced in this lesson are 8 classic dessert sauces which will add greatly to your everyday desserts, and add a very special appeal to the steamed puddings in the Desserts section.

Generally, accompanying dessert sauces are a matter of personal choice. However, for a simple dessert, most homemakers prefer a sauce which contrasts sharply in flavor and richness. Basic Lemon Sauce, for example, has

very robust flavor that ideally contrasts with the more subtle flavor of Black Cap Pudding (Desserts, pg. 110) On the other hand, for a richer dessert, a mild-flavored, delicate sauce is preferred. Escoffier's Christmas Plum Pudding (Desserts, pg. 112) is delicious topped with a mild-flavored buttery sauce. Sauces made with liquor are favorites at dinner parties. Stewed fruits, ice cream and bread puddings are unusually good topped with sauces made of brandy, rum, sherry, or liqueur.

So many dessert sauces can be made ahead of time and kept on hand in the refrigerator. Drop-in guests will be surprised and delighted when, on a minute's notice, you magically produce a delicious dessert topped with a luscious sauce.

LEMON CURD

¾ c. unsalted butter
1 tsp. grated lemon rind
⅔ c. lemon juice
2 c. sugar
6 eggs

Place the butter, rind, juice and sugar in the top of a double boiler. Cook, stirring constantly, over hot water on low heat until the sugar is dissolved. Beat the eggs for 5 minutes with an electric mixer. Stir a small amount of the hot mixture into the eggs, then pour the egg mixture into the hot mixture. Cook, stirring with a whisk, until thick and creamy. This makes 3 cups of sauce.

PUNCH SAUCE

2 tbsp. cornstarch
⅓ c. lemon juice
1¼ c. Sauterne
Grated rind of 1 lemon
1 1-in. piece of stick cinnamon
¼ c. unsalted butter
⅓ c. sugar
2 tbsp. rum

Combine the cornstarch and the lemon juice, stirring until well blended. Combine the Sauterne, lemon rind, cinnamon stick and butter in the top of a double boiler. Place over hot water and cook until the butter is melted. Blend in the cornstarch mixture and cook, stirring constantly, until thickened and clear. Add the sugar and rum, stirring until the sugar is dissolved. Remove the cinnamon stick. Serve with steamed puddings, gingerbread or nut breads. This makes about 2 cups of sauce.

JELLY SAUCE

1 c. red currant jelly
¼ c. port
2 tbsp. sweet white wine
2 tbsp. lemon juice

Combine all the ingredients in a small saucepan and heat, stirring, until the jelly is melted and the sauce is hot. This makes about 1½ cups of sauce.

BASIC LEMON SAUCE

⅓ c. sugar
2 tbsp. cornstarch
⅓ c. lemon juice
1¼ c. water
½ tsp. grated lemon rind
Pinch of salt
¼ c. butter

Combine the sugar and cornstarch in a small saucepan. Stir in the lemon juice and water, then add the lemon rind and salt. Place over medium heat and cook, stirring constantly, until thickened and clear. Remove from heat and stir in the butter. This makes about 1½ cups of sauce.

LEMON MOUSSELINE SAUCE

1 recipe Basic Lemon Sauce
1 c. whipping cream, whipped

Prepare Basic Lemon Sauce and cool completely. Fold in the whipped cream carefully. This makes about 3 cups of sauce.

BASIC HARD SAUCE

1 c. butter, softened
1 1-lb. box confectioners' sugar, sifted
¼ c. brandy

Cream the butter with an electric mixer until light. Add the sugar gradually and beat until fluffy. Add the brandy and blend well. Serve immediately and store any remaining sauce in the refrigerator. Bring to room temperature before serving. This makes about 3 cups of sauce.

VARIATION:

CALVADOS SAUCE

Prepare Basic Hard Sauce omitting the brandy and substituting an equal amount of Calvados or strong cider.

STRAWBERRY DRINGER

1 qt. large fresh strawberries
Sifted confectioners' sugar
2½ c. whipping cream

Remove the hulls from the strawberries, then cut the strawberries in quarters. Place ¼ of the strawberries in a straight-sided glass container and sprinkle with confectioners' sugar. Whip the cream until soft peaks form. Cover the strawberries with ¼ of the whipped cream. Repeat layers of strawberries and cream, sprinkling each layer of strawberries with sugar. Let stand for several hours, then serve over pound cake or angel food cake. This makes about 8 to 10 servings.

BRANDY SAUCE

1½ c. sugar
2 tbsp. cornstarch
½ tsp. salt
2¼ c. boiling water
2 eggs
3 tbsp. butter
½ c. brandy

Combine the sugar, cornstarch and salt in the top of a double boiler. Add the boiling water gradually, stirring constantly, then cook until sugar is dissolved. Beat the eggs until foamy, then stir in a small amount of the hot mixture. Stir the egg mixture back into the sauce. Cook, stirring constantly, over hot water for about 5 minutes or until thickened. Remove from heat and stir in the butter and brandy. This makes about 3 cups of sauce.

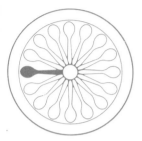

three italian dessert sauces

Italian cuisine is so often confined in our thinking to concoctions of pasta, tomato sauce, and cheese, that it is refreshing to consider another fascinating and delicious aspect of Italian cooking: tempting Italian dessert sauces. Each of the three sauces below has a distinct and unusual flavor and an amazing degree of versatility. With Basic Caramel Sauce, you may choose the consistency that best suits your dessert — it may be anywhere from thin to syrupy, depending upon the length of cooking time. Serve it on ice creams, plain cakes, puddings and custards to transform an everyday dessert to a sublime one. If you prefer a tangy topping for ice cream or cake, Kumquat Sauce will add not only zesty flavor but smashing color as well. Marsala Sweet Sauce, in which the wine flavor is very distinct, is best suited to rice or bread puddings, pound cake or any fresh fruit.

BASIC CARAMEL SAUCE

¼ c. butter
1 c. sugar
½ c. (packed) dark brown sugar
½ c. half and half cream
1 tsp. vanilla extract

Melt the butter in a small saucepan over medium heat. Stir in the sugar, brown sugar and cream and bring to a boil, stirring constantly, until the sugar is dissolved. Reduce heat and simmer for 1 to 2 minutes. Sauce should be thin. Remove from heat and stir in the vanilla. Cool. Serve over ice cream or pudding. This makes about 1½ cups of sauce.

KUMQUAT SAUCE

8 kumquats
1 c. sugar

Peel the kumquats and cut fruit into quarters. Remove seeds, then place the kumquats in a medium-sized saucepan. Stir in the sugar and ½ cup of water. Bring to a boil, stirring constantly, until sugar is dissolved. Reduce the heat and simmer for 15 minutes, stirring occasionally. Cool, then chill. This may be served over ice cream or plain cake. This makes about 1 cup of sauce.

MARSALA SWEET SAUCE

¼ c. cornstarch
1 c. Marsala Wine
2 tbsp. butter
½ c. sugar

Mix the cornstarch with ⅓ cup of Marsala until smooth. Pour 1 cup of water into a small saucepan and bring to a boil. Stir in the cornstarch mixture and bring to a boil again, stirring constantly. Add the butter and sugar, then cook for 5 minutes. Stir in the remaining Marsala and heat through. This sauce may be served over bread pudding, rice pudding, plain cake or fresh fruits. This makes about 1½ cups of sauce.

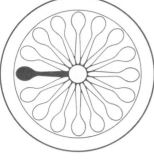

basic dill sauce

1 Melt the butter in a medium-sized saucepan over medium heat. Mix the flour and pepper and stir into the butter with a wire whisk until smooth.

Basic Dill Sauce is certain to challenge your imagination . . . It adapts to so many uses that its only limitation is the number of ways you will think of to serve it. The sauce is delicious on vegetable fritters, baked potatoes, Potato Flan, baked fish, chicken, broccoli, green beans — the list could go on and on. You can serve it as a dipping sauce for *hors d' oeuvres*, serve it cold on cold cuts or warmed on hot meats. To complete its list of commendable qualities, it is truly a good looking sauce: thin, smooth, and cream colored with flecks of green dill.

Fresh dill is the key to the success of this sauce. Although dried dill could be used in an emergency, only fresh dill will fully develop the sauce's delightfully different flavor.

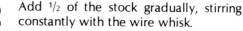

2 Add ½ of the stock gradually, stirring constantly with the wire whisk.

BASIC DILL SAUCE

¼ c. butter
¼ c. all-purpose flour
⅛ tsp. white pepper
2 c. Basic Chicken Stock *(Soups, pg. 2)*
¼ c. half and half cream
Salt to taste
1½ tsp. sugar
1 tbsp. cider vinegar
¼ c. chopped fresh dill

3 Blend the stock with the flour mixture until the sauce is smooth and thickened.

4 Stir in the remaining stock gradually, then bring to a boil, stirring constantly. Reduce heat and simmer for 10 minutes, stirring frequently.

6 Add the salt, sugar and vinegar and stir until the salt and sugar have dissolved.

5 Add the cream slowly to the sauce, stirring constantly with the wire whisk.

7 Stir in the dill and simmer for 5 minutes longer to blend the flavors. Beginners should prepare this sauce in a double boiler to insure smoothness. This makes about 2½ cups of sauce.

sauces
for game birds

SAVORY PÂTÉ DE FOIE CREAM

If you are searching for the perfect sauce for chicken or game birds — one that will accent rather than disguise the bird's flavor — Savory Pâté de Foie Cream is an excellent one. Be certain the sauce is set <u>around</u> the hot fowl, since it will melt if piped directly onto it.

SAVORY PÂTÉ DE FOIE CREAM

1 3-oz. package cream cheese, softened
Whipping cream

1 2¾-oz. can pâté de foie gras
1 tbsp. Madeira

Place the cream cheese in small mixing bowl and beat with a fork until smooth, adding just enough cream to moisten. Break up the *pâté* with a fork and add the Madeira gradually, blending well. Combine the cream cheese mixture and the *pâté* thoroughly. This mixture may be used to pipe designs over cold meats, or around game birds or chicken. It may also be served as a spread or garnish for *hors d'oeuvres*. This makes about ¾ cup of savory cream.

cranberry-orange sauce

Cranberry-Orange Sauce is very traditional and very American. Most frequently associated with holiday feasts, its flavor is one of which we never tire. The principal ingredients are fresh cranberries, sugar, and orange juice, and the addition of tawny Port adds zest and sparkle to its familiar taste.

Though it is most often served with chicken or turkey, don't overlook using it with wild game and game birds, ham and pork.

CRANBERRY-ORANGE SAUCE

1 lb. fresh cranberries
2 c. sugar
½ c. orange juice
⅛ tsp. salt
¼ c. tawny Port

Wash and pick over the cranberries. Combine the cranberries, sugar, orange juice, salt and Port in a large saucepan. Bring to a boil, then cover. Reduce heat and simmer until the cranberry skins pop and the cranberries are soft. Serve warm or cold with game or poultry. This makes about 3½ cups of sauce.

lemon and parsley sauce

Tang and pungence are mutually complementary and delectably "married" in Lemon and Parsley Sauce. Marvelous accompaniment for cold meats (especially cold, sliced beef tongue), this lemon-fragrant sauce will also evoke nonstop compliments when served over fish, chicken, new potatoes, asparagus, broccoli — nearly any meat or vegetable you choose.

LEMON AND PARSLEY SAUCE

2 c. chicken broth
2 tbsp. cornstarch

2 tbsp. lemon juice
1 tbsp. finely chopped parsley
Salt and pepper to taste
2 drops of yellow food coloring

Pour the broth into the top of a double boiler over hot water and place over medium heat. Dissolve the cornstarch in a small amount of water and add to the stock. Cook, stirring constantly, until thickened. Add the lemon juice, parsley and seasonings. Cook for 2 minutes longer. Add the food coloring, mixing well. This sauce may be served with cold sliced meat or fish. This makes about 2 cups of sauce.

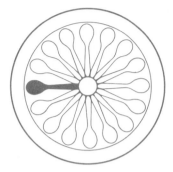

basic oriental sauces

Master the art of sauce making, oriental or occidental, and you can turn any dish into a special treat. A sauce provides the crowning glory to any dish and enhances both flavor and appearance. Sauces should be varied according to the dishes they accompany. They should be at the same time a subtle contrast and complement to the dish.

As a sauce is only as good as the ingredients used and the care taken in preparation, basic sauce recipes should be followed closely until original variations may safely be tried.

Basic Chinese Sweet and Sour Sauce adds a sunny tang to a wide variety of foods. This classic oriental sauce uses simple yet flavorful ingredients. Water and wine vinegar are used for the liquid base; cornstarch is used as the thickening agent; and soy sauce and brown sugar are used as flavoring.

It is the simplicity of this sauce which makes it distinctive. Sweet and sour sauce is typical of Chinese cuisine which is famed for brief cooking methods that yield a high nutritional value. As this sweet and sour sauce blends best with meat, it may be served with chicken, pork, beef, or seafood for an oriental flavoring. For example, one method for preparing shrimp calls for deep-fat frying until the outside is crisp and the inside soft. When the fried shrimp are combined with the sweet and sour sauce, the dish is a perfect combination of complementary flavors.

Another classic example of oriental sauces is Duk Sauce. Duk (or Duck) Sauce, a tart blend of jam and chutney, is also known as plum sauce, and is best when accompanied by a peppery, hot combination of dry mustard and wine. It is delicious when served with egg rolls, tempura, fried seafood, and pork.

BASIC CHINESE SWEET AND SOUR SAUCE

3/4 c. sugar
2 tbsp. soy sauce
1 tbsp. dry white wine
3 tbsp. wine vinegar
3 tbsp. catsup
2 tbsp. cornstarch
1/2 c. water

Combine the sugar, soy sauce, wine, vinegar and catsup in a saucepan and bring to a boil. Dissolve the cornstarch in the water and add to the sauce. Cook over low heat, stirring, until sauce has thickened. This makes about 1 to 1 1/4 cups of sauce.

DUK SAUCE

1 c. red plum jam
1 c. chutney
6 tbsp. dry mustard
1/4 c. Sauterne

Combine the jam and the chutney in a small bowl and blend thoroughly. The Duk Sauce may be served hot or cold. Place the dry mustard in a small bowl and stir in a small amount of the Sauterne until smooth. Add the remaining Sauterne gradually and blend thoroughly. Serve the sauce and hot mustard separately in small individual bowls. This makes 2 cups Duk Sauce and about 1/2 cup hot mustard.

TARTAR SAUCE SUPREME

1 c. Basic Blender Mayonnaise (Sauces, pg. 3)
1 1/2 tbsp. minced dill pickle
1 1/2 tbsp. minced fresh parsley
1 1/2 tbsp. capers
1 1/2 tbsp. grated onion
1 1/2 tbsp. minced green olives

Place the mayonnaise in a mixing bowl and stir in the pickle, parsley, capers, onion and olives. Chill the sauce for several hours, then serve with seafood. This makes about 1 1/2 cups of sauce.

CREOLE RÉMOULADE SAUCE

3 tbsp. drained capers
1/2 tsp. hot sauce
1/4 c. lemon juice
3/4 c. minced celery
1/2 c. minced parsley
1/4 c. minced green onions
1 tbsp. prepared horseradish
1 tbsp. Worcestershire sauce
1/4 c. catsup
1/2 c. Dijon mustard
2 c. Basic Mayonnaise (Sauces, pg. 3)

Combine all ingredients in a mixing bowl and chill well. This makes about 3 3/4 cups of sauce.

OYSTER COCKTAIL SAUCE

1 c. catsup
1 sm. onion, grated
2 tbsp. finely chopped celery
2 tsp. lemon juice
1 tbsp. Worcestershire sauce
Prepared horseradish to taste

Combine the catsup, onion, celery, lemon juice, Worcestershire sauce and horseradish in a mixing bowl, blending well. Chill for at least 30 minutes. Serve with fresh, raw oysters or Oyster Puffs (Seafood, pg. 30). This makes about 1¼ cups of sauce.

HORSERADISH SAUCE FOR SEAFOOD

1 c. sour cream
1 tsp. seasoned salt
¼ tsp. paprika
2 tsp. lemon juice
2 tbsp. prepared horseradish
1 tbsp. instant minced onion

Combine all of the ingredients in a mixing bowl, and chill well for the flavors to blend. This makes about 1¼ cups of sauce.

MEXICALI SAUCE

1 c. chili sauce
2 tbsp. lemon juice
¼ tsp. salt
1 tbsp. prepared horseradish
1 tbsp. instant minced onion
2 tbsp. Worcestershire sauce
1 tbsp. chopped chives

Combine all of the ingredients in a mixing bowl, then chill well for the flavors to blend. This makes about 1½ cups of sauce.

seafood sauce supreme

seafood sauce supreme

This tempting sauce is made with creamy Chef's Mayonnaise (pg. 34), chopped watercress, lemon juice, minced onion and Worcestershire sauce. It is an unusually delicious sauce for hot, crispy, fried shrimp.

Seafood Sauce Supreme is made with either homemade mayonnaise (Chef's Mayonnaise, pg. 34) or salad dressing, both delicious in their own right. It is quickly prepared, especially when the mayonnaise is made ahead of time.

This delicious seafood sauce is complementary to a variety of seafood dishes. However, it is particularly good with fried seafood.

SEAFOOD SAUCE SUPREME

1 c. Chef's Mayonnaise (pg. 34) or salad dressing
1 bunch of watercress, chopped
1 tbsp. lemon juice
1 tbsp. instant minced onion
1 tsp. Worcestershire sauce

Place all of the ingredients in a bowl and mix well. Chill to allow the flavors to blend. This makes about 2 cups of sauce.

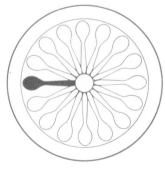

special lemon mayonnaise

SPECIAL LEMON MAYONNAISE

1 recipe Basic Mayonnaise *(pg. 3)*
Strained juice of 1 lemon
1 tsp. dry mustard
1 lemon, sectioned *(General Information, pg. 13)*

Place the mayonnaise in a large bowl. Combine the lemon juice and dry mustard in a small bowl and stir until well blended. Fold the lemon juice mixture into the mayonnaise until blended. Chop the lemon segments fine and fold into the mayonnaise. This makes about 2 cups of mayonnaise.

chef's mayonnaise

The ingredients in creamy Chef's Mayonnaise are similar to those in Basic Mayonnaise (pg. 3) and Basic Blender Mayonnaise (pg. 3). However, while Basic Blender Mayonnaise is mixed in a blender and Basic Mayonnaise is prepared with a mixer, Chef's Mayonnaise is mixed by hand with a wire whisk which produces a very thick mayonnaise. Follow the step-by-step illustrations for perfect results.

CHEF'S MAYONNAISE

2 eggs
1 tsp. salt
⅛ tsp. freshly ground white pepper
2 tbsp. wine vinegar
1 ¾ c. vegetable oil

1 Separate the eggs and place the egg yolks in a medium-sized bowl. Reserve the egg whites and refrigerate for use in other recipes.

2 Add the salt, pepper and ½ tablespoon of the vinegar to the egg yolks and beat well with a wire wisk.

3 Add ¼ cup of the oil, a drop or two at a time, beating well after each addition.

4 Add the remaining vinegar very slowly, beating until well blended.

5 Add the remaining oil, gradually increasing the amounts added and beating well after each addition.

6 The mayonnaise will be thick and glossy. This makes about 2 cups of mayonnaise.

breads

table of contents

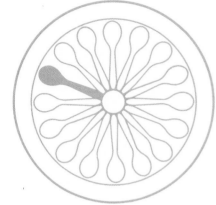

the key to
homemade breads

Home-baked bread prompts the image of a faraway time when Grandmother, in her clean white apron, began baking at four in the morning. She had golden-crusted loaves waiting for her husband and her children — and her children's children — when they came in from the fields. In addition to years of practice, a significant ingredient of Grandma's bread was the "tender loving care" she put into it — but sometimes loving care is not enough. Grandma's creative urge was limited by her cranky old wood stove, which was probably why she didn't bake the excitingly different kinds of breads we can make today. (Grandma would have loved them!)

You will learn how to bake BASIC bread like Grandma's, but this is only a beginning. Just think how much farther you can go when Grandma's kind of love is combined with your modern oven and the different types of handy utensils available today. We'll be using quite a few neat tricks Grandma would love to have known. Let's begin by getting down to our BASICS, such as how to bake, glaze, serve and store fresh breads.

You'll first meet a Basic White Bread recipe and a BASIC technique for preparing it. After you've learned these, you'll prepare four classic glazes. They will be used not only in baking breads, but later in cooking vegetables and other foods.

Then comes a zesty variation of Basic White Bread — Cheese Bread. After that, your new technique will be applied to Basic Whole Wheat Bread. And you will be able to make a three- and five-strand braid using either Basic White or Whole Wheat Bread.

Finally, you'll learn how to bake fancy bread shapes using unusual containers, such as ring molds and fluted pie pans — containers you've probably used often but may never have considered for breads. Less-sweet breads include not only the Basic White and Whole Wheat Breads, but fruit breads, waffles and pancakes, to mention several.

After mastering the BASIC recipes and techniques for preparing the *less-sweet* breads, you'll go on to some of the classic *sweet* breads such as *brioches* and *Savarins*. Obviously, sweet breads have more sugar or other sweet flavorings than less-sweet ones. They are therefore usually served as dessert or as coffee or tea-time treats.

There is still another distinction: most breads are classified as *yeast* — such as the breads in this lesson — or as *quick*. Quick breads include waffles, pancakes, some rolls, muffins and scones, which you'll learn to make in later lessons. *The type of leavening determines whether a bread is called yeast or quick.*

Quick breads usually contain baking powder or baking soda as a raising agent. As the name implies, they do not require a prolonged period of rising before baking. In almost all recipes for quick breads, the leavening takes place in the oven during baking. A few quick breads, such as biscuits, may require a small amount of kneading.

Yeast breads rise from the chemical action that occurs when the yeast mixes with some or all of the other ingredients. These breads need at least one period of rising before being baked; recipes for yeast breads almost always specify kneading. You'll learn how to handle yeast and yeast doughs with confidence, and to knead your breads until they are feather-light.

Yeast is usually available dried, in envelopes, for easy storage on the cupboard shelf. An expiration date is stamped on the outside of the package. For best results,

use it before that date. You may also substitute one cake compressed yeast for one package dried. Crumble yeast cake into warm liquid and proceed as recipe directs. An improved type yeast, recently developed, is called Rapid-mix. It is added to the dry ingredients instead of being dissolved in the liquid, making it more convenient.

Water is frequently used in making breads but it is sometimes used in combination with other liquids. Milk is often specified, particularly with sandwich breads, to give tender, small-crumbed loaves.

Flour for bread-making may be enriched white, rye, corn or wheat. We use all-purpose, enriched white flour in our BASIC recipes because the nutrients the mill grinds out when white flour is prepared have been restored (hence, the name). Enriched flour insures your family of the vitamins and minerals it needs.

While enriched white flour is available in almost all grocery stores, some other flours are not quite so easy to find. Most larger supermarkets and health food stores usually have rye and whole wheat flours, as well as some other flours you might want to try.

After you have purchased your flour, we recommend immediately placing it in a tightly-covered container. The standard flour canister holds about five pounds. For a larger quantity, earthenware jars, screwcap sealed jars or old-fashioned flour bins are good containers.

Salt is added to bread dough to enhance the flavor and to help the rising process. It is important that you never mix salt directly with yeast or add it to the yeast-and-water mixture — it retards the action of the yeast.

Two other ingredients are sometimes added to yeast breads: shortening and sugar. *Shortening* helps create a loaf or roll which breaks and crushes easily and has a soft, velvety crumb. It also helps bread stay fresh longer.

Sugar provides an immediate source of food for the yeast, assisting a quick raising action. It also introduces a touch of sweetness to your breads and helps create an appetizing, gold-colored crust.

Before you turn the page and begin preparing our remarkably simple Basic White Bread, we'd like you to look at pages 6 and 7 marked General Information. There you'll find an array of bakers' tools pictured and described.

Actually, bread can be baked with very simple equipment you probably already have in your kitchen. But it's fun to see the many intricate and unusual utensils that can be used — and especially the different pans shown.

basic
white bread

basic white bread

Here are four possible shapes of Basic White Bread. At the back is hexagon-shaped bread crossed with a very sharp knife before baking. Middle left: We baked this bread in a fluted mold after snipping the top, to form peaks, with a pair of very large scissors. Middle right: This bread was baked in a Savarin or ring mold; after cooking, it was turned upside down on a baking sheet and brushed with Anglais Glaze, (Breads, pg. 6). We returned it to the oven to brown for a few minutes. Front: Some trick of our camera has made this bread look flatter than it actually is. It was baked in the mold it sits on.

how to make your own bread

1 Put the yeast mixture on the top of your stove while the oven is in use or has been heated. Cover the top with a kitchen towel and let stand for 15 minutes. Add first batch of flour as recipe directs and let rise for 30 minutes.

2 After adding milk mixture as recipe directs, add in enough of remaining flour to make a soft dough. Work up a smooth dough using your hands or a wooden spoon. Turn the dough onto a lightly floured table surface for kneading.

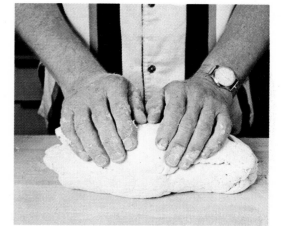

3 Knead the dough for a minimum of 10 minutes. To knead, pull the dough toward you with fingers close together . . .

BASIC WHITE BREAD

1½ c. lukewarm water
2 pkg. yeast
7½ c. all-purpose flour
3 tbsp. sugar
1 c. milk
1 tbsp. salt
¼ c. butter
1 recipe Anglais Glaze (Breads, pg. 6)

Place lukewarm water in a large warm bowl or crock. Sprinkle the yeast over water, stirring until dissolved. Cover and let stand for 15 minutes. Combine 1½ cups flour and 2 tablespoons sugar. Beat the flour mixture carefully into the yeast mixture with a wooden spoon until free from lumps. Cover with a towel and let rise in a warm place for 30 minutes. Scald the milk, then stir in the salt and remaining sugar. Add the butter and stir until dissolved. Cool to lukewarm. Add to the yeast mixture, then add enough of the remaining flour to make a soft dough. Turn out on a lightly floured board and knead for 10 minutes or until smooth and elastic, adding flour if needed. Place in a greased bowl, turning dough to grease the top. Cover with a towel and let rise in a warm place for an hour or until doubled in bulk. Turn dough out on a lightly floured board and divide in half. Shape into loaves and place in 2 well-greased 9 x 5-inch loaf pans or 3 smaller shaped molds as shown in our step-by-step illustrations. Cover and let rise for an hour or until doubled in bulk. Bake at 400 degrees for 10 minutes. Brush tops with *Anglais* Glaze, using pastry brush. Bake for 15 minutes longer. Turn loaves out on wire racks to cool.

4 . . . then press down and forward with the heels of your hands. The dough has been kneaded enough when small bubbles rise beneath the surface or when it is smooth and elastic. Place in greased bowl and follow recipe instructions.

5 Here are three types of pans we like to use for bread-making. Place dough into 2 or 3 loaf pans or molds. The one into which we are pressing dough is a shallow *Savarin* or ring mold. This kind of pan can be filled higher than either of the other two. As a rough guide to filling your pan, remember that bread dough doubles in rising.

6 Place the dough-filled pans on top of your warm oven. Cover the pans as before and let rise until bread looks like the one in the ring mold on the right of our picture. This takes about 1 hour or until doubled in bulk. We show you how to snip the tip of one loaf with a pair of clean kitchen scissors. The top of the bread in the hexagon mold was scored with a sharp knife before baking. Place pans in preheated 400-degree oven for 10 minutes.

7 Then, take one or two loaves out at a time and brush the tops with *Anglais Glaze* (pg. 6) and return pans to oven as soon as possible to finish baking. This will take 15 minutes longer. The best test for doneness is to rap bread tops lightly with your knuckles. If bread sounds hollow, it is done. If it does not, give it a minute or two more and test again for doneness.

four
classic glazes

Glazing is "the icing on the cake" for almost all foods. It entails simply the technique of adding flavor and a glossy coating to foods by brushing them with a liquid. It adds luster to the appearance of breads, pastry, lamb, veal, pork, poultry, vegetables and desserts.

There are four classic glazes. For savory, or non-sweet foods, we recommend *Anglais* Glaze. It contains egg, olive oil, salt and pepper and is applied with a soft-bristled brush.

Plain Glaze is similar to *Anglais* Glaze but lacks the seasonings. Brush it over most sweet items, except those you want to have a crisp finish (see below). Again, we recommend a soft-bristled brush.

Another classic coating is Egg White Glaze. It should be applied to sweet foods to produce a crisp top.

Finally there's Egg Wash — nothing more elaborate than egg white and salt. We like to use it for crisp tops on savory breads.

ANGLAIS GLAZE

1 egg
1 tsp. olive oil
½ tsp. salt
¼ tsp. white pepper

Combine all ingredients and beat well. Strain before using.

PLAIN GLAZE

1 egg
1 tsp. olive oil

Combine all ingredients and beat well. Strain before using.

EGG WHITE GLAZE

1 egg white
Extra fine sugar

Brush egg white over surface of food to be glazed and sprinkle with sugar.

EGG WASH

1 egg white
1 tsp. salt

Combine egg white and salt. Beat mixture with a fork until foamy.

storing
home-baked breads

It is disheartening to spend a couple of hours baking golden-brown, crusty bread only to have it go stale in a day. That's what will occur, however, in the absence of artificial preservatives, unless you follow the proper storage methods.

Before we explain our storage procedure, a word of caution: be absolutely certain your bread has completely cooled before wrapping it.

Recall what we said about foil when preparing chicken for roasting (Poultry, pg. 5): tightly folded foil insulates and protects; loosely folded foil allows air to penetrate.

Wrap your bread up as if it were never to come undone again. After two to five days — and in some instances up to a week, depending on the bread and on the weather conditions — it will still be perfectly fresh. If you want to store bread for a longer period of time, seal and date the package and freeze. Breads can be frozen up to six months, but the flavor begins to fade after two months.

When you're ready to thaw the bread, remove it from the freezer and dry the outside carefully to prevent the melting frost from making it soggy. Loosen the foil and let it stand at room temperature for about an hour or until thawed. It may then be reheated in the oven to restore the crusty top.

If despite your best intentions, you allow the bread to go stale, you can revitalize it somewhat by wrapping it loosely in foil and steaming it in a colander over boiling water for about 15-30 minutes. Then reheat as we have explained above.

The Creative Homemaker's Academy © MCMLXXIII
Selected Illustrations © B.P.C. Publishing Limited MCMLXX ·

cheese bread

The simple addition of cheese makes a whole new creation out of our Basic White Bread (pg. 4-5). The same recipe and techniques plus a blending of 2 distinctive cheeses, Emmenthal and Parmesan, produces a sharp and savory bread. Emmenthal, often called Switzerland Swiss, is the original, mild-flavored Swiss cheese with holes. (It is often confused with Gruyère, which is more expensive, but remember Emmenthal has bigger holes and a smaller price than Gruyère.) Parmesan, a sharply flavored Italian cheese, has a taste familiar to most of us.

For a truer flavor, we recommend buying cheeses in their original form and grating them yourself. You get a more natural taste than from the packaged, grated kinds usually found in the supermarket. It may be necessary to ask your supermarket manager to order it for you or to check out your nearest specialty food store.

CHEESE BREAD

1 recipe Basic White Bread *(pg. 4)*
1¾ c. freshly grated Parmesan cheese
2 tbsp. freshly grated Emmenthal or Swiss Cheese
1 recipe Anglais Glaze

Prepare the Basic White Bread according to the recipe direction, adding 1½ cups Parmesan cheese to the yeast mixture with the second addition of flour. Place in 2 prepared loaf pans. Bake at 400 degrees for 10 minutes. Brush with *Anglais* Glaze and bake for 10 minutes longer. Brush with *Anglais* Glaze, then sprinkle mixture of remaining Parmesan cheese and the Emmenthal cheese over the top of loaves. Bake for 5 minutes longer. Remove from pan and cool on wire rack.

cheese bread

Notice the fine texture of the sliced loaf. The cheese flavor is definite, but not overwhelming. Served with butter and a glass of milk, it makes an excellent snack.

basic whole wheat bread

basic whole wheat bread

On the left is a loaf made with two strands of Basic Whole Wheat and three strands of Basic White Bread (illustrated instructions for shaping a five-strand braid on pages 9 and 10). On the right, baked in a smaller-than-standard loaf pan, is whole wheat bread with its top snipped with a pair of large kitchen scissors. (You can review the technique for this on page 5.)

BASIC WHOLE WHEAT BREAD

¾ c. milk
¼ c. brown sugar (firmly packed)
1 tbsp. salt
⅓ c. butter
⅓ c. molasses
1½ c. lukewarm water
2 pkg. yeast
6 c. stone-ground whole wheat flour
1½ c. flour
1 recipe Egg Wash *(pg. 6)*

Scald the milk in a small saucepan. Add the brown sugar, salt, butter and molasses, then stir until dissolved. Let stand until lukewarm. Pour the water in a warm, large mixing bowl, then sprinkle the yeast over the water, stirring until dissolved. Pour in the milk mixture, stirring constantly. Stir in 4 cups of whole wheat flour, 1 cup at a time, mixing until smooth. Stir in the remaining whole wheat flour. Sprinkle with part of the regular flour, then turn out the dough onto a floured surface. Knead in the remaining flour for about 10 minutes or until the dough is smooth and elastic. Place the dough in well-buttered bowl, turning the dough to grease top. Cover with a towel and let it rise in a warm place for an hour or until doubled in bulk. Turn the dough onto a lightly floured surface and divide in half. Shape into loaves and place in two well-greased 9 x 5-inch loaf pans. Cover and let rise in a warm place for about an hour or until doubled in bulk. Bake at 400 degrees for 10 minutes. Brush with Egg Wash (pg. 6). Bake for 15 minutes longer.

three-& five-strand braids

We will now learn to make two classic braided bread shapes. We're using Basic White Bread to make our braid, but you can prepare it equally well with whole wheat bread dough. You can even use a combination of the two for an interesting effect as shown in the photograph on page 8.

Right now, follow our step-by-step illustrated instructions to make a three-strand braid. After you've made the three-strand braid, progress to the five-strand.

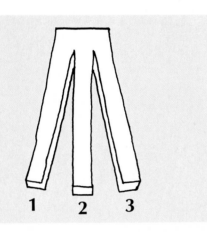

1 To make a three-strand braid, arrange strands as in the diagram. The sequence will be 1 over 2, 3 over 2; repeat.

2 This is the completed three-strand braid. Follow the diagram and remember that making this braid is simply a matter of weaving left over center, right over center, repeating to the end, and neatly tucking in the ends.

how to make a five-strand braided loaf

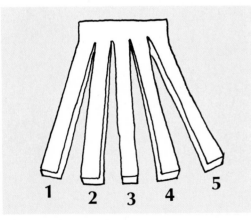

1 To make a five-strand braid, arrange five strands as shown in the diagram. We recommend that you always visualize the number of a strand by checking its position. As you face the bread, 1 will always be farthest left and 5 will always be farthest right. Your sequence here is 2 over 3, 5 over 2, 1 over 3, repeat.

2 How to make a five-strand braided loaf. Refer to diagrams and be certain you understand them thoroughly. It will help, too, if you have made a three-strand braid before attempting five-strands. Roll dough into a long, half-inch thick rectangle 7½ x 15 inches. Mark off top ends into five equal 1½-inch wide divisions. We're using a professional pastry cook's scraper, but a sharp kitchen knife does very well.

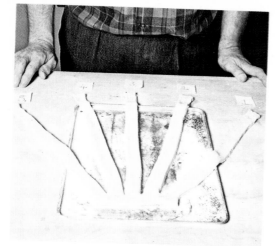

3 Divide the dough as shown, being careful to leave it joined at the end. Lay it on a lightly floured board with the five strips spread out. Never stretch the dough. Remember the strip on your left will always be 1, the strip on your right will always be 5, and those in the middle will be 2, 3, and 4 from left to right.

6 Cross 1 over 3 and repeat from beginning in the same sequence until. . .

4 Cross 2 over 3.

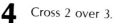

7 The braid is completed. When you reach the end of the strands, dab all five with cold water, pinch together, and tuck underneath the braid. (See left side of loaf.) Place on well-buttered baking sheet. Cover and let rise in a warm place for about an hour or until doubled in bulk. Bake at 400 degrees for 10 minutes. Brush with Egg Wash (pg. 6). Bake for 15 minutes longer or until bread tests done.

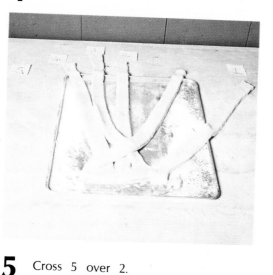

5 Cross 5 over 2.

fancy bread shapes

All of the shapes we're going to show you can be made with either Basic White Bread dough or Basic Whole Wheat Bread dough.

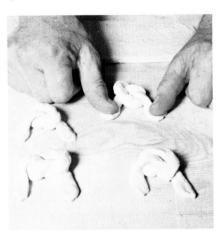

1 Knot rolls. Cut dough into 7-inch strips, ½ inch wide. Knot them in the center.

2 Pull out the ends, and flatten each end to ensure a good finished shape.

3 Twists. Cut 7-inch strips, 1¼ inches wide. Just twist, as we do above, using one hand to hold the dough steady and the other to twist.

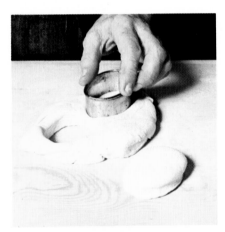

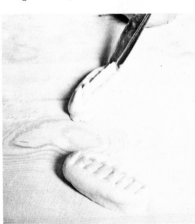

4 Oval rolls. With an oval pastry cutter cut out dough.

5 Use your hands to form the ovals into rolls with sharp ends.

6 With a pair of kitchen scissors, snip the top of each roll into a high, centered line of spikes.

7 Our small bread shapes are ready for rising on a lightly floured baking sheet. Let them rise until doubled in bulk. Brush with *Anglais* Glaze (pg. 6) and bake on a lightly floured baking sheet at 400 degrees for 12 to 15 minutes or until lightly browned.

brioches and savarins

Don't worry if your friends look askance when you refuse their invitation to go adventuring in baking shops, choosing instead to bake your own bread. When they sample the delectable *brioches* and rum-sprinkled *Savarins* you've created, they won't question your choice. We will start you on the road to exciting breads with a little BASIC training in the art of baking a couple of elegant breads from France.

Basically, a *brioche* is a light, rich roll made with flour, butter, eggs and yeast. It is cleverly shaped like a muffin with a top hat to be doffed, revealing many unusual fillings. For variety, specially made *brioche* pans with fluted sides come in individual, medium and large sizes. *Savarins* are equally versatile. Baked in a ring-type pan with a hole in the center, these soaked-in-syrup, dashed-with-rum creations can be filled imaginatively to make a variety of tea dessert breads.

Whether you're a beginner or an ambitious cook, we urge you to study carefully the BASIC *brioche* recipe. In the beginning, we promised that cooking would be a fun-filled adventure. The experience you are about to enjoy with *brioches* should again prove our claim.

individual brioche

Variations of our BASIC brioche *recipe, made in (left) individual* brioche *pans and (right) in a special pan called* dariole *pans. If you don't have* dariole *pans, you will have equally good results with 6-ounce, oven-proof glass, custard cups.*

BRIOCHE FOR SAVORY FILLINGS

½ c. butter, softened
2 c. sifted all-purpose flour
1 tbsp. extra fine sugar
1 tsp. salt
2 eggs
2 tbsp. milk
1 pkg. yeast
1 recipe Egg Wash *(pg. 6)*

To make the paste: beat the butter in a small bowl with a wooden spoon until creamy. Combine 1½ cups flour, sugar and salt in large mixing bowl. Make a well in the flour mixture, then place the eggs in the well. Stir eggs in a circular motion with a wooden spoon and work in flour gradually, adding milk as needed to make a smooth paste. Beat vigorously for 2 minutes or until glistening and smooth, scraping side of bowl frequently. Add the butter, and work into the paste until absorbed. To make the starter: combine the remaining flour and yeast in a small bowl. Mix in 2 to 2½ tablespoons warm water to form a soft ball. Cut a cross in the top of the ball of starter with scissors. Drop into a 2-quart bowl of warm water. Ball will sink to bot-

tom. Let stand for 7 to 8 minutes. Ball will rise to surface and double in bulk. Lift the starter carefully from the water with your hand and drain off excess water. Place in the bowl of paste. Work in the starter, beating vigorously until the consistency of whipped cream. The resulting dough may be slightly lumpy. Turn into well-buttered mixing bowl. Cover and chill for at least 1 hour. Knead dough with floured hands, shaping into a ball. Remove ¾ of the dough and shape into a ball. Place in well-buttered, fluted *brioche* mold. Snip cross in center with scissors and push the dough to the side to form a well. Roll the remaining dough into the shape of a pear and push the pointed end well into center of large ball. Cover and let rise in a warm place for 1 hour and 20 minutes or until doubled in bulk. Bake in preheated 375-degree oven for 40 minutes or until *brioche* tests done. Brush with Egg Wash 5 minutes before removing from oven. An aluminum foil tent may be placed over the top of the *brioche* if it browns too quickly. Remove from the oven and turn out on a wire rack to cool. Slice off head with a sharp knife. Hollow out center of *brioche*, leaving a shell about ¾ to 1 inch thick. Fill as desired.

FOR INDIVIDUAL BRIOCHES:

Shape dough into 24 small *brioches*, by the same method as for the large one. Place in buttered, individual, fluted *brioche* tins. Bake at 400 degrees for 15 to 20 minutes.

BASIC LARGE SWEET BRIOCHE

¹/₂ c. butter
¹/₃ c. extra fine sugar
1¹/₂ tsp. salt
1 pkg. yeast
¹/₄ c. warm water
¹/₂ c. warm milk
4 eggs
3¹/₂ c. all-purpose flour
1 recipe Egg Wash *(pg. 6)*

Beat the butter in a large mixing bowl with a wooden spoon or electric mixer until creamy, then add the combined sugar and salt gradually. Cream until well blended. Sprinkle yeast over warm water in small bowl and stir until dissolved. Add milk, yeast, eggs and flour to creamed mixture. Beat vigorously with a wooden spoon for 2 minutes or until smooth, scraping side of bowl frequently. Cover and let rise in warm place for about 2 hours or until doubled in bulk. Stir down and beat vigorously with wooden spoon for 2 minutes. Cover with aluminum foil and refrigerate overnight. Stir down and turn out on a lightly floured surface, then with floured hands shape ³/₄ of the dough into a ball. Place in a well-buttered, fluted *brioche* mold. Snip a cross in the center with scissors and push the dough to the side to form a well. Moisten inside of well with water. Shape the remaining dough into a pear shape to form head. Push the pointed end into the well in the center of

the large ball. Cover and let rise in a warm place for 1 hour and 20 minutes or until doubled in bulk. Bake in a preheated 400-degree oven for an hour or until cake tester comes out clean. Brush with Egg Wash 5 minutes before removing from oven. An aluminum foil tent may be placed over *brioche* if it browns too quickly. Remove from the oven and turn out on a wire rack to cool. To fill *brioche* with sweet or savory filling remove head and trim. Pull out dough in center of *brioche* to leave shell ¹/₂ to ³/₄ inch thick. Fill as desired.

Whether you have prepared individual, medium, or large *brioches*, you can treat all three as edible containers for either savory or sweet fillings.

SWEET FILLING FOR BRIOCHE

Apricot Jam
1 recipe Basic Confectioners' Custard
    (Desserts, pg. 19)
1 recipe Basic Chantilly Cream *(Desserts, pg. 19)*
Slivered almonds

Brush inside of *brioche* shell with a thick coating of apricot jam. Spoon confectioners' custard into *brioche* shell and fill remainder of the shell with chantilly cream. Sprinkle with almonds.

basic large sweet brioche

Basic is beautiful, as you can see from our elegant Basic Large Sweet Brioche. We simply dusted it with sifted confectioners' sugar, but you can go one step farther and try our suggested sweet filling.

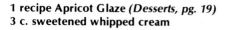

savarins

The *Savarin* takes its name from the famous French jurist and gourmet, Jean Anthelm Brillat-Savarin, who wrote *The Physiology of Taste (La Physiologie dû Gout)*, a classic on the art of eating and drinking.

There is a strange story about Brillat-Savarin's two spinster sisters. At the height of his career, these ladies would spend one month preparing for their brother's annual one-month visit, one month after his visit cleaning the house and covering the furniture and the remaining nine months in bed. If catering to their brother's special tastes took that much out of the poor ladies, the man must have truly been an exacting gourmet.

These rich breads, baked in special *Savarin* or ring molds well deserve his name. They are soaked in syrup, sprinkled with rum and often decorated and glazed. The hollow center of the *Savarin* is frequently filled with whipped cream or Confectioners' Custard and fruit.

BASIC SAVARIN

1 pkg. yeast
¼ c. lukewarm water
¼ c. lukewarm milk
2 c. all-purpose flour
4 eggs, lightly beaten
½ tsp. salt
1 tbsp. extra fine sugar
¾ c. unsalted butter, softened
1 recipe Basic Sugar Syrup
¼ c. dark rum

1 recipe Apricot Glaze (Desserts, pg. 19)
3 c. sweetened whipped cream

Sprinkle yeast into water in a small bowl and let it soften for 5 minutes. Add milk and stir to mix well. Sift the flour into a mixing bowl. Make a well in the center and pour in the yeast mixture and eggs. Mix together to make a soft, sticky dough, adding more lukewarm milk if needed. Beat the dough vigorously with a wooden spoon for 2 minutes. Cover and let stand in a warm place for 1 hour or until doubled in bulk. Stir down with a wooden spoon and sprinkle with salt and sugar. Spread with butter and beat for 3 to 4 minutes or until glistening and elastic. Spread dough in a buttered *Savarin* ring. Cover and let stand in a warm place until dough rises to the top of the mold. Bake in a 400-degree oven for 10 minutes. Reduce oven temperature to 350 degrees and bake for 30 minutes longer or until cake tester inserted in center comes out clean. Dilute Basic Sugar Syrup with 3 cups of water in a kettle large enough to hold the *Savarin* mold, then heat to lukewarm. Place hot *Savarin* in mold into kettle. Let stand for 1 to 2 minutes or just until *Savarin* begins to pull away from the side of the mold. Immediately remove from the syrup with tongs and invert onto a serving platter. Drizzle rum over and around the *Savarin*. Garnish the top with wedges of orange peel. Spoon Apricot Glaze over the top and brush carefully to cover the Savarin evenly and completely. Cool, then pipe whipped cream around the *Savarin*, then fill the center with remaining cream

BASIC SUGAR SYRUP

6 c. water
8½ c. sugar

Place water and sugar in a large pot over low heat. Heat until sugar is dissolved. Raise to a slow, rolling boil, then reduce temperature and simmer for 3 minutes. Chill, bottle and store.

Alternate Method of Introducing Syrup and Rum Into *Savarin*: Remove baked *Savarin* from pan and pierce top with the tines of a fork. Combine 1 cup Sugar Syrup and ¼ cup rum in a small saucepan and heat until warm. Spoon the rum-syrup mixture over the *Savarin* until all is absorbed.

basic savarin

After baking, we immersed our BASIC Savarin in a sugar syrup, sprinkled it with rum and used orange peel and candied cherries to decorate the top. We then covered the entire Savarin with Apricot Glaze (Desserts, pg. 19). A pyramid of whipped cream and grapefruit segments provide additional garnish.

cooking with breads

If you're surprised at the idea of cooking *with* breads, think again. You'll be amazed at how often you depend on breads in the preparation of other dishes. Bread can be rolled, crumbed, molded, dipped, toasted, fried, stuffed and cut in more ways than we could list here.

There are several Basic techniques involved in cooking with bread which we will explain on the following pages. After trying our suggestions, let your imagination create more. You will discover how delighted your guests are when served mushrooms in a *croustade* (bread shell); and how elegantly bread crumbs finish a casserole.

BREAD CRUMBS

As we mentioned earlier, an *au gratin* dish is technically one which is topped with bread crumbs and butter, with cheese being optional. To make your own bread crumbs, use bread that is 1 or 2 days old. Naturally, homemade bread is preferable.

For soft bread crumbs, break the stale bread into manageable chunks, about 1 inch square, place them in a clear plastic bag, and crush with your fingers. If you have a mortar and pestle handy, use that. After you've crumbled the bread crumbs as finely as possible, run them through a blender for uniform size. Just place the crumbs in the blender and blend until the bread crumbs are the size you want. These crumbs may be used fresh or stored in an airtight container in the freezer for several weeks.

For *dry* bread crumbs, spread stale bread slices on a baking sheet and place them in a slow oven (about 200 degrees) for 1½ hours until they are dried out and lightly browned. Then crush or blend them into fine crumbs. Store them in a tightly lidded jar in the freezer and they will be good for months. Try using leftover dry toast to have a ready supply of bread crumbs at all times.

CROUTONS, CROÛTES AND CROUSTADES

Popular forms of bread for an accompaniment with various foods include croutons, *croûtes* and *croustades*.

Croutons are most familiar as the tiny cubes of baked or fried bread which are tossed into salads and floated on soups as garnish. They are made by successively slicing, stripping and cubing the bread to a size of about ³/₈ to ¹/₂ inch and preparing according to our instructions on the next page. But these tiny tidbits are only the beginning. The photograph on the next page is a representative sampling of the many exciting shapes you can use — circles, squares, hearts and crescents — stamped out with cookie cutters. A doughnut cutter, dipped in cold water, works well for the standing rings.

Croûtes are similar to croutons but they are usually larger and are used as part of the dish as well as garnish. You'll see them later supporting foods such as game, poultry and fish.

Croustades are larger bread shells or cases used to hold creamed vegetables, meats and fish. They are made by hollowing out 2-inch slices of bread to a ¹/₄-inch shell, or by hollowing out loaves of bread. Then the bread shell is baked until browned and crisp.

croutons and bread shells

FRIED CROUTONS

For small croutons, cut the crust from dried slices of day-old bread, then cut the slices into about 1/2-inch squares. Melt 1/4 cup butter for each 2 cups bread squares in a heavy saucepan or skillet. Toss the bread squares in the butter to coat evenly, using a pancake turner. Fry over medium heat until croutons are golden, tossing continuously. Turn out on paper toweling to drain and to cool. Use in salads or soups. May be stored in an airtight container for several days.

BAKED CROUTONS OR CROÛTES

Cut fancy shapes from dried slices of day-old bread, using cookie cutters dipped in cold water. Brush both sides with melted butter and place on a baking sheet. Bake in a preheated 350-degree oven for 30 minutes or until golden. May be used for garnish or *canapé* bases. The larger croutons or croûtes are made the same way.

CROUSTADES

Cut the top from a loaf of unsliced day-old bread, then, with fingers, remove the center of the bread, leaving a smooth shell 1/2 to 3/4 inch thick. Brush the inner sides, bottom and top edge generously with melted butter. This will take about 1/2 cup butter. Place shell on a baking sheet. Bake in a preheated 250-degree oven for 1 hour and 15 minutes or until dry. Increase the oven temperature to 350 degrees and bake for 10 minutes longer or until golden. This shell may be filled with various creamed meats, seafoods and vegetables, such as mushrooms (*Vegetables, pg. 24*).

croutons and croûtes

Here is a representative sampling of the many possible shapes of croutons and croûtes.

The Creative Homemaker's Academy © MCMLXXIII
Selected Illustrations © B.P.C. Publishing Limited MCMLXX

hot garlic loaf

In the foreground is a French loaf, sliced, spread with the butter and crisped in the oven. Behind it is a thinly sliced regular loaf. Note that the bottom crust is not cut, allowing the slices to be spread with butter and clamped back together to heat. The result is a soft, delicious inside and a crisp outer crust.

HOT GARLIC LOAF

1 loaf unsliced bread
1 recipe Basic Garlic Butter *(General Information, pg. 30)*

Slice bread from the top almost to the bottom crust. You may spread softened garlic butter on each slice on both sides. Place on foil and wrap securely, then place on baking sheet. Bake in a pre-heated 300-degree oven for 20 minutes or until heated through. May spread garlic butter on thick slices of French bread and bake until browned. Serve immediately.

HERB BREAD

1 crescent of Vienna bread
¼ c. butter
3 tbsp. olive oil
1 clove of garlic, pressed
1 tsp. finely chopped fresh parsley
1 tsp. thyme leaves
1 tsp. tarragon leaves
1 tsp. oregano
1 tsp. chopped chives

Slice the bread in ½ to ¾-inch slices almost to bottom crust. Soften butter in a small bowl. Blend in the olive oil, a small amount at a time, with a small wooden spoon. Stir in the garlic and herbs. Spread between slices of bread. Wrap in aluminum foil. Bake in a preheated 300-degree oven for 20 minutes or until heated through. Serve immediately. Do not use powdered herbs; use only fresh or dried. French bread may be used, if desired.

1 Using a sharp knife, make crosswise cuts, ½ inch apart down the length of a crescent-shaped loaf or a thin loaf of French bread, being careful not to cut through the bottom crust.

2 Spread the butter and herb mixture on both sides of each slice and press the loaf back together tightly. Wrap in foil and place in a 300-degree oven for 10 minutes. Serve the bread very hot.

how to
cut paper-thin bread

Serving the paper-thin rolls of bread and butter shown in the pictures on this page will add considerably to your reputation as a hostess, for they show painstaking care in preparation. But they look much more difficult than they are, as you'll discover when you follow our step-by-step instructions on this page.

The main things to keep in mind are that the slices really are paper thin, the butter is soft, the knife *very* sharp, and the water boiling hot.

The bread slices should be thin enough to roll like the one in our pictures. After the bread is sliced, remove the crust from each slice. Fill them with asparagus or paper thin meat slices. Roll it up like a jelly roll. Dip the ends into chopped parsley or other herbs and secure the rolls with a toothpick. You may use one of the basic or savory butters (General Information, pg. 30). Bread and butter rolls may be prepared several hours in advance and will keep fresh if you store them in an airtight container.

1 You'll need a pot of boiling water, a loaf of unsliced bread, butter, a table knife for spreading butter and a very sharp kitchen knife. Spread butter on the end of the loaf of bread. Keep the kitchen knife in the pot of water when not using it.

2 Remove the knife from the water and shake off excess drops but do not wipe it dry.

3 Now cut paper-thin slices of bread and butter with the moist, hot knife.

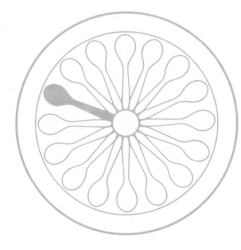

introducing
croissants

A *croissant* (French for crescent) is a delicate, buttery, flaky pastry roll baked in the shape of a crescent. When freshly baked, there is nothing quite like a *croissant*.

The invention of *croissants* in 1683, is attributed to Viennese bakers. Reportedly, in an attempt to ingratiate themselves with invading Turkish forces, these bakers prepared rolls called *kipfels*, in the shape of the national symbol of Turkey. (The bakers vehemently denied this report, claiming that they created the *kipfels* in honor of Vienna's finest hour, after the Turkish army had retreated.) A century later when the Austrian princess Marie Antoinette became queen of France, she introduced the *kipfels* to French chefs who devised their own recipe for them, using flaky pastry instead of plain dough and dubbed them *"croissants."*

The French, Swiss, Austrians and other central Europeans eat freshly-baked, flaky *croissants* for breakfast. This traditional breakfast bread is enthusiastically enjoyed by foreigners who visit these countries. They are excellent served with jam for tea or with any meal as a bread.

Using Cold Yeast Dough, believe it or not, *croissants* are really quite simple to make. However, the method for making them is more complicated to describe than it is to carry out. You will find the recipe and the step-by-step illustrations for Cold Yeast Dough used in this course to be very different from the usual method of preparing *croissants*. The rising steps for the dough are eliminated as are the long periods of chilling. It takes approximately forty-five minutes to prepare the dough up to the chilling stage.

Cold Yeast Dough must be chilled for a minimum of forty-five minutes or it may be for several hours. You <u>cannot</u> return trimmings or scraps to the unrolled dough and remember that you cannot re-roll the trimmings and produce successful *croissants*. You <u>can</u>, however, use the trimmings just as you would use puff pastry, to make little sweet or savory tidbits to serve as snacks or *canapés*.

(A little bit of thrifty ingenuity on your part can eliminate the necessity of discarding even the smallest scrap of this delicious pastry dough!)

This recipe is fun to make and the finished "made from scratch" rolls will be far superior to the crescent rolls available at the bakery.

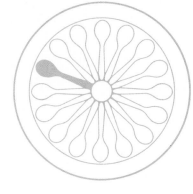

how to make basic cold yeast dough for croissants

1 Let butter come to room temperature and cut in the 4 tablespoons of flour thoroughly with 2 forks or a pastry blender.

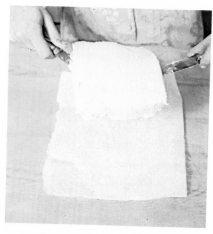

2 Shape the butter mixture into a rectangle, about ½ inch thick. Place the butter between sheets of waxed paper and refrigerate while preparing the Yeast Dough Mixture.

3 Place yeast and sugar in a bowl. Add a small amount of the water and stir until smooth, adding remaining water. Add beaten egg and blend well.

4 Combine flour and salt. Shape the flour into a ring on working surface, making a well in center. Pour a small amount of the yeast mixture into the well.

5 Begin working the flour into the liquid with 2 knives or pastry blender, adding liquid as needed. Do not break the flour wall.

6 When all the yeast mixture has been added, work the remaining flour into mixture with pastry scrapers or with hands if necessary. Work until smooth and shape dough into a ball.

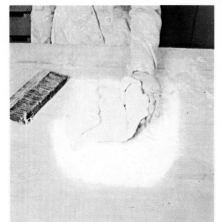

7 Lightly flour your hands. Slap the dough from palm to palm, across a space of about 20 inches. Count up to about 100 times, reshaping the dough into a ball when necessary. Slap the dough onto the counter and when it <u>breathes</u> perceptibly for a second or two it is active and ready.

8 Roll out the dough, on lightly floured board, into a 15 X 17-inch rectangle. Place the chilled butter mixture in the center.

9 Begin folding the dough with the end nearest you. Fold just over the center of butter mixture. Bring the opposite end up over center, making ends overlap. Then fold sides to center. Turn the folded dough over, on a lightly floured board, so that edges are underneath.

10 Roll out the dough into a long, narrow rectangle, using pressing, bumpy movements with the rolling pin. You will notice bubbles on the surface, as in the picture, which indicates the dough is springy and active.

11 Fold end of dough nearest you just over center. Bring opposite end over this fold. Give the dough a half turn so that a folded edge is toward you.

12 Turn the dough over, on lightly floured board, so that folded edges are underneath as shown in picture. Roll out the dough two more times the same size making the same folds and half turns in between each roll out. Place the dough on a lightly floured tea towel, then wrap and refrigerate for a minimum of 45 minutes. The dough is ready to roll out and use as each recipe directs.

**BASIC
COLD YEAST DOUGH**

Butter Mixture:
   1½ c. butter
   4 tbsp. all-purpose flour

Yeast Dough Mixture:
   2 pkg. dry yeast   1 egg, beaten
   1 tbsp. sugar   3⅓ c. sifted all-purpose flour
   1 c. water   ½ tsp. salt.

how to cut and roll croissants

CROISSANTS

1 recipe Cold Yeast Dough *(pg. 20)*
1 egg
1 tbsp. water

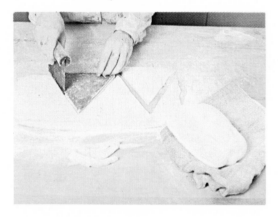

1 Cut out a cardboard triangle with a 6-inch base and 6½-inch sides. Roll out dough into a long strip about 6 inches wide and ¼ inch thick. Lay the cardboard triangle on the dough and cut out a triangle with a sharp knife. Reverse the cardboard triangle on the dough each time to ensure minimum amount of waste.

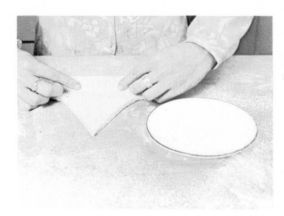

2 Place the base of each triangle of dough toward you; wet each tip with cold water. Holding the base with fingers as in picture, pull slightly to extend, then begin rolling towards the point.

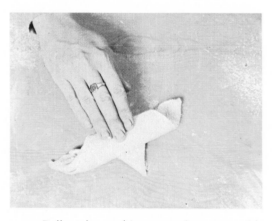

3 Roll up by pushing away from you with fingers. Then turn the roll around so that the tip overlaps away from you.

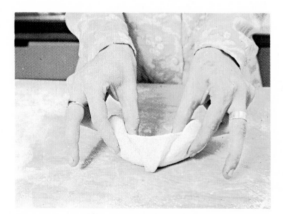

4 Curve the roll into a crescent shape. Flatten the two corners slightly. Beat the egg with the water. Brush egg mixture lightly over each roll. Place on an ungreased baking sheet. Bake in a preheated 400-degree oven, 1 shelf above center, for about 20 minutes or until richly browned. This makes about 12 large *croissants*.

croissants

Displayed here are 4 delectable variations of croissants. From left to right are anchovy croissants made with anchovy fillets rolled up inside, almond croissants made with almond paste, cheese croissants made with Emmenthal cheese, and jam and custard croissants.

SHOEBUCKLES

Shoebuckles, originally named for Henry VIII, are pinwheels of deliciously light and flaky yeast dough, puffed full of custard and just a hint of jam. During the 1500's, when Henry ruled, the fashion of the day was to wear large, ornate and often heavily jeweled shoebuckles. This fashion, plus Henry's tremendous appetite (he was most decidedly a horrendous glutton) led his chefs and pastry cooks to heights of ingenuity and cleverness. Henry often enjoyed massive seven-hour feasts, but quickly tired of eating "the same old thing". He was, however, enraptured with the smell and taste of freshly baked yeast breads and rolls. To curry his favor (and in those days, an unhappy Henry VIII often meant a short walk to the hangman's noose) Henry's pastry cooks, using scraps of left-over *croissant* dough, cleverly twisted the dough into shoebuckles. Henry was delighted and the cooks didn't let a speck of the *croissant* dough go to waste.

SHOEBUCKLES

1 recipe Cold Yeast Dough *(pg. 20)*
1 recipe Basic Confectioners' Custard *(Desserts, pg. 19)*
Red currant jelly or apricot jam
1 egg, beaten with 1 tbsp. water
1½ c. confectioners' sugar

Prepare Cold Yeast Dough. While dough is chilling for a minimum of 45 minutes, prepare Basic Confectioners' Custard and let cool. Roll out dough to ¼ inch thickness and cut in 4½-inch squares as shown in diagram. Cut from each corner toward center about 2 inches, as shown by dotted lines, leaving a circle in center. Place a heaping teaspoonful of Basic Confectioners' Custard in center (on X). Dollop about a teaspoon of jelly on top of the custard. Moisten all 8 corner tips with water. Lift corner A all the way over the center (covering custard and jelly). Skip corner B, and lift C over center and press lightly to make corner stick. Continue with corners E and then G, pressing tips together. Repeat with remaining squares. Brush each Shoebuckle lightly with the egg and water mixture. Place Shoebuckles on a lightly floured baking sheet. Bake in a preheated 400-degree oven, one shelf above center, for about 18 minutes or until golden brown. Remove from oven and cool on a rack. Mix confectioners' sugar with enough water to make a thin icing. Drizzle a small amount of icing over each Shoebuckle. This makes about 12 Shoebuckles.

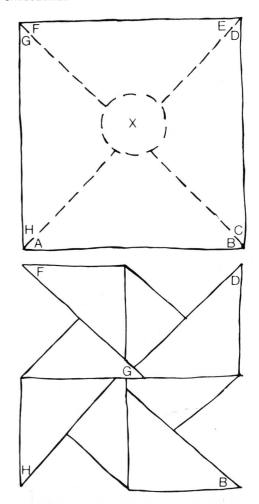

viennese coffee braid

Lightly dusted with confectioner's sugar, this coffee braid is one of the most spectacular breads that can be made. A three-strand braid, this bread can be served at breakfast with jelly or afternoon coffee. Viennese Coffee Braid can easily serve 20 people and can be made several days ahead of the serving time. When making this bread, the amount of raisins and almonds may be increased to please personal tastes.

VIENNESE COFFEE BRAID

2 pkg. dry yeast
4 tbsp. sugar
2⅓ c. milk, warmed
7 c. sifted all-purpose flour
2 c. seedless raisins
1½ tsp. salt
1 c. sliced almonds, crushed
6 tbsp. butter, softened
3 eggs
1 egg yolk
½ recipe Basic Confectioners' Icing (Desserts, pg. 8)

Combine yeast with 1 tablespoon sugar in a 1-pint bowl. Add ⅔ cup of warmed milk gradually, stirring until smooth. Add ⅓ cup flour, a small amount at a time, and stir until smooth. Cover with a cloth. Set in a warm place and let rise for 30 minutes. Place remaining flour, sugar, raisins, salt, and almonds in an extra large mixing bowl. Blend with a wooden spoon until raisins are well coated. Add 4 tablespoons softened butter and yeast mixture and mix well. Stir in eggs. Add remaining milk gradually, working into a dough. When thoroughly mixed, turn out onto a floured surface, preferably wooden or marble. Knead with the heel of your hand as shown in illustration No. 4, page 5. Alternate kneading with slapping the dough hard with

palm of hand. Continue kneading and slapping for about 10 minutes until dough is smooth and soft. Return dough to large bowl. Cover and let rise in a warm place for 1 hour. Turn out again onto floured surface and punch down the dough hard with your fist. Return to bowl. Cover and let rest for 30 minutes. Divide the dough into 3 parts, graduated in size. The three pieces, from small to large, will weigh about 15, 20, and 28 ounces. Roll out large piece about 19 inches long. Cut into three 2-inch wide strips. Melt remaining butter. Dab a little butter on one end of each strip of dough and pinch together. Make a 3-strand braid (page 9). Lift braid onto a floured, 16-inch long baking sheet. Brush top of braid with melted butter. Roll out second largest piece of dough into a 17-inch long strip. Cut in three 2-inch wide strips. Pinch together at one end as with first braid. Repeat braiding and place this braid on top of first, then brush with butter. Repeat procedure with smallest piece of dough, cutting 14-inch long strips. Braid and place on top. Brush with additional melted butter. Mix egg yolk with 1 tablespoon water and brush over the completed coffee braid. Cover lightly with tea towel, then set in warm place and let rise for 1 hour. Place in preheated 350-degree oven, one shelf above center, and bake for 1 hour. Remove from oven and place on cooling rack. Dust liberally with confectioners' sugar or drizzle with ½ recipe Basic Confectioners' Icing, (Desserts, pg. 8).

sweet fruit breads

All three of these hard-to-resist sweet breads are year-round favorites, but are particularly popular at holiday gatherings. Starting from the top of the photo, the first is French Fruit Bread, brushed with Apricot Glaze and sprinkled with confectioners' sugar. In the center, Simple Fruit Bread is brushed with the same glaze, then topped with crystallized fruits and nuts for holiday fare. Gingerbread, always a hit with children, is in the lower corner, capped with honey and crystallized fruits.

fruit breads

FRUIT BREADS

Moist and full of color, fruit breads look festive and appetizing whatever the occasion — or non-occasion! Fruit breads are made with delicious blends of candied lemon and orange peels, nuts, raisins, dates and fragrant spice combinations. These taste-tempting breads are frequently brushed with a glaze and topped with confectioners' sugar. Fruit breads may be wrapped and stored successfully for many weeks, ready to be served at a moments notice. With piping hot coffee, they are a treat for guests.

FRENCH FRUIT BREAD

4 eggs
³/₄ c. sugar
1¹/₂ c. sifted self-rising flour
1 tsp. cinnamon
¹/₂ tsp. salt
¹/₂ c. chopped blanched almonds
¹/₂ c. chopped blanched hazelnuts
1¹/₄ c. golden raisins
¹/₄ c. diced candied lemon peel
1 tsp. lemon juice
2 tbsp. rum
1 recipe Apricot Glaze (Desserts, pg. 19)
Confectioners' sugar

Beat eggs and sugar together until thick and lemon colored. Sift flour, cinnamon and salt into a medium bowl, then stir in nuts and fruits. Combine lemon juice and rum in a small bowl. Add flour mixture to egg mixture alternately with rum mixture, folding carefully after each addition. Blend well. Pour into greased and floured round or 9 x 5-inch loaf pan. Bake in a preheated 350-degree oven for 45 minutes or until bread tests done. Remove to wire rack and cool for 5 minutes, then remove from pan and cool completely. Brush top with Apricot Glaze and sprinkle with confectioners' sugar. You may substitute ³/₄ cup chopped dates for the lemon peel, if desired. This will make 10 to 12 servings.

SIMPLE FRUIT BREAD

1 lb. mixed dried fruits, diced
1 c. (firmly packed) brown sugar
1¹/₄ c. cold tea
2 c. sifted self-rising flour
Pinch of salt
1 egg, lightly beaten
1 recipe Apricot Glaze (Desserts, pg. 19)

Combine the dried fruits and brown sugar in a large mixing bowl. Pour the tea over the fruit mixture and let stand for 15 minutes. Add the flour, salt and egg and mix well. Turn into a well-greased and floured round mold or loaf pan. Bake in a preheated 375-degree oven on the middle shelf for 45 minutes. Cool for 10 minutes, then remove from pan and cool completely on a rack. Wrap tightly in aluminum foil. Store for 24 hours. Brush with the Apricot Glaze and garnish with diced mixed candied fruits and nuts. This makes about 9 servings.

GINGERBREAD

¹/₂ c. sugar
¹/₂ c. butter
¹/₂ c. molasses
1 egg, beaten
1³/₄ c. all-purpose flour
1 tsp. soda
Pinch of salt
1 tsp. ginger
1 tsp. cinnamon
³/₄ c. boiling water
Honey
¹/₂ c. chopped nuts

Combine the sugar, butter, molasses and egg in a large mixing bowl and beat until well mixed. Sift the flour, soda, salt, ginger and cinnamon together. Add to the molasses mixture, then mix well. Stir in the boiling water. Place in a greased loaf pan or 9-inch square baking pan. Bake in a preheated 350-degree oven for 45 minutes or until Gingerbread tests done. Remove from oven and brush top with honey. Sprinkle with candied fruits and nuts. Cool. This makes about 9 servings.

FRUIT LOAF

2 c. finely chopped mixed dried fruits
1½ c. sifted all-purpose flour
3 tsp. baking powder
½ tsp. salt
¾ c. sugar
¾ c. butter
2 eggs, beaten
1 tbsp. milk
¼ tsp. almond extract

Soak the dried fruits in enough boiling water to cover for 10 minutes, then drain well. Sift the flour, baking powder, salt and sugar together into a mixing bowl. Cut in the butter with a pastry blender until the mixture is the consistency of fine bread crumbs. Stir in the dried fruits until evenly distributed. Add the eggs, milk and almond extract and beat thoroughly. The batter will be very stiff. Spread the batter in a well-greased loaf pan. Bake in a preheated 350-degree oven for 1 hour or until the bread tests done. Cool slightly, then remove from pan. Serve warm with butter, if desired. This makes 10 to 12 servings.

fruit loaf

This tantalizing and easy-to-make Fruit Loaf may be wrapped tightly in foil and left for at least 24 hours before serving.

walnut brown bread

*This moist Walnut Brown Bread was
brushed with maple syrup and topped
with walnuts. It is so simple to prepare you
won't mind when your family asks for it
again and again. As a refreshment for
company, you need only put on the coffee
to produce a most satisfying treat.*

WALNUT BROWN BREAD

1 c. sifted all-purpose flour
¹/₂ c. sugar
2 tsp. soda
¹/₂ tsp. salt

1¹/₂ c. graham flour
1¹/₂ c. coarsely chopped walnuts
1 6-oz. can evaporated milk
¹/₂ c. water
1 tbsp. vinegar
1 egg, well beaten
1 c. dark molasses
Maple syrup

Sift the flour, sugar, soda and salt together into a
large mixing bowl, then stir in the graham flour and
1 cup walnuts. Mix the milk and water, then stir in
the vinegar. Add to the flour mixture. Add the egg
and molasses and beat until well mixed. Place in a
greased loaf pan. Bake in a preheated 325-degree
oven for 1 hour and 15 minutes or until the bread
tests done. Cool for 10 minutes, then remove from
pan. Place on wire rack and cool completely. Brush
the top lightly with maple syrup, then sprinkle the
remaining walnuts over the syrup. Wrap in
aluminum foil and store for at least 24 hours before
serving. This makes about 9 servings.

dutch
easter bread

dutch easter bread

Although this traditional Dutch bread is served on Easter Sunday morning in the land of its origin, by no means should you feel compelled to serve it only once a year! Its golden crust is deliciously crunchy and the filling, made of ground almonds and fruits, eliminates the need for any spread other than butter. We suggest serving your Dutch Easter Bread at breakfast time the way the folk in Amsterdam do it — accompanied with thin slices of cheese and rolled-up ham.

DUTCH EASTER BREAD

¹/₂ **recipe Basic White Bread** *(pg. 4)*
³/₄ **c. ground almonds**
¹/₂ **c. sifted confectioners' sugar**
¹/₄ **c. chopped candied cherries**
¹/₂ **c. chopped golden raisins**
2 egg whites
¹/₄ **c. unsalted butter, softened**
1 beaten egg, strained
Sugar

Prepare the dough and let rise until doubled in bulk. Combine the almonds, confectioners' sugar, cherries, raisins and egg whites and set aside. Punch the dough down. Roll out on lightly floured surface to a ¹/₂-inch thick rectangle. Cream the butter and spread over entire surface of the dough. Spoon the almond mixture lengthwise down center of rectangle to within 1 inch of ends. Fold the dough over filling in half lengthwise and press to seal edges. Fold in half lengthwise again. Taper the ends, sealing securely, and place, seam side down, on lightly floured baking sheet. Score the top diagonally with a sharp knife. Cover the loaf with a towel and let rise for about 1 hour and 15 minutes or until doubled in bulk. Brush top of loaf with beaten egg and sprinkle generously with sugar. Bake in a preheated 400-degree oven for 25 minutes. This makes 10 to 12 servings.

polish coffee cake

polish coffee cake

Another delectable Old World fruit bread is Polish Coffee Cake, or Babka as it is called, with raisins and almonds in every bite. Although this bread is delicious served plain, it may also be dusted with confectioners' sugar for further appeal.

POLISH COFFEE CAKE

1 c. milk, scalded
¾ c. sugar
1 tsp. salt
¼ c. butter
½ c. lukewarm water
2 pkg. dry yeast
4½ c. all-purpose flour
1 c. raisins
4 eggs, lightly beaten
1 tsp. grated lemon rind
Cinnamon
¼ c. chopped almonds

Combine the milk, sugar, salt and butter in a large mixing bowl and stir until the butter is melted. Cool to lukewarm. Pour the warm water into a small, warm bowl and sprinkle the yeast over the water then stir gently until yeast is dissolved. Stir into the milk mixture. Combine ¼ cup flour with the raisins and set aside. Add the eggs and 2 cups flour to the yeast mixture and beat until smooth. Add the remaining flour and lemon rind and mix well. Cover and let rise in a warm place until doubled in bulk. Punch the dough down, then add the raisins and knead into the dough. Grease a brioche pan well, then sprinkle with cinnamon. Scatter the almonds over bottom of pan. Shape the dough into a roll and seal ends together then place in pan. Cover and let rise for 1 hour or until doubled in bulk. Bake in a preheated 350-degree oven for 45 minutes or until coffee cake tests done. Cool for 10 minutes, then remove from pan onto wire rack. This makes about 12 servings.

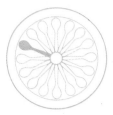

pancakes and waffles

Pancakes and waffles are the first of the quick breads in our cooking course — the world's oldest form of bread. The earliest ones were simple grain and water cakes dried on rocks in the sunshine. Today, their forms are so varied, they are appropriate at any meal of the day and in any role from the Russian *blini*, usually served as an appetizer, to the French *crêpes*.

BASIC PANCAKE BATTER

2 c. all-purpose flour, sifted
2 tsp. baking powder
1 tsp. soda
½ tsp. salt
2 tbsp. sugar
2 eggs, lightly beaten
¼ c. vegetable oil
1¾ c. buttermilk

Sift the flour, baking powder, soda, salt and sugar together into a mixing bowl. Combine the eggs, oil and buttermilk and stir into the flour mixture until just moistened. Drop from spoon onto hot greased griddle. Cook until bubbles rise and burst on top and bottom is browned. Turn and brown other side. This makes about 4 servings or about 20 small pancakes.

RAISIN PANCAKES WITH CHERRIES

1 can pitted black cherries
2 tsp. cornstarch
½ c. raisins
1 recipe Basic Pancake Batter
Butter

Drain the cherries and pour the juice into a small saucepan. Stir in the cornstarch and cook over low heat, stirring constantly, until thickened. Add the cherries and heat through. Stir the raisins into the pancake batter and cook as directed. Serve butter and hot cherry sauce over the pancakes. This makes 4 servings.

raisin pancakes with cherries

An inviting dish for fruit and pancake lovers, Raisin Pancakes With Cherries is easy to prepare, yet lovely to look at and full of exciting fruit flavor. A generous portion of bright, juicy cherries tumbles over each stack of pancakes, served with a pitcher of additional cherry sauce.

russian blinis

Through the years almost every country has developed a version of hot cakes distinctly its own and typical of the tastes of its people. Russia's classic contribution, the *blini*, has become the most famous of all appetizer pancakes.

Made from a batter very similar to American buckwheat cake batter, *blinis* are small, yeast pancakes which are eaten with caviar, smoked salmon, cheese, sour cream, melted butter, or any smoked fish. Each diner is served a plain *blini*, then allowed to choose the filling that suits his fancy. Most commonly, *blinis* are buttered, dabbed with sour cream, topped with the selected fish, then folded.

Although *blinis* are best known as a first course, they are also a perfect snack or brunch dish.

russian blinis

Russian Blinis are ordinarily served plain, as shown. Then various fillings are offered so that each diner may prepare his pancake according to personal preference. The three bowls contain sour cream, chopped onion, and red caviar.

RUSSIAN BLINIS

1
2 c. milk
½ cake or 1 pkg. dry yeast
½ c. warm water
2 c. sifted all-purpose flour
½ c. sifted buckwheat flour
3 eggs, separated
2 tsp. sugar
¾ tsp. salt
3 tbsp. sour cream
3 tbsp. melted butter

4 Scald the remaining milk and cool to lukewarm. Stir the dough down and stir in the milk, lightly beaten egg yolks, sugar, salt, sour cream and butter. Beat until smooth. Beat the egg whites until stiff but not dry, then fold ⅓ of the egg whites into the batter. Fold in the remaining egg whites carefully. Cover and let stand for 30 minutes.

2 Scald 1 cup of the milk and set aside to cool to lukewarm. Dissolve the yeast in the water, then add the lukewarm milk.

5 Ladle 1 to 4 tablespoons of batter, according to desired size of blini, onto hot greased griddle and cook until bottom is brown and the top bubbles. Turn and brown other side. Serve with red or black caviar and sour cream. You may omit the buckwheat flour and substitute all-purpose flour, if desired. This makes about 6 cups of batter.

3 Stir in 1½ cup all-purpose flour and ¼ cup buckwheat flour. Cover with towel and let stand in warm place for 2 hours and 30 minutes to 3 hours. Stir down and add the remaining ½ cup all-purpose flour and remaining ¼ cup buckwheat flour. Cover and let rise for 2 hours.

puffed pancakes

We prepared two versions of Puffed Pancakes, one mildly spicy, the other sweet. In the background, the pancakes are filled with bacon and dressed with Tomato Fondue Sauce (Sauces, pg. 15) for hearty flavor. The sweet version in the foreground was made with chocolate chips in the batter and served with plenty of maple syrup and seeded raisins.

PUFFED PANCAKES

2½ c. all-purpose flour, sifted
1 tbsp. sugar
¼ tsp. salt
2 eggs, lightly beaten
1⅓ c. milk
1¼ tsp. cream of tartar
2 tbsp. oil

Sift the flour, sugar and salt together into a mixing bowl. Beat the eggs and milk together until blended. Add the egg mixture to the flour mixture, blending well. Sift the cream of tartar over the surface of the batter and fold in gently. Heat the oil on a heavy griddle until a drop of water sizzles when sprinkled on the griddle. Drop the batter by spoonfuls onto the hot griddle. Cook until lightly browned, then turn and brown the other side. Stack the hot pancakes on a serving platter and serve with crisp-fried bacon and Tomato Fondue Sauce (Sauces, page 15). One-fourth cup chocolate chips may be added to the batter before baking and the pancakes may be served with 1 cup raisins heated in 1½ cups of maple syrup. This makes about 24 small pancakes.

DOUBLE BLUEBERRY PANCAKES

1 c. milk
2 tbsp. light corn syrup
1 tbsp. corn oil
1 egg, lightly beaten
1 c. pancake mix
¾ c. blueberries
⅓ c. cottage cheese
Blueberry syrup

Combine the milk, corn syrup, corn oil and egg in a mixing bowl. Add the pancake mix and stir until dry ingredients are moistened. The batter will be lumpy. Stir in the blueberries and cottage cheese carefully. Pour ¼ cup of the batter onto a hot griddle and cook until brown, turning once. Repeat cooking until all the batter is used. Serve with blueberry syrup. This makes 8 pancakes.

QUICK LEMON PANCAKES

2 c. pancake mix
2 tbsp. melted butter
1 1-pt. block lemon ice cream
Grated rind of 1 lemon
2 tbsp. sugar

Prepare the pancake mix and cook according to package directions. Drizzle with the butter and keep warm. Cut the ice cream into ¼-inch slices and place a slice on each pancake. Roll the pancakes and place on a platter. Sprinkle with the mixed lemon rind and sugar and serve immediately This makes about 8 pancakes.

double blueberry pancakes

Double Blueberry Pancakes — who can resist them when the berries are so moist and inviting? And the particularly attractive aspect of these pancakes, from a homemaker's point of view, is that they take only minutes to prepare with the aid of a commercial mix. The secret of their homemade flavor is the addition of cottage cheese to the batter. Now, even on a hurried morning your family may enjoy a delicious pancake breakfast.

BELLINI PANCAKES WITH CHEESE SAUCE SUPREME

4 eggs, separated
¾ c. all-purpose flour, sifted
½ c. half and half cream
¼ c. beer
¼ tsp. salt
Grated rind of 1 lg. lemon
2 tbsp. melted butter
Vegetable oil
1 recipe Cheese Sauce Supreme

Beat the egg yolks in a medium-sized mixing bowl with the electric mixer at medium speed for 5 minutes or until thick and creamy. Add the flour alternately with cream and beer, a small amount at a time, beating well after each addition. Add the salt, lemon rind and butter and mix well. Beat the egg whites until stiff, then fold ¼ of the egg whites into the batter. Fold in the remaining egg whites gently. Brush a hot griddle with oil, then cook the pancakes, using about ¼ cup of batter for each pancake. Cover each pancake with a thick layer of Cheese Sauce Supreme and stack in threes on an ovenproof serving dish. Broil until sauce is browned and bubbly and serve immediately. This makes 12 pancakes.

CHEESE SAUCE SUPREME

3 tbsp. butter
3 tbsp. all-purpose flour
¾ c. Chablis
¾ c. half and half cream
½ c. freshly grated Parmesan cheese
⅓ c. grated Gruyère cheese
1 3-oz. package cream cheese, softened
⅛ tsp. white pepper

Melt the butter in the top of a double boiler over hot but not boiling water. Stir in the flour to make a smooth paste. Pour in the Chablis gradually, stirring constantly, and cook until smooth and thick. Stir in the cream and Parmesan cheese and mix well. Combine the cream cheese and the Gruyère cheese in a small bowl and mix cheese with a wooden spoon until the cream cheese is smooth. Stir into the sauce mixture and cook until all cheese is melted and the sauce is smooth. This makes about 2 cups of sauce.

bellini pancakes with cheese sauce supreme

Cheese fans may prepare for something special when pancakes with cheese are the bill of fare. Light, puffy pancakes are made from an unusual foamy batter. Then the cheese excitement comes with the thick, creamy sauce, a combination of several types of cheese. The sauce is layered between and around the pancakes. Parmesan cheese may be sprinkled over individual servings as desired.

waffles

Crisp, tender, tempting waffles are served here with butter curls and maple syrup. Waffles needn't be square, as you see; there are numerous irons on the market in pretty and unusual shapes to add interest to the appearance of your meal.

BASIC WAFFLES

2 c. all-purpose flour
3 tsp. baking powder
³/₄ tsp. salt
2 tbsp. sugar
3 eggs, separated
1³/₄ c. milk
¹/₂ c. vegetable oil

Sift the flour with the baking powder, salt and sugar 3 times and place in a mixing bowl. Beat the egg yolks until frothy, then stir in the milk and oil. Pour into the flour mixture and beat with a rotary beater until smooth. Beat the egg whites until stiff peaks form, then fold into the batter. Pour enough batter for each waffle onto a hot waffle iron and bake until golden. Serve immediately with butter and syrup or honey. This makes about 8 waffles.

SOUR CREAM WAFFLE HEARTS

1 c. fresh raspberries
2 c. sweetened whipped cream
³/₄ c. strong brewed coffee
³/₄ c. milk
1 c. sour cream
1 egg
¹/₄ c. vegetable oil
1¹/₂ c. pancake mix

Fold the raspberries into the whipped cream and chill. Combine the coffee, milk, sour cream, egg and oil in a bowl and blend well. Add the pancake mix and beat with an electric mixer until smooth. Pour enough batter onto a hot waffle iron to spread to 1 inch from the edge. Bake until steaming stops. Repeat with the remaining batter. Trim waffles into heart shapes if heart-shaped waffle iron is not available. Serve immediately with the whipped cream mixture. One-half cup of raspberry jam may be substituted for the fresh raspberries. This makes about 4 servings.

melba toast

Melba Toast teams happily with nearly any meat or salad. And since it takes only minutes to prepare, you may add this bit of flare to your everyday meals as often as you like. Though it is served cold in most restaurants, you will find the taste of Melba Toast is infinitely better when brought to the table hot.

Melba Toast, frequently served in elegant napkin water lilies in fine restaurants, should hold no awe for you as it is quite easy to prepare at home. Begin with an ordinary, thinly sliced (¼ inch thick) loaf of sandwich bread. Toast both sides of the desired number of slices. Then, with a sharp knife, divide each through the middle, making two slices out of one. Now retoast the bread — and you have Melba Toast.

HOW TO MAKE MELBA TOAST

Trim the crusts from thin-sliced sandwich bread. Toast the bread in an electric toaster or in the oven.

1 Place the toast on a cutting board and slice through the toast very carefully.

2 The toast is now ready to be placed in the oven and the cut side browned.

introducing hot cross buns, crumpets and english muffins

The word crumpets usually brings to mind an elegant British drawing room filled with Victorian furniture, a silver tea service and well-dressed ladies regally sipping tea. Tea is an important British refreshment enjoyed periodically throughout the day, and commonly associated with the Britisher's tea are small cakes of spongy yeast bread called crumpets.

Crumpets are made by pouring a thick batter into buttered crumpet rings on a hot griddle. (If crumpet rings are unavailable, a tuna can, with both top and bottom removed, makes an excellent substitute.) When browned on both sides, the crumpets are taken up and the rings removed. The heavy consistency of the batter makes the cakes form perfectly and pop out easily.

Crumpets are delicious when split in half and spread with butter and jelly or rich marmalade. Of course they should be served hot.

hot cross buns and muffins

English Muffins, like Crumpets, are cooked in a crumpet ring on a griddle or in a greased skillet. Though Crumpets and English Muffins have the same porous appearance, their textures differ somewhat because English Muffins are made of a dough instead of a batter, and they are also rolled in cornmeal before cooking.

Unlike Crumpets and English Muffins, Hot Cross Buns are baked in the oven. The cross cut in the dough before baking, which gives them their name, is symbolic of Easter. In 18th Century England, Hot Cross Buns were the traditional bread for Good Friday, and were sold only on that day.

English Muffins and Hot Cross Buns are a delicious addition to any meal, particularly good at breakfast or as a mid-morning snack.

Cornmeal Muffins are, in the American sense, a true muffin. The method of cooking, ingredients, texture and appearance are entirely different from English Muffins. Cornmeal muffins contain baking powder as a leavening agent rather than yeast and they are baked in true muffin pans.

Any of the following recipes are so easily mastered that serving homemade bread will be both a convenience and a pleasure.

HOT CROSS BUNS

4 to 5 c. all-purpose flour
1/3 c. sugar
3/4 tsp. salt
1 1/2 tsp. cinnamon
2 pkg. dry yeast
1/4 c. butter
1 c. milk, scalded
2 eggs, slightly beaten
3/4 c. currants
1 recipe Egg Wash *(Breads, pg. 6)*
1 c. Basic Confectioners' Icing *(Desserts, pg. 8)*

Combine 1 1/4 cups of flour, sugar, salt, cinnamon and yeast in a large bowl. Add the butter to the milk, then cool to lukewarm. Pour the butter mixture into the flour mixture gradually, beating with an electric mixer until blended. Scrape the bowl occasionally. Add the eggs and about 1/2 cup of flour or enough to make a thick batter. Beat at high speed for 2 minutes. Stir in enough of the remaining flour to make a soft dough. Knead for 8 to 10 minutes on lightly floured surface until smooth and elastic. Place the dough in a greased bowl, turning to grease top. Cover with a towel and let rise for about 1 hour or until doubled in bulk. Punch down the dough and turn out on a lightly floured surface. Knead the currants into the dough. Divide the dough into 18 equal parts, then roll into balls. Place the balls in two 8-inch buttered cake pans. Brush with Egg Wash and cover. Let rise for 1 hour in a warm place until doubled in bulk. Cut a cross on the top of each bun with a sharp knife. Bake in a preheated 375-degree oven for 20 to 25 minutes. Remove the buns from the pans and cool on wire racks. Fill the crosses on top of the buns with confectioners' icing. You may reheat the buns before serving, if desired. This makes 18 buns.

ENGLISH MUFFINS

1 c. milk, scalded
2 tbsp. sugar
1 tsp. salt
1/4 c. butter
2 pkg. dry yeast
1 c. warm water
5 1/2 c. (about) all-purpose flour
Cornmeal

Combine the hot milk, sugar, salt and butter, stirring until the sugar is dissolved and the butter is melted. Place in a large mixing bowl and cool to lukewarm. Dissolve the yeast in warm water, stirring well, then add to the milk mixture. Beat in 3 cups of flour until smooth, then add enough of the remaining flour to make a soft dough. Place the dough on a lightly floured surface and knead for about 8 to 10 minutes or until smooth and elastic. Place the dough in a greased bowl, turning to grease the top. Cover and let the dough rise in a warm place for 1 hour or until doubled in bulk. Punch down and divide in half. Roll each dough section out to 1/2-inch thickness on a cornmeal-covered surface. Cut into circles with a 3-inch cookie cutter. Cover the circles with a towel and let rest for 30 minutes. Place the circles, cornmeal sides down, in a greased skillet over medium heat. Cook for about 15 minutes or until bottoms are well browned. Turn over and cook the other side for about 15 minutes longer or until brown. This makes about 20 muffins.

CORNMEAL MUFFINS

1/2 c. cornmeal
1/2 c. all-purpose flour
2 tbsp. sugar
1/2 tsp. salt
2 tsp. baking powder
1 egg, beaten
1/2 c. milk
2 tbsp. bacon drippings

Sift the cornmeal, flour, sugar, salt and baking powder together into a mixing bowl. Stir in the egg, milk and bacon drippings, mixing well. Fill 8 greased muffin cups 2/3 full with batter. Bake in a preheated 425-degree oven for 15 minutes or until browned. This makes 8 muffins.

DARBY CRUMPETS

2 c. milk, scalded
1/2 c. butter
1 1/2 tsp. salt
2 pkg. dry yeast
1 1/2 tsp. sugar
3 3/4 c. all-purpose flour

Combine the milk, butter and salt in a large bowl and stir until butter is melted. Cool to lukewarm. Dissolve yeast in 1/4 cup warm water and stir into milk mixture. Stir in sugar and flour and beat with a wooden spoon to a smooth, thick batter. Let rise, covered, in a warm place for 1 hour or until doubled in bulk. Place well-buttered crumpet rings on a well-buttered hot griddle. Fill rings almost half full with batter and smooth surface with a wet spoon. Cook over medium heat until batter has risen and bottoms are lightly browned. Turn crumpets and rings and cook until browned on the other side. Split in half and serve buttered. This makes 16 to 18 Crumpets.

hot cross buns, crumpets, english muffins

Homemade Hot Cross Buns, Crumpets, and English Muffins are perfect for breakfast or coffee break. Easy to make, they are also a pleasant change of fare from the more ordinary toast or bakery doughnuts.

introducing
biscuits

Biscuits, an American classic, were first originated by the colonists. This speciality was used to take the place of bread. They started as little dough cakes which were quickly kneaded and baked. Interestingly enough, what the English call biscuits, we call cookies. The English version of our American biscuits would be called scones or tea cakes.

For perfect biscuits, proper measuring of ingredients is essential. Be sure to use the exact amount of shortening specified in a given recipe to avoid those classic "bride's" biscuits. Baking powder or baking soda and sour milk are quick-acting leavening agents which facilitate fast cooking and which produce light biscuits. A slower acting agent, such as yeast, will produce biscuits which require longer preparation time and which are firmer in texture.

Once the dough is mixed and kneaded, biscuits should be cut not more than three inches in diameter nor more than one third of an inch thick. For special occasions, such as party luncheons, biscuits may be cut very small. Handle the dough as little as possible in the rolling out process, as excessive handling tends to toughen the dough. Always roll out biscuits on a well-floured surface.

Baked biscuits can be used in a variety of delicious ways. Hot, buttered biscuits may be served with any meal. Breakfast biscuits are usually accompanied by jams or jellies; biscuits may be used in a main dish as the base for creamed meats or seafood. Bite-sized, filled biscuits are served as hors d' oeuvres.

Regardless of how you serve them, homemade biscuits should be mastered by every cook.

SOUR MILK BISCUITS

3 c. all-purpose flour
4 tsp. baking powder
Pinch of soda
1 tsp. salt
1/2 c. vegetable shortening
1 1/2 c. sour milk or buttermilk
Melted butter

Sift the flour, baking powder, soda and salt together in a large bowl. Cut in the shortening with 2 knives or a pastry blender to make a coarse crumb-like consistency. Add the milk, blending well. Place the dough on a lightly floured surface and knead until smooth. Roll out to 1/2-inch thickness and cut into rounds with a biscuit cutter. Place on a greased baking sheet and brush with melted butter. Bake in a preheated 450-degree oven for 12 to 15 minutes or until golden brown. This makes about 2 dozen biscuits.

MARYLAND BEATEN BISCUITS

5 c. all-purpose flour
2 tsp. salt
1/2 tsp. baking powder
1 c. lard

Combine the flour, salt and baking powder in a mixing bowl. Cut in the lard to make a fine crumb-like consistency. Add enough water to make a stiff dough, then knead until the dough holds together. Place on a heavy table or chopping block. Beat with a hammer for 30 minutes or until the dough is blistered. Shape into small biscuits and place on a baking sheet, then prick tops with fork. Bake in a preheated 400-degree oven for about 15 minutes or until lightly browned. This makes 35 to 40 biscuits.

soda breads

Bread, by definition, is a baked product made of dough that has been raised by yeast or other gas-forming (leavening) agents. Soda Breads, introduced here, are among those breads *not* leavened by yeast. They belong to the category of Quick Breads, so named because their dough is not made with yeast, and therefore does not require additional time to rise before baking.

soda scones

Soda Scones, made from a basic soda bread recipe, have a biscuit-like texture. Instead of being made in a loaf, Soda Scones are made by cutting the dough in triangles and brushing the tops with a raw, beaten egg for a glossy appearance.

The ingredients baking powder, baking soda, and buttermilk leaven soda breads and give them a biscuit-like texture. Because they are without yeast, they do not rise as much as yeast breads. However, they are equally delicious and much easier to prepare. Many sweet and savory varieties can be made from a basic recipe, and the three breads which follow, Sweet Soda Bread, Cheese Soda Bread and Onion Soda Bread, are excellent examples.

Sweet Soda Bread is given its mildly sweet flavor with a small amount of sugar and 1½ cups of seedless raisins. This quick and easy recipe, which requires only 2 or 3 minutes of kneading, makes two loaves, delicious when sliced and buttered.

The recipes for Cheese Soda Bread and Onion Soda Bread are simple variations of Sweet Soda Bread. The sugar and raisins have been omitted, and savory cheese and onions added. These breads are a flavorful attraction at any meal.

SODA SCONES

3 c. sifted all-purpose flour
½ tsp. soda
2 tsp. cream of tartar
½ c. butter, softened
1 tbsp. sugar
¼ c. milk
¼ c. water
1 egg, beaten

Sift the flour, soda and cream of tartar into a large bowl, then work in the butter with fingers until of a fine meal consistency. Add the sugar and blend thoroughly. Combine the milk and water and stir into the flour mixture to form a medium-soft dough. Press the dough lightly into a 10 x 8-inch rectangle on a lightly floured surface, then cut into 1 x 3-inch triangles. Brush the tops with the egg and place on a baking sheet. Bake in a preheated 400-degree oven for 20 minutes or until lightly browned. Serve hot with butter and jam. This makes 16 scones.

SWEET SODA BREAD

4 c. sifted all-purpose flour
1 tbsp. baking powder
2 tsp. salt
1 tsp. soda
¼ c. butter
¼ c. sugar
1½ c. raisins
1 egg, beaten well
1¾ c. buttermilk

Sift the flour, baking powder, salt and soda together into a large bowl. Add the butter and cut in with 2 knives until the mixture is of a fine crumb consistency. Add the sugar and raisins and mix well. Combine the egg and buttermilk, then add to the dry mixture. Stir with a spoon, adding more flour if needed to make a soft dough. Turn out on a floured surface and knead for 2 or 3 minutes or until smooth. Divide the dough in half and shape into 2 round loaves on a large baking sheet. Cut a deep cross in each loaf with a sharp knife. Bake in a preheated 375-degree oven for 40 to 45 minutes. This makes about 20 servings.

Variations:

CHEESE SODA BREAD

Prepare the recipe for Sweet Soda Bread dough, omitting the sugar and raisins and adding 2 cups of grated sharp Cheddar cheese. Follow the recipe instructions for mixing, shaping and baking as for Sweet Soda Bread.

ONION SODA BREAD

Prepare the recipe for Sweet Soda Bread dough, omitting the sugar and raisins and adding 1½ cups of chopped onions. Follow the recipe instructions for mixing and shaping the bread. Saute 3 thin slices of onion in about 2 tablespoons of vegetable oil until just tender, but not brown. Drain on absorbent towels. Separate the onion slices into rings and arrange on top of the loaves. Follow instructions for baking Sweet Soda Bread.

The Creative Homemaker's Academy © MCMLXXIII
Selected Illustrations © B.P.C. Publishing Limited MCMLXX

raised doughnuts

What could be more inviting at breakfast than these sugarcoated Raised Doughnuts? The ones shown are filled with apricot jam, but you may choose your favorite jam filling for your Raised Doughnuts.

raised doughnuts

Doughnuts, a favorite breakfast food and coffee break snack among Americans, come in several varieties.

Raised Doughnuts are given their extravagant puff by the addition of yeast. They are also given set amounts of time to rise, before frying, to achieve their attractive "raised" appearance. To make them especially delicious, their centers are filled with rich jam before cooking. For the ultimate in flavor, roll them in sugar after frying.

Doughnuts raised with baking powder, such as the recipe for Fried Cake Doughnuts, page 46 will have a cake-like consistency. These doughnuts are distinctly different from the typical bakery doughnuts and are decidedly better.

French doughnuts are still another variety and can best be described as being like a *chou* pastry doughnut.

RAISED DOUGHNUTS

1 pkg. yeast
1 c. warm milk
1 tsp. salt
5 tbsp. sugar
4¼ c. (about) all-purpose flour
6 egg yolks
6 tbsp. butter, softened
1 tbsp. dark rum
1 tsp. grated lemon rind
Apricot or other jam
1 egg white

Dissolve the yeast in ¼ cup of the milk, then stir in the salt, 1 tablespoon of sugar and ¼ cup of flour until smooth and well blended. Let rise, covered, in a warm place for 30 minutes or until doubled in bulk. Place the egg yolks and remaining sugar in a medium-sized mixing bowl, then place bowl in large bowl of hot water. Beat until thick, then blend in the butter. Add the rum and lemon rind and beat until smooth. Add the egg mixture and remaining milk to the yeast mixture and blend well. Add 2 cups of flour and beat to a smooth light dough. Let rise for 30 minutes or until doubled in bulk. Punch down and turn out on a well-floured surface. Knead until smooth, working in enough of the remaining flour to make an easily handled dough. Roll out the dough on a lightly floured surface to ⅓-inch thickness, then cut into 4 x 3-inch rectangles. Spread 1 heaping teaspoon of jam along the 4-inch side of each rectangle. Roll as for jelly roll, then brush edge with egg white and pinch to seal. Place, seam side down, on a lightly floured towel and cover. Let rise for 30 minutes or until doubled in bulk. Fry in deep fat at medium heat for about 5 minutes or until brown on all sides. Drain on absorbent toweling, then roll in additional sugar. This makes 24 doughnuts.

cake doughnuts

FRIED CAKE DOUGHNUTS

3 c. all-purpose flour
2 tbsp. baking powder
¼ tsp. cinnamon
¼ tsp. nutmeg
¼ c. butter
⅔ c. sugar
2 eggs, beaten
¼ c. (about) milk
Vegetable oil

Sift the flour, baking powder and spices together in a large bowl. Blend in the butter with fingers to a fine crumb consistency. Add the sugar and mix well. Make a well in the center of the flour mixture and pour in the beaten eggs, mixing with a fork. Add enough milk to make of pastry consistency. Break off pieces of dough and shape into 1½-inch balls, then flatten to a 3-inch diameter. Heat oil in a deep fat fryer until just medium hot. The doughnuts will brown too fast and be doughy in the centers if the oil is too hot. Drop the doughnuts into the hot oil and fry for about 5 to 7 minutes or until golden brown. Drain on paper towels and roll in additional sugar. These doughnuts may be filled with jelly, if desired. Flatten out the balls to a 3-inch diameter and make a slight indentation in the centers. Fill the indentations with jelly and moisten the edges with water. Shape the dough over the jelly, pressing the moistened edges together and sealing well. Drop into the hot oil and fry as instructed. This makes about 24 doughnuts.

BEATEN FRENCH DOUGHNUTS

1 c. water
½ tsp. salt
2 tbsp. butter
1 c. sifted all-purpose flour
3 eggs
Confectioners' sugar

Place the water, salt and butter in a saucepan and bring to a boil, stirring, until the butter is melted. Add the flour gradually, stirring until smooth. Add the eggs, one at a time, beating well after each addition, then beat for 5 minutes. Cover and chill for 2 hours. Place dough in a pastry tube with a ½-inch plain tube affixed and pipe in the shape of small doughnuts onto a floured baking sheet. Let stand for 1 to 2 hours to dry. Drop into 375-degree deep fat and fry until brown. Drain on paper toweling, then roll in confectioners' sugar. This makes about 1½ dozen doughnuts.

fried cake doughnuts

These sugary treats are Fried Cake Doughnuts, which delicately conceal centers of rich raspberry jam. Served hot, they are perfect for breakfast or coffee breaks, and they make a luscious dessert at any meal.

PLAIN CAKE DOUGHNUTS

4 eggs
Sugar
⅓ c. milk
⅓ c. melted vegetable shortening
3½ c. sifted all-purpose flour
3 tsp. baking powder
¾ tsp. salt
2 tsp. cinnamon
½ tsp. nutmeg

Place the eggs in a mixer bowl and beat with an electric mixer until foamy, then add ⅔ cup of sugar. Beat for about 5 minutes. Add the milk and shortening and beat until blended. Sift the flour, baking powder, salt, 1 teaspoon of cinnamon and the nutmeg together, then add to the egg mixture and mix thoroughly. Chill for at least 2 hours. Roll out ⅜ inch thick on a lightly floured surface and cut with a floured doughnut cutter, then let stand for 15 minutes. Fry in deep fat at 375 degrees until brown, turning once. Remove and drain on paper toweling. Combine ½ cup of sugar and the remaining 1 teaspoon of cinnamon in a paper bag, then drop the doughnuts in the sugar mixture and shake until coated. This makes about 2 dozen doughnuts.

CHINESE HONEY SHORTBREAD

Chinese Honey Shortbread is a delicious variation of plain shortbread with a distinctive honey flavor. The recipe has been traced back to a 12th century cookbook of Chinese origin. In it, a certain Madam Wu is quoted as saying, "Make these into cakes and bake them on top of the stove." The following recipe, however, specifies that they be baked in the oven for a more uniform texture. The resulting fan-shaped, buttery cookies are excellent served with tea and would be a most appropriate dessert to follow an oriental meal.

CHINESE HONEY SHORTBREAD

2 1/2 c. all-purpose flour
Pinch of salt
1/2 c. butter
1/2 c. honey

Place the flour and salt in a medium-sized bowl, then add the butter. Rub the butter into the flour with the fingers until mixture is the consistency of very fine meal. Add the honey gradually and, working with the fingers, blend until dough is smooth and leaves the side of the bowl. Cut a 2 1/2 x 2-inch fan-shaped pattern from cardboard. Roll out the dough on a lightly floured surface to 1/4-inch thickness and cut into fan shapes. Place on a lightly floured baking sheet and cut 6 deep slashes lengthwise in the fans as shown in the illustration. Bake in preheated 350-degree oven for 15 minutes or until lightly browned. This makes about 30 pieces of shortbread.

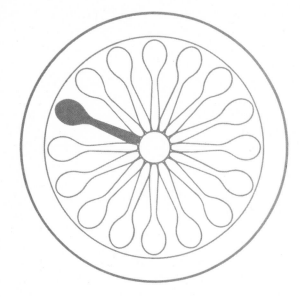

coffee breads

The following recipe for yeast dough yields enough for two coffee breads (or two cinnamon rings) and is one of the easiest and best you'll find for making a smooth, elastic dough every time. The dough kneads very well, and is easily cut and braided into a uniform shape which rises perfectly and bakes into a very professional looking loaf. The candied fruit adds a colorful and festive garnish, transforming this smooth-textured bread into a holiday treat.

The dough may be divided into two parts with one portion used for a coffee bread and the other used for the Cinnamon Ring.

COFFEE BREAD DOUGH

2 pkg. yeast
2¹/₂ c. lukewarm milk
³/₄ c. sugar
1 egg, beaten
1 tsp. salt
¹/₂ c. melted butter
1 tsp. ground cardamom
8¹/₂ c. all-purpose flour

Dissolve the yeast in ¹/₄ cup of milk. Combine remaining milk with the sugar, egg, salt, butter, cardamom and 2 tablespoons of flour in a large bowl. Beat with a wooden spoon until smooth, then beat in the yeast mixture until well blended. Beat in half of the remaining flour until well blended, then work in the remaining flour with the hands until smooth. Place the dough in a large, well-greased bowl, turning to grease the top. Cover and let rise in a warm place for 2 hours or until doubled in bulk. Turn the dough out onto a lightly floured surface and knead for 10 minutes or until the dough is smooth and elastic. This makes enough dough for 2 braids, 2 rings or 1 of each.

COFFEE BRAID

¹/₂ of the Coffee Bread Dough
1 recipe Egg Wash *(pg. 6)*

Roll out the dough on a lightly floured surface to an 18 x 6 x ¹/₂-inch rectangle. Braid according to the instructions for three-strand braid on page 9, brushing the edges and ends of each strip with the Egg Wash. Place on a lightly floured baking sheet and cover. Let rise for 30 minutes. Brush the top of the bread with the remaining Egg Wash. Bake in a preheated 375-degree oven for 25 minutes. Test for doneness according to the instructions in illustration 7 on page 5. Remove from the oven and place on a wire rack. Sprinkle with cinnamon and sugar and garnish with candied cherries, if desired. This makes 1 large Coffee Braid.

CINNAMON RING

¹/₂ of the Coffee Bread Dough
¹/₂ c. sifted confectioners' sugar
2 tsp. cinnamon
¹/₂ c. melted butter
1 recipe Egg Wash *(pg. 6)*

Roll out the dough on a lightly floured surface to a 36 x 8 x ¹/₈-inch rectangle. Mix the sugar and cinnamon well. Brush the entire surface of the dough with half the butter, then sprinkle with half the cinnamon mixture. Drizzle the remaining butter over the cinnamon mixture and top with the remaining cinnamon mixture. Roll the dough tightly as for jelly roll, starting at the long edge, then seal seam side with some of the Egg Wash. Shape into a circle, brushing ends with Egg Wash before joining. Place on a lightly floured baking sheet, seam side down, and snip the top of the dough with scissors at ¹/₂-inch intervals. Cover and let rise for 30 minutes. Brush the entire surface of the dough with the remaining Egg Wash. Bake in a preheated 375-degree oven for 25 minutes. Test for doneness according to the instructions in illustration 7 on page 5. Remove from the oven and place on a wire rack. This makes 1 large Cinnamon Ring.

batter curls

An excellent pastime to amuse young children on a rainy afternoon is making Batter Curls. These "squiggly cookies" are of Spanish origin (they're called *Churros* in Spanish) and are very simple to make. Using a pastry bag with a small nozzle, the thin batter which consists of egg, flour and milk, is piped with a spiral motion into hot fat and quickly deep fried. After draining well, they may be heaped on a plate and dusted with confectioners' sugar. A word of caution: because of the hot frying fat, if the aspiring young chefs in your household wish to assist in the preparation of Batter Curls, it is best to let them mix the batter and not participate in the actual frying process.

BATTER CURLS

3/4 c. all-purpose flour
1/8 tsp. salt
2 eggs
2 tbsp. milk
Confectioners' sugar

Combine the flour and salt in a mixer bowl. Combine the eggs and milk and beat well. Add to the flour mixture and beat with an electric mixer until smooth and blended. Pour the batter into a pastry bag with a 1/4-inch writing tube affixed. Hold a finger over the tip of the writing tube and release the batter with a circular motion, making 3 or 4-inch designs, directly into hot oil in a deep fat fryer. Fry until lightly browned, then drain on paper toweling. Sprinkle with confectioners' sugar.

batter curls

These "squiggly cookies" are light, airy and make delightful snack food. Children, especially, love their crisp goodness and unusual curly shapes. Like snowflakes, there are never two that are exactly alike!

The Creative Homemaker's Academy © MCMLXXIII
Selected Illustrations © B.P.C. Publishing Limited MCMLXX

austrian kugelhopf

Kugelhopf or Alsatian pastry is a classic sweet bread made from yeast risen dough. Prior to its introduction to France, this bread was made in Austria and Poland with leaven other than yeast. It was Queen Marie Antoinette's fondness for sweet pastries that made Kugelholpf a favorite. This elegantly molded Kugelholpf makes a delicious breakfast bread or a perfect addition for tea or coffee breaks.

AUSTRIAN KUGELHOPF

¾ c. chopped almonds
½ c. raisins
1½ tsp. grated lemon rind

6 c. all-purpose flour, sifted
1 c. sugar
1 tsp. salt
2 env. yeast
¼ c. lukewarm water
2 c. lukewarm milk
2 eggs, well beaten
⅓ c. melted butter
1 tsp. vanilla extract

Combine the almonds, raisins and lemon rind with ½ cup of the flour, then toss until well coated. Combine the sugar, salt and 2½ cups of the flour in a large mixing bowl. Sprinkle the yeast over the water, then stir until dissolved. Add the milk to the sugar mixture, stirring until well mixed. Add the yeast mixture and beat with a wooden spoon until smooth. Beat in the eggs thoroughly. Add the butter gradually, beating constantly. Stir in the vanilla extract. Add the remaining flour and beat until smooth and satiny. Add the raisin mixture and mix thoroughly. Cover with a towel. Let rise in a warm place for 1 hour and 30 minutes or until doubled in bulk. Stir down the dough and turn into a large, buttered bundt pan. Cover with a towel and let rise for 1 hour. Bake in a preheated 350-degree oven for about 50 minutes or until an inserted cake tester comes out clean. Remove from the pan and cool on a wire rack. Cover and let stand for 1 day. Sprinkle with confectioners' sugar before slicing. This makes about 20 servings.

austrian kugelhopf

This enticing Austrian Kugelholpf is most delicious served hot with butter. The perfectly browned crust has been lightly dusted with icing sugar. Note the golden cake-like texture of the bread which indicates proper dough preparation and correct baking technique.

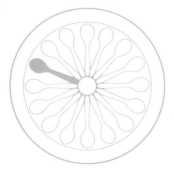

swedish crown

Unusual in taste, intricate in design, Swedish Crown bread will delight and please anyone. This very rich bread is prepared from Basic Cold Yeast Dough (pg. 20 & 21) to which egg white and sugar are added. The mixture is then filled with nuts, brown sugar, currants and butter. Shaped into dainty swirls and baked, Swedish Crown bread is a festive fare for any occasion.

SWEDISH CROWN

1 c. softened butter
1¼ c. (packed) brown sugar
2½ c. ground pecans
1½ c. currants
1 recipe Cold Yeast Dough *(pg. 21)*
1 egg white
½ c. sugar

Cream the butter in a large mixer bowl until light, then beat in the brown sugar until creamy. Stir in the pecans and currants. Divide the dough in half. Roll out half the dough on a lightly floured surface into a 20 x 12-inch rectangle, then spread with half the pecan mixture to within 1 inch of the edges. Roll up tightly as for jelly roll, starting at the long edge. Place on a lightly floured baking sheet, seam side down, and shape into a ring, sealing the ends together with a small amount of water. Make deep cuts with sharp scissors at ½-inch intervals all around the ring to within ½ inch of the base. Twist alternate sections of the dough toward the center and outer edge of the ring as shown in the illustration. Beat the egg white lightly with 1 tablespoon of water. Brush the surface of the ring with the egg white and sprinkle with 2 tablespoons of the sugar. Bake in a preheated 400-degree oven for 25 minutes or until golden brown, then sprinkle around the center of the ring with 2 tablespoons of the sugar. Repeat the procedure to make second ring, using the remaining dough, pecan mixture, egg white and sugar. Wrap tightly in foil and freeze. Each ring makes 8 to 10 servings.

swedish crown

Before baking the Swedish Crown, scissor snips are made in the uncooked dough. The rich, buttery cold yeast dough combined with currants, pecans and brown sugar makes this sweet bread unsurpassed in flavor. The baked Swedish Crown has been lavishly sprinkled with sugar.

torrijas

On a nippy evening, ward off the chill with a cup of hot coffee and Torrijas, (pronounced toe-ree-haas), Spain's form of French Toast. This delectable hot sweet bread is made from ingredients that normally are always on hand, making it a convenient snack choice.

Torrijas, Spain's tempting version of French Toast, are made from rounds of bread, cut from either one-inch or half-inch slices. The thicker type must be cut from an unsliced large loaf of bread; the thick Torrijas will be crisp on the outside, soft on the inside, and taste very much like French Toast. The thinner, half-inch rounds can be cut from standard sliced bread, and will be crisp throughout. Which is better? *Both* are delicious, so the choice is yours!

TORRIJAS

8 to 10   ¹/₂ or 1-in. thick bread slices
1 c. sifted confectioners' sugar
1 ¹/₂ tsp. cinnamon
2 eggs
2 tbsp. sherry

Cut 2 circles from each large slice of bread with a 2 ¹/₄-inch round cookie cutter. Sift the sugar and cinnamon together and set aside. Place the eggs in a small mixer bowl and beat with an electric mixer until fluffy. Strain the eggs, then stir in the sherry. Dip each bread round into the egg mixture. Fry in 380-degree oil in a deep fat fryer until lightly browned on each side. Watch carefully as the Torrijas brown quickly. Remove from the oil with a slotted spoon and drain on absorbent paper. Coat well with the sugar mixture and serve immediately. This makes 16 to 20 Torrijas.

SAFFRON COFFEE CAKE

1 tsp. saffron shreds
1 pkg. yeast
3 ³/₄ c. all-purpose flour
1 tsp. salt
¹/₂ c. vegetable shortening
¹/₄ c. butter, softened
¹/₄ c. sugar
¹/₂ c. lukewarm milk
1 egg, lightly beaten
¹/₂ c. currants
¹/₂ c. raisins
¹/₄ c. chopped mixed candied peel
Sifted confectioners' sugar

Place the saffron in a small bowl. Add ¹/₂ cup of boiling water and let stand for 15 minutes. Strain the water and cool to lukewarm. Add the yeast and stir until dissolved. Set aside. Place the flour and salt in a large bowl. Add the shortening and butter and work with the fingers until the mixture is the consistency of fine meal. Add the sugar and work until well blended. Make a well in the center of the flour mixture and pour in 3 tablespoons of the milk and the yeast mixture. Cover the milk mixture in the well with a thin layer of the flour mixture and let stand until the liquid bubbles through the flour layer. Mix until smooth, adding the remaining milk gradually. Add the egg and mix well. Mix the currants, raisins and mixed peel. Dust lightly with additional flour, then mix into the dough until evenly distributed. Cover and let rise in a warm place for 1 hour or until doubled in bulk. Punch down, then place in a 10-inch greased and lightly floured tube pan. Cover and let rise for 15 minutes. Bake in a preheated 400-degree oven for 45 minutes to 1 hour or until the coffee cake tests done and the top is golden. Dust with confectioners' sugar before serving. This dough may be baked in muffin pans for 15 to 20 minutes, if desired. This makes 15 to 20 servings.

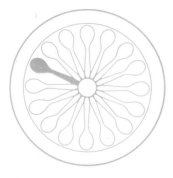

soufflé puffs

AUSTRIAN SOUFFLÉ PUFFS

4 eggs, separated
¼ c. sugar
2 tbsp. all-purpose flour
Pinch of salt
2 tbsp. water
1 tsp. vanilla extract

Beat the egg yolks in a large bowl until lemon colored, then add the sugar gradually, beating well after each addition. Sprinkle the flour and salt on the egg yolk mixture and beat until smooth, then beat in the water and vanilla extract. Beat the egg whites in a large bowl until stiff peaks form. Fold ¼ of the egg whites into the sugar mixture thoroughly, then fold in the remaining egg whites gently until well blended. Cook according to the step-by-step illustrations. You may serve the puffs with fresh fruits. This makes 8 servings.

2 Slide an oiled pancake turner under each can and place an oiled metal spatula over the top. Turn the cans over carefully. Cook until just set, then loosen the cooked mixture around the cans and remove the cans.

1 Remove the bottoms from 3 used 3 x 3-inch metal cans, then wash and dry well. Place a well-oiled griddle over medium heat. Oil the inside of each can very heavily and arrange the cans on the hot griddle. Spoon the soufflé mixture into the cans to within 1 inch of the top and cook for 5 to 8 minutes or until golden brown.

3 Cook for 5 minutes longer or until golden brown. Remove the puffs from the griddle with the pancake turner and place on a serving plate. Repeat with remaining soufflé mixture.

4 Dust generously with sifted confectioners' sugar and serve immediately.

austrian soufflé puffs

Austrian Soufflé Puffs are a variation of a fluffy, sweet classic called *Salzburger Nockerl*. Instead of the traditional baked-in-the oven method, we "baked" our puffs on a hot griddle and used cylindrical tins (made from empty fruit cans!) to assure perfectly molded shapes. This dessert or breakfast dish is lavishly coated with confectioners' sugar and true to the Austrian reputation for luscious extravagance. Tart, fresh fruits are served with the puffs, making a contrast to its sweetness.

FRESH POTATO COFFEE CAKE

1 ½ c. cubed fresh potatoes
1 c. scalded milk
½ c. vegetable shortening
Sugar
2 tsp. salt
2 pkg. dry yeast
2 lg. eggs, lightly beaten
8 ½ c. (about) sifted all-purpose flour
6 tbsp. melted butter
1 c. diced mixed candied fruits
¾ tsp. cinnamon
1 lg. egg white

Place the potatoes in a saucepan and cover with water. Bring to a boil, then reduce heat. Simmer until the potatoes are tender, then drain and mash. Measure 1 cup of mashed potatoes and place in a large mixing bowl. Add the milk, shortening, ⅓ cup of sugar and salt and mix well. Cool to lukewarm. Add the yeast to ½ cup of warm water and stir until dissolved. Pour into the potato mixture, then add the eggs and stir until mixed. Add 1 ½ cups of the flour and mix well. Cover and let rise in a warm place for 30 minutes or until bubbly. Add 5 cups of the flour, 1 cup at a time, mixing well after each addition. Spread ½ cup of the flour on a board. Place the dough on the flour, then sprinkle ½ cup of the flour over the dough. Knead for 10 minutes, adding the remaining flour as needed. Place in a lightly greased bowl, turning to grease the surface, then cover. Place in the refrigerator overnight. Roll out on a lightly floured board to 1-inch thickness and cut with a 2-inch biscuit cutter. Dip each round into the melted butter, then into the mixed fruits. Combine ¾ cup of sugar and the cinnamon. Dip the rounds in the cinnamon mixture, then stand the rounds up in 2 greased 8-inch ring molds. Beat the egg white until foamy and brush on the coffee cakes. Let rise in a warm place for about 1 hour and 30 minutes or until doubled in bulk. Bake in a preheated 350-degree oven for 40 minutes or until golden brown.

FRESH POTATO ROLLS OR FRESH POTATO BREAD

1 ½ c. cubed fresh potatoes
⅔ c. scalded milk
½ c. vegetable shortening
¼ c. sugar
2 tsp. salt
2 pkg. dry yeast
3 lg. eggs, lightly beaten
8 ½ c. (about) sifted all-purpose flour
3 tbsp. melted butter

Place the potatoes in a small saucepan and add enough water to cover. Bring to a boil, then reduce heat and simmer until the potatoes are tender. Drain the potatoes, then mash. Measure 1 cup of the mashed potatoes and place in a large bowl. Add the milk, shortening, sugar and salt and mix well. Cool to lukewarm. Add the yeast to ½ cup of warm water and stir until dissolved. Add to the potato mixture, then add the eggs and mix well. Add 1 ½ cups of the flour and stir until well combined. Cover and let rise in a warm place for about 30 minutes or until bubbly. Stir in 5 cups of the flour, 1 cup at a time, mixing well after each addition. Spread ½ cup of the flour on a board. Place the dough on the flour, then sprinkle 2 cups of the flour over the dough. Knead for 10 minutes, adding the remaining flour as needed. Place the dough in a lightly greased bowl, turning to grease the surface, then cover. Place in refrigerator overnight. Grease about 36 muffin cups. Shape the dough into small balls, then place 3 balls in each muffin cup. Brush with the butter. Let rise in a warm place for 1 hour and 30 minutes or until doubled in bulk. Bake in a preheated 425-degree oven for 15 minutes or until golden brown. The refrigerated dough may be divided in half and placed in 2 greased loaf pans, then brushed with butter. Let rise until doubled in bulk and bake at 350 degrees for about 40 minutes or until brown. This makes about 36 rolls or 2 loaves.

SWEET BREADS

Dried Fruit Coffee Cake is an unusually delicious sweet bread, made with dried fruit and brandy. This coffee cake has an outer dough case surrounding an inner dough containing the fruit. Appropriate garnishes for this coffee cake are apple rings, raisins and Apricot Glaze. However, if you wish to try a different glaze for the surface, melt a small amount of red currant jam and pour over the top.

DRIED FRUIT COFFEE CAKE

2½ c. dried apple rings
1 c. milk
1 env. dry yeast
3 tbsp. melted butter
1⅓ c. sugar
1 egg, beaten
4⅓ c. sifted all-purpose flour
1 tsp. salt
1 c. chopped dates
1 c. coarsely chopped dried figs
⅔ c. raisins
¼ c. chopped candied peel
½ c. chopped walnuts
2 tsp. cinnamon
1 tbsp. grated lemon rind
¾ c. brandy
½ c. hot Basic Sugar Syrup *(pg. 14)*
½ c. Apricot Glaze *(Desserts, pg. 19)*

Reserve 8 apple rings for garnish. Place the remaining apple rings in a small amount of water in a small saucepan and cook until just tender. Drain the apples and chop coarsely. Pour the milk into a small saucepan and bring just to a boil, then cool to lukewarm. Add the yeast to the milk and stir until dissolved. Pour the yeast mixture into a large mixer bowl, then beat in the butter, sugar and egg with a wooden spoon. Mix the flour and salt and add to the yeast mixture gradually, mixing until the dough is easily handled. Turn out onto a lightly floured surface and knead for 10 minutes, adding more flour as needed. Place in a large bowl, then cover with a cloth and let rise for 1 hour and 30 minutes. Punch the dough down and let rise for 45 minutes longer. Combine the chopped apples, dates, figs, ⅓ cup of raisins, the candied peel, walnuts, cinnamon, lemon rind and brandy in a large bowl, then add ⅓ of the dough and mix thoroughly. Roll out the remaining dough on a lightly floured surface to a circle about 15 inches in diameter. Fit the dough into a buttered 9-inch cake pan with removable bottom or a flan pan with removable bottom, letting the excess hang over the side. Place the fruit mixture in the center and pat out to the side of the pan, then cover with the overlapping dough. Seal the edges together with water. Let stand for 20 minutes. Bake in a preheated 350-degree oven on the center rack for 1 hour to 1 hour and 15 minutes or until brown. While the coffee cake is baking, pour the hot sugar syrup into a small bowl and add the reserved apple rings and the remaining raisins. Let stand until all the liquid is absorbed. Remove the coffee cake from the oven and brush with part of the Apricot Glaze. Garnish with the apple rings and raisins as shown in the illustration and pour the remaining glaze over the fruits. This makes 8 to 10 servings.

dried fruit coffee cake

Apricot Glaze gives this Dried Fruit Coffee Cake its beautiful, shiny appearance. Garnish it attractively with apple rings and raisins.

german beer coffee cake

german beer coffee cake

German Beer Coffee Cake is not actually a cake, but a delicious sweet bread and is best sliced and buttered. With hot coffee, it makes a wintertime treat.

GERMAN BEER COFFEE CAKE

2 c. (packed) dark brown sugar
1 c. butter, softened
2 eggs
1 tsp. cinnamon
1/2 tsp. allspice
1/2 tsp. ground cloves
3 c. sifted all-purpose flour
2 tsp. soda
1/2 tsp. salt
1 c. chopped walnuts
2 c. chopped dates
2 c. beer
Confectioners' sugar

Combine the brown sugar and the butter in a mixing bowl and cream until smooth and well blended. Add the eggs, one at a time, beating well after each addition. Sift the cinnamon, allspice, cloves, flour, soda and salt together. Dust the walnuts and dates with a small amount of the flour mixture. Add the remaining flour mixture to the creamed mixture alternately with the beer, blending well after each addition. Stir in the walnuts and dates. Spoon the batter into a large well-buttered and floured tube or bundt pan. Bake in a preheated 350-degree oven for 1 hour and 15 minutes or until an inserted cake tester comes out clean. Let stand for 5 minutes, then invert on a wire rack. Sprinkle with confectioners' sugar, then place on a serving plate. This makes 18 to 20 servings.

NOTE: The finished coffee cake should be very moist. It is best when wrapped in aluminum foil and stored for 1 day, then sliced and buttered.

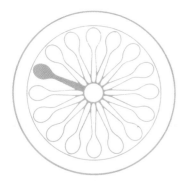

spiced rye loaves

spiced rye loaves

These Spiced Rye Loaves contain molasses, caraway seed and rye flour. Hot from the oven, sliced and buttered, the flavor is memorable.

SPICED RYE LOAVES

3 env. dry yeast
1/4 c. melted butter
2 1/2 c. lukewarm milk or water
2 tsp. salt
6 tbsp. dark molasses or corn syrup
1 tbsp. wine vinegar
2 tbsp. caraway seed
4 c. rye flour
4 c. all-purpose flour

Place the yeast in a large mixing bowl. Mix the butter, milk and salt, then pour over the yeast and stir until the yeast is dissolved. Add the molasses, vinegar and caraway seed and mix until blended. Add the rye flour and half the all-purpose flour and mix well. Add enough of the remaining all-purpose flour to make a stiff dough, then mix until smooth. Cover and let rise until doubled in bulk. Bake in a preheated 325-degree oven for about 1 hour or until the bread sounds hollow when tapped with the fingers, then brush with water. Remove loaves from the pans and cool on wire racks. One tablespoon aniseed or grated orange rind may be substituted for the caraway seed. This makes 2 loaves.

onion bread

ONION BREAD

1 c. milk, scalded
3 tbsp. sugar
1 tbsp. salt
1 1/2 tbsp. vegetable oil
2 env. dry yeast
3/4 c. warm water

1/2 c. minced onion
6 c. all-purpose flour

Pour the milk into a large mixing bowl. Add the sugar, salt and oil and mix until the sugar is dissolved. Cool until lukewarm. Dissolve the yeast in the warm water, then stir into the milk mixture. Add the onion and 4 cups of the flour and mix until blended. Add enough of the remaining flour, a small amount at a time, to make a stiff dough. Cover and let rise for 45 minutes. Punch down, then place in 2 greased loaf pans. Let rise until doubled in bulk. Bake in a preheated 350-degree oven for 1 hour or until the bread sounds hollow when tapped with the fingers. Remove from the pans and place on wire racks to cool. This makes 2 loaves.

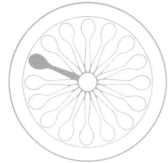

health buns

HEALTH BUNS

2 env. dry yeast
¼ c. melted butter
2 c. lukewarm skim milk
2 tsp. salt
1 tbsp. molasses or corn syrup
2¾ c. whole wheat flour
1¾ c. graham flour
3¼ c. all-purpose flour

Place the yeast in a large mixing bowl. Mix the butter, milk and salt. Pour over the yeast and stir until the yeast is dissolved. Add the molasses and mix well. Add the whole wheat flour and graham flour and stir until mixed. Add 2¾ cups of the all-purpose flour and mix until smooth. Cover and let rise until doubled in bulk. Knead on a lightly floured surface, adding the remaining flour as needed, for 10 minutes or until smooth and elastic, then shape into large, oblong buns. Place on a greased baking sheet and let rise until doubled in bulk. Bake in a preheated 400-degree oven for about 15 minutes or until browned. This makes 18 to 20 buns.

health buns

Health Buns, made with whole wheat flour, are naturally good for you, but they are so delicious, you will want to serve them for their flavor alone.

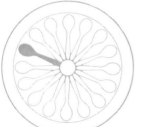

horseradish bread

HORSERADISH BREAD

½ c. butter
¼ tsp. salt
Pinch of freshly ground pepper
2 tbsp. prepared horseradish
1 long loaf of French bread

Place the butter in a small mixing bowl and let stand at room temperature until softened. Cream the butter until light and fluffy. Add the salt, pepper and horseradish and beat until well mixed. Cut the French bread crosswise into diagonal slices to within ½ inch of the base. Spread both sides of each slice generously with the butter mixture, then press the bread back into a loaf. Cut a sheet of aluminum foil 8 inches longer than the loaf and place the bread lengthwise on the foil. Bring the sides of the foil together, then fold over the bread loosely. Fold the ends of the foil to seal, then, if desired, refrigerate until needed. Place the loaf on a baking sheet. Bake in a preheated 300-degree oven, 1 shelf above center, for 10 to 15 minutes or until heated through, then serve immediately. This bread may be served with your choice of *pâté*, other spreads, or with a salad, if desired. This makes 10 to 12 slices.

STOLLEN

2 pkg. dry yeast
¼ c. warm water
1 c. scalded milk
½ c. butter
¼ c. sugar
1 tsp. salt
¼ tsp. ground cardamom
4 ½ c. sifted all-purpose flour
1 egg, slightly beaten
1 c. seedless raisins
¼ c. currants
¼ c. chopped mixed candied fruits
2 tbsp. grated orange rind
1 tbsp. grated lemon rind
¼ c. chopped blanched almonds
2 tbsp. melted butter
Confectioners' sugar

Dissolve the yeast in the warm water. Combine the milk, butter, sugar, salt and cardamom in a large bowl and cool to lukewarm. Stir in 2 cups of the flour and mix well. Add the yeast and egg and mix until blended. Stir in the fruits, grated rinds and almonds, then stir in enough of the remaining flour to make a soft dough. Turn out on a lightly floured surface and knead for 10 minutes or until smooth and elastic, adding more flour as needed. Place in a greased bowl, turning to grease the surface, and cover. Let rise in a warm place for 1 hour and 45 minutes or until doubled in bulk. Punch down and turn out onto a lightly floured surface. Cover and let rest for 10 minutes. Shape into a long, oval loaf and place on a greased baking sheet. Cover and let rise in a warm place for 1 hour or until doubled in bulk. Bake in a preheated 375-degree oven for 20 minutes. Reduce the oven temperature to 350 degrees and bake for about 40 minutes longer or until lightly browned. Brush with the melted butter, then place on a rack to cool. Sprinkle with confectioners' sugar, then with additional candied fruits. This makes about 15 servings.

DANISH CHRISTMAS BREAD

2 pkg. dry yeast
¼ c. lukewarm water
½ c. milk, scalded
⅓ c. sugar
1 tsp. salt
⅔ c. butter
5 c. sifted all-purpose flour
1 ½ tsp. vanilla extract
4 eggs, beaten
¼ c. warm water
2 tbsp. dark corn syrup
Confectioners' sugar
¼ c. chopped mixed candied fruits

Dissolve the yeast in the lukewarm water. Mix the milk, sugar, salt and butter in a large bowl and cool to lukewarm. Add 2 cups of the flour and mix well. Add the yeast, vanilla and eggs and mix until blended. Add enough of the remaining flour to make a soft dough and mix well. Knead on a lightly floured surface, adding more flour as needed, for 10 minutes or until smooth and elastic. Place in a greased bowl, turning to grease the surface. Cover and let rise in a warm place until doubled in bulk. Punch down, then shape into a round loaf. Place on a greased baking sheet. Cover and let rise until doubled in bulk. Bake in a preheated 350-degree oven for 20 minutes. Mix the warm water and syrup and brush on the bread. Bake for about 30 minutes longer or until well browned. Brush with the syrup mixture again, then place the bread on a rack to cool. Sprinkle with confectioners' sugar, then with the candied fruits. This makes about 15 servings.

stollen and danish christmas bread

Pictured here are two homemade sweet breads, traditionally baked for holiday occasions. On the left is a Stollen, containing candied fruit peel and chopped almonds. On the right is a round loaf of Danish Christmas Bread which has been brushed with a dark, corn syrup glaze.

RUM-YEAST CAKE

2 cinnamon sticks
1 c. boiling water
¼ c. milk, scalded
2 pkg. dry yeast
½ c. butter
¾ c. sugar
3 eggs, beaten
½ c. mashed potatoes
2 tbsp. rum
¼ tsp. baking powder
½ c. raisins
5 to 6 c. all-purpose flour
Confectioners' sugar

Place the cinnamon sticks in the boiling water in a saucepan and boil for 5 minutes. Cool to lukewarm and remove the cinnamon sticks. Cool the milk to lukewarm. Add the yeast and stir until dissolved. Mix the butter and sugar in a bowl until well blended. Add the eggs and blend thoroughly. Stir in the yeast mixture. Add the potatoes and mix thoroughly. Stir in the cinnamon water and rum. Add the baking powder, raisins and enough flour to make a soft dough and mix well. Knead on a lightly floured surface until smooth, adding more flour as needed. Place in a large, greased bowl, turning to grease the surface, and cover. Let rise until doubled in bulk.

Punch down, then place in a large, well-greased mold. Let rise until doubled in bulk. Bake in a preheated 350-degree oven for 1 hour or until a cake tester inserted in the center comes out clean. Let cool for 10 minutes, then remove from the pan and cool on a wire rack. Place on a cake plate and sprinkle with confectioners' sugar. Garnish with candied cherries and crystallized fruits. This makes about 15 servings.

ORANGE MUFFINS

2 c. sifted all-purpose flour
1 tsp. soda
1 tsp. salt
½ c. vegetable shortening
Grated rind of 1 orange
1 sq. unsweetened chocolate, grated
1 ½ c. (about) buttermilk

Sift the flour, soda and salt together into a bowl. Cut in the shortening until mixture is the consistency of cornmeal. Add the grated rind and chocolate, then stir in enough buttermilk to make a soft dough. Place on a floured board and knead lightly. Roll out ½ inch thick and cut with a floured round cutter the size of the muffin cups, then place in greased muffin cups. Bake in a preheated 475-degree oven for about 15 minutes. This makes about 12 muffins.

rum-yeast cake

This Rum-Yeast Cake was baked in a fluted, tube mold which gives it a very attractive shape. However, you may use any cake or loaf pan.

desserts

table of contents

When you are ready to learn the BASICS of cake decorating, we'll show you how to apply our butter cream frosting and confectioners' icing. Moreover, because the techniques we are developing are BASICS, you can easily move on to preparing gourmet cakes and thus build a complete repertoire of dessert recipes.

The most distinguishing feature of sponge cakes is their feathery-light, springy texture—their sponginess—that is created as much by the combination of ingredients as by technique. Sponge cakes should pass the following test: pinch the cake firmly, release and then watch whether it springs back to its original shape. If it doesn't, the texture is too dense. If it does, you have a perfect cake.

There is one exception—the Close-Textured Sponge Cake. As the name implies, it will not conform to the test.

Let's examine the "whats" and "hows" of sponge cakes. First, what goes into a perfect sponge cake? Eggs; extra fine or confectioners' sugar; cake flour; self-rising flour; and, for a richer sponge cake, butter. Ingredients causing cakes to rise are known as leavening agents. The natural leavening agent in sponge cake is *eggs.* Long ago, they were found to leaven cakes successfully whereas the only other natural leavening agent, yeast, would not produce a proper cake texture. When beaten, the egg foam contains countless air bubbles. During baking the moisture within each bubble vaporizes into steam and causes the cake to swell, hence to rise.

Sugar, of course, sweetens the sponge cake. We recommend extra fine sugar. Fine-grained sugar dissolves more quickly in beaten egg whites and contributes to the overall lightness of the cake. Even though the cost may be somewhat higher, the chances of success are greater if you choose extra fine sugar.

Flour adds bulk and body to your cake. We recommend any good brand of packaged cake flour. It is already sifted for you, thus it is more porous and has a greater volume and therefore adds lightness, fluffiness, and tenderness to a cake. (Throughout our recipes when you see the direction "sift flour X times," follow the directions

the key to perfect sponge cakes every time

Desserts—the most creative and beautiful area of cooking. Most renowned cooks of the world gained fame creating magnificent desserts. The *Creative Cooking Course* will show you how to prepare gorgeous concoctions with the skill and ease of a master chef. Let's begin with sponge cakes, which are easier to make than you ever imagined and are excellent dessert foods to demonstrate the essential steps of cake baking. You'll learn the BASICS of handling and mixing cake ingredients, preparing your baking pans, and how to turn finished cake out with a perfect surface for decorating.

exactly. And don't be surprised if in some recipes we call for a combination of self-rising and cake flours. Self-rising flour contains a chemical leavening agent, and we may want to include it in order to add height to the sponge cake and prevent it from becoming too heavy.)

NATURAL FLAVORING

True, natural flavoring is superior to artificial or imitation essences. Preparing your own flavorings is simple, and fun. For example, when many recipes call for vanilla you may heat some of the liquid listed in the recipe and steep a vanilla pod in it for about 20 minutes to obtain a delicious natural flavoring. Store the pod in a glass container for reuse. After several uses, the pod will lose some of its strength, but don't discard it. Quarter it and bury the four pieces in a canister of extra fine sugar for two or three weeks. The sugar absorbs the vanilla flavor. Use it when a recipe calls for both sugar and flavoring.

PREPARING YOUR INGREDIENTS

Now for the "how" of making sponge cakes. The first step is to set out all your refrigerated ingredients ahead of time, allowing them to warm to room temperature. An exception is when your recipe requires separated eggs. This is easier to do when the eggs are still cold. Then allow them to come to room temperature. Egg whites whip to a greater volume at room temperature.

When you see explicit instructions in BASIC recipes, follow the exact directions. For example, the correct handling of eggs is an assurance the sponge cake will rise properly and have a delicately light and airy texture. Also, egg beating must be thorough, as we previously explained, to incorporate all the tiny air bubbles which help leaven the cake.

To fold in dry ingredients, take a rubber spatula or wire whisk (we prefer the whisk) and, using an over-and-under motion, bring some of the mixture from the bottom of the container, folding it over dry ingredients on top. Then, moving down the side of the container, repeat the procedure until all the ingredients are well blended. Do this thoroughly but gently to break as few air bubbles as possible.

BAKING YOUR SPONGE CAKE

Prepare your pan exactly according to the recipe. Then, pour the sponge cake batter into your baking pan and bake the cake for the correct amount of time. When you are ready to test for doneness, press your knuckles gently into the center of the cake. If it springs back, the cake is done. If your knuckles make a slight indentation which does not spring back, give it a minute or so longer in the oven. You don't want it to fall in the middle, which it may well do if underbaked.

After removing a sponge cake from the oven, place the pan on a wire rack for 1 minute or until the cake has cooled enough so that it contracts slightly from the sides of the pan. The cake rack allows for the proper circulation of air to cool your cake quickly and evenly. When cooled, gently run a sharp knife around the edge and turn the cake out onto the rack.

basic rolled sponge cake

Here we present to you our 3-egg, butterless, crackless rolled sponge cake that has been filled with a fluffy butter cream (Desserts, pg. 7) and elegantly dusted with sifted confectioners' sugar.

We're ready to tackle our first BASIC recipe in the Desserts category—the Basic Rolled Sponge Cake. This elegant culinary creation, often known as a jelly roll, forms the basis of a complete collection of rolled sponge cake desserts. Our technique in preparing Basic Rolled Sponge Cake is unusual. Unlike what might have happened when you tried other methods, we can *promise* you a rolled sponge cake without cracks. Follow the explicit directions given below each step-by-step picture on how to prepare the sponge cake for baking and how to roll it up with expertise and confidence. For this BASIC the only special equipment you'll need is a 15 ½ x 10 ½ x 1-inch baking pan commonly marketed as a jelly roll pan.

BASIC ROLLED SPONGE CAKE

½ c. sifted extra fine granulated sugar
3 lg. eggs
¾ c. sifted cake flour
Confectioners' sugar

See our step-by-step illustrations for preparing cake.

1 To prepare your jelly roll pan, mark a base-fitting piece of waxed paper or aluminum foil as we're doing. Cut around the penciled line and turn the paper over so that the markings do not come in direct contact with the sponge cake batter.

2 Lay the waxed paper or foil in your baking pan and brush it thoroughly with cooking oil. Brush the sides of the pan as well.

3 To prepare the board or table surface on which you will turn out the finished sponge cake, spread a sheet of newspaper, somewhat larger than the baking pan, on your working surface and cover it with waxed paper or foil. Dust the waxed paper or foil lightly with cake flour. Many cookbooks will instruct you to use extra fine or confectioners' sugar instead of cake flour. However, we recommend cake flour because sugar will melt on contact with the hot sponge cake and cause it to stick and tear when you roll it. Cake flour will not stick.

4 Now we can begin to cook. Set all your ingredients out to warm to room temperature before beginning to work. Measure ½ cup sifted extra fine sugar onto a heat-resistant plate. Place it in the oven and bake at 425 degrees F., one shelf above the center, for 4 minutes. The sugar should be piping hot but not melted by then.

5 While you are waiting for the sugar to heat, break 3 large eggs into a large mixing bowl. Into a separate bowl place ¾ cup sifted cake flour. Now you have all the ingredients on hand so that when the sugar is piping hot you can pour it quickly onto the eggs, as shown above. Begin beating immediately, using an electric hand mixer set at medium speed.

6 Continue beating until your mixture resembles ours, for about 6 or 7 minutes. It should turn to a pale foam and double in bulk.

7 Stop beating. Shake the flour very lightly over the surface of the sponge cake mixture.

8 With a rubber spatula, fold and turn your mixture with an occasional cutting movement until every bit of flour has disappeared.

9 Pour the mixture into the prepared pan and with the spatula spread it evenly over the surface of the oiled paper. Very carefully push the mixture into the corners or the sponge cake may be difficult to roll.

10 Place the pan in the oven and bake at 425 degrees F., one shelf above center, for 9 minutes or until golden brown.

11 Run a metal spatula around the sides of the pan. Turn onto working surface, allow to cool slightly; remove waxed paper. Trim the edges lengthwise as shown and spread with desired filling. If you're using butter cream frosting instead of jelly as we are here, spread over sponge cake, and even out with a metal spatula.

12 With both hands, pick up the papers along the edge nearest you. Hold them exactly as we're showing you. Press the uncut edge of the cake firmly down onto the filling.

13 Put one hand behind the papers while holding them up with the other hand, as shown. Roll them away from you. Push with the hand at the back. You may find it easier to place one hand on top of the cake itself to guide it as you roll. The faster you go the easier to roll.

14 Our perfect rolled sponge cake! Just remember to lightly brush off the surplus flour from your completed sponge cake before covering it with icing or dusting it with sifted confectioners' sugar.

The Creative Homemaker's Academy © MCMLXXIII
Selected Illustrations © B.P.C. Publishing Limited MCMLXX

basic
six-egg
sponge cake

Our Basic Six-Egg Sponge Cake is impressively rich. While making it, you will learn a slightly different and very important technique for sponge cakes—working with egg whites. The whipping method employed here is valuable, since you'll be relying on it again and again in preparing meringues, sweet and savory soufflés and omelets. Follow the instructions carefully and you will produce stiffly-beaten egg whites that are satiny smooth, free of granules and firm enough to stand in peaks when the beater is removed.

First separate the eggs, removing every trace of egg yolk from the whites. If the slightest trace of fatty yolk remains it will inhibit whipping and the whites will probably not advance past the frothy stage. It is easier to separate yolks from the whites while the eggs are still cold. Then allow the whites to warm to room temperature so they whip to a greater volume. If there is any grease on the beaters or any water in the mixing bowl, the whites will not whip stiffly. An electric hand mixer will help whip the whites fast and furiously. A rotary beater will take more time and requires more muscle on your part. That we don't need. We suggest using a bowl of stainless steel, glass or glazed pottery. Aluminum tends to discolor the egg whites, and plastic retains a greasy film that will inhibit the volume of the beaten whites.

Perhaps the best advice on beating egg whites is to have patience and continue whipping until peaks begin to form. You may discover, as many cooks have, that adding a pinch of salt or cream of tartar will speed the whipping and stabilize the mixture. That is your decision—just remember a little goes a long way.

BASIC SIX-EGG SPONGE CAKE

1 c. cake flour
¼ tsp. salt
6 eggs, separated
1 c. extra fine sugar
1 tbsp. lemon juice
Grated rind of 1 lemon
Confectioners' sugar

Grease and lightly flour the bottom of a 9¼ x 5¼ x 2¾-inch loaf pan. Sift flour and salt together. Beat the egg yolks until thick and lemon-colored. Beat the egg whites in a large mixing bowl with an electric mixer at high speed until stiff but not dry. Add extra fine sugar, about 2 tablespoons at a time, beating thoroughly after each addition. Beat in the lemon juice and rind. Fold in egg yolks with a rubber spatula or wire whisk. Cut and fold in flour mixture, a small amount at a time. Continue folding for 2 minutes after last addition. Fill prepared pan ¾ full, smoothing batter evenly into the corners and over the top. (You will have batter left over.) Bake in a preheated 350-degree oven for 30 to 35 minutes or until cake tests done. Let cake cool in the pan for about 5 minutes. Turn out on rack to cool completely. Sprinkle with confectioners' sugar. Pour remaining batter into 12 cupcake liners in muffin pan, filling about ½ full. Bake at 350 degrees for about 18 minutes or until lightly browned.

basic six-egg sponge cake

Deliciously light and satisfying, Basic Six-Egg Sponge Cake stands out all by itself. It can be complemented with a serving of fruit or a dip of ice cream. We've baked the sponge cake in a standard 9 x 5 inch loaf pan, and liberally sprinkled sifted confectioners' sugar over it.

basic close-textured sponge cake

Our Basic Close-Textured Sponge Cake recipe is distinctive because it uses butter, cornstarch and milk in addition to the standard sponge cake ingredients of flour (we use both cake flour and self-rising flour here), eggs and extra fine sugar. To prepare this sponge cake, you'll "cream" the butter, or beat it with a rotary beater or electric mixer until it is smooth, creamy and pale. Three extra ingredients—creamed butter, cornstarch and milk—make this sponge cake more compact and close-textured than our other basic sponge cakes, therefore, its descriptive name. It is less crumbly than the other basic sponge cakes, and makes an ideal cake to finish with a frosting and an icing.

BASIC CLOSE-TEXTURED SPONGE CAKE

1 c. sifted cake flour
1 c. sifted self-rising flour
¾ c. cornstarch
1 c. butter
1 c. extra fine sugar
4 lg. eggs
½ c. milk

Use two 9-inch or one 12-inch removable or sliding based cake pans. Butter and lightly flour bases; do not prepare sides. Sift flours and cornstarch together twice. Cream the butter in a large mixing bowl with electric mixer at medium speed for about 2 minutes or until creamy and smooth. Add the sugar; cream for 2 minutes or until light and fluffy. Beat in 2 heaping tablespoons flour mixture. Add 1 egg; beat until smooth. Continue adding part of the flour mixture, then 1 egg until all ingredients are used. Add milk; beat until well mixed. Spoon batter equally and evenly into prepared pans. Bake in preheated 350-degree oven for 25 minutes. Cool on racks for about 5 minutes; remove layers from pans and let cool completely on cake racks. Frost as shown in our step-by-step illustrations.

applying butter cream frosting and confectioners' icing

A cake may be finished with a simple, smooth, glossy icing or with more decorative borders, swirls and rosettes. An uncooked butter cream frosting covered with a final uncooked confectioners' icing (pg. 8) makes a simple but elegant finish for the Basic Close-Textured

Sponge Cake given here. Our finishing provides BASIC decorating skills essential to creative cooking. At the risk of repetition, we again promise you'll later be finishing cakes with much more embellishment. But first let's master the BASIC frosting and icing techniques and recipes given here.

You're probably wondering why we make a difference between *frosting* and *icing.* We have a reason. If you look at our basic recipes for butter cream frosting and confectioners' icing, you'll notice a difference in ingredients. The two versions of butter cream frosting use confectioners' sugar, egg yolks and butter. The glacé icing requires only confectioners' sugar and water. The difference in ingredients makes a difference in consistency: the butter cream frosting is thicker than the thin confectioners' icing. We apply the thicker frosting to the cake first for a firm base on which the thin icing can be spread, obtaining a delicate, glossy, eye-appealing "polish."

Preparing the smooth butter cream surface first eliminates undesirable loose cake crumbs and conceals possible cracks in the cake that would undermine its appearance. Both butter cream frosting and confectioners' icing work together to provide attractiveness and, of course; flavor. (Later we'll learn how to add different ingredients to the Basic Butter Cream recipe given here for coffee, mocha and orange butter cream flavors.)

When making the butter cream frosting and the confectioners' icing use only confectioners' sugar. It alone produces the best texture, flavor and "look." Please notice the recipes for both butter cream frosting and confectioners' icing call for sifted confectioners' sugar. Don't skip the sifting even if it seems insignificant to you—only sifted confectioners' sugar gives frosting or icing the desired volume and fine texture. You can sift it with your flour sifter—just be sure it's clean.

Speaking of equipment, you'll need a flat, narrow metal spatula to spread both butter cream frosting and confectioners' icing on your sponge cake. Frosting and icing spread evenly and easily if you dip the spatula in very hot water before and during application. Shake off excess drops of water from the spatula to avoid "watering down" the consistency of your frosting or icing.

With these suggestions and reminders behind us, let's finish the close-textured sponge cake—one of the loveliest desserts you'll ever see.

After removing your cake from the oven, allow it to cool before taking out of the baking pan. (Remember, when cooled, it will contract slightly from the sides of the pan.) Simply invert the cake over a plate so that the cake is on the plate with the even side up. This is the surface you'll want to frost. Apply the butter cream frosting to the *completely* cooled and even surface. (On even a

The Creative Homemaker's Academy © MCMLXXIII
Selected Illustrations © B.P.C. Publishing Limited MCMLXX

slightly warm cake the frosting will soften and run down the sides.) Spread the top and sides with a thick, generous layer of frosting. You'll want a flawless, smooth, surface on which to apply the final confectioners' icing. Refrigerate the frosted cake for about 30 minutes or until the butter cream hardens, at which time you can even out any wrinkles and creases in the frosting. Here we demonstrate how to frost the sponge cake we baked in a round pan 12 inches in diameter. To finish a cake baked in two 9-inch pans, follow the same basic procedure in this order: frost the top of one layer, place the second layer on top of the first, frost the surface and sides, refrigerate for about 30 minutes and finally apply the icing.

1 Dip a metal spatula into very hot water and then shake off excess drops.

2 Following our example, slide the hot moistened spatula over the surface and sides of the sponge cake until it is smooth and even. If the frosting should soften while you are smoothing it, place the sponge cake in the refrigerator for a few minutes. When the surface is as flawless as an ice skating rink, put the cake in the refrigerator while you prepare the final confectioners' icing. Refrigerating the frosted cake before applying the icing makes spreading fast and easy—the icing will glide right over the top.

BASIC BUTTER CREAM NO. 1

¾ c. unsalted butter, softened
3 ¾ c. (scant) sifted confectioners' sugar
1 egg yolk
1 tsp. orange flower water
1 tsp. rose water

Cream the butter in a medium-sized mixing bowl with electric mixer at medium speed for 2 minutes or until light and fluffy. Add half the confectioners' sugar and the egg yolk and beat thoroughly. Add the remaining sugar, orange flower water and rose water, then beat until thoroughly combined.

Orange flower water and rose water are elegant flavorings usually obtainable in specialty food shops and some better supermarkets. Don't make the mistake of picking up orange flower *skin tonic* and rose *flower skin lotion* in a drugstore. These cosmetic preparations are not the same thing at all, and could be distasteful.

BASIC BUTTER CREAM NO. 2

3 egg yolks
1 ¼ c. sifted confectioners' sugar
½ c. butter, softened

Place the egg yolks in a medium-sized mixing bowl. Add the confectioners' sugar and blend well with a wooden spoon. Place the bowl with the egg mixture over hot water at medium heat and stir until it is very thick and creamy and free from any streaks. Remove from hot water. Place bowl in pan of ice and continue stirring until cool. Cream the butter until smooth, then whip into the sugar mixture, a spoonful at a time, with an electric mixer at medium speed until well blended.

adding final icing

After you have frosted your sponge cake as directed on page 6, you're ready to add the final Basic Confectioners' Icing. Note: The icing must be spread at the right consistency. When making the confectioners' icing, add the water sparingly and slowly, and watch the consistency carefully. If you add too much water and the icing becomes runny, work in more sifted confectioners' sugar to thicken it. Constantly check for spreading consistency by lifting your spoon with some of the icing on it. At proper spreading consistency, the icing is neither so thin that it runs off the spoon nor so thick that it sticks to the spoon.

We have added blue food coloring to our confectioners' icing for color contrast to show our icing technique. If you want a tinted icing, place a small amount of your icing in a cup, adding enough chosen food coloring to create a bright color. Blend the colored icing into the uncolored icing a little at a time until you obtain a *delicate tint.* Icing that is too brightly colored is not appealing.

1 Remove the frosted sponge cake from the refrigerator. Pour the confectioners' icing from the bowl onto the center of the sponge cake, as we are doing here.

2 Dip your metal spatula into hot water (don't forget to shake off excess drops) and work the icing evenly over the frosted surface of the sponge cake.

3 Wipe the spatula clean and dip it once more into hot water for the final touches. Smooth the remaining icing around the side of the cake. When finished, the sponge cake will have a smooth, flawless surface with a lovely sheen. It should be stored in the refrigerator until you're ready to serve it.

BASIC CONFECTIONERS' ICING

5 c. sifted confectioners' sugar
Water
Food Coloring

Place the sugar in a large mixing bowl, then stir in a small amount of water at a time to reach an easy spreading consistency. If your icing becomes too thin, add more sugar to thicken. Stir in desired food coloring as explained on page 7.

add flavor variety to sponge cupcakes

Our recipe for Sponge Cupcakes makes about 18 individual cakes. The Sponge Cupcakes, like the Basic Close-Textured Sponge Cake on page 6, use butter and milk for a firmer and more compact texture than standard sponge cakes not including these ingredients. Again you'll be creaming the butter, but this time with extra fine granulated sugar. To cream butter beat it by hand or with an electric mixer until smooth and soft.

Take a look at the picture on the next page and you'll see some suggestions for varying your cupcakes. We added currants, chopped candied cherries, chocolate chips, grated coconut and raisins for five different flavor variations. You can easily follow our example using any one of these extra ingredients, or another that you, as a creative cook, choose. Just add ½ cup of your chosen fruit or nuts in place of the raisins in our recipe.

You will need a cupcake or muffin pan to bake the cupcakes. To save some cleanup time, line the cupcake or muffin pan with fluted paper cups available in most grocery stores. Cupcakes baked in these paper cups will hold their shape better. Fill the cups no more than ½ full with the cupcake mixture, to allow rising during baking.

The Creative Homemaker's Academy © MCMLXXIII
Selected Illustrations © B.P.C. Publishing Limited MCMLXX

SPONGE CUPCAKES

1 c. cake flour
1 c. self-rising flour
½ c. butter, softened
1 c. extra fine sugar
2 eggs
½ c. raisins
1 tbsp. milk
1 tsp. vanilla

Combine the flours. Cream the butter with sugar in a large mixing bowl with electric mixer at medium speed. Add ½ cup of the flour mixture and 1 egg, then beat well. Add another ½ cup flour mixture and remaining egg, beating until well blended. Dust the raisins lightly with a small amount of the remaining flour. Add the remaining flour gradually, beating after each addition until well blended. Add milk and vanilla, mixing well. Stir in the raisins. Spoon into paper-lined muffin cups, filling ½ full. Bake in 375-degree oven on middle shelf for 18 to 20 minutes. To test for doneness insert a toothpick in the center of the cupcake; when the toothpick comes out clean, the cupcake is done. Chopped candied cherries, grated coconut, currants or chocolate chips may be substituted for the raisins. Yield: 18 cupcakes.

the simplicity of making meringue

A meringue is a delicate mixture of stiffly whipped egg whites and extra fine (granulated) sugar. It can be dropped or piped in a variety of shapes onto a baking sheet or spread over pies, cakes and pastries as a topping. The meringue should be placed in a very low oven to dry out, or, when used as a topping, to brown very lightly. We begin with a very simple meringue recipe—light and chewy cookies often known as kisses. In subsequent Desserts lessons, you'll rely on your mastery of the Basic Meringue recipe and technique to prepare more elaborate meringue desserts, such as superb French Meringue Cake and Baked Alaska.

To say making meringue is a hit or miss job, one day yielding beautifully risen products and the next day flops, is just another old wives' tale—like the one telling you to wrap a rolled sponge cake in a damp kitchen towel before filling it. All it takes to make perfect meringue is an understanding of and a familiarity with the BASIC preparation. Before going ahead with the basic recipe, you'll want to review the professional tricks on whipping egg whites given for the Basic Six-Egg Sponge Cake on page 5 of this Desserts section.

The success of meringue often depends on humidity. Some experts claim meringue can be made only on clear, dry days. To be perfectly honest, we've found it difficult to work with meringue on especially humid or rainy days. With heavy moisture in the air, egg whites will not stiffen sufficiently, however long you whip them. As simple as this may sound, the only solution to the problem of humidity we've found is to wait for a drier day!

Now proceed with the recipe. Follow the instructions carefully, adding only the specified amount of extra fine sugar. Excess sugar whipped into the meringue is likely to produce "beads" on the surface (sometimes referred to as "weeping") and a "gummy" texture.

Aside from whipping the egg whites, a 250-degree oven temperature is very important. Heat higher than 250 degrees will cause the meringue to brown before the egg whites have sufficiently dried out. After your cookies have dried out in the oven, find a warm, draft-free area in which to cool them completely or they may shrink. After all your pains, that would be a shame.

FREEZER TIP . . .

A wonderful feature of these meringue cookies is they freeze and thaw beautifully. After baking the cookies, cool them. *Gently* wrap each one in clear plastic, then in foil. Tuck them away in your home freezer for as long as a month. Thawing is a snap: remove the protective foil wrapping and allow the meringues to stand at room temperature for about three hours before serving.

Once you've proven to yourself how easy it is to make perfect meringue, try varying our BASIC recipe with the addition of chocolate chips. As your last step before preparing to bake, fold chocolate chips very gently into the meringue mixture, using a plastic or rubber spatula. Cook according to the Basic Meringue recipe. The chips will hold their shape perfectly in spite of the oven temperature, and you'll have no drippy chocolate mess to clean out of your oven. In the picture (on this page) you see an assortment of delicious, melt-in-your-mouth cookies.

BASIC MERINGUES

5 lg. egg whites
1 c. extra fine sugar

Beat the egg whites in a large mixing bowl with electric mixer at high speed for 5 minutes or until stiff, but not dry. Sprinkle ¼ cup sugar over egg whites and beat for 3 minutes longer. Sprinkle the remaining sugar 1 tablespoon at a time, over egg white mixture and fold in gently but thoroughly, using a rubber spatula. Drop by heaping tablespoonfuls, 2 inches apart, onto oiled brown paper over cookie sheets. Bake in preheated 250-degree oven for 55 minutes. Take from oven and immediately remove from paper onto cooling racks.

VARIATIONS:

CHOCOLATE MERINGUES

Combine 1½ tablespoons cocoa with the sugar and beat into egg whites as directed. Bake for 1 hour.

CHOCOLATE CHIP MERINGUES

Fold in ½ cup chocolate chips into Basic Meringue just before dropping onto prepared cookie sheets.

In the background, chocolate meringue cookies sandwiched together in pairs using softened chocolate chips.

In front, meringue cookies piped and slightly hollowed out to hold vanilla ice cream slices, then sandwiched together in pairs with whipped cream and topped with ground pistachio nuts.

On the right, rounded meringue cookies were dropped by spoonfuls onto a baking sheet to dry.

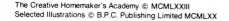

basic short pastry

PIE, FLAN AND TART PASTRY

You are about to start the journey through one of the most exciting areas of cooking — that of pastry making. Many good cooks have built their reputations on their ability to make feather-light, flaky crusts, and so can you. Granted, good pastry making *is* an art, but it's easily acquired by following faithfully our simple step-by-step instructions for pastry making.

A certain mystique surrounds the whole subject of pastries — a mystique which probably began centuries ago in France. The first pastry trade union, called a guild, was formed in Paris in 1270, but real stature was accorded pastry making in 1566 when King Charles IX granted guild members the title, "Master Pastry Cook." For hundreds of years closely guarded recipes were refined and handed down from father to son. But the specialties of Master Chefs are no longer closely guarded family secrets. And we are now going to hand them to you.

You'll discover that making good pastry is amazingly simple once you learn the proper techniques. We will show you how to blend the ingredients correctly and how to roll out the dough and place it in the pan so your pies, flans and tartlets look as good as they taste. Best of all, we'll be right there in the kitchen beside you with step-by-step instructions and pictures of the finished desserts.

We'll begin with short pastry, a rich dough used primarily to make crusts for pies, flans and tartlets. The term "short pastry" comes from the large amount of shortening or butter required to make it. While shortening is the most important *ingredient* in a crisp, tasty crust, there are two other important factors — blending the ingredients and chilling them properly.

BLENDING THE DOUGH

You'll want to avoid handling the dough whenever possible, because the heat from your hands can cause the shortening to melt slightly and blend with the flour before the crust is baked. (This could cause the finished product to be tough.) A truly light crust is the result of small particles of shortening melting *very* quickly and blending with the flour under great heat (this is why you should *always* preheat the oven).

STORAGE TIP

Wrap uncooked short pastry in waxed paper, then place in a plastic bag. It can be refrigerated for three to four days.

The ingredients in *sweet* short pastry and *savory* short pastry are somewhat different, but the methods of preparation are similar. The *sweet* pastry recipe makes an unusual cake-like, tender pastry. It calls for sugar and goes best with a sweet filling. *Savory* short pastry, requiring no sugar, produces a non-sweet crust that is perfect for meat, seafood and vegetable dishes.

1 Here you can see how to mix Basic *Sweet* Short Pastry (the procedure is the same for Basic *Savory* Short Pastry). We've already formed a ring with sifted flour and placed the egg yolks, sugar and softened butter in the middle. With two table knives, we work the flour into the center mixture, adding water to form a smooth, thick paste. In the foreground of this picture are two professional pastry cook's scrapers. We like to use them in our next step.

2 The completed pastry was placed on a floured cloth. Slide a pastry cook's scraper over your working surface to pick up flour and dough scraps. Shake the flour and scraps into a small sieve held over a bowl — the extra flour passing through the sieve can be used again in baking. A special pastry sweeper, pictured in the right foreground above, is useful for brushing up every bit of flour. If you don't own a scraper and brush like ours, use a knife or rubber scraper and a damp cloth to clean your surface.

BASIC SWEET SHORT PASTRY

4 c. self-rising flour
1 c. butter, softened
½ c. extra fine sugar
2 egg yolks
¼ c. cold water

Sift the flour into a mound on a clean working surface. Shape the flour into a large ring, forming a high wall, as shown in our step-by-step illustrations. Place the butter, sugar and egg yolks in the center of the ring, then add the water and work up central mixture with 2 table knives or pastry scrapers to form a smooth paste. Work in the flour carefully from the inside of the ring, adding more water if needed. Mix until pastry is thick and light. Gather the dough into a ball, place on lightly floured cloth and cover loosely. Refrigerate for at least 1 hour before using. It may be wrapped securely and stored in the refrigerator for up to a week. Instructions for oven temperature and length of baking time are included in the Apricot Flan recipe *(pg. 19)* which calls for this pastry.

BASIC SAVORY SHORT PASTRY

4 c. self-rising flour
½ c. butter, softened
½ c. vegetable shortening
1 c. freshly grated Parmesan cheese
1 tsp. salt
¼ tsp. fresh ground pepper
1 c. cold water

Sift the flour into a mound on a clean working surface. Shape the flour into a large ring, forming a high wall. Place the butter, vegetable shortening, cheese, salt and pepper in the center of the ring, then add half the water and work up the central mixture with 2 table knives using a cutting motion. Work in the flour carefully from the inside of the ring, adding more water if needed. Mix until all the flour is added and the dough holds together. Gather the dough into a ball. Place in a bowl and cover with a towel. Refrigerate for at least an hour. May be wrapped securely in plastic wrap or aluminum foil and stored in the refrigerator for a week. Instructions for oven temperature and length of baking time are included in the recipes which call for this pastry.

how to roll out pastry and line a pie pan, flan ring or tartlet pan

The art of whetting your guests' appetites begins with pleasing their eyes. A rich, flaky crust will do this for your pies and flans. The instructions on this page show you how to roll out the dough and to line your baking utensil neatly to produce an attractive, appealing dish that will draw raves.

EQUIPMENT

Naturally you'll need a rolling pin. The one we're using in our pictures is a classic — a chef's handleless rolling pin. Because of its extra length, it is ideal for working with large pieces of pastry. However, you may use a standard rolling pin with handles. A stockinette covering is nice to have, but not mandatory. The covering distributes the extra flour evenly as the dough is rolled out. A large, thin wooden board or special muslin pastry cloth, available in most department stores and grocery stores, makes a good working surface.

The type and size baking utensil needed for pastry dishes depends on whether you are preparing a pie or a flan, so let's first define our terms. We all know what a pie is. It may have either a top or a bottom crust — or both — and it has sloping sides. Our pie recipes call for 9-or 10-inch aluminum or oven-proof glass pie pans. We always serve pies from the baking dish. A flan is a similar concoction, always having a bottom crust. However, it is served in its own shell without the pan. It often has a thicker crust than a pie and several complementary layers of filling. The word "flan" originated in France and is generally interchangeable with the English word "tart."

Flans may be baked either in a springform pan or in a flan ring. The former consists of a circular metal ring (fluted or plain) with *vertical* sides and a removable bottom, making it easy to remove the flan to a serving platter. The flan ring is identical except it has no bottom and is placed on a cookie sheet for baking (see next page and General Information, pg. 8, for illustration of flan ring).

A cleanup tip while making flans is to wipe the flan ring and bottom with a dry cloth after the pastry has been removed and the cooking utensils are still hot. This eliminates scrubbing off sticky pastry scraps later.

ROLLING OUT THE PASTRY

Before you start to roll out the pastry, pop it into the refrigerator for at least 20 minutes or as recipe directs. This chilling step makes the dough more manageable and less sticky; it helps keep the heat of your hands from melting the shortening; and it makes the finished crust flakier. While the dough is being chilled, prepare your working surface by lightly dusting it (as well as the rolling pin) with flour to prevent sticking. Don't add too much flour — it may result in a tough, heavy crust.

Roll out the dough in all directions, from the center to the outer edges, so it forms a circle. The circle should be somewhat larger than your pie pan, flan ring or tartlet mold to ensure a proper fit. You might want to hold the baking utensil directly over the dough to measure.

LINING YOUR PAN OR RING

Now you're ready to line your baking utensil with the rolled out pastry. Below we illustrate the lining procedure with a flan ring. If you're making a pie, follow the same steps until you get to no. 4. Then leave an overlap around the rim of the pan. Flute the edges by placing your right index finger on the inside of the edge. With your left thumb and index finger, pinch the dough around your right index finger. Repeat all the way around the edge of the pan for an attractive, decorative finish. Trim.

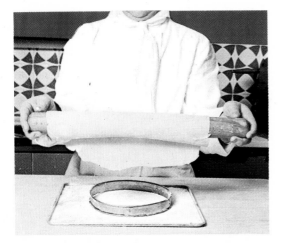

1 Place flan ring on a lightly floured baking sheet. To transfer the pastry to the flan ring, roll it loosely around your rolling pin.

2 Hold the rolling pin covered with pastry over the flan ring. Unroll the pastry over the ring exactly as the picture shows. You may be familiar with other methods for transferring the pastry to the baking utensil, but we've always had more professional results with this procedure.

3 With your knuckles, gently and neatly press the pastry against the sides of the flan ring. If you're lining a fluted flan ring, be careful in pressing the pastry against the ribbed edges.

4 Use your rolling pin again, rolling it over the pastry to cut a neat sharp edge. The excess pastry will fall away from the snugly-lined ring, which is now ready for filling and baking, or baking and filling, as needed.

how to bake a pastry shell without filling

In the previous section we discussed the BASIC technique for rolling out pastry and demonstrated how to line a flan ring. In this sequence of photographs you will see our method of baking a flan crust or pie shell without a filling. The technique, called "baking blind," will be used for two BASIC methods of preparing short pastry dishes.

In the first method, the pastry crust is baked alone and the filling is added afterwards. Use it for cream, pudding and custard fillings requiring no baking.

The second method, most often employed when the filling is especially juicy, involves partially baking the crust, filling the shell and returning the assembled pastry to the oven to continue baking. This helps prevent a soggy crust.

With this in mind you can now turn to our step-by-step pictures below. You should have no trouble mastering the fundamental steps of baking (or partially baking) an unfilled pastry shell. Just one final word — although we are demonstrating our method with a flan ring, the procedure is the same if you are working with a pie pan or tartlet mold.

1 The fluted flan ring, sitting on a heavy metal baking sheet, has been lined with Basic Sweet Short Pastry. Notice our circle of waxed paper is cut considerably larger than the size of the flan ring. (Lightweight foil may be used instead.)

2 Place the circle of paper on the flan crust (or pastry shell) and ladle in dried beans, peas, lentils or rice to fill the shell partially. The weight of the beans on the crust will prevent the sides of the pastry from collapsing and the bottom from swelling up.

3 Your flan ring should look similar to this when the beans are in place. There should be enough dried beans on the paper to hold the pastry against the container during baking. Then pop the flan ring into the oven for the length of time specified in your recipe.

4 Remove the pan from the oven and gently lift out the paper still containing the beans (save the beans for re-use). Place the shell back in the oven for 4 to 5 minutes to brown lightly. Remove from oven and cool. Next remove the flan ring from the pastry crust, which is now ready for filling or for storing in your freezer.

CHOCOLATE MOCHA MERINGUE PIE

2¾ c. milk
2 sq. semisweet chocolate, chopped
1½ tsp. instant coffee powder
⅓ c. all-purpose flour
¾ c. sugar
¼ tsp. salt
4 egg yolks, beaten
2 tbsp. butter
1 tsp. vanilla extract
1 9-in. baked Royal Short Pastry Shell *(pg. 16)*
1 recipe Basic Meringues mixture *(pg. 10)*

Scald 2½ cups of the milk in a double boiler over hot water on low heat, stirring constantly. Add the chocolate and coffee powder. Combine the flour and remaining milk in a small bowl and mix until smooth. Add the sugar and salt. Stir into the chocolate mixture in double boiler. Cook, stirring constantly, for 15 minutes. Stir a small amount into the egg yolks, then stir egg yolk mixture back into the chocolate mixture. Cook, stirring, for 8 minutes or until thickened and smooth. Add the butter, then remove from heat and beat with a wooden spoon until thick. Stir in the vanilla. Cool completely. Pour into the pie shell, then cover with Basic Meringues mixture, sealing edge. Bake at 350 degrees for 15 minutes or until lightly browned. Chill thoroughly. Garnish with grated chocolate. It may be refrigerated overnight and the pastry will remain crisp.

chocolate mocha meringue pie

Baked Royal Short Pastry shell filled with sweet, creamy chocolate mixture, topped with piped Basic Meringue mixture, (pg. 10) and then sprinkled with grated chocolate.

classic apple pie

Americans have enjoyed apple pie since the 17th Century, when apple orchards planted by the early colonists bore their first fruit. Today golden-crusted pies, extravagantly filled with thick, sweet apple slices, are a strong tradition in American cooking. Therefore, we had no second thoughts when choosing the kind of fruit pie to include first in this section.

Our recipe for Classic Apple Pie is accompanied by two new short pastry recipes, both of which are variations of the Basic Sweet Short Pastry (pg. 12). The recipes for Royal Short Pastry and Never-Fail Short Pastry are included to enrich your treasury of pastry knowledge while providing additional practice. Each recipe makes enough pastry for a two-crust pie.

When you make crusts for pies rather than flans, you may prefer to use one of these two pastry variations. The dough rolls out and cooks thinner, which is more desirable for a piecrust.

ROYAL SHORT PASTRY

2 c. all-purpose flour
1 tsp. salt
¼ c. vegetable shortening
1 tsp. vinegar
1 egg
1 to 2 tbsp. water

Sift the flour and salt together into a bowl. Add the shortening and blend with a pastry blender until the mixture resembles meal. Add the vinegar and egg and mix. Add water, a tablespoon at a time, until the ingredients hold together. Roll out the pastry on a floured surface to fit two 9-inch pie pans. Place in pans and crimp or flute the edges. Prick the sides and bottoms well with a fork. Bake in a preheated, 400-degree oven for 15 to 17 minutes or until lightly browned. Makes pastry for two 9-inch pie crusts.

NEVER-FAIL SHORT PASTRY

1 c. vegetable shortening
½ c. boiling water
1 tsp. salt
3 c. sifted all-purpose flour

Cream the shortening with boiling water until well mixed, either by hand or with an electric mixer. Add the salt and flour all at once and stir until thoroughly mixed. Form into a ball and chill in a covered container for at least an hour. Roll out half the dough for a single shell. Fit into a pie pan and then prick generously with a fork around edges and on bottom. Bake at 450 degrees for 15 minutes for a single crust. Dough may be kept for at least 3 weeks in the refrigerator. Makes pastry for two 9-inch pie crusts.

CLASSIC APPLE PIE

1 recipe Royal Short Pastry or Never-Fail Short Pastry
¾ c. sugar
1 tbsp. all-purpose flour
½ tsp. ground cinnamon
¼ tsp. ground nutmeg
⅛ tsp. salt
1 tbsp. grated lemon rind
5 c. Washington State apple slices
1 tbsp. lemon juice
2 tbsp. butter or margarine

Preheat oven to 425 degrees. Roll out half the pastry and line a 9-inch pie plate. Combine the sugar, flour, cinnamon, nutmeg, salt and lemon rind in a bowl. Add the apples and toss to coat evenly. Arrange the apples in the pastry-lined pie plate. Sprinkle with lemon juice and dot with butter. Roll out the remaining pastry and place over the apples. Cut air vents in the top. Trim the pastry and flute the edge, trimming any excess pastry. Bake for 40 to 45 minutes or until the crust is golden brown.

combining basics for an apricot flan

The incredibly lovely and appetizing Apricot Flan pictured on this page is made from BASICS — and is thus much easier to prepare than you may think at first glance. To make it, use the already familiar formula for Basic Sweet Short Pastry (pg. 12). To fill it, use two new simple and versatile recipes: Basic Confectioners' Custard and Basic Chantilly Cream, both of which you'll be meeting again in other recipes.

We've also included a recipe for Red Currant Jelly Glaze. This quick, uncomplicated glaze is brushed across the top surface of the flan's fruit filling. It adds a special polish to the Apricot Flan, keeps the fruit from "wrinkling" and provides a pleasant, flavorful contrast to the sweet custard, fruit and cream.

Basic Confectioners' Custard is used as the custard layer of our Apricot Flan. It prevents moisture in the fruit filling from seeping into the bottom crust, making it damp and soggy. Later we will use it as a filling for éclairs and cream puffs. Professional confectioners — makers of candies, cakes, pastries and ice creams — use custards such as this in preparing many of their sweet products.

apricot flan

A baked sweet short pastry shell is first filled with Basic Confectioners' Custard, then bright, sweet apricots. The dessert is spread with Red Currant Jelly Glaze and garnished with piped Basic Chantilly Cream and slivered almonds.

In cooking circles, "chantilly" refers to a culinary concoction containing fresh whipped cream, usually with flavoring added. We believe you'll agree our Basic Chantilly Cream is more delicious than plain whipped cream. The addition of egg white not only increases the volume of whipped cream, but helps it maintain a stable consistency for at least 24 hours. Using an icing bag, we'll pipe the Basic Chantilly Cream around the flan's edges to make a decorative border and then tuck slivers of almonds into the border, completing the garnish.

BASIC CHANTILLY CREAM

1 c. whipping cream
2 tbsp. confectioners' sugar
1 tsp. apricot or peach brandy (opt.)
1 egg white, stiffly beaten

Whip the cream with an electric mixer until stiff peaks form. Add confectioners' sugar, 1 tablespoon at a time, beating in gently. Add the brandy, a small amount at a time. Fold in the egg white gently but thoroughly.

BASIC CONFECTIONERS' CUSTARD

1 c. milk
1 vanilla pod or 1 teaspoon vanilla extract
¼ c. all-purpose flour
½ c. extra fine sugar
3 egg yolks

Combine the milk and the vanilla pod in a small saucepan. Cook over medium heat to just below the boiling point. Combine the flour and sugar in a medium mixing bowl, blending well. Add the egg yolks and beat thoroughly with an electric mixer. Remove the vanilla pod from the milk (then dry and store for later use). Pour the milk slowly into the flour mixture, stirring constantly with a wooden spoon until well blended. Pour the milk mixture into the top of a double boiler. Cook over boiling water, stirring constantly, until the custard is thick and smooth. Cool to lukewarm.

RED CURRANT JELLY GLAZE

1 10-oz. jar red currant jelly
¼ c. ruby port

Combine jelly and port in a small saucepan. Place over low heat and stir until the jelly is melted.

APRICOT GLAZE

1 c. apricot jam
1¼ c. water
¾ c. extra fine sugar

Combine all ingredients in a small, heavy saucepan and heat until the jam is dissolved, stirring constantly. Bring to a slow, rolling boil and cook until thickened, measuring occasionally until reduced to 1⅓ cups of glaze. Strain through a sieve.

APRICOT FLAN

½ recipe Basic Sweet Short Pastry *(pg. 12)*
1 recipe Basic Confectioners' Custard
2 1-lb. 1-oz. cans apricot halves, drained
1 recipe Red Currant Jelly Glaze
1 recipe Basic Chantilly Cream

Roll out enough pastry ⅛ to ¼ inch thick on a lightly floured surface to line a 9-inch flan ring. Place the flan ring on a lightly floured baking sheet. Line the ring with pastry. Bake blind as shown in our step-by-step illustrations *(pg. 14)* at 400 degrees for 10 minutes. Reduce the oven temperature to 375 degrees and bake for 15 minutes longer or until golden brown. Remove from oven, remove the paper and peas and place the shell back in the oven for 4 to 5 minutes to brown lightly. Remove from oven and let cool. Remove from the pan and place on a serving plate. Fill the flan case with cooled confectioners' custard, evenly smoothing the top. Place the apricots on absorbent paper and pat dry. Arrange the apricot halves, cut side down, close together over the custard. Spoon a thick coating of warm Red Currant Jelly Glaze over the apricots, letting the glaze run into the empty spaces between the pieces of fruit. Chill until ready to use. Using an icing bag fitted with a large star tube, pipe the chantilly cream around the pastry rim just before serving.

basic short pastry tartlets

Would you believe it if we said that you are about to make dessert tartlets rivaling those you look at so enviously on dessert wagons in elegant restaurants? If you've already tried your hand at the beautiful Apricot Flan featured on page 18, then you know it's possible. The wonder of it is how easy they are to prepare.

As we've mentioned before, tartlets are baked in muffin pans or small, individual tartlet molds with either fluted or plain sloping sides. The pans, of course, give the desserts their attractive shapes. Since they are removed from the utensils after cooking, the pans do not detract from the eye appeal of the finished products. Cherry Tartlets, which you will meet first, have an especially charming appearance, as the picture on this page shows. They are also delicious to eat.

Like the Apricot Flan, Cherry Tartlets are made from Basic Sweet Short Pastry (pg. 12). The pastry shells art baked before being layered with Basic Confectioners' Custard (pg. 19), and the fruit filling of your choice. The surface is brushed with Red Currant Jelly Glaze (pg. 19). Finally, the tartlets are served with Basic Chantilly Cream (pg. 19) or Basic Orange Cream Sauce (Sauces, pg. 6).

As you already know, you'll be relying heavily on BASIC recipes and techniques presented before, so you might want to review the pertinent preceding pages. A quick glance at the sections on mixing short pastry, lining the baking utensil with it and baking the shell without the filling (baked blind) would be helpful.

CHERRY TARTLETS

1 can red sour cherries
1 c. Basic Sugar Syrup *(Breads, pg. 14)*
Red food coloring
1 can dark, sweet, pitted cherries
½ recipe Basic Sweet Short Pastry *(pg. 12)*
1 recipe Basic Confectioners' Custard *(pg. 19)*
1 recipe Red Currant Jelly Glaze or Apricot Glaze
  (pg. 19)
1 recipe Basic Chantilly Cream *(pg. 19)*

Drain the red sour cherries and place them in a small saucepan. Add the sugar syrup and food coloring to tint to desired color. Bring to a boil, then set aside to cool. Drain the dark sweet cherries and set aside. Roll out the pastry on a floured surface, then cut into 5-inch circles. Place in tartlet pans and flute the edges. Arrange grease-proof paper and peas in the tartlet pans according to our step-by-step illustrations for baking without filling *(pg. 14)*. Bake at 400 degrees for 14 to 15 minutes or until edges are lightly browned. Take out of the oven and remove the paper and peas from the pans immediately. Place the shells back in the oven for 4 to 5 minutes to brown lightly. Remove from oven and cool completely. Remove from the pans. Drain the red and dark sweet cherries again thoroughly. Spoon confectioners' custard into the tartlet shells. Arrange the dark and red cherries over the custard. Spoon warm glaze over the cherries. Serve with chantilly cream.

cherry tartlets

Appealingly arranged for serving, black cherry tartlets alternate with red cherry tartlets. They are made from baked Basic Sweet Short Pastry shells, Basic Confectioners' Custard, fruit filling and Red Currant Jelly Glaze. A bowl of Basic Chantilly Cream for topping the tartlets sits in the center of our arrangement.

the importance of assembling and preparing ingredients and equipment before cooking

An illustration of the importance of organization in cooking is the following story: A newlywed had just moved into a small apartment. She was having her mother-in-law, who was a fantastic cook, to dinner for the first time. Wanting to impress her with her own baking skills, she decided to attempt making a fancy pastry dessert. She had never done much cooking before, but she was of the opinion that if she could read, she could cook. Armed with recipe and piles of ingredients she settled down to cooking. Things were going all right until she got to the part of her pastry recipe which called for six cups of flour. She had not thought to check her flour supply before beginning or to read her recipe through. So, when she started to measure her flour she found to her dismay she was two cups short. She headed for the supermarket leaving all the half-mixed ingredients on the kitchen counter. When she returned she found, to her horror, the butter had melted in the warm kitchen and blended with her flour, making a gooey mess. There was no way to salvage it and no time to begin again before her company came. That night, a very contrite hostess served bought pastry to her guests.

The newlywed learned a hard lesson of the importance of organization in cooking. To avoid this disaster in your kitchen, let's take a moment off to discuss the ins and outs of organization, one of the keys to success in our adventure into creative cooking. By organization we mean careful planning and preliminary preparation — reading your recipe and getting all the necessary ingredients out of cupboards and ready for use before actually beginning to cook. Although this applies to everything you cook from appetizers to entrées, the following desserts lesson is a good one with which to practice and get into the habit of organizing.

Once you acquire the tricks of planning and preparation, you'll have greater success with just about everything you make in the kitchen. Also, by being organized, you'll derive the full pleasure and enjoyment that cooking can bring to you.

There's little worse than discovering, like the new-lywed, that you're missing an important ingredient after you've begun to cook. To avoid this, read your recipe carefully before doing anything else because it will tell you which ingredients you'll need and the required amount of each. Next, take them out of the cupboard and line them up on your counter, so you'll know exactly where everything you'll need is. Because many dessert recipes call for refrigerated items, you'll want to be sure to assemble your ingredients in plenty of time for them to come to room temperature or for butter to soften.

There may have been many times when you have complained of anxiously looking for a wire whisk, for example, while trying to follow a recipe's instructions. To keep this from happening be sure to assemble all the needed equipment on your working space before beginning. If you have to wash any pieces of equipment, take care of this job next. Also be sure to assemble any large pieces of equipment, such as your electric mixer or blender, so they're ready for use the minute you need them. If your recipe calls for a greased baking pan, you might want to perform this step before going any farther.

You'll want to be sure to measure your dry and liquid ingredients before starting to cook (except such small liquid quantities as a teaspoon of vanilla flavoring). One of the advantages of doing this is that ingredients, such as flour, can be premeasured, set on waxed paper, and then put aside until needed so that your measuring utensil will once again be ready for immediate use.

Advance preparation does not stop with the assembling of ingredients and equipment as outlined above. Your ingredients, in particular, need a little more preliminary attention. If, for example, your recipe calls for egg whites, separate the eggs and then set the whites aside until time to whip them or mix them with the other ingredients. Or when cooking with chopped vegetables be sure to cut them up in advance and set them aside on a piece of waxed paper.

As you prepare our dessert recipes on the following pages try our suggestions for organized cooking. You'll be amazed at the time you'll save and pleased with the end results of the desserts.

how to make basic puff pastry

In an eighteenth century restaurant of great fame, the master chef ordered a young apprentice to prepare a batch of buttery pastry. The chef then left and the boy went right to work. He mixed the dough, rolled it into a ball, and got ready to wrap it for storage when, to his horror, he realized he had forgotten the butter! Hastily he flattened the dough with a rolling pin, slapped a pound of butter into the middle of it, and, to conceal the butter, folded the pastry over it.

Unfortunately the butter showed right through the dough. So the boy again rolled out the dough and folded it, becoming more and more frantic as he tried to distribute the butter. He went on rolling and folding until, at last, the butter disappeared.

When the chef returned he asked for the pastry. He rolled it out, shaped it, glazed it, and put it in the hottest of his coal ovens. As the pastry baked it rose several inches in height and was composed of a myriad of thin, golden brown layers. Swinging around to face the boy, the chef demanded to know what had happened. The apprentice burst into tears and confessed his mistake. Then, to his astonishment, the chef kissed him on both cheeks, and exclaimed, "C'est magnifique, c'est pâte feuilletée."

Our recipe for making *pâte feuilletée*, or puff pastry, is far less haphazard than the method above. In our dessert category we have already met and worked with one basic type of pastry — short pastry. Puff pastry is lighter, flakier, and more delicate than short pastry. The difference is due primarily to the unique method of mixing and handling puff pastry dough. When mixed, shaped as desired, and baked, the dough for puff pastry rises several times its original height and forms crisp, tissue-thin layers. From these layers comes the French name for puff pastry, *pâte feuilletée* meaning "leaved pastry."

In the next few pages you'll be making basic puff pastry and then using it to prepare a variety of sweet baked products that emulate those made by the world's greatest pastry chefs. Part of the success of puff pastry depends on your making sure the butter *doesn't* soften at any time during the procedure. You'll have no trouble keeping your butter from softening if you chill the ingredients, your hands, and your working surface. A cold marble working surface is ideal because marble holds a cold temperature better than any other material. If you don't have one, use a formica kitchen counter, but if your kitchen is warm be sure to rub ice over the working surface and then dry it thoroughly. To keep your hands cold dip them in ice water when working the butter into the flour.

Your success at puff pastry also depends on the incorporation of as much air as possible into the dough when mixing it. When the dough is baked at a high temperature, the air inside expands and causes it to rise. Our step-by-step directions will show you how to roll the dough to trap the air inside and cause the pastry to puff.

BASIC PUFF PASTRY

2 c. butter
3¾ c. 3-time sifted all-purpose flour
½ tsp. salt
2 tbsp. chilled lemon juice
¾ c. ice water

1 Place 1¼ cups butter in large mixing bowl filled with ice water. Knead with hands until butter has the consistency of soft dough and is free from lumps. Your hands will get so cold that you will have to remove them from the icy water several times during the kneading process. Place butter in double thickness of muslin or tea towel and squeeze to remove excess water.

2 Rub ice cubes over working surface to chill thoroughly. Place butter on cold surface; shape evenly into rectangle, about ½ inch thick. Place on dry piece of muslin or towel. Wrap and refrigerate.

3 Chill working surface again thoroughly with ice. Sift flour with salt onto cold surface. With fingers, work flour from center to form ring. Cut remaining ³/₄ cup butter into small pieces in center of ring.

4 Chill working hand in ice water until cold; dry. Mix flour, a small amount at a time, with the butter inside the ring. Do this process by rubbing the flour with the butter between your thumb and first 2 fingers.

5 This breaks down the butter to form small granules as shown. Chill and dry hand frequently during this process.

6 Reshape ring; pour chilled lemon juice and ¹/₄ cup ice water in center. Work flour mixture from inner ring into liquid using 2 knives; continue adding small amounts of water and working in flour mixture until all ingredients are moistened.

7 Shape into smooth ball. Sprinkle ball with additional sifted flour; wrap in cloth. Chill for 30 minutes.

8 Ice cleaned working surface again. Place dough on chilled, floured surface; roll out into long narrow ¹/₂-inch thick rectangle. Remove butter from muslin; place in center of rectangle.

9 Bring the edge nearest to you up and over to center of butter, brushing off excess flour; press down gently. Fold left, then right sides to center, brushing again and pressing down gently. Bring top flap over and press down gently. Lift dough and reflour surface, if necessary.

10 We are now starting the all important part of making puff pastry, blending the butter into the dough. In all rolling and handling of dough we must be very careful not to let the butter break through dough or the air trapped between layers will escape. If this should happen, then pat a small amount of flour over hole to patch. The air trapped between layers will expand when baked and cause the pastry to puff. Roll out gently, keeping rectangular shape; do not roll over ends.

11 Fold edge nearest to you to the center, then fold top edge to center. Now fold top over to bottom edge. Make ½ turn to right; stick finger in top edge of dough to indicate starting position for next rolling step. Wrap securely in waxed paper; refrigerate for 30 minutes.

12 Remove dough from refrigerator; place on iced, floured surface with finger mark at top of working surface. Repeat 3 rolling, folding and turning procedures as before, chilling 30 minutes after 2nd, 3rd and 4th rolling. After 5th roll, wrap and chill for at least 3 hours. Roll out the 6th and final roll as recipe directs and bake immediately. After 5th roll, dough may be chilled overnight. Let stand at room temperature for 30 minutes before rolling.

ECCLES PIES

3 oranges
2 lemons
2 c. raisins
¾ c. (packed) brown sugar
2 tbsp. lemon juice
1 recipe Basic Puff Pastry *(pgs. 22-24)*
1 egg white
Sugar

eccles pies

*From Eccles, a borough in Lancashire, England
come these delectable little pies made of a puff
pastry shell filled with a rich raisin mixture.*

Cut thin layer of peeling from oranges and lemons, being careful not to cut into white membrane. Cut peeling into slivers. Measure 1 cup combined orange and lemon peelings. Place in small saucepan; cover with water. Bring to a boil over medium heat; boil for 2 minutes. Drain well. Cover with water again; bring to a boil and boil for 2 minutes longer. Drain well. This process removes the bitterness from peelings. Combine raisins, mixed peelings, brown sugar and lemon juice in a medium saucepan. Cook over medium heat until brown sugar is dissolved, stirring constantly. Reduce heat to low; cook for 10 minutes, stirring frequently. Let cool. Roll puff pastry dough out thin, working on iced, floured surface. Cut into 5-inch rounds. Spread raisin mixture to within ½ inch of edge on ½ of each pastry circle. Brush entire circle edge with cold water. Fold pastry over filling. Pinch edges together securely. Brush tops of the pies with egg white; sprinkle generously with sugar. Make 3 slits on top of each pie, 1 inch apart. Wet baking sheet with cold water; shake off excess water. Moistening the baking sheet aids in the rising process. Place pies on baking sheet. Place in preheated 425-degree oven on shelf above center for 10 minutes. Reduce temperature to 350 degrees and bake for 15 to 20 minutes longer or until puffed and golden.

how to make rectangular puff pastry shells

In the section on salads in this lesson we discover that cucumbers and other vegetables can be used as "cups" for delicious salad mixtures. Here, let's see what unusual containers can be made of pastry to hold various delicious fillings. The step-by-step pictures presented here show you how to make rectangular-shaped puff pastry shells. You can make them of either Basic Puff Pastry (see page 22) or Rough Puff Pastry (see page 27) — whichever you feel most comfortable using.

We feel you'll enjoy making these shells as they're not difficult and can be filled with a great variety of mixtures. We'll be making them frequently throughout your CREATIVE COOKING COURSE to hold both sweet and savory fillings.

To make the shell, you'll need a rolling pin, a sharp knife for cutting the dough frames, one or two forks for pricking the bottom of the pastry to keep it from rising during baking, a ruler to measure the rectangle for the frames, a lightly floured baking sheet, and a pastry brush. When making your shell, don't be alarmed if the frame of dough slips from the base and the case doesn't end up a perfect rectangle. This may happen when the pastry puffs, but it will taste just as delicious and look equally attractive even if it isn't exactly rectangular.

To get an idea of just how luscious these shells can look, turn to page 28 of this lesson where you'll see the first dessert using a rectangular puff pastry shell.

1 Set your Rough Puff Pastry or Basic Puff Pastry on a lightly floured working surface. With a rolling pin, roll out the dough into a rectangular shape that is ½ inch thick, slightly longer than 12 inches and slightly wider than 8 inches, as shown above. Then with a knife neatly trim your dough to form a perfect rectangle.

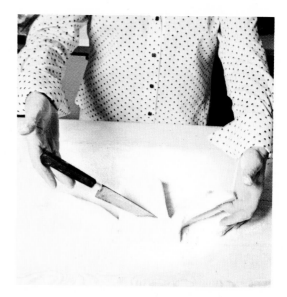

2 Now fold the dough lengthwise away from you. Using a sharp knife, cut a one-inch wide "frame" of dough from around the double layer edges, leaving the folded edges nearest you alone. (Later this frame will be opened as shown in picture four.)

3 Roll out the rectangle of dough to 1 inch larger than your frame. The frame is going to be positioned inside the edges of your rectangle — a glance at picture four will show you the completed rolled out dough. Prick the entire surface with a fork. Now brush the edges of the rectangle of dough with cold water. Next transfer your rectangle of dough to a lightly floured baking sheet. Place the cutout frame on the rectangle. Turn up the outer rim and pinch to the frame at the top. We are not moistening the baking sheet as we did for the Eccles pies on page 25 because we don't want the pastry to rise so much that there will be no space for filling.

4 With a knife make crisscross cuts on the top of the frame. Brush the top edge of the frame with an egg that has been beaten until blended. Bake the pastry shell in a preheated oven at 425 degrees for 10 minutes, then reduce temperature to 350 degrees and bake for 35 to 40 minutes longer.

POINTS TO REMEMBER WHEN MAKING ROUGH PUFF PASTRY

Our Rough Puff Pastry recipe is a variation of our Basic Puff Pastry. Generally, Rough Puff Pastry is used in the same way as Basic Puff Pastry, but instead of being flaky it is biscuit-like. It is delicious as a shell for a wide variety of dessert mixtures and fabulous as a crust for fruit, meat or vegetable pies. It's just the recipe you need when you're short of time but want to make a special delicacy.

Rough Puff Pastry is less time-consuming to make than Basic Puff Pastry. You do not turn the dough as many times and you skip the in between refrigeration steps. Don't be disappointed when your Rough Puff Pastry doesn't rise quite as high as Basic Puff Pastry. The short-cuts in handling the dough make this difference in the finished product.

To mix the ingredients for Rough Puff Pastry, follow our detailed recipe on this page. Be sure, as you did when working with Basic Puff Pastry, to keep your working surface cold. After making your dough, wrap and store in your refrigerator for a minimum of 24 hours or up to seven days.

ROUGH PUFF PASTRY

3½ c. sifted all-purpose flour
1 tsp. salt
1 c. butter
¾ c. vegetable shortening
1 c. ice water

Sift flour with salt into mound on clean working surface. Shape into large ring, forming high wall. Place butter, shortening and half the water in center. Work central mixture together with cutting motion, using 2 table knives or pastry scrapers. Work in flour carefully from inside of ring, adding more water as needed. Work with knives until all flour is added and dough holds together. Gather dough into a ball. Chill working surface thoroughly with ice; dust with flour. Roll out pastry into long thin rectangle. Fold top edge down to center, then bring bottom edge to top fold. Fold bottom to top again, making 5 layers. Turn pastry clockwise ½ turn, so edges on left and right are now at top and bottom. Repeat rolling and folding steps 2 more times. Wrap folded pastry securely in plastic wrap. Store in refrigerator for at least 24 hours before using. This pastry will keep in the refrigerator up to 7 days. Bake as directed in each individual recipe.

rectangular pastry shell of glazed mixed fruit

This tender flaky puff pastry shell is layered with delicious Basic Confectioners' Custard and heaped to well above the pastry's rim with juicy colorful mixed fruits. Warm Red Currant Jelly Glaze is spooned around and over it. Then bright red and green maraschino cherries are placed on top for decoration.

RECTANGULAR SHELL OF GLAZED MIXED FRUITS

1 med. can pear halves
1 sm. can sliced peaches
1 sm. can apricot halves
1 med. can sliced pineapple
2 fresh plums, seeded and halved
Red and green maraschino cherries
1 recipe Rough Puff Pastry *(pg. 27)*
1 recipe Basic Confectioners' Custard *(pg. 19)*
1 recipe Red Currant Jelly Glaze *(pg. 19)*
1 egg, well beaten

Drain liquid from fruits and place fruits on absorbent toweling. Roll and shape pastry to a 12 x 8-inch rectangle, working on a floured surface. We are now going to make a rectangular pastry shell as shown in the step-by-step illustrations on page 26. Bring edge nearest to you over to top edge. Cut an outer frame 1 inch wide, using sharp knife. Set frame aside. Unfold remaining dough; roll out and shape to 13 x 9-inch rectangle. Move carefully to floured baking sheet, turning topside down. You may roll lightly again to retain given size. Prick generously with fork over entire surface. Moisten pricked edges well with cold water. Place frame, topside down, over wet edges, 1/2 inch in from sides. Turn up the outer rim and pinch to the frame at the top. With wet spatula, press inside frame edges gently down into base dough, holding outer edge in place with hand. Make diagonal cross cuts on frame with pointed knife; brush top frame edges carefully with beaten egg. Bake in preheated 425-degree oven for 10 minutes. Reduce oven temperature to 350 degrees; bake for 35 to 40 minutes longer. Remove baking sheet from oven; place on rack until pastry shell is cool. Transfer pastry shell carefully to serving plate. Spread confectioners' custard evenly into center of shell. Arrange fruits over custard. Spoon warm glaze over and between fruits, spreading evenly. Garnish with additional cherries. Cut into squares to serve.

german plum pastry

If you're in a hurry and don't have the time to make puff pastry, you might try ordering it from your local bakery. This is just a substitute for homemade and can be bought by the pound. You must refrigerate puff pastry until you are ready to use it. Just be sure to order in plenty of time, so your baker will have a supply available. Try using the bought puff pastry to create this delicious and simple dessert called Meringue Puff Pastries.

MERINGUE PUFF PASTRIES

1 lb. bought puff pastry
1 egg white
Sugar or vanilla sugar *(pg. 2)*
1/2 recipe Basic Meringues mixture *(pg. 10)*

Let puff pastry come to room temperature. Roll out on floured surface to a 1/2-inch thick rectangle. Cut into 4-inch squares, then cut each square in half, diagonally. Let stand for 15 to 20 minutes. Brush

german plum pastry

The German name for this appetizing plum pastry is Zwetschgenkuchen. To make it we've created a flaky puff pastry with a special plum filling. Before baking the pastry, we brushed it with beaten egg white and sprinkled it with sugar for a special glazed quality and heightened flavor.

with egg white, then sprinkle generously with sugar. Place triangles on wet baking sheets. Bake in preheated 400-degree oven for 20 minutes. Spoon meringue into icing bag fitted with a large star tube. Remove pastries from oven and pipe the meringue in strips over tops of each triangle. Reduce the oven temperature to 350 degrees and continue baking pastries for 15 to 20 minutes longer. Remove from oven and serve hot or cold. May split and serve with fruits, jams or marmalades.

GERMAN PLUM PASTRY

2 17-oz. cans plums
1 recipe Basic Puff Pastry *(pg. 22)*
Grated rind of 1/2 lemon
1/4 c. (packed) brown sugar
3/4 tsp. cinnamon
1 egg white, beaten
Sugar

Drain the plums; cut into halves and remove pits. Roll out half the pastry to an 8 x 12-inch rectangle, working on marble or a floured board. Place on lightly floured baking sheet. Roll out remaining pastry on lightly floured board. Fold in half lengthwise; cut through the folded edge in 3/4-inch strips to within 1 inch of the edge. Overlap plum halves on base rectangle to within 1/2 inch of the edges. Combine lemon rind, brown sugar and cinnamon; sprinkle over the plums. Brush pastry edges with cold water. Place cut pastry over half the rectangle; unfold and fit over remaining rectangle. Pinch edges together securely. Brush top liberally with egg white and sprinkle generously with sugar. Bake in preheated 425-degree oven for 10 minutes. Reduce oven temperature to 350 degrees and bake for 25 to 30 minutes or until golden brown. Serve hot or cold. Variation: Substitute sliced fresh peaches for plums, using 1/3 cup brown sugar; follow all other directions.

how to make a puff pastry galette

The French word *galette* (pronounced Ga let) refers to a flat, round cake usually made of *pâté feuilletée,* or puff pastry. In most of the provinces of northern France, the *galette* is the cake eaten on Twelfth Night. A symbolic bean, either real or a small porcelain model, is baked into the dough of the *galette.* Today cooks of all nations take liberties with the meaning of *galette* using the word frequently to describe a food — either sweet or savory — that has a flat round shape. In the vegetable category of your CREATIVE COOKING COURSE one of the small shaped Duchess potatoes were called *galettes* (see Vegetables, pg. 4). In this dessert section we return to the true French meaning of the word as we show you in step-by-step illustrations how to make a puff pastry *galette* using either Basic Puff Pastry (pg. 22) or Rough Puff Pastry (pg. 27).

The *galette* is a very versatile type of pastry. It can be split in half and filled with sweetened cream or custard and soft fruit. It is then reassembled and dusted with confectioners' sugar for a marvelous dessert. Or, it can be split in half and filled with meat, seafood, poultry or vegetable leftovers that have been mixed with Basic White Sauce (see Sauces, pg. 4), then reassembled for a delicious entrée.

You can probably think of many other interesting ways to use puff pastry *galettes.* One which we're particularly fond of is the exquisite Pyramid *Galette* pictured on page 31 of this desserts section. This out-of-the ordinary dessert has for its base a puff pastry *galette.* This is topped with rings made of Basic Puff Pastry or Rough Puff Pastry that have been shaped with a plain pastry cutter.

When making the *galette* base, it is important to crisscross the top with a large sharp knife and then brush it with a beaten egg mixture. This crisscrossing will control the rising of the puff pastry, giving you a flat surface no matter how high the pastry rises in the oven.

After baking the *galette,* slice into two layers and fill it with Basic Confectioners' Custard, apricot jam and whipped cream. Place the top half of the *galette* over the filling and brush the sides with apricot jam, then sprinkle pistachio nuts over this. Brush the apricot glaze over the top of the *galette,* then place the puff pastry rings (that have been brushed with apricot glaze) in a pyramid shape on top. At the moment of serving dust overall with powdered confectioners' sugar. This delicious dessert is designed for special eye appeal. It will look fantastic as a centerpiece on a buffet dinner table.

The Creative Homemaker's Academy © MCMLXXIII
Selected Illustrations © B.P.C. Publishing Limited MCMLXX

1 Roll out your Basic Puff Pastry or Rough Puff Pastry to ¼-inch thickness. Cut two circles of dough (exact size will often depend on your recipe; see recipe for Pyramid *Galette*) using the removable bottom of a cake pan or similar circular object to ensure perfect roundness.

2 Stack and transfer the circles of dough onto your baking sheet (remember to first rinse the sheet in cold water and then shake off excess drops). Crisscross the top of your circle of dough with a large knife, as we're doing above. This crisscrossing helps keep the pastry level on top as it rises during baking. Brush with beaten egg.

3 Bake according to recipe instructions. This is what your finished puff pastry *galette* will look like when it comes out of the oven.

PYRAMID GALETTE

1 recipe Basic Puff Pastry *(pg. 22)*
1 egg, beaten
1 15-oz. jar apricot jam
¼ c. Chablis
1 recipe Basic Confectioners' Custard *(pg. 19)*
½ c. whipping cream, whipped
½ c. chopped pistachio nuts
Confectioners' sugar

Roll out ⅔ of the puff pastry to ¼-inch thickness, working on an iced, floured surface. Cut two 9-inch circles from the pastry; stack on baking sheet, rinsed with cold water. Crisscross the top with even cuts, using a large sharp knife. Brush gently with well-beaten egg. Bake in preheated 425-degree oven for 15 minutes. Reduce oven temperature to 350 degrees and bake for 10 minutes longer. Remove and cool on rack. Roll out remaining pastry to ⅛-inch thickness. Cut into fifty 2½-inch circles, then stamp out 1½-inch inner rounds from these circles. Place rings on wet baking sheet; brush with beaten egg. Bake in preheated 425-degree oven for 8 to 10 minutes or until golden brown. Place rings on rack to cool. Remove top layer of *galette* carefully and set aside. Place bottom layer on large round serving dish. Combine apricot jam and Chablis in a small heavy saucepan for glaze; stir over low heat until the jam is melted. Cool apricot glaze to lukewarm. Spread confectioners' custard evenly over bottom layer; drizzle a thin layer of glaze over custard. Spoon on whipped cream, spreading evenly. Replace top half of *galette*, then brush side with apricot glaze. Press pistachio nuts around side; pat gently until nuts stick. Brush the top generously with glaze, then brush the rings. Stack the rings pyramid-fashion on top of *galette* as shown in our illustration. Sift confectioners' sugar over rings. To serve, remove the rings with tongs to another serving plate. Cut *galette* into wedges and serve each wedge topped with several rings.

pyramid galette

This splendid dessert pyramid is made from apricot-glazed rings of puff pastry stacked on a galette base. The galette has been split in the middle and filled with Basic Confectioners' Custard, apricot jam and whipped cream. It almost looks too good to eat, but you'll find its taste is delicious.

coconut meringue pie

Coconut lovers will thrill to this delectable pie. It's made with a Basic Sweet Short Pastry Shell (page 12) filled with a creamy coconut filling, then topped with meringue. We've scattered grated, oven-browned coconut over the top.

COCONUT MERINGUE PIE

½ recipe Basic Sweet Short Pastry (*pg. 12*)
8 egg yolks
1 c. sugar
½ c. flour
2½ c. milk
1 vanilla pod or 1 tsp. vanilla extract
1 c. (lightly packed) frozen grated coconut
2 tbsp. butter

Roll out pastry to fit a 9-inch pie pan, working on floured surface. Place pastry carefully in pan. Flute edge; prepare for baking blind as shown in step-by-step illustrations (pg. 14). Bake in preheated 400-degree oven for 10 minutes. Reduce oven temperature to 375 degrees and bake for 15 minutes longer or until golden brown. Remove from oven, remove paper and peas and place shell back in oven for 4 to 5 minutes to brown lightly. Remove from oven; let cool thoroughly. Combine egg yolks, sugar and flour in large mixing bowl; beat with electric mixer at medium speed until creamy. Place milk in top of double boiler over hot water; add vanilla pod (if using vanilla extract, add after heating milk). Heat slowly until just below boiling point. Remove vanilla pod; dry and store for further use. Pour milk slowly into egg mixture, stirring constantly with wooden spoon. Add coconut; blend thoroughly. Return to top of double boiler; cook, stirring constantly, for about 10 minutes or until mixture thickens and coats a wooden spoon. Stir in butter; cook for 5 minutes longer or until filling is thick. Turn into pie shell; chill for 45 minutes or until cold and firm.

MERINGUE

¼ c. (lightly packed) frozen grated coconut
4 egg whites
¾ c. sugar

Place coconut between two sheets of paper toweling and pat out excess moisture. Beat egg whites in large mixing bowl with electric mixer at high speed until stiff peaks form. Sprinkle with 2 tablespoons sugar; beat for 3 minutes longer. Fold in coconut and remaining sugar with wire whisk until thoroughly blended. Spoon onto pie; spread evenly over top with tines of fork, sealing to edge. Bake in preheated 350-degree oven for 15 minutes or until lightly browned. Cool thoroughly before serving.

TURKISH ORANGES IN SUGAR SYRUP

4 oranges
1 c. sugar
Triple Sec or Curacao Liqueur to taste

Remove peel from oranges, using a lemon stripper as explained in General Information on page 11. Set the orange peel strips aside for use in Candied Orange Strips. Remove all pith from oranges, using a small sharp knife. Place oranges in a small heavy saucepan; add enough water to cover. Bring to a boil, then reduce heat and simmer for 15 minutes or until oranges are soft but not collapsed. Remove oranges; set aside. Add sugar to water; stir until dissolved. Bring to a slow, rolling boil; boil until liquid thickens to a light syrup. Place oranges in syrup, simmer for 7 to 10 minutes, basting frequently.

Remove oranges from syrup, using slotted spoon; arrange on a narrow serving dish. Drizzle with Triple Sec.

CANDIED ORANGE STRIPS

1 c. orange peel strips
1½ c. Basic Sugar Syrup (Breads, pg. 14)

Remove any remaining white membrane from orange peel strips with sharp knife. Place orange peel strips in a small saucepan; cover with cold water. Bring to a boil; pour off water. Repeat 2 more times to remove all bitterness from orange peel. Pour Basic Sugar Syrup over orange peel strips; bring to a boil. Reduce heat; simmer for about 45 minutes. Spoon candied orange strips over oranges; pour syrup over top.

turkish oranges in sugar syrup

Whole peeled oranges are simmered until soft, then resimmered in sugar syrup. We've spooned Candied Orange Strips over them, poured sugar syrup on top and garnished with bright green orange leaves. Around the serving dish we've draped strips of candied orange to create a festive air.

Take a delicate fluffy meringue shell, pile it high with rich whipped cream, garnish generously with tangy candied orange strips and you have a glorious dessert to make any occasion a special event. Desserts made from meringues have been prized highly since the first meringue was made in 1720 by a Swiss pastry cook named Gasparini. When the first meringues came to France, King Stanislaus considered them a royal treat. It is said that Marie-Antoinette had a craving for meringues and made her own at her Trianon palace.

Meringues are made of sugar and egg whites thoroughly beaten to form stiff peaks. Up until the 1800's meringues were shaped with a spoon. Today cooks use pastry bags or icing bags to shape them. We've made our beautiful meringue shell by piping the meringue through an icing bag in four circles.

To many cooks the word meringue is associated only with tops of pies such as our coconut pie on page 32 of this lesson. But there are several different types and uses of meringues. The type which we use for our meringue shell in this dessert recipe is called hard meringue and requires more sugar and more beating than soft meringue, which is usually used as a topping. After hard meringues have been baked and cooled they can be kept for several days in airtight containers. Another type is Italian meringue, which will be introduced in a later lesson. It is made with a hot sugar syrup instead of granulated sugar. Because of this it does not require baking and it is not as stiff as hard meringue.

Our dessert made with hard meringue can be prepared almost completely in advance. The only thing you need to do immediately before serving is whip the cream.

orange meringue dessert

This elegant and delectable dessert should be placed in a conspicuous place on your dinner or party table. Family and friends will delight in the light meringue shell filled with airy whipped cream and garnished with candied orange strips. Fill a sauce bowl with extra orange strips and syrup so your guests can add more to their servings. Everything except the whipped cream can be prepared ahead of time and stored until ready for use.

ORANGE MERINGUE

1 recipe Basic Meringues mixture *(pg. 10)*
2 c. whipping cream
1 c. cut Candied Orange Strips in syrup *(pg. 33)*

Draw a 7-inch diameter circle on oiled brown paper and place on baking sheet. Place part of the meringue mixture in icing bag; do not affix piping nozzle. Pipe meringue around edge of circle; continue piping in circles toward center until base layer is formed. Pipe a circle on outer edge of base layer to form wall. Place is preheated 275-degree oven, one shelf below center. Bake for 10 minutes or until a light crust forms. Fill icing bag with remaining meringue mixture; pipe two additional circles on outer edge, building the wall higher. Reduce oven temperature to 250 degrees; bake meringue for 1 hour and 15 minutes or until dry. Place baking sheet on rack until meringue is completely cooled. Remove meringue case carefully;

place on serving dish. Whip cream until stiff; pile into center of meringue case. Arrange Candied Orange Strips over top of whipped cream and drizzle with the syrup. Additional canelled orange strands may be used as garnish, if desired. Meringue case may be wrapped securely in foil and stored in airtight container until needed.

decorating techniques

If you've ever bought a bakery cake because "theirs look so much nicer" than one you could make, you know that those elegant rosettes, garlands and trellises don't compensate for the too sugary icing and the too dry cake you sometimes get. Now you can make those same elegant decorations, following the easy instructions we provide, and *know* that the cake will meet your standards of quality and taste. Soon you'll be adding unique decorative touches that even a professional baker will envy. Just as important, you'll have fun doing it.

You are already one step ahead in the decorating process. Remember the Duchess Potatoes in the Vegetables section (pg. 3)? The icing bag was used there to make decorative potatoes, and here you'll use it to make decorative rosettes and trellises for cakes. The only difference is that you'll be creating on a more delicate scale. Below you see the techniques for practicing with the icing bag and writing tubes, and on the next pages you'll see them put to work to achieve elaborate special-occasion cakes.

First you'll need to make a paper icing bag, which you'll find instructions for on page 22, General Information. (Or, use a canvas or plastic one if you have one among your equipment.) We'll use two tubes, a medium-sized plain writing tube for trellising and a medium star tube for the rosettes.

Next, prepare the icing, using the Basic Butter Cream Frosting on page 7. We will also pipe with Basic Royal Icing but butter cream is easier to learn with because it is thicker. If you want to add a tint to the decorative icing, don't add it to the entire batch at once — you're likely to end up with uneven dollops of color in the finished product. Instead, place a spoonful or so of the icing in a separate dish and work two or three drops of food coloring into it with a spatula. Then add the colored icing to the original mixture a little at a time.

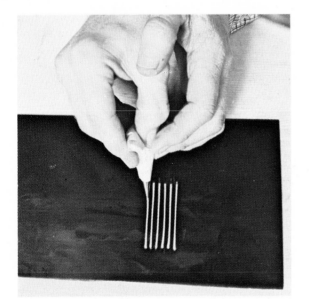

1 To get the feel of using the icing bag, play around a little each time you begin. Here we show you how to lay down lines using the plain writing tube. Note that the tube is not placed on the surface but is held a fraction above it. This is very important in controlling the line. Squeeze with an even, steady pressure to make a line that is consistent in size.

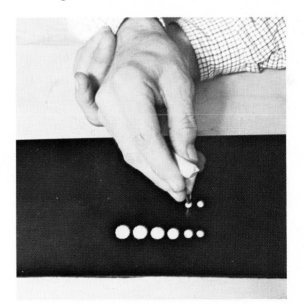

2 It is easy to achieve a professional touch with artistic rosettes. They are very effective yet simple to make. Using the medium star tube you can make varying sizes by using different amounts of pressure on the icing bag. The pressure of the hand gripping the icing bag determines the size of each rosette. Allow the icing mixture to touch the decorating surface, push in gently, then pull the bag back quickly, leaving the rosette on your cake.

1 Starting with a set of the lines you practiced on the previous page, form a trellis by crossing the lines. Note that the hands are clear of the working surface. Do not drag the tube through the other lines.

2 Here we see how the design looks when it is completed. If you like, you can now put tiny "dots" at each intersection of the lines for an even more decorative look.

trellis and rosette techniques

Now that you have practiced the trellises and rosettes used in cake decorating and found that they aren't nearly as difficult as they look let's put them to use and create a beautiful cake!

The Basic Close-Textured Sponge Cake introduced on page 6 of this section is an excellent choice for a first attempt at decorating because of its smooth finish. However, if you've already made this cake, you may want to try something different, so we are giving you two variations on the basic recipe. The Coffee Sponge Cake and the Lemon Sponge Cake add flavor variety but are as easy to decorate as the first cake.

We also offer two additional butter cream frosting recipes which complement the two new cakes — Basic Coffee Butter Cream and Basic Orange Butter Cream. Also included is a Basic Coffee Syrup recipe for adding a delicious coffee flavor to your desserts.

BASIC COFFEE SYRUP NO. 1

5 c. brewed coffee

Place coffee in a heavy saucepan and bring to a vigorous boil. Reduce heat slightly and let coffee boil slowly for 25 to 30 minutes or until reduced to 1/2 cup syrup. Cool and store in covered jar to use as needed.

BASIC COFFEE SYRUP NO. 2

2 tbsp. instant coffee
1/2 c. boiling water

Dissolve coffee in boiling water. Cool and store as directed above.

COFFEE SPONGE CAKE

1 recipe Basic Close-Textured Sponge Cake *(pg. 6)*
2 tbsp. Basic Coffee Syrup
1 recipe Basic Coffee Butter Cream *(pg. 37)*
1/2 c. slivered almonds

Prepare the sponge cake according to recipe directions, substituting the coffee syrup for 2 tablespoons of the milk. Bake in a preheated 350-degree oven for 35 minutes or until cake tests done. Cool on racks for 5 minutes, then remove from pans and cool *completely*. Brush off crumbs and place 1 layer, topside-up, on cake plate. Spread thickly with the butter cream, then sprinkle with almonds. Spread a small amount of butter cream over bottom of top layer and place the butter cream side down over the almonds. Spread butter cream smoothly over top of cake, then around the side. Chill for 15 minutes. Smooth the butter cream according to our step-by-step illustrations for applying butter cream on page 7. Pipe the trellis with a medium writing tube over the top of cake according to our step-by-step illustrations. Then begin piping medium-sized rosettes around bottom of cake. Continue with rows of rosettes to top edge of cake as shown in our illustration.

BASIC COFFEE BUTTER CREAM

1 c. unsalted butter, softened
5 c. sifted confectioners' sugar
2 egg yolks
¼ c. Basic Coffee Syrup *(pg. 36)*

Cream the butter in a large mixing bowl with electric mixer until light and fluffy. Add half the confectioners' sugar and beat until smooth. Add egg yolks and blend well, then mix in the remaining confectioners' sugar. Pour in coffee syrup and beat until well combined and fluffy. This will make enough frosting to fill, frost and decorate a 9-inch, 2 layer cake.

LEMON SPONGE CAKE

1 recipe Basic Close-Textured Sponge Cake *(pg. 6)*
Grated rind of 1 lemon
2 tbsp. lemon juice
Basic Orange Butter Cream

Prepare the sponge cake according to recipe directions, adding the lemon rind and substituting the lemon juice for 2 tablespoons of the milk. Bake in a preheated 350-degree oven for 35 minutes or until

cake tests done. Frost and decorate with Basic Orange Butter Cream according to the decorating directions for Coffee Sponge Cake.

BASIC ORANGE BUTTER CREAM

1 c. unsalted butter, softened
5 c. sifted confectioners' sugar
2 egg yolks
Grated rind of 1 orange
3 tbsp. strained orange juice
1 tsp. orange flower water

Cream the butter in a large mixing bowl with electric mixer until light and fluffy. Add half the confectioners' sugar and beat until smooth. Add egg yolks and blend well, then mix in the remaining confectioners' sugar. Add grated rind, orange juice and orange flower water and beat until well combined and fluffy. This will make enough frosting to fill, frost and decorate a 9-inch, 2 layer cake.

coffee sponge cake

Here you see the decorating techniques you have practiced being put to use. A bouquet of rosettes covers the sides and edges of the cake, while tiny "dots" were piped with the writing tube onto the intersections of the trellis lines. In the background is an uniced layer showing the texture of this delicious cake.

basic fruitcake

Winter has been a time of merrymaking throughout the history of Western culture. Our winter holidays today, Thanksgiving, Christmas and the New Year, incorporate many traditions from past celebrations — greenery, orna-

ments, exchanging gifts and, of course, food. Fruitcake is especially associated with the holiday season.

Fruitcakes probably originated because fresh fruits were unavailable in winter. By adding just enough batter to hold the preserved fruits together, enterprising cooks discovered an elegant yet hearty dessert.

We present here the two Basic types of fruitcake — dark and white — and offer simple as well as more elaborate ways of decorating them.

decorative white fruitcake

Using the decorating techniques presented on previous pages, we have piped green-tinted icing to make the trellis and rosettes for this cake. We used Basic Royal Icing, which you'll find on page 43, but you may also use Basic Butter Cream Frosting, page 7. To carry out a holiday motif, we encircled it with a paper frill and a great big bow and topped it with a tiny Christmas tree.

basic white fruitcake

*Elegant in its simplicity, this delicious fruitcake will
fill your house with Christmas memories.
Presented here with nothing more elaborate than a
snowy covering of sifted confectioners' sugar,
the cake is filled with pecans, walnuts,
glacéed cherries and pineapple. A mixture of
brandy, rosewater, orange flower water and orange
juice provides its distinctive taste.*

BASIC WHITE FRUITCAKE

1 8-oz. package red candied cherries
1 4-oz. package green candied cherries
1 8-oz. package diced candied pineapple
1 2½-oz. package chopped walnuts
1 3-oz. package chopped pecans
1 4-oz. package diced mixed fruits
1½ c. golden raisins
2½ c. sifted self-rising flour
¼ c. brandy
Juice of 1 orange
1 tsp. orange flower water (optional)
1 tsp. rose water (optional)
4 eggs, separated
1 c. unsalted butter, softened
Grated rind of 1 orange
2¼ c. sifted confectioners' sugar

Prepare a 9 x 3-inch round cake pan with removable bottom as explained in General Information on page 20. Cut the red and green cherries into
eighths and place in a large bowl. Add pineapple,
walnuts, pecans, mixed fruits, raisins and ½ cup

flour; mix well. Mix the brandy, orange juice,
orange flower water and rose water in a small
bowl. Add the egg yolks and beat well. Cream the
butter and grated rind in a very large bowl with an
electric mixer until butter is very light, scraping
side of bowl and beaters frequently. Stir in the
sugar, a small amount at a time, beating well with
the beater or a wooden spoon after each addition.
Add remaining flour alternately with brandy mixture, beating well after each addition. Add the fruit
mixture and mix well. Whip the egg whites with an
electric mixer until stiffly beaten. Add to the cake
mixture and cut in with the wooden spoon until
well combined. Turn into prepared pan; smooth
top. Place cake pan on 4 folds of brown paper on a
baking sheet. Bake in a preheated 325-degree oven
for 1 hour and 30 minutes. Reduce oven temperature to 275 degrees and bake for 45 minutes
longer or until cake tests done. Remove from oven
and place pan, right side up, on rack to cool. Remove from pan; remove paper. Sift confectioners'
sugar over top or frost and decorate cake with
Basic Butter Cream (page 7) or Basic Royal Icing
(page 43) according to our illustrations.

applying almond paste to dark fruitcake

The bane of a cake maker's existence is that inevitable crumb showing through when you cover a dark cake with a white or lightly tinted icing — no matter how carefully you cool the cake and brush away the crumbs. Well, don't despair. There *is* a solution! By covering a cake with almond paste before adding icing you can make its top and sides smooth enough to apply even the most delicate icing without a single crumb showing through.

Almond paste is a mixture of almonds, confectioners' sugar and egg whites which behaves much like pie pastry. It is so versatile you'll use it again and again in other recipes.

1 Brush top of fruitcake generously with your favorite jam.

2 Roll out almond paste about ⅛-inch thick on cold surface covered with a light sifting of confectioners' sugar.* Place cake, jam side down, on paste.

3 Press the cake on almond paste so that it adheres to the top and cut around it with a sharp knife. The almond paste will adhere to the cake.

4 Measure the circumference of the cake and the depth. Reroll the almond paste trimmings into a strip a fraction longer than the circumference and trim to exactly the depth. Brush the cake side with jam and press the strip around it.

5 Smooth the edges together and the cake is ready to apply the final icing.

bowl. Add the cherries, mixed fruits, golden and chopped raisins, currants, almonds and walnuts, then stir until well mixed. Combine the brandy, Madeira, port, orange flower water, rose water, Noyaux, fruit juices and rinds. Combine the molasses and golden syrup in a saucepan and heat just until warm. Cream the butter thoroughly in a very large bowl with a wooden spoon until light and fluffy. Add the sugar gradually, mixing well. Beat the eggs well and stir in the syrup mixture. Add the flour mixture to butter mixture alternately with the wine mixture, beating after each addition until well blended. Turn into the prepared cake pan (General Information, pg. 20) and smooth top, packing well. Bake in a preheated 325-degree oven, 1 shelf below center, for 1 hour. Reduce oven temperature to 300 degrees and bake for 2 hours longer or until cake tests done. Cool on a rack, right side up, for about 30 minutes. Remove cake from pan, then remove brown paper. Cool cake thoroughly. Brush cake with apricot jam. Cover with Basic Almond Paste. Frost with Basic Royal Icing according to our step-by-step illustrations.

*NOTE
Use confectioners' sugar instead of flour because if flour has any raising power, it may "work" under the almond paste and cause lumps or bubbles; confectioners' sugar will not.

BASIC DARK FRUITCAKE

1³/₄ c. sifted self-rising flour
¹/₂ tsp. nutmeg
¹/₂ tsp. ginger
¹/₂ tsp. cloves
¹/₂ tsp. cinnamon
1 4-oz. package red candied cherries, chopped
1 4-oz. package diced mixed fruits
2¹/₄ c. golden raisins
1 c. chopped raisins
3 c. currants
1 3¹/₂-oz. package chopped almonds
1 2¹/₂-oz. package chopped walnuts
¹/₄ c. brandy
¹/₄ c. Madeira
¹/₄ c. port
1 tsp. orange flower water
1 tsp. rose water
1 tbsp. Crème de Noyaux liqueur
Grated rind and strained juice of 1 orange
Grated rind and strained juice of 1 lemon
2 tbsp. molasses
2 tbsp. golden syrup
1 c. butter, softened
1¹/₂ c. (packed) dark brown sugar
3 eggs
1 12-oz. jar apricot jam, sieved
1 recipe Basic Almond Paste
1 recipe Basic Royal Icing *(pg. 43)*

Prepare a 9 x 3-inch round cake pan with removable bottom as explained in General Information on page 20. Sift the flour, nutmeg, ginger, cloves and cinnamon together in a large mixing

BASIC ALMOND PASTE NO. 1

2¹/₄ c. sliced, blanched almonds
1 lb. confectioners' sugar, sifted
2 egg whites
1 tsp. almond extract

Place about ¹/₂ cup of the almonds in blender. Set blender at grind and grind the almonds until very fine and mealy. Remove almonds from blender and repeat the same until all the almonds are ground to a fine, mealy texture. Combine ground almonds and confectioners' sugar in a large bowl. Work together with finger tips until well blended. Beat the egg whites with a fork until slightly frothy. Add ¹/₂ of the beaten egg whites to the almond mixture and mix to a paste. Add the almond extract, mixing thoroughly. Add enough of the remaining egg whites to make the mixture the consistency of pie pastry. Place on a cold surface and knead as with bread dough until it is smooth. When ready to roll out, dust your surface and rolling pin with additional confectioners' sugar.

BASIC ALMOND PASTE NO. 2

2 8-oz. cans almond paste
1 egg white
1 tsp. rose water (optional)
1 tsp. orange flower water (optional)

Place the almond paste in a mixing bowl and work with a wooden spoon until creamy. Add 1 teaspoon egg white and remaining ingredients and mix until combined, adding more egg white, if needed. Turn out on a cold surface covered with confectioners' sugar and knead until smooth and of pastry consistency.

basic
royal icing

Now that you have a smooth cake covered with almond paste according to our instructions on the previous page, you are ready to add the crowning touch — elegant Basic Royal Icing. This icing is a classic among professional cooks, because it is simple to make, it looks and tastes good and it is versatile for decorating. If desired, you may use it to make trellises and rosettes. You may add a tint, following the directions on page 7. It's sure to become a classic at your house, too.

Basic Royal Icing is a no-cook confection requiring ingredients you probably have in your kitchen: confectioners' sugar, lemon juice and egg whites. Although we recommend in our recipe that you use 3 egg whites, you may need more or less, depending on the spreading consistency you prefer. Be careful, though, to add it sparingly so you don't start an endless circle of adding more confectioners' sugar because the mixture is too thin, then adding more egg white because it is too thick.

In the picture strip below and on the next page, you'll learn the icing techniques for a perfectly smooth cake.

1 Spoon part of the royal icing onto the almond paste-covered cake.

2 Spread it out with a cake spatula to cover the entire top of the cake.

3 Working with a backward/forward wrist movement, smooth out the top. The blade of the spatula being worked with the wrist action will expel any air bubbles which may have become trapped in the icing.

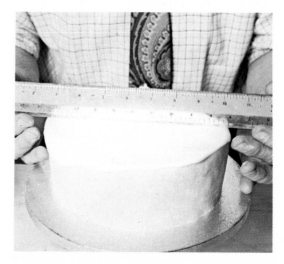

4 Gently slide a clear plastic ruler over the top to make the icing perfectly smooth. This professional procedure is technically called "combing."

5 Now begin applying royal icing liberally to the sides with the spatula.

6 Continue applying icing until the cake is covered all around.

7 Using a "comb" or ruler here (General Information, pg. 21), smooth the sides by turning the cake while holding the comb steady. Cross your hands as shown, holding the comb against the side of the cake in one hand and the turntable in the other. Pull the turntable around to achieve smooth sides.

8 The hands uncross themselves as the turntable moves around. *Try to keep the turning movement continuous.* Your smooth cake is now ready for further decorating, if you wish.

BASIC ROYAL ICING

7 c. sifted confectioners' sugar
Juice of 1 lemon
3 egg whites

Combine the sugar, lemon juice and 1 unbeaten egg white in a large bowl. Stir with a wooden spoon until the mixture is of spreading consistency, adding unbeaten egg white, a small amount at a time, as needed. Part of the icing may be tinted with food coloring for trellising and rosetting.

ice cream sponge

The beautiful Ice Cream-Filled Party Cake, pictured on this page, is so simple to prepare you won't believe it — and neither will the people you serve it to. To make it, you'll rely on the Basic Rolled Sponge Cake, page 2. You will fill this basic cake with peach preserves and your favorite ice cream flavors. Then you'll use another BASIC, Chantilly Cream, page 19, and the decorating methods you practiced on page 35 to pipe rows of large rosettes on the top. Finish it by topping with more peach preserves or sprinkling with pistachio nuts.

If you prefer a less elaborate cake for family occasions, leave off the piping and simply spread the top with Basic Chantilly Cream.

ice cream-filled party cake

We used the Basic Rolled Sponge Cake mixture introduced at the beginning of this section, page 2, as the basis for this beautiful dessert. But instead of rolling it, it is cut in rectangles. Cake layers are alternated with ice cream and topped with peach preserves and rosettes of Basic Chantilly Cream, page 19.

ICE CREAM-FILLED PARTY CAKE

2 recipes Basic Rolled Sponge Cake *(pg. 2)*
1 1-lb. jar peach preserves
1/2 gal. brick vanilla ice cream
1/2 gal. brick strawberry ice cream
Ground pistachio nuts
1 recipe Basic Chantilly Cream *(pg. 19)*

Prepare and bake sponge cakes according to recipe directions. Let cool, then cut each cake in half, crosswise. Place first layer on a chilled serving plate. Spread preserves over the top. Cover with 1/2-inch thick slices of vanilla ice cream. Top with second cake layer and spread with preserves. Cover with 1/2-inch thick slices of strawberry ice cream. Top with the third cake layer and spread on preserves. Cover with 1/2-inch thick slices of vanilla ice cream. Spread the remaining cake layer with preserves, then place preserve side down, over the vanilla ice cream. Place cake in freezer to harden ice cream. Spread the pistachio nuts on waxed paper. Cut slices of vanilla ice cream to fit ends of cake. Lay the ice cream on the nuts and press slightly so nuts will adhere to the ice cream. Press the ice cream quickly against the ends of the cake and return to the freezer. Just before serving, spoon the chantilly cream into an icing bag with a No. 4 (large) star tube. Pipe rosettes over the top as shown in our illustration. Drizzle additional peach preserves over top of chantilly cream, if desired. At the table, cut into slices to serve.

mastering
dessert soufflés

Basically, a soufflé, whether an entrée or a dessert, is made by incorporating stiffly beaten egg whites into a mixture of milk, flour, egg yolks and flavorings. The soufflé mixture is then poured into a baking dish or mold and baked until it puffs and browns on top.

The success of a soufflé depends largely on how stiffly the egg whites have been beaten and how lightly they have been folded into the other ingredients. The air bubbles incorporated into the egg whites expand as the soufflé is cooked and force it up into a puff. If the egg whites have been beaten correctly, they rise to several times their original volume and when lifted with the wires of a whisk, they stand in upright peaks. As we mentioned earlier, on page 5, if the egg whites contain any trace of egg yolk, or if the utensils with which they're beaten are the least bit moist or greasy, the egg whites will not increase their volume properly. In addition, it's very important that the egg whites be at room temperature.

BEATING METHODS

Hand beating is the classic method for obtaining perfectly beaten egg whites and is the one preferred by most serious cooks. Use a bowl of unlined copper if possible; the slight acidity of the copper helps to stabilize the beaten egg whites and prevents them from turning granular or "weeping." If you don't have a copper bowl, use one of stainless steel, glass, or pottery; never use aluminum, as it turns the egg whites grey. Egg whites actually increase faster and higher when beaten by hand with a large wire whisk than with an electric mixer. The whisk measures about 3 inches across and is larger than the beaters of an electric mixer. Thus, the whisk keeps all the egg whites in motion at the same time which results in faster beating, not to mention the superior texture of hand beaten egg whites.

If using the hand beating method, start by beating the whites for about twenty seconds until they are foamy. Increase the beating speed, trying to incorporate as much air into the whites as possible. When the whites form stiff peaks they are ready.

If using an electric mixer, start beating at low speed for about a minute until the whites become foamy, then slowly increase the speed to high and tilt the bowl to circulate the beater around the sides and up from the bottom of the bowl. This helps get more air into the whites. When stiff peaks form, they are ready to fold into the other soufflé ingredients.

Folding the stiffly beaten egg whites into the soufflé mixture must be done carefully so as to retain as much volume as possible. Using a rubber spatula or wire whisk, stir a spoonful of the egg whites into the other mixture to lighten it. Then gently fold in the rest of the whites, cutting down from the center of the mixture to the bottom of the bowl, then draw up against the side of the bowl to the center of the mixture and down again. Continue until all the egg whites are incorporated into the other ingredients. This procedure should not take more than a minute at the most. If you spend too much time on the folding process, the air bubbles in the egg whites tend to break down and all your care in producing perfectly beaten egg whites will have been for nothing. Instead of a high, light, velvety-textured soufflé, you'll have a very tasty baked pudding, which is not what was originally intended.

Pour the mixture into a well-greased porcelain mold, (preferably one that is made for soufflés) or into what the French call a *Charlotte mold*. Place the soufflé on the middle rack in a preheated oven. Do not be tempted to open the oven door to peek during the baking period or the cold draft caused by opening the oven door might cause the soufflé to fall. The soufflé will rise several inches over the rim of the baking mold by the end of the cooking time and will be golden brown on top. It is cooked when a toothpick stuck into the center of the soufflé comes out clean. A completely cooked soufflé will not fall for about five minutes if it is left in a warm oven till served. After five minutes, however, you must serve it immediately for it to be at the peak of perfection.

Do not be distressed if the soufflé begins to deflate as it is served. This is not an unusual occurrence . . . and the flavor and texture will still be lovely.

This section begins with a simple, BASIC soufflé recipe and, building on BASICS, graduates on to more elaborate soufflés.

basic four-egg soufflé

BASIC FOUR-EGG SOUFFLÉ

4 eggs, separated
4 tbsp. sugar
1 tsp. vanilla extract

Beat the egg yolks, sugar and vanilla together in a small mixing bowl, using an electric mixer, until creamy and very thick. Beat the egg whites in a large mixing bowl, using an electric mixer or a wire whisk, until dry and stiff peaks form. Fold the egg yolk mixture into the egg whites carefully with a wire whisk or rubber spatula. Pour into a well-buttered 6-inch soufflé dish; smooth the top, then dome the soufflé mixture slightly in the center. Bake in a preheated 425-degree oven on 1 shelf

A beautiful, fluffy soufflé — its elegance is in its plainness and simplicity. You'll need no elaborate equipment or hours of free time to create this delicious dessert, for this is the quickest and most basic soufflé of them all. Just dust the top with confectioners' sugar and serve it with pride.

above center for 13 minutes. Sprinkle top generously with confectioners' sugar, if desired. Serve immediately. May be served with Basic Vanilla Sauce *(Sauces, pg. 6)* or other dessert sauces. This will make from 4 to 6 servings.

VANILLA SOUFFLÉ

2 c. milk
¹/₂ c. sugar
¹/₂ vanilla pod or 1 tsp. vanilla extract
¹/₄ c. butter
¹/₃ c. all-purpose flour
6 egg whites, stiffly beaten

Combine milk, sugar and the vanilla pod in a small heavy saucepan and bring to a boil. Remove from heat and let stand for 30 minutes. Remove the vanilla pod; dry and store for future use. If using vanilla extract, add after scalding milk. Return the milk to a boil, then remove from heat. Melt the butter in a double boiler over medium heat. Stir in the flour to make a smooth paste, using a wooden spoon. Add the milk gradually, stirring constantly; cook until thickened. Pour the thickened mixture into a large mixing bowl. Cool slightly. Fold in ¹/₄ of the egg whites thoroughly, using a wire whisk. Add the remaining egg whites; fold in thoroughly. Pour into a well-buttered 6 or 7-inch soufflé dish; smooth the top, then dome the mixture slightly in the center. Bake in a preheated 425-degree oven on 1 shelf above center for about 25 minutes or a little longer for a drier soufflé. Serve immediately. This will make about 4 servings.

la soufflé

...delicious sweet soufflé will rise
...ur oven to a fluffy delicate
...everal times its original height.
...an bake it in a mold or in a
...seven-inch soufflé dish as
...n here. Be sure to serve it
...diately after removing from the
...as with other soufflés.

GRAND MARNIER SOUFFLÉ

12 sm. macaroons
6 tbsp. Grand Marnier liqueur
½ c. milk
1 1-in. piece of vanilla pod or 1 tsp. vanilla extract
¼ c. butter
⅓ c. all-purpose flour
½ c. vanilla sugar *(Desserts, pg. 2)*
1¼ c. half and half cream
3 egg yolks, lightly beaten
6 egg whites, stiffly beaten
½ c. whipping cream
1 tbsp. confectioners' sugar

Arrange the macaroons in a shallow dish and sprinkle with 4 tablespoons Grand Marnier. Let soak for 10 minutes or until soft. Remove with spatula and spread over bottom of buttered and lightly sugared 6 or 7-inch soufflé dish. Scald the milk with the vanilla pod, then remove from heat. Remove the vanilla pod, dry and store for future use. If using vanilla extract, add after scalding the milk. Melt the butter in the top of a double boiler. Stir in the flour to make a smooth paste. Add the scalded milk and vanilla sugar alternately, stirring constantly to keep a smooth paste. Pour in the half and half gradually, stirring constantly until smooth and creamy. Remove from heat. Pour about ¼ of the hot mixture slowly into the egg yolks, stirring constantly. Stir egg yolks into the hot mixture. Add 1 tablespoon Grand Marnier, mixing well. Cool mixture. Fold in ¼ of the egg whites thoroughly, using a wire whisk. Add the remaining egg whites and fold in thoroughly but carefully. Pour over the macaroons in the soufflé dish. Bake in preheated 425-degree oven for 25 to 30 minutes or until soufflé has puffed and browned. While the soufflé is baking, whip the cream with the confectioners' sugar until soft peaks form. Beat in the remaining 1 tablespoon Grand Marnier. Remove the soufflé from the oven and serve immediately with a dollop of whipped cream. Each serving may be sprinkled with confectioners' sugar, if desired. This will make about 6 servings.

CRYSTALLIZED FRUIT SOUFFLÉ

¼ c. diced crystallized mixed fruit
2 tbsp. brandy
1 recipe Vanilla Soufflé mixture *(pg. 47)*
2 c. half and half cream

Combine fruit and brandy in a small bowl; let stand for at least 30 minutes. Prepare the soufflé mixture using half and half cream in place of the milk. Sprinkle the fruit mixture over the soufflé mixture and fold in carefully, using a rubber spatula. Turn into a buttered 1½-quart baking dish. Bake in a preheated 425-degree oven on 1 shelf above center for 18 minutes. Sprinkle with additional diced mixed fruit if desired, then serve immediately. This will make 4 to 6 servings.

crystallized fruit soufflé

Why not serve a dessert soufflé for your next special occasion? A festive dessert, perfect for holiday entertaining, this Crystallized Fruit Soufflé is a variation of the Vanilla Soufflé, page 47. The gaily colored candied fruits and the silver leaves used for garnish make this soufflé picture-pretty.

cooking with chocolate

Chocolate is probably the most popular flavor of all. There are several different types of chocolate which are used in cooking. All of them are derived from the evergreen trees of the genus *Theobroma*, "Food of the Gods," although they are more commonly referred to as cacao trees. The cacao beans produced by these trees are hulled and from the hulled beans or "nibs" a chocolate liquor is extracted. The liquor is then molded into solid squares and, at this point, the squares are ready to be processed into different types of chocolate. Some of the chocolate squares have part of their cocoa butter content removed. They are then pulverized into a powder which is the cocoa we use to make hot chocolate. The extracted cocoa butter is then added to other squares of chocolate, the result being the bitter chocolate we know as unsweetened cooking chocolate.

Bitter Chocolate is used for many cooking and baking purposes; it is sold in packages of eight 1-ounce squares. This type of chocolate is also available in semi-liquid form which obliviates the need to melt the chocolate before using in a recipe. The semi-liquid is sold in 1-ounce packets.

Cocoa, a chocolate powder which can be sifted, is sold in several varieties: sweetened, unsweetened and Dutch Process Cocoa, the latter having a stronger chocolate flavor. All of these types of cocoa are used in beverages and baking.

Sweet Chocolate is very good to eat as well as to use in dessert and candy recipes. It is made from chocolate liquor with sugar and extra cocoa butter added.

Semisweet Chocolate, manufactured like sweet chocolate, has a stronger chocolate flavor. It is sold in 1-ounce squares and 8-ounce packages of chocolate chips.

Milk chocolate is most frequently sold as "eating chocolate" and is similar to semisweet chocolate but has milk or cream added. Whichever you use, remember that it is best not to substitute one type of chocolate for another. Always use the type of chocolate called for in that particular recipe.

Since chocolate scorches easily, it is best to melt it in a double boiler, which takes only ten to twelve minutes. In many recipes the chocolate can be melted in milk, butter or water over very low direct heat while stirring constantly. Another method of melting is to place the un-wrapped squares or chips in a small saucepan in a warm oven until they are melted.

Chocolate should be stored in a cool, dry place (never hotter than 78 degrees) or it may melt and lose some of its flavor. High temperatures cause it to turn grey, due to the fat content rising to the surface. If this happens, it is still perfectly usable, although its appearance is not as appealing. German's Sweet Chocolate is conditioned against heat, and, incidentally, does not derive its name from the country. It was invented in 1852 by a man named Samuel German who concocted a special blend of chocolate with sugar and cocoa butter added. He intended it to be used for candy bars but of course, it is now the most important flavoring ingredient in that famous dessert, German's Sweet Chocolate Cake.

how to melt chocolate chips

1 Pour a package of chocolate chips into an ovenproof bowl or pan. Place them in a warm oven at about 150-degrees F.

2 Leave oven door slightly open. When the chocolate chips have melted sufficiently, take them out of the oven. Softened, they will still have their original shape. Vigorously beat them until they look like the ones above.

HOW TO CUT CHOCOLATE CURLS

Pour softened chocolate chips as thinly as possible, 1/8 to 1/4 inch, onto a very cold surface. Marble is best, but if not available, ice down a kitchen counter or table. Let chocolate harden for about 2 hours or until it has lost its gloss. Hold a knife at a slight angle as shown in the picture, and pull it across the chocolate surface, using a pivot-like motion. The result will be beautiful chocolate curls which may be used to decorate cakes or other desserts.

CHOCOLATE CHIP POUND CAKE

3 c. sifted all-purpose flour
1 tsp. salt
1/4 tsp. soda
1/2 tsp. mace
1 c. butter, softened
3 c. sugar
6 eggs
1 c. sour cream
2 tbsp. brandy
1 c. chocolate chips

Prepare a 9 x 3-inch round cake pan with removable bottom by buttering and flouring bottom. Sift flour, salt, soda and mace together. Cream butter in a large mixing bowl with electric mixer until light and fluffy. Add sugar gradually, stirring constantly; beat until well combined. Add eggs, 2 at a time, beating well after each addition. Add sour cream; mix well. Add flour mixture slowly, beating constantly at low speed; blend in the brandy. Stir in chocolate chips, using a wooden spoon, then pour batter into prepared pan. Bake in a preheated 325-degree oven for 2 hours or until cake tests done. Let cool on rack for about 10 minutes, then remove from pan to cool completely. Place on serving dish in upright position. Top may crack slightly. Garnish with chocolate curls as shown in illustration.

chocolate chip pound cake

This moist pound cake was made with whole chocolate chips. Try tying a ribbon around it and decorate the top with chocolate curls or shavings.

how to make chocolate leaves

1 Wash rose leaves. Melt chocolate chips as instructed on page 49. Pull a single leaf, upside down, over the surface of the melted chocolate.

2 Remove any extra chocolate by tapping leaf against the side of the bowl. Then place leaf, chocolate side up, on a cookie sheet and place in refrigerator to harden.

3 When the chocolate has chilled and hardened, just peel off the leaves. You'll have perfect chocolate leaves with the veins from the real leaf imprinted in the chocolate.

MOCHA BUTTER CREAM

1 c. butter, softened
6 c. sifted confectioners' sugar
3 egg yolks
¼ c. Basic Coffee Syrup *(pg. 36)*
2 sq. semisweet chocolate, melted

Cream the butter in a large mixing bowl with electric mixer until light and fluffy. Add half the sugar and beat until smooth. Add egg yolks and blend well, then mix in the remaining confectioners' sugar. Add the coffee syrup and chocolate and beat until well combined and fluffy. This will make enough frosting to fill, frost and decorate a 2-layer, 9-inch cake.

CHOCOLATE GÂTEAU

3 c. sifted all-purpose flour
1½ tsp. soda
¾ tsp. salt
2¼ c. sugar
¾ c. butter
1½ tsp. vanilla extract
3 eggs
3 sq. unsweetened chocolate, melted
1½ c. ice water
1 recipe Mocha Butter Cream *(pg. 51)*
Chocolate Leaves *(pg. 51)*

Butter and flour the bottoms of two 9-inch square cake pans. Sift the flour, soda and salt together. Cream the sugar, butter and vanilla together in a large mixing bowl. Add eggs, then beat until light and fluffy. Stir in the chocolate. Add the flour mixture and ice water alternately, beating after each addition until smooth. Pour into prepared pans. Bake in a preheated 350-degree oven for 35 to 40 minutes or until cake tests done. Remove from oven and let cool for 10 minutes. Remove from pans and cool completely on cake racks. Place 1 layer of cake on serving plate, top side down, then spread with Mocha Butter Cream. Place second layer, top side down, over frosting. Cover top and sides with a very thin layer of Mocha But-ter Cream. Spoon half the remaining frosting into an icing bag with a No. 30 star tube affixed. Pipe rosettes around sides and over top as shown in our illustration, refilling icing bag as needed. Chill icing bag in freezer for 1 or 2 minutes if frosting becomes too soft. Using the largest chocolate leaves, stick leaves into top of cake to form outer petals of flower. Continue adding graduated leaves to form flower, ending with smallest leaves in center. Let cake stand in refrigerator until frosting and flower have set.

chocolate gâteau

This is a delicious devils food cake baked in a square pan. It is then placed on a square cake board and piped with mocha butter cream in the shape of rosettes over the top and sides. Chocolate leaves are then placed in the center to form a blooming rose.

Chocolate leaves are tucked under each of the four corners of the cake. This is an elegant party dessert, and not at all difficult to create.

HOW TO DOODLE SHAPES IN CHOCOLATE

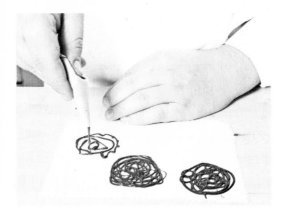

1 Make paper icing bags, (General Information, pg. 22) and fill with melted chocolate chips. Take the end of icing bag in two fingers and squeeze the chocolate through onto a piece of waxed paper, creating your own designs. Chill.

2 Lift the chilled doodles of chocolate from the waxed paper. Your hands should be cool when performing this step or the chocolate will melt. Rinsing hands in cold water will cool them sufficiently for handling the chilled doodles.

3 Next, place the doodle onto the dessert to be garnished. This one is placed into a mound of whipped cream. Doodles can be stored in airtight containers and refrigerated for several weeks.

doodling a dragonfly

The elegant dragonfly pictured on page 54 in this section is made of chocolate doodles. To create it, follow the diagram pictured, or if preferred, create your own pattern. Using a pencil, trace the outline onto a piece of waxed paper. Melt chocolate chips as directed on page 49, and beat with a wooden spoon. Next, make several paper icing bags, (General Information, pg. 22), then cut a little piece off the pointed end of each one. When the chocolate has cooled and gotten a little thicker, pour two spoonfuls into each paper icing bag. Fold the broad bottom end over several times to keep the chocolate from coming out. Turn the waxed paper over so that the dragonfly outline shows through on back. Take the chocolate-filled icing bags and doodle in and around the outlines. Doodle the chocolate in wiggles over the middle spaces and make sure that each wiggle touches the chocolate outline at some point so that the wings will look like the ones in the picture on page 54. Refrigerate the doodled dragonfly on the waxed paper until set and hardened. When the wings are hardened, peel the waxed paper off the wings. With a small table knife, fill in the two body outlines with lots of melted chocolate. Refrigerate until set; peel off the waxed paper and place dragonfly on the cake. Complete the dragonfly by adding antennaes made of fine strips of angelica and bits of glacéed cherries for the eyes.

dragonfly diagram

This diagram may be used as the outline for a dragonfly doodle. Or, if desired, create your own pattern for any size dragonfly.

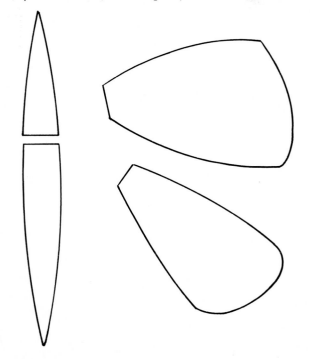

FRESH COCONUT CAKE

1 c. shortening
2 c. sugar
1 tsp. vanilla extract
3 c. sifted cake flour
3 tsp. baking powder
1 tsp. salt
½ c. milk
½ c. coconut milk
1 c. freshly grated coconut
6 egg whites, stiffly beaten

Grease and flour the bottoms of two 9-inch layer cake pans with removable bottoms. Cream the shortening and sugar together in the large mixer bowl, then add the vanilla extract. Combine the flour, baking powder and salt and sift. Add to the creamed mixture alternately with the milk and coconut milk, beating well after each addition. Stir in 1 cup coconut, then fold in the egg whites carefully but thoroughly. Turn into the prepared pans. Bake in a preheated 375-degree oven for 30 minutes or until cake tests done. Cool in pans for 10 minutes, then turn out on wire racks to cool completely.

Fresh Coconut Icing

Sugar
¼ c. coconut milk
¼ tsp. salt
½ tsp. cream of tartar
2 egg whites
1 tsp. vanilla extract
2 c. freshly grated coconut

Stir in 1 teaspoon sugar into the coconut milk, then spoon over the cake layers. Combine 1 cup sugar, salt, cream of tartar, egg whites, 3 tablespoons water and the vanilla extract in the top of a double boiler and stir until blended. Place over boiling water and cook for 7 minutes, beating constantly at high speed with an electric hand mixer. Stir in 1 cup coconut. Frost between layers and over top and side of cake. Sprinkle half the remaining coconut over top of cake, then press remaining coconut lightly around side of cake. Garnish with chocolate dragonfly.

HOW TO PREPARE FRESH COCONUT

There are 3 eyes in a coconut, 2 hard and 1 soft. Punch the soft eye with an ice pick and work it around to enlarge the hole. Place over measuring cup and drain out the milk. Break open shell and remove the meat from shell. Peel off the brown peeling and then grate the white meat.

fresh coconut cake

This Fresh Coconut Cake is decorated with doodled dragonflies. To create the twig holding the flying dragonfly, page 53, an extra doodling was added on the back. The baby dragonflies are attached with a little melted chocolate.

basic
chou pastry

Chou Pastry (which translated literally from the French, means "cabbage") is a very versatile and useful preparation which every cook should include in his or her basic repertoire. To explain the different spellings that we will use, *Choux* is the French plural of *Chou*. This pastry may be prepared very quickly, baked into the desired shapes and then frozen or refrigerated for later use. It may be baked into *choux* puffs or *éclairs* of any size, depending upon their use. Small ones may be filled with savory morsels of fish, chicken or ham to become tasty, bite-sized *canapés*. Larger ones may contain creamed poultry, meat, fish or mushrooms and be used as a hot entrée for a luncheon or light supper. In this section, there are several recipes for *chou* pastry, only one of which contains sugar. Basic *Chou* Pastry contains no sugar; however, it is used for sweet as well as savory fillings.

Chou pastry is simply a very, very thick paste made of flour, water (or milk), butter and seasonings into which whole eggs are beaten. Unlike puff and short pastry, *chou* pastry is cooked on top of the stove, allowed to cool, and then piped (through a pastry tube) or spooned onto a cookie sheet and baked. There is no need to ice surfaces or utensils, nor is it necessary to roll out the pastry with a rolling pin as part of its preparation. The eggs act as the leavening agent, causing the puffs to rise to several times their original volume during the baking time. When removed from the oven, slits may be cut into the puffs, allowing steam to escape, which helps to prevent the puffs from turning soggy. *Chou* pastry is usually baked into puffs or *éclairs* soon after it has been cooked on top of the stove. It is possible, though, to refrigerate it before baking. If this procedure is used, be sure to rub the surface of the *chou* pastry with butter and cover with waxed paper before refrigerating, to prevent a hard outer layer from forming. After removing it from the refrigerator, let the pastry come to room temperature before baking into puffs. *Choux* shells, or puffs which have been baked, freeze very nicely. Before using frozen *choux* puffs, place in a 425-degree oven for three to four minutes to thaw and crisp them.

At this point, the puffs or *éclairs* are ready to be filled with the desired mixture. The filling may be as simple as chilled whipped cream, or more elaborate, such as confectioners' custard or a savory filling. *Éclairs* are long, oval-shaped puffs, which are filled and iced.

In this section, you'll find recipes for Basic *Chou* Pastry made with cold water and Basic Sweet *Chou* Pastry made with milk. Cheese *Chou* Pastry Puffs, a savory recipe, is presented in the Appetizers section. The following pages provide imaginative uses for *chou* pastry which will help to provide new interest to your desserts.

BASIC SWEET CHOU PASTRY

¾ c. milk
2 tbsp. butter
1 tbsp. sugar
⅛ tsp. salt
¾ c. sifted all-purpose flour
3 eggs

Combine milk, butter, sugar and salt in a heavy saucepan. Cook over medium heat until the butter is melted and the sugar is dissolved, stirring constantly. Beat in the flour and eggs according to the step-by-step illustrations, *page 56*. Pipe out as desired on a lightly-greased baking sheet. Bake in a preheated 450-degree oven for 8 minutes. Reduce the oven temperature to 350 degrees and bake for 20 to 40 minutes longer, depending on the size of the puffs or *éclairs*, until dry. Cool on wire racks. Fill as desired.

BASIC CHOU PASTRY

1 c. water
½ c. butter
1 c. sifted all-purpose flour
⅛ tsp. salt
4 eggs

1 Combine water and butter in a heavy saucepan and place over medium heat. Cook until butter is melted and water comes to a boil.

2 Add all the flour and salt.

3 Stir vigorously with a wooden spoon until mixture is smooth and leaves side of pan, forming a ball.

4 Turn off heat and add first egg. Beat until well mixed.

5 Continue adding eggs, one at a time, beating well after the addition of each egg.

6 Beat until smooth. Cover lightly and let stand until cool. Spoon pastry into icing bag with a 1-inch plain piping tube attached and pipe into desired shapes on a lightly-greased baking sheet. Do not place too close together. Bake in a pre-heated 450-degree oven on shelf above center for 8 minutes. Reduce oven temperature to 350 degrees and bake for 20 to 40 minutes longer, depending on size of puffs, until dry and browned. Remove from baking sheet immediately and let cool on racks. Fill as desired. You may use an electric mixer to beat in eggs.

how to pipe
éclairs and cream puffs

For extra special occasions and dinners, it's important to serve an elegant dessert as the final touch. Why not prepare a compote piled high with luscious cream puffs? Or how about chocolate covered *éclairs* filled with coffee-flavored custard? The following pages contain recipes for these and other delightful desserts. They're not difficult and are sure to please your family and friends.

Éclairs and cream puffs are made with the same *chou* pastry. The only difference between the two is the shape; cream puffs are round, *éclairs* are long and slender.

After preparing *chou* pastry, the *éclairs* and cream puffs are piped through an icing or pastry bag onto a greased cookie sheet. The *éclairs* are piped in the shape of fingers, the cream puffs in the shape of small mounds. To make miniature *éclairs* and puffs, use a 1/4-inch tube; medium-sized *éclairs* and puffs require a 1/2-inch tube and the large ones will take a 1-inch tube. It is important to remember that it takes a good deal of practice to make puffs and *éclairs* uniform in size. If your first attempt to make these pastries results in a batch of varied sizes, don't be disappointed — they'll taste fine, and with practice, you'll be producing *éclairs* and puffs that look as though they were made by a master chef.

The length of baking time for *éclairs* and puffs depends on their size — about 25 minutes for small ones and as long as 50 minutes for the larger sizes. Care must be taken to bake them until they are browned and *completely* done; if the *éclairs* and puffs are taken from the oven before thoroughly cooked, they will fall exactly the way an undercooked soufflé falls. And, once they have fallen, they will not rise even if placed back into the oven immediately. If not certain whether the puffs are done, remove one puff from the oven, cut a slit in the side and let it cool for a minute or two. Then open it to test for doneness. The inside should be soft, but not doughy.

As soon as the *éclairs* and puffs have been removed from the oven, make a slit in one side of each, then allow to cool. Using an icing bag, pipe in desired filling. There are many possibilities for fillings — either use the suggested fillings in this section or create your own culinary masterpiece. You can even make *éclairs* or cream puffs for a diabetic member of the family, simply by using the Basic *Chou* Pastry recipe (which contains no sugar) and filling with your favorite dietary pudding.

Why not add a special touch to your next tea or wedding reception by serving Iced Miniature Cream Puffs and *Éclairs*? You'll be glad you did and so will your friends!

1 *Éclairs* are piped onto an oiled baking sheet. An ordinary butter knife, dipped in cold water, is used to smooth the first end of the *éclair* for a neat, uniform shape. If preferred, use a teaspoon instead of a pastry bag to spoon out *éclairs* or puffs.

2 The *éclair* is then pulled down to the required length, and the knife is again dipped into the cold water and used to cut off the opposite end of the *éclair*. The *éclairs* are then ready to be baked.

3 For puffs, the procedure is the same, except that on large and medium-sized puffs, more pressure is applied. The large puffs shown are made with a 1″ plain round tube, medium puffs take a 1/2″ tube and miniature puffs a 1/4″ tube. Hold the tube vertically above the baking sheet and squeeze the pastry bag until the desired size puff is pressed out, then cut off the tip with a knife dipped in cold water.

old-fashioned cream puffs

OLD-FASHIONED CREAM PUFFS

1 c. water
½ c. butter
1¼ c. sifted all-purpose flour
¼ tsp. salt
5 eggs
1 egg white
4 c. whipped cream
Sifted confectioners' sugar

Prepare the *chou* pastry according to the step-by-step illustrations, *page 56,* adding the egg white last. Cool, then pipe out onto a lightly greased baking sheet in large puffs. Bake in a preheated 450-degree oven for 8 minutes. Reduce the oven temperature to 350 degrees and bake for 45 minutes longer or until dry. Let cool thoroughly on wire racks. Make a small hole in the side of each puff with the tip of small knife. Pipe whipped cream into each puff. Dust generously with confectioners' sugar. This will make about 2 dozen puffs.

old-fashioned cream puffs

These pale golden, light cream puffs are easy to make and wonderful to eat. They are prepared with an exceptionally good, old-fashioned chou pastry and filled with whipped cream, then heavily dusted with confectioners' sugar. The fact that these Old-Fashioned Cream Puffs require only a little effort in their preparation certainly isn't reflected in the end result, as you can see in the illustration.

profiteroles
in chocolate sauce

Generally speaking, profiteroles are really just miniature cream puffs. They are made from Basic *Chou* Pastry or Basic Sweet *Chou* Pastry and baked into plain little puffs. There is an endless variety of uses for these tiny puffs. For hot or cold *hors d'oeuvres*, they may be stuffed with various kinds of *pâté*, meat or seafood salad, cheese mixtures, hot creamed meat or seafood, or anything else your imagination might suggest to you. For desserts they may be filled with pudding, ice cream, whipped cream, Chantilly cream, sweet custard, or even jam — anything you and your family would prefer.

Use an icing or pastry bag with a 1/2-inch tube and pipe 1½-inch puffs onto a lightly greased baking sheet. When baked, the puffs will expand to about the size of large eggs. They are then ready for use in the recipe.

The recipe for profiteroles, which we are suggesting, is a popular one, especially in Europe: a simple but classic presentation of tiny *choux* puffs heaped in a bowl, covered with chocolate sauce and served, rather like a cake. Some very fine restaurants fill each one with sweet custard before covering with chocolate sauce, but an easier approach, and an effective one, is simply fill with sweetened whipped cream or vanilla ice cream.

PROFITEROLES IN CHOCOLATE SAUCE

1 recipe Basic Sweet Chou Pastry *(pg. 55)*
2 c. sweetened whipped cream
1 recipe Basic Chocolate Sauce *(Sauces, pg. 16)*

Prepare and pipe out the *chou* pastry in 1½-inch puffs, then bake according to recipe directions. Let cool on wire racks. Pipe the whipped cream into the puffs by making a hole in the bottom of each puff using a plain tube. Place filled puffs in a serving bowl. Pour chocolate sauce over all just before serving. May be filled with vanilla ice cream if desired. This will make about 18 puffs.

profiteroles in chocolate sauce

This is one of the most delicious ways to serve choux puffs. Bake them in small puffs, fill with delicate whipped cream, then heap them in a bowl and cover with Basic Chocolate Sauce (Sauces, pg. 16). A variation of this method calls for filling the puffs with vanilla ice cream before covering with the chocolate sauce.

CHOCOLATE-FILLED ÉCLAIRS

1 recipe Basic Chou Pastry *(pg. 56)*
1⅓ c. chocolate chips, melted
1 recipe Basic Confectioners' Custard *(pg. 19)*
1 c. stiffly whipped cream
⅓ c. butter

Prepare the *chou* pastry and pipe out into *éclairs*, using a 1-inch plain piping tube, as shown in the step-by-step illustrations on *page 57*. Bake as directed for about 40 minutes and let cool. Stir 2 tablespoons melted chocolate chips into the hot confectioners' custard, then cool custard. Fold whipped cream into the cooled custard. Split the *éclairs* on one side and fill with the custard mixture. Mix the butter with the remaining chocolate chips and place over low heat, stirring constantly, until melted. Spread frosting over *éclairs* and chill until ready to serve. This will make 12 to 16 *éclairs*.

COFFEE-FILLED ÉCLAIRS

1 recipe Basic Chou Pastry *(pg. 56)*
4 tbsp. Basic Coffee Syrup *(pg. 36)*
⅛ tsp. salt
1 recipe Basic Confectioners' Custard *(pg. 19)*
2½ c. sifted confectioners' sugar

Prepare the *chou* pastry and pipe out into *éclairs*, using a 1-inch plain piping tube, as shown in the step-by-step illustrations on *page 57*. Bake as directed for about 40 minutes and let cool. Stir salt and 2 tablespoons coffee syrup into the cooled confectioners' custard. Split the *éclairs* on one side and fill with the custard mixture. For frosting, mix remaining coffee syrup into the confectioners' sugar, adding enough warm water, several drops at a time, to make of spreading consistency. Spread frosting over *éclairs* and chill until ready to serve. This makes 12 to 16 *éclairs*.

éclair pyramid

The wise hostess knows that a good way to make a special dinner party a memorable one is to serve a dramatic and elegant dessert. An excellent choice is an *Éclair Pyramid* which combines the two preceeding recipes — Chocolate-Filled *Éclairs* and Coffee-Filled *Éclairs*. This dessert is not quickly prepared, so allow extra time in the cooking schedule. However, making the pyramid is simply a matter of assembling the two kinds of *éclairs*. This may be done several hours before serving.

When preparing the component parts of the *Éclair Pyramid*, remember that you may make the pyramid any size desired, large or small. Take into consideration the size dish on which the pyramid is to be served and work from there. A large pyramid will require no more than eight *éclairs* (about six inches long) and two cream puffs, one larger than the other. If you have more *éclairs* than needed for the pyramid, these extras may be frozen unfilled, for later use, or filled and refrigerated.

The *Éclair Pyramid* is assembled by placing an ice cream cone in the center of a base of Basic Sweet Short Pastry. Arrange filled, iced *eclairs* around the cone with the ends perpendicular to the edge of the pastry base (see illustration). Next, place a chocolate cream puff on top of the cone and on top of that, a smaller one with coffee icing. Garnish the finished pyramid with sweetened whipped cream and *voila* — a beautiful dessert worthy of praise.

ÉCLAIR PYRAMID

½ recipe Basic Sweet Short Pastry *(pg. 12)*
½ recipe Basic Chocolate Sauce *(Sauces, pg. 16)*
1 ice cream cone
4 Chocolate-Filled Éclairs, chilled
4 Coffee-Filled Éclairs, chilled
1 lg. chocolate-filled cream puff, chilled
1 sm. coffee-filled cream puff, chilled
2 c. whipped cream

Roll out the pastry on a lightly floured board to 8½ inches in diameter. Fit into an 8-inch flan pan and press around bottom edge to allow pastry to extend half way up side of pan. Trim evenly and prick the bottom generously with a fork. Place on baking sheet. Bake in a preheated 400-degree oven for 8 minutes. Reduce the oven temperature to 350 degrees and bake for 20 minutes longer or until lightly browned. Let cool. Remove pyramid base carefully from pan and place on serving plate. Spread chocolate sauce over bottom of base. Place ice cream cone in center of base and frost with any remaining sauce. Arrange the *éclairs* around the cone as shown in the illustration. Place the chocolate cream puff on top of the cone, then place the coffee cream puff on top. Pipe the whipped cream between the *éclairs* with a No. 47 ribbon tube. Pipe rosettes around base and cream puffs with a No. 27 star tube. Chill until ready to serve. Will keep for several hours. You may spread any leftover coffee filling over chocolate sauce on pyramid base.

éclair pyramid

This elegantly dramatic chou pastry pyramid originated in Paris. Classically called Gâteau Réligeuse, it is created by arranging filled puffs and éclairs on a base of Basic Sweet Short Pastry, page 12, and garnishing with rosettes of whipped cream. The éclairs are iced alternately with coffee and chocolate frosting. To complete this aristocratic dessert, two small cream puffs are placed on top as the crowning effect.

iced miniature cream puffs and éclairs

ICED MINIATURE CREAM PUFFS AND ÉCLAIRS

1 recipe Basic Chou Pastry *(pg. 56)*
1 recipe Basic Confectioners' Custard *(pg. 19)*
1 recipe Basic Confectioners' Icing *(pg. 8)*
1 recipe Basic Butter Cream No. 1 *(pg. 7)*

Prepare pastry according to the step-by-step illustrations, *page 56*, and pipe out miniature cream puffs and *éclairs* using a small, plain, ¼-inch tube. Bake in a preheated 450-degree oven for 5 minutes. Reduce the oven temperature to 350 degrees and bake for 15 minutes or until dry and browned. Cool thoroughly. Pipe the confectioners' custard into the miniature puffs and *éclairs*. Divide the icing into small bowls and color each one with food coloring as desired. Spread carefully over each puff and *éclair*, then chill until icing has hardened. Divide the butter cream into small bowls and color each one with food coloring as desired. Decorate the puffs and *éclairs* with tiny dots, rosettes and wavy lines, using small paper icing bags *(General Information, pg. 22)*.

iced miniature cream puffs and *éclairs*

These tiny, delicate, pastel-colored cream puffs and éclairs would be very appropriate to serve at a wedding reception, an afternoon tea, or similar type of gathering — if served for a baby shower, they could be iced in pink and blue. Both the éclairs and puffs are filled with Basic Confectioners' Custard, page 19, covered with Basic Confectioners' Icing and decorated with tinted butter cream.

chantilly cream puffs

If you are searching for the perfect dessert to serve at a club meeting or during an afternoon of bridge, Chantilly Cream Puffs would be an elegant choice. They will turn any meal — brunch to Sunday evening supper for example — into a truly festive occasion.

Chantilly Cream Puffs are a richer and more elaborate version of Old-Fashioned Cream Puffs, page 58. They are 3-inch rings of *chou* pastry (3-inch outside diameter) which are baked, cooled and generously filled with Basic Chantilly Cream, page 19. The same filling is used to garnish the tops. Finally, they are topped with toasted almonds and dusted with confectioners' sugar.

For those who are diet-conscious, these cream puffs could be filled with a non-dairy dessert topping as a substitute for Basic Chantilly Cream; just by using a little ingenuity, even those in your family who are "calorie-counters" can enjoy these luscious cream puffs!

This recipe takes very little time to prepare for your family but it is also creative and elegant enough for company fare.

CHANTILLY CREAM PUFFS

1 recipe Basic Sweet Chou Pastry *(pg. 55)*
1 recipe Basic Chantilly Cream *(pg. 19)*
1 c. toasted sliced almonds
Sifted confectioners' sugar

Prepare the *chou* pastry and pipe out into 3-inch circles on a lightly greased baking sheet, using a ½ inch, plain tube. Bake in a preheated 450-degree oven for 5 minutes. Reduce the oven temperature to 350 degrees and bake for 12 to 15 minutes longer. Cool on wire rack. Split in half and fill bottom halves with Chantilly cream. Replace tops and pipe on remaining Chantilly cream. Sprinkle with almonds and dust with confectioners' sugar. This makes about 10 to 12 rings.

chantilly cream puffs

A delightful variation, these Chantilly Cream Puffs are rings of Basic Sweet Chou Pastry generously filled and topped with Basic Chantilly Cream. The toasted almonds on the tops provide eye appeal as well as flavor.

caramel-glazed cream puffs

caramel-glazed cream puffs

*The classic name of this cream puff dessert is
Gâteau St. Honoré. The base is made of Basic
Sweet Short Pastry, page 12. Here it is prepared
with two rings of caramel-glazed, cream-filled puffs
piled high for a most dramatic effect. Whipped
cream rosettes provide an elegant garnish.*

CARAMEL-GLAZED CREAM PUFFS

½ recipe Basic Sweet Short Pastry *(pg. 12)*
1 recipe Basic Chou Pastry *(pg. 56)*
1 recipe Caramel Glaze (Sauces, pg. 16)
3 recipes Basic Chantilly Cream *(pg. 19)*

Roll out pastry on a lightly floured board to 8
inches in diameter and ½ inch thick. Place on a
baking sheet. Bake in a preheated 400-degree oven
for 8 minutes. Reduce oven temperature to 350
degrees and bake for 20 minutes longer or until
golden. Let cool thoroughly, then place the pastry
base on serving dish. Prepare and bake medium-
sized cream puffs according to the step-by-step
illustrations, *page 57.* Prepare the Caramel Glaze
while the puffs are cooling. Dip the tops of the
puffs into the hot glaze, holding the puffs securely
with tongs. Place on foil to cool, being careful not
to touch the hot glaze. Drizzle glaze quickly over
the pastry base. Make a small hole in the side of
each cooled puff with the tip of a small knife. Pipe
Chantilly cream into each puff. Stack the puffs on
the pastry base as shown in the illustration.
Decorate with large piped rosettes of Chantilly
cream. This dessert will keep well for about 1 hour
without refrigeration.

The Creative Homemaker's Academy © MCMLXXIII
Selected Illustrations © B.P.C. Publishing Limited MCMLXX

how to make vol-au-vent shells

These "light as the wind" patty shells are made by first cutting out circles of puff pastry, page 22, with a fluted or plain pastry cutter. Then, half of the circles are stamped out in the center with a smaller cutter, as if you were making doughnuts. Step-by-step illustrations and instructions tell you how to place the rings on top of the circles and pinch both together. After the *vol-au-vents* are baked, the centers will pull right out, leaving a lovely shell to contain your choice of fillings. The most important thing to remember about *vol-au-vents* is that they *are puff pastry*, so avoid handling them (and thus warming them) as much as possible. However, when you are stamping out the circles, dip the cutter in hot water each time for smoother cutting, and also place the shells on a wet baking sheet for cooking.

The completed *vol-au-vents* may have savory fillings, since the pastry itself contains no sugar. However, they are delicious when filled with Basic Confectioners' Custard, page 19, frozen strawberries or raspberries and a topping of Basic Chantilly Cream, page 19. Other dessert ideas for fillings include the fruit mixtures used for tartlets, page 20, or ice cream topped with a dessert sauce.

HOW TO MAKE VOL-AU-VENTS

Prepare 1 recipe Basic Puff Pastry, page 22.

1 Roll out puff pastry (for 6th or final roll) to about ½ inch thick. Dip a 3-inch pastry cutter into very hot water and shake off the excess.

2 Cut all the pastry into 3-inch rounds, cutting close to avoid wasting pastry. Place half the rounds, topside down, on a wet baking sheet for bases.

3 Cut centers from the remaining rounds with a 2¼-inch cutter, as for doughnuts, and lift out centers with the tip of a knife making rings.

(Continued on next page)

4 Make an indentation about ½ way through each base on baking sheet with a 2¼-inch cutter, then using finger, wet around outside of indentation with cold water. Place rings, topside down, over bases. Pinch base and ring together, holding inner edge in place with finger and smoothing outer seam with wet finger. Place cutout centers inside the rings.

5 Bake in preheated 425-degree oven, one shelf above center, for 10 minutes. Reduce temperature to 350 degrees and bake for 20 minutes or until golden brown. Remove from oven and place on cooling rack. Cut around and lift out centers carefully with pointed knife. Lift out any doughy centers leaving hollow shell as shown. This makes about 10 *vol-au-vents*.

RASPBERRY VOL-AU-VENTS

2 c. fresh or 1 10-oz. package frozen raspberries
1 recipe Basic Confectioners' Custard (pg. 19)
8 vol-au-vent shells
1 recipe Basic Chantilly Cream (pg. 19)

Wash and drain the fresh raspberries or thaw and drain the frozen raspberries. Spoon confectioners' custard into the shells, then top with the raspberries. Place a dollop of Chantilly cream over the raspberries. Serve immediately.

> **NOTE**
>
> Miniature *vol-au-vent* shells are called *petits bouchées,* or literally "small mouthfuls." They are made exactly like the larger shells except that smaller cutters are used. These may be shaped either round or oval, fluted or plain.

bouchée shells

1 Roll out pastry and cut as for *vol-au-vents* using a 2¼-inch cutter. Cut centers from half the rounds with a 1½-inch cutter. Assemble and bake following the same procedure as for *vol-au-vents*.

2 Here are three sizes of *bouchées*, oval and round, baked and hollowed out for sweet or savory fillings.

presenting
ice creams and ices

According to legend, the Italians developed "iced cream" in the 14th century. Marco Polo brought tales from the Orient of slant-eyed men sitting on embroidered cushions eating dishes of ice flavored with exotic fruits. Later, "iced cream" was introduced to France by the Florentine chefs of Catherine de Médici. For the wedding festivities of her marriage to Henry II of France, a different flavor of ice cream was served each day. However, the Parisian public did not receive the new delicacy until 1660 when a Sicilian, Francisco Procopio, opened an ice cream shop. Ice cream was quickly the rage of Paris.

The simplest ices are still made from sugar, water and fruit juice. However, the original idea has been expanded and modified to include rich, custard-based ice creams with a seemingly endless variety of presentations.

TYPES OF ICE CREAM

As we said before, there are three basic types of ice cream, all of which depend on milk for body. French ice cream is a rich mixture based on an egg yolk custard. American ice cream is less rich but also uses a custard base. Philadelphia ice cream is even lighter because it contains no eggs. Sherbets contain some milk but a larger proportion of fruit juices. They may also contain egg whites or gelatin.

The ingredients combined for making ice cream must be chosen with regard to freezing characteristics, texture and flavor. The basic ingredients are milk, eggs, sugar, fruits or other flavorings. Milk or cream gives the mixture body, flavor and helps prevent crystallization; eggs act as a binder and thickener. Sugar provides sweetness and also helps prevent crystallization, although if too much is used, it retards freezing. In commercial ice cream, gelatin is sometimes used as a stabilizer. Flavorings have no effect on the freezing process. Cornstarch and flour are sometimes used to hold the ice crystals apart. They act as stabilizers to promote a smooth texture.

PREPARING ICE CREAM

Whole milk should always be scalded, that is, heated to just below the simmering point to reduce the water content and concentrate the protein. Evaporated or condensed milk needs no preparation. Whipping cream should be beaten until it is fluffy but not stiff; otherwise, it will not combine well. Since whipped cream as well as egg whites are added to incorporate air into ice cream and ices, fold them into the other ingredients gently. After preparing the ingredients for ice cream, be sure to chill any hot mixtures before the final mixing. In other words, do not mix hot custard with whipped cream or fruit.

For instructions on how to freeze ice cream, see General Information, page 34.

BASIC VANILLA ICE CREAM

2 recipes Basic Confectioners' Custard (pg. 19)
1/8 tsp. salt
1/2 tsp. vanilla extract
1 pt. whipping cream
4 tbsp. sugar

Prepare confectioners' custard in a large saucepan. Add salt and vanilla; mix well. Chill custard. Pour cream into a large bowl. Whip cream with an electric mixer until soft peaks form. Add sugar to cream, 1 tablespoon at a time, beating until sugar is blended. Add several mixing spoons of whipped cream to the chilled confectioners' custard and fold in to lighten mixture. Then pour custard mixture into whipped cream and fold until well blended. Pour mixture into a 1 1/2-quart ice cream mold or plastic container lined with plastic wrap. Wrap with 2 layers of aluminum foil and place top of container over the foil. Make sure the cream mixture is thoroughly covered and that the top is on securely. Place container in freezer and freeze until firm. May be frozen in an electric or manual ice cream maker if desired. (General Information, page 34). This makes 8 to 10 servings.

chocolate ice cream bombe

Basic Chocolate Ice Cream was placed in a bombe mold, page 71, turned out and decorated with rosettes of whipped cream and triangles of chocolate.

BASIC CHOCOLATE ICE CREAM

3 1/2 c. chocolate chips
2/3 c. water
5 c. milk
1 1/2 c. sugar
8 egg yolks
2 tsp. vanilla extract
1 pt. whipping cream

This ice cream is made in an ice cream maker. Combine 2 cups chocolate chips and water in small saucepan. Place over low heat, stirring until chips are melted. Heat milk, to just below boiling, in top of 2 1/2-quart double boiler over direct heat. Remove from heat and stir in melted chocolate. Combine 1 1/4 cups of sugar and egg yolks in large mixer bowl. Beat with electric mixer on low speed until mixture is pale yellow and fluffy. Add chocolate milk mixture gradually to sugar mixture, beating until well blended. Add vanilla extract. Pour mixture back into top of double boiler and place over boiling water. Cook, stirring constantly, for about 10 minutes until mixture is thickened and smooth. Place in refrigerator or freezer until thoroughly cooled. Whip cream with electric mixer or wire whisk until soft peaks form. Add remaining 1/4 cup sugar, beating until blended. Fold cream into cooled chocolate mixture. Pour into can of an electric or manual ice cream maker. Freeze according to instructions in General Information, page 34.

TO MAKE CHOCOLATE ICE CREAM *BOMBE*
Spoon frozen ice cream into a 1 1/2 quart mold lined with plastic wrap. Cover all over with 2 layers of aluminum foil. Place in freezer until ready to decorate and serve. Melt remaining 1 1/2 cups chocolate chips, page 49. Pour melted chocolate onto a foil-lined jelly roll pan and spread smooth with pastry scraper to about 1/8 inch thickness. Place in freezer to harden. Cut small triangular shapes in chocolate with a paring knife; return to freezer for about 5 minutes. Peel off foil and break chocolate triangles apart. Place back in freezer until ready to use. Unmold frozen Chocolate Ice Cream *Bombe* onto serving dish. Place chocolate triangles around mold and pipe with rosettes of additional whipped cream as shown in illustration.

MOCHA ICE CREAM

**2 recipes Basic Confectioners' Custard
(pg. 19)**
⅛ tsp. salt
¼ c. freeze-dried coffee
1 c. chocolate chips, melted (pg. 49)
1 c. milk
1 pt. whipping cream
4 tbsp. sugar

Prepare confectioners' custard in a large double boiler. Add salt, coffee and chocolate to hot custard mixture. Blend thoroughly. Stir in milk and place custard mixture in refrigerator or freezer compartment until completely cooled. Whip cream until soft peaks form. Add sugar, a tablespoon at a time, and blend well. Fold 1 cup of whipped cream into custard mixture. Add remaining whipped cream, blending thoroughly. This makes 2 quarts of custard mixture. Pour mixture into can of ice cream maker and freeze according to instructions in General Information, page 34. An electric ice cream maker will take about 35 minutes freezing time. Ice cream may be served immediately, packed or placed in a prepared mold and kept in freezer until ready to serve.

COFFEE ICE CREAM

**2 recipes Basic Confectioners' Custard
(pg. 19)**
⅓ c. Basic Coffee Syrup (pg. 36)
⅛ tsp. salt
½ tsp. vanilla extract
1 pt. whipping cream
4 tbsp. sugar

Prepare confectioners' custard, omitting ⅓ cup of the given amount of milk and substituting ⅓ cup Basic Coffee Syrup. Add salt and vanilla. Chill custard, stirring occasionally. Whip cream until soft peaks form. Add sugar and continue whipping for several seconds. Add cream to custard and fold in thoroughly. Pour mixture into ice cube trays or mold, then cover with 2 layers of foil and freeze until slightly frozen around edges. Remove from freezer and whip with electric mixer until smooth. Repeat this process of partially freezing and whipping. Pour mixture into an oiled mold or container lined with plastic wrap. Place aluminum foil over mold, covering completely, and place container cover over foil. Place in freezer for several hours or until frozen firm. This may be made in a manual or an electric ice cream maker (General Information, pg. 34).

SOFT FRUIT ICE CREAM

**2 10-oz. packages frozen sweetened
raspberries or strawberries**
½ c. sugar
½ c. water
2 egg whites
½ pt. whipping cream

Thaw raspberries or strawberries and place in blender. Blend to a purée. Combine sugar and water in a small saucepan. Heat, without stirring, until all sugar is dissolved. Bring to a slow boil for 8 to 9 minutes. While sugar syrup is boiling, beat egg whites with electric mixer until stiff peaks form. Pour hot sugar syrup into egg whites, beating constantly until mixture holds a stiff peak. Let egg white mixture stand until cool, then fold into fruit purée in a large bowl. Whip cream until soft peaks form, then fold into puréed fruit mixture until thoroughly mixed. Pour mixture into ice cube trays or bowl, then cover with 2 layers of foil and freeze until slightly frozen around edges. Remove from freezer and whip with electric mixer until smooth. Repeat this process of partially freezing and whipping. Quickly spoon mixture into lightly oiled or lined 1½-quart mold or into a plastic carton. Cover with two layers of foil and container top, then place in freezer. Freeze until firm (about 6 hours, depending on freezer) or overnight. May be frozen in an electric or manual ice cream maker. Three to 4 cups of sweetened, fresh fruit may be substituted for the frozen fruit. This will make about 6 servings.

LIQUEURS AND SPIRITS WITH
ICE CREAM

Many people enjoy ice cream served with just the slightest hint of alcohol flavoring — about a teaspoonful is sufficient. The most popular flavorings are either liqueurs or spirits such as brandy and *eaux de vie*, terms which will be explained in detail later under Beverages. Listed below are combinations you may wish to try.

WITH . . .	SERVE . . .
Mocha	Crème de Cacao or Tia Maria with equal proportions of Brandy
Chocolate	Crème de Cacao or Tia Maria with half as much Brandy
Coffee	Brandy, Kirsch or both
Orange	Orange Curacao and/or Brandy
Pistachio	Maraschino
Almond	Crème de Noyaux
Pineapple	Kirsch
Peach	Peach Brandy
Apricot	Apricot Brandy
Strawberry	Eau de Vie des Fraises
Raspberry	Bénédictine
Loganberry	Kirsch
Chestnut	Maraschino
Black Plum	Kirsch

orange ice cream

For this beautiful presentation, Orange Ice Cream has been placed in a hollowed-out orange, topped with Basic Meringues mixture, page 10, then lightly browned in a preheated broiler . . . an elegant but easy way to serve ice cream.

ORANGE ICE CREAM

8 lg. thick-skinned oranges
1¼ c. water
½ c. sugar
2½ tsp. grated orange rind
1 egg yolk
6 tbsp. frozen orange juice concentrate, thawed
1½ c. whipping cream
½ recipe Basic Meringues mixture *(pg. 10)*

Cut off about ⅓ of each orange at the top. Remove all fruit pulp and juice. Set orange cups aside. Place water, ⅓ cup sugar and orange rind in saucepan over medium heat. Let sugar dissolve, then bring mixture to a slow boil for about 9 minutes to form a thin syrup. Let syrup cool slightly. Beat egg with a fork. Add to softened frozen orange juice. Add egg mixture into syrup, stirring until well blended. Place over medium heat and cook, stirring constantly, for 6 to 7 minutes. Pour mixture into ice cube trays and freeze in freezer to a mushy consistency. Remove from freezer. Scrape into mixer bowl and beat for about 4 minutes until smooth. Repeat half-freezing and beating 2 more times. Whip cream until soft peaks form. Add remaining sugar to cream and beat for several seconds until blended. Fold cream into whipped orange mixture. Pour into orange cups or prepared mold. Cover with 2 layers of aluminum foil and freeze until firm. Prepare Basic Meringues mixture. Spoon meringue into icing bag with a large star tube affixed. Pipe meringue, in circular motion, over tops of frozen, ice cream-filled orange cups. Place in preheated oven, on middle shelf, at 400 degrees until meringue is lightly browned. Serve immediately.

how to
layer and mold ice creams

The variety of shapes and flavor combinations for molding ice cream is as infinite as your imagination — as a quick look at the photographs in this section will attest. The photographs on the following page are good examples of two ways of layering and molding frozen ice cream in ordinary pans. The three-tiered ice cream ring is layered so that all three flavors are visible, while in the orange and vanilla ice cream ring, only the vanilla ice cream is visible.

MOLDING AND UNMOLDING ICE CREAM

No matter what method of layering you use, begin by chilling the pan and brushing the inside lightly with vegetable oil. After freezing according to instructions below, remove the mold from the freezer and run the tip of a knife around the outside edge. Wait 2 or 3 minutes, then dip the mold into a pan of warm water for a few seconds, being careful not to get any water inside. Turn over onto a dish, wait another 2 minutes, and shake vigorously. The ice cream will slide right out.

If you prefer, you may place a doily on the dish to prevent the ice cream from slipping. Also, rather than dipping the mold in warm water, you may place the mold on the dish and wipe it with a cloth dipped in hot water.

After unmolding, garnish the ice cream quickly with whipped cream, chocolate leaves page 51, cutouts, or bits of glacéed fruit. Then make a tent of aluminum foil to cover the mold completely and return to freezer until about 10 minutes before serving time. Do not attempt to serve it directly from the freezer.

METHODS OF LAYERING

To make the three-tiered ice cream ring with all layers visible, pack the slightly softened ice cream into a mold or pan, one layer at a time, about 1 inch thick. Freeze hard, for about 30 minutes, between additions. Remember that the layer which will be on top of your ice cream dessert will be placed in the pan first.

To make molded ice cream with only 1 flavor visible, spread the entire exposed surface of the mold with a 1/2- to 1-inch layer of the ice cream flavor which will be on the outside. Freeze solid, and layer a second flavor about the same width inside the first layer. By now, there should be a narrow trench remaining to be filled, if the mold is ring-shaped. Again refreeze, and finish filling with a third flavor of ice cream. If you prefer, you may use only two flavors of ice cream, as we did for our orange

and vanilla ring — simply adjust the width of the layers accordingly.

BOMBE MOLDS

Because of the shape of the *bombe* mold, it must stand on its base during freezing. There are two ways to handle the layering procedure. The first is to fill the entire mold with the ice cream which will be on the outside, freeze hard and scrape out the center, leaving a 1/2- to 1-inch outside lining. Then fill the cavity with the second flavor and freeze. If making a three-layer *bombe*, again scrape out the center, leaving 1/2- to 1-inch of the second flavor. Fill with a third flavor of ice cream and freeze.

The other way to fill the mold requires fast work. Spread the layers of ice cream into the mold, one at a time, without freezing between layerings. Whichever method you use, seal the *bombe* mold by placing plastic wrap over the surface, putting on the cover and wrapping the edge with tape. Now place the mold in the freezer until the ice cream hardens.

These are ice cream combinations you may want to try in layers: vanilla, chocolate and pistachio; chocolate, vanilla and coffee or mocha; vanilla and raspberry; strawberry, vanilla and raspberry; peach, almond and pineapple; mocha, vanilla and apricot; almond, orange and vanilla. After you have some idea of which combinations taste good to you, invent your own.

BLACK CHERRY ICE CREAM

1 1-lb. can pitted black cherries in heavy syrup
2 recipes Basic Confectioners' Custard *(pg. 19)*
1/4 tsp. salt
2 tbsp. fresh lemon juice
1 pt. whipping cream
1/2 c. sugar

Pour cherries and syrup in blender container and process to chop coarsely. Prepare custard omitting the vanilla extract and adding the salt. Remove from heat and place in refrigerator to cool completely. Stir in the cherries and lemon juice. Whip the cream with electric mixer or wire whisk until soft peaks form. Add sugar slowly, beating constantly, until just blended. Add half the whipped cream to the custard mixture, then fold in thoroughly. Fold in remaining whipped cream gently. Pour into container of electric or manual ice cream maker and freeze according to instructions in General Information, page 34. May be served immediately or packed into molds, wrapped tightly and stored in freezer. This makes about 4 1/2 quarts ice cream.

PISTACHIO ICE CREAM

2 c. toasted pistachio nuts or pecans
2 c. sugar
1/4 c. all-purpose flour
1/4 tsp. salt
6 egg yolks
2 whole eggs
1 qt. milk, scalded
1 c. half and half cream
1 1/2 tsp. vanilla extract
1 pt. whipping cream

Chop the nuts finely in blender and set aside. Combine sugar, flour and salt in large bowl of electric mixer. Add egg yolks and whole eggs, then beat until fluffy and pale yellow. Add hot milk slowly and beat just until thoroughly mixed. Pour into large boiler and cook over medium to low heat, stirring constantly with a wooden spoon, for 10 minutes. Caution must be taken not to scorch the custard as it thickens. Remove from heat. Stir in nuts, half and half cream and vanilla. Chill until completely cooled. Whip cream until soft peaks form: Fold into chilled custard. Pour into container of electric or manual ice cream maker and freeze according to instructions in General Information, page 34. This will make about 3 quarts of ice cream.

three-tiered ice cream ring

This appetizing ice cream dessert, prepared in a ring mold or tube pan, includes Almond Ice Cream on the bottom layer, Black Cherry in the middle and Pistachio on top. Spirals of whipped cream and alternating sugar wafers and rolled cookies make this an altogether irresistible cool treat.

orange and vanilla ice cream ring

For a variety of design, this tasty dessert was prepared in a Savarin mold by first filling halfway with Basic Vanilla Ice Cream, freezing until set then adding Orange Ice Cream. To serve, drop orange segments (General Information, pg. 13) in the center and surround with rolled cookies.

ALMOND ICE CREAM

2 recipes Basic Confectioners' Custard *(pg. 19)*
1 tsp. almond extract
1/4 tsp. salt
2 3 1/2-oz. packages slivered almonds, toasted
1 c. half and half cream
2 c. milk
1/2 pt. whipping cream
1/4 c. sugar

Prepare the confectioners' custard omitting the vanilla and adding the almond extract and the salt. Place the almonds in the blender container and chop finely. Add the almonds to hot confectioners' custard and mix well. Stir in the half and half cream and the milk. Cool. Whip the cream until soft peaks form and add the sugar. Fold the whipped cream into the custard mixture, then turn into container of ice cream maker. Freeze according to instructions in General Information, page 34. This makes about 3 quarts.

molded tomato ice cream

tomato ice cream

This Tomato Ice Cream was packed into the two molds while it was still soft. The two halves were frozen separately, turned out and placed together. Garnish with fresh mint leaves and serve Tomato Ice Cream with a fresh fruit plate!

TOMATO ICE CREAM

1 recipe Basic Confectioners' Custard (pg. 19)
¹⁄₈ tsp. salt
1¹⁄₂ c. tomato purée
¹⁄₂ tbsp. fresh lemon juice
¹⁄₂ pt. whipping cream
¹⁄₄ c. sugar

Prepare Basic Confectioners' Custard omitting vanilla extract. Let custard cool slightly, then add salt, purée and lemon juice and blend thoroughly.

Place custard mixture in refrigerator to cool completely. Whip cream until soft peaks form. Add sugar and continue beating for several seconds until blended. Freeze in ice cream maker according to instructions in General Information, page 34. After freezing, ice cream may be packed into two pint molds lined with transparent wrap. Wrap molds tightly with aluminum foil and place in deep freezer until ready to unmold. Unmold and place two halves together as shown in illustration to form ball or melon shape. Garnish with mint leaves. This makes about 1 quart of ice cream.

FRESH PEACH ICE CREAM

3 c. mashed, ripe peaches
2 c. sugar
1 qt. milk
2 c. half and half cream
1/8 tsp. salt
1/2 pt. whipping cream

Have peaches, milk and creams chilled. Combine peaches and sugar and stir until well blended. Pour milk and half and half cream into can of ice cream maker. Add salt and stir until blended. Add peach mixture and stir just until blended. Whip cream until soft peaks form. Pour whipped cream into peach mixture in can and stir for several seconds to blend slightly. Freeze immediately according to freezing instructions in General Information, page 34. This is a Philadelphia type ice cream which should always be frozen in an electric or manual ice cream maker. This makes about 3 1/2 quarts of ice cream.

BLACK PLUM ICE CREAM

1 1-lb. can black or purple plums in heavy syrup
2 recipes Basic Confectioners' Custard (pg. 19)
1/4 tsp. salt
2 tbsp. fresh lemon juice
1 pt. whipping cream
1/2 c. sugar

Remove pits from plums and place plums and syrup in blender container. Process to chop coarsely. Prepare custard omitting the vanilla extract and adding the salt. Remove from heat and place in refrigerator to cool completely. Stir in the plums and lemon juice. Whip the cream until soft peaks form. Add sugar slowly, beating constantly, until just blended. Add half the whipped cream to the custard mixture, then fold in thoroughly. Fold in remaining whipped cream gently. Pour into ice cream maker and freeze according to instructions in General Information, page 34. May be served immediately or packed into molds, wrapped tightly and stored in the freezer. This makes about 4 1/2 quarts ice cream.

fresh pineapple and pineapple ice cream

The Pineapple Ice Cream in the background has been sprinkled with ground pistachio nuts. The fresh pineapple was sliced and coated with sugar. Serve these two dishes together for a special occasion.

FRESH PINEAPPLE

1 fresh pineapple
1 1/2 c. sugar

Cut top off pineapple, then slice pineapple in 1 1/2 inch slices. Remove all peeling from pineapple slices and cut out little brown spots with the point of a sharp knife or scissors. Remove center core and cut slices into quarters. Turn each quarter in sugar, then stack or reassemble quarters in shape of pineapple as shown in illustration. Garnish top with slender spikes of candied angelica or garnish with several spikes cut from pineapple top. Serve with Pineapple Ice Cream.

PINEAPPLE ICE CREAM

2 recipes Basic Confectioners' Custard (pg. 19)
1/4 tsp. salt
3 c. crushed pineapple
2 tbsp. fresh lemon juice
1 pt. whipping cream
1/2 c. sugar

Prepare Basic Confectioners' Custard omitting vanilla extract. Remove from heat. Add salt, pineapple and lemon juice to custard. Place custard mixture in refrigerator to cool completely. Whip cream with electric mixer or wire whisk until soft peaks form. Add sugar slowly and continue beating until just blended. Add half the whipped cream to cooled custard, then fold in all until thoroughly blended. Pour into freezer can of ice cream maker and freeze according to instructions in General Information, page 34. Ice cream may be served immediately or packed into molds, wrapped tightly and stored in deep freezer. May be served with fresh pineapple, as shown in illustration, if desired. This makes about 4 1/2 quarts of ice cream.

apricot ice cream coupes

A perfect compromise for those who like the taste of ice cream cones but not the inconvenience. Apricot coupes begin with a scoop of Apricot Ice Cream. Candied Orange Strips, page 33, are added before the whipped cream rosettes and cone "hats".

APRICOT ICE CREAM

2 recipes Basic Confectioners' Custard (pg. 19)
1/4 tsp. salt
3 c. chopped, canned or sweetened fresh apricots
2 tbsp. fresh lemon juice
1 pt. whipping cream
1/2 c. sugar

Prepare custard omitting the vanilla extract and adding the salt. Remove from heat and place in refrigerator to cool completely. Stir in the apricots and lemon juice. Whip the cream with electric mixer or wire whisk until soft peaks form. Add sugar slowly, beating constantly until just blended. Add half the whipped cream to the custard mixture, then fold in thoroughly. Fold in remaining whipped cream gently. Pour into ice cream maker and freeze according to instructions in General Information, page 34. May be served immediately or packed into molds, wrapped tightly and stored in the freezer. This makes 4 1/2 quarts of ice cream.

introducing ices

Ices are among the simplest of desserts to prepare, having a base of sugar syrup and fruit juices. Some recipes call for stiffly beaten egg whites and gelatin as a stabilizer for the mixture.

On the next three pages you'll find a variety of fruit ices and numerous attractive ways to serve them. Light and refreshing, these desserts are the perfect complement for a heavier entrée. Not so rich in calories as ice cream, they're sure to find favor with weight watchers.

Making fruit ices in your freezer requires special attention. The large liquid content of fruit ices encourages crystallization and an undesirable consistency. Care must be taken to prevent this from happening. As soon as ice crystals begin to form around the outside edges of the container, remove it from the freezer and beat or whip until smooth, being sure to chill the beaters first. Return to freezer and repeat the process periodically as the recipe directs. Wrap the container in aluminum foil to keep frost from collecting, as the ice must remain in the freezer for several hours before serving.

If you are making a fruit ice in an electric or manual ice cream maker, follow directions in General Information, page 34. The continuous "stirring" of the dasher assures a perfectly smooth consistency.

STRAWBERRY ICE

3 1-lb. packages sliced frozen strawberries
2 packages unflavored gelatin
1 c. Basic Sugar Syrup *(Breads, pg. 14)*
2 egg whites

Let strawberries stand at room temperature until partially thawed. Soften gelatin in 1/2 cup cold water, then dissolve in hot syrup. Place 1/3 of the strawberries and 1/3 of the syrup in blender container, then process until puréed. Pour into a large mixing bowl. Repeat blending process two more times with remaining strawberries and syrup. Pour half the strawberry mixture into ice cream maker container. Beat egg whites until soft peaks form, then turn into freezer container. Add the remaining strawberry mixture. Three pints of puréed fresh

strawberries may be substituted for the frozen strawberries. Fresh strawberries must be sweetened generously. Freeze according to instructions in General Information, page 34. This makes about 1/2 gallon of Strawberry Ice.

TANGERINE ICE

1 env. unflavored gelatin
2 c. Basic Sugar Syrup *(Breads, pg. 14)*
3 6-oz. cans frozen tangerine juice, thawed
4²/₃ c. water
1¹/₂ tbsp. lemon juice
1 egg white

Soften the gelatin in 1/4 cup cold water, then add to the hot sugar syrup and stir until dissolved. Combine all the ingredients except the egg white in ice cream maker container and mix. Freeze according to instructions in General Information, page 34, for about 8 minutes. Beat the egg white until soft peaks form. Remove top and lid of ice cream maker and add the egg white. Replace lid and top and freeze for about 30 minutes longer. Tangerine Ice may be served immediately or packed into containers, sealed and stored in the freezer. This makes about 3 quarts.

BLACKBERRY-RASPBERRY ICE

1 1-lb. package frozen blackberries
2 10-oz. packages frozen, sweetened raspberries
2 c. Basic Sugar Syrup *(Breads, pg. 14)*
2 egg whites

Partially thaw blackberries and raspberries, then purée in blender. Add hot sugar syrup while puréeing. Pour fruit purée into ice cream maker container. Beat egg whites until soft peaks form then lightly fold into cold fruit purée. Freeze immediately, according to directions in General Information, page 34. After freezing, you may spoon the Blackberry-Raspberry Ice into a prepared mold or plastic carton and store in deep freezer. This makes an attractive molded dessert. Mold or carton must be wrapped in foil and covered securely. If desired, you may serve with a teaspoon of *Crème de Cassis* liqueur spooned over top of each serving. Three cups of fresh blackberries and 3 cups fresh raspberries may be substituted for frozen fruit if desired. Fresh fruits must be sweetened generously. This makes about 3 quarts of Blackberry-Raspberry Ice.

LEMON ICE

1 can frozen lemonade concentrate
1 c. fresh lemon juice
2 env. unflavored gelatin
2 c. Basic Sugar Syrup *(Breads, pg. 14)*
2 egg whites

Combine the lemonade, lemon juice and 4 cups water in a large bowl. Soften the gelatin in 1/2 cup cold water, then dissolve in the hot sugar syrup. Add to the lemon mixture. Pour into the ice cream maker container. Freeze according to instructions in General Information, page 34, for about 8 minutes. Beat the egg whites until soft peaks form. Remove top and lid of ice cream maker carefully and add the egg whites to lemon mixture. Replace lid and top and freeze for about 30 minutes longer. This makes about 1/2 gallon of Lemon Ice.

lemon ices

Using egg whites and gelatin for stability, Lemon Ice holds its shape well when spooned into parfait glasses. Garnish with fresh strawberries to enhance the flavor and add stunning color contrast.

orange-lemon ice

Tangy segments of fresh orange and grapefruit are alternated in parfait glasses and topped with thick spirals of Orange-Lemon Ice to make this luscious dessert.

ORANGE-LEMON ICE

1 pkg. unflavored gelatin
2¼ c. water
½ c. sugar
1 tbsp. grated lemon rind
1 6-oz. can frozen lemonade concentrate
1 6-oz. can frozen orange juice concentrate
1 egg white

Soften gelatin in ¼ cup cold water. Combine remaining 2 cups water, sugar and lemon rind in small saucepan. Bring to a slow boil for 5 minutes to make a syrup. Dilute lemonade and orange juice in a large bowl according to can directions. Add softened gelatin to hot sugar syrup, stirring until dissolved, then add to orange-lemonade mixture. Pour into ice cream maker container and freeze according to instructions in General Information, page 34 for about 8 minutes. Beat egg white until soft peaks form. Open the freezer can and add egg white to mixture. Continue freezing for about 35 minutes. This may be packed in a covered, plastic container and stored in freezer. This makes about 3 quarts of Orange-Lemon Ice.

The Creative Homemaker's Academy © MCMLXXIII
Selected Illustrations © B.P.C. Publishing Limited MCMLXX

introducing custards

Hot or cold, spicy or sweet, custards are delectably light and refreshing. Topped with exotic sauces, custards are suitable for gourmet dining, or combined with fresh summer fruits, they are a classically simple, light dessert.

Custards have a pleasing, delicate texture which may vary slightly with the method in which they are prepared. If cooked on the stove in a double boiler, the custard will be especially soft and creamy, but if it is baked in the oven, the texture will be somewhat firmer and jelly-like.

The softer custards blend particularly well with fruits, make excellent bases for ice creams, and they are absolutely delicious as fillings for elegant desserts. Baked custards can be served straight from the oven, topped with a dab of whipped cream or dressed up with luxurious sauces. In fact, custards can be prepared in such a variety of ways we can make them as simple or as lavish as we want.

SMOOTH CUSTARD

For either baked or soft custard, the basic recipe ordinarily calls for slightly beaten eggs. The result is a fine-grained custard with a smooth top. However, a baked custard is equally delectable with a thinly crusted top, and this is easily obtained by beating the eggs thoroughly. A foam will rise to the surface of the cup when the custard is poured in, and this foam will brown beautifully while baking. Well-beaten eggs produce a custard that is just as creamy and smooth to the taste, but not quite as fine-grained as custard made with slightly-beaten eggs.

"BOILED" CUSTARD: A MISNOMER

Softer, top-of-the-stove custards are cooked over hot water in a double boiler. Inappropriately nicknamed "boiled" custards, neither the custard nor the water should be allowed to boil. If at any time the water gets too hot or comes to a boil, quickly remove the top section of the boiler and set it in cold water. Stir the mixture continuously while cooking. The custard is done when it coats a spoon smoothly and the watery appearance changes to a velvety, opaque one. To avoid the formation of a "skin" over the top, the custard may be stirred occasionally until it cools. If there are any lumps, simply strain the mixture.

BAKED CUSTARD

There need be no doubt in determining whether a baked custard is done. Insert a knife approximately one inch from the edge of the mold; if the blade comes out clean, remove the custard from the oven to cool. Although the center often appears to be less firm than the edge, the stored heat in the baking dish finishes the cooking process. You may invert it onto the serving platter when the dish is cool enough to handle easily.

If the custard is prepared the day before needed, cover and refrigerate it. At serving time, set the cooking-storage dish in warm water for about five minutes before transferring it to the serving platter.

The recipes in this section illustrate the remarkable versatility of custards, and each is certain to please and tempt those to whom it is served.

 ### BASIC EGG CUSTARD

2 eggs
2 egg yolks
½ c. sugar
3 c. milk
1 vanilla pod or 1 tsp. vanilla extract

Beat eggs, egg yolks and sugar together using an electric mixer at medium speed, for about 5 minutes or until thick and doubled in bulk. Heat milk with vanilla pod in a heavy saucepan slowly until hot, but not boiling. Remove pod and stir milk into egg mixture. Pour into top of large double boiler, then add the vanilla pod. Cook over hot water, stirring constantly, for about 20 minutes or until thickened. Remove vanilla pod, then rinse pod and pat dry for future use. This makes about 3 cups thin custard which may also be used as a sauce.

swiss roll and custard

Vanilla custard, cake and jelly are three favorite desserts. By combining two BASICS, a delightfully simple Egg Custard with the moist rolled sponge cake recipe, the result is this splendid dessert, Swiss Roll and Custard.

swiss roll and custard

SWISS ROLL AND CUSTARD

1 recipe Basic Rolled Sponge Cake *(pg. 3)*
1 7½-oz. jar blackberry jam
2 pkg. unflavored gelatin
½ c. cold water
1 recipe Basic Egg Custard *(pg. 79)*

Prepare sponge cake and spread evenly with blackberry jam. Roll up and let stand until ready to use. Sprinkle gelatin over cold water and let stand 3 minutes to soften. Prepare custard in double boiler, then stir in the softened gelatin until dissolved. Place double boiler in a bowl filled with ice and let stand for 5 minutes, stirring occasionally. Cut rolled sponge cake into 10 even slices. Place 1 slice in center of oiled 2-quart mold, then arrange 3 slices evenly around side of mold. Pour in custard slowly to half the depth of the 3 slices. Place another slice in the center of the custard and arrange 3 more slices around the side in between the first 3 slices. Pour in more custard to half the depth of the last 3 slices added. Place another slice in the center of the custard. Cut the remaining slice into thirds so that each third has a curved side and place around side of mold, straight edge down. Pour in remaining custard. Chill for several hours or until firm. Unmold and cut in wedges to serve. The rolled sponge cake may be made the day ahead and wrapped in plastic wrap, if desired. This makes 6 to 8 servings.

crème brûlée

CRÈME BRÛLÉE

6 egg yolks
6 tbsp. sugar
3 c. half and half cream
1 vanilla pod or 1 tsp. vanilla extract
½ c. light brown sugar

Beat the egg yolks slightly, then add the sugar. Beat for 5 minutes or until eggs are lemon-colored. Place the cream and the vanilla pod in the top of a double boiler, then bring to a boil. Pour a small amount of the hot mixture over the egg mixture, beating constantly. Return to the remaining hot mixture and cook over hot water for 3 to 4 minutes or until slightly thickened. Remove the vanilla pod and pour into a heat resistant serving dish. Chill for 6 to 8 hours or until set. Sift the brown sugar and sprinkle evenly over the custard. Place under the broiler about 4 inches from the source of heat. Broil, watching carefully, for 3 to 4 minutes or until the brown sugar melts. Chill before serving. This makes 6 servings.

crème brûlée

In the Northeastern United States, this creamy smooth confection with its caramelized sugar glaze is called Vermont Baked Custard. An extremely old dish, it is a specialty of Trinity College, Cambridge, England, and is known as "Cambridge Cream" or Burnt Cream. But in France, where Catherine de Médici probably ate it in the 1500's, Boiled Custard with brown sugar is known by the elegant title, Crème Brûlée.

malaysian coconut custard

MALAYSIAN COCONUT CUSTARD

2 c. coconut flakes
2 c. milk
4 eggs
½ c. sugar

Place ½ cup coconut flakes on a baking sheet. Broil about 4 to 6 inches from the source of heat until golden brown, watching carefully. Set aside. Combine remaining coconut and milk in a saucepan and bring to a boil. Remove from heat and cover. Let steep for 20 minutes. Line a large strainer with muslin or 2 layers of cheesecloth and pour the milk mixture into the muslin. Let drain, then wring out muslin until the coconut is dry. Discard the coconut. Beat the eggs and sugar together for 5 minutes or until thick. Stir in the coconut milk gradually until well mixed. Pour into 6 well-buttered custard cups and cover with aluminum foil. Place the cups in a shallow pan and fill the pan ⅓ full with boiling water. Place the pan in pre-heated 350-degree oven, 1 shelf above center. Bake for 5 minutes. Reduce oven temperature to 275 degrees and bake for 1 hour longer. Unmold onto serving dish and sprinkle the toasted coconut over the tops. Chill custard before serving. This makes about 6 servings.

malaysian coconut custard

With toasted grated coconut piled on top of each individual custard mound, this appetizing dessert can be served on one serving dish or on individual plates. Very slightly toasted "ribbons" of coconut may be piled over and around each custard for an appealing garnish.

FRIED CUSTARD

2 tbsp. cornstarch
¼ c. all-purpose flour
½ c. sugar
2 c. milk
4 egg yolks, beaten
Dash of nutmeg
Dash of salt
1 tsp. vanilla extract
Fine cracker crumbs
1 egg, beaten
Confectioners' sugar

Combine the cornstarch, flour and sugar in the top of a double boiler. Then add the milk gradually, stirring constantly. Cook over boiling water until thickened, then cook for 5 minutes longer, stirring constantly. Stir part of the hot mixture gradually into the egg yolks, then stir the egg yolks in the hot mixture. Add nutmeg and salt and cook for about 1 minute longer. Remove from heat and stir in the vanilla extract. Pour into an oiled 8-inch square pan and let stand in refrigerator for 4 to 5 hours or overnight. Cut firm custard into rounds, using a biscuit cutter. Dredge in cracker crumbs. Dip in egg, then dredge in crumbs again. Fry in deep hot fat at 380 degrees until golden brown. Sprinkle with confectioners' sugar and serve hot. Strained orange juice may be poured over each serving, if desired. Hot custard may be poured into an oiled 8 X 4-inch loaf pan and after chilling cut into 6 strips for frying, if desired. This makes 6 servings.

fried custard

Placed on a pedestal dish, Fried Custard makes a lovely centerpiece. Perhaps for a tea table at a bridal shower or at bridge luncheon? Included with these 'fritters' are matching glass containers, one containing fruit juice and the other sifted confectioners' sugar. One or both may be served with the custard.

fresh fruits luxembourg

FRESH FRUITS LUXEMBOURG

1 pt. fresh raspberries
1 pt. fresh strawberries
Sugar to taste
3 fresh pears, peeled and quartered
Lemon juice
1 recipe Luxembourg Sauce *(Sauces, pg. 20)*

Sprinkle the raspberries and strawberries with sugar, then sprinkle pears with lemon juice to prevent discoloration. Arrange the fruits in 6 serving dishes and top with sauce. This makes 6 servings.

fresh fruits luxembourg

A marvelous summer brunch begins with fresh summer fruit — fragrant, ripe strawberries, raspberries and pears. Add a sweet Luxembourg Sauce to the berries or fruit. Bon Appétit!

LITTLE CHOCOLATE POTS

1½ c. milk
2 c. chocolate chips
2 eggs
¼ c. sugar
Pinch of salt

Pour milk in heavy saucepan and heat to boiling point. Combine remaining ingredients in blender container. Pour in the hot milk, then blend at low speed for 1 minute or until smooth. Pour into 6 custard cups, then chill for at least 2 hours before serving. This makes 6 servings.

little chocolate pots

A rich French-style custard, Little Chocolate Pots or Petits Pots de Chocolat, is delicious as is, but outstanding when topped with spirals of whipped cream, sprinkled with chopped pistachio nuts and tipped with delicate chocolate leaves.

german custard

raspberries with german custard

GERMAN CUSTARD (SAUCE ALLEMANDE)

2½ c. milk
1 tbsp. potato flour
1 vanilla pod or 1 tsp. vanilla extract
Sugar to taste
3 eggs, separated

Make a paste with a small amount of the milk and the potato flour. Combine remaining milk and the vanilla pod in the top of a double boiler and bring to boiling point. Stir in the paste until smooth. Remove the vanilla pod, then rinse and dry for future use. Stir in sugar until well mixed. Beat the egg yolks thoroughly, then stir in a small amount of the hot mixture. Return egg mixture to the double boiler and cook, stirring constantly, until sauce is smooth. Remove from heat and let cool to luke-warm. Beat egg whites until stiff peaks form. Fold ⅓ of the egg whites into the custard until thoroughly blended, then fold in the remaining egg whites carefully. Chill until ready to serve. This makes 6 to 8 servings.

Raspberries with German Custard is a fitting finale to any menu , perhaps one featuring lamb with fresh artichokes. German Custard, also known as Sauce Allemande, is a very fluffy, foamy "stirred" custard made very much like a soufflé.

RASPBERRIES WITH GERMAN CUSTARD

1 qt. fresh raspberries
1 pt. fresh currants (opt.)
Sugar to taste
1 recipe German Custard

Combine raspberries, currants and sugar in a large bowl, then chill until ready to serve. Spoon raspberry mixture into serving dishes, then top with a generous amount of custard. Three 10-ounce packages frozen raspberries may be substituted for the fresh raspberries, if desired. This makes 6 servings.

banana chocolate cream

BANANA CHOCOLATE CREAM

8 coconut macaroons
Juice of 2 oranges, strained
1 tbsp. rum (opt.)
6 bananas
Grated rind of 1 orange
1 recipe Basic Confectioners' Custard *(pg. 19)*
¾ c. whipping cream, whipped
¼ c. coarsely grated sweet chocolate
Skinless sections of 2 oranges

Arrange the macaroons in 2 serving dishes. Combine orange juice and rum, then drizzle over the macaroons. Let stand for 20 minutes. Mash bananas with a fork. Stir orange rind into the confectioners' custard, then fold in the bananas. Fold in the whipped cream, then mound the banana mixture over the macaroons. Sprinkle evenly with grated chocolate. May be refrigerated for 3 to 4 hours before serving, if desired. Arrange orange sections around side of each dish as a border just before serving. This makes 4 to 6 servings.

banana chocolate cream

Garnished with mandarin orange slices, Banana Chocolate Cream is a delicious creation mixing fresh fruit tastes with Basic Confectioners' Custard, sweet chocolate and crisp macaroons. Shown here in two flute-edge crystal dishes, this custard may be served in individual cups for easier serving.

ratafia and rum custard

Delicate lemon and lime tinted whipped cream is piped over almond cookies and orange custard. Garnish with Crystalized Citrus Peel. This custard is accompanied by a bowl of Luxembourg Sauce (Sauces, pg. 20).

RATAFIA AND RUM CUSTARD

3 lg. oranges
Peel of 1 lg. lemon
1/2 c. rum
1 1/4 c. sweet white wine
2 tbsp. brandy
3/4 lb. ratafia cookies or almond cookies
1 recipe Orange Confectioners' Custard
1 c. whipping cream
Yellow and green food coloring

Remove the peel from the oranges carefully and set aside for crystallizing. Separate the oranges into sections. Store the sections in a covered plastic container in the refrigerator until ready to use. Cut the orange and lemon peels into long, tapering petals. Crystallize as instructed below. Combine rum, wine and brandy. Arrange ratafia cookies in a large serving dish, then pour the rum mixture carefully over the cookies. Let stand until the cookies are moistened. Drain the stored orange sections. Spread custard over the cookies, then arrange the orange sections evenly over the custard. Whip the cream until stiff and divide in half. Tint half the cream pale yellow and the other half pale green. Spoon whipped cream into icing bags with No. 3 star tube affixed to each and pipe rosettes over top of orange sections. Decorate with crystallized petals and chill until ready to serve. This makes 10 to 12 servings.

CRYSTALLIZED CITRUS PEEL

1 c. citrus peel
2 c. Basic Sugar Syrup (Breads, pg. 14)
1/2 c. sugar
1 tsp. cream of tartar

Cut citrus peel into desired shapes. Remove excess white membrane with sharp knife. Place peel in a medium saucepan and cover with cold water. Bring to a boil, then drain off the water. Repeat 2 more times to remove all bitterness from the peel. Pour syrup over the peel and bring to a boil. Reduce heat and simmer for about 45 minutes or until transparent. Remove the peel with a slotted spoon and let drain. Sift the sugar and cream of tartar together, then dredge the peel in the sugar mixture. Place on a rack to dry. Store in an airtight container between layers of waxed paper.

ORANGE CONFECTIONERS' CUSTARD

3 egg yolks
1/2 c. sugar
3 tbsp. all-purpose flour
3/4 c. strained fresh orange juice
1/2 c. water

Combine egg yolks, sugar and flour in a medium mixing bowl and beat thoroughly with an electric mixer. Combine the orange juice and water in a small saucepan, then cook over medium heat to just below boiling point. Pour the orange juice slowly into the egg yolk mixture, stirring constantly with a wooden spoon until well blended. Pour orange juice mixture into the top of a double boiler. Cook over boiling water, stirring constantly, until the custard is thick and smooth. Cool before serving. This makes about 1 1/2 cups of custard and may be used plain or as a sauce.

NORMANDY SAND CAKE

1 1/2 c. cake flour, sifted
1 tsp. baking powder
1/8 tsp. nutmeg
1/2 c. unsalted butter, softened
1 c. sugar
3 eggs
6 tbsp. Madeira
1/2 tsp. grated lemon rind

Sift the flour, baking powder and nutmeg together. Cream butter and sugar together, using electric mixer at medium speed, for 5 minutes or until thick and creamy. Add eggs, one at a time, beating well after each addition. Add the flour mixture alternately with the Madeira, beginning and ending with the flour mixture and beating well after each addition. Stir in the lemon rind. Pour batter into a well-greased and floured loaf pan. Bake in a preheated 350-degree oven for 25 to 30 minutes or until cake tests done. Let cake cool in pan for 5 minutes, then turn out on rack to cool completely. Dust with sifted confectioners' sugar before serving. This makes 6 to 8 servings.

normandy sand cake

This delicate cake, flavored with Madeira, dates back to Victorian times and is a perfect match to another Victorian favorite, Basic Sabayon Sauce (Sauces, pg. 20).

SWISS CARROT CAKE

2 c. sifted all-purpose flour
2 tsp. baking powder
1½ tsp. soda
1 tsp. salt
2 tsp. cinnamon
1½ c. salad oil
2 c. sugar
4 eggs
2 c. grated carrots
1 sm. can crushed pineapple
1½ c. chopped walnuts or pecans
1 tsp. vanilla extract

Sift flour, baking powder, soda, salt and cinnamon together. Combine oil and sugar in a large mixing bowl, then beat thoroughly with electric mixer. Add eggs, one at a time, beating well after each addition. Sift flour mixture into egg mixture and beat thoroughly. Stir in remaining ingredients. Spread batter evenly into well-greased and floured 9 X 13-inch pan or 2 loaf pans. Bake in a preheated 350-degree oven for 1 hour or until cake tests done. Let cool in pan for 5 minutes, then turn out on cake rack to finish cooling. Dust with sifted confectioners' sugar to serve. May be served with Orange Confectioners' Custard if desired. This makes 12 to 15 servings.

swiss carrot cake

Molded almond paste "carrots" with fringed angelica "leaves" decorate the top of this delicious Swiss Carrot Cake which has been liberally dusted with powdered confectioners' sugar. Chilled Orange Confectioners' Custard sauce spooned over a slice of warm Swiss Carrot Cake is an appetizing way to bring an informal dinner to a close.

presenting cheesecake

Cheesecake is a luscious, creamy dessert which seems to have just the right combination of tart and sweetness to please anyone's taste. The popularity of cheesecake dates back to ancient Greece, where the word meant anything from a honey-sweetened mold of cream cheese chilled in the snow to a small, hot, cheese-filled pastry. In fact, the word seemed to refer to any cheese dessert.

Today's cheesecakes do not cover quite that large a field, but they are still one of the most versatile desserts a modern homemaker can prepare. There are two basic categories of cheesecakes: baked and refrigerated. Depending upon the choice of cheese, a cheesecake may be soufflé-light, firm and rich, or creamy. You have only to thumb through the dessert section of any recipe book to see that cheesecakes can be combined and topped with an endless variety of fruits, nuts and toppings. Like a basic dress, cheesecake can be dressed up or down, but either way it has classic elegance.

Cheesecake is a somewhat confusing term because, actually it isn't a *cake* of any sort. So, if you search through the cake section of dessert recipes, you will most likely not see it. Look for it, instead, as a separate category.

Cheesecake is delicious and remarkably easy to prepare. Remember that since it is cheese-based, it should be baked at moderate temperatures. Some shrinkage is to be expected, but a great deal will occur if the temperature is too high.

In this lesson are a variety of cheesecakes . . . one to suit everyone's taste.

sour cream cheesecake

Firm, rich and creamy, this Sour Cream Cheesecake has a bottom crust of crumbled shortbread cookies. Chou pastry strips were piped over the top before baking.

baked cheesecake in pastry

SOUR CREAM CHEESECAKE

1½ c. shortbread cookie crumbs
½ c. unsalted butter, melted
1 12-oz. carton cottage cheese
1 tbsp. lemon juice
¼ tsp. grated lemon rind
1 egg, beaten
¼ c. sifted confectioners' sugar
⅛ tsp. vanilla extract
1 c. sour cream

Line the bottom of a 10 x 4-inch loaf pan with removable sides with greased and floured aluminum foil. Combine cookie crumbs and melted butter, mixing well. Press the crumb mixture firmly over the bottom of the prepared pan. Drain the cottage cheese well and place in blender container. Blend until free of large lumps. Combine cottage cheese, lemon juice, lemon rind, egg, confectioners' sugar and vanilla extract in a mixing bowl and mix well. Fold in the sour cream. Spoon the cheese mixture evenly over the crumb mixture and smooth the top. May pipe with ¼ recipe of Basic Sweet Chou Pastry, page 55, if desired. Bake at 350 degrees for about 50 minutes or until the cheesecake tests done. Cool well. Refrigerate overnight. You may add ¼ cup chocolate chips or raisins to cheese mixture before baking, if desired. This makes about 8 servings.

BAKED CHEESECAKE IN PASTRY

½ recipe French Lining Pastry (Pork, pg. 7)
Sugar
1 c. milk
2 8-oz. packages cream cheese
¼ c. all-purpose flour
½ tsp. salt
2 tsp. grated lemon rind
3 egg yolks
¼ c. melted butter
3 egg whites, stiffly beaten

Prepare French Lining Pastry, adding 2 tablespoons of sugar. Roll out paper-thin on lightly floured surface and line well-greased *brioche* pan. Bake blind as instructed (page 14) at 400 degrees for 20 minutes. Remove peas and reduce oven temperature to 375 degrees. Bake for 10 minutes longer or until golden brown. Scald the milk and cool to lukewarm. Beat the cream cheese in a large mixing bowl until light and fluffy, then beat in the flour, salt and lemon rind. Add egg yolks, one at a time, beating well after each addition. Beat in ¾ cup sugar. Add butter and milk and blend well. Fold in egg whites. Pour into pastry shell. Bake in a preheated 300-degree oven for 1 hour or until filling is set. Cool on a wire rack for 10 minutes, then loosen crust carefully and remove from pan. Chill well before serving. This makes 6 to 8 servings.

baked cheesecake in pastry

Notice the beautiful texture of this Baked Cheesecake In Pastry. Made with cream cheese, it is delectably moist and rich. A brioche mold, buttered and then thinly lined with pastry, was used to give it a beautiful appearance; however, a plain cake pan with a sliding base will serve equally well. Sweetened fresh fruits may be served with this cheesecake.

chilled cheesecake

CHILLED CHEESECAKE

3 tbsp. melted butter
¾ c. graham cracker crumbs
Sugar
¼ tsp. cinnamon
¼ tsp. nutmeg
2 env. unflavored gelatin
2 eggs, separated
1 c. milk
1 tsp. grated lemon rind
1 tbsp. lemon juice
1 tsp. vanilla extract
3 c. creamed cottage cheese
1 c. whipping cream, whipped

Combine the butter, graham cracker crumbs, 2 tablespoons of sugar, cinnamon and nutmeg in a bowl. Press ½ cup of the crumb mixture into an 8 or 9-inch springform pan. Combine the gelatin and ¾ cup of sugar in a medium saucepan. Beat the egg yolks, then stir in the milk gradually. Stir into the gelatin mixture and place over low heat. Cook, stirring constantly, for 3 to 5 minutes or until gelatin dissolves and mixture is slightly thickened. Remove from heat and stir in the lemon rind, lemon juice and vanilla extract. Beat the cottage cheese with an electric mixer at high speed for 3 to 4 minutes or until smooth. Stir into the gelatin mixture, then chill, stirring occasionally, until mixture mounds slightly when dropped from a spoon. Beat the egg whites until stiff but not dry. Add ¼ cup of sugar gradually and beat until very stiff. Fold into the gelatin mixture, then fold in the whipped cream. Turn into the prepared pan and sprinkle with remaining crumb mixture. Chill for 3 to 4 hours or until firm. Loosen side of pan with a sharp knife and release springform. An 8-cup loaf pan may be used instead of the springform pan. Grease the loaf pan lightly. Cut waxed paper to fit pan and line loaf pan. Invert onto serving plate to unmold then remove waxed paper. This makes 12 servings.

chilled cheesecake

Chilled Cheesecake, made with cottage cheese, has an easy-to-prepare graham cracker crumb crust.

PINEAPPLE CHEESECAKE

3 8-oz. packages cream cheese
16 graham crackers, crushed
1 c. drained crushed pineapple
1 c. sugar
4 eggs
1 tsp. vanilla extract
1 pt. sour cream

Have the cream cheese at room temperature. Sprinkle the graham cracker crumbs in bottom of a springform pan, then place the pineapple over the crumbs. Place the cream cheese in a large mixing bowl and beat until smooth. Add the sugar gradually, beating constantly. Add the eggs, one at a time, beating well after each addition. Add the vanilla extract and sour cream and beat until smooth. Place over the pineapple. Bake in a preheated 350-degree oven for 1 hour, then cool. Loosen side of the pan with a sharp knife and release springform. This makes 12 servings.

The Creative Homemaker's Academy © MCMLXXIII
Selected Illustrations © B.P.C. Publishing Limited MCMLXX

sweet cream cheese gâteau

sweet cream cheese gâteau

A scene-stealer, the Sweet Cream Cheese Gâteau is guaranteed to delight everyone who tastes it. After the cream cheese mixture is set, it is turned onto sponge cake (see the recipe that follows), heaped about the edges with Basic Chantilly Cream, page 19, and beautifully garnished with fresh strawberries. Cool and refreshing, it is a particularly welcome summer treat.

SWEET CREAM CHEESE GÂTEAU

1 recipe Easy Jam Sponge Cake *(pg. 96)*
2 egg yolks
¹/₂ c. confectioners' sugar
1¹/₂ tsp. kirsch
4 3-oz. packages cream cheese, softened
Juice of 1 orange, strained
1 recipe Basic Chantilly Cream *(pg. 19)*
1 pt. whole strawberries

Prepare the cake as instructed. Let cool but do not slice and fill. Combine the egg yolks and sugar in a mixer bowl and beat with an electric mixer until thick and creamy. Pour in the kirsch gradually, beating well. Cut the cream cheese into small cubes and add to the egg yolk mixture gradually, beating well after each addition. Beat for 10 minutes or until smooth. Line a small mold with plastic wrap, letting the wrap extend over the edge of the mold. Spoon the cream cheese mixture into the mold and place in the freezer for 2 hours. Trim the edge from the cake to fit the mold and place on a serving dish. Sprinkle the cake with orange juice. Lift the cheese mixture in the plastic wrap from the bowl and invert onto the cake. Remove plastic wrap carefully. Spread the rim of the cake with Chantilly cream. Serve with strawberries and remaining Chantilly cream. This makes 8 servings.

easy jam sponge cake

easy jam sponge cake

The Easy Jam Sponge Cake is as delicious as it is simple to prepare, and a perfect treat for the children. After the cake cools, merely slice through the center to make two layers and lavishly spread your favorite jam between (black currant jam was used in this cake). Dust the top with confectioners' sugar for a finishing touch.

EASY JAM SPONGE CAKE

2 eggs
1 egg yolk
⅔ c. confectioners' sugar
½ c. cake flour
¼ tsp. salt
¼ tsp. vanilla extract
1 12-oz. jar black currant jam

Line the bottom of a 9-inch layer cake pan with buttered waxed paper and sprinkle with flour.

Combine eggs, egg yolk and sugar in mixing bowl. Beat with electric mixer until very thick and creamy. Sift the flour and salt together. Fold the mixture into the egg mixture carefully. Add the vanilla extract. Turn the batter in the prepared pan. Bake in a preheated 350-degree oven for 30 minutes. Cool the cake on a rack for 5 minutes. Turn out and cool completely. Split the cake in half crosswise and spread the jam between layers. Sprinkle the top of the cake generously with additional confectioners' sugar. This makes about 8 servings.

stacked chocolate cake

The cocoa beans from which chocolate is made are a product of the Americas, where the Aztec emperors drank a chocolate liquid from golden ceremonial goblets, declaring it the royal drink. Doubtless your family will give chocolate a royal welcome, too, especially in the form of an extravagant chocolate cake.

Luscious and irresistible, a chocolate cake is a traditional welcome sign to guests and a special favorite with children. Generally, the more chocolate, the better — lavish rich chocolate icing over dark devil's food layers is nearly impossible to match.

Our cake was baked in a sheet cake pan, then divided into three separate sections. Each section was generously spread with Mocha Butter Cream and stacked to make 3 layers. Special Chocolate Icing was poured over the top as a glaze.

STACKED CHOCOLATE CAKE

1½ c. milk
4 sq. unsweetened chocolate
1½ c. sugar
½ c. butter
1 tsp. vanilla extract
2 eggs
2 c. sifted all-purpose flour
¾ tsp. salt
1 tsp. soda
1 recipe Mocha Butter Cream *(pg. 51)*
½ recipe Special Chocolate Icing

Line the bottom of a 13 x 8 x 2-inch baking pan with waxed paper, then grease and flour the waxed paper. Place 1 cup of milk, chocolate and ½ cup of sugar in the top of a double boiler. Place over boiling water and cook, stirring constantly, until chocolate is melted. Remove from boiling water and cool. Cream the butter and remaining sugar in a large mixing bowl with an electric mixer. Add the vanilla extract and eggs and beat well. Beat in the chocolate mixture. Sift the flour with the salt, then add to the chocolate mixture alternately with remaining milk. Beat for 2 minutes with the mixer at medium speed. Dissolve the soda in 3 table-spoons of boiling water. Add to the cake batter and beat for 1 minute longer. Pour into the prepared pan. Bake at 350 degrees for 30 to 35 minutes or until cake tests done. Cool in the pan for 10 minutes, then remove from the pan and cool on a rack. Trim edges from the cake and cut the cake cross-wise into 3 equal portions. Cover 2 portions with Mocha Butter Cream, then stack one on top of the other. Place on a cake plate. Top with the remaining portion. Spread top and sides with thin layer of Mocha Butter Cream. Pour most of the icing over top and sides of the cake and chill until firm. Drizzle remaining icing over top of the cake, if desired and chill until firm. This makes about 12 servings.

SPECIAL CHOCOLATE ICING

½ c. light corn syrup
6 tbsp. water
5 tbsp. butter
1 12-oz. package semisweet chocolate bits

Combine the corn syrup, water and butter in a saucepan. Bring to a rapid boil, stirring until butter is melted. Remove from heat and add the chocolate. Stir until the chocolate is completely melted. Cool to room temperature before pouring over cake, *petits fours* or desired dessert to glaze, then chill until set. This makes about 2½ cups of icing.

angel food cake

ANGEL FOOD CAKE

1 c. sifted cake flour
1½ c. sugar
¼ tsp. salt
12 egg whites
1¼ tsp. cream of tartar
1¼ tsp. almond extract
Toasted slivered almonds
Confectioners' sugar

Sift flour with ¾ cup of sugar and salt 4 times. Beat the egg whites with the cream of tartar until soft peaks form. Add remaining sugar, 2 tablespoons at a time, beating well after each addition. Sift ¼ cup of the flour mixture over egg whites and fold in carefully, then fold in the remaining flour mixture by fourths. Turn into a 10-inch tube pan. Bake in a preheated 375-degree oven for 35 to 40 minutes or until cake tests done. Invert the pan on a funnel and cool completely. Remove from pan. Scatter almonds on top and sprinkle with confectioners' sugar.

angel food cake

Soft, white and light as a feather, Angel Food Cake is deliciously delicate. It possesses a typical spongy texture with fine even holes, and a light brown crust that is tender but not sticky. Cover the top with slivered almonds and sifted confectioners' sugar. However, with the plain crust, it is wonderful with ice cream or fresh fruits and whipped cream.

mincemeat roll

MINCEMEAT ROLL

1 recipe Basic Rolled Sponge Cake (pg. 3)
1 1-lb. 2-oz. jar mincemeat
Sifted confectioners' sugar

Prepare the cake as instructed but do not roll. Place the mincemeat in a saucepan and heat through. Spread on the cake, then roll as for jelly roll. Sprinkle with confectioners' sugar. Slice and place on a serving platter. Garnish as desired. This makes 8 to 10 servings.

mincemeat roll

Mincemeat Roll, attractive and appetizing, was sliced and decorated with holly leaves of almond paste for Christmas festivities. A Basic Sponge Cake was spread with mincemeat, rolled up and dusted with confectioners' sugar. The old-fashioned glass sherry shaker in the background is filled with rum for sprinkling over the dessert. Although the Mincemeat Roll is shown in a holiday setting, it is a treat any time of the year. Served with piping hot coffee, family and friends will be delighted with its flavor and texture.

italian trifle

sprinkle ¹/₃ of the mixture over the cake layer. Spread ¹/₂ of the custard over the layer, then spread ¹/₂ of the glaze over the custard. Add second cake layer and sprinkle with ¹/₂ of the remaining wine mixture. Spread with remaining custard, then with remaining glaze. Add remaining cake layer and sprinkle with remaining wine mixture. Spread a thin layer of meringue over tops and sides of cake. Place remaining meringue in an icing bag with No. 4 star tube affixed and pipe onto top and sides of the cake as shown in the illustration. Bake in a pre-heated 350-degree oven for about 15 minutes or until golden brown. Cool, then chill. Decorate as desired. This makes 10 to 12 servings.

ITALIAN TRIFLE

1 recipe Basic Rolled Sponge Cake *(pg. 3)*
³/₄ c. sweet white wine
¹/₂ tsp. Strega
1 recipe Basic Confectioners' Custard *(pg. 19)*
1 recipe Apricot Glaze *(pg. 19)*
1 recipe Basic Meringues mixture *(pg. 10)*

Prepare the sponge cake but do not roll. Cut the sponge cake into 3 equal layers and place 1 layer on a cookie sheet. Mix the wine and Strega and

italian trifle

A Basic Rolled Sponge Cake was cut into three parts, custard and jelly filling spread between the layers, then mounds of luxurious meringue swirled over all to form this elegant Italian Trifle. Classic and extravagant in appearance, it will lend flair to any occasion.

introducing
fabulous crêpes

Anyone who can perfect the ability to make *crêpes* (thin French pancakes) has the foundation for creating many luscious and economical dishes. The possibilities range from first course recipes through desserts.

There are three important factors to consider when preparing *crêpes*. 1. The proper consistency of the batter depends on not overbeating. Beat the batter just until the dry ingredients are moistened and the batter is smooth. The best results will be achieved if the batter is mixed, covered, and stored for at least 30 minutes before cooking. 2. The surface of the *crêpe* pan, griddle or suitable skillet must be lightly and uniformly oiled. Re-oil the cooking surface as needed. 3. A source of even heat is important when cooking *crêpes*. The heat must constantly remain at the proper temperature.

Crêpes differ from their lower echelon cousin, the pancake, in that they are very thin and light. They may be spread with fruit or jam, rolled up and served as a dessert. Frequently, as in *Crêpes Suzette*, they are doused with Cognac, ignited, and brought flaming to the table. *Crêpes* may also be filled with savory meat, seafood or poultry mixtures and served as a first course or a light entrée for a luncheon. The variety of ways *crêpes* may be used is endless. The chafing dish is the perfect way to serve *crêpes*.

how to make basic crêpes

BASIC CRÊPE BATTER

6 eggs
¼ tsp. salt
2 tbsp. water
¼ c. all-purpose flour
3 tbsp. confectioners' sugar

Combine the eggs, salt and water in a mixer bowl and beat thoroughly with an electric mixer. Sift the flour and sugar together, then beat into the egg mixture gradually until smooth. Cook as instructed in the step-by-step illustrations and serve immediately with desired sauce or filling or store for later use, if desired. This makes enough batter for ten 6-inch *crêpes*.

SAVORY CRÊPE BATTER:

Prepare the Basic *Crêpe* Batter, omitting the sugar. Cook according to the step-by-step illustrations. Serve with seafood, poultry or meat fillings and desired sauces.

1 Place a large piece of waxed paper on a clean surface or cookie sheet, then brush with oil on both sides.

2 Place a *crêpe* or omelet pan over medium low heat, then brush with oil.

3 Lift pan from the heat and pour the batter on the side in a very thin layer.

4 Swirl the pan so the batter completely covers the bottom thinly. Return to heat and cook until set and edge is dry.

5 Slide a knife or spatula under the edge of *crêpe* to loosen.

6 Lift carefully with a spatula and turn over gently, then cook just for several seconds.

7 Remove from heat, then shake pan to loosen and slide out onto oiled paper. Continue cooking *crêpes* until all the batter is used.

8 Cut the oiled paper between *crêpes* and stack. This is the reason for oiling both sides of the waxed paper.

9 Seal the *crêpes* in aluminum foil and store in the refrigerator until ready to use. Loosen foil and place on cookie sheet in a 275-degree oven to reheat.

STORING CRÊPES

One convenient feature of *crêpes* is that they may be made ahead and stored in the refrigerator or freezer for later use. It is important to wrap the *crêpes* properly in waxed paper or aluminum foil with a sheet of paper separating each *crêpe.* When ready to use, place in warm oven until heated through.

filled loganberry crêpes

These paper-thin crêpes are filled with sweetened loganberries (raspberries may be used instead), rolled up and garnished with a dusting of confectioners' sugar. They are best served warm.

filled crêpes

FILLED LOGANBERRY CRÊPES

1 10-oz. package frozen loganberries
    or raspberries, thawed
1½ tbsp. cornstarch
⅓ c. Sauterne
1 tbsp. butter
10 Basic Crêpes (pg. 102)
Confectioners' sugar

Place the loganberries in a saucepan and stir in the cornstarch and Sauterne. Add the butter, then cook, stirring constantly, until thickened. Spoon about 2 tablespoons of the sauce on one side of a crêpe, then roll. Repeat with remaining crêpes. Place on ovenproof platter. Pour the remaining sauce over top. Place in a warm oven until ready to serve. Dust with confectioners' sugar just before serving. This makes 10 crêpes.

FILLED PINEAPPLE CRÊPES

20 Basic Crêpes (pg. 102)
2 c. canned or sweetened fresh pineapple pieces
½ c. apricot jam
¼ c. melted butter
Confectioners' sugar
Whipped cream

Prepare 2 recipes of Basic Crêpes Batter and cook according to step-by-step illustrations. Dice the pineapple pieces finely and combine with the apricot jam and butter. Spread a tablespoon of the pineapple mixture on each crêpe and roll up. Place crepes on an ovenproof platter. Brush with additional melted butter and sprinkle with confectioners' sugar. Place under broiler until lightly browned. Serve with whipped cream if desired. This makes about 10 servings.

CHOCOLATE CRÊPES

2 tbsp. cocoa
1 c. sifted all-purpose flour
¼ c. sugar
¼ tsp. salt
3 eggs
1 c. milk
½ tsp. vanilla
2 tbsp. melted butter

Sift the cocoa, flour, sugar and salt together into a medium-sized mixing bowl. Beat the eggs with an electric mixer at medium speed for 5 minutes or until thick. Stir the milk, vanilla and butter into the eggs. Blend the egg mixture into the flour mixture until smooth. Cook as instructed in the step-by-step illustrations No. 2 through No. 7 for Basic *Crêpes*, page 102, using butter to grease pan. Fold the *crêpes* into quarters and dust with confectioners' sugar. May top with sweetened whipped cream flavored with Crème de Cacao, if desired. This makes about 20 *crêpes*.

chocolate crêpes

Here is the perfect dessert for chocolate lovers. These delicate Chocolate Crêpes, shown here with a liberal dusting of confectioners' sugar, would team beautifully with vanilla ice cream or more elegantly with whipped cream and Crème de Cacao.

CRÊPES SUZETTE BATTER

When making dessert *crêpes*, many individuals use ordinary Basic *Crêpes* Batter, page 102, with good results. There are those cooks, however, who prefer the lightest possible texture in dessert *crêpes*. The following recipe for a delicate *crêpes* batter will satisfy the requirements of the most finicky chef.

CRÊPES SUZETTE

1 c. sifted all-purpose flour
3 tbsp. sugar
4 eggs
1 c. milk
¹/₂ c. water
Brandy
Orange Sauce

Sift the flour and sugar together. Beat the eggs in a medium-sized mixing bowl with an electric mixer at medium speed for 5 minutes or until thick. Add the flour mixture gradually, beating constantly until smooth. Add the milk, water and 2 tablespoons of brandy gradually and stir until the batter is smooth. Let stand for 30 minutes before using. Cook as instructed in the step-by-step illustrations No. 2 through No. 7 for Basic *Crêpes*, page 102, using butter to grease the pan. Turn very carefully as the *crêpes* are delicate. Grease the pan with additional butter as needed. *Crêpes* may be kept warm in a 250-degree oven until ready to serve. Fold *crêpes* into quarters and place in hot Orange Sauce in a chafing dish or heated serving dish. Drizzle with ¹/₂ cup of heated brandy and ignite. Serve the *crêpes* flaming. This makes about 24 *crêpes*.

Orange Sauce For Crêpes Suzette

12 sugar cubes
2 oranges
¹/₂ c. butter
²/₃ c. sifted confectioners' sugar
2 tsp. grated orange rind
1 c. orange juice
2 tsp. lemon juice
¹/₄ c. Grand Marnier or orange Curaçao liqueur

Rub the sugar cubes over the orange skins until each cube is yellow. Set aside. Melt the butter in a small saucepan over low heat and stir in the confectioners' sugar until blended, using a wooden spoon. Stir in the rind, orange juice and lemon juice. Add the sugar cubes, then cook over very low heat, pressing with the back of the spoon until dissolved. Add the Grand Marnier liqueur and cook until syrupy, stirring constantly. This makes 2 cups of sauce.

crêpes suzette

Whenever the word "crêpes" is mentioned, someone is bound to think "Suzette" because of the fame and popularity of this elegant dessert. French pancakes are heated in a tangy orange and butter sauce, folded in quarters like handkerchiefs, then flamed in brandy or orange liqueur.

The Creative Homemaker's Academy © MCMLXXIII
Selected Illustrations © B.P.C. Publishing Limited MCMLXX

HOW TO FILL AND COVER LEMON-SOUFFLÉED CRÊPES

Lemon-Souffléed *Crêpes* do require some last-minute preparation but they are guaranteed to draw raves from everyone who has a love for lemon. Basically, this dessert combines very thin *crêpes* with a light, airy lemon soufflé mixture. They are baked until puffed and browned, then heavily dusted with confectioners' sugar.

LEMON-SOUFFLÉED CRÊPES

3 tbsp. butter
3 tbsp. all-purpose flour
¼ c. lemon juice
Grated rind of 1 lemon
⅓ c. sugar
Dash of salt
½ c. Sauterne
¾ c. water
2 egg yolks, lightly beaten
4 egg whites
6 Basic Crêpes *(pg. 102)*
Confectioners' sugar

Melt the butter in the top of a double boiler over hot water. Stir in the flour until smooth. Add the lemon juice, lemon rind, sugar and salt and stir until well blended. Blend in the Sauterne, then the water gradually, stirring constantly until thickened. Remove from heat. Stir, a small amount at a time, into the egg yolks, then stir the egg yolks gradually into the sauce mixture. Return to heat and cook, stirring constantly, until thick. Remove from heat and cool. Beat the egg whites in a mixer bowl with an electric mixer until stiff peaks form. Stir in ¼ of the egg whites into the sauce, then fold in the remaining egg whites gently. Assemble according to the step-by-step illustrations. Bake in a preheated 425-degree oven, one shelf above center, for about 10 minutes or until puffed and golden. Dust generously with confectioners' sugar and serve immediately. This makes 6 servings.

2 Fold the *crêpe* over carefully.

3 Spoon soufflé mixture thickly over the filled *crêpes*.

1 Place enough of the soufflé on half of each *crêpe* for the filling.

4 Spread to edge to cover completely. Place carefully on a baking pan.

carnival crêpes

The next time you want to make a festive occasion even more special, prepare a stack of Carnival *Crêpes* for dessert. Carnival *Crêpes*, which are traditionally served in Switzerland at carnival time, are not really true *crêpes* at all but are more like deep-fried cookies.

These unusual "crêpes" are not made from a batter but from a thinly rolled dough. The dough is cut into rounds which are plunged individually into hot fat and fried until puffed-up and browned. They are then well drained, dusted with confectioners' sugar and stacked. Be sure to pass extra sugar in a bowl when serving. You may be concerned about the unusual ingredient, ammonium carbonate, but this may be found at your pharmacy.

carnival crêpes

Here's a delicious, towering dessert that will make a fitting finale for any teen-age party. But don't wait for special occasions as the excuse to make these tasty treats. Please your family and show them how special they really are. Prepare a stack of Carnival Crêpes just for them. They'll be so glad you did.

CARNIVAL CRÊPES

2½ c. sifted all-purpose flour
¼ tsp. salt
½ c. butter, softened
3 eggs
⅛ tsp. crushed ammonium carbonate
Vegetable oil
Confectioners' sugar

Combine the flour and salt in a mixing bowl, then add the butter. Rub the butter into the flour until the mixture is of a mealy consistency. Add the eggs, one at a time, and cut into the flour mixture with the side of a wooden spoon until the eggs are absorbed and the dough is smooth, thick and difficult to work with. Sprinkle with the ammonium carbonate and work into the dough. Pinch off walnut-sized pieces of dough and roll between palms of hands until round. Roll each ball until paper-thin on a heavily floured marble, enameled or other cold surface, being careful not to lift or turn while rolling. These are not difficult to roll paper-thin if surface is cold and well floured and rolling pin is well floured. Heat oil in deep fat fryer over medium high heat until very hot. Drop 1 circle at a time into hot oil and, using the handles of 2 wooden spoons, press gently and quickly around inside edge as the bubbles rise. This disperses the larger bubbles into smaller bubbles and causes the edges to flute. Turn quickly as soon as bottom is golden, being careful not to break the bubbles. Remove to paper towels to drain, then dust heavily with confectioners' sugar. This makes about 26 *crêpes*.

presenting steamed puddings

black cap pudding

Black Cap Pudding, is steamed with currants in the bottom of the mold to form the "cap." This pudding is deliciously accompanied by Basic Lemon Sauce (Sauces, pg. 25).

Introduced in this lesson is a very unique type of dessert prepared in what is perhaps an unfamiliar manner — steamed pudding. This dessert is regarded as an Englishman's heritage and an integral part of his way of life! This inherited love of the steamed pudding has always been strong in the New England states, but comparatively lost to other parts of the country. Although most Americans generally think of pudding as sweet, soft, creamy food of custard consistency, the steamed pudding of New England fame has either a spongy or cake-like texture.

The technique of steaming, though it may be unfamiliar, is simple. Generously butter a pudding mold, using more butter than the term "generously" normally implies (at least one to two tablespoons). This will assure perfect unmolding. After mixing the ingredients as called for in the chosen recipe, pour the batter into the mold and secure the lid. (If your mold has no lid, a few layers of waxed paper and a sheet of aluminum foil may be tied tightly over the top.) Now set the mold on a trivet inside a kettle or steamer, allowing at least one inch of clearance from the sides, top and bottom of the kettle, and pour in boiling water. Then tightly cover the kettle and steam the pudding over low heat. Water in the bottom of the steamer should be replaced as it evaporates.

BLACK CAP PUDDING

¾ c. currants
½ c. sugar
3 eggs
¾ c. sifted all-purpose flour
2 pinches of salt
¼ tsp. vanilla extract
Grated rind of 1 lemon
2 tbsp. butter, softened

Grease a 1-quart metal mold generously with 1 to 2 tablespoons butter. Add the currants and press down carefully but firmly. Combine the sugar and eggs in a medium-sized mixing bowl and place in a large mixing bowl, filled ⅓ full with boiling water. Beat with electric mixer at medium speed for about 5 minutes or until thick and foamy. Remove bowl from water. Mix the flour and salt, then fold in the flour, a very small amount at a time. Add the vanilla extract and lemon rind. Drop the soft butter over the top in small pieces, then fold in carefully. Butter should be very soft but not melted. Turn into prepared mold. Cover with a double thickness of buttered waxed paper, then cover with top of mold or with a double thickness of heavy-duty foil. Tie this on tightly with heavy string. Trim off paper and foil, leaving about 1 inch overhang. Place rack in steamer pan and add boiling water just to bottom of rack. Place the mold on the rack. Bring to a boil, then cover with lid. Reduce heat to low and cook at a low boil for 1 hour and 20 minutes. Add water, as needed, to keep water level just below rack. Remove mold from steamer and let rest for 2 minutes. Remove the covers and unmold. Serve with a lemon sauce (Sauces, pg. 25.) This makes about 8 servings.

HOW TO PLACE PUDDINGS INTO STEAMER

Make a simple strap with a 24-inch long strip of heavy-duty aluminum foil. Fold the foil into a 2½-inch wide strip.

1 Place the pudding mold on the strap, lift carefully and lower into the steamer.

2 Fold the ends of the strap over the pudding before placing the lid on the steamer.

3 When the pudding is done, lift from the steamer with ease — no burned fingers!

STEAMED COCONUT CAKES

½ c. sugar
3 eggs
¾ c. sifted all-purpose flour
2 pinches of salt
¼ tsp. vanilla extract
2 tbsp. butter, softened
1 c. red currant jelly
1 c. freshly grated coconut

Combine sugar and eggs in a medium-sized mixing bowl. Place the medium-sized bowl in a larger mixing bowl, filled ⅓ full with boiling water. Beat eggs and sugar with an electric mixer at medium speed for about 5 minutes or until thick and foamy. Remove bowl from water. Combine the flour and salt, then fold into the egg mixture, a very small amount at a time. This must be done very slowly and carefully. Fold in the vanilla extract. Drop the soft butter over the top in small pieces and fold in carefully. Butter should be very soft but not melted. Spoon into 6 very heavily buttered, individual molds or custard cups. Cover with buttered waxed paper and aluminum foil. Place on rack in steamer and add boiling water to just below rack. Cover and steam for 30 minutes. Remove covers and unmold. Melt the jelly in a small saucepan and place the coconut in a shallow bowl. Dip the cakes in the jelly to coat the top and side, then roll in the coconut. Garnish as desired. This makes 6 servings.

steamed coconut cakes

These Steamed Coconut Cakes were cooked in special dariole molds, ideally sized for individual servings. The use of small molds shortens the steaming time considerably. Alternative molds are everyday custard cups. The large copper chocolatière is filled with German Custard, page 86, to spoon over the dessert.

plum pudding

escoffier's christmas plum pudding

Escoffier's Christmas Plum Pudding is filled with the moisture and flavor of several fruits. Imagine apples, sultanas, raisins, currants, orange juice, and lemon juice steamed into one lovely concoction custom-tailored to crown your Christmas dinner. Accompanying it is holiday-right Brandy Butter (General Information, pg. 38), tinted with a few drops of green food coloring.

ESCOFFIER'S CHRISTMAS PLUM PUDDING

1 1-lb. loaf day-old bread
½ lb. suet, ground
1¾ c. all-purpose flour
½ c. (firmly packed) brown sugar
1 cooking apple, peeled and chopped
1½ c. golden raisins
1½ c. raisins
1¾ c. currants
2 tbsp. minced crystallized ginger
2 tsp. ground allspice
¼ c. flaked almonds
2 eggs
¾ c. brandy
Juice of 2 oranges
Juice of 1 lemon
Grated rind of 1 orange
Grated rind of 1 lemon
¼ c. whipping cream

Process the bread in a blender to make fine crumbs. Place in a large mixing bowl. Add the prepared suet, flour, brown sugar, apple, raisins, currants, ginger, allspice and almonds to bread crumbs, then mix well. Beat the eggs and add the brandy, juices and rinds. Blend into the crumb mixture, mixing well, then mix in the cream. Cover with plastic wrap and refrigerate overnight. Pack into two 1-quart pudding molds. Cover with buttered waxed paper and foil. Tie securely with string and trim off excess paper and foil. Cover with the pudding mold lid. Place in steamer and pour boiling water into steamer, halfway up side of mold. Cover with lid. Steam for 6 hours, adding water to maintain water level, as necessary. Serve with Brandy Butter (General Information, pg. 38). This makes about 15 servings.

HOW TO PREPARE SUET

Tear the suet into small pieces, discarding any stringy membranes. Chop the suet, a small amount at a time, in a blender or grind the suet in a meat grinder using the fine blade.

christmas cranberry pudding

christmas cranberry pudding

The spirit of yuletide is beautifully captured in Christmas Cranberry Pudding. Bright dots of color, provided by juicy, red cranberries, spark the holiday mood. And the accompanying Eggnog Dessert Sauce is as delicious as it is traditional.

CHRISTMAS CRANBERRY PUDDING

6 tbsp. butter
³/₄ c. sugar
2 eggs
2¹/₄ c. sifted all-purpose flour
2¹/₂ tsp. baking powder
¹/₄ tsp. salt
¹/₂ c. milk
2 c. cranberries
¹/₂ c. chopped pecans
Eggnog Dessert Sauce

Cream the butter and sugar in a large mixing bowl. Add eggs, one at a time, beating well after each addition. Sift the flour, baking powder and salt together and add to the creamed mixture alternately with milk. Stir in the cranberries and pecans. Turn into a greased 6-cup pyrex bowl or mold and cover with foil. Press foil tightly around edge and secure with string. Place mold on a rack in a kettle and pour enough water into kettle to come halfway up on mold. Bring water to a boil and cover tightly. Reduce heat to simmer. Steam for 2 hours. Let stand for 10 minutes, then unmold. Serve with Eggnog Dessert Sauce. Pudding may be refrigerated for several days or cooled, wrapped and frozen for several months. Thaw in refrigerator, if frozen, then wrap in foil. Bake at 325 degrees for about 45 minutes. This makes 10 to 12 servings.

EGGNOG DESSERT SAUCE

1 c. butter
1¹/₂ c. sugar
1 c. commercial eggnog
1 tbsp. rum

Combine the butter, sugar and eggnog in a saucepan, then simmer until heated through, stirring occasionally. Stir in rum. This makes 3 cups of sauce.

HOW TO FLAME A PUDDING

Flaming a steamed pudding is easy and failure-proof if you follow our simple procedure. Warm one part brandy to two parts vodka in a small saucepan over low heat. Then pour it over your dessert, set it alight and carry your pudding to the table in soft blue flames. The vodka, quite high in alcoholic content facilitates the flaming procedure and does not detract from the taste of the brandy in the pudding. Don't despair if your brandy/vodka mixture overheats and sets fire to itself in the saucepan. Just pour it on the dessert flaming. Please be careful when pouring the flaming mixture.

Cream Caramel Pudding is a delectable steamed dessert that is in actuality a basic sweet custard recipe. It is a contrast to the steamed puddings presented to this point, both of which have had cake textures.

Perhaps a few reminders are needed. First, do not worry about the omission of a butter coating on the mold; although the previous dishes necessitated a thick buttering, this pudding will come out of the mold quite easily without it.

Second, work with the caramelized sugar very carefully. Stir the sugar while heating, just as the recipe directs, over very low heat. When the sugar liquid is clear, transfer it quickly to the mold — because it will harden almost instantaneously if allowed to cool!

Finally, (and most important!) during steaming the water underneath the pudding must not be allowed to boil, for it will cause holes in the finished pudding. The water should be kept steaming gently. Although very simple, this is considered a very sophisticated dessert.

CREAM CARAMEL PUDDING

2¼ c. milk
1 c. sugar
1 vanilla pod or ½ tsp. vanilla extract
2 eggs
4 egg yolks
Pinch of salt

Combine the milk, ½ cup sugar and the vanilla pod in a heavy saucepan. Bring to a boil, then remove from heat. Let stand for 20 minutes, then remove the vanilla pod. Add vanilla extract if not using vanilla pod. Place the remaining sugar in a small saucepan. Place over very low heat and do not stir until sugar begins to brown, then stir very gently with back of wooden spoon until all sugar is dissolved and lightly browned. Pour quickly into a 1-quart ceramic pudding mold or terrine and swirl to cover bottom. Combine the eggs, egg yolks and salt in a mixer bowl and beat with an electric mixer until well mixed. Beat in the milk. Strain to remove foam. Pour into the caramelized sugar-lined mold. Cover with buttered waxed paper and foil. Tie securely with string and trim off excess paper and foil. Cover with pudding mold lid. Pour boiling water in steamer pan to just below rack. Place mold on rack and cover steamer with lid. Simmer for 1 hour and 15 minutes. Remove from the steamer and remove covers. Let stand until completely cooled. Invert onto serving dish. This makes about 6 servings.

cream caramel pudding

The perfect Cream Caramel Pudding is buttery smooth and free of holes. The luscious "juice" at the base of the pudding is actually the caramelized sugar that was poured into the mold before steaming. As the pudding is unmolded, the sugary liquid coats the custard. To add more richness to individual servings, spoon extra caramel over each.

ORANGE AND LEMON CURD PUDDING

1 recipe Basic Suet Crust
1 c. Lemon Curd *(Sauces, pg. 25)*
2 c. well-drained orange sections

Roll out the dough on floured surface to ¼-inch thickness and large enough to completely line a 1½-quart mold. Reroll the leftover scraps ⅛ inch thick and cut 1 circle to fit top of mold and set aside. Use the remaining pieces of dough for layers in the pudding. Spoon ¼ cup curd onto bottom of crust, then add ¼ cup of the orange slices. Add a layer of the dough. Add another ¼ cup curd and ¼ cup orange slices, then cover with layer of dough. Add the remaining orange slices and the remaining curd. Cover with the top circle and pinch edges together to seal. Cover with a double thickness of buttered waxed paper, then with heavy-duty foil. Tie securely with string. Trim off excess paper and foil. Place on rack of steamer pan. Pour in enough boiling water to come halfway up the side of the mold. Bring to a boil and cover steamer. Steam over low heat for 3 hours. Unmold and dust with confectioners' sugar. This makes a dumpling-like dessert. You may serve it with various dessert sauces such as Lemon Mousseline Sauce or Punch Sauce *(Sauces, pg. 25)*. This makes 6 to 8 servings.

basic suet crust and orange and lemon curd pudding

This unusual pudding begins with Basic Suet Crust, used to line the pudding mold. A mixture of orange segments and Lemon Curd is layered with pastry within the lined mold, then steamed. The finished product is actually a fruit dumpling, tastes like a deep dish cobbler but is called a pudding!

BASIC SUET CRUST

1¾ c. sifted all-purpose flour
½ tsp. salt
1½ tsp. baking powder
½ lb. suet, ground

Combine the flour, salt and baking powder in the sifter and sift onto cold working surface. Add the suet and work into the flour with 2 table knives until crumbly. Add enough cold water, about 6 to 7 tablespoons, to hold dough together. Gather into ball and roll according to recipe instructions.

sultana pudding

Sultana Pudding mixture was turned into two molds, steamed, and then stacked to produce this unique shape . . . but, of course, the choice of molds is optional. Lemon Curd (Sauces, pg. 25) is a flavorful companion for the fruit-filled dessert.

SULTANA PUDDING

2 c. fine bread crumbs
¼ c. all-purpose flour
¼ c. flaked almonds
½ c. golden raisins
½ c. raisins
½ c. currants
¼ tsp. allspice
1 tsp. grated lemon rind
1 tsp. grated orange rind
½ c. chopped peeled apple
⅓ c. chopped candied cherries
¼ c. butter
2 tbsp. (packed) light brown sugar
2 eggs
⅓ c. orange juice
¼ c. lemon juice
1 tbsp. molasses

Combine the bread crumbs, flour, almonds, raisins, currants, allspice, rinds, apple and cherries in a large bowl and blend thoroughly. Place the butter in a small mixer bowl and cream with electric mixer until smooth. Add the brown sugar and eggs, then beat until fluffy. Stir in the juices and molasses. Add the molasses mixture to the fruit mixture and toss with 2 forks until all the dry ingredients are moistened. Pack into a heavily buttered mold. Cover with buttered waxed paper, then with heavy-duty foil. Tie with string and trim off excess paper and foil. Place in steamer and pour boiling water in steamer, halfway up side of mold. Place the lid on the steamer and steam for 3 hours, adding water as necessary to maintain water level. Serve with Lemon Curd (Sauces, pg. 25) or German Custard (Desserts, pg. 86). Recipe may be doubled and half the recipe baked in a cone-shaped mold, if desired. This makes about 12 servings.

austrian nusspudding

Delicately sweetened and light, Austrian Nusspudding is much like a moist, rich, nut bread. And the secret of turning it out perfectly is to refrain from "peeking" inside the mold before the entire steaming time has elapsed — or the penalty will be a hole right in the center of the pudding. Nusspudding is delicious served warm with only a light dusting of confectioners' sugar. However, don't hesitate to serve it with Basic Chocolate Sauce (Sauces, pg. 16). A metal stencil was used for the white confectioners' sugar design on this Nusspudding. A paper doily makes a good substitute for the stencil.

AUSTRIAN NUSSPUDDING

4 c. fine soft bread crumbs
1 c. water
½ c. butter
¾ c. sugar
5 eggs, separated
2 c. ground walnuts or pecans
¼ tsp. salt
1 tsp. vanilla

Place the bread crumbs in a large bowl and pour the water over top, then let stand until bread crumbs are thoroughly moistened. Place the butter in a large bowl and cream with an electric mixer for about 5 minutes or until light. Add the sugar and beat until fluffy. Beat the egg yolks slightly and add a small amount at a time to the butter mixture alternately with the bread crumbs. Beat until smooth. Add the walnuts, salt and vanilla and blend well. Beat the egg whites until stiff peaks form. Stir ¼ of the egg whites into walnut mixture, then fold in the remaining egg whites very gently. Turn into a heavily buttered 7-inch soufflé dish. Cover the top with buttered waxed paper, then cover with heavy-duty foil. Tie securely with string and trim off excess paper and foil. Place in the steamer on rack and pour boiling water into steamer to just below rack. Cover steamer with lid and steam for 3 hours and 30 minutes. Unmold onto serving dish. Serve with a chocolate sauce or whipped cream, or both if desired. This makes 8 servings.

STEAMED CHOCOLATE PUDDING

1/2 c. butter, softened
3/4 c. sugar
3/4 c. all-purpose flour
3 tbsp. cocoa
1/8 tsp. salt
3 eggs
1/2 tsp. vanilla extract
1/4 c. half and half cream
Confectioners' sugar

Cream the butter in mixer bowl with electric mixer until light and fluffy. Add the sugar and beat for about 5 minutes. Sift the flour, cocoa and salt together. Beat in the flour mixture and eggs alternately, beginning and ending with the flour mixture. Add the vanilla extract and cream and beat in thoroughly. Turn into a very heavily buttered 1 to 1 1/2-quart metal mold or pyrex dish. Use 1 to 2 tablespoons butter to grease mold. Place a double thickness of buttered waxed paper over top, then cover with a double thickness of heavy-duty foil. Tie this tightly with heavy string. Trim paper and foil, leaving only about 1 inch overhang. If mold has a lid, place on top. Place rack in steamer and add boiling water just to bottom of rack. Place the mold on the rack. Bring to a boil, then cover with lid. Reduce heat to low and cook at a low boil for 2 hours, adding boiling water occasionally to keep water level just below rack. Remove mold from steamer. Let rest for about 2 minutes, then remove covers and un-mold. Dust generously with confectioners' sugar. Serve plain, with whipped cream, a chocolate sauce or Brandy Butter. This makes about 8 servings.

STEAMED MOLASSES CRANBERRY PUDDING

1 1/3 c. all-purpose flour
1 c. chopped fresh cranberries
1 tsp. baking powder
1/2 c. molasses
2 tsp. soda
1/2 c. hot water

Place 1/3 cup flour in a small mixing bowl, then add the cranberries. Stir until cranberries are well coated with the flour and set aside. Combine the remaining flour with the baking powder in a separate mixing bowl. Combine the molasses, soda and hot water and stir into the flour mixture. Mix until thoroughly blended. Fold in the cranberries. Spoon into a heavily buttered pudding mold. Cover with pudding mold lid or with a double thickness of buttered waxed paper and a double thickness of aluminum foil. Tie securely with string. Place on rack in steamer pan. Add boiling water to halfway of depth of mold. Cover steamer. Steam for 2 hours, adding boiling water as needed to maintain water level. Remove from steamer. Unmold and serve with Basic Hard Sauce or Brandy Sauce (Sauces, pages 25 and 26). This makes about 6 servings.

steamed chocolate pudding

The deliciousness of Steamed Chocolate Pudding lies in its airy, light texture which seems to disappear instantly in your mouth. Because it is so light, it seems the appetite always allows "room" for a slice, even at the finish of a very filling meal. Top it with Basic Chocolate Sauce (Sauces, pg. 16).

moor in a shirt

Here is a rich dessert you may serve with pride. Moor In A Shirt is an Austrian pudding and (typical of Austrian cuisine) the recipe calls for a lavish amount of butter, cream and eggs. The pudding may be served as shown with sifted confectioners' sugar and stiffly whipped cream.

MOOR IN A SHIRT

4 slices bread, crusts removed
1/2 c. whipping cream
1/3 c. butter, softened
2 eggs
2 egg yolks
3/4 c. sifted confectioners' sugar
1/4 c. ground toasted almonds
1/3 c. chocolate chips, melted
1/8 tsp. almond extract

Break the bread into small pieces and place in a bowl. Pour the cream over the bread, then mix with a wooden spoon until cream is absorbed. Place the butter in the small mixer bowl and cream with the electric mixer for about 5 minutes or until light and creamy. Add the bread mixture and beat until light and fluffy. Combine the eggs and egg yolks and beat lightly with a fork. Add the eggs and sugar alternately to the bread mixture, a small amount at a time, beating well after each addition. Add the almonds, chocolate and almond extract and beat until well blended. Turn into a heavily buttered 1 to 1 1/2-quart pudding mold. Cover with buttered waxed paper and heavy-duty foil, then tie securely with string. Trim off excess paper and foil. Place on rack in steamer and pour boiling water just to bottom of rack. Cover with lid and steam for 2 hours. Remove from steamer and let rest for 2 minutes. Unmold onto serving dish and dust with additional confectioners' sugar. Serve with whipped cream or a chocolate sauce, if desired. This makes 4 servings.

RICH MAN

3 tbsp. brandy
3 tbsp. Basic Sugar Syrup *(Breads, pg. 14)*
8 to 10 almond macaroons
¾ c. unsalted butter
1 c. sifted confectioners' sugar
¼ c. sherry
2 egg yolks
¼ c. ground toasted almonds
2 hard-boiled egg yolks, sieved
1 recipe Basic Chantilly Cream *(pg. 19)*

Combine the brandy and sugar syrup. Place the macaroons in a pie plate and pour the brandy mixture over top. Let soak until soft. Lift carefully with spatula and arrange in a well-buttered 1-quart mold. Place the butter in the small mixer bowl and cream with electric mixer for about 5 minutes or until light and fluffy. Add the sugar and beat until smooth. Add the sherry, egg yolks, almonds and hard-boiled egg yolks, then beat for about 5 minutes. Spoon carefully over the macaroons and pack down smoothly. Cover with plastic wrap and chill overnight. Dip in hot water and unmold in serving dish. Pipe the Chantilly Cream around the edge and on the top as desired. This makes 8 servings.

rich man

Rich Man, another flamboyantly delicious Austrian creation, is a chilled dessert. Its name alludes to the extravagant ingredients which include brandy, sherry, macaroons, almonds and generous measures of butter and eggs. For a serving variation, the dessert may be turned upside down after chilling and decorated, as shown, with whipped cream.

charlotte russe

Fancifully decorated with glacé fruit, whipped cream and ribbon, this classically elegant "lady" is Charlotte Russe. Ladyfingers are stood on end and fixed into place in a springform pan to form a border. Then a sumptuous cream filling is poured in and the dessert is refrigerated. The ribbon, optional of course, is not only for looks — it prevents the dessert from collapsing in a heated room! Decorative crystallized fruit may be used as a garnish.

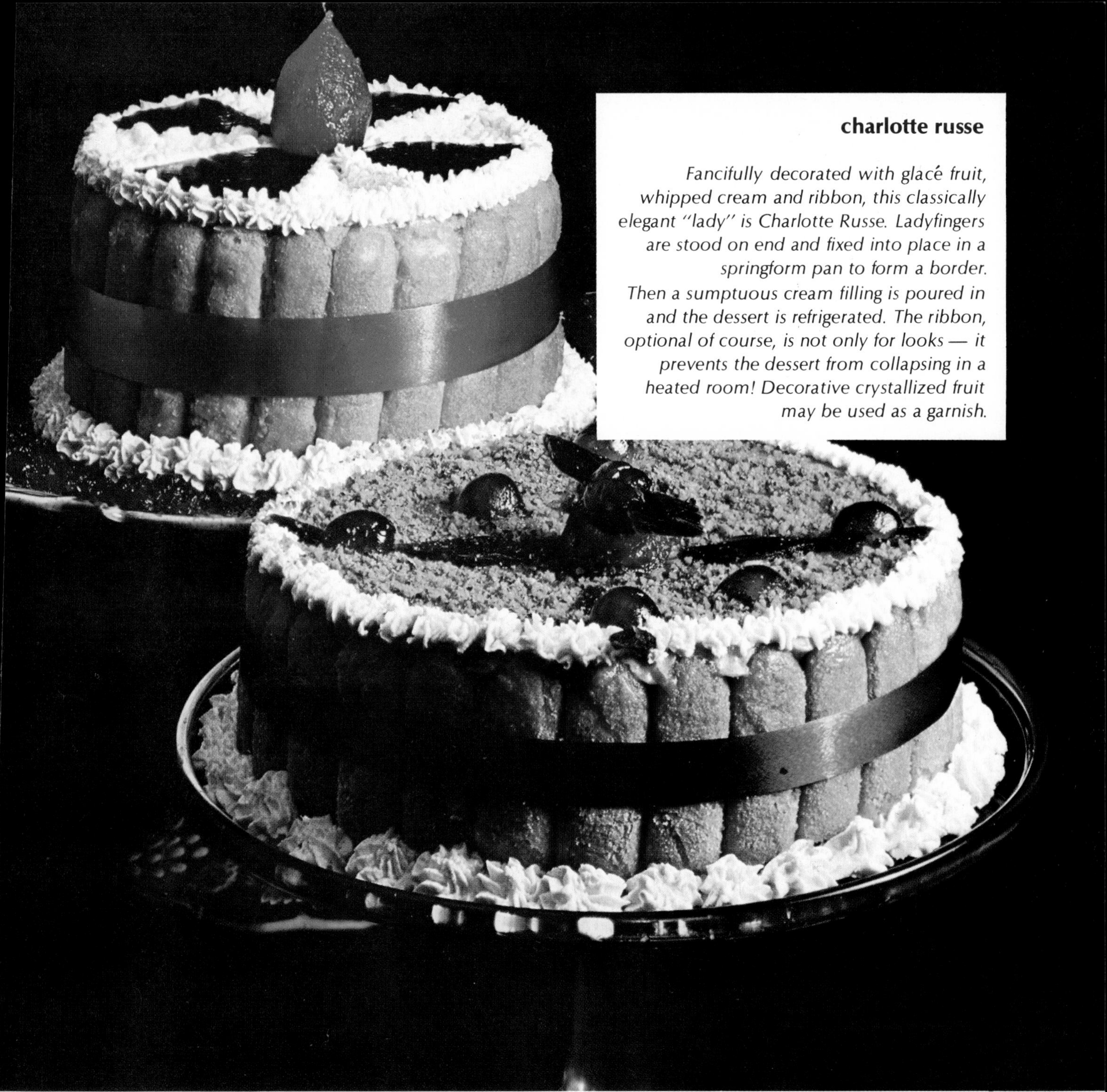

CHARLOTTE RUSSE

12 ladyfingers
Light corn syrup
2 env. unflavored gelatin
1 c. sugar
1/4 tsp. salt
4 eggs, separated
2 1/2 c. milk
2 tbsp. brandy or sherry
1 c. whipping cream, whipped

Wet the base of an 8-inch springform pan. Split the ladyfingers and cut off 1/2-inch tip of each half. Coat the side of the springform pan with corn syrup and place the ladyfinger halves around side of the pan, curved end up, to stand upright. Mix the gelatin, 1/2 cup sugar and salt in a 2-quart saucepan. Beat the egg yolks, then stir in the milk. Stir into the gelatin mixture and cook over low heat, stirring constantly, for about 6 minutes or until the gelatin is dissolved. Remove from heat. Add the brandy and mix well. Chill until mixture mounds slightly when dropped from a spoon. Beat the egg whites until stiff, but not dry, then beat until very stiff, adding remaining sugar gradually. Fold into the gelatin mixture. Fold in the whipped cream and turn into the prepared pan. Chill until firm. Release the spring to unmold and remove side of pan carefully. Place on a serving platter. Pipe additional whipped cream around the top edge and base of the Charlotte Russe and garnish as desired. This makes 12 servings.

ELEGANT STRAWBERRY WHIP

1 pt. fresh strawberries
1 c. whipping cream
½ c. confectioners' sugar, sifted
1 egg white
1 tsp. maraschino liqueur
1 tsp. kirsch

Remove the hulls from the strawberries and set aside 6 of the largest. Place the remaining strawberries in blender container and process until puréed. Whip the cream until soft peaks form, then beat in half the sugar. Beat the egg white until stiff but not dry, then fold into the whipped cream gently with the maraschino. Blend the kirsch and remaining sugar into the strawberry purée, then fold into the cream mixture. Spoon into 6 individual serving dishes and chill thoroughly. Garnish with the reserved strawberries. This makes 6 servings.

elegant strawberry whip

This light and appetizing summer treat has been aptly named Elegant Strawberry Whip. Puréed strawberries flavored with kirsch and maraschino liqueur are folded into whipped cream and egg whites for a pretty, chilled delight.

petits fours candies

The most thoughtful and meaningful gifts are those that you make yourself. Almost everyone indulges in a taste for sweets now and then, especially if the sweet is home-made candy. No matter what kind of candy is being made, there are a few basic rules that must be kept in mind if professional results are to be achieved. Use a large heavy saucepan with a capacity at least four times as large as the amount of candy mixture being cooked in it. It should have straight sides. Stir the candy mixture constantly until the sugar dissolves; then stir only as needed to prevent the mixture from sticking and scorching. Always use a wooden spoon — it will not heat up during the cooking time. If the recipe calls for butter, it is best to use unsalted butter. If sugar crystals form on the side of the pan, *do not* stir them into candy mixture. They may be removed with a basting brush rinsed in cold water. The most important piece of equipment to invest in for successful candymaking is an accurate candy thermometer — it is not expensive and can make the difference between grainy, rough-textured candy and smooth, creamy-textured treats that would rival any professional confectioner's product.

petits fours candies

Develop your skill at making candies and confections and you'll never again be at a loss for gift ideas (or something fun to do). A colorful, art-fully arranged assortment of homemade candies is a lovely present to give for almost any occasion.

Fondant is a creamy, soft mixture consisting of sugar, water, cream of tartar and flavorings. It is the foundation for many different candies that are not called fondant, but have fondant centers, stuffings or coatings. Chocolate creams, for example, are really fondants that have been dipped in chocolate. The pastel mints that frequently appear on the table at wedding receptions are pure fondant. Almonds and raisins are sometimes coated with creamy, smooth fondant. Dates and prunes may be stuffed with it, transforming the plain fruit into an unusual confection. Another popular use for fondant is for icing cakes and cookies.

The recipe for Basic Fondant adapts itself to many flavor variations. The water called for in the list of ingredients for Cooked Fondant may be replaced with strong coffee to give it a completely different flavor. The possibilities for using fondant are endless — most cooks find that once they have mastered the basic technique for making this useful confection, their culinary resources are endless.

BASIC FONDANT

1 1-lb box confectioners' sugar
1/4 c. light corn syrup
1 egg white

Combine the sugar, syrup and egg white in a bowl. Stir with a wooden spoon until mixture holds together, then turn out on a surface dusted with additional sifted confectioners' sugar. Knead for several minutes until the mixture is no longer sticky. Add desired flavoring, then roll out and cut into desired shapes. Place on a rack to dry, then store between waxed paper in a covered container. This makes about 1 1/2 cups of fondant.

VARIATIONS:
PEPPERMINT FONDANT

Add 5 or 6 drops of peppermint oil to Basic Fondant and knead until the flavoring is thoroughly blended into the mixture. Food coloring may be added with the oil of peppermint.

RASPBERRY FONDANT

Add about 2 tablespoons of raspberry-flavored powdered drink mix to Basic Fondant and knead until well blended.

COOKED FONDANT

2/3 c. sugar
1/3 c. light corn syrup

1/2 c. water
1/8 tsp. cream of tartar

Combine the sugar, syrup, water and cream of tartar in a heavy 2-quart saucepan. Stir until the sugar is dissolved, then cook over medium heat, stirring constantly, until the mixture comes to a boil. Cover the saucepan and cook for 3 minutes, then remove the cover and cook, without stirring, to 240 degrees on a candy thermometer. Remove from heat and pour at once onto a damp marble slab. Let set until just warm to the touch. Beat the fondant briskly with a metal spatula by turning in all the edges and continue until the mixture begins to thicken and turns creamy white. Do not become discouraged, as this process takes time. Store in a covered container at room temperature for 2 or 3 days to mellow. The fondant will change in consistency during this period. Remove the portion needed and add desired flavoring. Food coloring may also be added at this point. Knead until flavoring and coloring is thoroughly blended. Turn out on a marble slab dusted lightly with confectioners' sugar and roll out. Cut in desired shapes. This makes about 1 1/2 cups of fondant.

DIVINITY

2 1/2 c. sugar
1/2 c. light corn syrup
2/3 c. water
2 egg whites
2 tsp. vanilla extract

Place the sugar, syrup and water in a heavy 2-quart saucepan. Bring to a boil, stirring constantly, until sugar is completely dissolved, then wipe the side of pan with damp cloth wrapped around spoon. Cover the pan and cook for 1 minute. Uncover and cook the syrup to 232 degrees on a candy thermometer. Place the egg whites in a mixer bowl while syrup is cooking and beat with an electric mixer until stiff but not dry. Pour 1/3 of the syrup in a thin stream over the egg whites while beating constantly. Cook the remaining syrup to 244 degrees on the candy thermometer. Add to the egg white mixture in a thin stream, beating constantly. Add the vanilla extract and beat for 12 to 15 minutes or until the candy holds a peak when dropped from a spoon. Spoon the candy in mounds onto waxed paper, using 2 teaspoons. This makes about 60 pieces of divinity.

CHOCOLATE CHERRY CORDIALS

1 12-oz. package chocolate chips, melted (pg. 49)
3 tbsp. kirsch
1 1/2 tbsp. grenadine syrup
24 candied cherries

Spoon a small amount of melted chocolate into each of 24 paper or foil candy cases, coating sides and bottoms well. Chill for not more than 5 minutes to set chocolate. Combine the kirsch and grenadine syrup and chill well. Place a cherry in each case. Drizzle enough of the kirsch mixture over each cherry to cover halfway. Spoon melted chocolate over each cherry to fill case. Chill for 5 minutes or until chocolate is set. Place in airtight container and let stand for at least 24 hours before using. Peel casings from candy and eat carefully as the syrup will drip. This makes 24 cordials.

The Creative Homemaker's Academy © MCMLXXIII
Selected Illustrations © B.P.C. Publishing Limited MCMLXX

basic swiss chocolate mixture

One of the most delicious of all candies is Basic Swiss Chocolate Mixture, also called *Canache*. This combination of melted semisweet chocolate and heavy cream is well blended, allowed to cool and cut into small fancy shapes. This may be done either with a sharp paring knife or with candy cutters, if they are available in a local gourmet shop. The candy shapes may then be coated with chocolate drink powder, creamy fondant or melted chocolate chips. Or, more simply, they may be garnished with candy decorations and bits of nutmeats. Let your imagination be your guide!

BASIC SWISS CHOCOLATE MIXTURE (CANACHE)

³/₄ c. whipping cream
1 12-oz. package chocolate chips, melted
  (pg. 49)

Heat the cream in a double boiler until bubbling steadily. Pour the cream into the melted chocolate gradually, beating vigorously with a wooden spoon until dark and glossy. Return the chocolate mixture to the double boiler. Cook over medium heat, stirring constantly, for about 25 minutes or until the mixture is thick and falls heavily from the spoon. Cool for 5 minutes. Spread quickly in a buttered 8-inch square pan. Chill for 2 hours or until firm enough to handle easily. Cut the candy into squares, triangles or desired shapes. You may also break off pieces and roll them into balls. These pieces may be dipped in melted chocolate chips, chocolate drink powder or chocolate decorettes.

1 Dip the *Canache* pieces into instant chocolate drinking powder mix.

2 Roll the *Canache* balls in chocolate decorettes for Chocolate Truffles.

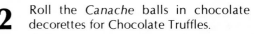

chocolate-coconut dips

1 recipe Basic Fondant *(pg. 124)*
¾ c. flaked coconut
1 12-oz. package chocolate chips, melted
    (pg. 49)
Sifted confectioners' sugar

1 Combine the fondant and the coconut and knead until well blended. Roll small pieces of the mixture between the palms of your hands to shape as shown in the illustration. Let them dry on racks for about 1 hour.

2 Drop 1 or 2 pieces at a time into the chocolate and turn with a wire loop until completely coated.

3 Drop the chocolate-coated pieces of candy into a jelly roll pan filled with sifted confectioners' sugar.

4 Roll in the confectioners' sugar with a fork until thickly coated. Sift confectioners' sugar into a serving dish and arrange the candy in the sugar. This makes 2½ to 3 dozen pieces of candy.

COCONUT PYRAMIDS

5½ c. freshly grated coconut
1 c. vanilla sugar *(Desserts, pg. 2)*
2 eggs, well beaten

Combine the coconut and sugar in a large mixer bowl and blend well with an electric mixer. Add the eggs and blend thoroughly. Pinch off a small amount of the mixture and roll into balls the size of a walnut, then shape into cones. Place the cones on waxed paper on a baking sheet. Bake in a preheated 350-degree oven for about 15 minutes or until top is lightly browned. Place the baking sheet on a wet towel and remove the cones immediately with a wet spatula. Cool on wire racks. You may divide the coconut mixture in half and tint ½ with red food coloring, if desired. These may be stored for several days in an airtight container. This makes about 24 pyramids.

coconut pyramids

Little kitchen helpers can take part in the preparation of these colorful Coconut Pyramids. They are chewy, sweet, simple to make, and guaranteed to please the "coconut lover".

ORANGE TWIGS

5 or 6 thin-skinned oranges
2 c. Basic Sugar Syrup *(Breads, pg. 14)*
½ c. sugar
1 tsp. cream of tartar
1 6-oz. package chocolate chips, melted *(pg. 49)*

Score the oranges with a sharp knife at ½-inch intervals at widest point, starting at stem end. Cut the peeling from the oranges and trim the ends, making twig-shaped pieces. Scrape some of the white membrane from the orange peelings and discard. Place the peelings in a medium saucepan and cover with cold water. Bring to a boil, then drain off the water. Repeat the boiling and draining process 2 more times to remove the bitterness from the peelings. Pour the sugar syrup over the peelings in the saucepan and bring to a boil. Reduce the heat and simmer for about 1 hour or until peelings are transparent. Remove the peelings with a slotted spoon and drain on waxed paper. Cool until easily handled. Sift the sugar and cream of tartar together. Dredge the peelings in the sugar mixture. Place on a rack and let stand overnight. Dip the peelings in the melted chocolate with tweezers and drain on waxed paper. Chill for no longer than 5 minutes to set chocolate. Trim off excess chocolate with a sharp knife. This makes about 70 twigs.

introducing
cookies

One of the most welcoming aromas is the fragrant smell of cookies baking in the oven. A treat to anyone who enjoys sweets, cookies are a favorite snack food. All cookies, no matter what shape or flavor, fall into one of five categories: drop, rolled, refrigerator, shaped or bar.

Drop cookies such as chocolate chip, are, as their name suggests, dropped by spoonfuls onto a cookie sheet. The resulting shape is irregular and round. The dough for drop cookies is soft and expands during baking. Allow 2 inches between each spoonful of dough on the cookie sheet.

Rolled cookies are made from a fairly stiff dough which is rolled out to a thickness of about ¼ inch and cut into the desired shapes. These cookies are usually crisp and tend to break fairly easily. They do not mail well.

Refrigerator cookies are a great convenience for busy homemakers. A rich thick dough can be made, shaped into rolls about 2 inches in diameter, and chilled in the refrigerator. When needed, small rounds are cut off and baked. They are easy and delicious.

CHOCOLATE-DIPPED ALMOND MACAROONS

Shaped cookies are of two types. The first is made with a very stiff dough, put into a cookie press and squeezed out into attractive shapes on a cookie sheet. One example of this kind of cookie is Maryses. The second type of shaped cookie is also made with a stiff dough. It is shaped into small balls which are then pressed into flat cookies with the tines of a fork or the bottom of a drinking glass. Peanut butter cookies are made by this method.

Bar cookies are quick, easy and good. Brownies fall into this category which includes any cookie that is made from a soft, cake-like dough and baked in a shallow square or rectangular pan. These cookies are then cut into bars or squares.

FRENCH COCONUT MACAROONS

4 egg whites
1 tsp. vanilla extract
1 c. confectioners' sugar
2 c. flaked coconut
½ c. all-purpose flour

Beat the egg whites with an electric mixer until stiff peaks form. Add the vanilla and mix well. Add the confectioners' sugar gradually, beating well after each addition. Beat until stiff and glossy. Fold in the coconut and flour, mixing well. Drop from a teaspoon onto a buttered and floured cookie sheet. Bake in a preheated 325-degree oven for 25 minutes or until lightly browned. This makes 2 dozen macaroons.

french coconut macaroons

French Coconut Macaroons with their crisp-chewy outsides and soft centers are popular with children and grown-ups alike. For perfect results, they are baked on a buttered and floured cookie sheet to prevent them from sticking.

almond macaroons

Real Almond Macaroons, made with almond paste, may be served with cold custard or ice cream for a luncheon or dinner dessert.

ALMOND MACAROONS

1 c. sugar
1 8-oz. can almond paste
2 egg whites

Combine the sugar and almond paste in a large bowl and mix with fingers until well blended. Add the egg whites gradually, using just enough to moisten, mixing with a wooden spoon. Roll lightly into walnut-sized balls and flatten slightly. Place about 2 inches apart on brown paper on a baking sheet. Bake in a preheated 325-degree oven for about 12 minutes or until very lightly browned. Remove from the oven and slide the paper onto a damp towel. Cool slightly, then remove macaroons with a spatula. This makes about 2 dozen macaroons.

refrigerator cookies

Because of their convenience, refrigerator cookies have become a favorite filler for cookie jars. These cookies are more delicate in texture than many other kinds of cookies as they require less flour. Refrigerator cookies are also more quickly prepared than other types of cookies because of the technique used to make them. Ingredients should be stirred together thoroughly to form a soft, workable dough. Care should be taken when dough is mixed to avoid overworking it. As with any cookie recipe, proper consistency of the dough should be maintained in order to avoid toughness. After dough has been correctly prepared, it should be shaped into a 2-inch roll and sealed tightly in waxed paper. The roll should then be placed in the coldest part of the refrigerator and chilled until firm. This process usually takes between 12 to 24 hours. Once the dough roll is chilled and firm, it should be sliced very thinly for baking.

There are many wonderful advantages in preparing refrigerator cookies. If you're in a particular hurry, the dough may be spooned straight from the mixing bowl onto the baking sheet without a great loss in texture or flavor. Likewise, cookie dough may be prepared ahead of time and frozen until ready for use.

The variety of refrigerator cookies is almost endless. A good standard recipe may be varied by the addition of different flavors and ingredients. The popular variations use chocolate, butterscotch, oatmeal, honey and nuts. Regardless of the recipe, delicious refrigerator cookies are always a welcome snack or dessert. For holidays or special occasions, gaily wrapped refrigerator cookies make a wonderful gift with a homemade touch.

CHOCOLATE AND VANILLA REFRIGERATOR COOKIES

1 c. butter, softened
1 c. sugar
3 eggs
4 c. sifted all-purpose flour
½ tsp. salt
1 tsp. soda
1 tsp. baking powder
1 tsp. vanilla extract
1 1-oz. square unsweetened chocolate, melted

Combine the butter and sugar in a large bowl and beat with the electric mixer until creamy. Add the eggs, one at a time, beating after each addition until thoroughly blended. Sift the flour, salt, soda and baking powder together, then add to the creamed mixture gradually, mixing well. Divide the dough in half. Add the vanilla to 1 portion and blend thoroughly. Add the chocolate to the remaining portion and mix well. Proceed with the following step-by-step illustration.

1 Shape each portion into 2 rolls 1 inch in diameter. Place a vanilla and a chocolate roll side by side and reverse for the upper pair. Press all 4 rolls together and wrap in waxed paper. Chill in the refrigerator overnight.

2 Cut in ¼-inch slices and place on a lightly floured baking sheet. Bake in a preheated 400-degree oven for 10 to 12 minutes or until the vanilla portion is lightly browned.

3 Remove from baking sheet immediately and cool on a rack. This makes 40 cookies.

nutmeg refrigerator cookies

Nutmeg and orange juice add spice and flavor to these crisp, flaky Nutmeg Refrigerator Cookies. The convenience of make-ahead, bake-when-needed dough is part of their appeal. If desired, these cookies may be iced or dusted with confectioners' sugar.

NUTMEG REFRIGERATOR COOKIES

1/2 c. butter
1/2 c. sugar
6 tbsp. half and half cream
3 tbsp. orange juice
Grated rind of 1 orange
3 c. all-purpose flour
1 1/2 tsp. nutmeg
1/2 tsp. salt

Cream the butter with the sugar in a bowl. Combine the cream, orange juice and rind and blend well. Sift the flour with nutmeg and salt, then add to the butter mixture alternately with the orange juice mixture. Add more flour, if needed, to form a stiff dough. Shape into a roll and wrap in waxed paper. Chill overnight. Slice 1/8 inch thick and cut a small hole with a piping tube or thimble in one side of each cookie. Place on a greased baking sheet. Bake in a preheated 375-degree oven for 8 to 10 minutes or until lightly browned. This will make 4 to 5 dozen cookies.

ALMOND TRIANGLES

1/2 c. butter
1 c. sugar
6 tbsp. whipping cream
3 eggs
1/2 tsp. salt
2 c. flour
Chopped almonds

Combine the butter and sugar in a mixer bowl, then cream until smooth. Beat in the cream and 2 of the eggs. Add the salt and flour and blend well. Wrap in waxed paper and chill overnight. Roll out on a lightly floured surface and cut into triangles. Beat the remaining egg slightly and brush over top surfaces of the triangles. Sprinkle with the almonds. Place the triangles on a greased baking sheet. Bake in a preheated 375-degree oven for 8 to 10 minutes or until golden brown. This makes 3 to 4 dozen cookies.

almond triangles

Almond Triangles are not only delicious but extremely attractive looking. These flaky cookies have been brushed with beaten eggs and sprinkled with chopped almonds. They are shown here in the shape of triangles though they may be baked in other desired shapes.

long-keeping assorted cookies

Cookies are wonderfully versatile. Here is an assortment of several varieties, all of which keep beautifully in a closed container. From left to right: Nantes Cookies, Chocolate-Wine Cookies, Maryses Fingers, Chocolate-Topped Macaroons and Plain Macaroons, and Paired Chocolate Cookies which have been heavily dusted with confectioners' sugar.

NANTES COOKIES

1 1/2 c. all-purpose flour
1 tsp. baking powder
2 eggs, well beaten
1/2 c. butter, softened
1/2 c. sugar
2 tbsp. Basic Sugar Syrup *(Breads, pg. 14)*
1/4 c. finely chopped slivered almonds
1 6-oz. package chocolate chips, melted *(pg. 49)*

Sift the flour and baking powder together into a mound on a clean working surface, then shape into a ring. Pour the eggs into the center, then add the butter and sugar. Blend well with 2 pastry scrapers until smooth dough is formed. Roll the dough to 1/8 inch thickness on a lightly floured surface. Cut with a floured 1 1/2-inch round cutter. Brush the cookies with sugar syrup and sprinkle with almonds. Make a firm indentation in the center of each cookie with finger. Place the cookies on a buttered and floured cookie sheet. Bake in a preheated 350-degree oven for 18 to 20 minutes or until lightly browned. Cool the cookies on a wire rack. Drop a small amount of melted chocolate onto the center of each cookie from a demitasse spoon. Chill the cookies for no longer than 5 minutes to set the chocolate. This makes about 3 1/2 dozen cookies.

CHOCOLATE-WINE COOKIES

1 1/2 c. all-purpose flour
1 tsp. baking powder
1/2 tsp. cinnamon
1 egg, beaten
1 c. ground pecans
1/2 c. butter, softened
1/2 c. sugar
1 tsp. sherry
1 6-oz. package chocolate chips, melted *(pg. 49)*
Almond slivers

Sift the flour, baking powder and cinnamon together onto a clean working surface, then shape into a ring. Place the egg, pecans, butter, sugar, sherry and 1/2 cup of melted chocolate in the center. Blend the mixture with pastry scrapers until a smooth dough is formed. Roll the dough out on a floured surface to 1/8 inch thickness. Cut into circles with a 1 1/2-inch cookie cutter. Press the circles into miniature cupcake pans, forming a very shallow shell. Bake in a preheated 350-degree oven for about 20 to 22 minutes. Cool on a wire rack. Fill the centers with remaining melted chocolate. Insert an almond sliver in each dab of chocolate. Chill for 5 minutes to set the chocolate. This makes about 3 1/2 dozen cookies.

MARYSES

1 c. butter, softened
½ c. sifted confectioners' sugar
1½ c. all-purpose flour

Place the butter in a large mixing bowl and cream with an electric mixer until light and smooth. Add the sugar and mix until blended. Add the flour gradually, mixing to a stiff dough. Place the dough in a pastry bag with a large star tube affixed. Pipe rosettes according to the illustration. Bake in a preheated 375-degree oven for about 10 minutes or until golden brown. Remove from baking sheet and place on rack to cool. These may be put together in pairs with melted chocolate chips, if desired. This makes about 6 dozen cookies.

HOW TO PIPE MARYSES ROSETTES

Hold the bag vertically over the buttered and floured baking sheet and squeeze into uniform rosettes, making a slight twisting motion to finish according to the illustration.

MARYSES FINGERS

Pipe the Maryses dough into 3-inch lengths with the large star tube onto a buttered and floured baking sheet. Bake as for Maryses. This makes about 5 dozen fingers.

MARYSES FINGERS WITH BUTTER CREAM AND NUTS

1 recipe Maryses mixture
1 cup Basic Butter Cream No. 2 (pg. 7)
1 tsp. lemon juice
Finely chopped pecans

Prepare the Maryses fingers according to instructions and cool. Combine the Butter Cream and lemon juice and spread a small amount on the top of each finger, then sprinkle with pecans.

CHOCOLATE-TOPPED MACAROONS

1 recipe Almond Macaroons (pg. 129)
Chocolate chips, melted (pg. 49)
24 candied cherries
¼ c. sugar

Prepare and bake macaroons and let them cool according to instructions. Spread each macaroon with chocolate. Roll the cherries in sugar and press into the soft chocolate. Set in the refrigerator for no longer than 5 minutes for the chocolate to set. This makes 24 cookies.

PAIRED CHOCOLATE COOKIES

2¾ c. all-purpose flour
1 tsp. baking powder
½ tsp. salt
⅔ c. vegetable shortening
⅔ c. sugar
2 eggs
1 tsp. vanilla extract
Chocolate chips, melted (pg. 49)
Confectioners' sugar

Sift the flour, baking powder and salt together. Combine the shortening and sugar in the large mixer bowl and cream with an electric mixer until smooth. Add the eggs and beat until light and fluffy. Stir in the vanilla and the flour mixture until blended. Shape into a ball and chill in the refrigerator. Roll small portions at a time of chilled dough to ⅛-inch thickness. Cut in rounds or desired shapes. Place on a baking sheet. Bake in a preheated 350-degree oven for 12 to 15 minutes or until golden brown. Remove to a rack to cool. Spread 1 cookie with chocolate and top with another cookie, then dust with confectioners' sugar. Placing a round cookie on a shaped cookie makes a novel variation. This makes about 36 paired, chocolate cookies.

basic shortbreads

Although the term rolled cookie is familiar to almost every cook, not many associate the term shortbread with cookies. This elegant morsel is indeed a rolled cookie with a distinctive difference. A shortbread recipe uses a basic rolled cookie recipe but the measure of ingredients differs. Popular additions are almonds, brown sugar, grated citrus rind, and sour cream. Shortbread cookies may be filled or dusted with confectioners' sugar to add a special finishing touch.

BASIC SCOTCH SHORTBREAD

2 c. sifted self-rising flour
1 c. unsalted butter
3/4 c. sugar

Place the flour in a large mixing bowl. Dice the butter and add to the flour. Blend with fingers until all the butter is absorbed in the flour. Add the sugar gradually, mixing with a wooden spoon until well blended. Knead the dough on a floured surface until smooth. The dough will be very soft. Divide the dough in half. Press each half into a 9 x 5-inch rectangle on a 15½ x 10½-inch ungreased cookie sheet with sides. Bake in a preheated 350-degree oven for about 22 minutes or until just set but not browned. Cool in pan for 5 minutes, then loosen around the edges carefully. Place a sheet of aluminum foil over the pan and invert carefully. Dust with confectioners' sugar, if desired. Cut into squares to serve. This makes about 30 squares.

DATE AND WALNUT SHORTBREAD SANDWICH

1 recipe Basic Scotch Shortbread
¼ c. chopped walnuts
1 c. chopped dates
2 tbsp. strained lemon juice
1 tbsp. (packed) brown sugar
¼ c. dark rum
Confectioners' sugar

Bake the shortbread according to the instructions. Combine the remaining ingredients except confectioners' sugar in a double boiler. Cook, stirring, until thickened and of spreading consistency. Place 1 layer of the shortbread on a serving platter and spread evenly with the date filling. Place remaining layer over the filling. Dust with confectioners' sugar and garnish as desired. Cut into small squares to serve. This makes about 15 squares.

date and walnut shortbread sandwich

This unusual dessert is made by filling two rectangles of baked shortbread with a tangy mixture of chopped dates and walnuts flavored with brown sugar, rum and lemon juice. A faint dusting of confectioners' sugar provides the background for the attractive garnish — a flower of date petals with angelica stem and leaves. The center of the flower is a walnut half.

introducing
dessert fritters

Dessert fritters, often called by their French name *beignets*, (pronounced bayn-yay) are fruit or other sweets coated in dessert fritter batter or pastry, and fried in deep fat. In this section we present recipes for three fruit fritters: Strawberry, Pineapple and Cherry Fritters. Strawberry Fritters are made with Basic Chou Pastry (pg. 56), while Pineapple and Cherry Fritters are made with Basic Fruit Fritter Batter, introduced in this section. All of these bite-sized delicacies make marvelous dessert treats.

STRAWBERRY FRITTERS

1 recipe Basic Chou Pastry *(pg. 56)*
1 qt. (about) large fresh strawberries
Sifted confectioners' sugar

Cover each strawberry with as thin a layer of *chou* pastry as possible. Place the strawberries on a platter until all are coated. Drop the pastry-covered strawberries, several at a time, into 350-degree oil in a deep fat fryer. Cook for 1 minute or until the pastry is golden brown, then remove from the oil with a slotted spoon. Drain on paper toweling for several seconds. Dust the fritters generously with confectioners' sugar. This makes 6 to 8 servings.

strawberry fritters

Strawberry Fritters or beignets as they are called in France, make marvelous party delicacies. Each strawberry is enveloped in a coating of Basic Chou Pastry (pg. 56) and rolled generously in confectioners' sugar.

BUGNES

Bugnes (pronounced buns) are small, specially shaped sweets made of rolled dough which is fried in deep fat. The dough is rolled out thin, cut into sections, and each section is tucked in a traditional pattern as the recipe instructs. Bugnes, often called fritters, have a light, crisp texture and a slightly spicy flavor.

BUGNES

1 pkg. yeast
5 c. all-purpose flour
1/2 tsp. salt
3 tbsp. sugar
1/2 c. butter, softened
6 eggs
2 tbsp. brandy
2 c. confectioners' sugar
2 tsp. nutmeg
2 tsp. cinnamon

Dissolve the yeast in 1 cup of lukewarm water. Combine 1 cup of flour and the yeast mixture to form a starter. Shape the starter into a ball and cut a cross on top with scissors. Place the starter in a 2-quart bowl of warm water. The starter will sink to the bottom. Let stand for about 5 to 7 minutes or until the ball rises to the top of the water. While the starter is standing, prepare the dough. Sift the remaining 4 cups of flour, the salt and sugar together into a large bowl and make a well in the center. Beat the butter until creamy and place in the well. Add the eggs, one at a time, beating well after each addition. Add the brandy and mix the dough well. Shape into a ball on a heavily floured surface and knead until elastic. Lift the starter from the bowl of water with your hands and let the excess water drip off. Place the starter on a piece of waxed paper. Flatten the dough with your hands and place the starter on the dough, then work the two mixtures together with the pastry scrapers until the 2 mixtures hold together. Knead on a heavily floured board only until well combined. The dough will be sticky. Place the dough in a greased bowl and cover with a towel. Let rise in a warm place for about 1 hour and 30 minutes or until doubled in bulk. Punch down the dough. Roll out the dough to 1/16-inch thickness on a heavily floured surface, then cut and shape according to the diagram instructions. Place the pieces on a lightly floured baking sheet and let rise for about 30 minutes or until doubled in bulk. Drop into hot fat in a deep fat fryer and cook quickly until lightly browned on each side. Drain on absorbent paper. Combine confectioners' sugar and spices in a paper bag and add the fried bungnes, shaking to coat well. You may serve these with Luxembourg Sauce (Sauces, pg. 20), Lemon Mousseline or Basic Lemon Sauce (Sauces, pg. 25). This makes about 100 Bugnes.

how to fold bugnes

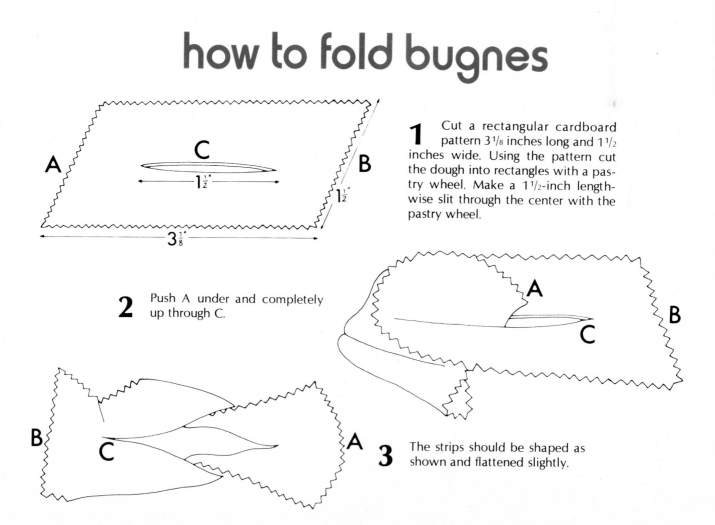

1 Cut a rectangular cardboard pattern 3 1/8 inches long and 1 1/2 inches wide. Using the pattern cut the dough into rectangles with a pastry wheel. Make a 1 1/2-inch lengthwise slit through the center with the pastry wheel.

2 Push A under and completely up through C.

3 The strips should be shaped as shown and flattened slightly.

bugnes

Bugnes are fried quickly in hot oil to a light golden brown. Pictured on the pedestal dish are Bugnes heavily dusted with confectioners' sugar. On the platter below, they are served plain.

BASIC FRUIT FRITTER BATTER

1½ c. all-purpose flour
½ tsp. salt
⅔ c. beer
1 tbsp. melted butter
1 egg white, stiffly beaten

Sift the flour and salt together into a large bowl, then stir in the beer until smooth. Do not beat. Add only enough lukewarm water to make a thick batter, then stir in the butter. If you do not wish to use this immediately, cover and set aside (no longer than 30 minutes) until ready to use, then fold in the egg white. This makes about 2½ cups of batter.

PINEAPPLE FRITTERS

2 1-lb. cans pineapple sticks
1 recipe Basic Fruit Fritter Batter

Drain the pineapple and place on paper toweling. Dip the pineapple sticks, one at a time, into the fritter batter and shake off any excess batter. Drop the fritters into hot oil at 375 degrees in deep fat fryer and fry until golden brown on all sides. Remove and drain on paper toweling. This makes about 8 servings.

CHERRY FRITTERS

Fresh cherries with stems
1 recipe Basic Fruit Fritter Batter

Hold the cherries by the stems and dip into the fritter batter. Fry in hot oil in deep fat fryer until brown. Remove with a slotted spoon and drain on paper toweling. One recipe of fritter batter is enough to coat about 2 pounds of cherries. If using only 1 pound of cherries, then the remaining batter may be used for other fruits.

pineapple fritters

Juicy pineapple fingers fill the centers of these crisp fritters. A lavish dusting of confectioners' sugar adds a final, flavorful touch.

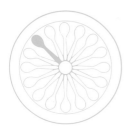

how to make practice roses

Elaborate cake decorating allows a homemaker to express the utmost in creativity. In learning and experimenting with techniques, enjoy practicing leisurely before actually designing and decorating your masterpiece. This section introduces Almond Paste Roses, so beautifully designed that you'll be anxious to try them right away. We suggest you practice with children's modeling compound, which we use to show you the different stages in making roses. Modeling compound is easy to work with, as it is pliable and can be used over and over again until you have mastered the proper techniques. Use the diagram as a guide for petal sizes and shapes.

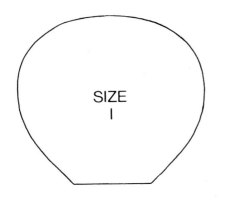

SIZE
1

Cut three petals the size of the diagram; cut remaining petals slightly larger than the first.

1 Beginning at the left side of the picture, we are showing you the 6 stages of making a rose. The first stage shows the bud with 1 petal laid over the tip of the peak and around the fat middle. The second stage is the first turned round to the opposite side with the second petal laid over the first and closed up. The third stage is the first of the remaining petals pressed in reverse position and curled over at the edge. The fourth stage has the fourth petal placed halfway from the center of the third petal. The fifth stage has the next petal placed halfway over the fourth and so on. The sixth stage shows the completed rose.

2 A center must be shaped, even if it is a 3 petaled rose. Take a walnut-sized piece of the compound, then pinch and shape until tapered into a bud with a base. You will need 3 sizes of petals. Cut 3 cardboard patterns in the shape of the petal diagram, increasing the size of each pattern by 1/4 inch. Mash the compound out thin and cut several petals of each size.

3 Start with a small petal. Attach the petal to the bottom of the bud, then wrap the petal around the bud. Continue with small petals, then with the second size petals, pressing the petal out thin at edges and curving it out as in the illustration. Continue with the larger petals, spreading edges outward to form a full-blown rose.

making and storing almond paste roses

Now that you have acquired the art of shaping roses, you are ready to perform with almond paste. Unlike the children's modeling compound, almond paste requires a great deal of care because it is sticky and dries out quickly. When not being worked, it should be kept covered with a piece of plastic wrap or a damp cloth. Dipping your fingers in flour before working the paste eliminates sticking problems.

In coloring the almond paste, be sure you reach the desired color by following these simple instructions: Take a portion of the paste about the size of a large pea. Dip a cocktail stick or other handy utensil into the chosen food coloring. Then drip the coloring on the small portion of paste, while working it around in your hand, until it is about 3 tones deeper than you wish to have. Then work the small portion back into the remainder of your paste for perfect coloring.

The thinner the edge of the petals, the more beautiful the rose, so pat each petal edge paper thin. When pressing the base edges of the petals together, do so with floury finger tips so that they blend well. Make sure your work is flawless by carefully following the six step-by-step illustrations.

It's so nice to know that these delicate Almond Paste Roses can be stored for long periods of time, even up to a year. Once the roses have been made and sufficiently hardened, they can be conveniently stored in a covered container and placed in the refrigerator. With this in mind, you can plan weeks ahead for those very special occasions.

In order to see how very lovely these creations look on a festively decorated cake, see the Bridesmaids Basket Cake on page 144.

making almond paste roses

1 Have a bowl of sifted flour and a bowl of cold water ready before beginning. Keep the almond paste and any trimming wrapped in plastic wrap while you work as the paste dries quickly. To begin your rose, shape a bud with lightly floured cold hands, pinching the base of bud and tapering the tip to complete shape.

2 Use a small knife to trim the base as much as possible yet leave the shape standing erect.

3 Flour the fingers of one hand and the palm of the other before starting the petals. Roll out a small ball, about the size of a cherry, then press down in the center of this ball with floured thumb. Pat out the pressed down ball with the first 2 fingers until the ball is a paper-thin, blunt-based rose petal.

5 Attach the second petal behind the first one with the edges facing toward you.

4 Pat each petal paper thin. Make the first 3 petals the same size. Brush the base and 1/3 of the way up the bud lightly with cold water. Place the first petal over the middle of the bud so that the bud tip is just a fraction under the petal. Press down the moistened base edges of petals with floured fingertip.

6 Brush again with water and attach the third petal. This is the first petal that you curve outward at the edges. Now add as many petals as desired in the same manner. Cut away the base and place the rose on lightly floured surface to dry completely. Brush away the surplus flour with a slightly dampened pastry brush when roses are dry. You may wish to brush with egg white and sprinkle immediately with sugar for a frosted effect.

pipe flowers
with basic royal icing

With Basic Royal Icing and an icing petal tube, you can produce beautiful, flowery creations which will give you great satisfaction. By simply taking a flower pin, as shown in picture one, covering it with a square of waxed paper and turning it in your left hand, you can complete these gorgeous flowers in shamefully little time. Follow the simple picture illustrations carefully.

Like Almond Paste Roses, once these colorful flowers are dry and hardened, they can be stored in an airtight container for an indefinite period of time.

After you have acquired all the perfected skills of making roses and piping flowers, don't limit yourself to icing and almond paste. Try out your talents on savory treats as well, using Savory Pâté de Foie Cream (Sauces, pg. 30) or other cream cheese mixtures for unusually creative *hors d'oeuvres*.

PETAL-SHAPING TUBES

2 Dab a small amount of icing on the pin, then press a waxed paper square on the iced pin. Place the remaining icing in the pastry bag with a petal tube affixed. Squeeze the icing bag with one hand and rotate the pin with the other hand. Pipe a bud in center of pin for a base. Hold the tube stationary with the large end pointed downward and encircle the bud with petals, working the tube in a curving, downward motion. Continue until the bud is covered with petals, each overlapping the other.

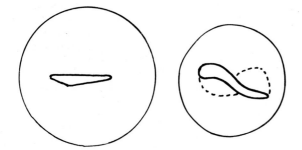

1 Place your flower pins in a piece of styrofoam, then cut 1 inch squares of waxed paper equal to the number of pins you have.

3 Remove the paper from the pin and place on working surface to dry completely. Store in airtight containers until ready to use.

bridesmaid basket cake

There is an interesting story behind the making of a bridesmaid cake. In a small bakeshop in England, a lady was asked to bake a bride's cake, which she did. But she also baked one for each of the bridesmaids. When asked why, she replied that maybe if each bridesmaid were given a cake, each might come back to order a wedding cake for her own wedding.

The Bridesmaid Basket Cake on the following page is a culinary masterpiece, one which will likely never be forgotten, but certainly not beyond the realm of reality for your own kitchen. With all the know-how you have attained, plus the easy-to-follow instructions following, this creation, soon to be your own, will bring you compliments long after the festive occasion is over.

BRIDESMAID BASKET CAKE

**2 recipes Basic Close-Textured Sponge Cake *(pg. 6)*
2 recipes Basic Royal Icing *(pg. 43)*
Red and blue food coloring
Almond Paste Roses *(Pg. 140)***

For this cake you will need three 9-inch layers of the sponge cake, 1 recipe pink icing, 1 recipe white icing, four 18-inch pieces florist wire and tape. Prepare 1 recipe icing, adding 8 drops of red food coloring and 1 drop of blue. Spread a thin layer of icing between the 3 layers. Ice the 3-layer cake on a foil-covered piece of heavy cardboard. Place on a turntable and smooth top and side with a hot, wet spatula (pg. 7). Let the icing harden. Place remaining pink icing in a small icing bag with writing tube affixed. Mark side of cake at 1-inch intervals for guide of vertical staves. The first stave may need additional guidelines 1/2 inch to either side. Combine ingredients for second recipe of icing in large mixer bowl, omitting lemon juice and adding 2 teaspoons of cream of tartar. Beat with an electric mixer until well combined and fluffy. Place in another icing bag with serrated tube affixed. Pipe pink staves and white wickers to form basket around cake according to the step-by-step illustrations. Wrap each wire with tape, then tape wires together at ends. Bend wires to form handle and spread apart at center. Spread icing liberally over the handle to within 1 inch of ends. Insert ends of handle into the cake about 1/2 inch from side. Finish icing the handle, covering any exposed wires. Extend the icing down the sides to hold the handle in position in a decorative manner. Attach pink-tinted almond roses to top of cake with a dab of pink icing. Decorate with greenery and a ribbon bow, if desired.

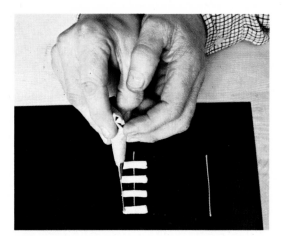

1 Place a small amount of icing in icing bag with a No. 6 writing tube affixed. Keep remaining icing covered with damp cloth. Pipe a vertical line for a stave as shown in the illustration. Place a small amount of icing in another icing bag with a No. 48 serrated tube affixed. Pipe wickers over the stave, 1/2 inch on each side, keeping serrated edge up and leaving enough space between wickers for alternate row. Pipe another stave along edges.

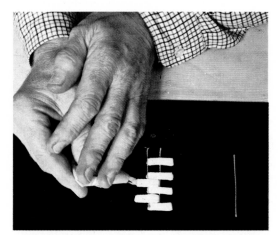

2 Pipe between the first set of wickers over the second stave, 1/2 inch on each side. This set of wickers will begin at the first stave, cross over the second stave and end at the next 1 inch guide line. Wipe icing tube tips frequently with wet cloth to remove hardened icing.

3 Continue piping staves and filling in with wickers as described until you have gone all around the cake. This is a simple procedure but takes patience and a steady hand.

bridesmaid basket cake

There simply are no words to appropriately describe the beauty of this masterpiece. We can say only that it is a work of art, worth the effort for those very special occasions. What bride or bridesmaid would not be happy with such a presentation?

introducing rice desserts

Rice is certainly best known served as a cereal, but many of us know how good rice can be combined with fruits and sauces and served as a dessert. Rice makes a wonderful dessert course after light meals and is so good with lemony sauces such as Basic Lemon Sauce (Sauces, pg. 25) or Lemon Mousseline Sauce (Sauces, pg. 25). Of course you may choose your own favorite sauce from the excellent variety in the Sauces section.

Throughout this section you will discover how versatile rice can be with such treats as Eight-Treasure Rice Pudding, Raisin and Rice Mold, Creamy Rice with Meringue Crown, and Sweet Rice Fritters.

RAISIN AND RICE MOLD

1 c. brown rice
¹⁄₂ c. raisins
Grated rind of 1 med. orange
¹⁄₄ c. honey
1 recipe Orange Confectioners' Custard
  (pg. 88)
¹⁄₂ recipe Red Currant Jelly Glaze (pg. 19)

Prepare the rice with the raisins as instructed in Basic Boiled Rice (Cereals, pg. 3), increasing the cooking time to about 40 minutes or until the rice is tender. Drain well and place in a large bowl. Add the grated rind and honey, then stir in just enough of the custard to hold rice mixture together. Place in a lightly greased 1¹⁄₂-quart mold and press down firmly. Chill well. Chill remaining custard. Turn the rice mold out onto a serving platter and pour the glaze over the rice mold. Garnish as desired. Serve with remaining custard. This makes 6 servings.

raisin and rice mold

Here are two very attractive ways to present Raisin and Rice Mold. In the background, the mold is coated with red currant glaze and topped with a cherry and angelica. In the foreground, the raisin and rice mixture was shaped in a savarin ring and topped with glazed pears and angelica prongs.

rice pudding

Eight-Treasure Rice Pudding is delightfully different from our traditional American rice pudding. It is a special Chinese version, richly filled with dates and pineapple. This oriental treat, topped with a rich syrup, is a perfect ending to a light meal.

EIGHT-TREASURE RICE PUDDING

½ c. rice
½ c. sugar
¼ c. butter
2 eggs, beaten
3 c. milk
1½ c. crushed pineapple, drained
½ c. chopped dates
½ tsp. salt
Nutmeg

Bring 2 cups of salted water to a boil, then stir in the rice. Reduce the heat and cover. Simmer for 20 minutes or until all water is absorbed. Add the sugar and butter and stir until the butter is melted. Combine the eggs and milk, then stir into the rice mixture. Add the pineapple, dates and salt and mix well. Pour into a buttered 1½-quart baking dish and sprinkle with nutmeg. Bake in a preheated 325-degree oven for 50 minutes. May be served with Almond Sauce (Sauces, pg. 20), if desired. This makes 4 to 6 servings.

CREAMY RICE WITH MERINGUE CROWN

½ c. long grain rice
1 c. milk
¼ c. butter
¾ c. (packed) light brown sugar
Juice of 1 sm. lemon
Juice of 1 sm. orange
2 tbsp. rum
1 recipe Apricot Glaze (Desserts, pg. 19)
½ recipe Basic Meringues mixture (Desserts, pg. 10)

Pour 2 cups water into the top of a double boiler and bring to a boil. Place over hot water, then stir in the rice. Cover and cook, stirring occasionally, until all of the water is absorbed. Stir in the milk and cover. Cook until all of the milk is absorbed, stirring occasionally. The rice should be very tender. Remove from the hot water and cool. Melt the butter in a small saucepan over low heat. Add the sugar and stir until dissolved. Add the lemon and orange juices and mix well. Simmer until thickened, then remove from heat and stir in the rum. Add to the rice and mix well. Cool. Grease a 7-inch soufflé dish with additional butter. Cut a 5-inch strip of aluminum foil 2 inches longer than the circumference of the soufflé dish, then fold in half to make a 2½-inch strip. Place around the outside of the soufflé dish, lapping over 1 inch, then tie with string. Place ⅓ of the rice mixture in the soufflé dish and press down evenly. Spoon ⅓ of the glaze over the rice mixture. Repeat the layers twice, then refrigerate until cold. Place the meringue mixture in a pastry bag with a No. 4 star tube affixed and pipe onto top of the rice mixture. Broil under low heat until lightly browned, watching closely so that meringue browns evenly. Remove the aluminum foil collar and place the soufflé dish on a serving platter. This makes about 6 servings.

creamy rice with meringue crown

Creamy Rice with Meringue Crown will be a "crowning" glory when this dessert treat is presented to family or dinner guests. Rice, brown sugar, lemon, orange and rum make an irresistible flavor combination, topped with fluffy, browned meringue.

rice fritters

sweet rice fritters

Served from an elegant tiered dish, these Sweet Rice Fritters are party fare. They are flavored with lemon rind, chopped almonds and cinnamon, then dusted with confectioners' sugar.

SWEET RICE FRITTERS

3 c. cold cooked rice
¹/₂ c. confectioners' sugar
Grated rind of 1 lemon
¹/₂ c. chopped almonds or pine nuts
¹/₂ tsp. cinnamon
1 egg, well beaten
6 tbsp. butter
1 recipe Basic Lemon Sauce (Sauces, pg. 25)

Combine the rice, sugar, lemon rind, almonds and cinnamon in a large bowl. Add the egg and mix well. Shape into small rolls, then flatten slightly. Place on a platter and chill well. Melt 3 tablespoons butter in a large skillet over medium heat. Add half the rice rolls and cook until lightly browned, turning once. Drain on paper toweling. Melt remaining butter in the skillet, then brown and drain remaining rice rolls. Sift additional confectioners' sugar over the rolls generously, then place on a serving dish. Serve with the lemon sauce. This makes about 14 fritters.

grand rice

Grand Rice, although it is made from ordinary rice pudding ingredients (sugar, rice, vanilla, eggs and milk), does not look or taste like ordinary rice pudding. However, this presentation, garnished with mandarin orange sections, is a "grand" rice dessert.

GRAND RICE

½ c. long grain rice
4 c. milk
1 vanilla pod or 1 tsp. vanilla extract
2 env. unflavored gelatin
½ c. sherry
3 egg yolks
1½ c. confectioners' sugar
½ c. whipped cream
Mandarin orange sections

Place the rice in the top of a double boiler over boiling water, then add 1 cup of milk and the vanilla pod or vanilla extract. Cover and cook, stirring occasionally, until all the milk is absorbed. Repeat the process, adding 1 cup of milk at a time and cooking each time until the milk is absorbed. The rice grains should have no hard centers. Remove the vanilla pod. Soften the gelatin in the sherry. Place the rice mixture in a blender container and process until the consistency of boiled custard. Blend the gelatin mixture into the rice mixture. Return the rice mixture to the top of the double boiler and place over hot water. Add the egg yolks, one at a time, beating with a whisk after each addition until smooth, then cook for 5 minutes, stirring constantly. Remove from hot water and stir in the confectioners' sugar. Cool to room temperature. Fold in the whipped cream thoroughly. Turn into a well-oiled 6-inch soufflé dish and chill until firm. Unmold onto a serving dish and garnish with orange sections. This makes 6 to 8 servings.

almond princes

ALMOND PRINCES

½ **recipe Basic Sweet Short Pastry** *(pg. 12)*
Sifted confectioners' sugar
¾ **c. ground almonds**
1 egg white, slightly beaten

Roll out the pastry on a lightly floured surface until very thin. Cut into 24 circles with a 2½-inch cookie cutter, then press into miniature cupcake pans. Prick the bottoms and sides of the shells. Combine 1½ cups of sugar and the almonds in a medium-sized bowl. Stir in enough egg white to make the mixture the consistency of thick paste. Fill the tart shells to just below the rims with the almond mixture, then sprinkle generously with confectioners' sugar. Bake in a preheated 350-de-

Almond Princes are a rich blend of ground almonds and sweet short pastry, dusted with confectioners' sugar. They are ideal served with hot tea or coffee.

gree oven until the filling is rounded and the tarts are golden brown. Remove the tarts from the pans and place on a wire rack until completely cooled. Place 2 skewers evenly over the tarts, and sift with confectioners' sugar to make a design. Serve with Japanese Tea (Beverages, pg. 36). This makes 24 tarts.

cream horns

These pretty little Cream Horns are puff pastry — light and flaky. They are filled with a rich combination of confectioners' custard, jam, and stiffly whipped cream.

Cream Horns are delicately feminine — and, because they are made with real Basic Confectioners' Custard and whipped cream, are much more delicious than those found in bake shops. The horns, or cornets, are made by wrapping strips of Rough Puff Pastry around cone-shaped metal forms. These forms may be bought at bakery supply houses in a choice of sizes. (We recommend 5-inch cones, as they are a perfect one-serving size.) If the forms are not available, make your own by cutting a double thickness of extra-heavy aluminum foil in 9-inch squares; then fold each square into a triangle and roll it into a cone, leaving a small opening at the pointed end. The extra foil at the wide end can be folded over for added strength.

CREAM HORNS

1 recipe Rough Puff Pastry *(pg. 27)*
1 beaten egg, strained
½ c. apricot jam
1 recipe Basic Confectioners' Custard *(pg. 19)*
1 c. whipping cream, whipped

Divide the pastry in half and roll out, ½ at a time, on a cold floured surface into a ⅛-inch thick and 18-inch long rectangle. Cut into strips 1¼ inches wide and 18 inches long. Wrap around horn molds as instructed in the step-by-step illustrations. Place, short side down, on a floured baking sheet. Brush the tops lightly with egg. Bake in a preheated 400-degree oven for 20 minutes or until browned. Remove from oven and slip the pastry from the molds immediately. Cool on racks. Stir the jam into the cool custard, then fold in ¾ cup of the whipped cream. Fill the horns ⅔ full with the custard mixture, then pipe the remaining whipped cream in the top. Garnish with ground pistachio nuts and dust with confectioners' sugar, if desired. Serve on cake plates. This makes about 22 horns.

how to make cream horns

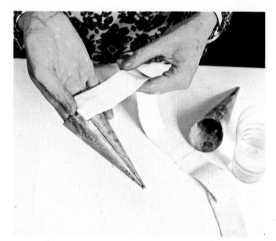

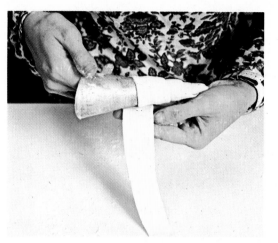

1 There are 2 ways to wrap the pastry around the cream horn molds. You may start at the top on the shallow side and wind over and over, making sure that each overlap is ⅓ over the previous one.

3 Wind upward, overlapping each time ⅓ of the way over previous lap.

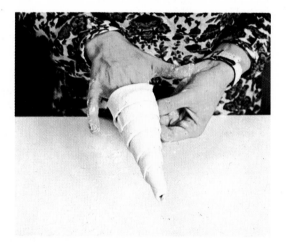

2 You may like to start at the bottom of the horn and wind the pastry to the top.

4 Brush the end of the pastry with water and pinch together firmly to seal.

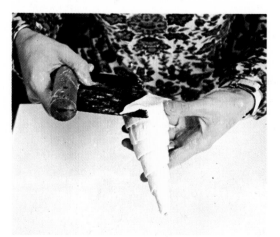

5 Cut the surplus pastry off the top. Place, short side down, on floured baking sheet.

BASIC ITALIAN MERINGUE

For Meringue Cake with Three Cream Fillings which will be introduced shortly, you will learn to make Basic Italian Meringue. Unlike the Basic Meringues mixture (pg. 10) previously introduced, Basic Italian Meringue need not be baked. It obtains its "cooked" texture from boiling sugar syrup which is poured hot into stiffly beaten egg whites. Then the mixture is spooned or piped out into shape on pieces of waxed paper and left to dry, preferably overnight.

This meringue cake is similar to a torte, which is by definition 3 or more layers of cake or pastry with rich filling between the layers. The rich custard fillings used with this recipe are delectable flavored with coffee, kirsch and ground pistachio nuts.

BASIC ITALIAN MERINGUE

2½ c. sugar
1¾ c. water
4 egg whites

Combine the sugar and water in a large saucepan over low heat and heat, without stirring, until all the sugar is dissolved. Bring to a boil and cook to medium soft-ball stage or 240 degrees on a candy thermometer. Beat the egg whites with an electric beater until stiff peaks form. Pour the hot syrup in a thin steady stream into the egg whites, beating constantly. Then beat until the mixture holds a firm peak and is cool. Use as recipe directs. The meringue may be covered and refrigerated overnight before using, if desired. Meringue may be piped when cold. This makes about 4 cups of meringue.

MERINGUE CAKE WITH THREE CREAM FILLINGS

1 recipe Basic Italian Meringue
2 recipes cold Basic Confectioners' Custard *(pg. 19)*
1 c. stiffly whipped cream
2 c. unsalted butter, softened
1 tbsp. kirsch
⅓ c. finely ground pistachio nuts
Green food coloring
2 tbsp. Basic Coffee Syrup No. 1 *(pg. 36)*

Draw an 8-inch circle on each of four 10-inch waxed paper squares, then turn waxed paper squares over. Divide the meringue into 4 equal parts and spread smoothly over the circles with a damp spatula. Let meringue circles dry overnight or until firm but not brittle. Combine the custard and whipped cream and blend thoroughly. Beat the butter with an electric mixer until the consistency of heavy cream. Add the custard mixture gradually, beating constantly until smooth and thickened, then divide into 3 equal parts. Stir the kirsch into the first part, the pistachio nuts and enough food coloring to tint light green into the second part, and the coffee syrup into the third part. Place 1 meringue circle in the center of a serving dish and spread with ⅔ of the kirsch filling. Place another meringue circle over the kirsch filling. Repeat layers, using ⅔ of the pistachio and coffee fillings, then top with the remaining meringue circle. Mark the top layer into thirds, then, using No. 4 star tube and a pastry bag, pipe the remaining fillings over the 3 sections as shown in the illustration. Any remaining filling may be piped into rosettes around the meringue circles. Chill for at least 6 hours before serving. Cut and serve the cake in small wedges. This makes 10 to 12 small servings.

meringue cake with three cream fillings

Before serving this delightful meringue cake, wait several hours, if possible, after it is prepared so that the rich filling will have time to soften the crisp Basic Italian Meringue. If, however, you prefer to serve it immediately, dip a sharp knife into boiling water before cutting, and each slice will come out smoothly.

glazed pears in syrup

These baked pears are lusciously coated in syrup made of red currant jelly. You may wish to add just a touch of your favorite liqueur to make them exceptionally flavorful. Serve them hot or chilled.

GLAZED PEARS IN SYRUP

6 firm ripe pears
1 4-oz. jar red currant jelly
3 c. Basic Sugar Syrup *(Breads, pg. 14)*
Red food coloring
1 tbsp. cornstarch
¼ c. Cointreau

Peel the pears, leaving the stems intact, then place the pears, stem end up, in a deep 8-inch round casserole. Melt the currant jelly in the sugar syrup in a saucepan over medium heat, then bring to a boil. Add enough food coloring for a deep red shade and pour over the pears. Bake, covered, in a preheated 275-degree oven for 1 hour or until the pears are just tender. Remove the pears carefully with a slotted spoon to a serving dish. Pour the syrup into a saucepan and bring to a boil. Mix the cornstarch with the Cointreau and stir into the syrup. Cook, stirring, until clear and thickened, then pour over the pears. Serve hot or cold. You may serve them with whipped cream, if desired. This makes 6 servings.

PEARS IN GINGER SAUCE

1 1-lb. 13 oz. can pear halves
1 lg. piece of preserved citron
¼ recipe Red Currant Jelly Glaze *(pg. 19)*
2 tbsp. preserved ginger slivers
2 tbsp. preserved ginger syrup
1 tbsp. cornstarch
2 tbsp. lemon juice

Drain the pears, reserving the syrup. Arrange the pear halves, cut side down, around the edge of a round serving platter. Cut the citron into slivers to resemble stems, then stick 1 sliver into the stem end of each pear half. Combine the reserved pear syrup, jelly glaze, preserved ginger and ginger syrup in a saucepan and bring to a boil over medium heat, stirring frequently. Mix the cornstarch with the lemon juice until smooth. Stir into the syrup mixture and cook, stirring constantly, until clear and thickened. Cool, then spoon over the pears. Fill the center of the platter with the remaining syrup mixture. Chill thoroughly. This makes about 6 servings.

POACHED EMPRESS PEACHES

6 lg. firm ripe peaches
Basic Sugar Syrup (*Breads, pg. 14*)
1 vanilla pod or 1 tsp. vanilla extract
2 c. hulled strawberries, puréed
1/2 c. sifted confectioners' sugar
3 tbsp. brandy
1/2 c. whipping cream, whipped

Place the peaches in a large saucepan and add enough boiling water to cover. Let stand for about 2 minutes, then lift the peaches out and dip into ice water. Slip the skins from the peaches and place the peaches in a large saucepan. Pour enough syrup over the peaches to cover and place the vanilla pod in the syrup. Simmer until the peaches are just tender, turning once. Drain the peaches, reserving the vanilla pod for later use. Cool the peaches, then chill. Combine the strawberries, sugar and brandy, then fold in the whipped cream. Place the peaches in a serving dish and spoon the strawberry mixture over the peaches. This makes 6 servings.

specialties for children

CANDY THERMOMETER TEMPERATURES

SOFT BALL	234° to 240°
HARD BALL	250° to 268°
SOFT CRACK	270° to 290°
HARD CRACK	300° to 310°
CARAMELIZED SUGAR	310° to 338°

Nearly all children eagerly finish meals in anticipation of desserts and sweet treats of all kinds, and the two which follow are especially welcomed by youngsters. First is Toffee Apples which are dipped in lemon juice, then coated with a hot syrup. Next, Peanut And Sesame Brittle, made of roasted peanuts, sesame seed and a rich syrup, makes a popular sweet snack for children and adults alike. Both recipes require the sugar syrup to be cooked to the hard-crack stage. This is a stage in candy making when a small amount of boiling syrup dropped in ice water will form hard threads which are very brittle. The table below lists some stages and temperatures on the candy thermometer.

TOFFEE APPLES

¼ c. lemon juice
3 med. Winesap apples
1 c. butter
1 c. sugar
⅓ c. (packed) brown sugar
½ tsp. soda

Mix the lemon juice with 1 cup water. Peel and core the apples, then cut each apple into eighths. Stick a colored cocktail pick into one end of each apple wedge. Dip into the lemon mixture and place on paper toweling, turning to drain well on all sides. Melt the butter in a medium-sized saucepan. Add the sugars and 3 tablespoons water and mix well. Bring to a boil, stirring constantly. Then cook, without stirring, to the hard-crack stage or 300 degrees on a candy thermometer. Remove from heat and stir in the soda quickly. Hold each apple wedge by the pick and dip into the hot syrup to coat well. Place on waxed paper to cool and harden. This makes 24 wedges.

PEANUT AND SESAME BRITTLE

1   1-lb. box light brown sugar
¼ c. white wine vinegar
3 tbsp. vegetable oil
½ c. toasted sesame seed
1½ c. shelled roasted Spanish peanuts

Combine the brown sugar, vinegar, oil and 2 tablespoons of water in a medium-sized saucepan and mix well. Bring to a boil over low heat, stirring to dissolve the sugar completely. Simmer, without stirring, to 300 degrees on a candy thermometer or to the hard-crack stage. Combine half the sesame seed with the peanuts and spread evenly in a well-greased cookie pan or on a marble slab. Pour the hot syrup over the peanut mixture and sprinkle with remaining sesame seed. Cool until hard. Break into bite-sized pieces and store in an airtight container. This makes about 2 pounds of brittle.

introducing
dessert omelets

The art of cooking a delectable omelet requires both imagination and skill. Omelets can be as delicious as they are economical, but proper preparation is essential.

Almost any cook can create an impressive dish once the skill of basic omelet preparation has been mastered. As you have already learned, a Basic French Omelet provides the cornerstone from which other omelets have evolved (Eggs and Cheese, pg. 4). These guidelines may be varied by both cooking methods and addition of ingredients. Before any omelet is cooked, it is essential that omelet pans be prepared correctly to insure best results (Eggs and Cheese, pg. 3).

One of the most delicious and versatile of all omelets is the omelet *sucree* or dessert omelet. Most sweet omelets are variations of the Basic Belgian Soufflé Omelet to which sugar, fruits, jam and a flavoring are folded in the omelet.

As a rule, omelet *sucree* is not served as the main course of a meal; however, a jam omelet might be served at breakfast just as sweet rolls are served for breakfast. In accordance with the French view, omelet *sucree* should be served only as a dessert or after the theatre fare. There are several reasons for this viewpoint. These omelets contain ingredients such as liqueurs, flavorings, and fruits; they are decorative and unusual, all of which makes them suitable for special occasions. Try the dessert omelet, find the one that is most pleasing to your taste, then serve it at brunch or for a late evening supper-breakfast.

JAM OMELET

3 eggs, separated
1½ tsp. sugar
1½ tbsp. half and half cream
2 tbsp. butter
¾ c. strawberry jam, heated
2 tsp. confectioners' sugar

Combine the egg yolks, sugar and cream in a small bowl and beat until lemon colored. Beat the egg whites until stiff peaks form, then fold in the egg yolk mixture slowly. Melt the butter in a skillet and add the egg mixture, spreading it over the skillet with a spoon. Cover and cook over low heat, removing the skillet from the heat occasionally, if needed, until the omelet is cooked through. Broil in the oven about 8 inches from the source of heat until lightly browned. Spread the jam on half the omelet, then fold remaining omelet over the jam. Lightly score the top of the omelet with a knife, then sprinkle confectioners' sugar over the top. This makes about 4 servings.

jam omelet

This Jam Omelet is sprinkled with confectioners' sugar and browned to a golden perfection. Strawberry jam has been folded into the warm, fluffy omelet, and it is garnished with an extra portion of jam for appealing color and flavor.

basic
belgian soufflé omelet

BASIC BELGIAN SOUFFLÉ OMELET

¾ c. tart jelly
4 eggs, separated
¼ c. cold water
Pinch of salt
2 tbsp. butter
Confectioners' sugar

Spoon the jelly into a small bowl and break it up with a fork, then set aside. Place the egg yolks in a small bowl and beat lightly with a fork. Add the water and salt and beat until blended. Beat the egg whites until very stiff. Fold the egg yolk mixture slowly into the egg whites until the mixture is a pale yellow foam. Melt the butter in a heated 9-inch omelet pan until butter just begins to brown. Pour the egg mixture into the pan and cook slowly, pulling the edge away from the side of pan and leveling the top to the side with a spatula. Pierce through the omelet with the tip of the spatula occasionally to allow the heat to rise through the omelet. Cook until the base is a light golden brown and set but the top is still foamy. Remove from the heat and place, about 6 to 8 inches from source of heat, in a preheated broiler. Broil for about 4 minutes or until top is lightly browned. Remove from the oven and spread the jelly over the top. Fold the omelet in half and slide out on a heated platter. Dust generously with confectioners' sugar. If a design is desired on the top, then heat a metal skewer on a stove burner and press quickly over the sugar. This makes 4 servings.

griddle soufflé omelet

This omelet is an egg dessert with a foreign flair. Fresh fruit has been used as a filling. Note the puffy appearance of this omelet. This is the essential feature which gives the omelet its name — soufflé.

GRIDDLE SOUFFLÉ OMELETS

Griddle Soufflé Omelets are unique individual omelets. Unlike the Basic Belgian Soufflé Omelet, this omelet is cooked entirely on top of the stove. The foamy egg mixture is shaped into ovals and gently browned on a hot griddle. Before removing from the griddle, soft fruits may be added. The finished omelets are lightly dusted with confectioners' sugar and should be served immediately.

GRIDDLE SOUFFLÉ OMELETS

4 eggs, separated
Pinch of salt
¼ c. confectioners' sugar
Butter
1 c. fresh fruit

Combine the egg yolks, salt and confectioners' sugar in a small mixer bowl. Beat with an electric mixer for about 5 minutes or until very thick and lemon colored. Beat the egg whites in a large bowl until stiff. Push the whites to one side of the bowl, then turn the egg yolk mixture into the bowl next to the whites. Cut and fold the two mixtures together with a rubber spatula until well blended. Cook according to the step-by-step illustrations. Place on a serving dish. Slide an oiled spatula under the top of each omelet and lift, then spoon in the raspberries. Dust with additional confectioners' sugar. Any soft fruit such as strawberries, loganberries or sliced peaches may be used, if desired. This makes 4 servings.

2 Reduce the heat slightly, then shape into neat ovals with a knife.

1 Melt a small amount of butter on the griddle over medium heat. Spoon half the omelet mixture onto the hot griddle to form an oblong loaf, then repeat with the remaining omelet mixture.

3 Cook until the bottoms are browned and set. Turn the omelets with a spatula and cook until lightly browned and set.

dessert omelets

An easy to prepare yet unusual dish, Apple Omelet is a fluffy dessert omelet the family is sure to enjoy. Eggs, sugar, cinnamon, and canned applesauce are combined and cooked until crusty-brown. The finished omelet may be dusted with sugar and quickly grilled for a crunchy glaze. This fruit filled dessert is perfect for a brunch.

APPLE OMELET

½ c. canned applesauce
½ tsp. cinnamon
4 tsp. sugar
4 eggs
Salt to taste
3 tbsp. butter
Confectioners' sugar

Place an omelet pan over very low heat. Combine the applesauce, cinnamon and sugar and mix well. Beat the eggs with a fork until well mixed and season with the salt. Stir in the applesauce mixture, blending well. Cut 2 tablespoons of the butter into small pieces and add to the egg mixture. Cook the omelet according to illustrations No. 5 through No. 10 (Eggs, pg. 5), adding the remaining 1 tablespoon of butter. Sprinkle with confectioners' sugar and serve immediately. This makes about 4 servings.

CHOCOLATE SOUFFLÉ OMELET

3 egg yolks
Pinch of salt
¼ c. chocolate chips, melted *(pg. 49)*
4 egg whites
⅓ c. sugar
¼ tsp. vanilla extract
2 tbsp. butter
Confectioners' sugar

Combine the egg yolks and salt in a small mixer bowl and beat with electric mixer for about 5 minutes or until thick. Blend in the chocolate. Beat the egg whites with electric mixer until very stiff, adding the sugar gradually. Blend in the vanilla extract. Fold ¼ of the egg whites into the chocolate mixture, then fold in the remaining egg whites carefully but thoroughly. Melt the butter over low heat in an omelet pan, swirling to coat the bottom of the pan. Turn the omelet mixture into the pan and level the top with a spatula. Cook over low heat until the bottom is set but top is still soft. Remove from heat and place in a preheated broiler, about 6 to 8 inches from source of heat, for about 8 minutes or until top is set. Fold in half and slide out on heated platter. Dust with confectioners' sugar and serve immediately. This makes about 4 servings.

apple omelet

This golden brown Apple Omelet is a spicy way to brighten menus. A rich apple filling is hidden beneath the glazed crust. The attractive serving platter with a fresh apple garnish enhances the simplicity of this omelet.

BELGIAN SOUFFLÉ OMELET IN MERINGUE

1 recipe Basic Italian Meringue (pg. 153)
Red food coloring
1 c. sliced fresh strawberries
½ c. sugar
¼ c. Grand Marnier
4 eggs, separated
Pinch of salt
1 tsp. water
2 tbsp. butter

Prepare the meringue and add about 4 drops of food coloring to tint a light pink. Cover with a damp towel until ready to use. Sprinkle the strawberries with ¼ cup of the sugar and 2 teaspoons of the Grand Marnier. Let stand for no longer than 10 minutes. Combine the egg whites, salt and water in a large mixer bowl and beat with an electric mixer until very stiff. Combine the remaining ¼ cup of sugar, 2 tablespoons of Grand Marnier and the egg yolks and beat until thoroughly mixed. Fold the egg yolk mixture slowly into the egg whites. Melt the butter in an omelet pan until foamy. Turn the egg mixture into the omelet pan and cook slowly, pulling the edge away from side of pan and leveling the top to the side with a spatula. Pierce through the omelet with the tip of the spatula occasionally to allow the heat to rise through the omelet. Cook until the base is a light golden brown and set but the top is still foamy. Remove from heat and place, about 6 to 8 inches from source of heat, in a pre-heated broiler. Broil for about 4 minutes or until top is set and lightly browned. Remove from the oven and spoon the strawberries over the top. Fold in half and slide out onto a heatproof dish. Place ⅓ of the meringue in a pastry bag with a large star tube affixed. Cover the omelet completely with the remaining meringue. Pipe around the edge and over the top, then pipe rosettes in a decorative manner. Place under the broiler for about 4 minutes or until lightly tinged with brown. Remove from the oven and serve immediately. This makes about 8 servings.

belgian soufflé omelet in meringue

Hidden under this luscious covering of pink meringue and fresh strawberries is a Belgian soufflé omelet. Cold Italian meringue is spread lavishly over the omelet and shaped into decorative rills. Once the meringue covered omelet has been quickly set in the oven, strawberries and flowers may be used for a fresh, colorful touch.

special pies

STRAWBERRY-LIME PIE

2 env. unflavored gelatin
1 6-oz. can frozen limeade concentrate
1/3 c. sugar
1 tsp. grated lime rind
1 c. diced fresh California strawberries
1 c. whipping cream, whipped
Green food coloring
1 baked 9-in. pie shell

Soften the gelatin in 1/2 cup of cold water. Combine the limeade concentrate, sugar and 3/4 cup of water in a small saucepan and cook over low heat, stirring constantly, until the concentrate melts and the sugar dissolves. Add the gelatin and stir until dissolved. Chill until syrupy, then stir in the lime rind and strawberries. Fold in the whipped cream until blended, then tint a pale green with food coloring. Chill until mixture mounds when dropped from a spoon, then place in the pie shell. Chill for 2 to 3 hours or until firm. Garnish with additional sliced strawberries. This makes about 6 to 8 servings.

strawberry-lime pie

This delicious and refreshing Strawberry-Lime Pie is a cool summertime treat. Its tangy lime flavor, combined with whipped cream and whole fresh strawberries is certain to draw enthusiastic compliments from family and guests.

NEW ORLEANS PECAN PIE

3 eggs, separated
1 c. sour cream
1 c. sugar
4 tbsp. cornstarch
1/4 tsp. grated lemon rind
Pinch of salt
1 baked 9-in. pie shell, cooled
1 c. (packed) brown sugar
1 c. chopped pecans

Mix the egg yolks, sour cream, sugar, cornstarch, lemon rind and salt in top of a double boiler and cook over boiling water until thick, stirring constantly. Pour into pie shell. Beat the egg whites until stiff, adding brown sugar slowly. Fold in pecans and spread over filling. Bake at 425 degrees until lightly browned. Refrigerate for several hours before serving. One-fourth teaspoon lemon extract may be substituted for grated lemon rind.

KEY LIME PIE

1 tbsp. unflavored gelatin
1 c. sugar
1/4 tsp. salt
4 eggs, separated
1/2 c. lime juice
1/4 c. water
1 tsp. grated lime peel
Green food coloring
1 c. whipping cream, whipped
1 baked 9-in. pie shell

Mix the gelatin, 1/2 cup sugar and salt in a saucepan. Beat egg yolks, lime juice and water together and stir into gelatin mixture. Cook over medium heat, stirring constantly, until mixture comes to a boil. Remove from heat and stir in grated peel. Add enough food coloring for a pale green color. Chill, stirring occasionally, until thickened. Beat egg whites until soft peaks form. Add remaining sugar gradually and beat until stiff peaks form. Fold gelatin mixture into egg whites and fold in whipped cream. Spoon into pastry shell and chill until firm. Spread with additional whipped cream and sprinkle additional grated lime peel around edge of pie.

BOUFFANT LEMON MERINGUE PIE

1/2 recipe Basic Sweet Short Pastry *(pg. 12)*
8 egg yolks
1 1/2 c. sugar
2/3 c. fresh lemon juice
2 env. unflavored gelatin
1 tsp. grated orange rind
2 tbsp. grated lemon rind
4 egg whites
1 tsp. cream of tartar
1 recipe Meringue Topping

Roll out the pastry on a lightly floured surface to a 1/8-inch thick circle. Line a greased 10-inch pie pan with the pastry and trim along the inside rim of the pie pan. Roll out the pastry trimmings into a long strip 1 inch wide. Make folds in the strip at 1-inch intervals, then place upright along the edge of the pastry in the pie pan, overlapping 1/2 inch. Seal the strip to the pastry with water. Bake blind as shown in the step-by-step illustrations (pg. 14) in a pre-heated 400-degree oven for 10 minutes. Reduce the oven temperature to 375 degrees and bake for 15 minutes longer. Remove from the oven and remove the peas and paper. Bake for 4 to 5 minutes longer or until lightly browned, then cool. Beat the egg yolks in a mixer bowl with an electric mixer until lemon colored. Add 1 cup of sugar gradually, then beat until well blended. Beat in the lemon juice gradually, then pour into the top of a double boiler over hot water. Cook, beating constantly, until thickened and foamy. Soften the gelatin in 1/4 cup of water, then stir into the egg yolk mixture until dissolved. Place the top of the double boiler in a bowl of iced water and stir until cooled. Stir in the orange and lemon rinds. Beat the egg whites and cream of tartar in a large mixer bowl until soft peaks form. Add remaining 1/2 cup of sugar gradually, beating constantly, then beat until stiff peaks form. Fold 1/4 of the egg white mixture into the gelatin mixture with a wire whisk or spatula to loosen the gelatin mixture. Fold in the remaining egg white mixture until well blended, then turn into the pie crust. Spoon the Meringue Topping over the filling carefully, sealing to the crust. Bake in a preheated 400-degree oven for 5 to 8 minutes or until the meringue is golden brown. Cool thoroughly. This pie may be chilled until served. This makes 6 to 8 servings.

MERINGUE TOPPING

5 egg whites
1 tsp. cream of tartar
3/4 c. sugar

Beat the egg whites and cream of tartar in a large mixer bowl until frothy. Beat in the sugar, 1 table-spoon at a time, then beat until stiff peaks form. Use as recipe directs. This makes enough meringue for one 10-inch pie or two 8-inch pies.

bouffant lemon meringue pie

Almost everyone enjoys lemon meringue pie. Fresh lemons are used to make the delicious filling. The Meringue Topping, which incorporates cream of tartar in egg whites, is the perfect meringue mixture for topping pies. The richness of this real, honest-to-goodness lemon pie will satisfy every connoisseur of pie!

mincemeat flan

COVERED MINCEMEAT FLAN

3 c. mincemeat
2 tbsp. brandy or rum
1 recipe Basic Sweet Short
    Pastry *(pg. 12)*

2 Push the pastry around the side of the ring over the mincemeat and brush with cold water.

1 Combine the mincemeat and the brandy and set aside. Roll out half the pastry on a lightly floured board. Cut a 10 to 11-inch circle. Place a 9-inch flan ring on a floured baking sheet, then place the pastry in the ring. Press the pastry slightly around the bottom and side of the ring, bringing the pastry to the top. Spoon the mincemeat into the pastry.

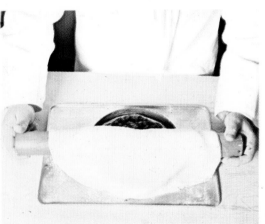

3 Roll out the remaining pastry on a lightly floured board into a circle and place over the top of the flan ring.

4 Cut off the surplus pastry by rolling the pin over the rim of ring.

5 Pinch the edges of the pastry together to seal securely. Bake in a preheated 375-degree oven for about 50 minutes or until top is browned. Remove the ring. Dust generously with confectioners' sugar and decorate with Almond Paste Holly Leaves. A 9-inch cake pan with removable bottom may be used, if desired. This makes about 8 servings.

making almond paste holly leaves

½ **recipe Basic Almond Paste**
No. 2 (pg. 41)
Green food coloring
Confectioners' sugar

Combine the almond paste and enough food coloring for desired tint and blend thoroughly. Roll out the almond paste to ⅛-inch thickness on a working surface dusted with confectioners' sugar.

1 Cut a single crescent from the almond paste at a slight angle, using a small, fluted pastry cutter. Cut the flutes outwards from the shape to be made each time.

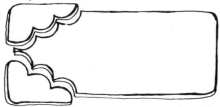

2 Cut again in the same way to make the point of the holly leaf.

3 Cut the third side to match the second side of the leaf.

4 Cut the fourth side to match the first side of the leaf.

5 Pinch 1 point of the leaf to form a stem.

tarts

MINCEMEAT TARTE TATIN

½ **recipe Basic Sweet Short Pastry** *(pg. 12)*
1 **1-lb. 2-oz. jar mincemeat with**
  brandy and rum

Roll out the pastry on a lightly floured surface to a ¼-inch thick circle. Place the bottom of a cake pan with removable bottom on the pastry and cut around the edge with a sharp knife. Place the bottom back in the pan. Grease and flour the cake pan, then spoon the mincemeat into the pan, spreading evenly. Place the pastry circle over the mincemeat and press down firmly. Bake in a preheated 375-degree oven for about 45 minutes or until the pastry is lightly browned. Invert the pan onto a serving platter and remove the bottom of the pan. Dust with confectioners' sugar and sprinkle with drops of brandy or rum, if desired. This makes 8 to 10 servings.

TARTE FLEURETTE

½ **recipe Basic Sweet Short Pastry** *(pg. 12)*
1 **recipe cold Basic Confectioners' Custard** *(pg. 19)*
1 **10-oz. jar plum jam**
2 **c. sweetened whipped cream**
½ **c. coarsely grated milk chocolate**

Prepare and chill the pastry according to the instructions. Roll out the pastry ¼ inch thick on a lightly floured surface to fit a 9-inch flan ring. Place the flan ring on a lightly floured baking sheet and line the ring with the pastry. Bake blind according to the step-by-step illustrations, (pg. 14) in a preheated 400-degree oven for 10 minutes. Reduce the oven temperature to 375 degrees and bake for 15 minutes longer or until golden. Remove the paper and peas and bake for 4 to 5 minutes longer to brown lightly. Let stand until cool and remove the ring. Place the custard in the flan and smooth the top. Spread the jam over the custard. Place the whipped cream in a pastry bag with a large star tube affixed and pipe over the jam. Sprinkle with the grated chocolate. This makes 8 servings.

mincemeat tarte tatin

For a traditional holiday treat, mincemeat tarts are a must. As a variation of the classic mincemeat pie, this tart is similar in flavor yet different in preparation and appearance. After the pastry has been rolled, it is placed on top of the mincemeat mixture and baked. The finished tart is then inverted onto a serving dish. This spicy mincemeat tart picks up an added flavor when sprinkled with a few drops of brandy or rum.

PORTUGUESE ALMOND PASTRY

1½ c. all-purpose flour
½ c. butter
½ c. sugar
¼ c. water
2 egg yolks, beaten
Almond Filling

Sift the flour onto a clean working surface and make a well in the center. Cut the butter into small pieces and place in the well. Add the sugar, water and egg yolks. Blend with 2 pastry scrapers, gathering flour from the ring, until of fine crumb consistency. Shape the pastry into a smooth ball, working in additional flour, if necessary. Divide the pastry into 2 parts. Roll out 1 part on a lightly floured surface to ¼-inch thickness and cut into a circle, using the bottom of a cake pan with removable bottom for a pattern. Fit the circle into the pan and spoon the Almond Filling over the pastry. Roll out the remaining pastry to ¼-inch thickness and cut a circle slightly larger than the bottom circle. Place the top pastry over the filling. Bake in a preheated 375-degree oven for 45 to 50 minutes or until the top crust is lightly browned. Cool for 5 minutes, then remove from the pan. Garnish with sliced toasted almonds, then with confectioners' sugar. This makes about 8 to 10 servings.

ALMOND FILLING

1½ c. ground almonds
¾ c. sugar
1½ tbsp. grated lemon rind
¼ c. butter, softened
3 eggs, slightly beaten

Combine the almonds and sugar in a medium-sized bowl and stir in the lemon rind. Work in the butter with the fingers until well blended. Add the eggs and blend thoroughly with a wire whisk. The consistency of the filling will be runny when mixed, but it will be firm when baked.

portuguese almond pastry

This almond pie is unusual in preparation and unusually good in taste. Almond Filling, with a zest of lemon, is placed on a base of uncooked pastry and then covered with a pastry top. The technique creates an unusual sandwich-like effect. Once baked and cooled, the pie is dusted with sugar and covered with toasted almonds.

strawberry and cream gâteau

Although *gâteau* is the French word for a stacked cake, the term may also be applied to any layered dish which resembles a cake. In this Strawberry and Cream Chou Pastry Gâteau, layers of pastry, strawberries, and cream combine to yield a deliciously different dessert. For the *gâteau*, a basic recipe and technique of making chou pastry (pg. 55) is used. Once the pastry has been baked, imagination becomes the key factor in creating a memorable *gâteau*. A variety of fresh fruits may be used.

STRAWBERRY AND CREAM CHOU PASTRY GÂTEAU

1 recipe Basic Sweet Chou Pastry *(pg. 55)*
1 recipe Basic Chantilly Cream *(pg. 19)*
1 c. crushed strawberries
3 c. whole strawberries
Confectioners' sugar

Spoon the pastry onto a lightly greased baking sheet in large dollops, forming a ring. Smooth the top with a small spatula, filling in between the dollops. Bake in a preheated 450-degree oven for 8 minutes. Reduce the oven temperature to 350 degrees and bake for 30 to 40 minutes longer or until dry. Cool on a wire rack, then split in half crosswise. Place the bottom half of the ring on a serving dish and spread with about 1/2 of the Chantilly cream. Cover with the crushed strawberries. Place the top half of the ring over the strawberries. Spoon the remaining Chantilly cream into a pastry bag with a large star tube affixed. Pipe around the base, then pipe dollops of cream over top. Arrange whole strawberries around the base and inside edge. Dust with confectioners' sugar. Place the remaining whole strawberries in the center. Serve immediately. This makes 8 to 10 servings.

danish cornet wafers

A skillful blending of ingredients and good preparation technique make Danish Cornet Wafers a dessert with a flair. Eggs, sugar, and flour are mixed into a soft dough, shaped into circles, and quickly baked in a hot oven. The circles are then placed into metal horns utilizing a similar technique to that which is used for making cream horns on page 152. When finished, the crispy cones are filled with custard. A plump topping of stiffly whipped cream completes this dessert.

DANISH CORNET WAFERS

2 eggs
¹⁄₃ c. sugar
¹⁄₂ c. sifted all-purpose flour
¹⁄₈ tsp. salt
¹⁄₄ tsp. almond extract
Butter
1 recipe Orange Confectioners' Custard *(pg.88)*
1 c. sweetened whipped cream

Beat the eggs until light, then add the sugar gradually, beating until thick and of a batter-like consistency. Fold in the flour gradually until smooth and well blended, then stir in the salt and almond extract. Place 3 widely spaced mounds, using 3 level tablespoons of batter for each, on a heavily greased baking sheet. Spread each mound with a metal spatula to a 4¹⁄₂-inch circle. Do not bake more than 3 circles at a time. Grease 3 horn molds heavily with butter. Bake in a preheated 400-degree oven for 4 to 5 minutes or until just set and the edges are lightly tinged with brown. Loosen the circles quickly with a spatula, leaving on the baking sheet. Place a horn mold in the center of each circle and roll the wafers around the molds as quickly as possible, overlapping as shown in the illustration. Place on a wire rack until cooled and just set, then remove the molds. Grease the molds again. Repeat until all the batter is baked greasing the horn molds each time. Fill each wafer with the custard. Garnish with whipped cream. This makes 12 wafers.

danish cornet wafers

Served in your special dishes, these Danish Cornet Wafers make a truly elegant dessert. The very delicate pastry has been filled with rich Orange Confectioners' Custard and then topped with whipped cream. Chocolate pretzels garnish each filled wafer with traditional Danish flair.

HOT CHOCOLATE SOUFFLÉ

Butter
Sugar
¾ c. chocolate chips
4 egg yolks
1 c. sifted confectioners' sugar
5 egg whites, at room temperature
½ tsp. cream of tartar

Grease a 6-inch soufflé dish generously with butter and coat the inside with sugar, shaking out the excess. Combine 2 tablespoons of cold water and the chocolate chips in the top of a double boiler. Place over hot water until the chocolate chips are melted, then beat with a wire whisk until blended. Cut 2 tablespoons of butter into small pieces and add to the chocolate, 1 piece at a time, beating until the butter is melted. Cool slightly. Place the egg yolks in a large mixer bowl and beat with an electric mixer until lemon colored. Add the confectioners' sugar gradually and beat until thick. Add ¼ of the chocolate mixture and beat with a wire whisk until blended. Add the remaining chocolate mixture and beat until well mixed. Beat the egg whites and cream of tartar with the electric mixer until stiff peaks form. Fold ¼ of the egg whites into the chocolate mixture, blending well. Fold in the remaining egg whites until well mixed. Spoon in the prepared soufflé dish and smooth the top. Bake in a preheated 400-degree oven for 35 minutes or until set. Dust with additional confectioners' sugar, if desired, and serve immediately. This makes about 6 servings.

hot chocolate soufflé

This Hot Chocolate Soufflé is just bursting with rich flavor. The key to the success of this luscious dessert depends on well-beaten egg yolks and stiffly beaten whites. This soufflé puffs beautifully, and is very suitable for special occasions.

INDIVIDUAL RED CURRANT SOUFFLÉS

1 c. red currant jelly
6 stiffly beaten egg whites
Confectioners' sugar

Place the jelly in the blender container and process until liquefied, then pour into a large mixing bowl. Fold 1/4 of the beaten egg whites into the jelly, mixing well. Add the remaining egg whites and fold in until well blended. Spoon into 4 buttered individual baking dishes. Bake in a preheated 425-degree oven for 8 to 9 minutes or until the tops are golden brown. Sprinkle with confectioners' sugar and serve immediately. The soufflés may be baked in 8 buttered custard cups, if desired. This makes 4 generous servings.

individual red currant soufflés

A simple blending of egg whites and red currant jelly combines to make these soufflés. The mixture is placed in these individual heat resistant dishes and quickly baked. This recipe may be easily varied by using another flavor of jelly.

cumberland soufflé pudding

Cumberland Soufflé Pudding is a delicious light dessert. The basis for this dish is a layer of apple slices, jam, butter and bread crumbs. Care should be taken to slice the apples paper thin. The mixture is then covered with Vanilla Soufflé and baked until golden brown.

CUMBERLAND SOUFFLÉ PUDDING

2 med. cooking apples
1 c. red raspberry jam
3 c. fine soft bread crumbs
½ c. butter, cut into sm. pieces
1 recipe Vanilla Soufflé mixture (pg. 47)

Pare and core the apples and cut into paper-thin slices. Place the jam in a blender container and process until of easy spreading consistency. Sprinkle half the bread crumbs over the bottom of a well-greased 10-inch baking dish, then cover with half the butter. Arrange half the apple slices over the butter and spread half the jam over the apples. Repeat the layers, then spoon the soufflé mixture over the top, mounding slightly in the center. Bake in a preheated 400-degree oven for 35 minutes or until set and golden brown. Serve with Punch Sauce (Sauces, pg. 25). Apples will not be tender unless sliced paper thin. A potato or vegetable slicer may be used for slicing. This makes 8 servings.

cumberland soufflé pudding

A clever combination of contrasting textures makes this Cumberland Soufflé Pudding a special dessert. The golden brown soufflé topping perfectly complements the crunchy apple filling hidden beneath it. Serve with a bowl of sweetened whipped cream or vanilla ice cream.

creamed cheese pudding

CREAMED CHEESE PUDDING

2 env. unflavored gelatin
2 eggs, separated
1 ¼ c. sugar
1 c. milk
¼ tsp. salt
2 tsp. grated lemon rind
3 c. creamed cottage cheese
Lemon juice
1 c. whipping cream, whipped
½ c. ground toasted almonds

3 c. confectioners' sugar
20 ladyfingers

Sprinkle the gelatin over ½ cup of water and let stand for 5 minutes to soften. Beat the egg yolks slightly in the top of a double boiler, then stir in 1 cup of the sugar, the milk and salt. Cook over hot water, stirring constantly, until thick. Stir in the gelatin, then remove from the heat. Combine the lemon rind, cottage cheese and ¼ cup of the lemon juice, then stir into the gelatin mixture. Refrigerate until the mixture mounds slightly when dropped from a spoon. Beat the egg whites until frothy, then add the remaining ¼ cup of sugar gradually, beating until stiff peaks form. Fold the egg whites into the cottage cheese mixture carefully, then fold in the whipped cream and almonds. Turn into a 9-inch springform pan and chill until firm. Sift the confectioners' sugar into a bowl, then add enough lemon juice gradually to make the icing of spreading consistency. Release the spring and remove the side. Place the pudding on a serving dish. Trim one end from the ladyfingers. Spread the icing on the ladyfingers, one at a time, and place around the pudding as each one is iced. Garnish top with rosettes of additional whipped cream. You may tint the icing, if desired. This makes about 15 servings.

creamed cheese pudding

This lovely Creamed Cheese Pudding is a light dessert that will serve many guests. It is quite similar to an lemon-flavored cheesecake and it may be conveniently prepared well in advance of serving.

crème marie louise

CRÈME MARIE LOUISE

1 recipe Basic Rolled Sponge Cake *(pg. 3)*
1   12-oz. package chocolate chips
1 recipe Filling
1 recipe Basic Chantilly Cream *(pg. 19)*

Prepare and bake the cake according to the instructions, using 2 round 9-inch cake pans. To make the chocolate case you will need a piece of heavy cardboard, a piece of very thin, smooth poster paper and an 8 to 9-inch springform pan. Cut a circle of the heavy cardboard to fit the bottom of the springform pan, then cut a circle of waxed paper about 1 inch larger. Tape the waxed paper to the cardboard, clipping around the edges of the waxed paper and taping securely to the bottom of the cardboard. Cut a strip of the poster paper to fit snugly around the inside rim of the pan. Tape ends together securely to form a ring. Place the heavy cardboard bottom in the pan, then place the poster paper ring inside the pan. Tape to the pan on 2 sides. Melt the chocolate according to instructions on page 49. Spread a layer of chocolate with a rubber spatula, about 1/8 inch thick, over the bottom. Refrigerate for about 30 minutes or until firm. Remove from the refrigerator and spread chocolate around the side evenly, also about 1/8 inch thick, making sure there are no holes where the bottom and side meet. Chill until firm. Cut the tape and release the spring, then remove the shell, as shown in the illustrations. Place on serving dish and place 1 layer of the cake in the bottom. Spread a layer of the Filling over the cake, then add the second layer. Spoon the remaining Filling over the cake and smooth the top with a spatula. This may stand in a cool room for about 2 hours or may be refrigerated for several hours. If refrigerated, you must remove from refrigerator about 2 hours before serving. Pipe the Chantilly cream around the edge just before serving. This makes about 15 servings.

FILLING

4 egg yolks
1 ½ c. whipping cream
1   12-oz. package chocolate chips, melted
    (pg. 49)
1 tbsp. dark rum
1 tsp. orange flower water
1 tsp. rose water

Place the egg yolks in a large mixer bowl and beat lightly. Whip the cream with an electric mixer until very soft peaks form, then add to the eggs and stir until just combined. Beat the chocolate with a wooden spoon until smooth, glossy and cool. Add the chocolate to the cream mixture with the electric mixer, beating at medium speed, then increase speed to high. Beat until chocolate is blended in, then add the flavorings. Beat until the consistency

of whipped cream. Use in the chocolate case or fill individual serving dishes for *Pots de Crème Marie Louise.*

HOW TO REMOVE CHOCOLATE CASE FROM PAN

1 Loosen the springform pan and remove carefully.

2 Cut the tape securing the ring of poster paper and peel off gently.

3 Remove the cardboard from the bottom and place case on dish.

crème marie louise

This luscious chocolate dessert is Crème Marie Louise, set in an elegant chocolate case. The top is attractively bordered with rich Chantilly cream.

HAZELNUT CREAM

1 recipe Basic Confectioners' Custard *(pg. 19)*
1 env. unflavored gelatin
2 tbsp. rum
1 c. ground toasted hazelnuts or pecans
1 c. whipping chream

Prepare the custard. Soften the gelatin in ¼ cup of water, then stir into the custard until dissolved before cooling the custard to lukewarm. Add the rum to the lukewarm custard mixture and mix well. Chill until partially set. Add the hazelnuts and mix until well blended. Beat the cream until stiff peaks form, then fold into the hazelnut mixture until blended. Turn into a lightly oiled 6-cup mold and chill until firm. Unmold onto a serving dish. Additional whipped cream may be piped in rosettes around the mold and each rosette topped with a whole toasted hazelnut, if desired. This makes about 8 servings.

hazelnut cream

Hazelnut Cream is a light, creamy dessert, similar to a mousse. It may be prepared in a mold, as shown, or if desired, served in individual molds or little pots. Rich with egg yolks, whipped cream, and hazelnuts, this dish may be made several days ahead of time and stored tightly covered in the refrigerator.

green grape gelatin

Summer is the time to serve a cool, shimmering molded gelatin dessert full of plump, green grapes. The wise hostess will choose seedless grapes for this recipe, which eliminates the problem of having to remove the seeds from the grapes!

GREEN GRAPE GELATIN

1   3-oz. package lime gelatin
1 env. unflavored gelatin
2 ½ c. white grape drink
1 c. Sauterne
1 lb. seedless green grapes

Combine the lime gelatin and the unflavored gelatin in a medium-sized mixing bowl and mix well. Bring 1 ½ cups of the grape drink to a boil, then add to the gelatin and stir until gelatin is dissolved. Stir in the remaining grape drink and the Sauterne. Chill until syrupy. Pour enough gelatin mixture into a ring mold to fill ½ inch deep, then chill in the refrigerator until almost set. Place the remaining gelatin over a bowl of ice to keep at syrupy stage, stirring occasionally. Arrange a layer of grapes over the gelatin mixture in the mold, then add enough gelatin mixture to just cover the grapes. Chill until firm, then pour enough syrupy gelatin over the grapes to cover ½ inch. Chill until firm. Add another layer of grapes and enough syrupy gelatin mixture to just cover. Chill again until firm, then add the remaining gelatin mixture. Chill until firm and ready to serve. Unmold on serving platter and garnish with Tokay grapes, if desired. Serve with Basic Chantilly Cream (pg. 19). This makes about 8 servings.

BAVAROIS CREAM WITH RASPBERRIES

1 ½ env. unflavored gelatin
3 tbsp. lemon juice
1 ¼ c. puréed raspberries
1 c. Basic Sugar Syrup *(Breads, pg. 14)*
1 c. whipping cream, whipped

Pour ½ cup of water into a small saucepan. Add the gelatin and let stand for 5 minutes. Stir in the lemon juice, then place over low heat, stirring constantly until the gelatin is dissolved. Cool to room temperature. Combine the puréed raspberries, sugar syrup and gelatin mixture, blending well. Fold in the whipped cream until well blended. Pour into an oiled 6-cup mold and chill until firm. Puréed strawberries or loganberries may be substituted for the raspberries. This makes about 6 servings.

bavarois cream with raspberries

This beautiful jewel-like dessert is shown in both large and individual servings. Other berries in season can be used in place of the raspberries, and fresh whole berries may be used for garnish, if desired.

frozen christmas custard

frozen christmas custard

This festive holiday dessert is comparable to homemade ice cream that is prepared in freezer trays. Cool, rich and creamy, it has its own multicolored decorations: currants, candied cherries, candied ginger and candied pineapple.

FROZEN CHRISTMAS CUSTARD

2 tbsp. chopped candied cherries
2 tbsp. chopped candied ginger
2 tbsp. chopped candied pineapple
2 tbsp. raisins
2 tbsp. currants
2 tbsp. chopped mixed candied peel
²/₃ c. Sauterne
2 recipes Basic Confectioners' Custard *(pg. 19)*
2 c. whipping cream, stiffly beaten

Combine the cherries, ginger, pineapple, raisins, currants and mixed peel in a small bowl and pour the Sauterne over the mixture. Let stand for 1 hour, then drain. Add the fruit mixture to the custard, then fold in the whipped cream until well blended. Place in a lightly oiled 8-cup soufflé dish and freeze until hard. Unmold according to the step-by-step illustrations. This makes about 10 to 12 servings.

The Creative Homemaker's Academy © MCMLXXIII
Selected Illustrations © B.P.C. Publishing Limited MCMLXX

1 Let the custard stand at room temperature for 10 minutes, then dip into hot water and turn out onto a platter.

2 Pour boiling water into a bowl, then dip a sharp knife into the water.

3 Cut the custard into wedges, dipping the knife into the water before cutting each slice, and place on a serving platter.

The Frozen Christmas Custard may be shaped into balls by dipping an ice cream scoop, which has been dipped in boiling water, into the custard.

frozen christmas custard snowballs

These Frozen Christmas Custard Snowballs are made with the same custard mixture as the Frozen Christmas Custard on the preceding page, but here they are served as gaily decorated snowballs with artificial holly leaves for garnish. (Note: Holly berries are poisonous, so be sure to use only artificial holly as a garnish for food.)

baked alaska

The famous and unusual dessert known as Baked Alaska is an exceptionally fancy creation and will mark any event as a very special occasion. The following recipe combines three Basic recipes already presented in the Desserts Section: ice cream, meringue and Sponge Cake. The entire preparation and assembly (except for the final baking of the meringue) may be completed well in advance and placed unbaked in the freezer until it is ready to be served. At this point, simply run it under a broiler until the meringue is delicately colored. Baked Alaska maý be prepared from commercial ice cream and cake, but nothing can compare with the superior taste and texture of made-from-scratch sponge cake and homemade ice cream.

The Creative Homemaker's Academy © MCMLXXIII
Selected Illustrations © B.P.C. Publishing Limited MCMLXX

baked alaska

This exciting tour de force, will draw an enthusiastic reception from family and guests. It is not unusually difficult to prepare, but be advised to allow plenty of time to assemble the component parts: sponge cake, ice cream and smoothly applied meringue. The meringue is a special one — it is made with confectioners' sugar rather than granulated sugar which makes it drier than some meringue. For added drama and elegance, place the Baked Alaska on a stainless steel platter before baking; when ready to serve, quickly decorate with greenery, blossoms amd candied violets.

BAKED ALASKA

½ **gallon ice cream**
1　**9-in. layer Basic Close-Textured Sponge Cake**
　　(pg. 6)
8 **egg whites**
⅛ **tsp. salt**
½ **tsp. cream of tartar**
1 ½ **c. sifted confectioners' sugar**
1 **tsp. vanilla extract**

Soften the ice cream. Line a 2-quart mold with plastic wrap. Pack the ice cream in the mold and freeze until firm. Place the cake layer on a stainless steel platter, then trim the edge to within ½ to ¾ inch larger than top of ice cream mold. Remove the ice cream from the mold and invert onto the cake. Remove the plastic wrap. Place the platter in the freezer until the ice cream is very firm.　Combine the egg whites and salt in a large mixer bowl and beat with an electric mixer at high speed until foamy. Add the cream of tartar and beat until soft peaks form. Beat until stiff peaks form, adding the sugar, 1 tablespoon at a time, and beating well after each addition. Beat in the vanilla. Place about ⅓ of the meringue in a pastry bag with a large star tube affixed and set aside. Remove the ice cream from freezer and spread the meringue very thickly over the entire surface, sealing well around the bottom of the cake. Pipe swirls and rosettes of meringue over the Alaska in a decorative manner. At this point the Alaska may be returned to the freezer until just before serving time. Bake in a preheated 450-degree oven for about 2 to 3 minutes or until the meringue is lightly tinged with brown. Serve immediately. Any flavor of ice cream may be used. This makes about 16 servings.

baked alaska (cut for serving)

Here the Baked Alaska has been cut revealing a cross section of the finished dessert. The illustrated dessert used grape flavored ice cream, although any kind of ice cream may be used. Let your imagination and creative instincts be your guide!

STRAWBERRY DESSERT SANDWICH

1 recipe Basic Confectioners' Custard *(pg. 19)*
1 recipe Basic Rolled Sponge Cake *(pg. 3)*
¼ c. whipping cream, whipped
3 pt. large fresh strawberries, cleaned

Prepare and chill the confectioners' custard. Prepare the sponge cake according to the step-by-step illustrations No. 1 through No. 11, omitting the filling. Cut the cake into identical triangles or squares. Fold the whipped cream into the custard until well blended, then spread over half the cake triangles. Slice enough of the strawberries to completely cover the custard mixture on each triangle, then place on the custard mixture. Place the remaining cake triangles over the strawberries and press lightly. Arrange the remaining strawberries in a bowl and place the bowl in the center of a large serving plate. Place the cake triangles around the bowl. Serve the strawberries with sugar and additional whipped cream, if desired. This makes about 12 servings.

strawberry dessert sandwich

Here is a wonderful and versatile dessert, suitable for any occasion. Its easy preparation is but one of the many charms of this simple, elegant dessert.

SPANISH SPONGE CAKE WITH FRUIT AND NUTS

1 ¼ c. butter, softened
1 tbsp. grated lemon rind
1 c. sugar
3 eggs
1 ½ c. sifted all-purpose flour
¼ tsp. salt
½ c. blanched sliced almonds
½ c. chopped candied cherries

Combine the butter and lemon rind in a large bowl, then beat with an electric beater until light and fluffy. Add ¾ cup of the sugar gradually, beating after each addition until smooth. Add 1 egg, 1 tablespoon of the flour and the salt and beat until smooth. Add the remaining eggs alternately with the flour, beating thoroughly after each addition. Spoon into a well-greased and floured 9-inch square cake pan and spread evenly. Combine the almonds and cherries and sprinkle over the cake mixture, then sprinkle with the remaining sugar. Bake in a preheated 350-degree oven for 35 minutes or until golden brown. This makes about 9 servings.

spanish sponge cake with fruit and nuts

Spanish sponge cake, with its flavorful topping of fruit and nuts, is perfect to serve at a tea or luncheon. The faint hint of lemon adds a marvelous flavor to the sponge cake, and a light dusting of sugar adds the finishing touch. This dessert may be baked and frozen for later use.

sweetheart spice cake

SWEETHEART SPICE CAKE

Butter
1 c. sugar
3 eggs
1/2 c. light molasses
2 3/4 c. sifted cake flour
1 tsp. soda
1 tsp. cinnamon
3/4 tsp. salt
Milk
1 1/2 tbsp. grated orange rind
3/4 c. cherry preserves
1 recipe Sweetheart Frosting
1 c. shredded coconut
Red food coloring

Cut 2 pieces of waxed paper to fit the bottom of 2 heart-shaped cake pans that measure 9 inches at the widest part and 1 1/2 inches in depth. Grease the bottoms of the pans with butter, then place the waxed paper over the butter. Grease the waxed paper with butter, then coat lightly with flour. Place 3/4 cup of butter in a large mixer bowl and beat with an electric mixer until light. Add the sugar gradually, beating until smooth after each addition. Add the eggs, one at a time, beating well after each addition. Stir in the molasses until well blended. Sift the flour with the soda, cinnamon and salt, then add to the egg mixture alternately with 1 cup of milk, beating well after each addition. Stir in the orange rind. Pour the batter into the prepared pans. Bake in a preheated 350-degree oven for 30 to 35 minutes or until a cake tester inserted in the center comes out clean. Cool in the pans for 5 minutes, then invert onto wire racks and remove the waxed paper carefully. Cool completely. Spread cherry preserves between the layers, then frost sides and top of cake with Sweetheart Frosting. Place the coconut in a pint jar. Add 1/2 teaspoon of milk and enough food coloring for desired tint. Cover the jar and shake vigorously until the coconut is tinted. Decorate the top edge and base of the cake with the coconut. This makes 12 to 15 servings.

sweetheart spice cake

For sentimental occasions, such as wedding anniversaries or Valentine's Day, nothing could be as appropriate as a heart cake served for dessert. The spices and cherry preserves in the cake will lead right to a man's heart!

SWEETHEART FROSTING

1 1/2 c. sugar
1/2 c. water
3 egg whites
1/8 tsp. cream of tartar
1 tsp. vanilla extract
Red food coloring

Combine the sugar and water in a heavy saucepan and stir well. Bring to a boil and cook, without stirring, to the hard-ball stage or 250 degrees on a candy thermometer. Place the egg whites and cream of tartar in a large mixer bowl and beat until stiff peaks form. Pour the hot syrup into the egg whites very gradually, beating constantly, then beat for 7 minutes or until stiff peaks form. Beat in the vanilla and enough food coloring for desired tint.

pêche melba

A French cook in an English kitchen was responsible for creating the luscious dessert known as *Pêche Melba*. *Georges Auguste Escoffier* combined his love for cooking and his adoration of music to create *Pêche Melba*. Enchanted with her operatic performance *Escoffier* honored Dame Nellie Melba with this elegant creation of fresh peaches on a mound of ice cream topped with ripe raspberry purée. He then placed the dish between swan wings made from a block of ice.

HOW TO BLANCH FRUIT TO REMOVE THE SKIN

Plunge the fruit into boiling water for several seconds to loosen the skin. Cool in ice water, then slip off the skin.

PÊCHE MELBA

4 lg. firm fresh peaches, blanched
1 c. Basic Sugar Syrup (*Breads, pg. 14*)
1 vanilla pod or 1 tsp. vanilla extract
1 recipe Basic Vanilla Ice Cream (*Desserts, pg. 67*)
    or 1 qt. commercial ice cream
1 recipe Melba Sauce

Cut the peaches in half and remove the seeds. Combine the syrup and vanilla pod and boil for 5 minutes, then remove the pod. Poach the peaches in the syrup for 10 minutes or until just tender, then remove from the syrup. Chill the peaches thoroughly. Place scoops of ice cream in 8 sherbet dishes, then place the peach halves over the ice cream, cut side down. Top with Melba Sauce. Garnish with whole raspberries, if desired. This makes 8 servings.

MELBA SAUCE

1 qt. fresh red raspberries, puréed
¼ c. red currant jelly
2 tsp. cornstarch
Sugar to taste
Brandy to taste (opt.)

Combine the raspberries and jelly in a heavy saucepan over low heat and stir gently until the jelly is melted. Dissolve the cornstarch in 2 tablespoons of water and add to the raspberry mixture, stirring constantly until smooth and clear. Stir in the sugar and brandy. This makes about 3 cups of sauce.

pêche melba

Elegant simplicity is the best description for this dessert. Only the best of ingredients are used to create an authentic Pêche Melba. Firm, fresh peaches are always used and fresh raspberries are preferred though not a must. Always use homemade vanilla ice cream, if possible, or another good quality. The dessert is topped with bright raspberry purée and served in clear crystal coupes.

gelatin
boats

orange currant boats

These shimmering Orange Currant Boats are deceptively easy to prepare. Ripe oranges have been hollowed out and filled with wine-flavored red currant gelatin. When set, the oranges are sliced into quarters. For a charming centerpiece, an extra orange shell has been filled with sparkling gelatin.

ORANGE CURRANT BOATS

2 env. unflavored gelatin
2   10-oz. jars red currant jelly
2 tbsp. lemon juice
¼ c. Port
6 med. oranges

Soften the gelatin in ½ cup of water for 5 minutes. Combine the gelatin, jelly and ½ cup of water in a small saucepan. Place over low heat and stir until the jelly is melted and the gelatin is dissolved. Stir in the lemon juice and Port and set aside. Prepare the orange shells, fill with the gelatin mixture, chill, and cut according to the step-by-step illustrations. Place on a serving plate. Any remaining gelatin may be congealed, then broken up and placed in half of a grapefruit shell. Place in the center of the plate. This makes 6 servings.

1 Cut a hole in the stem end of each orange and remove all of the pulp with a grapefruit knife, or, if preferred, cut the orange in half and remove pulp.

2 Place the orange pulp in a bowl and reserve for future use.

3 Place the orange shells in a foil-lined pan, then spoon enough of the gelatin mixture into each shell to fill to the top.

4 Chill until firm, then cut into halves, or quarters according to the size of the oranges.

classic mille-feuille

For a dessert with a difference, *Mille-Feuille* is a classic. *Mille-Feuille* (meaning "a thousand layers") is flaky layers of pastry filled with custard, cream or fruit. Because of the delicacy of this dessert, care in preparation is essential. A pastry dough is rolled to an even consistency, placed in oblong flan frames and baked until lightly browned. Each pastry strip is spread with custard, whipped cream and fruit in alternating layers. The finished dish is topped with a simple glaze to which a touch of chocolate or other flavoring may be added.

mille-feuille

This is a classic French pastry dessert. Alternating layers of custard, strawberry jam and whipped cream are sandwiched between thin layers of golden pastry. The Basic Confectioners' Icing has been marbled with softened chocolate which adds a colorful contrast.

CLASSIC MILLE-FEUILLE

1 recipe Basic Cold Yeast Dough (*Breads, pg. 21*)
2 c. strawberry jam
1/2 c. whipping cream, whipped
1 recipe Basic Confectioners' Custard (*pg. 19*)
1 c. Basic Confectioners' Icing (*pg. 8*)
2 squares unsweetened chocolate, melted

Roll out half the chilled dough at a time on a floured board to 1/2-inch thickness and cut 2 strips from each half to fit into a 12 x 3 1/2-inch metal flan frame as shown in illustration No. 1. Place 1 strip in the frame on a lightly floured baking sheet, placing remaining strips in the refrigerator until just before baking. Bake in a preheated 400-degree oven for 12 minutes or until golden brown. Repeat with remaining 3 strips, then cut strips in half lengthwise as shown in illustration No. 2. Place on racks to cool. Alternate method: Lacking a metal flan frame, roll out 1/3 of the dough on a floured board to about 3/8-inch thickness. Cut two 12 x 3 1/2-inch strips and place on a baking sheet. Repeat rolling the dough

and cutting strips 2 more times. Bake in a pre-heated 400-degree oven for 10 minutes or until golden brown. Lift with wide spatulas and place on racks to cool. Place 1 baked layer on a serving platter and spread with 1 cup of strawberry jam. Top with the second layer and spread with the whipped cream. Add the third layer, then spread with half the confectioners' custard. Top with the fourth layer and spread with the remaining cup of strawberry jam. Place the fifth layer over the jam and spread with the remaining confectioners' custard. Place the sixth layer on the top and cover with the icing. Drizzle the melted chocolate in 2 thin lines lengthwise over the icing, then pull the chocolate over the icing as shown in illustration No. 3, using a small skewer. Any remaining split layers may be cut into finger-sized strips and topped with additional filling or icing. Cut the layered mixture in half lengthwise carefully, then cut crosswise at 2 inch intervals. This makes 12 servings.

1 A metal flan frame is used as a pattern and then as a baking frame to hold the edges of the pastry strips in position.

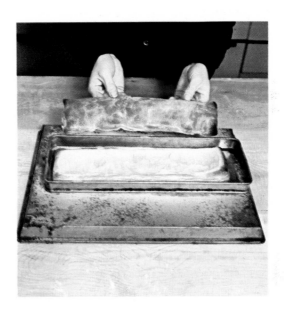

2 Cut the strips in half carefully, using a sharp knife.

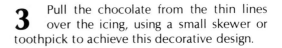

3 Pull the chocolate from the thin lines over the icing, using a small skewer or toothpick to achieve this decorative design.

PINEAPPLE DESSERT PIZZA

½ recipe Rough Puff Pastry *(pg. 27)*
1 recipe Egg Wash *(Breads, pg. 6)*
1 recipe Apricot Glaze *(pg. 19)*
7 pineapple rings
5 pitted sweet dark cherries

Roll out the pastry to a 15-inch circle and center in a lightly floured 12-inch pizza pan. Turn edge toward center and press gently into base dough. Make diagonal cuts around the edge with a sharp knife, then brush the edge with the Egg Wash. Bake in a preheated 425-degree oven for 10 minutes. Reduce the oven temperature to 350 degrees and bake for 35 to 40 minutes longer. Remove from oven and cool thoroughly. Transfer the pastry shell carefully to a serving plate. Spread the Apricot Glaze generously over the bottom of the shell. Arrange 5 pineapple rings over the glaze. Divide remaining pineapple rings into quarters and arrange among the rings, as shown in the illustration. Center the rings with the cherries and spread additional glaze evenly over the fruits. This makes 8 servings.

pineapple dessert pizza

The combination of pineapple and puff pastry is very delicious. After baking the pastry it is cooled, then covered with Apricot Glaze. Whole and quartered sections of pineapple are arranged over the jam. Although this dessert is exceptional when made with fresh pineapple, slices of canned pineapple may be substituted. Cherries placed inside the pineapple rings make a colorful garnish.

VIENNESE SACHERTORTE

1 c. chocolate chips
8 egg yolks, slightly beaten
½ c. unsalted butter, melted
1 tbsp. vanilla extract
10 egg whites
¼ tsp. salt
¾ c. sugar
1 c. sifted cake flour
1 recipe Apricot Glaze *(pg. 19)*
½ recipe Special Chocolate Icing *(pg. 97)*

Butter and lightly flour the bottoms of two 9-inch sliding-based cake pans. Melt the chocolate chips as instructed on page 49. Cool slightly. Combine the egg yolks with the chocolate chips in a small mixer bowl and blend well. Add the melted butter and vanilla extract, stirring until smooth and thoroughly blended. Beat the egg whites and salt until frothy. Add the sugar, 1 tablespoon at a time, beating well after each addition and continue beating until stiff peaks form. Fold ⅓ of the egg whites into the chocolate mixture thoroughly, then fold the chocolate mixture gently into egg whites. Fold flour gradually into the chocolate mixture until smooth and just blended, using a rubber spatula. Pour the batter into the prepared cake pans. Bake in a preheated 350-degree oven for 25 to 30 minutes or until the layers test done. Remove from oven and cool on wire racks for 1 minute. Remove the layers from the pans and let cool completely. Spread the Apricot Glaze between the layers and over the top of the cake. Pour chocolate icing over all, smoothing with a wet spatula. Chill the cake for 3 hours or until the glaze is set. Remove from the refrigerator 30 minutes before serving. The sachertorte may be piped with Basic Chantilly Cream (pg. 19). Each layer may be glazed individually, if desired. This makes 20 to 24 servings.

viennese sachertorte

Viennese Sachertorte is a famous chocolate dessert. The cut piece illustrates the rich, light texture of the cake which results from a skillful blending of ingredients. Melted chocolate chips are added to the batter. Stiffly beaten egg whites folded into the mixture add a fluffy consistency. When baked and cooled, the cake is brushed with Apricot Glaze (pg. 19). Special Chocolate Icing (pg. 97) makes a beautiful glaze on the cake.

fondant shapes

Basic Fondant Icing may be used in a variety of ways. It makes a delicious icing for cakes, nuts, cookies and candied fruit, as well as for candies. When worked into a stiff paste, this fondant can be rolled out on a cornstarch-dusted surface and cut into attractive shapes by using pastry cutters. As an added advantage, the stamped fondant shapes can be left on a tray for 24 hours to dry, then stored for an indefinite period of time. For storage, place them between layers of waxed paper in an airtight container.

BASIC FONDANT ICING

2   1-lb. boxes confectioners' sugar
1/2 c. white corn syrup
2 egg whites
1 tsp. vanilla extract
Cornstarch

Sift the sugar into a large bowl. Heat the syrup in a small pan over hot water. Make a well in the sugar, then add the syrup, egg whites and vanilla. Mix with a wooden spoon until smooth. Sift additional confectioners' sugar on a clean working surface. Place the fondant on the sugar and knead until of a smooth dough-like consistency. Add sugar as needed to keep fondant from sticking. Sift cornstarch over the working surface, then roll out the fondant to 1/4-inch thickness. Trim to fit the cake and place over the top. Decorate with desired cut out designs. For the green peppermint icing, add 4 drops of peppermint oil and 6 drops of green food coloring when the vanilla is added. This makes enough icing for a 2 layer cake or 2 rolls.

basic fondant icing

Pretty as a picture, this Fondant Iced Cake is a festive dessert for any occasion. A basic fondant recipe has been used for both icing the cake and decorating it. Because of the flexibility of flavoring fondant icing, it combines deliciously with any cake. As an extra benefit, fondant icing will keep for several weeks when properly covered and refrigerated, making it possible to prepare both the icing and cake well ahead of serving time.

how to
roll out and apply fondant icing

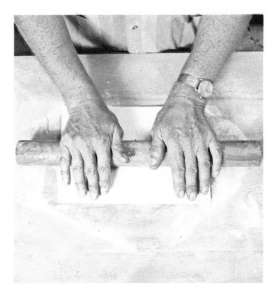

1 Roll out the fondant ¼ inch thick on a cornstarch-dusted surface.

2 The fondant can be picked up and rolled over the top of rolling pin if the surface has been sufficiently dusted with cornstarch.

3 Place the fondant over the roll, covering completely. Cut 2 pieces of the fondant to fit the ends. Dampen the edges with water and place on the ends, pinching to hold together. Decorate with desired shapes of fondant.

HOW TO CUT FONDANT SHAPES

Roll out fondant and cut with fluted pastry cutter or canapé cutters for desired shapes.

PETITS FOURS

Dainty Iced *Petits Fours* are as colorful as they are delicious. They are made with miniature rounds of sponge cake cut with a pastry cutter and topped with creamy, rich butter cream icing.

(Hint: If you freeze sponge cake before cutting, you will find it cuts into shapes beautifully. You must first dip your pastry cutters in warm water.)

Butter cream icing blends well with many flavors. Other than the liqueurs specified in the following recipe, try several flavors of brandy, also. Peach, apricot and apple brandy, for example, may be used with butter cream.

ICED PETITS FOURS

1 recipe Basic Close-Textured Sponge Cake *(pg. 6)*
2 recipes Basic Butter Cream No. 1 *(pg. 7)*
4 1-lb. boxes confectioners' sugar
Kirsch, Cointreau, Grand Marnier or Crème de Menthe
Food Coloring

Prepare the cake and bake in a jelly roll pan according to the instructions. Cut into rounds with a wet 1-inch cutter. The butter cream and icing may be divided and flavored with various liqueurs and tinted as desired or one flavor may be used. Icing *petits fours* is a time-consuming job. Keep the cake rounds covered to keep them from drying out. Make a small amount of icing at a time, because it dries quickly. Combine 2 cups of sifted confectioners' sugar with 1 teaspoon of desired liqueur, food coloring and enough water to make a dipping consistency. Dip the cake rounds into the icing, then place on wire racks over jelly roll pans to harden. Continue making icing and dipping the cakes until all have been covered. Prepare 1 recipe of butter cream at a time, then pipe a large rosette on the top of each iced cake. Prepare more icing as before and spoon carefully in a circular motion over the rosette of each cake, letting the icing flow evenly to coat completely. If a heavier coating is desired, then spoon another coat of icing over the cakes. Let stand until the icing has hardened. Store in airtight containers or freeze until ready to use. This makes about 100 *petits fours*.

iced petits fours

Iced Petits Fours make an elegant dessert for the most special occasions, and they are particularly appropriate for wedding festivities, teas and other large parties.

DIPLOMAT CAKES

Diplomat Cakes, which are perfect for any party menu, are both delicious and delightfully easy to prepare. They are made simply by cutting thin sponge cake into small circles and covering the circles of cake with Basic Butter Cream. A special whipped cream flavored with kirsch is mounded on top. You may make them in an array of beautiful colors with tinted butter cream.

LITTLE DIPLOMAT CAKES

1 recipe Basic Close-Textured Sponge Cake *(pg. 6)*
1 recipe Basic Butter Cream No. 1 *(pg. 7)*
1 tsp. kirsch
1 recipe Crème Jacqueline

Prepare the cake and bake in a jelly roll pan according to the instructions. Cut the cake into rounds with a 1½-inch wet cutter. Cover and set aside. Prepare the butter cream and add the kirsch. Frost the rounds on tops and sides with the butter cream. At this stage the cakes may be stored in an airtight container for several days. Prepare the *Crème Jacqueline*, folding in about ⅔ of the cherries and pineapple. Reserve the remaining fruits for garnish. Mound the *crème* on the top of the cakes, then garnish tops with the reserved cherries and pineapple. This makes about 50 little cakes.

CRÈME JACQUELINE

1½ c. whipping cream
6 tbsp. sifted confectioners' sugar
4 tsp. kirsch
⅔ c. chopped candied cherries
⅔ c. slivered candied green pineapple

Place the cream in the small mixing bowl and beat at high speed with an electric mixer until fluffy. Add the sugar gradually, beating constantly, until stiff. Add the kirsch and beat until well combined. Fold in the candied fruits. This makes about 4 cups of crème.

little diplomat cakes

A colorful blend of slivered pineapple and cherries gives a festive flair to these very rich and very special Diplomat Cakes.

FROZEN RASPBERRY SOUFFLÉ

1 recipe Basic Confectioners' Custard *(pg. 19)*
1 10-oz. package frozen raspberries, thawed
6 egg whites
½ c. sugar
1 c. whipping cream, whipped

Make a collar of thin poster paper to fit around the entire depth and 2 inches higher than a 6-inch soufflé dish. Tape together securely around the outside of the dish. Prepare the Confectioners' Custard. Pour the raspberries into a sieve placed over a bowl and press the berries through the sieve with the back of a wooden spoon until only the seeds remain. Discard the seeds and set the pulp aside. Place the egg whites in a large mixer bowl and beat at high speed until fluffy. Add the sugar gradually, beating until stiff peaks form. Place the cool custard in a large bowl, then add the whipped cream and fold in gently until well combined. Fold in the raspberry pulp, then add ⅓ of the egg whites. Fold in with a rubber spatula. Add the remaining egg whites and fold in completely. Turn into the mold and freeze for about 4 hours and 30 minutes. The side and top will be firm but the center will be soft. Remove the paper collar and serve immediately. This makes about 12 servings.

REMOVING PAPER COLLAR FROM SOUFFLÉ

1 Cut the tape securing the collar of poster paper.

2 Pull the poster paper off gently to reveal this frozen delight.

orange cheesecake

A moist, creamy cheesecake is a favorite dessert of nearly everyone. Here is a tangy variation on that theme: an Orange Cheesecake which has been garnished with orange slices and a sprig of mint.

ORANGE CHEESECAKE

1 c. sifted all-purpose flour
¼ c. sugar
1 tbsp. grated orange rind
½ c. butter
1 egg yolk
½ tsp. vanilla extract

Combine the flour, sugar and orange rind. Add the butter to the flour mixture and cut in with a pastry blender until of a course meal consistency. Add the egg yolk and vanilla and blend well. Place ⅓ of the dough on the bottom of a 9-inch springform pan, then pat out evenly to cover bottom. Bake in a pre-heated 400-degree oven for 5 minutes or until golden brown. Remove from the oven and cool. Pat the remaining dough evenly around sides to ½ inch from top. Set aside and prepare filling.

ORANGE CHEESE FILLING

5   8-oz. packages cream cheese, softened
1¾ c. sugar
3 tbsp. all-purpose flour
1 tbsp. grated orange rind
¼ tsp. salt
¼ tsp. vanilla extract
5 eggs
2 egg yolks
¼ c. frozen Florida orange juice concentrate, thawed

Combine the cream cheese, sugar, flour, orange rind, salt and vanilla in a large mixer bowl. Beat with an electric mixer at low speed until smooth. Add the eggs and egg yolks, one at a time, beating well after each addition. Stir in the orange juice concentrate, then pour into the prepared pan. Place on a cookie sheet. Bake in a preheated 400-degree oven for 8 to 10 minutes or until the crust is lightly browned. Reduce the oven temperature to 225 degrees and bake for 1 hour and 20 minutes longer. Cool to room temperature, then refrigerate until well chilled. Garnish with fresh orange sections (General Information, pg. 13). This makes 12 to 18 servings.

italian meringue with fruit and chantilly cream

Anyone who enjoys creating spectacular dishes will want to try this beautiful dessert with its combination of meringue, selected fruits and Chantilly cream. The meringue may be made a day in advance of serving and the fruits prepared ahead, leaving only the Chantilly cream and final assembly to be completed just before service. All ingredients should be well chilled.

ITALIAN MERINGUE WITH FRUIT AND CHANTILLY CREAM

1 recipe Basic Italian Meringue *(pg. 153)*
1 recipe Basic Confectioners' Custard *(pg. 19)*
2 fresh pears
2 fresh peaches
3 fresh apricots
3 canned pineapple slices
Red Currant Jelly Glaze *(pg. 19)*
Chopped pistachio nuts

Currant jelly
1 recipe Basic Chantilly Cream *(pg. 19)*

Cut a 9-inch circle of waxed paper, then spread enough of the meringue over the circle to make a ³/₄-inch deep layer. Let stand at room temperature until top is set. Place the remaining meringue in a pastry bag with a medium-sized star tube affixed and pipe a border around the edge of the circle. Make the peak for the center by holding the tube in a vertical position over waxed paper and pipe the remaining meringue, pulling the tube up as the meringue is piped. Allow the peak to dry at room temperature. Remove the waxed paper from the dried meringue shell, then place the meringue shell on a serving plate. Cover the bottom of the circle with the custard and chill. Peel the pears and cut in half, removing the cores. Peel the peaches and apricots and cut in half, removing the seeds. Arrange the fruits as shown in the illustration, then brush the pear halves with glaze and sprinkle with pistachio nuts. Fill the center of the pineapple stack with currant jelly, then place the meringue peak on top of the pineapple stack. Place the Chantilly cream in a pastry bag with a medium-sized star tube affixed, then pipe rosettes around the edge of the custard inside the meringue border and between the fruits. This makes about 18 servings.

FRENCH MERINGUE CAKE

The elegant appearance of a completed French Meringue Cake can be somewhat deceptive because its preparation is so simple. It may be placed in the category of those extra special dishes which are as easy and convenient to make (it can be made several days in advance) as they are impressive — a perfect company dessert. Due to its richness, serve French Meringue Cake in small portions accompanied by hot *demitasse*.

FRENCH MERINGUE CAKE

1 recipe Basic Meringues mixture *(pg. 10)*
1 recipe Basic Coffee Butter Cream *(pg. 37)*
Toasted sliced almonds
Sifted confectioners' sugar

Drop the meringue mixture by heaping tablespoonfuls onto cookie sheets lined with oiled brown paper. Bake in a preheated 250-degree oven for 55 minutes. Remove from the paper onto racks and cool, then crumble into a large bowl. Add 2 cups of the butter cream to the meringue crumbs and mix until the crumbs hold together, then divide into 2 equal parts. Place each part between 2 sheets of waxed paper and pat out into 7 x 8-inch rectangles. Chill for about 20 minutes or until layers are firm. Remove both sheets of waxed paper from 1 rectangle and place the rectangle on a serving platter. Spread with a thin layer of butter cream. Remove 1 sheet of waxed paper from remaining rectangle. Place the rectangle, waxed paper side up, over the butter cream-covered rectangle, then remove the waxed paper. Spread the remaining butter cream over the top and sides of the cake. Arrange the almonds over the top and sprinkle with confectioners' sugar just before serving. The sides may be piped with the remaining butter cream, if desired. This makes 20 servings.

french meringue cake

This is an elegant, delicious and extravagantly rich dessert. It is called Pave d'Orbec in Normandy, where it originated. Serve this dessert in small servings.

palmiers

Palmiers, a Paris specialty, are crisp palm leaf-shaped cookies which are made from puff pastry dough. They may be either sweet or savory, depending on their intended use. Tiny sweet palmiers are appropriate for teas or luncheons while the small savory ones make excellent party snacks. Larger palmiers of the sweet variety may be served as dessert pastries; those in the savory category would be good to accompany soups or stews. The imagination of the cook can determine the many uses and serving ideas for these versatile and delicious cookie-like pastries.

Homemade palmiers are invariably superior to those which are store bought, even those purchased in French bakeries. Leftover puff pastry may be used in the recipe, which makes them even more appealing — they're economical as well as delectable! Their finished size depends on the thickness and width of the dough after it has been rolled out. The suggested proportions in the following instructions may be altered or modified according to the desires of the cook.

Note: Savory Palmiers are obviously not dessert fare. However, since the preparation of both Sweet and Savory Palmiers is identical except for the filling, both recipes have been presented in the dessert section under the same step-by-step illustrations.

palmiers

A delicious French cookie made of puff pastry, these palmiers are excellent served with coffee or tea. Those shown above have been coated with an apricot glaze, but any similar seedless fruit preserve or glaze may be substituted if desired.

SWEET PALMIERS

½ recipe Basic Puff Pastry *(pg. 22)*
1 egg, well beaten
¼ c. sugar
1 recipe Apricot Glaze *(pg. 19)*
½ c. finely chopped nuts *(opt.)*

SAVORY PALMIERS

½ recipe Basic Puff Pastry *(pg. 22)*
¼ c. melted butter
¾ c. freshly grated Parmesan cheese
1 egg, well beaten

Roll out the pastry and follow the step-by-step illustrations for Sweet Palmiers, brushing with the butter and sprinkling with the cheese instead of using the ingredients in illustration No. 1. After baking, leave on the baking sheet and brush with egg, then sprinkle with additional cheese. Toast until golden brown.

1 Roll out the pastry on a lightly floured surface to about ⅛-inch thickness and cut into a 10 x 18-inch rectangle, trimming the edges with a sharp knife. Brush the entire surface with egg, then sprinkle with sugar. Brush with the glaze and sprinkle with nuts.

2 Roll one of the 10-inch sides tightly to the center, then roll the other side to the center.

3 Brush the rolls at the center with egg as shown in the illustration, then turn the twin roll over.

4 Cut into ¼-inch thick slices and place on a wet baking sheet. Bake in a preheated 400-degree oven, 1 shelf above center, for 25 minutes or until lightly browned.

heart-shaped peach pie

An ordinary heart-shaped cake pan is all that is needed to bake and serve this beautiful peach pie. A truly delicious flaky crust encases the freshly peeled peaches, which have been partially cooked in syrup before placing in the crust. Delicious peach syrup flavored with peach brandy is poured over each serving, adding a very special flavor. The paper frill covering the pan edge may be purchased in some specialty or gourmet shops.

HEART-SHAPED PEACH PIE

½ recipe Basic Cold Yeast Dough *(Breads, pg. 21)*
12 sm. firm fresh peaches, blanched *(pg. 185)*
1 tsp. vanilla extract
½ tsp. almond extract
1½ c. Basic Sugar Syrup *(Breads, pg. 14)*
1 egg, beaten
1 tbsp. peach or apricot brandy

Draw an outline of a heart-shaped cake pan on a piece of paper. Roll out half the dough on a lightly floured surface to ⅛-inch thickness and cut out a heart shape about 1½ inches larger than the pan. Fit the cutout dough into the pan, allowing the sides to hang over about ¼ inch. Trim off any excess dough with kitchen scissors. Cut the peeled peaches in half and remove the seeds. Place the peach halves, vanilla and almond extracts and the sugar syrup in a shallow saucepan and bring to a boil. Reduce heat and simmer for 5 minutes or until the peaches are tender. Drain the peaches and reserve the syrup. Cool the peaches and place, cut side down, in the pie shell. Pour about ½ cup of reserved sugar syrup over the peaches. Bring the overhanging dough over the peaches and brush the edge of the dough with cold water. Roll out the remaining dough and cut a heart-shaped piece, using the paper pattern. Place over the peaches and seal the top dough to the dough over the peaches, then brush with egg. Bake in a preheated 400-degree oven on the center rack for 35 to 40 minutes or until golden brown. Pour the remaining syrup into a small saucepan and add the brandy. Bring to a boil, then pour into a small pitcher. Serve with the pie. The syrup may be served cold, if desired. This makes 8 to 10 servings.

frangipane flan

This delicious apricot-flavored pastry is wonderful to serve for a leisurely breakfast or brunch. It is at its best when served still warm from the oven. The finished flan may be frozen for later use, if desired.

FRANGIPANE FLAN

¹/₂ **recipe Basic Sweet Short Pastry** *(pg. 12)*
2 **eggs**
2 **egg yolks**
3 **tbsp. all-purpose flour**
3 **tbsp. sugar**
1 **c. milk**
1 **tsp. vanilla extract**
¹/₈ **tsp. salt**
1 **tbsp. butter**
1 **macaroon**
1 **tbsp. Madeira**
³/₄ **c. apricot jam**
¹/₂ **c. sifted confectioners' sugar**

Roll out half the dough into a 12-inch circle and line a 9-inch flan ring according to the instructions and illustrations on pages 12 and 13. Chill the remaining dough. Place the eggs and egg yolks in a small mixer bowl and beat with an electric mixer until light, then beat in the flour and sugar until well blended. Combine the milk, vanilla and salt in the top of a double boiler and place over boiling water. Cook until the milk mixture is just below boiling point. Stir a small amount of the milk mixture into the egg mixture, then stir back into the milk mixture until smooth. Reduce heat until the water is hot, not boiling, and cook, stirring constantly with a wooden spoon, until mixture coats the spoon thickly. Remove from the water. Add the butter and stir until the butter is melted. Crumble the macaroon into a small bowl and add the Madeira, then stir until the consistency of paste. Stir the macaroon mixture into the custard until well blended. Spread the jam over the bottom of the prepared pastry and spoon the custard over the jam evenly. Roll out the remaining chilled dough into a rectangle and cut into ¹/₂-inch strips. Place the strips, lattice fashion, over the custard, sealing the edges to the pastry rim with a small amount of water. The pastry top may be made according to the instructions for trellised pastry (Vegetables, pg. 77). Bake in a preheated 375-degree oven for 35 to 40 minutes or until the filling is set and the crust is golden brown. Place the flan on a serving plate and remove the flan ring. Combine the confectioners' sugar with enough warm water to make a thin glaze, then drizzle it over the hot flan. This makes 6 to 8 servings.

upside-down apple cake

upside-down apple cake

Tart green apples are used in this tangy, moist Upside-Down Apple Cake. You will make this cake often because it is quick to make and it is always welcomed with enthusiasm by family or guests. Confectioners' sugar may be dusted over each serving, if desired.

UPSIDE-DOWN APPLE CAKE

4 or 5 tart cooking apples
Lemon juice
2 tbsp. butter
1 c. (packed) light brown sugar, sifted
1 egg
1 c. sugar
1 c. whipping cream
1 tsp. vanilla extract
2 c. all-purpose flour
2 tsp. baking powder
Confectioners' sugar

Peel the apples and remove the cores. Slice the apples paper-thin on a mandoline (General Information, pg. 32), then sprinkle lightly with lemon juice to keep from discoloring. Place the butter in a 9-inch round, shallow baking dish. Place in a preheated 325-degree oven until melted, then remove from oven. Do not turn off heat. Sprinkle the brown sugar over the butter. Overlap the apple slices in the baking dish, working from the center to the outside with only 1/4 inch between each overlap, until the bottom is covered. Place the egg in a medium-sized mixing bowl and beat well with an electric mixer. Add the sugar gradually and beat until mixed. Mix the cream and vanilla. Sift the flour with the baking powder, then add to the egg mixture alternately with the cream mixture, beating well after each addition. Pour over the apples. Bake for about 35 minutes or until a cake tester inserted in the center comes out clean. Let cool for 10 minutes, then turn out onto a rack and cool. Place on a cake plate and cut into servings. Sprinkle each serving with confectioners' sugar and if desired serve with Basic Chantilly Cream. This makes 6 to 8 servings.

QUICK APPLE CAKE

1¾ c. sifted cake flour
1 tsp. baking powder
½ tsp. soda
½ tsp. salt
Sugar
½ c. melted butter
1 egg
Buttermilk
1 tsp. vanilla extract
2 tart apples, peeled and thinly sliced
1 tsp. cinnamon

Sift the flour, baking powder, soda, salt and 1 cup of sugar into a mixing bowl. Pour ¼ cup butter into a 1 cup measuring cup, then add the egg. Fill the cup with buttermilk. Pour into the flour mixture and beat vigorously for 1 minute or until the batter is smooth. Stir in the vanilla. Pour the remaining butter into an ovenproof skillet or baking dish. Pour the batter into the skillet, then arrange the apples over the top. Combine the cinnamon with 2 tablespoons of sugar and sprinkle over the apples. Bake in a preheated 350-degree oven for 35 to 40 minutes. Serve hot from the skillet or cool for 5 minutes, then invert onto a rack. Slide onto a serving dish. This makes 8 to 10 servings.

BASIC STRUDEL PASTRY

1½ c. all-purpose flour
¼ tsp. salt
1½ tsp. butter, softened
1 tsp. lemon juice
½ c. lukewarm water
Melted butter

Sift the flour and salt together onto a pastry board and shape into a ring. Add the butter and lemon juice to the inside of the ring and cut into the flour with 2 table knives or pastry blenders. Add the water gradually, working in the flour from the inside of the ring. Use pastry scrapers to work the dough until all the flour is moistened. Gather into a ball. Sift additional flour lightly over the board, then knead the dough with the heel of your hand for 15 minutes. Dust a warm baking sheet with flour. Place the ball of dough on the baking sheet and invert a warm bowl over the dough. Let stand for 30 minutes. Place a sheet or tablecloth on a card table or a kitchen table. Dust generously with flour. Dust the dough lightly with flour on all sides. Roll out thin on a lightly floured board, then lift carefully on the back of hands to the center of the floured cloth on the table. Brush the dough lightly with melted butter. Place the hands under the dough and start working from the center, palms downward, folding your hands into a loose fist. With slightly raised knuckles, pull gently and evenly from the center to the edge until tissue paper thin. The dough will be thicker at the edge. Two people, working together, can do this easily but one person can stretch the dough properly. Be sure to work with palms down to avoid making holes in the dough. Brush with butter and let stand for 15 minutes to dry. Trim off the thicker edge before using as needed. This makes enough dough for 1 large strudel.

AUSTRIAN APPLE STRUDEL

1 recipe Basic Strudel Pastry
Melted butter
2 c. soft bread crumbs
4 c. thin-sliced tart apples
1 c. raisins
1 c. (packed) brown sugar

Pull the strudel pastry to paper thinness, then brush with melted butter and let dry for about 15 minutes, as instructed. Sauté the bread crumbs in ¼ cup of melted butter until golden. Combine the apples, raisins and brown sugar in a large mixing bowl, stirring together gently. Trim off the thicker edge of the pastry, then sprinkle the hot bread crumbs over the pastry to within 1 inch of the edge. Spoon the apple mixture over half the pastry, then roll the strudel, starting at the filled end. Slide the filled strudel onto a buttered baking sheet and bend into a horseshoe shape. Brush with melted butter. Bake in a preheated 375-degree oven for 40 minutes or until golden brown. Sprinkle generously with confectioners' sugar, if desired. This makes 8 servings.

quick apple cake

Quick Apple Cake, made with butter, sugar, cinnamon and apples, is baked in an ovenproof skillet or baking dish. Serve it hot straight from the skillet or on a serving dish.

mocha refrigerator cake

MOCHA REFRIGERATOR CAKE

1 Basic Rolled Sponge Cake *(pg. 3)*
1 doz. ladyfingers, split
1/2 c. unsalted butter, softened
1 egg yolk
4 c. sifted confectioners' sugar
1 tsp. orange flower water
1 tsp. rose water
1 6-oz. package chocolate chips, melted *(pg. 49)*
1 tbsp. Basic Coffee Syrup No. 1 *(pg. 36)*
1 tbsp. Tia Maria
1 tbsp. brandy
Chocolate Curls *(pg. 50)*
1/2 c. whipping cream, whipped

Prepare the sponge cake according to illustrations No. 1 through No. 11, omitting the filling, then cut the cake crosswise into 3 equal pieces. Cut the rounded tip off one end of each ladyfinger half, then line the sides of a 10 3/4 x 5 1/2 x 3-inch deep springform pan with ladyfingers, rounded side up. Place 1 piece of the cake in the bottom of the pan. Place the butter in a large mixing bowl and beat with an electric mixer at medium speed for 2 minutes or until light and fluffy, then beat in the egg yolk. Add the confectioners' sugar alternately with the orange flower and rose waters, beating constantly. Add the melted chocolate and beat constantly until well mixed, adding the coffee syrup, Tia Maria and brandy gradually. Chill for about 10 minutes or until mixture is of spreading consistency. Spread half the chocolate mixture over the sponge cake in the pan, then cover with a second piece of the cake. Spread the remaining chocolate mixture over the second layer and top with the remaining piece of sponge cake. Chill until firm, then remove the springform and place the cake on a serving dish. Decorate the top with Chocolate Curls. Place the whipped cream in a pastry bag with a star tube affixed and pipe rosettes around the base of the cake. Cake may be frozen before removing the springform, if desired. *Crème de Cacao* may be substituted for the Tia Maria. This makes about 8 servings.

mocha refrigerator cake

This Mocha Refrigerator Cake, so rich with chocolate goodness is a wonderful choice of dessert for a party or buffet dinner. It is really a rolled sponge cake filled with a delicious mocha cream. Lady fingers, whipped cream rosettes, and chocolate shavings add the finishing touches.

black cherry cream & macaroon mousse

BLACK CHERRY CREAM

1 1-lb. can pitted dark sweet cherries
2 env. unflavored gelatin
¹/₂ c. sweet white wine
1¹/₂ c. whipping cream, whipped
1 tbsp. kirsch

Drain the cherries well and reserve the juice. Soften the gelatin in ¹/₄ cup of water. Pour the reserved juice into a saucepan and bring just to a boil. Remove from the heat and stir in the gelatin until dissolved. Stir in the wine and cool to room temperature, then chill until slightly thickened. Fold in the whipped cream until evenly mixed and pour into a lightly oiled ring mold. Chill until firm, then unmold onto a serving plate. Fill the center of the ring with the cherries, then sprinkle the cherries with the kirsch. Garnish with additional whipped cream, if desired. This makes 8 to 10 servings.

MACAROON MOUSSE

4 egg yolks
¹/₂ c. sifted confectioners' sugar
¹/₂ c. rum
4 c. crushed Almond Macaroons (pg. 129)
2 c. whipping cream, whipped

Place the egg yolks in a large mixer bowl and beat with an electric mixer until light and fluffy. Add the sugar alternately with the rum and beat until well blended. Add the macaroons and mix well. Cover the bowl with aluminum foil and let stand for 15 minutes. Fold the whipped cream into the macaroon mixture gradually and blend well. Spoon the mixture into a wet mold and chill for about 3 hours or until set. Dip the mold into warm water, then unmold onto a serving dish and serve immediately. This makes about 10 to 12 servings.

macaroon mousse

Here is an unusual and delightful dessert which can be "whipped up" in a hurry and refrigerated until needed. It may be chilled in a large mold or, if desired, in small ones for individual servings. The combined flavors of the macaroons, rum and cream is superb.

chocolate cream coupes

Chocolate Cream *Coupes* are a simple-to-make but exceedingly elegant dessert and are certain to please even the most jaded palates. The chocolate cream mixture is a smooth creamy, deep chocolate-flavored pudding comparable to a mousse. It is important to use bitter chocolate in this recipe in order to achieve the rich chocolate taste that makes this an outstanding dessert. It is best if prepared a day in advance which makes it very convenient when serving the dessert for a company dinner.

The chocolate dragonflies may be made from semisweet chocolate chips according to the directions for Doodling Shapes In Chocolate on page 53. Any design, such as flowers, leaves or any appropriate motif, may be used instead of the butterflies merely by drawing your own pattern on waxed paper and then proceeding according to the instructions for the dragonfly doodles.

CHOCOLATE CREAM COUPES

3 1-oz. squares unsweetened chocolate
2 egg yolks
⅛ tsp. salt
¾ c. white corn syrup
2 c. whipping cream
1 tsp. vanilla extract

Place the chocolate in the top of a double boiler over hot, not boiling, water. If the water is too hot the chocolate will become lumpy and hard. Heat until chocolate is melted. Combine the egg yolks and salt in a small mixer bowl and beat until light and lemon colored. Add the corn syrup and beat until well combined. Pour the egg mixture slowly into the chocolate, beating constantly. Cook over hot water, stirring constantly, until thickened. Remove from heat and beat until cold. Whip the cream until fluffy, then add the vanilla and beat until stiff. Fold ⅓ of the whipped cream into the chocolate, then fold in the remaining whipped cream. Chill for at least 4 hours. Spoon into serving dishes, mounding as in illustration, if desired. Garnish each serving with a chocolate dragonfly (pg. 53). This makes 6 to 8 servings.

ORANGE-YOGURT CHIFFON PIE

1 ⅓ c. vanilla wafer crumbs
¼ c. melted butter
2 env. unflavored gelatin
Sugar
2 c. yogurt
1 6-oz. can frozen orange juice concentrate, thawed
2 egg whites
Toasted coconut

Combine the crumbs and butter, blending well, then press the mixture firmly and evenly over the bottom and side of a pie plate, building up around the rim. Chill. Combine the gelatin and ½ cup of sugar in a 1-quart saucepan, then stir in 1 cup of water. Cook over low heat, stirring constantly, until the gelatin is dissolved. Place the yogurt in a bowl. Add the orange juice concentrate gradually, then stir in the gelatin mixture until smooth. To make the meringue, beat the egg whites until frothy, then beat until stiff peaks form, adding 2 tablespoons of sugar gradually. Fold ¼ of the meringue into the orange mixture, then fold in the remaining meringue. Chill until the mixture mounds when dropped from a spoon. Turn into the prepared crust and chill until firm. Garnish with toasted coconut. This makes 6 to 8 servings.

orange-yogurt chiffon pie

Orange-Yogurt Chiffon Pie is a chilled dessert made with yogurt and frozen orange juice. A delicious crumb crust of vanilla wafers and a sprinkling of toasted coconut give an unexpected blend of flavors.

chocolate-mocha log cake

Chocolate-Mocha Log Cake is a delicious variation of Basic Rolled Sponge Cake (pgs. 3 and 4). To give the sponge cake a chocolatety flavor, substitute cocoa for two tablespoons of flour. Mocha Butter Cream (pg. 51) is used to frost the surface. Simply by imprinting the frosting with the tines of a fork, you can give this chocolate delicacy the appearance of a log, which is so attractive for special holiday occasions.

CHOCOLATE-MOCHA LOG CAKE

1 recipe Basic Rolled Sponge Cake *(pg. 3)*
2 tbsp. cocoa
1 recipe Mocha Butter Cream *(pg. 51)*
Confectioners' sugar
Chocolate Leaves *(pg. 51)*
Chocolate Curls *(pg. 50)*
Doodled shapes of chocolate *(pg. 53)*

Prepare the sponge cake according to the step-by-step illustrations, substituting the cocoa for 2 tablespoons of the flour and spreading the cake (before rolling it) with a thin layer of the Mocha Butter Cream. Place the rolled cake on a board lightly dusted with confectioners' sugar and frost the roll and ends with most of the remaining Mocha Butter Cream. Cut three 1 ¼-inch pieces from one of the trimmed edges of the cake, joining the pieces with some of the remaining butter cream to form a small cylinder. Make a design on the surface of the cake with the tines of a fork to resemble tree bark. Arrange the cylinder of cake on top to form a stump, then press the cylinder into the butter cream. Frost with Mocha Butter Cream as for the cake and seal with the remaining butter cream. Smooth the ends of the log with a small spatula dipped into boiling water, leaving the outer edges rough. Draw concentric circles, starting in the center of each end, to resemble the rings of the tree. Garnish with the Chocolate Leaves, Chocolate Curls and doodled chocolate vines as shown in the illustration. This makes about 10 servings.

chocolate-mocha log cake

For special holiday flair, serve this rich Chocolate-Mocha Log Cake doodled with chocolate vines. Chocolate Curls, dusted with confectioners' sugar, are placed around the cake.

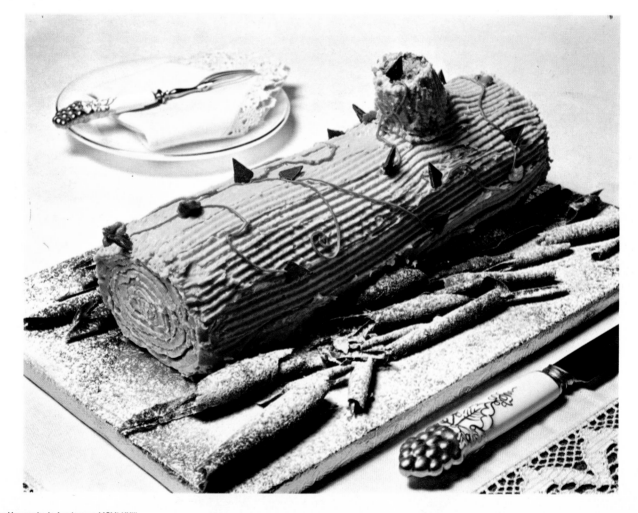

chocolate roulage

Chocolate *Roulage* is truly one of the most elegant chocolate desserts one can prepare. This rolled master-piece appears to be a time-consuming, complicated task, too demanding for most occasions. However, it is not that difficult to prepare, and the praises it earns will be more than worth the time spent.

Chocolate Roulage, sometimes called *Roulé* (both of which mean "rolled"), is baked in a jelly roll pan, similar to a Rolled Sponge Cake (pg. 3). It is then spread with vanilla-flavored whipped cream and then gently rolled. Follow the simple instructions for perfect results.

chocolate roulage

This beautiful rolled chocolate dessert is richly filled with vanilla-flavored whipped cream. Its elegant appearance is matched by its excellent flavor and soufflé-like texture.

CHOCOLATE ROULAGE

1   **4-oz. bar sweet cooking chocolate**
4   **1-oz. squares semisweet chocolate**
1/3 **c. cold water**
8 **eggs, separated**
1 **c. sugar**
Cocoa
1 1/2 **c. whipping cream**
3 **tbsp. sifted confectioners' sugar**
1 **tsp. vanilla extract**

Oil the bottom of a 15 1/2 x 10 1/2 x 1-inch jelly roll pan. Cut a piece of waxed paper to fit the width of pan and extend about 1 inch over ends. Place the chocolates and the water in the top of a double boiler over hot water. Stir with a wooden spoon until the chocolate is melted, then cool. Place the egg yolks in a large mixer bowl and beat slightly with the mixer. Add the sugar gradually, beating constantly until all the sugar is dissolved and the mixture is thick and of a batter consistency. Stir in the chocolate with a rubber spatula until well com-bined and free of streaks. Beat the egg whites until stiff peaks form. Fold about 1/3 of the egg whites into the chocolate mixture thoroughly to lighten, then fold in the remaining egg whites carefully but completely with a rubber spatula. Spread the batter evenly in the prepared pan. Bake in a preheated 350-degree oven for 18 minutes. Remove from oven and cover top with damp towels. Let stand for 30 minutes or until cooled. Remove the towels carefully, then loosen by lifting the extending ends of waxed paper. Place cocoa in a fine sieve and dust top generously. Place a piece of waxed paper over the top, then place a cookie sheet on top and invert. Peel the waxed paper carefully from the cake. Place the cream in a large mixer bowl and beat with an electric mixer until soft peaks form. Sprinkle in the confectioners' sugar and beat until stiff. Stir in the vanilla. Spread the whipped cream evenly over the cake. Roll the cake from the long side, as for a jelly roll, directly onto a serving tray. Roll with care as this cake is extremely tender. Dust the top generously with cocoa. You may refrigerate the roll for several hours before serving. Cut into slices to serve. This makes 10 to 12 servings.

special yellow cake

The idea for creating Farmer's Butter Cream Cake was conceived quite by accident. In the 19th Century, a farmer's wife, who had made and taken her own butter to market, was decorating the tops of her butter pat displays in her market stall. She found that by using a curved piece of tin, she could create beautiful curls of butter. Suddenly she thought how lovely her home-baked cakes would look decorated with these attractive curls. So the next time she baked a cake, she divided butter cream frosting into two parts, colored each in a pastel shade, and put them on a stone slab in the dairy to harden. When the butter cream had sufficiently hardened, she made a number of tiny rolls with her butter curler and used them to decorate her cake.

Whether the lovely story is fact or fiction, we have borrowed this idea for the following recipe. With two basic recipes, Basic Fondant Icing (pg. 192) and Basic Butter Cream (pg. 7), try this unique decoration.

BUTTER CREAM ROLLS

Dip the butter curler into lukewarm water, then hold upright on the butter cream and pull with a slight downward stroke to form a curl. Clean the curler well after each curl, as perfect curls are made with a clean, wet curler.

FARMER'S BUTTER CREAM CAKE

2 ½ c. sifted cake flour
1 tbsp. baking powder
½ tsp. salt
¾ c. butter, softened
1 ½ c. sugar
½ tbsp. vanilla extract
8 egg yolks
¾ c. milk
1 recipe Golden Lemon Filling
1 recipe Basic Fondant Icing *(pg. 192)*
Green and yellow food coloring
1 recipe Basic Butter Cream No. 1 *(pg. 7)*

Butter and flour the removable bottoms of two round 9-inch cake pans. Sift the flour, baking powder and salt together. Place the butter in a large mixing bowl, then beat in the sugar gradually, beating constantly. Beat for 3 minutes or until fluffy and the sugar is dissolved. Beat in the vanilla extract, then add the egg yolks and beat until light and fluffy. Still beating, add the flour mixture and milk alternately to the egg mixture, beginning and ending with the flour mixture. Beat just until smooth, then pour into prepared cake pans. Bake in a preheated 350-degree oven for 35 minutes or until the layers test done when a cake tester is inserted and comes out clean. Remove from oven and let cool for 5 minutes, then turn out on wire racks to cool completely. Place 1 layer on a serving dish and spread the lemon filling evenly over the top. Arrange the second layer over the filling. Prepare the fondant as instructed, substituting 1 tablespoon of lemon juice for the vanilla extract and adding green food coloring. Roll out ⅓ of the icing on a corn-starch-dusted board to ⅛-inch thickness. Cut into a 9½-inch circle large enough to fit over the top of the cake and extend ½ inch over the sides, then place on the cake top. Roll out the remaining icing into a long strip. Cut the strip long and wide enough to cover around the side of the cake, then place this strip around the side, being careful not to stretch the icing. Moisten the edges with water to seal well. Repair any tears with pieces of icing, then smooth with a wet spatula. The side strip may be textured with a special metal trellised roller, if available. Gather up the fondant trimmings into a ball and wrap in plastic wrap for future use. Prepare the butter cream, substituting 2 teaspoons of lemon juice for the orange flower water and the rose water. Tint half the butter cream with green food coloring and the remaining half with yellow food coloring. Pack into two 3-inch tart pans and level tops evenly. Refrigerate until hard or ready to use. Make butter cream rolls as shown in the illustration, placing each one directly onto the cake to form rows. This cake may be baked in 3 layers for 25 minutes and filled with 2 recipes of the filling, if desired. For an elegant white frosted cake, Basic Italian Meringue (pg. 153) may be used for frosting instead of the Basic Fondant Icing. This makes about 20 servings.

GOLDEN LEMON FILLING

¼ c. butter
½ c. sugar
3 egg yolks
¼ c. strained fresh lemon juice
1 tbsp. grated lemon rind

Combine all the ingredients in the top of a double boiler, then place over hot water. Cook, stirring constantly, until thick. Let cool. This makes enough filling for a 2-layer cake.

FONDANT TRIMMINGS

Trimmings of Basic Fondant Icing may be flavored with peppermint oil for mints. Roll out and cut with *canapé* cutters, then place on wire racks for about 5 hours or until dry. Store in an airtight container until ready to use.

ice cream bombes

Ice cream bombes are made with alternate layers of delicious homemade ice cream. These are set on a chocolate base and topped with milled pistachio nuts. Serve them for any festive occasion.

MULTIFLAVORED ICE CREAM BOMBES

Ice cream bombes are given this name because they are shaped in special spherical or bombe molds. They are traditionally made with concentric layers of ordinary ice cream mixtures, mousse or custard mixtures enclosed in ice cream. The special bombe mold, with both ends removable, permits easy unmolding of frozen mixtures.

Our ice cream bombes are made with Pistachio Ice Cream (pg. 72), Coffee Ice Cream (pg. 69), Basic Vanilla Ice Cream (pg. 67) and Mocha Ice Cream (pg. 69). Alternating layers of each in a mold, allowing each layer to harden before adding the next, creates this lovely, colorful dessert.

Each ice cream bombe is unmolded and served on an attractive chocolate base made with chocolate chips, first melted, then chilled. Follow the simple instructions to create this colorful dessert.

MULTIFLAVORED ICE CREAM BOMBES

Vegetable oil
1 qt. Pistachio Ice Cream *(pg. 72)*
1 pt. Coffee Ice Cream *(pg. 69)*
1 pt. Mocha Ice Cream *(pg. 69)*
1 pt. Basic Vanilla Ice Cream *(pg. 67)*
2 Chocolate Bases
Ground pistachio nuts

Oil 2 tall 6-cup molds. Soften each of the ice creams slightly before using. Pack half of 1 pint of the Pistachio Ice Cream into the base of each mold and freeze until firm. Pack 1/2 pint of the Coffee Ice Cream into each mold and freeze until firm. Repeat the process with the mocha, remaining pistachio and vanilla ice creams, freezing each layer until firm before adding the next layer. Place the Chocolate Bases on serving dishes. Unmold the bombes carefully and place over the bases. Sprinkle each bombe generously with pistachio nuts. Serve immediately. Other molds may be used, if desired. This makes about 14 servings.

CHOCOLATE BASE

Draw the outline of the mold to be used on waxed paper. Pour a layer of melted chocolate chips (pg. 49) onto the waxed paper and spread to the edge with a knife. Chill until firm. Add another layer of melted chocolate and spread evenly, then chill until firm. Pull off the waxed paper and store until used.

ICE CREAM SNOWBALL

Vegetable oil
1 recipe Almond Ice Cream *(pg. 72)*
Green food coloring
1 recipe Basic Italian Meringue *(pg. 153)*
Crystallized violets

Oil a 3-quart ball mold or metal bowl. Soften the ice cream slightly, then pack firmly into the mold. Freeze until very hard. Add enough food coloring to the meringue for desired tint. Unmold the ice cream onto a serving dish, then spread with a thin layer of the meringue. Return to the freezer until the ice cream is firm. Place the remaining meringue in a pastry bag with a large star tube affixed and pipe rosettes over the entire surface of ice cream ball. Return the ice cream ball to the freezer and freeze until firm if the ice cream becomes soft during the piping. Freeze the snowball until ready to serve. Garnish with crystallized violets and serve immediately. This makes about 20 servings.

ice cream snowball

This pretty dessert requires no more than your favorite ice cream and a batch of Basic Italian Meringue. Tint the Basic Italian Meringue and decorate the finished dessert with crystallized violets.

SWISS CREAM CHEESE PUDDING

1   1-lb. can crushed pineapple
1 env. unflavored gelatin
3   3-oz. packages cream cheese, softened
1/4 c. rum
1/2 c. chopped maraschino cherries
1 c. whipping cream, whipped

Drain the pineapple and reserve the juice. Soften the gelatin in 1/4 cup of cold water, then stir into the reserved juice. Place over low heat and stir until the gelatin is dissolved. Let cool for several minutes. Place the cream cheese in a mixer bowl and beat with an electric mixer until fluffy. Add the gelatin mixture slowly, beating constantly, until well combined. Stir in the rum, then chill until syrupy. Fold in the pineapple, cherries and whipped cream. Turn into a wet mold and chill until firm. Unmold onto a serving dish and garnish with piped Basic Chantilly Cream (pg. 19) and maraschino cherries. This makes 8 to 10 servings.

PEARS DE CACAO

12 canned pear halves
3 tbsp. cocoa
1/4 c. sugar
3/4 c. whipping cream, whipped
Dash of salt
1/2 tsp. vanilla extract
1/4 tsp. mint extract
1 tsp. unflavored gelatin
1/3 c. Crème de Cacao

Drain the pears thoroughly on paper toweling. Combine the cocoa and sugar in a mixer bowl, then blend into the cream. Add the salt, vanilla and mint extracts. Soften the gelatin in 1 tablespoon of cold water, then dissolve over hot water. Add the gelatin to the cream mixture and stir until smooth. Chill until of spreading consistency. Fill the cavities of the pears and spread the cut sides with the chocolate mixture. Place 2 pear halves together to form whole pears, then place in a shallow dish. Chill for at least 1 hour. Arrange each pear in a stemmed compote and spoon the *Crème de Cacao* over the pears. Garnish with Chocolate Leaves (page 51) and chill until ready to serve. This makes 6 servings.

swiss cream cheese pudding

This pudding, with its light, frothy texture, is generously filled with fruits and flavored with rum. A luscious piped topping of whipped cream and a border of chopped cherries make it elegant enough for very special occasions.

The Creative Homemaker's Academy © MCMLXXIII
Selected Illustrations© B.P.C. Publishing Limited MCMLXX

stuffed baked apples

stuffed baked apples

Stuffed Baked Apples are perfect for Fall days at apple harvest time. These are filled with chopped cherries, walnuts, almonds and honey. They are given a shimmering coating of hot, red currant glaze.

STUFFED BAKED APPLES

6 lg. cooking apples
3 tbsp. finely chopped candied cherries
2 tbsp. finely chopped walnuts
1 tbsp. finely chopped almonds
¼ c. honey
½ recipe Red Currant Jelly Glaze *(pg. 19)*

Core the apples. Cut a thin line through the peeling around the center of each apple, using a sharp knife. Place the cherries, walnuts, almonds and honey in a small bowl and mix well. Arrange the apples in a shallow baking pan, then fill the apple cavities with the cherry mixture. Bake in a preheated 375-degree oven for about 45 minutes or until the apples are tender. Remove from the oven and slip the upper halves of the peeling from the apples. Place the apples in a serving dish and spoon any pan juices into the cavities. Spoon the glaze over the apples. This makes 6 servings.

FIGS IN BRANDY

¾ c. sugar
4 cardamom seeds
¾ c. Cognac
½ c. raisins
½ c. blanched toasted almonds
1   1-lb. 4-oz. can Kadota figs, drained

Combine the sugar, cardamom seeds and ½ cup of the Cognac in a saucepan and cook, stirring constantly, until the sugar is dissolved. Stir in the raisins and almonds and heat through. Place the figs in a chafing dish, then pour the sugar mixture over the figs. Place over a low flame until the figs are heated through, spooning the sugar mixture over the figs frequently. Heat the remaining Cognac in a small saucepan, then ignite and pour over the figs. Serve immediately. This makes about 4 servings.

how to make
a chocolate easter egg

CHOCOLATE EASTER EGG

Vegetable Spray-on Coating
Chocolate chips, melted *(pg. 49)*
¹⁄₃ recipe Basic Royal Icing *(pg. 43)*
Small Chocolate Leaves *(pg. 51)*

Prepare the chocolate egg according to the step-by-step illustrations. Place the icing in a pastry bag with a medium writing tube affixed, then pipe the trellis as instructed on page 36. Let the icing dry. Prepare Chocolate Leaves but make them very small. Place a small amount of melted chocolate on the back of each leaf to hold firmly when pressed on the seam of the chocolate egg. Any shallow mold may be used for this process.

1 Be sure that the egg molds are thoroughly dry. Coat each mold generously with the vegetable spray about 3 times. Liquid paraffin may be used, if available.

2 Begin spreading the melted chocolate at the top of the mold.

3 Work slowly, spreading the chocolate evenly to at least ¹⁄₄-inch thickness.

4 Clean off the edges, if necessary, then refrigerate for several hours or overnight.

5 Loosen the chocolate carefully with the tip of a sharp knife, then tap the mold gently on the table.

6 Lift carefully or invert the mold to remove chocolate egg.

7 Smooth any rough edges from the egg with a very sharp knife, then spread the edge of one half with softened chocolate.

8 Press the 2 halves together to join the edges evenly.

9 Hold the egg together just until the edges are sealed.

chocolate easter egg

Here is a special Easter delight for children. Follow the simple instructions to create this marvelous Chocolate Easter Egg. It is decorated with piped Basic Royal Icing (pg. 43) and bordered with small Chocolate Leaves.

choux pastry fritters

Basic Chou Pastry is fun to work with because of its simplicity and versatility. Fried chou pastry makes a delicious, crisp puff which may be served alone or used to accompany fresh fruits, custards, Cremes or perhaps a favorite cheese. Puff Fritters will serve nicely for a variety of needs from coffee breaks to party desserts.

puff fritters

Puff Fritters are light textured, golden brown dessert treats made with Basic Chou Pastry (pg. 56). A light sweetness is added by dusting them with confectioners' sugar. These are delicious served warm.

PUFF FRITTERS

1 recipe Basic Chou Pastry (pg. 56)
Confectioner's sugar

Place the chou pastry in a pastry bag with a ½-inch writing tube affixed and pipe onto an oiled baking sheet into puffs according to illustration No. 3 on page 57. Remove from the baking sheet with a wet spatula. Drop into deep fat at 340 degrees and fry until golden on all sides, turning as necessary. Drain on paper toweling and dust with confectioners' sugar. This makes about 30 fritters.

DRUM CAKE WITH DRUMSTICKS

1 recipe Chocolate Gâteau batter *(pg. 52)*
2 recipes Basic Royal Icing *(pg. 43)*
1 recipe Basic Fondant Icing *(pg. 192)*
Red and blue paste food colorings
2 artificial holly berries
2 drinking straws
Narrow red ribbon

Prepare and bake the chocolate batter in two 9-inch round cake pans. Cool. Place 1 cake layer on a serving tray or foil-covered styrofoam base. Cover the layer with royal icing. Place the remaining cake layer on top. Spread a thin layer of royal icing over the top layer. Divide the fondant icing and color half with red paste, and the other half with blue paste food coloring. Roll out the blue icing ¼ inch thick. Cut into a strip the height of the cake and long enough to fit around the side. Fit around the side and seal with water. Roll out the red icing ¼ inch thick and cut two 1-inch strips to fit around the top and the bottom edge of the side. Brush lightly with water. Fit around the top and bottom edge and seal with water. Place the remaining royal icing in a pastry bag with a small star tube affixed. Pipe rosettes over the top of the cake. Place a small writing tube on the pastry bag and pipe design on side as shown in the illustration. Color any remaining royal icing blue and pipe rosettes at the ends and center of crosses on the side of cake. Glue the holly berries in the ends of the straws, then wrap the ribbon around the straws and place on the cake as shown. This makes about 20 slices.

drum cake with drumsticks

This colorful Drum Cake complete with drumsticks would gladden the heart of any little boy (or girl) on his birthday! It would also be very appropriate to serve in honor of a patriotic holiday such as Veteran's Day or Independence Day. Note: Any round fruitcake or two round layers of Basic Close-Textured Sponge Cake (page 6) may be used in this recipe.

CROQUEMBOUCHE

The word *croquembouche* may be literally defined as a "crunchy mouthful". It is a type of dessert which is crunchy and crumbly when chewed. Although a *croquembouche* may be constructed in any size with a variety of filled and coated *chou* puffs the classic one is made by arranging tiny custard-filled profiteroles (pg. 59) (usually around a metal *croquembouche* cone or flower pot) one on top of the other until they form a conical shaped tower. These little cream puffs are first quickly dipped into caramelized sugar before being set into place around the *croquembouche* cone. The sugar hardens almost instantly and holds the puffs in position. This towering cream puff dessert is easy and fun to make and the result is always spectacular — it may even be used as a centerpiece. NOTE: If the *croquembouche* is to be assembled hours ahead of time, it is best to keep it in as dry a place as possible to prevent the sugar from becoming sticky.

CROQUEMBOUCHE

- **2 recipes Basic Butter Cream No. 2 *(pg. 7)* or Mocha Butter Cream *(pg. 51)***
- **3 recipes Basic Chou Pastry *(pg. 56)***
- **4 recipes Basic Confectioners' Custard *(pg. 19)***
- **2 recipes Caramel Glaze *(Sauces, pg. 16)***
- **1 recipe Spun Sugar**

Prepare the butter cream and chill. Prepare 1 recipe of *chou* pastry and bake according to instructions for medium-sized puffs. Prepare the 2 remaining recipes of *chou* pastry and bake in small 1 1/2-inch puffs. Place the puffs on wire racks to cool. Do not split the puffs. You will need about 100 puffs to completely cover a 15-inch tall *croquembouche* cone. Prepare the confectioners' custard, making only 2 recipes at a time, and chill until cool. Fill a pastry bag, with a 1/4-inch writing tube affixed, with confectioners' custard. Hold a puff in one hand, then stick the writing tube in the side of the puff and fill the puff with custard. Do not overfill the puffs. This method eliminates splitting the puffs. Continue until all puffs are filled. Grease the outside of the *croquembouche* cone, or the form you are using, with butter. Set the cone on a large serving dish. Prepare 1 recipe of Caramel Glaze, following directions carefully and making sure that it cooks long enough to spin a brittle thread. The glaze will be straw-colored but not brown. Remove from the heat and place the saucepan in a pan of boiling water. Begin building the *Croquembouche* with the medium-sized puffs. Hold a puff with tongs and dip the top of the puff and 1 side into the Caramel Glaze. Quickly place the puff at the base of the cone, glazed side down and with the bottom of the puff against the cone, then continue around the base of the cone with more puffs. Make the second row, dipping each puff and stacking them as close together as possible on top of the bottom row. Use all of the medium puffs, reserving 1 for the top. Prepare additional Caramel Glaze as needed. Continue building the *Croquembouche* with the small puffs until all spaces are filled as closely as possible. Place the reserved puff on top. Place the butter cream in a pastry bag with a large star tube affixed, then pipe rosettes into the spaces between the puffs. Place the Spun Sugar over the *Croquembouche* or spin directly onto the *Croquembouche*. You may serve individual puffs from the *Croquembouche* with silver tongs. Spun Sugar may be omitted, if desired.

The Creative Homemaker's Academy © MCMLXXIII
Selected Illustrations © B.P.C. Publishing Limited MCMLXX

HOW TO SPIN SUGAR

Spun Sugar is not difficult to make and the professional results shown in the illustration may be achieved if a few basic rules are carefully observed. It is also a good idea to practice your "spinning" technique once or twice before making spun sugar for a special occasion.

1. You will need an old broom handle or two long handled wooden spoons. Protect the floor around the work area where the sugar is to be spun with plenty of newspapers or a plastic drop cloth which can be discarded.

2. Grease the broom handles or wooden spoon handles so that the Spun Sugar may more easily be removed. Suspend the broom handle or, if using wooden spoons, tape the spoons to a counter top, about 12 inches apart, with masking tape, letting the handles extend out over the floor.

3. Pay *very close* attention to the temperature of the sugar syrup as it boils. If cooked over a burner which is too hot, the syrup can progress from the not-fully-cooked stage to a burned-beyond-repair state in an exceedingly short time.

SPUN SUGAR

1/3 c. water
1/4 c. white corn syrup
1 c. sugar

Combine the water, corn syrup and sugar in a small saucepan. Bring to a boil over medium heat, stirring gently but constantly until the sugar is dissolved. Boil, without stirring, until the syrup reaches 310 degrees on a candy thermometer or until a small amount dropped into ice water forms hard, brittle threads. The syrup will be straw-colored. Remove from heat. Spin the sugar according to the illustration. If the syrup hardens before spinning the desired amount, reheat to the syrupy stage over medium heat. Use the Spun Sugar within 3 or 4 hours, as it melts at room temperature or in high humidity.

Hold 2 forks back to back. Dip the forks into the syrup and, as the syrup runs off, flick the forks back and forth over the broom handle or 2 wooden spoon handles, letting the threads spin down. Lift the cool Spun Sugar carefully from the handle and use for decoration as desired.

croquembouche

A *croquembouche* is the acme of French desserts. It is shown here with tiny butter cream rosettes piped around each puff giving a very professional and finished effect. A delicate veil of *Spun Sugar* floats from the top and tiny gladiolus, ferns, satin ribbons and lilies add a final touch of glory.

LEMON CLOUD PIE

1/2 **recipe Royal Short Pastry** *(pg. 16)*
1 **env. unflavored gelatin**
3/4 **c. sugar**
1/4 **tsp. salt**
1 **c. water**
1/3 **c. lemon juice**
2 **egg yolks, slightly beaten**
1 1/2 **tsp. grated lemon rind**
2 **c. frozen whipped topping, thawed**

Prepare the pastry for 1 pie crust according to the instructions, then cool. Combine the gelatin, sugar and salt in a saucepan. Add the water, lemon juice and egg yolks and blend well. Place over medium heat and cook, stirring constantly, for about 5 minutes or until the gelatin is dissolved. Remove from the heat and stir in the lemon rind. Turn into a mixing bowl and chill until thickened. Place the mixing bowl in a larger mixing bowl containing ice and water. Beat with an electric mixer until doubled in volume. Blend in 1 1/2 cups of the whipped topping, then spoon into the pie crust. Chill for 3 to 4 hours or until firm. Place the remaining whipped topping in the center of the pie and garnish with a twisted lemon slice, if desired. This makes 6 to 8 servings.

lemon cloud pie

Lemon Cloud Pie is, as its name implies, heavenly light and airy with the tang of lemon as the main flavor ingredient. This dessert is simple to make and can be prepared several days in advance of serving.

beverages

table of contents

introducing wines & spirits

The tasteful selection and serving of beverages — both alcoholic and non-alcoholic — is an area which, for one reason or another, many otherwise competent and confident cooks avoid or come close to ignoring. Undoubtedly, many people become so involved with planning and preparing the rest of the meal they simply overlook beverage selection until the last minute. At that point, they unimaginatively serve whatever is available. Still others are intimidated by the "right" choice of wines, but they needn't be — which is our theme in this introductory section on beverages.

In later lessons you'll learn the BASICS of brewing good coffee, and then put them to use in preparing iced and frozen coffee, and that magnificent after-dinner drink, cafe brulot. Teas, punches and even health food cocktails will be discussed. But for now let's concentrate on wines.

Our philosophy is simply this: The wine you like is a good wine for you, whether or not it is always "classically proper." But we're not going to leave you hanging with only that. We will supply the guidelines for beginning your own wine stock, making suggestions on selections for you to follow until your own tastes are developed. Just remember, food and wine are partners and must be complementary.

Of course, it would take volumes to explain *all* there is to know about this fascinating subject, but knowing all is not necessary. Here you'll acquire a depth of knowledge enabling you to converse with wine "experts." In particular, we'll examine several types of wine, domestic as well as imported, and learn where and how they are produced. You will discover the secret of identifying wines by the shape and color of the bottles. You'll learn the proper temperature for serving certain wines, and the recommended glass shape and size. We will also suggest appropriate wines to serve with various meals.

The distinction among wines, spirits and liqueurs will be pointed out. And you'll find recipes using all three as party, holiday and dessert beverages as well as traditional summer and winter drinks.

The following list represents an adequate, nice-to-have wine stock that will provide for a number of occasions and satisfy most individual tastes. We've divided the list into *Apéritifs*, light, flavorful wines served alone before dinner or with appetizers; *Table Wines*, served during dinner; and *After-Dinner Wines*, served alone following the meal or with dessert. A note: We've listed Champagne in the last two categories, but it is an excellent wine for any occasion and may be appropriately served throughout a meal.

APÉRITIFS

Dry Sherry
Medium Sherry
Dry Madeira (Sercial)
Dry white Port
Dry Vermouth
Sweet Vermouth

TABLE WINES

Dry white Burgundy
Red Burgundy
Dry white Bordeaux
Sweet white Bordeaux

Red Bordeaux (Claret)
Dry Moselle
Dry Hock
Dry white Italian
Champagne
Tawny Port

AFTER-DINNER WINES

Champagne
Ruby Port
Sweet Madeira
**   (Malvazia)**
Sparkling Burgundy

storing wines

Don't let our suggested wine list on the preceding page throw you off. Rather than attempting to purchase your entire stock at once, why not buy a few wines at a time so you can become familiar with each one? Your first purchase might include a red and a white Burgundy, a dry and a sweet white Bordeaux, and a light and a more lusty claret (Red Bordeaux).

A special storage area for your wines is advantageous: it provides easy access; it permits you to take advantage of sales because you have storage space on hand; and, when well-stocked, it gives you a large selection of wines for different occasions.

You don't have to have an old-fashioned wine cellar to enjoy these advantages. You can set up and stock your own storage space in other parts of your house, such as under the stairs or in an extra closet or cupboard.

When choosing your storage area, keep in mind that wine is sensitive to extreme temperatures, sudden temperature changes, sunlight and violent vibrations. Look for a well-ventilated area, preferably where the temperature ranges from 50 to 55 degrees. A much higher temperature will cause the wine to age more quickly than is desirable. Make sure there are not heating units nearby and that cold drafts — which might reduce the temperature suddenly — do not blow into the area.

Choose a dark place; exposure to sunlight causes most wines to become flat. And finally, vibrations are apt to disturb the "resting" wine and damage its quality.

You can make your wine cellar a do-it-yourself construction project, as we've done in our pictures. Or, simply purchase special "pigeonhole" or similar type wine racks that allow the bottles to lie horizontally.

These racks are easily obtainable in department stores and places where housewares are sold. They come in a variety of shapes and sizes and hold from a half dozen bottles up.

Wines in corked bottles should always be stored horizontally. This position keeps the corks moist — if allowed to dry out, the corks shrink, permit air to enter the bottles and thus cause the wine to spoil. Wines that are not corked may be stored upright and whiskey, gin, vodka and rum should always be stored upright. The stronger alcohol will destroy the cork.

1 As you can see, a wine storage area may be as simple or as elaborate as you like. This under-the-stairs version can hold a more-than-adequate wine supply.

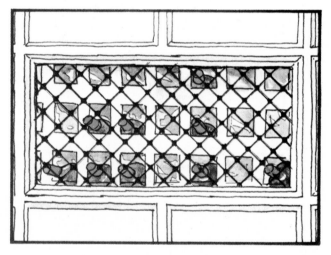

2 Ventilation and proper circulation are important aspects of a storage area. If your storage area is in a closet or similar *closed* space, you will need a vent as pictured here.

chilled fruit cocktails

*Thrill your guests and children
by treating them to these appetizing
chilled fruit cocktails. They're made of
refreshing fruit juices and various other
healthful ingredients. The
recipes are on the following page.*

chilled fruit cocktails

In the days of the early Manhattan settlers, cocktails were literally the tail feathers of cocks, dipped in a pimento concoction then used to tickle men's throats to entice them to drink. When most people think of cocktails today, they think of various mixed drinks made with liquor. But, cocktails aren't necessarily made with an alcoholic beverage. In this section we've included several beautiful cocktails made of such delicious ingredients as chilled fruit juices, ginger ale, sugar, milk and egg yolks.

These cool-tasting lovely drinks are perfect to serve to your non-drinking friends. They'll appreciate your thoughtfulness and be thrilled with the beauty and healthful qualities of these drinks. Or, if you're having alcoholic cocktails, serve these delightful fruit cocktails to your children and make them feel a part of the festivities. They are very good for youngsters, because they're full of vitamins and they have the extra bonus of tasting and looking marvelous.

You'll have no trouble making these elegant cocktails. Aside from the ingredients called for in our recipes, you'll only need a pitcher and a cocktail shaker to create them.

When making these beverages, remember that the look of your finished product is very important. Because of this we've garnished one of ours with tangy canelled orange strips (General Information, page 11-12), spooned foamy ice milk into another and added zapp to the third with soda water. Color is also an important element in making these cocktails truly enticing. To create really super effects we've used various colored fruit juices.

APPLE-GINGER COCKTAIL

2 cans frozen apple juice
4 juice cans chilled ginger ale
5 tbsp. lime juice

Thaw the apple juice until mushy. Pour the apple juice into a pitcher, then add the ginger ale and lime juice. Stir until blended. Pour into serving glasses. Garnish with canelled orange strip (General Information, page 11-12). This makes four servings.

PUSSY FOOT

Juice of ⅓ lemon, strained
Juice of 1 lime, strained
Juice of 1 chilled orange, strained
2 tsp. confectioners' sugar
1 egg yolk
Chilled soda water

Combine 1 tablespoon crushed ice, the strained fruit juices, sugar and egg yolk in cocktail shaker. Cover and shake vigorously to blend well. Strain into a serving glass; fill glass with soda water. This makes one serving.

PINK LADY COCKTAIL

¾ c. sugar
2 c. chilled cranberry juice
2 c. chilled pineapple juice
4 c. chilled ginger ale
Vanilla ice milk

Place the sugar in a pitcher, then add the cranberry juice slowly, stirring until sugar is dissolved. Add the pineapple juice and chill thoroughly. Add the ginger ale and pour into serving glasses. Add 1 serving spoon of ice milk to each glass and stir until foamy. Serve immediately. This makes about 8 servings.

CRANBERRY EGGNOG

3 eggs, separated
½ c. sugar
1 pt. cranberry juice
½ pt. whipping cream

Beat egg yolks with a wire whisk or fork until thick and lemon-colored. Add half the sugar and blend thoroughly. Begin adding the cranberry juice, a small amount at a time, beating with the whisk until all is blended into the egg mixture. Add remaining sugar and stir until dissolved. Whip the egg whites with an electric mixer, in a medium-sized mixer bowl, until stiff peaks form. Whip cream in a small mixer bowl until it is stiff. Fold cream into egg whites with a rubber spatula until blended. Then fold egg white mixture into cranberry juice mixture using a wire whisk or rubber spatula. Fold until just blended then ladle into eggnog cups or tumblers. Makes about 6 servings.

The Creative Homemaker's Academy © MCMLXXIII
Selected Illustrations © B.P.C. Publishing Limited MCMLXX

1 First, remove the metal capsule covering the cork by cutting it just below the rim of the bottleneck. Be sure the capsule doesn't come in contact with the contents because it's treated with lead and will taint the wine.

2 Peel away the capsule as shown.

3 After the capsule is removed, wipe the bottleneck with a clean napkin.

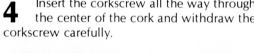

4 Insert the corkscrew all the way through the center of the cork and withdraw the corkscrew carefully.

5 Remove the corkscrew and cork.

6 Finally, wipe the inside of the bottleneck with one finger covered with the napkin and the wine is ready to serve.

introducing
wine glasses

The classic shapes of wine glasses came about in the regions where the various types of wine originated. It is nice to serve each wine from its specific type glass, but this is by no means essential. All the types of glasses are available, however, and collecting them is an exciting, if rather expensive, hobby. We have illustrated a complete collection below, but we suggest the all-around favorite, either no. 9, the 6²/₃-ounce tulip, or no. 8, the 10-ounce tulip, correct for anything you serve. When you start "collecting," make no. 6, a 5-ounce tulip, your second choice. This glass is preferable for fortified wines (explained later) such as port, sherry and Madeira, which are served in smaller quantities than table wines. For Cham-

pagne, you may of course use your tulip, or you may invest in a Champagne "flute," no. 2. This is also called a "cone Champagne." But don't waste your money on shallow bowl glasses which dissipate all the characteristic bubbles so carefully put there by the maker.

The glasses shown in the collection below, reading from left to right, are as follows: 1. hock glass; 2. Champagne flute, shaped to hold the bubbles in; 3. small brandy glass; 4. large brandy glass; 5. sherry glass or "copita"; 6. 5-ounce tulip for fortified wines; 7. Burgundy glass; 8. the 10-ounce tulip, a very popular size; 9. the 6²/₃-ounce tulip, the favorite size wine glass; and 10. claret (Bordeaux) glass.

Connoisseurs have spent centuries defining the certain subtle characteristics of each variety of wine and learning how best to enhance them. The wines have been tasted at various temperatures, with different types of food, and with different courses of meals. The "rules" regarding wine drinking and serving, then, are based on what reputable wine connoisseurs have found to be the ideal conditions for drinking each type of wine.

We'd like to share with you here a few of the generally accepted ideas about serving wine. But keep in mind that the "rules" are meant to increase your enjoyment, not restrict it. So, as always, your taste preferences will decide whether you follow them.

It has been found, for example, that a white wine may be poured directly from the bottle immediately after opening it. A red wine, on the other hand, may need to be decanted, especially if it has "thrown a deposit" — that is, if particles of sediment have settled to the bottom of the liquid. Since wine is stored on its side (label side up for easy identification), the fine particles will fall to the bottom *side* rather than the bottom of the bottle.

A deposit is by no means bad — in fact it is proof that the wine is alive. But it does require special handling, since, if the sediment is allowed to cloud the wine, it will spoil the flavor.

To an oenophile — wine lover — the color and bouquet of the beverage are as important as its taste. Selecting the right wine glass, then, is essential for the full enjoyment of wine.

The first essential of a proper wine glass is that it be of a good size. In fact, it is better to have one that is too large and fill it only a third full than to have it too small and overfill it.

One who appreciates wine first notices the color of the wine, which gives an indication of its age. Blood red wines are usually younger than those of a russet hue. White wines with a slight golden color are older than those of lighter color. For the visually sensitive, nothing is quite so beautiful as the candlelight reflection of wine through clear crystal. But the pleasure of studying the various shades of the beverage is definitely limited if the glass is tinted or patterned, so it should always be clear and plain. An old tradition of using colored glasses for German wines originated during an era when poor methods of treatment in the cask of these delicate wines often resulted in their being cloudy. Today's clear wines make these colored glasses unnecessary — although if you should be in possession of your great-grandmother's prized colored Venetian wine glasses, we certainly don't suggest you discard them!

The most conveniently shaped wine glass is the "tulip." For good balance a tulip glass should have a stem approximately the same length as the bowl and the stem should be solid rather than hollow. The stem prevents the brightness of the wine from being sullied by the smear of fingerprints on the bowl. If the stem were hollow, a chilled wine would be overly warmed by the heat transferred from the hands.

The second quality to appreciate in a good wine is its bouquet or aroma, and the bowl is designed to further

this appreciation. Its shape should be roundish, and narrower at the top than in the middle. This design allows the bouquet to concentrate at the lip of the glass — the rendezvous point for the appreciative nose — so the delicate odor doesn't drift away before you can enjoy it.

The bowl should never be filled more than half full so there is room to swirl the wine, coating the upper part of the glass with a winy film. As this film evaporates, its vapor concentrates in the narrowing chimney.

Even the taste of wine is enhanced by a good wine glass — anything which looks and smells good will always taste better.

basics of serving wines

DECANTING

Decanting is simply transferring the wine to a different container, leaving the sediment behind. Keeping the bottle always on its side so as not to disturb the sediment, place it gently in a cradle or on another steady surface which won't allow it to roll, and withdraw the cork as smoothly as possible. Have a decanter ready to catch the wine. Carefully pour the wine from the bottle to the decanter, tipping the bottle slightly when necessary, but taking care that no deposit goes through the wine.

LETTING THE WINE BREATHE

Another characteristic of red wines which calls for special care is that some of them, especially young ones, need time to "breathe" before being served. The reason is that a substance called tannin develops during production of red wine. Tannin ensures that the wine is sturdy enough to age properly and develop its flavors and bouquet. However, if a wine with tannin is drunk "young" (before it has had time to mature), the taste of the tannin will mask the flavors of the wine unless it is treated properly. Decanting the wine is one way to let it breathe. If it is not to be decanted, open the wine and pour off a glass so the wine level is below the neck of the bottle, allowing the air to reach a broader surface. (Air seems to soften the taste of tannin.) The wine should be allowed to breathe for about two hours before serving.

Red wines which have very little tannin, such as some Burgundies and very old clarets, do not need to breathe. In fact, they will begin to die as soon as they are exposed to a large quantity of air.

TABLE SERVICE OF WINE

For proper placement of the wine glass in the table setting see General Information, page 24.

There are two ways of serving the wine. *The host should always fill his own glass first and taste the wine — a formality to ensure that the wine is a good one and any bits of cork will be drawn into his glass.* Then he serves his guests. After the first glass, it is acceptable to pass the wine bottle and let guests help themselves.

TEMPERATURE OF WINE

All wines deserve to be served with care and that includes serving them at a proper temperature. The temperatures we recommend have been found to bring out the full flavor and bouquet of the particular wine.

Sparkling Wines such as Champagne and Sparkling Burgundy should be iced, preferably in an ice bucket.
White Wines — for example, Hocks, Moselles, Alsatians, White Burgundies and White Bordeaux — should be served chilled, but not iced, to about 40 degrees. It will remain cool longer after serving if the glass is held by the stem.
Rosé Wines should be chilled, but not over-chilled, to about 45 degrees.
Red Wines such as Red Burgundy and Red Bordeaux (Claret) should be served at low room temperature, about 65 degrees. Hold the glass by the bowl when you are drinking red wine to warm it slightly with your hand.

the many shapes of wine

No study of wines would be complete without an explanation of the bottles they come in. Learning the shapes and colors of wine bottles, which are governed by long tradition, will help you recognize the wine types. In addition, there is valuable information on the labels.

Pictured on this page is a sampling of classic wine bottle shapes accompanied by the glass the wine is traditionally served in. At left is the dark green Burgundy bottle, which slopes gently to the neck, with a Burgundy tulip in front. Next to it is a dark green claret bottle with a rounded slope and vertical neck, accompanied by a smaller tulip. The tall slender Moselle bottle is always green and the hock or Rhine wine bottle is always brown. Both are served in a hock glass. The last two bottles, with a flute between them, are Champagne, although in this size they are properly referred to as magnums. The Champagne magnum at left is the exclusive shape of a specific vineyard where a Bénédictine monk, *Dom Pérignon*, reportedly discovered the process for making Champagne.

READING THE WINE LABEL

Knowing how to read the labels will help you in selecting wines. By U.S. law, the label must specify the net contents and the country of origin. As a general rule, the more specific the origin is, the more pride it reflects. For example, beginning with the least specific: country (France), region (Bordeaux), area of a region (Graves), a specific wine-growing town (Margeaux) or, noblest of all, a chateau-bottled wine from a specific vineyard (Château d'Yquem). It will also be helpful if you learn to recognize the names of respected *négociants* (wine merchants and shippers as well. Usually, the label will specify the vintage, such as 1964, unless the bottle contains a blend of several years' growth.

In 1935, after a period of growing dishonesty in labeling practices, standards of production were set up to ensure that the bottle contained what its label said it did. The terms *Appellation Contrôlée* or *V.D.Q.S.* now afford proof that these standards have been met.

V.D.Q.S. (Vin Délimités de Qualité Supérieur — wines of superior quality) covers areas that produce good, sound wines of pronounced regional characteristics. They may be a blend, and they are often bottled without a vintage date, but they have passed strict regulations as to how they were made.

The label *Appellation Contrôlée* covers the major wine regions and vineyards producing wines aspiring to excellence. Each region has its own standards of what makes an above-average wine and the *Appellation Contrôlée* laws are based on these.

wine terminology

It seems simple enough to define wine as the fermented juice of the grape, but such a definition only begins to describe this interesting beverage. For example, a wine may be sweet or dry, still, fortified or sparkling, or red, rosé or white. However, since you've undoubtedly heard these words used to describe wine, it won't be difficult to clarify the terminology with a few simple explanations.

Except for certain wines produced in the Eastern United States, all wines are made from varieties of the particular grape *Vitis vinifera*. The grapes of California are of the European stock, having been brought over early in the Spanish settlement of the area. The climate of the East is unsuitable for *Vitis vinifera*, so wines there are made either from a cultivated wild grape native to this continent or from hybrids of the two. The distinctive taste of the native wine is often described as "foxy" or "grapey." New York and Ohio are the largest wine producers in the East.

SWEET OR DRY?

The classification of *sweet* and *dry* wines came about because dry seems to be the only acceptable opposite for sweet in describing the taste of wine, since sour wine refers to spoilage. If a wine is said to have a "dry finish," it means the aftertaste removes the effect of sweetness. Whenever more than one wine is served during a meal, a dry one should be served first, for the human sense of taste begins to tire after a while, and the taste for distinguishing sweets lasts longest. Also, a sweet wine before a dry one causes the dry wine to seem tasteless. Incidentally, many bottles will have the French terms *brut* (very dry) or *sec* (dry) on the label for this identification.

The distinctions among *still* (or table) *wines, fortified wines* and *sparkling wines* have to do with wines' production. Still wines are allowed to ferment naturally, with the possible addition of controlled amounts of yeast, sulfur or sugar (the last process being called chaptalization). Fortified wines such as sherry and port have a controlled amount of alcohol, usually grape brandy, added during vinification (transformation into wine), producing a higher alcohol content. Sparkling wines such as Champagne are fermented twice, the second time after they are bottled.

WINE NAMES

The wines of France and Germany are described by their region of origin — for example, Burgundy, Bordeaux or Rhine — for the same grape, when grown in a different soil or climate, will produce a different tasting wine.

California wines usually carry "varietal" labels (that is, the variety of *Vitis vinifera* that was used) rather than European district or even California district names. Thus, a Burgundy-type wine is labeled Pinot Noir; a Claret type, Cabernet Sauvignon; and a Beaujolais type, Gamay. Other red wine varietals are Barbera, Grenache, Grignolino and Zinfandel. White wines follow the same terminology other wine-producing countries use: Chardonnay, Riesling, Pinot Blanc, Traminer, Sylvaner, Folle Blanche, Semillon, Sauvignon Blanc and Johannisberg. Grape names to look for on *rosé* wines are Grenache, Gamay, Pinot Noir and Cabernet. Champagne is sold under the title "California Champagne," and port and sherry are sold under the same names as the European ones.

Eastern U.S. wines carry such varietal names as Scuppernong, Duchess, Delaware, Catawba, Elvira, Diana and Moore's Diamond.

A final classification, applicable only to table wines, is the division into red, white and *rosé*. These will be explained in greater detail later. Briefly, red wines get their color from the grape juice staying in contact with the grape skins for several days. *Rosés* are in contact only a few hours, while for white wines, the juice is removed immediately from the skins. Red wines are prized for their heartiness, whites for their delicacy and lightness.

introducing white burgundy

INTRODUCING WHITE BURGUNDY

Mention the word "Burgundy" to a wine connoisseur and watch his eyes light up with pleasure at the fond memories it conjures. For Burgundy is the world's best-known wine, with the possible exception of Bordeaux. Burgundy's white table wines are considered by some to be the world's finest. About one-fourth of all Burgundy wine is white.

Burgundy-the-wine is named after Burgundy-the-area of France where it is produced. Interestingly enough, Burgundy is no longer a political entity of any sort, having been divided into five different political *départments* in 1798 after the French Revolution.

However, Burgundy's name lives on in its most important product, and more important for our purposes than its political divisions are its wine-making districts, of which there are six. Chablis is off to itself, and the other five form a long chain down the southeastern flank of the Morvan hills facing out over the river Saône. The northernmost two, Côte de Nuits and Côte de Beaune, are collectively called Côte d'Or or "hill of gold." The other three are Côte Chalonnaise, Maconnais and Beaujolais. The specific characteristics of the white wines of each region will be discussed on these pages, but first we will tell you something about the making of white wine.

HOW WHITE WINE IS MADE

The term "white" wine is almost as confusing as the term "dry," for wines of this description may range from almost clear to pale gold, from greenish to almost brown. White wine may be made from either dark or light grapes. The juice is removed immediately from contact with the grape skins, so it does not have time to absorb their color, tannin or flavor. Since white wines have no tannin, they mature much faster than red wines. They are kept in the wooden barrels from 12 to 20 months; then they are bottled to continue their maturation.

Most white wines come to a peak after about 2 to 4 years in the bottle; usually they may be kept up to 7 years without deterioration. Of course, some will deteriorate faster, and a few exceptions may still be good after 50 years. If you wish to take your study of wines further, there are wine charts that list each year's growth, giving the quality and the years it is at its peak. However, your best bet is a good wine proprietor, a label you've learned to trust, and a willingness to take your chances now and then in experimentation.

WINE MAKING IN BURGUNDY

Wine making in Burgundy is quite different from that, for example, in Bordeaux. As a result of land reform following the French Revolution, vineyards were divided into small ownership plots, and one owner may have several plots widely separated. Since there are no large ownerships, few growers bottle their own wine. Mainly, they sell to a wine merchant, or *négociant*, who, if he is honest, keeps the varieties pure. Of course, blending is common among even good quality wines, but one would hope that the quality levels would be maintained and that care is taken in selecting wines as nearly alike as possible. The smaller merchants, in turn, may sell to a shipper, whose integrity is also an important factor in the resulting wine. In this country and in France, the terms *Appellation Contrôlée* and *V.D.Q.S.* may be relied upon to determine the quality of the wine.

Although there is no official classification of vineyards by quality in Burgundy, there is an unofficial standard of comparative excellence. The finest vineyard of each parish is called *tête de cuvée* ("the best of the batch") or *Grand Cru*. There may be several or no vineyards of this title in a parish. The second-best vineyards are known, confusingly enough, as *Premiers Crus* (first-growths) and third-ranked vineyards, second-growths. In practice, any growth below *Premier* will use only the regional name, such as Chablis or, if of lesser quality, Petit Chablis.

CHABLIS

Chablis is probably the best-known white Burgundy and has long enjoyed a great reputation as the perfect accompaniment to shellfish, especially oysters. The grapes are grown in hilly vineyards clustering around the little town of Chablis.

The taste of a great Chablis is very dry but by no means thin, although in a good year there is more body than usual. Chablis is pale in color with a slight tint of green. Its bouquet is powerful and its flavor slightly mineral or "steely." It is an agreeable blend of acidity and fruit, with its acidity ensuring a life of many years. It is usually at its best at 4 to 7 years of age.

These are characteristics of all Chablis, right down to the lowest Petit Chablis, although less marked in the lower echelons. What you pay for in a superior growth is a quality of many things, not just alcohol. Quality wines have greater strength of character, scent and taste, as well as greater length of rich, lingering aftertaste.

CÔTE D'OR

The northern area of the Côte d'Or, Côte de Nuits, is almost exclusively a red wine district. The few white wines produced there are excellent but seldom seen.

Further south, in the Côte de Beaune, are three of Burgundy's finest white wine vineyards: Corton-Charlemagne, Meursault and Montrachet. However, there are many other excellent white wines produced in this district.

Corton-Charlemagne can be described as a "big" wine, with a savor that tends to linger in your mouth after you have swallowed it. It smells somewhat like cinnamon, with a taste that suggests flint or steel.

Meursault is a consistently marvelous wine, very dry but at the same time soft and mellow. Its color is pale gold with a suggestion of green. It ages remarkably well for a white wine.

And then there is Montrachet (pronounced Mon-Rä-Shá)—the wine Alexandre Dumas claimed should only be drunk kneeling, with head bared. In its best years, this wine has no comparison. Wine connoisseurs describe it as completely balanced: sweet in nature, with no spare sugar, it is best described as dry and lively.

CÔTE CHALONNAISE, MÂCONNAIS AND BEAUJOLAIS

Côte Chalonnais produces good white wines which are light, pale and clean-tasting; they also age well. They are excellent, except when compared with their neighbors directly to the north.

Further south, in Mâconnais, most of the wines are good, though not outstanding, with the exception of one which stands equal to the best wines of Chablis and Côte de Beaune — Pouilly-Fuissé. This wine name is used by five villages, and is best characterized as dry and gentle.

In the southernmost tip of Burgundy, Beaujolais produces some small quantities of adequate white wine, but there is little reason to produce it since Beaujolais' red wines are of more importance.

In California, the Pinot Chardonnay produces a wine to be seriously compared with the white Burgundies of France. The major growing areas are the Napa and Sonoma valleys, the Livermore valley, Santa Clara and San Benito.

The light, delicate taste of white Burgundy is especially suited to lighter foods such as seafoods, poultry, ham or veal — in fact, almost anything except beef and game.

introducing red burgundies

On preceding pages, we have discussed the white wines of Burgundy. You may now want to review those pages for information about the region itself. Here we will discuss red Burgundies, considered by many people to be the world's finest red wines.

Usually made from dark grapes, red wine gets its striking color from the grape skins. To break their skins, the grapes are placed in giant vats and mashed slightly. Sweet juice, called *must*, then seeps out of the broken grapes and comes in contact with the natural yeast on the skins. A chemical reaction between the sugar in the juice and the yeast forms alcohol. This reaction is called *fermentation*.

Grapes for red wine are fermented for several days. During this time, the *must* absorbs the flavor, tannin and color of the skins. The wine is then transferred to barrels where it is kept for about two years. As it ages, all the sugar in the wine is converted to alcohol. Most natural wines, therefore, are relatively dry. When bad weather conditions cause a reduction in the sugar content of the grape crops, the government often decrees that the wine may be chaptalized; that is, controlled amounts of sugar are added to produce the correct proportion of alcohol in the wine. Because they absorb tannin from grape skins, red wines usually take longer to mature than whites. When first bottled, red wine is barely drinkable; within two years, it is drinkable but harsh. So, to be sure that the wine is fully mature — and at its peak of flavor — the wine should be carefully and patiently stored for longer periods. Some wines may take as few as six years to mature, while others may take as many as 16. On the assumption they will be stored by the buyer until mature, fine red wines are often sold after only two years in the bottle.

Different production methods are used to make fine wines and ordinary wines *(vin ordinaire)*. If the wine is not to be a great one, the long aging process is not required. Thus, *vin ordinaire* does not stay with the skins long enough to develop the strong taste of tannin. While lacking the depth of flavor found in a fine wine, *vin ordinaire* is refreshing and perfectly acceptable as a table wine.

BURGUNDY'S RED WINES — CÔTE D'OR

Burgundy is divided into two parts, the Côte d'Or (the golden hill) and southern Burgundy. With the exception of Chablis, all five wine districts in Burgundy are known for their red wines. Since so many excellent red Burgun-

dies are made, we will concentrate mainly on the *têtes de curvées* (page 14) of each region.

Because of such factors as type of grape used, soil acidity, climate and location of the vine, wines vary in taste from one region or even from one vineyard to the next. Knowledge of the type wine produced in each region will help you learn how to add to your wine stock according to your personal taste preference.

The northern section of the Côte d'Or is known as the Côte de Nuits. Here, all red wine is made from the Pinot Noir grape. In the Côte de Nuits, Gevrey-Chambertin is the northernmost commune from which wines are exported. The addition of the name "Chambertin" to the name of the village was in honor of the village's greatest

Burgundy

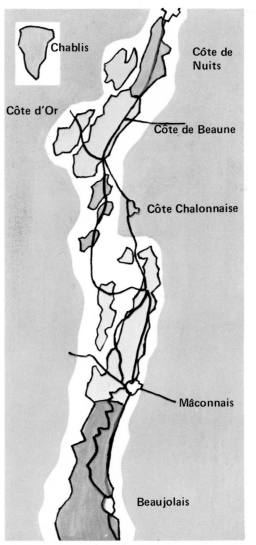

vineyard. Chambertin and Chambertin Clos de Bèze are the two vineyards in this region classified as *têtes de cuvées*. Though the Burgundies produced from these vineyards are the most vigorous and powerful, they still have a marked finesse and delicacy of flavor.

To the south, the commune of Chambolle-Musigny produces lighter, more delicate wines that have less body and robustness — but a noticeably fine bouquet. Two great wines come from this commune: Musigny, considered to be one of the finest wines in Burgundy, and Bonnes-Mares.

The most famous vineyard in Burgundy is located at Vougeot. Known as the Clos de Vougeot, this great vineyard comprises 125 acres that are entirely enclosed by a wall. The vineyard and the wall, which took 200 years to build, date back to the 12th century.

As a result of the French Revolution, the Clos de Vougeot vineyard was split up, and today it is divided among 70 owners. Because the vineyard is so large, the taste of the wines vary. To balance the taste, wines from different parts of the vineyard are blended. At its best, Vougeot is velvety, rich and truly one of the great wines.

Some of the greatest wines in Burgundy, as well as the most expensive, are found in the commune of Vosne-Romanée. Because the vineyard here is only 4¹/₂ acres, fewer grapes are available to produce wine. Thus, the size of the vineyard affects the price of the wine. The seven *têtes de cuvée* of this area are Romanée-Conti, La Tâche, La Romanée, Richebourg, Romanée-Saint-Vivant, Grands-Echézeaux and Echézeaux. The wines have a delicate yet fragrant bouquet, and the taste is rich but light. All of these wines are bottled *en domaine*.

The commune of Beaune is the most important wine city in the Côte d'Or, chiefly because of the famous Hospices de Beaune. This charity hospital for the elderly is financed through the sale of wine from vineyards donated to it. A total of 23 red wines bear the notation that they are Hospices wine. Though the Côte de Beaune does produce some excellent red wines, the region is better known for its white which are *Grand Cru* wines.

Other communes in the Côte d'Or which produce good red wines, either *Premiers Crus* or excellent *vin ordinaire*, include Morey-Saint Denis, Nuits-Saint Georges, Savigny-Lès-Beaune, Pommard, Volnay, Chassagne-Montrachet and Santenay.

CÔTE CHALONNAIS AND MACONNAIS

The two red wine communes of Côte Chalonnais are Mercurey and Givry. Both produce light, rich wines of finesse. Mâconnais begins the southern portion of Burgundy. About one-third of its wine is red. In this area, both Pinot Noir and Gamay grapes are used to produce the wine. In red wine, Mâconnais produces large quantities of agreeable *vin ordinaire*. This wine matures early, often at less than two years old, and so may be drunk when it is relatively young.

BEAUJOLAIS

Beaujolais, the largest and most productive region of Burgundy, produces the most delightful, quick-maturing red wines in the world. Made from the Gamay grape, these light, fruity wines are soft and easy to drink. They keep just a touch of acidity to make them refreshing. Beaujolais wines are to be quaffed rather than sipped, especially when served at low room temperature on hot summer days.

Nine communes are entitled to use their own names on their wines. They are: St. Amour, Juliénas, Chénas, Moulin'a Vent, Fleurie, Chiroubles, Morgon, Brouilly and Côte de Brouilly. These wines have the notation *Growth Beaujolais*. The others, if produced in the northern part of the region, are classified as *Beaujolais Villages*. In the south, they carry the notation *Beaujolais Supérieur* or *Beaujolais*.

THE WINES OF CALIFORNIA

Most California wine districts produce red, white and *rosé* wines. The grapes grown to most successfully produce wines comparable to their French counterparts are the Pinot Chardonnay (white Burgundy type) and Cabernet Sauvignon (red Bordeaux or claret type). Red Burgundy type wines produced from the Pinot Noir are less successful than blends that use a proportion of the Petite Syrah grape. These "burgundies" are simple, clean and dry wines. Their quality is at least as high as the French *vin ordinaire* and is generally higher. California's closest counterpart to a Beaujolais is made from the Zinfandel grape, a grape unknown in Europe.

The best way to discover which California wines you prefer is to try them. Compare the taste of red wines from the Napa Valley with those of Alameda, the wines of Modesto with those of Sonoma, and so forth. The following list identifies the California red wine names with their European counterparts:

CALIFORNIA RED WINES	EUROPEAN
Cabernet Sauvignon Zinfandel	Claret or Bordeaux Types
Pinot Noir	Burgundy Type
Chianti Barbera Grignolina	Italian Types

introducing coffee

When George III of England imposed a "tea tax" on the American colonists during the 1770's, undercurrents of culinary change were fast developing. Coffee, and desserts made with coffee became fashionable and those who wanted to appear not only patriotic but knowledgeable socially, cultivated a taste for this potable brew. In Boston, patriots and sympathizers gathered at the Union Street Coffee House for coffee and exciting conversation or "kaffeeklatsches."

In the years after the War of Independence, Americans returned to drinking tea — which continued to outsell coffee throughout most of the nineteenth century.

Inflated food prices from 1914-1919 and the National Prohibition Act gave coffee a big boost in the United States. In 1919, a cup of coffee could still be bought for a nickel. This, and the ban on the sale of alcoholic beverages, led millions to drink "a mild stimulant and morning eye-opener" — coffee.

In the following pages, there are several exciting dessert coffee recipes, coffee that is cool, refreshing and bittersweet, delicious coffee ices that are sweetened and flavored with milk and vanilla. Some are garnished with a flourish of whipped cream. Party, picnic or dessert, any occasion is just the right time for these elegant but simple beverages.

HOW TO MAKE DELICIOUS REAL COFFEE

This may be the first time you have ever seen coffee made this way. Coffee was brewed using an open kettle, an enameled jug and sieve before the advent of percolators. This method is still used in Europe and many claim it is more flavorful and aromatic than perked coffee.

1 Measure 2 tablespoons of regular grind coffee for each 8-ounce cup of water into a scalded enameled pot and add a pinch of salt.

2 Measure the briskly boiling water and pour it over the coffee. Stir thoroughly.

3 Cover and let stand for 3 to 4 minutes.

4 Pour through a cloth or fine sieve into coffee service. Serve immediately.

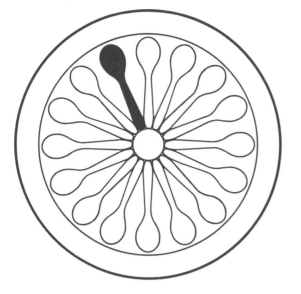

frozen black coffee

The Creative Homemaker's Academy © MCMLXXIII
Selected Illustrations © B,P.C. Publishing Limited MCMLXX

frozen black coffee

A summer-time dessert such as this delicious coffee-ice will provide the raison d'être for new rituals of hospitality. Frozen Black Coffee may be served as a dinner dessert, a luncheon beverage or a mid-afternoon refresher.

FROZEN BLACK COFFEE

2 ¹/₂ c. strong coffee
1 ¹/₄ c. Basic Sugar Syrup *(Breads, pg. 14)*
1 recipe Basic Chantilly Cream *(Desserts, pg. 19)*
Sugar

Combine the coffee and syrup, mixing well. Pou
into refrigerator trays and freeze until icy crysta
form. Dip the edges of tall glasses in cold wate
and then into sugar to frost. Spoon the coffee mix
ture into the glasses and top with Chantilly cream
Serve immediately. This makes 4 servings.

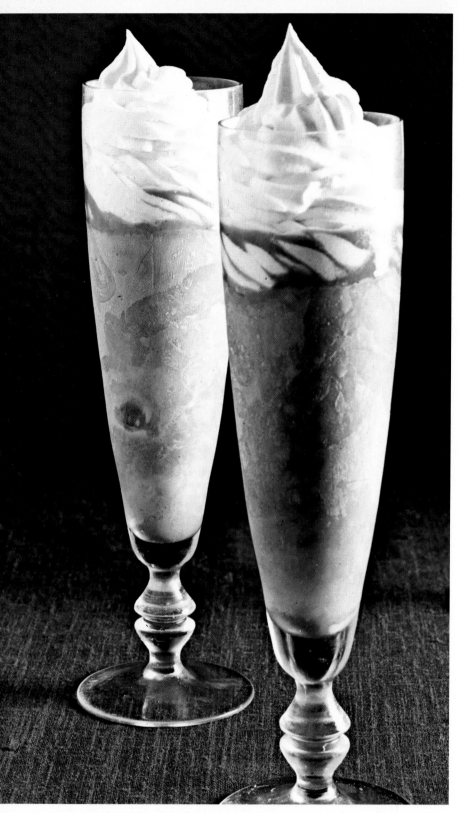

ICED COFFEE WITH WHIPPED CREAM

1 c. sugar
1½ c. milk
1 vanilla pod
1½ c. cold coffee
¾ c. whipping cream
Unsweetened whipped cream

Combine sugar, milk and vanilla pod in a heavy saucepan and bring to a boil, stirring until sugar is dissolved. Remove from heat and let stand until cold. Remove vanilla pod, then rinse and dry for future use. Combine milk mixture, coffee and whipping cream, mixing well, then pour into refrigerator trays. Place in freezing compartment and let stand until partially frozen. Stir and pour into tall glasses, filling ⅔ full. Top with spirals of whipped cream and serve immediately. Coffee mixture may be made ahead and frozen. Let thaw until mushy. This makes 6 servings.

ICED RUM COFFEE CREAM

½ c. (packed) brown sugar
¾ c. water
3 tbsp. instant coffee
8 ice cubes
2½ c. milk
1 pt. Basic Vanilla Ice Cream (Desserts, pg. 67)
¾ c. half and half cream
2 tbsp. rum

Combine brown sugar, water and coffee in a small heavy saucepan. Bring to a boil, stirring constantly until sugar is dissolved. Place ice cubes in a large mixing bowl. Pour coffee mixture over ice cubes and stir with a wooden spoon until ice cubes are melted. Stir in the milk. Cut ice cream into small pieces and add to coffee mixture. Crush until mixture is smooth, using wooden spoon. Stir in half and half cream and rum. Pour into pitcher and keep chilled until ready to serve. This makes 9 to 10 servings.

iced coffee with whipped cream

Two tall glass coupes are filled to within 2 inches of the top with a sweet confection of coffee, vanilla and milk then topped with a flourish of whipped cream. When coffee became fashionable in the late 1660's, iced coffee with whipped cream was served in Vienna which was to become the great European entrepôt of coffee and coffee-flavored desserts.

PICNIC COFFEE

1¼ c. regular grind coffee
18 c. cold water
2 eggs

Combine coffee and 16 cups water in a heavy saucepan. Beat eggs slightly, then stir eggs and crushed shells into water. Bring to a boil, then reduce heat and let simmer for 10 minutes. Remove from heat and pour in remaining water to settle grounds. Strain coffee into serving pot and keep hot, but do not boil. This makes 24 servings.

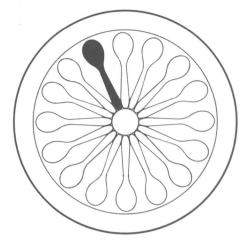

introducing port wines

In the Douro mountains of northern Portugal, there are tiered slopes alive with vines of grapes from which are made the richest Port wines in the world. At harvest, the approaching pickers sing and dance to the native music of small bands as they come to gather grapes. With them they bring the colorful tradition of making wine. They rise daily with the sun and sing as they climb the steep slopes. Cheerful women carefully cut grape bunches, removing the defective grapes and placing the round, plump ones in their small baskets. Rhythmically they move down the rows of vines until their small baskets are full. The women then empty the grapes into very large baskets which suntanned men load on their strong backs and carry down to spacious storehouses. Unexhausted after a long day, the men and women gather at night to dance in and around the home of the vineyard or *quinta* owner. After a night of laughter and song, they rise early to start the procedure all over again.

When the owner's large storage vats are full with rich grapes, the crushing process is begun. In a few areas the traditional foot treading method is still used. Although in most areas, machines have taken over this function. These full vats hold the embryo of the richest Port wine in the world.

Among the many varieties of grapes grown in the Douro, there are the very sweet, not so sweet, white and purple grapes. These large baskets are filled with freshly picked purple grapes, as rich in taste as they are in color.

The most famous of Portuguese wines is red Port, a medium sweet wine that is fortified with grape brandy during fermentation. Its name "Port" comes from the town of Oporto in the Douro Valley of Northern Portugal where it originated.

The actual fortification of Port was begun by the British around the 18th century when they found that imported Portuguese wine was much too harsh for their sensitive taste buds. The Portuguese peasants had never minded the harshness, but when the strong wine began to be imported into Britain, the British sought a method to make it more palatable. Had other imported wines been as cheap and accessible as Portuguese wines, they probably would not have bothered. However, because the Portuguese wines were more available, due to trade agreements, the British were anxious to experiment. They found that by adding a little brandy to the wine, they made it not only drinkable, but also quite delicious.

The Portuguese wine makers could not understand the British complaints about the harshness of Portuguese wine. They had always considered their grapes to be the richest and sweetest. What they failed to consider, however, was the effect the extremely warm Portuguese climate had on the wine during fermentation. The heat was causing all the sugar in the grapes to turn to alcohol, and none was retained in the wine. For this reason, they began adding brandy during fermentation.

The brandy served to maintain the sweetness of the grapes throughout fermentation, and the resulting wine was delectable.

Wine purists of the era opposed this procedure, claiming that the Portuguese wine makers were "tampering with nature." Great wine, in their opinion, was supposed to ferment naturally. However, all their bickering made little difference to the British wine lovers. They became staunch patrons of this delicious wine and called for it as often or more often than they did the unfortified (without the addition of brandy) varieties from neighboring countries. Port wine was not imported to any other country except Great Britain until the 19th century, and Britain is still its greatest consumer.

These are the steep terraced slopes in the Douro mountains of northern Portugal, filled with the vines of rich grapes. At harvest, the workmen travel up and down these slopes while taking the grapes to the storage vats.

types of port

Although all Port wines are allowed to mature in wooden casks for the first two or three years and all are marketed for sale in bottles, they are divided into the following two categories: Wood Port and Bottled Port. The terms "wood" and "bottled" do not indicate age or manner in which they are sold, but rather the manner in which they are matured. Wood Port spends not only the first three years in wooden casks, but also the remainder of its maturation period (from 5 to 15 years or longer). When Wood Port is bottled, it is ready for consumption. Bottled Port, on the other hand, is removed from the wooden casks at the end of the first three years, corked and bottled for the remainder of its maturation (anywhere from 5 to 40 years or longer).

Ruby Port is a ruby red Bottled Port. Age determines its flavor. As a youthful wine (aged only 5 to 10 years), it has a robust, fruity flavor. As an older wine (aged over 10 years), it has a much more mellow taste. Neither flavor is necessarily inferior to the other. The choice depends strictly on the individual's taste or whatever flavor is desired for a certain occasion. However, please note that the longer a wine is aged, the more expensive it will be.

Tawny Port is a Wood Port. Although it also is red before it matures, it turns a tawny russet color during maturation — a result of its storage in wooden casks over the years. It is mellow flavored and usually more expensive because it ordinarily matures for a much longer period of time than Ruby.

White Port can be Wood or Bottled. It begins and remains white in color because it is made from white grapes. Generally, white Port is not as sweet as the red. It is never considered to be as "high-classed" as Ruby or Tawny. The Portuguese frequently refer to it as a breakfast wine. Americans often serve dry white Port as an *aperitif*, and it is very popular when served as a substitute for sherry or Madeira.

When all the conditions for a particular year promise an especially good wine, the wine shippers declare a vintage year. The wine produced from that chosen year's harvest is expected to be of the highest quality, and it is treated with the greatest care and respect from the very beginning of fermentation, through years of aging, until it is opened and served. After Vintage Port is kept in wooden casks for two or three years, it is fortified a final time and bottled. All red wines form some sediment in the bottle, but Port forms an actual crust due to the absorption of so much brandy. Crusted Port, which ranks with Vintage Port, is so called because it throws a particularly heavy crust. To shake or upset the bottles causes the crust to re-mix with the wine. For this reason, shippers and consumers frequently mark the top of Port bottles with white paint so that, when moved, the wine will be placed on the same side and the crust will not be disturbed. In fact, wine consumers make a special attempt not to move the wine at all because the longer it lies still, the better it will be. Vintage Port is frequently cradled quietly and left undisturbed from 10 to 40 years, or even longer. This specially treated Vintage Port is the finest and most expensive Port available. It is proper to decant these wines in order to eliminate the crust or deposits. The wine should be carefully poured from the bottle into a decanter leaving the crust in the bottle.

Before Port wine can be exported, its quality must be tested and approved by the *Instituto of Portugal*, a governing body made up of official tasters who decide whether or not a wine is suitable for shipping. If the wine meets the approval of the institute, it is given the Certificate of Origin which corresponds to the French Appéllation Controlée.

HOW AND WHEN TO SERVE PORT

The British have always been most dedicated to Port wine. They think of Port strictly as an elegant dessert wine. To serve it any other time, in their opinion, is practically unlawful. When an Englishman serves his best Port wine, it is frequently a ceremonious affair and an awesome custom. Usually a British host who has just served an elaborate dinner to several distinguished guests will motion the servants to clear the table. Then he will solemnly light candles and have a decanter of his best Port placed in front of him. Slowly he will pour himself a glass and pass the bottle clockwise (never counterclockwise) around the table. All the guests are expected to enjoy the fragrance, taste and smoothness, and to indulge themselves totally in the ceremony.

After the wine decanter has made one complete trip around the table, the host frequently starts the cycle over, this time offering cigarettes and cigars to accompany the wine. (The host expects his guests to refrain from smoking with their first glass of wine so that they may appreciate to the fullest the taste and aroma of the rich Port.)

The British would probably be horrified at the "uncouth" Americans who drink Port whenever and wherever they feel like it. A knowledgeable and gracious hostess may serve Port as a part of the dessert course with cheese and nuts. However, many Americans find a bottle of good Port enjoyable both before or during dinner. Some even mix it with carbonated water or ginger ale and drink it over ice on summer outings, much to the Britisher's disgust. But even Americans are not likely to swig down a $35 or $40 bottle of Vintage Port on a picnic.

CALIFORNIA PORT

Although Port wine is associated most frequently with Portugal (and it is quite true that the best Port *does* come from this area), Port wine similar to Portuguese Port is made in almost every wine-making area of the world, including those in the United States. Imported wine has great prestige, but don't underestimate the excellent wine produced here in the United States. Maybe California wine does not have the romantic appeal of Portuguese imports, but wine experts say that some of the best wine in the world is made from California grapes.

The California wine maker adds pure grape brandy in the fashion of the famous Portuguese Port. The added brandy helps retain the sugar and regulate the alcohol content. Ruby, Tawny and White Port are all produced in California. Tinta and Tinta Madeira are varietal Ports (named for the grapes used) which are especially flavorful and fruity.

introducing rosé wines

Vin rosé (pronounced VANH-RO-ZAY) is a delicate, delightful beverage. Its taste is as light as its pale rose color. It is usually produced from dark grapes. The juice — obtained either from natural methods or from mashing — is left in contact with the skins about 24 hours. Following this short period in the vats, the grape skins are pressed dry, and the resulting juice is added to that obtained earlier.

Since the juice of the grapes is removed so early, the wine does not have time to absorb the full color, flavor or tannin from the grapes. Thus, a *rosé* is not as fullbodied as a red wine.

In France, the Loire River Valley region is known for its slightly sweet *rosés*. The area west of the Rhône River produces a fairly dry *rosé* of exceptional character. In Bordeaux, where *rosés* are light and dry, production of the wine is increasing. However, in comparison to the reds and whites, quantities produced are still miniscule. From the Jura comes a *rosé* deeper in color than most and slightly sweet. A *rosé* of merit that is dry and fresh is produced in southern Burgundy. In the United States, most California winemakers include *rosés* among their selections.

Though red wines are usually served at room temperature and whites are always served well chilled, *rosé* wines are always served slightly chilled. They are particularly refreshing as an accompaniment for simple hot weather meals.

Rosés are delicious when served with veal, since the meat also is delicate in flavor. However, *rosés* are appropriate with almost any food.

wine cellar

Pictured here is a large wine storage cellar. These two men are carefully inspecting the empty vats to make sure they are clean and ready to receive new wine. If the barrels pass this inspection, they are marked with the seal of approval.

presenting brandy

Brandy, called the most noble spirit of them all, is best known as an afterdinner drink. It is — quite simply stated — distilled wine. It may be the distillate of nearly any fruit: peaches, apricots, blackberries, grapes, apples and so on; but it is more generally taken to mean the "spirit (distilled fermented juice) of the grape."

To speak of brandy, we have to speak of the most exquisite example of spirits of this type . . . Cognac. Cognac is unequivocally and universally accepted at the greatest of brandies! It is prized all over the world and is a word known among people who may know no other French word!

This matchless brandy is produced in the quiet but busy town of Cognac, located on the Charente River, 70 miles north of Bordeaux, France. Charming and provincial, the town is nestled among low, rolling hills covered with trees, vineyards, and occasional chateaux. Cognac is dedicated completely to the making of the brandy for which it is famous.

The secret of great Cognac brandy is, paradoxically, the acidic, weak, almost undrinkable white wine from which it is made. And it was in search of a remedy for this terrible wine that Cognac came into being. In the 1600's, facing ruin, the farmers in the Cognac region discovered the technique of twice distilling their ill-tasting wine. The resulting product was found to be pleasing in taste, easy to handle, and — most exciting of all — aromatic.

Though brandy may be made anywhere that grapes grow, Cognac brandy must be made within a limited area in and surrounding Cognac, the town. The exclusivity of Cognac — the grapes used and the manner of distillation — is stipulated by French law.

The French call this heart drawn from the wine *Eau-de-Vie* or Water of Life. It is high in alcohol — about 70 percent! — and the remaining 30 percent consists of the finest elements from the wine. This precious 30 percent gives Cognac its rich bouquet. Now, white and clear like pure spring water, the *bonne chauffe* is ready to begin the marriage of raw alcohol and wood essences that will take place in aging.

It is important to understand at this point that Cognac does not improve in the bottle because of its high alcoholic content (which preserves the brandy in its same state, once cut off from air). For this reason it is aged in oaken barrels which allow air to siphon through the pores in the wood. It is contact with the air that, with time, causes the alcohol and wine elements to combine. (This means that an 1820 Cognac bottled in 1850 is the same "age" as a 1920 Cognac bottled in 1950.)

The type of wood used for the cask is as important to producing Cognac as the kind of wine and the manner of distillation. Cognac is aged only in barrels hewn (*not* sawed, for sawdust would ruin the taste!) from Limousin oaks of the Charente region. The rule is new barrels for new brandy. Only the Limousin oaks will do, for the essences of this wood blend perfectly with the brandy inside. In general, up to about 40 years, the longer the brandy remains in the cask, the finer the bouquet and the deeper the brownish color derived from the oak's tannin.

pot-still

This is one of the old copper pot-stills, required by French law to be used to distill Cognac. The brouillis dripping from the spout will be collected and aged in barrels made from Limousin oak.

After 40 years, it depends upon the brandy and how it is stored as to whether further benefit will result from aging.

Throughout the aging, continual evaporation (mostly of the alcohol) is taking place. Five to ten percent of the brandy will be lost to evaporation the first two years, then the rate will decrease. Ten casks of wine will, after aging, produce one cask of Cognac! Only in this extravagant way can nature produce this great brandy — and now we understand the high cost of Cognac.

AREA DISTINCTIONS

The Cognac-producing region along the Charente River is delimited by the French government and carefully subdivided according to soil characteristics and quality of brandy yielded in each subarea. These subdivisions are no arbitrary matter — they are based on the fact that the amount of calcium or chalk in the soil has a very definite effect upon the grape vines. The more chalk, the better the quality of grapes for Cognac-destined white wine.

This was vividly illustrated by an experiment in 1860 by a French geologist named *Coquand*. *Coquand*, with a friend who was a professional wine taster, made a trip to the Charente region. Visiting vineyard after vineyard in the area, the geologist went directly to the fields and analyzed the chalk content of the soil, while his friend stayed inside and merely sniffed and tasted his host's brandy. They took notes separately, each evaluating the quality and characteristics of the Cognac brandies — one from the soil, the other directly from the grape, so to speak. At the end of the trip when they compared their findings, their notes tallied perfectly.

So this changing relationship of the soil to the brandy each area produces accounts for the division of the region into six zones. The grapes yielded in each zone have varying qualities of body, aroma and maturation time after distillation. The zones are the basis of categorizing Cognac.

The very best Cognac is called *Grande Champagne* (not to be confused with the sparkling Champagne wine, for the word Champagne originally meant "chalky soil"); the zone which produces it lies south of Cognac, the town. *Grande Champagne* Cognac ages slowly and is therefore expensive. At its peak it is heavy and has a strongly fragrant aroma and great depth of character, yet remains subtle on the palate.

The second zone lies to the south of *Grande Champagne* and surrounds the town of Jarnac. This zone and the Cognac it produces are called *Petite Champagne*. This Cognac ages more quickly and is for this reason less expensive than *Grande Champagne*. The majority of firms blend *Petite Champagne* and *Grande Champagne* in a prescribed ratio (a minimum of 60% *Grande Cham-*

pagne) and sell this blend under the name *Fine Champagne*. These two regions produce the very worst-tasting white wine in the region — and the very best Cognac! It seems the harsher the wine, the better the brandy.

The other four zones, the excellence of whose brandy runs in the order named, are *Borderies, Fins Bois, Bons Bois,* and *Bois Ordinaires.* This is also the order in which the Cognacs age more and more rapidly. The Cognac of *Borderies* is soft and full-bodied; those of the three *Bois* zones are lusty but lack a strong bouquet.

To provide variously priced Cognacs with balanced characteristics of body and finesse, firms blend the lesser and higher quality brandies. The produce of good years is retained to blend with that of poor years. And, as with *Fine Champagne,* this is regulated and labeled. The quality of the brandy product in large part depends upon the skill of the blender. Each firm tries to keep its Cognac the same over the years, making blending truly an art.

HOW COGNAC IS MADE

There are three factors which are the secret of fine brandy: the wine from which it is distilled, the mode of distillation (the best brandy is made in pot-stills), and the manner and type of wood in which it is aged. As we have said, Cognac is made from the most perfectly suited white wine ever used in brandy making. Now let's explore the manner of distillation and aging, for this process is very strictly defined for Cognac.

The brandymaker begins with white wine made from the acidic grapes of the region (*St. Emilion, La Folle Blanche,* and *Comombar* grapes). Then, by French law, Cognac brandy must be distilled in a pot-still. This is a turnip-shaped copper kettle set atop a brick oven.

Knowing that alcohol boils at a lower temperature than water, he slowly heats the wine in the pot. The alcohol boils and vaporizes; this vapor rises through a swan-necked tube, leaving the water behind. Passing through a condenser, the vapor is collected in another vessel where it cools and becomes liquid again.

The first of the distillation that comes through the still, called the head or *tête*, is too pungent to be used. This is also the case with the last of the distillation, called the tail or *queue*. The head and tail are discarded. Only the center, called the heart or *coeur*, is saved.

At this point the cloudy distilled liquid (*brouillis*) is absolutely undrinkable, and contains "only" 20 to 30 percent alcohol. So the brandymaker passes the *brouillis* through the pot-still a second time, again discarding the head and tail and retaining the heart. The second distillation is the *bonne chauffe* ("good distillate").

SELECTION OF COGNAC

There are symbols and abbreviations used to indicate the quality of a Cognac and guide you in selection. However, these symbols are rather loosely defined, and each blending firm defines them according to its own standards.

Three Star (★★★) designates the youngest and cheapest Cognac (remembering that age refers to length of time in *cask*). Three Star Cognac is generally aged three to six years. V.O. for Very Old, or V.E. for Very Extra, is usually seven to twelve years old. A better quality of Cognac is the V.S.O.P., which stands for Very Special Old Pale, aged 18 to 25 years. (Pale in this case is a contradictory name, since the older a Cognac is . . . that is, the longer it is in the barrel . . . the darker it is. Very Superior Old Brown would be more appropriate!) The very finest and oldest Cognac is labeled V.V.S.O.P. standing for Very Very Superior Old Pale. This brandy is at least 25 years old, and up to forty.

Because the interpretation of the symbols is up to the firms, the house brand is actually more important than the symbols. A reliable firm will have high standards and maintain uniformity in its blends. Therefore it is wise to buy well-known brands.

Ninety percent of the Cognac sold is Three Star. But you might consider it a better investment to buy V.S.O.P. or the other older Cognacs since casing, bottling, duty, and so on, cost the same for all . . . making the higher cost of a much finer brandy comparatively little in terms of the greater enjoyment you are certain to derive.

U.S. BRANDY

You may be surprised to learn that California produces more brandy than the whole of France! Most of the United States' grape brandy is distilled in continuous or column stills which are more modern, fast and mechanized than the old-fashioned pot-stills used to make Cognac. Unfortunately, this type of distillation eliminates many of the elements that give character and flavor to Cognac brandies. But body and smoothness are given to the final product through the addition of sugar, syrup and wine.

California brandy is aged about four to six years, in either new or used white oak barrels. Unlike the French brandies, no old stocks from "good years" are kept on hand for blending. Don't let this discourage you from trying the American brandies, especially for use in mixed, long drinks. They are also quite acceptable for cooking purposes.

Body, finesse, and age are the criterion in selecting brandy. If a brandy has body, the flavor expands on the palate but does not burn the tongue. Finesse refers to the fragrance or bouquet. (An easy way to test the finesse of a brandy is to thoroughly wet the inside of a glass with the brandy, then empty it. With fine Cognac, the fragrant aroma will cling to the glass for hours — or even days — after emptied.) In reference to age, most Cognac producers agree that Cognac reaches perfection at about 40 years in the cask. Of course in most cases you will not be able to buy a brandy that is purely 40 years old, for most Cognacs are blends of different types and years. However, V.V.S.O.P. of a good house brand may be relied upon to assure a well-aged brandy.

HOW TO SERVE BRANDY

There is no doubt that the drinking of a fine old brandy is one of the most pleasurable ways to climax a meal. It is also a wonderful nightcap or bracer.

You should serve your brandy in medium-sized, narrow-necked glasses called balloons or tulips. Both (especially the balloon) are shaped deliberately to preserve and "show off" the fragrance of the brandy.

Warming the brandy before drinking releases the bouquet, but the manner of warming is important to attain full pleasure. Although you may see it done in some restaurants, it is an injustice to warm your brandy over a flame. This will shock the bouquet into rapid dispersal, shortening your enjoyment. Instead, cradle the glass in both hands, "nursing" it and warming it with the warmth of your hands. Within a few minutes, you will no longer feel the glass because it and the brandy will have reached the temperature of your hands. Now you are ready to bury your nose in the matchless aroma, savor the fragrance and then sip.

Because brandy loses its delicate quality when exposed to the air too long, it is best not to keep it long in a decanter or open bottle.

champagne

Champagne is one of France's many contributions to civilization. There is a certain mystique which surrounds this clear, effervescent wine — it is inevitably served on special occasions such as weddings, anniversaries, christenings, even the launching of ships. Unfortunately, due to its association with gay celebrations, many individuals forget to appreciate the qualities that can make Champagne a fine or great wine. Consequently, it is often not treated with the same solemn respect that a still wine of the same quality is likely to receive.

Champagne has the delicate, fresh flavor of vine-ripened grapes. It is a dry wine, having a very low sugar content — just enough to counteract its slight acidity. When a bottle of Champagne is opened, its distinctive bouquet is unmistakable even from some distance, yet its pungent aroma retains the subtlety of the lightest of wines. Its columns of minute bubbles race from the bottom of the glass upward, releasing a rich, full-bodied flavor not usually found in still wines. Many sparkling wines attempt to compete with Champagne, but there are very few that can match the inimitable qualities of this delicious effervescent wine.

The Small Province of Champagne is in Northern France and, like Burgundy or Cognac, only wine produced there should be called by the name of the province. However, the universal popularity of this wine has created such a demand for it that vineyards the world over produce it in vast quantities, calling it "Champagne" with impunity.

The chalky soil of Champagne province is ideal for growing the grapes necessary to make a clean, dry white wine. The gently sloping hills are protected from the north and expose the ripening fruit to the sun, which is necessary for the proper development of sugar in the grapes. Since the vineyards of Champagne are so far north (they are the closest to England of all French vineyards) the harvest comes late in the season and the grapes have a smaller amount of sugar than those grown further to the south. Because of the low sugar content of the pressed grapes, the fermenting process takes longer — hence, with the onset of the cold winter months, the fermentation is interrupted. The arrival of spring and warmer weather, triggers another fermentation period. This so-called "second fermentation" is responsible for the formation of carbon dioxide gas, producing the bubbles in Champagne which improve the flavor and delight the eye as well.

Dom Pérignon, a monk at the Abbey of Hautvillers in Champagne, is credited with the discovery of champagne about 1700. He actually did not discover the wine, but devised a method of bottling it which preserved its effervescence by sealing the bottles with tightly fitting corks during the second fermentation period. The corks were securely wired in place so the pressure built up by the carbon dioxide did not force them out, and thick-walled bottles were used to prevent explosion. The pressure inside an unopened champagne bottle can reach more than 120 pounds per square inch.

Prior to the time *Dom Pérignon* served as cellarmaster of the Abbey, the champagne bottles were stopped with rags soaked in olive oil to keep out vinegar bacteria. Of course the fizzy quality of the wine escaped into the air and the champagne was merely a still, dry, white wine. Some modern experts feel that *Dom Pérignon*'s most important contribution was his blending technique. By carefully combining the wines of several different vineyards in the area, he found that a superior wine could be created. The practice of blending has been continued into modern times in order to produce Champagne of consistent quality and character. Thus, strictly speaking, there is no such thing as "vintage Champagne."

Thanks to the ingenuity of *Dom Pérignon* and his innovations of blending and cork bottle stoppers, the monks at Hautvillers found to their extreme delight that instead of the frail, tart, still white wine to which they were accustomed, they now had a full-bodied, sparkling wine, more delicious than any they had tasted.

There was still one serious problem yet to be solved. One of the by-products of the second fermentation was a sediment which collected in the Champagne bottles; it was simply a collection of dead yeast cells which made the otherwise clear wine, cloudy and dark. Eighteenth century wine glasses were even constructed of frosted glass which hid the unappetizing appearance of the sediment-filled Champagne. Filtering the Champagne was found to be unsuccessful, since all the bubbles escaped during the filtering process, leaving a clear but flat wine. The problem was to devise a way of extracting the sediment while the wine was under pressure or with the pressure released only for a moment.

A clever genius of a woman, *Madame Clicquot*, was responsible for solving the problem of ridding the Champagne of its unwanted sediment without losing its sparkling quality. After the death of her husband, who owned a vineyard, she carried on the business, building a fine reputation for the wine bearing her husband's name. *Madame Clicquot* pondered the problem at length and finally arrived at a solution — invert the bottles and allow the sediment to collect on the cork. To do this, she had a

long table bored with holes large enough to accomodate the inverted Champagne bottles. She found it necessary to give a gentle shake to some of the bottles which served to jar the sediment off the insides. This procedure was called *remuage* or moving. The next stage was the actual removal of the cork and sediment, called *dégorgement*. This was achieved by holding the bottle upside down, cutting the string or wire, removing the cork and pouring off the first two inches of wine containing the sediment. A small amount of still wine was then added or "topped up" to replace the wine which had been removed and a new clean cork forced into the bottle to be secured with string or wire. Since many people preferred the Champagne sweeter than in its natural state (it was completely sugarless and dry at the end of the second fermentation period), the topping-up wine was mixed with sugar and a stabilizing drop or two of brandy. This mixture became known as the *dosage*. The degree of sweetness of Champagne was easy to control, since it depended on the amount of sugar in the *dosage*. *Brut*, the driest Champagne, had almost no sugar added to the topping-up wine; *sec* had a small amount, *demi-sec* slightly more; and *doux* a generous amount. The sweeter Champagnes were generally less expensive, as the sugar helped to conceal inferior qualities.

The grapes used in making Champagne are usually taken from three varieties: Pinot Noir, Pinot Blanc, and Pinot Chardonnay. The rich and full-bodied Pinot Noir is perhaps one of the most versatile grapes in common use. Its excellence is always recognized in the finest of the red wines of Burgundy. On the other hand, it is the basis for the palest of Champagnes. Although the outside of the Pinot Noir skin is a deep blue-black, the inner surface is red and the natural juice white and clear. For Champagne, therefore, the skins must be removed as quickly as possible after crushing as in the production of any white wine, since the liquid begins to take on the tint of the grape skins when the tannin is released during fermentation. Eventually, the juices of both white-skinned and black-skinned grapes are blended to achieve the delicate balance of flavor and shading which are the hallmark of this pinnacle of the vintner's art.

The exact proportions of the Champagne blends vary from brand to brand, for it is customary for each winery to attempt to preserve the distinctiveness of its product. To accomplish this, vats of older wine are maintained, eventually to be mixed with new wine. Batches of wine which are produced by these blendings, called *cuvées*, are the basis for nearly all the Champagne intended for commercial distribution. There is, however, one exception to this procedure. The most expensive Champagnes — though some doubt the qualities attributed to them — are made from the first and gentlest pressing of the grapes, or the *tête de cuvée*. These are mixed in the usual way, except that they remain unblended with older vattings.

Clearly one of the most delicate and important stages in the production of Champagne is the blending of the *cuvée*, whose character and excellence eventually will be tested in the account books of the firm selling the Champagne. Accordingly, in the spring of each year the directors and professional tasters of the firm meet in the winery's tasting room to judge the several pressings and to establish the blend which will represent their name in the wineshops of the world. At this point the wines are quite different in flavor and appearance from the sparkling wine they will become. Professional expertise is required in sampling these rather acidic and often unpalatable liquids as the quality of the final product will depend on how well these ingredients are selected and proportioned. But this is only the beginning of a complex and costly process which will result in the most versatile and one of the most delicious of wines.

Since the time of *Dom Pérignon* and *Madame Clicquot*, the manufacture of Champagne, universally referred to as *la methode Champenoise*, has changed very little in principle. Modern machinery and scientific technology have, of course, introduced refinements and streamlined some of the steps, but none of these innovations can surpass the skill and patience of the solitary laborers working down in the chilly, chalk-lined wine cellars of Champagne. There are, of course, other ways of making effervescent wines, but these produce Champagnes of decidedly inferior quality. The tank method, which is similar in principle to the brewing of beer, and impregnation, in which carbon dioxide gas is injected into a strong white wine before bottling, are cheaper ways of manufacturing sparkling wines in large quantities. Technically, wines produced by these methods should not be called "Champagnes" at all.

HOW TO SERVE CHAMPAGNE

Champagne should be served well chilled, but it should never be frozen. Wine, like all "living things" should never be made to withstand temperature extremes or violent shocks. When opening the bottle do not allow the cork to fly across the room — too much wine and sparkle will escape. Wrap the neck of the bottle in a napkin or towel and tilt the bottle about 45 degrees. Grasp the cork in the other hand and slowly twist the cork out of the bottle. An audible pop will accompany the release of the cork from the bottle and the Champagne is ready to pour.

One common mistake made by many restaurants is to serve Champagne in a wide-mouthed, shallow, stemmed glass. This type of glass aids and abets the escape of the bubbles which the vintners took such pains to put into their wine in the first place. The most appropriate glass (and one that helps to retain the sparkle) in which to serve Champagne is a clear, tulip shaped goblet with the rim bent slightly toward the center. It should be chilled and filled not more than two-thirds full.

CHAMPAGNE PUNCH

1 c. orange juice, chilled
2 c. lemon juice, chilled
2 ½ c. Basic Sugar Syrup *(Breads, pg. 14)*
1 qt. Sauterne, chilled
2 qt. soda water, chilled
1 qt. Champagne, chilled
Ice Ring

Combine juices, sugar syrup and Sauterne and pour into the punch bowl. Just before serving pour the soda water into the punch mixture, then add the Champagne. Stir the punch once or twice, just to mix. Float the ice ring in the punch. Serve in Champagne glasses. This makes about 20 cups of punch.

How To Make An Ice Ring:

Bring enough water to fill desired mold to a boil, then let stand until cool. This will remove air from the water and makes a crystal clear ice. Prepare fresh fruit slices or pieces, sprigs of mint or other green leaves, grapes or any desired decorative foods to place in the mold. Partially freeze a layer of the boiled water in your chosen mold. Chill remaining water. Layer the decorative fruits and greenery on the first slush-like layer. Partially cover this layer with very cold boiled water and freeze thoroughly. Fill mold with remaining water and freeze. Wrap a hot, wet towel around the mold to unmold and float the ice ring on top of prepared drink or punch.

HOW TO MAKE ICE BUCKETS FOR CHAMPAGNE

Select a plastic bucket of the desired size and shape for the mold, making certain that the finished ice buckets will be capacious enough to accommodate the size Champagne bottle being served. Fill the bucket with cold water. If you wish to tint your ice buckets, stir in vegetable food coloring, drop by drop, until the desired shade is achieved. Freeze until only the center remains soft and the water walls are hard. Remove from the freezer and scoop out enough of the central semi-ice to allow an empty quart beer bottle (securely wrapped in three thicknesses of aluminum foil) to be sunk in. Weight the beer bottle with enough pebbles or dry beans to keep it steadily in place. Return to freezer. On the day before the bucket is to be used, immerse the plastic mold to within 1/2 inch from the top rim in hot water until the ice (with the bottle still in the center) slides out of the plastic. Firmly grasp the foil-covered bottle and gently pull until the bottle slides out. Stuff the centers with foil and return to the freezer until the last possible moment. Make certain that the tray you use to hold the ice bucket has enough depth to catch the runoff as the ice bucket begins to melt. Insert the chilled bottle of Champagne in the Ice Bucket just before serving

how to make
a champagne
fountain

Champagne is considered by many to be an indispensable part of any special occasion. Why not add drama and excitement to the service of the Champagne by creating a Champagne Fountain? This will not involve any extra expense at all (all that is necessary is 23 wine glasses) and the spectacular effect is certain to turn the celebration into a gala event!

A Champagne Fountain is a pyramid of tiered wine glasses arranged contiguously. The bottom tier of the fountain as shown in the illustration has twelve glasses, the next has seven, the third has four and the top has one. The following rules must be followed to ensure a successful result:

1. Choose identical glasses without defects. If even one is slightly different from the rest, the fountain will not work.
2. The glasses from the bottom up must be placed as closely together as the widest central area of the Champagne glasses or tulips will permit.
3. The fountain should be poured by an individual with an absolutely firm hand. The pouring must be slow, deliberate and steady.
4. For obvious reasons, the wise person will first practice pouring the fountain with plain tap water.

It is not essential to use only 23 glasses for this pyramid structure. If you wish to increase the numbers, keep in mind that you must have the glasses bowl to bowl so that there is a 1/4-inch gap left between the rims of every pair of glasses at the point where the bowls are touching. Place the center of the base of each glass in the next tier directly over this 1/4-inch gap.

The last point to remember is to pour the Champagne into the very center of the glass in the uppermost tier. This is extremely important in order that the wine (or whatever potable is chosen to be served in the fountain) may cascade evenly into the tier of glasses below. They in turn will overflow into the next tier, and so on until the liquid has filled the bottom tier 2/3 full which is the correct amount for any wine glass to be filled. At this point, stop pouring! To avoid spills when serving the completely filled glasses of champagne (on the upper tiers,) it is a wise precaution to pour the surplus wine into empty glasses which have been discreetly placed within reach of the fountain.

champagne fountain

A sure way to turn a party or reception into a festive gala is to serve the Champagne or punch in this delightful Champagne Fountain. While not a terribly difficult trick to master, it is wise to rehearse with tap water the day before you plan to display your newly acquired skill.

presenting
red wines of bordeaux

Red Bordeaux wine (also called Claret by the British) is known as the queen of wines because of its characteristic delicate, feminine qualities. These attributes are not born with the wine but develop gradually as the wine ripens into maturity. Generally speaking, a young Red Bordeaux is a sturdy, almost brash wine which, given time, softens into serene and gentle authority with a velvety, subtle — yet full — flavor and bouquet.

Bordeaux is considered by most wine experts to be the most important wine region in France. Over half of the world's fine wines come from France and approximately one-half of these are produced in Bordeaux. This fertile section, located in the southwestern part of the country produces every type of unfortified wine — both light and robust reds, sweet as well as dry whites and some *rosés*. These wines range from the highest quality vintages (with commensurate price tags) to the most humble of the local pressings which are sold for pennies per bottle and are considered *vin très ordinaire*, not worth shipping out of the district.

There are several distinct varieties of grapes which are grown for the production of Red Bordeaux wine. These include Cabernet Sauvignon and Cabernet Franc, the Merlot and, of less importance, the Malbec and the Petit Verdot.

Cabernet Sauvignon is the classic variety of grape used in making red wine although the Cabernet Franc yields a greater volume of juice. The Merlot is also a prolific producer of wine and it has the added advantage of being an early ripener. The Malbec and Petit Verdot are less significant than either of the Cabernets or the Merlot but the inclusion of a small percentage of them in the total planting is considered beneficial to the vintage.

In the production of Red Bordeaux wine, most vintners do not plant just one type of vine, but a combination of several varieties. By adjusting the proportions of the different strains of grapes being planted, the characteristics of the wine can, to a large extent, be regulated. For example, a vintage consisting of 75 percent Cabernet Sauvignon, 10 percent Cabernet Franc, 10 percent Merlot and five percent Malbec will produce a wine quite different from a vintage of 60 percent Cabernet Sauvignon, 30 percent Merlot and 10 percent Petit Verdot. Each vintner has his own method of mixing the grape strains when planting vines, hence, the distinctive qualities of the wine produced in one vineyard will be markedly different from those of the wine grown in a neighboring château, even though the soil, climate and general layout of the land is identical.

To a novice, becoming familiar with the red wines of Bordeaux seems at first to be an impossible task. The endless array of names of châteaux and the infinite variety of labels may appear to be a hopelessly complex system to master. Actually, it's much simpler than it looks.

Any wine produced within the boundaries of the Bordeaux region as specified by the *appellation contrôlée* laws may be called Bordeaux. This primary step in nomenclature, however, only guarantees the origin of the wine — it says nothing of the quality.

In order to procure a really excellent Claret, the buyer must have more specific information than just the point of origin. Bordeaux is divided by law into two dozen districts. Some of these sections produce mediocre-to-fair wines, the majority produce average-to-good, but there are five which are renowned for consistently yielding some of the world's greatest wines. They are: Médoc, Graves, St.-Émilion and Pomerol, all famous for their red wines, and Sauternes, especially noted for its superior white dessert wines.

Médoc. A bottle of wine labeled with the name of a reliable shipper and the name Médoc is certain to be a satisfactory wine possessed with individual qualities which set it apart from wines of other districts. The Médoc is divided into two sections, the Haut-Médoc (high-Médoc) and the Médoc (which used to be called "low" or Bas-Médoc). Of the two sections, most experts agree that the best wines come from the Haut-Médoc.

The Haut-Médoc is subdivided into 28 municipalities referred to as communes. Four of the most famous of these communes are Margaux, Pauillac, St.-Estèphe and St.-Julien. Thus, a wine labeled *appellation contrôlée* and Pauillac stipulates that the wine comes from a small but excellent commune in the Haut-Médoc district of Bordeaux, France.

The final bit of information needed to classify a bottle of fine Bordeaux wine is the name of the specific vineyard in the commune which produced it. Individual vineyards in Bordeaux are traditionally called châteaux (pronounced sha-tō). The châteaux owners protect the reputation of their name with the utmost care. Some are so guarded about this that during those vintage years they consider to be inferior, they will not allow their name to appear on the wine label, or will simply sell the entire crop under the shield of anonymity. Château wine is always marked with the vintage year and is never blended with wines grown outside the boundaries of the château — it is always wine from the same year and harvest.

Graves. Unfortunately, red Graves is often treated with mild disinterest because people confuse it with a sweetish and undistinguished mass-produced white wine which is also marketed under the name Graves. The true red Graves are very fine, comparable to many of the top wines of Médoc. There are also excellent white wines grown in this district.

St.-Émilion produces a greater volume of wine than the Médoc and a good deal of it is marketed under the name of St.-Émilion, without the name of a particular château. There are, however, several very famous châteaux in this district, including Châteaux Cheval-Blanc and Ausone. St.-Émilion is held in high esteem in England where its wines are thought to be the most full-flavored and richest of all the Bordeaux red wines.

Pomerol. Some individuals judge the wines grown in Pomerol to be similar to those grown in the neighboring district of St.-Émilion. However, the most discriminating wine connoisseurs insist that Pomerol wines have their own distinctive characteristics, including a very subtle underlying flavor described as "truffle taste."

It is widely agreed that the very finest red wines of Bordeaux are produced by Médoc, Graves, St.-Émilion and Pomerol. There are, however, other sections of Bordeaux which also produce red wines and while they may not be of the same supreme quality as those mentioned above, they are good, adequate *vin ordinaire*, perfectly acceptable to be drunk as table wine.

The art of producing fine Red Bordeaux or Claret is no longer a monopoly of the French. In the past, the California wine industry has not often been credited with producing fine or great wines comparable to those of France. However, much progress has been made over the last four decades in perfecting wine-making techniques and the result has been an overall improvement in the quality of the table wines produced in this fertile state. After Prohibition ended in 1933, laws were passed to regulate the industry and a highly developed wine technology evolved, largely under the sponsorship of the University of California. Through this expanded knowledge of wine production, the previously undistinguished *vin ordinaire* (generally intended for immediate consumption on the domestic market) was transformed into excellent table wines, a few of which rival some of France's fine vintages.

The best California Red Bordeaux or Claret-type wines are grown in the cool climate of the area around San Francisco near the Pacific Ocean. These wines are marketed under the name of the grape, not the French wine names or the name of the district in which they are grown. Accordingly, Red Bordeaux that is manufactured in California will be labeled Cabernet Sauvignon or, in some instances, Claret.

introducing tea

A small oriental bush provides modern man with a refreshing beverage. The young leaves of the tea plant, an evergreen shrub native to the Orient, when picked and dried, make a beverage that is enjoyed as a refreshing summertime lift or a warm winter restorative.

The name "tea" comes from the Chinese word "Tay." The origin of the beverage can be traced to the necessity in many countries of boiling water to make it suitable for drinking. Boiling the water makes it flat and tasteless, however, the addition of tea leaves yields a warm and stimulating drink.

Tea has been a popular beverage in many countries for many years. It originated in China about 800 A.D. and the beverage soon was passed to neighboring Japan. In Japan, serving tea became an elaborate ritual, the tea ceremony. Tea was introduced in Europe in the early seventeenth century by Dutch tradesmen. The English custom of afternoon tea — high tea or low tea — became world famous. The American Colonies, as part of the British Empire, imported tea from England until the War of Independence. Even though it was several years after 1776 before tea drinking again became stylish in America, the practice did resume and today drinking tea is a common American custom.

The types of tea vary with both geographical location and method of preparation. Green tea or "bancha," associated with Japan, makes a light, slightly bitter brew. Oolong, another oriental tea, is a semifermented aromatic tea. Black tea is the most common and popular of all teas. The leaves are completely dried and fermented before processing. It is graded according to both flavor and size of leaf. The types of black teas include Ceylon, Darjeeling, Souchang and Sumatra.

The best tea is made with freshly drawn water which is boiled and poured over a measured amount of tea leaves then allowed to steep for 5 minutes. It is preferable to use a china or pottery teapot. Instant tea, which consists of pulverized tea with malto dextrin added as a preservative, is also available. Tea has no nutritive value. It does contain *theine*, a stimulant which is similar to the caffeine in coffee.

chinese tea

According to Chinese custom, only the freshest, most flavorful tea leaves available should be used in the making of tea. Here are three beautiful Chinese teapots filled with delicate Chinese tea. The dainty handleless teacups are typically oriental.

CHURCHWARDEN

1 lemon
6 cloves
1 bottle red Bordeaux
½ recipe Japanese Tea
Sugar to taste

Stud the lemon with the cloves and place in a small baking dish. Bake in a preheated 225-degree oven until the lemon is lightly browned. Heat the Bordeaux in a large saucepan. Do not boil. Place the lemon in the Bordeaux, then stir in the tea and sugar until the sugar is dissolved. Bring just to the boiling point and serve immediately. This makes about 8 servings.

JAPANESE TEA

Boiling water
2 tbsp. green tea

Fill a china or enameled teapot with boiling water and let stand for several minutes to heat. Pour all the water out of the teapot. Place the tea in a tea ball*, then place in the teapot. Pour 6 cups boiling water into the teapot. Cover and let steep for 5 minutes. Remove tea ball, then serve the tea immediately. The tea may be served with sugar, if desired. This makes 6 servings. (*A tea ball is a perforated metal container with a screw-on lid and a hanging chain.)

HOW TO MAKE MINT TEA

1 Assemble the teapot, green tea, lumps of sugar, rose water and tea glasses on a tray. Heat the teapot. Place 2 heaping teaspoons of green tea in the teapot and pour 1 cup of boiling water over the tea. Stir well.

2 Bruise 6 large sprigs of mint with your hands and pack the mint into the teapot. Pour enough boiling water into the teapot to fill nearly to the top.

3 Add desired amount of sugar and 2 teaspoons of rose water and stir until the sugar is dissolved. Lift the teapot high in the air and fill 1 tea glass with tea. Pour back into the teapot, then repeat the process 3 times. Serve immediately. Tea may be served in teacups, if desired.

introducing sherry

Of all the wines produced in Spain, sherry is the most famous. Sherry is also produced outside Spain in such countries as South Africa, Australia and the United States (some California sherries are excellent), but many connoisseurs insist that no one can successfully duplicate the delicate, unforced and appealing wine that comes from southern Spain. Spanish sherry is produced only in the triangle formed by three towns in southern Spain: Jerez (or Jerez de la Frontera), Sanlúcar de Barrameda and Puerto de Santa Maria. The Spanish government does not allow any wine to be labeled sherry except that which is grown within this area.

Sherry is a fortified wine — brandy is added after the fermentation period to increase the alcoholic content to between 15½ and 18% . There are two main categories of sherry — *fino* and *oloroso*. *Finos* are the lightest in color of all the sherries, a pale, golden wine with a bouquet that is reminiscent of a freshly picked apple, with just the suggestion of the flavor of almonds. A *fino* sherry is less robust than an *oloroso*, and has a delicate and subtle quality. It is ideal to serve as an *aperitif* or with the soup course of a formal dinner. It is also a suitable accompaniment for a fish course featuring a rich fish, such as salmon, swordfish or eel.

Olorosos are the sweet or dessert sherries. Although the word *oloroso* is Spanish for fragrant, the natural *oloroso* sherries in fact have considerably less bouquet and flavor than the *finos*. Consequently, they are sweetened and blended before they are sold, some are made into Cream Sherry, others into Brown Sherry and still others into Golden Sherry. Sweet sherry is best at the end of a meal with cheese or nuts. (A dessert sherry is not appropriate with a rich, heavy, sweet dessert.)

The grapes from which sherry is produced are always of the white varieties. About ninety percent of the sherry grapes are of the Palomino variety; the other 10% includes Pedro Ximénez, Mantúo, Albillo and Cañocazo. The chalky soil of the sherry-growing region is excellent for producing these fresh, clean tasting grapes. It is perhaps surprising that even in the intense heat of summer in southern Spain, the vines remain lush and green in spite of the fact that the fields are not irrigated and there is little or no rain. All the moisture needed for the growth of the vines is obtained from the subsoil. The sunbaked earth of the vineyards is plowed to a depth of three feet before the grapes are planted. Constant cultivation of the soil is necessary so that the moisture will rise from the subsoil to nourish the roots of the vines, thus ensuring a healthy, bountiful crop.

By harvest time, the grapes are plump, golden and very sweet, a result of the abundant warm sunshine common to this area of Spain. The high concentration of sugar is not quite enough to produce a strong wine, so after being harvested, the grapes are carefully laid out on grass mats in the sun to allow further development of the sugar content of the grapes. This may last only a few hours for a light sherry, to a week or more for the heavy, dark, dessert wines.

The grapes are still sometimes pressed by the centuries-old method of men treading them by foot, but more often than not this task is accomplished by machines. As soon as the juice referred to as *must* (*mosto* in Spanish) starts to run, it is channeled into waiting barrels (called butts). The high sugar level of the *must*, combined with the warm weather and the abundance of yeast cells, produces the immediate onset of fermentation. The butts of fermenting *must* are quickly transported to the *bodegas* where the *must* will live and grow into sherry. The *bodegas* are huge white sheds, whose tall gothiclike arches inevitably invite comparison to cathedrals. Inside, among the cool dim shadows of these immense storage sheds, the butts are stacked three high, in long rows that extend from one end of the *bodega* to the other.

After several months of fermentation, the wine is ready to be classified by type. It is tasted by experts who determine whether the wine in each cask will be light, a *fino*, or heavy, an *oloroso*. Incredible as it seems, prior to this time, the vintner cannot be certain what type of sherry will be produced from the vintage. For example, from two casks of wine, the contents of each yielded by the same grapes which were harvested on the same day in one particular field, one cask might offer the promise of delicacy, full flavor and bouquet, while the other contains a wine which is dull and flat, not likely to be worth marketing without the addition of strong brandy to improve its poor quality. The first cask will be declared to be a *fino* and the second, after being blended with brandy and sugar, will become an *oloroso*. Although the riddle of *olorosos* and *finos* has been somewhat exaggerated (vintners know from experience what type

of sherry is most likely to be produced from a given area) there is always the element of chance to be reckoned with — until the wine is tasted after the fermentation period, no one can be positive about the exact type of sherry contained in each cask. One fascinating characteristic of a *fino* is its tendency to grow *flor*, a white yeast growth that develops on the surface of the wine as long as it remains in the cask. The *olorosos* develop little or no *flor* and no one seems to know exactly why — it's almost certain, however, that the mysterious *flor* is the key to the difference between *finos* and *olorosos*. After classification, the wine is poured off into clean casks, slightly fortified with pure alcohol and stored in separate "nurseries" according to their type, until aged.

In order to maintain uniform standards of quality from one year to the next, sherry vintners use a system of blending called the *solera* system. A *solera* is a group of barrels of wine arranged in a particular order according to age. Part of the contents of the oldest barrel is drawn out to be bottled and is replaced by some of the wine from the second oldest barrel which is refilled from the third oldest barrel and so on, until all the barrels are full again. The wine is continually processed through the *solera* system with new wine going in at one point and the aged wine coming out from the other end to be bottled. The wine selected to replenish the wine in the youngest barrel will be taken from a nursery of sherry deemed to be the closest in character to that particular *solera*. A direct result of the *solera* system is that sherry is never identified by vintage year.

When wine is blended in this manner, the raw, young wine gradually assumes the character and refinements of the older wine with which it is mixed. It takes only a minute amount of old sherry to effect the desired improvements in a much larger quantity of new wine. After years of successive drawing off and adding to the sherry barrels in a *solera*, there will still be traces of the original wine contained in the *solera* at its inception, enough so that subsequent wines added decades later will inherit those fine qualities that only age can bestow.

At the time the sherry is to be bottled, it is generally too dry to be drunk as is, especially in the case of the *olorosos*. Thus further blending is necessary to transform it into the sweet, nut-like wine that sherry lovers enjoy. This final blending may involve the addition of a very sweet, almost molasses-like sherry made from grapes which had turned to raisins before being pressed, and/or a very old sherry, too strong to be drunk by itself, but somehow able to add a mellowness and discipline which is essential to all fine sherries. Because the demand for sweeter sherries is prevalent in the United States and Britain, while many Europeans generally prefer the lighter drier types of the *fino* variety, the blending techniques and practices of each vintner depends on the market he intends to reach.

INTRODUCING RUM

Because Christopher Columbus established the sugarcane plantations in the West Indies, it is a logical conclusion that he was indirectly responsible for the invention of rum, an important by-product of the sugarcane industry. Rum is an alcoholic beverage, distilled from the fermented juice of sugarcane syrup or molasses. There are many varieties of this popular liquor ranging from the very light Puerto Rican rum to the heavy dark Jamaican rum. Light, dry rums come from Puerto Rico, the Virgin Islands and the United States; these are always sold under a silver or white label. A golden or amber label or a rum bottle indicates a darker, sweeter rum, generally manufactured in Jamaica, Barbados, Martinique, Demerara or New England. An easy rule of thumb for serving rum is to use the lighter types for cocktails and heavy dark rum for tall drinks.

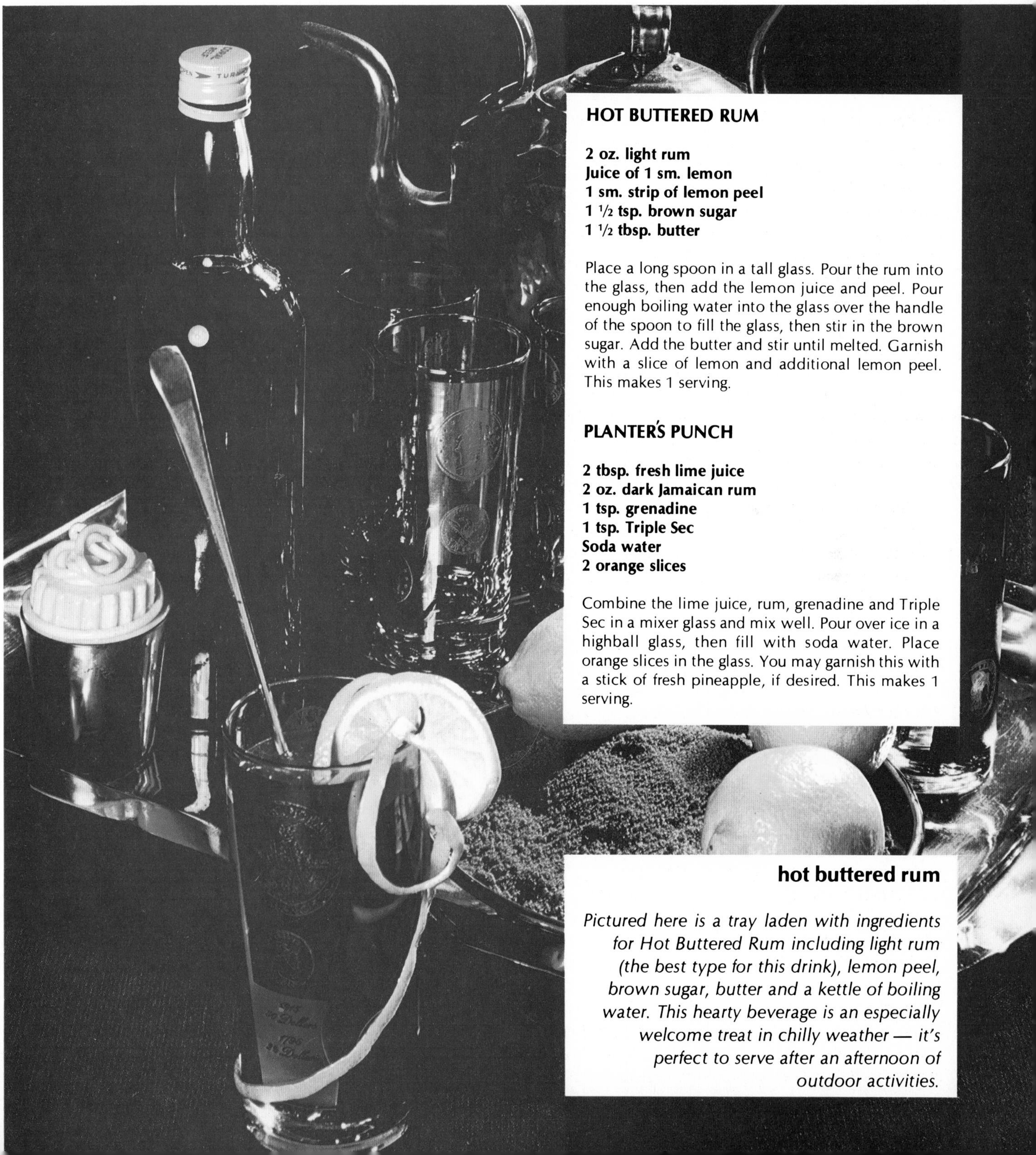

HOT BUTTERED RUM

2 oz. light rum
Juice of 1 sm. lemon
1 sm. strip of lemon peel
1 ½ tsp. brown sugar
1 ½ tbsp. butter

Place a long spoon in a tall glass. Pour the rum into the glass, then add the lemon juice and peel. Pour enough boiling water into the glass over the handle of the spoon to fill the glass, then stir in the brown sugar. Add the butter and stir until melted. Garnish with a slice of lemon and additional lemon peel. This makes 1 serving.

PLANTER'S PUNCH

2 tbsp. fresh lime juice
2 oz. dark Jamaican rum
1 tsp. grenadine
1 tsp. Triple Sec
Soda water
2 orange slices

Combine the lime juice, rum, grenadine and Triple Sec in a mixer glass and mix well. Pour over ice in a highball glass, then fill with soda water. Place orange slices in the glass. You may garnish this with a stick of fresh pineapple, if desired. This makes 1 serving.

hot buttered rum

Pictured here is a tray laden with ingredients for Hot Buttered Rum including light rum (the best type for this drink), lemon peel, brown sugar, butter and a kettle of boiling water. This hearty beverage is an especially welcome treat in chilly weather — it's perfect to serve after an afternoon of outdoor activities.

HAPPY MARRIAGE

2 c. Hot Chocolate, cooled
1 c. cold strong coffee
Sugar to taste
¾ c. brandy
¾ c. whipping cream, whipped

Combine the chocolate and coffee in a mixing bowl, then sweeten to taste. Whip vigorously with a wire whisk until frothy. Stir in the brandy, then pour into 2 tall glasses. Spoon whipped cream on top and serve with long spoons for stirring. This may be served hot in mugs, if desired. This makes 3 servings.

HOT CHOCOLATE

4 c. milk
1 vanilla pod or 1 tsp. vanilla extract
1   6-oz. package chocolate chips
½ c. sugar
Pinch of salt
1 ½ c. boiling water

Scald the milk with the vanilla pod, then remove the vanilla pod. Place the chocolate chips in the top of a double boiler and melt according to the instructions (Desserts, pg. 49). Stir in the sugar and salt and place the top of the double boiler over hot, not boiling, water. Add the boiling water slowly, stirring constantly, then stir until blended. Add the milk gradually, stirring constantly, then leave over the hot water for 1 minute. Remove the top of the double boiler from the hot water. Beat the Hot Chocolate with a large wire whisk until frothy. Pour into cups and garnish with dollops of whipped cream. This makes about fourteen ½-cup servings.

The Creative Homemaker's Academy © MCMLXXIII
Selected Illustrations © B.P.C. Publishing Limited MCMLXX

introducing liqueurs

A liqueur or cordial (the term preferred by connoisseurs) is a sweetened spirit such as brandy, flavored with herbs, bark, fruits, nuts, seeds, leaves, flowers, or even honey. Artificial coloring in a solution of alcohol is frequently added to liqueurs to give a color suggestive of the flavoring agents used. For example, green coloring is often added to normally white (mint-flavored) Crème de Menthe and green Chartreuse; yellow coloring is added to Pineapple Brandy and yellow Chartreuse.

The word 'liqueur' is derived from the Latin liquefacere which means "to make liquid, dissolve or melt." The flavoring agents of liqueurs are in fact, macerated (melted) in distilled spirits such as brandy, whiskey or rum and then sweetened and redistilled. Because some flavorings are too delicate to withstand the heat of distillation, they are merely infused (steeped) into the spirits and then bottled. This method of producing liqueurs is considered by most experts to be inferior to the distilling method. A third means of producing a liqueur is similar to percolating coffee. The flavoring elements such as seeds, leaves, etc., are placed in the top section of a machine that operates on the same principle as an electric coffee percolator. An alcoholic spirit such as brandy is poured in the lower section which is then heated causing the spirit vapors to rise to the upper level containing the flavoring substances. The vapors thus become instilled with the essence of the flavoring elements. The vapors then condense in the lower section of the apparatus ready to be redistilled and/or bottled.

When the infused or flavored spirits are distilled, the liquid becomes clear and water white. This clarity has led to a great deal of confusion when distinguishing the difference between liqueurs and the clear white brandies or eaux-de-vie (waters-of-life), distilled from cherries (Kirsch), raspberries (Framboise), strawberries (Fraise), plums (Mirabelle, Quetsch, Slivovitz), and pears (eau-de-vie de Poires). These potent fruit brandies are not true liqueurs, though they may be served in their stead. Each one is distilled from a single fruit, is completely dry (no additional sweetening is added) nor do they have extra flavoring agents. Unlike eau-de-vie, a liqueur must contain two and one-half percent sugar and, like spirits, it must have an alcoholic volume of over 24 percent with the proof varying from 49° proof for Cherry Heering to 110° proof for green Chartreuse. Another term sometimes

used to refer to liqueurs is **ratafia.** At one time this word applied to any liqueur drunk at the ratification of a treaty or agreement. Today it usually is used to describe sweetened apéritifs, often homemade, based on wines.

Liqueurs are generally served with coffee at the end of a meal at which time they are supposed to act as an aid to digestion. For this reason, the French refer to them as un digestif. The glass is which a liqueur is served should be thin (preferably stemware), clear, to enjoy the visual beauty of the liquid, and capacious, to allow the flavor and bouquet to expand in the glass, thus ensuring the fullest appreciation of the cordials fine qualities. Liqueurs should be served in small portions — they are intended to be sipped, slowly savored on the palate, then swallowed, leaving a pleasant aftertaste and producing an agreeable sense of satisfaction.

The records of history show that methods of distilling water and aromatic liquids had probably been developed by the time of Hippocrates (400 B.C.). However, it was not until 900 A.D. that recorded instances of the distilling of alcoholic spirits occur, a technique practiced chiefly by the Arabs. Some experts argue that alcoholic distillates may have been made from grains in Northern Europe. The advent of liqueurs was probably the direct result of two factors: the widespread experimentation of European monks and alchemists who cultivated bark, leaves, roots and herbs for use in medicinal potions, and the popular practice of using wines and spirits as antiseptic agents for cleansing wounds.

Arnáu de Valanova, a 13th century Spanish physician and chemist was the first to write about combining spirits with herbs. He went on to publicize recipes for healing liqueurs, and is accredited, by some, with the distinction of actually inventing the first "tincture of alcohol and herbs possessed of curative powers." Arnáu based his mixture on a sweetened distillate to which he added extract of lemon, rose petals and orange blossoms. He later added tiny particles of gold, thought to be a reliable remedy for many ills. In time, Arnáu (who was considered a "radical") was thoroughly investigated by the Spanish Inquisition and condemned. Only through the intervention of the Pope, whose life had been saved by some of Arnáu's potions, was the sentence lifted.

Following Arnáu's death, liqueurs increased in popularity. During the 14th century, when the Black Death appeared in Europe, liqueurs and spirit tonics became highly prized. By the turn of the 15th century, Italy had become the leading center of liqueur manufacturing. Catherine de Médici's entourage of Florentine chefs took some of their favorite liqueur recipes with them to France, thus spreading the popularity of these cordials. In the 17th and 18th centuries, ladies of the English court began the tradition of serving imported French liqueurs as a post-prandial libation. They used small cordial pots which were often miniature replicas of their own silver teapots. The 19th century witnessed a dramatic increase in the consumption of liqueurs which has continued into modern times.

types or categories of liqueurs

Although there are hundreds of liqueurs in existence today, no attempt will be made to mention them all, since many are obscure types which are not available on the American market. The following are some of the very well-known and popular liqueurs which are listed by category.

HERB LIQUEURS

Bénédictine, one of the best-known of the herb liqueurs was invented in 1510 at the Bénédictine monastery in Fecamp, France, by Dom Bernardo Vincelli who was trying to perfect a tonic to restore and fortify the monks after their strenuous daily labors. In 1534, Francois I, King of France, honored the liqueur with his official approval. The monastery was destroyed in the French Revolution and Bénédictine was subsequently not seen for some 70 years. Its formula eventually was discovered by Alexandre Le Grand, a scholar who, quite by accident, found the priceless recipe while researching old manuscripts and records. Le Grand perceived the possibility of marketing the liqueur and established the company which today continues to manufacture and sell Bénédictine on a secular basis. It is an amber liqueur based on cognac and flavored with a number of herbs and essences.

The label contains the letters D.O.M., for the Latin, *Deo Optimo Maximo*, meaning 'to God, most good, most great.' A variation of this cordial is called *B and B* which identifies it as a blend of Bénédictine and brandy. It has more appeal to those individuals who prefer a drier liqueur than Bénédictine, and it was enormously popular with the Victorians.

In 1605, the recipe for Chartreuse (which is still a highly guarded secret) was given to the Carthusian monks of the Grande Chartreuse Monastery at Voiron near Grenoble, France by the *Maréchal d'Estrées*. They perfected the formula which called for 130 herbs, flowers, and secret ingredients combined with a brandy base. In 1793, the monks, who were to experience many unpredictable changes of fortune, were expelled from France, resulting in the interruption of the manufacture of Chartreuse. Several years later they were allowed to return to their monastery, only to be expelled again in 1903. Finding refuge in Tarragona, Spain, they began producing Chartreuse under a different name. Because the French government had confiscated most of the possessions of the Order, including the trademark *Chartreuse*, the monks began inscribing the labels on the bottles *Liquor fabriquée à Tarragone par les Peres Chartreux*. In 1938, the monks were allowed to return to their old monastery in Voiron and resumed production of Chartreuse under the original name. There are two kinds of Chartreuse: green (colored with chlorophyll) which is stronger at 110° proof and yellow (colored with saffron), which is sweeter and less potent at 75° proof.

La Vieille Cure, a golden liqueur similar to Bénédictine, is extremely popular in France. It is made of various brandies combined with 52 different herbs, at Cenon near Bordeaux, France, where it has been produced since the Middle Ages.

Mille Fiori, a pale gold Italian liqueur, is, as its name implies, made from a thousand Alpine flowers. It is sold in tall thin bottles, each containing a small twig. The twig usually will have sugar crystals adhering to it due to the high sugar content of the liqueur.

Izarra is a Basque liqueur which was originally manufactured in an attempt to duplicate Chartreuse. Like Chartreuse, two types are produced: green at 85° proof and yellow at 64° proof. The spirit base is Armagnac brandy and the flavor is derived from several herbs and plants including lavender and sage.

Raspail, said to have been originated by Franĉôis Raspail in 1847, is a French herb liqueur manufactured at Cenon. Its ingredients include a great many natural essences including myrrh, angelica and calamus which is an Eastern aromatic plant.

Drambuie is one of the three most popular liqueurs in the United States. In has a Scotch whiskey base sweetened with heather blossom honey, and is flavored with various herbs according to a secret formula given to the MacKinnon family by Bonnie Prince Charlie as a reward for saving his life. The name 'Drambuie' is derived from the

The Creative Homemaker's Academy © MCMLXXIII
Selected Illustrations © B.P.C. Publishing Limited MCMLXX

Gaelic *An Dram Buidheach*, meaning 'the drink that satisfies.' This delicious liqueur is still produced by the MacKinnon Clan descendants near Edinborough, Scotland.

Glen Mist, a much more recent invention than Drambuie, is made of Scotch whiskey, honey and sugar. Created by Hector MacDonald, its production was halted in Scotland during World War II due to the shortage of Scotch whiskey, sugar and honey. For a brief time it was manufactured in Eire, using Irish whiskey as a base, but in 1963, S. F. Hallgarten resumed production in Scotland where its manufacture (using Scotch whiskey again) has continued to the present.

Irish Mist is nearly identical to Glen Mist except that it is based on Irish whiskey.

LIQUEURS WITH ONE PREDOMINANT HERB

Annisette, another liqueur flavored with sweetened aniseed, is compounded according to a secret formula confided to Marie Brizard by a traveler from the West Indies. There are several versions of Annisette available today but the popular one is manufactured by the Brizard distillery in Bordeaux, France.

Kummel is a sweet, white caraway-flavored liqueur, distilled from grain alcohol. The well-known Bols distillery was producing Kummel as long ago as 1575. Some manufacturers allow sugar crystallization to take place after bottling which results in a product called **Kummel Crystalize.** This liqueur is especially popular in Russia, Poland and the Baltic countries.

Danziger Goldwasser, a clear cordial flavored with the essence of caraway and aniseed, sparkles with tiny flecks of gold which are added at the time of bottling. The addition of the golden flecks dates back to the Middle Ages when gold was thought to be a panacea for all ills.

Pernod, an anis-flavored green liqueur, is extremely popular as an *apéritif* in France. Similar to absinthe (which has been banned in France since 1915) it is safe to drink since it does not contain wormwood, one of the key ingredients in absinthe. Pernod is usually combined with water when it is served, giving it a cloudy appearance.

Crème de Menthe is one of the best known liqueurs, appearing on most beverage menus. Most firms that manufacture liqueurs produce a *Crème de Menthe* because of the popular demand for it. Based on mint flavoring, it is either green or white.

FRUIT LIQUEURS

One of the most delicious of all the fruit liqueurs is **Cherry Heering** which was first marketed during the 19th century in Copenhagen, Denmark by a young grocer's assistant named Peter Heering. Its true cherry flavor is not overpowered by excessive sweetness because of the large number of cherry stones used in the distilling process. Cherry Heering, which is extremely popular in the United States, is often served over crushed ice as a dessert liqueur.

Maraschino, another cherry liqueur, is widely used for cooking purposes, although it also flavors some mixed drinks.

Other stone fruit liqueurs include **Peach Brandy, Apricot Brandy** and **Crème de Prunelle** (plum brandy). All of these are made by methods employing the use of the stone kernels to obtain the best flavor.

Soft fruit liqueurs are comprised of two groups: berries and tropical fruits. The berry liqueurs include Blackberry, Raspberry (*Crème de Framboise*), Strawberry (*Crème de Fraises*), Wood Strawberry (*Crème de Fraises de Boises*), and Blackcurrant (*Crème de Cassis*, first produced in the 16th century by the monks near Dijon). The tropical fruits

distillery and museum at fécamp, france

The distillery and museum at Fécamp, France, where the world famous Bénédictine liqueur is made, was originally the site of the Bénédictine Monastery. The magnificently ornate architecture is in contrast to the Spartan lifestyle which prevailed at the monastery where the liqueur was invented by Dom Bernardo Vincelli in 1510.

used to flavor liqueurs include Banana (*Crème de Banane*), and Pineapple (*Crème d'Ananas*), which is based on rum. Note: These soft fruit liqueurs are not to be confused with the *eaux-de-vie*, which have almost identical French names, in that each liqueur has "crème de' as part of its descriptive title, indicating that it has been sweetened. *Eaux-de-vie* are never sweetened, hence are not classified as liqueurs.

CITRUS FRUIT LIQUEURS

Curaçao, a term which applies to most orange-flavored liqueurs, was originally made in Holland from the dried peel of bitter oranges imported from the island of Curaçao. Its popularity rapidly spread and soon many firms began producing *Curaçao* under various names such as *Triple Sec*, *Grand Marnier* and *Cointreau*. *Curaçaos* are generally clear white.

BEAN AND KERNEL LIQUEURS

The best known bean and kernel liqueurs are those based on coffee and chocolate flavorings. Not generally served as straight cordials, they are most often used as the flavoring ingredients in mixed drinks. *Crème de Cacao* and Royal Mint Chocolates (which can best be described as an alcoholic afterdinner mint in liquid form) are produced from cocoa beans. **Tia Maria, Kahlua, Kona Coffee Liqueur** and **Luana** are derived from the coffee bean. Noyaux has a pleasant almond flavor which comes from the peach and apricot kernels used in its distilling process.

MISCELLANEOUS

In a category unto itself is a mild Dutch liqueur known as **Advocaat,** made from egg yolks and brandy. Low in alcoholic content (between 15 and 18 percent) it is so thick it may be eaten with a spoon. It is often compared to eggnog.

distillation room at fécamp

The modern distillation room at the Bénédictine distillery is something of an anachronism in its location in the Fécamp museum. The ornate Renaissance architecture of the museum does not hint of the 20th century distillery located within its antiquated walls. These facilities are typical of most present-day liqueur distilleries.

château monbousquet

Château Monbousquet which is located just outside St.-Émilion, Bordeaux, France, is a typical example of a spacious château nestled among the lush green vineyards. The pastoral setting is peacefully reflected in the clear water of the small lake.

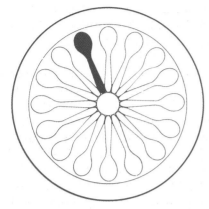

introducing
white wines
of bordeaux

The great wine-growing region of France known as Bordeaux, is unique compared to the other wine-growing areas — the quality of wine grown here is consistently good to excellent and the vines produce a yield of great magnitude: 130 million gallons or about one-half billion bottles of wine per year! Bordeaux is renowned for its supremely excellent red wines, known also as claret (see page 33). On a par with the finest of the clarets are the incredibly delicious sweet white dessert wines which come from Sauternes, the fifth of the five major wine-growing districts of the Bordeaux region. (The other four districts are Médoc, Graves, St.-Émilion and Pomerol. See page 34).

These rich, sweet white wines vary in color from the pale straw of a young Sauternes to the darker, almost brownish tinge of an aged Sauternes from Château d'Yquem, the undisputed monarch of all Sauternes-producing vineyards. It is important to realize that there is no such thing as a dry Sauternes — it is a contradiction in terms. There are many white wines produced in the United States which are labeled "sauterne" (a corruption of Sauternes) which is something of a misnomer. These wines are frequently of good to excellent quality but are comparatively dry, therefore, not a true Sauternes.

Anyone who is a lover of fine wines but has never before tasted a genuine Sauternes is bound to be surprised and delighted by its full, sweet, rich flavor. Quite unlike any of the sweetened fortified wines, Sauternes is a completely natural wine which derives all of its sweetness from the pressed grapes. There are no additives as there are, for example, in sherry or port which are fortified with a mixture of brandy and sugar. This fortifying process adds extra sweetness, checks the fermentation and increases the alcoholic content to about 20 percent. The alcoholic content of Sauternes is by nature fairly high, ranging from 13 percent to as high as 17 percent.

The key factor which is directly responsible for placing Sauternes in a distinctly different category from other white Bordeaux wines is called *pourriture noble* which is French for "noble rot." This rather unelegant but very descriptive name refers to the fungus *Botrytis cinerea*, which appears in late Autumn and "attacks" the sweet, ripe, juicy grapes, causing them to crack open and shrivel into raisins while still on the vine. With the onset of the shriveling process, the water content of the grapes is reduced and the sugar becomes highly concentrated. The juice pressed from these shriveled grapes is exceptionally sweet, a quality essential to making a fine Sauternes.

The mild damp September climate of Sauternes encourages the growth of the fungus which also appears in sections of Germany where Trockenbeerenaulsese, a wine quite similar to Sauternes is made, and the Tokay region of Hungary. The *pourriture noble* has never been seen in the California wine-growing valleys, which explains why most domestic sauterne bears only a faint resemblence to French Sauternes.

At harvest time, because the fungus does not do its work uniformly, only those grapes which have become shrivelled are picked, leaving the whole, unblemished ones to eventually wither and sweeten, at which time they, too, will be gathered for pressing. These conditions necessitate careful selection on the part of the workers who do the harvesting. The grapes must be picked individually, not in bunches as in other wine regions. Sometimes a field may be picked over five or six times before all the grapes are finally harvested. This extra time and effort which is so necessary to a good vintage will eventually be reflected in the price — an excellent Sauternes can be costly.

Weather conditions play an important role in the proper development of the *pourriture noble* as well as how it affects the grapes. Prolonged periods of rain or other weather-related disasters can completely inhibit the growth of the fungus which is so vital in the development of the sweet concentrated juice that is essential to a great Sauternes. Occasionally, a vintage is considered so inferior (due to the lack of sugar in the grapes) that the wine growers will sell their entire crop to shippers who then market the wine without the name of the château where it was grown, but simply labeled "Sauternes." In view of this, the most reliable rule to follow when looking for a superb Sauternes is to purchase a château-bottled wine from one of the highly rated châteaux. The owners of these vineyards jealously guard their reputations and permit only the best Sauternes to bear their names. (NOTE: It must be remembered that some of the lesser known vintners *do* sell very fine wine to shippers who market it without the name of a château on the label. Therefore, it is not always a valid assumption that Sauternes sold by a shipper will be of inferior quality.)

Some labels on Sauternes intended for the United States market are marked *Haut-Sauternes* rather than *Sauternes*. *Haut* (pronounced *oh*) is French for "upper" or "top" and its inclusion on a label implies that the contents of the bottle are of a better quality than a bottle marked only "Sauternes." The term is really quite ambiguous. In France, Sauternes is never labeled *haut* because there is no region called *Haut-Sauternes* (as there is in Médoc), nor are the grapes gathered from the tops of the vines. The conclusion that may be drawn is that the *haut* on a Sauternes label will command a higher price than a label without it, all other criteria being equal. Therefore, the same rule as before applies once again: ignore those

labels which distinguish between *Haut-Sauternes* and *Sauternes* and simply purchase a bottle which has been château-bottled. In the long run, it will probably be the most satisfactory and possibly less expensive.

The most important wine-producing châteaux in Sauternes were classified in 1855 as were those in the Médoc. There are five main communes which are most often found on French Sauternes labels. They are: *Sauternes*, (the same name as the district), *Bommes, Fargues, Preignac* and *Barsac*. The characteristics of the wines do not differ appreciably from one commune to another with the possible exception of Barsac where the wines tend to be somewhat fruitier. In fact, the novice wine drinker would find it difficult to distinguish the difference between wines from the different communes. Under the terms of the *appellation contrôlée* laws, only wines from these five communes may be labeled Sauternes. Wine grown in Barsac may be called either "Barsac" or "Sauternes" but most shippers prefer to use "Sauternes" on the label because it is more widely recognized by the wine-buying public, particularly outside France.

Most experts in culinary matters agree that a French Sauternes is most appropriately served well-chilled at the end of a meal with dessert, especially fruit and cheese. Some of the more enthusiastic devotees even go so far as to suggest omitting the dessert course entirely and serving an excellent sweet Sauternes as dessert in its own right. In their opinion, this luscious wine can best be appreciated when it is drunk by itself in order to fully comprehend its unique, fine qualities.

In addition to the sweet white wines of the Sauternes district, there are some very fine dry white wines produced in Bordeaux. Most people immediately think of Graves when dry white Bordeaux wine is mentioned, although almost all sections of Bordeaux produce some dry, medium-dry or medium-sweet white wine. The white Graves are generally very good to excellent. The *appellation contrôlée* laws specify that wines must contain 10 percent alcohol to be labeled "Graves" and 12 percent alcohol to merit the name "Graves *Supérieures*." The wine is dry and flinty with a mellow but full flavor. Some of the finest white Graves come from Château Haut-Brion which is also very famous for its claret.

Other districts in Bordeaux which are noted for good white wines are the Médoc (Château Talbot, and Chateau Latour are two of the best châteaux of the district), and *Entre-Deux-Mers* (meaning "between two seas") where the delicious plump oysters found along the shores of the area are perfectly complemented by the white wine produced there.

sangría
sauternes

SANGRÍA

1 lg. orange
1 lg. lemon
1/8 tsp. cinnamon
1/8 tsp. nutmeg
Sugar to taste
1 1/2 oz. brandy
1 fifth of claret
1 c. chilled club soda

Cut 2 thick slices from the center of the orange, then from the center of the lemon. Remove the seeds from all slices and set slices aside. Squeeze the juice from the remaining parts of the orange and lemon and strain into a 2-quart container. Add the spices, sugar, brandy, claret and orange and lemon slices and mix well. Cover and let stand for 1 hour. Pour the claret mixture and soda into a large decanter or serving pitcher. Pour over ice in tall, chilled glasses and garnish each glass with an orange slice. White Bordeaux wine may be used instead of claret, if desired. This makes about 6 servings.

sangría

This delicious refreshing drink is a perfect summer cooler. Red table wine, sugar syrup, sparkling water and fresh fruit are combined and served ice cold in clear frosty glasses. This drink is a favorite in Spain.

ICED SAUTERNES CUP

1 fifth of Sauterne
5 oz. sherry
2 1/2 oz. brandy
Rind of 1 lemon
3 slices of orange
3 slices of lemon
1 slice of cucumber peel

Place all of the ingredients in a serving pitcher. Add 3 cups of crushed ice and stir well. Serve in champagne glasses. This makes about 10 servings.

introducing spirits

A spirit is an alcoholic liquor which is distilled from a liquid containing alcohol (such as wine) or from fermented mash made from fruit, grain or molasses. Brandy (page 25) and Liqueurs (page 41) are examples of spirits as are rum (page 39), whiskey, gin and vodka. The characteristics of individual spirits are varied. Bourbon and Scotch whiskey are distilled at a fairly low alcoholic proof and therefore improve considerably in flavor with aging in charred casks. Vodka and gin are distilled at a relatively high proof and do not benefit much by aging. *Bourbon*, America's most popular whiskey, must have at least 51 percent corn in its mash content. It may not be distilled above 160 proof, and the required aging gives it a pleasant robust flavor. Scotch whiskey is a blend of some 20 malt whiskeys and grain whiskeys which is aged in former sherry casks. Scotch must be at least four years old before it can be imported into the United States. *Gin*, a nearly pure alcohol, distilled from various grains, is flavored with juniper berries. Sometimes other herbs or fruits are included among the flavoring ingredients. *Vodka* is Russian in origin. It is clear, water-white, practically odorless and has virtually no taste. It was originally made of rye or wheat mash but today it may be produced from various grains or potatoes.

introducing vermouth

Vermouth, often called an *apéritif*, is a fortified wine into which the essence of certain bitter, aromatic herbs is infused. The wine base is sweetened with sugar and pure alcohol is added, increasing the alcoholic content to around 20 percent. The flavoring agents may be a combination of any number of herbs and spices, but the most popular ones include essence of wormwood (the German word for wormwood is *vermuth*, hence the name), anise, cinnamon, cloves and quinine.

Vermouth dates back to medieval times when wine which had soured (and, consequently, was no longer drinkable), was salvaged by adding honey and herbs. The popularity of the drink gradually spread and demand for it in modern times has turned the manufacture of vermouth into a major industry, particularly in France and Italy. The United States also produces some very acceptable vermouth, both dry and sweet.

Dry white vermouth is generally thought of as being a French invention while Italy is considered to be responsible for sweet vermouth production, but, in reality, the Italians now produce more of both types than do their French neighbors. Sweet Italian vermouth is made in two colors: bianco (white) and rosso (red). Sweet vermouth is the main flavoring ingredient in a Manhattan cocktail and is also a very popular *apéritif* served over ice with a twist of lemon. It is made the same way as dry vermouth but has more sweetening added than the dry. The sweet red vermouth derives its color from the addition of caramel coloring.

Dry white vermouth is an important ingredient in some mixed cocktails, most notably the gin or vodka martini. The proportion of vermouth to gin is a matter of widely varying opinion (every martini expert has his own preferred formula) but a good quality dry vermouth is essential to produce a good martini. In addition to its use in mixed drinks, dry white vermouth is also a popular *apéritif* (considered very chic in some circles) when served over ice with a twist of lemon.

In cooking, when a recipe specifies using a dry white wine it is very important to use either the correct kind or none at all. Usually a Chablis or domestic Sauterne (which, unlike French Sauternes, tend to be fairly dry) are excellent for use in cooking. However, a dry white vermouth may be used as a very satisfactory substitute in any recipe that calls for a dry white wine.

CAFÉ BRÛLOT

3 tbsp. sugar
Thinly peeled rind of 1 sm. orange
1 vanilla pod or 1 tsp. vanilla extract
1 ½ c. brandy
6 c. piping hot black coffee

Place the sugar, orange rind and vanilla pod in a heatproof bowl and bruise the rind with a wooden spoon. Pour the brandy into a small saucepan, then place over low heat until heated through. Pour over the sugar mixture, then ignite and stir constantly for 30 seconds. Extinguish the flames with the hot coffee, then remove the orange rind and vanilla pod. Serve in coffee cups. Do not serve with cream or additional sugar. This makes about 20 demitasse cups.

café brûlot

One of the most extravagant and luxurious ways to end an elegant meal is to serve Café Brûlot in delicate demitasse cups. This delicious spiced beverage was created by the master French chef, Brillat-Savarin, who combined steaming black coffee, sugar, spices, orange and lemon peel and cognac, which he ignited before presenting it to the guests being served. You may add to the drama by dimming the lights before igniting the brandy so the flaming liquid may be more easily seen.

caribbean punch

A pleasant alternative to the traditional before-dinner cocktail is to serve a Caribbean Punch. A tangy combination of orange and lemon juice and white rum, its flavor is further enhanced with mint, cloves, cinnamon, nutmeg and ginger. Fresh pineapple chunks on a skewer and fancy-cut orange slices add an edible garnish. This delicious and festive drink is ideal to serve at patio parties or as a refreshing summer cooler.

CARIBBEAN PUNCH

Juice of 12 oranges
Juice of 12 lemons
3 c. white rum
½ c. (packed) brown sugar
1 tsp. cinnamon
1 tsp. cloves
1 tsp. nutmeg
1 tsp. ginger
12 c. crushed ice

Mix the orange juice, lemon juice, rum, brown sugar and the spices. Place the crushed ice in a punch bowl, then pour the rum mixture over the ice. Cover with a cloth and let stand for 10 minutes. Remove the cloth. Stir the rum mixture well, then add 2 trays of ice cubes and garnish with canelled orange slices (General Information, pg. 11). Dip the rims of the glasses in ice water, then in sugar for a frosted effect, if desired. Ladle the punch into the glasses, then garnish each glass with a canelled orange slice and long orange peel strip (General Information, pg. 12). This makes about twenty ¾-cup servings.

The Creative Homemaker's Academy © MCMLXXIII
Selected Illustrations © B.P.C. Publishing Limited MCMLXX

INDEX TO THE
CREATIVE COOKING COURSE

HOW TO USE THIS INDEX
Your cooking course is divided into 16 different categories of food. Following the recipes listed in this index you will find a reference that guides you to the correct category and the page number within that category. All Basic recipes are indexed under BASIC.

INDEX/2

▌General Information ▌Appetizers & Soups ▌Salads & Relishes ▌Eggs & Cheese ▌Beef ▌Pork ▌Lamb ▌Variety Meats & Game ▌Poultry ▌Seafood ▌Pasta & Cereals ▌Vegetables ▌Sauces ▌Breads ▌Desserts ▌Beverages

The Creative Homemaker's Academy © MCMLXXIII
Selected Illustrations © B.P.C. Publishing Limited MCMLXX

▌ General Information ▌ Appetizers & Soups ▌ Salads & Relishes ▌ Eggs & Cheese ▌ Beef ▌ Pork ▌ Lamb ▌ Variety
Meats & Game ▌ Poultry ▌ Seafood ▌ Pasta & Cereals ▌ Vegetables ▌ Sauces ▌ Breads ▌ Desserts ▌ Beverages

3/INDEX

INDEX/4

▓ General Information ▓ Appetizers & Soups ▓ Salads & Relishes ▓ Eggs & Cheese ▓ Beef ▓ Pork ▓ Lamb ▓ Variety
Meats & Game ▓ Poultry ▓ Seafood ▓ Pasta & Cereals ▓ Vegetables ▓ Sauces ▓ Breads ▓ Desserts ▓ Beverages

▉ General Information ▉ Appetizers & Soups ▉ Salads & Relishes ▉ Eggs & Cheese ▉ Beef ▉ Pork ▉ Lamb ▉ Variety
Meats & Game ▉ Poultry ▉ Seafood ▉ Pasta & Cereals ▉ Vegetables ▉ Sauces ▉ Breads ▉ Desserts ▉ Beverages

5/INDEX

INDEX/6

▮ General Information ▮ Appetizers & Soups ▮ Salads & Relishes ▮ Eggs & Cheese ▮ Beef ▮ Pork ▮ Lamb ▮ Variety
Meats & Game ▮ Poultry ▮ Seafood ▮ Pasta & Cereals ▮ Vegetables ▮ Sauces ▮ Breads ▮ Desserts ▮ Beverages

▌ General Information ▌ Appetizers & Soups ▌ Salads & Relishes ▌ Eggs & Cheese ▌ Beef ▌ Pork ▌ Lamb ▌ Variety
Meats & Game ▌ Poultry ▌ Seafood ▌ Pasta & Cereals ▌ Vegetables ▌ Sauces ▌ Breads ▌ Desserts ▌ Beverages

7/INDEX

INDEX/8

▌General Information ▌Appetizers & Soups ▌Salads & Relishes ▌Eggs & Cheese ▌Beef ▌Pork ▌Lamb ▌Variety Meats & Game ▌Poultry ▌Seafood ▌Pasta & Cereals ▌Vegetables ▌Sauces ▌Breads ▌Desserts ▌Beverages

▌General Information ▌ Appetizers & Soups ▌ Salads & Relishes ▌ Eggs & Cheese ▌ Beef ▌ Pork ▌ Lamb ▌ Variety
Meats & Game ▌ Poultry ▌ Seafood ▌ Pasta & Cereals ▌ Vegetables ▌ Sauces ▌ Breads ▌ Desserts ▌ Beverages

9/INDEX

INDEX/10

▌General Information ▌Appetizers & Soups ▌Salads & Relishes ▌Eggs & Cheese ▌Beef ▌Pork ▌Lamb ▌Variety
Meats & Game ▌Poultry ▌Seafood ▌Pasta & Cereals ▌Vegetables ▌Sauces ▌Breads ▌Desserts ▌Beverages

The Creative Homemaker's Academy © MCMLXXIII
Selected Illustrations © B.P.C. Publishing Limited MCMLXX

▌General Information ▌Appetizers & Soups ▌Salads & Relishes ▌Eggs & Cheese ▌Beef ▌Pork ▌Lamb ▌Variety
Meats & Game ▌Poultry ▌Seafood ▌Pasta & Cereals ▌Vegetables ▌Sauces ▌Breads ▌Desserts ▌Beverages

11/INDEX

INDEX/12

❚ General Information ❚ Appetizers & Soups ❚ Salads & Relishes ❚ Eggs & Cheese ❚ Beef ❚ Pork ❚ Lamb ❚ Variety Meats & Game ❚ Poultry ❚ Seafood ❚ Pasta & Cereals ❚ Vegetables ❚ Sauces ❚ Breads ❚ Desserts ❚ Beverages

▌General Information ▌Appetizers & Soups ▌Salads & Relishes ▌Eggs & Cheese ▌Beef ▌Pork ▌Lamb ▌Variety Meats & Game ▌Poultry ▌Seafood ▌Pasta & Cereals ▌Vegetables ▌Sauces ▌Breads ▌Desserts ▌Beverages

13/INDEX

The Creative Homemaker's Academy © MCMLXXIII
Selected Illustrations © B.P.C. Publishing Limited MCMLXX

INDEX/16

▌ General Information ▌ Appetizers & Soups ▌ Salads & Relishes ▌ Eggs & Cheese ▌ Beef ▌ Pork ▌ Lamb ▌ Variety
Meats & Game ▌ Poultry ▌ Seafood ▌ Pasta & Cereals ▼ Vegetables ▌ Sauces ▌ Breads ▌ Desserts ▌ Beverages

■ General Information ■ Appetizers & Soups ■ Salads & Relishes ■ Eggs & Cheese ■ Beef ■ Pork ■ Lamb ■ Variety
Meats & Game ■ Poultry ■ Seafood ■ Pasta & Cereals ■ Vegetables ■ Sauces ■ Breads ■ Desserts ■ Beverages

17/INDEX

INDEX/18

■ General Information ■ Appetizers & Soups ■ Salads & Relishes ■ Eggs & Cheese ■ Beef ■ Pork ■ Lamb ■ Variety
Meats & Game ■ Poultry ■ Seafood ■ Pasta & Cereals ■ Vegetables ■ Sauces ■ Breads ■ Desserts ■ Beverages

INDEX/20

▌General Information ▌Appetizers & Soups ▌Salads & Relishes▐Eggs & Cheese▐Beef▐Pork▐Lamb▐Variety
Meats & Game ▌Poultry ▌Seafood ▌Pasta & Cereals ▐Vegetables ▐Sauces▐Breads▐Desserts▐Beverages

PHOTOGRAPHY CREDITS:
Standard Brands Products: Planter's Peanut Oil; Olive Administration Committee; Pineapple Growers Association; South African Rock Lobster Service Corporation; United Fresh Fruit and Vegetable Association; Knox Gelatine; Florida Citrus Commission; National Association of Frozen Food Packers; Sterno, Inc.; National Broiler Council; National Fisheries Institute; Ball Corporation; Apple Pantry: Washington State Apple Commission; Rice Council; Sugar Information, Inc.; California Avocado Advisory Board; American Dairy Association; Florida Fruit and Vegetable Association; American Spice Trade Association; American Mushroom Institute; American Lamb Council; Brussels Sprouts Marketing Program; Louisiana Yam Commission; National Macaroni Institute; Artichoke Advisory Board; California Strawberry Advisory Board; Turkey Information Service; Best Foods, a Division of CPC International, Inc.; U.S. Department of Commerce: National Marine Fisheries Service; Booth Fisheries; Brer Rabbit Molasses; General Foods Kitchens.

NOTES

NOTES

NOTES

NOTES

NOTES

NOTES

NOTES

NOTES